| | |
|---|---|
| PMT | Periodic level payment of an annuity |
| PP | Purchase price per unit |
| PV | Present value |
| $PVA_n$ | Present value of an annuity for n years |
| PVP | Present value of a perpetuity |
| Q | Quantity produced or sold |
| $Q_{OpBE}$ | Operating breakeven in units |
| r | (1) A percentage discount rate, or cost of capital; also referred to as i |
| | (2) Required rate of return |
| $\ddot{r}$ | Historic or realized rate of return |
| $\bar{r}$ | "r bar," historic, or realized, average rate of return |
| $\hat{r}$ | "r hat," an expected rate of return |
| r* | Real risk-free rate of interest |
| $r_d$ | Cost of debt |
| $r_{dT}$ | After-tax cost of debt $= r_d(1-T)$ |
| $r_e$ | Cost of new common stock (equity) |
| $r_j$ | Cost of capital for an individual firm or security |
| $r_m$ | Cost of capital for "the market," or an "average" stock |
| $r_{PER}$ | Interest rate per compounding period |
| $r_{SIMPLE}$ | Nominal risk-free rate of interest |
| $r_{ps}$ | Cost of preferred stock |
| $r_{RF}$ | Rate of return on a risk-free security |
| $r_s$ | (1) Cost of retained earnings |
| | (2) Required return on a stock |
| $\rho$ | Correlation coefficient |
| ROA | Return on assets |
| ROE | Return on equity |
| RP | Risk premium |
| $RP_M$ | Market risk premium |
| S | Sales in dollars |
| $S_{OpBE}$ | Operating breakeven in dollars |
| SML | Security market line |
| $\Sigma$ | Summation sign (capital sigma) |
| $\sigma$ | Standard deviation (lowercase sigma) |
| $\sigma^2$ | Variance |
| t | Time period |
| T | (1) Marginal tax rate |
| | (2) Total demand or units sold |
| TIE | Times interest earned |
| v | Variable cost as a percent of selling price |
| V | Variable cost per unit |
| $V_d$ | Bond value |
| $V_{ps}$ | Preferred stock value |
| VC | Total variable costs |
| WACC | Weighted average cost of capital |
| YTC | Yield to call |
| YTM | Yield to maturity |

**DON'T THROW THIS CARD AWAY!**
**THIS MAY BE REQUIRED FOR YOUR COURSE!**

**THOMSON ONE** | Business School Edition

# Congratulations!

Your purchase of this NEW textbook includes complimentary access to THOMSON ONE – Business School Edition for Finance. THOMSON ONE – Business School Edition is a Web-based portal product that provides integrated access to Thomson Financial content for the purpose of financial analysis. This is an educational version of the same financial resources used by Wall Street analysts on a daily basis!

For hundreds of companies, this online resource provides seamless access to:

- **Current and Past Company Data:** Worldscope which includes company profiles, financials and accounting results, market per-share data, annual information, and monthly prices going back to 1980.

- **Financial Analyst Data and Forecasts:** I/B/E/S Consensus Estimates which provides consensus estimates, analyst-by-analyst earnings coverage, and analysts' forecasts.

- **SEC Disclosure Statements:** Disclosure SEC Database which includes company profiles, annual and quarterly company financials, pricing information, and earnings.

- **And More!**

**THOMSON**
**SOUTH-WESTERN**

**THOMSON ONE**
Business School Edition

**SERIAL NUMBER**

PRDDC00PP1SSF0

**HOW TO REGISTER YOUR SERIAL NUMBER**

1. Launch a web browser and go to **http://tabsefin.swlearning.com**

2. Click the "Register" button to enter your serial number.

3. Enter your serial number **exactly** as it appears here and create a unique User ID, or enter an existing User ID if you have previously registered for a different South-Western product via a serial number.

4. When prompted, create a password (or enter an existing password, if you have previously registered for a different product via a serial number.) Submit the necessary information when prompted. **Record your User ID and password in a secure location.**

5. Once registered, return to the URL above and select the "Enter" button; have your User ID and password handy.

For technical support, contact 1-800-423-0563 or email **tl.support@thomson.com**

# *Essentials of*
# Managerial Finance

14e

# *Essentials of*
# Managerial Finance

**14e**

**SCOTT BESLEY**

*University of South Florida*

**EUGENE F. BRIGHAM**

*University of Florida*

**THOMSON**

——————✳——————™

**SOUTH-WESTERN**

Australia · Brazil · Canada · Mexico · Singapore · Spain · United Kingdom · United States

THOMSON
™
SOUTH-WESTERN

**Essentials of Managerial Finance, Fourteenth Edition**
Scott Besley and Eugene F. Brigham

**VP/Editorial Director:**
Jack W. Calhoun

**Publisher:**
Alex von Rosenberg

**Executive Editor:**
Mike Reynolds

**Sr. Developmental Editor:**
Elizabeth Thomson

**Editorial Assistant:**
Adele Scholtz

**Content Project Manager:**
Elycia Arendt

**Manager of Technology, Editorial:**
John Barans

**Sr. Technology Project Manager:**
Matt McKinney

**Marketing Manager:**
Jason Krall

**Sr. Marketing Communications Manager:**
Jim Overly

**Sr. Manufacturing Coordinator:**
Sandee Milewski

**Printer:**
R R Donnelley
Willard Manufacturing Division
Willard, OH

**Art Director:**
Bethany Casey

**Cover and Internal Designer:**
Red Hanger Design, LLC

**Cover Images:**
Veer Incorporated/Artist:
Neil Brennan

**Compositor:**
International Typesetting
and Composition

**Project Management:**
Graphic World, Inc.

Library of Congress Control Number:
2007925965

For more information about our
products, contact us at

Thomson Learning Academic
Resource Center

1-800-423-0563

**Thomson Higher Education**
5191 Natorp Boulevard
Mason, OH 45040
USA

# Brief Contents

# Contents

## PART III   VALUATION—FINANCIAL ASSETS   181

# PART IV     VALUATION—REAL ASSETS (CAPITAL BUDGETING)     353

## PART V    COST OF CAPITAL, LEVERAGE, AND DIVIDEND POLICY    447

## PART VI    WORKING CAPITAL MANAGEMENT    563

# Preface

*Essentials of Managerial Finance* is intended for use in introductory finance courses. The book begins with a discussion of basic concepts, including financial statements, security markets, time value of money, interest rates, basic valuation, and risk analysis. Subsequent chapters explain how financial managers can help maximize their firms' values by improving decisions in such areas as capital budgeting, choice of capital structure, and working capital management. This organization has three important advantages:

1. Early in the book we explain how financial markets operate and how security prices are determined. This shows students how managerial finance can affect the value of the firm. Also, early coverage of key concepts such as valuation techniques and risk analysis permits their use and reinforcement throughout the remainder of the book.

2. The book is structured around markets and valuation, which helps students see how the various topics relate to one another.

3. Most students—even those who do not plan to major in finance—are interested in stock and bond valuation, rates of return, and other similar topics. Because learning is a function of interest and motivation, and because *Essentials* begins by showing the relationships among security markets, stock and bond values, and managerial finance, this organization works well from a pedagogic standpoint.

Now in its fourteenth edition, *Essentials* has grown through time, especially with respect to the long list of practical and theoretical developments it covers. Because the primary goal of financial managers should be to maximize the values of their firms, the focus of the book is still on valuation concepts. However, on the recommendations of reviewers, we have restructured the discussions of a few topics. In addition, because it has proven to be a useful pedagogy in the classroom, we have included discussions about how managerial finance concepts relate to personal financial decisions.

## RELATIONSHIP WITH *PRINCIPLES OF FINANCE*

As with *Essentials, Principles of Finance* (third edition) is intended for use in introductory finance courses. *Principles,* however, provides a more general coverage of the subject of finance than *Essentials. Principles of Finance* gives a survey of finance as a field of study by covering three major subject areas: (1) financial markets and institutions; (2) investments; and (3) managerial finance. Each of these areas is covered to some extent in *Essentials;* however, the primary emphasis is on managerial finance. *Principles* takes a more eclectic approach to the coverage of finance than does *Essentials.*

## INTENDED MARKET AND USE

As noted earlier, *Essentials* is intended for use as an introductory textbook. The key chapters can be covered in a one-term course, or, supplemented with cases and some outside readings, the book can also be used in a two-term course. If it is used in a one-term course, the instructor probably will cover only selected chapters, leaving the others for students either to examine on their own or to use as references in conjunction with work in later courses. Also, we wrote the chapters in a flexible, modular format to help instructors cover the material in a different sequence should they choose to do so.

## MAJOR CHANGES IN THE FOURTEENTH EDITION

In this book, we provide the reader with the tools needed to gain a good understanding of managerial finance, which is a requisite for success in business. Working with a team of reviewers, listening to students, and observing what works in the classroom, we continuously search for ways to improve the book in terms of clarity and understanding. As a result, some important changes appear in this edition, the most important of which are discussed here.

### Financial Markets, Interest Rates, and Valuation Concepts

In the thirteenth edition, topics relating to interest rates and financial markets were discussed in one chapter. In this edition, these topics are covered in two chapters. Discussions of the characteristics of and the participants in the financial markets are covered in one chapter (Chapter 3); the determinants of interest rates, the concept of yield, and the impact interest rates have on value are discussed in a separate chapter (Chapter 5). In addition, in the thirteenth edition valuation of financial assets was included in a single chapter. The fourteenth edition includes one chapter that describes the characteristics of debt and how to value debt (Chapter 6), and another chapter that describes the characteristics of equity and how to value equity (Chapter 7). Not only do we cover the traditional dividend discount model for stock valuation, but we also discuss and provide examples of how stocks can be valued using P/E ratios and the economic value added (EVA) approach, which are two valuation methods investors commonly use.

### Learning Objectives and End-of-Chapter Summary

Each chapter now begins with a section called Chapter *Essentials*—The Questions, which includes a set of questions, representing the learning objectives for the chapter, that students should be able to answer when they are finished reading the chapter. At the end of the chapter these questions are answered in a section called Chapter *Essentials*—The Answers, which replaces the typical end-of-chapter summary. This feature helps students connect the material covered in the chapter with questions that instructors often ask during class or on exams.

### Spreadsheets

This edition contains expanded coverage of spreadsheets. The application of spreadsheets to solve financial problems is prominent in the chapter that covers time value of money concepts (Chapter 4) and the chapter that describes capital budgeting techniques (Chapter 9). The interest tables have been taken out of the book because financial calculators and spreadsheets make them obsolete. Because students must use spreadsheets in the business world, they should be exposed to the benefits of this important business tool early in their business curriculum.

## Personal Finance

In the years we have taught the basic course in finance that all business majors are required to complete, we have noticed that most students seem uninterested. In fact, many admit that they would not take the course if it was not required. As a result, we have tried various methods to get the uninterested students more interested in finance. It seems that one way to get the attention of students is to relate managerial finance topics to personal financial decisions that everyone is exposed to at some point in their lives. Therefore, we added a new feature in each chapter that is titled Chapter *Essentials*—Personal Finance. This section contains discussions that relate the topics covered in the chapter to personal financial decisions. Our hope is that students make the connection between financial concepts presented in the course and the application to decisions that they will face with their personal finances. Perhaps this pedagogy will help students become more interested in learning some of the important financial concepts.

## Ethical Dilemmas

We feel that it is crucial for students who will some day be decision makers in the business world to be exposed to ethical situations to improve their critical thinking skills. For this reason, we began including ethical dilemma vignettes in *Essentials* more than a decade ago. In this edition, we have expanded the ethical dilemmas so that an ethical dilemma box is contained in each chapter. Each ethical dilemma vignette is related to the material covered in the chapter and is based on real-world circumstances. These ethical dilemmas (1) expose the students to the relationship between ethics and business, (2) promote the development of critical-thinking and decision-making skills, and (3) provide a vehicle for lively class discussion.

## OTHER FEATURES OF THE FOURTEENTH EDITION

### Multinational Finance Coverage

Coverage of multinational finance is still included in the chapters where the specific topics are covered rather than in a separate chapter devoted to multinational managerial finance. This placement allows students to better understand how the application of the material presented in the chapter differs in domestic and international settings.

### A Managerial Perspective and Industry Practice

Although boxed business anecdotes are not new to this edition of *Essentials*, we want to draw attention to them because each is either new to this edition or has been updated since the previous edition. Each chapter leads off with "A Managerial Perspective," which can be used for student reading, class lecture, or both. The "Industry Practice" boxes, which show the application of the concepts in real-world situations, are now available on the Website. The "Industry Practice" boxes give an indication as to the extent that the methods discussed in the chapters are actually used by businesses in the "real world."

## Thomson ONE

Nearly every chapter includes a problem from Thomson ONE, a powerful interactive database of financial information developed by Thomson Financial. These problems require students to apply the concepts discussed in the chapter using real-world data, which helps them to develop real-world critical-thinking skills.

## Assurance of Learning Outcomes

Recently imposed assurance of learning outcomes have spawned a multitude of efforts on campuses across the country to begin the process of defining program goals, embedding assessments, and measuring results. One of the initiatives that we have undertaken is to tag test items to measurable learning outcomes for a basic course in finance. To meet higher-level assessment needs such as measuring the ability of students to communicate effectively, different measurement tools are needed. To help faculty meet these needs, we have developed rubrics to help in the scoring of the certain problems. These problems can be assigned as a written or oral presentation for assessing student progress toward program goals. Rubrics are scoring tools that make explicit how students will be assessed. They also detail the specific attributes of different levels of proficiency within an assigned task.

## ANCILLARY MATERIALS

A number of items are available free of charge to adopting instructors:

1. **Instructor's Manual.** The comprehensive manual contains answers to all text questions and problems, detailed solutions to integrative problems, and suggested course outlines.

2. **Lecture Presentation Software.** To facilitate classroom presentations, computer graphics slide shows written in Microsoft PowerPoint are available. One set of slides features the essential topics presented in each chapter and the other set includes more detailed lecture notes.

3. **Test Bank.** The Test Bank contains more than 1,000 class-tested questions and problems, many of which are new. True/false questions, multiple-choice conceptual questions, multiple-choice problems (which can be easily modified to short-answer problems by removing the answer choices), and financial calculator problems are included for every chapter. For this version of the test bank, we have developed learning objectives and outcomes assessment criteria that satisfy AACSB requirements. Questions that can be used for assessment of outcomes are identified in the test bank. These questions were selected by a committee.

4. **Problem Spreadsheet.** Spreadsheets that contain models for the computer-related end-of-chapter problems are also available.

5. **Website.** A book-designated Website with numerous resources for instructors and students can be accessed through http://www.thomsonedu.com/finance/besley.

6. **WebTutor Toolbox.** WebTutor Toolbox provides instructors with text-specific content that interacts in the two leading Course Management Systems available in Higher Education—WebCT and Blackboard.

A number of additional items are available for purchase by students:

1. **Cases.** Cases in Financial Management, TextChoice by Thomson Custom Publishing, authored by Lin Klein and Eugene F. Brigham, is well-suited for use with *Essentials*. The cases provide real-world applications of the methodologies and concepts developed in this book. In addition, all of the cases are available in a customized format, so your students pay only for the cases you decide to use.

2. **Spreadsheet Analysis Book.** *Financial Analysis with Microsoft Excel* by Timothy Mayes and Todd Shank fully integrates the teaching of spreadsheet analysis with the basic finance concepts. This book makes a good companion to *Essentials* in courses in which computer work is highly emphasized.

3. **Aplia.** Student effort is the key determinant of student success. Aplia offers highly engaging, auto-graded homework assignments to ensure students put forth genuine effort throughout the term. The *Essentials* course in Aplia includes the following assignments:

   a. Problem Sets: Students stay on top of their work by regularly completing problem sets written specifically for *Essentials*. Every chapter includes a practice and a graded problem set with each question providing detailed feedback.

   b. News Analyses: Students learn to connect course theories to real-world events by reading relevant news articles and answering piece-specific recall and analysis questions.

   c. Tutorials: Students prepare themselves to learn finance at the start of the course by using interactive tutorials to overcome deficiencies in course prerequisites. These tutorials identify students who are unprepared for a finance course and require them to address any deficiency before it becomes a problem. Tutorials include instruction on accounting, math, statistics, and economics, as well as financial calculators.

## ACKNOWLEDGMENTS

This book reflects the efforts of a great many people over a number of years. For the fourteenth edition, we are indebted to the following professors who provided their input for improving the book:

Lyle Bowlin—Southeastern University

Michael Kinsman—Pepperdine University

Elisa Muresan—Long Island University

James Murtagh—Rensselaer Polytechnic Institute

Armand Picou—University of Central Arkansas

Robert Puelz—Southern Methodist University

Charles Rayhorn—Northern Michigan University

John Schatzberg—University of New Mexico

Zekiye Selvili—Cal State Fullerton

Gary Walker—Cleveland State University

Paul Weinstock—Ohio State University

Next, we would like to thank the following professors whose reviews and comments have helped prior editions and our companion books: Mike Adler, Syed Ahmad, Ed Altman, Bruce Anderson, Ron Anderson, George Andrea, Bob Angell, Vince Apilado, Henry Arnold, Bob Aubey, Gil Babcock, Peter Bacon, Kent Baker, William Baker, Robert Balik, Dean Balm, Tom Bankston, Les Barenbaum, Charles Barngrover, Bill Beedles, Yvett M. Bendeck, Moshe Ben-Horim, Bill Beranek, Tom Berry, Will Bertin, Dan Best, Roger Bey, Douglas Bible, Dalton Bigbee, John Bildersee, Russ Boisjoly, Keith Boles, Geof Booth, Jerry Boswell, Kenneth Boudreaux, Helen Bowers, Oswald Bowlin, Don Boyd, G. Michael Boyd, Pat Boyer, Joe Brandt, Elizabeth Brannigan, Greg Brauer, Mary Broske, Dave Brown, Kate Brown, Bill Brueggeman, Stephen G. Buell, Ted Byrley, Bill Campsey, Stephen Caples, Bob Carlson, Severin Carlson, David Cary, Steve Celec, Don Chance, Antony Chang, Susan Chaplinsky, Jay Choi, S. K. Choudhary, Shin-Herng Michelle Chu, Lal Chugh, Maclyn Clouse, Margaret Considine, Paul F. Conway, Phil Cooley, Joe Copeland, David Cordell, Marcia Cornett, M. P. Corrigan, Bruce Costa, John Cotner, Charles Cox, David Crary, John Crockett, Jr., Roy Crum, Ed Daley, Brent Dalrymple, Bodie Dickerson, Bernard Dill, J. David Diltz, Gregg Dimkoff, Les Dlabay, Mark Dorfman, Gene Drzycimski, Dean Dudley, David Durst, Ed Dyl, Richard Edelman, Charles Edwards, John Ellis, Dave Ewert, John Ezell, Michael Ferri, Jim Filkins, John Finnerty, Susan Fischer, Steven Flint, Russ Fogler, Gordon Foster, Dan French, Michael Garlington, David Garraty, Jim Garven, Adam Gehr, Jr., Jim Gentry, Philip Glasgo, Rudyard Goode, Walt Goulet, Bernie Grablowsky, Theoharry Grammatikos, Reynold Griffith, Ed Grossnickle, John Groth, Alan Grunewald, Manak Gupta, Sam Hadaway, Don Hakala, Paul Halpern, Gerald Hamsmith, William Hardin, John Harris, Paul Hastings, Bob Haugen, Steve Hawke, Del Hawley, Robert Hehre, George Hettenhouse, Hans Heymann, Kendall Hill, Roger Hill, Tom Hindelang, Linda Hittle, Ralph Hocking, J. Ronald Hoffmeister, Robert Hollinger, Jim Horrigan, John Houston, John Howe, Keith Howe, Robert M. Hull, Steve Isberg, Jim Jackson, Kose John, Craig Johnson, Keith Johnson, Ramon Johnson, Keith Jokob, Ray Jones, Frank Jordan, Manual Jose, Alfred Kahl, Gus Kalogeras, Mike Keenan, Bill Kennedy, James Keys, Carol Kiefer, Joe Kiernan, Rick Kish, Don Knight, Dorothy Koehl, Jaroslaw Komarynsky, Duncan Kretovich, V. Sivarama Krishnan, Harold Krogh, Gregory Koutmous, Charles Kroncke, Don Kummer, Joan Lamm, Larry Lang, P. Lange, Howard Lanser, John Lasik, Edward Lawrence, Martin Lawrence, Douglas Leary, Wayne Lee, Jim LePage, Jules Levine, John Lewis, Jason Lin, Chuck Linke, Bill Lloyd, Susan Long, Judy Maese, Bob Magee, Ileen Malitz, Phil Malone, Lewis Mandell, Terry Maness, Chris Manning, S. K. Mansinghka, Iqbal Mansur, Terry Martell, D. J. Masson, John Mathys, John McAlhany, Andy McCollough, Ambrose McCoy, Thomas McCue, Bill McDaniel, John McDowell, Charles McKinney, Robyn McLaughlin, Jamshid Mehran, Iihan Meric, Larry Merville, Massoud Metghalchi, Rick Meyer, Jim Millar, Ed Miller, John Mitchell, Carol Moerdyk, Bob Moore, Barry Morris, Gene Morris, Fred Morrissey, Chris Muscarella, David Nachman, Tim Nantell, Charlie Narron, Don Nast, Bill Nelson, Bob Nelson, Bob Niendorf, Gladson Nwanna, Tom O'Brien, William E. O'Connell, Jr., Dennis O'Connor, John O'Donnell, Jim Olsen, Robert Olsen, Jim Pappas, Stephen Parrish, Phil Pennell, Glenn Petry, Jim Pettijohn, Rich Pettit, Dick Pettway, Hugo Phillips, H. R. Pickett, John Pinkerton, Gerald Pogue, Eugene Poindexter, Ralph Pope, R. Potter, Franklin Potts, R. Powell, Chris Prestopino, Jerry Prock, Howard Puckett, Herbert Quigley, George Racette, Bob Radcliffe, Murli Rajan, Jim Reinemann, Bill Rentz, Ken Riener, Charles Rini, John Ritchie, Robert Ritzcovan, Pietra Rivoli, Antonio Rodriguez, James Rosenfeld, E. N. Roussakis, Dexter Rowell, Jim Sachlis, Abdul Sadik, Rakash Sah, Thomas Scampini, Kevin Scanlon, Frederick Schadler, John D. Schatzberg, Mary Jane Scheuer, Carl Schweser,

David Scott, John Settle, Alan Severn, Ramesh Shah, Sol Shalit, Hersh Shefrin, Frederic Shipley, Dilip Shome, Ron Shrieves, Neil Sicherman, J. B. Silvers, Clay Singleton, Joe Sinkey, Stacy Sirmans, Jaye Smith, Patricia Smith, Steve Smith, Don Sorensen, David Speairs, Andrew Spieler, Ken Stanly, Ed Stendardi, Alan Stephens, Don Stevens, Jerry Stevens, Glen Strasburg, David Suk, Philip Swensen, Ernest Swift, Paul Swink, Gary Tallman, Dular Talukdar, Dennis Tanner, Craig Tapley, Russ Taussig, John Teall, Richard Teweles, Ted Teweles, Francis C. Thomas, Andrew Thompson, John Thompson, Dogan Tirtiroglu, Marco Tonietti, William Tozer, George Trivoli, Randy Trostle, George Tsetsekos, Ricardo Ulivi, David Upton, Howard Van Auken, Pretorious Van den Dool, Pieter Vandenberg, Paul Vanderheiden, JoAnn Vaughan, Jim Verbrugge, Patrick Vincent, Steve Vinson, Susan Visscher, Gautam Vora, John Wachowicz, Mike Walker, Sam Weaver, Kuo-Chiang Wei, Bill Welch, Robert J. Wiley, Norm Williams, Tony Wingler, Ed Wolfe, Don Woods, Sally Jo Wright, Michael Yonan, David Zalewaki, Dennis Zocco, and Kent Zumwalt.

Special thanks are due to Rosemary Carlson, Morehead State University, who developed the Thomson ONE problems that are included at the ends of the chapters, and Louis Gapenski, who helped develop the integrative problems.

## ERRORS IN THE TEXT

At this point, most authors make a statement like this: "We appreciate all the help we received from the people listed above, but any remaining errors are, of course, our own responsibility." And generally there are more than enough errors remaining! Having experienced difficulty with errors ourselves, both as students and as instructors, we resolved to avoid this problem in *Essentials*. As a result of our error-detection procedures, we are convinced that it is relatively free of significant mistakes that either confuse or distract readers.

Partly due to our confidence that there are few errors in this book, but primarily because we want to correct any errors that might exist in this printing of the book, we offer a reward of $10 per error to the first person who reports it to us. For purposes of this reward, errors are defined as misspelled words, computation errors (not including rounding differences), errors in finance content and facts, and other errors that inhibit comprehension. Typesetting errors, such as spacing, or differences in opinion concerning grammatical or punctuational convention do not qualify for the reward. Also, because Internet addresses sometimes change, changes in Web addresses do not qualify as errors. However, we would like to know about such changes, so please send them to us. Updated Web addresses are regularly posted to the book's Website at www.thomsonedu.com/finance/besley. Finally, any qualifying error that has a follow-through effect is counted as two errors only. Errors should be reported to Scott Besley either via e-mail at sbesley@coba.usf.edu or by regular mail at the address given later.

## CONCLUSION

Finance is, in a real sense, the cornerstone of the enterprise system—good financial management is vitally important to the economic health of business firms, and hence to the nation and the world. Because of its importance, finance should be widely and thoroughly understood, but this is easier said than done. The field is relatively complex, and it is undergoing constant change in response to shifts in economic conditions. All of this makes finance stimulating and exciting but also challenging and sometimes perplexing. We sincerely hope that *Essentials* will meet its own challenge by contributing to a better understanding of our financial system.

Scott Besley
College of Business Administration, BSN3403
University of South Florida
4202 E. Fowler Avenue
Tampa, FL 33620-5500

Eugene F. Brigham
College of Business
University of Florida
Gainesville, FL 32611-7160

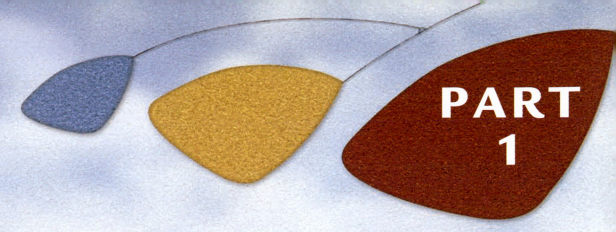

# Introduction to Managerial Finance

**CHAPTER 1**
An Overview of Managerial Finance

# An Overview of Managerial Finance

## A MANAGERIAL PERSPECTIVE

**W**hen you invest in the common stock of a company, what do you hope (expect) to gain? Rational investors would answer this question with a single word—wealth. As you will discover in this chapter, a corporation acts in the best interests of its stockholders when decisions are made that increase the value of the firm, which translates into an increase in the value of the company's stock.

The managers of large corporations generally are encouraged to "act in the best interests" of the firms' stockholders through executive compensation packages that reward "appropriate behavior"—that is, actions that increase firms' values. When managers act in their own best interests and stockholders believe that value is not being maximized, these executives often are ousted from their very lucrative positions. Sounds like a good plan, doesn't it?

Although it seems like a good idea to reward managers who run firms with the best interests of the stockholders (owners) in mind, in recent years stockholders have complained that executive compensation plans in many large corporations provide excessive rewards to executives who are interested only in increasing their own wealth positions. Consider, for example, that the CEO of Pfizer was paid $79 million during the period 2001–2005 and the CEOs of Home Depot and Verizon Communications were paid $27 million and $50 million, respectively, during the period from 2004–2005, even though at the same time these same firms produced negative returns for stockholders.[1] According to Paul Hodgson, senior research associate at The Corporate Library, this is evidence "that the link between long-term value growth and long-term incentive awards is broken at too many companies—if it was ever forged properly in the first place."[2]

In recent years, investors have said, "Enough is enough." Stockholders are now demanding, and more boards of directors are imposing, tougher rules with regard to compensation packages, making it more difficult for executives to earn excessive salaries. In 2006, for example, the shareholders of Pfizer, Merrill Lynch, Morgan Stanley, General Electric, Citigroup, and Raytheon, among others, became much more active in expressing their feelings about "excessive" executive pay plans.[3]

---

[1]Alan Murray, "CEOs of the World, Unite? When Executive Pay Can Be Truly Excessive," *The Wall Street Journal,* April 26, 2006, A2.

[2]"Pay for Failure," The Corporate Library, http://thecorporatelibrary.blogspot.com/. The Corporate Library provides articles and information about corporate governance and executive compensation. Additional reports about CEO compensation can be found by searching http://money.cnn.com/ using the key words "CEO pay."

[3]"Getting Active," *The Wall Street Journal Online,* May 4, 2006.

A compensation plan that has received a great deal of attention recently is the policy of offering "golden parachute" packages that provide executives with excessive payments when they are dismissed from their firms. In the past, a *golden parachute*, which gets its name from the fact that a significant severance pay permits an executive to easily "land on his or her financial feet" after dismissal from the company, often had to be honored no matter the reason for dismissal; one exception would be if a criminal offense was committed by the executive. More companies are now limiting the amount of the severance pay that executives can earn. In addition, large corporations, including ImClone Systems, NCR Corporation, and Walt Disney Company, are revising their policies so that it is easier to fire executives without having to pay excessive severance pay. More boards of directors are redefining what it means to be fired for "just cause" to include a wider range of actions or nonactions for which executives can be dismissed without severance pay. Firms now are including poor firm performance as a justifiable reason for dismissing executives without severance. It seems that stockholders are "speaking their minds," and the boards of directors of many companies are listening.[4]

As you read this chapter, think about the issues raised here: As a stockholder in a company, what goal(s) would you like to see pursued? To what extent should top managers let their own personal goals influence the decisions they make concerning how the firm is run? What factors should management consider when trying to "boost" the value of the firm's stock?

## Chapter *Essentials*
### —The Questions

After reading this chapter, you should be able to answer the following questions:

- What is finance, and why should everyone understand basic financial concepts?
- What are the different forms of business organization? What are the advantages and disadvantages of each?
- What goal(s) should firms pursue? Do firms always pursue appropriate goals?
- What is the role of ethics in successful businesses?
- How do foreign firms differ from U.S. firms?

"Why should I study finance?" You probably are asking yourself this question right now. To answer this question, we need to answer another question: What is finance?

## WHAT IS FINANCE?

In simple terms, finance is concerned with decisions about money, or more appropriately, cash flows. Finance decisions deal with how money is raised and used by businesses, governments, and individuals. To make rational financial decisions, you must understand three general, yet reasonable, concepts: Everything else equal, (1) more value is preferred to less; (2) the sooner cash is received, the more valuable it is; and (3) less risky assets are more valuable than (preferred to) riskier assets.

In this book, we will show that a firm that practices sound financial management can provide better products to its customers at lower prices, pay higher salaries to its employees, and still provide greater returns to investors who put up the funds needed to form and operate the business. Because the economy—both national and worldwide—consists of customers, employees, and investors, sound financial management contributes to the well-being of both individuals and the general population.

Although the emphasis in this book is business finance, you will discover that the same concepts that firms apply when making sound business decisions can be used to make informed decisions relating to personal finances. For example, consider the decision you might have to make if you won a state lottery worth $105 million. Which

---

[4]Joann Lublin, "Just Cause: Some Firms Cut Golden Parachute," *The Wall Street Journal*, March 13, 2006, B3, and "Getting Active," *The Wall Street Journal Online*, May 4, 2006.

*would* you choose, a lump-sum payment of $54 million today or a payment of $3.5 million each year for the next 30 years? Which *should* you choose? In Chapter 4 we will show that time value of money techniques that firms use to make business decisions can be used to answer this and other questions that relate to personal finances. In fact, in each chapter, we will show how the general business finance concepts that are presented apply to decisions about personal financial management.

### Self-Test Question
What are some common personal finance decisions that individuals face?

## GENERAL AREAS OF FINANCE

The study of finance consists of four interrelated areas: (1) *financial markets and institutions,* (2) *investments,* (3) *financial services,* and (4) *managerial finance.* Although our concern in this book is primarily with managerial finance, because these four areas are interrelated, an individual who works in any one area should have a good understanding of the other areas as well.

### Financial Markets and Institutions

Financial institutions, which include banks, insurance companies, savings and loans, and credit unions, are an integral part of the general financial services marketplace. The success of these organizations requires an understanding of factors that cause interest rates to rise and fall, regulations to which financial institutions are subject, and the various types of financial instruments, such as mortgages, auto loans, and certificates of deposit, that financial institutions offer.

### Investments

This area of finance focuses on the decisions made by businesses and individuals as they choose securities for their investment portfolios. The major functions in the investments area are (1) determining the values, risks, and returns associated with such financial assets as stocks and bonds and (2) determining the optimal mix of securities that should be held in a portfolio of investments.

### Financial Services

Financial services refers to functions provided by organizations that operate in the finance industry. In general, financial services organizations deal with the management of money. People who work in these organizations, which include banks, insurance companies, brokerage firms, and other similar companies, provide services that help individuals (and companies) determine how to invest money to achieve such goals as home purchase, retirement, financial stability and sustainability, budgeting, and related activities. The financial services industry is one of the largest in the world.

### Managerial (Business) Finance

Managerial finance deals with decisions that all firms make concerning their cash flows. As a consequence, managerial finance is important in all types of businesses, whether they are public or private, deal with financial services, or manufacture products. The types of duties encountered in managerial finance range from making decisions about plant expansions to choosing what types of securities to issue to finance such expansions. Financial managers also have the responsibility for deciding the credit terms under which customers can buy, how much inventory the firm should carry, how much cash to keep on hand, whether to acquire other firms (merger analysis), and how much of the firm's earnings to reinvest in the business and how much to pay out as dividends.

If you pursue a career in finance, you will need some knowledge of each of the areas of finance, regardless of which area you might enter. For example, a banker lending to a business must have a good understanding of managerial finance to judge how well the borrowing company is operated. The same holds true for a securities analyst. Even stockbrokers must understand general financial principles if they are to give intelligent advice to their customers. At the same time, corporate financial managers need to know what their bankers are thinking about and how investors are likely to judge their corporations' performances and thus determine their stock prices.

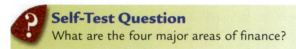

**Self-Test Question**
What are the four major areas of finance?

## THE IMPORTANCE OF FINANCE IN NONFINANCE AREAS

Believe it or not, everyone is exposed to finance concepts almost every day. For example, when you borrow to buy a car or house, finance concepts are used to determine the monthly payments you are required to make. When you retire, finance concepts are used to determine the amount of the monthly payments you receive from your retirement plan. If you want to start your own business, an understanding of finance concepts is essential for survival. Thus, even if you do not intend to pursue a career in a finance-related profession, it is important that you have some basic understanding of finance concepts. Similarly, if you pursue a career in finance, it is important that you have an understanding of other areas in the business, including marketing, accounting, production, and so forth, to make more informed financial decisions.

Let's consider how finance relates to some of the nonfinance areas in a business.

### Management

When we think of management, we often think of personnel decisions and employee relations, strategic planning, and the general operations of the firm. Strategic planning, which is one of the most important activities of management, cannot be accomplished without considering how such plans impact the overall financial well-being of the firm. Such personnel decisions as setting salaries, hiring new staff, and paying bonuses must be coordinated with financial decisions to ensure that any needed funds are available. For these reasons, managers must have at least a general understanding of financial management concepts to make informed decisions in their areas.

### Marketing

If you have taken a basic marketing course, probably one of the first things you learned was that the *four Ps of marketing*—product, price, place, and promotion—determine the success of products that are manufactured and sold by companies. Clearly, the price that should be charged for a product and the amount of advertising a firm can afford for the product must be determined in consultation with financial managers because the firm will lose money if the price of the product is too low or too much is spent on advertising. Coordination of the finance function and the marketing function is critical to the success of a company, especially for a small, newly formed firm, because it is necessary to ensure that sufficient cash is generated to survive. For these reasons, people in marketing must understand how marketing decisions affect and are affected by such issues as funds availability, inventory levels, and excess plant capacity.

## Accounting

In many firms (especially small ones), it is difficult to distinguish between the finance function and the accounting function. Often, accountants make finance decisions, and vice versa, because the two disciplines are closely related. In fact, you might recognize some of the material in this book from accounting courses that you have already taken. As you will discover, financial managers rely heavily on accounting information because making decisions about the future requires information about the past. As a consequence, accountants must understand how financial managers use accounting information in planning and decision making so that it can be provided in an accurate and timely fashion. Similarly, accountants must understand how accounting data are viewed (used) by investors, creditors, and other outsiders who are interested in the firm's operations.

## Information Systems

Businesses thrive by effectively collecting and using information, which must be reliable and available when needed for making decisions. The process by which the delivery of such information is planned, developed, and implemented is costly, but so are the problems caused by a lack of good information. Without appropriate information, decisions relating to finance, management, marketing, and accounting could prove disastrous. Different types of information require different information systems, so information system specialists work with financial managers to determine what information is needed, how it should be stored, how it should be delivered, and how information management will affect the profitability of the firm.

## Economics

Finance and economics are so similar that some universities and colleges offer courses related to these areas in the same department or functional area. Many tools used to make financial decisions evolved from theories or models developed by economists. Perhaps the most noticeable difference between finance and economics is that financial managers evaluate information and make decisions about cash flows associated with a particular firm or a small group of firms, whereas economists analyze information and forecast changes in activities associated with entire industries and the economy as a whole. It is important that financial managers understand economics and that economists understand finance—economic activity and policy impact financial decisions, and vice versa.

Finance will be a part of your life no matter what career you choose. There will be a number of times during your life, both in business and in a personal capacity, when you will make finance-related decisions. It is therefore important that you have some understanding of general finance concepts. *There are financial implications in virtually all business decisions, and nonfinancial executives must know enough finance to incorporate these implications into their own specialized analyses.* For this reason, every student of business, regardless of his or her major, should be concerned with finance.

## Finance in the Organizational Structure of the Firm

Although organizational structures vary from company to company, Figure 1-1 presents a fairly typical picture of the role of finance and its relationship with other areas within a firm. The chief financial officer (CFO), who often has the title of vice president of finance, reports to the president. The financial vice president's key subordinates are the treasurer and the controller. In most firms, the treasurer has direct responsibility for managing the firm's cash and marketable securities, planning how the firm is financed and when funds are raised, managing risk, and overseeing the corporate pension fund. The treasurer also supervises the credit manager, the inventory manager, and the director of capital budgeting, who analyzes decisions related to investments in fixed assets. The controller is responsible for the activities of the accounting and tax departments.

**Self-Test Questions**

Why do people in areas outside financial management need to know something about managerial finance?

Identify the two subordinates who report to the firm's chief financial officer and indicate the primary responsibilities of each.

## ALTERNATIVE FORMS OF BUSINESS ORGANIZATION

There are three main forms of business organization: (1) proprietorships, (2) partnerships, and (3) corporations. In terms of numbers, approximately 72 percent of businesses are operated as proprietorships, 8 percent are partnerships, and the remaining 20 percent are corporations. Based on the dollar value of sales, however, almost 85 percent of all business is conducted by corporations, while the remaining 15 percent is generated by both proprietorships (4 percent) and partnerships (11 percent).[5] Because most business is conducted by corporations, we will focus on that form in this book. However, it is important to understand the differences among the three major forms of business, as well as the popular "hybrid" forms of business that have evolved from these major forms.

## Proprietorship

**proprietorship**
An unincorporated business owned by one individual.

A **proprietorship** is an unincorporated business owned by one individual. Starting a proprietorship is fairly easy—just begin business operations. In many cases, however, even the smallest business must be licensed by the municipality (city, county, or state) in which it operates.

The proprietorship has three important advantages:

1. It is easily and inexpensively formed.
2. It is subject to few government regulations. Large firms that potentially threaten competition are much more heavily regulated than small "mom-and-pop" businesses.
3. It is taxed like an individual, not a corporation; thus, earnings are taxed only once.

---

[5]The statistics provided in this section are based on business tax filings reported by the Internal Revenue Service (IRS) in 2006. Additional statistics can be found on the IRS website at http://www.irs.ustreas.gov/tax_stats.

**FIGURE 1-1**  Role of Finance in a Typical Business Organization

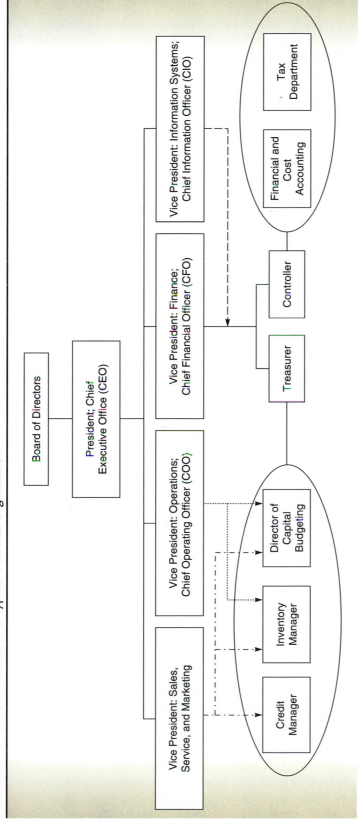

The proprietorship also has four important limitations:

1. The proprietor has *unlimited personal liability* for business debts. With unlimited personal liability, the proprietor (owner) can potentially lose all of his or her personal assets, even those assets not invested in the business; thus, losses can far exceed the money that he or she has invested in the company.

2. A proprietorship's life is limited to the time the individual who created it owns the business. When a new owner takes over the business, technically the firm becomes a new proprietorship (even if the name of the business does not change).

3. Transferring ownership is somewhat difficult. Disposing of the business is similar to selling a house in that the proprietor must seek out and negotiate with a potential buyer.

4. It is difficult for a proprietorship to obtain large sums of capital because the firm's financial strength generally is based on the financial strength of the sole owner.

For the reasons mentioned here, individual proprietorships are confined primarily to small business operations. In fact, only about 1 percent of all proprietorships have assets that are valued at $1 million or greater; nearly 90 percent have assets valued at $100,000 or less. However, most large businesses start out as proprietorships and then convert to corporations when their growth causes the disadvantages of being a proprietorship—namely, unlimited personal liability—to outweigh the advantages.

## Partnership

**partnership**
An unincorporated business owned by two or more people.

A **partnership** is the same as a proprietorship, except that it has two or more owners. Partnerships can operate under different degrees of formality, ranging from informal, oral understandings to formal agreements filed with the secretary of the state in which the partnership does business. Most legal experts recommend that partnership agreements be put in writing.

The advantages of a partnership are the same as for a proprietorship:

1. Formation is easy and relatively inexpensive.
2. It is subject to few government regulations.
3. It is taxed like an individual, not a corporation.

The disadvantages are also similar to those associated with proprietorships:

1. Owners have unlimited personal liability.
2. The life of the organization is limited.
3. Transferring ownership is difficult.
4. Raising large amounts of capital is difficult.

Under partnership law, each partner is liable for the debts of the business. Therefore, if any partner is unable to meet his or her pro rata claim in the event the partnership goes bankrupt, the remaining partners must make good on the unsatisfied claims, drawing on their personal assets if necessary. Thus, the business-related activities of any of the firm's partners can bring ruin to the other partners, even though those partners are not a direct party to such activities.

The first three disadvantages—unlimited liability, impermanence of the organization, and difficulty of transferring ownership—lead to the fourth, the difficulty partnerships have in attracting substantial amounts of funds. This is not a major problem for a slow-growing business. But if a business's products really catch on and it needs to raise large amounts of funds to capitalize on its opportunities, the difficulty in attracting funds becomes a real drawback. For this reason, growth companies such as Microsoft Corporation and Dell Inc. generally begin life as proprietorships or partnerships, but at some point they find it necessary to convert to corporations.

## Corporation

A **corporation** is a legal entity created by a state. It is separate and distinct from its owners and managers. This separateness gives the corporation four major advantages:

**corporation**
A legal entity created by a state, separate and distinct from its owners and managers, having unlimited life, easy transferability of ownership, and limited liability.

1. A corporation can continue after its original owners and managers no longer have a relationship with the business; thus, it is said to have *unlimited life*.

2. Ownership interests can be divided into shares of stock, which in turn can be *transferred far more easily* than can proprietorship or partnership interests.

3. A corporation offers its owners *limited liability*. To illustrate the concept of limited liability, suppose you invested $10,000 to become a partner in a business that subsequently went bankrupt, owing creditors $1 million. Because the owners are liable for the debts of a partnership, as a partner, you would be assessed for a share of the company's debt; you could even be held liable for the entire $1 million if your partners could not pay their shares. This is the danger of unlimited liability. On the other hand, if you invested $10,000 in the stock of a corporation that then went bankrupt, your potential loss on the investment would be limited to your $10,000 investment.[6]

4. The first three factors—unlimited life, easy transferability of ownership interest, and limited liability—make it much easier for corporations than for proprietorships or partnerships to raise money in the financial markets.

Even though the corporate form of business offers significant advantages over proprietorships and partnerships, it does have two major disadvantages:

1. Setting up a corporation, as well as subsequent filings of required state and federal reports, is more complex and time consuming than for a proprietorship or a partnership. When a corporation is created, (a) a **corporate charter,** which provides general information, including the name of the corporation, types of activities it will pursue, amount of stock, and so forth, must be filed with the secretary of the state in which the firm incorporates; and (b) a set of rules, called **bylaws,** that specifies how the corporation will be governed must be drawn up by the founder.

2. Corporate earnings are subject to double taxation—the earnings of the corporation are taxed at the corporate level, and then any earnings paid out as dividends are again taxed as income to stockholders.[7]

**corporate charter**
A document filed with the secretary of the state in which a business is incorporated that provides information about the company, including its name, address, directors, and amount of capital stock.

## Hybrid Business Forms—LLP, LLC, and S Corporation

Alternative business forms that include some of the advantages, as well as avoid some of the disadvantages, of the three major forms of business have evolved over time. These alternative forms of business combine some characteristics of proprietorships

**bylaws**
A set of rules drawn up by the founders of the corporation that indicate how the company is to be governed; includes procedures for electing directors, the rights of the stockholders, and how to change the bylaws when necessary.

---

[6]In the case of small corporations, the limited liability feature is often a fiction because bankers and credit managers frequently require personal guarantees from the stockholders of small, weak businesses.

[7]There was a push in Congress in 2003 to eliminate the double taxation of dividends by either treating dividends paid by corporations the same as interest—that is, making them a tax-deductible expense—or allowing dividends to be tax exempt to stockholders. Congress passed neither; instead, the tax on dividends received by investors was reduced from the ordinary tax rate to the capital gains rate. Taxes will be discussed briefly later in this book.

and partnerships with some characteristics of corporations. In this section, we provide a brief description of three popular *hybrid business forms* that exist today.

## Limited Liability Partnership (LLP)

**limited liability partnership (LLP)**
A partnership wherein one (or more) partner is designated the *general partner(s)* with unlimited personal financial liability and the other partners are limited partners whose liability is limited to amounts they invest in the firm.

In the earlier discussion of a partnership, we described the form of business that generally is referred to as a *general partnership*, where each partner is personally liable for the debts of the business. It is possible to limit the liability faced by some of the partners by establishing a **limited liability partnership (LLP),** wherein one (or more) partner is designated the *general partner(s)* and the others are *limited partners*. The general partner(s) remains fully personally liable for all business debts, whereas the limited partners are liable only for the amounts they have invested in the business. Only the general partners can participate in the management of the business. If a limited partner becomes involved in the day-to-day management of the firm, then he or she no longer has the protection of limited personal liability. The LLP form of business allows people to invest in partnerships without exposure to the personal financial liability that general partners face.

## Limited Liability Company (LLC)

**limited liability company (LLC)**
Offers the limited personal liability associated with a corporation, but the company's income is taxed like a partnership.

A **limited liability company (LLC)** is a legal entity that is separate and distinct from its owners and managers. An LLC offers the limited personal liability associated with a corporation, but the company's income is taxed like a partnership in that it passes through to the owners (it is taxed only once). The structure of the LLC is fairly flexible— owners generally can divide liability, management responsibilities, ownership shares, and control of the business any way they please. Like a corporation, paperwork (articles of organization) must be filed with the state in which the business is set up, and there are certain financial reporting requirements after the formation of an LLC.[8]

## S Corporation

**S corporation**
A corporation with no more than 75 stockholders that elects to be taxed the same as proprietorships and partnerships so that business income is taxed only once.

A domestic corporation that has no more than 75 stockholders and only one type of stock outstanding can elect to file taxes as an **S corporation.** If a corporation elects the S corporation status, then its income is taxed the same as income earned by proprietorships and partnerships—that is, income "passes through" the company to the owners so that it is taxed only once. The major differences between an S corporation and an LLC is that an LLC can have more than 75 stockholders and more than one type of stock.

For the following reasons, the value of any business, other than a very small concern, probably will be maximized if it is organized as a corporation:

1. Limited liability reduces the risks borne by investors. Other things held constant, *the lower the firm's risk, the higher its market value.*
2. *A firm's current value is related to its future growth opportunities,* and corporations can attract funds more easily than can unincorporated businesses to take advantage of growth opportunities.
3. Corporate ownership can be transferred more easily than ownership of either a proprietorship or a partnership. Therefore, all else equal, investors would be willing to pay more for a corporation than a proprietorship or partnership,

---

[8] Some states designate the types of businesses that can be LLCs. For example, often law firms and accounting firms can be formed as LLCs.

which means that the corporate form of organization can *enhance the value* of a business.

Most firms are managed with value maximization in mind, and this in turn has caused most large businesses to be organized as corporations.

**Self-Test Questions**

What are the key differences among proprietorships, partnerships, and corporations?

Explain why the value of any business (other than a small firm) will be maximized if it is organized as a corporation.

## WHAT GOAL(S) SHOULD BUSINESSES PURSUE?

Depending on the form of business, the primary goal of a firm might differ somewhat. But in general, every business owner wants the value of his or her investment in the firm to increase. The owner of a proprietorship has direct control over his or her investment in the company because it is the proprietor who runs the business. As a result, a proprietor might choose to work three days per week and play golf or fish the rest of the week as long as the business remains successful and he or she is satisfied living this type of life. On the other hand, the owners (stockholders) of a large corporation have very little control over their investments because they generally do not run the business. Because they are not involved in the day-to-day decisions, these stockholders expect that the managers who run the business do so with the best interests of the owners in mind.

Investors purchase the stock of a corporation because they expect to earn an acceptable return on the money they invest. Because we know investors want to increase their wealth positions as much as possible, all else equal, then it follows that managers should behave in a manner that is consistent with enhancing the firm's value. For this reason, throughout this book we operate on the assumption that management's primary goal is **stockholder wealth maximization,** which, as we will see, translates into maximizing the value of the firm as measured by the price of its common stock. Firms do, of course, have other objectives: In particular, managers who make the actual decisions are interested in their own personal satisfaction, in their employees' welfare, and in the good of the community and of society at large. Still, *stock price maximization is the most important goal of most corporations.*

If a firm attempts to maximize its stock price, is this good or is this bad for society? In general, it is good. Aside from such illegal actions as attempting to form monopolies, violating safety codes, and failing to meet pollution control requirements, *the same actions that maximize stock prices also benefit society.* First, note that stock price maximization requires efficient, low-cost plants that produce high-quality goods and services that are sold at the lowest possible prices. Second, stock price maximization requires the development of products that consumers want and need, so the profit motive leads to new technology, new products, and new jobs. Finally, stock price maximization necessitates efficient and courteous service, adequate stocks of merchandise, and well-located business establishments. These factors all are necessary to maintain a customer base that is required for producing sales and thus profits. Therefore, most actions that help a firm increase the price of its stock also are beneficial to society at large. This is why profit-motivated, free-enterprise economies have been so much more successful than socialistic and

**stockholder wealth maximization**
The appropriate goal for management decisions; considers the risk and timing associated with expected cash flows to maximize the price of the firm's common stock.

communistic economic systems. Because managerial finance plays a crucial role in the operation of successful firms, and because successful firms are necessary for a healthy, productive economy, it is easy to see why finance is important from a social standpoint.[9]

 **Self-Test Questions**

What should be management's primary goal?

How does the goal of stock price maximization benefit society at large?

## MANAGERIAL ACTIONS TO MAXIMIZE SHAREHOLDER WEALTH

How do we measure value, and what types of actions can management take to maximize value? Although we will discuss valuation in much greater detail later in the book, we introduce the concept of value here to give you an indication of how management can affect the price of a company's stock. First, the value of any investment, such as a stock, is based on the amount of cash flows the asset is expected to generate during its life. Second, investors prefer to receive a particular cash flow sooner rather than later. And, third, investors generally are risk averse, which means that they are willing to pay more for investments with more certain future cash flows than investments with less certain, or riskier, cash flows, everything else equal. For these reasons, we know that managers can increase the value of a firm by making decisions that increase the firm's expected future cash flows, generate the expected cash flows sooner, increase the certainty of the expected cash flows, or produce any combination of these actions.

The financial manager makes decisions about the expected cash flows of the firm, which include decisions about how much and what types of debt and equity should be used to finance the firm **(capital structure decisions)**, what types of assets should be purchased to help generate expected cash flows **(capital budgeting decisions)**, and what to do with net cash flows generated by the firm—reinvest in the firm or pay dividends **(dividend policy decisions)**. Each of these topics will be addressed in detail later in the book. But at this point, it should be clear that the decisions financial managers make can significantly affect the firm's value because they affect the amount, timing, and riskiness of the cash flows the firm produces.

Although managerial actions affect the value of a firm's stock, external factors also influence stock prices. Included among these factors are legal constraints, the general level of economic activity, tax laws, and conditions in the financial markets. Working within the set of external constraints, management makes a set of long-run strategic policy decisions that chart a future course for the firm. These policy decisions, along with the general level of economic activity and government regulations and rules (for instance, tax payments), influence the firm's expected

**capital structure decisions**
Decisions about how much and what types of debt and equity should be used to finance the firm.

**capital budgeting decisions**
Decisions as to what types of assets should be purchased to help generate future cash flows.

**dividend policy decisions**
Decisions concerning how much of current earnings to pay out as dividends rather than retain for reinvestment in the firm.

[9]People sometimes argue that firms, in their efforts to raise profits and stock prices, increase product prices and gouge the public. In a reasonably competitive economy, which we have, prices are constrained by competition and consumer resistance. If a firm raises its prices beyond reasonable levels, it will simply lose its market share. Even giant firms like General Motors lose business to the Japanese and Germans, as well as to Ford and Chrysler, if they set prices above levels necessary to cover production costs and earn a "normal" profit. Of course, firms want to earn more, and they constantly try to cut costs or develop new products and thereby to earn above-normal profits. Note, though, that if they are indeed successful and do earn above-normal profits, those very profits will attract competition that will eventually drive prices down, so again the main long-term beneficiary is the consumer.

**FIGURE 1-2**  Value of the Firm

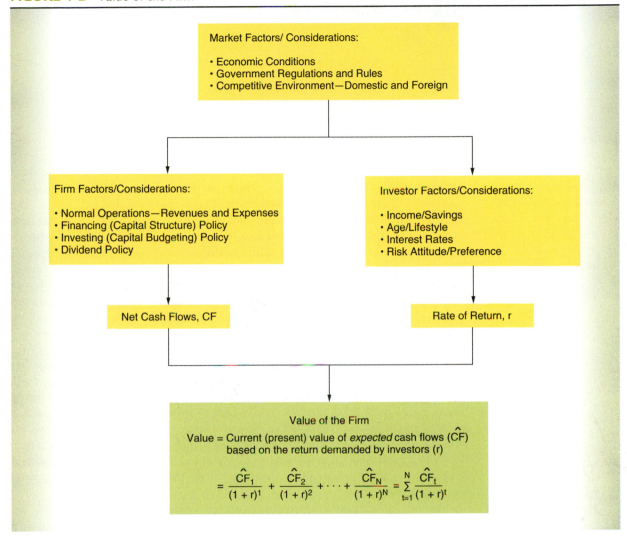

cash flows, the timing of these cash flows and their eventual transfer to stock-holders in the form of dividends, and the degree of risk inherent in the expected cash flows.

Figure 1-2 diagrams the general relationships involved in the valuation process. As you can see, and we will discuss in much greater detail throughout the book, a firm's value is ultimately a function of the cash flows it is expected to generate in the future and the rate of return at which investors are willing to provide funds to the firm for the purposes of financing operations and growth. Many factors, including conditions in the economy and financial markets, the competitive environment, and the general operations of the firm, affect the determination of the expected cash flows and the rate people demand when investing their funds. As we progress through the book, we will discuss these and other factors that affect a firm's value. For now, however, it is important to know that when we refer to **value,** we mean the worth of the expected future cash flows stated in current dollars—that is, the present, or current, value of the future cash flows associated with an asset.

**value**

The present, or current, value of the cash flows an asset is expected to generate in the future.

**Self-Test Questions**

Identify some decisions made by financial managers that affect the firm's value.

Identify some factors beyond a firm's control that influence its stock price.

## SHOULD EARNINGS PER SHARE (EPS) BE MAXIMIZED?

**profit maximization**
Maximization of the firm's net income.

**earnings per share (EPS)**
Net income divided by the number of shares of common stock outstanding.

Will **profit maximization** also result in stock price maximization? In answering this question, we introduce the concept of **earnings per share (EPS),** which equals net income (NI) divided by the number of outstanding shares of common stock (Shares)—that is, NI/Shares. Many investors use EPS to gauge the value of a stock. A primary reason EPS receives so much attention is the belief that net income, and thus EPS, can be used as a barometer for measuring the firm's potential for generating future cash flows. Although current earnings and cash flows are generally highly correlated, as we mentioned earlier, a firm's value is determined by the cash flows it is expected to generate in the future as well as the risk associated with these expected cash flows. Thus, financial managers who attempt to maximize earnings might not maximize value because earnings maximization is a shortsighted goal. Most managers who focus solely on earnings generally do not consider the impact that maximizing earnings in the current period has on either future earnings (timing) or the firm's future risk position.

First, think about the *timing of the earnings.* Suppose Xerox has a project that will cause earnings per share to rise by $0.20 per year for five years, or $1 in total, whereas another project would have no effect on earnings for four years but would increase EPS by $1.25 in the fifth year. Which project is better—in other words, is $0.20 per year for five years better or worse than $1.25 in Year 5? The answer depends on which project contributes the most to the value of the firm, which in turn depends on the time value of money to investors. Thus, timing is an important reason to concentrate on wealth as measured by the price of the stock rather than on earnings alone.

Second, consider *risk.* Suppose one project is expected to increase EPS by $1, while another is expected to increase earnings by $1.20 per share. The first project is not very risky. If it is undertaken, earnings will almost certainly rise by approximately $1 per share. However, the other project is quite risky. Although our best guess is that earnings will rise by $1.20 per share, we must recognize the possibility that there might be no increase whatsoever, or the firm might even suffer a loss. Depending on how averse stockholders are to risk, the first project might be preferable to the second.

In many instances, firms have taken actions that increased earnings per share, yet the stock price decreased because investors believed that either the higher earnings would not be sustained in the future or the riskiness of the firm would be increased substantially. Of course, the opposite effect has been observed as well. We see, then, that the firm's stock price, and thus its value, is dependent on (1) the cash flows the firm is expected to provide in the future, (2) when these cash flows are expected to occur, and (3) the risk associated with these cash flows. As we proceed through the book, you will discover that, everything else equal, the firm's value increases if the cash flows the firm is expected to provide increase, they are received sooner, their risk is lowered, or some combination of these actions occurs. Every significant corporate decision should be analyzed in terms of its effect on the firm's value, and hence the price of its stock.

**Self-Test Questions**

Will profit maximization always result in stock price maximization?

Identify three factors that affect the value of the firm, and explain the effects of each.

## MANAGERS' ROLES AS AGENTS OF STOCKHOLDERS

Because they generally are not involved in the day-to-day operations, stockholders of large corporations "permit" (empower) the managers to make decisions as to how the firms are run. Of course, the stockholders want the managers to make decisions that are consistent with the goal of wealth maximization. However, managers' interests can potentially conflict with stockholders' interests.

An *agency relationship* exists when one or more individuals, who are called the *principals*, hire another person, the *agent*, to perform a service and delegate decision-making authority to that agent. An **agency problem** arises when the agent makes decisions that are not in the best interests of the principals.

If a firm is a proprietorship managed by the owner, the owner-manager will presumably operate the business in a fashion that will improve his or her own welfare, with welfare measured in the form of increased personal wealth, more leisure, or perquisites.[10] However, if the owner-manager incorporates and sells some of the firm's stock to outsiders, a potential conflict of interest immediately arises. For example, the owner-manager might now decide not to work as hard to maximize shareholder wealth because less of the firm's wealth will go to him or her or might decide to take a higher salary or enjoy more perquisites because part of those costs will fall on the outside stockholders. This potential conflict between two parties—the principals (outside shareholders) and the agents (managers)—is an agency problem.

The potential for agency problems is greatest in large corporations with widely dispersed ownership—for example, IBM and General Motors—because individual stockholders own very small proportions of the companies and managers have little, if any, of their own wealth tied up in these companies. For this reason, managers might be more concerned about pursuing their own agendas, such as increased job security, higher salary, or more power, than maximizing shareholder wealth.

What can be done to ensure that management treats outside stockholders fairly at the same time the goal of wealth maximization is pursued? Several mechanisms are used to motivate managers to act in the shareholders' best interests. These include the following:

1. **Managerial compensation (incentives).** A common method used to motivate managers to operate in a manner consistent with stock price maximization is to tie managers' compensation to the company's performance. Such compensation packages should be developed so that managers are rewarded on the basis of the firm's performance over a long period of time, not on the performance in any particular year. For example, Dell uses performance targets based on growth in sales and profit margins relative to industry measures and such nonfinancial factors as customer satisfaction and product leadership. If the company achieves a targeted average growth in earnings per share, managers earn 100 percent of a specified reward. If the performance is above the target, higher rewards can

**agency problem**
A potential conflict of interest between outside shareholders (owners) and managers who make decisions about how to operate the firm.

---

[10]Perquisites are executive fringe benefits, such as luxurious offices, use of corporate planes and yachts, personal assistants, and general use of business assets for personal purposes.

be earned, whereas managers receive lower rewards when performance is below the target. Often the reward that managers receive is the stock of the company. If managers own stock in the company, they are motivated to make decisions that will increase the firm's value and thus the value of the stock they own.

All incentive compensation plans are designed to accomplish two things: (a) provide inducements to executives to act on those factors under their control in a manner that will contribute to stock price maximization and (b) attract and retain top-level executives. Well-designed plans can accomplish both goals.

2. **Shareholder intervention.** More than 25 percent of the individuals in the United States invest *directly* in stocks. Along with such institutional stockholders as pension funds and mutual funds, individual stockholders are "flexing their muscles" to ensure that firms pursue goals that are in the best interests of shareholders rather than managers (where conflicts might arise). Many institutional investors, especially pension funds such as TIAA-CREF and Laborers International Union of North America, routinely monitor top corporations to ensure that managers pursue the goal of wealth maximization. When it is determined that action is needed to "realign" management decisions with the interests of investors, these institutional investors exercise their influence by suggesting possible remedies to management or by sponsoring proposals that must be voted on by stockholders at the annual meeting. Stockholder-sponsored proposals are not binding, but the results of the votes are surely noticed by corporate management.

In situations where large blocks of the stock are owned by a relatively few large institutions, such as pension funds and mutual funds, and they have enough clout to influence a firm's operations, these institutional owners often have enough voting power to overthrow management teams that do not act in the best interests of stockholders. Examples of major corporations whose managements have been ousted in recent years include Coca-Cola, General Motors, IBM, Lucent Technologies, United Airlines, and Xerox.

**hostile takeover**
The acquisition of a company over the opposition of its management.

3. **Threat of takeover. Hostile takeovers,** instances in which management does not want the firm to be taken over, are most likely to occur when a firm's stock is undervalued relative to its potential, which often is caused by poor management. In a hostile takeover, the managers of the acquired firm generally are fired, and those who do stay on typically lose the power they had prior to the acquisition. Thus, managers have a strong incentive to take actions that maximize stock prices. In the words of one company president, "If you want to keep control, don't let your company's stock sell at a bargain price."

Wealth maximization is a long-term goal, not a short-term goal. For this reason, when executives are rewarded for maximizing the price of the firm's stock, the reward should be based on the long-run performance of the stock. Because the goal of wealth maximization is achieved over time, management must be able to convey to stockholders that their best interests are being pursued. As you proceed through the book, you will discover that many factors affect the value of a stock, which makes it difficult to determine precisely when management is acting in the stockholders' best interests. However, a firm's management team will find it difficult to "fool" investors, both in general and for a long period—stockholders can generally differentiate when a firm makes a major decision that is value increasing, and vice versa.

**Self-Test Questions**

What is an agency relationship?

Give some examples of potential problems between stockholders and managers.

List some factors that motivate managers to act in the best interests of stockholders.

## BUSINESS ETHICS

The word *ethics* can be defined as "standards of conduct or moral behavior." **Business ethics** can be thought of as a company's attitude and conduct toward its employees, customers, community, and stockholders. High standards of ethical behavior demand that a firm treat each party with which it deals in a fair and honest manner. A firm's commitment to business ethics can be measured by the tendency of the firm and its employees to adhere to laws and regulations relating to such factors as product safety and quality, fair employment practices, fair marketing and selling practices, the use of confidential information for personal gain, community involvement, bribery, and illegal payments to foreign governments to obtain business.

Although most firms have policies that espouse ethical business conduct, there are many instances of large corporations that have engaged in unethical behavior. For example, companies such as Arthur Andersen, Enron, and WorldCom MCI have fallen or been changed significantly as the result of unethical, and sometimes illegal, practices. In some cases, employees (generally top management) have been sentenced to prison for illegal actions that resulted from unethical behavior. In recent years, the number of high-profile instances in which unethical behavior has resulted in substantial gains to executives at the expense of stockholders' positions has increased to the point where public outcry resulted in legislation aimed at arresting the apparent tide of unethical behavior in the corporate world. As a result of the large number of recent scandals disclosed by major corporations, Congress passed the Sarbanes-Oxley Act of 2002. A major reason for the legislation was that accounting scandals caused the public to be skeptical of accounting and financial information reported by large U.S. corporations. Simply put, the public no longer trusted what managers said. Investors felt that executives were pursuing interests that too often resulted in large gains for themselves and large losses for stockholders.

The 11 "titles" in the Sarbanes-Oxley Act of 2002 establish standards for accountability and responsibility of reporting financial information for major corporations. The act provides that a corporation must (1) have a committee that consists of outside directors to oversee the firm's audits, (2) hire an external auditing firm that will render an unbiased (independent) opinion concerning the firm's financial statements, and (3) provide additional information about the procedures used to construct and report financial statements. In addition, the firm's CEO and CFO must certify financial reports submitted to the Securities and Exchange Commission. The act also stiffens the criminal penalties that can be imposed for producing fraudulent financial information and provides regulatory bodies with greater authority to enact prosecution for such actions.

Despite the recent decline in investor trust of financial reporting by corporations, the executives of most major firms in the United States believe their firms should, and do, try to maintain high ethical standards in all of their business dealings. Further, most executives believe that there is a positive correlation between ethics and long-run profitability because ethical behavior (1) prevents fines and legal expenses, (2) builds

**business ethics**
A company's attitude and conduct toward its stakeholders—employees, customers, stockholders, and so forth; ethical behavior requires fair and honest treatment of all parties.

public trust, (3) attracts business from customers who appreciate and support ethical policies, (4) attracts and keeps employees of the highest caliber, and (5) supports the economic viability of the communities where these firms operate.

Today most firms have in place strong codes of ethical behavior, and they conduct training programs designed to ensure that all employees understand the correct behavior in different business situations. It is imperative that top management—the company's chairman, president, and vice presidents—be openly committed to ethical behavior and that they communicate this commitment through their own personal actions as well as through company policies, directives, and punishment/reward systems. Clearly, investors expect nothing less.

**Self-Test Questions**

How would you define *business ethics?*

Is "being ethical" good for profits and firm value in the long run? In the short run?

## CORPORATE GOVERNANCE

**corporate governance**
The "set of rules" that a firm follows when conducting business; these rules identify who is accountable for major financial decisions.

**stakeholders**
Those who are associated with a business; stakeholders include mangers, employees, customers, suppliers, creditors, stockholders, and other parties with an interest in the firm.

The term *corporate governance* has become a regular part of business vocabulary in recent years. As a result of the scandals uncovered at Arthur Andersen, Enron, WorldCom MCI, and many other companies, stockholders, managers, and Congress have become quite concerned with how firms are operated. **Corporate governance** deals with the "set of rules" that a firm follows when conducting business. Together these rules provide the "road map" that managers follow to pursue the various goals of the firm, including maximizing its stock price. It is important for a firm to clearly specify its corporate governance structure so that individuals and entities that have an interest in the well-being of the business understand how their interests will be pursued. A good corporate governance structure should provide those who have a relationship with a firm—that is, the **stakeholders**—with an understanding as to how executives run the business and who is accountable for important decisions. As a result of the Sarbanes-Oxley Act of 2002 and increased stockholder pressure, firms are revising their corporate governance policies so that all stakeholders—managers, stockholders, creditors, customers, suppliers, and employees—better understand their rights and responsibilities.[11] And, from our previous discussions, it should be clear that maximizing shareholder wealth requires the fair treatment of all stakeholders.

Studies show that firms that follow good corporate governance generate higher returns to stockholders. Good corporate governance includes a board of directors with members that are independent of the company's management. An independent board generally serves as a "checks and balances" system that monitors important management decisions, including executive compensation. It has also been shown that firms that develop governance structures that make it easier to identify and correct accounting problems and potentially unethical or fraudulent practices perform better than firms that have poor governance policies (internal controls).[12]

---

[11]Broadly speaking, the term *stakeholders* should include the environment in which we live and do business. It should be apparent that a firm cannot survive—that is, remain sustainable—unless it fairly treats both human stakeholders and environmental stakeholders. A firm that destroys either the trust of its employees, customers, and shareholders or the environment in which it operates, destroys itself.

[12]See, for example, Reshma Kapadia, "Stocks Reward Firms' Good Behavior," *The Wall Street Journal Online,* March 18, 2006, and David Reilly, "Checks on Internal Controls Pay Off," *The Wall Street Journal,* May 8, 2006, C3.

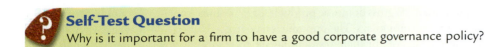

**Self-Test Question**
Why is it important for a firm to have a good corporate governance policy?

## FORMS OF BUSINESSES IN OTHER COUNTRIES

U.S. corporations can best be described as "open" companies because they are publicly traded organizations that, for the most part, are independent of each other and of the government. As we described earlier, such companies offer limited liability to owners who usually do not participate in the day-to-day operations and who can easily transfer ownership by trading stock in the financial markets. While most developed countries with free economies have business organizations that are similar to U.S. corporations, some differences exist relating to ownership structure and management of operations. Although a comprehensive discussion is beyond the scope of this book, this section provides some examples of differences between U.S. companies and non-U.S. companies.

Firms in most developed economies, such as corporations in the United States, offer equities with limited liability to stockholders that can be traded in domestic financial markets. However, such firms are not always called corporations. For instance, a comparable firm in England is called a *public limited company,* or PLC, while in Germany it is known as an *Aktiengesellschaft,* or AG. In Mexico, Spain, and Latin America, such a company is called a *Sociedad Anónima,* or SA. Some of these firms are publicly traded, whereas others are privately held.

Like corporations in the United States, most large companies in England and Canada are "open," and their stocks are widely dispersed among a large number of different investors. Of note, however, is that two-thirds of the traded stocks of English companies are owned by institutional investors rather than individuals. On the other hand, in much of continental Europe, stock ownership is more concentrated; major investor groups include families, banks, and other corporations. In Germany and France, for instance, corporations represent the primary group of shareholders, followed by families. Although banks do not hold a large number of shares of stock, they can greatly influence companies because many shareholders assign banks their **proxy votes** for the directors of the companies. Also, often the family unit has concentrated ownership and thus is a major influence in many large companies in developed countries such as these. The ownership structures of these firms and many other non-U.S. companies, including very large organizations, often are concentrated in the hands of a relatively few investors or investment groups. Such firms are considered "closed" because shares of stock are not publicly traded, relatively few individuals or groups own the stock, and major stockholders often are involved in the firms' daily operations.

The primary reason non-U.S. firms are likely to be more closed, and thus have more concentrated ownership, than U.S. firms results from the "universal" banking relationships that exist outside the United States. Financial institutions in other countries generally are less regulated than in the United States, which means foreign banks, for instance, can provide businesses a greater variety of services, including short-term loans, long-term financing, and even stock ownership. These services are available at many locations, or branches, throughout the country. As a result, non-U.S. firms tend to have close relationships with individual banking organizations that also might take ownership positions in the companies. What this means is that banks in countries like Germany can meet the financing needs of family-owned businesses, even if they are very large. Therefore, such companies need not "go public," and thus relinquish control, to finance additional growth. Consider the fact that in both France and Germany approximately

**proxy votes**
Voting power that is assigned to another party, such as another stockholder or institution.

75 percent of the gross domestic product (GDP) comes from firms not publicly traded—that is, closed businesses. The opposite is true in the United States, where large firms do not have "one-stop" financing outlets; hence, their growth generally must be financed by bringing in outside owners, which results in more widely dispersed ownership.

**industrial groups**
Organizations composed of companies in different industries with common ownership interests, which include firms necessary to manufacture and sell products—a network of manufacturers, suppliers, marketing organizations, distributors, retailers, and creditors.

In some parts of the world, firms belong to **industrial groups,** which are organizations composed of companies in different industries with common ownership interests and, in some instances, shared management. Firms in the industrial group are "tied" by a major lender, typically a bank, which often also has a significant ownership interest along with other firms in the group. The objective of an industrial group is to include firms that provide materials and services required to manufacture and sell products—that is, to create an organization that ties together all the functions of production and sales from start to finish. Thus, an industrial group encompasses firms involved in manufacturing, financing, marketing, and distribution of products, which includes suppliers of raw materials, production organizations, retail stores, and creditors. A portion of the stocks of firms that are members of an industrial group might be traded publicly, but the "lead" company, which is typically a major creditor, controls the management of the entire group. Industrial groups are most prominent in Asian countries. In Japan, an industrial group is called a *keiretsu,* and it is called a *chaebol* in Korea. Well-known *keiretsu* groups include Mitsubishi, Toshiba, and Toyota, while the best-known *chaebol* probably is Hyundai. The success of industrial groups in Japan and Korea has inspired the formation of similar organizations in developing countries in Latin America and Africa as well as other parts of Asia.

The differences in ownership concentration of non-U.S. firms might cause the behavior of managers, and thus the goals they pursue, to differ. For instance, often it is argued that the greater concentration of ownership of non-U.S. firms permits managers to focus more on long-term objectives, especially wealth maximization, than short-term earnings because firms have easier access to credit in times of financial difficulty. In other words, creditors who also are owners generally have greater interest in supporting short-term survival. On the other hand, it also has been argued that the ownership structures of non-U.S. firms create an environment in which it is difficult to change managers, especially if they are significant stockholders. Such entrenchment could be detrimental to firms if management is inefficient. Consider, for example, firms in Japan that generally are reluctant to fire employees because losing one's job is a disgrace in the Japanese culture. Whether the ownership structure of non-U.S. firms is an advantage or a disadvantage is debatable. But we do know that the greater concentration of ownership in non-U.S. firms permits greater monitoring and control by individuals or groups than the more dispersed ownership structures of U.S. firms.

**Self-Test Questions**

What is the primary difference between U.S. corporations and non-U.S. firms?

What is an industrial group?

What are some of the names given to firms in other countries?

## MULTINATIONAL CORPORATIONS

Large firms, both in the United States and in other countries, generally do not operate in a single country; rather, they conduct business throughout the world. In fact, the largest firms in the world truly are multinational rather than domestic operations. Managers of such multinational companies face a wide range of issues that are not present when a company operates in a single country. This section highlights the key differences between multinational and domestic corporations and the impacts these differences have on managerial finance for U.S. businesses.

The term **multinational corporation** is used to describe a firm that operates in two or more countries. Rather than merely buying resources from foreign concerns, multinational firms make direct investments in fully integrated operations, with worldwide entities controlling all phases of the production process, from extraction of raw materials, through the manufacturing process, to distribution to consumers throughout the world. Today, multinational corporate networks control a large and growing share of the world's technological, marketing, and productive resources.

> **multinational corporation**
> A firm that operates in two or more countries.

U.S. and foreign companies "go international" for the following major reasons:

1. **To seek new markets.** After a company has saturated its home market, growth opportunities often are better in foreign markets. As a result, such homegrown firms as Coca-Cola and McDonald's have aggressively expanded into overseas markets, and foreign firms such as Sony and Toshiba are major competitors in the U.S. consumer electronics market.

2. **To seek raw materials.** Many U.S. oil companies, such as ExxonMobil, have major subsidiaries around the world to ensure they have continued access to the basic resources needed to sustain their primary lines of business.

3. **To seek new technology.** No single nation holds a commanding advantage in all technologies, so companies scour the globe for leading scientific and design ideas. For example, Xerox has introduced more than 80 different office copiers in the United States that were engineered and built by its Japanese joint venture, Fuji Xerox.

4. **To seek production efficiency.** Companies in countries where production costs are high tend to shift production to low-cost countries. For example, General Motors has production and assembly plants in Mexico and Brazil, and even Japanese manufacturers have shifted some of their production to lower-cost countries in the Pacific Rim. The ability to shift production from country to country has important implications for labor costs in all countries. For example, when Xerox threatened to move its copier rebuilding work to Mexico, its union in Rochester, New York, agreed to work rule and productivity improvements that kept the operation in the United States.

5. **To avoid political and regulatory hurdles.** Many years ago, Japanese auto companies moved production to the United States to get around U.S. import quotas. Now, Honda, Nissan, and Toyota all assemble automobiles or trucks in the United States. Similarly, one of the factors that prompted U.S. pharmaceutical maker SmithKline and UK drug company Beecham to merge in 1989 was the desire to avoid licensing and regulatory delays in their largest markets. Now, GlaxoSmithKline, as the company is known, can identify itself as an inside player in both Europe and the United States.

Since the 1980s, investments in the United States by foreign corporations have increased significantly. This "reverse" investment has created concerns for U.S. government officials, who contend it could erode the doctrine of independence and self-reliance that has traditionally been a hallmark of U.S. policy. Just as U.S. corporations with extensive overseas operations are said to use their economic power to exert substantial economic and political influence over host governments around the world, it is feared that foreign corporations might gain similar influence over U.S. policy. These developments also suggest an increasing degree of mutual influence and interdependence among business enterprises and nations, to which the United States is not immune. Political and social developments that influence the world economy also influence U.S. businesses and financial markets.

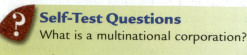

**Self-Test Questions**

What is a multinational corporation?

Why do companies "go international"?

## MULTINATIONAL VERSUS DOMESTIC MANAGERIAL FINANCE

In theory, the concepts and procedures discussed in the remaining chapters of this book are valid for both domestic and multinational operations. However, several problems uniquely associated with the international environment increase the complexity of the manager's task in a multinational corporation, and they often force the manager to change the way alternative courses of action are evaluated and compared. Six major factors distinguish managerial finance as practiced by firms operating entirely within a single country from management by firms that operate in several different countries:

1. **Different currency denominations.** Cash flows in various parts of a multinational corporate system often are denominated in different currencies. Hence, an analysis of **exchange rates** and the effects of fluctuating currency values must be included in all financial analyses.

**exchange rates**
The prices at which the currency from one country can be converted into the currency of another country.

2. **Economic and legal ramifications.** Each country in which the firm operates has its own unique political and economic institutions, and institutional differences among countries can cause significant problems when a firm tries to coordinate and control the worldwide operations of its subsidiaries. For example, differences in tax laws among countries can cause a particular transaction to have strikingly dissimilar after-tax consequences, depending on where it occurred. Also, differences in legal systems of host nations complicate many matters, from the simple recording of a business transaction to the role played by the judiciary in resolving conflicts. Such differences can restrict multinational corporations' flexibility to deploy resources as they wish and can even make procedures illegal in one part of the company that are required in another part. These differences also make it difficult for executives trained in one country to operate effectively in another.

3. **Language differences.** The ability to communicate is critical in all business transactions. People born and educated in the United States often are at a disadvantage because they generally are fluent only in English, whereas European and Japanese businesspeople usually are fluent in several languages, including English. As a result, it is often easier for international companies to invade U.S. markets than it is for Americans to penetrate international markets.

4. **Cultural differences.** Even within geographic regions long considered fairly homogeneous, different countries have unique cultural heritages that shape values and influence the role of business in the society. Multinational corporations find that such matters as defining the appropriate goals of the firm, attitudes toward risk taking, dealing with employees, and the ability to curtail unprofitable operations can vary dramatically from one country to the next.

5. **Role of governments.** Most traditional models in finance assume the existence of a competitive marketplace in which the terms of trade are

determined by the participants. The government, through its power to establish basic ground rules, is involved in this process, but its participation is minimal. Thus, the market provides both the primary barometer of success and the indicator of the actions that must be taken to remain competitive. This view of the process is reasonably correct for the United States and a few other major industrialized nations, but it does not accurately describe the situation in most of the world. Frequently, the terms under which companies compete, the actions that must be taken or avoided, and the terms of trade on various transactions are determined not in the marketplace but by direct negotiation between the host government and the multinational corporation. This is essentially a political process, and it must be treated as such.

6. **Political risk.** The distinguishing characteristic that differentiates a nation from a multinational corporation is that the nation exercises sovereignty over the people and property in its territory. Hence, a nation is free to place constraints on the transfer of corporate resources and even to *expropriate*—that is, take for public use—the assets of a firm without compensation. This is political risk, and it tends to be largely a given rather than a variable that can be changed by negotiation. Political risk varies from country to country, and it must be addressed explicitly in any financial analysis. Another aspect of political risk is terrorism against U.S. firms or executives abroad. For example, in the past, U.S. executives have been captured and held for ransom in several South American and Middle Eastern countries.

These six factors complicate managerial finance within multinational firms and they increase the risks these firms face. However, prospects for high profits often make it worthwhile for firms to accept these risks and to learn how to minimize or at least live with them.

### Self-Test Question

Identify and briefly explain the major factors that complicate managerial finance within multinational firms.

To summarize the key concepts, let's answer the questions that were posed at the beginning of the chapter:

- **What is finance, and why should everyone understand basic financial concepts?** Finance deals with decisions about money—that is, how money is raised and used by companies and individuals. Everyone deals with financial decisions, both in business and in their personal lives. For this reason, and because *there are financial implications in nearly every business-related decision*, it is important that everyone has at least a general knowledge of financial concepts so that they can make informed decisions about their money.

- **What are the different forms of business organization? What are the advantages and disadvantages of each?** The three main forms of business organization are the *proprietorship*, the *partnership*, and the *corporation*. Although proprietorships and partnerships are easy to start, the major disadvantage to these forms of business is that the owners have unlimited personal liability for the debts of the businesses. On the other hand, a corporation is more difficult to start than the other forms of business, but owners have limited liability. Most business is conducted by corporations because this organizational form maximizes firms' values.

## Chapter *Essentials*
—The Answers

- **What goal(s) should firms pursue? Do firms always pursue appropriate goals?** The primary goal of management should be to maximize stockholders' wealth, which in turn means maximizing the price of the firm's stock. Further, actions that maximize stock prices also increase social welfare. The price of a firm's stock depends on the firm's projected cash flows and the timing and riskiness of these cash flows.

  There are times when managers might be tempted to act in their own best interests rather than pursue the goal of wealth maximization. The potential for such an *agency problem,* or conflict of interest, can be lessened by providing managers with incentives, or motivations, to act in the best interests of the stockholders.

- **What is the role of ethics in successful businesses?** Most firms have established strict *codes of conduct,* or guidelines, to ensure that managers "behave" ethically when dealing with stakeholders. Executives believe that there is a positive correlation between business ethics and the long-run success of their firms—that is, "ethical firms" survive, whereas "unethical firms" do not.

- **How do foreign firms differ from U.S. firms?** Non-U.S. firms generally have more concentrated ownership than U.S. firms. International operations have become increasingly important to individual firms and to the national economy. Companies go "international" to seek new markets, seek raw materials, seek new technology, seek production efficiency, and avoid trade barriers.

  The major factors that distinguish managerial finance as practiced by domestic firms from that of multinational companies include (1) different currency denominations, (2) economic and legal ramifications, (3) language differences, (4) cultural differences, (5) role of governments, and (6) political risk.

## Chapter *Essentials*
### —Personal Finance

The basic knowledge you learn in this book will help you understand how to (1) review companies and industries to determine their prospects for future growth and ability to maintain the safety of the funds you invest, (2) determine how much risk you are willing to take with your investment position, and (3) evaluate how well your investments are performing so that you can better ensure your funds are invested "appropriately."

Following are the general concepts presented in this chapter as they relate to personal financial decisions.

## Valuation

Throughout the book we will show that the concept of value is fairly easy to grasp—that is, value is based on the future cash flows an asset is expected to produce (both the amount and the timing) and the risk associated with those cash flows. If you can apply this concept, you should be able to estimate the values of investments and make informed decisions about these investments based on their current selling prices.

## Investment Goals

When you invest your money in a company's stock, you hope that the value of the stock increases significantly—that is, you want the value of the stock to be maximized. Thus, you want managers to make decisions that maximize the value of the firm. When managers make decisions that are in their own best interests rather than the best interests of stockholders—that is, an agency problem exists—you will have a tendency to sell the stock of that firm and invest in firms where managers "do the right thing."

## Ethics

When investing, you should behave ethically—that is, your interaction with and conduct toward other investors should be fair and honest. Also, you will tend to invest in firms that are considered ethical because firms that have good corporate governance policies have proven to be better investments than firms that have poor corporate governance policies.

### ETHICAL DILEMMA

## Chances Are What They Don't Know Won't Hurt Them!

Futuristic Electronic Technologies (FET) recently released a new advanced electronic micro system to be used by financial institutions, large corporations, and governments to process and store financial data, such as taxes and automatic payroll payments. Even though FET developed the technology used in the creation of the product, FET's competitors are expected to possess similar technology soon. To beat the competition to the market, FET introduced its new micro system a little earlier than originally planned. In fact, laboratory testing had not been fully completed before the product reached the market. The tests are complete now, and the final results suggest the micro system might be flawed with respect to how some data are retrieved and processed. The tests are not conclusive, though, and even if additional testing proves a flaw does exist, according to FET, it is of minuscule importance because the problem seems to occur for only one out of 100 million retrieval and processing attempts. The financial ramifications associated with the flaw are unknown at this time.

Assume you are one of FET's senior executives whose annual salary is based on the performance of the firm's common stock. You realize that if FET recalls the affected micro system, the stock price will suffer; thus, your salary for the year will be less than you expected. To complicate matters, you just purchased an expensive house based on your salary expectations for the next few years—expectations that will not be realized unless the new micro system is a success for FET. As one of the senior executives, you will help determine what course of action FET will follow with respect to the micro system. What should you do? Should you encourage FET to recall the micro system until further testing is completed? Or can you suggest another course of action?

## QUESTIONS

**1-1**  What are the three principal forms of business organization? What are the advantages and disadvantages of each?

**1-2**  Would the role of the financial manager be likely to increase or decrease in importance relative to other executives if the rate of inflation increased? Explain.

**1-3**  What does it mean to maximize the value of a corporation?

**1-4**  In general terms, how is value measured? What are the three factors that determine value? How does each factor affect value?

**1-5**  Should stockholder wealth maximization be thought of as a long-term or a short-term goal? For example, if one action would probably increase the firm's stock price from a current level of $20 to $25 in six months and then to $30 in five years, but another action would probably keep the stock at $20 for several years but then increase it to $40 in five years, which action would be better? Can you think of some specific corporate actions that might have these general tendencies?

**1-6**    Drawing on your background in accounting, can you think of any accounting procedure differences that might make it difficult to compare the relative performance of different firms?

**1-7**    Would the management of a firm in an oligopolistic or in a competitive industry be more likely to engage in what might be called "socially conscious" practices? Explain your reasoning.

**1-8**    What is the difference between stock price maximization and profit maximization? Under what conditions might profit maximization not lead to stock price maximization?

**1-9**    If you were the president of a large publicly owned corporation, would you make decisions to maximize stockholders' welfare or your own personal interests? What are some actions stockholders can take to ensure that management's interests and those of stockholders coincided? What are some other factors that might influence management's actions?

**1-10**    The president of United Semiconductor Corporation made this statement in the company's annual report: "United's primary goal is to increase the value of the common stockholders' equity over time." Later on in the report, the following announcements were made:

**a.**    The company contributed $1.5 million to the symphony orchestra in San Francisco, where it is headquartered.

**b.**    The company is spending $500 million to open a new plant in Mexico. No revenues will be produced by the plant for four years, so earnings will be depressed during this period in comparison to earnings had the decision not been made to open the new plant.

**c.**    The company is increasing its relative use of debt. Whereas assets were formerly financed with 35 percent debt and 65 percent equity, henceforth the financing mix will be 50-50.

**d.**    The company uses a great deal of electricity in its manufacturing operations, and it generates most of this power itself. Plans are to use nuclear fuel rather than coal to produce electricity in the future.

**e.**    The company has been paying out half of its earnings as dividends and retaining the other half. Henceforth, it will pay out only 30 percent as dividends.

Discuss how United's stockholders, customers, and labor force will react to each of these actions and then how each action might affect United's stock price.

**1-11**    What is corporate governance? Does a firm's corporate governance policy relate to whether it conducts business in an ethical manner? Explain.

**1-12**    Can a firm sustain its operations by maximizing stockholders' wealth at the expense of other stakeholders?

**1-13**    Why do U.S. corporations build manufacturing plants abroad when they could build them at home?

**1-14**    Compared to the ownership structure of U.S. firms, which are "open" companies, what are some advantages of the ownership structure of non-U.S. firms, many of which are "closed" companies? Can you think of any disadvantages?

**1-15**    Compared to purely domestic firms, what are some factors that make financial decision making more complicated for firms that operate in foreign countries?

## SELF-TEST PROBLEM

*Solution appears in Appendix B*

**ST-1** Define each of the following terms:                                               key terms

    **a.** Proprietorship; partnership; corporation

    **b.** Corporate charter; bylaws

    **c.** Stockholder wealth maximization

    **d.** Capital structure decisions; capital budgeting decisions; dividend policy decisions

    **e.** Value

    **f.** Profit maximization; earnings per share

    **g.** Agency problem

    **h.** Hostile takeover

    **i.** Business ethics; corporate governance

    **j.** Stakeholders

    **k.** Multinational corporation

    **l.** Industrial group; *chaebol; keiretsu*

    **m.** Exchange rate

## PROBLEM

### Integrative Problem

**1-1**    Marty Kimble, who "retired" many years ago after winning a huge lottery        **forms of business**
jackpot, wants to start a new company that will sell authentic sports memorabilia. He plans to name the company Pro Athlete Remembrances, or PAR for short. Marty is still in the planning stages, so he has a few questions about how PAR should be organized when he starts the business and what he should do if the company becomes very successful in the future. Marty has little knowledge of finance concepts. To answer his questions and learn more about finance in general, Mr. Kimble has hired Sunshine Business Consultants (SBC). Assume you are a new employee of SBC and your boss has asked you to answer the following questions for Mr. Kimble.

    **a.** What is finance? Why is the finance function important to the success of a business?

    **b.** Why is it important for people who work in other areas in a business to have an understanding of finance? Do you think it is more important for Marty Kimble to have a basic understanding of all the areas in a business than it is for a person who works for a large national corporation?

    **c.** What are the alternative forms of business organization? What are the advantages and disadvantages of each?

    **d.** What form of business organization do you recommend that Mr. Kimble use when starting PAR? Why?

**e.** Assume that PAR is organized as a proprietorship when it starts business. If PAR becomes extremely successful and grows substantially, would you recommend that Mr. Kimble change the business organization to either a partnership or a corporation? Explain your answer.

**f.** What goal should Mr. Kimble pursue when operating PAR?

**g.** Assume that PAR is organized as a proprietorship when it starts business and that Mr. Kimble plans to convert the business to a corporation at some point in the future. What are some potential problems that Mr. Kimble as one of the owners might face after converting to a corporation? Discuss some solutions to these potential problems.

**h.** Mr. Kimble would like PAR to grow so that at some point in the future the company can conduct business in other countries. Why do firms "go global"?

**i.** Discuss any differences and problems that Mr. Kimble should be aware of when conducting business in foreign markets.

**GET REAL WITH    THOMSON ONE | Business School Edition**

**organizational structure**

**1-1** Adobe Systems Inc. [NASNM:ADBE] makes the popular Adobe Acrobat software for creating PDF-formatted files. Symantec Corporation [NASNM: SYMC] produces the popular Norton Security software for computer virus protection.

These firms are peers, operating in the same industry—the technology industry—as well as the same market sector—the software sector. Using the Thomson One database, answer the following questions:

**a.** According to the Overview section, who are the key executives, based on their titles, in each firm?

**b.** You can access the firms' websites from their Overview section. Go to their corporate websites and find the corporate executive structure. Create an organizational chart for each firm.

**c.** Point out the similarities and differences for these firms, which are in the same market sector and industry, with regard to their organizational structure.

**d.** Where does the chief financial officer fit on the organizational charts of these two firms?

**multinational business**

**1-2** Using the Thomson One database, find a multinational firm that is based in the United States. Answer these questions:

**a.** What is the name and ticker symbol of the company you selected?

**b.** What is the industry and market sector in which the firm is classified?

**c.** What is the firm's major line of business?

**d.** In what countries does the firm operate?

**e.** Why, in your opinion, do overseas operations help the firm you selected to maximize shareholder wealth? Be specific in your answer.

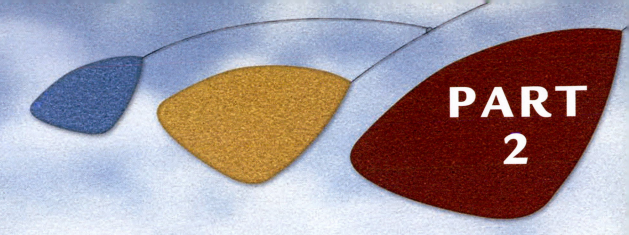

# PART 2

# Essential Concepts in Managerial Finance

# 2

# Analysis of Financial Statements

## A MANAGERIAL PERSPECTIVE

Firms in the United States are required to make "full and fair" disclosure of their operations by publishing various financial statements and other reports required by the Securities and Exchange Commission (SEC), the Financial Accounting Standards Board (FASB), and the American Institute of Certified Public Accountants (AICPA). One such report that firms publish is the annual report, which is often used to convey more than financial results. For example, some corporations view the annual report as an opportunity to showcase top management and sell the future of the company, without regard to the financial information. It is not unusual for work on the report to begin as much as six months before its publication, and many firms hire professional designers and writers to ensure that the final product looks sharp and reads well. Some firms pride themselves on the unique packaging designs used for their annual reports. For example, since 1977 McCormick & Company has used one of the spices and seasonings it produces to scent the paper on which its annual report is printed—the scent for 2006 was nutmeg.

In many instances, the puffery contained in an annual report detracts from the report's nominal purpose of providing objective financial information about the firm. Of course, some companies use the annual report as originally intended—to communicate the financial position of the firm. One such firm is Berkshire

Hathaway, whose legendary chairman Warren Buffett says, "I assume I have a very intelligent partner who has been away for a year and needs to be filled in on all that's happened." Consequently, in his letters, he often admits mistakes and emphasizes the negative. Buffett also uses his letters to educate his shareholders and to help them interpret the data presented in the rest of the report. Berkshire Hathaway's annual reports contain little, if any, puffery, freeing readers to focus on the company's financial statements and Buffett's interpretation of them. Some CEOs might contend that such a bare-bones approach is too dull for the average stockholder and that some readers might actually be intimidated by an overload of financial information. The manner in which Buffett presents financial information for Berkshire Hathaway seems to work, however, because the firm's stockholders are considered more sophisticated than the average investor. If you would like to examine some of the statements made by Warren Buffett, visit Berkshire Hathaway's website at http://berkshirehathaway.com; even the company website lacks glitter.

More and more, firms are recognizing that the "slick" annual report has lost its credibility with serious seekers of financial information and has become ever more expensive to produce. With the growth in electronic communications, the trend in recent years has been to post annual reports, devoid of the traditional "frills," on the company's website and refer stockholders to that location.

As you read this chapter, think about the kinds of information that corporations provide to their stockholders. Do you think the basic financial statements provide adequate data for making investment decisions? What other information might be helpful? Also, consider the pros and cons of Buffett's decision to include frank, and frequently self-critical, letters in his company's annual reports. Would you suggest that other companies follow suit?

## Chapter *Essentials*
### —The Questions

After reading this chapter, you should be able to answer the following questions:

- What financial statements do corporations publish, and what information does each statement provide?
- How do investors use financial statements?
- What is ratio analysis and why are the results of such an analysis important to both managers and investors?
- What are some potential problems (caveats) associated with financial statement analysis?
- What is the most important ingredient (factor) in financial statement analysis?

In Chapter 1, we stated that managers should strive to maximize the value of the firm's stock. We also noted that a stock's value is determined by the cash flows that the firm is expected to generate in the future. Thus, to estimate value, both managers and investors must be able to estimate future cash flows. In this chapter, we give some indication as to how financial statements that are constructed by firms can be used to accomplish this task.

Financial statement analysis involves analysis of a firm's financial position to identify its current strengths and weaknesses and to suggest actions that the firm might pursue to take advantage of those strengths and correct any weaknesses. In this chapter, we discuss how to evaluate a firm's current financial position using its financial statements. In later chapters, we will examine the types of actions that a firm can take to improve its financial position in the future, thereby increasing the price of its stock.

## RECORDING BUSINESS ACTIVITY—FINANCIAL STATEMENTS

A brief discussion of the history and evolution of accounting and the production of financial statements provides an indication as to why such records are needed and how they are used.[1] Many people believe that the birth of accounting took place more than 4,000 years ago in ancient Mesopotamia as the result of the Code of Hammurabi, which required merchants to provide prices of goods and services in writing so that sales agreements were recorded. Merchants also kept written histories of transactions to ensure that disputed sales could be settled; without written proof of the terms, transactions often were invalidated. As a result, it was very important for merchants to keep accurate records of their transactions, which included prices, quantity and quality of the products sold, and so forth.

As societies became more sophisticated and governments provided more and more services to the citizens, "accountants" became an important factor in the determination and collection of the taxes that were used to finance government services. Bookkeepers kept the tax records during these times. The penalties for "accounting

---

[1]Much of the information provided in this section can be found in the History of Accounting page on the website of the Association of Chartered Accountants in the United States (ACAUS), which is located at http://www.acaus.org/acc_his.html. For much more information about the history of accounting, visit this website.

irregularities" included fines, disfigurement, or even death. As a result, bookkeepers/accountants were motivated to provide reliable, accurate records.

According to all accounts, it wasn't until the fifteenth century that the birth of modern accounting began when Benedetto Cotrugli introduced the double-entry bookkeeping system, which was more formally developed by Luca Pacioli a few decades later. In his writings, Pacioli stated that to be successful, a merchant must have access to funds (cash or credit) to support daily operations and a system that permits the merchant to easily determine his financial position. He also recommended that merchants record all assets and liabilities, both personal and business, before starting business, and he noted that these records should be kept current.

As you can see from this brief history lesson, "financial books" have historically provided important information about the financial well-being of businesses. Today, financial statements provide similar information, which is important to a firm's stakeholders. Information that is included in these statements can be used by managers to improve the firm's performance and by investors (either stockholders or creditors) to evaluate the firm's financial position when making investment decisions.

**Self-Test Question**

Why is it important to maintain financial records?

## FINANCIAL REPORTS

Of the various reports that corporations provide to their stockholders, the **annual report** probably is the most important. This report provides two types of information. First, it includes a verbal section, often presented as a letter from the chairman, that describes the firm's operating results during the past year and discusses new developments that will affect future operations. Second, the annual report presents four basic financial statements: *the balance sheet, the income statement, the statement of cash flows,* and *the statement of retained earnings.* Taken together, these statements give an accounting picture of the firm's operations and financial position. Detailed data are provided for the two most recent years, along with historical summaries of key operating statistics for the past five or 10 years.[2]

The quantitative information and verbal information contained in the annual report are equally important. The financial statements indicate what actually happened to the firm's financial position and to its earnings and dividends over the past few years, whereas the verbal statements attempt to explain why things turned out the way they did. To illustrate how annual reports can prove helpful, we will use data taken from a fictitious company called Unilate Textiles. Unilate is a manufacturer and distributor of a wide variety of textiles and clothing items that was formed in 1990 in North Carolina. The company has grown steadily and has earned a reputation for selling quality products. In the most recent annual report, management reported that earnings dropped 8.5 percent due to losses associated with a poor cotton crop and from increased costs caused by a three-month employee strike and a retooling of the factory. Management then went on to paint a more optimistic picture for the future, stating that full operations had been resumed, several unprofitable businesses had been eliminated, and profits were expected to rise sharply next year. Of course, an increase in profitability might not

**annual report**
This report describes the firm's operating results during the past year and discusses new developments that will affect future operations and gives an accounting picture of the firm's operations and financial position.

[2]Firms also provide quarterly reports, but they are much less comprehensive than the annual reports. In addition, larger firms file even more detailed statements, giving breakdowns for each major division or subsidiary, with the SEC. These reports, called *10-K reports,* are made available to stockholders upon request to a company's corporate secretary. Many companies also post these reports on their websites. Finally, many larger firms also publish *statistical supplements,* which give financial statement data and key ratios going back 10 to 20 years.

occur, and analysts should compare management's past statements with subsequent results to determine whether this optimism is justified. In any event, *investors use the information contained in an annual report to form expectations about future earnings and dividends.* Clearly, then, investors are quite interested in the annual report.

Because this book is intended to provide an introduction to managerial finance, Unilate's financial statements are constructed so that they are simple and straightforward. At this time, the company uses only debt and common stock to finance its assets—that is, Unilate does not have outstanding preferred stock, convertible financing instruments, or derivatives. Also, the company has only the basic assets that are required to conduct business, including cash and marketable securities, accounts receivable, inventory, and ordinary fixed assets. For this reason, Unilate does not have assets that require complex accounting applications.

 **Self-Test Questions**

Identify the two types of information given in the annual report.

Why are investors interested in a firm's annual report?

## FINANCIAL STATEMENTS

**balance sheet**
This financial statement represents a picture taken at a specific point in time (date) that shows a firm's assets and how those assets are financed (debt or equity).

Before we analyze how Unilate's financial position compares with other firms, let's take a look at the financial statements the company publishes. Information contained in the financial statements is used by investors to estimate the cash flows that the company is expected to generate in the future.

### The Balance Sheet

The **balance sheet** represents a picture taken *at a specific point in time (date)* that shows a firm's assets and how those assets are financed (debt or equity). Figure 2-1

**FIGURE 2-1    Simple Balance Sheet**

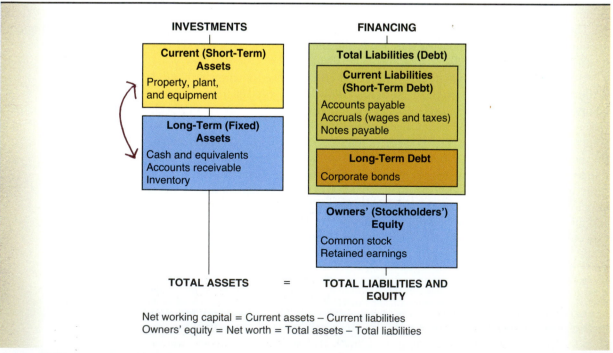

**TABLE 2-1**  Unilate Textiles: December 31 Balance Sheets ($ millions, except per-share data)

| | 2009 | | 2008 | |
|---|---|---|---|---|
| | Amount | Percent of Total Assets | Amount | Percent of Total Assets |
| **Assets** | | | | |
| Cash and equivalents | $ 15.0 | 1.8% | $ 40.0 | 5.4% |
| Accounts receivables | 180.0 | 21.3 | 160.0 | 21.3 |
| Inventory | 270.0 | 32.0 | 200.0 | 26.7 |
| Total current assets | $465.0 | 55.0%[b] | $ 400.0 | 53.3%[b] |
| Net plant and equipment[a] | 380.0 | 45.0 | 350.0 | 46.7 |
| Total assets | $845.0 | 100.0% | $ 750.0 | 100.0% |
| | | | | |
| **Liabilities and Equity** | | | | |
| Accounts payable | $ 30.0 | 3.6% | $ 15.0 | 2.0% |
| Accruals | 60.0 | 7.1 | 55.0 | 7.3 |
| Notes payable | 40.0 | 4.7 | 35.0 | 4.7 |
| Total current liabilities | $130.0 | 15.4% | $ 105.0 | 14.0% |
| Long-term bonds | 300.0 | 35.5 | 255.0 | 34.0 |
| Total liabilities (debt) | $430.0 | 50.9% | $ 360.0 | 48.0% |
| Common stock (25 million shares) | 130.0 | 15.4 | 130.0 | 17.3 |
| Retained earnings | 285.0 | 33.7 | 260.0 | 34.7 |
| Total common equity | $415.0 | 49.1% | 390.0 | 52.0 |
| Total liabilities and equity | $845.0 | 100.0% | $ 750.0 | 100.0% |
| | | | | |
| Book value per share | $ 16.60 | | $ 15.60 | |
| = (Common equity)/Shares | | | | |
| Market value per share (stock price) | $ 23.00 | | $ 25.00 | |
| | | | | |
| **Additional information:** | | | | |
| Net working capital | $335.0 | | $ 295.0 | |
| = Current assets − Current liabilities | | | | |
| Net worth = Total assets − Total liabilities | 415.0 | | 390.0 | |

[a]Breakdown of net plant and equipment account:

| | | | | |
|---|---|---|---|---|
| Gross plant and equipment | $680.0 | | $600.0 | |
| Less: Accumulated depreciation | (300.0) | | (250.0) | |
| Net plant and equipment | $380.0 | | $350.0 | |

[b]Rounding difference.

shows the general setup for a simple balance sheet. Table 2-1 shows Unilate's balance sheets on December 31 for the years 2008 and 2009. December 31 is the end of the fiscal year, which is when Unilate "takes a snapshot" of its existing assets, liabilities, and equity to construct the balance sheet. In this section, we concentrate on the more recent balance sheet—that is, December 31, 2009.

Assets, which represent the firm's investments, are classified as either short term (current) or long term (see Figure 2-1). Current assets generally include items that will be liquidated and thus converted into cash within one year, whereas long-term, or fixed, assets include investments that help generate cash flows over longer periods. As Table 2-1 shows, at the end of 2009, Unilate's current assets, which include cash and equivalents, accounts receivable (amounts due from customers), and inventory, totaled $465 million; its long-term assets, which include the building and equipment used to manufacture the textile products, had a net value equal to $380 million; thus, its total assets were $845 million. Table 2-1 shows that 55 percent of Unilate's assets were in the form of current, or short-term, assets, whereas the remaining 45 percent were in the form of plant and equipment (long-term assets).

To finance its assets, the firm "issues" debt, equity (stock), or both forms of financing. Debt represents the loans the firm has outstanding, and it generally is divided into two categories—short-term debt and long-term debt (see Figure 2-1). Short-term debt, which is labeled *current liabilities*, includes accounts payable (amounts owed to suppliers), accruals (amounts owed to employees and state and federal governments), and notes payable (amounts owed to the bank). Current liabilities represent debt that is due within one year—that is, these debts are paid off within 12 months. Table 2-1 shows that Unilate's short-term debt totaled $130 million. Long-term debt includes the bonds and similar debt instruments that the firm has issued that are paid off over a period longer than one year. At the end of 2009, Unilate had outstanding bonds equal to $300 million. In combination, then, the total amount of debt Unilate used to finance its assets was $430 million. Thus, according to Table 2-1, about 51 percent of the firm's assets were financed using debt, most of which was in the form of long-term bonds (70 percent of total liabilities).

**common stockholders' equity or net worth**
The total assets minus total liabilities.

Equity represents stockholders' ownership, which, unlike debt, does not have to be "paid off." Total equity is the amount that would be paid to stockholders if the firm's assets could be sold at the values reported on the balance sheet and its debt is paid off in the amounts reported on the balance sheet. Thus, the firm's **common stockholders' equity,** or **net worth,** equals total assets minus total liabilities. Table 2-1 shows that Unilate's net worth was $415 million at the end of 2009. This implies, but does not mean, that common stockholders would receive $415 million if Unilate liquidates its assets at the values reported on the balance sheet and pays off all of its outstanding debt. However, suppose that all of the accounts receivable cannot be collected or some inventory had to be sold for less than the amount shown on the balance sheet. If liabilities remain constant, the value of the stockholders' equity must decline because the firm's creditors (debt holders) would want to be paid the full amount they are owed before stockholders got paid anything. For example, if Unilate could collect only $800 million by liquidating all of its assets today, then the amount that would be left over and could be distributed to stockholders after paying off its debts would be $370 million ($800 million liquidation proceeds minus $430 million needed to pay off liabilities), not $415 million. This simple example shows that the risk of asset value fluctuations is borne by the stockholders. Note, however, that if asset values rise, these benefits will accrue exclusively to the stockholders. The change in the firm's net worth is reflected by changes in the retained earnings account; if bad debts are written off in the asset section of the balance sheet, the retained earnings balance is reduced in the equity section.

**retained earnings**
An account that effectively represents the total amount of income a company has saved and reinvested in assets since it started business. It shows the cumulative amount of income the company has kept rather than paid out as dividends over the years.

Notice that the common equity section shown in Table 2-1 is composed of two accounts—common stock and retained earnings. The common stock account shows the amount that stockholders paid to Unilate when the company issued stock to raise funds. Unilate has issued stock only once—when it was formed in 1990—so the amount shown in the common stock account has remained constant at $130 million since that time. The amount shown in the **retained earnings** account effectively represents the total amount of income that Unilate has saved and reinvested in assets since the firm started business. It is important to note that the amount reported on the balance sheet in the retained earnings account shows the cumulative amount of income the company has kept rather than paid out as dividends over the years. According to Table 2-1, Unilate has kept $285 million of all the income generated since 1990. This amount could have been paid to stockholders as dividends over the years, but Unilate instead decided to use these funds to finance some of its investment in assets.

Note that in Table 2-1 the assets are listed in order of their "liquidity," or the length of time it typically takes to convert them to cash. The claims (liabilities and equity) are listed in the order in which they must be paid. Accounts payable generally must be paid within 30 to 45 days, accruals are payable within 60 to 90 days, and so on, down to the stockholders' equity accounts, which represent ownership and need never be "paid off." The practice of listing assets and liabilities in this order began in the fifteenth century when Luca Pacioli suggested that items should be listed based on "mobility" such that cash and other assets that can be converted to cash easily should be listed first on the financial books.[3]

Notice that the assets, liabilities, and equity reported on the balance sheets in Table 2-1 are stated both in dollars and as a percent of total assets. When items on a balance sheet are stated as percentages, it is termed a **common size balance sheet.** The resultant percentage statement can be easily compared with statements of larger or smaller firms, or with those of the same firm over time. For example, we noted that 51 percent of Unilate's assets were financed with debt in 2009. We can compare this percent with other textile firms to determine whether Unilate has too much debt. We discuss such comparisons later in the chapter.

Some additional points about the balance sheet are worth noting:

**common size balance sheet**
Items on a balance sheet that are stated as percentages.

1. *Cash and equivalents versus other assets.* Although the assets are all stated in terms of dollars, only the cash and equivalents account represents actual money that can be spent. Receivables are bills that others owe to Unilate; inventories show the dollars that the company has invested in raw materials, work-in-process, and finished goods available for sale; and net fixed assets reflect the amount of money that Unilate paid for its plant and equipment when it acquired those assets less the amount that has been written off (depreciated) since the assets' acquisitions. The noncash assets should produce cash over time, but they do not represent cash in hand. The amount of cash they would bring in if sold today could be either higher or lower than the values that are reported on the balance sheet (their *book values*). At the end of 2009, Unilate had $15 million cash and equivalents that could be used to pay the bills. Of course, in 2010, most customers that owe Unilate money at the end of 2009 will pay their bills, Unilate will sell some inventory for cash, and Unilate will pay most of its bills. As a result, the amount in the cash and equivalents account will vary throughout the year. It is important that Unilate has enough cash on hand to pay bills when they are due, but Unilate doesn't want to keep too much cash because cash is an idle asset in the sense that it does not earn a positive return for the firm.

2. *Accounting alternatives.* Not every firm uses the same method to determine the account balances shown on the balance sheet. For instance, Unilate uses the FIFO (first-in, first-out) method to determine the inventory value shown on its balance sheet. It could have used the LIFO (last-in, first-out) method instead. During a period of rising prices, compared with LIFO, FIFO will

---

[3]See the History of Accounting that is discussed on the website of the Association of Chartered Accountants in the United States (ACAUS), which is located at http://www.acaus.org/acc_his.html.

produce a higher balance sheet inventory value but a lower cost of goods sold, and thus a higher net income.

In some cases, a company might use one accounting method to construct financial statements provided to stockholders and another accounting method for tax purposes, internal reports, and so forth. For example, companies generally use the most accelerated method permissible to calculate depreciation for tax purposes because accelerated methods lower taxable incomes and thus taxes that must be paid. The same companies might use straight-line depreciation for constructing financial statements reported to stockholders because this method results in higher net incomes. There is nothing illegal or unethical with this practice, but when evaluating firms, users of financial statements must be aware that more than one accounting alternative is available for constructing financial statements.

3. *Breakdown of the common equity account.* The equity section of Unilate's balance sheet contains two accounts: common stock and retained earnings. The common equity sections of some firms include three accounts: common stock at par, paid-in capital, and retained earnings. We mentioned earlier that the retained earnings account is built up over time as the firm saves, or reinvests, a part of its earnings rather than paying everything out as dividends. The other two accounts arise from the issuance of stock to raise funds (capital). When a firm issues common stock to raise funds to invest in assets, the amount that investors pay for the stock must be reported in the equity section of the balance sheet. For example, Unilate issued 25 million shares of stock at $5.20 to raise $130 million when it started business. Thus, Unilate's stockholders provided the company with $130 million of funds to invest in its assets. Because Unilate's common stock does not have a par value, the entire amount of the issue is reported in the common stock account.

If Unilate's common stock had a par value equal to $2 per share, then the funds raised through the stock issue would have to be reported in two accounts: common stock at par and paid-in capital. The amount reported in the common stock at par account would equal the total value of the stock issue stated in terms of its par value, and it would be computed as follows:

$$\text{Common stock at par} = \text{Total shares issued} \times \text{share par value}$$
$$= 25{,}000{,}000 \times \$2 = \$50{,}000{,}000$$

The amount that was paid above the par value is reported in the paid-in capital account. In this case, because the total value of the issue was $130 million, the remaining $80 million would be reported in the paid-in capital account. This amount can also be computed by multiplying the portion of the selling price per share that exceeds the stock's par value by the number of shares that were issued. If Unilate's stock had a par value equal to $2 and each share was issued at $5.20, then the additional $3.20 per share is considered paid-in capital. Therefore, the amount reported in the paid-in capital account would be $80 million = ($5.20 − $2.00) × 25 million shares.

The breakdown of the common equity accounts shows whether the company actually earned the funds reported in its equity accounts or if the funds came mainly from selling (issuing) stock. This information is important to both creditors and stockholders. For instance, a potential creditor would be interested in the amount of money that the owners put up, and stockholders would want to know the form of stockholders' funds.

**4.** *Book values versus market values.* The values, or accounting numbers, that are reported on the balance sheet are called *book values,* and they are generated using generally accepted accounting principles (GAAP). In many cases, these book values are not the same as the prices (values) for which the assets can actually be sold in the marketplace. That is, the **book values** of assets often do not equal their **market values.** For example, when Unilate built its original distribution center in 1990, the value of the building was $90 million, which represented the market value at the time. Today, in 2009, the book value of the building is $33 million because $57 million has been depreciated over the years. However, the appraised (market) value of the building is $60 million. Thus, the market value of the building ($60 million) is greater than its book value ($33 million).

Whereas the book values of assets often are not equal to their market values, the book values of a firm's debt generally are either equal to or very close to the market values of the firm's liabilities. Because most debt represents a contractual obligation to pay a certain amount at a specific time, the amounts reported on the balance sheet normally are the amounts that the firm owes its creditors.

The equity section of the balance sheet must equal the book value of assets minus the book value of liabilities (see Figure 2-1). As we mentioned, it is likely that book values of assets *differ from* their market values, but it is likely that the book values of liabilities are *close to* their market values. As a result, the difference between the book value and market value of equity primarily depends on the differences between the book values and market values of the firm's assets. If the aggregate book value of the firm's assets is much lower than their aggregate market value, then the book value of equity will be much lower than the market value of the firm's common stock, and vice versa.

**5.** *The time dimension.* The balance sheet can be thought of as a snapshot of the firm's financial position *at a point in time.* The balance sheet changes every day as inventories are increased or decreased, as fixed assets are added or retired, as liabilities are increased or decreased, and so on. Companies whose businesses are seasonal experience especially large changes in their balance sheets during the year. For example, most retailers have large inventories just before Christmas but low inventories and high accounts receivable just after this holiday. As a result, firms' balance sheets will change over the year, depending on the date on which the statements are constructed.

> **book values**
> The values, or accounting numbers, that are reported on the balance sheet and are generated using generally accepted accounting principles (GAAP).

> **market values**
> The prices (values) for which assets can actually be sold in the marketplace.

## The Income Statement

The **income statement,** which is also referred to as the profit and loss statement, presents the results of business operations *during a specified period of time* such as a quarter or a year. It summarizes the revenues generated and the expenses incurred by the firm during the accounting period. Table 2-2 gives the 2008 and 2009 income statements for Unilate Textiles. Net sales are shown at the top of the statement, followed by various costs, including income taxes, that are subtracted to determine the net income (earnings) available to common stockholders. A report on earnings and dividends per share appears at the bottom of the statement. In managerial finance, earnings per share (EPS) is called "the bottom line" because EPS is often considered the most important item on the income statement. Unilate earned $2.16 per share in 2009, down from $2.36 in 2008, but it still raised the per-share dividend from $1.08 to $1.16.

> **income statement**
> Also referred to as the profit and loss statement. It presents the results of business operations *during a specified period of time* such as a quarter or a year and summarizes the revenues generated and the expenses incurred by the firm during the accounting period.

**TABLE 2-2** Unilate Textiles: Income Statements for Years Ending December 31 ($ millions, except per-share data)[a]

| | 2009 | | 2008 | |
|---|---|---|---|---|
| | Amount | Percent of Total Sales | Amount | Percent of Total Sales |
| Net sales | $1,500.0 | 100.0% | $1,435.0 | 100.0% |
| Variable operating costs (82% of sales) | (1,230.0) | 82.0 | (1,176.7) | 82.0 |
| Gross profit | $ 270.0 | 18.0 | $ 258.3 | 18.0 |
| Fixed operating costs except depreciation | ( 90.0) | 6.0 | ( 85.0) | 5.9 |
| Earnings before interest, taxes, depreciation, and amortization (EBITDA) | $ 180.0 | 12.0 | 173.3 | 12.1 |
| Depreciation | ( 50.0) | 3.3 | ( 40.0) | 2.8 |
| Net operating income (NOI) = | | | | |
| Earnings before interest and taxes (EBIT) | $ 130.0 | 8.8 | 133.3 | 9.3 |
| Interest | ( 40.0) | 2.7 | ( 35.0) | 2.4 |
| Earnings before taxes (EBT) | $ 90.0 | 6.0 | 98.3 | 6.9 |
| Taxes (40%) | ( 36.0) | 2.4 | ( 39.3) | 2.7 |
| Net income | $ 54.0 | 3.6 | $ 59.0 | 4.1 |
| Preferred dividends | 0.0 | | 0.0 | |
| Earnings available to common stockholders (EAC) | $ 54.0 | | 59.0 | |
| Common dividends | ( 29.0) | | ( 27.0) | |
| Addition to retained earnings | $ 25.0 | | 32.0 | |
| | | | | |
| **Per-share data (25 million shares):** | | | | |
| Earnings per share = (Net income)/Shares | $ 2.16 | | $ 2.36 | |
| Dividends per share = (Common dividends)/Shares | $ 1.16 | | $ 1.08 | |

[a]The parentheses in this statement and subsequent statements indicate a negative value.

## Should identical firms report the same net income?

The obvious answer is yes. However, even though two firms have identical operating structures—that is, facilities, employees, and production methods—they might be financed differently. For example, one firm might be financed with a substantial amount of debt, whereas the other firm is financed only with stock. Interest payments to debt holders are tax deductible; dividend payments to stockholders are not. The firm that is financed with debt will have greater tax-deductible expenses as a result of the interest expense and thus will report a lower net income than the firm that is financed with equity only. For this reason, when comparing the operations of two firms, analysts often examine the *net operating income (NOI)*, also known as the *earnings before interest and taxes (EBIT)*, because this figure represents the result of normal operations before considering the effects of the firm's financial structure. Unilate's EBIT was $130 million in 2009. A firm that has the same operating structure (and follows the same accounting procedures) as Unilate should have reported EBIT equal to $130 million as well, even if it does not use the same amount of debt as Unilate to finance its assets.

## Does net income determine value?

Investors often focus on the net income that a firm generates when determining how well the firm has performed during a particular time period. But if investors are concerned with whether management is pursuing the goal of maximizing the firm's stock price, net income might not be the appropriate measure to examine.

Recall from your accounting courses that, for most corporations, the income statement is generated using the accrual method of accounting. That is, revenues are recognized when they are earned, not when the cash is received, and expenses are recognized when they are incurred, not when the cash is paid. As a result, not all of the amounts shown on the income statement represent cash flows. But remember that the value of an investment, such as the firm's stock price, is determined by the cash flows it generates. Therefore, although the firm's net income is important, cash flows are even more important because cash is needed to continue normal business operations, such as the payment of financial obligations, the purchase of assets, and the payment of dividends. As a result, in finance we focus on *cash flows* rather than net income.

One item on Unilate's income statement that we know is a noncash item is depreciation. The cash payment for a fixed asset, such as a building, occurs when the asset is originally purchased. But because the asset is used to generate revenues and its life extends for longer than one year, depreciation is the method that is used to *match* the expense associated with the decrease in the value of the asset with the revenues that the asset helps to generate. For example, Table 2-2 shows that Unilate's net income for 2009 was $54 million and the depreciation expense for the year was $50 million. Because depreciation was not an expense that required a cash payment, Unilate's net cash flow must be at least $50 million higher than the $54 million that is reported as net income. If the only noncash item on its income statement is depreciation, then the net cash flow that Unilate generated in 2009 was $104 million.

When a firm sells its products for cash and pays cash for all of the expenses reported on its income statement, except depreciation and amortization, its net cash flow can be computed using this simple equation:

| Net cash flow = Net income + Depreciation and amortization | **2–1** |
| --- | --- |

$$= \$54 \text{ million} + \$50 \text{ million} = \$104 \text{ million}$$

Managers and analysts often use this equation to estimate the net cash flow generated by a firm, even when some customers have not paid for their purchases or the firm has not paid all of the bills for supplies, employee salaries, and the like. In such cases, Equation 2–1 can be used only to estimate the net cash flow generated by the firm. To get a better estimate of net cash flow, as well as to examine in detail which of the firm's actions provided cash and which actions used cash, a statement of cash flows should be constructed. We discuss the statement of cash flows in the next section.

For our purposes, it is useful to divide cash flows into two categories: (1) *operating cash flows* and (2) *other cash flows*. **Operating cash flows** arise from normal operations, and they represent, in essence, the difference between cash collections and cash expenses, including taxes paid, associated with the manufacture and sale of inventory. Other cash flows arise from borrowing, from the sale of fixed assets, or from the repurchase of common stock. Our focus here is on operating cash flows.

We know that operating cash flows can differ from **accounting profits** (or operating income) for two primary reasons: (1) a firm sells on credit, and (2) some operating expenses are not cash costs. For example, we know that depreciation and

**operating cash flows**
Arise from normal operations, and represent the difference between cash collections and cash expenses, including taxes paid, associated with the manufacture and sale of inventory.

**accounting profits**
The operating income of a company.

amortization expenses are costs that do not use cash. For this reason, analysts often compute a firm's *earnings before interest, taxes, depreciation, and amortization (EBITDA)* when evaluating its operations. Because both depreciation, which recognizes the decline in the values of tangible assets, and amortization, which recognizes the decline in the values of intangible assets (patents, trademarks, and so forth) are noncash expenses, EBITDA provides an indication of the cash flows that are generated by normal operations. Unilate's EBITDA was $180 million in 2009. This is higher than the reported EBIT of $130 million because the depreciation expense was $50 million; Unilate has no amortization expense.

## Statement of Cash Flows

**statement of cash flows**
Shows how the firm's operations have affected its cash position by examining the firm's investment decisions (uses of cash) and financing decisions (sources of cash).

The **statement of cash flows** is designed to show how the firm's operations have affected its cash position by examining the firm's investment decisions (uses of cash) and financing decisions (sources of cash). The information contained in the statement of cash flows can help answer questions such as the following: Is the firm generating the cash needed to purchase additional fixed assets for growth? Does it have excess cash flows that can be used to repay debt or to invest in new products? This information is useful for both financial managers and investors, so the statement of cash flows is an important part of the annual report.

Constructing a statement of cash flows is relatively easy. First, to some extent, the income statement shows the cash flow effects of a firm's operations. For example, Unilate reported its 2009 net income as $54 million, which we know includes a $50 million depreciation expense that is a noncash operating cost. As reported earlier, if the $50 million depreciation expense is added back to the $54 million net income, we *estimate* that the cash flow generated from normal operations is $104 million. For most firms, however, some of the reported revenues have not been collected and some of the reported expenses have not been paid at the time the income statement is constructed. To adjust the *estimate* of cash flows obtained from the income statement and to account for cash flow effects not reflected in the income statement, we need to examine the implications of changes in the balance sheet accounts during the period in question (fiscal year 2009 for Unilate). Looking at the changes in the balance sheet accounts from the beginning to the end of the year, we want to identify which items provided cash (a source) and which items used cash (a use) during the year. To determine whether a change in a balance sheet account was a source or a use of cash, we follow these simple rules:

| Sources of Cash | Uses of Cash |
| --- | --- |
| ***Increase in a Liability or Equity Account***<br>Borrowing funds or selling stock provides the firm with cash. | ***Decrease in a Liability or Equity Account***<br>Paying off a loan or buying back stock uses cash. |
| ***Decrease in an Asset Account***<br>Selling inventory or collecting receivables provides cash. | ***Increase in an Asset Account***<br>Buying fixed assets or buying more inventory uses cash. |

Using these rules, we can identify which changes in Unilate's balance sheet accounts provided cash and which changes used cash during 2009. Table 2-3 shows the results of this identification. In addition, the table includes the cash flow information contained

**TABLE 2-3**  Unilate Textiles: Cash Sources and Uses, 2009 ($ millions)

| | Account Balances as of: | | Change | |
| --- | --- | --- | --- | --- |
| | 12/31/09 | 12/31/08 | Sources | Uses |
| **Balance Sheet Effects (Adjustments)** | | | | |
| Cash and marketable securities | $ 15.0 | $40.0 | $ 25.0 | |
| Accounts receivable | 180.0 | 160.0 | | $( 20.0) |
| Inventory | 270.0 | 200.0 | | ( 70.0) |
| Gross plant and equipment | 680.0 | 600.0 | | ( 80.0) |
| Accounts payable | 30.0 | 15.0 | 15.0 | |
| Accruals | 60.0 | 55.0 | 5.0 | |
| Notes payable | 40.0 | 35.0 | 5.0 | |
| Long-term bonds | 300.0 | 255.0 | 45.0 | |
| Common stock (25 million shares) | 130.0 | 130.0 | | |
| **Income Statement Information** | | | | |
| Net income | $ 54.0 | | | |
| Add: Depreciation | 50.0 | | | |
| Gross cash flow from operations | $104.0 | | 104.0 | |
| Dividend payment | 29.0 | | | ( 29.0) |
| Totals | | | $199.0 | $(199.0) |

in Unilate's 2009 income statement. This information can be used to construct the statement of cash flows that is shown in Table 2-4.[4]

Each balance sheet change in Table 2-4 is classified as resulting from (1) operations, (2) long-term investments, or (3) financing activities. Operating cash flows are those associated with the production and sale of goods and services. The *estimate* of cash flows obtained from the income statement is the primary operating cash flow, but changes in accounts payable, accounts receivable, inventories, and accruals are also classified as operating cash flows because these accounts are directly affected by the firm's day-to-day operations. Investment cash flows arise from the purchase or sale of plant, property, and equipment. Financing cash inflows result when the firm issues debt or common stock. Financing cash outflows occur when the firm pays dividends, repays debt (loans), or repurchases stock. The cash inflows and outflows from these three activities are summed to determine their effect on the firm's liquidity position, which is measured by the change in the cash and equivalents account from one year to the next.

The top part of Table 2-4 shows cash flows generated by and used in operations. For Unilate, operations provided net cash flows of $34 million. The operating cash flows are generated principally from the firm's day-to-day operations, and this amount can be determined by adjusting the net income figure to account for noncash items. In 2009, Unilate's day-to-day operations provided $104 million of funds ($54 million net income plus $50 million depreciation), but the increase in

---

[4]The cash flow statement is presented in either of two formats. The method used here is called the *indirect method.* Cash flows from operations are calculated by starting with net income, adding back expenses not paid out of cash, and subtracting revenues that do not provide cash. With the *direct method,* operating cash flows are found by summing all revenues that provide cash and then subtracting all expenses that are paid in cash. Both formats produce the same result, and both are accepted by the Financial Accounting Standards Board.

**TABLE 2-4**   Unilate Textiles: Statement of Cash Flows for the Period Ending December 31, 2009 ($ millions)[a]

| | | |
|---|---|---|
| ***Cash Flows from Operating Activities*** | | |
| Net income | 54.0 | |
| *Additions (adjustments) to net income* | | |
| Depreciation[b] | 50.0 | |
| Increase in accounts payable | 15.0 | |
| Increase in accruals | 5.0 | |
| *Subtractions (adjustments) from net income* | | |
| Increase in accounts receivable | (20.0) | |
| Increase in inventory | (70.0) | |
| Net cash flow from operations | | $ 34.0 |
| ***Cash Flows from Long-Term Investing Activities*** | | |
| Acquisition of fixed assets | | $ (80.0) |
| ***Cash Flows from Financing Activities*** | | |
| Increase in notes payable | $ 5.0 | |
| Increase in bonds | 45.0 | |
| Dividend payment | (29.0) | |
| Net cash flow from financing | | $ 21.0 |
| Net change in cash | | $ (25.0) |
| Cash at the beginning of the year | | 40.0 |
| Cash at the end of the year | | $ 15.0 |

[a]The parentheses indicate a negative value—that is, a cash outflow.

[b]Depreciation is a noncash expense that was deducted when calculating net income. It must be added back to show the correct cash flow from operations.

inventories and investment in receivables during the year accounted for a combined use of funds equal to $90 million, whereas increases in accounts payable and accruals provided only $20 million in additional operating (short-term) funds. The second section in Table 2-4 shows the company's long-term investing activities. Unilate purchased fixed assets totaling $80 million, which was its only investment activity during 2009. Unilate's financing activities, shown in the bottom section of Table 2-4, included borrowing from banks (notes payable), selling new bonds, and paying dividends to its common stockholders. The company raised $50 million by borrowing, but it paid $29 million in dividends, so its net inflow of funds from financing activities was $21 million.

When we total all of these sources and uses of cash, we see that Unilate had a $25 million cash shortfall during 2009—that is, Unilate's cash outflows were $25 million greater than its cash inflows. It met this shortfall by drawing down its cash and equivalents from $40 million to $15 million, as shown in Table 2-1 (the firm's balance sheet).

Unilate's statement of cash flows should raise some concerns for the financial manager and outside analysts. The company generated $34 million in cash from operations, it spent $80 million on new fixed assets, and it paid out another $29 million in dividends. These cash outlays were covered by borrowing heavily, selling off marketable securities (cash equivalents), and drawing down its bank account. Obviously, this situation cannot continue indefinitely, so something must be done. We will consider some of the actions that the financial manager might recommend later in this chapter.

**TABLE 2-5** Unilate Textiles: Statement of Retained Earnings for the Period Ending December 31, 2009 ($ millions)

| | |
|---|---|
| Balance of retained earnings, December 31, 2008 | $260.0 |
|    Add: 2009 net income | 54.0 |
|    Less: 2009 dividends paid to stockholders | (29.0) |
| Balance of retained earnings, December 31, 2009 | $285.0 |

## Statement of Retained Earnings

Changes in the common equity accounts between balance sheet dates are reported in the **statement of retained earnings.** Unilate's statement is shown in Table 2-5. Of the $54 million that it earned, Unilate decided to keep $25 million for reinvestment in the business. Thus the balance sheet item called "retained earnings" increased from $260 million at the end of 2008 to $285 million at the end of 2009.

It is important to realize that the retained earnings account represents a claim *against assets,* not assets per se. A firm retains earnings primarily to expand the business, which means funds are invested in plant and equipment, in inventories, and so forth, *not* necessarily in a bank account (cash). Changes in retained earnings represent the recognition that income generated by the firm during the accounting period was reinvested in various assets rather than paid out as dividends to stockholders. *As a result, the amount of retained earnings as reported on the balance sheet does not represent cash and is not "available" for the payment of dividends or anything else.*[5]

**statement of retained earnings**
Shows changes in the common equity accounts between balance sheet dates.

### Self-Test Questions

Describe the four basic financial statements: the balance sheet, the income statement, the statement of cash flows, and the statement of retained earnings.

Explain the following statement: "Retained earnings as reported on the balance sheet do not represent cash and are not 'available' for the payment of dividends or anything else."

Differentiate between operating cash flows and other cash flows.

List two reasons why operating cash flows might differ from net income.

In accounting, the emphasis is on the determination of net income. What is emphasized in finance, and why is that focus important?

Describe the general rules for identifying whether changes in balance sheet accounts represent sources or uses of cash.

---

[5]A positive number in the retained earnings account indicates only that in the past, according to generally accepted accounting principles, the firm has earned income, but its dividends have been less than its reported income. Even though a company reports record earnings and shows an increase in the retained earnings account, it still might be short of cash. The same situation holds for individuals. You might own a new BMW (no loan), lots of clothes, and an expensive stereo and, therefore, have a high net worth. If you had only 23¢ in your pocket plus $5 in your checking account, you would still be short of cash.

# HOW DO INVESTORS USE FINANCIAL STATEMENTS?

The previous section gives you an indication as to how accountants construct financial statements and some of the cautions that should be taken when interpreting the numbers contained on statements published by companies. In this section, we give you an indication as to how investors use financial statements to obtain useful information when attempting to determine the value of a company. Although this discussion is not meant to be exhaustive, it should give you an idea of some of the information that investors "glean" from financial statements.

## Working (Operating) Capital

The term *working capital* generally refers to a firm's current assets because investment in these assets is necessary to keep the firm's day-to-day operations "working." For example, without inventory, the firm has no products to sell, and a firm that does not permit customers to purchase on credit, which generates accounts receivable, might not be able to sell finished products. These "working assets" often are termed *spontaneous assets* because their values change on a daily basis as the result of the firm's normal operations, not because formal decisions were made to effect such changes. Although some of the financing of working capital assets is provided by outside investors, such as stockholders, much of the funding for these short-term assets is provided from "loans" provided by suppliers, employees, and the government. Suppliers provide funding by allowing the firm to purchase raw materials on credit; employees provide funding by allowing the firm to pay salaries once (twice) each week (month) rather than requiring payment at the end of each day; and the government provides funding by allowing the taxes the firm collects to be paid periodically rather than at the time of a sale or payment of salaries. These sources of funds are "free" in the sense that the firm does not have to pay interest to use them. In addition, these liabilities are often termed *spontaneously generated funds,* or *spontaneous liabilities*, because they change spontaneously as the firm's normal operations change, not because the firm makes a conscious effort or enters a contractual agreement to change these sources of short-term financing. On the other hand, more formal financing arrangements, such as bank loans, require specific, conscious actions by the firm, and rent, or interest, must be paid for using these funds.

Investors are interested in a firm's operating capital for two reasons: (1) short-term financing arrangements must be paid off in the short term, and (2) short-term investments generally earn a lower return than long-term investments. A couple of the measures used to evaluate a firm's working capital position include net working capital and net operating working capital. We briefly discuss each of these measures and show you the result of the computation for Unilate Textiles in 2009 (in millions).

**Net working capital** is defined as follows:

**Net working capital**
Calculated by subtracting the current liabilities from the current assets.

$$\text{Net working capital} = \text{NWC} = \text{Current assets} - \text{Current liabilities}$$
$$= \$465.0 - \$130.0 = \$335.0$$

This computation shows that of the $465.0 million in current assets, $130.0 million is financed with short-term financing arrangements and the remaining $335.0 million is financed with long-term funds, which include bonds and common stock.

Net operating working capital is defined as follows:

$$\begin{array}{c} \text{Net operating} \\ \text{working capital} \\ \text{(NOWC)} \end{array} = \left( \begin{array}{c} \text{Current assets} \\ \text{required for operations} \end{array} \right) - \left( \begin{array}{c} \text{Non-interest-bearing} \\ \text{current liabilities} \end{array} \right)$$

$$= \$465.0 - \$90.0 = \$375.0$$

Unilate's current assets include cash and equivalents, accounts receivable, and inventory. All of these assets are part of the firm's normal operations. Because the $40 million in notes payable represents interest-bearing short-term loans from the bank, non−interest-bearing current liabilities include only accounts payable ($30 million) and accruals ($60 million). In 2008, Unilate's NOWC was $330 million, so its NOWC increased by $45 million in 2009. Looking at Unilate's balance sheets for the two years, we see that operating assets increased by $65 million (primarily because inventory increased $70 million), whereas non-interest-bearing liabilities increased by only $20 million (from $70 million in 2008 to $90 million in 2009). We discuss the ramifications of this trend later in this chapter when we use ratio analysis to examine Unilate's financial position.

## Operating Cash Flows

Earlier we mentioned that when a firm sells its products for cash and pays cash for its expenses, except depreciation and amortization, we can compute the net cash flow by adding the depreciation and amortization expense to the net income amount shown on the income statement. As a result, Unilate's net cash flow in 2009 was $104 million. Another measure that managers and investors examine is the operating cash flow generated by a firm. The *operating cash flow* is defined as follows:

$$\text{Operating cash flow} = \text{NOI}(1 - \text{Tax rate}) + \begin{array}{c} \text{Depreciation and} \\ \text{amortization expense} \end{array}$$

$$= \begin{array}{c} \text{Net operating} \\ \text{profit after taxes} \end{array} + \begin{array}{c} \text{Depreciation and} \\ \text{amortization expense} \end{array}$$

$$= \$130.0(1 - 0.40) + \$50.0 = \$128.0$$

The operating cash flow represents the cash flow that the firm would have available for investing in assets if it has no debt. In other words, Unilate would generate $128 million if all of its assets are financed only with common stock and the funds were invested in only operating assets, which include current and fixed assets that are used in the normal operation of the firm. Looking at Unilate's balance sheet, we see that the company is financed with nearly 51 percent debt. The income statement shows that Unilate paid interest equal to $40 million in 2009. Because interest is a tax-deductible expense that reduces the total amount of taxes that must be paid, it really didn't cost Unilate $40 million for its outstanding debt. Rather, the net cash flow associated with the debt was $24 million = $40 million × (1 − 0.40). Thus, Unilate paid $24 million in "net interest" for its outstanding debt, which means that its net cash flow would have been $104 million = $128 million − $24 million if all sales were collected in cash and all expenses, except depreciation and amortization, were paid in cash during 2009. Clearly, this was not the case, as the statement of cash flows given in Table 2-4 shows.

## Free Cash Flow

We mentioned earlier that depreciation is used to recognize the decline in the value over time of an asset that has a life longer than one year. Because such assets are required to maintain normal operations, the firm must be able to replace worn-out assets at some time in the future. If the costs of these long-term assets do not change significantly over time, then the firm should be able to put aside cash in the amount of the depreciation expense each year and have sufficient funds to replace the assets when they wear out. Even if they don't put aside cash each year, managers recognize that plans must be made to replace "used up" assets at some point in time if the firm is going to remain in business. If the firm pays out the net cash flows generated each year to investors, it might not be able to replace necessary assets. For this reason, investors are concerned with the *free cash flow* that a firm generates.

**Free cash flow**

Measures the cash flow that the firm is *free* to pay to investors (both bondholders and stockholders) after considering the cash investments that are needed to continue operations, including investments in fixed assets needed to man-ufacture products, working capital needed to continue operations, and new opportunities that will grow the stock price.

**Free cash flow** measures the cash flow that the firm is *free* to pay to investors (both bondholders and stockholders) after considering the cash investments that are needed to continue operations, including investments in fixed assets needed to manufacture products, working capital needed to continue operations, and new opportunities that will grow the stock price. We compute the free cash flow by subtracting the amount that is needed to fund investments during the year from operating cash flow:

$$\begin{aligned} \text{Free cash flow (FCF)} &= \text{Operating cash flow} - \text{Investments} \\ &= \text{Operating cash flow} - (\Delta \text{ in fixed assets} + \Delta \text{ NOWC}) \\ &= \$128.0 - (\$80.0 + \$45.0) = \$3.0 \end{aligned}$$

We determined that Unilate's operating cash flow was $128 million in 2009 and the change in net operating working capital ($\Delta$ NOWC) was $45 million. Footnote *a* in Table 2-1 shows that the company purchased an additional $80 million of fixed assets in 2009. As a result, Unilate generated a free cash flow equal to $3 million during the year. According to its income statement, the company paid interest equal to $40 million and a common stock dividend equal to $29 million in 2009. These amounts were much greater than the free cash flow that was generated during the year. Although Unilate paid a dividend that was much greater than the free cash flow would suggest was appropriate, investors, especially bondholders, probably would not complain as long as the firm is experiencing robust, profitable growth in operations. We will evaluate Unilate's growth as well as its financial position later in this chapter.

## Economic Value Added (EVA)[6]

**economic value added (EVA)**

Based on the concept that the earnings from actions taken by a company must be suf-ficient to compensate the suppliers of funds—both the bondholders and the stockholders.

The **economic value added (EVA)** measure is based on the concept that the earnings from actions taken by a company must be sufficient to compensate the suppliers of funds—both the bondholders and the stockholders.

To determine a firm's EVA, we adjust the operating income reported on the income statement to account for the costs associated with both the debt and the equity that the firm has outstanding. Recall that the computation of net income includes interest expense, which is a reflection of the cost of debt, but the dividends paid to stockholders, which is an indication of the cost of equity, are recognized after net income is determined. The general concept underlying EVA is to determine how

---

[6]The basic EVA approach was developed by Stern Stewart Management Services. Another measure developed by Stern Stewart is market value added (MVA), which is the difference between the market value and book value of a firm's equity.

much a firm's economic value is increased by the decisions it makes. Thus we can write the basic EVA equation as follows:

$$\text{EVA} = \text{NOI}(1 - \text{Tax rate}) - [(\text{Invested capital}) \times (\text{After-tax cost of capital as a percent})]$$

Here, invested capital is the amount of funds provided by investors (both bondholders and stockholders) and the cost of capital is the rate of return associated with this capital.

The EVA measure gives an estimate of the true economic profit that is generated by a firm. If the EVA is positive, the actions of the firm should increase its value. Conversely, if the EVA is negative, the actions of the firm should decrease its value.

If we assume that Unilate's total capital, which includes its bonds and common stock, has an average cost equal to 10 percent, then the EVA would be

$$\text{EVA} = \$130.0(1 - 0.40) - [(\$845.0 - \$90.0) \times 0.10]$$
$$= \$78.0 - \$75.5 = \$2.5$$

To compute this value, we deducted the amount of "free" financing that is provided by spontaneous current liabilities from total liabilities and common equity to determine the amount of "costly" financing for which Unilate pays either interest or dividends. We discuss the concepts of capital financing and cost of capital in detail later in Chapters 11 and 12. At this point, we can say that according to the EVA computation, in 2009, Unilate generated $78.0 million net operating profit after taxes and the dollar cost associated with its financing structure was $75.5 million. As a result, the economic profit generated in 2009 was $2.5 million, which suggests that the value of the firm should have increased in 2009. Because investors consider other factors when estimating the firm's future cash flows, we will wait to pass judgment about Unilate's financial position until after the next section.

**Self-Test Questions**

What is net working capital and net operating working capital?

How is operating cash flow measured?

What is free cash flow, and why is it an important factor in determining the value of a firm?

What is EVA and how does it differ from accounting income?

Consider a firm that reported net operating income equal to $40,000 this year. Examination of the company's balance sheet and income statement shows that the tax rate was 40 percent, the depreciation expense was $5,000, $25,000 was invested in assets during the year, and invested capital equals $200,000. (1) What was the operating cash flow that the firm generated during the year? (2) What was the firm's free cash flow? (3) What was the firm's EVA if its average cost of funds is 8 percent after taxes? (*Answers:* $29,000; $74,000; and $8,000)

## FINANCIAL STATEMENT (RATIO) ANALYSIS

As we discovered in previous sections, financial statements provide information about a firm's position at a point in time as well as its operations over some past period. Nevertheless, the real value of financial statements lies in the fact that they can be used to help predict the firm's financial position in the future and to determine expected earnings and dividends. From an investor's standpoint, *predicting the future is the purpose of financial statement analysis;* from management's standpoint, *financial statement analysis is useful both as a way to anticipate future conditions and, more important, as a starting point for planning actions that will influence the future course of events.*

The first step in a financial analysis typically includes an evaluation of the firm's ratios. The ratios are designed to show relationships among financial statement accounts *within* firms and *between* firms. Translating accounting numbers into relative values, or ratios, allows us to compare the financial position of one firm with the financial position of another firm, even if their sizes are significantly different.

In this section, we calculate the 2009 financial ratios for Unilate Textiles and then evaluate those ratios in relation to the industry averages. Note that all dollar amounts used in the ratio calculations given here are in millions, except where per-share values are used. Also, note that there are literally hundreds of ratios that are used by management, creditors, and stockholders to evaluate firms. In this book, we show only a few of the most often-used ratios.

## Liquidity Ratios

**liquid asset**
An asset that can be easily converted to cash without significant loss of its original value.

A **liquid asset** is one that can be easily converted to cash without significant loss of its original value. Converting assets—especially current assets such as inventory and receivables—to cash is the primary means by which a firm obtains the funds needed to pay its current bills. Therefore, a firm's "liquid position" deals with the question of how well the company is able to meet its current obligations. Short-term, or current, assets are more easily converted to cash (more liquid) than are long-term assets. In general, then, one firm would be considered more liquid than another firm if it has a greater proportion of its total assets in the form of current assets.

According to its balance sheet, Unilate has debts totaling $130 million that must be paid off within the coming year—that is, current liabilities equal $130 million. Will it have trouble satisfying those obligations? A full liquidity analysis requires the use of cash budgets (described in Chapter 17). Nevertheless, by relating the amount of cash and other current assets to the firm's current obligations, ratio analysis provides a quick, easy-to-use measure of liquidity. Two commonly used **liquidity ratios** are discussed in this section.

**liquidity ratios**
A ratio analysis that provides a quick, easy-to-use measure of liquidity by relating the amount of cash and other current assets to the firm's current obligations.

### Current Ratio

**current ratio**
Calculated by dividing the current assets of a company by the current liabilities.

The **current ratio** is calculated as follows:

$$\text{Current ratio} = \frac{\text{Current assets}}{\text{Current liabilities}} = \frac{\$465.0}{\$130.0} = 3.6 \text{ times}$$

$$\text{Industry average} = 4.1 \text{ times}$$

Current assets normally include cash and equivalents, accounts receivable, and inventories. Current liabilities consist of accounts payable, short-term notes payable, long-term debt that matures in the current period (current maturities of long-term debt), accrued taxes, and other accrued expenses (principally wages).

When a company experiences financial difficulty, it pays its bills (accounts payable) more slowly, borrows more from its bank, and so forth. If current liabilities are rising more rapidly than current assets, the current ratio will fall, which could spell trouble. Because the current ratio provides the best single indicator of the extent to which the claims of short-term creditors are covered by assets that are expected to be converted to cash fairly quickly, it is the most commonly used measure of short-term solvency. You should be careful when examining the current ratio, however, just as you should when examining any ratio individually. For example, just because a firm has a low current ratio (even one less than 1.0), this does not mean that the current obligations cannot be met. Consider a firm with a current ratio equal to 0.9, which suggests that if all current assets are liquidated at their book values, only 90 percent of the current liabilities can be covered. If the firm manufactures and sells a substantial amount of inventory for cash and collects much of its current accounts receivables long before suppliers, employees, and short-term creditors need to be paid, then it really does not face a liquidity problem.

Unilate's current ratio of 3.6 is below the average for its industry, 4.1, so its liquidity position is somewhat weak. Because current assets are scheduled to be converted to cash in the near future, it is highly probable that they can be liquidated at close to their stated value. With a current ratio of 3.6, Unilate could liquidate current assets at only 28 percent of book value and still pay off its current creditors in full.[7]

Although industry average figures are discussed later in this chapter in some detail, at this point you should note that an industry average is not a magic number that all firms should strive to attain. In fact, some well-managed firms might be above the average and other good firms might be below it. If a firm's ratios are far removed from the average for its industry, however, an analyst should question why this deviation has occurred. A significant deviation from the industry average should signal the analyst (or management) to *check further*, even if the deviation is considered to be in the "good" direction. For example, we know that Unilate's current ratio is below average. But what would you conclude if Unilate's current ratio was nearly twice that of the industry—perhaps 8.0? Is this difference good? Maybe not. Because current assets, which are liquid, safe assets, generally generate lower rates of return than do long-term assets, it might be argued that firms with too much liquidity are not investing wisely.

## Quick (Acid Test) Ratio

The **quick,** or **acid test, ratio** is calculated as follows:

$$\text{Quick (acid test) ratio} = \frac{\text{Current assets} - \text{Inventory}}{\text{Current liabilities}}$$

$$= \frac{\$465.0 - \$270.0}{\$130.0} = \frac{\$195.0}{\$130.0} = 1.5 \text{ times}$$

$$\text{Industry average} = 2.1 \text{ times}$$

**quick, or acid test, ratio**
Calculated by subtracting the inventory from the current assets, then dividing by the current liabilities.

Inventories typically are the least liquid of a firm's current assets, so they are the assets on which losses are most likely to occur in the event of a "quick" liquidation. Therefore, a measure of the firm's ability to pay off short-term obligations without relying on the sale of inventories is important.

The textile industry's average quick ratio is 2.1, so Unilate's ratio value of 1.5 is low in comparison with the ratios of its competitors. This difference suggests that Unilate's level of inventories is relatively high. Even so, if the accounts receivable can be collected, the company can pay off its current liabilities even without having to liquidate its inventory.

---

[7]Unilate's current ratio is 3.577, and 1/3.577 = 0.2796, which is 28 percent when rounded to two decimal places. Note that 0.2796($465.0) = $130, which is the amount of current liabilities.

Our evaluation of the liquidity ratios suggests that Unilate's liquidity position currently is fairly poor. To get a better idea of why Unilate is in this position, we must examine its asset management ratios.

## Asset Management Ratios

**asset management ratios**
Measure how effectively the firm is managing its assets. These ratios are designed to answer the following question: Does the total amount of each type of asset as reported on the balance sheet seem reasonable, too high, or too low in view of current and projected sales levels?

The second group of ratios, the **asset management ratios,** measures how effectively the firm is managing its assets. These ratios are designed to answer the following question: Does the total amount of each type of asset as reported on the balance sheet seem reasonable, too high, or too low in view of current and projected sales levels?

Firms invest in assets to generate revenues both in the current period and in future periods. To purchase their assets, Unilate and other companies must borrow or obtain funds from other sources. If firms have too many assets, their interest expenses will be too high; hence, their profits will be depressed. On the other hand, because production is affected by the capacity of assets, if assets are too low, profitable sales might be lost because the firm is unable to manufacture enough products.

### Inventory Turnover Ratio

**inventory turnover ratio**
Calculated by dividing the cost of goods sold by the inventory.

The **inventory turnover ratio** is defined as follows:[8]

$$\text{Inventory turnover ratio} = \frac{\text{Cost of goods sold}}{\text{Inventory}} = \frac{\text{Variable operating costs}}{\text{Inventory}}$$

$$= \frac{\$1,230.0}{\$270.0} = 4.6 \text{ times}$$

$$\text{Industry average} = 7.4 \text{ times}$$

As a rough approximation, each item of Unilate's inventory is sold out and restocked, or "turned over," 4.6 times per year (every 79 days), which is considerably lower than the industry average of 7.4 times (every 49 days).[9] This ratio suggests that Unilate is holding excess stocks of inventory; excess stocks are, of course, unproductive and represent an investment with a low or zero rate of return. With such a low turnover, we must wonder whether Unilate is holding damaged or obsolete goods (for example, textile types, styles, and patterns from previous years) that are not actually worth their stated value.

You should use care when calculating and using the inventory turnover ratio because purchases of inventory (and thus the cost of goods sold) occur over the entire year, whereas the inventory figure applies to one point in time (perhaps December 31). For this reason, it is better to use an average inventory measure.[10] If the firm's business is highly seasonal, or if a strong upward or downward sales trend has occurred during the

---

[8]*Turnover* is a term that originated many years ago with the old Yankee peddler, who would load up his wagon with goods, then go off on his route to peddle his wares. The merchandise was his "working capital" because it was what he actually sold, or "turned over," to produce his profits. His "turnover" was the number of trips that he took each year. Annual sales divided by inventory equaled turnover, or trips per year. If the peddler made 10 trips per year, stocked 100 pans, and made a gross profit of $5 per pan, his annual gross profit would be $100 \times \$5 \times 10 = \$5,000$. If the peddler went faster and made 20 trips per year, his gross profit would double, other things held constant.

[9]Some compilers of financial ratio statistics, such as Dun & Bradstreet, use the ratio of sales to inventories carried at cost to depict inventory turnover. If this form of the inventory turnover ratio is used, the true turnover will be overstated because sales are given at market prices whereas inventories are carried at cost.

[10]Preferably, the average inventory value should be calculated by dividing the sum of the monthly figures during the year by 12. If monthly data are not available, you could add the beginning-of-year and end-of-year figures and divide by 2; this calculation will adjust for growth but not for seasonal effects. Using this approach, Unilate's average inventory for 2009 would be $235 = (\$200 + \$270)/2$, and its inventory turnover would be $5.2 = \$1,230/\$235$, which still is well below the industry average.

year, it is essential to make such an adjustment. To maintain comparability with industry averages, however, we did not use the average inventory figure in our computations.

## Days Sales Outstanding

**Days sales outstanding (DSO),** also called the *average collection period (ACP),* is used to evaluate the firm's ability to collect its credit sales in a timely manner. DSO is calculated as follows:[11]

**days sales outstanding (DSO)**
Also called the *average collection period (ACP).* It is used to evaluate the firm's ability to collect its credit sales in a timely manner.

$$\text{Days sales outstanding(DSO)} = \frac{\text{Accounts Receivable}}{\text{Average daily sales}} = \frac{\text{Accounts Receivable}}{\left[\frac{\text{Annual sales}}{360}\right]}$$

$$= \frac{\$180.0}{\left[\frac{\$1,500.0}{360}\right]} = \frac{\$180.0}{\$4.17} = 43.2 \text{ days}$$

$$\text{Industry average} = 32.1 \text{ days}$$

The DSO represents the average length of time that the firm must wait after making a credit sale before receiving cash—that is, its average collection period. Unilate has about 43 days of sales outstanding, somewhat higher than the 32-day industry average. The DSO also can be evaluated by comparing it with the terms on which the firm sells its goods. For example, Unilate's sales terms call for payment within 30 days, so the fact that sales are outstanding an average of 43 days indicates that customers generally are not paying their bills on time. If the trend in DSO over the past few years has been rising, but the credit policy has not been changed, it would be even stronger evidence that the company should take steps to improve the time it takes to collect accounts receivable. This situation seems to be the case for Unilate because its 2008 DSO was 40 days.

## Fixed Assets Turnover Ratio

The **fixed assets turnover ratio** measures how effectively the firm uses its plant and equipment to help generate sales. It is computed as follows:

**fixed assets turnover ratio**
Measures how effectively the firm uses its plant and equipment to help generate sales. It is calculated by dividing the sales by the net fixed assets.

$$\text{Fixed assets turnover ratio} = \frac{\text{Sales}}{\text{Net fixed assets}} = \frac{\$1,500.0}{\$380.0} = 3.9 \text{ times}$$

$$\text{Industry average} = 4.0 \text{ times}$$

Unilate's ratio of 3.9 is almost equal to the industry average, indicating that the firm is using its fixed assets about as efficiently as the other members of its industry. Unilate seems to have neither too many nor too few fixed assets in relation to other similar firms.

Take care when using the fixed assets turnover ratio to compare the performance of different firms. Recall from accounting that most balance sheet accounts are stated in terms of historical costs. Inflation might cause the value of many assets that were purchased in the past to be seriously understated. Therefore, if we are comparing an old firm that acquired many of its fixed assets years ago at low prices with a new company that acquired its fixed assets only recently, we probably would find that the

---

[11]To compute DSO using this equation, we must assume that all of the firm's sales are on credit. We usually compute DSO in this manner because information on credit sales is rarely available. Because all firms do not have the same percentage of credit sales, the days sales outstanding could be misleading. Also, note that by convention, much of the financial community uses 360 rather than 365 as the number of days in the year for purposes such as this. The DSO is discussed further in Chapters 14 and 15.

old firm has a higher fixed assets turnover ratio. Because financial analysts typically do not have the data necessary to make inflation adjustments to specific assets, they must simply recognize that a problem exists and deal with it judgmentally. In Unilate's case, the issue is not a serious one because all firms in the industry have been expanding at about the same rate; in this instance, the balance sheets of the comparison firms are indeed comparable.

## Total Assets Turnover Ratio

**total assets turnover ratio**
Measures the turnover of all of the firm's assets. It is calculated by dividing the sales by the total assets.

The **total assets turnover ratio** measures the turnover of all of the firm's assets. It is calculated as follows:

$$\text{Total assets turnover ratio} = \frac{\text{Sales}}{\text{Total assets}} = \frac{\$1,500.0}{\$845.0} = 1.8 \text{ times}$$

$$\text{Industry average} = 2.1 \text{ times}$$

Unilate's ratio is somewhat lower than the industry average, indicating that the company is not generating a sufficient volume of business given its investment in total assets. To become more efficient, Unilate should increase its sales, dispose of some assets, or pursue a combination of these steps.

Our examination of Unilate's asset management ratios shows that its fixed assets turnover ratio is very close to the industry average, but its total assets turnover is below average. The fixed assets turnover ratio excludes current assets, whereas the total assets turnover ratio includes them. Therefore, comparison of these ratios confirms our conclusion from the analysis of the liquidity ratios: Unilate seems to have a liquidity problem. The fact that the company's inventory turnover ratio and average collection period are worse than the industry averages suggests, at least in part, that the firm might have problems with inventory and receivables management. Slow sales and tardy collections of credit sales suggest that Unilate might rely more heavily on external funds, such as loans, than the industry to pay current obligations. Examining the debt management ratios will help us to determine whether this assessment actually is the case.

## Debt Management Ratios

The extent to which a firm uses debt financing has three important implications:

**financial leverage**
Borrowing that affects the expected rate of return realized by stockholders because the interest on debt is tax deductible whereas dividends are not, so paying interest lowers the firm's tax bill, everything else equal. Also, the rate a firm earns from its investments in assets usually differs from the rate at which it borrows.

1. By raising funds through debt, the firm avoids diluting stockholder ownership.

2. Creditors look to the equity, or owner-supplied funds, to provide a margin of safety. If the stockholders have provided only a small proportion of the total financing, the risks of the enterprise are borne mainly by its creditors.

3. If the firm earns more on investments financed with borrowed funds than it pays in interest, the return on the owners' capital is magnified, or "leveraged."

**Financial leverage,** or borrowing, affects the expected rate of return realized by stockholders for two reasons. First, the interest on debt is tax deductible whereas dividends are not, so paying interest lowers the firm's tax bill, everything else equal. Second, the rate a firm earns from its investments in assets usually differs from the rate at which it borrows. If the firm has healthy operations, it typically invests the funds it borrows at a rate of return that is greater than the interest rate on its debt. In combination with the tax advantage that debt offers compared with stock, the higher investment rate of return produces a magnified positive return to the stockholders. Under these conditions, leverage works to the advantage of the firm and its stockholders.

Unfortunately, financial leverage is a double-edged sword. When the firm experiences poor business conditions, typically sales are lower and costs are higher than expected, but the cost of borrowing, which generally is fixed, still must be paid. The *costs* (interest payments) associated with borrowing are contractual and do not vary with sales, and they must be paid to avoid the threat of bankruptcy. Therefore, the required interest payments might impose a very significant burden on a firm that has liquidity problems. In fact, if the interest payments are high enough, a firm with a positive operating income could end up with a negative return to stockholders. Under these conditions, leverage works to the detriment of the firm and its stockholders.

Detailed discussions of financial leverage are given in Chapters 12 and 17. For the purposes of ratio analysis in this chapter, we need to understand that firms with relatively high debt ratios have higher expected returns when business is normal or good, but they are exposed to risk of loss when business is poor. Thus, firms with low debt ratios are less risky, but they also forgo the opportunity to "leverage up" their return on equity. The prospects of high returns are desirable, but the average investor is averse to risk. Therefore, decisions about the use of debt require firms to balance the desire for higher expected returns against the increased risk that results from using more debt. Determining the optimal amount of debt for a given firm is a complicated process, and we will defer discussion of this topic until Chapter 12. Here, we will simply look at two procedures that analysts use to examine the firm's debt in a financial statement analysis: (1) They check balance sheet ratios to determine the extent to which borrowed funds have been used to finance assets, and (2) they review income statement ratios to determine how well operating profits can cover fixed charges such as interest. These two sets of ratios are complementary, so analysts use both types.

## Debt Ratio

The **debt ratio** measures the percentage of the firm's assets financed by creditors (borrowing). It is computed as follows:

$$\text{Debt ratio} = \text{Debt-to-total-assets ratio} = \frac{\text{Total liabilities}}{\text{Total assets}}$$

$$= \frac{\$430.0}{\$845.0} = 0.509 = 50.9\%$$

$$\text{Industry average} = 42.0\%$$

**debt ratio** Measures the percentage of the firm's assets financed by creditors (borrowing). It is calculated by dividing the total liabilities by the total assets.

Total debt includes both current liabilities ($130 million) and long-term debt ($300 million). Creditors prefer low debt ratios because the lower the ratio, the greater the cushion against creditors' losses in the event of liquidation. The owners, on the other hand, can benefit from leverage because it magnifies earnings, thereby increasing the return to stockholders. Too much debt often leads to financial difficulty, which eventually could cause bankruptcy.

Unilate's debt ratio is almost 51 percent, which means that its creditors have supplied slightly more than half of the firm's total financing. Because the average debt ratio for the industry is 42 percent, Unilate might find it difficult to borrow additional funds without first raising more equity capital through a stock issue. Creditors might be reluctant to lend the firm more money, and management might be subjecting the firm to a greater chance of bankruptcy if it sought to increase the debt ratio much further by borrowing additional funds.[12]

## Times-Interest-Earned Ratio

**times-interest-earned (TIE) ratio**
Calculated by dividing the earnings before interest and taxes by the interest charges.

The **times-interest-earned (TIE) ratio** is defined as follows:

$$\text{Times interest earned (TIE) ratio} = \frac{\text{Earnings before interest and taxes}}{\text{Interest charges}}$$

$$= \frac{\text{EBIT}}{\text{Interest charges}} = \frac{\$130.0}{\$40.0} = 3.3 \text{ times}$$

$$\text{Industry average} = 6.5 \text{ times}$$

The TIE ratio measures the extent to which a firm's earnings before interest and taxes (EBIT), also called *net operating income (NOI),* can decline before these earnings are unable to cover annual interest costs. Failure to meet this obligation can bring legal action by the firm's creditors, possibly resulting in bankruptcy. Note that EBIT, rather than net income, is used in the numerator. Because interest is paid with pretax dollars, the firm's ability to pay current interest is not affected by taxes.

Unilate's interest is covered 3.3 times. Because the industry average is 6.5 times, compared with firms in the same business, Unilate is covering its interest charges by a low margin of safety (about one-half of the industry average). Its TIE ratio reinforces our conclusion based on the debt ratio that Unilate probably would face difficulties if it attempted to borrow additional funds.

## Fixed Charge Coverage Ratio

**fixed charge coverage ratio**
Similar to the TIE ratio, but more inclusive because it recognizes that many firms lease rather than buy assets and also must make sinking fund payments

The **fixed charge coverage ratio** is similar to the TIE ratio, but it is more inclusive because it recognizes that many firms lease rather than buy assets and also must make sinking fund payments.[13] Leasing is widespread in certain industries, making this ratio preferable to the TIE ratio for many purposes. Unilate's annual long-term lease payments total $10 million, and the company must make an annual $8 million required payment to help retire its debt. Because sinking fund payments must be paid with after-tax dollars, whereas interest and lease payments are paid with pretax dollars, the sinking fund payments must be divided by (1 − Tax rate) to find the before-tax income required to pay taxes and still have enough left to make the sinking fund payment. In this case, $8/(1 − 0.4) = $13.33. Therefore, if the company had pretax income of $13.33 million, it could pay taxes at a 40 percent rate and have $8 million left to make the sinking fund payment.

---

[12]The ratio of debt to equity also is used in financial analysis. The debt-to-assets (D/A) and debt-to-equity (D/E) ratios are simply transformations of each other because total debt plus total equity must equal total assets:

$$D/E = \frac{D/A}{1 - D/A}, \text{ and } D/A = \frac{D/E}{1 - D/E}$$

[13]Generally, a long-term lease is defined as one that extends for more than one year. Thus, rent incurred under a six-month lease would not be included in the fixed charge coverage ratio, but rental payments under a one-year or longer lease would be defined as a fixed charge and would be included. A sinking fund is a required annual payment designed to reduce the balance of a bond or preferred stock issue.

Fixed charges include interest, annual long-term lease obligations, and sinking fund payments. The fixed charge coverage ratio is calculated as follows:

$$\text{Fixed charge coverage ratio} = \frac{\text{EBIT} + \text{Lease payments}}{\begin{array}{c}\text{Interest} \\ \text{charges}\end{array} + \begin{array}{c}\text{Lease} \\ \text{payments}\end{array} + \left[\dfrac{\text{Sinking fund payments}}{(1 - \text{Tax rate})}\right]}$$

$$= \frac{\$130.0 + \$10.0}{\$40.0 + \$10.0 + \left[\dfrac{\$8.0}{(1 - 0.4)}\right]} = \frac{\$140.0}{\$63.33} = 2.2 \text{ times}$$

$$\text{Industry average} = 5.8 \text{ times}$$

In the numerator of the fixed charge coverage ratio, the lease payments are added to EBIT because we want to determine the firm's ability to cover its fixed financing charges from the income generated before any fixed financing charges are considered (deducted). The EBIT figure represents the firm's operating income net of lease payments, so the lease payments must be added back.

Unilate's fixed charges are covered only 2.2 times, compared with the industry average of 5.8 times. Again, this difference indicates that the firm is weaker than average, and it points out the difficulties that Unilate probably would encounter if it attempted to increase its debt or other fixed financial obligations.

Our examination of Unilate's debt management ratios indicates that the company has a debt ratio that is *higher than* the industry average, and it has coverage ratios that are substantially *lower than* the industry averages. This finding suggests that Unilate is in a somewhat dangerous position with respect to leverage (debt). In fact, the firm might have great difficulty borrowing additional funds until its debt position improves. If the company cannot pay its current obligations, it might be forced into bankruptcy. To see how Unilate's debt position has affected its profits, we next examine its profitability ratios.

## Profitability Ratios

Profitability is the net result of a number of policies and decisions. The ratios examined thus far provide some information about the way the firm is operating, but the **profitability ratios** show the combined effects of liquidity management, asset management, and debt management on operating results.

### Net Profit Margin

The **net profit margin,** which gives the profit per dollar of sales, is calculated as follows:

$$\text{Net profit margin} = \frac{\text{Net profit}}{\text{sales}} = \frac{\$54.0}{\$1,500.0} = 0.036 = 3.6\%$$

$$\text{Industry average} = 4.9\%$$

Unilate's net profit margin is lower than the industry average of 4.9 percent, indicating that its sales might be too low, its costs might be too high, or both. Recall that, according to its debt ratio, Unilate has a greater proportion of debt than the industry average, and the TIE ratio shows that Unilate's interest payments on its debt are not covered as well as in the rest of the industry. This partly explains why Unilate's profit margin is low. To see this fact, we can compute the ratio of EBIT (operating income) to sales, which is called the *operating profit margin.* Unilate's operating profit margin of 8.7 percent is exactly the same as the industry average, so the cause of its low net profit margin is the relatively high interest attributable to the firm's higher-than-average use of debt.

**profitability ratios**
Show the combined effects of liquidity management, asset management, and debt management on operating results.

**net profit margin**
Gives the profit per dollar of sales and is calculated by dividing the net profit by the sales.

### Return on Total Assets

**return on total assets (ROA)**
Calculated by dividing the net income by the total assets.

The **return on total assets (ROA)** is computed as follows:

$$\text{Return on total asset (ROA)} = \frac{\text{Net income}}{\text{Total assets}} = \frac{\$54.0}{\$845.0} = 0.064 = 6.4\%$$

$$\text{Industry average} = 10.3\%$$

Unilate's 6.4 percent return is well below the 10.3 percent average for the textile industry. This low return results from the company's higher-than-average use of debt.

### Return on Common Equity

**return on common equity (ROE)**
The *rate of return on stockholders' investment.* It is calculated by dividing the net income available to common stockholders by the common equity.

The **return on common equity (ROE),** or the *rate of return on stockholders' investment,* is computed as follows:[14]

$$\text{Return on equity (ROE)} = \frac{\text{Net income available to common stockholders}}{\text{Common equity}}$$

$$= \frac{\$54.0}{\$415.0} = 0.130 = 13.0\%$$

$$\text{Industry average} = 17.7\%$$

Unilate's 13.0 percent return is lower than the 17.7 percent industry average. This result follows from the company's greater use of debt (leverage), a point that is analyzed further later in this chapter.

Our examination of Unilate's profitability ratios shows that the company's operating results have suffered because of its poor liquidity position, its poor asset management, and its above-average debt. In the final group of ratios, we will examine Unilate's market value ratios to see how investors feel about the company's current position.

## Market Value Ratios

**market value ratios**
Relate the firm's stock price to its earnings and book value per share. They give management an indication of what investors think of the company's future prospects based on its past performance.

The **market value ratios** relate the firm's stock price to its earnings and book value per share. They give management an indication of what investors think of the company's future prospects based on its past performance. If the firm's liquidity ratios, asset management ratios, debt management ratios, and profitability ratios are all good, then its market value ratios will be high, and its stock price will probably be as high as can be expected. Of course, the opposite also is true.

### Price/Earnings Ratio

**price/earnings (P/E) ratio**
Shows how much investors are willing to pay per dollar of reported profits.

The **price/earnings (P/E) ratio** shows how much investors are willing to pay per dollar of reported profits. To compute the P/E ratio, we need to know the firm's earnings per share (EPS):

$$\text{Earnings per share (EPS)} = \frac{\text{Net income available to common stockholders}}{\text{Number of common shares outstanding}}$$

$$= \frac{\$54.0}{25.0} = \$2.16$$

---

[14]Net income available to common stockholders is computed by subtracting preferred dividends from net income. Because Unilate has no preferred stock, its net income available to common stockholders is the same as its net income.

Unilate's stock sells for $23. With an EPS of $2.16, its P/E ratio is therefore 10.6:

$$\text{Price/Earnings (PE) ratio} = \frac{\text{Market price per share}}{\text{Earnings per share}} = \frac{\$23.00}{\$2.16} = 10.6 \text{ times}$$

$$\text{Industry average} = 15.0 \text{ times}$$

Other things held constant, P/E ratios are higher for firms with high growth prospects and lower for riskier firms. Because Unilate's P/E ratio is lower than those of other textile manufacturers, it suggests that the company is regarded as being somewhat riskier than most of its competitors, as having poorer growth prospects, or both. From our analysis of its debt management ratios, we know that Unilate has higher-than-average risk associated with leverage. However, we do not know whether its growth prospects are poor.

## Market/Book Ratio

The ratio of a stock's market price to its book value gives another indication of how investors regard the company. The stocks of companies with relatively high rates of return on equity generally sell at higher multiples of book value than those with low returns. First, we find Unilate's book value per share:

$$\text{Book value per share} = \frac{\text{Common equity}}{\text{Number of common shares outstanding}}$$

$$= \frac{\$415.0}{25.0} = \$16.60$$

Next, we divide the market value per share by the book value per share to get a **market/book (M/B) ratio** of 1.4 times for Unilate:

$$\text{Market/book (M/B) ratio} = \frac{\text{Market price per share}}{\text{Book value per share}} = \frac{\$23.00}{\$16.60} = 1.4 \text{ times}$$

$$\text{Industry average} = 2.5 \text{ times}$$

**market/book (M/B) ratio** Calculated by dividing the market value per share by the book value per share.

Investors are willing to pay less for Unilate's book value than for that of an average textile manufacturer. This finding should not be surprising because, as we discovered previously, Unilate has generated below-average returns with respect to both total assets and common equity. Generally, the stocks of firms that earn high rates of return on their assets sell for prices well in excess of their book values. For very successful firms, the market/book ratio can be as high as 10 to 15.

Our examination of Unilate's market value ratios indicates that investors are not excited about the future prospects of the company's common stock as an investment. Perhaps they believe that Unilate is headed toward bankruptcy unless the firm takes action to correct its liquidity and asset management problems and to improve its leverage position. One approach used to determine the direction in which a firm is headed is to evaluate the trends of the ratios over the past few years and thereby answer the following question: Is the firm's position improving or deteriorating?

## Trend Analysis

Our analysis of Unilate's ratios indicates that the firm's current financial position is poor compared with the industry norm. Note, however, that this analysis does not tell us whether the company is in a better or a worse financial position than it was in

**FIGURE 2-2**   Rate of Return on Common Equity (ROE), 2005–2009

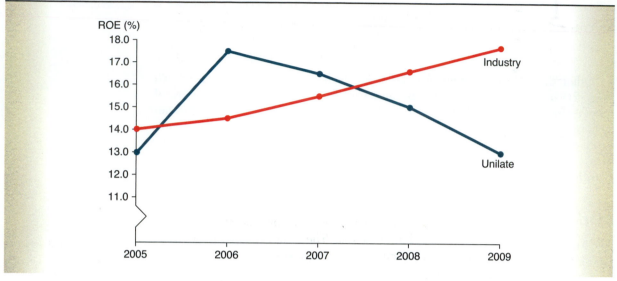

**trend analysis**
Examines the paths taken in the past to provide information about whether the firm's financial position is more likely to improve or deteriorate in the future.

previous years. To determine the direction in which the firm is headed, we must analyze trends in ratios. By examining the paths taken in the past, **trend analysis** provides information about whether the firm's financial position is more likely to improve or deteriorate in the future.

A simple approach to trend analysis is to construct graphs containing both the firm's ratios and the industry averages for the past five years. Using this approach, we can examine both the direction of the movement in, and the relationships between, the firm's ratios and the industry averages.

Figure 2-2 shows that Unilate's return on equity has declined since 2005, even though the industry average has steadily increased at a moderate rate. We could analyze other ratios in a similar fashion. If we were to compare Unilate's ratios from 2009 with those from 2008, we would discover that Unilate's financial position has deteriorated, not strengthened—not a good trend.

**Self-Test Questions**

Identify two ratios that are used to analyze a firm's liquidity position, and write out their equations.

Identify four ratios that are used to measure how effectively a firm is managing its assets, and write out their equations.

Identify three ratios that are used to measure the extent to which a firm uses debt financing, and write out their equations.

Identify three ratios that show the combined effects of liquidity, asset management, and debt management on profitability, and write out their equations.

Identify two ratios that relate a firm's stock price to its earnings and book value per share, and write out their equations.

# SUMMARY OF RATIO ANALYSIS: THE DuPONT ANALYSIS

Management and analysts often evaluate ratios using the DuPont approach, named after the company whose managers developed the evaluation technique. The idea is to attain greater detail by dissecting a single ratio into two or more related ratios. Using the basic approach, we compute the return on assets (ROA) by multiplying the net profit margin by the total assets turnover. The formula, which is called the **DuPont equation,** is as follows:

**2–2**

$$\text{ROA} = \text{Net profit margin} \times \text{Total assets turnover}$$
$$= \frac{\text{Net income}}{\text{Sales}} \times \frac{\text{Sales}}{\text{Total assets}}$$

**DuPont equation**
Used to attain greater detail by dissecting a single ratio into two or more related ratios. In the basic approach, we compute the return on assets (ROA) by multiplying the net profit margin by the total assets turnover.

In 2009, Unilate made 3.6 percent, or 3.6 cents, on each dollar of sales, and assets were "turned over" nearly 1.8 times during the year. The company earned a return of 6.4 percent on its assets. Using the DuPont equation, we have

$$\text{ROA} = \frac{\$54}{\$1,500} \times \frac{\$1,500}{\$845} = 0.036 + 1.775 = 0.0639 = 6.4\%$$

If the company were financed only with common equity—that is, if it had no debt, the ROA and the ROE would be the same because total assets would equal the amount of common equity. But nearly 51 percent of Unilate's capital consists of debt, both long term and short term. Thus, as earlier computations show, the ROA and ROE are not equal. Instead, because ROA is defined as *net income available to common stockholders* divided by total assets, the ROA of 6.4 percent all goes to common stockholders. Because the common equity represents less than 100 percent of Unilate's capital, the return to the common stockholders, ROE, must be greater than the ROA of 6.4 percent. To translate the ROA into the ROE, we must multiply ROA by the *equity multiplier,* which is the ratio of assets to common equity, or the number of times that the total assets exceed the amount of common equity (it is also the inverse of the percent of total assets that is financed with equity). Using this approach, we can write ROE as follows:

**2–3**

$$\text{ROE} = \text{ROA} \times \text{Equity multiplier} = \frac{\text{Net income}}{\text{Sales}} \times \frac{\text{Total assets}}{\text{Common equity}}$$

$$= 6.4\% \times \frac{\$845.0}{\$415.0} = 6.4\% \times 2.036 = 13.0\%$$

We can combine Equation 2–2 and Equation 2–3 to form the *extended* DuPont equation, which is written as follows:

**2–4**

$$\text{ROE} = \left[ \left( \frac{\text{Profit}}{\text{margin}} \right) \times \left( \frac{\text{Total assets}}{\text{turnover}} \right) \right] \times \left( \frac{\text{Equity}}{\text{multiplier}} \right)$$
$$= \left[ \frac{\text{Net income}}{\text{Sales}} \times \frac{\text{Sales}}{\text{Total assets}} \right] \times \frac{\text{Total assets}}{\text{Common equity}}$$

$$\text{ROE}_{\text{Unilate}} = 3.6\% \times 1.775 \times 2.036 = 13.0\%$$
$$\text{ROE}_{\text{Industry}} = 4.9\% \times 2.100 \times 1/(1 - 0.42) = 17.7\%$$

Note that the equity multiplier for the industry is computed as the inverse of the equity to total assets ratio ($= 1 -$ Debt ratio). Thus, the industry's equity multiplier is $1/[1 - (\text{Debt ratio})] = 1/(1 - 0.42) = 1.72$.

The DuPont computation shows that Unilate's ROE is lower than that of the industry because Unilate's profit margin and total assets turnover (efficiency) are lower than those of the industry. Unilate's management can use the DuPont system to analyze ways of improving the firm's performance. Focusing on the net profit margin, Unilate's marketing personnel can study the effects of raising prices (or lowering them to increase volume), of selling new products or moving into markets with higher margins, and so forth. The company's cost accountants can study various expense items and, working with engineers, purchasing agents, and other operating personnel, seek ways of holding down costs. To improve the assets turnover, Unilate's financial analysts, working with both production and marketing personnel, can investigate ways of minimizing the investment in various types of assets. At the same time, its treasury staff can analyze the effects of alternative financing strategies, seeking to hold down interest expense and the risk of debt while still using leverage to increase the rate of return on equity.

As a result of a DuPont analysis, Sally Anderson, Unilate's president, recently announced a series of moves designed to cut the company's operating costs by more than 20 percent per year. Anderson also announced that the company intends to concentrate its capital in markets in which profit margins are reasonably high. If competition increases in certain product markets (such as the low-price end of the textiles market), Unilate will withdraw from those segments. The company is seeking a high return on equity, and Anderson recognizes that if competition drives profit margins too low in a particular market, it becomes impossible to earn high returns on the capital invested to serve that market. To achieve a high ROE, Unilate might have to develop new products and shift capital into new areas. The company's future depends on this type of analysis, and if the firm succeeds in the future, then the DuPont system will have helped Unilate achieve that success.

### Self-Test Questions

Explain how the DuPont equation combines multiple ratios to reveal the basic determinants of ROA and ROE.

Suppose that a firm has determined that its ROA is 10 percent and its total assets turnover ratio is 4. What is the firm's net profit margin? (*Answer:* 2.5%)

Suppose that ratio analysis shows that a firm has an ROE equal to 18 percent, total assets turnover equal to 3 times, and a net profit margin equal to 4 percent. What is the firm's debt to total assets (debt) ratio? (*Answer:* The equity multiplier is 1.5, so the percent of total assets financed with equity is 67 (0.67 $= 1/1.5$); thus the debt ratio equals 33% $= 100\% - 67\%$.)

## COMPARATIVE RATIOS (BENCHMARKING)

**comparative ratio analysis**
The ratios calculated for a particular company compared with those of other firms in the same industry.

The preceding analysis of Unilate Textiles involved a **comparative ratio analysis**—that is, the ratios calculated for Unilate were compared with those of other firms in the same industry. Comparative ratios for a large number of industries are available from several sources, including Dun & Bradstreet (D&B), Robert Morris Associates, and the U.S. Department of Commerce. Trade associations and individual firms' credit departments also compile industry average financial ratios. Finally, financial statement data for thousands of publicly owned corporations are

**TABLE 2-6**  Unilate Textiles: Summary of Financial Ratios ($ millions, except per-share dollars)

| Ratio | Formula for Calculation | Calculation | Ratio Value | Industry Average | Comment |
|---|---|---|---|---|---|
| **_Liquidity_** | | | | | |
| Current | $= \dfrac{\text{Current assets}}{\text{Current liabilities}}$ | $\dfrac{\$465.0}{\$130.0}$ | $= 3.6\times$ | $4.1\times$ | Low |
| Quick, or acid, test | $= \dfrac{\text{Current assets} - \text{Inventory}}{\text{Current liabilities}}$ | $\dfrac{\$195.0}{\$130.0}$ | $= 1.5\times$ | $2.1\times$ | Low |
| **_Asset Management_** | | | | | |
| Inventory turnover | $= \dfrac{\text{Cost of goods sold}}{\text{Inventory}}$ | $\dfrac{\$1,230.0}{\$270.0}$ | $= 4.6\times$ | $7.4\times$ | Low |
| Days sales outstanding (DSO) | $= \dfrac{\text{Accounts Receivable}}{\left[\dfrac{\text{Annual sales}}{360}\right]}$ | $\dfrac{\$180.0}{\$4.17}$ | $= 43.2 \text{ days}$ | $32.1 \text{ days}$ | Poor |
| Fixed assets turnover | $= \dfrac{\text{Sales}}{\text{Net fixed assets}}$ | $\dfrac{\$1,500.0}{\$380.0}$ | $= 3.9\times$ | $4.0\times$ | OK |
| Total assets turnover | $= \dfrac{\text{Sales}}{\text{Total assets}}$ | $\dfrac{\$1,500.0}{\$845.0}$ | $= 1.8\times$ | $2.1\times$ | Low |
| **_Debt Management_** | | | | | |
| Debt to total assets | $= \dfrac{\text{Total liabilities}}{\text{Total assets}}$ | $\dfrac{\$430.0}{\$845.0}$ | $= 50.9\%$ | $42.0\%$ | Poor |
| Times interest earned (TIE) | $= \dfrac{\text{EBIT}}{\text{Interest charges}}$ | $\dfrac{\$130.0}{\$40.0}$ | $= 3.3\times$ | $6.5\times$ | Low |
| Fixed charge coverage | $= \dfrac{\text{EBIT} + \text{L}}{\text{Interest charges} + \text{L} + \left[\dfrac{\text{SF}}{(1-\text{T})}\right]}^{a}$ | $\dfrac{\$140.0}{\$63.33}$ | $= 2.2\times$ | $5.8\times$ | Low |
| **_Profitability_** | | | | | |
| Net profit margin | $= \dfrac{\text{Net profit}}{\text{Sales}}$ | $\dfrac{\$54.0}{\$1,500.0}$ | $= 3.6\%$ | $4.9\%$ | Poor |
| Return on total assets (ROA) | $= \dfrac{\text{Net income}}{\text{Total assets}}$ | $\dfrac{\$54.0}{\$845.0}$ | $= 6.4\%$ | $10.3\%$ | Poor |
| Return on equity (ROE) | $= \dfrac{\text{Net income available to common stockholders}}{\text{Common equity}}$ | $\dfrac{\$54.0}{\$415.0}$ | $= 13.0\%$ | $17.7\%$ | Poor |
| **_Market Value_** | | | | | |
| Price/Earnings (P/E) | $= \dfrac{\text{Market price per share}}{\text{Earnings per share}}$ | $\dfrac{\$23.00}{\$2.16}$ | $= 10.6\times$ | $15.0\times$ | Low |
| Market/Book (M/B) | $= \dfrac{\text{Market price per share}}{\text{Book value per share}}$ | $\dfrac{\$23.00}{\$16.60}$ | $= 1.4\times$ | $2.5\times$ | Low |

[a]L, lease payments; SF, sinking fund payments; T, tax rate.

available from various databases. Because brokerage houses, banks, and other financial institutions have access to these data, security analysts can and do generate comparative ratios tailored to their specific needs. Table 2-7 provides a sample of the ratios provided by the _Almanac of Business and Industrial Financial Ratios for selected industries._

**TABLE 2-7**   Ratios for Selected Industries

| NAICS Code,[a] Line of Business (Number of Firms) | Type of Operations | Current Ratio (×) | Quick Ratio (×) | Debt Ratio (%) | TIE Ratio (×) | DSO (days) | Inventory Turnover (×) | Total Assets Turnover (×) | Profit Margin (%) | Return on Assets (%) | Return on Equity (%) |
|---|---|---|---|---|---|---|---|---|---|---|---|
| 325410 Pharmaceuticals (1,508) | Manufacturing | 1.0 | 0.6 | 68.0 | 3.9 | 112.5 | 4.3 | 0.5 | 13.9 | 9.0 | 13.1 |
| 325600 Soaps, Cleaners, & Toilet Goods (3,147) | Manufacturing | 0.9 | 0.5 | 62.7 | 3.5 | 36.0 | 9.6 | 0.8 | 8.1 | 9.6 | 12.1 |
| 335310 Electrical Equipment (820) | Manufacturing | 1.3 | 0.9 | 38.9 | 2.5 | 109.1 | 6.0 | 0.6 | 5.6 | 5.3 | 3.2 |
| 421300 Lumber & Construction (14,986) | Wholesale | 1.7 | 0.9 | 61.9 | 2.7 | 39.6 | 2.7 | 8.0 | 1.9 | 8.4 | 11.8 |
| 422700 Petroleum & Products (5,322) | Wholesale | 1.5 | 1.2 | 48.4 | 3.0 | 43.4 | 37.5 | 1.9 | 1.6 | 4.7 | 6.1 |
| 444130 Hardware Stores (10,391) | Retail | 2.5 | 0.9 | 57.3 | 2.4 | 18.8 | 3.5 | 2.3 | 1.5 | 7.9 | 7.0 |
| 445310 Beer, Wine, & Liquor Stores (15,364) | Retail | 2.2 | 0.6 | 77.6 | 2.9 | 2.4 | 7.2 | 3.6 | 1.3 | 7.4 | 19.3 |
| 541700 Scientific Research (8,352) | Retail | 3.0 | 2.1 | 41.2 | 4.3 | 83.7 | 11.4 | 0.4 | — | — | — |

[a]NAICS is the North American Industry Classification System, which replaced the Standard Industrial Classification (SIC) codes in 1997. NAICS is the result of efforts by the United States, Canada, and Mexico to provide comparable statistics about business activity throughout North America.

**Source:** 2005, CCH Incorporated. All rights reserved. Reprinted with permission from *Almanac of Business and Industrial Financial Ratios, 2005 Edition.*

Each of the data-supplying organizations uses a somewhat different set of ratios designed for its own purposes. For example, D&B deals mainly with small firms, many of which are proprietorships, and it sells its services primarily to banks and other lenders. Therefore, D&B is concerned largely with the creditor's viewpoint, and its ratios emphasize current assets and liabilities, not market value ratios. When you select a comparative data source, make sure your emphasis is similar to that of the agency whose ratios you plan to use. Additionally, there are often definitional differences in the ratios presented by different sources, so before using any source, verify the exact definitions of the ratios to ensure consistency with your work.

**Self-Test Questions**

How is comparative ratio analysis carried out?

How does comparative ratio analysis compare with trend analysis?

## USES AND LIMITATIONS OF RATIO ANALYSIS

As noted earlier, three main groups use ratio analysis:

- *Managers,* who employ ratios to help analyze, control, and thus improve the firm's operations
- *Credit analysts,* such as bank loan officers or bond rating analysts, who analyze ratios to help ascertain a company's ability to pay its debts
- *Security analysts (or investors),* including stock analysts, who are interested in a company's efficiency and growth prospects, and bond analysts, who are concerned with a company's ability to pay interest on its bonds and the liquidation value of the firm's assets in the event that the company fails

Although ratio analysis can provide useful information concerning a company's operations and financial condition, it does have inherent problems and limitations that necessitate care and judgment. Some potential problems follow:

1. Many large firms operate a number of divisions in very different industries. In such cases, it is difficult to develop a meaningful set of industry averages for comparative purposes. Consequently, ratio analysis tends to be more useful for small, narrowly focused firms than for large, multidivisional ones.

2. Most firms want to be better than average, so merely attaining average performance is not necessarily good. As a target for high-level performance, it is best to focus on the industry leaders' ratios.

3. Inflation might distort firms' balance sheets. For example, if recorded values are historical, they could be substantially different from the "true" values. Furthermore, because inflation affects both depreciation charges and inventory costs, it also affects profits. For these reasons, a ratio analysis for one firm over time, or a comparative analysis of firms of different ages, must be interpreted with judgment.

4. Seasonal factors can distort a ratio analysis. For example, the inventory turnover ratio for a textile firm will be radically different if the balance sheet figure used for inventory is the one just before the fall fashion season versus the one just after the close of the season. You can minimize this problem by

using monthly averages for inventory (and receivables) when calculating ratios such as turnover.

**"window dressing" techniques**
Techniques used to make financial statements look stronger.

5. Firms can employ **"window dressing" techniques** to make their financial statements look stronger. To illustrate, consider a Chicago builder that borrowed on a two-year basis on December 28, 2008, held the proceeds of the loan as *cash* for a few days, and then paid off the loan ahead of time on January 2, 2009. This activity improved the company's current and quick ratios, and it made the firm's year-end 2008 balance sheet look good. The improvement was strictly window dressing, however; a week later, the balance sheet was back at the old level.

6. Different accounting practices can distort comparisons. As noted earlier, inventory valuation and depreciation methods can affect financial statements and thus the fact that different methods can be used makes comparisons among firms difficult.

7. It is difficult to generalize about whether a particular ratio is "good" or "bad." For example, a high current ratio might indicate a strong liquidity position, which is good, or excessive cash, which is bad (because excess cash in the bank is a nonearning asset). Similarly, a high fixed assets turnover ratio might denote either a firm that uses its assets efficiently or one that is undercapitalized and cannot afford to buy enough assets.

8. A firm might have some ratios that look "good" and others that look "bad," making it difficult to tell whether the company is on balance, strong, or weak. Statistical procedures can be used to analyze the net effects of a set of ratios and thereby clarify the situation. Many banks and other lending organizations use statistical procedures to analyze firms' financial ratios and, on the basis of their analyses, classify companies according to their probability of getting into financial trouble.[15]

Ratio analysis is useful, but analysts should be aware of these problems and make adjustments as necessary. When conducted in a mechanical, unthinking manner, however, this type of analysis is dangerous. Used intelligently and with good judgment, it can provide useful insights into a firm's operations. Probably *the most important and most difficult input to successful financial statement (ratio) analysis is the judgment used when interpreting the results to reach an overall conclusion about the firm's financial position.*

 **Self-Test Questions**
Name three types of users of ratio analyses. What type of ratio does each group emphasize?

## Chapter *Essentials*
### —The Answers

To summarize the key concepts, let's answer the questions that were posed at the beginning of the chapter:

- **What financial statements do corporations publish, and what information does each statement provide?** A company publishes a number of financial statements— including a balance sheet, income statement, statement of cash flows, and

[15]The technique used is called discriminant analysis. For a discussion of this technique, see Edward I. Altman, "Financial Ratios, Discriminant Analysis, and the Prediction of Corporate Bankruptcy," *Journal of Finance,* September 1968, 589–609, or Eugene F. Brigham and Phillip R. Daves, *Intermediate Financial Management,* 9th ed. (Cincinnati, OH: South-Western College Publishing, 2007), Chapter 25.

statement of retained earnings—to provide management and investors with information about the firm's operations. The balance sheet shows a "snapshot" at one point in time of the firm's assets and how those assets are financed (debt, equity, or both). The income statement reports the effects of the firm's operations during an accounting period; the revenues that were earned and the expenses that were incurred are netted out to compute the bottom-line net income figure. The statement of cash flows shows the activities that generated funds and the activities that used funds during the accounting period—it shows how and why the firm's cash position changed during the period. The statement of retained earnings shows what caused changes in the firm's common equity during the accounting period—that is, it shows whether new stock was issued or outstanding stock was repurchased and whether dividends were paid.

- **How do investors use financial statements?** The information contained in the financial statements helps investors (both debt holders and stockholders) determine the financial position of a firm, which helps them to estimate the cash flows the firm will generate in the future. Debt holders want to estimate future cash flows to determine whether the debt contracts will be fully honored; stockholders estimate future cash flows to determine the value of the firm's common stock.

- **What is ratio analysis and why are the results of such an analysis important to both managers and investors?** Ratio analysis is used to evaluate a firm's current financial position and the direction this position is expected to take in the future. By determining the firm's financial position, investors form opinions about future conditions of the firm and the safety of their investments. Managers use the information provided by ratio analyses to plan actions that will correct the firm's weaknesses and take advantage of its strengths.

- **What are some potential problems (caveats) associated with financial statement analysis?** Limitations to financial statement analysis include problems associated with classifying a large conglomerate firm into a particular industry or finding firms that can be used for comparative analysis; distortion of some of the numbers reported on financial statements because of inflation; wide swings in the operating accounts of seasonal firms; use of different generally accepted accounting principles to "manipulate" financial numbers; and difficulty in making general conclusions when some ratios look good and others look bad.

- **What is the most important ingredient (factor) in financial statement analysis?** To form general impressions about a firm's financial position, judgment must be used when interpreting financial ratios. Because judgment is involved, conclusions will not always be correct.

 **ETHICAL DILEMMA**

### Hocus-Pocus—Look, An Increase in Sales!

Dynamic Energy Wares (DEW) manufactures and distributes products that are used to save energy and to help reduce and reverse the harmful environmental effects of atmospheric pollutants. DEW relies on a relatively complex distribution system to get the products to its customers. Large companies, which account for nearly 30 percent of the firm's total sales, purchase directly from DEW. Smaller companies and retailers that sell to individuals are required to make their purchases from one of the 50 independent distributors that are contractually obligated to exclusively sell DEW's products.

DEW's accountants have just finished the firm's financial statements for the third quarter of the fiscal year, which ended three weeks ago. The results are terrible. Profits are down 30 percent from this time last year, when a downturn in sales began. Profits are depressed primarily because DEW continues to lose market share to a competitor that entered the field nearly two years ago.

Senior management has decided it needs to take action to boost sales in the fourth quarter so that year-end profits will be "more acceptable." Starting immediately, DEW will (1) eliminate all direct sales, which means that large companies must purchase products from DEW's distributors just as the smaller companies and retailers do; (2) require distributors to maintain certain minimum inventory levels, which are much higher than previous levels; and (3) form a task force to study and propose ways that the firm can recapture its lost market share.

The financial manager, who is your boss, has asked you to attend a hastily called meeting of DEW's distributors to announce the implementation of these operational changes. At the meeting, the distributors will be informed that they must increase inventory to the required minimum level before the end of DEW's current fiscal year or face losing the distributorship. According to your boss, the reason for this requirement is to ensure that distributors can meet the increased demand they will face when the large companies are no longer permitted to purchase directly from DEW. The sales forecast you have been developing over the past few months, however, indicates that distributors' sales are expected to decline by almost 10 percent during the next year. As a consequence, the added inventories might be extremely burdensome to the distributors. When you approached your boss to discuss this potential problem, she said, "Tell the distributors not to worry! We won't require payment for six months, and any additional inventory that remains unsold after nine months can be returned. But they must take delivery of the inventory within the next two months."

It appears that the actions implemented by DEW will produce favorable year-end sales results for the current fiscal year. Do you agree with the decisions made by DEW's senior management? Will you be comfortable announcing the changes to DEW's distributors? How would you respond to a distributor who says, "DEW doesn't care about us. The company just wants to look good no matter who gets hurt—that's unethical"? What will you say to your boss? Will you attend the distributors' meeting?

## Chapter *Essentials*
### —Personal Finance

The concepts presented in this chapter should help you understand how to evaluate your own financial position to determine your "operating cash flow," "free cash flow," and whether your debt position is appropriate given your income.

## Disposable Income (Operating Cash Flow)

An individual's after-tax income is called *disposable income* because this is the amount that is left to pay current bills, spend on groceries, save or invest for future spending, and so forth. Disposable income is effectively your "take-home" pay (from all income sources) because it can be "disposed of" in whatever manner you choose. It is important for you to know how much income you have at your disposal so that you can determine how much you can afford to pay for housing, food, and transportation. You must "live within your means"—that is, you cannot buy a house or drive a car that cannot be supported on your income. Disposable income is the key input to constructing a financial budget that can be used to guide spending and investment.

## Discretionary Income (Free Cash Flow)

Because you *must* pay certain bills for necessities, including housing, utilities, food, and transportation, you cannot spend all of your disposable income as you please.

*Discretionary income* is the amount of disposable income that can be spent for things you want rather than for things you need. If you know how much of your disposable income is discretionary, you can plan better for retirement by determining how much of your income can be contributed to a retirement fund each year. If you develop a personal financial budget, you will find that any discretionary income that remains after planned savings (e.g., for retirement) represents funds that can be used to pay for entertainment, to buy nonessential items, and so forth.

## Debt Position (Ratios)

Lenders consider many factors when they decide whether to grant loans (especially mortgages) to individuals. Some key ratios that are evaluated include the debt to income ratio, housing expense ratio, and loan to value ratio. The *debt to income ratio* is computed by dividing monthly debt payments (mortgage, automobile, credit cards, and other loans) by disposable income. Many mortgage lenders require this ratio to be less than 35 percent. Mortgage lenders also prefer that your total monthly house payment (principal, interest, property taxes, and insurance) be less than 25 to 30 percent of your gross monthly income—that is, your *housing expense ratio* should not exceed about 30 percent. The *loan to value (LTV) ratio* is computed by dividing the amount that is owed on the mortgage by the market value of a house or other property. An LTV equal to 70 percent indicates that the borrower has 30 percent equity in the property. Many mortgage lenders want the LTV to be less than 80 percent.

Just as managers and investors use financial statements and ratio analysis to evaluate the financial position of a firm, you should use personal financial ratios to evaluate your financial position. You should apply the same concepts that we discussed in this chapter to your personal finances—that is, you should determine what your current financial position is and forecast what you expect your financial position to be in the future. Living within your financial means and planning for your financial future are key ingredients to sustaining a happy and successful "financial" life.

## QUESTIONS

**2-1**  What four financial statements appear in most annual reports?

**2-2**  If a "typical" firm reports $20 million of retained earnings on its balance sheet, could its directors declare a $20 million cash dividend without any qualms? Explain why or why not.

**2-3**  Describe the changes in balance sheet accounts that would constitute sources of funds. What changes would be considered uses of funds?

**2-4**  Financial ratio analysis is conducted by four types of analysts: managers, equity investors, long-term creditors, and short-term creditors. What is the primary emphasis of each of these groups in evaluating ratios?

**2-5**  What are some steps that must be taken when using ratio analysis? What is the most important aspect of ratio analysis?

**2-6**  Profit margins and turnover ratios vary from one industry to another. What differences would you expect to find between a grocery chain, such as Safeway, and a steel company? Think particularly about the turnover ratios and the profit margin, and consider the effect on the DuPont equation.

**2-7**    If a firm's ROE is low and management wants to improve it, explain how using more debt might help. Could using too much debt prove detrimental?

**2-8**    How might (a) seasonal factors and (b) different growth rates distort a comparative ratio analysis? Give some examples. How might these problems be alleviated?

**2-9**    Explain the difference between net income, or accounting profit, and net cash flow. Why do these numbers generally differ?

**2-10**    Explain the difference between net cash flow and operating cash flow. What causes these two numbers to differ?

**2-11**    What is *free cash flow*? Can a company have a negative free cash flow and still be considered successful?

**2-12**    Following are the balance sheets for Batelan Corporation for the fiscal years 2008 and 2009. In the column to the right of the balance sheet amounts, indicate whether the change in the account balance represents a source or a use of cash for the firm. Place a (+) in the space provided to indicate a source of funds, a (−) to indicate a use of funds, and a (0) if the effect cannot be determined with the information provided.

|                               | 2009     | 2008     | Source (+) or Use (−)? |
|-------------------------------|----------|----------|------------------------|
| Cash                          | $  400   | $  500   |                        |
| Accounts receivable           | 250      | 300      |                        |
| Inventory                     | 450      | 400      |                        |
| Current assets                | $1,100   | $1,200   |                        |
| Net property and equipment    | 1,000    | 950      |                        |
| Total assets                  | $2,100   | $2,150   |                        |
|                               |          |          |                        |
| Accounts payable              | $  200   | $  400   |                        |
| Accruals                      | 300      | 250      |                        |
| Notes payable                 | 400      | 200      |                        |
| Current liabilities           | $  900   | $  850   |                        |
| Long-term debt                | 800      | 900      |                        |
| Total liabilities             | $1,700   | $1,750   |                        |
| Common stock                  | 250      | 300      |                        |
| Retained earnings             | 150      | 100      |                        |
| Total equity                  | $  400   | $  400   |                        |
| Total liabilities and equity  | $2,100   | $2,150   |                        |

From these balance sheets, can you tell whether Batelan generated a positive or negative net income during 2009? Can you tell whether dividends were paid? Explain.

**2-13**    Indicate the effects of the transactions listed in the following table on total current assets, current ratio, and net income. Use (+) to indicate an increase, (−) to indicate a decrease, and (0) to indicate either no effect or an indeterminate effect. Be prepared to state any necessary assumptions, and assume the initial current ratio is greater than 1.0. (*Note:* A good accounting background is necessary to answer some of these questions; if yours is not strong, just answer the questions you can handle.)

| | Total Current Assets | Current Ratio | Effect on Net Income |
|---|---|---|---|
| **a.** Cash is acquired through issuance of additional common stock. | _____ | _____ | _____ |
| **b.** Merchandise is sold for cash. | _____ | _____ | _____ |
| **c.** Federal income tax due for the previous year is paid. | _____ | _____ | _____ |
| **d.** A fixed asset is sold for less than its book value. | _____ | _____ | _____ |
| **e.** A fixed asset is sold for more than its book value. | _____ | _____ | _____ |
| **f.** Merchandise is sold on credit. | _____ | _____ | _____ |
| **g.** Payment is made to trade creditors for previous purchases. | _____ | _____ | _____ |
| **h.** A cash dividend is declared and paid. | _____ | _____ | _____ |
| **i.** Cash is obtained through short-term bank loans. | _____ | _____ | _____ |
| **j.** Marketable securities are sold below cost. | _____ | _____ | _____ |
| **k.** Advances are made to employees. | _____ | _____ | _____ |
| **l.** Current operating expenses are paid. | _____ | _____ | _____ |
| **m.** Short-term promissory notes are issued to trade creditors in exchange for past due accounts payable. | _____ | _____ | _____ |
| **n.** Long-term bonds are issued to pay accounts payable. | _____ | _____ | _____ |
| **o.** Accounts receivable are collected. | _____ | _____ | _____ |
| **p.** Equipment is purchased with short-term notes | _____ | _____ | _____ |
| **q.** Merchandise is purchased on credit. | _____ | _____ | _____ |

## SELF-TEST PROBLEMS

*(Solutions appear in Appendix B at the end of the book.)*

**ST-1** Define each of the following terms:                     key terms

    **a.** Annual report; income statement; balance sheet; common size balance sheet

    **b.** Stockholders' equity, or net worth; paid-in capital; retained earnings

    **c.** Statement of retained earnings; statement of cash flows

    **d.** Book value; market value

    **e.** Operating cash flows; accounting profits

    **f.** Net working capital; net operating working capital

    **g.** Free cash flow; economic value added (EVA)

    **h.** Liquidity ratios: current ratio; quick, or acid test, ratio

    **i.** Asset management ratios: inventory turnover ratio; days sales outstanding (DSO); fixed assets turnover ratio; total assets turnover ratio

    **j.** Financial leverage: debt ratio; times-interest-earned (TIE) ratio; fixed charge coverage ratio

    **k.** Profitability ratios: net profit margin; return on total assets (ROA); return on common equity (ROE)

    **l.** Market value ratios: price/earnings (P/E) ratio; market/book (M/B) ratio; book value per share

    **m.** Trend analysis; comparative ratio analysis

    **n.** DuPont analysis; DuPont equation

    **o.** "Window dressing"; seasonal effects on ratios

**debt ratio**    **ST-2** K. Billingsworth & Company had earnings per share of $4 last year, and it paid a $2 dividend. Total retained earnings increased by $12 million during the year, and book value per share at year-end was $40. Billingsworth has no preferred stock, and no new common stock was issued during the year. If the company's year-end debt (which equals its total liabilities) was $120 million, what was its year-end debt/assets ratio?

**cash flows**    **ST-3** Refreshing Pool Corporation reported net operating income equal to $120,000 this year. Examination of the company's balance sheet and income statement shows that the tax rate was 40 percent, the depreciation expense was $25,000, $150,000 was invested in assets during the year, and invested capital equals $500,000. The firm's average after-tax cost of funds is 12 percent. What was the firm's (1) operating cash flow, (2) free cash flow, and (3) economic value added (EVA)?

**ratio analysis**    **ST-4** The following data apply to A.L. Kaiser & Company ($ millions):

| | |
|---|---:|
| Cash and equivalents | $ 100.00 |
| Fixed assets | $ 283.50 |
| Sales | $1,000.00 |
| Net income | $ 50.00 |
| Quick ratio | 2.0× |
| Current ratio | 3.0× |
| DSO | 40.0 days |
| ROE | 12.0% |

Kaiser has no preferred stock—only common equity, current liabilities, and long-term debt.

    **a.** Find Kaiser's (1) accounts receivable (A/R), (2) current liabilities, (3) current assets, (4) total assets, (5) ROA, (6) common equity, and (7) long-term debt.

    **b.** In part a, you should have found Kaiser's accounts receivable (A/R) to be $109.6 million. If Kaiser could reduce its DSO from 40 days to 30 days while holding other things constant, how much cash would it generate? If this cash were used to buy back common stock (at book value) and thereby reduce the amount of common equity, how would this action affect the company's (1) ROE, (2) ROA, and (3) total debt/total assets ratio?

## PROBLEMS

**2-1**  Hindelang Corporation has $1,312,500 in current assets and $525,000 in current liabilities. Its initial inventory level is $375,000, and it will raise funds through additional notes payable and use them to increase inventory. How much can Hindelang's short-term debt (notes payable) increase without pushing its current ratio below 2.0? What will be the firm's quick ratio after Hindelang has raised the maximum amount of short-term funds?

**liquidity ratio**

**2-2**  W. F. Bailey Company had a quick ratio of 1.4, a current ratio of 3.0, an inventory turnover ratio of 5, total current assets of $810,000, and cash and equivalents of $120,000 in 2009. If the cost of goods sold equaled 86 percent of sales, what were Bailey's annual sales and DSO?

**ratio calculations**

**2-3**  Wolken Corporation has $500,000 of debt outstanding, and it pays an interest rate of 10 percent annually. Wolken's annual sales are $2 million, its average tax rate is 20 percent, and its net profit margin is 5 percent. If the company does not maintain a TIE ratio of at least 5, its bank will refuse to renew the loan, and bankruptcy will result. What is Wolken's TIE ratio?

**TIE ratio**

**2-4**  Coastal Packaging's ROE last year was only 3 percent, but its management has developed a new operating plan designed to improve things. The new plan calls for a total debt ratio of 60 percent, which will result in interest charges of $300 per year. Management projects an EBIT of $1,000 on sales of $10,000, and it expects to have a total assets turnover ratio of 2.0. Under these conditions, the average tax rate will be 30 percent. If the changes are made, what return on equity (ROE) will Coastal earn? What is the ROA?

**return on equity**

**2-5**  Barbell Corporation's income statement reports that the company's "bottom line" was $180,000 in 2008. The statement also shows that the company had depreciation and amortization expenses equal to $50,000 and taxes equal to $120,000. What was Barbell's net cash flow?

**net cash flow**

**2-6**  Last year Z&B Paints reported its net income as $650,000. A review of its income statement shows that Z&B's operating expenses (fixed and variable), excluding depreciation and amortization, were $1,500,000; its depreciation and amortization expense was $300,000; and its tax rate was 35 percent. Z&B has no debt—that is, the firm is financed with stock only.

a. What were Z&B's sales revenues last year?

b. What was Z&B's net cash flow last year?

c. What was Z&B's operating cash flow last year?

**net cash flow**

**2-7**  Psyre Company reported net operating income (NOI) equal to $150,000 this year. Examination of the company's balance sheet and income statement shows that the tax rate was 40 percent, the depreciation expense was $40,000, $120,000 was invested in assets during the year, and invested capital currently is

**economic value**

$1,100,000. If Psyre's average after-tax cost of funds is 10 percent, what is the firm's EVA?

**ratio calculation**    **2-8**    Assume you are given the following relationships for Zumwalt Corporation:

| | |
|---|---|
| Sales/total assets | 1.5× |
| Return on assets (ROA) | 3.0% |
| Return on equity (ROE) | 5.0% |

Calculate Zumwalt's net profit margin and debt ratio.

**return on equity**    **2-9**    Earth's Best Company has sales of $200,000, a net income of $15,000, and the following balance sheet:

| | | | |
|---|---|---|---|
| Cash | $ 10,000 | Accounts payable | $ 30,000 |
| Receivables | 50,000 | Other current liabilities | 20,000 |
| Inventories | 150,000 | Long-term debt | 50,000 |
| Net fixed assets | 90,000 | Common equity | 200,000 |
| Total assets | $300,000 | Total liabilities and equity | $300,000 |

a. The company's new owner thinks that inventories are excessive and can be lowered to the point at which the current ratio is equal to the industry average, 2.5, without affecting either sales or net income. If inventories are sold off and not replaced so as to reduce the current ratio to 2.5, if the funds generated are used to reduce common equity (stock can be repurchased at book value), and if no other changes occur, by how much will the ROE change?

b. Now suppose we wanted to take this problem and modify it for use on an exam—that is, to create a new problem that you have not seen to test your knowledge of this type of problem. How would your answer change if we made the following changes: (1) We doubled all of the dollar amounts? (2) We stated that the target current ratio was 3.0? (3) We said that the company had 10,000 shares of stock outstanding, and we asked how much the change in part a would increase EPS? (4) What would your answer to (3) be if we changed the original problem to state that the stock was selling for twice book value, so common equity would not be reduced on a dollar-for-dollar basis?

c. Explain how we could have set the problem up to have you focus on changing accounts receivable, or fixed assets, or using the funds generated to retire debt (we would give you the interest rate on outstanding debt), or how the original problem could have stated that the company needed *more* inventories and it would finance them with new common equity or with new debt.

**statement of cash flows**    **2-10**    The consolidated balance sheets for Lloyd Lumber Company at the beginning and end of 2009 follow. The company bought $50 million worth of fixed assets. The charge for depreciation in 2009 was $10 million. Net income was $33 million, and the company paid out $5 million in dividends.

a. Fill in the amount of the source or use in the appropriate column.

## Lloyd Lumber Company: Balance Sheets at Beginning and End of 2009 ($ million)

| | Jan. 1 | Dec. 31 | Source | Use |
|---|---|---|---|---|
| | **Change** | | | |
| Cash | $ 7 | $ 15 | | |
| Marketable securities | 0 | 11 | | |
| Net receivables | 30 | 22 | | |
| Inventories | 53 | 75 | | |
| Total current assets | $90 | $123 | | |
| Gross fixed assets | 75 | 125 | | |
| Less: Accumulated depreciation | (25) | (35) | | |
| Net fixed assets | $ 50 | $ 90 | | |
| Total assets | $140 | $213 | | |
| | | | | |
| Accounts payable | $ 18 | $ 15 | | |
| Notes payable | 3 | 15 | | |
| Other current liabilities | 15 | 7 | | |
| Long-term debt | 8 | 24 | | |
| Common stock | 29 | 57 | | |
| Retained earnings | 67 | 95 | | |
| Total liabilities and equity | $140 | $213 | | |

**Note:** Total sources must equal total uses.

 

**b.** Prepare a statement of cash flows.

**c.** Briefly summarize your findings.

**2-11** Montejo Corporation expects 2010 sales to be $12 million. Operating costs other than depreciation are expected to be 75 percent of sales, and depreciation is expected to be $1.5 million in 2010. All sales revenues will be collected in cash, and costs other than depreciation must be paid during the year. Montejo's interest expense is expected to be $1 million, and it is taxed at a 40 percent rate.

*income and cash flow analysis*

**a.** Set up an income statement and a cash flow statement (use two columns on one page) for Montejo. What is the expected cash flow from operations?

**b.** Suppose Congress changed the tax laws so that Montejo's depreciation expenses doubled in 2010, but no other changes occurred. What would happen to the net income and cash flow from operations expected in 2010?

**c.** Suppose that Congress, rather than increasing Montejo's 2010 depreciation, reduced it by 50 percent. How would the income and cash flows be affected?

**d.** If this company belonged to you, would you prefer that Congress increase or decrease the depreciation expense allowed your company? Explain why.

**2-12** Data for Unilate Textiles' 2008 financial statements are given in Table 2-1 and Table 2-2 in the chapter.

*ratio analysis*

**a.** Compute the 2008 values of the following ratios:

|  | | **2008 Values** | |
| Ratio | | Unilate | Industry |
| --- | --- | --- | --- |
| Current ratio | | _____ | 3.9× |
| Days sales outstanding | | _____ | 33.5 days |
| Inventory turnover | | _____ | 7.2× |
| Fixed assets turnover | | _____ | 4.1× |
| Debt ratio | | _____ | 43.0% |
| Net profit margin | | _____ | 4.6% |
| Return on assets | | _____ | 9.9% |

**b.** Briefly comment on Unilate's 2008 financial position. Can you see any obvious strengths or weaknesses?

**c.** Compare Unilate's 2008 ratios with its 2009 ratios, which are presented in Table 2-6. Comment on whether you believe Unilate's financial position improved or deteriorated during 2009.

**d.** What other information would be useful for projecting whether Unilate's financial position is expected to improve or deteriorate in the future?

**ratio analysis**    **2-13**    Data for Campsey Computer Company and its industry averages follow.

**a.** Calculate the indicated ratios for Campsey.

**b.** Construct the DuPont equation for both Campsey and the industry.

**c.** Outline Campsey's strengths and weaknesses as revealed by your analysis.

**d.** Suppose Campsey had doubled its sales as well as its inventories, accounts receivable, and common equity during 2009. How would that information affect the validity of your ratio analysis? (*Hint:* Think about averages and the effects of rapid growth on ratios if averages are not used. No calculations are needed.)

### Campsey Computer Company: Balance Sheet as of December 31, 2009

| | | | |
| --- | --- | --- | --- |
| Cash | $ 77,500 | Accounts payable | $129,000 |
| Receivables | 336,000 | Notes payable | 84,000 |
| Inventories | 241,500 | Other current liabilities | 117,000 |
| Total current assets | $655,000 | Total current liabilities | $330,000 |
| Net fixed assets | 292,500 | Long-term debt | 256,500 |
| | | Common equity | 361,000 |
| Total assets | $947,500 | Total liabilities and equity | $947,500 |

### Campsey Computer Company: Income Statement for Year Ended December 31, 2009

| | |
| --- | --- |
| Sales | $1,607,500 |
| Cost of goods sold | (1,353,000) |
| Gross profit | $ 254,500 |
| Fixed operating expenses except depreciation | ( 143,000) |
| Earnings before interest, taxes, depreciation, and amortization (EBITDA) | $ 111,500 |
| Depreciation | ( 41,500) |
| Earnings before interest and taxes (EBIT) | $ 70,000 |

| | |
|---|---|
| Interest | ( 24,500) |
|    Earnings before taxes (EBT) | $ 45,500 |
| Taxes (40%) | ( 18,200) |
|    Net income | $ 27,300 |

| Ratio | Campsey | Industry Average |
|---|---|---|
| Current ratio | _____ | 2.0× |
| Days sales outstanding | _____ | 35.0 days |
| Inventory turnover | _____ | 5.6× |
| Total assets turnover | _____ | 3.0× |
| Net profit margin | _____ | 1.2% |
| Return on assets (ROA) | _____ | 3.6% |
| Return on equity (ROE) | _____ | 9.0% |
| Debt ratio | _____ | 60.0% |

**2-14** Complete the balance sheet and sales information in the table that follows for Isberg Industries using the following financial data:    **balance sheet**

Debt ratio: 50%
Quick ratio: 0.80×
Total assets turnover: 1.5×
Days sales outstanding: 36.5 days
Gross profit margin on sales: (Sales − Cost of goods sold)/Sales = 25%
Inventory turnover ratio: 5.0×

### Balance Sheet

| | | | | |
|---|---|---|---|---|
| Cash | _____ | Accounts payable | _____ |
| Accounts receivable | _____ | Long-term debt | $60,000 |
| Inventories | _____ | Common stock | _____ |
| Fixed assets | _____ | Retained earnings | $97,500 |
| Total assets | $300,000 | Total liabilities and equity | _____ |
| Sales | _____ | Cost of goods sold | _____ |

**2-15** The Finnerty Furniture Company, a manufacturer and wholesaler of high-quality home furnishings, has experienced low profitability in recent years. As a result, the board of directors has replaced the president of the firm with a new president, Elizabeth Brannigan, who has asked you to make an analysis of the firm's financial position using the DuPont chart. The most recent industry average ratios and Finnerty's financial statements are as follows:    **DuPont analysis**

### Industry Average Ratios

| | | | |
|---|---|---|---|
| Current ratio | 2.0× | Fixed assets turnover | 6.0× |
| Debt ratio | 30.0% | Total assets turnover | 3.0× |
| Times interest earned | 7.0× | Profit margin on sales | 3.0% |
| Inventory turnover | 8.5× | Return on total assets | 9.0% |
| Days sales outstanding | 24.0 days | Return on common equity | 12.9% |

| Finnerty Furniture Company: Balance Sheet as of December 31, 2009 ($ millions) | | | |
|---|---|---|---|
| Cash | $ 45 | Accounts payable | $ 45 |
| Marketable securities | 33 | Notes payable | 45 |
| Net receivables | 66 | Other current liabilities | 21 |
| Inventories | 159 | Total current liabilities | $111 |
| Total current assets | $303 | Long-term debt | 24 |
| | | Total liabilities | $135 |
| Gross fixed assets | 225 | Common stock | 114 |
| Less depreciation | (78) | Retained earnings | 201 |
| Net fixed assets | $147 | Total stockholders' equity | $315 |
| Total assets | $450 | Total liabilities and equity | $450 |

| Finnerty Furniture Company: Income Statement for Year Ended December 31, 2009 ($ millions) | |
|---|---|
| Net sales | $795.0 |
| Cost of goods sold | (660.0) |
| Gross profit | $135.0 |
| Selling expenses | ( 73.5) |
| Depreciation expense | ( 12.0) |
| Earnings before interest and taxes (EBIT) | $ 49.5 |
| Interest expense | ( 4.5) |
| Earnings before taxes (EBT) | $ 45.0 |
| Taxes (40%) | ( 18.0) |
| Net income | $ 27.0 |

a. Calculate those ratios that you think would be useful in this analysis.

b. Construct a DuPont equation for Finnerty, and compare the company's ratios to the industry average ratios.

c. Do the balance sheet accounts or the income statement figures seem to be primarily responsible for the low profit?

d. Which specific accounts seem to be most out of line compared with those of other firms in the industry?

e. If Finnerty had a pronounced seasonal sales pattern, or if it grew rapidly during the year, how might that affect the validity of your ratio analysis? How might you correct for such potential problems?

**ratio analysis**    **2-16**    Cary Corporation's forecasted 2010 financial statements follow, along with industry average ratios.

a. Calculate Cary's 2010 forecasted ratios, compare them with the industry average data, and comment briefly on Cary's projected strengths and weaknesses.

b. What do you think would happen to Cary's ratios if the company initiated cost-cutting measures that allowed it to hold lower levels of inventory and substantially decrease the cost of goods sold? No calculations are necessary. Think about which ratios would be affected by changes in these two accounts.

### Cary Corporation: Forecasted Balance Sheet as of December 31, 2010

| | | | |
|---|---|---|---|
| Cash | $ 72,000 | Accounts and notes payable | $ 432,000 |
| Accounts receivable | 439,000 | Accruals | 170,000 |
| Inventories | 894,000 | Total current assets | $ 602,000 |
| Total current assets | $1,405,000 | Long-term debt | 404,290 |
| Land and building | 238,000 | Common stock | 575,000 |
| Machinery | 132,000 | Retained earnings | 254,710 |
| Other fixed assets | 61,000 | Total liabilities and equity | $1,836,000 |
| Total assets | $1,836,000 | | |

### Cary Corporation Forecasted Income Statement for 2010

| | |
|---|---|
| Sales | $4,290,000 |
| Cost of goods sold | (3,580,000) |
| Gross operating profit | $ 710,000 |
| General administrative and selling expenses | ( 236,320) |
| Depreciation | ( 159,000) |
| Miscellaneous | ( 134,000) |
| Earnings before taxes (EBT) | $ 180,680 |
| Taxes (40%) | ( 72,272) |
| Net income | $ 108,408 |
| Number of shares outstanding | 23,000 |
| **Per-Share Data** | |
| EPS | $ 4.71 |
| Cash dividends per share | $ 0.95 |
| P/E ratio | 5.0× |
| Market price (average) | $ 23.57 |

### Industry Financial Ratios (2010)[a]

| | |
|---|---|
| Quick ratio | 1.0× |
| Current ratio | 2.7× |
| Inventory turnover[b] | 5.8× |
| Days sales outstanding | 32.0 days |
| Fixed assets turnover[b] | 13.0× |
| Total assets turnover[b] | 2.6× |
| Return on assets | 9.1% |
| Return on equity | 18.2% |
| Debt ratio | 50.0% |
| Profit margin on sales | 3.5% |
| P/E ratio | 6.0× |

[a]Industry average ratios have been constant for the past four years.

[b]Based on year-end balance sheet figures.

## Integrative Problem

**2-17** Donna Jamison was recently hired as a financial analyst by Computron Industries, a manufacturer of electronic components. Her first task was to

**financial statement analysis**

conduct a financial analysis of the firm covering the past two years. To begin, she gathered the following financial statements and other data.

| Balance Sheets | 2009 | 2008 |
|---|---|---|
| **Assets** | | |
| Cash | $ 52,000 | $ 57,600 |
| Accounts receivable | 402,000 | 351,200 |
| Inventories | 836,000 | 715,200 |
| Total current assets | $1,290,000 | $1,124,000 |
| Gross fixed assets | 527,000 | 491,000 |
| Less accumulated depreciation | (166,200) | (146,200) |
| Net fixed assets | $360,800 | $ 344,800 |
| Total assets | $1,650,800 | $1,468,800 |
| **Liabilities and Equity** | | |
| Accounts payable | $ 175,200 | $ 145,600 |
| Notes payable | 225,000 | 200,000 |
| Accruals | 140,000 | 136,000 |
| Total current liabilities | $ 540,200 | $ 481,600 |
| Long-term debt | 424,612 | 323,432 |
| Common stock (100,000 shares) | 460,000 | 460,000 |
| Retained earnings | 225,988 | 203,768 |
| Total equity | $ 685,988 | $ 663,768 |
| Total liabilities and equity | $1,650,800 | $1,468,800 |

| Income Statements | 2009 | 2008 |
|---|---|---|
| Sales | $3,850,000 | $3,432,000 |
| Cost of goods sold | (3,250,000) | (2,864,000) |
| Other expenses | ( 430,300) | ( 340,000) |
| Depreciation | ( 20,000) | ( 18,900) |
| Total operating costs | $3,700,300 | $3,222,900 |
| EBIT | $ 149,700 | $ 209,100 |
| Interest expense | ( 76,000) | ( 62,500) |
| EBT | $ 73,700 | $ 146,600 |
| Taxes (40%) | ( 29,480) | ( 58,640) |
| Net income | $ 44,220 | $ 87,960 |
| EPS | $ 0.442 | $ 0.880 |

## Statement of Cash Flows (2009)

**Operating Activities**

| | |
|---|---|
| Net income | $ 44,220 |
| *Other additions (sources of cash)* | |
| Depreciation | 20,000 |
| Increase in accounts payable | 29,600 |
| Increase in accruals | 4,000 |
| *Subtractions (uses of cash)* | |
| Increases in accounts receivable | ( 50,800) |
| Increase in inventories | (120,800) |
| Net cash flow from operations | $(73,780) |

**Long-Term Investing Activities**

| | |
|---|---:|
| Investment in fixed assets | $(36,000) |

**Financing Activities**

| | |
|---|---:|
| Increase in notes payable | $ 25,000 |
| Increase in long-term debt | 101,180 |
| Payment of cash dividends | ( 22,000) |
| Net cash flow from financing | $104,180 |
| Net reduction in cash account | $( 5,600) |
| Cash at beginning of year | 57,600 |
| Cash at end of year | $ 52,000 |

| Other Data | 2009 | 2008 |
|---|---|---|
| December 31 stock price | $ 6.00 | $ 8.50 |
| Number of shares | 100,000 | 100,000 |
| Dividends per share | $ 0.22 | $ 0.22 |
| Lease payments | $40,000 | $40,000 |

Industry average data for 2009:

| Ratio | Industry Average |
|---|---|
| Current | 2.7× |
| Quick | 1.0× |
| Inventory turnover | 6.0× |
| Days sales outstanding (DSO) | 32.0 days |
| Fixed assets turnover | 10.7× |
| Total assets turnover | 2.6× |
| Debt ratio | 50.0% |
| TIE | 2.5× |
| Fixed charge coverage | 2.1× |
| Net profit margin | 3.5% |
| ROA | 9.1 % |
| ROE | 18.2% |
| Price/earnings | 14.2× |
| Market/book | 1.4× |

Assume that you are Donna Jamison's assistant and that she has asked you to help her prepare a report that evaluates the company's financial condition. Answer the following questions:

**a.** What can you conclude about the company's financial condition from its statement of cash flows?

**b.** What is the purpose of financial ratio analysis, and what are the five major categories of ratios?

**c.** What are Computron's current and quick ratios? What do they tell you about the company's liquidity position?

**d.** What are Computron's inventory turnover, days sales outstanding, fixed assets turnover, and total assets turnover ratios? How does the firm's utilization of assets stack up against that of the industry?

e. What are the firm's debt, times-interest-earned, and fixed charge coverage ratios? How does Computron compare to the industry with respect to financial leverage? What conclusions can you draw from these ratios?

f. Calculate and discuss the firm's profitability ratios—that is, its net profit margin, return on assets (ROA), and return on equity (ROE).

g. Calculate Computron's market value ratios—that is, its price/earnings ratio and its market/book ratio. What do these ratios tell you about investors' opinions of the company?

h. Use the DuPont equation to provide a summary and overview of Computron's financial condition. What are the firm's major strengths and weaknesses?

i. Use the following simplified 2009 balance sheet to show, in general terms, how an improvement in one of the ratios—say, the DSO—would affect the stock price. For example, if the company could improve its collection procedures and thereby lower the DSO from 37.6 days to 27.6 days, how would that change "ripple through" the financial statements (shown in thousands below) and influence the stock price?

| Accounts receivable | $   402 | Debt | $   965 |
| Other current assets | 888 | | |
| Net fixed assets | 361 | Equity | 686 |
| Total assets | $1,651 | Total liabilities and equity | $1,651 |

j. Although financial statement analysis can provide useful information about a company's operations and its financial condition, this type of analysis does have some potential problems and limitations, and it must be used with care and judgment. What are some problems and limitations?

## Computer-Related Problem

*Work the problem in this section only if you are using the computer problem spreadsheet CD.*

**ratio analysis**   **2-18** Use the computerized model in the File C02 to solve this problem.

a. Refer to Problem 2–16. Suppose Cary Corporation is considering installing a new computer system that would provide tighter control of inventories, accounts receivable, and accounts payable. If the new system is installed, the following data are projected (rather than the data given in Problem 2-16) for the indicated balance sheet and income statement accounts:

| | |
|---|---|
| Accounts receivable | $  395,000 |
| Inventories | $  700,000 |
| Other fixed assets | $  150,000 |
| Accounts and notes payable | $  275,000 |
| Accruals | $  120,000 |
| Cost of goods sold | $3,450,000 |
| Administrative and selling expenses | $  248,775 |
| P/E ratio | 6.0× |

How do these changes affect the projected ratios and the comparison with the industry averages? (Note that any changes to the income statement will change the amount of retained earnings; therefore, the model is set up to calculate 2010 retained earnings as 2009 retained earnings plus net income minus dividends paid. The model also adjusts the cash balance so that the balance sheet balances.)

**b.** If the new computer were even more efficient than Cary's management had estimated and thus caused the cost of goods sold to decrease by $125,000 from the projections in part a, what effect would it have on the company's financial position?

**c.** If the new computer were less efficient than Cary's management had estimated and caused the cost of goods sold to increase by $125,000 from the projections in part a, what effect would it have on the company's financial position?

**d.** Change, one by one, the other items in part a to see how each change affects the ratio analysis. Then think about and write a paragraph describing how computer models such as this one can be used to help make better decisions about the purchase of such items as a new computer system.

**GET REAL WITH** **THOMSON ONE** Business School Edition

**2-19** Intel Corporation [INTC] designs, manufactures, and markets computer and communications products. Using the financial ratios discussed in the chapter, compare Intel with its peer firms, as designated by its industry group. Answer the following questions. [*Hint:* Click on Peers/Peer Sets/Peers by DJ Industry Group.] **comparative analysis**

**a.** How did Intel compare with its peers during the past three years with regard to liquidity, asset management, debt management, and profitability? [*Hint:* Click on Financials/Financial Ratios. You might have to calculate some of the ratios by clicking on Financial/Key Financials.] Explain your answers.

**b.** Based solely on your ratio analysis, if you had to recommend a firm in which to invest in this industry group, would you recommend Intel or another firm?

**2-20** Nextel Communications Inc. [NXTL] is a provider of digital wireless communication services. Using the information from the firm's cash flow statements, answer the following questions. [*Hint:* Click on Financials/Financial Statements/Thomson Financials/Cash Flow Statements.] **ratio analysis**

**a.** What conclusions can you make concerning the financial position of Nextel with regard to its operating, investing, and financing activities during the past five years?

**b.** How has Nextel improved over the five-year period? What problems has the company experienced?

# The Financial Markets and the Investment Banking Process

**D**o you like roller-coaster rides? Consider the ups and downs of the stock market in May and June of 2006. The following table gives an indication of the wild ride investors took if they owned stocks similar to those that make up the Dow Jones Industrial Average (DJIA).[1]

The DJIA decreased from 11,367.78 to 11,150.22 during May and June, a loss of nearly 2 percent for the 44-day trading period, which translates to a loss of about 12 percent for the year. As you can see, however, the decline was not steady—there were quite a few periods in which rather significant increases occurred. Was the stock market a lion or a lamb in May and June 2006? Clearly, many of the movements in the DJIA were extreme like a lion's roar, but the market could not decide which way to go, much like a lost lamb.

According to the pundits, the primary reasons for the turbulence in the market were the uncertainty of

| Period | Number of Trading Days | Actual Change in Points | Simple Percent Change[2] | |
| --- | --- | --- | --- | --- |
| | | | Per Period | Annualized |
| June 28–29 | 2 | 266.06 | 2.43% | 444.46% |
| June 14–15 | 2 | 309.05 | 2.89 | 526.82 |
| June 9–13 | 3 | −232.68 | −2.13 | −258.80 |
| June 2–7 | 4 | −329.38 | −2.93 | −266.92 |
| May 24–26 | 3 | 180.26 | 1.62 | 197.61 |
| May 11–23 | 9 | −544.30 | −4.68 | −284.40 |
| May 4–10 | 5 | 242.37 | 2.13 | 155.20 |

[1]The Dow Jones Industrial Average is an index that consists of stocks of the largest 30 industrial firms in the United States.

[2]These computations do not consider compounding. For example, if the daily change was 1 percent, the simple annual rate of return was computed as $1.0\% \times 365 = 365\%$. The concept of interest compounding is discussed in Chapter 4.

investors about the future of the economy due to the uncertainty about both the war in Iraq and fuel prices and the failure of many earnings reports announced by large firms at the time to meet investors' expectations. In addition, economists and investors were uncertain as to how Ben Bernanke, the new chairman of the Board of Governors of the Federal Reserve, would guide the monetary policy of the United States.

As the numbers presented here show, the stock market—indeed, any financial market—can send investors (and borrowers) along an exceedingly bumpy path. Consequently, both investors and businesspeople should be informed about why such movements occur in the financial markets. Consider, for example, a business that needs to raise funds for expansion. Should the firm raise the needed funds by issuing either stocks or bonds during periods of significant market fluctuations similar to what was exhibited in the stock market in May–June 2006? This chapter begins the process of answering questions such as this by describing the characteristics of the various financial markets. In addition, it provides an overview of how firms use the financial markets to raise funds. As you read this chapter, as well as related chapters later in the book, keep in mind this example of the May–June 2006 market and try to explain why markets experience such drastic changes at times.

## Chapter *Essentials*
### —The Questions

After reading this chapter, you should be able to answer the following questions:

- What are financial markets and what role do they play in improving the standard of living in an economy?
- Why is it important for financial markets to be somewhat efficient?
- Why are there so many different types of financial markets? How do we differentiate among various financial markets?
- What is an investment banking house and what role does an investment banking house play when firms want to raise funds in the financial markets?
- What is a financial intermediary and what role does a financial intermediary play in the financial markets? Why are there so many different types of intermediaries?
- How do the financial markets in the United States differ from financial markets in other parts of the world?

Financial markets are extremely important to the economic well-being of the United States.[3] For this reason, it is important that both investors and financial managers understand the environment and markets within which securities are traded and businesses operate. This chapter examines the markets in which firms raise funds, securities are traded, and the prices for stocks and bonds are established.

## WHAT ARE FINANCIAL MARKETS?

Businesses, individuals, and government units often need to raise funds to invest in assets. For example, suppose Florida Power & Light (FP&L) forecasts an increase in the demand for electricity in Florida, and the company decides to build a new power plant. Because FP&L almost certainly will not have the hundreds of millions of dollars necessary to pay for the plant, the company will have to raise these funds in the financial markets. Similarly, if you want to buy a house that costs $150,000, but you have only $40,000 in savings, where do you get the other $110,000 you need?

Whereas some individuals and firms need funds, others have incomes that are greater than their current expenditures. Thus, they have funds available to invest, or save. For

---

[3]Throughout much of this chapter, we primarily refer to corporations as the users, or issuers, of such financial assets as debt and equity. In reality, governments, government agencies, and individuals also issue debt. For example, an individual "issues" a mortgage when he or she finances the purchase of a house. Because corporations issue a variety of debt instruments and can also issue equity, we will identify them as the issuers more often than governments or individuals in the examples.

example, Alexandra Trottier has an annual income of $50,000, but her expenses (including taxes) are only $40,000. As a result, Alexandra has $10,000 to invest (save) this year.

People and organizations that need money are brought together with those that have surplus funds in the *financial markets*. Note that "markets" is plural—in a developed economy such as that of the United States, a great many different financial markets exist, each of which includes many institutions and individuals. Unlike *physical asset markets*, which deal with products such as wheat, autos, real estate, computers, and machinery, *financial asset markets* deal with stocks, bonds, mortgages, and other *claims on real assets* with respect to the distribution of future cash flows generated by such assets.

In a general sense, the term *financial market* refers to a conceptual "mechanism" rather than a physical location or a specific type of organization or structure. We usually define the **financial markets** as a system that includes individuals and institutions, instruments, and procedures that bring together borrowers and savers, no matter the location. If this financial system did not exist, you would not be able to buy the $150,000 house until you save $150,000, and Alexandra Trottier would not have the ability to grow her $10,000 through investment.

**financial markets**
A system consisting of individuals and institutions, instruments, and procedures that brings together borrowers and savers.

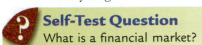

**Self-Test Question**
What is a financial market?

## IMPORTANCE OF FINANCIAL MARKETS

The primary role of financial markets is to *facilitate* the flow of funds from individuals and businesses that have surplus funds to individuals, businesses, and governments that have needs for funds in excess of their incomes. In developed economies, financial markets help efficiently allocate excess funds of savers to individuals and organizations in need of funds for investment or consumption. The more efficient the process of funds flow, the more productive the economy, both in terms of manufacturing and financing.

### Flow of Funds

By providing *mechanisms* by which borrowers and lenders get together to transfer funds, the financial markets allow us to consume amounts different from our current incomes.[4] In this way, these markets provide us with the ability to transfer income through time. When we borrow, for example, we sacrifice future income to increase current income; when we save, or invest, we sacrifice current income in exchange for greater expected income in the future. For example, young adults borrow funds to go to college or to buy such high-priced items as houses or cars, so they tend to save little or nothing. After they become established in their careers and reach or are near their peak income years, these same individuals generally save (invest) greater percentages of their incomes. Finally, when they retire, these individuals rely on funds accumulated from prior years' savings to provide their retirement income. Consequently, adults go through three financial phases that would not be possible without financial markets:

1. Young adults desire to consume more than their incomes, so they must borrow.

---

[4]Throughout this chapter, we often refer to the parties involved in financial market transactions as *borrowers* or *lenders*, which implies that only loans are traded in the financial markets. In reality, stocks, options, and many other financial assets also are traded in the financial markets. In our general discussions, we will use the term *borrowers* to refer to parties such as individuals and government units that raise needed funds through various types of loans as well as corporations that use both loans and stock issues to raise needed funds. We will use the term *lenders* to refer to those parties that provide funds, whether the medium is a loan or a stock.

**FIGURE 3-1    Diagram of the Capital Formation Process**

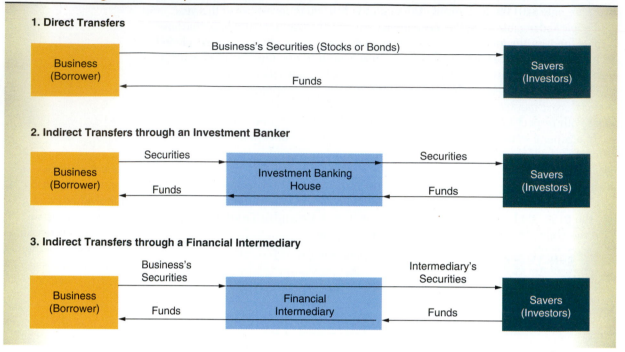

**1. Direct Transfers**

Business (Borrower) → Business's Securities (Stocks or Bonds) → Savers (Investors)

Savers (Investors) → Funds → Business (Borrower)

**2. Indirect Transfers through an Investment Banker**

Business (Borrower) → Securities → Investment Banking House → Securities → Savers (Investors)

Savers (Investors) → Funds → Investment Banking House → Funds → Business (Borrower)

**3. Indirect Transfers through a Financial Intermediary**

Business (Borrower) → Business's Securities → Financial Intermediary → Intermediary's Securities → Savers (Investors)

Savers (Investors) → Funds → Financial Intermediary → Funds → Business (Borrower)

2. Older working adults earn more than their consumption needs, so they save.

3. Retired adults use the funds accumulated in earlier years to at least partially replace income lost due to retirement.

Without financial markets, consumption would be restricted to income earned each year plus any amounts put aside (perhaps in a coffee can) in previous years. As a result, our standard of living would be much lower than is now possible.

Funds are transferred from those with surpluses (savers) to those with needs (borrowers) by the three different processes diagrammed in Figure 3-1:

1. A *direct transfer* of money and securities, as shown in the top section, occurs when a business sells its stocks or bonds directly to savers (investors) without going through any type of intermediary or financial institution. The business delivers its securities to savers, who in turn give the firm the money it needs.

2. As shown in the middle section, a transfer can also go through an *investment banking house,* which serves as a middleman that facilitates the issuance of securities. The company sells its stocks or bonds to the investment bank, which in turn sells these same securities to savers. The firm's securities and the savers' money merely "pass through" the investment banking house. For example, when IBM raises funds by issuing stock, it generally uses the services of an investment banker, such as Goldman Sachs or Merrill Lynch, to sell the issue in the financial markets. The investment banking process is described in greater detail later in this chapter.

3. Transfers can also be made through a *financial intermediary,* such as a bank or a mutual fund. In this case, the intermediary obtains funds from savers and then uses the money to lend out or to purchase another business's securities.

For example, when you deposit money in a savings account at your local bank, the bank takes those funds—along with other depositors' funds—and creates mortgages and business and automobile loans. The existence of intermediaries greatly increases the efficiency of the financial markets. More information concerning the roles and descriptions of financial intermediaries is provided later in this chapter.

For simplicity, Figure 3-1 assumes that the entity in need of capital is a business. Nevertheless, it is easy to visualize the demander of funds as being a home purchaser or a government unit. Direct transfers of funds from savers to borrowers are possible and do occur on occasion. Generally, however, corporations and government entities use investment bankers to help them raise needed capital in the financial markets, and individual savers use such intermediaries as banks and mutual funds to help them lend their funds or to borrow needed funds.

## Market Efficiency

If the financial markets did not provide efficient funds transfers, the economy simply could not function as it does now. Because Florida Power & Light would have difficulty raising needed capital, Miami's citizens would pay more for electricity. Likewise, you would not be able to buy the house you want when you want it, and Alexandra Trottier would have no place to invest her savings. Clearly, the level of employment and productivity, and hence our standard of living, would be much lower. Therefore, it is absolutely essential that our financial markets function efficiently—not only quickly but also at a low cost. When we speak of market efficiency, we generally mean either economic efficiency or informational efficiency.

### Economic Efficiency

The financial markets are said to have **economic efficiency** if funds are allocated to their optimal use at the lowest costs. In economically efficient markets, businesses and individuals invest their funds in assets that yield the highest returns, and the costs of searching for such opportunities are lower than those observed in less efficient markets. Often individuals hire brokers, who charge commissions, to help search for and then buy or sell investments in the financial markets. If the commissions and other costs associated with such transactions, which are called **transaction costs,** are very high, investments will not be as attractive as when transaction costs are low.

**economic efficiency**
Funds are allocated to their optimal use at the lowest costs in the financial markets.

**transaction costs**
Costs associated with buying and selling investments, including commissions, search costs, taxes, and so on.

### Informational Efficiency

The prices of investments bought and sold in the financial markets are based on available information. If these prices reflect existing information and adjust very quickly when new information becomes available, then the financial markets have achieved **informational efficiency.**

When the financial markets have a large number of participants in search of the most profitable investments, informational efficiency generally exists. For instance, in the United States, millions of individual investors and more than 100,000 highly trained professionals participate in the financial markets. As a consequence, you would expect investment prices to adjust almost instantaneously to new information because a large number of the market participants will evaluate the new information when it becomes known in an effort to find more profitable investments.

**informational efficiency**
The prices of investments reflect existing information and adjust quickly when new information enters the markets.

Informational efficiency generally is classified into one of the following three categories:

1. *Weak-form* efficiency states that all information contained in *past price movements* is fully reflected in current market prices. Therefore, information about recent, or past, trends in investment prices is of no use in selecting "winning" investments; the fact that an investment has risen for the past three days, for example, gives us no clues as to what it will do today or tomorrow.

2. *Semistrong-form* efficiency states that current market prices reflect all *publicly available information*. In this case, it does no good to scrutinize such published data as a corporation's financial statements because market prices will have adjusted to any good or bad news contained in such reports as soon as they were made public. Even under semistrong-form efficiency, insiders (for example, the executives of companies) can still earn **abnormal returns** on their own companies' investments (stocks). An investor earns an *abnormal return* when the return he or she receives is greater than is justified by the risk associated with the investment. If you and all of your friends invest in securities of similar risk, you should all earn about the same return. If the return you earn on your investment is 20 percent and the return your friends earn is 12 percent, the additional 8 percent is considered an abnormal return.

3. *Strong-form* efficiency states that current market prices reflect *all pertinent information*, whether it is publicly available or privately held. If this form of efficiency holds, even insiders would find it impossible to earn abnormal returns in the financial markets.[5]

**abnormal returns**
Returns that exceed those that are justified by the risks associated with the investments.

The informational efficiency of the financial markets has received a great deal of attention. The results of most market efficiency studies suggest that the financial markets are highly efficient in the weak form and reasonably efficient in the semistrong form, but strong-form efficiency does not appear to hold.

Financial markets that are informationally efficient also tend to be economically efficient. This situation arises because investors can expect prices to reflect appropriate information and thus make intelligent choices about which investments will likely provide the best returns.

> **? Self-Test Questions**
>
> What are the three methods by which funds are transferred from savers (lenders) to borrowers?
>
> Why do you think that most transfers of money and securities are indirect rather than direct?
>
> What does it mean to have economically efficient financial markets? What does it mean to have informationally efficient markets?
>
> What are the three forms (degrees) of informational efficiency?

---

[5]Several cases of illegal insider trading have made the news headlines in the past. In a famous case, Ivan Boesky admitted to making $50 million by purchasing the stocks of firms he knew were preparing to merge. Boesky went to jail and had to pay a large fine, but he helped disprove strong-form efficiency. More recently, Martha Stewart served time in jail because she was convicted of obstructing justice by lying to federal investigators about whether inside information was used to time the sale of stock she owned (ImClone Systems Inc.).

# TYPES OF FINANCIAL MARKETS

A number of different financial markets, with a variety of investments and participants, exist today. We generally differentiate among financial markets based on the types of investments, maturities of investments, types of borrowers and lenders, locations of the markets, and types of transactions. There are too many different types of financial markets to discuss here. Instead, we describe only the more common classifications and provide some indication of the function of each type of market.

## Money Markets versus Capital Markets

Some borrowers need funds for short periods; others need funds for extended periods. Similarly, some investors prefer to invest for short periods, but others prefer to invest for longer periods. The markets for short-term financial instruments are termed the *money markets,* and the markets for long-term financial instruments are called the *capital markets.* More specifically, the **money markets** include debt instruments that have maturities equal to one year or less when originally issued, and the **capital markets** include instruments with original maturities greater than one year. By definition, then, money markets include only debt instruments because equity instruments (that is, stocks) have no specific maturities, whereas capital markets include both equity instruments and such long-term debt instruments as mortgages, corporate bonds, and government bonds.

The primary function of the money markets is to provide liquidity to businesses, governments, and individuals so that they can meet their short-term needs for cash because, in most cases, the receipt of cash inflows does not coincide exactly with the payment of cash outflows. The existence of money market instruments with different maturities permits us to better match our cash inflows with cash outflows in the short run. Consider, for example, a corporation that needs to pay for the purchase of inventory today, but cash from sales of the inventories will not be received for another 30 days. The company has the opportunity to raise the needed funds through a 30-day loan, so it can match the timing of the cash outflow (payment for inventory) with the timing of the cash inflow (collection for inventory sales). Individuals, companies, and governments use the money markets similarly—to better align short-term cash flows. Thus, when cash surpluses exist for short periods, short-term investments are desirable; when cash deficits exist for short periods, short-term loans (debt instruments) are desirable.

The primary function of the capital markets is to provide us with the opportunity to transfer cash surpluses or deficits to future years—that is, transfer income through time. For example, without the availability of mortgages, most individuals could not afford to buy houses when they are young and just starting their careers because they have little or no savings and their incomes are not sufficient to pay for such houses. Based on our abilities to generate sufficient funds from future years' incomes to repay the debts, mortgages and other long-term loans permit us to borrow funds we do not have today. Similarly, corporations issue stocks and bonds to get funds to support such current investment needs as expansion, and investors who provide the funds receive promises that cash flows generated by these firms will be distributed at some point in the future. In essence, individuals, corporations, and governments use the capital markets either to spend more than the funds generated in the current period in exchange for their ability to replace (repay) the additional funds (with interest) in future periods or to invest current income to enable greater consumption in the future.

**money markets**
The segments of the financial markets in which the instruments that are traded have maturities equal to one year or less.

**capital markets**
The segments of the financial markets in which the instruments that are traded have maturities greater than one year.

## Debt Markets versus Equity Markets

**debt markets**
Financial markets in which loans are traded.

**equity markets**
Financial markets in which corporate stocks are traded.

Simply stated, the **debt markets** are markets in which loans are traded, and the **equity markets** are markets in which stocks are traded. A debt instrument is a contract that specifies the amounts, as well as the dates, a borrower must repay a lender. In contrast, equity represents "ownership" in a corporation; it entitles the stockholder to share in future cash distributions generated from income and from liquidation of the firm.

The debt markets permit individuals, companies, and governments to consume future income in the current period through such loans as mortgages and corporate bonds. These loans require repayment, with interest, from income (cash flows) generated during the loan period. Conversely, the equity markets permit corporations to raise funds by selling ownership interests, thereby transferring some risks associated with businesses to individuals and other companies. Purchasers of equity receive the right to distributions of cash flows made by the firm from income generated in the future. Unlike debt, however, equity is not a specific contract that guarantees that cash distributions will be made or that the investment will be repaid. Because debt typically has a maturity, it can be considered temporary funding; equity is more permanent because it has no specific maturity.

Equity markets, which also are called stock markets, are familiar to most people. In fact, nearly 50 percent of all Americans invest in stocks, either directly or through mutual funds. In addition, more than 10,000 institutions, such as pension funds and insurance companies, invest in the equity markets. Clearly, stock markets are very important in the United States. For that reason, we discuss the characteristics of stock markets in more detail in the next section.

Debt markets generally are described (labeled) according to the characteristics of the debt that is traded. Many different types of debt exist, which leads to many different types of debt markets. For example, short-term debt instruments, such as those issued by the U.S. Treasury, are traded in the *money markets.* Long-term debt instruments, such as corporate bonds and mortgages, are traded in the *capital markets.* In addition, the debt markets are clearly divided by the type of participant—issuer (borrower) or investor (lender). The portion of the debt markets in which government bonds are traded differs from the corporate bonds market, and the market for consumer debt differs from both of these segments. Thus the segmentation of the debt markets is based on the maturity of the instrument, the type of debt, and the participant (borrowers and investors).

## Primary Markets versus Secondary Markets

**primary markets**
Markets in which various organizations raise funds by issuing new securities.

**secondary markets**
Markets in which financial assets that have previously been issued by various organizations are traded among investors.

The *primary markets* are markets in which "new" securities are traded, and the *secondary markets* are markets in which "used" securities are traded.

**Primary markets** are the markets in which corporations raise new capital. If IBM were to sell a new issue of common stock to raise capital, this activity would be a primary market transaction. The corporation selling the newly created stock receives the proceeds from the sale in a primary market transaction.

**Secondary markets** are markets in which existing, previously issued securities are traded among investors. Thus, if Jessica Rogers decides to buy 1,000 shares of existing IBM stock, the purchase would occur in the secondary market. Secondary markets also exist for mortgages, other types of loans, and other financial assets. The corporation whose securities are traded in the secondary market is not involved in the transaction and therefore does not receive any funds from the transaction.

# Derivatives Markets

Options, futures, and swaps are some of the securities traded in the **derivatives markets.** These securities are called *derivatives* because their values are determined, or "derived," directly from other assets.

Let's consider an option that is known as a *call*. A **call option** allows the option buyer (owner) to purchase a certain number of shares of stock (or some other security) from the option seller at a prespecified price—say, $50—for a particular period of time—say, 60 days. Because the option contract fixes the purchase price of the stock, the value of the call option changes as the actual *market value* of the stock changes. For example, if the per-share price of the "underlying" stock increases to $60 (decreases to $45), the value of the option increases (decreases) because the person who owns the option can "exercise" his or her right to purchase the stock for the contracted $50 per share from the option seller regardless of the existing market price of the stock. A **put option** is a contract that gives the owner of the option the right to sell a stock (or some other security) at a specified price during some period in the future.

Another popular derivative is a **futures contract,** which is a contract for the "future" delivery of an item where the price, amount, delivery date, place of delivery, and so forth are specified. For example, a farmer in Nebraska might contract with General Mills to deliver 10,000 bushels of wheat in three months at a price of $3.25 per bushel. This contract requires the farmer to deliver 10,000 bushels of wheat to General Mills in three months, and General Mills will pay the farmer $32,500 when the wheat is delivered, regardless of what the market price of wheat is at the time of delivery.

Although many investors use derivatives to speculate about the movements of prices in the financial markets and the markets for such commodities as wheat and soybeans, these instruments are typically employed to help manage risk. That is, individuals, corporations, and governments use derivatives to *hedge* risk by contracting to set future prices, which offsets exposures to uncertain price changes in the future. We discuss derivatives in greater detail later in the book.

**derivatives markets**
Financial markets in which options and futures are traded.

**call option**
An option that allows the buyer to purchase stock (or some other security) from the option seller at a pre-specified price during a particular time period.

**put option**
An option that allows the buyer to sell stock (or some other security) from the option seller at a prespecified price during a particular time period.

**futures contract**
A contract for the "future" delivery of an item where the price, amount, delivery date, place of delivery, and so forth are specified.

**Self-Test Questions**

How are the financial markets differentiated?

What are the differences between (1) the money markets and the capital markets, (2) the primary markets and the secondary markets, and (3) the debt markets and the equity markets?

What types of assets are traded in the derivatives markets?

# STOCK MARKETS

In recent years, individuals have expressed greater interest in stocks than ever before. A major reason for this increased interest is the fact that the stock markets generated record-breaking returns during the 1990s. From 1995 to 1999, the annual returns in the stock markets averaged more than 20 percent—an unprecedented level. Much of the record upward movement in the markets was spurred by enthusiastic buying by individual investors who felt they had to join their neighbors in trying to "get rich" by trading stocks. Although the markets slowed and even turned around during the 2000–2006 period, the popularity and intrigue of the stock markets is still evident. This section describes the characteristics of stock markets.

## Types of General Stock Market Activities

We can classify general stock market activities into three distinct categories:

1. *Trading in the outstanding, previously issued shares of established, publicly owned companies: the secondary market.* If the owner of 100 shares of IBM sells his or her stock, the trade is said to have occurred in the *secondary market.* The company receives no new money when sales occur in this market.

2. *Additional shares sold by established, publicly owned companies: the primary market.* If IBM decides to sell (or issue) additional shares to raise funds for expansion, this transaction is said to occur in the *primary market.* The company receives the funds that are raised when its securities are sold (issued) in the primary market.

3. *New public offerings by privately held firms: the initial public offering (IPO) market; the primary market.* When Google decided to sell some stock to raise capital needed to grow and expand into new products, it took its stock public. Whenever stock in a privately held corporation is offered to the public for the first time, the company is said to be **going public.** The market for stock that has recently gone public is called the **initial public offering (IPO) market.**

Nearly all stock transactions occur in the secondary markets. Nevertheless, primary market transactions are very important to corporations that need to raise funds for capital projects. In this section, we examine the general characteristics of stock markets, which function principally as secondary markets; the next section considers how stocks and bonds are issued in the primary markets.

Traditionally, we have categorized stock markets in the United States into one of two basic types: (1) *physical stock exchanges,* which include the New York Stock Exchange (NYSE), the American Stock Exchange (AMEX), and several regional exchanges; and (2) the less formal *over-the-counter (OTC) market,* which consists of a network of dealers around the country and includes the well-known Nasdaq market. As a result of heated competition, stock markets have changed significantly in recent years through mergers and by introducing new, more efficient trading systems. As a result, it is now very difficult to differentiate between the two categories of stock markets. Even so, we generally still refer to stock markets as having the general characteristics of either a physical stock exchange or the OTC/Nasdaq market.

## Physical Stock Exchanges[6]

The **physical security exchanges** are tangible physical entities. The physical exchanges in the United States include national exchanges, such as the NYSE and the AMEX, and regional exchanges, such as the Philadelphia Stock Exchange (PHLX) and the Chicago Stock Exchange (CHX).[7] The prices of stocks listed on the physical stock exchanges are determined by auction processes in which investors (through their brokers) bid for stocks.

**going public**
The act of selling stock to the general public for the first time by a corporation or its principal stockholders.

**initial public offering (IPO) market**
The market consisting of stocks of companies that have just gone public.

**physical security exchanges**
Formal organizations with physical locations that facilitate trading in designated ("listed") securities. The two major U.S. stock exchanges are the New York Stock Exchange (NYSE) and the American Stock Exchange (AMEX).

---

[6]The statistics and other information that are provided in this section are based on information that is reported by the various stock exchanges. Additional statistics and information can be found on the websites of the exchanges: http://www.nyse.com, http://amex.com, http://www.chx.com, and http://www.archipelago.com.

[7]The NYSE, which is more than 200 years old, is the largest physical stock exchange in the world in terms of the total value of stocks traded. The PHLX, which was established in 1790, is the oldest physical exchange in the United States; the New York Stock Exchange was started a couple of years later in 1792.

Until the late 1990s, most stock exchanges were not-for-profit organizations that were owned by their members, who were said to hold "seats" on the exchanges (although everyone stood up). These seats, which were bought and sold, gave the holder the right to trade on the exchanges.[8] Organizations such as these that are owned and operated by their members are said to have *mutual ownership* structures.

The current trend of stock exchanges is to convert from not-for-profit mutual ownership organizations to for-profit organizations that are owned by stockholders and are publicly traded. The process of converting an exchange from a mutual ownership organization to a stock ownership organization is called **demutualization.** The first U.S. stock exchange to demutualize was the Pacific Exchange (PCX) in 2000. Not long after its conversion, PCX and Archipelago Holdings Inc. (Arca), which is an electronic communications network (ECN), merged to form ArcaEX. ArcaEX was the first totally electronic stock market in the United States. In March 2006, the largest merger of stock exchanges took place when the NYSE joined with ArcaEX to form the NYSE Group. When the merger took place, the ownership structure of the NYSE was demutualized. The previous owners of the NYSE—that is, the "seat" holders—were given stock ownership in the new organization, and *trading licenses* were auctioned off to those companies that wished to have either electronic or physical access to the exchange's facilities and trading services. This marked the end of the NYSE traditional seat membership (ownership) that had existed for more than 210 years.[9] Now, trading licenses are awarded to successful bidders through the SEATS (Stock Exchange Auction Trading System) auction.

At about the same time the NYSE merged with ArcaEX and became a for-profit organization, the Chicago Stock Exchange demutualized and the board of directors of the American Stock Exchange approved demutualization. Many foreign stock exchanges have also demutualized since the late 1990s, including the Australian Stock Exchange, Hong Kong Stock Exchange, Stock Exchange of Singapore, and Toronto Stock Exchange, to name a few. It is estimated that at least 80 percent of the world's developed stock exchanges will be demutualized within the next few years. Clearly, the ownership structure of the stock exchanges has changed dramatically in recent years. To trade on an exchange, however, membership similar to a "seat" is still required.

**demutualization**
The process of converting a stock exchange from a mutual ownership organization to a stock ownership organization.

## Exchange Members

Exchange members are charged with different trading responsibilities, depending on the type of license (trading permit) they own. For example, trading licenses on the NYSE are classified into one of two categories: floor brokers and specialists. The responsibilities of each NYSE member are given here:

1. *Floor brokers* act as agents for investors who want to buy or sell securities. *House brokers* are floor brokers who are employed by brokerage firms such as Merrill Lynch and Smith Barney to execute orders for the firms' clients. *Independent brokers* are freelance brokers who work for themselves or for firms that provide trading services to house brokers rather than for a

---

[8]NYSE stocks were not traded continuously until 1871. Prior to that time, stocks were traded sequentially according to their position on a stock roll, or roster, sheet. Members were assigned chairs, or "seats," in which to sit while the roll call of stocks proceeded. The number of "seats" changed as the number of members changed, until the number was fixed at 1,366 in 1868.

[9]The number of seats, or memberships, that were available on each exchange varied—the number of seats on the NYSE was fixed at 1,366, the AMEX had about 850 members, and the CHX had about 450 members. The cost of exchange membership also has varied considerably. For example, in 2005 a seat on the CHX cost about $19,000, whereas a seat on the NYSE sold for a record $4 million in December 2005.

brokerage firm. Independent brokers "farm out" their services to brokerage firms that need additional help because trading activity is too high for their house brokers to handle.

2. *Specialists* are considered the most important participants in NYSE transactions because their role is to bring buyers and sellers together. Each specialist oversees a particular group of stocks. Specialists are charged with ensuring that the auction process is completed in a fair and efficient manner. To accomplish his or her job, a specialist might have to buy stock when not enough sellers exist or sell stock when not enough buyers exist; he or she must be ready to *make a market* when either buyers or sellers are needed. To accomplish this task, a specialist must maintain inventories in the stocks he or she is assigned. The specialist posts a *bid price* (the price he or she will pay for the stock) and an *ask price* (the price at which shares will be sold out of inventory) in an effort to keep the inventory in balance. Bid prices are somewhat lower than ask prices, with the difference, or *spread,* representing the specialist's profit margin.[10] If many buy orders start coming in because of favorable developments or if many sell orders come in because of unfavorable events, the specialist will raise or lower prices to keep supply and demand in balance. On the NYSE, supply/demand imbalances require specialists to participate in buying or selling shares only about 10 percent of the time.

## Listing Requirements

**listing requirements**
Characteristics a firm must possess to be listed on an exchange.

For a stock to be traded on an exchange, it must be *listed.* Each exchange has established **listing requirements,** which indicate the quantitative and qualitative characteristics that a firm must possess to be listed. Table 3-1 provides examples of the listing requirements for some U.S. exchanges. The primary purpose of these requirements is to ensure that investors have some interest in the company so that the firm's stock will be actively traded on the exchange.

**TABLE 3-1**   Listing Requirements for Stock Exchanges and the Nasdaq

|  | NYSE | AMEX and Regional Exchanges[a] | Nasdaq |
|---|---|---|---|
| Round-lot (100 shares) shareholders | 2,000 | 800 | 400 |
| Number of public shares (millions) | 1.1 | 0.5 | 1.1 |
| Market value of public shares ($ millions) | $ 100 | $   3 | $   8 |
| Shareholders equity ($ millions) | — | $   4 | $  15 |
| Pretax income ($ millions) | $2.00 | $0.75 | $1.00 |

[a]These numbers are indicative of the listing requirements for larger regional stock exchanges, including the Chicago Stock Exchange, the Pacific Exchange, and the Philadelphia Stock Exchange. The listing requirements for smaller regional exchanges generally are not as restrictive.

---

[10]Special facilities are available to help institutional investors such as mutual funds or pension funds sell large blocks of stock without depressing their prices. In essence, brokerage houses that cater to institutional clients purchase blocks of stocks (defined as 10,000 or more shares) and then resell the stocks to other institutions or individuals. Also, when a firm is preparing to make a major announcement that will likely cause its stock price to fluctuate sharply, it will ask the exchanges to halt trading in its stock until the announcement has been made and digested by investors. For example, when Texaco announced that it planned to acquire Getty Oil, trading in both Texaco and Getty stocks was halted for one day.

Approximately 2,700 companies in the United States and worldwide have shares listed for trade on the NYSE, about 1,200 firms are listed on the AMEX, more than 150 firms are listed on the Chicago Stock Exchange, and the Philadelphia Exchange and Pacific Exchange have more than 2,400 listed companies each. The Nasdaq (which stands for the National Association of Security Dealers Automated Quotation) has the greatest number of *listed* companies—more than 3,300 firms. The Nasdaq evolved from the OTC market, as described in the next section.

A listed firm pays a relatively small annual fee to the exchange to receive such benefits as the marketability offered by continuous trading activity and the publicity and prestige associated with being an exchange-listed firm. Many people believe that listing has a beneficial effect on the sales of the firm's products, and it probably is advantageous in terms of lowering the return demanded by investors to buy its common stock. Investors respond favorably to a listed firm's increased information and liquidity, and they have confidence that its quoted price is not being manipulated. It is not required that a qualified firm be listed on an exchange—listing is the choice of the firm.

## The Over-the-Counter (OTC) Market and the Nasdaq

If a security is not traded on a physical exchange, it has been customary to say that it is traded in the **over-the-counter (OTC) market,** which is an intangible trading system that consists of a network of brokers and dealers around the country. An explanation of the term *over-the-counter* helps clarify how the market got its name.

The exchanges operate as auction markets: Buy and sell orders come in more or less simultaneously, and exchange members match these orders. If a stock is traded less frequently, perhaps because it is the stock of a new or a small firm, few buy and sell orders come in, and matching them within a reasonable length of time could be difficult. To avoid this problem, some brokerage firms maintain inventories of such stocks; they buy when individual investors want to sell and sell when investors want to buy. At one time, the inventory of securities was kept in a safe, and the stocks, when bought and sold, literally were passed *over the counter.*

Traditionally, the OTC market has been defined as including all facilities needed to conduct security transactions not conducted on the physical exchanges. These facilities consist of (1) the *dealers* who hold inventories of OTC securities and who are said to "make a market" in these securities, (2) the *brokers* who act as *agents* in bringing the dealers together with investors, and (3) the *electronic networks* that provide a communications link between dealers and brokers. Unlike physical exchanges, the OTC market does not operate as an auction market. The dealers who make a market in a particular stock continuously quote a price at which they are willing to buy the stock (the *bid price*) and a price at which they will sell shares (the *ask price*). Each dealer's prices, which are adjusted as supply and demand conditions change, can be read off computer screens across the country. The spread between the bid and ask price (the *dealer's spread*) represents the dealer's markup, or profit.

Brokers and dealers who participate in the OTC market are members of a self-regulating body known as the *National Association of Security Dealers* (NASD), which licenses brokers and oversees trading practices. The computerized trading network used by NASD is known as the NASD Automated Quotation system, or Nasdaq, and *The Wall Street Journal* and other newspapers provide information on Nasdaq transactions. Today, the Nasdaq is considered a sophisticated market of its own, separate from the OTC market. In fact, unlike the general OTC market, the Nasdaq includes *market makers* who continuously monitor trading activities in various stocks to ensure that such stocks are available to traders who want to buy or sell. The role of

**over-the-counter (OTC) market**

A collection of brokers and dealers, connected electronically by telephones and computers, that provides for trading in securities not listed on the physical stock exchanges.

**electronic communications networks (ECNs)**
Electronic systems that transfer information about securities transactions to facilitate the execution of orders by automatically matching buy and sell orders for a large number of investors.

the Nasdaq market maker is similar to that of the specialist on the NYSE. Also, companies must meet minimum financial requirements to be *listed*, or included, on the Nasdaq (see Table 3-1); the OTC market has no such requirements.

As information technology has evolved, so have the choices to investors as to how to trade securities. Today most stocks and bonds can be traded electronically using trading systems known as **electronic communications networks (ECNs).** ECNs, which are registered with the Securities and Exchange Commission (SEC), are electronic systems that transfer information about securities transactions to facilitate the execution of the orders. ECNs automatically match the buy and sell orders by price for a large number of investors. Investors use ECNs through accounts they have at brokerage firms, such as Charles Schwab, that offer online trading services and subscribe to ECNs. When an order (buy or sell) is placed electronically, the process is seamless in the sense that investors have no indication that an ECN is used to execute their transactions. In essence, ECNs allow investors to submit orders in an "electronic-exchange" market. Generally, the biggest users of ECNs are institutional investors such as mutual funds, pension funds, and so forth. ECNs provide an alternative trading medium, which has increased the competition with the stock exchanges. In fact, as a result of the increased competition and to improve its competitive position, the NYSE merged with the Archipelago Exchange (ArcaEX), an ECN, to form the NYSE Group.

According to a study published by the SEC, nearly all the transactions executed by ECNs in 1999 involved Nasdaq stocks (93 percent). The study also reported that few of these transactions (4 percent) occurred "after hours"—that is, after the physical stock exchanges had closed.[11] Today, approximately 50 percent of the total dollar volume of trades in Nasdaq stocks is executed using ECNs, whereas ECNs account for 5 percent of the dollar transactions of securities listed on the physical stock exchanges. As after-hour trading increases in the future, so will the use of ECNs.

In terms of *numbers of issues,* most stocks are traded over the counter. Even though the OTC market includes some very large companies, most of the stocks traded over the counter involve small companies that do not meet the requirements to be listed on a physical exchange. On the other hand, because the stocks of larger companies generally are listed on the exchanges, approximately two-thirds of the total *dollar volume of stock trading* takes place on the exchanges. In fact, the NYSE generates greater than 50 percent of the daily dollar trading volume with its listing of nearly 2,700 stocks.

## Competition Among Stock Markets

Competition among the major stock markets has become increasingly fierce in recent years. In the United States, the major stock markets, especially NYSE and Nasdaq, continuously explore ways to improve their competitive positions. Two factors have changed the competitive arena of the stock markets. First, whereas many years ago stocks could be traded only on the exchanges where they were listed, today many stocks are *dual listed*. A stock with a **dual listing** is eligible (registered) to be traded on more than one stock market (exchange). Dual listing increases liquidity because a stock has more exposure through a greater number of outlets than if it was listed on only one exchange. Various stock markets compete to list stocks that are very actively traded because increased trading activity translates into increased profits.

Second, in 2005 the Securities and Exchange Commission voted to adopt Regulation NMS (National Market Structure), which mandates that the "trade-through rule"

**dual listing**
When stocks are listed for trading in more than one stock market.

---

[11]Securities and Exchange Commission, "Special Study: Electronic Communications Networks and After-Hours Trading," June 2000. This study is available at the SEC website, which is located at http://www.sec.gov/.

be used when securities are traded. The "trade-through rule" states that a stock trade should be executed at the best price that is available in all of the stock markets. In other words, a trade order continues to "pass through" markets until the best price is reached; the order cannot be "traded though" to another market once the best trading price is found. The objective of the **"trade-through rule"** is to provide investors equal access to various stock markets so that they can trade at the best prices. Clearly, this rule requires all of the stock markets—that is, NYSE, Nasdaq, and regional markets—and ECNs to be "connected" electronically. Those markets that have electronic advantages, such as processing speed and cost efficiencies, will be most successful in this very competitive environment. Based on the recent changes that have been made by the NYSE and Nasdaq, it seems that Regulation NMS is producing the desired result—that is, increased competition among the stock markets, which ultimately benefits investors in the form of better prices and lower trading costs.

As a result of the increased competition among the stock markets, both the NYSE and Nasdaq have taken actions to improve their competitive positions. For example, we mentioned earlier that in 2006 the NYSE merged with ArcaEX to form the NYSE Group. The "new and improved" NYSE Group effectively consists of two distinct stock (securities) exchanges. The physical stock exchange called the NYSE still exists, and the products and services it offers continue to improve, but they are very similar to what was offered prior to the merger. In addition, the NYSE Group offers a fully electronic exchange through NYSE Arca, which was previously the ArcaEX that evolved from the Archipelago ECN. The NYSE Group was formed to improve the competitive position of the NYSE. For the same reason, later in the same year, the NYSE Group agreed to merge with Euronext, which operates the stock markets in Paris, Amsterdam, Brussels, and Lisbon. It is certain that the NYSE will continue such actions in an effort to improve its competitive position in financial markets around the world.

In an effort to become more competitive with other stock markets—especially the NYSE—the Nasdaq, the AMEX, and the Philadelphia Stock Exchange merged in 1998 to form the Nasdaq Amex Market Group. However, the merger did not produce the desired results, so AMEX members bought the exchange back from NASD in 2005. Even so, Nasdaq continues to explore ways to improve its competitive position. Soon after the announcement of the NYSE–ArcaEX merger agreement in 2005, Nasdaq acquired Instinet to improve its ability to compete with the NYSE as an electronic stock exchange. Instinet provided an "electronic exchange" that improved the technology and efficiency of Nasdaq trading. In 2006, Nasdaq tried to acquire the London Stock Exchange (LSE). Although the takeover attempt was originally rejected and had not taken place at the time of this writing (February 2007), it is clear that Nasdaq seeks ways to compete better with the NYSE Group.

Increased competition among global stock markets assuredly will result in similar alliances among various exchanges/markets in the future. Clearly, the playing field on which the exchanges compete will be much different in the future than it has been in the past. Many believe that the playing field is becoming more level for all players.

## REGULATION OF SECURITIES MARKETS

Sales of new securities, such as stocks and bonds, as well as operations in the secondary markets, are regulated by the **Securities and Exchange Commission (SEC)** and, to a lesser extent, by each of the 50 states. For the most part, the SEC regulations are intended to ensure that investors receive fair disclosure of financial and nonfinancial information from publicly traded companies and to discourage fraudulent and misleading behavior by firms' investors, owners, and employees to manipulate stock prices.

**trade-through rule**
Requires a trade order to continue to "pass through" markets until the best price is reached.

**Securities and Exchange Commission (SEC)**
The U.S. government agency that regulates the issuance and trading of stocks and bonds.

The primary elements of SEC regulations include (1) jurisdiction over most interstate offerings of new securities to the general investing public; (2) regulation of national securities exchanges; (3) the power to prohibit manipulation of securities' prices—deliberate manipulation of securities' prices is illegal; and (4) control over stock trades by corporate **insiders,** which include the officers, directors, and major stockholders of a company.[12]

**insiders**
Officers, directors, major stockholders, or others who might have inside information about a company's operations.

### Self-Test Questions

What are the two basic types of stock markets, and how do they differ?

Are the greatest number of stocks traded over the counter or on physical stock exchanges?

What are the two types of memberships available on the NYSE?

How do stocks traded on the Nasdaq differ from stocks traded on the NYSE?

What is the primary purpose for regulating securities trading?

## THE INVESTMENT BANKING PROCESS

**investment banker**
An organization that underwrites and distributes new issues of securities; it helps businesses and other entities obtain needed financing.

When a business needs to raise funds in the financial markets, it generally enlists the services of an **investment banker** (see Panel 2 in Figure 3-1). Merrill Lynch, Morgan Stanley, and Goldman Sachs are examples of companies that offer investment banking services. Such organizations perform three types of tasks: (1) They help corporations design securities with the features that are most attractive to investors given existing market conditions; (2) they buy these securities from the corporations; and (3) they resell the securities to investors (savers). Although the securities are sold twice, this process is actually one primary market transaction, with the investment banker acting as a middleman (agent) as funds are transferred from investors (savers) to businesses.

Investment banking has nothing to do with the traditional banking process as we know it; it deals with the issuance of new securities, not deposits and loans. The major investment banking houses often are divisions of large financial service corporations that engage in a wide range of activities. For example, Merrill Lynch has a brokerage department that operates thousands of offices worldwide as well as an investment banking department that helps companies issue securities, take over other companies, and the like. The firm's brokers sell previously issued stocks as well as stocks that are issued through their investment banking departments. Thus, financial service organizations such as Merrill Lynch sell securities in both the secondary markets and the primary markets.

This section briefly describes how securities are issued in the financial markets and explains the role of investment bankers in this process.

### Raising Capital: Stage I Decisions

The corporation that needs to raise funds makes some preliminary decisions on its own, including the following:[13]

**1.** *Dollars to be raised.* How much new capital do we need?

---

[12]Insiders must file monthly reports of changes in their holdings of the corporation's stock, and any *short-term* profits from trading in the stock must be handed over to the corporation.

[13]For the most part, the procedures described in this section also apply to government entities. Governments issue only debt, however; they do not issue stock.

2. *Type of securities used.* Should we use stock, bonds, or a combination of the two? And if stock is to be issued, should it be offered to existing stockholders or sold to the general public?

3. *Competitive bid versus negotiated deal.* Should the company simply offer a block of its securities for sale to the investment banker that submits the highest bid of all interested investment bankers or should it sit down and negotiate a deal with a single investment banker? These two procedures are called *competitive bids* and *negotiated deals (purchases),* respectively. Only a handful of the largest firms, whose securities are already well known to the investment banking community, are in a position to use the competitive bid process. The investment banks would have to do a large amount of investigative work to bid on an issue unless they were already quite familiar with the firm, and the costs involved would be too high to make it worthwhile unless the investment bank was sure of getting the deal. For these reasons, most offerings of stocks or bonds are made on a negotiated basis.[14]

4. *Selection of an investment banker.* If the issue is to be negotiated, which investment banker should the firm use? Older corporations that have "been to market" before will already have established a relationship with an investment banker, although it is easy enough to change investment bankers if the firm is dissatisfied. A firm that is just going public will have to choose an investment bank, and different investment banking houses are better suited for different companies. The older, larger "establishment houses," such as Morgan Stanley, deal mainly with large companies such as GM, IBM, and ExxonMobil. Other bankers specialize in more speculative issues such as initial public offerings.

## Raising Capital: Stage II Decisions

Stage II decisions, which are made jointly by the firm and its selected investment banker, include the following:

1. *Reevaluating the initial decisions.* The firm and its investment banker will reevaluate the initial decisions about the size of the issue and the type of securities to use. For example, the firm initially might have decided to raise $50 million by selling common stock, but the investment banker might convince the company's management that it would be better, in view of existing market conditions, to limit the stock issue to $25 million and then raise the other $25 million as debt.

2. *Best efforts or underwritten issues.* The firm and its investment banker must decide whether the investment banker will work on a best efforts basis or underwrite the issue. In an **underwritten arrangement,** the investment banker generally assures the company that the entire issue will be sold, so the investment banker bears significant risks in such an offering. With this type of arrangement, the investment banking firm typically buys the securities from the issuing firm and then sells the securities in the primary markets, hoping to make a profit. In a **best efforts arrangement,** the investment banker does not buy the securities from the issuing firm; rather, the securities are handled on a contingency basis, and the investment banker receives a commission based on the amount of the issue that is sold. The investment banker essentially promises to exert its best efforts when selling the

**underwritten arrangement**
Agreement for the sale of securities in which the investment bank guarantees the sale by purchasing the securities from the issuer, thus agreeing to bear any risks involved in the transaction.

**best efforts arrangement**
Agreement for the sale of securities in which the investment bank handling the transaction gives no guarantee that the securities will be sold.

[14]On the other hand, by law, most government entities are required to solicit competitive bids for bond issues.

**underwriter's spread**
The difference between the price at which the investment banking firm buys an issue from a company and the price at which the securities are sold in the primary market—it represents the investment banker's gross profit on the issue.

**flotation costs**
The costs associated with issuing new stocks or bonds.

**offering price**
The price at which common stock is sold to the public.

securities, which means that the issuing firm takes the chance the entire issue will not be sold and that all needed funds will not be raised.

3. *Issuance (flotation) costs.* The investment banker's fee must be negotiated, and the firm must estimate the other expenses that it will incur in connection with the issue, including lawyers' fees, accountants' costs, printing and engraving, and so forth. Usually, the investment banker will buy the issue from the company at a discount below the price at which the securities are to be offered to the public. This **underwriter's spread** covers the investment banker's costs and provides for a profit.

Table 3-2 gives an indication of the **flotation costs** associated with public issues of bonds and common stock. As the table shows, costs as a percentage of the proceeds are higher for stocks than for bonds, and they are also higher for small issues than for large issues. The relationship between the size of the issue and the flotation costs primarily reflects the existence of fixed costs: Certain costs must be incurred regardless of the size of the issue, so the percentage flotation cost is quite high for small issues.

4. *Setting the offering price.* If the company is already publicly owned, the **offering price** will be based on the existing market price of the stock or the yield on the firm's bonds. For common stock, the arrangement typically calls for the investment banker to buy the securities at a prescribed number of points below the closing price on the last day of registration, which is the day the issue is released for sale by the Securities and Exchange Commission. Investment bankers have an easier job if an issue carries a relatively low price, but the issuer of the securities naturally wants as high of a price as

**TABLE 3-2**   Flotation (Issuance) Costs for Issuing Debt and Equity[a]

| Issue Size ($ millions) | Bonds[b] | | Equity[c] | |
|---|---|---|---|---|
| | **Straight** | **Convertible** | **Seasoned Issues** | **IPOs** |
| Under 10.0 | 4.4% | 8.8% | 13.3% | 17.0% |
| 10.0– 19.9 | 2.8 | 8.7 | 8.7 | 11.6 |
| 20.0– 39.9 | 2.4 | 6.1 | 6.9 | 9.7 |
| 40.0– 59.9 | 2.3 | 4.3 | 5.9 | 8.7 |
| 60.0– 79.9 | 2.3 | 3.2 | 5.2 | 8.2 |
| 80.0– 99.9 | 2.2 | 3.0 | 4.7 | 7.9 |
| 100.0–199.9 | 2.3 | 2.8 | 4.2 | 7.1 |
| 200.0–499.9 | 2.2 | 2.2 | 3.5 | 6.5 |
| 500.0 and larger | 1.6 | 2.1 | 3.2 | 5.7 |

[a]The results provided in this table represent the direct costs as a percentage of the size of the issue. Direct costs include underwriting fees, registration fees, legal costs, auditing costs, and other costs directly related to the issue. The numbers presented in this table are intended to provide an indication of the costs associated with issuing debt and equity. Such costs increase somewhat when interest rates are cyclically high; when money is in relatively tight supply, the investment bankers will have a more difficult time placing issues. Thus, actual flotation costs will vary over time.

[b]A straight bond is the traditional type of bond discussed in Chapter 6, in which interest is paid periodically (perhaps every six months) and the principal amount is repaid at maturity. A convertible bond resembles a straight bond but can be converted into shares of common stock by the bondholder.

[c]Seasoned equity issues are issues of stock of publicly traded corporations. Initial public offerings (IPOs) are equity issues of privately held companies that are "going public" by offering shares of stock to the general public for the first time.

**Source:** Inmoo Lee, Scott Lochhead, Jay Ritter, and Quanshui Zhao, 1996, "The Costs of Raising Capital," *Journal of Financial Research*, 19 (Spring), 59–74.

possible. Therefore, an inherent conflict of interest on price exists between the investment banker and the issuer. If the issuer is financially sophisticated and makes comparisons with similar security issues, however, the investment banker will be forced to price the issue close to the market price.

A company that is going public for the first time (an IPO) will not have an established price (or demand curve). Consequently, the investment banker must estimate the equilibrium price at which the stock will sell after it is issued. If the offering price is set below the true equilibrium price, the stock price will rise sharply after issue, and the company and its original stockholders will have "given away" too many shares to raise the required capital. If the offering price is set above the true equilibrium price, either the issue will fail or, if the investment bankers succeed in selling the stock, their investment clients will be unhappy when the stock subsequently falls to its equilibrium level. For these reasons, it is important that the equilibrium price be estimated as accurately as possible.

## Selling Procedures

Once the company and its investment bankers have decided how much money to raise, the types of securities to issue, and the basis for pricing the issue, they will prepare and file a registration statement and prospectus with the SEC. The **registration statement** provides financial, legal, and technical information about the company, whereas the **prospectus** summarizes the information in the registration statement and is provided to prospective investors for use in selling the securities. Lawyers and accountants at the SEC examine both the registration statement and the prospectus; if the information is deemed inadequate or misleading, the agency can delay or stop the public offering. When the SEC approves the registration statement and the prospectus, it merely validates that the required information has been furnished. The SEC does not judge the quality or value of the issue; that task is left to potential investors.

The final price of the stock (or the interest rate on a bond issue) is set at the close of business on the day the issue clears the SEC, and the securities are then offered to the public on the following day. Typically, investment bankers sell the stock within a day or two after the offering begins. On occasion, however, they miscalculate, set the offering price too high, and are unable to move the issue. Alternatively, the market might decline during the offering period, which also would force the investment bankers to reduce the price of the stock. In either instance, on an underwritten offering the corporation would still receive the agreed-upon price, and the investment bankers would have to absorb any losses.

Because they are exposed to large potential losses, investment bankers typically do not handle the purchase and distribution of an issue alone unless it is fairly small. If the amount of money involved is large and the risk of price fluctuations is substantial, an investment banker will form an **underwriting syndicate,** where the issue is distributed to a number of investment firms in an effort to minimize the amount of risk carried by each firm. The investment banking house that sets up the deal is called the *lead,* or *managing, underwriter.*

In addition to the underwriting syndicate, larger offerings might require the services of still more investment bankers as part of a *selling group.* The selling group, which handles the distribution of securities to individual investors, includes all members of the underwriting syndicate plus additional dealers who take relatively small participations (or shares of the total issue) from the syndicate members. Members of the selling group act as selling agents and receive commissions for their efforts: They do not purchase the securities, so they do not bear the same risk that the underwriting

**registration statement**
A statement of facts filed with the SEC about a company that plans to issue securities.

**prospectus**
A document describing a new security issue and the issuing company.

**underwriting syndicate**
A group of investment banking firms formed to spread the risk associated with the purchase and distribution of a new issue of securities.

syndicate does. Thus, the underwriters act as wholesalers and bear the risk associated with the issue, whereas members of the selling group act as retailers. The number of investment banking houses in a selling group partly depends on the size of the issue.

## Shelf Registrations

The selling procedures just described, including a minimum waiting period (20 days) between registration with the SEC and sale of the issue, apply to many security sales. However, large, well-known public companies (seasoned companies) that frequently issue securities file a master registration statement with the SEC and then update it with a short-form statement just prior to each individual offering. In such a case, a company could decide at 10 A.M. to sell registered securities and have the sale completed before noon. This procedure is known as **shelf registration** because, in effect, the company puts its new securities "on the shelf" and then sells them to investors when it thinks the market is right.

**shelf registration**
Securities registered with the SEC for sale at a later date; the securities are held "on the shelf" until the sale.

## Maintenance of the Secondary Market

In the case of a large, established firm such as General Motors, the investment banking firm's job is finished once it has disposed of the stock and the net proceeds have been turned over to the company. Conversely, in the case of a company going public for the first time, the investment banker has an obligation to maintain a market for the shares after the issue has been completed. Such stocks typically are traded in the OTC market, and the lead underwriter generally agrees to "make a market" in the stock and keep it reasonably liquid. The company wants a good market to exist for its stock, as do its stockholders. Therefore, if the investment banking house wants to do business with the company in the future, keep its own brokerage customers happy, and have future referral business, it will hold an inventory of the shares and help maintain an active secondary market in the stock.

 **Self-Test Questions**

How does an investment bank differ from a "regular" bank?

What is the sequence of events that takes place when a firm decides to issue new securities?

What is an underwriting syndicate and why is it important in the investment banking process?

What type of firm would use a shelf registration? Explain.

## INTERNATIONAL FINANCIAL MARKETS

Financial markets have become much more global during the past few decades. As the economies of developing countries have grown, greater numbers of investors have provided funds to these financial markets. In 1970, U.S. stocks accounted for nearly two-thirds of the value of worldwide stock markets. Today, as Table 3-3 shows, U.S. stock markets represent less than 40 percent of the total value worldwide, but the markets in the United States still dominate the stock markets in other countries.[15] During the past decade, the areas of greatest worldwide growth have been in the emerging markets of Russia, China, and Saudi Arabia. More recently, the financial

---

[15]The value given for U.S. stock exchanges is based on the combined values of the New York Stock Exchange, the American Stock Exchange, and Nasdaq.

**TABLE 3-3**  Foreign Stock Market Values ($ billion)[a]

| | Year-End 1996 | | Year-End 2006 | | |
| --- | --- | --- | --- | --- | --- |
| | Market Value | Percent of Total | Market Value | Percent of Total | 10-Year Growth |
| **I. Developed Stock Markets** | | | | | |
| United States | $ 8,484.4 | 41.9% | $17,369.3 | 37.3% | 104.7% |
| Japan | 3,088.9 | 15.3 | 4,720.3 | 10.1 | 52.8 |
| United Kingdom | 1,740.2 | 8.6 | 3,653.2 | 7.8 | 109.9 |
| France | 591.1 | 2.9 | 2,248.7 | 4.8 | 280.4 |
| Canada | 486.3 | 2.4 | 1,520.1 | 3.3 | 212.6 |
| Germany | 671.0 | 3.3 | 1,461.4 | 3.1 | 117.8 |
| Switzerland | 402.1 | 2.0 | 1,231.6 | 2.6 | 206.3 |
| Italy | 258.2 | 1.3 | 1,023.6 | 2.2 | 296.4 |
| Australia | 312.0 | 1.5 | 1,003.0 | 2.2 | 221.5 |
| Netherlands | 378.7 | 1.9 | 656.4 | 1.4 | 73.3 |
| Hong Kong | 449.4 | 2.2 | 613.9 | 1.3 | 36.6 |
| Other developed markets | 1,144.7 | 5.7 | 3,447.8 | 7.4 | 201.2 |
| All developed markets | $18,007.0 | 88.9% | $38,949.2 | 83.6% | 116.3% |
| **II. Emerging Stock Markets** | | | | | |
| China | $ 113.8 | 0.6% | 1,844.5 | 4.0% | 1,520.8% |
| Russia | 37.2 | 0.2 | 905.5 | 1.9 | 2,334.2 |
| Korea | 138.8 | 0.7 | 732.5 | 1.6 | 427.7 |
| India | 122.6 | 0.6 | 670.1 | 1.4 | 446.6 |
| Saudi Arabia | 45.9 | 0.2 | 658.1 | 1.4 | 1,333.8 |
| Brazil | 217.0 | 1.1 | 636.4 | 1.4 | 193.3 |
| Taiwan, China | 273.6 | 1.4 | 604.8 | 1.3 | 121.0 |
| Mexico | 106.5 | 0.5 | 383.0 | 0.8 | 259.6 |
| South Africa | 241.6 | 1.2 | 370.0 | 0.8 | 53.2 |
| Malaysia | 307.2 | 1.5 | 188.0 | 0.4 | −38.8 |
| Other emerging markets | 641.4 | 3.2 | 647.8 | 1.4 | 1.0 |
| All emerging markets | 2,245.6 | 11.1 | 7,640.8 | 16.4 | 240.3 |
| All stock markets | $20,252.6 | 100.0% | $46,590.0 | 100.0% | 130.0% |

[a]All market value are stated in U.S. dollars. Some of the changes in market values from 1996 to 2006 resulted from changes in the value of the dollar relative to foreign currencies (exchange rate changes).

**Source:** *Standard & Poor's Global Stock Markets Factbook, 2006* and *Standard & Poor's Global Stock Market Review: The World By Numbers*, December 2006.

markets of both China and India have attracted a great deal of attention as a result of the unprecedented growth these countries have experienced during the past few years.

Even with the expansion of stock markets internationally, exchanges in the United States continue to account for the greatest numbers of trades, with respect to both volume and value. Stock trades in the United States are approximately seven times greater than the value of stocks traded in both Japan and the United Kingdom. In fact, U.S. trading activity accounts for approximately 50 percent of worldwide trading activity each year.

The international market for bonds has experienced growth similar to the international stock markets. Table 3-4 shows the values of some of the foreign bond markets in 2005. The value of the U.S. bond market is substantial ($20 billion), but the bond markets in Euroland, Japan, and the United Kingdom have a combined value that is nearly the same (about $18 billion).

**TABLE 3-4** Foreign Bond Market Values, 2005—Domestic Debt ($ billions)[a]

| Country | Total Bonds | Percentage of Total |
|---|---|---|
| **I. Developed Countries** | | |
| United States | $20,310.5 | 45.8% |
| Euroland[a] | 8,749.9 | 19.7 |
| Japan | 8,370.7 | 18.9 |
| United Kingdom | 1,002.8 | 2.3 |
| Canada | 793.5 | 1.8 |
| Other developed countries | 2,047.5 | 4.6 |
| Total developed countries | $41,274.9 | 93.1% |
| **II. Developing (Emerging) Regions** | | |
| Africa[b] | $96.2 | 0.2% |
| Asia[c] | 1,792.8 | 4.0 |
| Eastern Europe[d] | 342.9 | 0.8 |
| Latin America[e] | 807.8 | 1.8 |
| Total developing countries | $3,039.7 | 6.9% |
| Total domestic debt outstanding | $44,314.6 | 100.0% |

[a]Includes Austria, Belgium, Finland, France, Germany, Greece, Ireland, Italy, Netherlands, Portugal, and Spain.

[b]Includes South Africa.

[c]Includes China, India, Indonesia, Malaysia, Singapore, South Korea, and Thailand.

[d]Includes Czech Republic, Poland, and Turkey.

[e]Includes Argentina, Brazil, and Mexico.

**Source:** *Bank for International Settlements, BIS Quarterly Review,* June 2006. Data are available on the BIS website at www.bis.org.

**Euroland**

The countries that comprise the European Monetary Union (EMU).

The term **Euroland** refers to the countries that comprise the European Monetary Union (EMU), which officially was born on January 1, 1999, with 11 member countries. The members created a common currency (the euro) and a common debt instrument that is denominated in the euro and traded in a unified financial market called the Euromarket.[16] The emergence of Euroland was intended to reduce or eliminate country boundaries with respect to member countries' economic and trading policies. As the data in Table 3-4 show, in 2005 the size of the Euroland bond market was 43 percent of the size of the U.S. bond market. And the combination of the Euroland and Japanese markets is about 85 percent of the size of the U.S. bond market. Clearly, Euroland and Japan are important factors in international financial markets. The financial markets truly are global in nature, which means that events that influence the Asian and European markets also influence the U.S. markets.

Although the globalization of financial markets continues and international markets offer investors greater frontiers of opportunities, investing overseas can be difficult because of restrictions or barriers erected by foreign countries. In many cases, individual investors find it difficult or unattractive to invest directly in foreign stocks. Many countries prohibit or severely limit the ability of foreigners to invest in their financial markets, or they make it extremely difficult to access reliable information concerning the companies that are traded in the stock markets. For these reasons, most individuals interested in investing internationally do so indirectly, by purchasing financial

---

[16]The 11 countries included in Euroland are Austria, Belgium, Finland, France, Germany, Ireland, Italy, Luxembourg, the Netherlands, Portugal, and Spain.

instruments that represent foreign stocks, bonds, and other investments but that are offered by institutions in the United States. Investors can participate internationally by purchasing American depository receipts (ADRs), mutual funds that hold international stocks, or foreign securities certificates issued in dollar denominations.

## Self-Test Questions

Why should investors in the United States be concerned with financial markets in other countries?

How do you think the European Monetary Union will affect the international financial markets?

# FINANCIAL INTERMEDIARIES AND THEIR ROLES IN FINANCIAL MARKETS

Financial intermediaries include financial services organizations such as commercial banks, savings and loan associations, pension funds, and insurance companies. In simple terms, **financial intermediaries** facilitate the transfer of funds from those who have funds (savers) to those who need funds (borrowers) by *manufacturing* a variety of financial products that take the form of either loans or savings instruments. When intermediaries take funds from savers, they issue *securities*. These securities, which have names such as savings accounts, money market funds, and pension plans, represent claims, or liabilities, against the intermediaries. The funds received by intermediaries are, in turn, lent to businesses and individuals via debt instruments created by these institutions, which include automobile loans, mortgages, commercial loans, and similar types of debt. The process by which financial intermediaries transform funds provided by savers into funds used by borrowers is called **financial intermediation.** Figure 3-2 illustrates the financial intermediation process. The arrows at the top of the boxes (pointing to the right) show the flow of funds from savers to borrowers through intermediaries. The arrows at the bottom of the boxes (pointing to the left) indicate the changes in the balance sheets of savers, borrowers, and intermediaries that result from the intermediation process. In essence, savers *exchange* funds for claims, or liabilities, from intermediaries, which include deposits at banks, retirement plans, or money market funds. The intermediaries then *exchange* funds provided by savers for claims, or liabilities, from borrowers that are packaged as debt or other instruments created by the intermediaries, including mortgages, commercial loans, and many other types of loans.

Without financial intermediaries, savers would have to provide funds *directly* to borrowers, which would be a difficult task for those who do not possess such expertise; loans such as mortgages and automobile financing would be much more costly, so the

> **financial intermediaries** Specialized financial firms that facilitate the transfer of funds from savers to borrowers.

> **financial intermediation** The process by which financial intermediaries transform funds provided by savers into funds used by borrowers.

**FIGURE 3-2** The Financial Intermediation Process

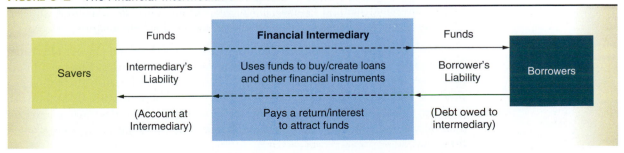

financial markets would be much less efficient. Clearly, the presence of intermediaries improves economic well-being. In fact, financial intermediaries were created to fulfill specific needs of both savers and borrowers and to reduce the inefficiencies that would otherwise exist if users of funds could get loans only by borrowing directly from savers.

Improving economic well-being is only one of the benefits associated with intermediaries. Following are other benefits:

1. *Reduced costs.* Without intermediaries, the net cost of borrowing would be greater and the net return earned by savers would be less because individuals with funds to lend would have to seek out appropriate borrowers themselves, and vice versa. Intermediaries are more cost efficient than individuals for two reasons: They create combinations of financial products that better match the funds provided by savers with the needs of borrowers, and they spread the costs associated with these activities over large numbers of transactions. Because intermediaries have expertise and achieve economies of scale that individuals cannot, the costs associated with transforming savings into loans are lower when financial intermediaries exist.

2. *Risk/diversification.* The loan portfolios of intermediaries generally are well diversified because they provide funds to a large number and variety of borrowers by offering many types of loans. Just like investors who purchase varied financial securities, intermediaries spread their risk by "not putting all their financial eggs in one basket."

3. *Funds divisibility/pooling.* Intermediaries can pool funds provided by individuals to offer loans or other financial products with different denominations. That is, an intermediary can offer a large loan to a single borrower by combining the funds provided by many small savers. In essence, intermediaries permit the "little guys" to be a part of large loans and the "big guys" to obtain large amounts of funds without having to find individuals with sufficient wealth.

4. *Financial flexibility.* Because intermediaries offer a variety of financial products, both savers and borrowers have greater choices, or financial flexibility, than can be achieved with direct placements. For instance, banks offer savers products such as regular passbook savings accounts, certificates of deposit, and money market accounts, and they offer borrowers products such as commercial loans, mortgages, and credit cards. In general, the financial products created by intermediaries are quite varied with respect to denominations, maturities, and other characteristics; hence, intermediaries attract many different types of savers and borrowers.

5. *Related services.* A system of specialized intermediaries offers more than just a network of "mechanisms" to transfer funds from savers to borrowers. Many intermediaries provide financial services in areas in which they achieve comparative advantages. For example, banks provide individuals with a convenient method to make payments through checking accounts, and life insurance companies offer financial protection for beneficiaries.

Think about the complications that would arise if we could not pay our bills using checks or we could not borrow funds to purchase cars or houses. Financial intermediaries increase the standard of living in the economy because their financial products help both individuals and businesses invest in opportunities that otherwise might be unreachable. For example, without the mortgages offered by savings and loan associations, individuals would find it much more difficult to purchase houses when they want.

**Self-Test Questions**

What is the principal role of financial intermediaries?

In what ways do financial intermediaries benefit society?

## Types of Financial Intermediaries

In the United States, a large set of specialized, highly efficient financial intermediaries has evolved. Competition and government policy have created a rapidly changing arena, however, such that different types of institutions currently create financial products and perform services that previously were reserved for others. This trend, which is destined to continue into the future, has blurred the lines among the various types of intermediaries. Still, some degree of institutional identity persists, and these distinctions are discussed in this section.

Each type of intermediary originated to satisfy a particular need in the financial markets. For this reason, it has been easy historically to distinguish among the various types of intermediaries based on the characteristics of their assets and liabilities. Even though such organizations are more alike today than at any time in modern history, differences in organizational structures persist among the intermediaries. For that reason, as we describe each type of intermediary, we indicate the *types* of loans, deposits, and other products it offers. Table 3-5 shows the total value of the assets of intermediaries in the United States. Comparison of the sizes of these institutions gives you an idea as to the importance each plays in the financial markets.

## Commercial Banks

Commercial banks, commonly referred to simply as banks, are the traditional "department stores of finance"—that is, they offer a wide range of products and services to a variety of customers. Historically, banks were the institutions that handled checking accounts and provided mechanisms for clearing checks. Also, they traditionally provided the medium through which the supply of money was expanded or contracted. Today, however, several other institutions provide checking and check-clearing services and significantly influence the money supply. Conversely, banking companies offer a greater range of services than before, including trust operations, stock brokerage services, and insurance.

Originally, banks were established to serve the needs of commerce, or business—hence the name "commercial banks." Today, commercial banks represent one of the

**TABLE 3-5**   Size of Financial Intermediaries, 2006 ($ billions)

|                               | Assets   |
|-------------------------------|----------|
| Commercial banks              | $9,333   |
| Mutual funds                  | 8,900    |
| Private pension funds         | 7,207    |
| Life insurance companies      | 4,772    |
| Savings and loan associations | 1,877    |
| Credit unions                 | 679      |

**Source:** Commercial banks and savings and loans, Federal Deposit Insurance Corporation (http://www.fdic.gov); mutual funds, Investment Company Institute (http://www.ici.org/stats/mf); pension funds, Federal Reserve Board (http://www.federalreserve.gov); life insurance, American Council of Life Insurers (http://www.acli.com); credit unions: National Credit Union Administration (http://www.ncua.gov).

largest groups of depository intermediaries. Most individuals have at least one checking or savings account at a commercial bank, and many people have borrowed from banks to finance automobile purchases or use bank-issued credit cards. In addition, commercial banks still represent the primary source of business loans.

## Credit Unions

A credit union is a depository institution that is owned by its depositors, who are members of a common organization or association, such as an occupation, a religious group, or a community. Credit unions operate as not-for-profit businesses and are managed by member depositors elected by other members.

The first credit unions can be traced to financial pools, or cooperatives, established in England about 200 years ago. The original purpose of these financial groups was to create savings pools that could be used to provide credit to neighboring farmers who suffered temporary losses of income due to crop failures or other catastrophes. The common bonds possessed by the members generated a "help thy neighbor" attitude within the savings pools.

Today, credit unions differ significantly from their earliest forms: They are much larger and hence less personal. Nevertheless, the spirit of credit unions remains unchanged—to serve depositor members. Members' savings are still loaned to other members, but the loans are primarily for automobile purchases, home improvements, and the like. Thanks to the common bond that members possess, loans from credit unions often are the cheapest source of funds for individual borrowers.

## Thrift Institutions

Thrift institutions cater to savers, especially individuals who have relatively small savings or need long-term loans to purchase houses. Thrifts, which include savings and loan associations, were originally established because the services offered by commercial banks were designed for businesses rather than individuals, whose needs differ greatly.

Historically, S&Ls have been viewed as places to obtain real estate mortgages. In fact, when these institutions were first established, depositors pooled their savings to create loans that were used to help other depositors build houses in a particular geographic area. Each savings association was eventually liquidated when the building goals were achieved and all of the loans were repaid.

Today, S&Ls take the funds of many small savers and then lend this money to home buyers and other types of borrowers. S&Ls provide savers with flexibility because funds do not have to be committed for long periods. In many cases, savings can be easily liquidated (withdrawn) with little or no restriction. As a result, S&Ls help "create liquidity" that otherwise would be lacking.

## Mutual Funds

Mutual funds are *investment companies* that accept money from savers and then use these funds to buy various types of financial assets, including stocks, long-term bonds, short-term debt instruments, and so forth. These organizations pool funds, reducing risks through diversification. They also achieve economies of scale, which lower the costs of analyzing securities, managing portfolios, and buying and selling securities.

Hundreds of different types of mutual funds exist, offering a variety of goals/ instruments to meet the objectives of different types of savers. Investors who prefer to receive current income can invest in *income funds*, which include financial instruments that generate fairly constant annual incomes (bonds with constant annual interest payments and stocks with constant dividend payments). Investors who are willing to accept higher risks in hopes of obtaining higher returns can invest in *growth funds,* which include investments that generate little or no income each year but exhibit high growth potential that could result in significant increases in the values of the investments (that is, capital gains) in the future. Funds with many other "objectives" are also available; investors can find a mutual fund to meet almost any financial goal.

One of the most popular savings instruments available in the financial markets is the *money market fund.* A **money market mutual fund** includes short-term, low-risk securities and generally allows investors to write checks against their accounts. From their beginning in the mid-1970s, money market funds have experienced unparalleled growth. In 1975 the total value of money market funds was less than $10 *million;* by 2006 this total value exceeded $2 *trillion.* Other mutual funds have shown similar, albeit somewhat slower, growth patterns. With nearly $9 trillion in assets at the beginning of 2006, mutual fund investment companies represented the second-largest financial institution in the United States; only commercial banks ($9.3 trillion in assets) had a greater amount of assets. Today, investment companies offer some 8,000 individual mutual funds. According to the Investment Company Institute (ICI), which monitors the performances of mutual funds, more than 80 million individuals own 90 percent of the mutual funds. The primary reason individuals invest in mutual funds is for retirement.

> **money market mutual fund**
> A mutual fund that invests in short-term, low-risk securities and allows investors to write checks against their accounts.

## Whole Life Insurance Companies[17]

Broadly speaking, the purpose of life insurance is to provide a beneficiary, such as a spouse or family members, with protection against financial distress or insecurity that might result from the premature death of a "breadwinner" or other wage earner. In a general sense, life insurance can be labeled either term insurance or whole life insurance. *Term life insurance* is a relatively short-term contract that provides protection for a temporary period—perhaps for one year or for five years at a time—and it must be renewed each period to continue such protection. *Whole life insurance* is a long-term contract that provides lifetime protection. Most whole life insurance companies also offer tax-deferred savings plans designed to provide benefits to participants when they retire.

The cost of term insurance, called the *premium,* generally increases with each renewal because the risk of premature death increases as the insured ages. In contrast, the premiums associated with whole life insurance policies are fixed payments computed as an average of the premiums required over the expected life of the insured person. As a consequence, the premiums in the early years exceed what is needed to cover the insured, and the premiums in the later years are less than what is needed. The excess amounts in the early years are invested to make up for the deficits in later years. These invested amounts provide savings features that create cash values for the whole life insurance policies. In contrast, term life insurance policies do not provide savings features because the premiums are fixed for only a short time period (generally five years or less); for this reason, the premiums are based on the existing risks only and change at renewal when risks

---

[17]Insurance is intended to reduce the consequences of risk by transferring some of the economic consequences to others—namely insurance companies—that are better able to absorb such risks. Insurance companies achieve risk reduction by pooling, or diversifying, the risks of individuals, companies, and governments.

change. Thus, whole life policies offer both insurance coverage and a savings feature, whereas term life policies do not.[18]

## Pension Funds

Pensions are retirement plans funded by corporations or government agencies for their workers. Pension plans are administered primarily by the trust departments of commercial banks or by life insurance companies. Probably the most famous pension plan is Social Security, which is a government-sponsored plan funded by tax revenues. Most state and municipal governments and large corporations offer pension plans to their employees. Many of these plans have been established to accept both employer and employee contributions, which often are shielded from taxes until the assets are withdrawn from the plan.

The earliest pensions in the United States were created by railroad companies more than a century ago. As the country became more industrialized, pension plans expanded greatly. The growing popularity of pensions was accompanied by new problems associated with managing such plans. Many pensions did not survive the financial turmoil of the 1920s and 1930s because they were "pay-as-you-go" plans with benefits paid out of the contributions made by the existing employees. "Pay-as-you-go" plans are termed *unfunded pensions.* Social Security, which was established in 1935 to supplement the retirement income provided by private pensions, is the largest unfunded pension. Since World War II, private pensions have grown significantly compared with government pensions. Today, they account for 62 percent of the total assets held in retirement plans.

### Self-Test Questions

List the major types of financial intermediaries, and briefly describe each one's function.

Why are mortgages the primary asset held by savings institutions?

## FINANCIAL ORGANIZATIONS IN OTHER PARTS OF THE WORLD

Two notable factors distinguish financial institutions in the United States from those in other countries. These differences can be traced to the regulatory climate that has existed historically in the United States. Generally speaking, U.S. financial institutions have been much more heavily regulated and have faced greater limitations than have their foreign counterparts with regard to expansion (branching), the services that could be offered, and relationships with nonfinancial businesses. Such regulations have imposed an organizational structure and competitive environment that have long curbed the ability of individual financial intermediaries in the United States to grow.

First, past regulation restricted the ability of financial institutions, especially intermediaries, to operate through branches. As a result, the U.S. "banking" system traditionally has been characterized by a large number of independent financial institutions of various sizes, rather than a few very large institutions that might exist if

---

[18]Premiums charged by other insurance companies, such as health insurance, property and casualty insurance, and the like, are based only on the risks faced and are changed over time as the risks change. In other words, they reflect the cost of the peril (risk) that is insured at the time that the premium is paid. There is no savings function because individuals pay only for the insurance services offered by such companies. Such insurance companies do not perform the same intermediary function as life insurance companies.

"branching" was not restricted. Consider, for example, that there are approximately 18,000 individual banks, credit unions, and thrift institutions in the United States; Japan has fewer than 160 such institutions, there are about 20 Australian-owned banks (four of which are considered large commercial banks), and Canada has only 70 chartered banks (seven of which operate nationally and internationally). Even India, which has a population nearly four times larger than that of the United States, has fewer than 300 individual banks (about 3.5 percent of the total number of U.S. banks). In India and other countries, however, each financial intermediary generally has many branches. For instance, the State Bank of India alone has more than 13,000 offices (branches). The financial institutions of nearly every other country in the world have been allowed to branch with few, if any, limitations, and as a result their banking systems include far fewer individual, or unit, institutions than exist in the United States.

Second, most foreign financial institutions are allowed to engage in nonbanking (nonfinancial) business activities whereas the nonbanking activities of U.S. intermediaries have been severely restricted until recently. Developed countries such as the United Kingdom, France, Germany, and Switzerland, to name a few, permit financial firms and commercial businesses to interact without restriction; banking firms can own commercial firms, and vice versa. Other countries, including Canada, Japan, and Spain, allow the mixing of financial institutions and commercial firms with some restrictions.

In the past, regulations that restricted the nonbanking activities of U.S. financial institutions put these organizations at a competitive disadvantage internationally. However, Congress has shown that it is willing to remove existing "competitive restraints" to allow U.S. institutions to better compete in the global financial arena. To be more like their international counterparts, U.S. financial intermediaries must have the ability to engage in more aspects of multilayer financial deals, which means that these organizations must be able to offer services such as investment banking, commercial lending, insurance, and other necessary financial services. In many countries, banking/financial organizations can maintain equity positions in companies to which they lend money. Being able to operate as a company's lender, owner, investment banker, and insurer permits foreign financial organizations to be a "one-stop shop" for financial services and products. Because a single financial institution can offer such financial products as a package, it is possible to reduce the aggregate costs associated with financial services.

Panel A in Table 3-6 lists the 10 largest banking organizations in the world. Notice that three of the banking institutions on the list are located in the United States and six are located in Europe. The three largest banking institutions in the United States—Bank of America, JP Morgan Chase, and Citibank—ranked seventh, 10th, and 18th in the world, respectively. It should not be surprising that foreign banks dominate international banking activities. Certainly, having to cope with fewer restrictions has helped these banks attain such dominance. In addition, such institutions have been involved in international banking much longer than have U.S. banks. So that you can compare U.S. banking organizations with foreign banking organizations, Panel B in Table 3-6 lists the 10 largest institutions in the United States. It is interesting that one of the 10 largest U.S. banking organizations, HSBC North America, actually is a subsidiary of a UK banking organization.

Even with the restrictions on U.S. banking operations carried out overseas, the presence of U.S. banks in international banking has grown rapidly in recent years. At the same time, the limitations that overseas banking operations face in the United States have not discouraged the entry of foreign banks, especially in California, where

**TABLE 3-6**    Largest Banking Organizations Ranked by Size of Assets, December 2005

*Panel A*                                                          *Largest Banking Organizations in the World*

| World Rank | Bank Name | Country | Total Assets ($ billions) |
|---|---|---|---|
| 1 | Barclays PLC | United Kingdom | $1,586.9 |
| 2 | UBS AG | Switzerland | 1,563.3 |
| 3 | BNP Paribas SA | France | 1,483.9 |
| 4 | The Royal Bank of Scotland Group PLC | United Kingdom | 1,300.1 |
| 5 | Crédit Agricole SA | France | 1,252.0 |
| 6 | Deutsche Bank AG | Germany | 1,170.3 |
| 7 | Bank of America NA | United States | 1,082.2 |
| 8 | ABN AMRO Holding NV | Netherlands | 1,038.9 |
| 9 | Credit Suisse Group | Switzerland | 1,016.1 |
| 10 | JPMorgan Chase Bank NA | United States | 1,014.0 |

*Panel B*                                                          *Largest Banking Organizations in the United States*

| U.S. Rank | Bank Name* | City | Total Assets ($ billions) |
|---|---|---|---|
| 1 | Bank of America NA (7) | Charlotte, NC | $1,082.2 |
| 2 | JPMorgan Chase Bank NA (10) | New York, NY | 1,014.0 |
| 3 | Citibank NA (18) | New York, NY | 706.5 |
| 4 | Wachovia Bank NA (36) | Charlotte, NC | 472.1 |
| 5 | Wells Fargo Bank NA (40) | San Francisco, CA | 403.3 |
| 6 | US Bank NA | Cincinnati, OH | 202.6 |
| 7 | SunTrust Bank | Atlanta, GA | 172.9 |
| 8 | HSBC Bank USA NA | Wilmington, DE | 154.0 |
| 9 | State Street Bank & Trust | Boston, MA | 89.2 |
| 10 | KeyBank NA | Cleveland, OH | 86.2 |

*The number in parentheses is the bank's world ranking. Only the top 50 banks in the world are ranked.

**Source:** *Bankers Almanac* at http://www.bankersalmanac.com/addcon/infobank/wldrank.aspx and the Federal Reserve at http://www.federalreserve.gov.

large Japanese banks have claimed significant market shares. As the world continues to become more globally oriented, so will the banking industry—U.S. banks are becoming more important internationally and foreign banks are increasing their presence in the United States.

**Self-Test Questions**

How do U.S. financial institutions differ from their counterparts in other countries?

What two factors distinguish the banking system in the United States from banking structures in other countries?

What changes are needed for U.S. financial institutions to become more competitive with financial institutions in other countries? Do you think such changes will occur in the near future?

To summarize the key concepts, let's answer the questions that were posed at the beginning of the chapter:

- **What are financial markets and what role do they play in improving the standard of living in an economy?** Financial markets are the "mechanisms" by which borrowers and lenders are brought together. Without financial markets, individuals (companies) with excess funds to invest would either have to personally seek out individuals (companies) who had a need for those funds or simply hold the funds until a future period. If savers had to seek out borrowers, the search costs would be higher and the net returns earned on investments would be lower.

- **Why is it important for financial markets to be somewhat efficient?** When financial markets are *economically efficient*, investors invest in financial assets that yield the highest returns at the lowest cost, and borrowers borrow money at the lowest costs. In both cases, transaction costs are lower than they would be if financial markets did not exist; thus money is efficiently distributed in the economy. When financial markets are *informationally efficient,* the prices of financial securities reflect available information. Depending on the amount of information that is reflected in securities' prices, the financial markets are considered to have achieved one of three degrees of informational efficiency: weak-form efficiency, semistrong-form efficiency, or strong-form efficiency.

- **Why are there so many different types of financial markets? How do we differentiate among various financial markets?** Different types of financial markets exist because savers (investors) and borrowers have different needs. Some investors (borrowers) want to invest for short periods, whereas others want to invest (borrow) for long periods. Financial markets are categorized according to the type of financial security that is traded, time to maturity, type of participant, location, and type of transaction.

- **What is an investment banking house and what role does an investment banking house play when firms want to raise funds in the financial markets?** An investment banking house is an organization that acts as a middleman, or agent, to help firms and governments raise funds by issuing financial instruments. The investment banker provides advice about the financial markets and helps to sell the securities that are issued. If investment banking houses did not exist, firms and governments would have to issue securities by themselves, which would be much more costly in most cases.

- **What is a financial intermediary and what role does a financial intermediary play in the financial markets? Why are there so many different types of intermediaries?** A financial intermediary is an organization that takes "deposits" and uses the money to generate returns by creating loans or other types of investments. There are many different types of financial intermediaries because individuals have different needs, and different intermediaries provide different services for individuals. Because intermediaries facilitate the process by which borrowers and lenders (investors) are brought together, they help to lower costs and provide the best rates to borrowers and lenders; thus, the standard of living in the economy is higher than if the intermediaries did not exist.

- **How do the financial markets in the United States differ from financial markets in other parts of the world?** The United States has the largest and most active financial markets in the world. There are more participants in the U.S. financial markets than in foreign financial markets. Also, most experts would agree that the

U.S. financial markets are generally more efficient than foreign financial markets. A primary difference between U.S. financial markets and foreign financial markets is the participation and structure of financial intermediaries. There are more independent financial intermediaries in the United States than in any country in the world. And although their competitive positions are improving, for the most part U.S. financial intermediaries are competitively disadvantaged because they face greater restrictions as to the types of business associations they can enter than do their foreign counterparts.

## ETHICAL DILEMMA

### Anything for (a) BUC?

The Bank of Universal City (BUC) is a medium-size state banking organization that is located in Louisiana. BUC offers a good variety of products and services, including checking and savings accounts, a bill-paying service, credit cards, business consulting, insurance, and investing services. The CEO of BUC, Chuck Charles, has publicly stated that he intends to grow the bank's assets by 15 percent annually for the next five years. Although 15 percent is a fairly robust growth rate, it is not an impossible goal for BUC. In fact, last year, which was the first year the plan was implemented, the bank's assets grew nearly 20 percent. However, much of the growth occurred because there was a significant increase in population when a large manufacturing firm relocated to Universal City 18 months ago.

With only three weeks remaining in the current fiscal year, Mr. Charles is concerned that actual growth for the year will fall well short of what is needed to keep the bank on track to achieve its overall growth projections. As a result, Mr. Charles has instructed the vice president in charge of Univest, which is the investment management division of BUC, to find a way to increase the amount of investment funds the bank currently manages.

As the assistant to the vice president of Univest, you are responsible for sales and thus get paid a commission for the funds the division manages. Your boss and the CEO of BUC have given you names (leads) of people and organizations they think are good prospects for Univest. After contacting the prospects, you discover that the only one who seems interested is Rudolph Radcliff, the head of a radical religious organization based in Universal City. It has been rumored that the organization, which is called Righteous Freedom Choice (RFC), funds foundations that are based in countries that are not friendly to the United States. It is suspected that some of the organizations RFC sponsors support terrorist activities around the world. A few days ago, a colleague told you that he thought RFC would be moving its funds to a new investment organization because the firm that currently manages the funds refused to continue as its investment adviser; it had been discovered that the funds had been received from organizations that are involved in illicit activities. This information was reported to your colleague during a conversation that he had with two prominent businesspeople at a charity gala the previous weekend. Your colleague noted, however, that the tone of the conversation suggested that the two businesspeople were not on friendly terms with Mr. Radcliff.

When your colleague relayed this information to you, you did not ask questions, such as the names of the businesspeople, because you didn't expect to be involved with RFC. Now, you need to make a decision as to whether to pursue RFC's funds to help Univest and BUC meet their growth objectives. Unfortunately, the colleague who told you the information about RFC is on vacation for the next few weeks and cannot be contacted to answer questions you might have. Univest's sales have been stagnant this year. As a result, if sales don't increase substantially during the next few weeks, your commission salary will be much lower than normal. And if your commission salary does not increase, you and your spouse will have to consider moving from the luxurious house that you purchased five years ago. What should you do?

The concepts presented in this chapter should help you understand what factors affect financial markets, the differences among the markets, in which markets you should invest your money, and the roles of financial intermediaries in the financial markets. If you understand the basic concepts contained in this chapter, you should be able to make more informed decisions about when and where to borrow (and invest).

## What do financial markets have to do with personal finance?

When you borrow money to purchase a house (or anything else) or you invest some of your income, the transactions take place in the financial marketplace. Because there are differences among financial markets, there are also differences among the interest rates that exist in these markets. When rates are higher in the stock markets than in the bond markets, investors tend to buy stocks rather than bonds, and vice versa. When rates on home equity loans are lower than rates on other consumer loans, individuals tend to borrow money through home equity loans. As a result, if you monitor financial markets on a fairly regular basis, you will make better decisions about borrowing and investing than if you have no knowledge of the activities in these markets; you should be able to plan better as to when to borrow (invest) to get the best interest rates. We detail the determination of, and factors that affect, interest rates in Chapter 5.

## How can knowledge (even a slight amount) of financial intermediaries help me make better decisions about my personal finances?

Different financial intermediaries specialize in different types of financial products. For example, commercial banks primarily service businesses, whereas credit unions primarily service consumers. Generally, you can find better rates and varieties of products/services at financial intermediaries that specialize in those particular products/services. For example, savings and loan associations often have better mortgage rates than commercial banks, and credit unions generally offer better rates on automobile loans than either of these institutions. In addition, intermediaries that specialize in particular financial products are better able to service those products because they employ people who are most familiar with all aspects of those products.

## QUESTIONS

**3-1**  What is a financial market? What is the role of a financial market?

**3-2**  What would happen to the standard of living in the United States if people lost faith in our financial markets? Why?

**3-3**  How does a cost-efficient capital market help to reduce the prices of goods and services?

**3-4**  The SEC attempts to protect investors who are purchasing newly issued securities by requiring issuers to provide relevant financial information to prospective investors. The SEC does not provide an opinion about the real value of the securities. Hence, an unwise investor might pay too much for some stock and consequently lose heavily. Do you think the SEC should, as a part of every new stock or bond offering, render an opinion to investors on the proper value of the securities being offered? Explain.

**3-5**    How do you think each of the following would affect a company's ability to attract new capital and the flotation (issuing) costs involved in doing so?

   **a.** The decision to list a company's stock on a physical stock exchange; the stock now trades in the over-the-counter market.

   **b.** The decision of a privately held company to go public.

   **c.** An increasing importance of institutions in the stock and bond markets.

   **d.** The trend toward financial conglomerates as opposed to stand-alone investment banking houses.

   **e.** An increase in the number of shelf registrations.

**3-6**    Before entering into a formal agreement, investment bankers carefully investigate the companies whose securities they underwrite, especially with issues of firms going public for the first time. Because the investment bankers themselves do not plan to hold the securities but intend to sell them to investors as soon as possible, why are they so concerned about making careful investigations?

**3-7**    Why would management be interested in getting a wide distribution of its stock?

**3-8**    Both physical stock exchanges and the OTC are markets for trading stocks. Why do you think companies want to be listed on physical exchanges rather than stay OTC?

**3-9**    Microsoft and Intel qualify to be listed on the New York Stock Exchange, but both have chosen to be traded on the Nasdaq market. Can you think of reasons why the companies would choose to be traded on the Nasdaq? (*Hint:* Both companies deal with products that relate to electronic/computer media.)

**3-10**    What types of companies enter the markets for initial public offerings? Why do companies choose to go public? Why not stay private?

**3-11**    What are financial intermediaries, and what economic functions do they perform?

**3-12**    In what ways do financial intermediaries improve the standard of living in an economy? What would happen to the standard of living in the United States if people lost faith in the safety of our financial institutions? Why?

**3-13**    The federal government has (1) encouraged the development of the savings and loan industry; (2) virtually forced the S&L industry to make long-term, fixed-interest-rate mortgages; and (3) forced S&Ls to obtain most of their capital as deposits that are withdrawable on demand.

   **a.** Would the S&Ls be better off if rates are expected to increase or to decrease in the future?

   **b.** Would the S&L industry be better off if the individual institutions sold their mortgages to federal agencies and then collected servicing fees or if the institutions held the mortgages that they originated?

**3-14**    What are some of the various types of financial intermediaries?

**3-15**    How has deregulation of the financial services industry affected the makeup of financial intermediaries? How do you think intermediaries' characteristics will change in the future?

**3-16**   How do financial intermediaries in the United States differ from their counterparts in other countries? Why are they different?

## SELF-TEST PROBLEMS

*(Solutions appear in Appendix B at the end of the book.)*

**ST-1** Define each of the following terms:                                          **key terms**

    **a.**  Informational efficiency; economic efficiency

    **b.**  Money market; capital market

    **c.**  Debt market; equity market

    **d.**  Primary market; secondary market

    **e.**  Over-the-counter (OTC) market; physical stock exchange; Nasdaq

    **f.**  Floor broker; house broker; independent broker; specialist

    **g.**  Investment banker

    **h.**  Going public; new issue market; initial public offering (IPO)

    **i.**  Prospectus; registration statement

    **j.**  Shelf registration

    **k.**  Best efforts arrangement; underwritten arrangement

    **l.**  Underwriter's spread; flotation costs; offering price

    **m.**  Underwriting syndicate; lead, or managing, underwriter; selling group

    **n.**  Securities and Exchange Commission (SEC); insiders

    **o.**  Financial intermediary; financial intermediation

    **p.**  Commercial bank; thrift institution; credit union

    **q.**  Mutual fund; money market mutual fund; pension fund

**ST-2** Global Geotell just hired InvestPro, a local investment banker, to help it issue      **flotation costs and**
common stock. The proceeds of the stock offering will be used for research      **net proceeds**
and development of a new satellite tracking system for the U.S. Navy. The
market value of the issue equals $150 million, direct costs incurred by Global
Geotell will amount to $225,000, and InvestPro charges a 7 percent fee for its
services.

    **a.**  What will be the net proceeds to Global Geotell from the $150 million equity issue? That is, how much of the issue will Global Geotell be able to use?

    **b.**  If the price per share of the common stock equals $25 at the time of the issue, how many shares of stock must be issued if the total value of the issue is $150 million?

    **c.**  How many shares of stock must be issued if Global Geotell actually needs $150 million for its research and development? Assume that the issue price is $25 per share.

## PROBLEMS

**3-1**   Security Brokers Inc. specializes in underwriting new stock issues of small      **profit (loss) on a new**
firms.      **stock issue**

      On a recent offering of Barenbaum Inc., the terms were

| Price to public | $7.50 per share |
| Number of shares | 3 million |
| Proceeds to Barenbaum | $21,000,000 |

Security Brokers incurred $450,000 in out-of-pocket expenses in the design and distribution of the issue. What profit or loss would Security Brokers incur if the issue we're sold to the public at an average price of

a. $7.50 per share?

b. $9.00 per share?

c. $6.00 per share?

**underwriting and flotation expenses**   **3-2**   The Taussig Company, whose stock price is currently $30, needs to raise $15 million by issuing common stock. Underwriters have informed Taussig's management that it must price the new issue to the public at $27.53 per share to ensure that all shares will be sold. The underwriters' compensation will be 7 percent of the issue price, so Taussig will net $25.60 per share. The company will also incur expenses in the amount of $360,000. How many shares must Taussig sell to net $15 million after underwriting and flotation expenses?

**size of equity issue**   **3-3**   Anderson Anchor Corporation needs to raise $54 million to support its expansion plans. Anderson's investment banker normally charges 10 percent of the market value to handle an equity issue. If the price of Anderson's stock is expected to be $12, how many shares of stock must be issued so that the company receives the needed $54 million?

**underwriting and flotation expenses**   **3-4**   WonderWorld Widgets (WWW) needs to raise $75 million in debt. To issue the debt, WWW must pay its underwriter a fee equal to 3 percent of the issue. The company estimates that other expenses associated with the issue will total $450,000. If the face value of each bond is $1,000, how many bonds must be issued to net the needed $75 million? Assume that the firm cannot issue a fraction of a bond—only "whole bonds" can be issued.

**debt issue**   **3-5**   Eagle Sports Products (ESP) is considering issuing debt to raise funds to finance its growth during the next few years. The amount of the issue will be between $35 million and $40 million. ESP has already arranged for a local investment banker to handle the debt issue. The arrangement calls for ESP to pay flotation costs equal to 7 percent of the total market value of the issue.

a. Compute the flotation costs that ESP will have to pay if the market value of the debt issue is $39 million.

b. If the debt issue has a market value of $39 million, how much will ESP be able to use for its financing needs? That is, what will be the net proceeds from the issue for ESP? Assume that the only costs associated with the issue are those paid to the investment banker.

c. If the company needs $39 million to finance its future growth, how much debt must ESP issue?

**equity issue**   **3-6**   Investment Bankers Association (IBA) has an agreement with Northern Airlines to underwrite an equity issue with a market value equal to $11 million.

a. If IBA's underwriting fee is 5 percent and its out-of-pocket expenses associated with the issue are $125,000, what is the net amount that IBA will receive under its agreement with Northern?

**b.** Assuming that the information in part a does not change and Northern incurs out-of-pocket expenses equal to $240,000 for items such as printing, legal fees, and so on, what will be the net proceeds from the equity issue for Northern?

**3-7**    The Sprite Toy Company needs to raise funds for a major expansion of its manufacturing operations. Sprite has determined that it will issue $100 million of financing, but it has not decided whether to issue debt or equity. The company is publicly traded.    **flotation costs**

**a.** Based on the information given in Table 3-2, compute the flotation costs that Sprite would incur if it raises the needed funds by issuing equity only.

**b.** Based on the information given in Table 3-2, compute the flotation costs that Sprite would incur if it raises the needed funds by issuing straight debt only.

**c.** If Sprite wants to keep its flotation costs low, which form of financing should it use? Discuss some factors other than flotation costs that the company should consider.

**3-8**    Bluesky.com, which currently is a privately held corporation, is making plans for future growth. The company's financial manager has recommended that Bluesky "go public" by issuing common stock to raise the funds needed to support the growth. The current owners, who are the founders of the company, are concerned that control of the firm will be diluted by this strategy. If Bluesky undertakes an IPO, it is estimated that each share of stock will sell for $5; the investment banking fee will be 15 percent of the total value of the issue; and the costs to the company for items such as lawyer fees, printing stock certificates, SEC registration, and so on will be approximately 1 percent of the total value of the issue.    **IPO and control**

**a.** If the market value of the stock issue is $42 million, how much will Bluesky be able to use for growth?

**b.** How many shares of stock will Bluesky have to issue to obtain $42 million for growth?

**c.** The founders now hold all of the company's stock—10 million shares. If the company issues the number of shares computed in part b, what proportion of the stock will the founders own after the IPO?

**d.** If the founders must issue stock to finance the growth of the firm, is there anything you can think of that they might be able to do to protect their controlling interest for at least a few years after the IPO?

## Integrative Problems

**3-9**    Kampfire Inc., a very successful manufacturer of camping equipment, is considering "going public" next month to raise funds to help finance the company's future growth. The financial manager of Kampfire has approached the investment banking firm where you work seeking help with its decision. Your boss has asked you to explain the nature of the U.S. financial markets and the process of issuing equity to the financial manager. To help with this task, your boss has asked you to answer the following questions in explaining the U.S. financial system to the financial manager.    **financial markets**

**a.** What is a *financial market?* How are financial markets differentiated from markets for *physical assets?*

**b.** Differentiate between *money markets* and *capital markets.*

**c.** Differentiate between a *primary market* and a *secondary market.* If Microsoft decided to issue additional common stock, and an investor purchased 1,000 shares of this stock from Merrill Lynch, the underwriter, would this transaction be a primary market transaction or a secondary market transaction? Would it make a difference if the investor purchased previously outstanding Microsoft stock in the Nasdaq market?

**d.** Describe the three primary ways in which capital is transferred between savers and borrowers.

**e.** Securities can be traded on *physical stock exchanges* or in the *over-the-counter market.* Define each of these markets, and describe how stocks are traded in each one.

**f.** Describe the *investment banking process* as it relates to initial public offerings.

**g.** Kampfire estimates that it needs $25 million to support its expected growth. The underwriting fees charged by the investment banking firm where you work are based on the schedule given in Table 3-2. In addition, it is estimated that Kampfire will incur $245,000 in other expenses related to the IPO. If your analysis indicates that Kampfire's stock can be sold for $8.20 per share, how many shares must be issued to net the company the $25 million it needs?

**financial intermediaries**    **3-10**    Assume you recently graduated with a degree in finance and have just reported to work as an investment adviser at the firm of Balik and Kiefer Inc. Your first assignment is to explain the roles financial intermediaries play in the U.S. banking system to Michelle Delatorre, a professional tennis player who has just come to the United States from Chile. Delatorre is a highly ranked tennis player who expects to invest substantial amounts of money through Balik and Kiefer. She is also very bright, and, therefore, she would like to understand in general terms what will happen to her money. Your boss has developed the following questions, which you must answer to help explain the nature of financial intermediaries in the U.S. banking system to Ms. Delatorre.

**a.** What is a *financial intermediary?* What is the *financial intermediation process?*

**b.** What *roles* do financial intermediaries fulfill? How have intermediaries helped improve our standard of living as well as the efficiency of the financial markets?

**c.** What are the different *types* of financial intermediaries? Give some characteristics that differentiate the various types of intermediaries.

**d.** How do U.S. financial intermediaries differ from financial intermediaries in other countries?

**e.** How have the U.S. financial intermediaries changed in recent years? What are the arguments for such changes? What changes are expected in the future?

**f.** How can Ms. Delatorre use the services provided by financial intermediaries?

GET REAL WITH    **THOMSON ONE** Business School Edition

**3-11**  The Dow Jones Industrial Average (DJIA), which is an index that includes the 30 largest industrial firms in the United States, is one of the most quoted financial market indexes in the world. Many investors use the DJIA as a barometer of the performance of the U.S. financial markets because it provides an indication as to how the U.S. economy is performing at any point in time.

**world stock markets**

As stated in the chapter, U.S. stock markets accounted for approximately two-thirds of the value of the world markets in 1970. Today, however, U.S. markets account for less than 45 percent of the total value of worldwide stock markets. One reason the U.S. markets account for a lower proportion of the value of all stock markets in the world is because emerging markets have expanded significantly in recent years. Countries along the Pacific Rim, including China and Korea, as well as South American countries and India, are responsible for much of the recent growth in world financial markets. Using the Thomson ONE database, compare the major market indexes of the following countries with regard to their changes in value during the past 12 months:

| | |
|---|---|
| Argentina | [ARGMERV] |
| France | [FRCAC40] |
| Germany | [DAXINDX] |
| Japan | [NIKI300] |
| South Korea | [KORCOMP] |
| United States | [DJIND] |

Go to the Thomson ONE database and click on Indices in the upper left corner of the screen. Enter the ticker symbols one at a time and find the change in price (index value) for the past 12 months. Compare the change in value for each market index and write a paragraph about the growth in the market in each country.

**CHAPTER**

**4**

# The Time Value of Money

**E**ven as a student, you should be thinking about retirement. Chances are that unless you create a savings plan for retirement as soon as you start your career, or soon afterward, either you will have to work longer than you had planned to attain the retirement lifestyle you desire or you will have to live below the standard of living you planned for your retirement years. According to the experts, it's never too soon to start saving for retirement. Unfortunately, most Americans are professional procrastinators when it comes to saving and investing for retirement. The savings rate in the United States is the lowest of any developed country. During the 1980s, individuals saved an average of approximately 9 percent of their income, during the 1990s the savings rate dropped to about 5 percent, and since 2000 the savings rate has averaged less than 2 percent. In fact, in 2005 the savings rate actually dipped below zero, which meant that, on average, people borrowed more than they saved.

Some people believe that they don't need to save much to live comfortably when they retire because they expect to receive Social Security benefits. But don't bet on it! The ratio of workers paying into Social Security to retirees receiving benefits, which was 16.5 in 1950, was down to 3.3 in 2006, and it is expected to be 2.1 by the year 2031. What does all this mean? Current projec-

tions are that the government retirement system will go bankrupt within the next 40 years. There are a number of reasons the future of Social Security is in doubt. First, the life expectancy of Americans has increased by more than 15 years, from 67 to more than 80, since the inception of Social Security in 1935, and it is expected to increase further in the future. Second, the number of elderly as a percent of the American population has increased substantially. By the year 2040, it is expected that 25 percent of the U.S. population will be age 65 or older, which is twice today's proportion. Third, more than 77 million baby boomers born between 1946 and 1964 are beginning to retire, which is adding a tremendous burden to the system. At some point in the future, there might be more retirees receiving Social Security benefits than there are workers making contributions to the plan because birthrates since the mid-1960s have fallen sharply. From 1946 to 1964, the average family had three children; from 1970 to 1990, the average number of children dropped to two.

What does the retirement plight of the baby boomers (and their children) have to do with the time value of money? Actually, a great deal. According to a survey conducted by the Employee Benefit Research Institute (EBRI), Americans are not very confident that they will have sufficient funds at retirement to live comfortably. And although most people indicate that they have saved for retirement, very few have any idea as to the amount they need to save to meet their retirement goals. To retire comfortably, 10 to 20 percent of your income should be set aside each year. For example, it is estimated that a 35-year-old who is earning $55,000 would need at least $1 million to retire at the current standard of living in 30 years. To achieve this goal, the individual would have to save about $10,500 each year at 7 percent return, which represents nearly a 20 percent annual savings. The annual savings would have been less than one-half of this amount if the individual had begun saving for retirement at age 25.

The techniques and procedures covered in this chapter are exactly the ones used by experts to forecast the boomers' retirement needs, their probable wealth at retirement, and the resulting shortfall. If you study this chapter carefully, perhaps you can avoid the trap into which many people seem to be falling—spending today rather than saving for the future.

**Source:** "The 2006 Annual Report of the Board of Trustees of the Federal Old-Age and Survivors Insurance and Disability Insurance Trust Funds" and other reports that are available at the website of the Social Security Administration, which is located at http://www.ssa.gov, and "Saving for Retirement in America" and other reports that are available at the Employee Benefit Research Institute website, which is located at http://www.ebri.org.

## Chapter *Essentials* — The Questions

After reading this chapter, you should be able to answer the following questions:

- Why is it important to understand and be able to apply time value of money concepts?
- What is the difference between a present value amount and a future value amount?
- What is an annuity? What are the two types of annuities, and how do their values differ?
- What is the difference between the annual percentage rate (APR) and the effective annual rate (EAR)? Which is more appropriate to use?
- What is an amortized loan? How are amortized loan payments and loan payoffs determined?
- How is the return (interest rate) on an investment (loan) determined?

In Chapter 1, we mentioned that, all else equal, a dollar received sooner is worth more (has more value) than a dollar received at some later date. The logic is simple—*the sooner a dollar is received the more quickly it can be invested to earn a positive return*. So does this mean that an investment that will return $7,023 in five years is more valuable than an investment that will return $8,130 in eight years? Not necessarily, because the eight-year investment promises a higher dollar payoff than the five-year investment. To determine which investment is more valuable, we need to compare the dollar payoffs for the investments at the same point in time. For example, we can compare these two investments by restating, or revaluing, their future payoffs in terms of current (today's) dollars. The concept used to revalue payoffs such as those associated with these investments is termed the **time value of money (TVM)**. It is essential that both financial managers and investors have a clear understanding of the TVM and its effect on the value of an asset. TVM concepts are discussed in this chapter, and we show how the timing of cash flows affects the values of assets and rates of return.

The principles of time value analysis that are developed in this chapter have many applications, ranging from setting up schedules for paying off loans to decisions about whether to acquire new equipment. In fact, *of all the techniques used in finance, none is more important than the concept of TVM*. Because this concept is used throughout the remainder of the book, it is vital that you understand the TVM principles presented here before you move on to other topics.

**time value of money (TVM)** The principles and computations used to revalue cash payoffs at different times so they are stated in dollars of the same time period; used to convert dollars from one time period to those of another time period.

# CASH FLOW TIME LINES

The first step in time value of money analysis is to construct a **cash flow time line,** which, much like a road map, is used to help visualize the situation that is being analyzed. To illustrate the time line concept, consider the following diagram:

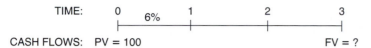

On the time line, Time 0 is today; Time 1 is one period from today, or the end of Period 1; Time 2 is two periods from today, or the end of Period 2; and so on. Often the periods are years; but other time intervals, such as semiannual periods, quarters, months, or even days, are also used. Note that each tick mark corresponds to the end of one period as well as the beginning of the next period—that is, the tick mark at Time 1 represents both the end of Year 1 and the beginning of Year 2.[1]

Cash flows are placed directly below the tick marks and the interest rate is shown directly above the time line. Unknown cash flows, which we are trying to determine in the analysis, are indicated by question marks. Here $100 is invested at Time 0, and we want to determine how much this investment will be worth in three years if it earns 6 percent interest each year.

The cash flow time line is an essential tool that will help you to better understand time value of money concepts—even experts use cash flow time lines to analyze complex problems. We will use cash flow time lines throughout the book, and you should get into the habit of using them when you work problems.

 **Self-Test Questions**

Why is it helpful to draw a cash flow time line when performing a time value of money analysis?

Draw a cash flow time line to illustrate the following situation: You invest $5,000 today in a four-year savings instrument that pays 7 percent interest each year.

# FUTURE VALUE

A dollar in hand today is worth more than a dollar to be received in the future because if you had the money now, you could invest it, earn interest, and end up with more than one dollar in the future. The process of converting a value stated as a current dollar amount, which is termed the **present value (PV),** to a **future value (FV)** is called **compounding.** To illustrate, suppose you deposit $100 in a bank account that pays 6 percent interest each year. This is the situation depicted on the cash flow time line in the previous section. How much would you have at the end of three years? To begin, we define the following terms:

**PV** = Present value, or beginning amount, that is invested (or received). Here PV = $100.

**cash flow time line**
An important tool used in time value of money analysis; it is a graphical representation used to show the timing of cash flows.

**present value (PV)**
The value today—that is, current value—of a future cash flow or series of cash flows.

**future value (FV)**
The amount to which a cash flow or series of cash flows will grow over a given period of time when compounded at a given interest rate.

**compounding**
The process of determining the value of a cash flow or series of cash flows at some time in the future when compound interest is applied.

---

[1]For our discussions, the difference between the end of one period and the beginning of the next period is the same as one day ending and the next day beginning—it occurs in less than one second.

**r** = Interest rate the bank pays on the account each year. The interest earned is based on the balance in the account at the beginning of each year, and we assume that it is paid at the end of the year. Here r = 6%, or, expressed as a decimal, r = 0.06.

**INT** = Dollars of interest you earn during the year = (Beginning-of-year amount) × r. Here INT = $100 × 0.06 = $6 in the first year.

$FV_n$ = Future value, or value of the account at the end of n periods (years, in this case), after the interest earned has been added to the account.

**n** = Number of periods interest is earned. Here n = 3.

When computing the future value of an amount invested today, we determine by how much the amount will increase as the result of the interest it earns each year. In our example, the $100 that you invest today will earn 6 percent interest each year for the next three years. So, to what amount will your $100 grow in three years if it is left in the bank account to earn interest? Following is a cash flow time line that is set up to show the amount that will be in the bank account at the end of each year. To compute the end-of-year balance, the amount that is in the bank account at the beginning of the year is multiplied by (1 + r) = 1.06, which accounts for the 6 percent increase that occurs as a result of the annual interest payment.

| Time (t): | 0 | | 1 | 2 | 3 |
|---|---|---|---|---|---|
| | | 6% | | | |
| Account balance: | 100.00 | × (1.06) | 106.00 × (1.06) | 112.36 × (1.06) | 119.10 |

Note the following points:

1. You start by depositing $100 in the bank account—this amount is shown at time t = 0.

2. You earn $100 × 0.06 = $6 of interest during the first year, so the amount at the end of Year 1 is $100 + $6 = $106 = $100(1.06).

3. You start the second year with $106. In the second year, you earn 6 percent interest both on the $100 you invested originally and on the $6 paid to you as interest in the first year—that is, $6.36 interest is earned in the second year. The $6.36 interest earned in the second year is higher than the first year's interest of $6 because you earn an additional $0.36 = $6 × 0.06 interest by leaving the $6 interest received in Year 1 in the account to earn interest in Year 2. This is an example of *compounding*, which occurs when interest is earned on interest.

4. This process continues. And because the beginning balance is higher in each succeeding year, the amount of interest earned increases each year.

5. The balance in the bank account at the end of Year 3 is $119.10.

As you can see, the total interest earned, $19.10, is greater than $6 per year ($18 for three years), which is 6 percent of the *original* $100 investment. Because the interest earned each year is left in the bank account to earn additional interest the following year, $1.10 = 19.10 − $18.00 was earned because previously paid interest earned an additional 6 percent interest. When interest is left in the account (or reinvested) to earn additional interest, as in our example, the investment is said to earn **compounded interest.**

In this chapter, we will show four different approaches to solve a time value of money problem. We will solve the problem using (1) the cash flow time line to compute the value at the end of each period, which we refer to as the *time line solution;* (2) the

**compounded interest**
Interest earned on interest that is reinvested.

appropriate equation, which we refer to as the *equation (numerical) solution;* (3) the time value of money functions that are programmed into a financial calculator, which we refer to as the *financial calculator solution;* and (4) the time value of money functions that are programmed into a spreadsheet, which we refer to as the *spreadsheet solution.* Each approach will give the same answer to a particular problem because each is performing the same computation—we simply use different approaches to perform the computation.

## Time Line Solution

We showed the time line solution to the current time value of money problem in the previous section. Based on the time line solution, we know that the end-of-the-year balances in the bank account will be $106.00, $112.36, and $119.10 in Year 1, Year 2, and Year 3, respectively.

## Equation (Numerical) Solution

According to the time line solution, we can compute the balance in the bank account by multiplying the balance at the beginning of each of the three years by $(1 + r) = (1.06)$. As a result, in our example, we would get the same ending balance of $119.10 if we multiplied the initial $100 investment by $(1.06)^3$. That is,

$$FV_3 = \$100(1.06)^3 = \$100(1.191016) = \$119.10$$

When this concept is generalized, the future value of an amount invested today can be computed by applying this equation:

$$FV_n = PV(1 + r)^n$$

**4–1**

According to Equation 4–1, to compute the future value (FV) of an amount invested today (PV) we need to determine by what multiple the initial investment will increase in the future. As you can see, the multiple by which any amount will increase depends on both the interest rate (r) and the length of time (n) interest is earned—that is, $(1 + r)^n$. The solution for $(1 + r)^n$ can be found with a regular calculator by using the exponential function to raise $(1 + r)$ to the nth power. To solve using the exponential function key on your calculator, which generally is labeled $\boxed{y^x}$, you would enter 1.06 into your calculator, press the $y^x$ function key, enter 3, and then press the $\boxed{=}$ key. The result displayed on your calculator should be 1.191016, which, when multiplied by $100, gives the final answer, $119.1016, or $119.10 when rounded.

## Financial Calculator Solution

Equation 4–1 and most other TVM equations have been programmed directly into *financial calculators,* and such calculators can be used to find future values. These calculators have five keys that correspond to the five most commonly used TVM variables:

      PMT  FV

These key designations correspond to the TVM keys that are on a Texas Instruments BAII PLUS financial calculator, which is the model we use throughout this book. Here

**N** = Number of periods; some calculators use n rather than N. This key corresponds to n in Equation 4–1.

**I/Y** = Interest rate per period; some calculators use I, INT, or I/YR rather than I/Y. This key corresponds to r in Equation 4–1.

**PV** = Present (today's) value. This key corresponds to PV in Equation 4–1.

**PMT** = Annuity payment. This key is used only if the cash flows involve a series of equal, or constant, payments (an annuity). If there are no periodic payments in the particular problem, then PMT = 0. We will use this key later in the chapter.

**FV** = Future (ending) value. This key corresponds to FV in Equation 4–1.

Throughout the book, we show the values that need to be entered into the financial calculator above the keys and the result of the computation below the keys. For the current example, the inputs and the result are

Financial calculators require that all cash flows be designated as either inflows or outflows because the computations are based on the fact that we generally pay, which is a **cash outflow,** to receive a benefit, which is a **cash inflow.** As a result, you must enter cash outflows as negative numbers. In our illustration, you deposit the initial amount, which is a cash outflow to you, and you take out, or receive, the ending amount, which is a cash inflow to you. Thus, for this problem, the PV should be entered as −100.[2] If you forget the negative sign and enter 100, then the calculator assumes that you receive $100 in the current period and that you must pay it back with interest in the future, so the FV appears as −119.10, a cash outflow. Sometimes the convention of changing signs can be confusing, but, if you think about what you are doing, you should not have a problem with whether the calculator gives you a positive or a negative answer.[3]

**cash outflow**

A payment, or disbursement, of cash for expenses, investments, and so forth.

**cash inflow**

A receipt of cash from an investment, an employer, or other sources.

## Spreadsheet Solution[4]

You probably will use a calculator to solve TVM problems that are assigned for homework and that appear on your exams. However, because most businesses use spreadsheets to solve these problems, you need to have some familiarity with the applications of the TVM functions that are programmed into spreadsheets. You should be able to understand the discussion that follows even if you have not used spreadsheets often.

To access the TVM functions that are programmed into Excel, you must click on the "*paste function*," which is designated $f_x$ and can be found in the "Insert" menu on

---

[2]To reduce clutter, we do not show the dollar signs for the time line solution or the financial calculator solution.

[3]We should note that financial calculators permit you to specify the number of decimal places that are displayed. For most calculators, at least 12 significant digits are used in the actual calculations. But for the purposes of reporting the results of the computations, generally we use two places for answers when working with dollars or percentages and four or five places when working with decimals. *The nature of the problem dictates how many decimal places should be displayed*—to be safe, you might want to set your calculator so that the floating decimal format is used and round the final results yourself.

[4]If you are not familiar with spreadsheets, Appendix A at the end of the book provides a short tutorial.

**FIGURE 4-1**   Using *Excel's FV Function* to Compute Future Value

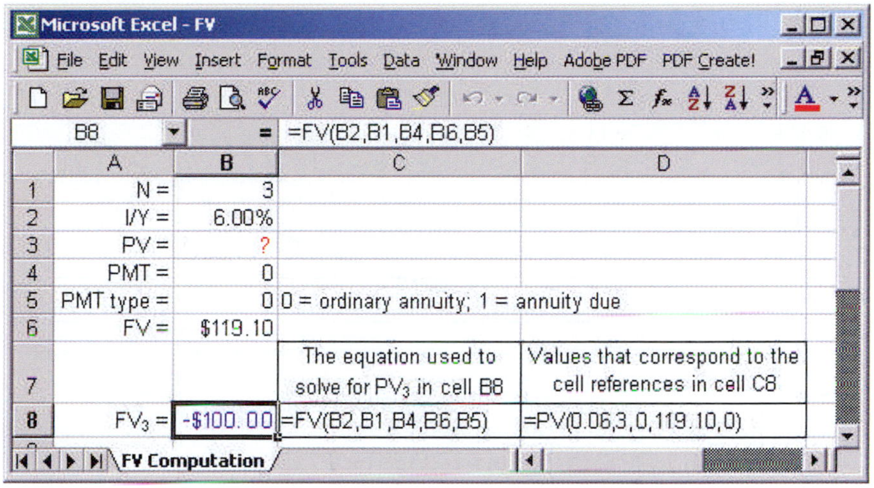

| | | | | |
|---|---|---|---|---|
| **Microsoft Excel - FV** | | | | _ □ × |
| File Edit View Insert Format Tools Data Window Help Adobe PDF PDF Create! | | | | _ 🗗 × |
| | B8 | = =FV(B2,B1,B4,B6,B5) | | |

| | A | B | C | D |
|---|---|---|---|---|
| 1 | N = | 3 | | |
| 2 | I/Y = | 6.00% | | |
| 3 | PV = | ? | | |
| 4 | PMT = | 0 | | |
| 5 | PMT type = | 0 | 0 = ordinary annuity; 1 = annuity due | |
| 6 | FV = | $119.10 | | |
| 7 | | | The equation used to solve for PV₃ in cell B8 | Values that correspond to the cell references in cell C8 |
| 8 | FV₃ = | -$100.00 | =FV(B2,B1,B4,B6,B5) | =PV(0.06,3,0,119.10,0) |

\ FV Computation /

**Note:** According to the equation shown in cell C8, the input values must be entered in a specific order: I/Y, N, PMT, PV, and PMT type (not used for this problem). It's a good idea to set up a table that contains the data needed to solve the problem, and then refer to the cell where each number is located when you apply the FV equation. If you follow this technique, you can change any number in the table you set up and the result of the change will immediately show in the cell where the equation is located. For example, if the current problem is changed so that $500 rather than $100 is deposited in a bank account, you would change the value in cell B3 to −$500, and the result of $595.51 would appear in cell B8.

the toolbar at the top of the spreadsheet. Each preprogrammed function is standardized so that numbers must be entered in a specific order to solve the problem correctly. In this chapter, we show the inputs, the format of the spreadsheet function, and the results. For a more detailed discussion of how to set up the spreadsheet to solve a TVM problem, see Appendix A at the end of the book.

Figure 4-1 shows the setup and the results of using the *FV function* to compute the future value in three years of $100 invested today at 6 percent. Because a financial calculator is programmed much like a spreadsheet to solve TVM problems, the labels given in rows 1 through 5 of column A correspond to the TVM keys on a financial calculator. Note that the $100 that is invested today is entered into the spreadsheet as a negative value, just as it is when using a financial calculator to solve the problem. When entering values, there is one difference between a financial calculator and a spreadsheet—the interest rate is entered as a percentage (6.0 in our example) in the financial calculator, whereas it is entered as a decimal (0.06 in our example) in the spreadsheet. (In Figure 4-1, even though 0.06 was entered in cell **B2** for the interest rate, it appears as 6.00% because the cell was formatted so that the number appears as a percent.)

## Graphic View of the Compounding Process: Growth

Figure 4-2 shows how $1 (or any other sum) grows over time at various interest rates. The data used to plot the curves were obtained by solving Equation 4–1 for different values of r and n. We used a spreadsheet to generate the values and draw the curves shown in Figure 4-2. The figure shows that (1) the future value of an amount invested at a positive interest rate today will grow to a higher amount the longer it is invested, and (2) the higher the rate of interest, the faster the rate of growth of an amount invested today. In other words, the higher the interest rate, the greater the effect of interest compounding. The *interest rate is,* in fact, *a growth rate:* If a sum is deposited and earns 6 percent interest, then the funds on deposit will grow at a rate of 6 percent per period.

**FIGURE 4-2**    Relationship among Future Value, Growth or Interest Rates, and Time

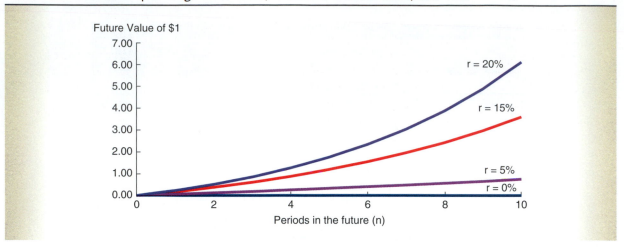

## PRESENT VALUE

In the example presented in the previous section, we saw that an initial amount of $100 invested at 6 percent per year would be worth $119.10 at the end of three years. This means that you should be indifferent between the choice of receiving $100 today or $119.10 at the end of three years if you have the opportunity to earn 6 percent interest per year. The $100 that would be invested today is defined as the present value, or PV, of $119.10 due in three years when the **opportunity cost rate** is 6 percent. Suppose someone offered to sell you an investment that promises to pay $119.10 in three years for $95 today. Should you buy this investment if your opportunity cost is 6 percent? You should definitely buy it because, as we discovered in the previous section, it would cost you exactly $100 to produce the $119.10 in three years if you earn a 6 percent return. Therefore, if you could find another investment with the same risk that would produce the same future amount—that is, $119.10—but its cost is less than $100 then you could earn a return higher than 6 percent by purchasing the investment. On the other hand, if the price of the security is greater than $100, you should not buy it because it would cost you only $100 to produce the same future amount at 6 percent per year.

   In general, *the present value of a cash flow due n years in the future is the amount that, if it were on hand today, would grow to equal the future amount at a particular rate of return.* Because $100 will grow to $119.10 in three years at a 6 percent interest

**opportunity cost rate**
The rate of return on the best available alternative investment of equal risk.

rate, $100 is the present value of $119.10 due three years in the future when the opportunity cost rate is 6 percent.

The process of finding present values is called **discounting.** Discounting simply is the reverse of compounding—that is, rather than adding interest to a current amount to determine its future value, we take interest out of a future amount to determine its present value. In essence, when we compute the present value of a future amount, we "strip out" the interest that the amount earns during the investment period. Consequently, if we solve for PV in Equation 4–1, we have an equation that can be used to solve for the present value of a future dollar amount:

**discounting**
The process of determining the present value of a cash flow or a series of cash flows received (paid) in the future; the reverse of compounding.

4–2

$$PV = FV_n \left[ \frac{1}{(1 + r)^n} \right]$$

**TIME LINE SOLUTION:**
Applying Equation 4–2 to the current situation gives the following:

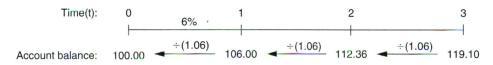

**EQUATION (NUMERICAL) SOLUTION:**
Applying Equation 4–2 to the current situation gives the following:

$$PV = \$119.10 \left[ \frac{1}{(1.06)^3} \right] = \$119.10(0.839619) = \$100.00$$

**FINANCIAL CALCULATOR SOLUTION:**
Enter N = 3, I/Y = 6, PMT = 0, and FV = 119.10; then solve for PV = −100.00

| Inputs: | 3 | 6 | ? | 0 | 119.10 |
|---|---|---|---|---|---|
| | N | I/Y | PV | PMT | FV |
| Output: | | | = −100.00 | | |

**SPREADSHEET SOLUTION:**
Figure 4-3 shows the setup and the results of using the spreadsheet's *PV function* to compute the present value of $119.10 to be received in three years if the interest rate is 6 percent. Note that the setup is the same as in Figure 4-1, except we now enter FV = $119.10 and we solve for PV rather than entering PV = −$100.00 and solving for FV.

## Graphic View of the Discounting Process

Figure 4-4 shows how the present value of $1 (or any other sum) to be received in the future diminishes as the time to receipt or the interest rate increases. Again, we used a spreadsheet to generate the values and draw the curves shown in Figure 4-4. The figure shows that (1) the present value of a sum to be received at some future date decreases and approaches zero as the payment date is extended further into the future, and (2) the present value of a future amount is lower the higher the interest (discount)

**FIGURE 4-3**   Using *Excel's PV Function* to Compute Present Value

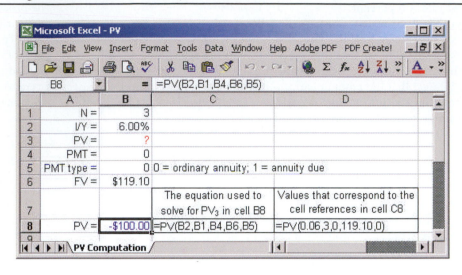

**Note:** According to the equation shown in cell C8, the input values must be entered in a specific order: I/Y, N, PMT, FV, and PMT type (not used in this computation).

rate. At relatively high interest rates, funds due in the future are worth very little today, and even at relatively low discount rates, the present value of an amount due in the very distant future is quite small. For example, at a 20 percent discount rate, $5 million due in 100 years is worth only 6¢ today; conversely, 6¢ would grow to approximately $5 million in 100 years if it is invested at 20 percent.

### Self-Test Questions

What is meant by the term *opportunity cost rate*?

What is discounting? How is discounting related to compounding?

Assume you have the opportunity to purchase an investment that promises to pay you $3,041.63 in five years and your opportunity cost is 4 percent. How much should you be willing to pay for this investment today? How would your answer change if your opportunity cost is 6 percent? (*Answers:* $2,500; $2,272.88)

## COMPARISON OF FUTURE VALUE WITH PRESENT VALUE

In the previous sections, we showed that $100 invested today at 6 percent will grow to $119.10 in three years, and an amount equal to $119.10 to be received in three years is worth $100 today if the opportunity cost is 6 percent. Let's assume that you win a raffle that allows you to choose one of two prizes—$100 that will be paid to you today or $119.10 that will be paid to you in three years. If your opportunity cost is 6 percent, which prize *should* you choose? Believe it or not, you should flip a coin to make your choice because both prizes are equally desirable. Whichever prize you receive can be used to create the other prize. For example, if you are given the prize that pays you $100 today, you can invest the money at 6 percent and it will grow to $119.10 in three years. Conversely, if you are given the prize that pays you $119.10 in three years, you can sell the prize for $100 today. What if you need money today to help pay your rent? Shouldn't you choose the prize that pays you $100 today? The answer is the same as

**FIGURE 4-4**   Relationship among Present Value, Growth or Interest Rates, and Time

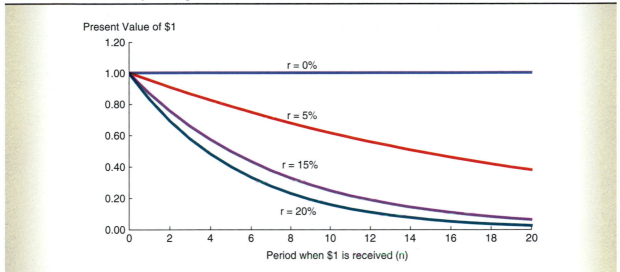

Present Value of $1

r = 0%
r = 5%
r = 15%
r = 20%

Period when $1 is received (n)

before—it doesn't matter which prize you choose because you can convert the payoff you receive from one prize into the payoff that you would receive from the other prize. In other words, even if you receive the prize with the future payoff, you should be able to turn it into cash today by selling it.

This simple example shows that when we work TVM problems, we simply restate dollars (values) from one time period into their *equivalent* values at some other point in time. Simply stated, when we determine the future value of a current amount, we add the interest that the amount will earn if it is invested today and then is liquidated at some future time. Conversely, when we determine the present value of a future amount, we take out the interest that the amount will earn during the time period to determine how much has to be invested today to create the same future amount—you might say that we "de-interest" the future amount. If you understand this concept, you will have little difficulty grasping the material presented in the rest of the book.

**Self-Test Question**

If your opportunity cost is 20 percent, which is better, receipt of $5,000 today or $10,368 in four years? Why? (*Answer:* You should be indifferent.)

## SOLVING FOR INTEREST RATES (r) AND TIME (n)

Equation 4–1 and Equation 4–2 are equivalent; they are simply arranged differently. Equation 4–1 is arranged to solve future value (FV) problems and Equation 4–2 is arranged to solve present value (PV) problems. These equations include four variables: PV, FV, r, and n. If we know the values of any three of these variables, we can solve for the value of the fourth. To this point, we have known the number of years, n, and the interest rate, r, plus either the PV or the FV. In many situations, however, we need to solve for either r or n.

### Solving for r

Suppose you can buy a security at a price of $78.35 that will pay you $100 after five years. What rate of return will you earn if you purchase the security? Here you know

PV, FV, and $n$, but you do not know $r$, the interest rate you will earn on your investment. We can solve this problem as follows:

## TIME LINE SOLUTION:

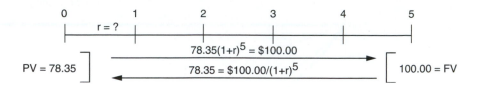

## EQUATION (NUMERICAL) SOLUTION:

Plugging the known values into Equation 4–1, we have

$$FV_n = PV(1 + r)^n$$

$$\$100.00 = \$78.35(1 + r)^5$$

In this case, solving for $r$ is not very difficult. However, because it is easier to solve for $r$ using either a financial calculator or a spreadsheet, we do not show the numerical solution here.[5]

## FINANCIAL CALCULATOR SOLUTION:

Enter the known values into the appropriate locations—that is, N = 5, PV = −78.35, PMT = 0, and FV = 100; then solve for the unknown value:

## SPREADSHEET SOLUTION:

Figure 4-5 shows how to use the RATE function that is built into Excel to solve for $r$ in our example. According to the answer, if you invest \$78.35 today at 5 percent, in five years your investment will be worth \$100—that is, $FV_5 = \$78.35(1.05)^5 = \$100$.

## Solving for n

Suppose you know that a security will provide a return of 10 percent per year, it will cost \$68.30, and you will receive \$100 at maturity. In how many years does the security mature? In this case, we know PV, FV, and $r$, but we do not know $n$, the number of periods.

## TIME LINE SOLUTION:

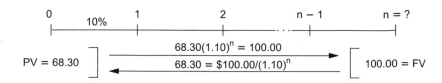

---

[5]If you are interested, we can solve for $r$ using simple algebra:

$$(1 + r)^5 = \frac{\$100.00}{\$78.35} = 1.27632$$

$$(1 + r) = (1.27632)^{1/5} = (1.27632)^{0.2} = 1.05$$

$$r = 1.05 - 1 = 0.05 = 5.0\%$$

**FIGURE 4-5**   Using *Excel's RATE Function* to Compute r for a Lump-Sum Amount

**Note:** According to the equation shown in cell C8, the input values must be entered in a specific order: N, PMT, PV, FV, and PMT type (not used in this computation).

## EQUATION (NUMERICAL) SOLUTION:

Plugging the known values into Equation 4–1, we have

$$FV_n = PV(1 + r)^n$$
$$\$100.00 = \$68.30(1.10)^n$$

One method of finding the value of n is to use a trial-and-error process in which you insert different values of n into the equation until you find a value that "works" in the sense that the right side of the equation equals $100. You would eventually find that the solution is n = 4—that is, it takes four years for $68.30 to grow to $100 if interest equal to 10 percent is paid each year[6]: $FV_4 = \$68.30(1.10)^4 = \$100$.

## FINANCIAL CALCULATOR SOLUTION:

Enter I/Y = 10, PV = −68.30, PMT = 0, and FV = 100; then solve for n = 4.

| Inputs: | ? | 10 | −68.30 | 0 | 100.00 |
|---------|---|-----|--------|---|--------|
| | N | I/Y | PV | PMT | FV |

Output: = 4.00

## SPREADSHEET SOLUTION:

Figure 4-6 shows how to use the NPER function that is built into Excel to solve for n in our example. Simply enter the required information into the NPER function and you will find that the answer is n = 4.

---

[6]The value of n also can be found as follows:

$$\$100 = \$68.30(1.10)^n$$
$$(1.10)^n = \frac{\$100}{\$68.30} = 1.46413$$
$$\ln[(1.10)^n] = n[\ln(1.10)] = \ln(1.46413)$$
$$n = \frac{\ln(1.46413)}{\ln(1.10)} = \frac{0.3813}{0.0953} = 4.0$$

You can use your calculator to find ln, which is the natural logarithm. For most calculators, you insert the number—in this case, 1.4641—and then press the LN key (or its equivalent). The result is 0.3813.

FIGURE 4-6   Using *Excel's NPER Function* to Compute n for a Lump-Sum Amount

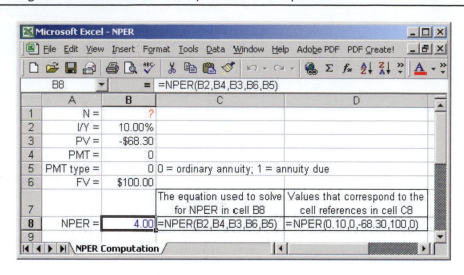

**Note:** According to the equation shown in cell C8, the input values must be entered in a specific order: I/Y, PMT, PV, FV, and PMT type (not used in this computation).

**Self-Test Questions**

Suppose you just called the East Key State Bank and found that the balance in your savings account is $1,269.50. If you deposited $800 six years ago, what rate of return have you earned on the savings account? (*Answer:* 8.0%)

Assume you can invest $1,000 today at 7 percent interest. If you plan to sell the investment when its value reaches $1,500, for how long will your money have to be invested? (*Answer:* 6 years)

## ANNUITY PAYMENTS

**annuity**
A series of payments of an equal amount at fixed, equal intervals for a specified number of periods.

**ordinary (deferred) annuity**
An annuity with payments that occur at the end of each period.

**annuity due**
An annuity with payments that occur at the beginning of each period.

In the previous sections, we showed how to find both the future value of a single amount invested today and the present value of a single amount to be received in the future. But many investments provide a series of cash flows over time—for example, if you buy a bond, you might receive a $100 interest payment every year for the life of the bond. When cash flows, such as interest payments on a bond, are constant and are received at equal time intervals, such as once every 12 months, the cash flow series is called an **annuity.** The annuity payments are given the symbol PMT, and they can occur either at the beginning or at the end of each period. If the payments occur at the end of each period, as they typically do in business transactions, the annuity is called an **ordinary,** or **deferred, annuity.** If payments are made at the *beginning* of each period, the annuity is an **annuity due.** Because ordinary annuities are more common in finance, when the term *annuity* is used in this book, you should assume that the payments occur at the end of each period unless otherwise noted.

Suppose Alice decides to deposit $100 each year for three years in a savings account that pays 5 percent interest per year. If Alice makes her first deposit one year from today, the series of deposits would be considered an *ordinary annuity*. The cash flow time line for this annuity is as follows:

## Ordinary Annuity Cash Flow Time Line (Alice's Deposits)

Suppose Alice's twin brother Alvin thinks that his sister's savings plan is a good idea, so he decides to copy her by also depositing $100 each year for three years in a savings account that pays 5 percent interest per year. But Alvin decides to make his first deposit today rather than one year from today. This series of deposits is an *annuity due,* and its cash flow time line is as follows:

## Annuity Due Cash Flow Time Line (Alvin's Deposits)

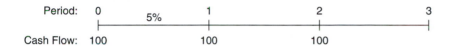

As you can see from these cash flow time lines, the only difference between an ordinary annuity (Alice's deposits) and an equivalent annuity due (Alvin's deposits) is the timing of the cash flows. Both annuities have the same total amount (cash flows) deposited over the three-year period, but each deposit is made earlier if the cash flow series represents an annuity due. Do you think that the values of these two annuities are the same? Based on what we covered earlier in the chapter, you should have answered "No!" to this question. We know that $100 deposited today is not the same as $100 deposited in one year. In our example, we know that the first $100 that Alvin deposits today has a different (higher) "time value" than the first $100 that Alice deposits in one year. Which annuity is the better annuity? We can answer this question by computing the future values of the two annuities.

In the sections that follow, we show you how to compute both the future value and the present value of an annuity. We also show you how to determine the interest rate you pay on annuities such as automobile loans and how much you have to invest each year (or other period) to achieve goals such as accumulating a specific amount—say, $2 million in a retirement plan. As you read this section, keep in mind that, to be considered an annuity, the series of cash flows must (1) be constant and (2) occur at equal intervals. If a cash flow series is lacking one or both of these requirements, then it is not an annuity, and the procedures used to determine the values of annuities do not apply.

 **Self-Test Questions**

What is the difference between an ordinary annuity and an annuity due?

Under what circumstances would you prefer a series of cash flows to be an annuity due? When would you prefer a series of cash flows to be an ordinary annuity? (*Hint:* Consider those instances when you receive the annuity payments versus when you pay the annuity payments.)

## FUTURE VALUE OF AN ANNUITY, FVA

In this section, we will use the example that was introduced in the previous section to show you how to compute the future values of the two annuities—that is, the ordinary annuity (Alice's deposits) and the annuity due (Alvin's deposits).

### Future Value of an Ordinary Annuity

Remember that Alice has chosen to deposit $100 each year for three years in a savings account that pays 5 percent interest per year, and the first deposit will be made one year from today. In this section, we show how to compute the amount that Alice will have in her savings account at the end of three years.

**TIME LINE SOLUTION:**

One way to determine the future value of an ordinary annuity, which we designate $FVA_n$, is to compute the future value of *each* annuity payment using Equation 4–1 and then sum the results. Using this approach, the computation of the future value of Alice's deposits (annuity) is as follows:

**$FVA_n$**
The future value of an *ordinary* annuity over n periods.

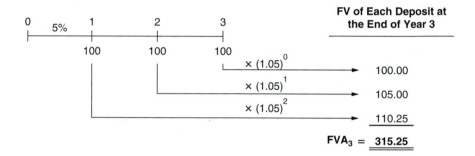

**EQUATION (NUMERICAL) SOLUTION:**

The time line solution shows that we can compute the future value of the annuity simply by determining the future values of the individual payments and then summing the results. Thus, we can write an equation for the future value of an ordinary annuity as a series of solutions to Equation 4–1:

**4–3**

$$FVA_n = PMT(1 + r)^0 + PMT(1 + r)^1 + PMT(1 + r)^2 + \cdots + PMT(1 + r)^{n-1}$$
$$= PMT[(1 + r)^0 + (1 + r)^1 + (1 + r)^2 + \cdots + (1 + r)^{n-1}]$$
$$= PMT\left[\sum_{t=0}^{n-1}(1 + r)^t\right]$$

The first line of Equation 4–3 presents the annuity payments in reverse order of payment, with the superscript in each term indicating the number of periods of interest is compounded (earned) for each payment. In the current example, Alice deposits the first $100 at the end of Year 1, so interest is earned in Year 2 and Year 3 only (see the cash flow time line). Note that the last $100 deposit is made at the same time the computation is made, so there is no time for this deposit to earn interest. Because the deposit each year (PMT) is the same—that is, $PMT_1 = PMT_2 = \ldots = PMT_n = PMT$—we can simplify the first line of Equation 4–3 to produce the next two

**FIGURE 4-7**  Using *Excel's FV Function* to Compute the Future Value of an Ordinary Annuity

| | A | B | C | D |
|---|---|---|---|---|
| | B8 | | = =FV(B2,B1,B4,B3,B5) | |
| 1 | N = | 3 | | |
| 2 | I/Y = | 5.00% | | |
| 3 | PV = | 0 | | |
| 4 | PMT = | -$100.00 | | |
| 5 | PMT type = | 0 | 0 = ordinary annuity; 1 = annuity due | |
| 6 | FV = | ? | | |
| 7 | | | The equation used to solve for FVA₃ in cell B8 | Values that correspond to the cell references in cell C8 |
| 8 | FV₃ = | $315.25 | =FV(B2,B1,B4,B3,B5) | =FV(0.05,3,-100,0,0) |

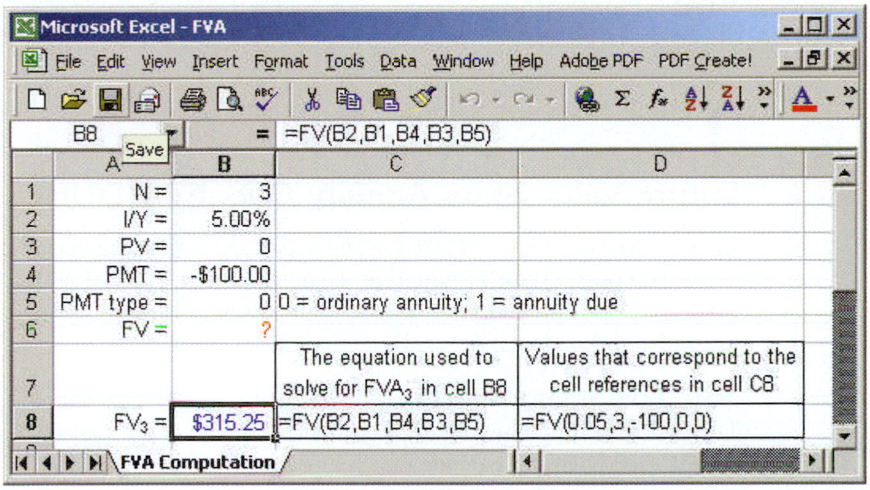

**Note:** According to the equation shown in cell C8, the input values must be entered in a specific order: I/Y, N, PMT, PV, and PMT type (0 = ordinary annuity).

lines. Further simplification of Equation 4–3 produces a general equation that can be used to solve for the future value of an ordinary annuity[7]:

$$\text{FVA}_n = \text{PMT}\left[\sum_{t=0}^{n-1}(1+r)^n\right] = \text{PMT}\left[\frac{(1+r)^n - 1}{r}\right] \qquad 4\text{–}4$$

Using Equation 4–4, the future value of $100 deposited at the end of each year for three years in a savings account that earns 5 percent interest per year is

$$\text{FVA}_3 = \$100\left[\frac{(1.05)^3 - 1}{0.05}\right] = \$100(3.15250) = \$315.25$$

**FINANCIAL CALCULATOR SOLUTION:**
To solve for FVA₃ using a financial calculator, we must use the PMT (annuity) key. In our example, because the annuity payment equals $100 per year, PMT = −100. Enter N = 3, I/Y = 5, PV = 0, and PMT = −100; then solve for FV:

| Inputs: | 3 | 5 | 0 | −100 | ? |
|---|---|---|---|---|---|
| | N | I/Y | PV | PMT | FV |
| Output: | | | | | = 315.25 |

**SPREADSHEET SOLUTION:**
Figure 4-7 shows how to set up and solve the current situation using an Excel spreadsheet. Notice that we use the same financial function that we used to solve

[7]The simplification shown in Equation 4-4 is found by applying the algebra of geometric progressions.

for the future value of a single payment, which is shown in Figure 4-1. But to solve for the future value of an annuity, we must enter a value for PMT so that the value in cell **B4** is −$100. Also, because we are solving for the future value of an ordinary annuity, the value in cell **B5** is 0. The value in cell **B5** is like an on-off switch that tells the FV function in the spreadsheet whether the annuity payment represents an ordinary annuity, in which case cell **B5** = 0, or an annuity due, in which case cell **B5** = 1.

## Future Value of an Annuity Due, FVA(DUE)

Because Alvin intends to make his deposits at the *beginning* of each year, his series of deposits represents an *annuity due*. To determine the future value of an annuity due, we must adjust our computation to recognize that each annuity payment earns interest for one additional year (period).

**TIME LINE SOLUTION:**
The cash flow time line that depicts Alvin's deposits is the same as for Alice's deposits except each payment is made one year earlier, which means that each deposit earns interest for an additional year.

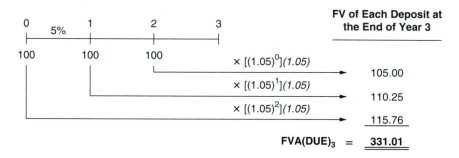

**FVA(DUE)ₙ**
**FVA(DUE)$_n$**
The future value of an annuity *due* over n periods.

Here we designate the future value of an annuity due as **FVA(DUE)$_n$**. As you can see, the future value of the annuity due ($331.01) is greater than the future value of the equivalent ordinary annuity ($315.25). As the time line shows, the future value of *each deposit* is greater for an annuity due than for an ordinary annuity because each deposit receives interest for one additional year.

**EQUATION (NUMERICAL) SOLUTION:**
The time line solution shows that the computation of the future value of the annuity due is the same as the computation of the future value of an ordinary annuity except that each deposit is multiplied by an additional $(1 + r) = (1.05)$ to account for the fact that interest is earned for one additional year. If we make this same adjustment to Equation 4–4, the numerical solution for FVA(DUE)$_n$ is

**4–5**

$$FVA(DUE)_n = PMT\left[\sum_{t=1}^{n}(1+r)^t\right] = PMT\left[\left\{\frac{(1+r)^n - 1}{r}\right\} \times (1+r)\right]$$

Using Equation 4–5, we find that FVA(DUE)$_n$ is

$$FVA(DUE)_3 = \$100\left[\left\{\frac{(1.05)^3 - 1}{0.05}\right\} \times (1.05)\right]$$

$$= \$100[3.15250 \times 1.05] = \$100[3.310125] = \$331.01$$

**FIGURE 4-8**   Using *Excel's FV Function* to Compute the Future Value of an Annuity Due

| | A | B | C | D |
|---|---|---|---|---|
| | | | =FV(B2,B1,B4,B3,B5) | |
| 1 | N = | 3 | | |
| 2 | I/Y = | 5.00% | | |
| 3 | PV = | 0 | | |
| 4 | PMT = | -$100.00 | | |
| 5 | PMT type = | 1 | 0 = ordinary annuity; 1 = annuity due | |
| 6 | FV = | ? | | |
| 7 | FVA(DUE) | | The equation used to solve for FVA(DUE)$_3$ in cell B8 | Values that correspond to the cell references in cell C8 |
| 8 | FV(DUE)$_3$ = | $331.01 | =FV(B2,B1,B4,B3,B5) | =FV(0.05,3,-100,0,1) |

FVA(DUE) Computation

**Note:** According to the equation shown in cell C8, the input values must be entered in a specific order: I/Y, N, PMT, PV, and PMT type (1 = annuity due).

**FINANCIAL CALCULATOR SOLUTION:**

Financial calculators have a switch, or key, generally marked DUE or BGN, that allows you to switch from end-of-period payments (ordinary annuity) to beginning-of-period payments (annuity due). When the beginning mode is activated, the display normally will show the word BEGIN, or the letters BGN. Thus, to deal with annuities due, switch your calculator to BEGIN and proceed as before:

|  |  |  |  |  | BGN |
|---|---|---|---|---|---|
| Inputs: | 3 | 5 | 0 | −100 | ? |
| | N | I/Y | PV | PMT | FV |
| Output: | | | | | = 331.01 |

Because most problems specify end-of-period cash flows—that is, ordinary annuities—*you should always switch your calculator back to the END mode after you work an annuity due problem.*

**SPREADSHEET SOLUTION:**

Figure 4-8 shows how to set up and solve the current situation using an Excel spreadsheet. Notice that inputs to the spreadsheet are the same as in Figure 4-7, where we computed the future value of an ordinary annuity, except that cell **B5** contains a 1 rather than a 0. Entering a 1 for the PMT type indicates to the spreadsheet that the cash flow series is an annuity due.

Because each of the payments from the annuity due (Alvin's deposits) is received one year earlier than the corresponding payment from the ordinary annuity (Alice's deposits), the annuity due payments earn greater total interest than the ordinary annuity. For this reason, everything else equal, *FVA(DUE)$_n$ will always be greater than FVA$_n$*—that is, FVA(DUE)$_n$ > FVA$_n$.

**Self-Test Questions**

How do you compute the future value of an annuity?

How do you modify your computations for determining the future value of an ordinary annuity to compute the future value of an annuity due?

Everything else equal, which annuity has the greater future value: an ordinary annuity or an annuity due? Why?

Suppose you want to start your own business in 10 years, and you plan to save funds to invest in the business. You have determined that you can save $5,000 per year for 10 years at 7 percent interest. If the first $5,000 deposit isn't made until one year from today, how much money will you have in 10 years when you start your business? How much would you have if you deposit the first $5,000 today? (*Answers:* $69,082; $73,918)

# PRESENT VALUE OF AN ANNUITY, PVA

Suppose Alice is trying to decide whether to make a single lump-sum deposit today rather than depositing $100 each year for the next three years. Alice's twin, Alvin, is also considering this option. How much must the lump-sum payment be so that it is equivalent to the $100 annuity? We can answer this question by computing the present value of the annuity. Remember that we compute the present value of a future amount by taking out interest that the amount earns during the investment period—that is, we discount the future amount by the interest it earns. We apply this concept when computing the present value of an annuity.

## Present Value of an Ordinary Annuity, PVA

Alice wants to know how much she has to deposit today as a lump-sum amount to end up with the same future value as she would have if she deposited $100 each year, beginning in one year, for the next three years in a savings account that pays 5 percent interest per year. Because the three $100 deposits represent an ordinary annuity, in this section we show how to compute present value of an ordinary annuity.

### TIME LINE SOLUTION:

**$PVA_n$**

The present value of an *ordinary* annuity with n payments.

One way to determine the present value of an ordinary annuity, which we designate $PVA_n$ is to compute the present value of *each* annuity payment using Equation 4–2 and then sum the results. Here is the computation of the present value of Alice's deposits (annuity):

### EQUATION (NUMERICAL) SOLUTION:

The time line solution shows that we can compute the present value of the annuity simply by computing the PVs of the individual payments and summing the results. The general equation used to find the PV of an ordinary annuity is a series of solutions to Equation 4–2, which can be written as follows:

**FIGURE 4-9**   Using *Excel's PV Function* to Compute the Present Value of an Ordinary Annuity

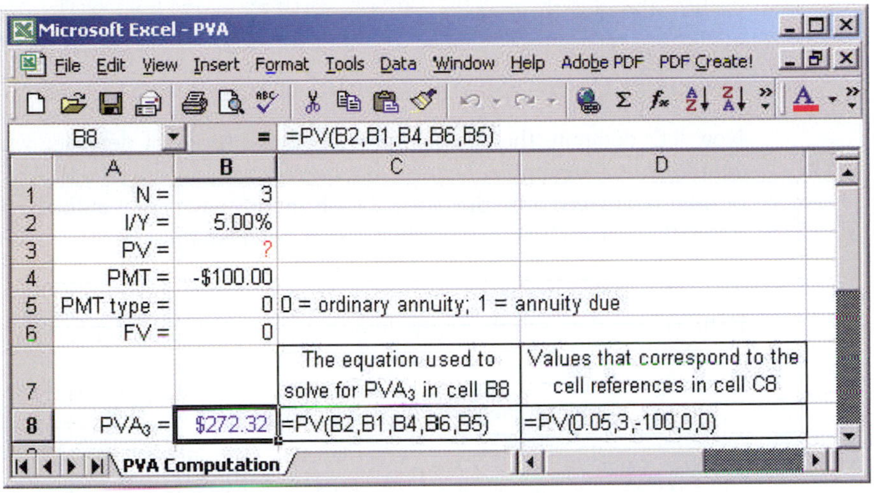

**Note:** According to the equation shown in cell C8, the input values must be entered in a specific order: I/Y, N, PMT, FV, and PMT type (0 = ordinary annuity).

$$PVA_n = PMT \left[\frac{1}{(1+r)^1}\right] + PMT \left[\frac{1}{(1+r)^2}\right] + \cdots + PMT \left[\frac{1}{(1+r)^n}\right]$$

$$= PMT \sum_{t=1}^{n} \left[\frac{1}{(1+r)^t}\right] = PMT \left[\frac{1 - \dfrac{1}{(1+r)^n}}{r}\right]$$

4–6

Using Equation 4–6, the PV of the three-year annuity with end-of-year payments of $100 and an opportunity cost of 5 percent is

$$PVA_3 = \$100 \left[\frac{1 - \frac{1}{(1.05)^3}}{0.05}\right] = \$100(2.72325) = \$272.32$$

**FINANCIAL CALCULATOR SOLUTION:**
Enter N = 3, I/Y = 5, PMT = −100, and FV = 0; then solve for PV:

| Inputs: | 3 | 5 | ? | −100 | 0 |
|---------|---|---|---|------|---|
|         | N | I/Y | PV | PMT | FV |
| Output: | | | = 272.32 | | |

**SPREADSHEET SOLUTION:**
Figure 4-9 shows how to set up and solve the current situation using an Excel spreadsheet. Notice that we use the same financial function that we used to solve for the present value of a single payment, which is shown in Figure 4-3. But to solve for the future value of an annuity, we enter a value for PMT so that the value in cell **B4** is −$100.

In this section, we found that the present value of a three-year $100 ordinary annuity that earns 5 percent interest each year is $272.32. As a result, if Alice deposits

$272.32 today and earns 5 percent interest for the next three years, her bank account will have the same balance in three years as it would if she deposits $100 at the end of each of the next three years—that is, $315.25 = 272.32(1.05)^3$.

## Present Value of an Annuity Due, PVA(DUE)

Now let's compute the present value of Alvin's series of deposits, which represent an *annuity due*. To compute the present value of an annuity due, the PVA$_n$ computation must be adjusted to recognize the fact that each annuity payment is at the beginning of the year rather than the end of the year—that is, each payment must be *discounted for one less year*.

**TIME LINE SOLUTION:**
Following is the cash flow time line that depicts Alvin's deposits:

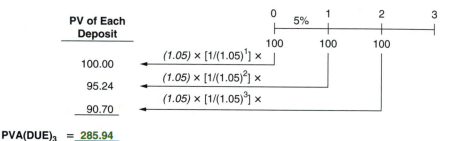

**FINANCIAL CALCULATOR SOLUTION:**
Switch to the beginning-of-period mode (BGN), and enter N = 3, I/Y = 5, PMT = −100, and FV = 0; then compute PV = 285.94. Again, because most problems deal with end-of-period cash flows, *don't forget to switch your calculator back to the END mode.*

**SPREADSHEET SOLUTION:**
The inputs to the spreadsheet are the same as in Figure 4-9, where we computed the present value of an ordinary annuity, except that cell **B5** contains a 1 rather than a 0, which indicates to the spreadsheet that the cash flow series is an annuity due. When you enter 1 in cell **B5,** you should see the result that was shown for the ordinary annuity in cell **B8** change to $285.94.

In this section, we found that the present value of a three-year $100 annuity that earns 5 percent annual interest is $272.32 if it is an ordinary annuity and $285.94 if it is an annuity due. These results tell us that Alice should be indifferent between making a single deposit of $272.32 today or depositing $100 at the end of each of the next three years. In a previous section, we found that the future value of the same three-year $100 ordinary annuity, FVA$_3$, is $315.25. If Alice chooses to deposit $272.32 today and this money earns 5 percent interest for the next three years, the value of this deposit in three years will also be $315.24 = $272.32(1.05)^3$. (There is a difference of $0.01 due to rounding.) This same logic applies to Alvin's situation. But why is the present value of Alvin's series of deposits ($285.94) greater than the present value of Alice's series of deposits ($272.32)? The answer is fairly simple: The future value of Alvin's annuity due in three years ($331.01) is greater than the future value of Alice's ordinary annuity ($315.25) at the same time period and the same interest rate. As a result, Alvin has to deposit a greater amount today to accumulate the higher future value.

The comparison of $PVA_n$ and **$PVA(DUE)_n$** can also be viewed from a slightly different standpoint. Suppose you are considering investing an amount today at 5 percent interest so that you can pay yourself $100 per year for the next three years. According to the solutions given here, you would have to invest $272.32 today if the first $100 withdrawal from the investment will be in one year (ordinary annuity). On the other hand, you would have to invest $285.94 today if the first $100 is withdrawn today (annuity due). It makes sense that the annuity due has the higher value today; because the first $100 annuity payment is today, only $185.94 = $285.94 − $100.00 will be available to earn 5 percent interest in the first year.

**$PVA(DUE)_n$**
The present value of an annuity due over n periods.

**Self-Test Questions**

How do you compute the present value of an annuity?

All else equal, which annuity has the greater present value: an ordinary annuity or an annuity due? Why?

Suppose you are considering an investment that pays $5,000 per year for 10 years and your opportunity cost is 7 percent interest. If you don't receive the first $5,000 payment until one year from today, what is the most you should be willing to pay for the investment? How much would you be willing to pay if you receive the first $5,000 payment today? (*Answers*: $35,118; $37,576)

# COMPUTING ANNUITY PAYMENTS (PMT), INTEREST RATES (r), AND TIME (n)

The equations used to solve for either FVA or PVA contain four variables: Either FVA or PVA, depending on whether we are looking for the future value or the present value of an annuity; n; r; and PMT. If we know the values of all the variables except one, we can solve for the value of the unknown variable. In this section, we set up three examples to show you how to solve for (1) annuity payments (PMT), (2) the annual interest rate that is earned (paid) on an annuity (r), and (3) how long it takes (n) to achieve a financial goal with an annuity. Because the solutions to these situations are fairly simple when we use either a financial calculator or a spreadsheet, we use only these approaches to solve the problems.

## Computing Annuity Payments, PMT

Suppose you want to start your own business in 10 years, and you plan to deposit an amount in a savings account every year so that you have sufficient funds to start the business. You have determined that you need $100,000 in 10 years, and you have decided to make the first deposit at the end of this year. If the savings account pays an annual interest rate equal to 5 percent, how much must you deposit each year to reach your $100,000 goal?

**FINANCIAL CALCULATOR SOLUTION:**
Enter N = 10, I/Y = 5, PV = 0, and FV = 100,000. Solving for PMT, we find that you must deposit $7,950.46 at the end of each year to have $100,000 in 10 years:

**FIGURE 4-10**    Using *Excel's PMT Function* to Compute the Annuity Payment for an Ordinary Annuity

**Note:** According to the equation shown in cell C8, the input values must be entered in a specific order: I/Y, N, PV, FV, and PMT type (0 = ordinary annuity).

Inputs:    10         5         0         ?         100,000
           N         I/Y       PV        PMT       FV

Output:                                  = −7,950.46

What would the answer be if you decided that the first deposit should be made today rather than one year from today? Switch your calculator to the BGN mode, and you should find that the answer is $7,571.86. Because each deposit is made one year earlier—that is, we now have an annuity due—each deposit earns more interest, and consequently the annual deposit needed to reach the goal of $100,000 in 10 years is lower than for the ordinary annuity.

### SPREADSHEET SOLUTION:

Figure 4-10 shows the setup and the inputs used to solve this problem using the PMT function that is available in Excel. The solution shown in Figure 4-10 assumes that the series of deposits represents an ordinary annuity. If the deposits are made at the beginning of the year such that the series is an annuity due, simply enter a 1 in cell **B5,** and the solution for an annuity due, $7,571.86, will appear in cell **B8.**

## Solving for r

Suppose you borrow $1,000, and the loan agreement requires you to pay $282 per year for the next four years. If the payments are made at the end of each year, what interest rate are you paying on the loan?

### FINANCIAL CALCULATOR SOLUTION:

Enter N = 4, PV = 1,000, PMT = −282, and FV = 0. Solving for I/Y, we find that r equals 5 percent.

Inputs:    4         ?         1,000     −282      0
           N         I/Y       PV        PMT       FV

Output:              = 5.0

In this problem, the information that was given included the amount of the annuity payment, the *present value* of the annuity, and the number of years the annuity payment is made. If the *future value* of the annuity is given instead of the present value, we would follow the same procedure outlined here to find r. Also, we follow the same steps to solve this problem if the loan payments are made at the beginning of the year (annuity due) rather than the end of the year (ordinary annuity). Simply switch your calculator to the BGN mode. You should find that I/Y equals 8.7 percent if the $282 payments represent an annuity due. Think about why the interest rate is much higher for the annuity due than for the ordinary annuity, everything else equal.

**SPREADSHEET SOLUTION:**
To solve this problem using an Excel spreadsheet, use the same RATE function that is described in Figure 4-5. Simply enter the values in the appropriate cells and the answer, 5.00%, will appear in cell **B8**.

# Solving for n

Suppose you borrow $18,000 to make home improvements. According to the loan agreement, the interest on the loan is 13 percent. If you can afford to pay only $4,070 at the end of each year, how many payments must you make to pay off the loan?

**FINANCIAL CALCULATOR SOLUTION:**
Enter I/Y = 13, PV = 18,000, PMT = −4,070, and FV = 0. Solving for N, we find that n equals 7 years.

| Inputs: | ? | 13.0 | 18,000 | −4,070 | 0 |
|---|---|---|---|---|---|
| | N | I/Y | PV | PMT | FV |

Output:  = 7.0

If you make the first loan payment immediately, it would take less time—only 5.8 years—to pay off the loan.

**SPREADSHEET SOLUTION:**
To solve this problem using an Excel spreadsheet, use the same NPER function that is described in Figure 4-6. Simply enter the values in the appropriate cells and the answer, 7 years, will appear in cell **B8**.

## Self-Test Questions

Suppose you just won a lottery prize equal to $100,000. You plan to use the winnings to help pay for your college education for the next five years (your plans include graduate school). If you can invest your winnings at 6 percent, how much can you withdraw from the investment each year to pay for your education? Assume that the withdrawals represent an annuity due—that is the first withdrawal is today. (*Answer:* $22,396)

Suppose you pay $846.80 for an investment that promises to pay you $250 per year for the next four years. If the payments are made at the end of each year, what interest rate (rate of return) will you earn on this investment? (*Answer:* 7.0%)

Suppose you pay $1,685 for an investment that promises to pay you $400 per year. If the payments are made at the end of each year, how many payments must you receive to earn a 6 percent return? (*Answer:* 5 payments)

**perpetuity**
A stream of equal payments expected to continue forever.

# PERPETUITIES

Most annuities call for payments to be made over some finite period of time—for example, $100 per year for three years. However, some annuities go on indefinitely, or perpetually. These *perpetual* annuities are called **perpetuities.** The present value of a perpetuity is found by applying the following equation:[8]

**4–7**

$$PVP = \frac{\text{Payment}}{\text{Interest rate}} = \frac{PMT}{r}$$

**consol**
A perpetual bond issued by the British government to consolidate past debts; in general, any perpetual bond.

Perpetuities can be illustrated by British securities that were issued after the Napoleonic Wars. In 1815 the British government sold a huge bond issue and used the proceeds to pay off many smaller bonds that were issued in prior years to pay for the wars. Because the purpose of the bonds was to consolidate past debts, the bonds were called **consols.** The consols paid constant interest but did not have maturities—that is, the consols were perpetuities. Suppose each consol promised to pay $100 per year in perpetuity. (Actually, interest was stated in pounds.) What would each bond be worth if the opportunity cost rate, or discount rate, was 5 percent? The answer is $2,000:

$$PVP = \frac{\$100}{0.05} = \$2,000$$

Suppose the interest rate increases to 10 percent. What would happen to the consol's value? The value would drop to $1,000:

$$PVP = \frac{\$100}{0.10} = \$1,000$$

We see that the value of a perpetuity changes dramatically when interest rates change. This example demonstrates an important financial concept: Everything else equal, when the *interest rate changes, the value of an investment changes in an opposite direction.* In our example, the value of the consol dropped dramatically when the interest rate increased from 5 percent to 10 percent. If in subsequent periods the interest rate declines, the value of the consol will increase. This is a fundamental valuation concept that we will discuss in greater detail in Chapter 6.

**Self-Test Questions**

What happens to the value of a perpetuity when interest rates increase? What happens when rates decrease?

What is the present value of a $3,500 annuity that will be paid forever beginning in one year if the interest rate is 7 percent? What is the value of this perpetuity if the interest rate increases to 10 percent? (*Answers:* $50,000; $35,000)

[8]The derivation of Equation 4–7 is given in the Web/CD Extension to Chapter 5 in Eugene F. Brigham and Phillip R. Daves, *Intermediate Financial Management*, 9th ed. (Cincinnati, OH: South-Western College Publishing, 2007).

# UNEVEN CASH FLOW STREAMS

The definition of an annuity includes the words *constant amount*—in other words, annuities involve payments that are the same for every period. Although many financial decisions do involve constant payments, some important decisions involve uneven, or nonconstant, cash flows. For example, common stocks typically pay an increasing stream of dividends over time, and fixed asset investments such as new equipment normally do not generate constant cash flows. Consequently, it is necessary to extend our TVM discussion to include **uneven cash flow streams.**

Throughout the book, we use the term **payment (PMT)** to identify annuity situations in which the cash flows are constant, and we use the term **cash flow (CF)** to denote a cash flow series in general, which includes both uneven cash flows and annuities. When all cash flows in a series are nonconstant, $CF_1 \neq CF_2 \neq CF_3 \neq \ldots \neq CF_n$, which represents an *uneven cash flow stream;* when all cash flows in a series are equal, $CF_1 = CF_2 = CF_3 = \ldots = CF_n = PMT$, which represents an annuity.

**uneven cash flow stream**
A series of cash flows in which the amount varies from one period to the next.

**payment (PMT)**
This term designates constant cash flows— that is, the amount of an annuity payment.

**cash flow (CF)**
This term designates cash flows in general, including uneven cash flows.

## Present Value of an Uneven Cash Flow Stream

To find the present value (PV) of an uneven cash flow stream, we must sum the PVs of the individual cash flows included in the stream. The PV is found by applying this general present value equation, which is simply a series of PV solutions to Equation 4–2:

$$PV = \frac{CF_1}{(1+r)^1} + \frac{CF_2}{(1+r)^2} + \cdots + \frac{CF_n}{(1+r)^n} = \sum_{t=1}^{n} \frac{CF_t}{(1+r)^t}$$

**4–8**

Note that Equation 4–8 is the same as Equation 4–6, which is used to compute PVA, except that CF is substituted for PMT. Unlike Equation 4–6, however, we cannot simplify Equation 4–8 further because the cash flows are not necessarily equal.

To illustrate the application of Equation 4–8, let's assume you are considering buying an investment that promises to pay $500, $800, and $300 over the next three years. The first payment will be received one year from today, and your opportunity cost is 8 percent. How much should you pay for this investment?

### TIME LINE SOLUTION:

One way to find the present value of the cash flow stream in our example is to compute the PV of each individual cash flow and then sum these values—that is, solve for PV using Equation 4–8.

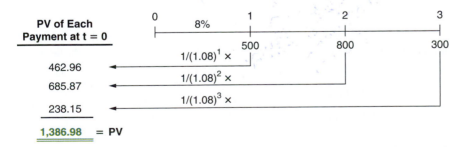

You can find the *present value of any cash flow stream by summing the present values of the individual cash flows* as shown here. When the cash flows are the same—that is, constant—we can simplify the computations by applying the annuity solutions discussed earlier. The annuity equations (solutions) can only be used to compute the present value of cash flows that are all the same, whereas Equation 4–8 can be used to find the present value for any cash flow stream (constant or nonconstant).

**FINANCIAL CALCULATOR AND SPREADSHEET SOLUTIONS:**

Problems involving uneven cash flows can be solved in one step with most financial calculators and spreadsheets. Using a financial calculator, you first input the individual cash flows in chronological order into the cash flow register. Cash flows usually are designated $CF_0$, $CF_1$, $CF_2$, $CF_3$, and so on. Next, you enter the interest rate. At this point, you have entered all the known values of Equation 4–8, so you need only press the NPV key to find the present value of the cash flow stream. The calculator has been programmed to find the PV of each cash flow, including $CF_0$, and then to sum these values to find the PV of the entire stream. To input the cash flows for this problem, enter 0 (because $CF_0 = 0$), 500, 800, and 300 in that order into the cash flow register, enter $I = 8$, and then compute the NPV to get the answer, $1,386.98. NPV stands for net present value.

Using a spreadsheet, you follow a similar procedure by setting up the spreadsheet so that the cash flows are ordered sequentially. Then using the NPV function, solve for the present value of the nonconstant cash flow series. Because we discuss the application of this function in much greater detail in Chapter 7 and Chapter 9, we will wait until then to describe in detail the process of solving for NPV using both a financial calculator and a spreadsheet.

## Future Value of an Uneven Cash Flow Stream

**terminal value**

The future value of a cash flow stream.

The future value of an uneven cash flow stream, sometimes called the **terminal value,** is found by compounding each payment to the end of the stream and then summing the future values.[9]

**TIME LINE SOLUTION:**

The future value of our illustrative uneven cash flow stream is $1,747.20.

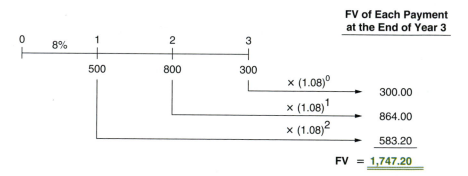

Alternatively, because we already know the present value of the cash flow series, we could have used Equation 4–1 to find the future value of the cash flows. The computation for our situation would be as follows:

$$FV_n = PV(1 + r)^n$$

$$= \$1,386.98(1.08)^3 = \$1,386.98(1.259712) = \$1,747.20$$

---

[9]Some financial calculators have a net future value (NFV) key that, after the cash flows and interest rate have been entered into the calculator, can be used to compute the future value of an uneven cash flow stream. In any event, it is easy enough to compound the individual cash flows to the terminal year and then sum them to find the FV of the stream.

We generally are more interested in the present value of an asset's cash flow stream than in the future value because the present value represents today's value, which we can compare with the price of the asset.

## Solving for r with Uneven Cash Flow Streams

To solve for r for an uneven cash flow stream without a financial calculator or a spreadsheet, you must go through tedious trial-and-error calculations. With a financial calculator, however, it is fairly easy to find the value of r. Simply input the CF values into the cash flow register and then press the IRR key. IRR stands for *internal rate of return,* which is the return on an investment. Spreadsheets have a built-in IRR function that can also be used to solve for r. We will defer further discussion of this calculation for now, but we will take it up later in the book (see Chapter 9).

### Self-Test Questions

Give two examples of financial decisions that would typically involve uneven flows of cash.

What is meant by the term *terminal value?*

Consider the following uneven cash flow stream: $1,000 at the end of Year 1, $5,000 at the end of Year 2, $800 at the end of Year 3, and $2,000 at the end of Year 4. If your opportunity cost is 10 percent, what is the most you should pay for an investment with these payoffs? If you were to invest each cash flow when you receive it, how much would your investment be worth at the end of four years? (*Answers:* $7,008.40; $10,261)

## SEMIANNUAL AND OTHER COMPOUNDING PERIODS

In all of our examples to this point, we have assumed that interest is compounded once per year, or annually. This is called **annual compounding.** Suppose, however, that you deposited $100 in a bank that pays a 6 percent annual interest rate, but that interest is paid every six months. This is called **semiannual compounding.** Note that financial institutions, such as banks and credit unions, generally pay interest more often than every six months; often interest is paid on a daily basis. But in our example, we assume interest is paid semiannually so that we can more easily illustrate the effect of multiple interest payments each year.

To illustrate semiannual compounding, let's return to the example we introduced at the beginning of the chapter: Assume that $100 is invested at an interest rate of 6 percent for a period of three years. First, consider again what happens when interest is *compounded annually.*

**annual compounding**
The process of determining the future (or present) value of a cash flow or series of cash flows when interest is paid once per year.

**semiannual compounding**
The process of determining the future (or present) value of a cash flow or series of cash flows when interest is paid twice per year.

### TIME LINE AND EQUATION SOLUTIONS—6 PERCENT INTEREST COMPOUNDED ANNUALLY:

Following is the cash flow time line with the future value computation using Equation 4–1:

| Time (t): | 0 | 6% | 1 | | 2 | | 3 |
|---|---|---|---|---|---|---|---|

Account balance: 100.00 $\xrightarrow{\times (1.06)}$ 106.00 $\xrightarrow{\times (1.06)}$ 112.36 $\xrightarrow{\times (1.06)}$ 119.10

$$FV_n = PV(1 + r)^n = 100(1.06)^3 = 119.10$$

**FINANCIAL CALCULATOR SOLUTION—6 PERCENT INTEREST COMPOUNDED ANNUALLY:**
Input N = 3, I/Y = 6, PV = −100, and PMT = 0; then compute FV = 119.10.

**SPREADSHEET SOLUTION—6 PERCENT INTEREST COMPOUNDED ANNUALLY:**
The spreadsheet solution is shown in Figure 4-1.

How would the future value change if interest is paid twice each year—that is, semiannually? To find the future value, we must make two adjustments: (1) convert the annual interest rate to a rate per period, which is called the *periodic rate,* and (2) convert the number of years to the total number of interest payments (compounding periods) during the life of the investment. These conversions are as follows:

**4–9**

$$\text{Periodic rate} = r_{PER} = \frac{\text{Stated annual interest rate}}{\text{Number of interest payments per year}} = \frac{r_{SIMPLE}}{m}$$

**4–10**

$$\begin{aligned}\text{Number of interest periods} &= n_{PER} = \text{Number of years} \times \text{Interest payments per year} \\ &= n_{YRS} \times m\end{aligned}$$

Here m is the number of interest compounding periods per year, $r_{SIMPLE}$ is the simple (noncompounded) annual interest rate, $r_{PER}$ is the rate of interest that is paid *each* compounding period, $n_{YRS}$ is the number of years interest is earned, and $n_{PER}$ is the total number of interest payments during the $n_{YRS}$ years. Note that $r_{PER} = r_{SIMPLE}$ and $n_{PER} = n_{YRS}$ only when interest is compounded annually.

In our current example, if interest is paid semiannually, there are $n_{PER} = 2 \times 3 = 6$ interest payments during the life of the investment, and interest is paid at a rate equal to $r_{PER} = r_{SIMPLE}/m = 6\%/2 = 3\%$ every six months. Here is the value of the $100 at the end of three years at 6 percent with semiannual compounding:

**TIME LINE AND EQUATION SOLUTIONS—6 PERCENT INTEREST COMPOUNDED SEMIANNUALLY:**
Following is the cash flow time line with the future value computation using Equation 4–1 after converting $r_{YRS}$ to $r_{PER}$ and $n_{YRS}$ to $n_{PER}$:

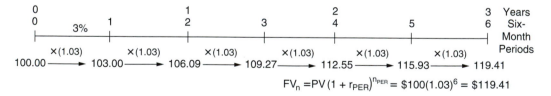

$$FV_n = PV(1 + r_{PER})^{n_{PER}} = \$100(1.03)^6 = \$119.41$$

**FINANCIAL CALCULATOR SOLUTION—6 PERCENT INTEREST COMPOUNDED SEMIANNUALLY:**
Input N = 3 × 2 = 6, I/Y = 6/2 = 3, PV = −100, and PMT = 0; then compute FV = 119.41.

**SPREADSHEET SOLUTION—6 PERCENT INTEREST COMPOUNDED SEMIANNUALLY:**
Make the same conversions as you do when entering the values into the financial calculator, and then input the converted values into the appropriate cells shown in Figure 4-1. The result that appears in cell **B8** will be $119.41.

The FV is larger under semiannual compounding because, compared with annual compounding, the first interest payment is sooner—that is, in six months rather than one year—and interest is compounded more often—that is, interest is earned on previously paid interest more frequently.

How would the result change if interest is paid quarterly? In this case, $r_{PER} = 6\%/4 = 1.5\%$ and $n_{PER} = 3 \times 4 = 12$ compounding periods. If you make these changes in your calculator—that is, $N = 12$ and $I/Y = 1.5$—you will find that the future value of the $100 deposit is $119.56. This amount is greater than the future value when interest is compounded semiannually. Our results show us that FV(quarterly compounding) = $119.56 > FV(semiannual compounding) = $119.41 > FV(annual compounding) = $119.10. This relationship demonstrates an important financial concept: Everything else equal, an amount invested today will be worth more in the future when compounding occurs more often than once per year; and *the more often compounding occurs each year, the higher the future value of a present value amount.*

The preceding discussion was concerned with finding the future value of a lump-sum amount that is invested today. The same adjustments must be made to compute the present value of a future amount when interest is compounded more than once per year. For example, let's compute the present value of a $500 obligation that must be paid in four years when the opportunity cost is 8 percent. If interest is compounded annually, to find the present value using a financial calculator, enter $N = 4$, $I/Y = 8$, $PMT = 0$, and $FV = -500$; the solution is $367.51. If interest is compounded quarterly, enter $N = 4 \times 4 = 16$, $I/Y = 8/4 = 2$, $PMT = 0$, and $FV = -500$; the solution is $364.22. This example shows that *when there is more interest compounding during the year, everything else equal, the present value of a future amount is lower.* More compounding generates greater interest, which means that less has to be put aside (invested) today to meet a specific future financial goal (obligation).

### Self-Test Questions

What changes must you make in your calculations to determine the future value of an amount that is compounded at 8 percent semiannually versus one that is compounded annually at 8 percent?

Why is semiannual compounding better than annual compounding from a saver's standpoint?

Suppose you have $1,000 that you want to invest today. How much would you have in 10 years if you put your money in a savings account that pays 10 percent compounded annually? How much would you have if the bank pays 10 percent compounded quarterly? (*Answers:* $2,593.74; $2,685.06)

## COMPARISON OF DIFFERENT INTEREST RATES

In the previous section, we showed that the dollar interest earned on an investment is greater when interest is computed (compounded) more than once per year. In simple terms, this means that the *effective* return earned on an investment is higher than the stated, or simple, return ($r_{SIMPLE}$) when there are multiple interest compounding periods during the year. For example, in the previous section we found that $100 invested for three years at 6 percent will grow to $119.10 when interest is compounded annually, whereas the same $100 will grow to $119.41 when interest is compounded semiannually. Because the $100 investment earns more interest (INT) when interest is compounded semiannually, the *effective* annual return is higher with semiannual compounding than with annual compounding. This important financial principle can be summarized as follows: Everything else equal, *the greater the number of compounding periods per year, the greater the effective rate of return on an investment.*

Different compounding periods are used for different types of investments. For example, banks generally compute interest on a daily, or even continuous, basis; most bonds pay interest semiannually; and stocks generally pay dividends quarterly.[10] If we are to properly compare the returns that are earned on investments with different compounding periods, we need to put them on a common basis. This requires us to distinguish between the *simple (or quoted) interest rate* and the *effective annual rate (EAR)*:

**simple (quoted) interest rate ($r_{SIMPLE}$)**
The rate quoted by borrowers and lenders that is used to determine the rate earned per compounding period (periodic rate, $r_{PER}$).

- The **simple,** or **quoted, interest rate ($r_{SIMPLE}$)** in our example is 6 percent. On all types of contracts, interest is always quoted as an annual rate, and if compounding occurs more frequently than once per year, that fact is stated along with the rate. In our example, the quoted rate is *6 percent, compounded semiannually.* The simple rate is also called the **annual percentage rate,** or **APR.** This is the rate that is reported to you by banks, credit card companies, automobile dealerships, student loan officers, and other lenders when you borrow money. The APR is a noncompounded interest rate because it does not consider the effect compounding has when interest is paid more than once per year. In other words, you could have two loans (or investments) that have the same stated APR—say, 6 percent—but you could actually be paying different effective rates because the number of loan payments per year differs (annual versus semiannual). As a result, to compare loans (or investments) for which interest is paid at different times during the year, we must compare the loans' (investments') effective annual interest rates, not their APRs.

**annual percentage rate (APR)**
Another name for the simple interest rate, $r_{SIMPLE}$; does not consider the effect of interest compounding.

**effective (equivalent) annual rate ($r_{EAR}$)**
The annual rate of interest actually being earned, as opposed to the quoted rate, considering the compounding of interest.

- The **effective (equivalent) annual rate ($r_{EAR}$)** is defined as the rate that would produce the same ending (future) value if annual compounding had been used. To find $r_{EAR}$, we adjust the APR to include the effect of interest compounding—that is, we convert the APR to its equivalent annual rate of return based on the number of interest payments (compounding periods) each year.

- If interest is computed once each year—that is, compounded annually—$r_{EAR} = r_{SIMPLE} = $ APR. But, *if compounding occurs more than once per year, the effective annual rate is greater than the simple, or quoted, interest rate*—that is, $r_{EAR} > r_{SIMPLE}$.

In our example, $r_{EAR}$ is the rate that will grow a $100 investment to $119.41 at the end of three years. This is the rate at which you would need to invest $100 today to produce $119.41 at the end of Year 3 if interest is paid one time each year—that is, when annual compounding exists. Here is the cash flow time line that shows this situation:

We can compute the effective annual rate, given the simple rate, $r_{SIMPLE}$, and the number of compounding periods per year, $m$, by solving the following equation:

**4–11**

$$\text{Effective annual rate (EAR)} = r_{EAR} = \left(1 + \frac{r_{SIMPLE}}{m}\right)^m - 1.0 = (1 + r_{PER})^m - 1.0$$

---

[10]For a discussion of continuous compounding, see the Web/CD Extension to Chapter 2 in Eugene F. Brigham and Michael Ehrhardt, *Financial Management*, 12th ed. (Fort Worth, TX: Harcourt College Publishers, 2008).

Here $r_{SIMPLE}$ is the simple, or quoted, interest rate—that is, the APR—and m is the number of compounding periods (interest payments) per year. For example, to find the effective annual rate if the simple rate is 6 percent and interest is paid semiannually, we find the following result:

$$\text{Effective annual rate (EAR)} = r_{EAR} = \left(1 + \frac{0.06}{2}\right)^2 - 1.0$$

$$= (1.03)^2 - 1.0 = 1.0609 - 1.0 = 0.0609 = 6.09\%$$

Using a financial calculator, enter N = 3, PV = −100, PMT = 0, and FV = 119.41; then solve for I/Y = 6.09.

Based on what we discussed here and the discussion in the previous section, semiannual compounding (or any nonannual compounding) can be handled in either of two ways:

### ALTERNATIVE 1:

*State everything on a periodic basis rather than on an annual basis.* As we showed in the previous section, we can compute the interest rate per period (periodic rate, $r_{PER} = r_{SIMPLE}/m$) and the total number of interest payments ($n_{PER} = n_{YRS} \times m$) during the life of the investment, or loan, when finding its present value or future value. In our example, you would use $n_{PER} = 3 \times 2 = 6$ periods rather than three years, and use $r_{PER} = 6/2 = 3$ interest rate per period rather than 6 percent interest per year.

### ALTERNATIVE 2:

*Find the effective annual rate ($r_{EAR}$) by applying* Equation 4–11, and then use this rate as an annual rate over the given number of years, $n_{YRS}$. In our example, use $r_{EAR} = 6.09\%$ and $n_{YRS} = 3$ years.

Here are the time line solutions and equation (numerical) solutions for the two alternatives that can be applied to compute the future value of $100 invested for three years at 6 percent interest compounded semiannually:

### ALTERNATIVE 1: USE THE RATE PER PERIOD ($r_{PER}$)—STATE EVERYTHING ON A PERIODIC BASIS

$$FV_n = PV(1 + r_{PER})^{n_{PER}} = \$100(1.03)^6 = \$119.41$$

Using a financial calculator, enter N = 6, I/Y = 3.0, PV = −100, and PMT = 0; then solve for FV = 119.41.

### ALTERNATIVE 2: USE THE EFFECTIVE ANNUAL RATE ($r_{EAR}$)—STATE EVERYTHING ON AN ANNUAL BASIS

$$FV_n = PV(1 + r_{EAR})^{n_{YRS}} = \$100(1.0609)^3 = \$119.41$$

Using a financial calculator, enter N = 3, I/Y = 6.09, PV = −100, and PMT = 0; then solve for FV = 119.41.

Both procedures give the same result: $119.41. Also, notice that the account balance at the end of each of the three years is the same regardless of which alternative is used. Thus, as these time lines show, 6 percent interest compounded semiannually is equivalent to 6.09 percent compounded annually.

Suppose you've decided to deposit $100 in a bank account that pays 6 percent interest compounded semiannually (the current situation), but you expect to leave the money in the bank account for 18 months rather than three years. What will the balance in the account be in 18 months? Either Alternative 1 or Alternative 2 can be used to solve this problem. Using Alternative 1, the equation (numerical) solution is as follows:

$$FV = \$100(1.03)^3 = \$100(1.092727) = \$109.27$$

In this case, $n_{PER} = 3$ because three interest payments are made during the 18-month period.

Converted into years, $n_{PER} = 3$ is the same as $n_{YRS} = 1.5$—that is, 18 months equates to 1.5 years. Therefore, using Alternative 2, the equation (numerical) solution is as follows:

$$FV = \$100(1.0609)^{1.5} = \$100(1.092727) = \$109.27$$

The solution given here illustrates the use of *fractional time periods* to compute the present value of a single payment, or lump-sum amount, using the effective annual rate ($r_{EAR}$). Using a financial calculator, enter N = 1.5, I/Y = 6.09, PV = −100, and PMT = 0; then compute FV = 109.27.

The points made in this section can be generalized for other situations when compounding occurs more frequently than once per year. When computing either the future value or the present value of a lump-sum amount, either (1) convert the simple annual interest rate (APR = $r_{SIMPLE}$) to the periodic interest rate ($r_{PER}$) and the number of years ($n_{YRS}$) to the total number of compounding periods ($n_{PER}$) during the life of the investment (loan), or (2) convert the APR to the effective annual rate ($r_{EAR}$) and use the number of years ($n_{YRS}$).

## Self-Test Questions

What changes must you make in your calculations to determine the future value of an amount that is compounded at 8 percent semiannually versus an amount that is compounded annually at 8 percent?

Why is semiannual compounding better than annual compounding from a saver's standpoint?

What are meant by the terms *annual percentage rate (APR)*, *effective annual rate ($r_{EAR}$)*, and *simple interest rate ($r_{SIMPLE}$)*?

How are the simple rate, the periodic rate, and the effective annual rate related? Can you think of a situation in which all three of these rates will be the same?

Suppose you are considering depositing $400 in one of two banks. Bank A offers to pay 12 percent interest compounded monthly, whereas Bank B offers to pay 12.5 percent compounded annually. Which bank offers the better effective rate? (*Answer:* $r_{EAR}$ at Bank A = 12.7%; $r_{EAR}$ at Bank B = 12.5%)

# AMORTIZED LOANS

One of the most important applications of compound interest involves loans that are paid off in installments over time. Included in this category are automobile loans, home mortgages, student loans, and some business debt. If a loan is to be repaid in equal periodic amounts (monthly, quarterly, or annually), it is said to be an **amortized loan.**[11]

To illustrate, suppose a firm borrows $15,000, and the loan is to be repaid in three equal payments at the end of each of the next three years. The lender will charge 8 percent interest on the loan balance that is outstanding at the beginning of each year. Our first task is to determine the amount the firm must repay each year—that is, the annual payment. To find this amount, recognize that the $15,000 represents the present value of an annuity (PVA) of PMT dollars per year for three years, discounted at 8 percent:

**amortized loan**
A loan that requires equal payments over its life; the payments include both interest and repayment of the debt.

Using a financial calculator, the solution is

Enter N = 3, I/Y = 8, PV = 15,000 (the firm receives the cash), and FV = 0; then compute PMT = 5,820.50.

Thus the firm must pay the lender $5,820.50 at the end of each of the next three years, in which case the percentage cost to the borrower, which is also the rate of return to the lender, will be 8 percent. Each payment consists partly of interest and partly of repayment of the amount borrowed (principal). This breakdown is given in the **amortization schedule** shown in Table 4-1. The interest component is largest in the first year, and it declines as the outstanding balance of the loan decreases. For tax purposes, a business borrower reports the interest component shown in column 3 as a deductible cost each year, whereas the lender reports this same amount as taxable income.

**amortization schedule**
A schedule showing precisely how a loan will be repaid. It gives the required payment on each payment date and a breakdown of the payment, showing how much is interest and how much is repayment of principal.

Column 5 in Table 4-1 shows the outstanding balance that is due for our illustrative loan at the end of each year. If you do not have an amortization schedule, such as the one shown in Table 4-1, you can still determine the outstanding balance of the loan by computing the present value of the *remaining* loan payments. For example, after the first loan payment of $5,820.50 is made at the end of Year 1, the loan agreement calls for two more payments equal to $5,820.50 each. If you compute the present value of the two remaining payments at 8 percent interest per year, you will find that $PVA_2 =$ $10,379.50, which is the remaining balance at the end of Year 1 that is shown in column 5 in Table 4-1 (calculator solution: N = 2, I/Y = 8, PMT = 5,820.50; PV = ? = 10,379.49). The same logic that is presented in Table 4-1 can be used to create amortization schedules for home mortgages, automobile loans, and other amortized loans.

---

[11]The word *amortized* comes from the Latin *mors,* meaning "death," so an amortized loan is one that is "killed off" over time.

**TABLE 4-1**    Loan Amortization Schedule; $15,000 Loan at 8 Percent Interest Rate

| Year | Beginning of Year Balance (1) | Payment (2) | Interest @ 8%[a] (3) = (1) × 0.08 | Repayment of Principal[b] (4) = (2) − (3) | Remaining Balance[c] (5) = (1) − (4) |
|------|------|------|------|------|------|
| 1 | $15,000.00 | $5,820.50 | $1,200.00 | $4,620.50 | 10,379.50 |
| 2 | 10,379.50 | 5,820.50 | 830.36 | 4,990.14 | 5,389.36 |
| 3 | 5,389.36 | 5,820.50 | 431.15 | 5,389.35 | 0.01 |

[a]Interest is calculated by multiplying the loan balance in Column 1 by the interest rate (0.08). For example, the interest in Year 2 is $10,379.50 × 0.08 = $830.36.

[b]Repayment of principal is equal to the payment of $5,820.50 in Column 2 minus the interest charge for each year in Column 3. For example, the repayment of principal in Year 2 is $5,820.50 − $830.36 = $4,990.14.

[c]The $0.01 remaining balance at the end of Year 3 results from a rounding difference.

Financial calculators and spreadsheets are programmed to calculate amortization tables—you simply enter the data and apply the appropriate built-in function. If you have a financial calculator, it is worthwhile to read the appropriate section of the manual and learn how to use its amortization feature. Similarly, it is worth your time to learn how to set up an amortization table using a spreadsheet. For the sake of brevity, we show the steps that are required to set up the amortization schedule in Table 4-1 using both a financial calculator and a spreadsheet in Appendix 4A at the end of this chapter.

 **Self-Test Questions**

To construct an amortization schedule, how do you determine the amount of the periodic payments?

How do you determine the portion of each payment that goes to interest and the portion that goes to repay the debt?

Suppose you have an outstanding automobile loan with two years remaining until it is paid off. The interest rate on the loan is 6 percent, and you are required to pay $452.07 *per month*. If you want to pay off the loan today, for how much should you write the check? (*Answer:* $10,200)

**Chapter *Essentials***

**—The Answers**

To summarize the key concepts, let's answer the questions that were posed at the beginning of the chapter:

- **Why is it important to understand and be able to apply TVM concepts?** It is essential that you have at least a basic understanding of TVM concepts so that you are able to compare various investments. When we apply TVM concepts, we restate dollars from one time period into equivalent dollars from another time period. Consider the question that was posed at the beginning of the chapter: Which is better, an investment that will return $7,023 in five years or an investment that will return $8,130 in eight years? If your opportunity cost is 5 percent, the two investments are identical because their present values are the same (PV = $5,502.70). Once the future values of these investments are translated into dollars at the same time period (Period 0 in this case), they can be compared. For these two investments, we could determine what the value of the five-year investment would be when the eight-year investment matures by restating the dollars at the end of Year 5—that is, $7,023—into equivalent dollars at the end of Year 8. In Year 8, the five-year investment would be worth FV = $7,023(1.05)^3 = $8,130, which is the same as the amount that the eight-year investment will return at the end of Year 8. A basic TVM concept or "rule" is that dollars are comparable only when they are stated at the same time period; *dollars from different time periods should never be compared because their values are not the same.* (The only exception to this rule is when the interest rate equals zero, which is highly unlikely.)

- **What is the difference between a present value amount and a future value amount?** When we compute the future value of an amount invested today, we add the interest that is earned during the investment period—that is, the current amount is compounded to a future period. When we compute the present value of a future amount, we take out the interest that is earned during the investment period—that is, we discount, or "de-interest," the future amount to restate it in current dollars.

- **What is an annuity? What are the two types of annuities, and how do their values differ?** An annuity is a series of equal payments that occur at equal time intervals. For example, a rent payment equal to $700 per month is an annuity. Further, the rent payment is called an *annuity due* because the payment is at the beginning of the period (month). If the annuity payment is at the end of the period, then it is called an *ordinary annuity*. Determining the present (future) value of an annuity is based on the same concept that is used to determine the present (future) value of a lump-sum, or single payment, amount. Because the annuity payments occur one period earlier, both the present value and the future value of an annuity due are greater than the present value and future value of an ordinary annuity.

- **What is the difference between the annual percentage rate (APR) and the effective annual rate (EAR)? Which is more appropriate to use?** The APR is a simple interest rate ($r_{SIMPLE}$) that is quoted on loans, certificates of deposit, and so forth; it does not consider the effects of compounded interest. The EAR, $r_{EAR}$, is the actual interest rate, or rate of return, that an investment (loan) earns (costs) considering the effects of interest compounding. If interest is compounded more than once per year, $r_{EAR} > r_{SIMPLE}$; if interest is compounded annually, $r_{EAR} = r_{SIMPLE}$.

  APR is used to compute $r_{PER}$ to determine the dollar amount of interest that is paid each interest payment period, whereas $r_{EAR}$ is used to determine the actual return that is earned (paid) on an investment (loan). If you want to know the "true" return (cost) on an investment (loan), you must compute $r_{EAR}$.

- **What is an amortized loan? How are amortized loan payments and payoffs determined?** An amortized loan is one that is paid off in equal payments over a specified period. Each payment consists partly of interest and partly of repayment of the amount borrowed. In the early years, a large portion of each payment represents the interest charge, whereas in later years a large portion of each payment represents the repayment of the amount borrowed. For an amortized loan, the amount that is owed at any point in time can be determined by computing the present value of the remaining loan (annuity) payments. An amortization schedule shows how much of each payment constitutes interest, how much is used to repay the debt, and the remaining balance of the loan at each point in time.

- **How is the return (interest rate) on an investment (loan) determined?** If we know both the cost of an investment and the amount to which the investment will grow in the future, we can determine its return. For example, suppose you just purchased an investment for $3,500 that promises to pay you $6,885 in 10 years. The return on this investment is 7 percent (using a financial calculator, enter N = 10, PV = −3,500, PMT = 0, and FV = 6,885; solve for I/Y = 7.0).

## ETHICAL DILEMMA

### It's All Chinese to Me!

Terry Zupita is considering how to invest the modest amount of money she recently inherited ($48,000). Based on her knowledge of different types of investments, as well as the advice of friends, Terry thinks that she should invest her inheritance in a long-term U.S. Treasury bond that promises to pay her $3,690 interest every six months for 10 years. However, today at lunch, Terry asked her best friend Mike how he would invest the money. Mike responded that he thought she could invest in something other than the T-bond and earn a much higher rate of return. In fact, he told Terry that he was at a company social a few nights ago where he overheard a few people talking about a U.S. automobile manufacturer that is partnering with the Chinese government to open a manufacturing operation in Shanghai. The firm, named Universal Autos (UA), would have exclusive rights to manufacture U.S. automobiles in China. One of the men involved in the conversation stated that he thought the arrangement presented a huge opportunity for UA to substantially increase its profits during the next 10 years, which should translate into significant increases in the company's stock price. All of the other people involved in the discussion agreed.

Intrigued, Terry thought it would be a good idea to investigate UA as a potential investment, so she sought advice from her friends and relatives. One friend advised against UA as an investment because she had heard from another friend that the company planned to use child labor in its Chinese manufacturing plant. Another friend advised against the investment because he had heard rumors that the workers in such plants are physically abused on a regular basis. And Terry's uncle, who works in the U.S. State Department, said he had heard that UA paid a huge bribe to the Chinese government before the deal was signed, and it is illegal to offer or pay such kickbacks. However, Terry's boyfriend, who happens to be Chinese, thinks that she should invest her money in UA. According to information provided by his family and friends in China, the agreement between UA and China represents a historic business deal that the Chinese government intends to support fully, so there is little risk associated with the investment. In fact, according to her boyfriend, Terry's $48,000 could grow to $112,500 in 10 years if she invests it in UA. If you were Terry, what would you do? Should you invest in a company that might knowingly use child labor, use workers who are abused, or pay bribes to foreign governments?

## Chapter *Essentials*
### —Personal Finance

Following are the general concepts presented in this chapter as they relate to personal financial decisions.

## Valuation

As was mentioned in Chapter 1, an asset's value is based on the future cash flows it is expected to produce (both the amount and the timing) during its life. In this chapter, we introduced the basic techniques used to determine value, which are based on time value of money concepts. You should now be able to determine the value of a stream of cash flows, regardless of whether the stream represents an annuity or an uneven cash flow series. Consider, for example, an investment that promises to pay investors $500 per year for the next four years. If investors demand a 6 percent annual return from this investment, what is its value? (*Answer:* $1,732.55.) We apply this basic technique to value other types of investments later in the book.

## Personal Loans

After reading this chapter, you should be able to determine the characteristics associated with loans that you will acquire in the future—that is, you should be able to compute the monthly (or any other period) payments, amount that needs to be borrowed, or interest rate when given enough information about a loan. For example, suppose your budget indicates that you can afford to make monthly payments equal to $400 to purchase an automobile, and you want to pay off the loan used for the purchase over four years. If the rate on automobile loans is 7 percent, "how much car can you buy"—that is, what is the maximum net purchase price you can afford? (*Answer:* $16,704.) If after three years you decide to pay off the automobile loan early, how much would you need? (*Answer:* $4,623.)

## Retirement Goals

You should now understand that it is important that you begin planning for retirement today. Suppose you have determined that you will need $1.5 million when you retire in 40 years so that you can live the lifestyle you desire after retirement. If your opportunity cost is 8 percent compounded annually, beginning in one year how much will you have to contribute each year to a retirement fund to reach your goal? (*Answer:* $5,790.) If you wait 20 years to start making contributions, how much will you have to invest each year to reach the same retirement goal? (*Answer:* $32,778.) As you can see, depending on when you start contributing to a retirement plan, there is quite a difference in the annual payments required to meet the same retirement goal. This simple example should show you that you should start planning for retirement today. The sooner you start investing for retirement, the sooner you start earning interest, and thus the lower the contributions that are needed to reach your particular retirement goal.

## QUESTIONS

**4-1** What is an *opportunity cost rate*? How is this rate used in time value analysis, and where is it shown on a cash flow time line? Is the opportunity rate a single number that is used in all situations?

**4-2** An *annuity* is defined as a series of payments of a fixed amount for a specific number of periods. Thus, $100 a year for 10 years is an annuity, but $100 in Year 1, $200 in Year 2, and $400 in Years 3 through 10 does *not* constitute an annuity. However, the second series *contains* an annuity. Is this statement true? Explain.

**4-3** If a firm's earnings per share grew from $1 to $2 over a 10-year period, the total *growth* would be 100 percent, but the *annual growth rate* would be *less than* 10 percent. True? Explain. Under what conditions would the annual growth rate *actually* be 10 percent per year?

**4-4** Would you rather have a savings account that pays 5 percent interest compounded semiannually or one that pays 5 percent interest compounded daily? Explain.

**4-5** Give a verbal definition of the term *present value,* and illustrate it using a cash flow time line with data from an example you construct. As a part of your answer, explain why present values are dependent on interest rates.

**4-6** To find the present value of an uneven series of cash flows, you must find the PVs of the individual cash flows and then sum them. Annuity procedures can never be of use, even if some of the cash flows constitute an annuity (for example, $100 each for Years 3, 4, 5, and 6) because the entire series is not an annuity. Is this statement true? Explain.

**4-7**    The present value of a perpetuity is equal to the payment on the annuity, PMT, divided by the interest rate, r: PVP = PMT/r. What is the *sum, or future value,* of a perpetuity of PMT dollars per year? (*Hint:* The answer is infinity, but explain why.)

**4-8**    When financial institutions, such as banks or credit unions, advertise the rates on their loans, they report the APR. If you wanted to compare the interest rates on loans from different financial institutions, should you compare the APRs? Explain.

**4-9**    Under what conditions would the simple interest rate, or APR (remember $r_{SIMPLE}$ = APR) equal the effective annual rate, $r_{EAR}$?

**4-10**    What is an amortized loan? What is an amortization schedule and how is it used?

## SELF-TEST PROBLEMS

*(Solutions appear in Appendix B at the end of the book.)*

key terms    **4-1**    Define each of the following terms:

a. PV; *r*; INT; $FV_n$; n; $PVA_n$; $FVA_n$; PMT

b. Opportunity cost rate

c. Annuity; lump-sum payment; cash flow; uneven cash flow stream

d. Ordinary (deferred) annuity; annuity due

e. Perpetuity; consol

f. Cash outflow; cash inflow; cash flow time line

g. Compounding; discounting

h. Annual, semiannual, quarterly, monthly, and daily compounding

i. m; simple (quoted) interest rate, $r_{SIMPLE}$; APR; effective annual rate, $r_{EAR}$; periodic rate, $r_{PER}$

j. Amortized loan; amortization schedule; principal component versus interest component of a payment

k. Terminal value

rates of return    **4-2**    Suppose you are evaluating two investments, both of which require you to pay $5,500 today. Investment A will pay you $7,020 in five years, whereas Investment B will pay you $8,126 in eight years.

a. Based only on the return you would earn from each investment, which is better?

b. Can you think of any factors other than the expected return that might be important to consider when choosing between the two investment alternatives?

future value    **4-3**    Assume it is now January 1, 2008. On January 1, 2009, you will deposit $1,000 into a savings account that pays 8 percent.

a. If the bank compounds interest annually, how much will you have in your account on January 1, 2012?

b. What would your January 1, 2012, balance be if the bank used quarterly compounding rather than annual compounding?

c. Suppose you deposited the $1,000 in four payments of $250 each on January 1 of 2009, 2010, 2011, and 2012. How much would you have in your account on January 1, 2012, based on 8 percent annual compounding?

**d.** Suppose you deposited four equal payments in your account on January 1 of 2009, 2010, 2011, and 2012. Assuming an 8 percent interest rate, how large would each of your payments have to be for you to obtain the same ending balance as you calculated in part a?

**4-4** Assume it is now January 1, 2008, and you will need $1,000 on January 1, 2012. Your bank compounds interest at an 8 percent annual rate.      **time value of money**

    **a.** How much must you deposit on January 1, 2009, to have a balance of $1,000 on January 1, 2012?

    **b.** If you want to make equal payments on each January 1 from 2009 through 2012 to accumulate the $1,000, how large must each of the four payments be?

    **c.** If your father were to offer either to make the payments calculated in part b ($221.92) or to give you a lump sum of $750 on January 1, 2009, which would you choose?

    **d.** If you have only $750 on January 1, 2009, what interest rate, compounded annually, would you have to earn to have the necessary $1,000 on January 1, 2012?

    **e.** Suppose you can deposit only $186.29 each January 1 from 2009 through 2012, but you still need $1,000 on January 1, 2012. At what interest rate, with annual compounding, must you invest to achieve your goal?

    **f.** To help you reach your $1,000 goal, your father offers to give you $400 on January 1, 2009. You will get a part-time job and make six additional payments of equal amounts each six months thereafter. If all of this money is deposited in a bank that pays 8 percent, compounded semiannually, how large must each of the six payments be?

    **g.** What is the effective annual rate being paid by the bank in part f?

**4-5** Bank A pays 8 percent interest, compounded quarterly, on its money market account. The managers of Bank B want the rate on its money market account to equal Bank A's effective annual rate, but interest is to be compounded on a monthly basis. What simple, or quoted, rate must Bank B set?      **effective annual rates**

## PROBLEMS

**4-1** If you invest $500 today in an account that pays 6 percent interest compounded annually, how much will be in your account after two years?      **FV—lump sum**

**4-2** What is the present value of an investment that promises to pay you $1,000 in five years if you can earn 6 percent interest compounded annually?      **PV—lump sum**

**4-3** What is the present value of $1,552.90 due in 10 years at (a) a 12 percent discount rate and (b) a 6 percent rate?      **PV—different interest rates**

**4-4** To the closest year, how long will it take a $200 investment to double if it earns 7 percent interest? How long will it take if the investment earns 18 percent?      **time to double a lump sum**

**4-5** Which amount is worth more at 14 percent: $1,000 in hand today or $2,000 due in six years?      **TVM comparisons**

**4-6** Martell Corporation's 2008 sales were $12 million. Sales were $6 million five years earlier. To the nearest percentage point, at what rate have sales grown?      **growth rate**

**4-7** Find the future value of the following *ordinary annuities:*      **FV—ordinary annuity**

    **a.** $400 per year for 10 years at 10 percent

    **b.** $200 per year for five years at 5 percent

**FV—annuity due**  **4-8**  Find the future value of the following *annuities due:*

  **a.** $400 per year for 10 years at 10 percent

  **b.** $200 per year for five years at 5 percent

**PV—ordinary annuity**  **4-9**  Find the present value of the following *ordinary annuities:*

  **a.** $400 per year for 10 years at 10 percent

  **b.** $200 per year for five years at 5 percent

**PV—annuity due**  **4-10**  Find the present value of the following *annuities due:*

  **a.** $400 per year for 10 years at 10 percent

  **b.** $200 per year for five years at 5 percent

**perpetuity**  **4-11**  What is the present value of a perpetuity of $100 per year if the appropriate discount rate is 7 percent? If interest rates in general were to double and the appropriate discount rate rose to 14 percent, what would happen to the present value of the perpetuity?

**PV—uneven cash flow stream**  **4-12**  Find the *present values* of the following cash flow streams under the following conditions:

| Year | Cash Stream A | Cash Stream B |
|------|---------------|---------------|
| 1 | $100 | $300 |
| 2 | 400 | 400 |
| 3 | 400 | 400 |
| 4 | 300 | 100 |

  **a.** The appropriate interest rate is 8 percent.

  **b.** What is the value of each cash flow stream at a zero percent interest rate?

**FV—lump sum, various compounding periods**  **4-13**  Find the amount to which $500 will grow in five years under each of the following conditions:

  **a.** 12 percent compounded annually

  **b.** 12 percent compounded semiannually

  **c.** 12 percent compounded quarterly

  **d.** 12 percent compounded monthly

**PV—lump sum, various compounding periods**  **4-14**  Find the present value of $500 due in five years under each of the following conditions:

  **a.** 12 percent simple rate, compounded annually

  **b.** 12 percent simple rate, compounded semiannually

  **c.** 12 percent simple rate, compounded quarterly

  **d.** 12 percent simple rate, compounded monthly

**FV—ordinary annuity, various compounding periods**  **4-15**  Find the future values of the following *ordinary* annuities:

  **a.** FV of $400 each six months for five years at a simple rate of 12 percent, compounded semiannually

  **b.** FV of $200 each three months for five years at a simple rate of 12 percent, compounded quarterly

  **c.** The annuities described in parts a and b have the same amount of money paid into them during the five-year period and both earn interest at the same simple rate, yet the annuity in part b earns $101.75 more than the one in part a over the five years. Why does this occur?

**4-16**   Find the present values of the following *ordinary* annuities:

    **a.** FV of $400 each six months for five years at a simple rate of 12 percent, compounded semiannually

    **b.** FV of $200 each three months for five years at a simple rate of 12 percent, compounded quarterly

    **c.** The annuities described in parts a and b have the same amount of money paid into them during the five-year period and both earn interest at the same simple rate, yet the present value of the annuity in part b is $31.46 greater than the one in part a. Why does this occur?

PV—ordinary annuity, various compounding periods

**4-17**   To complete your last year in business school and then go through law school, you will need $10,000 per year for four years, starting next year (that is, you will need to withdraw the first $10,000 one year from today). Your rich uncle offers to put you through school, and he will deposit a sum of money in a bank paying 7 percent interest. The sum is sufficient to provide the four payments of $10,000 each, and his deposit will be made today.

    **a.** How large must the deposit be?

    **b.** How much will be in the account immediately after you make the first withdrawal? After the last withdrawal?

required lump-sum payment

**4-18**   Sue wants to buy a car that costs $12,000. She has arranged to borrow the total purchase price of the car from her credit union at a simple interest rate equal to 12 percent. The loan requires quarterly payments for a period of three years. If the first payment is due three months (one quarter) after purchasing the car, what will be the amount of Sue's quarterly payments on the loan?

PMT—loan payments

**4-19**   While Steve Bouchard was a student at the University of Florida, he borrowed $12,000 in student loans at an annual interest rate of 9 percent. If Steve repays $1,500 per year, how long, to the nearest year, will it take him to repay the loan?

repaying a loan, n

**4-20**   You need to accumulate $10,000. To do so, you plan to make deposits of $1,750 per year, with the first payment being made one year from today, in a bank account that pays 6 percent annual interest. Your last deposit will be more than $1,750 if more is needed to round out to $10,000. How many years will it take you to reach your $10,000 goal, and how large will the last deposit be?

reaching a financial goal

**4-21**   Jack just discovered that he holds the winning ticket for the $87 million mega lottery in Missouri. Now he needs to decide which alternative to choose: (1) a $44 million lump-sum payment today or (2) a payment of $2.9 million per year for 30 years; the first payment will be made today. If Jack's opportunity cost is 5 percent, which alternative should he choose?

TVM comparisons—lottery winner

**4-22**   At the beginning of Chapter 1, we presented the following situation: "Consider the decision you might have to make if you won a state lottery worth $105 million. Which *would* you choose, a lump-sum payment of $54 million today or a payment of $3.5 million each year for the next 30 years? Which *should* you choose?" You should now be able to answer these questions.

    **a.** If your opportunity cost is 6 percent, which alternative should you select?

    **b.** At what opportunity cost would you be indifferent between the two alternatives?

TVM comparisons—lottery winner

**4-23**   Find the interest rates, or rates of return, on each of the following:

    **a.** You *borrow* $700 and promise to pay back $749 at the end of one year.

    **b.** You *lend* $700 and receive a promise to be paid $749 at the end of one year.

effective interest rate, $r_{EAR}$

     **c.** You borrow $85,000 and promise to pay back $201,229 at the end of 10 years.

     **d.** You borrow $9,000 and promise to make payments of $2,684.80 per year for five years.

**$r_{EAR}$ versus $r_{SIMPLE}$**    **4-24** The First City Bank pays 7 percent interest, compounded annually, on time deposits. The Second City Bank pays 6.5 percent interest, compounded quarterly.

     **a.** Based on effective interest rates, in which bank would you prefer to deposit your money?

     **b.** Assume that funds must be left on deposit during the entire compounding period to receive any interest. Could your choice of banks be influenced by the fact that you might want to withdraw your funds during the year rather than at the end of the year?

**$r_{EAR}$ and $r_{SIMPLE}$**    **4-25** Krystal Magee invested $150,000 18 months ago. Currently, the investment is worth $168,925. Krystal knows the investment has paid interest every three months (i.e., quarterly), but she doesn't know what the yield on her investment is. Help Krystal. Compute both the annual percentage rate (APR), $r_{SIMPLE}$, *and* the effective annual rate (EAR) of interest, $r_{EAR}$.

**effective rate of return**    **4-26** Your broker offers to sell you a note for $13,250 that will pay $2,345.05 per year for 10 years. If you buy the note, what rate of interest (to the closest percent) will you be earning?

**EAR, $r_{EAR}$**    **4-27** A mortgage company offers to lend you $85,000; the loan calls for payments of $8,273.59 per year for 30 years. What is the effective annual interest rate, $r_{EAR}$, that the mortgage company is charging you?

**loan evaluation—mortgage**    **4-28** Suppose you found a house that you want to buy, but you still have to determine what mortgage to use. Bank of Middle Texas has offered a 30-year fixed mortgage that requires you to pay 8 percent interest compounded monthly. If you take this offer, you will have to pay "3 points," which means you will have to make a payment equal to 3 percent of the amount borrowed at the time you sign the mortgage agreement. Bank of South Alaska has offered a 30-year fixed mortgage with no points but at an interest rate equal to 8.4 percent compounded monthly. For either mortgage, the first payment would not be made until one month after the mortgage agreement is signed. The purchase price of the house is $250,000, and you plan to make a down payment equal to $40,000.

     **a.** If you make a down payment equal to $40,000 and borrow the rest of the purchase price of the house from Bank of Middle Texas, how much will you have to pay for the "3 points" when you sign the mortgage agreement?

     **b.** Assume that the points charged by Bank of Middle Texas can simply be added to the mortgaged amount so that the total amount borrowed from the bank includes the points that must be paid at the time the mortgage is signed plus the net purchase price of the house (purchase price less the down payment). For example, the points that apply to a $100,000 mortgage would be $2,000, so the mortgage amount would be $102,000. Which bank offers the lower monthly payments?

     **c.** What would the points on the Bank of Middle Texas mortgage have to equal for you to be indifferent between the two mortgages?

**loan amortization**    **4-29** Assume that your aunt sold her house on January 1 and that she took a mortgage in the amount of $10,000 as part of the payment. The mortgage has a quoted (or simple) interest rate of 10 percent, but it calls for payments every six months, beginning on June 30, and the mortgage is to be amortized over 10 years. Now, one year later, your aunt must file a Form 1099 with the IRS and with the person who bought the house, informing them of the interest that was included in the two payments made during the year. (This interest will be income to your aunt and a deduction to the buyer of the house.) To the closest dollar, what is the total amount of interest that was paid during the first year?

**4-30** Lorkay Seidens Inc. just borrowed $25,000. The loan is to be repaid in equal installments at the end of each of the next five years, and the interest rate is 10 percent.

**amortization schedule**

    **a.** Set up an amortization schedule for the loan.

    **b.** How large must each annual payment be if the loan is for $50,000? Assume that the interest rate remains at 10 percent and that the loan is paid off over five years.

    **c.** How large must each payment be if the loan is for $50,000, the interest rate is 10 percent, and the loan is paid off in equal installments at the end of each of the next 10 years? This loan is for the same amount as the loan in part b, but the payments are spread out over twice as many periods. Why are these payments not half as large as the payments on the loan in part b?

**4-31** Assume that AT&T's pension fund managers are considering two alternative securities as investments: (1) Security Z (for zero intermediate year cash flows), which costs $422.41 today, pays nothing during its 10-year life, and then pays $1,000 at the end of 10 years, or (2) Security B, which has a cost today of $500 and pays $74.50 at the end of each of the next 10 years.

**effective rates of return**

    **a.** What is the rate of return on each security?

    **b.** Assume that the interest rate AT&T's pension fund managers can earn on the fund's money falls to 6 percent immediately after the securities are purchased and is expected to remain at that level for the next 10 years. What would be the price of each security after the change in the interest rate?

    **c.** Now assume that the interest rate rose to 12 percent (rather than fell to 6 percent) immediately after the securities are purchased. What would be the price of each security after the change in the interest rate? Explain the results.

**4-32** Jason worked various jobs during his teenage years to save money for college. Now it is his 20th birthday, and he is about to begin his college studies at the University of South Florida (USF). A few months ago, Jason received a scholarship that will cover all of his college tuition for a period not to exceed five years. The money he has saved will be used for living expenses while he is in college; in fact, Jason expects to use all of his savings while attending USF. The jobs he worked as a teenager allowed him to save a total of $10,000, which currently is invested at 12 percent in a financial asset that pays interest monthly. Because Jason will be a full-time student, he expects to graduate four years from today, on his 24th birthday.

**PMT—ordinary annuity versus annuity due**

    **a.** How much can Jason withdraw every month while he is in college if the first withdrawal occurs today?

    **b.** How much can Jason withdraw every month while he is in college if he waits until the end of this month to make the first withdrawal?

**4-33** Sue Sharpe, manager of Oaks Mall Jewelry, wants to sell on credit, giving customers three months in which to pay. However, Sue will have to borrow from her bank to carry the accounts payable. The bank will charge a simple

**r$_{SIMPLE}$, simple interest rate**

15 percent, but with monthly compounding. Sue wants to quote a simple rate to her customers (all of whom are expected to pay on time) that will exactly cover her financing costs. What simple annual rate should she quote to her credit customers?

**loan repayment— credit card**

**4-34**   Brandi just received her credit card bill, which has an outstanding balance equal to $3,310. After reviewing her financial position, Brandi has concluded that she cannot pay the outstanding balance in full; rather, she has to make payments over time to repay the credit card bill. After thinking about it, Brandi decided to cut up her credit card. Now she wants to determine how long it will take to pay off the outstanding balance. The credit card carries an 18 percent interest rate, which is compounded monthly. The minimum payment that Brandi must make each month is $25. Assume that the only charge Brandi incurs from month to month is the interest that must be paid on the remaining outstanding balance. Brandi plans to mail a payment tomorrow.

**a.** If Brandi pays $150 each month, how long will it take her to pay off the credit card bill?

**b.** If Brandi pays $222 each month, how long will it take her to pay off the credit card bill?

**c.** If Brandi pays $360 each month, how long will it take her to pay off the credit card bill?

**loan repayment—student loan**

**4-35**   Brandon just graduated from college. Unfortunately, Brandon's education was fairly costly; the student loans he took out to pay for his education total $95,000. The provisions of the student loans require Brandon to pay interest equal to the prime rate, which is 8 percent, plus a 1 percent margin—that is, the interest rate on the loans is 9 percent. Payments will be made monthly, and the loans must be repaid within 20 years. Brandon wants to determine how he is going to repay his student loans. His first payment is due in one month.

**a.** If Brandon decides to repay the loans over the maximum period—that is, 20 years—how much must he pay each month?

**b.** If Brandon wants to repay the loans in 10 years, how much must he pay each month?

**c.** If Brandon pays $985 per month, how long will it take him to repay the loans?

**financing alternatives— automobile loans**

**4-36**   Assume you are going to purchase a new car. You have already applied and been accepted for an automobile loan through your local credit union. The loan can be for an amount up to $25,000, depending on the final price of the car you choose. The terms of the loan call for monthly payments for a period of four years at a stated interest rate equal to 6 percent. After selecting the car you want, you negotiate with the sales representative and agree on a purchase price of $24,000, which does not include any rebates or incentives. The rebate on the car you chose is $3,000. The dealer offers "0% financing," but you forfeit the $3,000 rebate if you take the "0% financing."

**a.** What are the monthly payments you will have to make if you take the "0% financing"? (*Hint:* Because there is no interest, the total amount that has to be repaid is $24,000, which also equals the sum of all the payments.)

**b.** What are the monthly payments if you finance the car with the credit union loan?

**c.** Should you use the "0% financing" loan or the credit union loan to finance the car?

**d.** Assume it is one year later, and you have decided to repay the amount you owe on the automobile loan. How much must you repay if you chose the dealer's "0% financing"? The credit union loan?

**4-37** A father is planning a savings program to put his daughter through college. His daughter is now 13 years old. She plans to enroll at the university in five years, and it should take her four years to complete her education. Currently, the cost per year (for everything—food, clothing, tuition, books, transportation, and so forth) is $12,500, but these costs are expected to increase by 5 percent—the inflation rate—each year. The daughter recently received $7,500 from her grandfather's estate; this money, which was invested in a mutual fund that pays 8 percent interest compounded annually, will be used to help meet the costs of the daughter's education. The rest of the costs will be met by money that the father will deposit in a savings account. He will make equal deposits to the account in each year beginning today until his daughter starts college—that is, he will make a total of six deposits. These deposits will also earn 8 percent interest.

*reaching a financial goal—saving for college*

**a.** What will be the present value of the cost of four years of education *at the time the daughter turns 18*? (*Hint:* Calculate the cost [at 5 percent inflation, or growth] for each year of her education, discount three of these costs back [at 8 percent] to the year in which she turns 18, then sum the four costs, which include the cost of the first year.)

**b.** What will be the value of the $7,500 that the daughter received from her grandfather's estate *when she starts college at age 18*? (*Hint:* Compound for five years at 8 percent.)

**c.** If the father is planning to make the first of six deposits today, how large must each deposit be for him to be able to put his daughter through college? (*Hint:* Be sure to draw a cash flow time line to depict the timing of the cash flows.)

**4-38** As soon as she graduated from college, Kay began planning for her retirement. Her plans were to deposit $500 semiannually into an IRA (a retirement fund) beginning six months after graduation and continuing until the day she retired, which she expected to be 30 years later. Today is the day Kay retires. She just made the last $500 deposit into her retirement fund, and now she wants to know how much she has accumulated for her retirement. The fund has earned 10 percent compounded semiannually since it was established.

*reaching a financial goal—saving for retirement*

**a.** Compute the balance of the retirement fund assuming all the payments were made on time.

**b.** Although Kay was able to make all the $500 deposits she planned, 10 years ago she had to withdraw $10,000 from the fund to pay some medical bills incurred by her mother. Compute the balance in the retirement fund based on this information.

**4-39** Sarah is on her way to the local Chevrolet dealership to buy a new car. The list, or "sticker," price of the car is $13,000. Sarah has $3,000 in her checking account that she can use as a down payment toward the purchase of a new car. Sarah has carefully evaluated her finances, and she has determined that she can afford payments that *total* $2,400 per year on a loan to purchase the car. Sarah can borrow the money to purchase the car either through the dealer's "special financing package," which is advertised as 4.0 percent financing, or from a local bank, which has automobile loans at 12 percent interest. Each loan would be outstanding for a period of five years, and the payments would be made

*automobile loan computation*

quarterly (every three months). Sarah knows the dealer's "special financing package" requires that she will have to pay the "sticker" price for the car. But if she uses the bank financing, she thinks she can negotiate with the dealer for a better price. Assume Sarah wants to pay $600 per payment regardless of which loan she chooses, and the remainder of the purchase price will be a down payment that can be satisfied with any of the $3,000 in Sarah's checking account. Ignoring charges for taxes, tag, and title transfer, how much of a reduction in the "sticker price" must Sarah negotiate to make the bank financing more attractive than the dealer's "special financing package"?

**PMT—retirement plan**   **4-40**   Janet just graduated from a women's college in Mississippi with a degree in business administration, and she is about to start a new job with a large financial services firm based in Tampa, Florida. From reading various business publications while she was in college, Janet has concluded it probably is a good idea to begin planning for her retirement now. Even though she is only 22 years old and just beginning her career, Janet is concerned that Social Security will not be able to meet her needs when she retires. Fortunately for Janet, the company that hired her has a good retirement/investment plan that permits her to make contributions every year. So Janet is now evaluating the amount she needs to contribute to satisfy her financial requirements at retirement. She has decided that she would like to take a trip as soon as her retirement begins (a reward to herself for many years of excellent work). The estimated cost of the trip, including all expenses such as meals and souvenirs, will be $120,000, and it will last for one year (no other funds will be needed during the first year of retirement). After she returns from her trip, Janet plans to settle down to enjoy her retirement. She estimates she will need $70,000 each year to be able to live comfortably and enjoy her "twilight years." The retirement/investment plan available to employees where Janet is going to work pays 7 percent interest compounded annually, and it is expected this rate will continue as long as the company offers the opportunity to contribute to the fund. When she retires, Janet will have to move her retirement "nest egg" to another investment so she can withdraw money when she needs it. Her plans are to move the money to a fund that allows withdrawals at the beginning of each year; the fund is expected to pay 5 percent interest compounded annually. Janet expects to retire in 40 years, and, after looking at the life insurance actuarial tables, she has determined that she will live another 20 years after she returns from her "retirement trip" around the world. If Janet's expectations are correct, how much must she contribute to the retirement fund to satisfy her retirement plans if she plans to make her first contribution to the fund one year from today, and the last contribution will be made on the day she retires?

### Integrative Problem

**TVM analysis**   **4-41**   Assume that you are nearing graduation and that you have applied for a job with a local bank. As part of the bank's evaluation process, you have been asked to take an examination that covers several financial analysis techniques. The first section of the test addresses TVM analysis. See how you would do by answering the following questions:

   **a.** Draw cash flow time lines for (1) a $100 lump-sum cash flow at the end of Year 2, (2) an ordinary annuity of $100 per year for three years, (3) an uneven cash flow stream of −$50, $100, $75, and $50 at the end of Years 0 through 3.

**b. (1)** What is the future value of an initial $100 after three years if it is invested in an account paying 10 percent annual interest?

**(2)** What is the present value of $100 to be received in three years if the appropriate interest rate is 10 percent?

**c.** We sometimes need to find how long it will take a sum of money (or anything else) to grow to some specified amount. For example, if a company's sales are growing at a rate of 20 percent per year, approximately how long will it take sales to triple?

**d.** What is the difference between an ordinary annuity and an annuity due? What type of annuity is shown in the following cash flow time line? How would you change it to the other type of annuity?

**e. (1)** What is the future value of a three-year ordinary annuity of $100 if the appropriate interest rate is 10 percent?

**(2)** What is the present value of the annuity?

**(3)** What would the future and present values be if the annuity were an annuity due?

**f.** What is the present value of the following uneven cash flow stream? The appropriate interest rate is 10 percent, compounded annually.

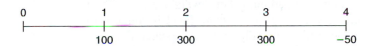

**g.** What annual interest rate will cause $100 to grow to $125.97 in three years?

**h. (1)** Will the future value be larger or smaller if we compound an initial amount more often than annually—for example, every six months, or semiannually—holding the stated interest rate constant? Why?

**(2)** Define the stated, or quoted, or simple, rate, ($r_{SIMPLE}$), annual percentage rate (APR), the periodic rate ($r_{PER}$), and the effective annual rate ($r_{EAR}$).

**(3)** What is the effective annual rate for a simple rate of 10 percent, compounded semiannually? Compounded quarterly? Compounded daily?

**(4)** What is the future value of $100 after three years with 10 percent semiannual compounding? Quarterly compounding?

**i.** Will the effective annual rate ever be equal to the simple (quoted) rate? Explain.

**j. (1)** What is the value at the end of Year 3 of the following cash flow stream if the quoted interest rate is 10 percent, compounded semiannually?

(2) What is the PV of the same stream?

(3) Is the stream an annuity?

(4) An important rule is that you should never show a simple rate on a time line or use it in calculations unless what condition holds? (*Hint:* Think of annual compounding, when $r_{SIMPLE} = r_{EAR} = r_{PER}$.) What would be wrong with your answer to parts (1) and (2) if you used the simple rate 10 percent rather than the periodic rate $r_{SIMPLE}/2 = 10\%/2 = 5\%$?

**k. (1)** Construct an amortization schedule for a $1,000 loan that has a 10 percent annual interest rate that is repaid in three equal install-ments.

**(2)** What is the annual interest expense for the borrower, and the annual interest income for the lender, during Year 2?

**l.** Suppose on January 1 you deposit $100 in an account that pays a simple, or quoted, interest rate of 11.33463 percent, with interest added (com-pounded) daily. How much will you have in your account on October 1, or after nine months?

**m.** Now suppose you leave your money in the bank for 21 months. Thus, on January 1 you deposit $100 in an account that pays 11.33463 percent compounded daily. How much will be in your account on October 1 of the following year?

**n.** Suppose someone offered to sell you a note that calls for a $1,000 payment 15 months from today. The person offers to sell the note for $850. You have $850 in a bank time deposit (savings instrument) that pays a 6.76649 percent simple rate with daily compounding, which is a 7 percent effective annual interest rate; and you plan to leave this money in the bank unless you buy the note. The note is not risky—that is, you are sure it will be paid on schedule. Should you buy the note? Check the decision in three ways: (1) by comparing your future value if you buy the note versus leaving your money in the bank, (2) by comparing the PV of the note with your current bank investment, and (3) by comparing the $r_{EAR}$ on the note with that of the bank investment.

**o.** Suppose the note discussed in part n costs $850 but calls for five quarterly payments of $190 each, with the first payment due in three months rather than $1,000 at the end of 15 months. Would it be a good investment?

## Computer-Related Problem

*Work the problem in this section only if you are using the problem spreadsheet*

amortization schedule    **4-42**   Use the computerized model in the File C04 to solve this problem.

**a.** Set up an amortization schedule for a $30,000 loan to be repaid in equal installments at the end of each of the next 20 years at an interest rate of 10 percent. What is the annual payment?

**b.** Set up an amortization schedule for a $60,000 loan to be repaid in 20 equal annual installments at an interest rate of 10 percent. What is the annual payment?

**c.** Set up an amortization schedule for a $60,000 loan to be repaid in 20 equal annual installments at an interest rate of 20 percent. What is the annual payment?

**4-43**  Starbucks Corporation [SBUX] does much more than make great latte. The company purchases, roasts, and markets coffee beans. Starbucks also sells such products as premium teas and coffee-related accessories through its retail stores. Imagine you are one of Starbucks' shareholders and you would like to estimate how much the stock will earn per share over the next three years. Using the Thomson ONE database, find the earnings estimates for Starbucks Corporation for the next three years, and then answer the following questions:

**a.** Calculate the present value of the mixed stream of cash flows you pulled from the database. Assume you own one share of the stock. In this case, the cash flows are the earnings per share (EPS) estimates, and the interest rate is 3 percent. (*Hint:* Click on the Estimates tab for SBUX to get the estimates.)

**b.** What is the present value of the cash flows if you own 100 shares of Starbucks stock?

**c.** If you own 100 shares of Starbucks stock and you want to hold the stock only if you expect to earn more than $3 in earnings per share over a three-year period, would you buy more of the stock or sell the shares you already own?

**d.** Calculate the present value of the cash flows if the interest rate rises to 5 percent.

**e.** Why does the present value change when the interest rate rises?

# Generating an Amortization Schedule—Financial Calculator Solution and Spreadsheet Solution

**APPENDIX 4A**

The amortization schedule shown in Table 4-1 was generated using a regular calculator to compute each value. Although there is nothing wrong with this procedure, it can be tedious and time consuming when there are numerous installment payments. Therefore, in this section, we show you how to generate an amortization schedule using both a financial calculator and a spreadsheet.

In the chapter, we assumed that a firm borrows $15,000, and the loan is to be repaid in equal payments at the end of each of the next three years. The interest on the loan is 8 percent. To set up the amortization schedule for this situation, we first determined the amount of the payment the firm must make each year. Using either a financial calculator or a spreadsheet, we found that the annual payment must be $5,820.50.

## FINANCIAL CALCULATOR SOLUTION

The following steps show you how to generate an amortization schedule using a Texas Instruments BAII PLUS. For more information or if you have a different type of calculator, refer to the manual that came with your calculator.

**1.** Enter the information for the amortized loan into the TVM registers as described in the chapter:

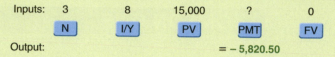

| Inputs: | 3 | 8 | 15,000 | ? | 0 |
|---------|---|---|--------|---|---|
|         | N | I/Y | PV | PMT | FV |

Output:                                            = − 5,820.50

2. Enter the amortization function by pressing 2nd PV, which has "Amort" written above it (a secondary function). P1 = 1 is displayed, which indicates that the starting point for the amortization schedule is the first period. Press ↓, and P2 = 1 is displayed, which indicates the ending point for the first set of computations is the first period.

3.  a. Press ↓, and BAL = 10,379.49729 is displayed. This result indicates that the remaining principal balance at the end of the first year is $10,379.50.

    b. Press ↓, and PRN = −4,620.502711 is displayed, which indicates that the amount of principal repaid in the first period is $4,620.50.

    c. Press ↓, and INT = −1,200 is displayed, which indicates that the amount of interest paid in the first period is $1,200.

4. Press ↓ CPT, and P1 = 2 is displayed. Next, press ↓, and P2 = 2 is displayed. This information indicates that the next series of computations relates to the second payment. Follow the procedures given in Step 3:

    a. Press ↓; display shows BAL = 5,389.354362

    b. Press ↓; display shows PRN = −4,990.142928

    c. Press ↓; display shows INT = −830.3597831

These values represent the ending loan balance, the amount of principal repaid, and the amount of interest paid, respectively, for the second year.

5. Press ↓ CPT, and P1 = 3 is displayed; then press ↓, and P2 = 3 is displayed. This information indicates that the next series of computations relates to the third payment. Follow the procedures given in Step 3:

    a. Press ↓; display shows BAL = −0.000000

    b. Press ↓; display shows PRN = −5,389.354362

    c. Press ↓; display shows INT = −431.1483489

These values represent the ending loan balance, the amount of principal repaid, and the amount of interest paid, respectively, for the third, and final, year.

If you combine the results from Steps 3 through 5 in a table, you would find that it contains the same values given in Table 4. If you use a calculator to construct a complete amortization schedule, you must repeat Step 3 for each year the loan exists—that is, Step 3 must be repeated 10 times for a 10-year loan. If you would like to know either the balance, principal repayment, or interest paid in a particular year, you need only set P1 and P2 equal to that particular year to display the desired values.

## SPREADSHEET SOLUTION

To set up the amortization schedule using Excel, we use two financial functions: IPMT and PPMT. IPMT gives the interest payment for a particular period, given the amount borrowed and the interest rate. PPMT gives the principal repayment for a particular period, given the amount borrowed and the interest rate. The following spreadsheet shows the content of each cell to construct an amortization schedule for our illustrative loan:

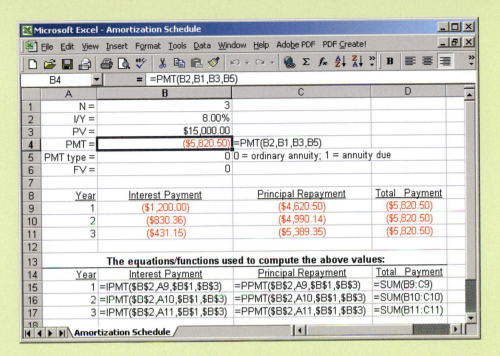

Note that the $ sign is used when referring to cells in the equations to fix the locations of the cells that contain common values required for each computation. Fixing the cell locations allows you to use the copy command to copy the relationships from row 9 to rows 10 and 11.

# PART 3

# Valuation—Financial Assets

# The Cost of Money (Interest Rates)

During the period from 2000 through 2004—that is, the beginning of the twenty-first century—for the most part, interest rates trended downward. For example, at the beginning of 2000, the rates on three-month Treasury bills and 20-year Treasury bonds were 5.4 percent and 6.7 percent, respectively. At the beginning of 2002, the rates on the same investments had dropped to 1.7 percent and 5.8 percent, respectively. And at the beginning of 2004, the rates had dropped further to 0.9 percent and 5.0 percent, respectively. One reason rates decreased during this period was the recession the U.S. economy experienced during 2001. In the years following the recession, the "investment" confidence of businesses and individuals was fairly low, so there was not much demand for funds to finance such investments as new growth in business or replacement of worn-out assets. Because rates were considered "too low," the Federal Reserve decided to increase rates. From July through December 2004, the Fed increased interest rates six times, such that the rate on three-month Treasury bills climbed to 2.4 percent. Fearing excessive economic growth and to control inflation, the Fed continued to increase interest rates throughout 2005 and during the first six months of 2006. At the time of this writing (July 2006), the rate on three-month Treasury bills was 4.9 percent and the rate on 20-year Treasury bonds was 5.3 percent. This suggests that the Fed's actions were more successful on short-term interest rates, which more than doubled since 2004, than on long-term interest rates, which increased less than 0.5 percent.

Other factors that affected market rates at the beginning of the twenty-first century included the "beating" technology stocks took in the stock markets, which resulted in a significant loss of value in the technology industry; uncertainty generated by news that a global economic crisis was imminent; and disclosures that the executives of some large U.S. firms approved the use of, or ignored, unethical accounting practices their firms were using to "cook the books." These factors resulted in investors losing confidence in the financial markets, and thus withdrawing their funds to what they considered safer havens, such as certificates of deposit and savings accounts at banks and savings and loan associations.

When the economy slipped into the 2001 recession and financial markets faltered, companies slowed expansion and borrowed less. To encourage a reversal of this trend and to attempt to prop up a declining economy, the Federal Reserve cut interest rates. The actions of the Fed and investors decreased interest rates to their lowest levels in 45 years in 2002 and 2003. Although the low interest rates were not attractive to investors, borrowers found the low rates very attractive. During this period, many borrowers—both individuals and businesses—refinanced their outstanding loans to reduce their interest costs. The increased demand for funds resulted in a moderate increase in interest rates from 2000–2006.

As companies become more confident that consumer demand will return to "normal," they will borrow additional amounts to replace deteriorating assets that probably should have been replaced years earlier. Clearly, the behavior of participants in the financial markets—businesses and individuals—is based on expectations about future interest rates. When rates are low, investors have little incentive to purchase stocks and bonds, but borrowers demand more loans, and vice versa.

Whether a business or an individual, when we borrow we would like interest rates to be low. When rates are low, as they were in 2002 and 2003, many firms and individuals refinance to replace higher-interest debt with lower-interest debt. But when interest rates are low, those who depend on the income from their investments suffer. It is a fact that interest rates affect all of us. Thus, as you read this chapter, think about (1) all the factors the Fed must consider before attempting to change interest rates and (2) the effects of interest rate changes on inflation, on the financial markets, on you as an individual (student), and on the economy as a whole.

## Chapter *Essentials*
### —The Questions

After reading this chapter, you should be able to answer the following questions:

- What is the cost of money, and how is it determined?
- What factors affect interest rates (costs of money)?
- What is a yield curve? Does the yield curve indicate future interest rates?
- How do government actions and business activity affect interest rates?
- How does the level of interest rates (returns) affect the values of stocks and bonds?

In Chapter 3, we stated that the primary role of the financial markets is to help bring together *borrowers* and *lenders* by facilitating the flow of funds from those who have surplus funds (investors) to those who need funds in excess of their current incomes (borrowers).[1] In a free economy such as that of the United States, the excess funds of lenders are allocated to borrowers in the financial markets through a pricing system that is based on the supply of, and the demand for, funds. This system is represented by interest rates, or the cost of money, such that those borrowers who are willing to pay the rates that prevail in the financial markets are able to use funds provided by others. This chapter describes the basic concepts associated with interest rates, including factors that affect rates (returns) and methods for forecasting them.

## REALIZED RETURNS (YIELDS)

Before analyzing the factors that affect interest rates, it will be helpful to understand how investors earn returns when providing (supplying) funds to borrowers. Whether the investment instrument is debt or equity, the dollar return earned by an investor can be divided into two categories: (1) income paid by the *issuer* of the financial asset and (2) the change in value of the financial asset in the financial market (capital gains) over some time period. Thus the dollar return on a financial asset can be stated as follows:

5–1

$$\text{Dollar return} = (\text{Dollar income}) + (\text{Capital gains})$$
$$= (\text{Dollar income}) + (\text{Ending value} - \text{Beginning value})$$

---

[1] Recall from Chapter 3 that savers (investors) and borrowers (issuers of financial assets) can be individuals, firms, and government units.

Here "Beginning value" represents the market value of the investment at the beginning of the period and "Ending value" represents its market value at the end of the period.

If the financial asset is debt, the income from the investment consists of the *interest paid* by the borrower. If the financial asset is equity, the income from the investment is the *dividend paid* by a corporation. Also, note that the amount of the capital gains can be negative if the value of the financial asset decreases during the period it is held.

To determine an investment's yield, we state the dollar return as a percentage of the dollar amount that was originally invested. Thus, the yield is computed as follows:

**5–2**

$$\text{Yield} = \frac{\text{Dollar return}}{\text{Beginning value}} = \frac{\text{Dollar income} + \text{Capital gains}}{\text{Beginning value}}$$

$$= \frac{\text{Dollar income} + (\text{Ending value} - \text{Beginning value})}{\text{Beginning value}}$$

To illustrate the concept of yield, consider the return that you would earn if you purchased a corporate bond on January 1, 2008 for $980.00 and sold it on December 31, 2008 for $990.25. If the bond paid $100.00 interest on December 31, 2008, the total dollar return on your investment would be $110.25; this amount includes $100.00 in interest income and $10.25 = $990.25 − $980.00 in capital gains. Thus the one-year yield, or percent return, would be

$$\text{Yield (\% return)} = \frac{\$100.00 + \$10.25}{\$980.00} = \frac{\$110.25}{\$980.00} = 0.1125 = 11.25\%$$

In this example, investors who purchased the bond at the beginning of 2008 and held it until the end of 2008 would have earned a one-year holding period return of 11.25 percent. If we assume that this is the same return that investors expected to earn when they purchased the bond at the beginning of the year, then this yield represents the average rate of return that investors required to provide their funds to the company that issued the bond. In this case, the "cost of money" for such a corporation was essentially 11.25 percent in 2008 because investors demanded the equivalent of a $110.25 return to invest $980.[2] In the remainder of the chapter, we discuss factors that determine the cost of money and examine what causes the cost of money to change.

## Self-Test Questions

What are the two sources of the dollar return associated with an investment?

How is the yield on an investment computed?

## FACTORS THAT AFFECT THE COST OF MONEY

Four fundamental factors affect the cost of money: (1) *production opportunities*, (2) *time preferences for consumption*, (3) *risk*, and (4) *inflation*. To see how these factors operate, imagine an isolated island community where the people survive by

---

[2]If we look at the same firm's stock, we would expect the yield, or "cost," to be different because stock has a different risk than debt (bonds). The effects of risk on return will be discussed in detail in Chapter 8.

eating fish. They have a stock of fishing gear that permits them to live reasonably well, but they would like to have more fish. Now suppose Mr. Crusoe has a bright idea for a new type of fishnet that would enable him to increase his daily catch substantially. It would take him a year to perfect his design, build his net, and learn how to use it efficiently. Mr. Crusoe probably would starve before he could put his new net into operation. Recognizing this problem, he might suggest to Ms. Robinson, Mr. Friday, and several others that if they would give him one fish each day for one year, he would return two fish per day during all of the next year. If someone accepted the offer, then the fish that Ms. Robinson or one of the others gave to Mr. Crusoe would constitute *savings*, these savings would be *invested* in the fishnet, and the extra fish the net produced would constitute a *return on the investment.*

**production opportunities**
The returns available within an economy from investment in productive (cash-generating) assets.

Obviously, the more productive Mr. Crusoe thought the new fishnet would be— that is, the higher the **production opportunity**—the higher his expected return on the investment would be, and the more he could afford to offer potential investors for their savings. In this example, we assume that Mr. Crusoe thinks he will be able to pay, and thus has offered, a 100 percent rate of return; he has offered to give back two fish for every one he receives. He might have tried to attract savings for less—say, 1.5 fish next year for every one he receives this year.

**time preferences for consumption**
The preferences of consumers for current consumption as opposed to saving for future consumption.

The attractiveness of Mr. Crusoe's offer for a potential saver would depend in large part on the saver's **time preference for consumption.** For example, Ms. Robinson might be thinking of retirement, and she might be willing to trade fish today for fish in the future on a one-for-one basis. Mr. Friday might be unwilling to "lend" a fish today for anything less than three fish next year because he has a wife and several young children to feed with his current fish. Mr. Friday is said to have a high time preference for consumption, whereas Ms. Robinson has a low time preference for consumption. Note also that if the entire population is living at the subsistence level, time preferences for current consumption would necessarily be high, aggregate savings would be low, interest rates would be high, and capital formation would be difficult.

**risk**
In a financial market context, the chance that a financial asset will not earn the return promised.

The **risk** inherent in the fishnet project, and thus in Mr. Crusoe's ability to repay the loan, also affects the return required by investors: The higher the perceived risk, the higher the required rate of return. For example, if Mr. Crusoe has a history of not always following through with his ideas, Ms. Robinson, Mr. Friday, and others who are interested in Mr. Crusoe's new fishnet would consider investment to be fairly risky, and thus they might provide Mr. Crusoe with one fish per day this year only if he promises to return four fish per day next year. Also, a more complex society includes many businesses like Mr. Crusoe's, many goods other than fish, and many savers like Ms. Robinson and Mr. Friday. Furthermore, people use money as a medium of exchange rather than barter with fish. When the society uses money, the value of money in the future, which is affected by inflation, comes into play. That is, the higher the expected rate of **inflation,** the greater the required return.

**inflation**
The tendency of prices to increase over time.

*This simple illustration shows that the interest rate paid to savers depends in a basic way on (1) the rate of return that producers expect to earn on their invested capital, (2) savers' time preferences for current versus future consumption, (3) the riskiness of the loan, and (4) the expected future rate of inflation.* The returns that borrowers expect to earn by investing borrowed funds set an upper limit on how much they can pay for savings. In turn, consumers' time preferences for consumption establish how much consumption they are willing to defer, and hence how much they will save at different levels of interest offered by borrowers. Higher risk and higher inflation also lead to higher interest rates.

**Self-Test Questions**

What do we call the price paid to borrow money?

What four fundamental factors affect the cost of money?

## INTEREST RATE LEVELS

Funds are allocated among borrowers by interest rates: Firms with the most profitable investment opportunities are willing and able to pay the most for capital, so they tend to attract it away from less efficient firms or from firms whose products are not in demand. Of course, our economy is not completely free in the sense of being influenced only by market forces. As a result, the federal government supports agencies that help designated individuals or groups obtain credit on favorable terms. Among those eligible for this kind of assistance are small businesses, certain minorities, and firms willing to build facilities in areas characterized by high unemployment. Even with these government interventions, most capital in the U.S. economy is allocated through the price system.

Figure 5-1 shows how supply and demand interact to determine interest rates in two capital markets. Markets A and B represent two of the many capital markets in existence. The going interest rate, which we designate as r for this discussion, initially is 6 percent for the low-risk securities in Market A. That is, borrowers whose credit is strong enough to qualify for this market can obtain funds at a cost of 6 percent, and investors who want to put their money to work without much risk can obtain a 6 percent return. Riskier borrowers must borrow higher-cost funds in Market B. Investors who are willing to take on more risk invest in Market B expecting to earn a 9 percent return, but they also realize that they might actually receive much less (or much more).

**FIGURE 5-1    Interest Rates as a Function of Supply and Demand**

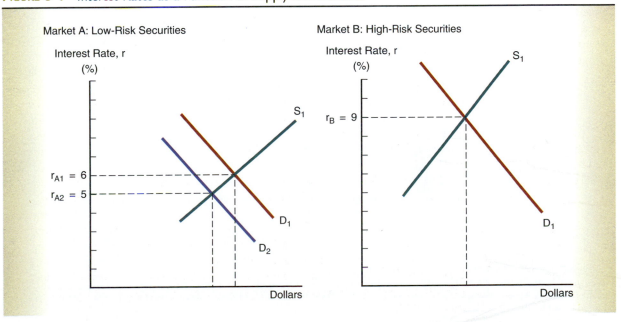

If the demand for funds declines, as it typically does during business recessions, the demand curves will shift to the left, as shown in Curve $D_2$ in Market A. The market-clearing, or equilibrium, interest rate in this example then falls to 5 percent. Similarly, you should be able to visualize what would happen if the supply of funds tightens: The supply curve, $S_1$, would shift to the left, which would raise interest rates and lower the level of borrowing in the economy.

Financial markets are interdependent. For example, if Markets A and B were in equilibrium before the demand shifted to $D_2$ in Market A, it means that investors were willing to accept the higher risk in Market B in exchange for a risk premium of 9% − 6% = 3%. After the shift to $D_2$, the risk premium would initially increase to 9% − 5% = 4%. In all likelihood, this larger premium would induce some of the lenders in Market A to shift to Market B, which in turn would cause the supply curve in Market A to shift to the left (or up) and the supply curve in Market B to shift to the right. The transfer of capital between markets would raise the interest rate in Market A and lower it in Market B, thereby bringing the risk premium closer to the original level, 3 percent. For example, when rates on Treasury securities increase, the rates on corporate bonds and mortgages generally follow suit.

As discussed in Chapter 3, many financial markets are found in the United States and throughout the world. There are markets for short-term debt, long-term debt, home loans, student loans, business loans, government loans, and so forth. Prices are established for each type of fund, and these prices change over time as shifts occur in supply and demand conditions. Figure 5-2 illustrates how long- and short-term interest rates to business borrowers have varied since 1975. Notice that short-term interest rates are especially prone to rise during booms and then fall during recessions. (The shaded areas of the chart indicate recessions.) When the economy is expanding, firms need capital, and this demand for capital pushes rates higher. Inflationary pressures are strongest during business booms, which also exert upward pressure on

**FIGURE 5-2** Long- and Short-Term Interest Rates, 1975–2006

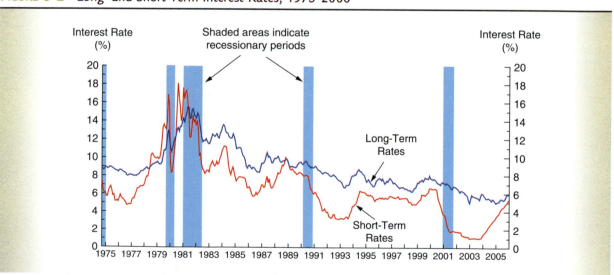

**Note:** Short-term interest rates are measured by three-month loans to very large, strong corporations, and long-term rates are measured by AAA corporate bonds.

Tick marks on the X axis represent the middle of the year—that is, July 1.

**Source:** Interest rates are found at the Federal Reserve Website at www.federalreserve.gov/; information about recessions can be found at the National Bureau of Economic Research Website at www.nber.org/cycles.html/, and CPI data are found at the Website of the U.S. Department of Labor, Bureau of Labor, at www.bls.gov.

FIGURE 5-3    Relationship between Annual Inflation Rates and Long-Term Interest Rates, 1975–2006

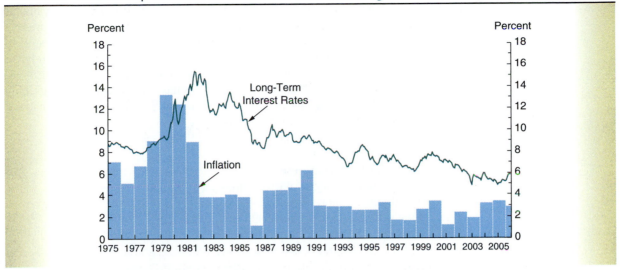

**Note:** Interest rates are those for AAA long-term corporate bonds.
Inflation is measured as the annual rate of change in the Consumer Price Index (CPI).

**Source:** Interest rates are found at the Federal Reserve Website at www.federalreserve.gov/; and CPI data are found at the Website of the U.S. Department of Labor, Bureau of Labor, at www.bls.gov.

rates. Conditions are reversed during recessions, such as the one during 1990–1991. In these periods, slack business reduces the demand for credit, the rate of inflation falls, and thus interest rates decline.

These tendencies do not hold exactly—just look at the period after 1984. The price of oil fell dramatically in 1985 and 1986, reducing inflationary pressures on other prices and easing fears of serious long-term inflation. In earlier years, these fears had pushed interest rates to record high levels. From 1984 to 1987, the economy was fairly strong, but dwindling fears about inflation more than offset the normal tendency of interest rates to rise during good economic times, and the net result was lower interest rates.[3]

Figure 5-3 highlights the relationship between inflation and long-term interest rates by plotting rates of inflation along with long-term interest rates. Prior to 1965 (not shown), when the average rate of inflation was approximately 1 percent, interest rates on the least risky bonds generally ranged from 4 percent to 5 percent. As the war in Vietnam accelerated in the late 1960s, the government's demand for funds to finance the war increased, the rate of inflation increased, and interest rates began to rise. The rate of inflation decreased after 1970, leading to a drop in long-term interest rates. The 1973 Arab oil embargo was followed by a quadrupling of oil prices in 1974, which caused a spurt in inflation. In turn, this increase drove interest rates to record highs in 1974 and 1975. Inflationary pressures eased in late 1975 and 1976, but then rose again after 1976. In 1980, inflation rates hit the highest level on record, and fears of continued double-digit inflation pushed interest rates to historic highs. From 1981 through 1986, the inflation rate dropped sharply. Indeed, in 1986, inflation was only 1.1 percent, the lowest level in 25 years. In 1993, interest rates

---

[3]Short-term rates respond to current economic conditions, whereas long-term rates primarily reflect long-run expectations for inflation. As a result, short-term rates are sometimes higher than and sometimes lower than long-term rates. The relationship between long-term and short-term rates is called *term structure of interest rates*. This topic is discussed later in the chapter.

dropped to historical lows: The Treasury bill yield actually fell below 3 percent. By 2001, rates had dropped further. By the end of the year, inflation was slightly higher than 1 percent, the Treasury bill rate was slightly lower than 2 percent, and interest rates charged to strong corporations for long-term loans were about 6 percent. In October 2006 (at the time this book was written), inflation was approximately 2.5 percent, the Treasury bill rate was about 5 percent, and the rate on AAA corporate bonds was about 6 percent. Although interest rates have varied since the beginning of the twenty-first century, a particular trend (either upward or downward) had not emerged in 2006.

 **Self-Test Questions**

How are interest rates used to allocate capital among firms?

What happens to market-clearing, or equilibrium, interest rates in a capital market when the demand for funds declines? What happens when inflation increases or decreases?

Why does the price of capital change during economic booms and recessions? How does risk affect interest rates?

How does a change in rates in one financial market affect the rates in other financial markets?

## THE DETERMINANTS OF MARKET INTEREST RATES

In general, the quoted (or nominal) interest rate on *any* security, r, is composed of a risk-free rate of interest plus a premium that reflects the riskiness of the security. This relationship can be expressed as follows:

**5–3**

$$\text{Rate of return} = r = \text{Risk-free rate} + \text{Risk premium}$$

This relationship is illustrated in Figure 5-4, which shows that investors require greater returns to invest in securities with greater risks. Although we discuss risk and return in detail in Chapter 8, the discussion in this section will give you an indication as to factors that affect interest rates on such debt securities as bonds. The interest on *debt* can be expressed as follows:

**5–4**

$$\text{Rate of return} = r = r_{RF} + RP = r_{RF} + [DRP + LP + MRP]$$

The variables in Equation 5–4 are defined as follows:

$r$ = Quoted, or *nominal,* rate of interest on a given security.[4] There are many different securities, hence many different quoted interest rates.

---

[4]The term *nominal* as it is used here means the *stated* rate as opposed to the *real* rate, which is adjusted to remove the effects of inflation. If you bought a 10-year Treasury bond in July 2006, the quoted, or nominal, rate was 5.1 percent, but because inflation was expected to average 2.5 percent over the next 10 years, the real rate was $2.6\% = 5.1\% - 2.5\%$.

**FIGURE 5-4   Rate of Return (Interest Rate)**

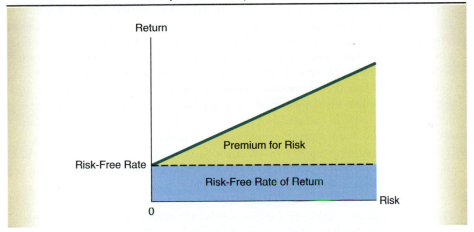

$r_{RF}$ = Quoted risk-free rate of return. Theoretically this rate is the return associated with an investment that has a guaranteed outcome in the future—that is, it has *no risk*. We generally use the return on U.S. Treasury bills as the risk-free rate because T-bills represent the short-term debt of the U.S. government that is very liquid and free of most risks. In other words, T-bills are considered very close to pure risk-free assets.

**RP** = Risk premium, which is the return that exceeds the risk-free rate of return, $r_{RF}$, and thus represents payment for the risk associated with an investment. RP = DRP + LP + MRP.

**DRP** = Default risk premium, which reflects the chance that the borrower—that is, the issuer of the security—will not pay the debt's interest or principal on time.

**LP** = Liquidity, or marketability, premium, which reflects the fact that some investments are more easily converted into cash on short notice at a "reasonable price" than are other securities.

**MRP** = Maturity risk premium, which accounts for the fact that longer-term bonds experience greater price reactions to interest rate changes than do short-term bonds.

We discuss the components that make up the quoted, or nominal, rate on a given security in the following sections.

## The Nominal, or Quoted, Risk-Free Rate of Interest, $r_{RF}$

The **nominal**, or **quoted, risk-free rate**, $r_{RF}$, is the interest rate on a security that has absolutely no risk at all—that is, one that has a guaranteed outcome in the future, regardless of the market conditions. No such security exists in the real world; hence, there is no observable, truly risk-free rate. However, there is one security that is free of most risks: a U.S. Treasury bill (T-bill), which is a short-term security issued by the U.S. government.

The nominal risk-free rate, $r_{RF}$, has two components: the *"real" risk-free rate,* which we designate $r^*$, and an adjustment for the average inflation that is expected during the life of the investment, which we designate IP, or the *inflation premium*. As a result, $r_{RF} = r^* + IP$ in Equation 5–4.

**nominal (quoted) risk-free rate, $r_{RF}$**
The rate of interest on a security that is free of all risk; $r_{RF}$ is proxied by the T-bill rate or the T-bond rate and includes an inflation premium.

**real risk-free rate of interest, r\***
The rate of interest that would exist on default-free U.S. Treasury securities if no inflation were expected.

The **real risk-free rate of interest, r\***, is defined as the interest rate that would exist on a security with a *guaranteed* payoff—that is, a risk-free security—*if inflation is expected to be zero* during the investment period. It can be thought of as the rate of interest that would exist on short-term U.S. Treasury securities in an *inflation-free world*. The real risk-free rate changes over time depending on economic conditions, especially (1) on the rate of return corporations and other borrowers are willing to pay to borrow funds and (2) on people's time preferences for current versus future consumption. It is difficult to measure the real risk-free rate precisely, but most experts think that $r^*$ fluctuates in the range of 2 percent to 4 percent in the United States.

No matter what investments they make, all investors are affected by inflation. For this reason, the minimum rate earned on any security, *no matter its risk*, must include compensation for the loss of purchasing power that is expected during the life of the investment due to inflation. Thus, $r_{RF}$ must include a component for the average inflation, or purchasing power loss, that investors expect in the future.

If the term *risk-free rate* is used without either the term *real* or the term *nominal*, people generally mean the quoted (nominal) rate, and we will follow that convention in this book. Therefore, when we use the term *risk-free rate*, we mean the nominal risk-free rate, $r_{RF} = r^* + IP$. Also, we generally use the T-bill rate to approximate the short-term risk-free rate and the T-bond rate to approximate the long-term risk-free rate. So whenever you see the term *risk-free rate*, assume that we are referring either to the quoted T-bill rate or to the quoted T-bond rate.

## Inflation Premium (IP)

Inflation has a major effect on interest rates because it erodes the purchasing power of the dollar and lowers the real rate of return on investments. To illustrate, suppose you saved $1,000 and invested it in a certificate of deposit that matures in one year and will pay 4.5 percent interest. At the end of the year, you will receive $1,045—your original $1,000 plus $45 of interest. Now suppose the inflation rate during the year is 10 percent, and it affects all items equally. If pizza had cost $1 per slice at the beginning of the year, it would cost $1.10 at the end of the year. Therefore, your $1,000 would have bought $1,000/$1 = 1,000 slices of pizza at the beginning of the year but only $1,045/$1.10 = 950 slices at year's end. *In real terms*, therefore, you would be worse off: You would receive $45 in interest, but that amount would not be sufficient to offset inflation. In this case, you would be better off buying 1,000 slices of frozen pizza (or some other storable asset such as land, timber, apartment buildings, wheat, or gold) than investing in the certificate of deposit.

**inflation premium (IP)**
A premium for expected inflation that investors add to the real risk-free rate of return.

Investors are well aware of the effect of inflation. When they lend money, therefore, they build in an **inflation premium (IP)** equal to the *average inflation rate expected over the life of the security*. Thus, if the real risk-free rate of interest, $r^\circ$, is 3 percent, and if inflation is expected to be 2 percent (and hence IP = 2%) during the next year, then the quoted rate of interest on one-year T-bills would be 3% + 2% = 5%.

It is important to note that the rate of inflation built into interest rates is the *rate of inflation expected in the future*, not the rate experienced in the past. Thus, although the rates reported by the government indicate that inflation is currently 3 percent, if investors expect inflation to average 5 percent over the next few years, then 5 percent would be built into current interest rates. Note also that the inflation rate reflected in the quoted interest rate of an investment is the *average inflation expected over the life of the investment*. Consequently, the inflation rate that is built into a one-year bond is the expected inflation rate for the next year, but the inflation rate built into a 30-year bond is the average rate of inflation expected over the next 30 years.

Generally, expectations of future inflation are closely correlated with rates experienced in the recent past. Thus, if the inflation rate reported for the month increased, people would tend to raise their expectations for future inflation. This change in expectations would, in turn, bring about an increase in interest rates.

## Default Risk Premium (DRP)

The *risk* that a borrower will *default* on a loan—that is, not pay the interest or the principal—also affects the market interest rate on a security: The greater the default risk, the higher the interest rate that lenders charge (demand). Treasury securities have no default risk because everyone believes that the U.S. government will pay its debt on time. As a result, U.S. Treasury securities (bills, notes, and bonds) generally carry the lowest interest rates on taxable securities in the United States. For corporate bonds, the better the bond's overall credit rating (AAA is the best), the lower its default risk and, consequently, the lower its interest rate.[5] Following are some representative interest rates on long-term (10-year) corporate bonds that existed in July 2006:

| Type of Debt | Amount of Risk | Rate, r | $DRP = r - r_{RF}$ |
|---|---|---|---|
| U.S. Treasury, $r_{RF}$ | No default risk | 5.1% | — |
| AAA corporate bond | Default risk greater than T-bonds | 5.8 | 0.7% |
| BBB corporate bond | Default risk greater than AAA corporate bonds | 6.5 | 1.4 |
| CCC corporate bond | Default risk much greater than BBB corporate bonds | 17.6 | 12.5 |

Assuming that these three bonds have identical provisions, the only reason their rates differ is because their default risks differ. As a result, the difference between the quoted interest rate on a T-bond and that on a corporate bond with similar maturity, liquidity, and other features is the **default risk premium (DRP)**. Thus, if the bonds listed in the table were *otherwise similar,* the default risk premium would be $DRP = r - r_{RF}$. Default risk premiums vary somewhat over time, but the July 2006 figures were fairly normal compared with levels in recent years.

## Liquidity Premium (LP)

Liquidity generally is defined as the ability to convert an asset into cash on short notice and "reasonably" capture the amount initially invested. The more easily an asset can be converted to cash at a price that substantially recovers the initial amount invested, the more liquid it is considered. Clearly, assets have varying degrees of liquidity, depending on the characteristics of the markets in which they are traded. For instance, such financial assets as government securities, stocks, and bonds trade in very active and efficient secondary markets, whereas the markets for real estate are much more restrictive. Also, it generally is easier to convert an asset into cash at a "good" price the closer the asset's life is to its maturity date. Thus, financial assets generally are more liquid than real assets, and short-term financial assets generally are more liquid than long-term financial assets.

**default risk premium (DRP)**
The difference between the interest rate on a U.S. Treasury bond and a corporate bond of equal maturity and marketability; compensation for the risk that a corporation will not meet its debt obligations.

---

[5]Bond ratings, and bonds' riskiness in general, are discussed in more detail in Chapter 6. For this example, note that bonds rated AAA are judged to have less default risk than are bonds rated AA, AA bonds are less risky than A bonds, and so on.

**liquidity premium (LP)**
A premium added to the rate on a security if the security cannot be converted to cash on short notice at a price that is close to the original cost.

Because liquidity is important, investors evaluate liquidity and include a **liquidity premium (LP)** when market rates of securities are established. Although it is very difficult to accurately measure liquidity premiums, a differential of at least 2 and perhaps 4 or 5 percentage points exists between the least liquid and the most liquid financial assets of similar default risk and maturity.

## Maturity Risk Premium (MRP)

**interest rate risk**
The risk of capital losses to which investors are exposed because of changing interest rates.

The prices of long-term bonds decline sharply whenever interest rates rise. Because interest rates can and do occasionally rise, *all* long-term bonds—even Treasury bonds—have an element of risk called **interest rate risk.** As a general rule, the bonds of any organization, from the U.S. government to General Motors, have more interest rate risk the longer the maturity of the bond.[6] Therefore, the required interest rate must include a **maturity risk premium (MRP),** which is higher the longer the time to maturity. Everything else being equal, maturity risk premiums raise interest rates on long-term bonds relative to those on short-term bonds. Such a premium, like the other types of premiums, is extremely difficult to measure. Nevertheless, two things seem clear: (1) The MRP appears to vary over time, rising when interest rates are more volatile and uncertain, then falling when interest rates are more stable; and (2) the maturity risk premium on T-bonds with 20 to 30 years to maturity normally is in the range of 1 or 2 percentage points.[7]

**maturity risk premium (MRP)**
A premium that reflects interest rate risk; bonds with longer maturities have greater interest rate risk.

To illustrate the effect of time to maturity on the prices of bonds, consider two investments that are identical except for their maturity dates. Both investments promise to pay $1,000 at maturity, but Investment A matures in two years whereas Investment B matures in 10 years. To simplify this example, let's assume that there is no maturity risk premium, so that the return on both investments is currently 10 percent. Under these conditions, the value of Investment A is $826.45 and the value of Investment B is $385.54. What will be the values of these investments if the return on the investments *immediately* increases to 12 percent? The following table shows the answer to this question as well as the changes in the investments' values stated both in dollars and in percentages.

| Investment | Maturity | Value @ 10% | Value @ 12% | $ Change in Value | % Change in Value |
|---|---|---|---|---|---|
| A | 2 years | $826.45 | $797.19 | $29.26 | 3.5% |
| B | 10 years | 385.54 | 321.97 | 63.57 | 16.5 |

Note that both the dollar change and the percentage change are greater for the investment with the longer term to maturity—that is, Investment B. This simple example, which illustrates the general concept of maturity risk, shows you why

---

[6]For example, if you had bought a 30-year Treasury bond for $1,000 in 1972, when the long-term interest rate was 7 percent, and held it until 1981, when long-term T-bond rates were 14.5 percent, the value of the bond would have declined to $514. That decrease would represent a loss of almost half the money, and it demonstrates that long-term bonds—even U.S. Treasury bonds—are not risk free. If you had purchased short-term T-bills in 1972 and subsequently reinvested the principal each time the bills matured, however, you would still have $1,000. This point will be discussed in detail in Chapter 6.

[7]The MRP has averaged 1.5 percentage points over the past 65 years. See *Stocks, Bonds, Bills, and Inflation: 2006 Yearbook* (Chicago: Ibbotson Associates, 2006).

investors normally demand higher MRPs for investments with longer terms to maturity.

Although long-term bonds are heavily exposed to interest rate risk, short-term investments are more vulnerable to **reinvestment rate risk.** When short-term investments mature and the proceeds are reinvested, or "rolled over," a decline in interest rates would necessitate reinvestment at a lower rate, and hence would lead to a decline in interest income. For example, suppose you invested $100,000 in one-year Treasury bills and you live on the income generated from this investment. In 1981, short-term rates were approximately 15 percent, so your investment would have provided roughly $15,000 in interest income. Because you would have to reinvest the $100,000 each year at the prevailing interest rate, however, your income would have declined to about $9,000 by 1983, to about $1,300 by 2003, and to about $5,000 by 2006. Had you invested your money in long-term—say, 30-year—Treasury bonds in 1981, you would have received a stable annual income of about $13,000.[8] Thus, although "investing short" preserves one's principal, the interest income provided by short-term investments varies from year to year, depending on reinvestment rates.

**reinvestment rate risk**
The risk that a decline in interest rates will lead to lower income when bonds mature and funds are reinvested.

### Self-Test Questions

Write an equation for the nominal interest rate on any debt security.

Distinguish between the *real* risk-free rate of interest, r*, and the *nominal,* or quoted, risk-free rate of interest, r.

How do investors deal with inflation when they determine interest rates in the financial markets? Explain.

Does the interest rate on a Treasury bond include a default risk premium? Explain.

Briefly explain the following statement: "Although long-term bonds are heavily exposed to interest rate risk, short-term Treasury bills are more vulnerable to reinvestment rate risk."

Suppose that economists have determined that the real risk-free rate of return is 3 percent and that inflation is expected to average 2.5 percent per year long into the future. What should the rate be on a one-year Treasury bond? Assume that there is no maturity risk premium associated with the bond. (*Answer:* 5.5%)

Suppose that economists have determined that the real risk-free rate of return is 3 percent and that inflation is expected to average 2.5 percent per year long into the future. In addition, Treasury bonds with terms to maturity greater than one year incur a maturity risk premium equal to 0.1 percent per year. What should the rate be on a five-year Treasury bond? (*Answer:* 6.0%)

---

[8]Long-term bonds also have some reinvestment rate risk. To earn the quoted rate on a long-term bond, the interest payments must be reinvested at the quoted rate. If interest rates fall, however, the interest payments must be reinvested at a lower rate. In such a case, the realized return would be less than the quoted rate. Note that the reinvestment rate risk is lower on a long-term bond than on a short-term bond because only the interest payments (rather than the interest plus principal) on the long-term bond are exposed to reinvestment rate risk. Only zero coupon bonds (which are discussed in Chapter 6 ) are completely free of reinvestment rate risk.

## THE TERM STRUCTURE OF INTEREST RATES

**term structure of interest rates**
The relationship between yields and maturities of securities.

A study of Figure 5-2 reveals that at certain times, such as in 2004 and 2005, short-term interest rates are lower than long-term rates. At other times, such as in 1980 and 1981, short-term rates are higher than long-term rates. The relationship between long- and short-term rates, which is known as the **term structure of interest rates,** is important to corporate treasurers, who must decide whether to borrow by issuing long- or short-term debt, and to investors, who must decide whether to buy long- or short-term bonds. For these reasons, it is important to understand (1) how long- and short-term rates are related and (2) what causes shifts in their relative positions.

The relationship between long- and short-term bonds varies and is generally dependent on the supply and demand relationship that exists for these bonds at a particular point in time. For example, the tabular section of Figure 5-5 includes interest rates for different maturities on three different dates. The set of data for a given date, when plotted on a graph such as that in Figure 5-5, is called the **yield curve** for that date. The yield curve provides a snapshot of the relationship between short- and long-term rates on a particular date. The yield curve changes in both position and slope over time. For example, in March 1980, all rates were relatively high, and short-term rates were higher than long-term rates, so the yield curve on that date was *downward sloping*. However, in July 2003, all rates were much lower, and long-term rates were higher than short-term rates, so the yield curve at that time was *upward sloping*. And in July 2006, all rates were higher than in 2003, and short- and long-term rates did not differ much, so the yield curve was fairly *flat*, or *horizontal*.

**yield curve**
A graph showing the relationship between yields and maturities of securities.

**"normal" yield curve**
An upward-sloping yield curve.

Historically, long-term rates have generally been higher than short-term rates, so the yield curve normally has been upward sloping. For this reason, people often refer to an upward-sloping yield curve as a **"normal" yield curve.** On the other hand, a downward-sloping yield curve is pretty rare, and thus we normally refer to this type of curve as an **inverted,** or **"abnormal" yield curve.** Thus, in Figure 5-5, the yield curve for March 1980 was inverted, but the yield curve for July 2003 was normal. In the next section, we discuss three explanations for the shape of the yield curve and explain why an upward-sloping yield curve is considered normal.

**inverted ("abnormal") yield curve**
A downward-sloping yield curve.

 **Self-Test Questions**

What is a yield curve, and what information would you need to draw this curve?

How does a "normal" yield curve differ from a flat yield curve and an inverted yield curve?

## WHY DO YIELD CURVES DIFFER?

It is clear from Figure 5-5 that the shape of the yield curve at one point in time can be significantly different from the yield curve at another point in time. For example, interest rates were much higher in 1980 than in 2003, and the yield curve was downward sloping in 1980 whereas it was upward sloping in 2003. Remember that interest rates consist of a risk-free return, $r_{RF}$, which includes the real risk-free return ($r^*$) and an adjustment for expected inflation (IP), and a risk premium that rewards investors for various risks, including default risk (DRP),

FIGURE 5-5  U.S. Treasury Bonds: Interest Rates on Different Dates

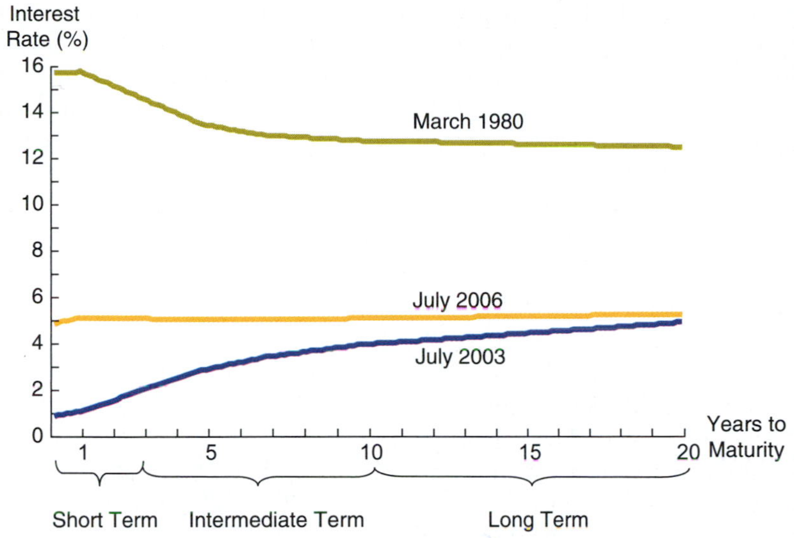

| Term to Maturity | Interest Rate | | |
|---|---|---|---|
| | March 1980 | July 2003 | July 2006 |
| 3 months | 15.7% | 0.9% | 4.9% |
| 1 year | 15.8 | 1.1 | 5.2 |
| 5 years | 13.5 | 2.9 | 5.1 |
| 10 years | 12.8 | 4.0 | 5.1 |
| 20 years | 12.5 | 4.9 | 5.3 |

**Source:** Federal Reserve, http//www.federalreserve.gov.

liquidity risk (LP), and maturity risk (MRP). Although the real risk-free rate of return, r*, does change at times, it generally is relatively stable from period to period. As a result, when interest rates shift to substantially different levels, it generally is because investors have changed either their expectations concerning future inflation or their attitudes concerning risk. Because changes in investors' risk attitudes generally evolve over time (years), *inflation expectations represent an important factor in the determination of current interest rates* and thus the shape of the yield curve.

To illustrate how inflation affects the shape of the yield curve, let's examine interest rates on U.S. Treasury securities. First, the rate of return on these securities can be written as follows:

$$r_{\text{Treasury}} = r_{\text{RF}} + \text{MRP} = [r^* + \text{IP}] + \text{MRP} \qquad \textbf{5–5}$$

This equation is the same as Equation 5–4, except the default risk premium (DRP) and the liquidity premium (LP) are not included because we generally consider Treasury securities to be very liquid (marketable), default-free investments. As a result, DRP = 0 and LP = 0. The maturity risk premium (MRP) is included in the equation because Treasury securities vary in maturity from as little as a few days to as much as 30 years. All else equal, *investors generally prefer to hold short-term securities* because such securities are less sensitive to changes in interest rates and provide greater investment flexibility than longer-term securities. Investors will, therefore, generally accept lower yields on short-term securities, and this leads to relatively low short-term rates. *Borrowers,* on the other hand, *generally prefer long-term debt* because short-term debt exposes them to the risk of having to refinance the debt under adverse conditions (e.g., higher interest rates). Accordingly, borrowers want to "lock into" long-term funds, which means they are willing to pay a higher rate, other things held constant, for long-term funds than for short-term funds, which also leads to relatively low short-term rates. Taken together, these two sets of preferences imply that under normal conditions, a positive maturity risk premium (MRP) exists, and the MRP increases with years to maturity, causing the yield curve to be upward sloping. In economics, the general theory that supports this conclusion is referred to as the **liquidity preference theory,** which simply states that long-term bonds normally yield more than short-term bonds, all else equal, primarily because MRP > 0 and MRP increases with time to maturity.

During the past few decades, we have observed three basic shapes to the yield curve associated with Treasury securities. Each of the three shapes is shown in Figure 5-5—that is, a normal, or upward sloping yield curve; an inverted, or downward sloping yield curve; and a flat yield curve. For this reason, although MRP > 0, which supports the *liquidity preference theory,* it appears that this theory does not fully explain the shape of the yield curve. Remember that the nominal risk-free rate of return consists of two components: the real risk-free rate of return, $r^*$, which is considered to be relatively constant from one year to the next, and an adjustment for the inflation expectations of investors, IP. Expectations about future inflation do vary over time. But the inflation premium, IP, that is included in interest rates is somewhat predictable because it is the average of the inflation rates that are expected to occur during the life of the investment (a Treasury security in this case). In fact, the yield curve is often used as an aid when forecasting future interest rates because both investors and borrowers base their current decisions on expectations regarding which way interest rates will move in the future. For example, interest rates were at such low levels in 2003 and 2004 (the lowest in 45 years) that most people believed that rates most certainly would have to increase in the future. The attitude was that rates could not possibly drop any lower. During this time, many homeowners refinanced their houses to take advantage of, and thus "lock in," the low rates, whereas most investors purchased short-term securities in hopes that rates would increase in the future, at which time they would be able to "lock in" the higher rates. Clearly, the expectations of the participants in the financial markets—that is, investors and borrowers—greatly impact interest rates. The **expectations theory** states that the yield curve depends on *expectations* concerning future inflation rates. We illustrate how expectations can be used to help *forecast* interest rates in the next section.

Let's consider the effect of inflation expectations and maturity on the determination of interest rates with two simple examples: (1) inflation is expected to increase in the future, and (2) inflation is expected to decrease in the future. Assume the real risk-free rate, $r^*$, is 2 percent and that investors demand a 0.1 percent maturity risk premium for each year remaining until maturity for any debt with a term to maturity greater than one year, with a maximum value of 1 percent. For example, if a Treasury bill matures in one year, MRP = 0; but, if a Treasury bond matures in five years, MRP = 0.5%, and bonds that mature in 10 years or longer will have MRP = 1.0%. Also, assume that inflation expectations are as follows for the two situations:

**liquidity preference theory**
The theory that, all else being equal, lenders prefer to make short-term loans rather than long-term loans; hence, they will lend short-term funds at lower rates than they lend long-term funds.

**expectations theory**
The theory that the shape of the yield curve depends on investors' expectations about future inflation rates.

| Year | Increasing Inflation | Decreasing Inflation |
|------|---------------------|----------------------|
| 1 | 1.0% | 5.0% |
| 2 | 1.8 | 4.2 |
| 3 | 2.0 | 4.0 |
| 4 | 2.4 | 3.4 |
| 5 | 2.8 | 3.2 |
| After Year 5 | 3.0 | 2.4 |

Note that these two situations are not related—that is, we are not assuming that the economic conditions in the first year in both cases are the same.

Using this information, we can compute the interest rates for Treasury securities with any term to maturity. To illustrate, consider a bond that matures in five years. For the case in which inflation is expected to *increase,* the interest rate, or yield, on this bond should be 4.5 percent: $r^* = 2\%$, IP = 2%, and MRP = 0.5%. Because IP is the average of the rate of inflation that is expected for each year during the life of the bond, IP = $(1.0\% + 1.8\% + 2.0\% + 2.4\% + 2.8\%)/5 = 2.0\%$. Also, MRP = 0.1% per year for this bond because its term to maturity is greater than one year; thus, MRP = $0.1\% \times 5$ years = 0.5%. As a result,

$$r = [r^* + IP] + MRP = [2\% + 2\%] + 0.5\% = 4.5\%$$

Figure 5-6 shows the yield curves for both inflationary situations. The yields are given in the tables below the graphs. As the graphs show, when inflation is expected to increase, the yield curve is upward sloping, and vice versa. In either case, economists often use the yield curve to form expectations about the future of the economy. For example, when inflation is high and expected to decline, as panel b of Figure 5-6 indicates, the yield curve generally is downward sloping. In many cases a downward-sloping yield curve suggests that the economy will weaken in the future: Consumers delay purchases because they expect prices to decline in the future, borrowers wait to borrow funds because they believe rates will be lower in the future, and investors provide more funds to the financial markets in an effort to capture higher current rates. All of these actions lead to lower long-term rates in the current period.

There are times when the yield curve exhibits either humps or dips for bonds in a particular range of terms to maturity. Figure 5-7 shows the yield curve for February 2006. The graph is "humped" for short-term bonds and then exhibits a somewhat normal upward slope for bonds with longer maturities. The shape of this yield curve suggests that the supply/demand conditions for bonds with short-term maturities were significantly different than for the longer maturity ranges in February 2006. When supply/demand conditions in one range of maturities are significantly different than in other maturity ranges, interest rates for bonds in that maturity range are either substantially higher or substantially lower than rates in the maturity ranges on either side. In such cases, the resulting yield curve is not smooth or uniform; rather, there is a hump in the yield curve if rates are higher and a dip if rates are lower. The reason these humps and dips occur is because there are instances when investors and borrowers prefer bonds with specific maturity ranges. For example, a person borrowing to buy a long-term asset like a house or an electric utility borrowing to build a power plant would want a long-term loan. However, a retailer borrowing in September to build its inventories for Christmas would prefer a short-term loan. Similar differences exist among savers. For example, a person

**FIGURE 5-6   Illustrative Yield Curves for Treasury Securities**

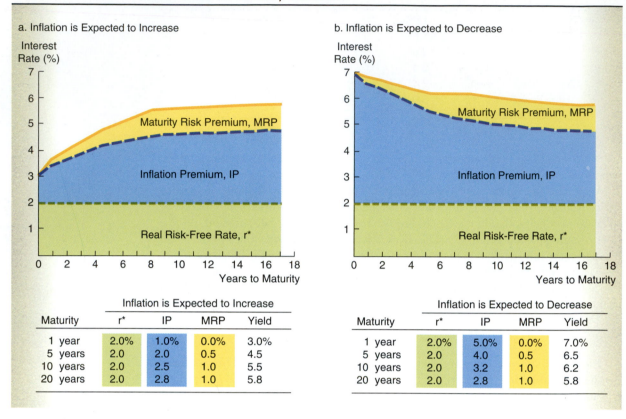

| Inflation is Expected to Increase | | | | |
|---|---|---|---|---|
| Maturity | r* | IP | MRP | Yield |
| 1 year | 2.0% | 1.0% | 0.0% | 3.0% |
| 5 years | 2.0 | 2.0 | 0.5 | 4.5 |
| 10 years | 2.0 | 2.5 | 1.0 | 5.5 |
| 20 years | 2.0 | 2.8 | 1.0 | 5.8 |

| Inflation is Expected to Decrease | | | | |
|---|---|---|---|---|
| Maturity | r* | IP | MRP | Yield |
| 1 year | 2.0% | 5.0% | 0.0% | 7.0% |
| 5 years | 2.0 | 4.0 | 0.5 | 6.5 |
| 10 years | 2.0 | 3.2 | 1.0 | 6.2 |
| 20 years | 2.0 | 2.8 | 1.0 | 5.8 |

**Note:** The inflation premium is the average of the expected inflation rates during the life of the security. Therefore, in the case where inflation is expected to increase, $IP_{10}$ is computed as follows:

$$IP_{10} = \frac{1.0\% + 1.8\% + 2.0\% + 2.4\% + 2.8\% + 3.0\% + 3.0\% + 3.0\% + 3.0\% + 3.0\%}{10}$$

$$= \frac{25\%}{10} = 2.5\%$$

saving to take a vacation next summer would want to lend (save) in the short-term market, but someone saving for retirement 20 years hence would probably buy long-term securities.

According to the **market segmentation theory** that has been developed by economists, the slope of the yield curve depends on supply/demand conditions in the long- and short-term markets. Thus, the yield curve could at any given time be flat, upward sloping, or downward sloping and have humps or dips. Interest rates would be high in a particular segment compared with other segments when there was a low supply of funds in that segment relative to demand, and vice versa. The hump in the curve shown in Figure 5-7 suggests that the demand for short-term loans was high relative to supply—that is, borrowers sought short-term loans rather than long-term loans, not many investors bought short-term investments so the supply of short-term funds was low, or both conditions existed.

In this section, we use Treasury securities to illustrate concepts relating to the shape of the yield curve. The same concepts apply to corporate bonds. To include corporate bonds in the illustration, however, we would have to determine the default risk premium (DRP) and the liquidity premium (LP) associated with these bonds. In

**market segmentation theory**

The theory that every borrower and lender has a preferred maturity and that the slope of the yield curve depends on the supply of and the demand for funds in the long-term market relative to the short-term market.

FIGURE 5-7    U.S. Treasury Bonds: Yield Curve, February 2006

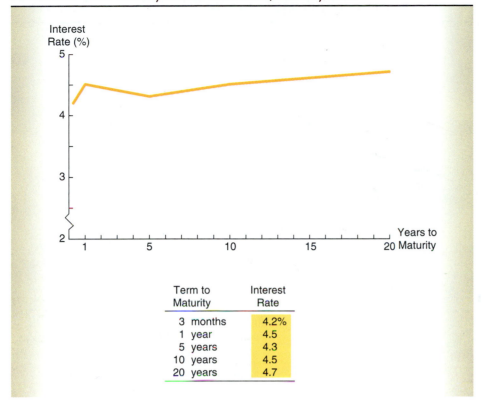

| Term to Maturity | Interest Rate |
| --- | --- |
| 3 months | 4.2% |
| 1 year | 4.5 |
| 5 years | 4.3 |
| 10 years | 4.5 |
| 20 years | 4.7 |

**Source:** Federal Reserve, http://www.federalreserve.gov.

other words, the interest rates on corporate bonds would be determined using Equation 5–6:

$$r = r_{RF} + [DRP + LP + MRP] = [r^* + IP] + [DRP + LP + MRP]$$    **5–6**

For corporate bonds, $DRP > 0$ and $LP > 0$, which means that interest rates on corporate bonds are greater than interest rates on Treasury securities with the same maturities. The risk-free rate of return for both types of securities is the same, $r_{RF} = r^* + IP$. But because corporate bonds have default risk, liquidity risk, and maturity risk, whereas long-term Treasury securities have only maturity risk, the risk premiums on corporate bonds $(MRP + DPR + LP)$ are greater than the risk premiums on Treasuries (MRP)—that is, $RP_{Corporate} > RP_{Treasury}$. As a result, if we plotted the yield curves for the bonds of a particular corporation, such as Wal-Mart or General Motors (GM), the curves would be higher than for Treasury securities, and the curves would be higher for riskier corporations. For instance, the yield curve for Wal-Mart's bonds would be below the yield curve for GM's bonds because GM had financial problems and was considered riskier than Wal-Mart; Wal-Mart's bonds were rated as investment grade because they had low default risk, whereas GM's bonds were rated as "junk bonds" because they had high default risk. Note that although GM's bonds were rated as "junk bonds" at the time of this writing, the rating might be different when you read this book.

**FIGURE 5-8**    Yield Curves, July 2006: Treasury Bonds, AAA-Rated Corporate Bonds, and BBB-Rated Corporate Bonds

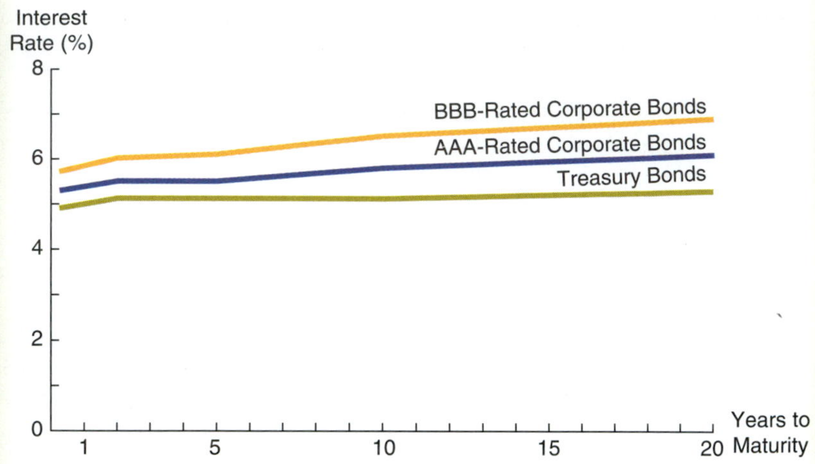

| Term to Maturity | Interest Rate, July 2006 | | |
| --- | --- | --- | --- |
| | Treasury Bond | AAA-Rated Corporate Bond | BBB-Rated Corporate Bond |
| 3 months | 4.9% | 5.3% | 5.7% |
| 1 year | 5.1 | 5.5 | 6.0 |
| 5 years | 5.1 | 5.5 | 6.1 |
| 10 years | 5.1 | 5.8 | 6.5 |
| 20 years | 5.3 | 6.1 | 6.9 |

**Source:** Federal Reserve, http://www.federalreserve.gov; Yahoo! Finance, http://finance.yahoo.com/bonds/composite_bond_rates.

Figure 5-8 shows the yield curves for T-bonds, AAA-rated corporate bonds, and BBB-rated corporate bonds in July 2006. The figure illustrates the relationships of the yields for bonds with different risks. Remember that BBB-rated corporate bonds have more risk than AAA-rated corporate bonds, which have more risk than T-bonds. Figure 5-8 verifies that the risk/return relationship shown in Figure 5-4 actually exists in the financial markets—that is, investors demand higher returns to purchase riskier investments such that $r_{BBB} > r_{AAA} > r_{Treasury}$.

**Self-Test Questions**

How do the various risk premiums affect the yield curve?

Discuss the validity of each of the three theories mentioned in this section that have been proposed to explain the shape of the yield curve.

The interest rate on Cloudy Sun Company's bonds is 8 percent. It has been determined that a portion of this return, equal to 3 percent, represents compensation for LP and MRP. If $r^* = 2.5\%$ and inflation is expected to be 2 percent every year in the future, what is the DRP associated with Cloudy Sun's bonds? What is $r_{RF}$? (*Answers:* 0.5%; 4.5%)

# DOES THE YIELD CURVE INDICATE FUTURE INTEREST RATES?

It was mentioned earlier that the *expectations theory* states that the shape of the yield curve depends on expectations concerning future inflation rates. It was also mentioned that the primary reason interest rates change is because investors change their expectations concerning future inflation rates. If this is true, can we use the yield curve to help forecast future interest rates? In this section, we examine Treasury securities to illustrate how interest rates might be forecasted using information provided by a yield curve. Because there exist many factors that affect interest rates in the real world, models that are used to forecast interest rates are very complex and not always very accurate. Therefore, the discussion in this section is very much oversimplified; significantly more analysis than examining a yield curve is needed to forecast interest rates.

Although we know that Treasury securities are exposed to maturity risk, to simplify the discussion here we assume that $MRP = 0$ in the determination of interest rates for these securities. If $MRP = 0$, then all Treasury securities have the same risk, regardless of their terms to maturity, and neither investors nor borrowers should have a preference for securities with particular maturities because all securities are interchangeable. In other words, if a person wants to invest for a five-year period, he or she would not care whether the funds are invested in a Treasury bond that matures in five years or in a Treasury bill that matures in one year and can be "turned over" for the next five years. The Treasury securities should be perfect substitutes for each other so that the investor earns the same return if the money is invested in one five-year Treasury bond or five one-year Treasury bills that mature one after the other. The reason for this is because the yield on the five-year T-bond is the average of the yields on the five one-year T-bills.

To illustrate, suppose that on January 1, 2008, the real risk-free rate of interest was $r^* = 3\%$ and expected inflation rates for the next three years were as follows:[9]

| Year | Expected Annual (1-year) Inflation Rate | Expected Average Inflation Rate from January 1, 2008, to December 31 of Indicated Year |
|------|------|------|
| 2008 | 2.0% | $IP_1 = (2\%)/1 = 2.0\%$ |
| 2009 | 4.0% | $IP_2 = (2\% + 4\%)/2 = 3.0\%$ |
| 2010 | 6.0% | $IP_3 = (2\% + 4\% + 6\%)/3 = 4.0\%$ |

Given these expectations, the following interest rate pattern should exist:

| Bond Type | Real Risk-free Rate ($r^*$) | | Inflation Premium: Average Expected Inflation Rate ($IP_t$) | | Nominal Treasury Bond Rate for Each Maturity ($r_{RF}$) |
|------|------|---|------|---|------|
| 1-year bond | 3.0% | + | 2.0 % | = | 5.0% |
| 2-year bond | 3.0% | + | 3.0 % | = | 6.0% |
| 3-year bond | 3.0% | + | 4.0 % | = | 7.0% |

---

[9]In this example, we compute simple *arithmetic* average. Technically, we should be using *geometric* average, but the differences are not material in this example.

If the yields on these hypothetical bonds were plotted, the yield curve would be upward sloping, similar to the July 2003 yield curve in Figure 5-5.

Had the pattern of expected inflation rates been reversed, with inflation expected to fall from 6 percent to 2 percent during the three-year period, the following situation would exist:

| Year | Expected Annual (1-year) Inflation Rate | Expected Average Inflation Rate from January 1, 2008, to December 31 of Indicated Year |
|------|------|------|
| 2008 | 6.0% | $IP_1 = (6\%)/1 = 6.0\%$ |
| 2009 | 4.0% | $IP_2 = (6\% + 4\%)/2 = 5.0\%$ |
| 2010 | 2.0% | $IP_3 = (6\% + 4\% + 2\%)/3 = 4.0\%$ |

Given these expectations, the following interest rate pattern should exist:

| Bond Type | Real Risk-Free Rate ($r^t$) | | Inflation Premium: Average Expected Inflation Rate ($IP_t$) | | Nominal Treasury Bond Rate for Each Maturity ($r_{RF}$) |
|------|------|------|------|------|------|
| 1-year bond | 3.0% | + | 6.0% | = | 9.0% |
| 2-year bond | 3.0% | + | 5.0% | = | 8.0% |
| 3-year bond | 3.0% | + | 4.0% | = | 7.0% |

In this case, the pattern of interest rates would produce an inverted yield curve like the March 1980 yield curve in Figure 5-5. According to the expectations theory, whenever the annual rate of inflation is expected to decline, the yield curve must be downward sloping, or inverted, and vice versa. This is illustrated in Equation 5–7.

We should also be able to forecast the interest rate each year by examining the yields that currently exist on bonds with various maturities. For example, if *The Wall Street Journal* reports that the yield on a one-year T-bill is 5 percent and the yield on a two-year T-bond is 6 percent, then, because the yield on any bond is the average of the annual interest rates during its life, we know the following relationship exists in this situation:

**5–7**

$$\text{Yield on a 2-year bond} = \frac{(\text{Interest rate in Year 1}) + (\text{Interest rate in Year 2})}{2}$$
$$= \frac{R_1 + R_2}{2}$$

Here $R_1$ is the expected interest rate during the first year only (Year 1) and $R_2$ is the expected interest rate during the second year only (Year 2). Plugging in the known information, we have

$$6\% = \frac{5\% + R_2}{2}$$

Solving for $R_2$, we have

$$5\% + R_2 = 6\%(2) = 12\%, \text{ so } R_2 = 12\% - 5\% = 7\%$$

This is the yield an investor would expect to earn during 2009 if a two-year bond is purchased. Therefore, according to this example, investors would expect the interest rate to equal 5 percent in 2008 and 7 percent in 2009. If this is true, then the average yield over the next two years is 6% = (5% + 7%)/2. You can see that the yield curve is upward sloping whenever interest rates are expected to increase in future years because the *average yield* increases as higher interest rates are included in the computation.

This information can also be used to determine the expected inflation rate. In the current example, the interest rate consists of the real risk-free rate, $r^*$, which is constant, and an adjustment for inflation. Therefore, to determine the expected inflation rate each year, we simply subtract $r^*$ from the nominal interest rate that is expected to occur during the year. Remember, we assumed that the real risk-free rate, $r^*$, is 3 percent per year. As a result, in the current example, investors expect inflation to be 2% = 5% – 3% in 2008 and 4% = 7% – 3% in 2009. These results are the same as the expected inflation rates that were reported earlier.

## Self-Test Questions

If interest rates are based solely on the expectations of investors and borrowers, how are long-term interest rates computed?

Suppose that the yield (interest) on a three-year Treasury bond is 4 percent and the yield (interest) on a four-year Treasury bond is 4.5 percent. The MRPs for these bonds equal zero. Using the rates on these bonds, estimate the one-year interest rate in Year 4. If $r^* = 2\%$ each year, what is the expected inflation rate in Year 4? (*Answers:* 6% = [4.5% × 4 years] – [4% × 3 years]; 4% = 6% – 2%)

## OTHER FACTORS THAT INFLUENCE INTEREST RATE LEVELS

Factors other than those discussed previously also influence both the general level of interest rates and the shape of the yield curve. The four most important factors are Federal Reserve policy, the level of the federal budget deficit, the foreign trade balance, and the level of business activity.

### Federal Reserve Policy

You probably learned two important points in your economics courses: (1) The money supply has a major effect on both the level of economic activity and the rate of inflation; and (2) in the United States, the Federal Reserve Board controls the money supply. If the Fed wants to control growth in the economy, it slows growth in the money supply. Such an action initially causes interest rates to increase and inflation to stabilize. The opposite effect occurs when the Fed loosens the money supply.

The most important tool used by the Fed to manage the supply of money is **open market operations,** which involve buying or selling U.S. Treasury securities to change bank reserves. When the Fed wants to increase the money supply, it purchases government securities from *primary dealers* who have established trading relationships with the Federal Reserve. The Fed pays for the securities by sending funds to the banks where the primary dealers have accounts. This action increases the deposit balances of the dealers, which in turn increases the overall reserves of the banking system. Banks have additional funds to lend, so the money supply increases. The Fed carries out "normal" open market operations on a continuous basis to maintain economic activity within defined limits, and it shifts its open market strategies toward heavier-than-normal buying or selling to make more substantial adjustments.

**open market operations** Operations in which the Federal Reserve buys or sells Treasury securities to expand or contract the U.S. money supply.

During periods when the Fed is actively intervening in the markets, the yield curve will be distorted. Short-term rates will be temporarily "too low" if the Fed is easing credit and "too high" if it is tightening credit. Long-term rates are not affected as much by Fed intervention as are short-term rates.

## Federal Deficits

If the federal government spends more than it takes in from tax revenues, it runs a deficit. Deficit spending must be covered either by borrowing or by printing money. If the government borrows, the added demand for funds pushes up interest rates. If it prints money, the expectation is that future inflation will increase, which also drives up interest rates. Thus, the larger the federal deficit, other things held constant, the higher the level of interest rates. Whether long- or short-term rates are affected to a greater extent depends on how the deficit is financed. Consequently, we cannot generalize about how deficits will influence the slope of the yield curve.

## International Business (Foreign Trade Balance)

Businesses and individuals in the United States buy from and sell to people and firms in other countries. If Americans buy more than we sell (that is, if Americans import more than we export), the United States is said to be running a *foreign trade deficit.* When trade deficits occur, they must be financed, and the main source of financing is debt.[10] Therefore, the larger the trade deficit, the more the United States must borrow. As the country increases its borrowing, interest rates are driven up. Also, foreigners are willing to hold U.S. debt only if the interest rate on this debt is competitive with interest rates in other countries. Therefore, if the Federal Reserve attempts to lower interest rates in the United States, causing U.S. rates to fall below rates abroad, then foreigners will sell U.S. bonds; this activity will depress bond prices and cause U.S. interest rates to increase. As a result, the existence of a deficit trade balance hinders the Fed's ability to combat a recession by lowering interest rates.

The United States has been running annual trade deficits since the mid-1970s, and the cumulative effect of these deficits has been to make the United States the largest debtor nation of all time. As a result, U.S. interest rates are very much influenced by interest rate trends in other countries (higher rates abroad lead to higher U.S. rates). For this reason, U.S. corporate treasurers—and anyone else who is affected by interest rates—must keep up with developments in the world economy.

We mentioned earlier that financial markets in the United States are interdependent in the sense that when rates in one market increase investors tend to take their funds out of other markets to capture the higher rates in the market where the rates first increased. For example, when interest rates increase significantly in the bond markets, investors generally sell their stocks and invest the proceeds in bonds. Of course, borrowers and other users of funds act differently because they want to use the cheaper source of funds—in this case, stocks. Clearly such actions affect both markets; the additional funds provided to, and the lower demand for funds in, the bond markets help to decrease interest rates on bonds, whereas the decrease in funds in the stock markets helps to increase rates on stocks. International financial markets are similarly interdependent—that is, when rates are higher in one country than in other countries,

---

[10]The deficit could also be financed by selling assets, including gold, corporate stocks, entire companies, and real estate. The United States has financed its massive trade deficits by all of these approaches, but the primary method has been by borrowing.

businesses tend stay away from the high-interest country when seeking to borrow funds, whereas investors tend to migrate to the high-interest country. As a result, when interest rates are not "properly aligned," investors and borrowers take actions that realign the rates, in both domestic financial markets and international financial markets.

## Business Activity

We can return to Figure 5-2 to see how business conditions influence interest rates. Here are the key points revealed by that graph:

1. Because inflation increased from the 1960s to 1981, the general tendency during this period was toward higher interest rates. Since the 1981 peak, the trend has generally been downward.

2. Until 1966, short-term rates were almost always lower than long-term rates. Thus, in those years, the yield curve was almost always "normal" in the sense that it was upward sloping.

3. The shaded areas in Figure 5-2 indicate recessions. During recessions, both the demand for money and the rate of inflation tend to fall, and, at the same time, the Federal Reserve tends to increase the money supply in an effort to stimulate the economy. As a result, interest rates typically decline during recessions. In 2004 and 2005, the U.S. economy showed signs of expanding, so any actions taken by the Fed to change interest rates constituted efforts to discourage too much expansion and to control future growth so that it did not result in high inflation.

4. During recessions, short-term rates decline more sharply than do long-term rates. This situation occurs for two reasons. First, the Fed operates mainly in the short-term sector, so its intervention has the strongest effect here. Second, long-term rates reflect the average expected inflation rate over the next 20 to 30 years. This expectation generally does not change much, even when the current rate of inflation is low because of a recession.

### Self-Test Questions

Other than inflationary expectations, liquidity preferences, and normal supply/demand fluctuations, name four additional factors that influence interest rates. Explain their effects.

How does the Fed stimulate the economy? How does it affect interest rates?

## INTEREST RATE LEVELS AND STOCK PRICES

Interest rates have two effects on corporate profits. First, because interest is a cost, the higher the rate of interest, the lower a firm's profits, other things held constant. Second, interest rates affect the level of economic activity, and economic activity affects corporate profits. Interest rates obviously affect stock prices because of their effects on profits. Perhaps even more important, they influence stock prices because of competition in the marketplace between stocks and bonds. If interest rates rise sharply, investors can obtain higher returns in the bond market, which induces them to sell stocks and transfer funds from the stock market to the bond market. A massive sale of stocks in response to rising interest rates obviously would depress stock prices. Of course, the reverse occurs if interest rates decline. Indeed, the bull market of December 1991, when the Dow Jones Industrial Average rose 10 percent in less than one month, was caused almost entirely by a sharp drop in long-term interest rates. On the other hand, at least to some extent, the poor performance exhibited by the market in 1994 and 2000, when the prices of common stocks declined, resulted from increases in interest rates.

Nevertheless, as interest rates decline, the stock market generally is the "hot" investment. In the 1990s, rates in the debt markets remained at relatively low to moderate levels, while rates in the stock markets reached historically high levels. In 2004, fearing that the economy would grow too quickly and inflation would escalate significantly, the Federal Reserve began increasing interest rates; in July 2006, the Fed was still increasing interest rates in an attempt to constrict inflationary pressures. At the time of this writing, in July 2006, it appeared that the Fed's actions had tempered investors' expectations of high inflation to the point that interest rates could be "left alone" for the first time in two years. During 2005 and 2006, because investors were uncertain as to the future direction of the economy and the level of inflation, they invested cautiously. As a result, the performance of the stock markets during this period was below average at best.

### ? Self-Test Question

In what two ways do changes in interest rates affect stock prices?

## THE COST OF MONEY AS A DETERMINANT OF VALUE

In this chapter, we discussed some of the factors that determine the cost of money. For the most part, these same factors also affect other rates of return, including rates earned on stocks and other investments. In Chapter 1, we mentioned that the value of an asset is a function of the cash flows it is expected to generate in the future and the *rate of return* at which investors are willing to provide funds to purchase the investment. We know that many factors, including conditions in the economy and financial markets, affect the determination of the expected cash flows and the rate people demand when investing their funds; thus, the process of determining value can be fairly complex. After reading Chapter 4, however, we know that the value of an asset can be stated in simple mathematical terms as the present value of the future cash flows that the asset is expected to generate during its life. Thus, to compute the value of an asset, we must solve this equation:

5–8

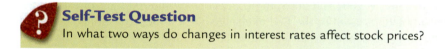

$$\text{Value of an asset} = \frac{\widehat{CF}_1}{(1+r)^1} + \frac{\widehat{CF}_2}{(1+r)^2} + \cdots + \frac{\widehat{CF}_n}{(1+r)^n} = \sum_{t=1}^{n} \frac{\widehat{CF}_t}{(1+r)t}$$

In this equation, r represents the cost of funds. You can see that mathematically, as r increases, the denominator in Equation 5–8 increases, which decreases the present value. In general, then, when the cost of money increases, the value of an asset decreases. Let's consider the logic of this statement with a simple example. Suppose that you are offered an investment that will pay you a constant $100 per year forever. If you want to earn a 10 percent return on this investment, you should be willing to pay $1,000 = $100/0.10 to purchase it. But would the amount you are willing to pay for the investment be different if interest rates on similar investments increase to 12 percent before you have a chance to purchase the perpetuity? Because the $100 annual payment that you will receive from the investment does not change, you must change the amount that you are willing to pay for the perpetuity if you want to earn the higher 12 percent return. To earn the higher return, you must lower the price you are willing to pay for the investment to $833.33 = $100/0.12. In other words, if you purchase the investment for $833.33, you will earn 12 percent because $100 is 12 percent of $833.33.

As you can see, the cost of money—that is, interest rates (returns)—affects the prices of investments. In fact, changes in interest rates can have a significant effect on the prices of stocks and bonds. In general, *when rates in the financial markets increase, the prices (values) of financial assets decrease.* In the next couple of chapters, we discuss the valuation of stocks and bonds to give you a better understanding of this fundamental valuation concept.

**Self-Test Question**

How does the cost of money affect the value of an asset?

**Chapter *Essentials***
**—The Answers**

To summarize the key concepts, let's answer the questions that were posed at the beginning of the chapter:

- **What is the cost of money, and how is it determined?** The "cost of money" is simply the interest rate that lenders charge borrowers. Interest rates and such other rates as stock returns are determined by the supply of funds and the demand for those funds. When the demand for borrowed funds increases (decreases) relative to the supply of funds provided by investors, interest rates increase (decrease).

- **What factors affect interest rates (costs of money)?** The major factors that influence interest rates include (1) production opportunities, (2) time preferences for consumption, (3) risk, and (4) inflation. Everything else equal, interest rates are higher when (1) borrowed funds can be invested in opportunities that provide higher payoffs because higher interest rates can be paid to attract such funds; (2) fewer people are willing to save because they either want or need to consume more of their incomes in the current period than normal; (3) risks associated with investing are higher because investors require higher returns to take on greater risks; and (4) inflation expectations increase because purchasing power losses are greater with higher inflation rates.

- **What is a yield curve? Does the yield curve indicate future interest rates?** A yield curve is a snapshot of the relationship between short- and long-term interest rates at a particular time period. Although a yield curve can be downward sloping or flat, it is normally upward sloping. We know that investors "set" interest rates based on their expectations about the period during which their money is going to be invested, and long-term interest rates represent averages of short-term interest rates. It makes sense then that many believe that the yield curve can be used to forecast future interest rates. According to the expectations theory, the direction of the shape of the yield curve indicates the direction interest rates will move in the future—that is, if the yield curve is upward sloping, interest rates are expected to increase in the future.

- **How do government actions and business activity affect interest rates?** When the federal government spends more than it earns (collects in taxes), the additional funds must be borrowed. Government borrowing exerts additional pressure on the demand for borrowed funds and perhaps inflates interest rates compared with what they would be if the government spent only what it collected in taxes. Businesses generally borrow more when interest rates are low, good investment opportunities are plentiful, or when both situations exist. Everything else equal, when businesses demand additional loans, whether through the bank or by issuing bonds, interest rates increase. The Federal Reserve carries out the monetary policy of the United States. As a result, when the general level of interest rates is either too high or too low, the Fed will take actions to adjust interest rates to a more "normal" level.

- **How does the level of interest rates (returns) affect the values of stocks and bonds?** Following is a fundamental concept that will be mentioned throughout the book: Changes in *prices of assets move opposite changes in rates of return—that is, when rates increase, the prices (values) of assets decrease*. We show examples of this concept in the next few chapters.

**Chapter *Essentials***
**—Personal Finance**

Compared with someone who "has no clue," if you have a basic understanding of interest rates and you plan well, you can possibly (1) lower the cost of borrowing to buy a house, a car, or other high-price item that generally requires a loan to purchase and (2) increase the average rate of return you earn when investing your money. Consider how you can make better decisions about investing and borrowing if you have a basic idea as to the role interest rates play in the financial markets. For example, if you have an indication, or feeling, as to the direction interest rates will change in the future, you will be able to make informed decisions about when to invest in long-term (short-term) securities and when to borrow money via long-term (short-term) loans.

Suppose you believe that general interest rates are going to increase during the next 12 to 18 months. What should be your investing strategy and what should be your borrowing strategy? How can some of the concepts presented in this chapter help you make decisions about your personal finances?

- If you are considering purchasing a house in the near future and you think interest rates are going to increase substantially, it probably would be better to buy now rather than wait until interest rates increase. If you buy now, the mortgage will have a lower interest rate than if you wait until interest rates are higher. In other words, if you need loans for a period longer than 12 to 18 months, you should borrow long term so that you "lock in" today's lower rates.

- On the other hand, if you want to invest money today, you don't want to "lock in" today's lower rates by investing in long-term securities. Instead, you should invest in short-term securities and wait until market rates increase before "locking in" the higher rates.

- From our brief discussion of risk, you should realize that you can possibly earn higher returns if you invest in riskier securities rather than "safer" securities; you can also lose more of your investment when you take greater risks. On the other hand, you can lower the interest rates you pay for loans by taking actions that lower your individual credit risk. Like investors, lending institutions charge higher rates to lend to, or invest in, individuals with greater credit risks. We discuss risk and return in greater detail in Chapter 8.

## ETHICAL DILEMMA

### Unadvertised Special: Is It a "Shark"?

Skip Stephens recently graduated from college with a degree in business administration. While attending college, Skip built up a large amount of debt, which currently includes student loans, outstanding credit card balances, bank loans, and so forth. Now that he has a good-paying job, Skip wants to clean up his debt position to improve his credit reputation so that he can qualify for a mortgage when he is ready to purchase a house in a few years.

As a result of a conversation with a financial planner, Skip decided that he should consolidate his debt into a single loan. Consolidation will help him monitor his debt better as he pays it off, and such an action probably will also decrease the interest rate that he is now paying. It took some effort, but Skip was able to find a financial institution that seems willing to offer him the type of loan he needs. The firm, which is named Syndicated Lending, is a new firm that specializes in loans to riskier borrowers, so it appears to be the right fit for Skip. Much of Syndicated's business is conducted electronically via the Internet. Although the company has a Website that gives some information about loans that Syndicated offers, there is not much information about interest rates, application fees, and other charges association with getting a loan. When Skip clicked on the "Interest Rate" icon on Syndicated's Website, a message appeared that said to contact the company directly. After many attempts, Skip was able to speak to a "real" person at Syndicated. When he asked why more information was not available on the Website, the employee stated that the company decided not to post interest rates because managers believed it was unfair to publicize low rates to lure customers knowing that most borrowers are unable to qualify for such loans. In other words, managers felt that using the "bait and switch" tactics like those used by competitors was

unethical. The employee gave Skip some general information about the loans that Syndicated offers, but she would not tell him interest rates because the company had a policy of not quoting a rate until a thorough credit check was completed. As a result, to get an interest quote, Skip would have to fill out and submit a loan application and he would have to pay a $100 application/credit check fee.

Skip decided that he wanted more information about Syndicated before deciding whether to apply for a loan, so he talked with people in the local area, searched chat boards and consumer opinion Websites on the Internet, and so forth. Although much of the information he collected was positive, many people complained that Syndicated was a "shady" organization that has a reputation of changing interest rates without notice and that it is not a customer-friendly firm. Some of the people whom Skip talked with went so far as to call Syndicated an unethical "loan shark" that could get away with unannounced interest rate hikes and other changes in loan agreements because the company knows that its customers cannot borrow from any other financial institution in the local area. Now Skip is wondering whether it is wise to apply for a consolidated loan from Syndicated, even though it appears that he can improve his credit rating and lower his interest payments. What should Skip do? Does it seem as though Syndicated follows unethical lending practices? Is it unethical to use "bait and switch" tactics like those that Syndicated accuses other institutions of using?[11] Should interest rates be posted on the company's Website?

---

[11]A firm uses a "bait and switch" practice when it advertises a product at a price that it doesn't intend to honor; rather, the company plans to sell either the same product or something else at a higher price.

## QUESTIONS

**5-1**  Explain why the return associated with an investment includes both the income paid by the issuer and the change in value associated with the investment.

**5-2**  Suppose interest rates on residential mortgages of equal risk were 8 percent in California and 10 percent in New York. Could this differential persist?

What forces might tend to equalize rates? Would differentials in borrowing costs for businesses of equal risk located in California and New York be more or less likely to exist than differentials in residential mortgage rates? Would differentials in the cost of money for New York and California firms be more likely to exist if the firms being compared were very large or very small? What are the implications of the trend for financial institutions to become large megabanking organizations and to engage in nationwide branching?

**5-3**   Which fluctuate more, long-term or short-term interest rates? Why?

**5-4**   Suppose a new process was developed that could be used to make oil out of seawater. The equipment required would be quite expensive but would, in time, lead to very low prices for gasoline, electricity, and other types of energy. What effect would this development have on interest rates?

**5-5**   Suppose a new, highly liberal Congress and presidential administration were elected. The first order of business for these bodies was to take away the independence of the Federal Reserve System and force the Fed to greatly expand the money supply. What effect would this change have on the level and slope of the yield curve

    **a.** immediately after the announcement?

    **b.** that would exist two or three years in the future?

**5-6**   Suppose interest rates on long-term Treasury bonds rose from 5 percent to 10 percent as a result of higher interest rates in Europe. What effect would this change have on the price of an average company's common stock?

**5-7**   How does the Federal Reserve change the money supply in the United States? What action would the Fed take to increase interest rates? To decrease interest rates?

**5-8**   How are the values of financial assets affected by changes in interest rates?

**5-9**   Suppose you believe that the economy is just entering a recession. Your firm must raise capital immediately using debt (bonds). Should you borrow on a long-term or a short-term basis? Why?

## SELF-TEST PROBLEMS

*(Solutions appear in Appendix B at the end of the book.)*

**key terms**   **ST-1**   Define each of the following terms:

    **a.** Dollar return on investment; percent return (yield) on investment

    **b.** Production opportunities; time preferences for consumption; risk

    **c.** Real risk-free rate of interest, $r^*$; nominal risk-free rate of interest, $r_{RF}$

    **d.** Inflation premium (IP)

    **e.** Default risk premium (DRP)

    **f.** Liquidity; liquidity premium (LP)

    **g.** Interest rate risk; maturity risk premium (MRP)

    **h.** Term structure of interest rates; yield curve

    **i.** "Normal" yield curve; "inverted" yield curve

    **j.** Market segmentation theory; liquidity preference theory; expectations theory

    **k.** Open market operations

**ST-2**   On January 1, 2008, Garrity Jones purchased 100 shares of Anchor
Concrete's common stock for $80 per share. By December 31, 2008, the
value of the stock had decreased to $75 per share. During the year, however,
Garrity received dividends that totaled $5 per share.

**realized return**

   **a.** What is the *dollar* return that Garrity earned during 2008?

   **b.** Compute the yield (percent return) associated with the investment for 2008.

**inflation rates**

**ST-3**   Assume that it is now January 1, 2008. The rate of inflation is expected to be
2 percent throughout 2008. In 2009 and after, increased government deficits
and renewed vigor in the economy are expected to push inflation rates higher.
Investors expect the inflation rate to be 3 percent in 2009, 5 percent in 2010,
and 6 percent in 2011. The real risk-free rate, r*, currently is 3 percent. Assume
that no maturity risk premiums are required on bonds with five years or less to
maturity. The current interest rate on five-year T-bonds is 8 percent.

   **a.** What is the average expected inflation rate over the next four years?

   **b.** What should be the prevailing interest rate on four-year T-bonds?

   **c.** What is the implied expected inflation rate in 2012, or Year 5, given that
bonds that mature in Year 5 yield 11 percent?

## PROBLEMS

**5-1**   Suppose it is now January 1, 2008, and you just sold an investment that you own
for $12,500. You purchased the investment four years ago for $10,500. During
the time you held the investment, it paid income equal to $1,000 each year.
What is the four-year holding period yield that you earned on your investment?

**investment yield**

**5-2**   A year ago, Melissa purchased 50 shares of common stock for $20 per share.
During the year, the value of her stock decreased to $18 per share. If the
stock did not pay a dividend during the year, what yield did Melissa earn on
her investment?

**investment yield**

**5-3**   Suppose the annual yield on a two-year Treasury bond is 7.5 percent, the
yield on a one-year bond is 5 percent, r* is 3 percent, and the maturity risk
premium is zero.

**expected rate of return**

   **a.** Using the expectations theory, forecast the interest rate on a one-year
bond during the second year. (*Hint:* Under the expectations theory, the
yield on a two-year bond is equal to the average yield on one-year bonds
in Year 1 and Year 2.)

   **b.** What is the expected inflation rate in Year 1? Year 2?

**5-4**   Assume that the real risk-free rate is 4 percent and the maturity risk
premium is zero. If the nominal rate of interest on one-year bonds is 11
percent and on comparable-risk two-year bonds it is 13 percent, what is the
one-year interest rate that is expected for Year 2? What inflation rate is
expected during Year 2? Why might the average interest rate during the two-
year period differ from the one-year interest rate expected for Year 2?

**expected rate of interest**

**5-5**   The rate of inflation for the coming year is expected to be 3 percent, and the
rate of inflation in Year 2 and thereafter is expected to remain constant at some
level above 3 percent. Assume that the real risk-free rate, r*, is 2 percent for all
maturities and the expectations theory fully explains the yield curve, so there are
no maturity premiums. If three-year Treasury bonds yield 2 percentage points
more than one-year bonds, what rate of inflation is expected after Year 1?

**inflation rates**

**expected inflation rate**    **5-6**    According to *The Wall Street Journal,* the interest rate on one-year Treasury bonds is 2.2 percent, the rate on two-year Treasury bonds is 3.0 percent, and the rate on three-year Treasury bonds is 3.6 percent. These bonds are considered risk free, so the rates given here are risk-free rates ($r_{RF}$). The one-year bond matures one year from today, the two-year bond matures two years from today, and so forth. The *real* risk-free rate ($r^*$) for all three years is 2 percent. Using the expectations theory, compute the expected inflation rate for the next 12 months (year).

**MRP and DRP**    **5-7**    Suppose that economists have determined that the real risk-free rate of return is 3 percent and that inflation is expected to average 2.5 percent per year long into the future. A one-year Treasury note offers a rate of return equal to 5.6 percent. You are evaluating two corporate bonds: (1) Bond A has a rate of return, $r_A$, equal to 8 percent; (2) Bond B has a rate of return, $r_B$, equal to 7.5 percent. Except for their maturities, these bonds are identical—Bond A matures in 10 years, whereas Bond B matures in five years. You have determined that both bonds are very liquid, and thus neither bond has a liquidity premium. Assuming that there is an MRP for bonds with maturities equal to one year or greater, compute the annual MRP. What is the DRP associated with corporate bonds?

**yield to maturity**    **5-8**    Today is January 1, 2009, and according to the results of a recent survey, investors expect the *annual* interest rates for the years 2012–2014 to be as follows:

| Year | One-Year Rate |
|------|---------------|
| 2012 | 5.0% |
| 2013 | 4.0 |
| 2014 | 3.0 |

The rates given here include the risk-free rate, $r_{RF}$, and appropriate risk premiums. Today a three-year bond—that is, a bond that matures on December 31, 2011—has an interest rate equal to 6 percent. What is the yield to maturity for bonds that mature at the end of 2012, 2013, and 2014?

**expected interest**    **5-9**    Suppose current interest rates on Treasury securities are as follows:

| Maturity | Yield |
|----------|-------|
| 1 year | 5.0 |
| 2 years | 5.5 |
| 3 years | 6.0 |
| 4 years | 5.5 |

Using the expectations theory, compute the expected interest rates (yields) for each security one year from now. What will the rates be two years from today and three years from today?

**yield curve**    **5-10**    Suppose you and most other investors expect the rate of inflation to be 7 percent next year, to fall to 5 percent during the following year, and then to remain at a rate of 3 percent thereafter. Assume that the real risk-free rate, $r^*$, is 2 percent and that maturity risk premiums on Treasury securities rise from zero on very short-term bonds (those that mature in a few days) by 0.2 percentage points for each year to maturity, up to a limit of 1.0 percentage point on five-year or longer-term T-bonds.

a. Calculate the interest rate on one-, two-, three-, four-, five-, 10-, and 20-year Treasury securities and plot the yield curve.

b. Now suppose IBM, a highly rated company, had bonds with the same maturities as the Treasury bonds. As an approximation, plot a yield curve for IBM on the same graph with the Treasury bond yield curve. (*Hint:* Think about the default risk premium on IBM's long-term versus its short-term bonds.)

c. Now plot the approximate yield curve of Long Island Lighting Company, a risky nuclear utility.

**5-11**  Assume that the real risk-free rate of return, r*, is 3 percent, and it will remain at that level far into the future. Also assume that maturity risk premiums on Treasury bonds increase from zero for bonds that mature in one year or less to a maximum of 2 percent, and MRP increases by 0.2 percent for each year to maturity that is greater than one year—that is, MRP equals 0.2 percent for a two-year bond, 0.4 percent for a three-year bond, and so forth. Following are the expected inflation rates for the next five years:

rate of interest

| Year | Inflation Rate |
|------|----------------|
| 2009 | 3.0% |
| 2010 | 5.0 |
| 2011 | 4.0 |
| 2012 | 8.0 |
| 2013 | 3.0 |

a. What is the average expected inflation rate for a one-, two-, three-, four-, and five-year bond?

b. What should be the MRP for a one-, two-, three-, four-, and five-year bond?

c. Compute the interest rate for a one-, two-, three-, four-, and five-year bond.

d. If inflation is expected to equal 2 percent every year after 2013, what should the interest rate be for a 10- and 20-year bond?

e. Plot the yield curve for the interest rates you computed in parts c and d.

**5-12**  Today's *Wall Street Journal* reports that the yield on Treasury bills maturing in 30 days is 3.5 percent, the yield on Treasury bonds maturing in 10 years is 6.5 percent, and the yield on a bond issued by Nextel Communications that matures in six years is 7.5 percent. Also, today the Federal Reserve announced that inflation is expected to be 2.0 percent during the next 12 months. There is a maturity risk premium (MRP) associated with all bonds with maturities equal to one year or more.

real risk-free rate, MRP, and DRP

a. Assume that the increase in the MRP each year is the same and the total MRP is the same for bonds with maturities equal to 10 years and greater—that is, MRP is at its maximum for bonds with maturities equal to 10 years and greater. What is the MRP per year?

b. What is the default risk premium associated with Nextel's bond?

c. What is the real risk-free rate of return?

**5-13**  A bond issued by Zephyr Balloons currently has a market price equal to $1,080. The bond pays $120 interest annually.

returns

a. If you buy the bond and its price does not change during the year, what is the total dollar return that you would earn if you sell the bond at the end of the year? Compute the yield for the year.

b. If the price of the bond increases to $1,100 during the year, what is the total dollar return that you would earn if you sell the bond at the end of the year? Compute the yield for the year.

c. If the price of the bond decreases to $1,000 during the year, what is the total dollar return that you would earn if you sell the bond at the end of the year? Compute the yield for the year.

**yield curves** 5-14 The following yields on U.S. Treasury securities were published in *The Wall Street Journal* on July 14, 2006:

| Term | Rate |
| --- | --- |
| 6 months | 5.0% |
| 1 year | 5.1 |
| 2 years | 5.1 |
| 3 years | 5.1 |
| 4 years | 5.2 |
| 5 years | 5.2 |
| 10 years | 5.3 |
| 20 years | 5.3 |
| 30 years | 5.0 |

Plot a yield curve based on these data. Discuss how each of the three term structure theories discussed in the chapter can explain the shape of the yield curve you plot.

**inflation and interest rates** 5-15 It is January 1, 2008. Inflation currently is about 2 percent; throughout 2007 the Fed took action to maintain inflation at this level. Now the economy is starting to grow too quickly, and reports indicate that inflation is expected to increase during the next five years. Assume that *at the beginning* of 2008, the rate of inflation *expected* for 2008 is 4 percent; for 2009 it is *expected* to be 5 percent; for 2010 it is *expected* to be 7 percent; and for 2011 and every year thereafter, it is *expected* to settle at 4 percent.

a. What is the average expected inflation rate over the five-year period 2008–2012? (Use the arithmetic average.)

b. What average nominal interest rate would, over the five-year period, be expected to produce a 2 percent real risk-free rate of return on five-year Treasury securities?

c. Assuming a real risk-free rate of 2 percent and a maturity risk premium that starts at 0.1 percent and increases by 0.1 percent *each year*, estimate the interest rate in January 2008 on bonds that mature in one, two, five, 10, and 20 years. Also, draw a yield curve based on these data.

d. Describe the general economic conditions that could be expected to produce an upward-sloping yield curve.

e. If the consensus among investors in early 2008 had been that the expected rate of inflation for every future year was 5 percent (that is, Inflation$_{2008}$ = Inflation$_{2009}$ −= ... = Inflation$_\infty$ = 5%), what do you think the yield curve would have looked like? Consider all factors that are likely to affect the curve. Does your answer here make you question the yield curve you drew in part c?

## Integrative Problem

**5-16**  In an effort to better understand how her investments are affected by market factors, Michelle Delatorre, the professional tennis player introduced in the Integrative Problem in Chapter 3, has posed some questions about yields and interest rates that she wants answered. Your boss at Balik and Kiefer has asked you to answer the following questions for Ms. Delatorre.

**yields and interest rates**

a. What is the difference between the *dollar return* and the *percentage return,* or *yield,* on an investment? Show how each return is computed.

b. Ms. Delatorre mentioned that she purchased a stock one year ago for $250 per share and that the stock has a current market value equal to $240. She knows she received a dividend payment equal to $25, but she doesn't know what rate of return she earned on her investment. Help Ms. Delatorre by showing her how to compute the rate of return on her investment.

c. What do you call the *price* that a borrower must pay for debt capital? What is the price of equity capital? What are the *four* fundamental factors that affect the cost of money, or the general level of interest rates, in the economy?

d. What is the *real risk-free rate of interest* ($r^*$) and the *nominal risk-free rate* ($r_{RF}$)? How are these two rates measured?

e. Define the terms *inflation premium (IP), default risk premium (DRP), liquidity premium (LP),* and *maturity risk premium (MRP).* Which of these premiums is included when determining the interest rate on (1) short-term U.S. Treasury securities, (2) long-term U.S. Treasury securities, (3) short-term corporate securities, and (4) long-term corporate securities? Explain how the premiums would vary over time and among the different securities.

f. What is the *term structure* of interest rates? What is a *yield curve?* At any given time, how would the yield curve facing a given company such as IBM or Microsoft compare with the yield curve for U.S. Treasury securities? Draw a graph to illustrate your answer.

g. Several theories have been advanced to explain the shape of the yield curve. The three major ones are the *market segmentation theory,* the *liquidity preference theory,* and the *expectations theory.* Briefly describe each of these theories. Do economists regard one as being "true"?

h. Suppose most investors expect the rate of inflation to be 1 percent next year, 3 percent the following year, and 4 percent thereafter. The real risk-free rate is 3 percent. The maturity risk premium is zero for bonds that mature in one year or less, and 0.1 percent for two-year bonds; the MRP increases by 0.1 percent per year thereafter for 20 years, then becomes stable. What is the interest rate on one-, 10-, and 20-year Treasury bonds? Draw a yield curve with these data. Is your yield curve consistent with the three term structure theories (see **"Why Do Yield Curves Differ?"**)?

**i.** Suppose current interest rates on treasury securities are as follows:

| Maturity | Yield |
|----------|-------|
| 1 year   | 4.4%  |
| 2 years  | 4.8   |
| 3 years  | 5.0   |
| 4 years  | 5.4   |
| 5 years  | 6.0   |

Using the expectations theory, compute the expected interest rates (yields) for each security one year from now. What will the rates be three years from today?

## Computer-Related Problem

*Work the problem in this section only if you are using the computer problem spreadsheet.*

yield curve     **5-17** The problem requires you to use File C05 on the computer problem spreadsheet.

**a.** Assume today is January 1, 2009, and the expected inflation rates for the next five years are as follows:

| Year | Inflation Rate |
|------|----------------|
| 2009 | 8.0% |
| 2010 | 6.0 |
| 2011 | 4.0 |
| 2012 | 3.0 |
| 2013 | 5.0 |

In 2014 and thereafter, inflation is expected to be 3 percent. The maturity risk premium is 0.1 percent per year to maturity for bonds with maturities greater than six months, with a maximum MRP equal to 2 percent. The real risk-free rate of return is currently 2.5 percent, and it is expected to remain at this level long into the future. Compute the interest rates on Treasury securities with maturities equal to one year, two years, three years, four years, five years, 10 years, 20 years, and 30 years. (The initial spreadsheet solution that you will see is for Problem 5-10.)

**b.** Discuss the yield curve that is constructed from the results in part a.

**c.** Rework part a assuming one year has passed—that is, today is January 1, 2010. All the other information given in part a is the same. Rework part a again assuming two, three, four, and five years have passed.

**d.** Assume that all the information given previously is the same and the default risk premium for corporate bonds rated AAA is 1.5 percent, whereas it is 4 percent for corporate bonds rated B. Compute the interest rates on AAA- and B-rated corporate bonds with maturities equal to one year, two years, three years, four years, five years, 10 years, 20 years, and 30 years.

# CHAPTER 6

# Bonds (Debt)—Characteristics and Valuation

## A MANAGERIAL PERSPECTIVE

In June 2003, 10-year Treasury bonds were selling at prices that promised investors an average return equal to 3.2 percent. As a result, a 10-year Treasury bond with a face, or par, value equal to $10,000 that paid $160 interest every six months had a market value equal to $10,000 at that time. One year later, in June 2004, the value of the same bond was $8,842 because the market interest rate on similar-risk investments had increased to 4.8 percent. Thus, if you had purchased the bond one year earlier, at least on paper, you would have incurred a capital loss equal to $1,158. Your "paper loss" would have shrunk somewhat if you still owned the bond in 2005 when its market value was $9,391 because the interest rate on similar-risk investments had decreased to 4.1 percent. Unfortunately, if you held on to the bond hoping that its price would increase, you would have been disappointed because in June 2006 its value declined to $8,785, when interest rates increased to 5.3 percent. Although you would have incurred a capital loss during this three-year period, you would have received interest payments equal to $160 every six months ($320 each year).

Why did the market value of the Treasury bond change? The primary reason the value of this investment, as well as other debt instruments, changed was that market interest rates changed several times during the 2003–2006 period. An investor who purchased a 10-year Treasury bond in June 2003, when interest rates were at historically low levels and then sold the same bond in July 2006, after interest rates had increased, would have earned an average annual return (noncompounded) equal to −0.9 percent. The return consisted of a capital loss equal to $1,215 = $8,785 − $10,000 and interest payments totaling $960 ($320 each year), which would have resulted in a net dollar *loss* equal to $255. If you continued to hold the bond, you would find that its value would change each time interest rates change. Whether the bond's value increases or decreases depends on the direction of the interest rate change.

As you read this chapter, think about why the value of the Treasury bonds decreased during the 2003–2006 period, which was characterized by generally increasing interest rates. What happens to the values of bonds when the returns demanded by investors—that is, interest rates—change? The concepts presented in this chapter will help you answer the question. The better you understand general valuation concepts, such as those presented in this chapter, the better financial decisions you will make, both in business and in your personal life (e.g., retirement planning).

Chapter *Essentials*
—The Questions

After reading this chapter, you should be able to answer the following questions:

- What is debt? What types of debt exist and what are some of the characteristics of debt?
- What are bond ratings? What information is provided by bond ratings?
- How are bond prices determined?
- How are bond yields (market rates) determined?
- What is the relationship between bond prices and interest rates? Why is it important for investors to understand this relationship?

In this chapter, we discuss debt. In the next few sections, we describe the general characteristics and features of debt. Then, we show how bonds are valued and discuss factors that affect the value of bonds. It is important to understand the valuation concepts presented in this chapter because they represent the primary foundation of finance.

# DEBT CHARACTERISTICS[1]

**debt**

A loan to a firm, government, or individual.

Simply stated, **debt** is a loan to a firm, government, or individual. Many types of debt instruments exist: home mortgages, commercial paper, term loans, bonds, secured and unsecured notes, and marketable and nonmarketable debt, among others. Often, we identify debt by describing three of its features: the principal amount that needs to be repaid, the interest payments, and the time to maturity. For instance, a $1,000, 10-year, 8 percent bond consists of debt with a $1,000 principal due in 10 years that pays interest equal to 8 percent of the principal amount, or $80, per year. In this section, we explain the meaning of these terms and describe some of the general features associated with debt.

## Principal Value, Face Value, Maturity Value, and Par Value

The principal value of debt represents the amount owed to the lender, which must be repaid at some point during the life of the debt. For much of the debt issued by corporations, the principal amount is repaid at maturity. Consequently, we also refer to the principal value as the *maturity value.* In addition, the principal value generally is written on the "face," or outside page, of the debt instrument, so it is sometimes called the *face value.* When the market value of debt is the same as its face value, it is said to be selling at *par;* thus, the principal amount is also referred to as the *par value.* For most debt, the terms *par value, face value, maturity value,* and *principal value* are used interchangeably to designate the amount that must be repaid by the borrower.

## Interest Payments

In many cases, owners of debt instruments receive periodic payments of interest, which are computed as a percentage of the principal amount. For example, if you buy a corporate bond that has a $1,000 face value and pays 8 percent interest, you will receive $80 interest per year from the company that issued the bond. Some debt does not pay interest; to generate a positive return for investors, such financial assets must sell for less than their par, or maturity, values. Securities that sell for less than their par values are said to be selling at a discount. Securities that sell at a discount when issued are

---

[1]In this chapter, we primarily discuss bonds (debt) from the perspective of a corporation. Most of the characteristics we describe for corporate debt also apply to government debt.

called **discounted securities.** Often, discounted debt securities have maturities of one year or less.

## Maturity Date

The maturity date represents the date on which the principal amount of a debt is due. As long as interest has been paid when due, once the principal amount is repaid, the debt obligation has been satisfied. Some debt instruments, called installment loans, require the principal amount to be repaid in several payments during the life of the loan. In such cases, the maturity date is the date the last installment payment of principal is due. The time to maturity varies—some debt has maturity as short as a few hours, while other debt has no specific maturity.

## Priority to Assets and Earnings

Corporate debt holders have priority over stockholders with regard to distribution of earnings and liquidation of assets. That is, they must be paid before stockholders can be paid. Interest on debt is paid before stock dividends are distributed, and any outstanding debt must be repaid before stockholders can receive any proceeds from liquidation of the company.

## Control of the Firm (Voting Rights)

Corporate debt holders do not have voting rights, so they cannot attain control of the firm. Nevertheless, debt holders can affect the management and the operations of a firm by placing restrictions on the use of the funds as part of the loan agreement.

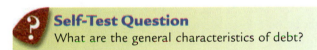

**Self-Test Question**
What are the general characteristics of debt?

## TYPES OF DEBT

Many different types of debt exist. In general, however, we categorize debt as being either short term or long term. In this section, we describe some common debt instruments. When reading this section, keep in mind that there are two participants in a debt arrangement: the borrower, who pays interest (or some similar cost) to use money provided by others, and the lender (investor), who provides money to the borrower for the "right price." We discuss factors that determine the "right price," or the cost of money, in Chapter 5. In this section, we discuss some of the different forms debt can take—that is, the different types of debt that are available to both borrowers and lenders (investors).

## Short-Term Debt

Short-term debt generally refers to debt instruments with maturities of one year or less. Some of the more common short-term debt instruments are described here.

### Treasury Bills

**Treasury bills (T-bills)** are discounted securities issued by the U.S. government to finance operations. When the U.S. Treasury issues T-bills, the prices are determined by an auction process: Interested investors and investing organizations submit competitive bids for the T-bills offered.[2] T-bills are issued electronically with face values ranging from $1,000 to $5 million and with maturities of four, 13, or 26 weeks at the time of issue.

## Repurchase Agreement (Repo)

**repurchase agreement**
An arrangement in which one firm sells some of its financial assets to another firm with a promise to *repurchase* the securities at a later date.

A **repurchase agreement** is an arrangement in which one firm sells some of its financial assets to another firm with a promise to *repurchase* the securities at a higher price at a later date. The price at which the securities will be repurchased is agreed to at the time the *repo* is arranged. One firm agrees to sell the securities because it needs funds, whereas the other firm agrees to purchase the securities because it has excess funds to invest. Thus, with this arrangement, the repo *seller* effectively borrows funds from the repo *buyer*. Often the parties involved in repurchase agreements are banks, and the securities that are sold and repurchased are government securities such as T-bills. Although some repos last for days or even weeks, the maturity for most repurchase agreements is overnight.

## Federal Funds

**federal funds**
Overnight loans from one bank to another.

Often referred to simply as "fed funds," **federal funds** represent overnight loans from one bank to another. Banks generally use the fed funds market to adjust their reserves: Banks that need additional funds to meet the reserve requirements of the Federal Reserve borrow from banks with excess reserves. The interest rate associated with such debt is known as the *federal funds rate.* Federal funds have very short maturities, often overnight.

## Banker's Acceptance

**banker's acceptance**
An instrument issued by a bank that obligates the bank to pay a specified amount at some future date.

A **banker's acceptance** might be best described as a postdated check. More accurately, a banker's acceptance is a time draft—an instrument issued by a bank that obligates the bank to pay a specified amount to the owner of the banker's acceptance at some future date. Generally used in international trade, a banker's acceptance arrangement is established between a bank and a firm to ensure the firm's international trading partner that payment for goods and services essentially is guaranteed at some future date, which is sufficient time to verify the completion of the transaction. A banker's acceptance is generally sold by the original owner before its maturity to raise immediate cash. Because a banker's acceptance does not pay interest, it is sold at a discount. Banker's acceptances generally have maturities of 180 days or less.

## Commercial Paper

**commercial paper**
A discounted instrument that is a type of promissory note, or legal IOU, issued by large, financially sound firms.

**Commercial paper** is a type of promissory note, or legal IOU, issued by large, financially sound firms. Like a T-bill, commercial paper does not pay interest, so it must be sold at a discount. The maturity on commercial paper varies from one to nine months, with an average of about five months.[3] Generally, commercial paper is issued in denominations of $100,000 or more, so few individuals can afford to *directly* invest in the commercial paper market. Instead, commercial paper is sold primarily to other businesses, insurance companies, pension funds, money market mutual funds, and banks.

---

[2]The Treasury also sells T-bills on a noncompetitive basis to investors or investment organizations offering to buy a certain dollar amount. In such cases, the purchase price is based on the average of the competitive bids received by the Treasury.

[3]The maximum maturity without SEC registration is 270 days. Also, commercial paper can be sold only to "sophisticated" investors; otherwise, SEC registration would be required even for maturities of less than 270 days.

## Certificate of Deposit (CD)

A **certificate of deposit** represents a time deposit at a bank or other financial intermediary. Traditional CDs generally earn periodic interest and must be kept at the issuing institution for a specified time period. To liquidate a traditional CD prior to maturity, the owner must return it to the issuing institution, which applies an interest penalty to the amount paid out.

**Negotiable CDs,** however, can be traded to other investors prior to maturity because they can be redeemed by whoever owns them at maturity. Often called jumbo CDs, these investments typically are issued in denominations of $1 million to $5 million, and they have maturities that range from a few months to a few years.

## Eurodollar Deposit

A **Eurodollar deposit** is a deposit in a bank outside the United States that is not converted into the currency of the foreign country; instead, it is denominated in U.S. dollars. Such deposits are not exposed to exchange rate risk, which is the risk associated with converting dollars into foreign currencies. Eurodollar deposits earn rates offered by foreign banks and are not subject to the same regulations imposed on deposits in U.S. banks. Consequently, the rate that can be earned on Eurodollars is sometimes considerably greater than the rate that can be earned in the United States.

## Money Market Mutual Funds

**Money market mutual funds** are investment funds that are pooled and managed by firms that specialize in investing money for others (called investment companies) for the purpose of investing in short-term financial assets, including those described here. These funds offer individual investors the ability to *indirectly* invest in such short-term securities as T-bills, commercial paper, Eurodollars, and so on, which they otherwise would not be able to purchase because such investments either are sold in denominations that are too large or are not sold to individuals.

# Long-Term Debt

Long-term debt refers to debt instruments with maturities greater than one year. Owners of such debt generally receive periodic payments of interest. This section describes some common types of long-term debt.

## Term Loans

A **term loan** is a contract under which a borrower agrees to make a series of interest and principal payments on specific dates to the lender. Term loans usually are negotiated directly between the borrowing firm and a financial institution, such as a bank, an insurance company, or a pension fund. For this reason, they are often referred to as private debt. Although term loans' maturities vary from two to 30 years, most maturities are in the three-year to 15-year range.[4]

Term loans have three major advantages over public debt offerings such as corporate bonds: *speed, flexibility,* and *low issuance costs.* Because they are negotiated

**certificate of deposit**
An interest-earning time deposit at a bank or other financial intermediary.

**negotiable CD**
Certificate of deposit that can be traded to other investors prior to maturity; redemption is made by the investor who owns the CD at maturity.

**Eurodollar deposit**
A deposit in a foreign bank that is denominated in U.S. dollars.

**money market mutual funds**
Pools of funds managed by investment companies that are primarily invested in short-term financial assets.

**term loan**
A loan, generally obtained from a bank or insurance company, on which the borrower agrees to make a series of payments consisting of interest and principal.

---

[4]Most term loans are amortized, which means they are paid off in equal installments over the life of the loan. Amortization protects the lender against the possibility that the borrower will not make adequate provisions for the loan's retirement during the life of the loan. (Chapter 4 reviews the concept of amortization.) Also, if the interest and principal payments required under a term loan agreement are not met on schedule, the borrowing firm is said to have *defaulted,* and it can then be forced into bankruptcy.

directly between the lender and the borrower, formal documentation is minimized. The key provisions of a term loan can be worked out much more quickly than can those for a public issue, and it is not necessary for the loan to go through the Securities and Exchange Commission (SEC) registration process. Another advantage of term loans relates to their future flexibility. If a bond issue is held by many different bondholders, it is virtually impossible to obtain permission to alter the terms of the agreement, even though new economic conditions might make such changes desirable. With a term loan, however, the borrower generally can sit down with the lender and work out mutually agreeable modifications to the contract.

The interest rate on a term loan can be either fixed for the life of the loan or variable. If a fixed rate is used, generally it will be set close to the rate on bonds of equivalent maturity and risk at the time of issue. If the rate is variable, usually it will be set at a certain number of percentage points above an index representing the prime rate, the commercial paper rate, the T-bill rate, or some other designated rate. When the index rate rises or falls, the rate charged on the outstanding balance of the term loan is adjusted accordingly at specified periods. Generally, when interest rates become more volatile, banks and other lenders are more reluctant to make long-term, fixed-rate loans, so variable-rate term loans become more common.

## Bonds

**bond**
A long-term debt instrument.

**coupon rate**
Interest paid on a bond or other debt instrument stated as a percentage of its face, or maturity, value.

**government bond**
Debt issued by federal, state, or local governments.

**municipal bond**
A bond issued by state or local governments.

**revenue bond**
A municipal bond that generates revenue, which in turn can be used to make interest payments and repay the principal.

**general obligation bond**
A municipal bond backed by the local government's ability to impose taxes.

**corporate bonds**
Long-term debt instruments issued by corporations.

A **bond** is a long-term contract under which a borrower agrees to make payments of interest and principal on specific dates to the bondholder (investor). The interest payments are determined by the *coupon rate* and the principal, or face, value of the bond. The **coupon rate** represents the total interest paid each year, stated as a percentage of the bond's face value. Typically, interest is paid semiannually, although bonds that pay interest annually, quarterly, and monthly also exist. For example, a 10 percent coupon bond with a face value equal to $1,000 would commonly pay $50 interest every six months, or a total of $100 each year.

Next, we describe some of the more common bonds issued by both governments and corporations.

1. **Government bonds** are issued by the U.S. government, state governments, and local or municipal governments. U.S. government bonds are issued by the U.S. Treasury and are called either *Treasury notes* or *Treasury bonds*. Both types of debt pay interest semiannually. The primary difference between Treasury notes and Treasury bonds is the maturity when the debt is issued: The original maturity on notes is from more than one year to 10 years, whereas the original maturity on bonds exceeds 10 years.

    **Municipal bonds**, or *munis*, are similar to Treasury bonds, except that they are issued by state and local governments. The two principal types of munis are revenue bonds and general obligation bonds. **Revenue bonds** are used to raise funds for projects that generate *revenues*, which contribute to payment of interest and the repayment of the debt. **General obligation bonds** are backed by the government's ability to tax its citizens; special taxes or tax increases are used to generate the funds needed to service such bonds. Generally, the income that an investor earns from munis is exempt from federal taxes.

2. As the name implies, **corporate bonds** are issued by businesses called corporations.[5] Although corporate bonds traditionally have been issued with

---

[5]The forms of business organizations—proprietorships, partnerships, and corporations—are described in Chapter 1. At this point, we need note only that corporate bonds are issued by businesses formed as corporations; proprietorships and partnerships cannot use corporate bonds to raise funds.

maturities of between 20 and 30 years, bonds with shorter maturities, such as seven to 10 years, are also common. Corporate bonds resemble term loans, but a bond issue generally is advertised, offered to the public, and sold to many different investors. Indeed, thousands of individual and institutional investors might purchase bonds when a firm sells a bond issue, whereas generally only one lender is involved with a term loan.[6] With corporate bonds, the interest rate typically remains fixed, although the popularity of floating-rate bonds has grown during the past couple of decades. In addition, several types of corporate bonds exist, the most important of which are discussed in the remainder of this section.

3. With a **mortgage bond,** the corporation pledges certain assets as security, or collateral, for the bond. To illustrate, in 2007 Muttle Furniture needed $30 million to build a major regional distribution center. The company issued bonds in the amount of $24 million, secured by a mortgage on the property. (The remaining $6 million was financed with stock, or equity capital.) If Muttle defaults on the bonds, the bondholders can foreclose on the property and sell it to satisfy their claims. At the same time, if Muttle so chooses, it can issue *second mortgage bonds* secured by the same $30 million facility. In the event of liquidation, the holders of these second mortgage bonds would have a claim against the property, but only after the first mortgage bondholders had been paid off in full. Second mortgages are sometimes called *junior mortgages* because they are junior in priority to the claims of *senior mortgages,* or *first mortgage bonds.*

**mortgage bond**
A bond backed by fixed assets. First mortgage bonds are senior in priority to claims of second mortgage bonds.

4. A **debenture** is an unsecured bond; as such, it provides no lien, or claim, against specific property as security for the obligation. Therefore, debenture holders are general creditors whose claims are protected by property not otherwise pledged as collateral. In practice, the use of debentures depends on the nature of the firm's assets as well as its general credit strength. An extremely strong company, such as IBM, will tend to use debentures; it simply does not need to put up property as security for its debt. Debentures also are issued by companies in industries in which it would not be practical to provide security through a mortgage on fixed assets. For example, large mail-order houses and commercial banks characteristically hold most of their assets in the form of inventories or loans, neither of which is satisfactory security for a long-term mortgage bond.

**debenture**
A long-term bond that is not secured by a mortgage on specific property.

A **subordinated debenture** is an unsecured bond that ranks below, or is "inferior to," other debt with respect to claims on cash distributions made by the firm. In the event of bankruptcy, for instance, *subordinated debt* has claims on assets only after senior debt has been paid off. Subordinated debentures might be subordinated either to designated notes payable (usually bank loans) or to all other debt.

**subordinated debenture**
A bond that has a claim on assets only after the senior debt has been paid off in the event of liquidation.

5. Several other types of corporate bonds are used sufficiently often to merit mention. First, **income bonds** pay interest only when the firm has sufficient income to cover the interest payments. As a consequence, missing interest payments on these securities cannot bankrupt a company. From an investor's standpoint these bonds are riskier than "regular" bonds.

**income bond**
A bond that pays interest to the holder only if the interest is earned by the firm.

---

[6]For very large term loans, 20 or more financial institutions might form a syndicate to grant the credit. Also, note that a bond issue can be sold to one lender (or to just a few); in this case, the issue is said to be "privately placed." Companies that place bonds privately do so for the same reasons that they use term loans—speed, flexibility, and low issuance costs.

**putable bond**
A bond that can be redeemed at the bond-holder's option when certain circumstances exist.

**indexed (purchasing power) bond**
A bond that has interest payments based on an inflation index to protect the holder from inflation.

**floating-rate bond**
A bond whose interest rate fluctuates with shifts in the general level of interest rates.

**zero coupon bond**
A bond that pays no annual interest but is sold at a discount below par, thus providing compensation to investors in the form of capital appreciation.

**junk bond**
A high-risk, high-yield bond used to finance mergers, leveraged buyouts, and troubled companies.

**Putable bonds** are bonds that can be turned in and exchanged for cash at the bondholder's option. Generally, the option to turn in the bond can be exercised only if the firm takes some specified action, such as being acquired by a weaker company or increasing its outstanding debt by a large amount.

**Indexed,** or **purchasing power, bonds** are popular in countries plagued by high rates of inflation. With such a bond, the interest payment is based on an inflation index such as the Consumer Price Index (CPI). The interest paid rises automatically when the inflation rate rises, thereby protecting bondholders against inflation.

**Floating-rate bonds** are similar to *indexed bonds* except the coupon rates on these bonds "float" with market interest rates rather than with the inflation rate. Thus, when interest rates rise, the coupon rates will increase, and vice versa. In many cases, limits are imposed on how high and low (referred to as "caps" and "collars," respectively) the rates on such debt can change, both during each period (year) and over the life of the bond.

6. During the 1980s, some interesting new debt instruments were introduced, which illustrates how flexible and innovative issuers can be. *Original issue discount bonds (OIDs)*, commonly referred to as **zero coupon bonds,** were created during this era. These securities were offered at substantial discounts below their par values because they paid little or no coupon interest. OIDs have since lost their attraction for many individual investors, primarily because the interest income that must be reported each year for tax purposes includes any cash interest actually received, which is $0 for zero coupons, plus the annual *prorated* capital appreciation that would be received if the bond was held to maturity. Thus capital appreciation is taxed before it is actually received. For this reason, most OID bonds currently are held by institutional investors, such as pension funds and mutual funds, rather than by individual investors.[7]

7. Another innovation from the 1980s is the **junk bond,** a high-risk, high-yield bond often issued to finance a management buyout (MBO), a merger, or a troubled company. In junk bond deals, firms generally have significant amounts of debt, so bondholders must bear as much risk as stockholders normally would. The yields on these bonds reflect this fact. For example, at the beginning of 2005, R. J. Tower Automotive, which produces structural components for automobiles, found itself in a troubled financial situation, so the company filed for bankruptcy. At the time, more than 75 percent of Tower's total financing consisted of debt, which the company was having difficulty servicing—that is, covering the required payments. At the beginning of 2006, even though it was fighting to emerge from bankruptcy, Tower's debt position had deteriorated such that its debt ratio—that is, total debt divided by total assets—was nearly 91 percent. In July 2006, its bond issue with a coupon rate equal to 12 percent was selling for 60.5 percent of face value, which meant that investors could buy an R. J. Tower bond with a $1,000 face value for $605 and earn nearly 25 percent if they held the bond

---

[7]Shortly after corporations began to issue zeros, investment firms figured out a way to create zeros from U.S. Treasury bonds, which are issued only in coupon form. In 1982, Salomon Brothers bought $1 billion of 12 percent, 30-year Treasuries. Each bond had 60 coupons worth $60 each, which represented the interest payments due every six months. Salomon then in effect clipped the coupons and placed them in 60 piles; the last pile also contained the "stripped" bond itself, which represented a promise to pay $1,000 in 2012. These 60 piles of U.S. Treasury promises were then placed with the trust department of a bank and used as collateral for "zero coupon U.S. Treasury Trust Certificates," which are, in essence, zero coupon Treasury bonds. A pension fund that expected to need money in 2007 could have bought 25-year certificates backed by the interest that the Treasury will pay in 2007. Treasury zeros are, of course, safer than corporate zeros, so they are very popular with pension fund managers.

until its 2013 maturity. At the time, the yield on average-risk corporate bonds with similar maturity dates was nearly 6 percent. The emergence of junk bonds as an important type of debt is another example of how corporations adjust to and facilitate new developments in the financial markets.[8]

## Rates of Return on Different Types of Debt

To give you some perspective as to how they relate, Table 6-1 lists some of the different types of debt we discussed in this section. The debt instruments are arranged from those with the shortest maturities to those with the longest maturities. Because short-term debt has greater liquidity and less maturity risk than long-term debt, everything else equal, we expect the rates on short-term debt to be lower than the rates on long-term debt. In other words, as we discussed in Chapter 5, the liquidity premium (LP) and the maturity risk premium (MRP) should be lower for short-term debt than long-term debt. The rates shown in Table 6-1 follow this pattern.

### Self-Test Questions

Differentiate between the characteristics of short-term debt and the characteristics of long-term debt.

What are the three major advantages that term loans have over public offerings?

Differentiate between term loans and bonds.

Differentiate between mortgage bonds and debentures.

Define income bonds, putable bonds, and indexed bonds.

What problem was solved by the introduction of long-term floating-rate debt, and how is the rate on such bonds actually set?

Why would you expect junk bonds to have higher yields than traditional bonds with similar coupons?

## BOND CONTRACT FEATURES

A firm's managers are concerned with both the effective cost of debt and any restrictions in debt contracts that might limit the firm's future actions. This section discusses features that generally are included in bond contracts, which can affect the firm's cost of debt and its future financial flexibility.

## Bond Indenture

Bondholders have a legitimate fear that once they lend money to a company and become "locked in" for a period as long as 30 years the firm will take some action that is designed to benefit stockholders but is harmful to bondholders. Bondholders attempt

---

[8]The development of junk bond financing has, as much as any other factor, helped to reshape the U.S. financial scene. The existence of these securities led directly to the loss of independence of Gulf Oil and hundreds of other companies, and it prompted major shake-ups in such companies as CBS, Union Carbide, and USX (formerly U.S. Steel). The phenomenal growth of the junk bond market was impressive but controversial. Significant risk, combined with unscrupulous dealings, produced substantial losses for investors. In 1990, for example, "junk bond king" Michael Milken was sent to jail for his role in misleading investors in this market. Additionally, the realization that high leverage can spell trouble—as when Campeau, with $3 billion in junk financing, filed for bankruptcy in early 1990—slowed the growth in the junk bond market from its glory days. Recent trends, however, indicate that a slight resurgence has begun.

**TABLE 6-1**   Summary of Debt Instruments

| Instrument | Market Participants | Riskiness | Maturity | Rates on 7/26/06[a] |
|---|---|---|---|---|
| Treasury bills | Sold to institutional investors by the Treasury to finance government operations | Default free | four to 26 weeks | 5.1% |
| Repurchase agreements | Used by banks to adjust reserves—sell investments with a repurchase promise | Low risk | Very short/overnight | 5.2% |
| Federal funds | Interbank loans used to adjust reserves | Low risk | Very short/overnight | 5.3% |
| Banker's acceptances | Firm's promise to pay (IOU); guaranteed by a bank | Low risk if bank is strong | Up to 180 days | 5.4% |
| Commercial paper | Issued by large, financially secure firms | Low default risk | Up to 270 days | 5.4% |
| Negotiable CDs | Issued by large, financially sound banks | Riskier than T-bills | Up to a few years | 5.5% |
| Eurodollars | Dollar-denominated deposits in foreign banks | Depends on strength of foreign bank | Up to 1 year | 5.6% |
| Money market funds | Invest in T-bills, CDs, and other short-term investments | Low risk | No specific maturity (instant liquidity) | 4.6% |
| Treasury notes/bonds | Issued by the U.S. government to finance expenditures | No default risk, but prices change when market rates change | 1 to 30 years | 5.2% |
| Municipal bonds | Issued by state and local governments | Riskier than Treasury bonds | Up to 30 years | 4.7% |
| Term loans | Issued by corporations; negotiated with financial institutions | Depends on borrower; riskier than government bonds | 2 to 30 years | 5.8% |
| Residential mortgages | Property loans from financial intermediaries | Risk depends on borrower; much riskier than government bonds | Up to 30 years | 6.4% |
| Corporate bonds | Debt issued by corporations | Depends on the company; riskier than government bonds; not as risky as stock | Up to 40 years | 5.9% |

[a]Interest rates are for the longest maturity securities of the type and for the strongest (safest) securities of a given type. Thus, the 5.9 percent interest rate shown for corporate bonds reflects that rate on 30-year, AAA bonds. Lower-rated bonds have higher interest rates.

**indenture**

A formal agreement (contract) between the issuer of a bond and the bondholders.

to reduce the potential for financial problems by use of legal restrictions designed to ensure, insofar as possible, that the company does nothing to cause the quality of its bonds to deteriorate after they have been issued. An **indenture** is a legal document that spells out any legal restrictions associated with the bond as well as the rights of the bondholders (lenders) and the corporation (bond issuer). A **trustee,** usually a bank, is assigned to represent the bondholders and to guarantee that the terms of the indenture are carried out. The indenture might be several hundred pages long, and it includes **restrictive covenants** that cover such points as the conditions under which the issuer can pay off the bonds prior to maturity, the level at which various financial measures (such as the ability to pay interest) must be maintained if the company is to sell additional bonds, and restrictions against the payment of dividends when earnings do not meet certain specifications. The Securities and Exchange Commission approves indentures for publicly traded bonds and verifies that all indenture provisions have been met before allowing a company to sell new securities to the public. The trustee is responsible for making sure that any covenants are not violated and for taking appropriate action if they are. What constitutes "appropriate action" varies with the circumstances. Perhaps insisting on immediate compliance would result in bankruptcy, which in turn might lead to large losses on the bonds. In such a case, the trustee might decide that the bondholders would be better served by giving the company a chance to work out its problems rather than by forcing it into bankruptcy.

**trustee**
An official who ensures that the bondholders' interests are protected and that the terms of the indenture are carried out.

**restrictive covenant**
A provision in a debt contract that constrains the actions of the borrower.

## Call Provision

Most corporate bonds contain a **call provision,** which gives the issuing corporation the right to call the bonds for redemption prior to maturity. A call provision generally states that the company must pay the bondholders an amount greater than the par value for the bonds when they are called. This additional sum, which is termed a *call premium,* typically equals one year's interest if the bonds are called during the first year in which a call is permitted; the premium declines at a constant rate each year thereafter. Bonds usually are not callable until several years (generally five to 10) after they are issued; bonds with such *deferred calls* are said to have *call protection.* Call provisions allow firms to refinance debt, much as individuals might refinance mortgages on their houses—when interest rates decline, firms can *recall* (refund) some existing debt and replace it with new, lower-cost debt.

**call provision**
A provision in a bond contract that gives the issuer the right to redeem the bonds under specified terms prior to the normal maturity date.

## Sinking Fund

A **sinking fund** is a provision that facilitates the orderly retirement of a bond issue. Typically, the sinking fund provision requires the firm to retire a portion of the bond issue each year. On rare occasions, the firm might be required to deposit money with a trustee, which invests the funds and then uses the accumulated sum to retire the bonds when they mature. Failure to meet the sinking fund requirement will throw the bond issue into default, which might force the company into bankruptcy. In most cases, the firm has the right to handle the sinking fund in two ways: by randomly calling for redemption (at par value) of a certain percentage of the bonds each year or by purchasing the required amount of bonds in the open market. The firm will choose the lower-cost method. If interest rates have risen, causing bond prices to fall, it will buy bonds in the open market at a discount; if interest rates have fallen, it will call the bonds. Note that a call for sinking fund purposes is quite different from a refunding call as discussed earlier. A sinking fund call does not require the company to pay a call premium, but only a small percentage of the issue is normally callable in any one year.

**sinking fund**
A required annual payment designed to amortize a bond issue.

## Convertible Feature[9]

A **conversion feature** permits the bondholder (investor) to exchange, or *convert,* the bond into shares of common stock at a fixed price. Investors have greater flexibility with *convertible bonds* than with straight bonds because they can choose whether to hold the

**conversion feature**
Permits bondholders to exchange their investments for a fixed number of shares of common stock.

---

[9]We discuss the characteristics of convertible securities in greater detail in Chapter 18.

| TABLE 6-2 | Moody's & Standard & Poor's (S&P) Bond Ratings | | | | | | | |
|---|---|---|---|---|---|---|---|---|
| | **High Quality** | | | **Investment Grade** | **Junk Bonds** | | | |
| | | | | | **Substandard** | | **Speculative** | |
| Moody's | Aaa | Aa | A | Baa | Ba | B | Caa | C |
| S&P | AAA | AA | A | BBB | BB | B | CCC | D |

**Note:** Both Moody's and S&P use "modifiers" for bonds rated below triple A. S&P uses a plus and minus system; that is, A$^+$ designates the strongest A-rated bonds and A– indicates the weakest. Moody' uses a 1, 2, or 3 designation, with 1 denoting the strongest and 3 the weakest; thus, within the double-A category, Aa1 is the best, Aa2 is average, and Aa3 is the weakest.

company's bond or convert into its stock. When the conversion takes place, the firm has effectively issued stock. Once the conversion is made, investors cannot convert back to bonds (preferred stock).

An important provision of a convertible bond is the conversion ratio, which is defined as the number of shares of stock that the bondholder receives upon conversion. Related to the conversion ratio is the conversion price, which is the effective price paid for the common stock obtained by converting a convertible bond. For example, a $1,000 convertible bond with a conversion ratio of 20 can be converted into 20 shares of common stock, so the conversion price is $50 = $1,000/20. If the market value of the stock rises above $50 per share, it would be beneficial for the bondholder to convert into stock (ignoring any costs associated with conversion).

### Self-Test Questions

How do trustees and indentures reduce potential problems for bond-holders?

What are the two ways in which a sinking fund can be handled? Which method will the firm choose if interest rates rise? If interest rates fall?

What is the difference between a call for sinking fund purposes and a refunding call?

Are securities that provide for a sinking fund regarded as riskier than those without this type of provision? Explain.

Why is a call provision so advantageous to a bond issuer? When will the issuer initiate a refunding call? Why?

## BOND RATINGS

**investment-grade bond**
A bond rated A or triple B; many banks and other institutional investors are permitted by law to hold only bonds rated investment-grade or better.

Since the early 1900s bonds have been assigned quality ratings that reflect their probability of going into default. The two major rating agencies are Moody's Investors Service (Moody's) and Standard & Poor's Corporation (S&P). Table 6-2 shows these agencies' rating designations.[10] The triple-A and double-A bonds are extremely safe. Single-A and triple-B bonds are strong enough to be called **investment-grade bonds;** they are the lowest rated bonds that many banks and other institutional investors are permitted by law to hold. Double-B and lower-rated bonds are speculative, or *junk bonds;* they have a significant probability of going into default, and many financial institutions are prohibited from buying them.

---

[10]In the discussion to follow, a reference to the S&P code is intended to imply the Moody's code as well. Thus "triple-B bonds" mean both BBB and Baa bonds, "double-B bonds" mean both BB and Ba bonds, and so on.

**FIGURE 6-1**   Yields on Selected Long-Term Bonds, 1990–2006

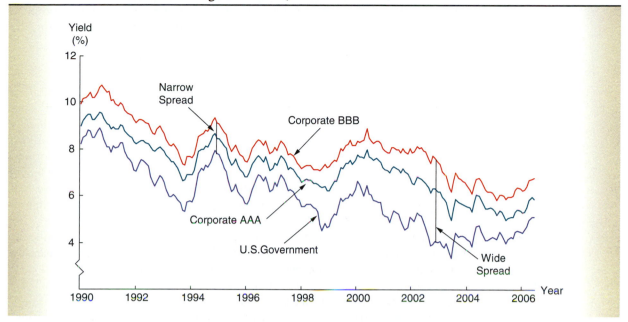

**Note:** The yields for the U.S. government bonds are based on bonds with 10-year maturities.

## Bond Rating Criteria

Bond ratings are based on both qualitative and quantitative factors. Factors considered by the bond rating agencies include the financial strength of the company as measured by various ratios, collateral provisions, the seniority of the debt, restrictive covenants, provisions such as a sinking fund or a deferred call, litigation possibilities, regulation, and so on. Representatives of the rating agencies have consistently stated that no precise formula is used to set a firm's rating; all the factors listed, plus others, are taken into account, but not in a mathematically precise manner. Statistical studies have borne out this contention. Indeed, researchers who have tried to predict bond ratings on the basis of quantitative data have found only limited success, indicating that the agencies use subjective judgment when establishing a firm's rating.[11]

## Importance of Bond Ratings

Bond ratings are important to both issuers and investors for several reasons. First, because a bond's rating serves as an indicator of its default risk, the rating has a direct, measurable influence on the bond's interest rate and the firm's cost of using such debt. As we discussed in Chapter 5, the greater a bond's default risk, the greater the default risk premium (DRP) associated with the bond. Second, most bonds are purchased by institutional investors rather than individuals, and many institutions are restricted to investment-grade, or high-quality, securities. If a firm's bonds fall below a BBB rating, it will therefore have a difficult time selling new bonds because many potential purchasers will not be allowed to buy them. As a result of their higher risk and more restricted market, lower-grade bonds offer higher returns than high-grade bonds. Figure 6-1 illustrates this point. In each of the years shown on the graph, U.S.

---

[11]See Ahmed Belkaoui, *Industrial Bonds and the Rating Process* (London: Quorum Books, 1983).

government bonds have the lowest yields, AAA-rated corporate bonds have the next lowest, and BBB-rated corporate bonds have the highest yields. The figure also shows that the gaps between yields on the three types of bonds vary over time, indicating that the cost differentials, or risk premiums, fluctuate as well.

## Changes in Ratings

Changes in a firm's bond rating affect both its ability to borrow long-term capital and the cost of such funds. Rating agencies review outstanding bonds on a periodic basis, occasionally upgrading or downgrading a bond as a result of its issuer's changed circumstances. For example, in June–July 2006, S&P downgraded the debt of Ford Motor Company from BB− to B+. The rating change was made to reflect poor sales and Ford's tenuous financial position. The bond ratings for both Ford and General Motors had slipped to "junk bond" status during the previous year because both companies were trying to reverse financial distress caused by substantial declines in sales of some of the models of automobiles that were previously popular with buyers (e.g., SUVs). At the same time, S&P upgraded the debt of defense contractor Lockheed Martin from BBB+ to A− because the outlook for improved earnings was good and the company took actions to stabilize its financial position.

### Self-Test Questions

Name the two major rating agencies and some factors that affect bond ratings.

Why are bond ratings important to both firms and investors?

## FOREIGN DEBT INSTRUMENTS

Like the U.S. debt markets, the international debt markets offer a variety of instruments with many different features. Here, we discuss a few of the more familiar types of debt that are traded internationally.

Any debt sold outside the country of the borrower (issuer) is called international debt. Two important types of international debt exist: foreign debt and Eurodebt.

**foreign debt**
Debt issued by a foreign borrower but denominated in the currency of the country in which it is sold.

**Foreign debt** is debt sold by a foreign borrower but denominated in the currency of the country in which the issue is sold. For instance, Bell Canada might need U.S. dollars to finance the operations of its subsidiaries in the United States. If it decides to raise the needed capital in the domestic U.S. bond market, the bond will be underwritten by a syndicate of U.S. investment firms, denominated in U.S. dollars, and sold to U.S. investors in accordance with SEC and applicable state regulations. Except for the foreign origin of the borrower (Canada), this bond is indistinguishable from bonds issued by equivalent U.S. corporations. Because Bell Canada is a foreign corporation, however, its bond is called a *foreign bond.* Foreign bonds generally are labeled according to the country in which they are issued. For example, if foreign bonds are issued in the United States, they are called *Yankee bonds;* if they are issued in Japan, they are called *Samurai bonds;* and if they are issued in the United Kingdom, they are called *Bulldog bonds.*

**Eurodebt**
Debt issued in a country other than the one in whose currency the debt is denominated.

The term **Eurodebt** is used to designate any debt sold in a country other than the one in whose currency the debt is denominated. Examples include *Eurobonds,* such as a British firm's issue of pound-denominated bonds sold in France or Ford Motor Company's dollar-denominated issue that is sold in Germany. The institutional arrangements by which Eurobonds are marketed are different from those for most other bond issues, with the most important distinction being a far lower level of required disclosure than normally applies to bonds issued in domestic markets, particularly in the United States. Governments tend to be less strict when regulating securities denominated in foreign currencies than they are on home-currency securities because the bonds' purchasers generally are more "sophisticated." The lower disclosure requirements result in lower total transaction costs for Eurobonds.

Eurobonds appeal to investors for several reasons. Generally, they are issued in bearer form rather than as registered bonds, so the names and nationalities of investors are not recorded. Individuals who desire anonymity, whether for privacy reasons or for tax avoidance, find Eurobonds to their liking. Similarly, most governments do not withhold taxes on interest payments associated with Eurobonds.

More than half of all Eurobonds are denominated in dollars; bonds in Japanese yen and Euros account for most of the rest. Although centered in Europe, Eurobonds truly are international. Their underwriting syndicates include investment firms from all regions of the world, and the bonds are sold to investors not only in Europe but also in such faraway places as Bahrain and Singapore. Until recently, Eurobonds were issued solely by multinational firms, international financial institutions, and national governments. Today, however, the Eurobond market is being tapped by purely domestic U.S. firms such as electric utilities, which find that borrowing overseas enables them to lower their debt costs.

Some other types of *Eurodebt* include the following:

1. *Eurocredits.* Eurocredits are bank loans that are denominated in the currency of a country other than that in which the lending bank is located. Many of these loans are very large, so the lending bank often forms a loan syndicate to help raise the needed funds and to spread out some of the risk associated with the loan.

   Interest rates on Eurocredits, as well as other short-term Eurodebt forms, typically are tied to a standard rate known by the acronym **LIBOR,** which stands for *London InterBank Offer Rate.* LIBOR is the rate of interest offered by the largest and strongest London banks on deposits of other large banks of the highest credit standing. In July 2006, the three-month LIBOR rate was 5.5 percent, which was the same as the rate offered by domestic U.S. banks on three-month certificates of deposit (CDs).

2. *Euro-commercial paper (Euro-CP).* Euro-CP is similar to commercial paper issued in the United States. This short-term debt instrument is issued by corporations, and it typically has a maturity of one, three, or six months. The principal difference between Euro-CP and U.S. commercial paper is that there is not as much concern about the credit quality of Euro-CP issuers.

3. *Euronotes.* Euronotes, which represent medium-term debt, typically have maturities ranging from one to 10 years. The general features of Euronotes closely resemble those of longer-term debt instruments such as bonds. The principal amount is repaid at maturity, and interest often is paid semiannually. Most foreign companies use Euronotes just as they would a line of credit, continuously issuing notes to finance medium-term needs.

**LIBOR**
The London InterBank Offer Rate; the interest rate offered by the best London banks on deposits of other large, very creditworthy banks.

**Self-Test Questions**

Differentiate between foreign debt and Eurodebt.

Why do Eurobonds appeal to investors?

What are Eurocredits, Euro-commercial paper, and Euronotes?

## VALUATION OF BONDS

As mentioned earlier, a bond's contract—the indenture—specifies such provisions as the principal amount (or par value) that must be repaid, the coupon interest rate, the maturity date, and any other features of the "loan." For example, suppose on January 2,

2007, Genesco Manufacturing borrowed $25 million by selling 25,000 individual bonds for $1,000 each. Genesco received the $25 million, and it promised to pay the holders of each bond annual interest equal to $100 per year and to repay the $25 million at the end of 15 years.[12] The lenders (investors), who wanted to earn a 10 percent return on their investment, were willing to give Genesco $25 million, so the value of the bond issue was $25 million. But how did investors decide that the issue was worth $25 million? Would the value have been different if they had demanded a different rate of return—say, 12 percent?

As we will see, a bond's market price is determined by the cash flows that it generates, both the interest that it pays, which depends on the coupon interest rate, and the principal amount that must be repaid. Other things held constant, *the higher the coupon rate, the higher the market price of the bond.* At the time a bond is issued, the coupon rate generally is set at a level that will cause the market price of the bond to equal its par value. With a lower coupon rate, investors would not be willing to pay $1,000 for the bond. With a higher coupon rate, investors would clamor for the bond and bid its price up over $1,000. Investment bankers can judge quite precisely the coupon rate that will cause a bond to sell at its $1,000 par value. A bond that has just been issued is known as a *new issue.* (*The Wall Street Journal* classifies a bond as a new issue for about one month after it has first been issued.) Once the bond has been on the market for a while, it is classified as an *outstanding bond,* or a *seasoned issue.* Newly issued bonds generally sell very close to their par values, but the prices of outstanding bonds can vary widely from their par values. Coupon interest payments are constant. Consequently, when economic conditions change, a bond that sold at par when it was issued will sell for more or less than par thereafter, depending on the relationship between the prevailing market rates and the bond's coupon rate.

## The Basic Bond Valuation Model[13]

The value of any financial asset is based on the cash flows that investors expect the asset to generate in the future. In the case of a bond, the cash flows consist of interest payments during the life of the bond plus a return of the principal amount borrowed (the par value) when the bond matures. In a cash flow time line format, here is the situation:

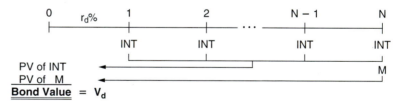

Here

$r_d$ = Average rate of return investors require to invest in the bond (the letter d stands for "debt"). For the Genesco Manufacturing bond issue, $r_d = 10\%$.[14]

N = Number of years before the bond matures. For the Genesco bonds, N = 15. Note that N declines each year the bond is outstanding, so a bond

---

[12]Actually, Genesco would receive some amount less than $25 million because of costs associated with issuing the bond, such as legal fees, investment banking fees, and so forth. For our discussion here, we choose to ignore issuing costs to simplify the explanations. Chapter 3 describes the topic of issuing costs and the investment banking process.

[13]In finance, the term *model* refers to an equation or a set of equations designed to show how one or more variables affect some other variable. A bond valuation model, then, shows the mathematical relationship between a bond's price and the set of variables that determines the price.

[14]The appropriate interest rate on debt securities was discussed in Chapter 5. The bond's riskiness, liquidity, and years to maturity, as well as supply and demand conditions in the capital markets, all influence the interest rate on bonds.

that had a maturity of 15 years when it was issued (original maturity = 15) will have N = 14 after one year, N = 13 after two years, and so on. Note also that at this point we assume that the bond pays interest once per year, or annually, so N is measured in years. Later, we will examine semiannual payment bonds—that is, interest is paid every six months.[15]

**INT** = Dollars of interest paid each year = Coupon rate × Par value. In our example, each bond issued by Genesco requires an interest payment equal to $100. The coupon rate for these bonds must be 10 percent because $100 = 0.10($1,000). In financial calculator terminology, INT = PMT = 100.

**M** = Par, or face, value of the bond = $1,000. This amount must be paid off at maturity.

We can now redraw the cash flow time line for Genesco's bond to show the numerical values for all variables except the bond's value:

The following general equation can be solved to find the value of any bond:

**6–1**

$$\text{Bond Value} = V_d = \left[\frac{\text{INT}}{(1+r_d)^1} + \frac{\text{INT}}{(1+r_d)^2} + \cdots + \frac{\text{INT}}{(1+r_d)^N}\right] + \frac{M}{(1+r_d)^N}$$

$$= \left[\sum_{t=1}^{N} \frac{\text{INT}}{(1+r_d)^t}\right] + \frac{M}{(1+r_d)^N} = \text{INT}\left[\frac{1 - \dfrac{1}{(1+r_d)^N}}{r_d}\right] + M\left[\frac{1}{(1+r_d)^N}\right]$$

Inserting the values relevant to Genesco's bond into Equation 6–1, we have[16]

$$V_d = \$100\left[\frac{1 - \dfrac{1}{(1.10)^{15}}}{0.10}\right] + \$1,000\left[\frac{1}{(1.10)^{15}}\right]$$

$$= \$100(7.60608) + \$1,000(0.23939) = \$1,000$$

The value of the bond can be computed using any of the three approaches discussed in Chapter 4: (1) equation (numerical) solution, (2) financial calculator solution, or (3) spreadsheet solution.

---

[15]Some bonds have been issued that either pay no interest during their lives (*zero coupon bonds*) or else pay very low coupon rates. Such bonds are sold at a discount below par, and so they are called *original issue discount bonds*. The "interest" earned on a zero coupon bond comes at the end when the company pays off at par ($1,000) a bond that was purchased for, say, $321.97. The discount of $1,000 − $321.97 = $678.03 substitutes for interest.

[16]The bond prices quoted by brokers are calculated as described. If you bought a bond between interest payment dates, however, you would have to pay the basic price plus accrued interest. Thus, if you purchased a Genesco bond six months after it was issued, your broker would send you an invoice stating that you must pay $1,000 as the basic price of the bond plus $50 interest, representing one-half of the annual interest of $100. The seller of the bond would receive $1,050. If you bought the bond the day before its interest payment date, you would pay $1,000 − (364/365)($100) = $1,099.73. Of course, you would receive an interest payment of $100 at the end of the next day. Throughout the chapter, we assume that the bond is being evaluated immediately after an interest payment date. The more expensive financial calculators include a built-in calendar that permits the calculation of exact values between interest payment dates.

**FIGURE 6-2**   Cash Flow Time Line for Genesco Manufacturing 10% Coupon Bonds, $r_d = 10\%$

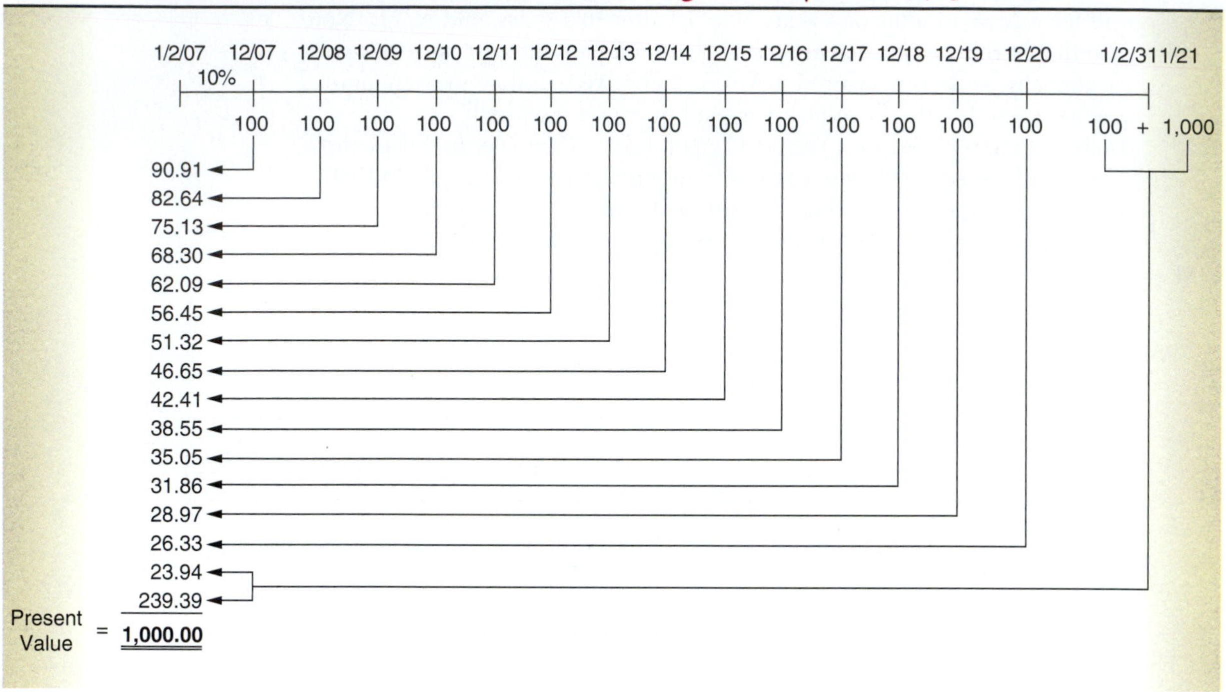

| 1/2/07 | 12/07 | 12/08 | 12/09 | 12/10 | 12/11 | 12/12 | 12/13 | 12/14 | 12/15 | 12/16 | 12/17 | 12/18 | 12/19 | 12/20 | 1/2/31 1/21 |
|---|---|---|---|---|---|---|---|---|---|---|---|---|---|---|---|

10%

100  100  100  100  100  100  100  100  100  100  100  100  100  100  100 + 1,000

90.91
82.64
75.13
68.30
62.09
56.45
51.32
46.65
42.41
38.55
35.05
31.86
28.97
26.33
23.94
239.39

Present Value = **1,000.00**

**Note:** The sum of the individual present values recorded at two decimal places (as they are here) actually is 999.99 due to rounding of the individual present value results.

## Equation (Numerical) Solution

We can discount each cash flow back to the present and sum these PVs to find the value of the bond. Figure 6-2 illustrates this process. This procedure is not very efficient, especially if the bond has many years to maturity. Alternatively, we can use Equation 6–1 to find the bond's value. Applying this approach, in the previous section we found that the value of the Genesco bond is equal to $1,000.

## Financial Calculator Solution

In Chapter 4, we worked problems in which we used only four of the five time value of money (TVM) keys. All five of these keys are used with bond problems. Here is the setup:

Input N = 15, I/Y = 10, PMT = 100, and FV = 1,000; then solve for PV = −1,000. Because the PV is an outflow to the investor, it is shown with a negative sign.

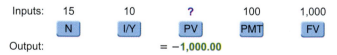

Inputs:  15   10   ?   100   1,000
         N    I/Y  PV  PMT   FV
Output:            = −1,000.00

## Spreadsheet Solution

Figure 6-3 shows the setup and the results of using the spreadsheet's PV function to compute the value of Genesco's bond. Note that the setup is the same as we used in Chapter 4 except that we must input values for four variables—N, I/Y, PMT, and FV—to compute the fifth variable, the value of the bond.[17]

---

[17]For a more detailed discussion about how to use a spreadsheet to solve time value of money problems, see Chapter 4.

**FIGURE 6-3**   Using Excel's *PV Function* to Compute the Value of a Bond

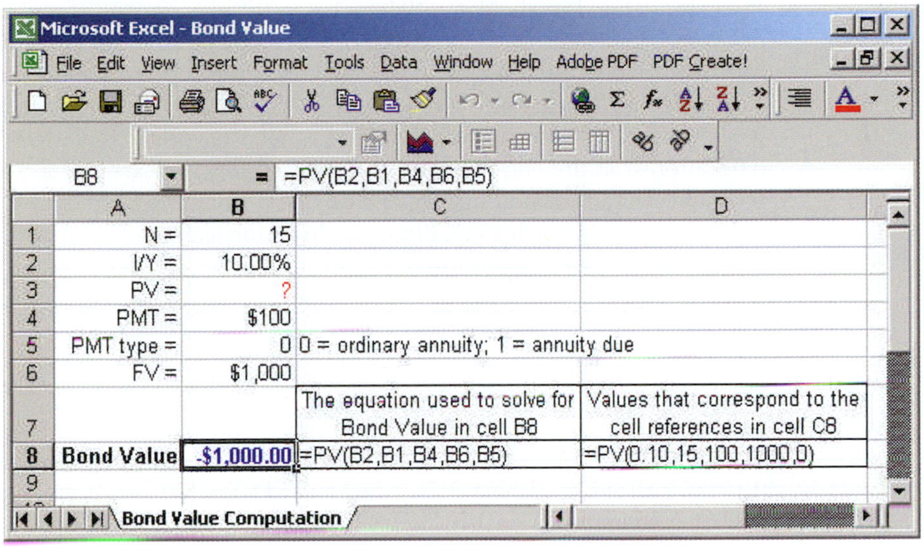

The spreadsheet shows:

| | A | B | C | D |
|---|---|---|---|---|
| | | | =PV(B2,B1,B4,B6,B5) | |
| 1 | N = | 15 | | |
| 2 | I/Y = | 10.00% | | |
| 3 | PV = | ? | | |
| 4 | PMT = | $100 | | |
| 5 | PMT type = | 0 | 0 = ordinary annuity; 1 = annuity due | |
| 6 | FV = | $1,000 | | |
| 7 | | | The equation used to solve for Bond Value in cell B8 | Values that correspond to the cell references in cell C8 |
| 8 | Bond Value | -$1,000.00 | =PV(B2,B1,B4,B6,B5) | =PV(0.10,15,100,1000,0) |

**Note:** According to the equation shown in cell C8, the input values must be entered in a specific order: I/Y, N, PMT, FV, and PMT type (equal to 0 in this computation).

To simplify the discussion, we solve the situations that we set up in the rest of the chapter using the financial calculator approach. Although we do not show the spreadsheet solutions, you can set up a spreadsheet as shown in Figure 6-3 and simply change the appropriate values to find the solution to the situation at hand. Likewise, if you prefer to use the equation (numerical) approach, you can set up an equation in the form shown in Equation 6–1 and plug in the appropriate values to determine the value of the bond being discussed.

**Self-Test Questions**

Write a formula that can be used to determine the value of a bond.

Acme Corporation's $1,000 face value bonds have a coupon rate equal to 6 percent. If the bonds mature in 10 years, for what price should they be selling in the financial markets if similar bonds offer an 8 percent rate of return? (*Answer:* $865.80)

# FINDING BOND YIELDS (MARKET RATES): YIELD TO MATURITY AND YIELD TO CALL

Suppose you were offered a 19-year, 7 percent coupon, $1,000 par value bond at a price of $821. What rate of interest, or yield, would you earn if you bought this bond? In this section, we show you how to compute the yield, or return, you would earn if you purchase a bond with these characteristics. Before we begin, we want to remind you that both the par, or principal, value of the bond and its coupon rate of interest are contractually set, so the cash flows provided by the bond do not change during its life.

## Yield to Maturity

**yield to maturity (YTM)**
The average rate of return earned on a bond if it is held to maturity.

If you buy a bond and hold it until it matures, the average rate of return you will earn per year is called the bond's **yield to maturity (YTM).** Generally, this is the rate of return, or yield, discussed by bond traders when they talk about rates of return. To find the yield to maturity, we solve Equation 6–1 for $r_d$. For the current situation, we know that investors expect the bond's dollar payoffs to include $70 = \$1,000 \times 0.07$ interest at the end of each year for the next 19 years and a $1,000 principal payment when the bond matures in 19 years. Investors have determined that this bond is currently worth $821. Plugging this information into Equation 6–1, we have

$$V_d = \frac{\$70}{(1+rd)^1} + \frac{\$70}{(1+rd)^2} + \cdots + \frac{\$70+\$1,000}{(1+rd)^{19}} = \$821$$

$$= \frac{\$70}{(1+YTM)^1} + \frac{\$70}{(1+YTM)^2} + \cdots + \frac{\$70+\$1,000}{(1+YTM)^{19}} = \$821$$

It is easy to solve for $YTM = r_d$ with a financial calculator. Input $N = 19$, $PV = -821$ (this is a cash outflow when you buy the bond), $INT = PMT = 70$, and $M = FV = 1,000$, and then compute $I/Y = 9.0$ (the yield to maturity, $r_d$).[18]

| Inputs: | 19 | ? | −821 | 70 | 1,000 |
|---|---|---|---|---|---|
| | N | I/Y | PV | PMT | FV |
| Output: | | = 9.0 | | | |

For this bond, the "going rate of return," or yield, currently is 9 percent. Thus, an investor who purchases this bond today for $821 and holds it until it matures in 19 years will receive an *average* of approximately 9 percent return each year.

Notice that $YTM = 9\% > Coupon = 7\%$. When the bond was issued, which might have been five to 10 years ago, the yield for similar bonds was 7 percent. We know that this is the case because a firm sets the coupon rate on a bond immediately before it is issued so that the bond's issuing price equals its face (par) value. But as market conditions change, the bond's yield to maturity changes, which causes its market price to change. In our example, market interest rates have increased since the time the bond was issued, so the price (value) of the bond has decreased below its face value. In reality, the calculated YTM, and thus the price of a bond, will change frequently before it matures because market conditions change frequently. We will discuss the relationship between YTM changes and price changes in greater detail later in the chapter.

---

[18]If you do not have a financial calculator, you can compute the *approximate* yield to maturity using the following equation:

$$\text{Approximate yield to maturity} = \frac{\left(\begin{array}{c}\text{Annual}\\\text{interest}\end{array}\right) + \left(\begin{array}{c}\text{Accrued}\\\text{capital gains}\end{array}\right)}{\text{Average value of the bond}} = \frac{INT + \left(\frac{M-V_d}{N}\right)}{\left[\frac{2(V_d)+M}{3}\right]}$$

This equation is based on the work of Gabriel A. Hawawini and Ashok Vora, "Yield Approximations: A Historical Perspective," *Journal of Finance,* March 1982, 145–156.

For the bond in our example, the approximate yield to maturity is

$$\text{Approximate yield to maturity} = \frac{\$70 + \left(\dfrac{\$1,000 - \$821}{19}\right)}{\left[\dfrac{2(\$821)+\$1,000}{3}\right]} = \frac{\$70 + \$9.42}{\$880.67} = 0.0902 \approx 9.0\% = r_d = YTM$$

As you can see, the result of this computation is close to the result we found using a financial calculator.

## Yield to Call

Bonds that contain call provisions (callable bonds) often are called by the firm prior to maturity. In cases in which a bond issue is called, investors do not have the opportunity to earn the yield to maturity (YTM) because the bond issue is retired before the maturity date arrives. Thus, for callable bonds, we generally compute the **yield to call (YTC),** rather than the YTM. The computation for the YTC is the same as that for the YTM except that we substitute the **call price** of the bond for the maturity (par) value, and the number of years until the bond can be called for the years to maturity. To calculate the YTC, then, we modify Equation 6–1 and solve the following equation for $r_d$:

**yield to call (YTC)**
The average rate of return earned on a bond if it is held until the first call date.

**call price**
The price a firm has to pay to recall a bond; generally equal to the principal amount plus some interest.

**6–2**

$$
\begin{aligned}
V_d &= \frac{INT}{(1+r_d)^1} + \frac{INT}{(1+r_d)^1} + \cdots + \frac{INT + Call\ price}{(1+r_d)^{N_c}} \\
&= \frac{INT}{(1+YTC)^1} + \frac{INT}{(1+YTC)^2} + \cdots + \frac{INT + Call\ price}{(1+YTC)^{N_c}}
\end{aligned}
$$

Here $N_c$ is the number of years until the company can call the bond, Call price is the price that the company must pay to call the bond on the first call date (it is often set equal to the par value plus one year's interest), and $r_d$ now represents the yield to call (YTC). To solve for the YTC, we proceed just as we did to solve for the YTM of a bond.

For example, suppose the bond we are currently examining has a call provision that "kicks in" nine years from today—that is, the bond is callable 10 years before it matures. If the firm calls the bond on the first date possible, it will have to pay a call price equal to $1,070. The setup for computing the YTC for this bond is

$$
\begin{aligned}
V_d &= \frac{\$70}{(1+r_d)^1} + \frac{\$70}{(1+r_d)^2} + \cdots + \frac{\$70 + \$1,070}{(1+r_d)^9} = \$821 \\
&= \frac{\$70}{(1+YTC)^1} + \frac{\$70}{(1+YTC)^2} + \cdots + \frac{\$70 + \$1,070}{(1+YTC)^9} = \$821
\end{aligned}
$$

Using your calculator, you would find the YTC equals 10.7 percent:

| Inputs: | 9 | ? | −821 | 70 | 1,070 |
|---|---|---|---|---|---|
|  | N | I/Y | PV | PMT | FV |
| Output: |  | = 10.7 |  |  |  |

Input N = 9, PV = −821 (this is a cash outflow when you buy the bond), INT = PMT = 70, and M = FV = 1,070, and then compute I/Y = 10.7 = YTC. Thus, investors who purchase the bond today will earn an average annual return equal to approximately 10.7 percent if the bond is called in nine years.

### Self-Test Questions

What does it mean when we say that a bond's yield to maturity is 10 percent?

What is the difference between a bond's coupon rate of interest and its yield to maturity?

> Write a formula that can be used to determine the yield to maturity of a bond. Can the same equation be used to compute the bond's yield to call?
>
> Prizor Corporation has an outstanding bond that has a face value equal to $1,000 and a 10 percent coupon rate of interest. The bond, which matures in six years, currently sells for $1,143. What is the bond's yield to maturity (YTM)? (*Answer:* 7%)

## INTEREST RATES AND BOND VALUES

Even though the interest payment, maturity value, and maturity date of a bond do not change, regardless of the conditions in the financial markets, the market values of bonds fluctuate continuously as a result of changing market conditions. To see why the values of bonds change, let's again examine Genesco's bonds to see what happens when market interest rates change.

First, let's assume you purchased one of Genesco's bonds on the day it was issued. Remember that the bond has 15 years remaining until maturity, a 10 percent coupon rate of interest, and the market interest rate at the time of issue was 10 percent. As we showed earlier, to purchase the bond you would have paid the market value of $1,000. Suppose *that immediately after you purchased the bond,* interest rates on similar bonds increased from 10 percent to 12 percent. How would the value of your bond be affected?

Because the cash flows associated with the bond—that is, interest payments and principal repayment—remain constant, the value of the bond will decrease when interest rates increase. In Equation 6–1, the values in the numerators do not change, but the values in the denominators increase, which results in a lower value for the bond. In present value terms, the decrease in value makes sense. If you want to mimic the Genesco bond—that is, pay yourself $100 each year for 15 years and then pay yourself $1,000 at the end of the 15th year—you must deposit $1,000 in a savings account that pays 10 percent interest annually. But if you found a savings account that pays 12 percent interest annually, you could deposit some amount less than $1,000 and pay yourself the same cash flows because your deposit would earn greater interest. As we show in the following calculations, at 12 percent, the amount you would have to deposit to provide the same cash flows as Genesco's bond is $863.78. The same logic applies when we consider how an interest rate change affects the value of Genesco's bond.

If market rates *increase* from 10 percent to 12 percent immediately after you purchase Genesco's bond, the value of the bond would decrease to $863.78:

| Inputs: | 15 | 12 | ? | 100 | 1,000 |
|---------|----|----|----|-----|-------|
|         | N  | I/Y | PV | PMT | FV |
| Output: |    |    | = −863.78 |     |       |

Input N = 15, I/Y = 12, INT = PMT = 100, and M = FV = 1,000; then compute PV = −$863.78.

What would be the price of Genesco's bond if interest rates had *decreased* from 10 percent to 8 percent immediately after it was issued?

| Inputs: | 15 | 8 | ? | 100 | 1,000 |
|---------|----|----|----|-----|-------|
|         | N  | I/Y | PV | PMT | FV |
| Output: |    |    | = −1,171.19 |     |       |

Input N = 15, I/Y = 8, INT = PMT = 100, and M = FV = 1,000; then compute PV = −$1,171.19.

The arithmetic of the bond value increase should be clear, but what sort of logic lies behind it? The fact that $r_d$ has declined to 8 percent means that if you had $1,000 to invest, you could buy *new* bonds such as Genesco's, except that these new bonds would pay $80 of interest each year rather than the $100 interest paid by Genesco. Naturally, you would prefer $100 to $80, so you would be willing to pay more than $1,000 for Genesco's bonds to get its higher coupons. Because all investors would recognize these facts, the Genesco Manufacturing bonds would be bid up in price to $1,171.19. At that point, they would provide the same rate of return to potential investors as the new bonds—8 percent.

Following is a table that summarizes the relationship between the value of Genesco's bond and its yield to maturity.

| Relationship of Market Rate, $r_d$, and Coupon Rate, C = 10% | Bond Value, $V_d$ (N = 15, PMT = 100, FV = 1,000, and I/Y = $r_d$) | Relationship of Market Price, $V_d$ and Maturity Value, M = $1,000 |
| --- | --- | --- |
| $r_d$ = 10% = C | $1,000.00 | $V_d$ = M; bond sells at par |
| $r_d$ = 12% > C | 863.78 | $V_d$ < M; bond sells at a discount |
| $r_d$ =  8% < C | 1,171.19 | $V_d$ > M; bond sells at a premium |

These same relationships exist for all bonds—that is, when the market yield (YTM) and the coupon rate of interest are equal, the bond sells for its *par value*; when the market yield is greater than the coupon rate of interest, the bond sells for less than its par value, or at a *discount*; and when the market yield is less than the coupon rate of interest, the bond sells for greater than its par value, or at a *premium*. A bond that sells for less than its face value is called a **discount bond,** whereas a bond that sells for greater than its face value is called a **premium bond.** This exercise demonstrates an important fundamental concept in finance that was mentioned earlier: When interest rates change, the values of bonds change in an opposite direction—that is, *when rates increase, bond prices decrease, and vice versa*.

**discount bond**
A bond that sells below its par value. This occurs whenever the going rate of interest rises above the coupon rate.

**premium bond**
A bond that sells above its par value. This occurs whenever the going rate of interest falls below the coupon rate.

### Self-Test Questions

What is the relationship between a bond's yield to maturity and its market value?

Terry's Towel Company has an outstanding bond that has a $1,000 face value and pays $80 interest per year. The bond's existing market rate is 10 percent and the bond matures in 12 years. What was the market interest rate when the bond was issued eight years ago? What will happen to the price of the bond if the interest rate on similar bonds decreases to 8 percent? (*Answers:* 8%, which is the coupon rate; market price will increase from $863.73 to $1,000)

## CHANGES IN BOND VALUES OVER TIME

Let's again assume that immediately after Genesco issued its bond, interest rates in the economy fell from 10 to 8 percent. In the previous section, we showed that the price of the bond would increase to $1,171.19. Assuming that interest rates remain constant at 8 percent for the next 15 years, what would happen to the value of Genesco's bond as time passes and the maturity date approaches? It would decrease gradually from $1,171.19 at present to $1,000 at maturity, when Genesco would redeem each bond for $1,000. We can illustrate this point by calculating the value of the bond one year from now, when it has 14 years remaining to maturity.

| Inputs: | 14 | 8 | ? | 100 | 1,000 |
|---------|-----|-----|-----|-----|-------|
|         | N   | I/Y | PV  | PMT | FV    |
| Output: |     |     | = −1,164.88 |     |       |

**interest (current) yield**
The interest payment divided by the market price of the bond.

As you can see, the value of the bond will decrease from $1,171.19 to $1,164.88, or by $6.31. If you were to calculate the bond's value at other future dates using $r_d = 8\%$, its price would continue to decline as the maturity date is approached—when $N = 13$, $V_d = \$1,158.08$, when $N = 12$, $V_d = \$1,150.72$, and so on. At maturity, the value of the bond would have to equal its par value of $1,000 (as long as the firm does not go bankrupt).

Suppose that Sherman Sheridan purchased a Genesco bond just after the market rate dropped to 8 percent, so he paid $1,171.19 for the bond. If he sold the bond one year later for $1,164.88, Sherman would realize a capital *loss* of $6.31, which would produce a total dollar return of $93.69 = $100.00 − $6.31. The percentage rate of return that Sherman earned on the bond would consist of an **interest yield** (also called a **current yield**) plus a **capital gains yield.** These yields are calculated as follows:

**capital gains yield**
The percentage change in the market price of a bond over some period of time.

**6–3**

$$\text{Bond yield} = \text{Current (interest) yield} + \text{Capital gains yield}$$
$$= \frac{\text{INT}}{V_{d,\text{Begin}}} + \frac{V_{d,\text{End}} - V_{d,\text{Begin}}}{V_{d,\text{Begin}}}$$

Here, $V_{d,\text{Begin}}$ represents the value of the bond at the beginning of the year (period) and $V_{d,\text{End}}$ is the value of the bond at the end of the year (period).

The yields for Genesco's bond after one year are computed as follows:

$$\text{Current yield} = \$100.00/\$1,171.19 = \quad 0.0854 = \quad 8.54\%$$
$$\text{Capital gains yield} = \quad -\$6.31/\$1,171.19 = -0.0058 = \underline{-0.54\%}$$
$$\text{Total rate of return (yield)} = \quad \$93.69/\$1,171.19 = \quad 0.0800 = \underline{8.00\%}$$

Had interest rates risen from 10 to 12 percent rather than fallen immediately after issue, the value of the bond would have immediately decreased to $863.78. If the rate remains at 12 percent, the value of the bond at the end of the year will be $867.44.

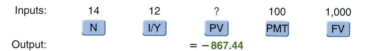

| Inputs: | 14 | 12 | ? | 100 | 1,000 |
|---------|-----|-----|-----|-----|-------|
|         | N   | I/Y | PV  | PMT | FV    |
| Output: |     |     | = −867.44 |     |       |

The total expected future yield on the bond would again consist of a current yield and a capital gains yield, but now the capital gains yield would be positive. The total yield on the bond would be 12 percent. The capital gain for the year is $867.44 − $863.78 = $3.66. The current yield, capital gains yield, and total yield are calculated as follows:

$$\text{Current yield} = \$100.00/\$863.78 = 0.1153 = 11.58\%$$
$$\text{Capital gains yield} = \quad \$3.66/\$863.78 = 0.0047 = \underline{0.42\%}$$
$$\text{Total rate of return (yield)} = \$103.66/\$863.78 = 0.1200 = \underline{12.00\%}$$

**TABLE 6-3**    Genesco Bonds: Coupon = 10%, $r_d$ = 12%

| Years to Maturity | Ending Value($) | Capital Gains ($) | Interest ($) | Capital Gains Yield (%) | + | Current Yield (%) | = | Total Yield (%) |
|---|---|---|---|---|---|---|---|---|
| 15 | $863.78 | | | | | | | |
| 14 | 867.44 | $3.66 | $100 | 0.42% | | 11.58% | | 12.00% |
| 13 | 871.53 | 4.09 | 100 | 0.47 | | 11.53 | | 12.00 |
| 12 | 876.11 | 4.58 | 100 | 0.53 | | 11.47 | | 12.00 |
| 11 | 881.25 | 5.14 | 100 | 0.59 | | 11.41 | | 12.00 |
| 10 | 887.00 | 5.75 | 100 | 0.65 | | 11.35 | | 12.00 |
| 9 | 893.44 | 6.44 | 100 | 0.73 | | 11.27 | | 12.00 |
| 8 | 900.65 | 7.21 | 100 | 0.81 | | 11.19 | | 12.00 |
| 7 | 908.72 | 8.07 | 100 | 0.90 | | 11.10 | | 12.00 |
| 6 | 917.77 | 9.05 | 100 | 1.00 | | 11.00 | | 12.00 |
| 5 | 927.90 | 10.13 | 100 | 1.10 | | 10.90 | | 12.00 |
| 4 | 939.25 | 11.35 | 100 | 1.22 | | 10.78 | | 12.00 |
| 3 | 951.96 | 12.71 | 100 | 1.35 | | 10.65 | | 12.00 |
| 2 | 966.20 | 14.24 | 100 | 1.50 | | 10.50 | | 12.00 |
| 1 | 982.14 | 15.94 | 100 | 1.65 | | 10.35 | | 12.00 |
| 0 | 1,000.00 | 17.86 | 100 | 1.82 | | 10.18 | | 12.00 |

What would happen to the value of the bond if market interest rates remain constant at 12 percent until maturity? Because the bond's value must equal the principal, or par, amount at maturity (as long as bankruptcy does not occur), its value will gradually increase from the current price of $867.44 to its maturity value of $1,000. For example, the value of the bond would increase to $871.53 at N = 13, its value would be $876.11 at N = 12, and so forth. Table 6-3 shows the value of Genesco's bond at the end of each year as it approaches the maturity date, assuming the market rate, $r_d$, remains at 12 percent.

Figure 6-4 graphs the value of Genesco's bond over time, assuming that interest rates in the economy (1) remain constant at 10 percent, (2) fall to 8 percent and then remain constant at that level, or (3) rise to 12 percent and remain constant at that level. Of course, if interest rates do not remain constant, then the price of the bond will fluctuate. *Regardless of what interest rates do in the future, the bond's price will approach its face value ($1,000) as it nears its maturity date* (barring bankruptcy, in which case the bond's value might drop to zero).

Figure 6-4 illustrates the following key points that we discussed in this section:

1. *Whenever the going rate of interest, $r_d$, equals the coupon rate, a bond will sell at its par value.*

2. Interest rates change over time, but the coupon rate remains fixed after the bond has been issued. *Whenever the going rate of interest is greater than the coupon rate, a bond's price will fall below its par value (a discount bond); whenever the going rate of interest is less than the coupon rate, a bond's price will rise above its par value (a premium bond).*

3. *An increase in interest rates will cause the price of an outstanding bond to fall, whereas a decrease in rates will cause it to rise.*

4. *The market value of a bond will always approach its par value as its maturity date approaches,* provided that the firm does not go bankrupt.

**FIGURE 6-4**    Time Path of the Value of Genesco's 10% Coupon, $1,000 Par Value Bond When Interest Rates Are 8%, 10%, and 12%

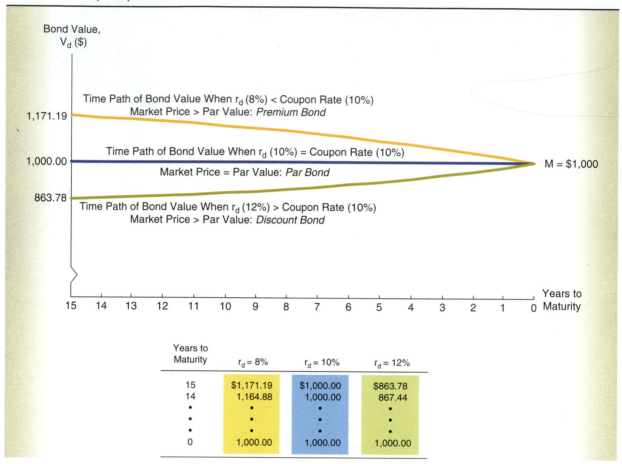

These points are important because they show that bondholders can suffer capital losses or make capital gains, depending on whether market interest rates rise or fall after the bond is purchased. Of course, as we saw in Chapter 5, interest rates do change over time.

 **Self-Test Questions**

Consider a bond that is currently selling at a premium. If market interest rates remain constant, what will happen to the bond's value as the maturity date approaches? What would happen to the bond's value if the bond is currently selling at a discount?

Suppose you purchase a 10-year bond that has a current market price equal to $929.76. The bond has a face value equal to $1,000, and it pays $60 interest each year. Assuming that the going rate of interest remains at its current level, which is 7 percent, what will be the value of bond at the end of the year? What will be its value five years from now? (*Answers:* $934.85; $959.00)

## BOND VALUES WITH SEMIANNUAL COMPOUNDING

Although some bonds pay interest annually, *most* pay interest semiannually. To evaluate semiannual payment bonds, we must modify the bond valuation equation just as we did in Chapter 4 when discussing interest compounding that occurs more than once per year. As a result, Equation 6–1 becomes

$$V_d = \left(\frac{INT}{2}\right)\left[\frac{1 - \dfrac{1}{(1 + r_d/2)^{2 \times N}}}{(r_d/2)}\right] + \frac{M}{(1 + r_d/2)^{2 \times N}}$$

**6–4**

To illustrate, assume that Genesco's bonds pay $50 interest every six months rather than $100 at the end of each year. Each interest payment is now only half as large as before, but there are twice as many payments. When the going (simple) rate of interest is 8 percent with semiannual compounding, the value of the bond when there are 14 years remaining until maturity is found as follows:[19]

| | | | | | |
|---|---|---|---|---|---|
| Inputs: | 28 | 4 | ? | 50 | 1,000 |
| | N | I/Y | PV | PMT | FV |
| Output: | | | = −1,166.63 | | |

Input N = 28 = 14 × 2, I/Y = 4 = 8/2, INT = PMT = 50 = 100/2, and M = FV = 1,000; compute PV = −$1,166.63.

The value with semiannual interest payments ($1,166.63) exceeds the value when interest is paid annually ($1,164.88). This higher value occurs because interest payments are received, and therefore can be reinvested, somewhat more rapidly under semiannual compounding.

Students sometimes want to discount the *maturity (par) value* at 8 percent over 14 years rather than at 4 percent over 28 interest (six-month) periods. This approach is incorrect. Logically, all cash flows in a given contract must be discounted at the same periodic rate—the 4 percent semiannual rate in this instance—because it is the investor's opportunity rate.

### Self-Test Questions

What adjustments must be made when using Equation 6–1 to compute the value of a bond that pays interest semiannually?

Suppose you are considering investing in a 20-year, 11 percent coupon bond that has a $1,000 face value and pays interest semiannually. If the market rate of return is 8 percent, what is the market value of the bond? (*Answer:* $1,296.89)

## INTEREST RATE RISK ON A BOND

As we saw in Chapter 5, interest rates change over time. Furthermore, changes in interest rates affect bondholders in two ways. First, an increase in interest rates leads to a decline in the values of outstanding bonds (at $r_d = 10\%$, the value of Genesco's 15-year bond was $1,000; at $r_d = 12\%$, $V_d = \$863.78$). Because interest

[19]We also assume a change in the effective annual interest rate, from 8 percent to EAR = $(1.04)^2 - 1 = 0.0816 = 8.16\%$. Most bonds pay interest semiannually, and the rates quoted are simple rates compounded semiannually. Therefore, effective annual rates for most bonds are somewhat higher than the quoted rates, which, in effect, represent the APRs for the bonds.

**interest rate price risk**
The risk of changes in bond prices to which investors are exposed due to changing interest rates.

rates can rise, bondholders face the risk of suffering losses in the values of their portfolios. This risk is called **interest rate price risk.** Second, many bondholders (including such institutional bondholders as pension funds and life insurance companies) buy bonds to build funds for some future use. These bondholders reinvest the cash flows; each interest payment is reinvested when it is received (generally every six months) and the principal repayment is reinvested when it is received at maturity (or when the bond is called). If interest rates decline—say, from 10 percent to 8 percent—the bondholders will earn a lower rate of return on *reinvested cash flows,* which will reduce the future values of their portfolios relative to the values they would have accumulated if interest rates had not fallen. This risk is called **interest rate reinvestment risk.**

**interest rate reinvestment risk**
The risk that income from a bond portfolio will vary because cash flows must be reinvested at current market rates.

We can see, then, that, any given change in interest rates has two separate effects on bondholders: It changes the current values of their portfolios (price risk), and it changes the rates of return at which the cash flows from their portfolios can be reinvested (reinvestment risk). These two risks tend to offset one another. For example, an increase in interest rates will lower the current value of a bond portfolio. But because the future cash flows produced by the portfolio will be reinvested at a higher rate of return, the future value of the portfolio will increase.

An investor's exposure to interest rate price risk is higher on bonds with long maturities than on those that will mature in the near future. We can demonstrate this fact by considering how the value of a one-year bond with a 10 percent coupon fluctuates with changes in $r_d$ and then comparing these changes with the effects on a

**FIGURE 6-5**    Value of Long- and Short-Term 10% Annual Coupon Rate Bonds at Different Market Interest Rates ($r_d$)

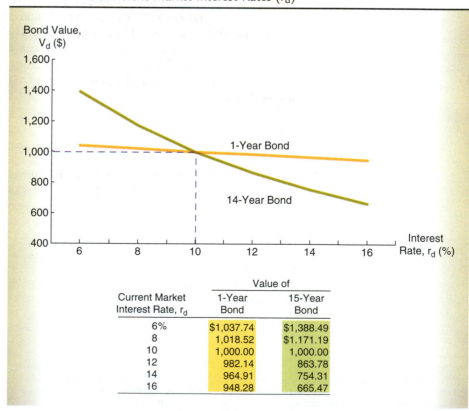

| Current Market Interest Rate, $r_d$ | Value of 1-Year Bond | 15-Year Bond |
|---|---|---|
| 6% | $1,037.74 | $1,388.49 |
| 8 | 1,018.52 | $1,171.19 |
| 10 | 1,000.00 | 1,000.00 |
| 12 | 982.14 | 863.78 |
| 14 | 964.91 | 754.31 |
| 16 | 948.28 | 665.47 |

15-year bond as calculated previously. Figure 6-5 shows the values for a one-year bond and a 15-year bond at several different market interest rates, $r_d$. The values for the bonds were computed by assuming that the coupon interest payments for the bonds occur annually. Notice how much more sensitive the price of the long-term bond is to changes in interest rates. At a 10 percent interest rate, both the long- and short-term bonds are valued at $1,000. When rates rise to 12 percent, the value of the long-term bond decreases to $863.78, or by 13.6 percent, but the value of the short-term bond falls to only $982.14, which is a 1.8 percent decline.

For bonds with similar coupons, this differential sensitivity to changes in interest rates always holds: *The longer the maturity of the bond, the more significantly its price changes in response to a given change in interest rates.* Thus, if two bonds have exactly the same risk of default, the bond with the longer maturity typically is exposed to more price risk from a change in interest rates.[20]

The logical explanation for this difference in interest rate price risk is simple. Suppose you bought a 15-year bond that yielded 10 percent, or $100 per year. Now suppose that interest rates on comparable-risk bonds increased to 12 percent. You would be stuck with only $100 of interest for the next 15 years. On the other hand, had you bought a one-year bond, you would have received a low return for only one year. At the end of the year, you would get your $1,000 back, and you could then reinvest it and receive 12 percent, or $120 per year, for the next 14 years. As you can see, interest rate price risk reflects the length of time one is committed to a given investment. As we described in Chapter 5, the longer a bond's term to maturity, the higher its maturity risk premium (MRP), which accounts for its higher interest rate risk.

Although a one-year bond has less interest rate price risk than a 15-year bond, the one-year bond exposes the buyer to more interest rate reinvestment risk. Suppose you bought a one-year bond that yielded 10 percent, and then interest rates on comparable-risk bonds fell to 8 percent such that newly issued bonds now pay $80 interest. After one year, when you got your $1,000 back, you would have to invest your funds at only 8 percent. As a result, you would lose $100 − $80 = $20 in annual interest. Had you bought the 15-year bond, you would have continued to receive $100 in annual interest payments even if rates fell. If you reinvested those coupon payments, you would have to accept a lower rate of return, but you would still be much better off than if you had been holding the one-year bond.

 **Self-Test Questions**

Differentiate between interest rate price risk and interest rate reinvestment risk.

When interest rates increase, which risk would be considered positive, interest rate price risk or interest rate reinvestment risk? Which risk is positive when interest rates decrease?

## BOND PRICES IN RECENT YEARS

From Chapter 5, we know that interest rates fluctuate. We have also just seen that the prices of outstanding bonds rise and fall inversely with changes in interest rates. When interest rates fall, many firms "refinance" by issuing new, lower-cost debt and using the proceeds to repay higher-cost debt. In 2003, interest rates dropped to levels that had

---

[20]If a 10-year bond were plotted in Figure 6-5, its curve would lie between the curves for the 15-year and one-year bonds. The curve of a one-month bond would be almost horizontal, indicating that its price would change very little in response to an interest rate change. A perpetuity would have a very steep slope.

**FIGURE 6-6**    Value of a $1,000 Bond Issued August 1, 1997, That Matures on July 31, 2012

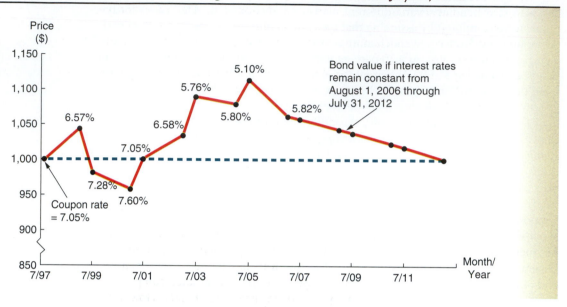

not been seen in more than 45 years. Not surprisingly, firms that had issued higher-cost debt in earlier years refinanced much of their debt at that time. Because rates have increased since 2003, many of the corporate bonds that exist today were issued in 2003.[21]

Let's assume a company issued a 15-year bond on August 1, 1997, when the market average interest rate on AAA-rated bonds was 7.05 percent. Assume further that this bond still existed in late July 2006. Figure 6-6 shows what has happened to the price since it was issued in 1997, as well as what will happen to the price if interest rates remain constant from August 1, 2006, until the bond matures on July 31, 2012. Because the interest rate on similar-risk bonds was 7.05 percent when the bond was originally issued in 1997, the coupon rate of interest was set at 7.05 percent so that the bond was issued at its par value—that is, $1,000. But as market interest rates changed, so did the value of the bond. Notice from Figure 6-6 that interest rates decreased in 1998 so that the bond was selling for $1,043 one year after its issue. In 1999 and 2000, rates increased to greater than the coupon rate of interest, so the bond was selling at a discount—$981 in 1999 and $958 in 2000. In 2001, rates began to decrease, and the bond price increased. Note from Figure 6-6 that when the market interest rates were (1) less than the bond's coupon rate—that is, $r_d < 7.05\%$— the plot of the price of the bond was above the $1,000 dashed horizontal line, which means the bond was selling at a premium ($V_d > M$); (2) greater than the bond's coupon rate—that is, $r_d > 7.05\%$—the plot of the price of the bond was below the $1,000 dashed horizontal line, which means the bond was selling at a discount ($V_d < M$); and (3) approximately equal to the bond's coupon rate—that is, $r_d = 7.05\%$—the plot of the price of the bond was nearly on the $1,000 dashed horizontal line, which means the bond was selling at par ($V_d = M$).

When you read this book, interest rates might be much higher or much lower than they were in July 2006. But as Figure 6-6 shows, the value of the bond that was

---

[21]In some cases, corporate bonds could not be refinanced at the lower rates because of restrictions that existed in the debt contracts or because firms were not financially sound.

issued in 1997 will continue to approach its par value of $1,000 until the maturity date, at which time the bond's price should be exactly $1,000. This is the case for any corporate bond as long as the issuing firm is financially strong enough to pay both the interest that is due and the face value of the debt on the maturity date. The prices of other bonds that existed during the period from 1997 through 2006 would have exhibited a similar pattern of changes as the prices of the bond discussed in this example.

> **? Self-Test Question**
> How have bond prices fluctuated in recent years?

## BOND QUOTES

In this section, we give a brief description of how to "read" the bond information that is published in financial publications such as *The Wall Street Journal*. First, we should note that most corporate bonds are traded in the over-the-counter (OTC) market because large institutional investors—that is, pension funds, insurance companies, and mutual funds—represent the primary investment group for bonds. However, information about bonds traded in the OTC market is not readily available. For this reason, we will examine the information that is published in *The Wall Street Journal*, which represents the quotations primarily for bonds traded on the New York Stock Exchange.

Figure 6-7 shows some of the bond quotes that were published in *The Wall Street Journal* on July 25, 2006. These quotes represent "prices" at the close of trading on Thursday, July 24, 2006. Following is a brief description of what information is provided in each of the columns in Figure 6-7.

**FIGURE 6-7**    Corporate Bond Quotations

## Corporate Bonds

Monday, July 24, 2006

Forty most active fixed-coupon corporate bonds

| COMPANY (TICKER) | COUPON | MATURITY | LAST PRICE | LAST YIELD | *EST SPREAD | UST† | EST $ VOL (000's) |
|---|---|---|---|---|---|---|---|
| Nextel Communications Inc (S) | 7.375 | Aug 01, 2015 | 102.313 | 6.822 | 178 | 10 | 70,397 |
| Credit Suisse (USA) Inc (CS) | 5.375 | Mar 02, 2016 | 96.032 | 5.922 | 88 | 10 | 63,300 |
| DaimlerChrysler North America Holding Corp (DCX) | 4.050 | Jun 04, 2008 | 96.890 | 5.842 | 76 | 2 | 62,926 |
| CIT Group Inc (CIT) | 5.200 | Nov 03, 2010 | 97.870 | 5.772 | 79 | 5 | 57,450 |
| Cisco Systems Inc (CSCO) | 5.500 | Feb 22, 2016 | 96.832 | 5.938 | 90 | 10 | 45,685 |
| Residential Capital Corp (RESCAP) | 6.375 | Jun 30, 2010 | 99.396 | 6.550 | 156 | 5 | 32,820 |
| Merrill Lynch Inc (MER) | 5.770 | Jul 25, 2011 | 100.154 | 5.734 | 74 | 5 | 30,740 |
| Sara Lee Corp (SLE) | 6.250 | Sep 15, 2011 | 100.343 | 6.169 | 118 | 5 | 30,016 |
| Anadarko Finance Co (APC) | 7.500 | May 01, 2031 | 109.332 | 6.720 | 156 | 30 | 30,000 |
| Verizon Wireless Capital LLC (VZW) | 5.375 | Dec 15, 2006 | 99.850 | 5.739 | n.a. | n.a. | 28,647 |
| Berkshire Hathaway Finance (BRK) | 3.400 | Jul 02, 2007 | 98.055 | 5.571 | n.a. | n.a. | 27,605 |

Volume represents total volume for each issue; price/yield data are for trades of $1 million and greater. * Estimated spreads, in basis points (100. basis points is one percentage point), over the 2, 3, 5, 10 or 30-year hot run Treasury note/bond. 2-year: 5.125 06/08; 3-year: 4.875 05/09; 5-year: 5.125 06/11; 10-year: 5.125 05/16; 30-year: 5.375 02/31. †Comparable U.S. Treasury issue.

Source: *The Wall Street Journal*, Dow Jones MarketAxess Corporate BondTicker.

**COMPANY (TICKER)**—provides the name of the company that issued the bond and the company's trading (ticker) symbol. For example, the quote that is highlighted is for Merrill Lynch, which provides securities brokerage services, investment banking, wealth and asset management, and other financial services. Merrill Lynch's ticker symbol is MER. You can use this symbol to look up quotes for the company's bonds and stocks at various sites on the Internet.

**COUPON**—bond's coupon rate of interest. The coupon rate for Merrill Lynch's bond is 5.77 percent, which means investors who own this particular bond issue will receive interest payments equal to $57.70 each year for every $1,000 face value bond they own ($57.70 = 0.0577 × $1,000).

**MATURITY**—the date the bond matures, which is July 25, 2011. Thus, the Merrill Lynch bond matures in five years (from July 24, 2006).

**LAST PRICE**—gives the "price" of the bond at the close of the market on the previous trading day stated as a *percent of its face value.* Each Merrill Lynch bond was selling for 100.154 percent of its face value at the end of trading on July 24, 2006. Thus, a $1,000 face value bond was selling for $1,001.54 = $1,000 × 1.00154.

**LAST YIELD**—the yield to maturity on the bond at the close of the previous trading day. Thus, at the end of trading on July 24, Merrill Lynch's bond had a yield to maturity (YTM) equal to 5.734 percent. With the information that is provided in the three previous columns—that is, the coupon interest rate, maturity date, and market price—we can use the methods described earlier in this chapter to compute the bond's YTM. Using a financial calculator, input N = 10 = 5 × 2, PV = −1,001.54, PMT = 28.85, and FV = 1,000; compute I/Y = 2.867, which is the six-month yield. (The bond pays interest every six months.) Thus, YTM = 2.867% × 2 = 5.734%, which is the YTM reported in *The Wall Street Journal.*

**EST SPREAD**—the estimated number of basis points (100 basis points equal 1 percent) the YTM on the company's bond issue exceeds a Treasury bond or note with a similar term to maturity. Thus, the YTM on Merrill Lynch's bond, which has a term to maturity equal to five years, exceeds the yield on a five-year Treasury bond by approximately 74 basis points, or by 0.74 percent. The July 24, 2006, quote reported in *The Wall Street Journal* for a five-year Treasury note was 4.99 percent, which is 0.74 percent lower than the 5.734 percent YTM reported for Merrill Lynch's five-year bond.

**UST**—the maturity of the Treasury bond or note with which the corporate bond's YTM is compared. The YTM on Merrill Lynch's bond was compared with the yield on a five-year Treasury.

**EST $ VOL (000's)**—gives the dollar volume of bonds that were traded the previous day. Thus, approximately $30,740,000 of the particular Merrill Lynch bond issue was traded on July 24, 2006.

The bond quotes shown in Figure 6-7 illustrate the valuation concepts we discussed in this chapter. For example, because the Merrill Lynch bond has a coupon rate equal to 5.77, we know that the going rate on similar bonds on the date this bond was issued was approximately 5.77 percent. Further, because the Merrill Lynch bond was selling for a premium on July 24, 2006, we know that interest rates on similar-risk bonds on this date were lower that the 5.77 percent coupon rate of interest on Merrill's bond. And the yield to maturity reported in *The Wall Street Journal* is equal to what we computed using the methods described in this chapter.

To summarize the key concepts, let's answer the questions that were posed at the beginning of the chapter:

- **What is debt? What types of debt exist and what are some of the characteristics of debt?** In simple terms, debt represents a loan. A debt agreement, which is called an *indenture*, specifies the principal amount that must be repaid, the amount of interest that is paid on specific dates, and the date the debt matures. There are many types of debt—short-term debt includes Treasury bills, repurchase agreements, federal funds, and commercial paper, to name a few; long-term debt generally includes term loans and bonds (corporate, government, and municipal). Bonds often include such provisions as a call, which allows the issuer to "call" the bond in for a refund prior to maturity; a sinking fund, which requires the issuer to repay portions of the bond each year; and a convertible feature, which allows bondholders to convert their bonds into common stock.

- **What are bond ratings? What information is provided by bond ratings?** A bond rating, which is based on both quantitative and qualitative factors, gives an indication of the default risk associated with a bond. Bonds with low ratings are perceived as having greater risk than bonds with high ratings; thus, to attract investors, low-rated bonds generally must have higher rates of return than high-rated bonds. Some organizations, such as pension funds and insurance companies (institutional investors) can invest only in high-rated bonds, which means that bond ratings are very important to these types of investors.

- **How are bond prices determined?** The price of a bond is computed as the present value of the cash flows the bond is expected to pay during its life. As a result, a bond's market price is determined by the interest paid during its life, which depends on the bond's coupon rate of interest, and the principal amount that must be repaid at maturity.

- **How are bond yields (market rates) determined?** A bond's yield to maturity (YTM) is the average annual rate of return that an investor will earn if he or she buys the bond at the current market price and holds it until it matures. A bond's yield to call (YTC) is the same as its yield to maturity, except the period that is examined ends on the first date that the bond can be called rather than the maturity date. To determine the YTM, we compute the rate that equates the market value of the bond to the present value of both the future dollar interest payments and the repayment of the principal amount. For example, if a bond currently sells for $950, the YTM is the rate at which the present value of all the future cash flows associated with the bond equals $950.

- **What is the relationship between bond prices and interest rates? Why is it important for investors to understand this relationship?** Bond prices and interest rates are negatively related—that is, when interest rates increase, bond prices decrease, and vice versa. Further, for a particular interest rate change, the prices of bonds with longer terms to maturity exhibit greater changes (both in dollar amounts and percentages) than prices of shorter-term bonds. Understanding these relationships is important to both investors and borrowers. If investors expect that interest rates will increase in the near term, then they should invest in short-term debt because the market values of bonds will decrease when interest rates increase, at which time longer-term bonds can be purchased for much lower prices. In addition, the values of the short-term bonds will decrease less than the values of long-term bonds. Borrowers would follow the opposite strategy—that is, they would borrow using long-term debt if they expected interest rates to increase in the near term.

## ETHICAL DILEMMA

### Which ARM Should You Choose—the Left or the Right?

Alan recently joined Friendly Investment and Financing Options (FIFO) as a loan officer. FIFO is a national company that specializes in mortgage lending. One of Alan's responsibilities is to increase the amount of mortgages FIFO initiates. In a meeting he had with the CEO yesterday, Alan was told about a new mortgage that FIFO intends to market. The new mortgage is called an option adjustable rate mortgage, or an option ARM for short, and its most attractive feature is that homeowners can choose to make relatively low monthly payments at the beginning of the mortgage period. However, the payments increase significantly later in the life of the mortgage. In fact, depending on the amount the borrower chooses to pay (hence, the term "option") early, the amounts that must be paid later could be substantial; as much as four to five times the initial payments. In many cases, when a homeowner chooses to pay the minimum amount or an amount that he or she can afford, the mortgage turns "upside down," which means that the amount due on the mortgage grows to an amount that is greater than the value of the house.

The primary benefit of option ARMs to borrowers is that such loans allow those who cannot afford the monthly payments associated with conventional mortgages the opportunity to purchase houses. A borrower with income that is lower than is needed to qualify for a conventional mortgage can borrow using option ARMs, choose an affordable (lower than conventional) payment in the early years of the mortgage, and then make the higher payments in later years when their incomes presumably will be higher. Thus, option ARMs permit those who can't afford conventional mortgages to buy houses today that they otherwise couldn't afford until years into the future.

Lenders such as FIFO like selling option ARMs because they can recognize as current revenues the monthly payments that would be required if the loans were conventional mortgages, regardless of the amounts that the borrowers opt to pay. In other words, companies can "book" revenues that will not be collected for a few years.

Unlike most people, including many professionals, Alan understands the complexities of option ARMs. He knows that many borrowers who choose such mortgages will lose their houses three to five years after buying them because the payments increase so significantly after the low-payment option period expires that these borrowers cannot afford the new monthly payments. And, although they would like to refinance with conventional mortgages, often these homeowners do not have good enough credit. This scenario is quite disturbing to Alan. He would like to explain to his customers in clear terms the possible pitfalls of option ARMs, but the CEO of FIFO has instructed Alan that he should provide only the information that is required by law and to follow company policy, which states that lending officers should provide basic printed material, give simple advice, and answer questions that might provide negative information only when asked.

Alan has a bad feeling about option ARMs. He knows that they are great lending/borrowing tools when used as intended. He is afraid, however, that FIFO is more concerned about booking revenues than the financial well being of its customers (borrowers). What should Alan do? How would you handle this situation if you were Alan?

---

### Chapter *Essentials*
—Personal Finance

Some of the concepts presented in this chapter reinforce and extend the concepts that are discussed in Chapter 5. In this chapter, we showed you how to value a bond or an investment with similar characteristics. We also showed you how changes in interest rates and risk affect bond values. Following are some questions you should be able to answer that will help you make better personal financial decisions.

- How can I use knowledge of, or expectations about, interest rate changes to help make investment decisions? *Answer:* We know that bond prices decrease (increase) when interest rates increase (decrease). As a result, if interest rates are expected to increase, investors generally wait to invest their money in ("lock into") long-term bonds until the rates peak. When interest rates are increasing, investors still want to "put their money to work," so they generally invest in short-term bonds (debt) until rates are finished increasing.

- How can I use bond ratings to help make investment decisions? *Answer:* Bond ratings provide an indication of the default risks associated with bond issues. Thus, if you don't mind risking your money to try to earn higher returns, you would invest in lower-rated bonds—that is, bonds with greater default risk. If you don't like taking much risk, then you should invest in high-rated bonds.

- How does knowledge of bond valuation help me to make investment decisions? *Answer:* If you understand why bond prices change, then you understand why the returns you earn via your bond investments change, and vice versa.

- How can I use the concepts discussed in this chapter to help make decisions about borrowing money? *Answer:* Individuals, like corporations, have credit ratings. The better an individual's credit rating, the lower the interest rate he or she is charged on loans, such as mortgages and automobile loans. To lower the interest you are charged, you need to improve your credit rating.

- How can I use knowledge of bond valuation to make decisions about whether to repay loans early? *Answer:* Most long-term consumer debt is paid off in installments; thus, each payment includes both interest that is due and repayment of some of the principal amount, or the outstanding balance. For such loans, you can determine the amount of principal you owe, which is the amount that would have to be paid off to liquidate the loan, by computing the present value of all the remaining payments using the loan's interest rate as $r_d$. As we showed in Chapter 4, you must "strip" the remaining loan payments of the interest charges—that is, you must "deinterest" the payments.

## QUESTIONS

**6-1**  The rate of return that you would earn if you bought a bond and held it to its maturity date is called the bond's yield to maturity (YTM). If interest rates in the economy rise after a bond has been issued, what will happen to the bond's price and to its YTM? Does the length of time to maturity affect the extent to which a given change in interest rates will affect the bond's price?

**6-2**  A bond that pays interest forever and has no maturity date is a perpetual bond. How is the yield to maturity on such a bond determined?

**6-3**  What effect do you think each of the following items should have on the interest rate that a firm must pay on a new issue of long-term debt? Indicate whether each factor would tend to raise, lower, or have an indeterminate effect on the interest rate, and then explain why.

   **a.** The firm uses bonds rather than a term loan.

   **b.** The firm uses debentures rather than first mortgage bonds.

   **c.** The firm makes its bonds convertible into common stock.

   **d.** If the firm makes its debentures subordinate to its bank debt, what will the effect be

      **(1)** on the cost of the debentures?

      **(2)** on the cost of the bank debt?

      **(3)** on the average cost of total debt?

   **e.** The firm sells income bonds rather than debentures.

**f.** The firm must raise $100 million, all of which will be used to construct a new plant, and it is debating the sale of first mortgage bonds or debentures. If it decides to issue $50 million of each type, rather than $75 million of first mortgage bonds and $25 million of debentures, how will this choice affect

   **(1)** the cost of debentures?

   **(2)** the cost of mortgage bonds?

   **(3)** the overall cost of the $100 million?

**g.** The firm puts a call provision on its new issue of bonds.

**h.** The firm includes a sinking fund on its new issue of bonds.

**i.** The firm's bonds are downgraded from A to BBB.

**6-4**   Rank the following securities from lowest (1) to highest (7) in terms of their riskiness for an investor. All securities (except the Treasury bond) are for a given firm. If you think two or more securities are equally risky, indicate so.

**a.** Income bond

**b.** Subordinated debentures—noncallable

**c.** First mortgage bond—no sinking fund

**d.** U.S. Treasury bond

**e.** First mortgage bond—with sinking fund

**f.** Subordinated debentures—callable

**g.** Term loan

**6-5**   A sinking fund can be set up in one of two ways:

**a.** The corporation makes annual payments to the trustee, who invests the proceeds in securities (frequently government bonds) and uses the accumulated total to retire the bond issue at maturity.

**b.** The trustee uses the annual payments to retire a portion of the issue each year, either by calling a given percentage of the issue through a lottery and paying a specified price per bond or by buying bonds on the open market, whichever is cheaper.

Discuss the advantages and disadvantages of each procedure from the viewpoint of both the firm and its bondholders.

**6-6**   Suppose a company simultaneously issues $50 million of convertible bonds with a coupon rate of 9 percent and $50 million of pure bonds with a coupon rate of 12 percent. Both bonds have the same maturity. Does the fact that the convertible issue has the lower coupon rate suggest that it is less risky than the pure bond? Would you regard the cost of the funds as being lower on the convertible security than on the pure bond? Explain. (*Hint:* Although it might appear at first glance that the convertible's cost is lower, it is not necessarily the case because the interest rate on the convertible understates its cost. Think about this point before answering the questions.)

**6-7**   In 1936 the Canadian government raised $55 million by issuing bonds at a 3 percent annual rate of interest. Unlike most bonds issued today, which have a specific maturity date, these bonds can remain outstanding forever; they are, in fact, perpetual.

   At the time of issue, the Canadian government stated in the bond indenture that cash redemption was possible at face value ($100) on or after

September 1966; in other words, the bonds were callable at par after September 1966. Believing that the bonds would actually be called, many investors purchased these bonds in 1965 with the expectation of receiving $100 in 1966 for each perpetual bond they had. In 1965 the bonds sold for $55. A rush of buyers, however, drove the price to slightly less than the $100 par value by 1966. But prices fell dramatically when the Canadian government announced that these perpetual bonds were indeed perpetual and would not be paid off. The bonds' market price declined to $42 in December 1966. Because of their severe losses, hundreds of Canadian bondholders formed the Perpetual Bond Association to lobby for face value redemption of the bonds, claiming that the government had reneged on an implied promise to redeem the bonds. Government officials in Ottawa insisted that claims for face value payment were nonsense—that the bonds were and always had been clearly identified as perpetuals. One Ottawa official stated, "Our job is to protect the taxpayer. Why should we pay $55 million for less than $25 million worth of bonds?"

The following questions relating to the Canadian issue will test your understanding of bonds in general:

**a.** Do you think it would it make sense for a business firm to issue bonds like the Canadian government bonds described here?

**b.** Suppose the U.S. government today sold $100 billion each of four types of bonds: five-year bonds, 50-year bonds, "regular" perpetual bonds, and Canadian-type perpetual bonds. Rank the bonds from the one with the lowest to the one with the highest expected interest rate. Explain your answer.

**c.** Do you think the Canadian government would have taken the same action with regard to retiring the bonds if the interest rate had fallen rather than risen after they were issued?

**d.** Do you think the Canadian government was fair or unfair in its actions? Give the pros and cons of its decision, and justify your reason for thinking that one outweighs the other. Would it matter if the bonds had been sold to "sophisticated" rather than "naive" purchasers?

## SELF-TEST PROBLEMS

*(Solutions appear in Appendix B at the end of the book.)*

**ST-1** Define each of the following terms:                                    **key terms**

    **a.** Bond; term loan; mortgage bond

    **b.** Debenture; subordinated debenture

    **c.** Convertible bond; income bond; putable bond; indexed (purchasing power) bond; floating-rate bond

    **d.** Indenture; restrictive covenant; trustee

    **e.** Call provision; sinking fund

    **f.** Zero coupon bond; original issue discount bond (OID)

    **g.** Junk bond; investment-grade bonds

    **h.** Eurodebt; foreign debt; LIBOR; Euronotes; Eurocredits

    **i.** Premium bond; discount bond

**j.** Current yield (on a bond); yield to maturity (YTM)

**k.** Interest rate price risk; interest rate reinvestment risk

**convertible bond**    **ST-2** Nickles Mining recently issued convertible bonds. Each convertible bond has a face value equal to $1,000 and can be converted into 50 shares of common stock.

  **a.** What would be the minimum price of the stock that would make it beneficial for bondholders to convert their bonds? Ignore the effects of taxes or other costs.

  **b.** Suppose the bond also has a call provision, which Nickles just exercised. The call price is $1,100. If the company's stock is currently selling for $20.50, should investors convert their bonds into common stock or redeem them for cash?

**bond valuation**    **ST-3** The Pennington Corporation issued a new series of bonds on January 1, 1983. The bonds were sold at par value, which is $1,000, have a 12 percent coupon, and mature in 30 years, on December 31, 2012. Coupon payments are made semiannually (on June 30 and December 31).

  **a.** What was the YTM on Pennington's bonds on January 1, 1983?

  **b.** What was the price of the bond on January 1, 1988 (five years later), assuming that the level of interest rates had fallen to 10 percent?

  **c.** Find the current yield and capital gains yield on the bond on January 1, 1988, given the price determined in part b.

  **d.** On August 1, 2008, Pennington's bonds sold for $916.42. What was the YTM at that date?

  **e.** What were the current yield and capital gains yield on July 1, 2008?

**sinking fund**    **ST-4** The Vancouver Development Company just sold a $100 million, 10-year, 12 percent bond issue. A sinking fund will retire the issue over its life. Sinking fund payments are of equal amounts and will be made *semiannually*, and the proceeds will be used to retire bonds as the payments are made. Bonds can be called at par for sinking fund purposes, or the funds paid into the sinking fund can be used to buy bonds in the open market.

  **a.** How large must each semiannual sinking fund payment be?

  **b.** What will happen, under the conditions of the problem stated to this point, to the company's debt service requirements (interest and sinking fund payments) per year for this issue over time?

  **c.** Now suppose that Vancouver Development sets up its sinking fund so that, at the end of each year, equal annual amounts are paid into a sinking fund trust held by a bank, with the proceeds being used to buy government bonds that pay 9 percent interest.

    **(1)** What is the amount of the payment that must be made to the sinking fund each year?

    **(2)** What are the annual cash requirements for covering bond service costs under this trusteeship arrangement? (*Note:* Interest must be paid on Vancouver's outstanding bonds but not on bonds that have been retired.)

  **d.** What would have to happen to bond prices to cause the company to buy bonds on the open market rather than call them under the original sinking fund plan?

# PROBLEMS

**6-1**  Filkins Farm Equipment needs to raise $4.5 million for expansion, and it expects that five-year zero coupon bonds can be sold at a price of $567.44 for each $1,000 bond.

    **a.** How many $1,000 par value zero coupon bonds would Filkins have to sell to raise the needed $4.5 million?

    **b.** What will be the burden of this bond issue on the future cash flows generated by Filkins? What will be the annual debt service costs?

    **c.** What is the yield to maturity (YTM) on the bonds?

*zero coupon bonds*

**6-2**  The Swift Company is planning to finance an expansion. The principal executives of the company agree that an industrial company such as theirs should finance growth by issuing common stock rather than by taking on additional debt. Because they believe that the current price of Swift's common stock does not reflect its true worth, however, they have decided to sell convertible bonds. Each convertible bond has a face value equal to $1,000 and can be converted into 25 shares of common stock.

    **a.** What would be the minimum price of the stock that would make it beneficial for bondholders to convert their bonds? Ignore the effects of taxes or other costs.

    **b.** What would be the benefits of including a call provision with these bonds?

*convertible bond*

**6-3**  Buner Corporation's outstanding bond has the following characteristics:

*bond valuation*

| | |
|---|---|
| Years to maturity | 6.0 |
| Coupon rate of interest | 8.0% |
| Face value | $1,000 |

If investors require a rate of return equal to 12 percent on similar-risk bonds and *interest is paid semiannually,* what should be the market price of Buner's bond?

**6-4**  Intercontinental Baseball Manufacturers (IBM) has an outstanding bond that matures in 10 years. The bond, which pays $25 interest every six months ($50 per year), is currently selling for $598.55. What is the bond's yield to maturity?

*yield to maturity*

**6-5**  A corporation has an outstanding bond with the following characteristics:

*yield to maturity*

| | |
|---|---|
| Coupon interest rate | 6.0% |
| Interest payments | semiannually |
| Face value | $1,000.00 |
| Years to maturity | 8 |
| Current market value | $ 902.81 |

What is the yield to maturity (YTM) for this bond?

**6-6**  Suppose Ford Motor Company sold an issue of bonds with a 10-year maturity, a $1,000 par value, a 10 percent coupon rate, and semiannual interest payments.

*bond valuation*

**a.** Two years after the bonds were issued, the going rate of interest on bonds such as these fell to 6 percent. At what price would the bonds sell?

**b.** Suppose the interest rate remained at 6 percent for the next eight years. What would happen to the price of the Ford Motor Company bonds over time?

**bond valuation    6-7**   Rick bought a bond when it was issued by Macroflex Corporation 14 years ago. The bond, which has a $1,000 face value and a coupon rate equal to 10 percent, matures in six years. Interest is paid every six months; the next interest payment is scheduled for six months from today. If the yield on similar-risk investments is 14 percent, what is the current market value (price) of the bond?

**bond valuation    6-8**   Suppose that five years ago Cisco Systems sold a 15-year bond issue that had a $1,000 par value and a 7 percent coupon rate. Interest is paid semiannually.

**a.** If the going interest rate has risen to 10 percent, at what price would the bonds be selling today?

**b.** Suppose that the interest rate remained at 10 percent for the next 10 years. What would happen to the price of the Cisco Systems bonds over time?

**bond valuation    6-9**   The Desreumaux Company has two bond issues outstanding. Both bonds pay $100 annual interest plus $1,000 at maturity. Bond L has a maturity of 15 years and Bond S has a maturity of one year. Interest is paid annually.

**a.** What will be the value of each of these bonds when the going rate of interest is (1) 5 percent, (2) 7 percent, and (3) 11 percent? Assume there is only one more interest payment to be made on Bond S.

**b.** Why does the longer-term (15-year) bond fluctuate more when interest rates change than does the shorter-term bond (one-year)?

**yield to maturity    6-10**   It is now January 1, 2008, and you are considering the purchase of an outstanding Puckett Corporation bond that was issued on January 1, 2006. The Puckett bond has a 9.5 percent annual coupon and a 30-year original maturity (it matures on December 31, 2037). Interest rates have declined since the bond was issued, and the bond is now selling at 116.575 percent of the par value, or $1,165.75. What is the yield to maturity in 2008 for the Puckett bond? (Interest is paid annually.)

**yield to maturity    6-11**   The Severn Company's bonds have four years remaining to maturity. Interest is paid annually, the bonds have a $1,000 par value, and the coupon interest rate is 9 percent.

**a.** Compute the yield to maturity for the bonds if the current market price is (1) $829 or (2) $1,104.

**b.** Would you pay $829 for one of these bonds if you thought that the appropriate rate of interest was 12 percent—that is, if $r_d = 12\%$? Explain your answer.

**yields    6-12**   Robert bought a new issue of 10-year bond with a coupon rate equal to 8 percent. If Robert sells the bond at the end of the year when its market price is $925, what return would he earn? What portion of the return is capital gains and what portion is the current yield?

**yields    6-13**   On January 2, 2007, a Sunny Communications $1,000 face value, six-year bond sold for $889. Investors who bought this particular bond will be paid interest equal to $40 every six months. Market interest rates did not change until December 31, 2007, when they decreased significantly. On January 2, 2008, the price of the bond was $1,042.

    **a.** What was the bond's yield to maturity on January 2, 2007?

    **b.** What was the bond's yield to maturity on January 2, 2008?

    **c.** What return did investors who bought the bond on January 2, 2007 earn if they sold the bond one year later? What were the capital gains yield and the current yield on the bond in 2007?

**6-14** Using the information provided in problem 6-13, compute the value of the bond on January 2, 2009, assuming interest rates do not change. What return would investors earn in 2008? What would be the capital gains yield and the current yield?

*valuation/yields*

**6-15** What will be the rate of return on a perpetual bond with a $1,000 par value, an 8 percent coupon rate, and a current market price of (a) $600, (b) $800, (c) $1,000, and (d) $1,500? Assume that interest is paid annually.

*rate of return for a perpetual bond*

**6-16** As investment manager of Pasco Electric Company's pension plan (which is exempt from income taxes), you must choose between IBM bonds and AT&T preferred stock. The bonds have a $1,000 par value, mature in 20 years, pay $40 every six months, and sell at a price of $897.40 per bond. The preferred stock is a perpetuity; it pays a dividend of $2 each quarter, and it sells for $95 per share. What is the effective annual rate of return (EAR) on the *higher-yielding* security?

*effective annual rate*

**6-17** Tapley Corporation's 14 percent coupon rate, semiannual payment, $1,000 par value bonds mature in 30 years. The bonds sell at a price of $1,353.54, and their yield curve is flat. Assuming that interest rates in the general economy are expected to remain at their current level, what is the best estimate of Tapley's simple interest rate on *new* bonds?

*simple interest rate*

**6-18** The bonds of the Lange Corporation are perpetuities with a 10 percent coupon. Bonds of this type currently yield 8 percent, and their par value is $1,000.

*perpetual bond valuation*

    **a.** What is the price of the Lange bonds?

    **b.** Suppose interest rate levels rise to the point where such bonds now yield 12 percent. What would be the price of the Lange bonds?

    **c.** At what price would the Lange bonds sell if the yield on them was 10 percent?

    **d.** How would your answers to parts a, b, and c change if the bonds were not perpetuities but rather had a maturity of 20 years?

**6-19** In January 2006, the yield on AAA-rated corporate bonds averaged approximately 5 percent; one year later, the yield on these same bonds had climbed to about 6 percent because the Federal Reserve increased interest rates during the year. Assume that IBM issued a 10-year, 5 percent coupon bond on January 1, 2006. On the same date, Microsoft issued a 20-year, 5 percent coupon bond. Both bonds pay interest *annually*. Also assume that the market rate on similar-risk bonds was 5 percent at the time that the bonds were issued.

*bond valuation; capital gains yield and current yield*

    **a.** Compute the market value of each bond at the time of issue.

    **b.** Compute the market value of each bond one year after issue if the market yield for similar-risk bonds was 6 percent on January 1, 2007.

    **c.** Compute the 2006 capital gains yield for each bond.

    **d.** Compute the current yield for each bond in 2006.

**e.** Compute the total return that each bond would have generated for investors in 2006.

**f.** If you invested in bonds at the beginning of 2006, would you have been better off if you held long-term or short-term bonds? Explain.

**g.** Assume that interest rates stabilize at the January 2007 rate of 6 percent, then they stay at this level indefinitely. What would be the price of each bond on January 1, 2012, after six years from the date of issue have passed? Describe what should happen to the prices of these bonds as they approach their maturities.

## Integrative Problem

bond valuation **6-20** Robert Campbell and Carol Morris are senior vice presidents of the Mutual of Chicago Insurance Company. They are codirectors of the company's pension fund management division, with Campbell having responsibility for fixed income securities (primarily bonds) and Morris being responsible for equity investments. A major new client, the California League of Cities, has requested that Mutual of Chicago present an investment seminar to the mayors of the represented cities. Campbell and Morris, who will make the actual presentation, have asked you to help them by answering the following questions.

**a.** What are the key features of a bond?

**b.** How do you determine the value of a bond?

**c.** What is the value of a one-year, $1,000 par value bond with a 10 percent annual coupon if its required rate of return is 10 percent? What is the value of a similar 10-year bond?

**d. (1)** What would be the value of the bond described in part c if, just after it had been issued, the expected inflation rate rose by 3 percentage points, causing investors to require a 13 percent return? Is the security now a discount bond or a premium bond?

**(2)** What would happen to the bond's value if inflation fell, and $r_d$ declined to 7 percent? Would it now be a premium bond or a discount bond?

**(3)** What would happen to the value of the 10-year bond over time if the required rate of return remained at (i) 13 percent or (ii) remained at 7 percent?

**e. (1)** What is the yield to maturity on a 10-year, 9 percent annual coupon, $1,000 par value bond that sells for $887.00? That sells for $1,134.20? What does the fact that a bond sells at a discount or at a premium tell you about the relationship between $r_d$ and the bond's coupon rate?

**(2)** What is the current yield, the capital gains yield, and the total return in each case in the preceding question?

**f.** Suppose that the bond described in part e is callable in five years at a call price equal to $1,090.00. What is the yield to call (YTC) on the bond if its market value is $887.00? What is the YTC on the same bond if its current market price is $1,134.20?

**g.** What is *interest rate price risk*? Which bond in part c has more interest rate price risk, the one-year bond or the 10-year bond?

**h.** What is *interest reinvestment rate risk*? Which bond in part c has more interest rate reinvestment rate risk, assuming a 10-year investment horizon?

**i.** Redo parts c and d, assuming that the bonds have semiannual rather than annual coupons.

**j.** Suppose you could buy, for $1,000, either a 10 percent, 10-year, annual payment bond or a 10 percent, 10-year, semiannual payment bond. Both bonds are equally risky. Which would you prefer? If $1,000 is the proper price for the semiannual bond, what is the proper price for the annual payment bond?

**k.** What is the value of a perpetual bond with an annual coupon of $100 if its required rate of return is 10 percent? 13 percent? 7 percent? Assess the following statement: "Because perpetual bonds match an infinite investment horizon, they have little interest rate price risk."

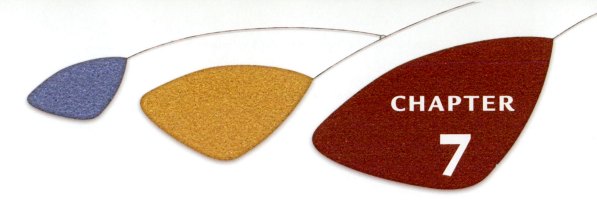

# Stocks (Equity)—Characteristics and Valuation

Throughout history, the investment adage "buy low, sell high" has been repeated again and again. Following this advice is not as difficult as it might seem because, historically, the stock market has trended upward over the long term. Thus, if you invest in a basket of securities today and you hold your position for a long period—say, 10 to 20 years—chances are that you will be able to sell the securities for much higher prices. In fact, if you earn the historical market average return, your original investment will double every six to seven years.

In today's world, the many technological advances that have been made in processing and delivering information have increased the interests of average individuals in managing their own investment portfolios. Of course, every person who manages his or her own investments wants to find stocks that will become "winners" after they are purchased, which will result in investment bonanzas. Some investors go to extreme measures in their attempts to identify such stocks. Recognizing this fact, perhaps the old adage should be revised to the following: "Beat the market—buy lower, sell higher."

Investors who try to "beat the market" on a risk-adjusted basis use various approaches in their attempts to identify stocks that are either mispriced or promise very high growth rates. These two groups of stock are referred to as *value stocks* and *growth stocks*, respectively. Value stocks are those that can be purchased for less than their "true" values, whereas growth stocks promise to provide strong growth in profits in the future. Investors generally identify growth and value stocks according to their price/earnings (P/E) ratios. Often stocks with high P/E ratios are labeled growth stocks because their market prices are high relative to their current earnings, which suggests that investors are willing to pay a premium for future earnings, or growth. On the other hand, stocks with low P/E ratios generally are considered value stocks because their prices are low relative to earnings, which suggests that their market values are currently, and hopefully temporarily, depressed. Both stocks offer higher potential capital gains to stockholders than "average" stocks.

Some professional investors believe that value stocks produce greater return potentials than growth stocks; other professionals believe just the opposite. Which side is correct? The answer is not clear-cut. Because some empirical evidence supports those who claim that value stocks outperform growth stocks while other empirical evidence disproves this claim, proponents of growth stocks and proponents of value stocks will remain on opposite sides of the fence for years to come.[1] Substantial returns can be made in either camp, and most professional advisers tell investors to look for both good growth prospects and bargains. Thus, it seems that every investor wants the same question answered: How can I pick the "winners"?

Unfortunately, there is no clear answer to this question. In fact, you might discover that it really cannot be answered. Even so, in this chapter, we attempt to give you an idea of some approaches used by investors to value and select stocks—that is, to pick the "winners."

## Chapter *Essentials*
### —The Questions

After reading this chapter, you should be able to answer the following questions:

- What is equity? What are some of the features/characteristics of equity?
- What factors affect stock prices?
- In general, how are stock prices determined?
- How are stock returns (yields) determined?
- What approaches (techniques) do investors use to value stocks?

As we saw in Chapter 2, corporations raise capital in two basic forms: debt and equity. In Chapter 6, we discussed the characteristics of debt and showed how to value corporate bonds. In this chapter, we discuss the characteristics of corporate equity and show some methods used to value stock.

Each corporation issues at least one type of stock, or equity, called *common stock.* Some corporations issue more than one type of common stock, and some issue *preferred stock* in addition to common stock. As the names imply, most equity takes the form of common stock, and preferred shareholders have preference over common shareholders when a firm distributes funds to stockholders. We discuss the general characteristics of both preferred and common stock in the next few sections.

## PREFERRED STOCK

Preferred stock often is referred to as a *hybrid* security because it is similar to bonds (debt) in some respects and similar to common stock in other respects. The hybrid nature of preferred stock becomes apparent when we try to classify it in relation to bonds and common stock. Like bonds, preferred stock has a par, or face, value. Preferred dividends are similar to interest payments in that they are fixed in amount and must be paid before common stock dividends can be distributed. If the preferred dividend is not earned, however, the directors can omit it (or "pass") without throwing the company into bankruptcy. Thus, although preferred stock has a fixed payment like bonds, a failure to make this payment will not lead to bankruptcy.

Accountants classify preferred stock as equity and report it in the equity portion of the balance sheet under "preferred stock" or "preferred equity." Financial analysts, on the other hand, sometimes treat preferred stock as debt and at other times treat it as equity, depending on the type of analysis involved. If the analysis is undertaken by a common stockholder, the key consideration is the fact that the preferred dividend is a fixed charge that reduces the amount that can be distributed to common shareholders and the preferred dividend must be paid before a common stock dividend can be paid; from the common stockholder's point of view, then, preferred stock is similar to debt. Suppose, however, that a bondholder is studying

---

[1]Examples of studies that address this issue can be found in James M. Clash and Mary Beth Grover, "The Wallflower Strategy," *Forbes,* February 9, 1998, 114–117; John C. Bogle, *Common Sense on Mutual Funds*, John Wiley & Sons, 1999; and Penelope Wang, "Value vs. Growth: The Unlikeliest Bubble," *Money*, September 2006, 65–71.

the firm's chance of failure in the event of a decline in sales and income. If the firm's income declines, the debt holders have a prior claim to the available income ahead of preferred stockholders. If the firm eventually fails, these debt holders have a prior claim to assets when the firm is liquidated. Thus, to a bondholder, preferred stock is similar to common equity.

From management's perspective, preferred stock falls between debt and common equity. Because failure to pay dividends on preferred stock will not force the firm into bankruptcy, this type of stock is safer to use than debt. At the same time, if the firm is highly successful, the common stockholders do not share that success with the preferred stockholders because preferred dividends are fixed. Remember, however, that the preferred stockholders do have a higher priority claim than the common stockholders. We see, then, that preferred stock shares some characteristics with debt and some characteristics with common stock, and it is used in situations in which neither debt nor common stock is entirely appropriate. For instance, a corporation might find preferred stock to be an ideal instrument when it needs to raise funds and already has a considerable amount of debt. In this situation, its creditors might be reluctant to lend more funds, and, at the same time, its common stockholders might not want their ownership shares diluted.

Preferred stock has a number of features, the most important of which are described next.

## Par Value

Most preferred stock has a par value or its equivalent under some other name—for example, liquidation value or liquidation preference. The par value is important for two reasons: (1) it establishes the amount due to the preferred stockholders in the event of liquidation, and (2) the preferred dividend generally is stated as a percentage of the par value. For example, Chesapeake Energy Corporation, a company that produces and distributes natural gas, has an issue of preferred stock with a liquidation "preference" (value) equal to $100 and a stated dividend of 5 percent. Investors who hold this issue of preferred stock receive a total annual dividend equal to $5 per share (5 percent of $100); a dividend equal to $1.25 is paid every January 15, April 15, July 15, and October 15. In the event that the firm is liquidated and sufficient funds are available after repaying creditors, each share of Chesapeake Energy Corporation's 5% preferred stock will be paid $100.

## Cumulative Dividends

Most preferred stock provides for **cumulative dividends;** that is, any preferred dividends not paid in previous periods must be paid before common dividends can be distributed. The cumulative feature acts as a protective device. If the preferred stock dividends were not cumulative, a firm could avoid paying preferred and common stock dividends for, say, 10 years, plowing back all of its earnings into the company, and then pay a huge common stock dividend but only the stipulated annual dividend to the preferred stockholders. Obviously, such an action would effectively void the preferential position that the preferred stockholders are supposed to enjoy. The cumulative feature helps prevent such abuses.[2] Chesapeake Energy Corporation's 5% preferred stock issue is cumulative. As a result, holders of this stock are ensured they will be paid

**cumulative dividends**
A protective feature on preferred stock that requires preferred dividends previously not paid to be disbursed before any common stock dividends can be paid.

---

[2]Most cumulative plans do not provide for compounding—in other words, the unpaid preferred dividends themselves earn no return. Also, many preferred issues have a limited cumulative feature; for example, unpaid preferred dividends might accumulate for only three years.

any missed preferred dividend payments, termed *dividends in arrears,* before common stockholders are paid any new dividends.

## Maturity

Preferred stock generally has no specific maturity date. But, as we describe later in this chapter, firms can essentially incorporate a maturity proviso by including a call provision with the preferred stock issue. The Chesapeake Energy Corporation 5% preferred stock issue is callable on April 15, 2010. Thus, although it has no specified maturity date, this preferred stock is expected to be called, or "mature," in 2010.

## Priority to Assets and Earnings

As mentioned previously, preferred stockholders have priority over common stockholders with regard to earnings and assets. Thus, dividends must be paid on preferred stock before they can be paid on the common stock, and, in the event of bankruptcy, the claims of the preferred shareholders must be satisfied before the common stockholders receive anything. To reinforce these features, most preferred stocks have coverage requirements similar to those placed on bonds, such as maintaining a times-interest-earned (TIE) ratio greater than 3. These restrictions limit the amount of preferred stock that a company can use, and they require a minimum level of retained earnings before the firm can pay any common dividends.

## Control of the Firm (Voting Rights)

Almost all preferred stock is nonvoting stock, which means that preferred stockholders neither elect the members of the board of directors nor vote on corporate issues. However, preferred stockholders often are given the right to vote for directors if the company has not paid the preferred dividend for a specified period, such as two years. For example, the Chesapeake Energy Corporation 5% preferred stock issue provides voting rights to these preferred stockholders after dividends have been missed for 18 months or more. This feature motivates management to make every effort to pay preferred dividends.

## Convertibility

Most preferred stock that has been issued in recent years is convertible into common stock. For example, each share of the Chesapeake Energy Corporation 5% preferred stock issue is convertible into 3.8811 shares of common stock at the *option of the preferred shareholders.* As a result, the **conversion price** for the preferred stock is $25.766, which is determined by dividing the stock's principal amount per share by the conversion ratio—that is $25.766 = $100/3.8811.

**conversion price**
A convertible stock's principal amount per share divided by the conversion ratio.

## Other Provisions

Some other provisions occasionally found in preferred stocks include the following:

1. *Call provision.* A call provision gives the issuing corporation the right to call in the preferred stock for redemption. As in the case of bonds, call provisions generally state that the company must pay an amount greater than the par value of the preferred stock, with the additional amount being dubbed a **call premium.** For example, Great Plains Energy has a preferred stock issue that has a $100 par value and a 4.50 percent coupon and is callable at $101. The call premium in this case is $1, or 10 percent of the stock's par value.

**call premium**
The amount in excess of par value that a company must pay when it calls a security.

2. *Sinking fund.* Most newly issued preferred stocks have sinking funds that call for the repurchase and retirement of a given percentage of the preferred stock each year.

3. *Participating.* A rare type of preferred stock is one that participates with the common stock in sharing the firm's earnings. Participating preferred stocks generally work as follows: (a) the stated preferred dividend is paid—for example, $5 per share; (b) the common stock is then entitled to a dividend in an amount up to the preferred dividend; (c) if the common dividend is raised to, say, $5.50, the preferred dividend must likewise be raised to $5.50.

**Self-Test Questions**

Explain the following statement: "Preferred stock is a hybrid."

Identify and briefly explain some of the key features of preferred stock.

## COMMON STOCK

We usually refer to common stockholders as the "owners" of the firm because investors in common stock have certain rights and privileges generally associated with property ownership. Common stockholders are entitled to any earnings that remain after interest payments are made to bondholders and dividends are paid to preferred stockholders. Because debt and preferred stock are generally "fixed-payment" securities, common stockholders do not have to share earnings that exceed the amounts that the firm is required to pay to bondholders and preferred stockholders. As a result, common stockholders benefit when the firm performs well. On the other hand, the payments due to bondholders and preferred stockholders do not change when the company performs poorly. In this case, payment of "mandatory" fixed financial obligations might reduce the common stockholders' (owners') equity. Thus, it is the common stockholders who bear most of the risk associated with a firm's operations.

The most common characteristics and rights associated with common stock are discussed next.

### Par Value

In many cases, common stock does not have a par value. But corporations that are chartered in certain states are required to assign par values to their common stocks. Legally, the par value of a common stock represents a stockholder's minimum financial obligation in the event the corporation is liquidated and its debts are repaid. For example, if a stock has a par value equal to $10, then the investor is obligated to contribute $10 per share to repay the firm's debt upon liquidation. If the stock is purchased for more than $10 per share, then the investor's obligation is satisfied; but if the stock is purchased for less than $10—say, for $6—then the stockholder is required to make up the difference—$4 in this case—if the firm goes bankrupt and additional funds are needed to repay creditors. In nearly every instance, common stock is sold for higher than its par value, so investors generally are not concerned with a stock's par value. As you will discover later in this chapter, the par value and market value of a common stock are not related—that is, *par value does not determine market value, and vice versa.*

### Dividends

The firm has no obligation, contractual or implied, to pay common stock dividends. Some firms pay relatively constant dividends year after year; other companies do not pay dividends at all. The return that investors receive when they own a company's common stock is based on both the change in the stock's market value (capital gain) and the dividend paid by the company. Some investors prefer current income to future capital gains, so they invest in firms that pay large dividends; thus, their returns are based primarily on the dividends earned from owning such stocks. These types of stocks traditionally are called **income stocks.** For example, stocks of utility companies often pay fairly constant dividends; thus, they are typically considered income stocks. On the other hand, some investors prefer capital gains to current income, so they invest in firms that pay little or no dividends; thus, their returns are based primarily on the capital gains earned from owning such stocks. Generally these types of firms retain most, if not all, of their earnings each year to help fund growth opportunities, so their stocks are referred to as **growth stocks.** Microsoft Corporation is a good example of a growth stock. Until 2003 the company did not pay a dividend, but the growth in net income averaged nearly 50 percent from 1995 to 1999. In 2000, a period of decrease for many companies, Microsoft's net income grew by 21 percent over the previous year. Even when it started paying dividends, the estimated growth for Microsoft was greater than 12 percent.

**income stocks**
Stocks of firms that traditionally pay large, relatively constant dividends each year.

**growth stocks**
Stocks that generally pay little or no dividends so as to retain earnings to help fund growth opportunities.

## Maturity

Like preferred stock, common stock has no specified maturity—that is, it is perpetual. At times, however, companies repurchase shares of their common stock in the financial markets. Stock repurchases might be undertaken when (1) the firm has excess cash but no "good" investment opportunities, (2) the price of the firm's stock is undervalued, or (3) management wants to gain more ownership control of the firm—by repurchasing the stock of other investors, the percentage owned by management increases.

## Priority to Assets and Earnings

Common stockholders can be paid dividends only after the interest on debt and the preferred dividends are paid. In the event of liquidation resulting from bankruptcy, common stockholders are last to receive any funds. Thus, as investors, the common stockholders are "last in line" to receive any cash distributions from the corporation.

## Control of the Firm (Voting Rights)

The common stockholders have the right to elect the firm's directors, who in turn appoint the officers who manage the business. Stockholders also vote on shareholders' proposals, mergers, and changes in the firm's charter. In a small firm, the major stockholder typically assumes the positions of president and chairperson of the board of directors. In a large, publicly owned firm, the managers typically own some stock, but their personal holdings are insufficient to provide voting control. Thus, stockholders can remove the managers of most large, publicly owned firms if they decide that a management team is not effective.

Numerous state and federal laws stipulate how stockholder control is to be exercised. Corporations must hold an election of directors periodically, usually once each year, with the vote taken at the annual meeting. In many firms, one-third of the directors are elected each year for a three-year term. Each share of stock normally has one vote, so the owner of 1,000 shares has 1,000 votes. Stockholders of large corporations, such as General Motors, can appear at the annual meeting and vote in person, but typically they transfer their right to vote to a second party by means of an instrument known as a **proxy.** The management of large firms always solicits, and thus usually gets, stockholders' proxies. If earnings are poor and stockholders are dissatisfied, however, an outside group

**proxy**
A document giving one person the authority to act for another, typically the power to vote shares of common stock.

might solicit the proxies in an effort to overthrow management and take control of the business. This kind of battle is known as a **proxy fight.**

The question of corporate control has become a central issue in finance. The frequency of proxy fights has increased, as have attempts by one corporation to take over another by purchasing a large amount of the outstanding stock. This action is called a **takeover.** Well-known examples of takeover battles include Chevron's acquisition of Gulf Oil (1984), Kohlberg Kravis Roberts & Company's (KKR) acquisition of RJR Nabisco (1989), AT&T's takeover of NCR (1991), and Nations-Bank's takeovers of both Barnett Banks and Bank America Corporation (1998). More recent examples include the mergers of Oracle and PeopleSoft (2005) and Hewlett-Packard and Compaq (2002).

Managers who do not have majority control (more than 50 percent of their firm's stock) are very much concerned about proxy fights and takeovers, and many attempt to get stockholder approval for changes in their corporate charters that would make takeovers more difficult. For example, in the past, companies have persuaded their stockholders to agree to the following provisions: (1) to elect only one-third of the directors each year (rather than electing all directors each year), (2) to require 75 percent of the stockholders (rather than 50 percent) to approve a merger, and (3) to approve a "poison pill" provision that would allow the stockholders of a firm that is taken over by another firm to buy shares in the second firm at a substantially reduced price. The third provision makes the acquisition unattractive and, therefore, wards off hostile takeover attempts. Managements seeking such changes generally cite a fear that the firm will be picked up at a bargain price, but it often appears that managers' concerns about their own positions might be an even more important consideration.

## Preemptive Right

Some common stockholders have the right, called a **preemptive right,** to purchase any additional shares of stock sold by the firm. The preemptive right requires a firm to offer existing stockholders shares of a new stock issue in proportion to their ownership holdings before such shares can be offered to other investors. Most common stock issues do not have preemptive rights because most states do not require such rights to be included in corporate charters.

The purpose of the preemptive right is twofold. First, it protects the power of control of current stockholders. If not for this safeguard, the management team of a corporation under criticism from stockholders could prevent stockholders from removing the managers from office by issuing a large number of additional shares and purchasing these shares themselves. Second, and more important, a preemptive right protects stockholders against the dilution of value that would occur if new shares were sold at relatively low prices.

## Types of Common Stock

Although most firms have only one type of common stock, in some instances **classified stock** is used to meet the special needs of the company. Generally, when special classifications of stock are used, one type is designated Class A, another Class B, and so on. Small, new companies seeking to obtain funds from outside sources frequently use different types of common stock. For example, when Genetic Concepts went public, its Class A stock was sold to the public and paid a dividend, but this stock did not have voting rights until five years after its issue. The company's Class B stock, which was retained by the organizers of the firm, had full voting rights for five years, but the legal terms stated that dividends could not be paid on the Class B stock until Genetic

**proxy fight**
An attempt by a person or group of people to gain control of a firm by getting its stockholders to grant that person or group the authority to vote their shares so as to change the management team.

**takeover**
An action whereby a person or group succeeds in ousting a firm's management and taking control of the company.

**preemptive right**
A provision in the corporate charter or bylaws that gives existing common stockholders the right to purchase on a pro rata basis new issues of common stock.

**classified stock**
Common stock that is given a special designation, such as Class A, Class B, and so forth, to meet special needs of the company.

**founders' shares**
Stock owned by the firm's founders that has sole voting rights but generally pays out only restricted dividends for a specified number of years.

**closely held corporations**
A corporation that is owned by a few individuals who are typically associated with the firm's management.

**publicly owned corporations**
A corporation that is owned by a relatively large number of individuals who are not actively involved in its management.

Concepts had established its earning power by building up retained earnings to a designated level. The use of classified stock thus enabled the public to take a position in a conservatively financed growth company without sacrificing income, while the founders retained absolute control during the crucial early stages of the firm's development. At the same time, outside investors were protected against excessive withdrawals of funds by the original owners. As is often the case in such situations, Genetic Concepts' Class B stock was called **founders' shares.**

Note that "Class A," "Class B," and so on have no standard meanings. One firm could designate its Class B shares as founders' shares and its Class A shares as those sold to the public, whereas another firm might reverse these designations. Still other firms could use stock classifications for entirely different purposes.[3]

Some companies are so small that their common stocks are not actively traded; they are owned by only a few people, usually the companies' managers. Such firms are said to be *privately owned,* or **closely held, corporations,** and their stock is called *closely held stock.* In contrast, the stocks of most larger companies are owned by a large number of investors who are not active in management. Such companies are said to be **publicly owned corporations,** and their stock is called *publicly held stock.*

### Self-Test Questions

Identify and briefly explain some of the key features of common stock.

Identify some actions that companies have taken to make takeovers more difficult.

What are the two primary reasons for the existence of the preemptive right?

What are some reasons that a company might use classified stock?

What is a closely held stock?

## EQUITY INSTRUMENTS IN INTERNATIONAL MARKETS

For the most part, the financial securities of companies in other countries are similar to those in the United States. Some differences do exist, however, as discussed in this section. Also, some financial securities have been created specifically to permit investors easier access to international investments, such as *American depository receipts.*

## American Depository Receipts

**American depository receipts (ADRs)**
"Certificates" created by organizations such as banks that represent ownership in stocks of foreign companies that are held in trust by a bank located in the country in which the stock is traded.

Ownership of foreign companies can be traded internationally through *depository receipts,* which represent shares of the underlying stocks of foreign companies. In the United States, most foreign stock is traded through **American depository receipts (ADRs).** ADRs are not foreign stocks; instead, they are "certificates" created by organizations such as banks. The certificates represent ownership in stocks of foreign

---

[3]When General Motors (GM) acquired Hughes Aircraft for $5 billion in 1985, it paid for the purchase in part with a new Class H common stock (designated as GMH). The GMH stock had limited voting rights and its dividends were tied to Hughes's performance as a GM subsidiary. The company created the new stock for the following reasons: (1) GM wanted to limit voting privileges on the new classified stock because of management's concern about a possible takeover, and (2) Hughes's employees wanted to be rewarded more directly based on Hughes's own performance than would have been possible with regular GM stock. GM's deal posed a problem for the New York Stock Exchange, which had a rule against listing any company's common stock if the firm had any nonvoting common stock outstanding. GM made it clear that it was willing to delist if the NYSE did not change its rules. The NYSE concluded that such arrangements as GM had made were logical and were likely to be made by other companies in the future, so it changed its rules to accommodate GM.

companies that are held in trust by a bank located in the country in which the stock is traded. ADRs provide U.S. investors with the ability to invest in foreign companies with less complexity and difficulty than might otherwise be possible.

Each ADR certificate represents a certain number of shares of stock of a foreign company, and it entitles the owner to receive any dividends paid by the company in U.S. dollars. ADRs are traded in the stock markets in the United States, which often are more liquid than foreign markets. All financial information, including values, is denominated in dollars and stated in English, thereby eliminating potential problems with exchange rates and language translations.

In many cases, investors can purchase foreign securities directly. Such investments might be complicated by legal issues, the ability to take funds such as dividends out of the country, and interpretation of value and information into domestic terms. Thus, ADRs enable investors to participate in the international financial markets without having to bear risks greater than those associated with the corporations in which the investments are made. The market values of ADRs move in tandem with the market values of the underlying stocks that are held in trust.

## Foreign Equity (Stock)

The equities of foreign companies resemble those of U.S. corporations. The primary difference between stocks of foreign companies and U.S. companies is that U.S. regulations provide greater protection of stockholders' rights than do the regulations of most other countries.

In the international markets, equity generally is referred to as either "Euro stock" or "Yankee stock." **Euro stock** is traded in countries other than the "home" country of the company, not including the United States. Thus, if the stock of a Japanese company is sold in Germany, it would be considered a Euro stock. On the other hand, **Yankee stock** is issued by foreign companies and traded in the United States. If a Japanese company sells its stock in the United States, it is termed a Yankee stock in the international markets.

**Euro stock**
Stock traded in countries other than the "home" country of the company, not including the United States.

**Yankee stock**
Stock issued by foreign companies and traded in the United States.

**Self-Test Questions**

What is an ADR? What are the advantages of investing in foreign stocks via an ADR?

What is the difference between a Yankee stock and a Euro stock?

## STOCK VALUATION—DIVIDEND DISCOUNT MODEL (DDM)

In this section, we examine the process used to value stock, both preferred and common. We begin by introducing a general stock valuation model, and we then apply this model to various scenarios. Later in the chapter, we show a couple of other methods investors use to evaluate the value of a stock.

## Definitions of Terms Used in the Stock Valuation Models

Stocks provide an expected future cash flow stream, and a stock's value is found in the same manner as the values of other assets—that is, the present value of the expected future cash flow stream. A stock's expected cash flows consist of two elements: the dividends expected in each year and the price that investors expect to receive when they sell the stock. The expected final stock price includes the return of the original investment plus a capital gain or loss. And as you will discover, the future selling price of a stock is a function of the cash flows (dividends) that investors expect the company to distribute from the point when the stock is sold through the rest of its life.

Before we present the general stock valuation model, let's define some terms and notations that we will use in the remainder of the chapter.

**$\hat{D}_t$**
The dividend that the stock is expected to pay at the end of Year t.

$\hat{D}_t$ = Dividend that the stockholder expects to receive at the end of Year t (pronounced "D 'hat' t"); we designate expected value by placing a "hat" (^) above the variable. $D_0$ is the most recent dividend, which already has been paid; $\hat{D}_1$ is the next dividend expected to be paid at the end of this year; $\hat{D}_2$ is the dividend expected at the end of two years; and so forth. $\hat{D}_1$ represents the first cash flow that a new purchaser of the stock expects to receive. Note that $D_0$, the dividend that was just paid, is known with certainty (which explains why there is no "hat" over the D). All future dividends are *expected* values, so the estimate of $\hat{D}_t$ might differ among investors.[4]

**market price, $P_0$**
The price at which a stock sells in the market.

$P_0 = V_s$ = Actual **market price (value)** of the stock today.

**intrinsic value, $\hat{P}_0$**
The value of an asset that, in the mind of a particular investor, is justified by the facts; $\hat{P}_0$ can be different from the asset's current market price, its book value, or both.

$\hat{P}_t$ = Expected price of the stock at the end of each Year t. $\hat{P}_0$ is the **intrinsic,** or **theoretical, value** of the stock today as seen by the particular investor doing the analysis; $\hat{P}_1$ is the price *expected* at the end of Year 1; and so on. Note that $\hat{P}_0$ is the intrinsic value of the stock today based on a particular investor's estimate of the stock's expected dividend stream and the riskiness of that stream. Whereas $P_0$ is fixed and is identical for all investors because it represents the actual price at which the stock currently can be purchased in the stock market, $\hat{P}_0$ can differ among investors depending on what they believe the firm actually is worth. An investor would buy the stock only if his or her estimate of $\hat{P}_0$ is equal to or greater than the current selling price, $P_0$.

Because many investors participate in the market, many values for $\hat{P}_0$ are possible. We can imagine there exists a group of "average," or "marginal," investors whose actions actually determine the market price. For these average investors, $P_0$ must equal $\hat{P}_0$; otherwise, a disequilibrium would exist, and buying and selling in the market would change $P_0$ until $P_0 = \hat{P}_0$.

**growth rate, g**
The expected rate of change in dividends per share.

g = Expected **growth rate** in dividends as predicted by an average investor. (If we assume that dividends are expected to grow at a constant rate, then g is also equal to the expected rate of growth in the stock's price.) Different investors might use different growth rates to evaluate a firm's stock, but the market price, $P_0$, reflects the value for g estimated by average investors.

**required rate of return, $r_s$**
The minimum rate of return on a common stock that stockholders consider acceptable.

$r_s$ = Minimum acceptable, or **required, rate of return** on the stock, considering both its riskiness and the returns available on other investments. Again, this term generally relates to average investors. The determinants of $r_s$ are discussed in detail in Chapter 8.

**dividend yield**
The expected dividend divided by the current price of a share of stock, $\hat{D}_1/P_0$.

$\dfrac{\hat{D}_1}{P_0}$ = Expected **dividend yield** on the stock during the coming year. If the stock is expected to pay a dividend of $1 during the next 12 months, and if its current price is $10, then the expected dividend yield is $1/$10 = 0.10 = 10%.

**capital gains yield**
The change in price (capital gain) during a given year divided by the price at the beginning of the year, $(\hat{P}_1 - P_0)/P_0$.

$\dfrac{\hat{P}_1 - P_0}{P_0}$ = Expected **capital gains yield** on the stock during the coming year; it is the expected change in the stock's value stated as a percent. If the stock sells for $10 today, and if its price is expected to rise to $10.50 at the end of one year, then the expected capital gain is

---

[4]Stocks generally pay dividends quarterly, so theoretically we should evaluate them on a quarterly basis. In stock valuation, however, most analysts work on an annual basis because the data generally are not precise enough to warrant refinement to a quarterly model.

$\hat{P}_1 - P_0 = \$10.50 - \$10.00 = \$0.50$, and the expected capital gains yield is $\$0.50/\$10 = 0.05 = 5\%$.

$\hat{r}_s = $ **Expected rate of return,** which is the return that an investor who buys the stock expects to receive. The value of $\hat{r}_s$ could be above or below the required rate of return, $r_s$, but an investor should buy the stock only if $\hat{r}_s$ is equal to or greater than $r_s$—that is, a stock is considered a good investment if $\hat{r}_s \geq r_s$. $\hat{r}_s = $ expected dividend yield plus expected capital gains yield; in other words,

$$\hat{r}_s = \frac{\hat{D}_1}{P_0} + \frac{\hat{P}_1 - P_0}{P_0}$$

In our example, the expected total return is $\hat{r}_s = 10\% + 5\% = 15\%$.

$\ddot{r}_s = $ **Actual,** or **realized,** *after-the-fact* **rate of return.** You might expect to obtain a return equal to 15 percent if you buy a stock today, but if the market goes down, you might end up next year with an actual realized return that is much lower—perhaps even negative. For example, if $\ddot{r}_s = 8\%$, then $\ddot{r}_s = 8\% < \hat{r}_s = 15\%$, and those who invested in this stock would be disappointed because the return they actually earned was lower than the return they expected.

**expected rate of return, $\hat{r}_s$**
The rate of return on a common stock that an individual stockholder expects to receive. It is equal to the expected dividend yield plus the expected capital gains yield, $\hat{r}_s = \hat{D}_1/P_0 + (\hat{P}_1 - P_0)/P_0$.

**actual (realized) rate of return, $\ddot{r}_s$**
The rate of return on a common stock actually received by stockholders; $\ddot{r}_s$ can be greater than or less than $\hat{r}_s$ and/or $r_s$.

## Expected Dividends as the Basis for Stock Values

Recall from our discussions in previous chapters that we determine the value of any asset by computing the present value of the cash flows that the asset is expected to generate in the future. In our discussion of bonds, we found that the value of a bond is the present value of the interest payments over the life of the bond plus the present value of the bond's maturity (par) value. Stock prices are likewise computed as the present value of a stream of cash flows, and the basic stock valuation equation resembles the bond valuation equation (see Equation 6–1).

What cash flows do corporations provide to their stockholders? First, think of yourself as an investor who buys a stock with the intention of holding it (in your family) forever. In this case, all that you (and your heirs) will receive is a stream of dividends. Thus, the value of the stock today is calculated as the present value of an infinite stream of dividends, which is depicted on a cash flow time line as follows:

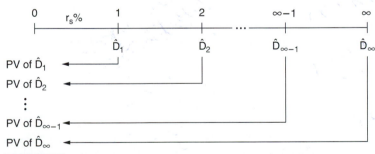

To compute the value of the stock, we solve this equation:

**7–1**

$$\text{Stock Value} = V_s = \hat{P}_0 = \frac{\hat{D}_1}{(1 + r_s)^1} + \frac{\hat{D}_2}{(1 + r_s)^2} + \cdots + \frac{\hat{D}_{\infty-1}}{(1 + r_s)^{\infty-1}} + \frac{\hat{D}_\infty}{(1 + r_s)^\infty}$$

$$= \sum_{t=1}^{\infty} \frac{\hat{D}_t}{(1 + r_s)^t}$$

How do you determine the value of $\hat{P}_0$ when you plan to hold the stock for a specific (finite) period and then sell it? This is the typical scenario followed by investors. Unless the company is likely to be liquidated and therefore disappear, *the value of the stock is still determined by Equation 7–1.* To see why, recognize that for any individual investor, the expected cash flows consist of expected dividends plus the expected price of the stock when it is sold. However, the sale price that the current investor receives depends on the dividends that the *future investor expects* to be paid by the company from that point forward. As a consequence, for all present and future investors, expected cash flows include *all* of the expected future dividends. Put another way, unless a firm is liquidated or sold to another concern, the cash flows that it provides to its stockholders will consist only of a stream of dividends. Therefore, the value of a share of stock must equal the present value of the dividend stream that the company is expected to pay throughout its life.

The general validity of Equation 7–1 can be confirmed by considering the following scenario: Suppose you buy a stock and expect to hold it for one year. You will receive dividends during the year plus the value of the stock when you sell it at the end of the year. What will determine the value of $\hat{P}_1$? $\hat{P}_1$ equals the present value of the dividends during Year 2 plus the stock price at the end of that year, which in turn is determined as the present value of another set of future dividends and an even more distant stock price. This process can be continued forever, with the ultimate result being Equation 7–1.

Equation 7–1 is a generalized stock valuation model in the sense that over time the value of $\hat{D}_t$ can follow any pattern: $\hat{D}_t$ can be rising, falling, or constant, or it can even be fluctuating randomly. In any event, Equation 7–1 will still hold. Often, however, the projected stream of dividends follows a systematic pattern, in which case we can develop a simplified (easier to apply) version of the stock valuation model expressed in Equation 7–1. In the following sections, we consider the cases of zero growth, constant growth, and nonconstant growth.

**zero growth stock**
A common stock whose future dividends are not expected to grow at all; that is, $g = 0$, and $D = \hat{D}_1 = \hat{D}_2 = \cdots = \hat{D}_\infty$.

## Valuing Stock with Zero Growth

Suppose a firm's dividends are expected to stay the same every year. In this case, we have a **zero growth stock,** for which the dividends expected in future years equal some constant amount—the current dividend. That is, $\hat{D}_1 = \hat{D}_2 = \cdots = \hat{D}_\infty = D_0 = D$. In this case, we can drop the subscripts and the "hats" on D (we are certain about the value of the future dividends) and rewrite Equation 7–1 as follows:

**7–2**

$$\hat{P}_0 = \frac{D}{(1 + r_s)^1} + \frac{D}{(1 + r_s)^2} + \cdots + \frac{D}{(1 + r_s)^{\infty-1}} + \frac{D}{(1 + r_s)^\infty}$$

As we noted in Chapter 4 in connection with the British consol bond, a security that is expected to pay a constant amount every year forever is called a perpetuity. *A zero growth stock is a perpetuity.* Recall that the value of any perpetuity is simply the cash payment divided by the discount rate. As a result, the value of a zero growth stock reduces to the following formula:

**7–3**

$$\text{Value of a zero growth stock} = \hat{P}_0 = \frac{D}{r_s}$$

Suppose we have a stock that is expected to always pay a dividend equal to $1.60, and the required rate of return associated with such an investment is 20 percent. The stock's value would be computed as follows:[5]

$$\hat{P}_0 = \frac{\$1.60}{0.20} = \$8.00$$

Generally, we can find the price of a stock and the most recent dividend paid to the stockholders by looking in a financial newspaper such as *The Wall Street Journal.* Therefore, if we have a stock with constant dollar dividends, we can solve for the expected rate of return by rearranging Equation 7–3 as follows:

$$\hat{r}_s = \frac{D}{P_0}$$

**7–4**

Because we are dealing with an *expected rate of return,* we put a "hat" on the r value. Thus, if we bought a stock at a price of $8 and expected to receive a constant dividend of $1.60, our expected rate of return would be

$$\hat{r}_s = \frac{\$1.60}{\$8.00} = 0.20 = 20\%$$

By now, you probably have recognized that Equation 7–3 can be used to value preferred stock. Recall that preferred stocks entitle their owners to receive regular, or fixed, dividend payments. If the payments last forever, the issue is a *perpetuity* whose value is defined by Equation 7–3. We can use Equation 7–3 to value any asset, including common stock, with expected future cash flows that exhibit the properties of a perpetuity—that is, constant cash flows forever.

## Valuing Stocks with Constant, or Normal, Growth

In general, investors expect the earnings and dividends of most companies to increase each year. Even though expected growth rates vary from company to company, it is not uncommon for investors to expect dividend growth to continue in the foreseeable future at about the same rate as that of the nominal gross national product (real GNP plus inflation). On this basis, we might expect the dividend of an average, or "normal," company to grow at a rate of 3 to 5 percent per year. Thus, if the last dividend paid by a normal, or constant, growth company was $D_0$, the firm's dividend in any future Year t can be forecasted as $\hat{D}_t = D_0(1 + g)^t$, where g is the constant expected rate of growth. For example, if a firm just paid a dividend of $1.60—that is, $D_0 = \$1.60$—and investors expect a 5 percent growth rate, then the estimated dividend one year hence would be $\hat{D}_1 = \$1.60(1.05) = \$1.68$; $\hat{D}_2$ would be $\$1.60(1.05)^2 = \$1.764$; and so on.

Using this method for estimating future dividends, we can determine the current stock value, $\hat{P}_0$, by using Equation 7–1. That is, we can find the dividend that is

[5]If you think that having a stock pay dividends forever is unrealistic, then think of it as lasting only for 50 years. Here you would have an annuity of $1.60 per year for 50 years. The PV of a 50-year annuity of $1.60 with an opportunity rate of interest equal to 20 percent would be 1.60(4.9995) = 7.999, which rounds to the same value as we computed for the perpetuity. Thus, the dividends from Year 51 to infinity contribute very little to the value of the stock.

expected to be paid each year in the future, calculate the present value of each dividend payment, and sum these present values to find the value of the stock. But because g is constant, we can rewrite Equation 7–1 as follows:[6]

**7–5**

$$\hat{P}_0 = \frac{D_0(1+g)^1}{(1+r_s)^1} + \frac{D_0(1+g)^2}{(1+r_s)^2} + \cdots + \frac{D_0(1+g)^{\infty-1}}{(1+r_s)^{\infty-1}} + \frac{D_0(1+g)^\infty}{(1+r_s)^\infty}$$

$$= \frac{D_0(1+g)}{r_s - g} = \frac{\hat{D}_1}{r_s - g} = \text{Value of a constant growth stock}$$

Inserting values into the last version of Equation 7–5, we find that the value of our illustrative stock is $11.20:

$$\hat{P} = \frac{\$1.60(1.05)}{0.20 - 0.05} = \frac{\$1.68}{0.15} = \$11.20$$

**constant growth model**
Also called the Gordon model, it is used to find the value of a stock that is expected to experience constant growth.

The **constant growth model** as set forth in the last term of Equation 7–5 is often called the Gordon model, after Myron J. Gordon, who did much to develop and popularize it.

Equation 7–5 is sufficiently general to encompass the zero growth case described earlier. If growth is zero, it is simply a special case of constant growth. Thus, Equation 7–5 simplifies to Equation 7–3 when $g = 0$. Note also that a necessary condition for the derivation of the simplified form of Equation 7–5 is that $r_s$ be greater than g. For situations in which $r_s$ is not greater than g, the results will be meaningless. For example, when $r_s < g$, the denominator in the simplified form of Equation 7–5 is negative, which gives a negative value for $\hat{P}_0$; $\hat{P}_0 < 0$ doesn't make sense in the world of finance.

Figure 7-1 illustrates the concept underlying the valuation process for a constant growth stock. Dividends are growing at the rate $g = 5\%$. Because $r_s > g$, however, the present value of each future dividend is declining. For example, the dividend in Year 1 is $\hat{D}_1 = D_0(1 + g)^1 = \$1.60(1.05) = \$1.68$. The present value of this dividend, discounted at 20 percent, is $PV(\hat{D}_1) = \$1.68/(1.20)^1 = \$1.40$. The dividend expected in Year 2 grows to $\$1.68(1.05) = \$1.764$, but the present value of this dividend falls to $\$1.225$. Continuing, $\hat{D}_3 = \$1.8522$ and $PV(\hat{D}_3) = 1.0719$, and so on. As you can see, the expected dividends are growing, but the present value of each successive dividend is declining because the dividend growth rate, 5 percent, is less than the rate used for discounting the dividends to the present, 20 percent.

If we summed the present values of each future dividend, this summation would equal the value of the stock, $\hat{P}_0$. When g is a constant, this summation is equal to $\hat{D}/(r_s - g)$, as shown in Equation 7–5. Therefore, if we extended the lower step function curve in Figure 7-1 to infinity and added up the present values of each future dividend, the summation would be identical to the value given by solving Equation 7–5, $11.20.

Growth in dividends occurs primarily as a result of growth in *earnings per share (EPS)*. Earnings growth, in turn, results from a number of factors, including inflation, the amount of earnings that the company retains and reinvests, and the rate of return that the company earns on its equity (ROE). Regarding inflation, if output (in units) remains stable and if both sales prices and input costs rise at the inflation rate, then EPS will also grow at the inflation rate. Likewise, EPS will grow as a result of the reinvestment, or plowback, of earnings. If the firm's earnings are not all paid out as

---

[6]The last term in Equation 7–5 is derived in the Extensions section of Chapter 5 in Eugene F. Brigham and Phillip R. Daves, *Intermediate Financial Management*, 9th ed. (Cincinnati, OH: South-Western College Publishing, 2007). In essence, the full-blown version of Equation 7–5 is the sum of a geometric progression, and the last term is the solution value of the progression.

**FIGURE 7-1**    Present Value of Dividends of a Constant Growth Stock: $D_0 = \$1.60$, $g = 5\%$, $r_s = 20\%$

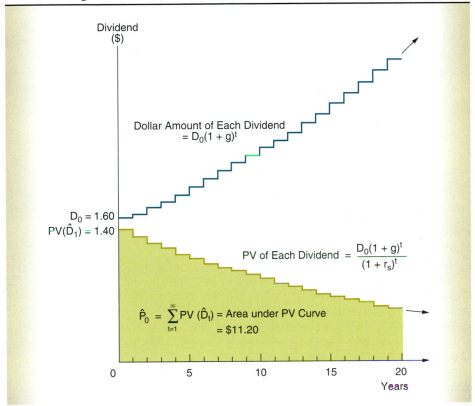

dividends (that is, if the firm retains some fraction of its earnings), the dollars of investment behind each share will increase over time, which should lead to growth in future earnings and dividends.

## Expected Rate of Return on a Constant Growth Stock

We can solve Equation 7–5 for $r_s$, again using the "hat" to denote that we are dealing with an expected rate of return:[7]

$$\hat{r}_s = \frac{\hat{D}_1}{P_0} + g$$

$$\begin{array}{ccc} \text{Expected rate} & = & \text{Expected} & + & \text{Expected growth rate,} \\ \text{of return} & & \text{dividend yield} & & \text{or capital gains yield} \end{array}$$

**7–6**

For example, imagine that you buy a stock for a price $P_0 = \$11.20$ and that you expect the stock to pay a dividend $\hat{D}_1 = \$1.68$ one year from now and to grow at a constant rate $g = 5\%$ in the future. In this case, your expected rate of return will be 20 percent:

$$\hat{r}_s = \frac{\$1.68}{\$11.20} + 0.05 = 0.15 + 0.05 = 0.20 = 20.0\%$$

[7]The $r_s$ value of Equation 7–5 is a *required* rate of return. When we transform this equation to obtain Equation 7–6, we are finding an *expected* rate of return. Obviously, the transformation requires that $r_s = \hat{r}_s$. This equality holds if the stock market is in equilibrium, a condition that will be discussed in Chapter 8.

In this form, we see that $\hat{r}_s$ is the *expected total return* and that it consists of an *expected dividend yield*, $\hat{D}_1/P_0 = 15\%$, plus an *expected growth rate or capital gains yield*, $g = 5\%$.

Suppose we had conducted this analysis on January 1, 2008. That is, $P_0 = \$11.20$ is the January 1, 2008, stock price and $\hat{D}_1 = \$1.68$ is the dividend expected at the end of 2008 (December 31). What is the expected stock price at the end of 2008 (or the beginning of 2009)? We would again apply Equation 7–5, but this time we would use the expected 2009 dividend, $\hat{D}_2 = \hat{D}_1(1 + g) = \hat{D}_{2009} = \hat{D}_{2008}(1 + g) = \$1.68(1.05) = \$1.764$, and solve for $\hat{P}_1$ as follows:

$$\hat{P}_1 = \hat{P}_{1/1/09} = \frac{\hat{D}_{12/31/09}}{r_s - g} = \frac{\$1.764}{0.20 - 0.05} = \$11.76$$

Notice that $\hat{P}_1 = \$11.76$ is 5 percent greater than $P_0$, the $\$11.20$ price on January 1, 2008—that is, $\hat{P}_{1/1/09} = \$11.20(1.05) = \$11.76$. In this case, we would expect to earn a capital gain of $\$0.56 = \$11.76 - \$11.20$ during the year. This amount represents a capital gains yield of 5 percent:

$$\text{Capital gains yield} = \frac{\text{Capital gains}}{\text{Beginning price}} = \frac{\hat{P}_1 - P_0}{P_0}$$
$$= \frac{\$11.76 - \$11.20}{\$11.20} = \frac{\$0.56}{\$11.20} = 0.05 = 5.0\%$$

Here $P_0$ represents the actual stock price at the beginning of the period and $\hat{P}_1$ represents the expected price of the stock at the end of one period (one year in this case).

We could extend this analysis further, if desired. In each future year, the expected capital gains yield would equal $g = 5\%$, the expected dividend growth rate. Continuing, we could estimate the dividend yield in 2009 as follows:

$$\text{Dividend yield}_{2009} = \frac{\hat{D}_1}{P_0} = \frac{\hat{D}_{12/31/09}}{P_{1/1/09}} = \frac{\$1.764}{\$11.76} = 0.15 = 15.0\%$$

We could also calculate the dividend yield for 2010, which would again be 15 percent. Thus, for a constant growth stock, the following conditions must hold:

1. The dividend is expected to grow forever at a constant rate, g. The stock price is expected to grow at this same rate, g. As a result, the expected capital gains yield is also constant, and it is equal to g.

2. The expected dividend yield, $\hat{D}_1/P_0$, is a constant.

3. The expected total rate of return, $\hat{r}_s$, is equal to the expected dividend yield plus the expected growth rate: $\hat{r}_s = \hat{D}_1/P_0 + g$.

We should clarify the meaning of the term *expected* here. It means expected in a probabilistic sense, as the statistically expected outcome. Thus, if we say the growth rate is expected to remain constant at 5 percent, we mean that the best prediction for the growth rate in any future year is 5 percent. We do not literally expect the growth rate to be exactly equal to 5 percent in each future year. In this sense, the constant growth assumption is a reasonable one for many large, mature companies.

## Valuing Stocks with Nonconstant Growth

Firms typically go through *life cycles*. During the early part of their lives, their growth greatly exceeds that of the economy as a whole. Later, their growth matches the economy's growth. In the final stage of its life, a firm's growth lags behind that of the

**FIGURE 7-2**    Illustrative Dividend Growth Rates

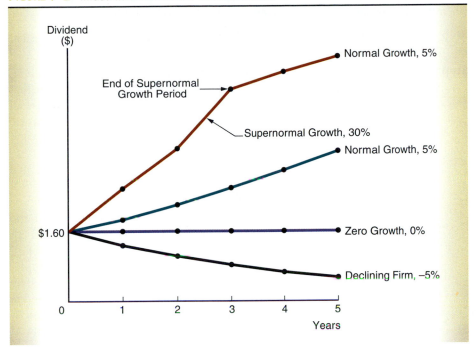

economy.[8] Automobile manufacturers in the 1920s; computer software firms such as Microsoft in the 1990s; and the Wi-Fi, which stand for *wireless fidelity*, industry in the 2000s are examples of firms in the early part of this cycle. Today, firms, such as those in the tobacco industry or coal industry, are in the waning stages of their life cycles; that is, their growth is not keeping pace with the general economic growth (in some cases, their growth actually is negative). Firms with growth rates that do not match the economy's growth are called **nonconstant growth** firms. Figure 7-2 illustrates nonconstant growth and compares it with constant growth (both positive and negative) and zero growth.[9]

In Figure 7-2 the dividends of the supernormal growth (growth much greater than the economy's growth) firm are expected to grow at a 30 percent rate for three years. The growth rate is then expected to fall to 5 percent, the assumed average for the economy, and remain at that level for the remainder of the firm's life. The value of this firm, like the value of any other firm, is the present value of its expected future dividends as determined by Equation 7–1. In the case in which $\hat{D}_t$ is growing at a constant rate, we discovered that Equation 7–1 can be simplified to $\hat{P}_0 = \hat{D}_1/(r_s - g)$. In the supernormal case, however, the expected growth rate is not a constant—it declines at the end of the period of

**nonconstant growth**
The part of the life cycle of a firm in which its growth either is much faster or is much slower than that of the economy as a whole.

---

[8]The concept of a life cycle could be broadened to include a *product cycle*, which would include both small, start-up companies and large companies such as IBM, which periodically introduce new products that boost sales and earnings. We should also mention *business cycles*, which alternately depress and boost sales and profits. The growth rate just after a major new product has been introduced, or just after a firm emerges from the depths of a recession, is likely to be much higher than the "expected long-run average growth rate," which is the proper value to use for evaluating the project.

[9]A negative growth rate indicates a declining company. A mining company whose profits are falling because of a declining ore body is an example. Someone buying such a company would expect its earnings, and consequently its dividends and stock price, to decline each year, which would lead to capital losses rather than capital gains. Obviously, a declining company's stock price will be relatively low, and its dividend yield must be high enough to offset the expected capital loss and still produce a competitive total return. Students sometimes argue that they would not be willing to buy a stock whose price was expected to decline. If the annual dividends are large enough to *more than offset* the falling stock price, however, the stock still could provide a good return.

supernormal growth. To find the value of such a stock, or of any nonconstant growth stock when the growth rate will eventually stabilize, we proceed in three steps:

**Step 1.** We compute the value of the dividends that are affected by nonconstant growth, and then find the present value of these dividends.

**Step 2.** *We find the price of the stock at the end of the nonconstant growth period, at which point it becomes a constant growth stock.* It is at this point that we can use a modified version of Equation 7–5 to compute $\hat{P}_t$ because all future dividends will grow at a constant rate, $g_{norm}$. In this case, the future stock price, $\hat{P}_t$ is computed as follows:

$$\hat{P}_t = \frac{\hat{D}_t(1 + g_{norm})}{r_s - g_{norm}} = \frac{\hat{D}_{t+1}}{r_s - g_{norm}}$$

Here $g_{norm}$ is the rate at which dividends will grow when constant, or normal, growth is attained. $\hat{P}_t$ represents the value in Year t of the dividends that are expected to be paid in Year $t + 1$ and beyond. In other words, $\hat{P}_t = (PV_t \text{ of } \hat{D}_{t+1}) + (PV_t \text{ of } \hat{D}_{t+2}) + \cdots + (PV_t \text{ of } \hat{D}_\infty)$, where $PV_t$ represents the present value in Year t. In our example, nonconstant growth ends at the end of Year 3, and thus dividends start growing at a constant rate ($g_{norm} = 5\%$) after the dividend for Year 3 is paid—that is, in Year 4. The constant growth model can be applied as soon as nonconstant growth ends. Because the first dividend to grow at the constant rate of 5 percent is the Year 4 dividend, $\hat{D}_4$, we can apply the constant growth model at the end of Year 3 to compute $\hat{P}_3$. After we compute $\hat{P}_t$ ($\hat{P}_3$ in our example), we discount this value to the present period—that is, Year 0. PV of $\hat{P}_t = \hat{P}_t / (1 + g)^t$.

**Step 3.** We add these two present value components to find the intrinsic value of the stock, $\hat{P}_0$. Thus, $\hat{P}_0 = (PV \text{ of nonconstant growth dividends}) + (PV \text{ of } \hat{P}_t)$.

To determine the value of the stock for our example, we assume the following conditions exist:

**$r_s$** = Stockholders' required rate of return; $r_s = 20\%$. This rate is used to discount the cash flows.

**$n_{super}$** = Number of years of supernormal growth; $n_{super} = 3$ years.

**$g_{super}$** = Rate of growth in both earnings and dividends during the supernormal growth period; $g_{super} = 30\%$. (*Note:* The growth rate during the supernormal growth period could vary from year to year.)

**$g_{norm}$** = Rate of normal (constant) growth after the supernormal period; $g_{norm} = 5\%$.

**$D_0$** = *Last* dividend paid by the company; $D_0 = \$1.60$.

To begin the valuation process, let's take a look at the cash flow time line for our situation:

Following the steps outlined earlier, we compute the value of our stock as

**Step 1.**   Calculate the dividends for each year during the nonconstant growth period—

$$\hat{D}_t = D_0(1+g_{super})^t.$$

$$\hat{D}_1 = D_0(1+g_{super})^1 = \$1.600(1.30)^1 = \$2.0800$$

$$\hat{D}_2 = D_0(1+g_{super})^2 = \$1.600(1.30)^2 = \hat{D}_1(1+g_{super})$$

$$= 2.0800(1.30) = \$2.7040$$

$$\hat{D}_3 = D_0(1+g_{super})^3 = \$1.600(1.30)^3 = \hat{D}_2(1+g_{super})$$

$$= 2.7040(1.30) = \$3.5152$$

Show these values on the cash flow time line as cash flows for Years 1 through 3.

**Step 2.**   The price of the stock is the PV of dividends from Year 1 to infinity ($\infty$). In theory, we could continue projecting each future dividend beyond Year 3, when normal growth of 5 percent occurs. In other words, we could use $g_{norm} = 5\%$ to compute $\hat{D}_4$, $\hat{D}_5$, and so on, with $\hat{D}_3 = \$3.5152$ being the base dividend for normal growth:

$$\hat{D}_4 = D_3(1+g_{norm})^1 = \$3.5152(1.05)^1 = \$3.6910$$

$$\hat{D}_5 = D_3(1+g_{norm})^2 = \$3.5152(1.05)^2 = \$3.8755$$

$$\vdots$$

$$\hat{D}_{20} = D_3(1+g_{norm})^{17} = \$3.5152(1.05)^{17} = \$8.0569$$

We can continue this process, and then find the PV of this stream of dividends. However, after $\hat{D}_3$ has been paid in Year 3, the stock becomes a constant growth stock. Thus, we can apply the constant growth formula at that point and find $\hat{P}_3$, which is the PV of the dividends from Year 4 through infinity as evaluated in Year 3. After the firm has paid the Year 3 dividend, all of the future dividends will grow at a constant rate equal to 5 percent, so

$$\hat{P}_3 = \frac{\hat{D}_4}{r_s - g_{norm}} = \frac{\$3.6910}{0.20 - 0.05} = \$24.6067$$

This $24.6067 appears on the cash flow time line as a *second cash* flow in Year 3. The $24.6067 is a Year 3 cash flow in the sense that the owner of the stock *could* sell it for $24.6067 at the end of Year 3, and also in the sense that $24.6067 is the present value equivalent of the dividend cash flows from Year 4 to infinity. Therefore, the *total cash flow* recognized in Year 3 is the sum of $\hat{D}_3 + \hat{P}_3 = \$3.5152 + \$24.6067 = \$28.1219$.

**Step 3.**   Figure 7-3 shows the cash flow time line with the actual cash flows we determined in Step 1 and Step 2. Now that we have included the cash flows on the cash flow time line, we need to discount each cash flow at the required rate of return, $r_s = 20\%$. To find the present value, we can either (1) compute the PVs directly or (2) use the cash flow function on a financial calculator. To compute the PVs directly, divide each cash flow by $(1.20)^t$, and you will get the results shown in Figure 7-3. If you use the cash flow function on your calculator, input $CF_0 = 0$, $CF_1 = 2.0800$, $CF_2 = 2.7040$, $CF_3 = 28.1219$, and $I = 20$; compute NPV = 19.8854. Using either method, you should find that the current price of the stock is $19.89, which is the result shown to the left below the cash flow time line in Figure 7-3.

**FIGURE 7-3    Determining the Value of a Nonconstant Growth Stock**

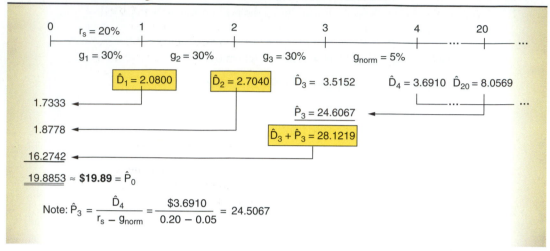

Note: $\hat{P}_3 = \dfrac{\hat{D}_4}{r_s - g_{norm}} = \dfrac{\$3.6910}{0.20 - 0.05} = 24.5067$

To give a different perspective of the valuation process presented in Steps 1 through 3, let's assume that the same situation exists for the stock that we are currently evaluating, except investors expect the company to pay dividends for the next 50 years and then go bankrupt rather than continue to pay dividends forever. Table 7-1 shows the dividend that would be paid each year as well as the present value of all of the dividends that would be paid during the 50-year period. Notice that the present value of the dividends equals $19.8584, which is about $0.03 less than the result we computed earlier (shown in Figure 7-3). Because the only difference between the result shown in Table 7-1 and the result shown in Figure 7-3 is that Table 7-1 excludes the dividends that would be received beyond Year 50, $0.03 represents the present value of the dividends from Year 51 to infinity. This is an extremely small value.

Clearly, it is very easy to compute the dividends and their present values for 50 years using a spreadsheet if we know the annual growth rates. But it is easier to compute the dividends during the nonconstant growth period, use the modified version of Equation 7–5 to compute the value of the stock at the point when nonconstant growth ends, and then add the present values of these future cash flows to determine $\hat{P}_0$.

## Self-Test Questions

In general, how should the value of a stock be determined?

Write out a simple equation that can be used to compute the value of a stock that exhibits constant dividend growth. Can this equation be used for stocks that exhibit zero growth in dividends?

What are the two elements of a stock's expected return?

How do you calculate the capital gains yield and the dividend yield of a stock?

How do you determine the value of a stock with nonconstant growth?

Suppose that the last dividend paid by a company was $3.00, dividends are expected to grow at a constant rate equal to 3 percent forever, and stockholders require 13 percent to invest in similar types of investments. What is the value of the company's stock? (*Answer:* $30.90)

Suppose Winding Road Map Company just paid a dividend equal to $5. For the past few years, the company has been growing at a rate equal to 20 percent. This growth is expected to continue for another two years, and then for every year thereafter the company's growth is expected to be 5 percent. If investors require a return equal to 14 percent to invest in Road Map, what is the value of its stock? (*Answer:* $75.44)

## APPLYING THE DDM TECHNIQUE IN THE REAL WORLD

In this section, we show how the DDM technique can be used to estimate the intrinsic value of stocks that currently exist. We show the application for two situations: (1) a dividend-paying stock, and (2) a non-dividend-paying stock.

**TABLE 7-1**    Present Value of the Dividends Received from a Stock Investment during a 50-Year Period

Information: Last dividend payment, $D_0 = \$1.60$
Dividend growth rates: $g_{super} = g_1 = g_2 = g_3 = 30\%$; $g_{norm} = g_4 = \cdots = g_\infty = 5\%$
Required rate of return, $r_s = 20\%$

| Year | Growth Rate, $g_t$ | Dividend $\hat{D}_t = \hat{D}_{t-1}(1+g_t)$ | PV of Dividend $= \hat{D}_t/(1.20)^t$ | Year | Growth Rate, $g_t$ | Dividend $\hat{D}_t = \hat{D}_{t-1}(1+g_t)$ | PV of Dividend $= \hat{D}_t/(1.20)^t$ |
|---|---|---|---|---|---|---|---|
| 1 | 30% | $2.0800 | $1.7333 | 26 | 5% | $10.7970 | $0.0943 |
| 2 | 30 | 2.7040 | 1.8778 | 27 | 5 | 11.3369 | 0.0825 |
| 3 | 30 | 3.5152 | 2.0343 | 28 | 5 | 11.9037 | 0.0722 |
| 4 | 5 | 3.6910 | 1.7800 | 29 | 5 | 12.4989 | 0.0632 |
| 5 | 5 | 3.8755 | 1.5575 | 30 | 5 | 13.1238 | 0.0553 |
| 6 | 5 | 4.0693 | 1.3628 | 31 | 5 | 13.7800 | 0.0484 |
| 7 | 5 | 4.2727 | 1.1924 | 32 | 5 | 14.4690 | 0.0423 |
| 8 | 5 | 4.4864 | 1.0434 | 33 | 5 | 15.1925 | 0.0370 |
| 9 | 5 | 4.7107 | 0.9130 | 34 | 5 | 15.9521 | 0.0324 |
| 10 | 5 | 4.9462 | 0.7988 | 35 | 5 | 16.7497 | 0.0284 |
| 11 | 5 | 5.1936 | 0.6990 | 36 | 5 | 17.5872 | 0.0248 |
| 12 | 5 | 5.4532 | 0.6116 | 37 | 5 | 18.4666 | 0.0217 |
| 13 | 5 | 5.7259 | 0.5352 | 38 | 5 | 19.3899 | 0.0190 |
| 14 | 5 | 6.0122 | 0.4683 | 39 | 5 | 20.3594 | 0.0166 |
| 15 | 5 | 6.3128 | 0.4097 | 40 | 5 | 21.3774 | 0.0145 |
| 16 | 5 | 6.6284 | 0.3585 | 41 | 5 | 22.4462 | 0.0127 |
| 17 | 5 | 6.9599 | 0.3137 | 42 | 5 | 23.5685 | 0.0111 |
| 18 | 5 | 7.3078 | 0.2745 | 43 | 5 | 24.7470 | 0.0097 |
| 19 | 5 | 7.6732 | 0.2402 | 44 | 5 | 25.9843 | 0.0085 |
| 20 | 5 | 8.0569 | 0.2102 | 45 | 5 | 27.2835 | 0.0075 |
| 21 | 5 | 8.4597 | 0.1839 | 46 | 5 | 28.6477 | 0.0065 |
| 22 | 5 | 8.8827 | 0.1609 | 47 | 5 | 30.0801 | 0.0057 |
| 23 | 5 | 9.3269 | 0.1408 | 48 | 5 | 31.5841 | 0.0050 |
| 24 | 5 | 9.7932 | 0.1232 | 49 | 5 | 33.1633 | 0.0044 |
| 25 | 5 | 10.2829 | 0.1078 | 50 | 5 | 34.8215 | 0.0038 |
| | | | | | | $\Sigma$ PV of dividends $=$ | $19.8584 |

## Dividend-Paying Stock—Altria Group

To illustrate the use of the DDM technique for stock valuation, let's consider Altria Group (formerly Philip Morris; ticker symbol MO). In 2006 the company paid a dividend equal to $3.00 per share. To evaluate Altria, let's assume that today's date is January 1, 2007, and that all dividend payments are made at the end of the year. Examining the past 10 years of growth in earnings and dividends, we find that the growth in both earnings and dividends has averaged approximately 10 percent each year. This growth rate most certainly will change somewhat in the future. Because Altria is currently restructuring its debt position, which has an estimated cost of $1.5 billion, let's make a simple assumption that the firm's earnings will continue to grow at 10 percent for the next five years and then decline by 1 percent each year until the pace settles at 3 percent, the rate at which earnings will continue to grow from that time on. An examination of the firm's dividend policy shows that Altria has consistently paid approximately 50 percent of earnings as dividends during the past five years. Thus, we assume this practice will continue. In addition, let's assume that future economic conditions will be such that the expected market returns will not differ significantly from the average during the past 10 years, and thus stockholders will demand a 9 percent return to invest in Altria's stock.[10] We now have sufficient information to apply the DDM method to value Altria stock. Table 7-2 shows the steps we took to value the stock and the results of the valuation.

Using the DDM technique, we estimate the value of Altria to be $72.17 at the beginning of 2007. The actual market price of Altria stock in August 2006 was about $80 per share. Does this price mean that the stock is incorrectly valued (overvalued) in the market? Perhaps. Of course, not everyone will predict the same growth rates as we did; thus, because different analysts might reach completely different conclusions, different forecasts are likely. If we find that analysts arrive at substantially different predictions, which one is most reliable? It is very difficult—if not impossible—to answer this question. We do know that valuation methods such as the DDM technique are most effective when forecasts of future dividends are accurate and when the assumptions associated with the DDM method are not violated. For example, to apply the constant growth model to find the price of Altria stock in 2017, we had to assume that dividends would grow at a constant rate of 3 percent from 2018 until infinity. Clearly, this assumption might not be reasonable. Even so, the DDM approach provides analysts with estimates of the values of common stocks. Professional analysts, however, employ much more complex computations than we used in our example; more detailed information is used to better predict the future performance of a firm.

## Non-Dividend-Paying Stock—Green Bay Packers

Everyone has heard of the Green Bay Packers, a famous National Football League team. Did you know, however, that the Green Bay Packers football team is owned by its fans? The team has issued stock four times—in 1923, 1935, 1950, and 1997. The funds received through the stock issues were primarily used to keep the team solvent and to make improvements both in the practice facilities and at Lambeau Field, which is the stadium where the Packers play their home games.

Although the stockholders literally own the team, other than voting rights, there is little benefit to owning Green Bay Packers stock. Dividends are not paid, the rights of the stock ownership cannot be transferred to other individuals, stockholders have no preference with respect to purchasing season tickets, and the stock can be redeemed

---

[10]We discuss how to determine this rate in the next chapter.

**TABLE 7-2**  Using the DDM Technique to Value Altria Group (formerly Philip Morris)

**Step 1.** Forecast the dividends based on the assumed future growth rates for the periods when nonconstant growth is expected. At the same time, we can find the present values of the dividends using the required return, $r_s = 9.0\%$.

| Year | Assumed Growth | Forecasted Earnings | Forecasted Dividend (50% of EPS) | PV of the Dividend at 9.0% |
|------|------|------|------|------|
| 2006 |       | $5.40  |                       |        |
| 2007 | 10.0% | 5.94   | $\hat{D}_1 = 2.97$    | $2.97  |
| 2008 | 10.0  | 6.53   | $\hat{D}_2 = 3.27$    | 2.75   |
| 2009 | 10.0  | 7.19   | $\hat{D}_3 = 3.60$    | 2.78   |
| 2010 | 10.0  | 7.91   | $\hat{D}_4 = 3.96$    | 2.81   |
| 2011 | 10.0  | 8.70   | $\hat{D}_5 = 4.35$    | 2.83   |
| 2012 | 9.0   | 9.48   | $\hat{D}_6 = 4.74$    | 2.83   |
| 2013 | 8.0   | 10.24  | $\hat{D}_7 = 5.12$    | 2.80   |
| 2014 | 7.0   | 10.95  | $\hat{D}_8 = 5.48$    | 2.75   |
| 2015 | 6.0   | 11.61  | $\hat{D}_9 = 5.81$    | 2.68   |
| 2016 | 5.0   | 12.19  | $\hat{D}_{10} = 6.10$ | 2.58   |
| 2017 | 4.0   | 12.68  | $\hat{D}_{11} = 6.34$ | 2.46   |

PV of dividends (2007–2017) = $29.99

**Step 2.** Compute the price of the stock *after* nonconstant growth ends in the year 2017.

$$\hat{P}_{2017} = \frac{\hat{D}_{2018}}{r_s - g_{norm}} = \frac{[\$12.68(1.03)]0.5}{0.09 - 0.03} = \frac{\$6.53}{0.06} = \$108.83$$

Find the present value of this future stock price:

$$\text{PV of } \hat{P}_{2017} = \frac{\$108.83}{(1.09)^{11}} = 42.18$$

**Step 3.** Compute the current price of the stock, which is the present value of the dividends computed in Step 1 plus the present value of the future price computed in Step 2.

$$\hat{P}_0 = \$29.99 + \$42.18 = \$72.17$$

only by returning it to the team, at which time a minimal price would be recovered. If the team is sold, the proceeds will be distributed to a designated charity, not to stockholders. Based on this information, what do you think is the "financial value" of the Green Bay Packers stock? Your answer should be "very little." Because the issuing company—that is, the Green Bay Packers—is not expected to pay stockholders cash flows in any form in the future, financially speaking the value of the stock is $0. In other words, if we apply the DDM technique literally, then the present value of all the future cash flows that investors expect the Green Bay Packers to pay its stockholders is $0.

In 1997, each share of stock issued by the Green Bay Packers was sold for $200, and the issue was quickly sold out. If the financial value of the stock equals $0, why would people pay $200 per share? Those who purchased the stock did so to support the team because they thought the stock might be valuable as a collector's item at a later date, or both. The reason we mention the Green Bay Packers stock here is to make the point that the value of an asset is based on the future cash flows it is expected to generate. Thus, if an asset, such as the Green Bay Packers stock, is not expected to provide any future cash flows, its value should be zero.

From this example, should we conclude that every stock that does not currently pay a dividend should have a value equal to $0? No, not if investors expect the stock to provide at least one cash flow in the future. Many small, growing firms do not pay dividends because their earnings are reinvested in the companies' operations. Investors in these firms expect that the stocks' values will increase as the companies grow and thus they will be able to capture substantial capital gains. But investors in general must also expect that the companies will pay dividends at some time in the future; otherwise, the stocks' prices should equal $0.

Suppose you are evaluating a company that has announced it will make only one cash distribution, which will be a liquidating dividend equal to $20,000 per share paid 40 years from today. How much should you be willing to pay for the stock of this company if the appropriate required rate of return for similar investments is 12 percent? The answer is $69.20, which is the present value of the $20,000 dividend that the firm is expected to pay in 50 years. Suppose you buy the stock and you plan to hold it for 10 years at which time you will sell it. At what price should you be able to sell the stock 10 years from today? The answer is $214.94, which is the present value of the $20,000 dividend that will be received 40 years later. If you compute the annual return on this investment during the 40-year period, you will discover that the stock's value will grow at 12 percent each year.

Although it is not as simple to value a stock that does not currently pay dividends, these exercises show that the value of a stock should be based on the cash flows investors expect to receive by owning the stock. At times people buy stocks even when the market prices exceed what investors think are reasonable prices for the stocks. In such instances, those who buy the stocks expect that they can sell the stocks to someone else for higher prices. These investors are said to be following the "bigger fool" theory of investment: They think that they might be a fool to buy a stock at an excessive price, but they also think that they can find an even bigger fool who will buy the stock for a higher price at some later date. Some believe that the bigger fool theory was widely followed at the end of 1999, just before the dot-com stocks lost much of their values, and many went bankrupt. Even the bigger fool theory suggests that investors who are the original "fools" make decisions about value based on what cash flows they expect to receive from the "bigger fools" they hope will buy the stock in the future.

## Self-Test Questions

To apply the DDM model, what assumptions must be made?

Do you believe that Altria's stock was overvalued in August 2006? Why or why not?

What is the value of a stock that is never expected to pay a dividend?

## OTHER STOCK VALUATION METHODS

Investors often use more than one method to determine the value of a stock. In this section, we describe two other valuation methods that are popular with investors. It is important to keep in mind that to apply any model literally, certain assumptions must be met. There are few, if any, instances in which all of the assumptions associated with a model are met in the real world. Therefore, models such as those described in this chapter should be used as guidance when determining the value of a stock—that is, the results should not be "taken literally" to mean that a stock should be selling for exactly the same price that a model predicts.

## Valuation Using P/E Ratios

Many analysts consider the P/E ratio, or earnings multiplier, to be a good indicator of the value of a stock in relative terms. The **P/E ratio** mentioned here is the same as that described in Chapter 2; it is computed by dividing the current market price per share, $P_0$, by the earnings per share, $EPS_0$. The higher (lower) the P/E ratio, the more (less) investors are willing to pay for each dollar earned by the firm.

In a sense, the P/E ratio gives an indication of a stock's "payback period." For example, if a firm's P/E ratio is 12, then, assuming that the firm distributes all of its earnings as dividends, it would take 12 years for an investor to recover his or her initial investment. If we view P/E ratios as measures of payback, all else being equal, lower earnings multipliers are better. In fact, it has been suggested that firms with low P/E ratios relative to other firms in their industries can earn above-average risk-adjusted returns, and vice versa. The rationale is that if a company's P/E ratio is too low relative to that of similar firms, its earnings have not been fully captured in the existing stock value; thus, the price will be bid up. Similarly, if the firm's P/E ratio is too high relative to that of similar firms, the market has overvalued its current earnings and its stock price should decrease.

How can we use P/E ratios to value common stocks? Generally speaking, we examine whether the stock's P/E ratio is considered to be higher or lower than "normal" to decide whether the price is too high or too low. If we can determine what value is appropriate for the P/E ratio, we can then multiply that value by the firm's EPS to estimate the appropriate stock price. Determining the appropriate P/E requires judgment, so analysts do not always agree about what the preferred P/E ratio for a firm should be.

Depending on an analysis of the company, such as evaluation of the firm's financial statements, the P/E ratio might need to be adjusted to reflect expectations about the firm's performance in the future. It might be adjusted downward if the firm's future is considered less promising than the recent past because investors might not be willing to pay the same multiple for the earnings expected to be generated in the future. Although the adjustment process is somewhat arbitrary, we know that P/E ratios are higher (lower) for firms with higher (lower) expected earnings growth and lower (higher) expected required rates of return. For example, investors will place a higher value on the current earnings if the firm is expected to grow at a higher-than-normal rate.

To illustrate the use of P/E ratios to determine the price of a stock, let's again examine Altria Group (MO). Financial sources, such as *The Wall Street Journal* and SmartMoney.com, reported that Altria had a P/E ratio equal to approximately 15 in August 2006, which was slightly lower than the industry average of 17. If we examine the firm's P/E ratios for the past five years, we find that Altria's values have ranged from 5 to 15, with an average of approximately 13. Because the most recent trend has been for the P/E ratio to move toward the industry average, we might assume that the appropriate future P/E ratio for Altria is between 13 and 15. Therefore, we can multiply the EPS expected for 2007 by 13 and 15 to estimate a price range for the stock. According to Zacks Investment Research, analysts estimated that the EPS should be about $5.94 in 2007. Thus, using the P/E ratio method to value Altria stock, we estimated the stock price to be between $77.22 = \$5.94 \times 13$ and $89.10 = \$5.94 \times 15$. The actual selling price of Altria stock in August 2006, $80, is within this estimated price range.

**P/E ratio**
The current market price of the stock divided by the earnings per share; $P_0/EPS_0$.

## Evaluating Stocks Using the Economic Value Added Approach

**economic value added (EVA)**
An analytical method that seeks to evaluate the earnings generated by a firm to determine whether they are sufficient to compensate the suppliers of funds—both the bondholders and the stockholders.

**Economic value added (EVA)** is a fairly new approach that is used to measure financial performance and thus evaluate the attractiveness of a firm's stock. The basic approach, which was developed by Stern Stewart Management Services, is to use basic financial principles to analyze a company's performance to value the firm. Companies that have used EVA include Coca-Cola, Eli Lily, AT&T, Sprint, and Quaker Oats, to name a few. Some companies, such as Coca-Cola, have used EVA since the early 1980s. So what is EVA and how is it applied to make investment decisions?

EVA is based on the concept that the earnings from actions taken by a company must be sufficient to compensate the suppliers of funds—both the bondholders and the stockholders. Using the EVA approach, we adjust a firm's earnings from operations to account for the costs associated with both the debt and the equity issued by the firm. The general concept underlying the EVA approach is a determination of how much a firm's economic value is increased by the decisions it makes. Thus we can write the basic EVA equation as

**7–7**

$$\text{Economic value added} = \text{EVA} = \text{EBIT}(1 - \text{T}) - \left[\begin{array}{c}(\text{Percent cost} \\ \text{of funds})\end{array} \times \begin{array}{c}(\text{Invested} \\ \text{capital})\end{array}\right]$$

In this equation, EBIT represents the earnings before interest and taxes as reported on the firm's income statement, T is the firm's marginal tax rate, invested capital is the amount of funds provided by investors (both debt and equity), and percent cost of funds is the average "interest rate" that the firm pays for its debt and equity (invested capital). We discuss the cost of funds in detail in Chapter 11. For the purposes of our discussion here, we simply define the percent cost of funds as the *average* rate of return that must be paid to investors—both bondholders and stockholders—who provide funds to the firm. As a result, when EVA is greater than zero, the firm's value should increase because it has earned more than needs to be paid to investors who have provided the funds that the firm invests.

To illustrate the use of the EVA approach, let's again examine Altria Group. First, we gathered the following information from the financial statements published by the company at the end of March 2006:

| | |
|---|---|
| Operating income, EBIT | $16.6 billion |
| Total capital = Long-term debt + Equity | $81.8 billion |
| Marginal tax rate | 30% |
| Debt/assets ratio | 67% |
| Number of outstanding shares of common stock | 2.81 billion |

To estimate percent cost of funds for Altria, we first computed (1) the ratio of interest expenses to total debt, which gives an indication of the average interest rate the company is paying and (2) the average return stockholders have earned during the past few years, which we use as the required rate of return demanded by stockholders. We then computed the weighted average of these two values, using the proportion of the firm that is financed with debt as the weight for the "cost of debt," and the proportion of the firm that is financed with equity as the weight for the "cost of equity." Based on information provided in Altria's financial statements, we estimated that the average interest rate on debt is about 5.5 percent. Market data show that the firm's return to common stockholders has averaged about 9 percent during the past few years. Using this information, we computed Altria's cost of funds as

$$\frac{\text{Cost}}{\text{of funds}} = \left(\frac{\text{After-tax cost}}{\text{of debt}} \times \frac{\text{Proportion}}{\text{of debt}}\right) + \left(\frac{\text{Cost of}}{\text{stock}} \times \frac{\text{Proportion}}{\text{of stock}}\right)$$
$$= [5.5\%(1 - 0.3) \times 0.67] + (9\% \times 0.33) = 5.5\%$$

We compute the cost of debt on an after-tax basis because interest is tax deductible to the firm; this adjustment is not made to the cost of stock because dividends are not tax deductible.

If we apply Equation 7–7, we find that Altria's EVA is

$$\text{EVA} = [\$16.6 \text{ billion} \times (1 - 0.3)] - (0.0555 \times \$81.8 \text{ billion})$$
$$= \$11.62 \text{ billion} - \$4.54 \text{ billion} = \$7.08 \text{ billion}$$

According to this computation, the EVA approach suggests that investors demanded $4.54 billion in compensation for providing funds to the firm. Because the firm generated $11.62 billion in net operating profits after taxes to cover the compensation associated with financing, we can conclude that Altria was able to use its funds to earn higher returns than those demanded by investors. Thus, the firm should be attractive to investors. Altria stock should be especially attractive to common stockholders because they have the right to any amounts earned in excess of their required rate of return.

We can use the EVA concept to determine the maximum dividend per share that can be paid to stockholders before we would expect the firm's value to be threatened. The computation is simple—just divide the computed EVA by the number of outstanding shares. In the case of Altria Group, the maximum dividend suggested by EVA is $2.52 = $7.08 billion/2.81 billion shares. In 2006, Altria paid a dividend equal to $3.20; thus, the actual dividend was greater than the EVA dividend. This finding might suggest that the firm was overvalued. Like the other analytical techniques discussed in this section, however, the EVA approach requires additional computations and predictions to achieve greater precision in the final result. For instance, Stern Stewart indicates that it has identified more than 160 possible adjustments to accounting values contained in financial statements that can be used to better estimate the true economic value of the firm's performance.

The EVA approach has gained attention as a valuation technique because it is based on the fundamental principle of wealth maximization, which should be the goal of every firm. It is also attractive because it allows us to outline the value creation process in simple terms: (1) changing the proportion of debt and equity that is used to finance a firm can change value because the "cost of funds" is affected, and (2) increasing the efficiency of the firm through reductions in operating expenses or increases in revenues will increase operating income and thus increase value. Prospective EVA users should be aware that to obtain a precise estimate of the economic performance of a firm, it might be necessary to make many adjustments to the accounting numbers contained in the firm's financial statements. Knowing how to apply such adjustments often takes considerable expertise.

## Self-Test Questions

How are P/E ratios used to estimate the value of common stock?

What is EVA? How can you use the EVA approach to determine the attractiveness of a firm?

In general, what are some of the difficulties associated with the application of valuation techniques described in this section?

## CHANGES IN STOCK PRICES

Stock prices are not constant. They sometimes change significantly, as well as very quickly. For example, on October 19, 1987, the Dow Jones Industrial Average (DJIA) dropped 508 points, and the average stock lost about 23 percent of its value in just one day. Some stocks lost more than half of their values on that day. More recently, from March 9, 2001, through March 22, 2001, the DJIA decreased by more than 1,255 points; the average stock lost nearly 12 percent of its value during that period. Not long after, during April 2001, the DJIA increased by almost 1,300 points and the value of the average stock increased by nearly 14 percent. To see how such changes can occur, assume you own the stock of a company that just paid a $2.50 dividend ($D_0 = \$2.50$). The company's growth has been constant for many years, so it is expected that the company will continue to grow at the same rate, 6 percent, in the future ($g = 6\%$). Currently, investors require a return equal to 15 percent for such investments. The expected value of the company's stock should therefore be

$$\hat{P}_0 = \frac{\$2.50(1.06)}{0.15 - 0.06} = \frac{\$2.65}{0.09} = \$29.44$$

Now consider what would happen to the stock price if the value of any of the variables used to compute the current price changes. For instance, how would the price be affected if investors demand a higher rate of return—say, 18 percent? If we change the value for $r_s$ to 18 percent in the previous equation, we find that the expected value of the stock would be

$$\hat{P}_0 = \frac{\$2.50(1.06)}{0.18 - 0.06} = \frac{\$2.65}{0.12} = \$22.08$$

The new price is lower because investors demand a higher return for receiving the same future cash flows.

How would the price change if the future cash flows differ from the expected cash flows, but the required return is 15 percent? Consider the effect if the company's growth rate is 4 percent rather than 6 percent:

$$\hat{P}_0 = \frac{\$2.50(1.04)}{0.15 - 0.04} = \frac{\$2.60}{0.11} = \$23.64$$

Again, the new price is lower than the original price of $29.44. In this case, however, the price is lower because the cash flows that the stock is expected to provide are smaller than expected previously.

From this simple example, you should have concluded that changes in stock prices occur for two reasons: (1) investors change the rates of return required to invest in stocks, and (2) expectations about the cash flows associated with stocks change. From the preceding example, we can generalize about how such changes would affect stock prices: *Stock prices move opposite changes in rates of return, but they move in the same direction as changes in cash flows expected from the stock in the future.* Therefore, if investors demand higher (lower) returns to invest in stocks, then prices should fall (increase). If investors expect their investments to generate lower (higher) future cash flows, then prices should also fall (increase).

Earlier in this chapter, we found that, according to the DDM valuation model, the value of Altria Group's stock should be $72.14. As an exercise, one at a time, change the value of each variable used in the computation of this stock's value to determine the impact such a change will have on the price of Altria's stock. If you set up a spreadsheet using a format similar to that shown in Table 7-2 you can change the value of a variable and see the effect on the "bottom line" result immediately. Everything else equal, you should conclude that (1) if $\hat{D}_1$ is higher (lower) than the original estimate, all future dividends will also be higher (lower), and the price of the stock will be higher (lower); (2) if any of the growth rates shown in Table 7-2 are higher (lower) than originally estimated, the stock price will be higher (lower) because the expected future cash flows will be higher; and (3) if the required rate of return is lower (higher) than originally estimated, the price will be higher (lower).

When a stock price is in "equilibrium," we should see that the actual price equals the expected price of the stock. As a result, according to the DDM valuation model, the stock of Altria Group is not in equilibrium because the actual price of the stock, $P_0$, was $80 in August 2006 whereas the DDM model indicated that the price should have been about $72. If investors believed that $\hat{P}_0 = \$72$ is the appropriate value for Altria's stock, potential investors will not buy the stock and existing stockholders will sell the stock they own. Because demand will decrease, the market price of Altria's stock will tend to decrease to its equilibrium value of $72. Of course, we generally do not know (cannot compute) the "true" equilibrium price of a stock because it is unlikely that (1) the company's future growth pattern is exactly as analysts forecast and (2) all the assumptions of the model that is used to estimate the equilibrium value are met. But the various valuation techniques we discussed in this chapter give at least an indication of a stock's equilibrium, or intrinsic, value.

Evidence suggests that stocks—especially those of large NYSE companies—adjust rapidly to disequilibrium situations. Consequently, equilibrium ordinarily exists for any given stock, and, in general, required and expected returns are equal. Stock prices certainly change, sometimes violently and rapidly, but these changes simply reflect different conditions and expectations. Of course, sometimes a stock continues to react for several months to a favorable or unfavorable development, but this reaction does not signify a long adjustment period; rather, it illustrates that as more new pieces of information about the situation become available, the market adjusts to them.

**Self-Test Questions**

All else being equal, how should prices change if investors demand lower rates of return to purchase stock?

What does it mean when a stock is "out of equilibrium"?

To summarize the key concepts, let's answer the questions that were posed at the beginning of the chapter:

**Chapter *Essentials***

—The Answers

- **What is equity? What are some of the features/characteristics of equity?** Equity generally is defined as the value of assets that are *owned* minus the amount of debt that is *owed*. Thus, if a firm's assets are sold at their *book values* and all debts are paid off, the amount remaining is the equity that can be paid to stockholders. Some firms have two types of stock (equity)—preferred stock and common stock. Preferred stock has preference when the firm distributes cash in the form of dividends or liquidation proceeds. Neither preferred stock nor common stock has a maturity date, thus both have infinite lives. Preferred stockholders generally are paid a constant dividend. Although some common stocks pay constant, or fairly constant, dividends, many common stocks either pay no dividends or pay variable dividends. Common stockholders elect the members of the board of directors, who then appoint the corporate officers who run the day-to-day operations; most preferred stockholders have no voting rights. Common stockholders generally are considered the owners of the firm because they bear most of the risks associated with the firm's operations. It is the common stockholders who benefit most when the firm performs very well, but it is the same stockholders who incur the greatest losses when the firm performs poorly.

- **What factors affect stock prices?** The primary reason that stock prices change is because investors change their expectations about the returns the firm will generate in the future. Stockholders earn returns in two forms: (1) dividends and (2) capital gains. If investors expect either of these components to increase (decrease), the market value of the stock increases (decreases). Stockholders also demand a minimum rate of return to invest in a company. If this return, which is termed the required rate of return, increases (decreases), the price of the company's stock decreases (increases). Both the return that investors expect to earn by investing in a stock and the return they require to invest in a stock are affected by business and economic conditions.

- **How are stock prices determined?** We mentioned in Chapter 4 that the value of any asset is equal to the present value of the future cash flows the asset is expected to generate. The same concept is used to determine stock prices. In other words, the price (value) of a stock is equal to the present value of the dividends stockholders expect to receive during the company's life. The model that we often use to determine the value of a stock is called the dividend discount model (DDM)—all the future dividends are discounted to the present period to determine the stock's current value. Even if an investor does not intend to hold a stock for the life of the company, its value is computed as the present value of the dividends the company is expected to pay in the future because the price the investor receives when the stock is sold at some later date is the present value of the dividends that the company is expected to pay from that date forward.

- **How are stock returns (yields) determined?** The total return that a stockholder earns each year is based on the dividend that the company pays and the change in the market value of the stock during the year. These two components of total return are referred to as the dividend yield and the capital gains yield, respectively. The dividend yield is computed by dividing the dividend received during the year by the beginning-of-year stock price—that is, Dividend yield $= \hat{D}_1/P_0$. The capital gains yield equals the change in the market value of the stock stated as a percent—that is, Capital gains yield $= (\hat{P}_1 - P_0)/P_0$. Some investors prefer stocks that pay high dividends and thus have high dividend yields, whereas other investors prefer stocks that produce large capital gains and thus have high capital gains yields.

- **What approaches (techniques) do investors use to value stocks?** In addition to the dividend discount model, two approaches that investors find easy to apply to determine the values of stocks are the price/earnings (P/E) ratio and the economic value added (EVA). If you know, or can determine, the appropriate P/E ratio for a firm, you can estimate the *intrinsic* market value of its stock by multiplying the firm's earnings per share (EPS) by the P/E ratio. This is a simple technique that many investors use to get a general idea as to the value of a stock. The EVA approach is based on the concept that an increase in the value of the firm is represented by earnings that remain after all investors—both debt holders and stockholders—are paid the proper amounts for the use of their funds. The "leftover earnings" represent the amount by which a firm's economic value is increased by the decisions that are made during the year.

## ETHICAL DILEMMA

### Too High Tech ("Smoke and Mirrors" or Real Sales)?

Staci Sutter works as an analyst for Independent Investment BankShares (IIBS), which is a large investment banking organization. She has been evaluating an initial public offering (IPO) that IIBS is handling for a technology company named ProTech Incorporated. Staci is essentially finished with her analysis, and she is ready to estimate the price for which the stock should be offered when it is issued next week. According to her analysis, Staci has concluded that ProTech is financially strong and is expected to remain financially strong long into the future. In fact, the figures provided by ProTech suggest that the firm's growth will exceed 30 percent during the next five years. For these reasons, Staci is considering assigning a value of $35 per share to ProTech's stock.

Staci, however, has an uneasy feeling about the validity of the financial figures she has been evaluating. She believes that Protech's CFO has given her what he believes are "quality financial statements." Yesterday Staci received an e-mail from a friend, who was an executive at ProTech until he was fired a few months ago, that suggests that the company has been artificially inflating its sales by selling products to an affiliate company and then repurchasing the same items a few months later. At the same time, Staci received a memo from her boss, Mr. Baker, who has made it clear that he thinks the ProTech IPO can be extremely profitable to top management "if it is handled correctly." In his memo, Mr. Baker indicates that the issue price of ProTech's stock must be at least $34 per share for the IPO to be considered successful by IIBS. Part of Staci's uneasiness stems from the fact that a cow-orker confided that she had seen the CEO of Pro-Tech and his wife at an amusement park with Mr. Baker and his wife last month. If she discovers that ProTech's sales figures are inflated, Staci surely would assign a different value to the company's stock for the IPO. But it will take her at least two weeks to completely reevaluate the company using different data. Staci knows that if she stays with her current analysis and she is wrong, the consequences can destroy IIBS because reputation is important in the investment banking business. If you were in Staci's situation, what would you do?

The concepts presented in this chapter should help you understand what factors affect stock prices and why stock prices change as investors' expectations change. If you understand the basic concepts we discussed, you should be able to determine a rough estimate for the value of stocks that you might be interested in purchasing (or you already own), and thus make more informed decisions about your investment positions.

**How can the concepts presented in the chapter help me to determine whether a stock's market value is appropriate?** There is no scientific process that can be used to value stock. However, we know that the market value of a stock is based on the future cash flows it is expected to provide investors. We also know that, theoretically, the "intrinsic" value of a stock can be determined by computing the present value of these expected future cash flows. Although it isn't always easy to forecast the future cash flows that a stock will generate, you can gather information from various sources—for example, investment sites on the Internet, professional analysts, knowledgeable friends, and so forth—to form your own opinions about a stock's potential cash flows. Using this information, you can use the techniques described in the chapter to get a "ballpark" estimate of the stock's value.

**Should I purchase regular preferred stock, convertible preferred stock, regular common stock, Class A common stock, or Class B common stock?** The answer to this question depends on the reason you want to invest in stocks. If you want to receive dividends (income) each year, then you would invest in income-producing stocks, such as preferred stock or the stock of large, well-established firms that pay

**Chapter *Essentials***
—Personal Finance

relatively constant dividends from year to year. But if you are willing to wait to receive capital gains at some later date, then you should purchase stocks of companies that pay little or no dividends because such firms invest current earnings to fund future growth. After reading the discussions of the characteristics of different types and classes of stocks given in this chapter, you should be more informed when making decisions about what kind of stock is appropriate to meet your investment needs.

**How do I know how well my investment in a stock is performing?** As we mentioned in the chapter, the return that is earned on an investment in a stock is a combination of the dividend that is paid by the company and the change in the market value of the stock. Thus, to determine how well your investment is performing, you should compute the total return that the stock provides—that is, the combination of the dividend yield and the capital gains yield. Some stocks generate high dividend yields along with low capital gains yields, whereas other stocks provide low dividend yields but produce high capital gains yields. Depending on your personal tax position, you might prefer to invest in a stock that generates either high dividend yields or high capital gains yields.

**How do expectations affect stock prices?** As we mentioned, the value of a stock is based on the cash flows it is expected to generate throughout its life. If investors change their expectations about a stock's future cash flows, then the market price of the stock changes. For example, if Pfizer announces that it has developed a drug that cures all types of cancers, investors view this event as good news in the sense that they expect the company's future earnings and thus payouts to stockholders to be greater than before the new drug was developed. As a result, the market price of Pfizer's stock should increase; the present value of the expected future cash flows, which are higher than before the development of the drug, is higher. Pay attention to announcements made by companies, and try to determine what impact such announcements will have on the companies' stock prices. Generally, when the announcement is considered "good news," the market price of a stock increases, and vice versa. To make your conclusions, consider whether the announcement suggests that the future cash flows generated by the firm will increase or whether they will decrease.

## Questions

**7-1**   In what respect is preferred stock similar to bonds, and in what respect is it similar to common stock?

**7-2**   Explain the following statement: "Whereas a bond contains a promise to pay interest, common stock provides an expectation but no promise of dividends."

**7-3**   Should preferred stock be classified as debt or equity? Does it matter if the classification is being made by the firm's (a) management, (b) creditors, or (c) equity investors?

**7-4**   What is the significance of the par value on a preferred stock? What is the significance of the par value on a common stock?

**7-5**   It is often said that the primary purpose of the preemptive right is to allow individuals to maintain their proportionate share of the ownership and control of a corporation.

   **a.** How important do you suppose this consideration is for the average stockholder of a firm whose shares are traded on the New York Stock Exchange?

   **b.** Is the preemptive right likely to be of greater importance to stockholders of publicly owned or closely held firms? Explain.

**7-6**    Evaluate the following statement: "Issuing convertible securities represents a means by which a firm can sell common stock at a price above the existing market price."

**7-7**    Two investors are evaluating IBM's stock for possible purchase. They agree on the expected value of $\hat{D}_1$ and on the expected future dividend growth rate. They also agree on the riskiness of the stock. One investor normally holds stocks for two years, and the other normally holds stocks for 10 years. On the basis of the type of analysis presented in this chapter, they should both be willing to pay the same price for IBM's stock. True? Explain.

**7-8**    If you bought a share of common stock, you would typically expect to receive dividends plus capital gains. Would you expect the distribution between the dividend yield and the capital gains yield to be influenced by the firm's decision to pay more dividends rather than to retain and reinvest more of its earnings?

**7-9**    How will the price of AT&T's stock change if investors decide they want to earn a higher return for purchasing the stock? Assume all else remains constant. Will the price of AT&T's stock change if the CEO announces that the company must pay a 10-year, $10 million fine for unfair trade practices? Explain your rationale.

**7-10**   How might an investor's tax situation affect his or her decision to purchase stocks of companies in the early stages of their lives, when they are growing rapidly and paying little or no dividends, versus stocks of older, more mature firms that provide relatively low capital gains?

**7-11**   How does the par value of common stock relate to its market value?

**7-12**   Everything else equal, how would each of the following affect the market value of a stock? Indicate by a plus (+), minus (−), or a zero (0) if the factor would increase, decrease, or have an indeterminate effect. Be prepared to justify your answer.

    **a.** Investors require a higher rate of return to buy the stock.   _____

    **b.** The company increases dividends.   _____

    **c.** The company's growth rate increases.   _____

    **d.** Investors become more risk averse.   _____

## SELF-TEST PROBLEMS

*(Solutions appear in Appendix B at the end of the book.)*

**ST-1**   Define each of the following terms:                **key terms**

    **a.** Common equity; preferred stock

    **b.** Cumulative dividends; call premium

    **c.** Income stocks; growth stocks

    **d.** Proxy; proxy fight; takeover

    **e.** Preemptive right

    **f.** Classified stock; founders' shares

    **g.** Closely held corporation; publicly owned corporation

    **h.** American depository receipt (ADR); Euro stock; Yankee stock

    **i.** Intrinsic value, $\hat{P}_0$; market price, $P_0$

    **j.** Growth rate, g; required rate of return, $r_s$; expected rate of return, $\hat{r}_s$; actual (realized) rate of return, $\ddot{r}_s$

    **k.** Capital gains yield; dividend yield

     **l.** Zero growth stock; normal (constant) growth; nonconstant growth

     **m.** P/E ratio; economic value added, EVA

**stock growth rates and valuation**

**ST-2** You are considering buying the stocks of two companies that operate in the same industry. Both firms have very similar characteristics except for their dividend payout policies, and both are expected to earn $6 per share this year. Company D (for "dividend") is expected to pay out all of its earnings as dividends, whereas Company G (for "growth") is expected to pay out only one-third of its earnings, or $2 per share. Company D's stock price is $40. Both firms are equally risky. Which of the following is most likely to be true?

    **a.** Company G will have a faster growth rate than Company D, so G's stock price should be greater than $40.

    **b.** Although G's growth rate should exceed D's growth rate, D's current dividend exceeds that paid by G, which should cause D's price to exceed G's price.

    **c.** An investor in Company D will get his or her money back faster because D pays out more of its earnings as dividends. Thus, in a sense, D is like a short-term bond, and G is like a long-term bond. If economic shifts cause $r_d$ and $r_s$ to increase, and if the expected streams of dividends from D and G remain constant, the stocks of both companies will decline, but D's price should decline more.

    **d.** Company D's expected and required rate of return is $\hat{r}_s = r_s = 15\%$. Company G's expected return will be higher because of its higher expected growth rate.

    **e.** On the basis of the available information, the best estimate of G's growth rate is 10 percent.

**constant growth stock valuation**

**ST-3** Ewald Company's current stock price is $36, and its last dividend was $2.40. In view of Ewald's strong financial position and its consequent low risk, its required rate of return is only 12 percent. If dividends are expected to grow at a constant rate, g, in the future, and if $r_s$ is expected to remain at 12 percent, what is Ewald's expected stock price five years from now?

**nonconstant growth stock valuation**

**ST-4** Snyder Computer Chips Inc. is experiencing a period of rapid growth. Earnings and dividends are expected to grow at a rate of 15 percent during the next two years, at 13 percent in the third year, and at a constant rate of 6 percent thereafter. Snyder's *last* dividend was $1.15, and the required rate of return on the stock is 12 percent.

    **a.** Calculate the value of the stock today.

    **b.** Calculate $\hat{P}_1$ and $\hat{P}_2$.

    **c.** Calculate the dividend yield and capital gains yield for Years 1, 2, and 3.

**EVA analysis**

**ST-5** American Transmitter (AT) is a telecommunications firm that currently does not pay a dividend. The following information about AT has been gathered from various sources:

| | |
|---|---:|
| Average cost of funds | 8.0% |
| EBIT | $600,000 |
| Total capital | $2,000,000 |
| EPS | $2.64 |
| Shares outstanding | 100,000 |
| Marginal tax rate | 40.0% |

a. Compute the economic value added (EVA) for AT in the current operating period. Is AT a good investment?

b. Given the answer from part a, compute the EVA dividend that AT could pay without harming the value of the firm.

c. Estimate the market price per share assuming that AT normally has a P/E ratio equal to 15. Assume that AT's annual interest expense is $80,000.

## PROBLEMS

**7-1**    Nancy Cotton bought NuTalk for $15 per share. One year later, Nancy sold the stock for $21 per share, just after she received a $0.90 cash dividend from the company. What total return did Nancy earn? What were the dividend yield and the capital gains yield?

**rates of return**

**7-2**    Ralph Rafferty purchased Gold Depot at the beginning of January for $25 per share. Ralph received a $1.25 dividend payment from the company at the end of December. At that time, the stock was selling for $27.50 per share. What is Ralph's return on his investment for the year? What portion of the total return is the dividend yield and what portion is the capital gains yield?

**rates of return**

**7-3**    Many years ago, Minnow Bait and Tackle issued preferred stock. The stock pays an annual dividend equal to $6.80. If the required rate of return on similar-risk investments is 8 percent, what should be the market value of Minnow's preferred stock?

**preferred stock valuation**

**7-4**    The Ape Copy Company's preferred stock pays an annual dividend equal to $16.50. If investors demand a return equal to 11 percent to purchase Ape's preferred stock, what is its market value?

**preferred stock valuation**

**7-5**    Jones Brothers Clothing just issued preferred stock with a face value equal to $80 that pays a 10 percent annual dividend. If the stock currently yields 8 percent, what is its market value?

**preferred stock valuation**

**7-6**    Advanced Corporation's growth has slowed to a constant rate during the past few years. As a result, the company expects its common stock dividend to grow at a constant 4 percent for the remainder of the company's life. A few days ago, Advanced paid common stockholders a $5 dividend. If the required rate of return on the company's stock is 12 percent, what is the value of the stock today?

**constant growth stock valuation**

**7-7**    Ms. Manners Catering (MMC) has paid a constant $1.50 per share dividend to its common stockholders for the past 25 years. Beginning with the next dividend, MMC expects to increase the dividend at a constant rate equal to 2 percent per year into perpetuity. Investors require a 12 percent rate of return to purchase MMC's common stock. What is the market value of MMC's common stock?

**constant growth stock valuation**

**7-8**    McCue Mining Company's ore reserves are being depleted, so the firm's sales are falling. Also, its pit is getting deeper each year, so its costs are rising. As a result, the company's earnings and dividends are declining at a constant rate of 5 percent per year. If $D_0 = \$5$ and $r_s = 15\%$, what is the value of McCue Mining's stock?

**constant growth stock valuation**

**7-9**    Your broker offers to sell you some shares of Wingler & Company common stock, which paid a dividend of $2 *yesterday.* You expect the dividend to grow at a rate of 5 percent per year into perpetuity. Given that the appropriate discount rate is 12 percent, what is the market value of Wingler's stock?

**constant growth stock valuation**

**constant growth dividend**    **7-10**    The common stock of Old Betsy Flags is currently selling for $28 per share. The company has been growing at a constant annual rate of 4 percent, and this growth is expected to continue for an infinite period. The required rate on the stock is 11 percent. If you buy the stock today, what is the next dividend you would receive?

**EVA analysis**    **7-11**    J.D. Agribusiness has $500,000 invested capital, 60 percent of which is in the form of debt. With this capital structure, the company's average cost of funds is 12 percent. According to J.D.'s latest income statement, the firm's operating income is $100,000 and its marginal tax rate is 40 percent. Under the EVA approach, is J.D. Agribusiness a good company in which to invest?

**EVA analysis**    **7-12**    RJS Foods reported that its net income was $65,000 last year. The firm's interest expense was reported to be $40,000, and its marginal tax rate was 35 percent. According to the company's balance sheet, invested capital equals $800,000.

**a.** Compute the operating income (EBIT) that RJS Foods generated last year.

**b.** If the average cost of the funds it uses is 12 percent, what was RJS's EVA last year?

**valuation using P/E ratios**    **7-13**    The stock of East/West Maps is currently selling for $122.40, which equates to a P/E ratio of 30×.

**a.** Using the P/E ratio, compute the current EPS of East/West.

**b.** Assume that earnings next year increase by 20 percent, but the P/E ratio drops to 25×, which is more in line with the industry average. What will be the price of East/West stock next year?

**c.** If an investor purchases the stock today for $122.40 and sells it in one year at the price computed in part b, what rate of return would be earned?

**cash flows and constant growth**    **7-14**    Assume you purchased the Wingler & Company stock described in Problem 7-9. When you purchased the stock, you decided that you would hold it for three years. If you plan to sell the stock in three years, what cash flows will you receive each year?

**nonconstant growth stock valuation**    **7-15**    Assume that the average firm in your company's industry is expected to grow at a constant rate of 6 percent, and its dividend yield is 7 percent. Your company is considered as risky as the average firm in the industry, but it has just successfully completed some R&D work that leads you to expect that its earnings and dividends will grow at a rate of 50 percent $[\hat{D}_1 = D_0(1 + g_{super}) = D_0(1.50)]$ this year and 25 percent the following year. After that period, growth should match the 6 percent industry average rate. The last dividend paid $(D_0)$ was $1. What is the value per share of your firm's stock?

**nonconstant growth stock valuation**    **7-16**    Microtech Corporation is expanding rapidly. Because it needs to retain all of its earnings, it does not currently pay any dividends. Investors expect Microtech to begin paying dividends eventually, with the first dividend of $1.00 coming three years from today. The dividend should grow rapidly—at a rate of 50 percent per year—during Years 4 and 5. After Year 5, the company should grow at a constant rate of 8 percent per year. If the required return on the stock is 15 percent, what is the value of the stock today?

**nonconstant growth stock valuation**    **7-17**    Bayboro Sails is expected to pay dividends of $2.50, $3.00, and $4.00 in the next three years—that is, $\hat{D}_1 = \$2.50, \hat{D}_2 = \$3.00,$ and $\hat{D}_3 = \$4.00,$ respectively. After three years, the dividend is expected to grow at a constant rate of 4 percent per year indefinitely. Stockholders require a return of 14 percent to invest in Bayboro's common stock. Compute the value of Bayboro's common stock today.

**7-18**  The Swift Company is planning to finance an expansion. The principal executives of the company agree that an industrial company such as theirs should finance growth by issuing common stock rather than by taking on additional debt. Because they believe that the current price of Swift's common stock does not reflect its true worth, however, they have decided to sell convertible preferred stock. Each share of stock has a face value equal to $100 and can be converted into five shares of common stock.

    **a.** What would be the minimum price of the stock that would make it beneficial for preferred stockholders to convert their shares into common stock? Ignore the effects of taxes or other costs.

    **b.** What would be the benefits of including a call provision with the preferred stock issue?

*convertible preferred stock*

**7-19**  Sanger Music Company's preferred stock, which currently sells for $105 per share, pays an annual dividend equal to $12.60. What is the yield—that is, the rate of return—that Sanger's preferred stockholders earn?

*return on preferred stock*

**7-20**  Tando Airlines has preferred stock outstanding that has a par value equal to $100. Preferred dividend payments equal 8 percent of the stock's par value. If Tando's preferred stock currently sells for $160, what is the rate of return that preferred stockholders earn? What portion of this return is the dividend yield and what portion is the capital gains yield? (*Hint:* Think about the growth rate that is associated with preferred stock.)

*return on preferred stock*

**7-21**  You buy a share of Damanpour Corporation stock for $21.40. You expect it to pay dividends of $1.07, $1.1449, and $1.2250 in Years 1, 2, and 3, respectively. You also expect to sell the stock at a price of $26.22 at the end of three years.

    **a.** Calculate the growth rate in dividends.

    **b.** Calculate the expected dividend yield.

    **c.** Assuming that the calculated growth rate is expected to continue, you can add the dividend yield to the expected growth rate to determine the expected total rate of return. What is this stock's expected total rate of return?

*return on common stock*

**7-22**  Investors require a 15 percent rate of return on Goulet Company's stock ($r_s = 15\%$).

    **a.** What will be Goulet's stock value if the previous dividend was $D_0 = \$2$ and if investors expect dividends to grow at a constant compound annual rate of (1) −5 percent, (2) 0 percent, (3) 5 percent, and (4) 10 percent?

    **b.** Using data from part a, calculate the value for Goulet's stock if the required rate of return is 15 percent and the expected growth rate is (1) 15 percent or (2) 20 percent. Are these results reasonable? Explain.

    **c.** Is it reasonable to expect that a constant growth stock would have $g > r_s$?

*constant growth stock valuation*

**7-23**  The stock of Gerlunice Company has a rate of return equal to 15.5 percent.

    **a.** If the last dividend the company paid, $D_B$, was $2.25, and if g remains constant at 5 percent, at what price should Gerlunice's stock sell?

    **b.** Suppose the Federal Reserve increases the money supply, causing the risk-free rate to drop. The return expected for investing in Gerlunice will fall to 13.5 percent. How should this change affect the price of the stock?

    **c.** In addition to the change in part b, suppose that investors' risk aversion declines; this fact, combined with the decline in $r_{RF}$, causes $r_s$ for Gerlunice's stock to fall to 12 percent. At what price would the stock sell?

*constant growth stock valuation*

**d.** Now suppose Gerlunice undergoes a change in management. The new group institutes policies that increase the expected constant growth rate to 6 percent. Also, the new management stabilizes sales and profits, which causes the return demanded by investors to decline to 11.6 percent. After all these changes, what is the firm's new equilibrium price?

**nonconstant growth stock valuation**

**7-24**  It is now January 1, 2008. Swink Electric Inc. has just developed a solar panel capable of generating 200 percent more electricity than any solar panel currently on the market. As a result, Swink is expected to experience a 15 percent annual growth rate for the next five years. When the five-year period ends, other firms will have developed comparable technology, and Swink's growth rate will slow to 5 percent per year indefinitely. Stockholders require a return of 12 percent on Swink's stock. The firm's most recent annual dividend $(D_0)$, which was paid yesterday, was $1.75 per share.

**a.** Calculate Swink's expected dividends for 2008, 2009, 2010, 2011, and 2012.

**b.** Calculate the value of the stock today. Proceed by finding the present value of the dividends expected at the end of 2008, 2009, 2010, 2011, and 2012, plus the present value of the stock price that should apply at the end of 2012. You can find the year-end 2012 stock price by using the constant growth equation (see Equation 7–5). To find the December 31, 2012, price, use the dividend expected in 2013, which is 5 percent greater than the 2012 dividend.

**c.** Calculate the expected dividend yield, $\hat{D}_1/P_1$, the capital gains yield expected in 2008, and the expected total return (dividend yield plus capital gains yield) for 2008. (Assume that $\hat{P}_0 = P_0$, and recognize that the capital gains yield is equal to the total return minus the dividend yield.) Calculate these same three yields for 2012.

**d.** Suppose your boss believes that Swink's annual growth rate will be only 12 percent during the next five years and that the firm's normal growth rate will be only 4 percent. Without doing any calculations, explain the general effect that these growth-rate changes would have on the price of Swink's stock.

**e.** Suppose your boss also regards Swink as being quite risky and believes that the required rate of return for this firm should be 14 percent, not 12 percent. Without doing any calculations, explain how the higher required rate of return would affect the price of the stock, its capital gains yield, and its dividend yield.

**supernormal growth stock valuation**

**7-25**  Tanner Technologies Corporation (TTC) has been growing at a rate of 20 percent per year in recent years. This same growth rate is expected to last for another two years.

**a.** If $D_0 = \$1.60$, $r_s = 10\%$, and $g_{norm} = 6\%$, what is TTC's stock worth today? What are its expected dividend yield and capital gains yield at this time?

**b.** Assume that TTC's period of supernormal growth lasts another five years rather than two years. Without doing any calculations, explain how this change would affect its price, dividend yield, and capital gains yield.

**c.** What will be TTC's dividend yield and capital gains yield once its period of supernormal growth ends? (*Hint:* These values will be the same regardless of whether you examine the case of two or five years of supernormal growth; the calculations are very easy.)

**d.** Of what interest to investors is the changing relationship between dividend yield and capital gains yield over time?

## Integrative Problem

**7-26**   Robert Campbell and Carol Morris are senior vice presidents of the Mutual of Chicago Insurance Company. They are codirectors of the company's pension fund management division. A major new client has requested that Mutual of Chicago present an investment seminar to illustrate the stock valuation process. As a result, Campbell and Morris have asked you to analyze the Bon Temps Company, an employment agency that supplies word processor operators and computer programmers to businesses with temporarily heavy workloads. You are to answer the following questions.

**stock valuation**

  **a.** What is the difference between common stock and preferred stock? What are some of the characteristics of each type of stock?

  **b.** What is the difference between a publicly held company and a privately held company? How can the two types of companies be identified?

  **c.** What is classified stock? When "going public," why might a small company designate some stock currently outstanding as "founders' shares"?

  **d.** **(1)** Write a formula that can be used to value any stock, regardless of its dividend pattern.

   **(2)** What is a constant growth stock? How do you value a constant growth stock?

   **(3)** What happens if the growth is constant, and $g > r_s$? Will many stocks have $g > r_s$?

  **e.** Bon Temps has an issue of preferred stock outstanding that pays stockholders a dividend equal to $10 each year. If the appropriate required rate of return for this stock is 8 percent, what is its market value?

  **f.** Assume that Bon Temps is a constant growth company whose last dividend ($D_0$, which was paid yesterday) was $2.00 and whose dividend is expected to grow indefinitely at a 6 percent rate. The appropriate rate of return for Bon Temps' stock is 16 percent.

   **(1)** What is the firm's expected dividend stream over the next three years?

   **(2)** What is the firm's current stock price?

   **(3)** What is the stock's expected value one year from now?

   **(4)** What are the expected dividend yield, the capital gains yield, and the total return during the first year?

  **g.** Assume that Bon Temps' stock is currently selling at $21.20. What is the expected rate of return on the stock?

  **h.** What would the stock price be if its dividends were expected to have zero growth?

  **i.** Assume that Bon Temps is expected to experience supernormal growth of 30 percent for the next three years, then to return to its long-run constant growth rate of 6 percent. What is the stock's value under these conditions? What are its expected dividend yield and its capital gains yield in Year 1? In Year 4?

**j.** Suppose Bon Temps is expected to experience zero growth during the first three years and then to resume its steady-state growth of 6 percent in the fourth year. What is the stock's value now? What are its expected dividend yield and its capital gains yield in Year 1? In Year 4?

**k.** Assume that Bon Temps' earnings and dividends are expected to decline by a constant 6 percent per year—that is, $g = -6\%$. Why might someone be willing to buy such a stock, and at what price should it sell? What would be the dividend yield and capital gains yield in each year?

**l.** Bon Temps' financial statements show the following information:

| | |
|---|---:|
| Average cost of funds | 10.0% |
| EBIT | $ 500,000 |
| Total capital | $1,250,000 |
| EPS | $ 2.00 |
| Shares outstanding | 150,000 |
| Marginal tax rate | 30.0% |

**(1)** Compute the company's economic value added (EVA).

**(2)** Interpret the EVA figure that you just computed.

**m.** Suppose that normally Bon Temps' P/E ratio is 20×. Using the information given in part l, estimate the market price per share for Bon Temps' common stock.

## Computer-Related Problems

*Work these problems in this section only if you are using the problem spreadsheet.*

**nonconstant growth stock valuation**

**7-27** Use the spreadsheet in File C07 to solve this problem.

**a.** Refer to Problem 7-24. Rework part d, using the computerized model to determine what Swink's expected dividends and stock price would be under the conditions given.

**b.** Suppose your boss regards Swink as being quite risky and believes the required rate of return should be higher than the 12 percent originally specified. Rework the problem under the conditions given in part d, except change the required rate of return to (1) 13 percent, (2) 15 percent, and (3) 20 percent to determine the effects of the higher required rates of return on Swink's stock price.

**EVA analysis**

**7-28** Rework Problem 7-11 using the changes that follow. Consider each change to be independent of the others; that is, in each case, assume all values except those to be changed remain the same as originally stated in Problem 7-11.

**a.** All else equal, except the debt/assets ratio is 70

**b.** All else equal, except the EBIT for each firm is $80,000

**c.** All else equal, except the marginal tax rate for each firm is 35 percent

**GET REAL WITH**    **THOMSON ONE** Business School Edition

**7-29**    Wachovia [WB] is a financial services company that is often held in the portfolios of investors who are interested in earning dividend income. These investors are interested in the expected growth rate in dividends for such companies because they often rely on dividends as part of their annual income.

**dividend growth rates**

  **a.** Find the last dividend paid by Wachovia. [*Hint:* Click on Overview/Full Reports/Thomson Reports/Stock Section.]

  **b.** Calculate the growth rate of the expected dividends for Wachovia using the forecasted figures for the next two years. [*Hint:* Click on Estimates and Consensus Estimates.]

  **c.** If you are a Wachovia stockholder and your required rate of return is 8 percent, what is the intrinsic value of the stock?

  **d.** What does the term *intrinsic value* mean?

  **e.** Bank of America [BAC] is a competitor of Wachovia. Calculate the growth rate of the expected dividends for Bank of America using the last dividend the company paid.

  **f.** Would you rather own Wachovia or Bank of America if you are primarily concerned with the expected growth in future dividends? Explain.

# Risk and Rates of Return

## A MANAGERIAL PERSPECTIVE

The performance of the major stock markets from 1995 through 1998 can best be described as remarkable—a period that investors would love to repeat again and again. During that four-year stretch, stocks traded on U.S. stock markets earned an average return greater than 20 percent per year. In 1998, companies such as Microsoft and WorldCom MCI more than doubled in value. The value of some Internet companies, such as America Online, Amazon.com, and Yahoo!, increased by more than 500 percent. Consider the return you would have earned in 1998 if you had purchased Amazon.com at the beginning of the year for $30.13 and then sold it at the end of the year for $321.25: a one-year return of 966 percent. On the other hand, if you had waited until January 2000 to buy Amazon.com and then held it until the end of the year, you would have lost approximately 80 percent of your investment because the company's stock decreased significantly during the year. In fact, during 2000 the values of most Internet company stocks declined significantly. Indeed, many Internet companies did not survive the "Internet skepticism" that existed during the year. By comparison, if you had purchased the stock of Enron at the beginning of 2000, your investment would have nearly doubled in value by the end of the year. But if you still held Enron in mid-2003, the value of your investment would have declined to $0.05 per share

because the company was in bankruptcy at that time. More recently, the price of Google increased 140 percent in 2005, but then it declined 28 percent in the first two months of 2006 before it recovered to generate a positive 9 percent return for the entire year.

If you had bet all your money on the stock of a single company, you would have essentially "put all your eggs in one basket" and faced considerable risk. For example, you would have won big if you chose to invest in Amazon.com for one year either in 1998 or 2002. But you would have lost big if you chose to invest in Amazon.com in 2000. Investors who diversified by spreading their investments among many stocks, perhaps through mutual funds, would have earned a return somewhere between the extraordinary increases posted by Amazon.com in 1998 and 2002 and the extraordinary decreases posted by Amazon.com and other Internet companies in 2000. Large "baskets" of such diversified investments would have earned returns fairly close to the average of the stock markets.

Investing is risky! Although the stock markets performed well from 1995 through 1998, they also go through periods characterized by decreasing prices or negative average returns. For instance, in 1990, 1994, and 2000, the average stock listed on the New York Stock Exchange decreased in value by 7.5 percent, 3.1 percent, and 5.9 percent, respectively. More recently,

305

during the first few months of 2006, the stock market was fairly fickle. At the beginning of the year, the Dow Jones Industrial Average (DJIA) was 10,718. One month later, the DJIA was at about the same level, which means investors earned an average rate of return of approximately 0 percent during the month of January. In mid-May, however, the DJIA was 11,630. Investors who "got in the market" in January and "got out of the market" in May earned an equivalent annual return equal to about 26 percent (noncompounded), and investors who waited to "get in the market" in February and then got out in May earned an equivalent annual return equal to about 34 percent. One month later, however, the DJIA was back to its beginning-of-the-year value. During 2006 the DJIA at times experienced periods of substantial increases and other times it decreased substantially, but by the end of the year the index had increased 16 percent, which represented a higher-than-average market return. What a roller-coaster ride! What risk!

Who knows what the stock market will be doing when you read this book. It could be an up market (referred to as a "bull" market) or it could be a down market (referred to as a "bear" market). Whatever the case, as times change, investment strategies and portfolio mixes need to be changed to meet new conditions. For this reason, you need to understand the basic concepts of risk and return and to recognize how diversification affects investment decisions. As you will discover, investors can create portfolios of securities to reduce risk without reducing the average return on their investments. After reading this chapter, you should have a better understanding of how risk affects investment returns and how to evaluate risk when selecting investments such as those described here.

## Chapter *Essentials*
### —The Questions

After reading this chapter, you should be able to answer the following questions:

- What does it mean to take risk when investing?
- How are the risk and return of an investment measured? How are the risk and return of an investment related?
- For what type of risk is an average investor rewarded?
- How can investors reduce risk?
- What actions do investors take when the return they require to purchase an investment is different from the return the investment is expected to produce?

In this chapter, we take an in-depth look at how investment risk should be measured and how it affects assets' values and rates of return. Recall that in Chapter 5, when we examined the determinants of interest rates, we defined the real risk-free rate, $r^*$, to be the rate of interest on a risk-free security in the absence of inflation. The actual interest rate on a particular debt security was shown to be equal to the real risk-free rate plus several premiums that reflect both inflation and the riskiness of the security in question. In this chapter, we define the term *risk* more precisely in terms of how it relates to investments, we examine procedures used to measure risk, and we discuss the relationship between risk and return. Both investors and financial managers should understand these concepts and use them when considering investment decisions, whether the decisions concern financial assets or real assets.

We will demonstrate that each investment—each stock, bond, or physical asset—is associated with two types of risk: diversifiable risk and nondiversifiable risk. The sum of these two components is the investment's total risk. Diversifiable risk is not important to rational, informed investors because they will eliminate its effects by diversifying it away. The really significant risk is nondiversifiable risk; this risk is bad in the sense that you cannot eliminate it, and if you invest in anything other than risk-free assets, such as short-term Treasury bills, you will be exposed to it. In the balance of the chapter, we will describe these risk concepts and consider how risk enters into the investment decision-making process.

# DEFINING AND MEASURING RISK

*Webster's Dictionary* defines *risk* as "a hazard; a peril; exposure to loss or injury." As this definition suggests, risk refers to the chance that some unfavorable event will occur. If you engage in skydiving, you are taking a chance with your life: Skydiving is risky. If you bet on the horses, you risk losing your money. If you invest in speculative stocks (or, really, *any* stock), you are taking a risk in the hope of receiving an appreciable return.

Most people view risk in the manner just described—as a chance of loss. In reality, however, *risk occurs any time we cannot be certain about the outcome of a particular activity or event,* so we are not sure what will happen in the future. Consequently, *risk results from the fact that an action such as investing can produce more than one outcome in the future.* When multiple outcomes are possible, some of the possible outcomes are considered "good" and some of the possible outcomes are considered "bad."

To illustrate the riskiness of financial assets, suppose you have a large amount of money to invest for one year. You could buy a Treasury security that has an expected return equal to 5 percent. This investment's anticipated rate of return can be determined quite precisely because the chance of the government defaulting on Treasury securities is negligible; the outcome is essentially guaranteed, which means that the security is a risk-free investment.

Alternatively, you could buy the common stock of a newly formed company that has developed technology that can be used to extract petroleum from the mountains in South America without defacing the landscape and without harming the ecology. The technology has yet to be proved economically feasible, so the returns that the common stockholders will receive in the future remain uncertain. Experts who have analyzed the common stock of the company have determined that the *expected*, or average long-run, return for such an investment is 30 percent. Each year, the investment could yield a positive return as high as 900 percent. Of course, there also is the possibility that the company might not survive, in which case the entire investment will be lost and the return will be −100 percent. The return that investors receive each year cannot be determined precisely because more than one outcome is possible; this stock is a risky investment. Because there is a significant danger of earning considerably less than the expected return, investors probably would consider the stock to be quite risky. There is also a very good chance that the actual return will be greater than expected, which, of course, is an outcome you would gladly accept. This possibility could not exist if the stock did not have risk.

Thus, when we think of investment risk, along with the chance of receiving less than expected, we should consider the chance of receiving more than expected. If we consider investment risk from this perspective, then we can define **risk** as the chance of receiving an actual return other than expected. This definition simply means that there is *variability in the returns* or outcomes from the investment. Therefore, investment risk can be measured by the variability of all the investment's returns, both "good" and "bad."

Investment risk, then, is related to the possibility of earning an actual return other than the expected one. *The greater the variability of the possible outcomes, the riskier the investment.* We can define risk more precisely, however, and it is useful to do so.

**risk**
The chance that an outcome other than the expected one will occur.

## Probability Distributions

An event's *probability* is defined as the chance that the event will occur. For example, a weather forecaster might state: "There is a 40 percent chance of rain today and a 60 percent chance that it will not rain." If all possible events, or outcomes, are listed, and

**probability distribution**
A listing of all possible outcomes, or events, with a probability (chance of occurrence) assigned to each outcome.

if a probability is assigned to each event, the listing is called a **probability distribution.** For our weather forecast, we could set up the following simple probability distribution:

| Outcome | Probability |
|---|---|
| Rain | 0.40 = 40% |
| No rain | 0.60 = 60 |
| | 1.00   100% |

Here the possible outcomes are listed in the left column, and the probabilities of these outcomes, expressed both as decimals and as percentages, are given in the right columns. Notice that the probabilities must sum to 1.0, or 100 percent.

Probabilities can also be assigned to the possible outcomes (or returns) from an investment. If you buy a bond, you expect to receive interest on it; those interest payments will provide you with a rate of return on your investment. This investment has two possible outcomes: (1) the issuer makes the interest payments, or (2) the issuer fails to make the interest payments. The higher the probability of default on the interest payments, the riskier the bond; the higher the risk, the higher the rate of return you would require to invest in the bond. If you invest in a stock instead of buying a bond, you will again expect to earn a return on your money. As we saw in Chapter 7, a stock's return includes dividends plus capital gains. Again, the riskier the stock—that is, the greater the variability of the possible payoffs—the higher the stock's expected return must be to induce you to invest in it.

With this idea in mind, consider the possible rates of return (dividend yield plus capital gains yield) that you might earn next year on a $10,000 investment in the stock of either Martin Products Inc. or U.S. Electric. Martin manufactures and distributes equipment for the data transmission industry. Because its sales are cyclical, the firm's profits rise and fall with the business cycle. Furthermore, its market is extremely competitive, and some new company could develop better products that could force Martin into bankruptcy. U.S. Electric, on the other hand, supplies electricity, which is considered an essential service. Because it has city franchises that protect it from competition, this firm's sales and profits are relatively stable and predictable.

Table 8-1 shows the rate-of-return probability distributions for these two companies. As shown in the table, there is a 20 percent chance of a boom, in which case both companies will have high earnings, pay high dividends, and enjoy capital gains. There is a 50 percent probability that the two companies will operate in a normal economy and offer moderate returns. There is a 30 percent probability of a recession, which will mean low earnings and dividends as well as potential capital losses. Notice, however, that Martin's rate of return could vary far more dramatically than that of U.S.

**TABLE 8-1**    Probability Distributions for Martin Products and U.S. Electric

| State of the Economy | Probability of This State Occurring | Rate of Return on Stock If Economic State Occurs | |
|---|---|---|---|
| | | Martin Products | U.S. Electric |
| Boom | 0.2 | 110% | 20% |
| Normal | 0.5 | 22 | 16 |
| Recession | 0.3 | −60 | 10 |
| | 1.0 | | |

**TABLE 8-2**   Calculation of Expected Rates of Return: Martin Products and U.S. Electric

| State of the Economy (1) | Probability of This State Occurring (2) | Martin Products | | U.S. Electric | |
|---|---|---|---|---|---|
| | | Return If This State Occurs (3) | Product: (2) × (3) = (4) | Return If This State Occurs (5) | Product: (2) × (5) = (6) |
| Boom | 0.2 | 110% | 22% | 20% | 4% |
| Normal | 0.5 | 22 | 11 | 16 | 8 |
| Recession | 0.3 | −60 | −18 | 10 | 3 |
| | 1.0 | | $\hat{r}_{US} = 15\%$ | | $\hat{r}_{US} = 15\%$ |

Electric. There is a fairly high probability that the value of Martin's stock will vary substantially, possibly resulting in a loss of 60 percent or a gain of 110 percent; conversely, there is no chance of a loss for U.S. Electric, and its maximum gain is 20 percent.[1]

**Self-Test Questions**

What does *investment risk* mean?

Set up illustrative probability distributions for (1) a bond investment and (2) a stock investment.

## EXPECTED RATE OF RETURN

Table 8-1 provides the probability distributions showing the possible outcomes for investing in Martin Products and U.S. Electric. We can see that the most likely outcome is for the economy to be normal, in which case Martin will return 22 percent and U.S. Electric will return 16 percent. Other outcomes are also possible, however, so we need to summarize the information contained in the probability distributions into a single measure that considers all these possible outcomes. That measure is called the expected value, or *expected rate of return,* for the investments.

Simply stated, the **expected value (return)** is the *weighted average* of the outcomes, with each outcome's weight being its probability of occurrence. Table 8-2 shows how we compute the expected rates of return for Martin Products and U.S. Electric. We multiply each possible outcome by the probability it will occur and then sum the results. We designate the expected rate of return, $\hat{r}$, which is termed "r hat."[2] We insert the "hat" over the r to indicate that this return is uncertain because we do not know when each of the possible outcomes will occur in the future. For example, Martin products will return its stockholders 110 percent when the economy is booming, but we do not know in which year the economy will be booming.

**expected value (return), $\hat{r}$**
The rate of return expected to be realized from an investment; the mean value of the probability distribution of possible results.

---

[1]It is, of course, completely unrealistic to think that any stock has no chance of a loss. Only in hypothetical examples could this situation occur.

[2]In Chapter 6, we used $r_d$ to signify the return on a debt instrument, and in Chapter 7, we used $r_s$ to signify the return on a stock. In this section, however, we discuss only returns on stocks; thus, the subscript "s" is unnecessary, and we use the term $\hat{r}$ rather than $\hat{r}_s$ to represent the expected return on a stock.

The expected rate of return can be calculated using the following equation:

**8–1**

$$\text{Expected rate of return} = \hat{r} = Pr_1 r_1 + Pr_2 r_2 + \cdots + Pr_n r_n$$

$$= \sum_{i=1}^{n} Pr_i r_i$$

Here $r_i$ is the ith possible outcome, $Pr_i$ is the probability that the ith outcome will occur, and n is the number of possible outcomes. Thus, $\hat{r}$ is a weighted average of the possible outcomes (the $r_i$ values), with each outcome's weight being its probability of occurrence. Using the data for Martin Products, we compute its expected rate of return as follows:

$$\hat{r} = Pr_1(r_1) + Pr_2(r_2) + Pr_3(r_3)$$
$$= 0.2(110\%) + 0.5(22\%) + 0.3(-60\%) = 15.0\%$$

Notice that the expected rate of return does not equal any of the possible payoffs for Martin Products given in Table 8-1. Stated simply, the expected rate of return represents the average payoff that investors will receive from Martin Products if the probability distribution given in Table 8-1 does not change over a long period of time. If this probability distribution is correct, then 20 percent of the time the future economic condition will be termed a boom, so investors will earn a 110 percent rate of return; 50 percent of the time the economy should be normal and the investment payoff will be 22 percent; and 30 percent of the time the economy should be in recession and the payoff will be a loss equal to 60 percent. On average, then, Martin Products' investors should earn 15 percent over some period of time.

We can graph the rates of return to obtain a picture of the variability of possible outcomes, as shown in Figure 8-1. The height of each bar in the figure indicates the probability that a given outcome will occur. The probable returns for Martin Products

**FIGURE 8-1    Probability Distribution of Martin Products' and U.S. Electric's Rate of Return**

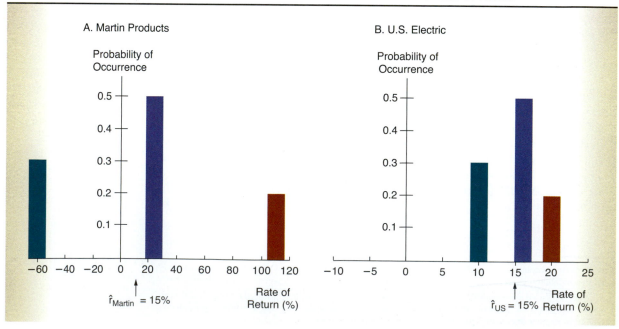

range from +110 percent to –60 percent, with an expected return of 15 percent. The expected return for U.S. Electric is also 15 percent, but its range is much narrower.

## Continuous versus Discrete Probability Distributions

So far, we have assumed that only three states of the economy can exist: recession, normal, and boom. Under these conditions, the probability distributions given in Table 8-1, are called **discrete** because the number of outcomes is limited, or finite. In reality, of course, the state of the economy could actually range from a deep depression to a fantastic boom, with an unlimited number of possible states in between. Suppose we had the time and patience to assign a probability to each possible state of the economy (with the sum of the probabilities still equaling 1.0) and to assign a rate of return to each stock for each state of the economy. We would then have a table similar to Table 8-1, except that it would include many more entries in each column. We could use this table to calculate the expected rates of return as described previously, and we could approximate the probabilities and outcomes by constructing continuous curves such as those presented in Figure 8-2. In this figure, we have changed the assumptions so that there is essentially a zero probability that Martin Products' return will be less than –60 percent or more than 110 percent, or that U.S. Electric's return will be less than 10 percent or more than 20 percent. Virtually any return within these limits is possible, however. Such probability distributions are called **continuous** because the number of possible outcomes is unlimited. For example, U.S. Electric's return could be 10.01 percent, 10.001 percent, and so on.

**discrete probability distribution**
The number of possible outcomes is limited, or finite.

**continuous probability distribution**
The number of possible outcomes is unlimited, or infinite.

**FIGURE 8-2**  Continuous Probability Distributions of Martin Products' and U.S. Electric's Rates of Return

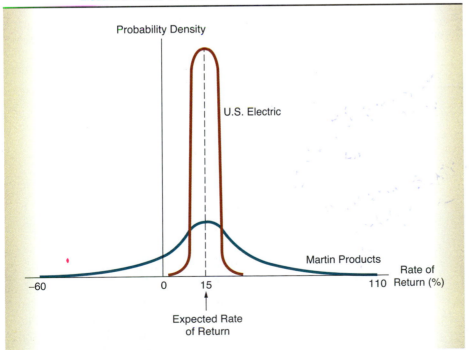

**Note:** The assumptions regarding the possibilities of various outcomes have been changed from those in Figure 8-1. There the probability of obtaining exactly 16 percent return for U.S. Electric was 50 percent; here it is *much smaller* because there are many possible outcomes instead of just three. With continuous distributions, it is more appropriate to ask what the probability is of obtaining at least some specified rate of return than to ask what the probability is of obtaining exactly that rate. This topic is covered in detail in statistics courses.

The *tighter the probability distribution, the less variability* there is and the more likely it is that the actual outcome will approach the expected value. Consequently, under these conditions, it becomes less likely that the actual return will differ dramatically from the expected return. Thus, *the tighter the probability distribution, the lower the risk assigned to a stock.* Because U.S. Electric has a relatively tight probability distribution, its *actual* return is likely to be closer to its 15 percent expected return than is that of Martin Products.

## Measuring Total (Stand-Alone) Risk: The Standard Deviation

**standard deviation, σ**
A measure of the tightness, or variability, of a set of outcomes.

Because we have defined risk as the variability of returns, we can measure it by examining the tightness of the probability distribution associated with the possible outcomes. In general, the width of a probability distribution indicates the amount of scatter, or variability, of the possible outcomes. To be most useful, any measure of risk should have a definite value; thus, we need a measure of the tightness of the probability distribution. The measure we use most often is the **standard deviation,** the symbol for which is σ, the Greek letter "sigma." The smaller the standard deviation, the tighter the probability distribution, and, accordingly, the lower the total risk associated with the investment. To calculate the standard deviation, we take the following steps, as shown in Table 8-3:

1. Calculate the expected rate of return using Equation 8–1. For Martin, we previously found $\hat{r} = 15\%$.

2. Subtract the expected rate of return, $\hat{r}$, from each possible outcome, $r_i$, to obtain a set of deviations from $\hat{r}$:

$$\text{Deviation}_i = r_i - \hat{r}$$

**variance, σ²**
The standard deviation squared; a measure of the width of a probability distribution.

The deviations are shown in column 3 of Table 8-3.

3. Square each deviation (shown in column 4), multiply the result by the probability of occurrence for its related outcome (column 5), and then sum these products to obtain the **variance, σ²,** of the probability distribution, which is shown in column 6:

**8–2**

$$\text{Variance} = \sigma^2 = (r_1 - \hat{r})^2 Pr_1 + (r_2 - \hat{r})^2 Pr_2 + \cdots + (r_n - \hat{r})^2 Pr_n$$

$$= \sum_{i=1}^{n} (r_i - \hat{r})^2 Pr_i$$

**TABLE 8-3**    Calculating Martin Products' Standard Deviation

| Payoff $r_i$ (1) | | Expected Return $\hat{r}$ (2) | | Deviation $r_j - \hat{r}$ (1) − (2) = (3) | $(r_j - \hat{r})^2 =$ (4) | Probability (5) | $(r_j - \hat{r})^2 Pr_i$ (4) × (5) | | $\sigma^2$ (6) |
|---|---|---|---|---|---|---|---|---|---|
| 110% | − | 15% | = | 95 | 9,025 | 0.2 | 9,025 × 0.2 | = | 1,805.0 |
| 22 | − | 15 | = | 7 | 49 | 0.5 | 49 × 0.5 | = | 24.5 |
| −60 | − | 15 | = | −75 | 5,625 | 0.3 | 5,625 × 0.3 | = | 1,687.5 |
| | | | | | | | Variance = $\sigma^2$ | = | 3,517.0 |

$$\text{Standard deviation} = \sigma = \sqrt{\sigma^2} = \sqrt{3,517} = 59.3\%$$

**4.** Take the square root of the variance to get the standard deviation shown at the bottom of column 6:

8–3

$$\text{Standard deviation} = \sigma = \sqrt{(r_1 - \hat{r})^2 Pr_1 + (r_2 - \hat{r})^2 Pr_2 + \cdots + (r_n - \hat{r})^2 Pr_n}$$

$$= \sqrt{\sum_{i=1}^{n} (r_i - \hat{r})^2 Pr_i}$$

As you can see, the standard deviation is a weighted average deviation from the expected value, and it gives an idea of how far above or below the expected value the actual value is likely to be. As shown in Table 8-3 Martin's standard deviation is $\sigma = 59.3\%$. Using these same procedures, we find U.S. Electric's standard deviation to be 3.6 percent. The larger standard deviation for Martin indicates a greater variation of returns for this firm, and hence a greater chance that the actual, or realized, return will differ significantly from the expected return. Consequently, Martin Products would be considered a riskier investment than U.S. Electric, according to this measure of risk.

To this point, the example we have used to compute the expected return and standard deviation is based on data that take the form of a known probability distribution. That is, we know or have estimated all of the future outcomes and the chances that these outcomes will occur in a particular situation. In many cases, however, the only information we have available consists of data over some *past period.* For example, suppose we have observed the following returns associated with a common stock:

| Year | $\hat{r}$ |
|------|------|
| 2008 | 15% |
| 2009 | −5 |
| 2010 | 20 |
| 2011 | 22 |

We can use this information to *estimate* the risk associated with the stock by estimating standard deviation of returns. The estimated standard deviation can be computed using a series of past, or observed, returns to solve the following formula:

8–4

$$\text{Estimated } \sigma = s = \sqrt{\dfrac{\displaystyle\sum_{t=1}^{n} (\ddot{r}_t - \bar{r})^2}{n - 1}}$$

Here $\ddot{r}_t$ represents the past realized rate of return in Period t, and $\bar{r}$ ("r bar") is the arithmetic average of the annual returns earned during the last n years. We compute $\bar{r}_t$ as follows:

8–5

$$\bar{r} = \dfrac{\ddot{r}_1 + \ddot{r}_2 + \cdots + \ddot{r}_n}{n} = \dfrac{\displaystyle\sum_{t=1}^{n} \ddot{r}_n}{n}$$

Continuing our current example, we would determine the arithmetic average and estimate the value for σ as follows:[3]

$$\bar{r} = \frac{15 + (-5) + 20 + 22}{4} = 13.0\%$$

$$\text{Estimated } \sigma = s = \sqrt{\frac{(15-13)^2 + (-5-13)^2 + (20-13)^2 + (22-13)^2}{4-1}}$$

$$= \sqrt{\frac{458}{3}} = 12.4\%$$

The historical standard deviation is often used as an estimate of the future standard deviation. Much less often, and generally incorrectly, $\bar{r}_t$ for some past period is used as an estimate of $\hat{r}_t$, the *expected* future return. Because past variability is likely to be repeated, s might be a good estimate of future risk. It is much less reasonable, however, to expect that the past *level* of return (which could have been as high as +100 percent or as low as –50 percent) is the best expectation of what investors think will happen in the future.

## Coefficient of Variation (Risk/Return Ratio)

**coefficient of variation (CV)**
A standardized measure of the risk per unit of return. It is calculated by dividing the standard deviation by the expected return.

Another useful measure to evaluate risky investments is the **coefficient of variation (CV),** which is the standard deviation divided by the expected return:

**8–6**

$$\text{Coefficient of variation} = CV = \frac{\text{Risk}}{\text{Return}} = \frac{\sigma}{\hat{r}}$$

The coefficient of variation shows the risk per unit of return. It provides a more meaningful basis for comparison when the expected returns on two alternatives differ. Because both U.S. Electric and Martin Products have the *same expected return, it is not necessary to compute the coefficient of variation* to compare the two investments. In this case, most people would prefer to invest in U.S. Electric because it offers the same expected return with lower risk. The firm with the larger standard deviation, Martin, must have the larger coefficient of variation because the expected returns for the two stocks are equal, but the numerator in Equation 8–6 is greater for Martin. In fact, the coefficient of variation for Martin is 59.3%/15% = 3.95; for U.S. Electric, CV = 3.6%/15% = 0.24. Thus Martin is more than 16 times riskier than U.S. Electric using this criterion.

The coefficient of variation is more useful when we consider investments that have different expected rates of return *and* different levels of risk. For example, Biobotics Corporation is a biological research and development firm that, according to stock analysts, offers investors an expected rate of return equal to 35 percent with a standard deviation of 7.5 percent. Biobotics offers a higher expected return than U.S. Electric, but it is also riskier. With respect to both risk and return, is Biobotics or U.S. Electric a better investment? If we calculate the coefficient of variation for Biobotics, we find that it equals 7.5%/35% = 0.21, which is slightly less than U.S. Electric's coefficient of variation of 0.24. Thus, Biobotics actually has less risk per unit of return than U.S. Electric, even though its standard deviation is higher. In this case, the additional return

---

[3]You should recognize from statistics courses that a sample of four observations is not sufficient to make a good estimate. We use four observations here only to simplify the illustration.

**FIGURE 8-3**   Comparison of Probability Distributions and Rates of Return for U.S. Electric and Biobotics Corporation

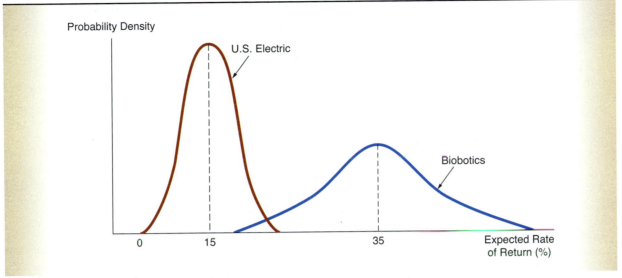

offered by Biobotics is more than sufficient to compensate investors for taking on the additional risk.

Figure 8-3 graphs the probability distributions for U.S. Electric and Biobotics. As you can see in the figure, U.S. Electric has the smaller standard deviation and hence the more peaked probability distribution. As the graph clearly shows, however, the chances of a really high return are much better with Biobotics than with U.S. Electric because Biobotics' expected return is so high. Because the coefficient of variation captures the effects of both risk and return, it is a better measure for evaluating risk in situations where investments differ with respect to both their amounts of total risk and their expected returns.

## Risk Aversion and Required Returns

Suppose you have worked hard and saved $1 million, which you now plan to invest. You can buy a 10 percent U.S. Treasury note, and at the end of one year you will have a sure $1.1 million—that is, your original investment plus $100,000 in interest. Alternatively, you can buy stock in R&D Enterprises. If R&D's research programs are successful, the value of your stock will increase to $2.2 million. Conversely, if the firm's research is a failure, the value of your stock will go to zero, and you will be penniless. You regard R&D's chances of success or failure as being 50-50, so the expected value of the stock investment is $0.5(\$0) + 0.5(\$2,200,000) = \$1,100,000$. Subtracting the $1 million cost of the stock leaves an expected profit of $100,000, or an expected (but risky) 10 percent rate of return:

$$\begin{aligned}
\text{Expected rate} \atop \text{of return} &= \frac{\text{Expected ending value} - \text{Beginning value}}{\text{Beginning value}} \\
&= \frac{\$1,100,000 - \$1,000,000}{\$1,000,000} = \frac{\$100,000}{\$1,000,000} = 0.10 = 10.0\%
\end{aligned}$$

In this case, you have a choice between a sure $100,000 profit (representing a 10 percent rate of return) on the Treasury note and a risky expected $100,000 profit (also representing a 10 percent expected rate of return) on the R&D Enterprises stock. Which one would you choose? If you choose the less risky investment, you are risk averse. Most investors are risk averse, and certainly the average investor is risk averse, at least with regard to his or her "serious money." Because this is a well-documented fact, we shall assume **risk aversion** throughout the remainder of the book.

**risk aversion**
Risk-averse investors require higher rates of return to invest in higher-risk securities.

What are the implications of risk aversion for security prices and rates of return? The answer is that, other things held constant, the higher a security's risk, the higher the return investors demand, and thus the less they are willing to pay for the investment. To see how risk aversion affects security prices, we can analyze the situation with U.S. Electric and Martin Products stocks. Suppose each stock sold for $100 per share and had an expected rate of return of 15 percent. Investors are averse to risk, so they would show a general preference for U.S. Electric because there is less variability in its payoffs (less uncertainty). People with money to invest would bid for U.S. Electric stock rather than Martin stock, and Martin's stockholders would start selling their stock and using the money to buy U.S. Electric stock. Buying pressure would drive up the price of U.S. Electric's stock, and selling pressure would simultaneously cause Martin's price to decline. These price changes, in turn, would alter the expected rates of return on the two securities. Suppose, for example, that the price of U.S. Electric stock was bid up from $100 to $125, whereas the price of Martin's stock declined from $100 to $75. This development would cause U.S. Electric's expected return to fall to 12 percent, whereas Martin's expected return would rise to 20 percent. The difference in returns, $20\% - 12\% = 8\%$, is a **risk premium (RP).** The risk premium represents the compensation that investors require for assuming the *additional* risk of buying Martin's stock.

**risk premium (RP)**
The portion of the expected return that can be attributed to the additional risk of an investment. It is the difference between the expected rate of return on a given risky asset and the expected rate of return on a less risky asset.

This example demonstrates a very important principle: In a market dominated by risk-averse investors, *riskier securities must have higher expected returns,* as estimated by the average investor, than less risky securities. If this situation does not hold, investors will buy and sell investments and prices will continue to change until the higher-risk investments have higher expected returns than the lower-risk investments. Figure 8-4 illustrates this relationship. We will consider the question of how much higher the returns on risky securities must be later in the chapter, after we examine how diversification affects the way risk should be measured.

**FIGURE 8-4    Risk/Return Relationship**

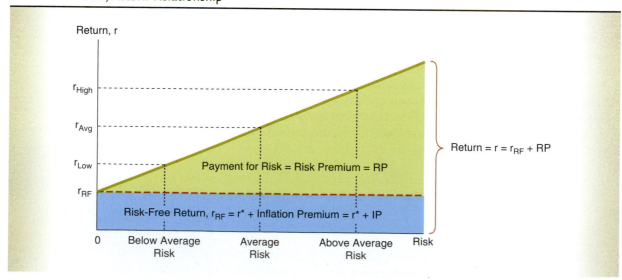

## PORTFOLIO RISK—HOLDING COMBINATIONS OF ASSETS

In the preceding section, we considered the riskiness of an investment held in isolation—that is, the *total* risk of an investment if it is held by itself. Now we analyze the riskiness of investments held in portfolios.[4] As we shall see, holding an investment—whether a stock, bond, or other asset—as part of a portfolio generally is less risky than holding the same investment all by itself. In fact, most financial assets are not held in isolation but rather as parts of portfolios. Banks, pension funds, insurance companies, mutual funds, and other financial institutions are required by law to hold diversified portfolios. Even individual investors—at least those whose security holdings constitute a significant part of their total wealth—generally hold stock portfolios rather than the stock of only one firm. From an investor's standpoint, then, the fact that a particular stock goes up or down is not very important. What is important is the return on his or her portfolio and the portfolio's risk. Logically, *the risk and return characteristics of an investment should not be evaluated in isolation; instead, the risk and return of an individual security should be analyzed in terms of how that security affects the risk and return of the portfolio in which it is held.*

To illustrate, consider an investment in Payco American, a collection agency company that operates several offices nationwide. The company is not well known, its stock is not very liquid, its earnings have fluctuated quite a bit in the past, and it doesn't even pay a dividend. This suggests that Payco is risky and that its required rate of return, r, should be relatively high. Even so, Payco's r always has been quite low relative to the rates of return offered by most firms with similar risk. This information indicates that investors regard Payco as being a low-risk company despite its uncertain profits and its nonexistent dividend stream. The reason for this somewhat counterintuitive fact relates to diversification and its effect on risk. Payco's stock price rises during recessions, whereas the prices of other stocks tend to decline when the economy slumps. Therefore, holding Payco in a portfolio of "normal" stocks tends to stabilize returns on the entire portfolio.

---

[4]A *portfolio* is a collection of investment securities or assets. If you owned some General Motors stock, some ExxonMobil stock, and some IBM stock, you would be holding a three-stock portfolio. For the reasons set forth in this section, the majority of all stocks are held as parts of portfolios.

**expected return on a portfolio, $\hat{r}_p$**
The weighted average expected return on stocks held in a portfolio.

## Portfolio Returns

The **expected return on a portfolio, $\hat{r}_p$**, is simply the weighted average of the expected returns on the individual stocks in the portfolio, with each weight being the proportion of the total portfolio invested in each stock:

8–7

$$\text{Portfolio return} = \hat{r}_p = w_1\hat{r}_1 + w_2\hat{r}_2 + \cdots + w_N\hat{r}_N = \sum_{j=1}^{N} w_j\hat{r}_j$$

Here the $\hat{r}_j$ values are the expected returns on the individual stocks, the $w_j$ values are the weights, and the portfolio includes N stocks. Note two points: (1) $w_j$ is the proportion of the portfolio's dollar value invested in Stock j, which is equal to the value of the investment in Stock j divided by the total value of the portfolio, and (2) the $w_j$ values must sum to 1.0.

Suppose security analysts estimate that the following returns could be expected on four large companies:

| Company | Expected Return, $\hat{r}$ |
|---|---|
| AT&T | 8% |
| Citigroup | 13 |
| General Electric | 19 |
| Microsoft | 16 |

If we formed a $100,000 portfolio, investing $25,000 in each of these four stocks, our expected portfolio return would be 14.0 percent:

$$\hat{r}_p = w_{ATT}\hat{r}_{ATT} + w_{Citi}\hat{r}_{Citi} + w_{GE}\hat{r}_{GE} + w_{Micro}\hat{r}_{Micro}$$
$$= 0.25(8\%) + 0.25(13\%) + 0.25(19\%) + 0.25(16\%) = 14.0\%$$

**realized rate of return, $\ddot{r}$**
The return that is actually earned. The actual return ($\ddot{r}$) usually differs from the expected return ($\hat{r}$).

Of course, after the fact and one year later, the actual **realized rates of return, $\ddot{r}$,** on the individual stocks will almost certainly differ from their expected values, so $\ddot{r}_p$ will be somewhat different from $\hat{r}_p = 14\%$. For example, Microsoft's stock might double in price and provide a return of $+100$ percent, whereas General Electric's stock might have a terrible year, see its price fall sharply, and provide a return of $-75$ percent. Note, however, that those two events would somewhat offset each other, so the portfolio's return might still approach its expected return, even though the individual stocks' actual returns were far from their expected returns.

## Portfolio Risk

As we just saw, the expected return of a portfolio is simply a weighted average of the expected returns of the individual stocks in the portfolio. Unlike returns, the riskiness of a portfolio ($\sigma_P$) generally is *not* a weighted average of the standard deviations of the individual securities in the portfolio. Instead, the portfolio's risk usually is *smaller* than the weighted average of the individual stocks' standard deviations. In fact, it is theoretically possible to combine two stocks that by themselves are quite risky as measured by their standard deviations and form a completely risk-free portfolio—that is, a portfolio with $\sigma_P = 0$.

To illustrate the effect of combining securities, consider the situation depicted in Figure 8-5. The bottom section of the figure gives data on the rates of return for Stock

**FIGURE 8-5**    Rate of Return Distribution for Two Perfectly Negatively Correlated Stocks ($\rho = -1.0$) and for Portfolio WM

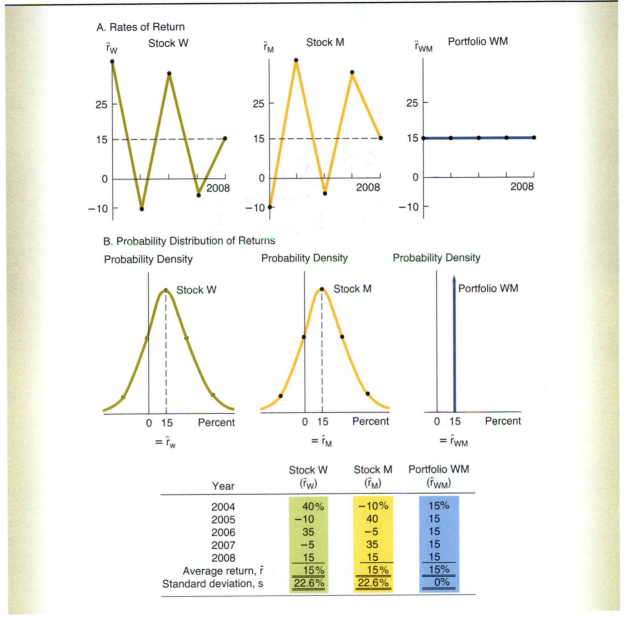

| Year | Stock W ($\ddot{r}_W$) | Stock M ($\ddot{r}_M$) | Portfolio WM ($\ddot{r}_{WM}$) |
|---|---|---|---|
| 2004 | 40% | −10% | 15% |
| 2005 | −10 | 40 | 15 |
| 2006 | 35 | −5 | 15 |
| 2007 | −5 | 35 | 15 |
| 2008 | 15 | 15 | 15 |
| Average return, $\bar{r}$ | 15% | 15% | 15% |
| Standard deviation, s | 22.6% | 22.6% | 0% |

**Note:** To construct Portfolio WM, 50 percent of the total amount invested is invested in Stock W and 50 percent is invested in Stock M.

W and Stock M individually as well as rates of return for a portfolio invested 50 percent in each stock. The three top graphs show the actual historical returns for each investment from 2004 to 2008, and the lower graphs show the probability distributions of returns, assuming that the future is expected to be like the past. The two stocks would be quite risky if they were held in isolation. When they are combined to form Portfolio WM, however, they are not risky at all. (*Note:* These stocks are called W and M because their returns graphs in Figure 8-5 resemble a W and an M.)

The reason Stocks W and M can be combined to form a risk-free portfolio is because their returns move in opposite directions. That is, when W's returns are low,

**correlation coefficient, ρ**
A measure of the degree of relationship between two variables.

M's returns are high, and vice versa. The relationship between any two variables is called *correlation*, and the **correlation coefficient, ρ,** measures the direction and the strength of the relationship between the variables.[5] In statistical terms, we say that the returns on Stock W and Stock M are perfectly negatively correlated, with $\rho = -1.0$.[6]

The opposite of perfect negative correlation—that is, $\rho = -1.0$—is perfect positive correlation—that is, $\rho = +1.0$. Returns on two perfectly positively correlated stocks would move up and down together, and a portfolio consisting of two such stocks would be exactly as risky as the individual stocks. This point is illustrated in Figure 8-6, in which we see that the portfolio's standard deviation equals that of the individual stocks. As you can see, there is no diversification effect in this case—that is, risk is not reduced if the portfolio contains perfectly positively correlated stocks.

Figure 8-5 and Figure 8-6 demonstrate that when stocks are perfectly negatively correlated ($\rho = -1.0$), all risk can be diversified away; conversely, when stocks are perfectly positively correlated ($\rho = +1.0$), diversification is ineffective. In reality, most stocks are positively correlated, but not perfectly so. On average, the correlation coefficient for the returns on two randomly selected stocks would be about +0.4. For most pairs of stocks, ρ would lie in the range of +0.3 to +0.6. *Under such conditions, combining stocks into portfolios reduces risk but does not eliminate it completely.* Figure 8-7 illustrates this point with two stocks for which the correlation coefficient is $\rho = +0.67$. Both Stock W and Stock Y have the same average return and standard deviation—$\bar{r} = 15\%$ and $s = 22.6\%$. A portfolio that consists of 50 percent of both stocks has an average return equal to 15.0 percent, which is exactly the same as the average return for each of the two stocks. The portfolio's standard deviation, however, is 20.6 percent, which is less than the standard deviation of either stock. Thus the portfolio's risk is *not* an average of the risks of its individual stocks—diversification has reduced, but not eliminated, risk.

From these two-stock portfolio examples, we have seen that risk can be completely eliminated in one extreme case ($\rho = -1.0$), whereas diversification does no good in the other extreme case ($\rho = +1.0$). In between these extremes, combining two stocks into a portfolio reduces, but does not eliminate, the riskiness inherent in the individual stocks.

What would happen if the portfolio included more than two stocks? *As a rule, the riskiness of a portfolio will be reduced as the number of stocks in the portfolio increases.* If we added enough stocks, could we completely eliminate risk? In general, the answer is no, but the extent to which adding stocks to a portfolio reduces its risk depends on the *degree of correlation* among the stocks: *The smaller the positive correlation among stocks included in a portfolio, the lower its total risk.* If we could find a set of stocks whose correlations were negative, we could eliminate all risk. *In the typical case, in which the correlations among the individual stocks are positive but less than +1.0, some—but not all—risk can be eliminated.*

---

[5]The *correlation coefficient*, ρ, can range from +1.0 (denoting that the two variables move in the same direction with exactly the same degree of synchronization every time movement occurs) to −1.0 (denoting that the variables always move with the same degree of synchronization, but in opposite directions). A correlation coefficient of zero suggests that the two variables are not related to each other—that is, changes in one variable occur *independently* of changes in the other.

[6]Following is the computation of the correlation coefficient that measures the relationship between Stock W and Stock M shown in Figure 8-5. The average return and standard deviation for both stocks are the same: $\bar{r} = 15\%$ and $s = 22.6\%$.

$$\text{Covariance} = \frac{(40-15)(-10-15) + (-10-15)(40-15) + (35-15)(-5-15) + (-5-15)(35-15) + (15-15)(15-15)}{5-1}$$

$$= -512.5$$

$$\text{Correlation} = \rho = \text{Covariance}/(s_W s_M) = -512.5/[(22.6)(22.6)] = -1.0$$

**FIGURE 8-6**   Rate of Return Distributions for Two Perfectly Positively Correlated Stocks ($\rho = +1.0$) and for Portfolio MM′

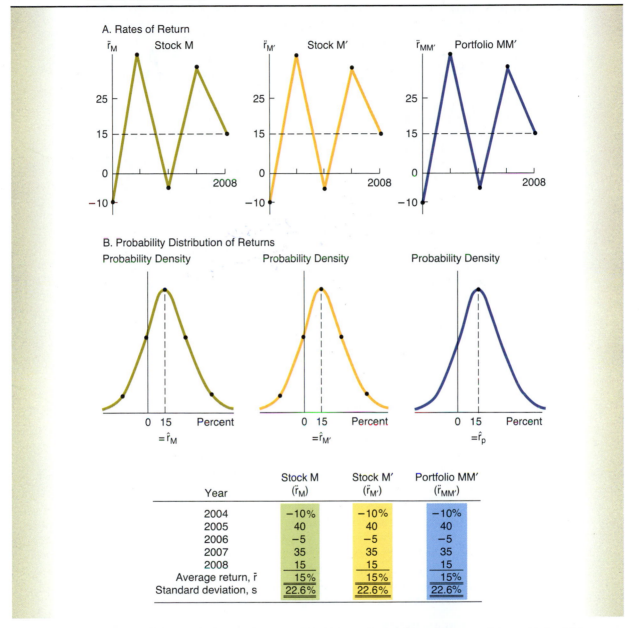

| Year | Stock M ($\ddot{r}_M$) | Stock M′ ($\ddot{r}_{M'}$) | Portfolio MM′ ($\ddot{r}_{MM'}$) |
|---|---|---|---|
| 2004 | −10% | −10% | −10% |
| 2005 | 40 | 40 | 40 |
| 2006 | −5 | −5 | −5 |
| 2007 | 35 | 35 | 35 |
| 2008 | 15 | 15 | 15 |
| Average return, $\bar{r}$ | 15% | 15% | 15% |
| Standard deviation, s | 22.6% | 22.6% | 22.6% |

**Note:** To construct Portfolio MM′, 50 percent of the total amount invested is invested in Stock M and 50 percent is invested in Stock M′.

To test your understanding, consider the following question: Would you expect to find higher correlations between the returns on two companies in the same industry or in different industries? For example, would the correlation of returns on Ford's and General Motors' stocks be higher, or would the correlation coefficient be higher between either Ford or GM and Procter & Gamble (P&G)? How would those correlations affect the risk of portfolios containing them?

*Answer:* Ford's and GM's returns have a correlation coefficient of approximately 0.9 with one another because both are affected by the factors that affect auto sales. They have a correlation coefficient of only 0.4 with the returns of P&G.

**FIGURE 8-7**   Rate of Return Distributions for Two Partially Correlated Stocks ($\rho = +0.67$) and for Portfolio WY

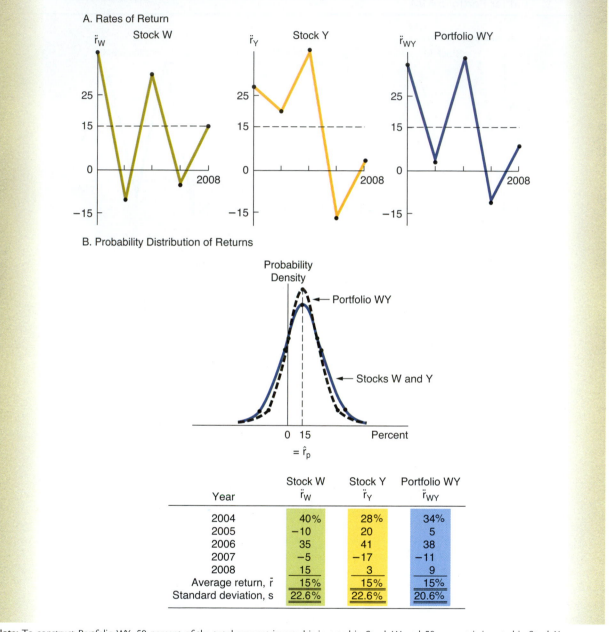

**Note:** To construct Portfolio WY, 50 percent of the total amount invested is invested in Stock W and 50 percent is invested in Stock Y.

*Implications:* A two-stock portfolio consisting of Ford and GM would be riskier than a two-stock portfolio consisting of either Ford or GM plus P&G. Thus, to minimize risk, portfolios should be diversified *across* industries.

## Firm-Specific Risk versus Market Risk

As noted earlier, it is very difficult—if not impossible—to find stocks whose expected returns are not positively correlated. Most stocks tend to do well when the national

**FIGURE 8-8**    Effects of Portfolio Size on Portfolio Risk for Average Stocks

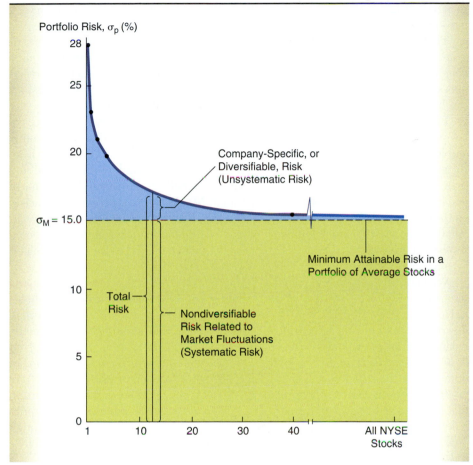

economy is strong and to do poorly when it is weak.[7] Thus, even very large portfolios end up with substantial amounts of risk, though the risks generally are less than if all of the money was invested in only one stock.

To see more precisely how portfolio size affects portfolio risk, consider Figure 8-8. This figure shows how portfolio risk is affected by forming ever-larger portfolios of randomly selected stocks listed on the New York Stock Exchange (NYSE). Standard deviations are plotted for an average one-stock portfolio, for a two-stock portfolio, and so on, up to a portfolio consisting of all common stocks listed on the NYSE. As the graph illustrates, the riskiness of a portfolio consisting of average NYSE stocks generally tends to decline and to approach some minimum limit as the size of the portfolio increases. According to the data, $\sigma_1$, the standard deviation of a one-stock portfolio (or an average stock), is approximately 28 percent. A portfolio consisting of all of the stocks in the market, which is called the *market portfolio*, would have a standard deviation, $\sigma_M$, of about 15 percent (shown as the horizontal dashed line in Figure 8-8).

Figure 8-8 shows that almost half of the riskiness inherent in an average individual stock can be eliminated if the stock is held as part of a reasonably well-diversified

---

[7]It is not too difficult to find a few stocks that happened to rise because of a particular set of circumstances in the past while most other stocks were declining. It is much more difficult to find stocks that could logically be *expected* to go up in the future when other stocks are falling. Payco American, the collection agency discussed earlier, is one of those rare exceptions.

portfolio—namely, a portfolio containing 40 or more stocks. Some risk always remains, so it is virtually impossible to diversify away the effects of broad stock market movements that affect almost all stocks.

That part of the risk of a stock that can be eliminated is called *diversifiable*, or *firm-specific*, or *unsystematic, risk;* that part that cannot be eliminated is called *nondiversifiable*, or *market*, or *systematic, risk.* Although the name given to the risk is not especially important, the fact that a large part of the riskiness of any individual stock can be eliminated through portfolio diversification is vitally important.

**Firm-specific,** or **diversifiable, risk** is caused by such things as lawsuits, loss of key personnel, strikes, successful and unsuccessful marketing programs, the winning and losing of major contracts, and other events that are unique to a particular firm. Because the actual outcomes of these events are essentially random (unpredictable), their effects on a portfolio can be eliminated by diversification—that is, bad events in one firm will be offset by good events in another. **Market,** or **nondiversifiable, risk,** on the other hand, stems from factors that *systematically* affect all firms, such as war, inflation, recessions, and high interest rates. Because most stocks tend to be affected similarly (negatively) by these *market* conditions, systematic risk cannot be eliminated by portfolio diversification.

We know that investors demand a premium for bearing risk. That is, the riskier a security, the higher the expected return required to induce investors to buy (or to hold) it. However, if investors really are primarily concerned with *portfolio risk* rather than the risk of the individual securities in the portfolio, how should we measure the riskiness of an individual stock? The answer is this: *The relevant riskiness of an individual stock is its contribution to the riskiness of a well-diversified portfolio.* In other words, the riskiness of General Electric's stock to a doctor who has a portfolio of 40 stocks or to a trust officer managing a 150-stock portfolio is the contribution that the GE stock makes to the entire portfolio's riskiness. The stock might be quite risky if held by itself, but if much of this total risk can be eliminated through diversification, then its **relevant risk**—that is, its *contribution to the portfolio's risk*—is much smaller than its total, or stand-alone, risk.

A simple example will help clarify this point. Suppose you are offered the chance to flip a coin once. If a head comes up, you win $20,000; if the coin comes up tails, you lose $16,000. This proposition is a good bet: The expected return is $2,000 = 0.5($20,000) + 0.5(−$16,000). It is a highly risky proposition, however, because you have a 50 percent chance of losing $16,000. For this reason, you might refuse to make the bet. Alternatively, suppose you were offered the chance to flip a coin 100 times; you would win $200 for each head but lose $160 for each tail. It is possible that you would flip all heads and win $20,000. It is also possible that you would flip all tails and lose $16,000. The chances are very high, however, that you would actually flip about 50 heads and about 50 tails, winning a net of about $2,000. Although each individual flip is a risky bet, collectively this scenario is a low-risk proposition because most of the risk has been diversified away. This concept underlies the practice of holding portfolios of stocks rather than just one stock. Note that all of the risk associated with stocks cannot be eliminated by diversification: Those risks related to broad, systematic changes in the economy that affect the stock market will remain.

Are all stocks equally risky in the sense that adding them to a well-diversified portfolio would have the same effect on the portfolio's riskiness? The answer is no. Different stocks will affect the portfolio differently, so different securities have different degrees of relevant (systematic) risk. How can we measure the relevant risk of an individual stock? As we have seen, all risk except that related to broad market movements can, and presumably will, be diversified away. After all, why accept risk that we can easily eliminate? *The risk that remains after diversifying is market risk*

---

**firm-specific (diversifiable) risk**
That part of a security's risk associated with random outcomes generated by events, or behaviors, specific to the firm. It *can* be eliminated by proper diversification.

**market (nondiversifiable) risk**
The part of a security's risk associated with economic, or market, factors that systematically affect firms. It *cannot* be eliminated by diversification.

**relevant risk**
The portion of a security's risk that cannot be diversified away; the security's market risk. It reflects the security's contribution to the risk of a portfolio.

*(that is, risk that is inherent in the market), and it can be measured by evaluating the degree to which a given stock tends to move up and down with the market.*

## The Concept of Beta (β)

Recall that the relevant risk associated with an individual stock is based on its systematic risk, which in turn depends on the sensitivity of the firm's operations to economic events such as interest rate changes and inflationary pressures. Because the *general movements in the financial markets reflect movements in the economy,* we can measure the market risk of a stock by observing its tendency to move with the market or with an average stock that has the same characteristics as the market. The measure of a stock's sensitivity to market fluctuations is called its **beta coefficient,** designated with the Greek letter β.

An *average-risk stock* is defined as one that tends to move up and down in step with the general market as measured by some index, such as the Dow Jones Industrial Average, the S&P 500 Index, or the New York Stock Exchange Composite Index. Such a stock will, *by definition,* have a beta (β) of 1.0. This value indicates that, in general, if the market moves up by 10 percent, the stock price will also increase by 10 percent; if the market falls by 10 percent, the stock price will decline by 10 percent. A portfolio composed of such β = 1.0 stocks will move up and down with the broad market averages, and it will be just as risky as the averages. If β = 0.5, the stock's relevant (systematic) risk is only half as volatile as the market, and a portfolio of such stocks will be half as risky as a portfolio that includes only β = 1.0 stocks—it will rise and fall only half as much as the market. If β = 2.0, the stock's relevant risk is twice as volatile as an average stock, so a portfolio of such stocks will be twice as risky as an average portfolio. The value of such a portfolio could double—or halve—in a short period of time. If you held such a portfolio, you could quickly become a millionaire—or a pauper.

Figure 8-9 graphs the relative volatility of three stocks. The data below the graph *assume* that in 2006 the "market," defined as a portfolio consisting of all stocks, had a total return (dividend yield plus capital gains yield) of $r_M = 14\%$, and Stocks H, A, and L (for high, average, and low risk) also had returns of 14 percent. In 2007 the market rose sharply, and the return on the market portfolio was $r_M = 28\%$. Returns on the three stocks also increased: the return on H soared to 42 percent; the return on A reached 28 percent, the same as the market; and the return on L increased to only 21 percent. In 2008 the market dropped, with the market return falling to $r_M = -14\%$. The three stocks' returns also fell, H plunging to −42 percent, A falling to −14 percent, and L declining to 0 percent. As you can see, all three stocks moved in the same direction as the market, but H was by far the most volatile; A was just as volatile as the market; and L was less volatile than the market.

The beta coefficient measures a stock's volatility relative to an average stock (or the market), which has β = 1.0. We can calculate a stock's beta by plotting a line like those shown in Figure 8-9. The slopes of these lines show how each stock moves in response to a movement in the general market. Indeed, *the slope coefficient of such a "regression line" is defined as a beta coefficient.* Betas for literally thousands of companies are calculated and published by Merrill Lynch, Value Line, and numerous other organizations. Table 8-4 provides the beta coefficients for some well-known companies. Most stocks have betas in the range of 0.50 to 1.50, and the average for all stocks is 1.0 by definition.[8]

**beta coefficient, β**
A measure of the extent to which the returns on a given stock move with the stock market.

---

[8]In theory, betas can be negative. For example, if a stock's returns tend to rise when those of other stocks decline, and vice versa, then the regression line in a graph such as Figure 8-9 will have a downward slope, and the beta will be negative. Note, however, that few stocks have negative betas. Payco American, the collection agency company, might have a negative beta.

FIGURE 8-9    Relative Volatility of Stocks H, A, and L

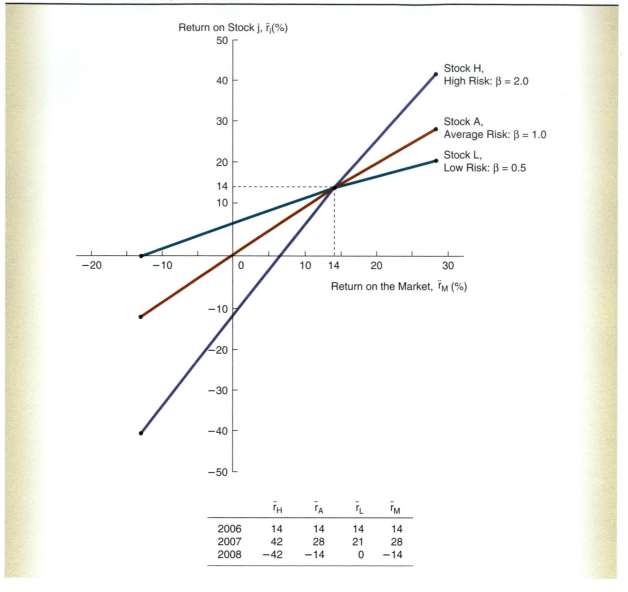

| | $\ddot{r}_H$ | $\ddot{r}_A$ | $\ddot{r}_L$ | $\ddot{r}_M$ |
|---|---|---|---|---|
| 2006 | 14 | 14 | 14 | 14 |
| 2007 | 42 | 28 | 21 | 28 |
| 2008 | −42 | −14 | 0 | −14 |

If we add a higher-than-average-beta stock ($\beta > 1.0$) to an average-beta ($\beta = 1.0$) portfolio, then the beta, and consequently the riskiness, of the portfolio will increase. Conversely, if we add a lower-than-average-beta stock ($\beta < 1.0$) to an average-risk portfolio, the portfolio's beta and risk will decline. *Thus, because a stock's beta measures its contribution to the riskiness of a portfolio, theoretically beta is the correct measure of the stock's riskiness.*

We can summarize our discussion to this point as follows:

1. A stock's risk consists of two components: *market risk* and *firm-specific risk*.

2. *Firm-specific risk* can be eliminated through diversification. Most investors do diversify, either by holding large portfolios or by purchasing shares in mutual funds. We are left, then, with *market risk*, which is caused by general movements in the stock market and which reflects the fact that most stocks

**TABLE 8-4**   Beta Coefficients for Selected Companies

| Company | Beta | Industry/Product |
|---------|------|------------------|
| **I. Above Average Market Risk: β > 1.0** | | |
| Nortel Networks Corporation | 4.18 | Communications equipment; telephone equipment |
| Yahoo! Inc. | 3.40 | Computer services/global Internet communications |
| E*TRADE Group Inc. | 2.87 | Investment services/online financial services |
| Sun Microsystems | 2.80 | Computers and peripherals |
| eBay | 1.76 | Retail (specialty nonapparel)/web-based auction |
| **II. Average Market Risk: β ≈ 1.0** | | |
| Dow Jones & Company | 1.02 | Publishing and printing (newspapers) |
| Ryland Group | 1.01 | Home building |
| Scotts Corporation | 0.99 | Pesticide, fertilizer, and agricultural chemicals |
| Krispy Kreme | 0.99 | Snack and nonalcoholic beverage bars |
| Toyota Motor Corporation | 0.99 | Auto and truck manufacturer |
| **III. Below Average Market Risk: β < 1.0** | | |
| Barnes & Noble | 0.75 | Specialty retailing; bookstores |
| Kroger Company | 0.50 | Food retailing; supermarkets |
| Walgreen Company | 0.28 | Retail drugs; pharmacies and drugstores |
| Gillette Company | 0.28 | Personal and household products |
| Progress Energy | 0.17 | Electric utilities; electric power generation |

**Source:** *Standard & Poor's Research Insight, 2006.*

are systematically affected by major economic events such as war, recessions, and inflation. Market risk is the only risk that is relevant to a rational, diversified investor because he or she should already have eliminated firm-specific risk.

3. Investors must be compensated for bearing risk. That is, *the greater the riskiness of a stock, the higher its required return.* Such compensation is required only for risk that cannot be eliminated by diversification. If risk premiums existed on stocks with high diversifiable risk, well-diversified investors would start buying these securities and bidding up their prices, and their final (equilibrium) expected returns would reflect only nondiversifiable market risk.

An example might help clarify this point. Suppose half of Stock A's risk is market risk (it occurs because Stock A moves up and down with the market). The other half of Stock A's risk is diversifiable. You hold only Stock A, so you are exposed to all of its risk. As compensation for bearing so much risk, *you want* a risk premium of 8 percent higher than the 5 percent Treasury bond rate. That is, you demand a return of 13 percent (= 5% + 8%) from this investment. But suppose other investors, including your professor, are well diversified; they also hold Stock A, but they have eliminated its diversifiable risk and thus are exposed to only half as much risk as you are. Consequently, their risk premium will be only half as large as yours, and they will *require* a return of only 9 percent (= 5% + 4%) to invest in the stock.

If the stock actually yielded more than 9 percent in the market, other investors, including your professor, would buy it. If it yielded the 13 percent you demand, you would be willing to buy the stock, but the well-diversified investors would compete with you for its acquisition.

They would bid its price up and its yield down, which would keep you from getting the stock at the return you need to compensate you for taking on its *total risk*. In the end, you would have to accept a 9 percent return or else keep your money in the bank. Thus, risk premiums in a market populated with *rational* investors—that is, those who diversify—will reflect only market risk.

4. The market (systematic) risk of a stock is measured by its *beta coefficient*, which is an index of the stock's relative volatility. Some benchmark values for beta follow:

$\beta = 0.5$: The stock's relevant risk is only half as volatile, or risky, as the average stock.

$\beta = 1.0$: The stock's relevant risk is of average risk.

$\beta = 2.0$: The stock's relevant risk is twice as volatile as the average stock.

5. *Because a stock's beta coefficient determines how the stock affects the riskiness of a diversified portfolio, beta ($\beta$) is a better measure of a stock's relevant risk than is standard deviation ($\sigma$), which measures total, or standalone, risk.*

## Portfolio Beta Coefficients

A portfolio consisting of low-beta securities will itself have a low beta because the beta of any set of securities is a weighted average of the individual securities' betas:

**8–8**

$$\text{Portfolio beta} = \beta_p = w_1\beta_1 + w_2\beta_2 + \cdots + w_N\beta_N$$

$$= \sum_{j=1}^{N} w_j\beta_j$$

Here $\beta_P$, the beta of the portfolio, reflects how volatile the portfolio is in relation to the market; $w_j$ is the fraction of the portfolio invested in the jth stock; and $\beta_j$ is the beta coefficient of the jth stock. For example, if an investor holds a $105,000 portfolio consisting of $35,000 invested in each of three stocks, and each of the stocks has a beta of 0.7, then the portfolio's beta will be $\beta_{P1} = 0.7$:

$$\beta_{P1} = (1/3)(0.7) + (1/3)(0.7) + (1/3)(0.7) = 0.7$$

Such a portfolio will be less risky than the market, which means it should experience relatively narrow price swings and demonstrate relatively small rate-of-return fluctuations. When graphed in a fashion similar to Figure 8-9 , the slope of its regression line would be 0.7, which is less than that for a portfolio of average stocks.

Now suppose one of the existing stocks is sold and replaced by a stock with $\beta_j = 2.5$. This action will increase the riskiness of the portfolio from $\beta_{P1} = 0.7$ to $\beta_{P2} = 1.3$:

$$\beta_{P2} = (1/3)(0.7) + (1/3)(0.7) + (1/3)(2.5) = 1.3$$

Had a stock with $\beta_j = 0.4$ been added, the portfolio beta would have declined from 0.7 to 0.6. Adding a low-beta stock, therefore, would reduce the riskiness of the portfolio.

## Self-Test Questions

Explain the following statement: "A stock held as part of a portfolio is generally less risky than the same stock held in isolation."

What is meant by perfect positive correlation, by perfect negative correlation, and by zero correlation?

In general, can we reduce the riskiness of a portfolio to zero by increasing the number of stocks in the portfolio? Explain.

What is meant by diversifiable risk and nondiversifiable risk? What is an average-risk stock?

Why is beta the theoretically correct measure of a stock's riskiness?

If you plotted the returns on a particular stock versus those on the Dow Jones Industrial Average index over the past five years, what would the slope of the line you obtained indicate about the stock's risk?

Suppose you have a portfolio that includes two stocks. You invested 60 percent of your total funds in a stock that has a beta equal to 3.0 and the remaining 40 percent of your funds in a stock that has a beta equal to 0.5. What is the portfolio's beta? (*Answer:* 2.0)

# THE RELATIONSHIP BETWEEN RISK AND RATES OF RETURN (CAPM)

In the preceding section, we saw that beta is the appropriate measure of a stock's relevant risk. Now we must specify the relationship between risk and return. For a given level of beta, what rate of return will investors require on a stock to compensate them for assuming the risk? To determine an investment's required rate of return, we use a *theoretical* model called the **Capital Asset Pricing Model (CAPM).** The CAPM shows how the relevant risk of an investment as measured by its beta coefficient is used to determine the investment's appropriate required rate of return.

Let's begin by defining the following terms:

$\hat{r}_j$ = *Expected* rate of return on the jth stock; is based on the probability distribution for the stock's returns.

$r_j$ = *Required* rate of return on the jth stock; $r_j$ is the rate that *investors demand* for investing in Stock j. If $\hat{r}_j < r_j$, you would not purchase this stock, or you would sell it if you owned it; if $\hat{r}_j > r_j$, you would want to buy the stock; and, you would be indifferent if $\hat{r}_j = r_j$.

$r_{RF}$ = Risk-free rate of return. In this context, $r_{RF}$ is generally measured by the return on long-term U.S. Treasury securities.

$\beta_j$ = Beta coefficient of the jth stock. The beta of an average stock is $\beta_A = 1.0$.

$r_M$ = Required rate of return on a portfolio consisting of all stocks, which is the market portfolio. $r_M$ is also the required rate of return on an average ($\beta_A = 1.0$) stock.

**Capital Asset Pricing Model (CAPM)**
A model used to determine the required return on an asset, which is based on the proposition that any asset's return should be equal to the risk-free return plus a risk premium that reflects the asset's nondiversifiable risk.

$$RP_M = (r_M - r_{RF}) =$$ Market risk premium. This is the additional return above the risk-free rate required to compensate an average investor for assuming an average amount of risk ($\beta_A = 1.0$).

$$RP_j = (r_M - r_{RF})\beta_j =$$ Risk premium on the jth stock $= (RP_M)\beta_j$. The stock's risk premium is less than, equal to, or greater than the premium on an average stock, depending on whether its relevant risk as measured by beta is less than, equal to, or greater than an average stock, respectively. If $\beta_j = \beta_A = 1.0$, then $RP_j = RP_M$; if $\beta_j > 1.0$, then $RP_j > RP_M$; and, if $\beta_j < 1.0$, then $RP_j < RP_M$.

**market risk premium (RP$_M$)**
The additional return over the risk-free rate needed to compensate investors for assuming an average amount of risk.

The **market risk premium (RP$_M$)** depends on the degree of aversion that investors on average have to risk.[9] Let's assume that at the current time, Treasury bonds yield $r_{RF} = 5\%$ and an average share of stock has a required return of $r_M = 11\%$. In this case, the market risk premium is 6 percent:

$$RP_M = r_M - r_{RF} = 11\% - 5\% = 6\%$$

It follows that if one stock is twice as risky as another, its *risk premium* should be twice as high. Conversely, if a stock's *relevant* risk is only half as much as that of another stock, its *risk premium* should be half as large. Furthermore, we can measure a stock's relevant risk by finding its beta coefficient. Therefore, if we know the market risk premium, $RP_M$, and the stock's risk as measured by its beta coefficient, $\beta_j$, we can find its risk premium as the product $RP_M \times \beta_j$. For example, if $\beta_j = 0.5$ and $RP_M = 6\%$, then $RP_j$ is 3 percent:

**8–9**
$$\text{Risk premium for stock } j = RP_M \times \beta_j$$

$$= 6\% \times 0.5 = 3.0\%$$

As Figure 8-4 shows, the required return for any investment j can be expressed in general terms as

**8–10**
$$\text{Required return} = \text{Risk-free return} + \text{Premium for risk}$$
$$r_j = r_{RF} + RP_j$$

Based on our previous discussion, Equation 8–10 can also be written as

**8–11**
$$r_j = r_{RF} + (RP_M)\beta_j = \text{Capital Assest Pricing Model (CAPM)}$$
$$= r_{RF} + (r_M - r_{RF})\beta_j$$

$$= 5\% + (11\% - 5\%)(0.5)$$
$$= 5\% + 6\%(0.5) = 8\%$$

---

[9]This concept, as well as other aspects of CAPM, is discussed in more detail in Chapter 3 of Eugene F. Brigham and Phillip R. Daves, *Intermediate Financial Management*, 9th ed. (Cincinnati, OH: South-Western College Publishing, 2007). Note that we cannot measure the risk premium of an average stock, $RP_M = r_M - r_{RF}$, with great precision because we cannot possibly obtain precise values for the expected future return on the market, $r_M$. Empirical studies suggest that where long-term U.S. Treasury bonds are used to measure $r_{RF}$ and where $r_M$ is an estimate of the expected return on the S&P 500, the market risk premium varies somewhat from year to year. It has generally ranged from 4 to 8 percent during the past 20 years. Chapter 3 of *Intermediate Financial Management* also discusses the assumptions embodied in the CAPM framework. Some of the assumptions of the CAPM theory are unrealistic. As a consequence, the theory does not hold exactly.

**Figure 8-10**    The Security Market Line (SML)

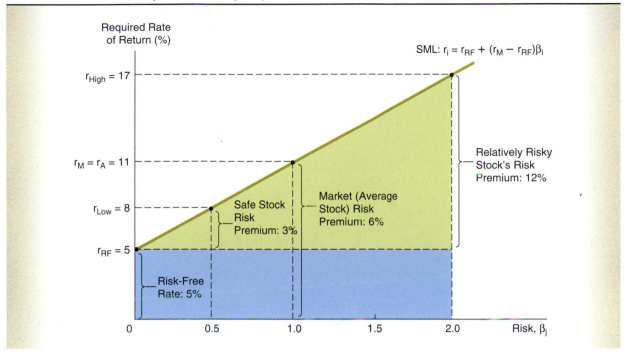

Equation 8–11, which is the CAPM equation for equilibrium pricing, is called the **security market line (SML).**

If some other stock were riskier than Stock j and had $\beta_{j2} = 2.0$, then its required rate of return would be 17 percent:

$$r_{j2} = 5\% + (6\%)2.0 = 17\%$$

An average stock, with $\beta = 1.0$, would have a required return of 11 percent, the same as the market return:

$$r_A = 5\% + (6\%)1.0 = 11\% = r_M$$

Equation 8–11 (the SML equation) is often expressed in graph form. Figure 8-10, for example, shows the SML when $r_{RF} = 5\%$ and $r_M = 11\%$. Note the following points:

1. *Required rates of return* are shown on the vertical axis, and risk (as measured by beta) is shown on the horizontal axis. This graph is quite different from the one shown in Figure 8-9, in which the returns on individual stocks are plotted on the vertical axis and returns on the market index are shown on the horizontal axis. The slopes of the three lines in Figure 8-9 represent the three stocks' betas. In Figure 8-10, these three betas are plotted as points on the horizontal axis.

2. Risk-free securities have $\beta_j = 0$; therefore, $r_{RF}$ appears as the vertical axis intercept in Figure 8-10.

3. The slope of the SML reflects the degree of risk aversion in the economy. The greater the average investor's aversion to risk, (a) the steeper the slope of the line, (b) the greater the risk premium for any stock, and (c) the higher the

**security market line (SML)**
The line that shows the relationship between risk as measured by beta and the required rate of return for individual securities.

**FIGURE 8-11**    Shift in the SML Caused by a 2 Percent Increase in Inflation

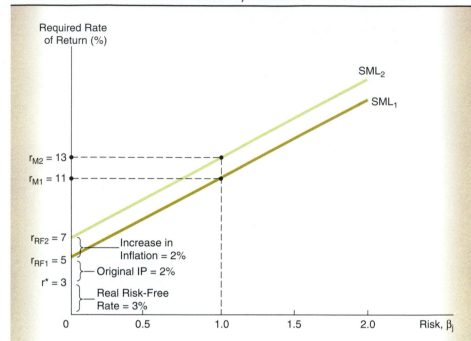

required rate of return on stocks.[10] These points are discussed further in a later section.

4. The values we worked out for stocks with $\beta_j = 0.5$, $\beta_j = 1.0$, and $\beta_j = 2.0$ agree with the values shown on the graph for $r_{Low}$, $r_A$, and $r_{High}$.

Both the SML and a company's position on it change over time because of changes in interest rates, investors' risk aversion, and individual companies' betas. Such changes are discussed in the following sections.

## The Impact of Inflation

As we learned in Chapter 5, interest amounts to "rent" on borrowed money, or the price of money. In essence, then, $r_{RF}$ is the price of money to a risk-free borrower. We also learned in Chapter 5 that the risk-free rate as measured by the rate on U.S. Treasury securities is called the *nominal*, or *quoted*, rate, and it consists of two elements: (1) a *real inflation-free rate of return*, $r^*$, and (2) *an inflation premium, IP*, equal to the anticipated average rate of inflation.[11] Thus, $r_{RF} = r^* + IP$.

If the expected rate of inflation rose by 2 percent, $r_{RF}$ would also increase by 2 percent. Figure 8-11 illustrates the effects of such a change. Notice that under the CAPM, the increase in $r_{RF}$ also causes an *equal increase in the rate of return on all*

---

[10]Students sometimes confuse beta with the slope of the SML. This is a mistake. The slope of any line is equal to the "rise" divided by the "run," or $(y_1 - y_0)/(x_1 - x_0)$. Consider Figure 8-10. If we let $y = r$ and $x = \beta$, and we go from the origin to $\beta_M = 1.0$, we see that the slope is $(r_M - r_{RF})/(\beta_M - \beta_{RF}) = (11\% - 5\%)/(1 - 0) = 6\%$. Thus, the slope of the SML is equal to $(r_M - r_{RF})$, the market risk premium. In Figure 8-10, $r_j = 5\% + (6\%)\beta_j$, so a doubling of beta (for example, from 1.0 to 2.0) would produce an 8-percentage-point increase in $r_j$. In this case, the total risk premium on Stock j would double—that is, $RP_j = (8\%)2.0 = 16\%$.

[11]Long-term Treasury bonds also contain a maturity risk premium (MRP). Here we include the MRP in $r^*$ to simplify the discussion.

**FIGURE 8-12    Shift in the SML Caused by Increased Risk Aversion**

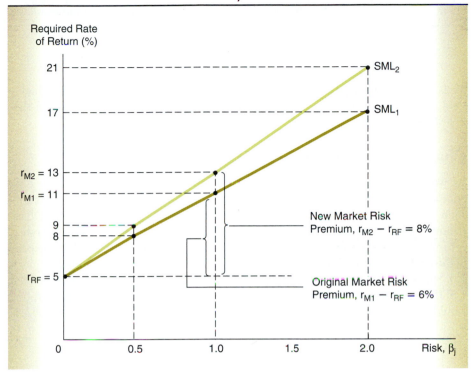

*risky assets* because the inflation premium is built into the required rate of return of both risk-free and risky assets.[12] For example, the risk-free return increases from 5 percent to 7 percent, and the rate of return on an average stock, $r_M$, increases from 11 percent to 13 percent. Thus, all securities' returns increase by 2 percentage points.

## Changes in Risk Aversion

The slope of the security market line reflects the extent to which investors are averse to risk. The steeper the slope of the line, the greater the average investor's risk aversion. If investors were *indifferent* to risk, and if $r_{RF}$ was 5 percent, then risky assets would also provide an expected return of 5 percent. If there was no risk aversion, there would be no risk premium, so the SML would be horizontal. *As risk aversion increases, so does the risk premium* and, therefore, so does the slope of the SML.

Figure 8-12 illustrates an increase in risk aversion. In this case, the *market* risk premium increases from 6 percent to 8 percent, and $r_M$ increases from $r_{M1} = 11\%$ to $r_{M2} = 13\%$. The returns on other risky assets also rise, with the effect of this shift in risk aversion being *more pronounced on riskier securities*. For example, the required return on a stock with $\beta_j = 0.5$ increases by only 1 percentage point, from 8 percent to 9 percent. By comparison, the required return on a stock with $\beta_j = 2.0$ increases by

---

[12]Recall that the inflation premium for any asset is equal to the average expected rate of inflation over the life of the asset. In this analysis, we must therefore assume either that all securities plotted on the SML graph have the same life or that the expected rate of future inflation is constant.

Also note that $r_{RF}$ in a CAPM analysis can be proxied by either a long-term rate (the T-bond rate) or a short-term rate (the T-bill rate). Traditionally, the T-bill rate was used, but a movement toward use of the T-bond rate has occurred in recent years because a closer relationship exists between T-bond yields and stocks than between T-bill yields and stocks. See *Stocks, Bonds, Bills, and Inflation, 2006 Yearbook* (Chicago: Ibbotson & Associates, 2007) for a discussion.

4 percentage points, from 17 percent to 21 percent. Because $\Delta RP_j = \Delta RP_M(\beta_j) = (13\% - 11\%)\beta_j = (2\%)\beta_j$, the changes in these risk premiums are computed as follows:

1. if $\beta_j = 0.5, \Delta RP_j = (2\%)0.5 = 1\%$

2. if $\beta j = 2.0, \Delta RP j = (2\%)2.0 = 4\%$

Thus, when the average investor's aversion to risk changes, investments with higher beta coefficients experience greater changes in their required rates of return than investments with lower betas.

## Changes in a Stock's Beta Coefficient

As we will see later in this book, a firm can affect its beta risk by changing the composition of its assets and by modifying its use of debt financing. External factors, such as increased competition within a firm's industry or the expiration of basic patents, can also alter a company's beta. When such changes occur, the required rate of return, r, changes as well, and, as we saw in Chapter 7, this change will affect the price of the firm's stock. For example, consider Genesco Manufacturing, with a beta equal to 1.0. Suppose some action occurred that caused this firm's beta to increase from 1.0 to 1.5. If the conditions depicted in Figure 8-10 held, Genesco's required rate of return would increase from

$$r_1 = r_{RF} + (r_M - r_{RF})\beta_j$$
$$= 5\% + (11\% - 5\%)1.0 = 11\%$$

to

$$r_2 = 5\% + (11\% - 5\%)1.5 = 14\%$$

Any change that affects the required rate of return on a security, such as a change in its beta coefficient or in expected inflation, will affect the price of the security.

## A Word of Caution

A word of caution about betas and the CAPM is in order here. First, the model was developed under very restrictive assumptions. Some of the assumptions include the following: (1) all investors have the same information, which leads to the same expectations about future stock prices; (2) everyone can borrow and lend at the risk-free rate of return; (3) stocks (or other security) can be purchased in any denomination or fraction of shares; and (4) taxes and transaction costs (commissions) do not exist.

Second, the entire theory is based on *ex ante*, or *expected*, conditions, yet we have available only *ex post*, or *past*, data. The betas we calculate show how volatile a stock has been in the past, but conditions could certainly change. The stock's *future volatility*, which is the item of real concern to investors, might therefore differ quite dramatically from its past volatility.

Although the CAPM represents a significant step forward in security pricing theory, it does have some potentially serious deficiencies when applied in practice. As a consequence, estimates of $r_j$ found through use of the SML might be subject to considerable error. For this reason, many investors and analysts use the CAPM and the concept of $\beta$ to provide "ballpark" figures for further analysis. The concept that investors should be rewarded only for taking relevant risk makes sense. And the CAPM provides an easy way to get a rough estimate of the relevant risk and the appropriate required rate of return of an investment.

## Self-Test Questions

Differentiate between the expected rate of return ($\hat{r}$) and the required rate of return (r) on a stock. Which would have to be larger to persuade you to buy the stock?

What are the differences between the relative volatility graph (Figure 8-9), in which "betas are made," and the SML graph (Figure 8-10), in which "betas are used"? Consider the methods of constructing the graphs and the purposes for which they were developed.

What happens to the SML graph (1) when inflation increases or (2) when inflation decreases?

What happens to the SML graph (1) when risk aversion increases or (2) when risk aversion decreases? What would the SML look like if investors were indifferent to risk—that is, had zero risk aversion?

How can a firm influence its market, or beta, risk?

Stock F has a beta coefficient equal to 1.2. If the risk-free rate of return equals 4 percent and the expected market return equals 10 percent, what is Stock F's required rate of return? (*Answer:* $r_F = 11.2\%$)

## STOCK MARKET EQUILIBRIUM

Based on our previous discussion, we know that we can use the CAPM to find the *required return* for an investment (say, Stock Q), which we designate as $r_Q$. Suppose the risk-free return is 5 percent, the market *risk premium* is 6 percent, and Stock Q has a beta of 1.5 ($\beta_Q = 1.5$). In this case, the marginal, or average, investor will require a return of 14 percent on Stock Q:

$$r_A = 5\% + 6\%(1.5) = 14\%$$

This 14 percent return is shown as a point Q on the SML in Figure 8-13.

The average investor will want to buy Stock Q if the expected rate of return exceeds 14 percent, will want to sell it if the expected rate of return is less than 14 percent, and will be indifferent (and therefore will hold but not buy or sell Stock Q) if the expected rate of return is exactly 14 percent. Now suppose the investor's portfolio contains Stock Q, and he or she analyzes the stock's prospects and concludes that its earnings, dividends, and price can be expected to grow at a constant rate of 4 percent per year forever. The last dividend paid was $D_0 = \$3$, so the next expected dividend is

$$\hat{D}_1 = \$3.00(1.04) = \$3.12$$

Our "average" (marginal) investor observes that the current price of the stock, $P_0$, is $34.67. Should he or she purchase more of Stock Q, sell the current holdings, or maintain the current position?

Recall from Chapter 7 that we can calculate Stock Q's *expected rate of return* as follows (see Equation 7–6):

$$\hat{r}_Q = \frac{\hat{D}_1}{P_0} + g = \frac{\$3.12}{\$34.67} + 0.04 = 0.09 + 0.04 = 0.13 = 13\%$$

**FIGURE 8-13   Expected and Required Returns on Stock Q**

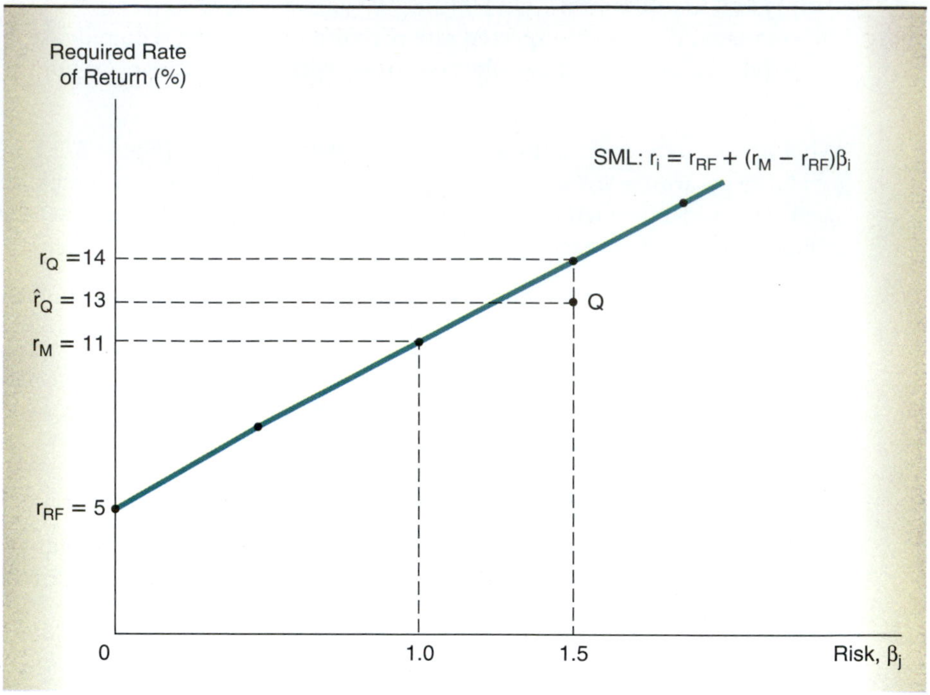

This value is plotted on Figure 8-13 as Point Q, which is below the SML. Because the expected rate of return, $\hat{r}_Q = 13\%$, is less than the required return, $r_Q = 14\%$, this marginal investor would want to sell the stock, as would other holders. Because few people would want to buy at the $34.67 price, the current owners would be unable to find buyers unless they cut the price of the stock. The price would therefore decline, and this decline would continue until the stock's price reaches $31.20. At that point, the market for this security would be in **equilibrium** because the expected rate of return, 14 percent, would be equal to the required rate of return:

**equilibrium**
The condition under which the expected return on a security is just equal to its required return, $\hat{r} = r$, and the price is stable.

$$\hat{r}_Q = \frac{\$3.12}{\$31.20} + 0.04 = 0.10 + 0.04 = 0.14 = 14\%$$

Had the stock initially sold for less than $31.20—say, $28.36—events would have been reversed. Investors would have wanted to buy the stock because its expected rate of return ($\hat{r} = 15\%$) would have exceeded its required rate of return, and buy orders would have driven the stock's price up to $31.20.

To summarize, two conditions must hold in equilibrium:

1. The expected rate of return as seen by the marginal investor must equal the required rate of return: $\hat{r}_j = r_j$.

2. The actual market price of the stock must equal its intrinsic value as estimated by the marginal investor: $P_0 = \hat{P}_0$.

Of course, some individual investors might believe that $\hat{r}_j > r_j$ and $\hat{P}_0 > P_0$ hence they would invest most of their funds in the stock. Other investors might ascribe to the opposite view and sell all of their shares. Nevertheless, it is the marginal investor who establishes the actual market price. For this investor, $\hat{r}_j = r_j$ and $P_0 = \hat{P}_0$. If these conditions do not hold, trading will occur until they do hold.

**Self-Test Questions**

When a stock is in equilibrium, what two conditions must hold?

If a stock is not in equilibrium, explain how financial markets adjust to bring it into equilibrium.

Suppose Porter Pottery's stock currently sells for $32. The company, which is growing at a constant rate, expects its next dividend to equal $3.20. Analysts have determined that the market value of the stock is currently in equilibrium and that investors require a rate of return equal to 14 percent to purchase the stock. If the price of the stock increases to $35.56 tomorrow after Porter's year-end financial statements are made public, what is the stock's expected return? Assume that the company's growth rate remains constant. (*Answer:* 13%)

## DIFFERENT TYPES OF RISK

In Chapter 5, we introduced the concept of risk in our discussion of interest rates, or the cost of money. At that point, we stated that the nominal, or quoted, rate of return, r, can be written as follows:

$$\text{Rate of return (interest)} = r = \text{Risk-free rate} + \text{Risk premium}$$
$$= \quad r_{RF} \quad + \quad RP$$
$$= \quad [r^* + IP] \quad + [DRP + LP + MRP]$$

Remember that here

     $r$ = Quoted, or *nominal*, rate of interest on a given security. There are many different securities, hence many different quoted interest rates.

  $r_{RF}$ = Nominal risk-free rate of return.

    $r^*$ = Real risk-free rate of interest, which is the interest rate that would exist on a security with a *guaranteed* payoff if inflation is expected to be zero during the investment period.

    $IP$ = Inflation premium, which equals the average inflation rate expected over the life of the security.

 $DRP$ = Default risk premium, which reflects the chance that the borrower will not pay the debt's interest or principal on time.

   $LP$ = Liquidity, or marketability, premium, which reflects the fact that some investments are more easily converted into cash on a short notice at a "reasonable price" than are other securities.

 $MRP$ = Maturity risk premium, which accounts for the fact that longer-term bonds experience greater price reactions to interest rate changes than do short-term bonds.

    The discussion in Chapter 5 presented an overall view of interest rates and general factors that affect these rates. But we did not discuss risk evaluation in detail; rather, we described some of the factors that determine the total risk associated with debt, such as default risk, liquidity risk, and maturity risk. In reality, these risks also affect other types of investments, including equity. Equity does not represent a legal contract that requires the firm to pay defined amounts of dividends at particular times or to "act" in specific ways. There is, however, an expectation that positive returns will be generated through future distributions of cash because dividends will be paid, capital gains will be generated through growth, or both. Investors also expect the firm to behave "appropriately." If these expectations are not met, investors generally consider the firm in "default" of their expectations. In such cases, as long as no laws have been broken, stockholders generally do not have legal recourse, as would be the case for a default on debt. As a result, investors penalize the firm by selling their stock holdings, which causes the value of the firm's stock to decline.

In this chapter, we build on the general concept that was introduced in Chapter 5 by showing how the risk premium associated with any investment should be determined (at least in theory). The basis of our discussion is Equation 5–3, which we develop further in this chapter as follows:

$$r_j = \text{Risk-free rate} + \text{Risk premium}$$
$$= \quad r_{RF} \quad + \quad (r_M - r_{RF})\beta_j = \text{CAPM}$$

According to the CAPM, investors should not expect to be rewarded for all of the risk associated with an investment—that is, its total, or stand-alone, risk—because some risk can be eliminated through diversification. The *relevant risk*, and thus the risk for which investors should be compensated, is that portion of the total risk that cannot be "diversified away." Thus, in this chapter we show the following:

$$
\begin{aligned}
\text{Total risk} = \sigma &= \text{Systematic risk} && + \text{Unsystematic risk} \\
&= \text{Market(economic)risk} && + \text{Firm-specific risk} \\
&= \text{Nondiversifiable risk} && + \text{Diversifiable risk} \\
&= \text{Cannot be eliminated} && + \text{Can be eliminated} \\
\text{Relevant risk} &= \text{Nondiversifiable risk} && + \sout{\text{Diversifiable risk}}\,(\text{eliminated}) \\
&= \text{Systematic risk}
\end{aligned}
$$

Systematic risk is represented by an investment's beta coefficient, $\beta$, in Equation 8–11.

The specific types and sources of risk to which a firm or an investor is exposed are numerous and vary considerably depending on the situation. A detailed discussion of all the different types of risks and the techniques used to evaluate risks is beyond the scope of this book. But you should recognize that risk is an important factor in the determination of the required rate of return (r), which, according to the following equation, is one of the two variables we need to determine the value of an asset:

$$\text{Value} = \frac{\hat{CF}_1}{(1+r)^1} + \frac{\hat{CF}_2}{(1+r)^2} + \cdots + \frac{\hat{CF}_n}{(1+r)^n} = \sum_{t=1}^{n} \frac{\hat{CF}_t}{(1+r)^t}$$

This equation was first introduced in Chapter 1, and it was discussed in greater detail in Chapter 6 and Chapter 7. What is important to understand here is that the value of an asset, which could be a stock or a bond, is based on the cash flows that the asset is expected to generate during its life and the rate of return investors require to "put up" their money to purchase the investment. In this chapter, we provide you with an indication as to how the required rate of return, r, should be determined, and we show that investors demand higher rates of return to compensate them for taking greater amounts of "relevant" risks.

Because it is an important concept and has a direct effect on value, we will continue to discuss risk in the remainder of the book. Although there are instances in which the discussions focus on the risk to which investors are exposed, most of the discussions

**TABLE 8-5**   Different Types (Sources) of Risk

| General Type of Risk | Name of Risk | Brief Description |
|---|---|---|
| **I. Systematic risks** (nondiversifiable risk; market risk; relevant risk) | Interest rate risk | When interest rates change, (1) the values of investments change (in opposite directions) and (2) the rate at which funds can be reinvested also changes (in the same direction). |
| | Inflation risk | The primary reason short-term interest rates change is because investors change their expectations about future inflation. |
| | Maturity risk | Long-term investments experience greater price reactions to interest rate changes than do short-term bonds. |
| | Liquidity risk | Reflects the fact that some investments are more easily converted into cash on a short notice at a "reasonable price" than are other securities. |
| | Exchange rate risk | Multinational firms deal with different currencies; the rate at which the currency of one country can be *exchanged* into the currency of another country—that is, the exchange rate—changes as market conditions change. |
| | Political risk | Any action by a government that reduces the value of an investment. |
| **II. Unsystematic risks** (diversifiable risk; firm-specific risk) | Business risk | Risk that would be inherent in the firm's operations if it used no debt—factors such as labor conditions, product safety, quality of management, competitive conditions, and so forth, affect firm-specific risk. |
| | Financial risk | Risk associated with how the firm is financed—that is, its credit risk. |
| | Default risk | Part of financial risk—the chance that the firm will not be able to service its existing debt. |
| **III. Combined risks** (some systematic risk and some unsystematic risk) | Total risk | The combination of systematic risk and unsystematic risk; also referred to as stand-alone risk, because this is the risk an investor takes if he or she purchases only one investment, which is tantamount to "putting all your eggs into one basket." |
| | Corporate risk | The riskiness of the firm without considering the effect of stockholder diversification; based on the combination of assets held by the firm (inventory, accounts receivable, plant and equipment, and so forth). Some diversification exists because the firm's assets represent a portfolio of investments in real assets. |

focus on risks that affect corporations. Because we discuss different types of risk throughout the book, we thought it might be a good idea to summarize and describe these risks in brief terms. Table 8-5 shows the risks that are discussed in the book and indicates whether each risk is considered a component of systematic (nondiversifiable) or unsystematic (diversifiable) risk. Note that (1) this table oversimplifies risk analysis because some risks are not easily classified as either systematic or unsystematic, and (2) some of the risks included in the table will be discussed later in the book. Even so, this table should show the relationships among the different risks discussed in the book.

**Self-Test Question**

Classify default risk, maturity risk, and liquidity risk as either diversifiable or nondiversifiable risk.

## Chapter *Essentials*
### —The Answers

To summarize the key concepts, let's answer the questions that were posed at the beginning of the chapter:

- **What does it mean to take risk when investing?** In finance, risk is defined as the chance of receiving a return other than the one that is expected. Thus, an investment is considered risky if more than one outcome (payoff) is possible. Every *risky* investment has both "bad" risk—that is, the chance that it will return less than expected—and "good risk"—that is, the chance that it will return more than expected. In simple terms, risk can be defined (described) using one word: variability.

- **How are the risk and return of an investment measured? How are the risk and return of an investment related?** An investment's risk is measured by the variability of its possible payoffs (returns). Greater variability in returns indicates greater risk. Investors require higher returns to take on greater risks. Thus, generally speaking, investments with greater risks also have higher returns. The expected return of an investment is measured as a weighted average of all of the possible returns the investment can generate in the future, with the weights being the probability that the particular return will occur.

- **How can investors reduce risk?** Risk can be reduced through diversification. Investors achieve diversification by forming portfolios that contain numerous financial securities (perhaps stocks and bonds) that are not strongly related to each other. For example, an investor can form a well-diversified portfolio by purchasing the stocks of 40 or more companies in different industries, such as transportation, utilities, health care, entertainment, food services, and so forth. Total risk, which is equal to market (systematic) risk plus firm-specific (unsystematic) risk, can be reduced through diversification because little or no unsystematic risk should exist in a well-diversified investment portfolio.

- **For what type of risk is an average investor rewarded?** Investors should be rewarded only for risk that they must take. Because firm-specific, or unsystematic, risk can be reduced or eliminated through diversification, investors who do not diversify their investment portfolios should not be rewarded for taking such risk. Consequently, an investment's *relevant* risk is its systematic, or market, risk, which is the risk for which investors should be rewarded. Systematic risk cannot be reduced through diversification. An investment's "irrelevant" risk is its firm-specific, or unsystematic, risk because it is this portion of the total risk that can be eliminated (at least theoretically) through diversification.

- **What actions do investors take when the return they require to purchase an investment is different from the return the investment is expected to produce?** Investors will purchase a security only when its expected return, $\hat{r}$, is greater than its required return, r. When $\hat{r} < r$, investors will not purchase the security and those who own the security tend to sell it, which causes the security's price to decrease and its expected return to increase until $\hat{r} = r$.

## ETHICAL DILEMMA

### RIP—Retire in Peace

Retirement Investment Products (RIP) offers a full complement of retirement planning services and a diverse line of retirement investments that have varying degrees of risk. With the investment products available at RIP, investors could form retirement funds with any level of risk preferred, from risk free to extremely risky. RIP's reputation in the investment community is impeccable because the service agents who advise clients are required to fully inform their clients of the risk possibilities that exist for any investment position, whether it is recommended by an agent or requested by a client. Since 1950, RIP has built its investment portfolio of retirement funds to $60 billion, which makes it one of the largest providers of retirement funds in the United States.

You work for RIP as an investment analyst. One of your responsibilities is to help form recommendations for the retirement fund managers to evaluate when making investment decisions. Recently, Howard, a close friend from your college days who now works for SunCoast Investments, a large brokerage firm, called to tell you about a new investment that is expected to earn very high returns during the next few years. The investment is called a "Piggy-back Asset Investment Device," or PAID for short. Howard told you that he really does not know what this acronym means or how the investment is constructed, but all the reports he has read indicate PAIDs should be a hot investment in the future, so the returns should be very handsome for those who get in now. The one piece of information he did offer was that a PAID is a rather complex investment that consists of a combination of securities whose values are based on numerous debt instruments issued by government agencies, including the Federal National Mortgage Association, the Federal Home Loan Bank, and so on. Howard made it clear that he would like you to consider recommending to RIP that PAIDs be purchased through SunCoast Investments. The commissions from such a deal would bail him and his family out of a financial crisis that resulted because they had bad luck with their investments in the 2001 financial markets. Howard has indicated that somehow he would reward you if RIP invests in PAIDs through SunCoast because, in his words, "You would literally be saving my life." You told Howard you would think about it and call him back.

Further investigation into PAIDs has yielded little additional information beyond what previously was provided by Howard. The new investment is intriguing because its expected return is extremely high compared with similar investments. Earlier this morning, you called Howard to quiz him a little more about the return expectations and to try to get an idea concerning the riskiness of PAIDs. Howard was unable to adequately explain the risk associated with the investment, although he reminded you that the debt of U.S. government agencies is involved. As he says, "How much risk is there with government agencies?"

The PAIDs are very enticing because RIP can attract more clients if it can increase the return offered on its investments. If you recommend the new investment and the higher returns pan out, you will earn a very sizable commission. In addition, you will be helping Howard out of his financial situation because his commissions will be substantial if the PAIDs are purchased through SunCoast Investments. Should you recommend the PAIDs as an investment?

The concepts presented in this chapter should help you to better understand the relationship between investment risk and return, which is an important concept in finance. If you understand the basic concepts we discussed, you should be able to construct an investment portfolio that has the level of risk with which you are comfortable.

**What important principles should I remember from this chapter when investing?** First, remember that risk and return are positively related. As a result, in most cases, when you are offered an investment that promises to pay a high return, you should conclude that the investment has high risk. When considering possible investments, *never* separate "risk" and "return"—that is, do not consider the return of an investment without also considering its risk. Second, remember that you can reduce some investment risk through diversification, which can be achieved by purchasing different investments that are not highly positively related to each other. In many instances, you can reduce risk without reducing the expected rate of return associated with your investment position.

**How can I diversify if I don't have enough money to purchase 40 different securities?** Mutual funds, which we briefly discussed in Chapter 3, provide investors with the opportunity to diversify their investment positions because these

**Chapter *Essentials***
—Personal Finance

investments consist of large portfolios often containing more than 50 to 100 securities that are well diversified. Many types of mutual funds with various investment objectives exist. Shares in most mutual funds can be purchased for as little as $500; thus, you don't have to be rich to diversify. Individuals are well advised to follow an old adage when investing: "Don't put all your eggs in one basket."

**How can I use the concepts presented in the chapter to construct a portfolio that has a level of risk with which I am comfortable?** Remember that (1) a stock's (investment's) beta coefficient gives a measure of its "relevant" risk, and (2) a portfolio's beta equals the weighted average of the betas of all of the investments contained in the portfolio. Thus, if you can determine their beta coefficients, you can choose those investments that provide the risk level you prefer when they are combined to form a portfolio. If you prefer lower risk to higher risk, you should purchase investments with low betas, and vice versa. In addition, you can adjust the riskiness of your portfolio by adding or deleting stocks with particular risks—that is, to reduce a portfolio's risk, you can either add securities with low betas or delete from the portfolio (sell) securities with high betas. Beta coefficients for most large companies' stocks are easy to find—they are posted on numerous Internet sites, contained in various financial publications that are available in public libraries, published by investment organizations, and so forth.

**How can I determine the required and expected rates of return for an investment?** Many investors examine the past performance of an investment to determine its expected return. Care must be taken with this approach because past returns often do not reflect future returns. However, you might be able to get a rough idea as to what you expect a stock's long-term growth will be in the future by examining its past growth, especially if the firm is fairly stable. Investors also rely on information provided by professional analysts to form opinions about expected rates of return.

To determine an investment's required rate of return, investors often evaluate the performances of similar-risk investments. In addition, as we discussed in this chapter, some investors use the CAPM to get a "ballpark figure" for an investment's required rate of return. The beta coefficients for most large companies can be obtained from many sources, including the Internet; the risk-free rate of return can be estimated using the rates on existing Treasury securities; and the expected market return can be estimated by evaluating market returns in recent years, the current trend in the market, and predictions made by economists and investment analysts.

When investing your money, keep these words of wisdom in mind: "If you lose sleep over your investments or are more concerned with the performance of your portfolio than with your job, then your investment position probably is too risky." If you find yourself in such a position, use the concepts discussed in this chapter to adjust the riskiness of your portfolio.

## QUESTIONS

8-1   "The probability distribution of a less risky expected return is more peaked than that of a riskier return." Is this a correct statement? Explain.

8-2   What shape would the probability distribution have for (a) completely certain returns and (b) completely uncertain returns?

8-3   Give some events that affect the price of a stock that would result from unsystematic risk. What events would result from systematic risk? Explain.

8-4   Explain why systematic risk is the "relevant" risk of an investment and why investors should be rewarded only for this type of risk.

**8-5**  Security A has an expected return of 7 percent, a standard deviation of expected returns of 35 percent, a correlation coefficient with the market of −0.3, and a beta coefficient of −0.5. Security B has an expected return of 12 percent, a standard deviation of returns of 10 percent, a correlation coefficient with the market of 0.7, and a beta coefficient of 1.0. Which security is riskier? Why?

**8-6**  Suppose you owned a portfolio consisting of $250,000 of long-term U.S. government bonds.

  **a.** Would your portfolio be risk-free?

  **b.** Now suppose you hold a portfolio consisting of $250,000 of 30-day Treasury bills. Every 30 days your bills mature and you reinvest the principal ($250,000) in a new batch of bills. Assume that you live on the investment income from your portfolio and that you want to maintain a constant standard of living. Is your portfolio *truly* risk-free?

  **c.** Can you think of any asset that would be completely risk-free? Could someone develop such an asset? Explain.

**8-7**  A life insurance policy is a financial asset. The premiums paid represent the investment's cost.

  **a.** How would you calculate the expected return on a life insurance policy?

  **b.** Suppose the owner of a life insurance policy has no other financial assets—the person's only other asset is "human capital," or lifetime earnings capacity. What is the correlation coefficient between returns on the insurance policy and returns on the policyholder's human capital?

  **c.** Insurance companies have to pay administrative costs and sales representatives' commissions; hence, the expected rate of return on insurance premiums is generally low, or even negative. Use the portfolio concept to explain why people buy life insurance despite the negative expected returns.

**8-8**  If investors' aversion to risk increased, would the risk premium on a high-beta stock increase more or less than that on a low-beta stock? Explain.

**8-9**  Do you think it is possible to construct a portfolio of stocks that has an expected return that equals the risk-free rate of return?

**8-10**  Suppose the beta coefficient of a stock doubles from $\beta_1 = 1$ to $\beta_2 = 2$. Logic says that the required rate of return on the stock should also double. Is this logic correct? Explain.

## SELF-TEST PROBLEMS

*(Solutions appear in Appendix B at the end of the book.)*

**ST-1**  Define the following terms, using graphs or equations to illustrate your answers whenever feasible:  **key terms**

  **a.** Risk; probability distribution

  **b.** Expected rate of return, $\hat{r}$; required rate of return, r

  **c.** Continuous probability distribution; discrete probability distribution

  **d.** Standard deviation, $\sigma$; variance, $\sigma^2$; coefficient of variation, CV

  **e.** Risk aversion; realized rate of return, $\bar{r}$

  **f.** Risk premium for Stock j, $RP_j$; market risk premium, $RP_M$

  **g.** Expected return on a portfolio, $\hat{r}_P$

    **h.** Correlation coefficient, $\rho$

    **i.** Market risk; company-specific risk; relevant risk

    **j.** Beta coefficient, $\beta$; average stock's beta, $\beta_M$

    **k.** Capital Asset Pricing Model (CAPM); security market line (SML); SML equation

    **l.** Slope of SML as a measure of risk aversion

**beta coefficient**   **ST-2** Of the $10,000 invested in a two-stock portfolio, 30 percent is invested in Stock A and 70 percent is invested in Stock B. If Stock A has a beta equal to 2.0 and the beta of the portfolio is 0.95, what is the beta of Stock B?

**required rate of return**   **ST-3** If the risk-free rate of return, $r_{RF}$, is 4 percent and the market return, $r_M$, is expected to be 12 percent, what is the required rate of return for a stock with a beta, $\beta$, equal to 2.5?

**realized rates of return**   **ST-4** Stock A and Stock B have the following historical returns:

| Year | Stock A's Returns, $\ddot{r}_A$ | Stock B's Returns, $\ddot{r}_B$ |
|------|-------------------|-------------------|
| 2004 | −10.00% | −3.00% |
| 2005 | 18.50 | 21.29 |
| 2006 | 38.67 | 44.25 |
| 2007 | 14.33 | 3.67 |
| 2008 | 33.00 | 28.30 |

    **a.** Calculate the average rate of return for each stock during the period 2004–2008. Assume that someone held a portfolio consisting of 50 percent Stock A and 50 percent Stock B. What would have been the realized rate of return on the portfolio in each year from 2004 through 2008? What would have been the average return on the portfolio during this period?

    **b.** Calculate the standard deviation of returns for each stock and for the portfolio. Use Equation 8–4.

    **c.** Looking at the annual returns data on the two stocks, would you guess that the correlation coefficient between returns on the two stocks is closer to 0.9 or to −0.9?

**ST-5** Stocks R and S have the following probability distributions of returns:

| Probability | Returns | |
|-------------|---------|---------|
| | **Stock R** | **Stock S** |
| 0.5 | −2% | 20% |
| 0.1 | 10 | 12 |
| 0.4 | 15 | 2 |

    **a.** Calculate expected return for each stock.

    **b.** Calculate the expected return of a portfolio consisting of 50 percent of each stock.

    **c.** Calculate the standard deviation of returns for each stock and for the portfolio. Which stock is considered riskier with respect to total risk?

    **d.** Compute the coefficient of variation for each stock. According to the coefficient of variation, which stock is considered riskier?

**e.** Looking at the returns in the probability distributions of the two stocks, would you guess that the correlation coefficient between returns on the two stocks is closer to 0.9 or to −0.9?

**f.** If you added more stocks at random to the portfolio, which of the following is the most accurate statement of what would happen to $\sigma_P$?

(1) $\sigma_P$ would remain constant, no matter how many stocks are added.

(2) $\sigma_P$ would approach 15 percent as more stocks are added.

(3) $\sigma_P$ would decline to zero if enough stocks were included

# PROBLEMS

**8-1**  Based on the following probability distribution, what is the security's expected return?

**expected return**

| State | Probability | r |
|-------|-------------|------|
| 1 | 0.2 | −5.0% |
| 2 | 0.4 | 10.0 |
| 3 | 0.5 | 30.0 |

**8-2**  What is the expected return of the following investment?

**expected return**

| Probability | Payoff |
|-------------|--------|
| 0.3 | 30.0% |
| 0.2 | 10.0 |
| 0.5 | −2.0 |

**8-3**  Susan's investment portfolio currently contains three stocks that have a total value equal to $100,000. The beta of this portfolio is 1.5. Susan is considering investing an additional $50,000 in a stock that has a beta equal to 3. After she adds this stock, what will be the portfolio's new beta?

**portfolio beta**

**8-4**  Suppose $r_{RF} = 5\%$, $r_M = 12\%$. What is the appropriate required rate of return for a stock that has a beta coefficient equal to 1.5?

**required return**

**8-5**  The current risk-free rate of return, $r_{RF}$, is 4 percent and the market *risk premium*, $RP_M$, is 5 percent. If the beta coefficient associated with a firm's stock is 2.0, what should be the stock's required rate of return?

**required return**

**8-6**  Following is information for two stocks:

**coefficient of variation**

| Investment | Expected Return, $\hat{r}$ | Standard Deviation, $\sigma$ |
|------------|---------------------------|------------------------------|
| Stock D | 10.0% | 8.0% |
| Stock E | 36.0 | 24.0 |

Which investment has the greater *relative* risk?

**8-7**  ZR Corporation's stock has a beta coefficient equal to 1.8 and a required rate of return equal to 16 percent. If the expected return on the market is 10 percent, what is the risk-free rate of return, $r_{RF}$?

**risk-free return**

**portfolio return**    **8-8**    Currently, the risk-free return is 3 percent and the expected market rate of return is 10 percent. What is the expected return of the following three-stock portfolio?

| Amount Invested | Beta |
|---|---|
| $400,000 | 1.5 |
| 500,000 | 2.0 |
| 100,000 | 4.0 |

**expected returns**    **8-9**    The market and Stock S have the following probability distributions:

| Probability | $r_M$ | $r_S$ |
|---|---|---|
| 0.3 | 15% | 20% |
| 0.4 | 9 | 5 |
| 0.3 | 18 | 12 |

**a.** Calculate the expected rates of return for the market and Stock S.

**b.** Calculate the standard deviations for the market and Stock S.

**c.** Calculate the coefficients of variation for the market and Stock S.

**portfolio return**    **8-10**    Marvin has investments with the following characteristics in his portfolio:

| Investment | Expected Return, $\hat{r}$ | Amount Invested |
|---|---|---|
| ABC | 30% | $10,000 |
| EFG | 16 | 50,000 |
| QRP | 20 | 40,000 |

What is the expected return of Marvin's portfolio of investments, $\hat{r}_p$?

**expected returns**    **8-11**    Stocks X and Y have the following probability distributions of expected future returns:

| Probability | $r_X$ | $r_Y$ |
|---|---|---|
| 0.1 | −10% | −35% |
| 0.2 | 2 | 0 |
| 0.4 | 12 | 20 |
| 0.2 | 20 | 25 |
| 0.1 | 38 | 45 |

**a.** Calculate the expected rate of return for Stock Y, $\hat{r}_Y$, ($\hat{r}_X = 12\%$).

**b.** Calculate the standard deviation of expected returns for Stock X ($\sigma_Y = 20.35\%$). Also, calculate the coefficient of variation for Stock Y. Is it possible that most investors might regard Stock Y as being less risky than Stock X? Explain.

**required return**    **8-12**    Yesterday Susan determined that the risk-free rate of return, $r_{RF}$, is 3 percent, the required return on the market portfolio, $r_M$, is 10 percent, and the required rate of return on Stock K, $r_K$, is 17 percent. Today Susan received new information that indicates investors are more risk averse than she thought, such that the market risk premium, $RP_M$, actually is 1 percent higher than she estimated yesterday. When Susan considers the effect of this change in risk premium, what will she determine the new $r_K$ to be?

**8-13**   Terry recently invested equal amounts in five stocks to form an investment portfolio, which has a beta equal to 1.2—that is, $\beta_P = 1.2$. Terry is considering selling the riskiest stock in the portfolio, which has a beta coefficient equal to 2.0, and replacing it with another stock. If Terry replaces the stock with $\beta = 2.0$ with a stock with $\beta = 1.0$, what will be the *new beta* of his investment portfolio? Assume that the equal amounts are invested in each stock in the portfolio.   **portfolio beta**

**8-14**   Thomas has a five-stock portfolio that has a market value equal to $400,000. The portfolio's beta is 1.5. Thomas is considering selling a particular stock to help pay some university expenses. The stock is valued at $100,000, and if he sells it the portfolio's beta will increase to 1.8. What is the beta of the stock Thomas is considering selling?   **portfolio beta**

**8-15**   Suppose $r_{RF} = 8\%$, $r_M = 11\%$, and $r_B = 14\%$.   **beta computation**

   **a.** Calculate Stock B's beta, $B_\beta$.

   **b.** If Stock B's beta were 1.5, what would be its new required rate of return?

**8-16**   Suppose $r_{RF} = 9\%$, $r_M = 14\%$, and $\beta_X = 1.3$.   **SML and CAPM**

   **a.** What is $r_X$, the required rate of return on Stock X?

   **b.** Now suppose $r_{RF}$ (1) increases to 10 percent or (2) decreases to 8 percent. The slope of the SML remains constant. How would each change affect $r_M$ and $r_X$?

   **c.** Assume $r_{RF}$ remains at 9 percent, but $r_M$ (1) increases to 16 percent or (2) decreases to 13 percent. The slope of the SML does not remain constant. How would these changes affect $r_X$?

**8-17**   Suppose you hold a diversified portfolio consisting of a $7,500 investment in each of 20 different common stocks. The portfolio beta is equal to 1.12. You have decided to sell one of the stocks in your portfolio with a beta equal to 1.0 for $7,500 and to use the proceeds to buy another stock for your portfolio. Assume that the new stock's beta is equal to 1.75. Calculate your portfolio's new beta.   **portfolio beta**

**8-18**   Stock R has a beta of 1.5, Stock S has a beta of 0.75, the expected rate of return on an average stock is 15 percent, and the risk-free rate of return is 9 percent. By how much does the required return on the riskier stock exceed the required return on the less risky stock?   **required rates of return**

**8-19**   Suppose you are the money manager of a $4 million investment fund. The fund consists of four stocks with the following investments and betas:   **portfolio required return**

| Stock | Investment | Beta |
|---|---|---|
| A | $ 400.000 | 1.50 |
| B | 600,000 | −0.50 |
| C | 1,000,000 | 1.25 |
| D | 2,000,000 | 0.75 |

If the market required rate of return is 14 percent and the risk-free rate is 6 percent, what is the fund's required rate of return?

**expected returns and risk**    **8-20** Following is information about Investment A, Investment B, and Investment C:

| | | Return on Investment | | |
|---|---|---|---|---|
| Economic Condition | Probability | A | B | C |
| Boom | 0.5 | 25.0% | 40.0% | 5.0% |
| Normal | 0.4 | 15.0 | 20.0 | 10.0 |
| Recession | 0.1 | −5.0 | −40.0 | 15.0 |
| $\hat{r}$ | | 18.0% | 24.0% | ? |
| $\sigma$ | | ? | 23.3% | 3.3% |

**a.** Compute the expected return, $\hat{r}$, for Investment C.

**b.** Compute the standard deviation, $\sigma$, for Investment A.

**c.** Based on total risk and return, which of the investments should a risk-averse investor prefer?

**expected returns**    **8-21** Suppose you win the Florida lottery and are offered a choice of $500,000 in cash or a gamble in which you would get $1 million if a head is flipped but zero if a tail comes up.

**a.** What is the expected value of the gamble?

**b.** Would you take the sure $500,000 or the gamble?

**c.** If you choose the sure $500,000, are you a risk averter or a risk seeker?

**d.** Suppose you take the sure $500,000. You can invest it in either a U.S. Treasury bond that will return $537,500 at the end of one year or a common stock that has a 50-50 chance of being either worthless or worth $1,150,000 at the end of the year.

   **(1)** What is the expected *dollar* profit on the stock investment? (The expected profit on the T-bond investment is $37,500.)

   **(2)** What is the expected *rate* of return on the stock investment? (The expected rate of return on the T-bond investment is 7.5 percent.)

   **(3)** Would you invest in the bond or the stock?

   **(4)** Exactly how large would the expected profit (or the expected rate of return) have to be on the stock investment to make you invest in the stock, given the 7.5 percent return on the bond?

   **(5)** How might your decision be affected if, rather than buying one stock for $500,000, you could construct a portfolio consisting of 100 stocks with $5,000 invested in each? Each of these stocks has the same return characteristics as the one stock—that is, a 50-50 chance of being worth either zero or $11,500 at year-end. Would the correlation between returns on these stocks matter?

**8-22**  The McAlhany Investment Fund has total capital of $500 million invested in five stocks:

| Stock | Investment | Stock's Beta Coefficient |
|-------|------------|--------------------------|
| A | $160 million | 0.5 |
| B | 120 million | 2.0 |
| C | 80 million | 4.0 |
| D | 80 million | 1.0 |
| E | 60 million | 3.0 |

The current risk-free rate is 8 percent. Market returns have the following estimated probability distribution for the next period:

| Probability | Market Return |
|-------------|---------------|
| 0.1 | 10% |
| 0.2 | 12 |
| 0.4 | 13 |
| 0.2 | 16 |
| 0.1 | 17 |

**a.** Compute the expected return for the market.

**b.** Compute the beta coefficient for the investment fund. (Remember, this problem involves a portfolio.)

**c.** What is the estimated equation for the security market line?

**d.** Compute the fund's required rate of return for the next period.

**e.** Suppose John McAlhany, the president, receives a proposal for a new stock. The investment needed to take a position in the stock is $50 million, it will have an expected return of 18 percent, and its estimated beta coefficient is 2.0. Should the firm purchase the new stock? At what expected rate of return should McAlhany be indifferent to purchasing the stock?

**8-23**  Stock A and Stock B have the following historical returns:

| Year | Stock A's Returns, $\ddot{r}_B$ | Stock B's Returns, $\ddot{r}_B$ |
|------|--------------------------------|--------------------------------|
| 2004 | −18.0% | −14.5% |
| 2005 | 33.0 | 21.8 |
| 2006 | 15.0 | 30.5 |
| 2007 | −0.5 | −7.6 |
| 2008 | 27.0 | 26.3 |

**a.** Calculate the average rate of return for each stock during the period 2004–2008.

**b.** Assume that someone held a portfolio consisting of 50 percent Stock A and 50 percent Stock B. What would have been the realized rate of return on the portfolio in each year from 2004 through 2008? What would have been the average return on the portfolio during this period?

c. Calculate the standard deviation of returns for each stock and for the portfolio. Use Equation 8–4.

d. Calculate the coefficient of variation for each stock and for the portfolio.

e. If you are a risk-averse investor, would you prefer to hold Stock A, Stock B, or the portfolio? Why?

## Integrative Problem

**risk and rates of return**

**8-24**  Assume you recently graduated with a major in finance, and you just landed a job in the trust department of a large regional bank. Your first assignment is to invest $100,000 from an estate for which the bank is trustee. Because the estate is expected to be distributed to the heirs in approximately one year, you have been instructed to plan for a one-year holding period. Furthermore, your boss has restricted you to the following investment alternatives, shown with their probabilities and associated outcomes. (For now, disregard the blank spaces in the table; you will fill in the blanks later.)

### Estimated Returns on Alternative Investments

| State of the Economy | Probability | T-Bills | High Tech | Collections | U.S. Rubber | Market Portfolio | Two-Stock Portfolio |
|---|---|---|---|---|---|---|---|
| Recession | 0.1 | 8.0% | −22.0% | 28.0% | 10.0% | −13.0% | |
| Below Average | 0.2 | 8.0 | −2.0 | 14.7 | −10.0 | 1.0 | |
| Average | 0.4 | 8.0 | 20.0 | 0.0 | 7.0 | 15.0 | |
| Above Average | 0.2 | 8.0 | 35.0 | −10.0 | 45.0 | 29.0 | |
| Boom | 0.1 | 8.0 | 50.0 | −20.0 | 30.0 | 43.0 | |
| $\hat{r}$ | | | | | | | |
| $\sigma$ | | | | | | | |
| CV | | | | | | | |

The bank's economic forecasting staff has developed probability estimates for the state of the economy, and the trust department has a sophisticated computer program that was used to estimate the rate of return on each alternative under each state of the economy. High Tech Inc. is an electronics firm, Collections Inc. collects past-due debts, and U.S. Rubber manufactures tires and various other rubber and plastics products. The bank also maintains an "index fund" that includes a market-weighted fraction of all publicly traded stocks; by investing in that fund, you can obtain average stock market results. Given the situation as described, answer the following questions.

a. (1) Why is the risk-free return independent of the state of the economy? Do T-bills promise a completely risk-free return? (2) Why are High Tech's returns expected to move with the economy whereas Collections' are expected to move counter to the economy?

b. Calculate the expected rate of return on each alternative and fill in the row for $\hat{r}$ in the table.

c. You should recognize that basing a decision solely on expected returns is appropriate only for risk-neutral individuals. Because the beneficiaries of the trust, like virtually everyone, are risk averse, the riskiness of each alternative is an important aspect of the decision. One possible measure of risk is the *standard deviation* of returns. (1) Calculate this value for each alternative, and fill in the row for σ in the table. (2) What type of risk does the standard deviation measure? (3) Draw a graph that shows *roughly* the shape of the probability distributions for High Tech, U.S. Rubber, and T-bills.

**d.** Suppose you suddenly remembered that the *coefficient of variation (CV)* is generally regarded as being a better measure of total risk than the standard deviation when the alternatives being considered have widely differing expected returns and risks. Calculate the CVs for the different securities, and fill in the row for CV in the table. Does the CV measure produce the same risk rankings as the standard deviation?

**e.** Suppose you created a two-stock portfolio by investing $50,000 in High Tech and $50,000 in Collections. (1) Calculate the expected return ($\hat{r}_p$), the standard deviation ($\sigma_p$), and the coefficient of variation ($CV_p$) for this portfolio and fill in the appropriate rows in the table. (2) How does the riskiness of this two-stock portfolio compare to the riskiness of the individual stocks if they were held in isolation?

**f.** Suppose an investor starts with a portfolio consisting of one randomly selected stock. What would happen (1) to the riskiness and (2) to the expected return of the portfolio as more randomly selected stocks are added to the portfolio? What is the implication for investors? Draw two graphs to illustrate your answer.

**g.** (1) Should portfolio effects influence the way that investors think about the riskiness of individual stocks? (2) If you chose to hold a one-stock portfolio and consequently were exposed to more risk than diversified investors, could you expect to be compensated for all of your risk? That is, could you earn a risk premium on the part of your risk that you could have eliminated by diversifying?

**h.** The expected rates of return and the beta coefficients of the alternatives as supplied by the bank's computer program are as follows:

| Security | Return ($\hat{r}$) | Risk (β) |
|---|---|---|
| High Tech | 17.40% | 1.29 |
| Market | 15.00 | 1.00 |
| U.S. Rubber | 13.80 | 0.68 |
| T-bills | 8.00 | 0.00 |
| Collections | 1.74 | −0.86 |

(1) What is a *beta coefficient*, and how are betas used in risk analysis? (2) Do the expected returns appear to be related to each alternative's market risk? (3) Is it possible to choose among the alternatives on the basis of the information developed thus far? (4) Use the data given at the beginning of the problem to construct a graph that shows how the T-bill's, High Tech's, and Collections' beta coefficients are calculated. Discuss what beta measures and explain how it is used in risk analysis.

**i.** (1) Write out the SML equation, use it to calculate the required rate of return on each alternative, and then graph the relationship between the expected and required rates of return. (2) How do the expected rates of return compare with the required rates of return? (3) Does the fact that Collections has a negative beta coefficient make any sense? What is the implication of the negative beta? (4) What would be the market risk and the required return of a 50-50 portfolio of High Tech and Collections? Of a 50-50 portfolio of High Tech and U.S. Rubber?

**j.** (1) Suppose investors raised their inflation expectations by 3 percentage points over current estimates as reflected in the 8 percent T-bill rate. What effect would higher inflation have on the SML and on the returns required on high- and low-risk securities? (2) Suppose instead that investors' risk aversion increased enough to cause the market risk premium to increase by 3 percentage points. (Inflation remains constant.) What effect would this change have on the SML and on returns of high- and low-risk securities?

## Computer-Related Problem

*Work the problem in this section only if you are using the problem spreadsheet.*

**realized rates of return**

**8-25**   Using File C08, rework Problem 8-23, assuming that a third stock, Stock C, is available for inclusion in the portfolio. Stock C has the following historical returns:

| Year | Stock C's Return, $r_c$ |
|------|-------------------------|
| 2004 | 32.00% |
| 2005 | −11.75 |
| 2006 | 10.75 |
| 2007 | 32.25 |
| 2008 | −6.75 |

**a.** Calculate (or read from the computer screen) the average return, standard deviation, and coefficient of variation for Stock C.

**b.** Assume that the portfolio now consists of 33.33 percent Stock A, 33.33 percent Stock B, and 33.33 percent Stock C. How does this composition affect the portfolio return, standard deviation, and coefficient of variation versus when 50 percent was invested in A and in B?

**c.** Make some other changes in the portfolio, making sure that the percentages sum to 100 percent. For example, enter 25 percent for Stock A, 25 percent for Stock B, and 50 percent for Stock C. (Note that the program will not allow you to enter a zero for the percentage in Stock C.) Notice that $\hat{r}_p$ remains constant and that $\sigma_p$ changes. Why do these results occur?

**d.** In Problem 8–23, the standard deviation of the portfolio decreased only slightly because Stocks A and B were highly positively correlated with one another. In this problem, the addition of Stock C causes the standard deviation of the portfolio to decline dramatically, even though $\sigma_C = \sigma_A = \sigma_B$. What does this change indicate about the correlation between Stock C and Stocks A and B?

**e.** Would you prefer to hold the portfolio described in Problem 8-23 consisting only of Stocks A and B or a portfolio that also included Stock C? If others react similarly, how might this fact affect the stocks' prices and rates of return?

# Valuation—Real Assets (Capital Budgeting)

# Capital Budgeting Techniques

I n the summer of 1990, after five years of planning and $3.5 billion in costs for development and for new factories and equipment, General Motors (GM) began production of a new compact car—the Saturn. The Saturn car was sold through special, "haggle-free" dealerships, which was a unique concept at the time, rather than the typical GM dealership. Now, more than 15 years later, it is safe to say that most people in the United States have heard of the Saturn car line. For it to have survived so long, you probably would expect that the Saturn has been a successful venture. Unfortunately for GM, however, the Saturn line never really reached the sales necessary for the project to be considered a success. Even though consumers seem to like the Saturn concept and it has a good service reputation, annual sales of less than 100,000 in recent years have been well below the amounts needed for GM to begin to call the project a viable investment. Some believe GM has used the Saturn project as a loss leader to attract first-time new car buyers and as a means to satisfy federal regulations concerning the average fuel economy of the line of cars it offers. Even so, Saturn cannot survive if sales continue to decline. Attempting to reverse the trend, a few years ago the Saturn division of GM introduced a new sedan called the Ion, a sport-utility vehicle called the Vue, and a convertible called the Saturn Sky. Unfortunately, these models have not

shown the success that was expected. In fact, GM has been losing approximately $1 billion annually in recent years (sales in 2004 and 2005 declined 22 percent and 24 percent, respectively). It is estimated that the losses associated with the Saturn line since 1990 total nearly $15 billion.

Do you think GM should scrap the Saturn line? Maybe. But GM planned to invest another $3 billion from 2005 through 2007 to save the Saturn line. Some people believe that attempts to save the Saturn line will prove futile, given the history of the brand. However, GM believes that the Saturn line has three characteristics that can prove successful in the future: (1) a reputable and recognizable brand name, (2) customer loyalty (70 percent of those who buy a Saturn return), and (3) high customer satisfaction. And in its attempt to salvage the Saturn division, GM plans to develop new models and manufacturing processes that are believed to have the potential to generate large profits. If the plans to revive the Saturn line prove to be unsuccessful, then the fact that GM used "good money" to invest in a "bad" project might prove to be the death of the company because GM's financial position in 2005 and 2006 was rather tenuous. As a result of its poor financial position, GM announced plans in June 2005 to reduce its workforce by 25,000, or 14 percent of its employees, by 2008. Eliminating jobs and closing inefficient plants is part of GM's strategy to restructure its financial position. In 2006, GM announced that it planned to introduce hybrid cars through the Saturn division. Company executives believe that providing more fuel-efficient cars that consumers demand will help increase Saturn sales in the future. However, it is doubtful that this line of cars will continue to exist unless it can make a positive contribution to the improvement of GM's financial position.

GM's Saturn project is an example of a massive capital budgeting venture that required a substantial amount of analysis and decision making before the billions of dollars required for development and implementation were spent. The firm wants to ensure that such a decision, which has long-term, far-reaching effects, is in the best interest of shareholders—that is, the investment contributes to increasing the value of the firm. The principles set forth in this chapter and the next offer insights into how capital budgeting decisions such as these are made.

**Source:** Various articles available on Dow Jones Interactive® Publications Library located at http://www.wsj.com.

## Chapter *Essentials*
### —The Questions

After reading this chapter, you should be able to answer the following questions:

- How do firms make decisions about whether to invest in costly, long-lived real assets such as buildings and equipment?
- How does a firm make a choice between two (or more) acceptable investments when only one can be purchased?
- How are different capital budgeting techniques related? Which technique is the best to use?
- Which capital budgeting methods do firms actually use?

In the previous three chapters, we showed how assets are valued and required rates of return are determined. Now we apply these concepts to investment decisions involving the fixed assets of a firm, or *capital budgeting*. Here the term *capital* refers to fixed assets used in production, whereas a *budget* is a plan that details projected inflows and outflows during some future period. Thus, the capital budget is an outline of planned expenditures on fixed assets, and **capital budgeting** is the process of analyzing projects and deciding (1) which are acceptable investments and (2) which actually should be purchased.

Our treatment of capital budgeting is divided into two chapters. First, this chapter gives an overview and explains the basic techniques used in capital budgeting analysis. In Chapter 10, we show how the cash flows associated with capital budgeting projects are estimated and how risk is considered in capital budgeting decisions.

**capital budgeting**
The process of planning and evaluating expenditures on assets whose cash flows are expected to extend beyond one year.

## IMPORTANCE OF CAPITAL BUDGETING

A number of factors combine to make capital budgeting decisions among the most important decisions financial managers must make. First, the impact of capital budgeting is long term; thus, the firm loses some decision-making flexibility when capital projects are purchased. For example, when a firm invests in an asset with a 10-year economic life, its operations are affected for 10 years. The firm is "locked in" by the capital budgeting decision. Further, because asset expansion is fundamentally related to expected future sales, a decision to buy a fixed asset that is expected to last 10 years involves an implicit 10-year sales forecast.

An error in the forecast of asset requirements can have serious consequences. If the firm invests too much in assets, it will incur unnecessarily heavy expenses. But if it does not spend enough on fixed assets, it might find that inefficient production and inadequate capacity lead to lost sales that are difficult, if not impossible, to recover.

Timing is also important in capital budgeting. Capital assets must be ready to come on line when they are needed; otherwise, opportunities might be lost. For example, consider what happened to Decopot, a decorative tile manufacturer with no formal capital budgeting process. Decopot attempted to operate at full capacity as often as possible. This was not a bad idea because demand for Decopot's product and services was relatively stable. A few years ago, however, Decopot began to experience intermittent spurts of additional demand for its products. Decopot could not satisfy the additional demand because it did not have the capacity to produce any more products, and customers had to be turned away. The spurts in demand continued, so senior management decided to add capacity to increase production so the additional orders could be filled in the future. It took nine months to get the additional capacity ready. Finally, Decopot was ready for the increased demand the next time it arrived. Unfortunately, the "next time" never came because competitors had expanded their operations six months earlier, which allowed them to fill customers' orders when Decopot could not. Many of Decopot's customers are now its competitors' customers. If Decopot had properly forecasted demand and planned its capacity requirements, it would have been able to maintain or perhaps even increase its market share; instead, its market share decreased.

Effective capital budgeting can improve both the timing of asset acquisitions and the quality of assets purchased. A firm that forecasts its needs for capital assets in advance will have an opportunity to purchase and install the assets before they are needed. Unfortunately, like Decopot, many firms do not order capital goods until they approach full capacity or are forced to replace worn-out equipment. If many firms order capital goods at the same time, backlogs result, prices increase, and firms are forced to wait for the delivery of machinery; in general, the quality of the capital goods deteriorates. If a firm foresees its needs and purchases capital assets early, it can avoid these problems.

Finally, capital budgeting is important because the acquisition of fixed assets typically involves substantial expenditures, and before a firm can spend a large amount of money, it must have the funds available. Large amounts of money are not available automatically. Therefore, a firm contemplating a major capital expenditure program must arrange its financing well in advance to be sure the required funds are available.

### Self-Test Questions

Why are capital budgeting decisions so important to a firm's success?

Why is the sales forecast a key element in a capital budgeting decision?

## GENERATING IDEAS FOR CAPITAL PROJECTS

The same general concepts that we developed for valuing financial assets are involved in capital budgeting. However, whereas a set of stocks and bonds already exists in the financial markets and investors select from this set, capital budgeting projects are created by the firm. For example, a sales representative might report that customers frequently ask for a particular product that the company does not currently produce. The sales manager then discusses the idea with the marketing research group to determine the size of the market for the proposed product. If it appears likely that a significant market does exist, cost accountants and engineers will be asked to estimate production costs. If those estimates show the product can be produced and sold at a sufficient profit, the project will be undertaken.

A firm's growth, and even its ability to remain competitive and to survive, depends on a constant flow of ideas for new products, ways to make existing products better, and ways to produce output at a lower cost. Accordingly, a well-managed firm will go to great lengths to develop good capital budgeting proposals. Some firms even provide incentives to employees to encourage suggestions that lead to beneficial investment proposals. If a firm has capable and imaginative executives and employees and its incentive system works properly, many ideas for capital investment will be advanced.

Because some capital investment ideas will be good and others will not, procedures must be established for evaluating the worth of such projects to the firm. Our topic in the remainder of this chapter is the evaluation of the acceptability of capital projects.

### Self-Test Question

How does a firm generate ideas for capital projects?

## PROJECT CLASSIFICATIONS

**replacement decisions**
Whether to purchase capital assets to take the place of existing assets to maintain or improve existing operations.

Capital budgeting decisions generally are termed either *replacement decisions* or *expansion decisions.* **Replacement decisions** involve determining whether capital projects should be purchased to take the place of existing assets that might be worn out, damaged, or obsolete. Usually the replacement projects are necessary to maintain or improve profitable operations using the *existing* production levels. On the other hand, if a firm is considering whether to *increase* operations by adding capital projects to existing assets that will help produce either more of its existing products or entirely new products, **expansion decisions** are made.

**expansion decisions**
Whether to purchase capital projects and add them to existing assets to increase existing operations.

Some capital budgeting decisions involve *independent projects,* whereas others will involve *mutually exclusive projects.* **Independent projects** are projects whose cash flows are not affected by one another, so the acceptance of one project does not affect the acceptance of the other project(s). *All independent projects can be purchased if they all are acceptable.* For example, if South-Western College Publishing, which publishes this book, decides to purchase the ABC television network, it still could publish new textbooks. Conversely, if a capital budgeting decision involves **mutually exclusive projects,** then when one project is taken on, the others must be rejected. *Only one mutually exclusive project can be purchased, even if they all are acceptable.* For example, Global Sports and Entertainment Ltd. has a parcel of land on which it wants to build either a children's amusement park or a domed baseball stadium. Because the land is not large enough for both alternatives, if Global chooses to build the amusement park, it cannot build the stadium, and vice versa.

**independent projects**
Projects whose cash flows are not affected by decisions made about other projects.

**mutually exclusive projects**
A set of projects in which the acceptance of one project means the others cannot be accepted.

In general, relatively simple calculations, and only a few supporting documents, are required for replacement decisions, especially maintenance-type investments in profitable plants. More detailed analysis is required for cost-reduction replacements, for expansion of existing product lines, and especially for investments in new products or areas. Also, within each category, projects are broken down by their dollar costs: Larger investments require both more detailed analysis and approval at a higher level within the firm.

### Self-Test Questions

What is the difference between replacement decisions and expansion decisions?

What is the difference between independent projects and mutually exclusive projects?

## SIMILARITIES BETWEEN CAPITAL BUDGETING AND ASSET VALUATION

To make capital budgeting decisions, we must value the assets, or projects, that are being evaluated. Not surprisingly, then, capital budgeting involves the same steps used in general asset valuation as described in the past few chapters:

1. Estimate the cash flows expected to be generated by the asset during its life. This is similar to estimating the future dividends that a stock will generate.

2. Evaluate the riskiness of the projected cash flows to determine the appropriate rate of return to use for computing the present value of the estimated cash flows.

3. Compute the present value of the expected cash flows—that is, compute the investment's value. This is equivalent to finding the present value of a stock's expected future dividends. In other words, solve the following equation:

$$\text{PV of CF} = \frac{\hat{CF}_1}{(1+r)^1} + \frac{\hat{CF}_2}{(1+r)^2} + \cdots + \frac{\hat{CF}_n}{(1+r)^n} = \sum_{t=1}^{n} \frac{\hat{CF}_t}{(1+r)^t}$$

4. Compare the present value of the future expected cash flows with the initial investment, or cost, required to acquire the asset. Alternatively, the expected rate of return on the project can be calculated and compared with the rate of return considered appropriate (required) for the project.

*If a firm identifies (or creates) an investment opportunity with a present value greater than its cost, the value of the firm will increase by purchasing the investment.* There is a direct link between capital budgeting and stock values: The more effective the firm's capital budgeting procedures, the higher the price of its stock.

### Self-Test Questions

List the steps in the capital budgeting process, and compare them with the steps in general asset valuation.

Explain how capital budgeting is related to the wealth-maximization goal that should be pursued by the financial manager of a firm.

## NET PRESENT VALUE (NPV)

Following the steps outlined in the previous section, to determine the acceptability of a capital budgeting project, we must determine its value and then compare this value with the project's purchase price. Remember from our previous discussions that the value of an asset can be determined by computing the present value of the cash flows it is expected to generate during its life. If we subtract (or add a negative cash flow) the purchase price of the asset from the present value of its expected future cash flows, the result is the net dollar value, or net benefit that accrues to the firm if the asset is purchased. This net benefit is called the asset's **net present value (NPV).** The NPV shows by how much a firm's value, and thus stockholders' wealth, will increase if a capital budgeting project is purchased. *If the net benefit computed on a*

**net present value (NPV)**
The present value of an asset's future cash flows minus its purchase price (initial investment).

**FIGURE 9-1   Net Cash Flows for Project S and Project L**

| | | Expected After-Tax Net Cash Flows, $\hat{CF}_t$ | |
|---|---|---|---|
| | Year (t) | Project S | Project L |
| | 0 | $(3,000) | $(3,000) |
| | 1 | 1,500 | 400 |
| | 2 | 1,200 | 900 |
| | 3 | 800 | 1,300 |
| | 4 | 300 | 1,500 |

| **Project S:** | 0 | 1 | 2 | 3 | 4 |
|---|---|---|---|---|---|
| Net cash flow | (3,000) | 1,500 | 1,200 | 800 | 300 |

| **Project L:** | 0 | 1 | 2 | 3 | 4 |
|---|---|---|---|---|---|
| Net cash flow | (3,000) | 400 | 900 | 1,300 | 1,500 |

*present value basis—that is, NPV—is positive, then the asset (project) is considered an acceptable investment.* In other words, to determine whether a project is acceptable using the NPV technique, we apply the following decision rule:

**NPV Decision Rule:** A project is acceptable if NPV > $0

We use the following equation to compute NPV:

**9–1**

$$NPV = \hat{CF}_0 + \frac{\hat{CF}_1}{(1+r)^1} + \frac{\hat{CF}_2}{(1+r)^2} + \cdots + \frac{\hat{CF}_n}{(1+r)^n} = \sum_{t=0}^{n} \frac{\hat{CF}_t}{(1+r)^t}$$

Here $\hat{CF}_t$ is the expected net cash flow at Period t, and r is the rate of return required by the firm to invest in this project.[1] Cash outflows (expenditures on the project, such as the cost of buying equipment or building factories) are treated as negative cash flows.

To illustrate the application of the NPV method and the other capital budgeting techniques discussed in this chapter, we use the cash flow data shown in Figure 9-1 for Project S and Project L. Throughout this chapter, we assume that these projects are equally risky and that their expected cash flows are known with certainty. In the next chapter, we discuss how these cash flows are determined and how risk should be considered in capital budgeting analyses. The expected cash flows, $\hat{CF}_t$, shown in Figure 9-1 are the "bottom line," after-tax cash flows, which we assume occur at the end of the designated year. For Project S and Project L, only $\hat{CF}_0$ is negative, but for many large projects such as the Alaska Pipeline, an electric generating plant, or Chevrolet's Saturn project, outflows occur for several years before operations begin and cash flows turn positive. Incidentally, the S stands for *short* and the L for *long:* Project S is a short-term project in the sense that its cash inflows tend to come in

---

[1]The rate of return required by the firm generally is termed the firm's *cost of capital* because it is the average rate the firm must pay for the funds used to purchase capital projects. The concept of cost of capital is discussed in Chapter 11.

sooner than those for Project L. We use these two illustrative projects to simplify our presentations.

At a 10 percent required rate of return, Project S's net present value, NPV$_S$, is $161.33:

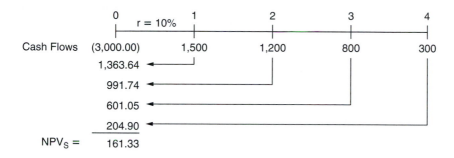

As the lower section of the cash flow time line shows, to find the NPV, we compute the present value of each cash flow, including $\hat{CF}_0$, and sum the results. Using Equation 9–1, the numerical solution for NPV$_S$ is

$$NPV_S = (3,000) + \frac{1,500}{(1.10)^1} + \frac{1,200}{(1.10)^2} + \frac{800}{(1.10)^3} + \frac{300}{(1.10)^4}$$
$$= (3,000) + 1,363.64 + 991.74 + 601.05 + 204.90$$
$$= 161.33$$

It is not difficult to calculate the NPV using Equation 9–1 and a regular calculator as we did here. Nevertheless, the most efficient way to find the NPV is by using a financial calculator. Different calculators are set up somewhat differently, but they all have a section of memory called the "cash flow register" that is used for computing the present value of uneven cash flows such as those in Project S (as opposed to equal annuity cash flows). As we saw in Chapter 4, a solution process for Equation 9–1 is literally programmed into financial calculators. Simply input the cash flows (being sure to observe the signs) in the order they occur, along with the value of I/Y = r. For Project S, enter $CF_0 = -3,000$, $CF_1 = 1,500$, $CF_2 = 1,200$, $CF_3 = 800$, $CF_4 = 300$, and I/Y = r = 10%. At this point, you have entered in your calculator the cash flows and the interest rate shown on the time line for Project S. There is one unknown—NPV. Now you just ask the calculator to solve the equation for you; the answer, 161.33, will appear on the screen.[2] Using this same process for Project L, we find NPV$_L$ = $108.67.[3] On this basis, both projects should be accepted if they are *independent*, but Project S should be the one chosen if they are *mutually exclusive* because NPV$_S$ = $161.33 > NPV$_L$ = $108.67.

The rationale for the NPV method is straightforward. An NPV of zero signifies that the project's cash flows are just sufficient to repay the invested capital and to provide the required rate of return (r) on that capital. If a project has a positive NPV, then it generates a return that is greater than is needed to pay for funds provided by investors, and this excess return accrues solely to the firm's stockholders. Therefore, if a firm takes on a project with a positive NPV, the position of the stockholders is improved

---

[2] Refer to the manual that came with your calculator to determine how the CF function is used.

[3] Appendix 9A at the end of this chapter shows how to compute the NPV for Project S using a spreadsheet. It also shows how to use a spreadsheet to compute the project's internal rate of return (IRR), which is discussed later in the chapter.

because the firm's value increases. In our example, shareholders' wealth would increase by $161.33 if the firm takes on Project S but by only $108.67 if it takes on Project L. Viewed in this manner, it is easy to see why Project S is preferred to Project L, and it also is easy to see the logic of the NPV approach. If the two projects are independent, both should be accepted because shareholders' wealth would increase by a total of $270 = $161.33 + $108.67. *In general, a project is considered acceptable if its NPV is positive; it is not acceptable if its NPV is negative.*[4]

 **Self-Test Questions**

What is the rationale for using the NPV method to evaluate a capital budgeting project?

Whole Wheat Bakery is considering purchasing a new machine that costs $75,000. The machine is expected to generate after-tax cash flows equal to $30,000, $38,000, and $28,000 during its three-year life. Whole Wheat requires such investments to earn a return equal to at least 12 percent. What is the machine's NPV? Should the bakery purchase the machine? (*Answers:* NPV = $2,009; purchase the project)

## INTERNAL RATE OF RETURN (IRR)

In Chapter 6, we present procedures for finding the yield to maturity (YTM), or rate of return, on a bond. Recall that if you invest in a bond and hold it to maturity, the average return you can expect to earn on the money you invest is the YTM. Exactly the same concepts are employed in capital budgeting to determine the **internal rate of return (IRR)**, which is the rate of return the firm expects to earn if a project is purchased and held for its economic life. The IRR is defined as the discount rate that equates the present value of a project's expected cash flows to the initial amount invested. *As long as the project's IRR, which is its expected return, is greater than the rate of return required by the firm for such an investment, the project is acceptable.* In other words, to determine whether a project is acceptable using the IRR technique, we apply the following decision rule:

**internal rate of return (IRR)**
The discount rate that forces the PV of a project's expected cash flows to equal its initial cost; IRR is similar to the YTM on a bond.

> **IRR Decision Rule:** A project is acceptable if IRR > r

where r is the firm's required rate of return.

We can use the following equation to solve for a project's IRR:

**9-2**

$$NPV = \hat{CF}_0 + \frac{\hat{CF}_1}{(1 + IRR)^1} + \frac{\hat{CF}_2}{(1 + IRR)^2} + \cdots + \frac{\hat{CF}_n}{(1 + IRR)^n} = \sum_{t=0}^{n} \frac{\hat{CF}_t}{(1 + IRR)^n} = 0$$

or

$$\hat{CF}_0 = \frac{\hat{CF}_1}{(1 + IRR)^1} + \frac{\hat{CF}_2}{(1 + IRR)^2} + \cdots + \frac{\hat{CF}_n}{(1 + IRR)^n}$$

---

[4]This description of the process is somewhat oversimplified. Both analysts and investors anticipate that firms will identify and accept positive NPV projects, and current stock prices reflect these expectations. Thus, stock prices react to announcements of new capital projects only to the extent that such projects were not already expected. In this sense, we can think of a firm's value as consisting of two parts: (1) the value of its existing assets and (2) the value of its "growth opportunities," or projects with positive NPVs.

For Project S, the cash flow time line for the IRR computation is as follows:

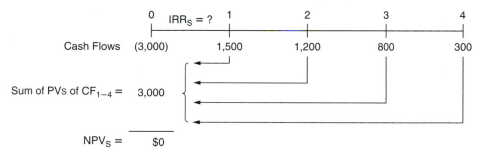

Using Equation 9–2, here is the setup for computing $IRR_S$:

$$(3,000) + \frac{1,500}{(1+IRR)^1} + \frac{1,200}{(1+IRR)^2} + \frac{800}{(1+IRR)^3} + \frac{300}{(1+IRR)^4} = 0$$

Although it is fairly easy to find the NPV without a financial calculator, the same is *not* true of the IRR. Without a financial calculator, you must solve Equation 9–2 by trial and error—that is, you must try different discount rates until you find the one that forces NPV equal to zero. This discount rate is the IRR. For a project with a fairly long life, the trial-and-error approach is a tedious, time-consuming task. Fortunately, it is easy to find IRRs with a financial calculator.

To solve for IRR using a financial calculator, follow the steps used to find the NPV. First, enter the cash flows as shown on the preceding cash flow time line into the calculator's cash flow register. For Project S, enter $CF_0 = -3,000$, $CF_1 = 1,500$, $CF_2 = 1,200$, $CF_3 = 800$, and $CF_4 = 300$. In effect, you have entered the cash flows into the equation shown below the cash flow time line. You now have one unknown, IRR, or the discount rate that forces NPV to equal zero. The calculator has been programmed to solve for the IRR, and you activate this program by pressing the key labeled "IRR." Following are the IRRs for Project S and Project L found using a financial calculator:

$$IRR_S = 13.1\%$$
$$IRR_L = 11.4\%$$

*A project is acceptable if its IRR is greater than the firm's* **required rate of return,** *or* **hurdle rate.** For example, if the hurdle rate required by the firm is 10 percent, then both Project S and Project L are acceptable. If they are mutually exclusive, Project S is more acceptable than Project L because $IRR_S > IRR_L$. On the other hand, if the firm's required rate of return is 15 percent, neither project is acceptable.

Notice from Equation 9–2 that *you do not need to know the firm's required rate of return (r) to solve for IRR*. However, you need the required rate of return to make a decision as to whether a project is acceptable once its IRR has been computed. Also, note that (1) the IRR is the rate of return that will be earned by anyone who purchases the project, and (2) the IRR is dependent on the project's cash flow characteristics— that is, the amounts and the timing of the cash flows—not the firm's required rate of return. As a result, *the IRR of a particular project is the same for all firms, regardless of their particular required rates of return*. A project might be acceptable to one firm (Project S would be acceptable to a firm that has a required rate of return equal to 10 percent) but not acceptable to another firm (Project S is not acceptable to a firm that has a required rate of return equal to 15 percent).

Why is a project acceptable if its IRR is greater than its required rate of return? Because the IRR on a project is the rate of return that the project is expected to generate,

**required rate of return, or hurdle rate**
The discount rate (cost of funds) that the IRR must exceed for a project to be considered acceptable.

and if this return exceeds the cost of the funds used to finance the project, a surplus remains after paying for the funds. This surplus accrues to the firm's stockholders. Therefore, *taking on a project whose IRR exceeds its required rate of return, or cost of funds, increases shareholders' wealth.* On the other hand, if the IRR is less than the cost of funds, then taking on the project imposes a cost on current stockholders that decreases wealth.

Consider what would happen if you borrow funds at a 10 percent interest rate to invest in the stock market. The 10 percent interest is your *cost of funds,* which is what you *require* your investments to earn to break even. You lose money if you earn less than 10 percent, and you gain money if you earn more than 10 percent. This break even characteristic makes the IRR useful in evaluating capital projects.

### Self-Test Questions

What is the rationale for using the IRR method to evaluate a capital budgeting project?

"The IRR on a capital budgeting project is the same as the YTM on a bond." Is this a correct statement?

Whole Wheat Bakery is considering purchasing a new machine that costs $75,000. The machine is expected to generate after-tax cash flows equal to $30,000, $38,000, and $28,000 during its three-year life. Whole Wheat requires such investments to earn a return equal to at least 12 percent. What is the machine's internal rate of return (IRR)? Should the bakery purchase the machine? (*Answers:* IRR = 13.6%; purchase the project)

## COMPARISON OF THE NPV AND IRR METHODS

We found the NPV for Project S is $161.33, which means that the firm's value will increase by $161.33 if the project is purchased. The IRR for Project S is 13.1 percent, which means that the firm will earn a 13.1 percent rate of return on its investment if it purchases Project S. We generally measure wealth in dollars, so the NPV method should be used to accomplish the goal of maximizing shareholders' wealth. In reality, using the IRR method could lead to investment decisions that increase but do not maximize wealth. We choose to discuss the IRR method and compare it with the NPV method because many corporate executives are familiar with the meaning of IRR, it is entrenched in the corporate world, and it does have some virtues. For these reasons, it is important to understand the IRR method and be prepared to explain why a project with *a lower IRR might sometimes be preferable to one with a higher IRR.*

### NPV Profiles

**net present value (NPV) profile**
A curve showing the relationship between a project's NPV and various discount rates (required rates of return).

A graph that shows a project's NPV at various discount rates (required rates of return) is termed the project's **net present value (NPV) profile.** Figure 9-2 shows the NPV profiles for Project L and Project S. To construct the profiles, we calculate the projects' NPVs at various discount rates—say, 0, 5, 10, and 15 percent—and then plot these values. The points plotted on our graph for each project are shown at the bottom of Figure 9-2.[5]

Because the IRR is defined as the discount rate at which a project's NPV equals zero, the point where its *NPV profile crosses the x axis indicates a project's internal rate of return.*

---

[5]Note that the NPV profiles are curved—they are *not* straight lines. Also, the NPVs approach the cost of the project as the discount rate increases without limit. The reason is that, at an infinitely high discount rate, the PV of the future cash flows would be zero, so NPV at $r = \infty$ is $CF_0$, which in our example is −$3,000.

**FIGURE 9-2**  NPV Profiles for Project S and Project L

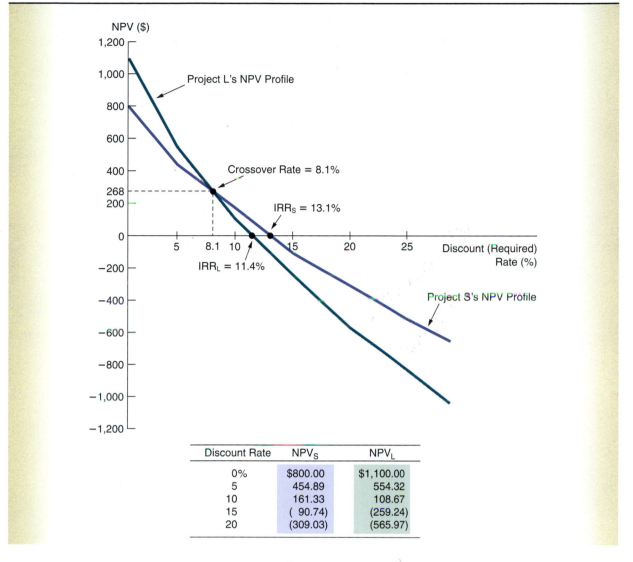

| Discount Rate | NPV$_S$ | NPV$_L$ |
|---|---|---|
| 0% | $800.00 | $1,100.00 |
| 5 | 454.89 | 554.32 |
| 10 | 161.33 | 108.67 |
| 15 | ( 90.74) | (259.24) |
| 20 | (309.03) | (565.97) |

## NPVs and the Required Rate of Return

Figure 9-2 shows that the NPV profiles for Project L and Project S decline as the discount rate (required rate of return) increases. Notice, however, that Project L has the higher NPV at low discount rates, whereas Project S has the higher NPV at high discount rates. According to the graph, NPV$_S$ = NPV$_L$ = $268 when the discount rate equals 8.1 percent. We call this point the **crossover rate** because below this rate NPV$_S$ < NPV$_L$, and above this rate, NPV$_S$ > NPV$_L$; but at this rate the NPVs are equal, and thus cross over, at 8.1 percent.[6]

**crossover rate**
The discount rate at which the NPV profiles of two projects cross and, thus, at which the projects' NPVs are equal.

---

[6]The crossover rate is easy to calculate. Simply go back to Figure 9-1, in which we first show the two projects' cash flows. Now calculate the difference in the cash flows for Project S and Project L in each year. The differences are computed as $\dot{CF}_S - \dot{CF}_L$. Thus, the cash flow differences for Projects S and L are CF$_0$ = $0, CF$_1$ = +$1,100, CF$_2$ = +$300, CF$_3$ = −$500, and CF$_4$ = −$1,200, respectively. To compute the crossover rate using a financial calculator, enter these numbers in the order given here into the cash flow register, and then ask the calculator to compute the IRR. You should find IRR = 8.11%.

Figure 9-2 also indicates that Project L's NPV is "more sensitive" to changes in the discount rate than is Project S's NPV. That is, Project L's NPV profile has the steeper slope, indicating that a given change in r has a larger effect on $NPV_L$ than on $NPV_S$. Project L is more sensitive to changes in r because the cash flows from Project L are received later than those from Project S. As a general rule, the impact of an increase in the discount rate is much greater on distant cash flows than on near-term cash flows.[7] Consequently, if a project has most of its cash flows coming in the early years, its NPV will not be lowered very much if the required rate of return increases. Conversely, a project whose cash flows come later will be severely penalized by high required rates of return. Accordingly, Project L, which has its largest cash flows in the later years, is hurt badly when the required rate of return is high, whereas Project S, which has relatively rapid cash flows, is affected less by high discount rates.

## Independent Projects

Note that the IRR formula, Equation 9–2, is simply the NPV formula, Equation 9–1, solved for the particular discount rate that forces the NPV to equal zero. Thus, the same basic equation is used for both methods. Mathematically, the NPV and IRR methods will *always* lead to the same accept/reject decisions for independent projects: *If a project's NPV is positive, its IRR will exceed r; if NPV is negative, r will exceed the IRR.* To see why this is so, look back at Figure 9-2, focus on Project L's profile, and note the following:

- The IRR criterion for acceptance is that the required rate of return is less than (or to the left of) the IRR (11.4 percent).
- Whenever the required rate of return is less than the IRR (11.4 percent), NPV > 0.

Thus, at any required rate of return less than 11.4 percent, Project L will be acceptable by both the NPV and the IRR criteria. Both methods reject the project if the required rate of return is greater than 11.4 percent. Project S—and all other independent projects under consideration—could be analyzed similarly, and *in every case, if a project is acceptable using the IRR method, then the NPV method also will show it is acceptable.*

## Mutually Exclusive Projects

If Project S and Project L are *mutually exclusive* rather than independent, then only one project can be purchased. If you use IRR to make the decision as to which project is better, you would choose Project S because $IRR_S = 13.1\% > IRR_L = 11.4\%$. If you use NPV to make the decision, you might reach a different conclusion depending on the firm's required rate of return. Note from Figure 9-2 that if the required rate of return is less than the crossover rate of 8.1 percent, $NPV_L > NPV_S$, but $NPV_S > NPV_L$ if the required rate of return is greater than 8.1 percent. As a result, Project L would be preferred if the firm's required rate of return is less than 8.1 percent, but Project S would be preferred if the firm's required rate of return is greater than 8.1 percent.

---

[7]To illustrate, consider the present value of $100 to be received in one year versus $100 to be received in 10 years. The present values of each $100 discounted at 10 percent and at 15 percent are as follows:

| Future Value | Year Received | PV @ 10% | PV @ 15% | Percent Difference |
|---|---|---|---|---|
| $100 | 1 | $90.91 | $86.96 | −4.3% |
| $100 | 10 | 38.55 | 24.72 | −35.9 |

As you can see, the farther into the future the cash flows are, the greater their sensitivity to discount rate changes.

As long as the firm's required rate of return is greater than 8.1 percent, using either NPV or IRR will result in the same decision—that is, Project S should be purchased—because $NPV_S > NPV_L$ and $IRR_S > IRR_L$. On the other hand, if the firm's required rate of return is less than 8.1 percent, a person who uses NPV will reach a different conclusion as to which project should be purchased: He or she will choose Project L because $NPV_L > NPV_S$. In this situation—that is, the required rate of return is less than 8.1 percent—*a conflict exists* because NPV says choose Project L over Project S, whereas IRR says just the opposite. Which answer is correct? Logic suggests that the NPV method is better because it selects the project that adds more to shareholder wealth.

Two basic conditions can cause NPV profiles to cross and thus lead to conflicts between NPV and IRR: (1) when *project size (or scale) differences* exist, meaning that the cost of one project is much larger than that of the other or (2) when *timing differences* exist, meaning that the timing of cash flows from the two projects differs such that most of the cash flows from one project come in the early years and most of the cash flows from the other project come in the later years, as occurs with Projects L and S.[8]

When either size or timing differences occur, the firm will have different amounts of funds to invest in the various years, depending on which of the two mutually exclusive projects it chooses. For example, if one project costs more than the other, then the firm will have more money at $t = 0$ to invest elsewhere if it selects the smaller project. Similarly, for projects of equal size, the one with the larger early cash inflows provides more funds for reinvestment in the early years. Given this situation, the rate of return at which differential cash flows can be invested is an important consideration.

The critical issue in resolving conflicts between mutually exclusive projects is this: How useful is it to generate cash flows earlier rather than later? The value of early cash flows depends on the rate at which we can reinvest these cash flows. *The NPV method implicitly assumes that the rate at which cash flows can be reinvested is the required rate of return, r, whereas the IRR method implies that the firm has the opportunity to reinvest at the project's IRR.* These assumptions are inherent in the mathematics of the discounting process. The cash flows can actually be withdrawn as dividends by the stockholders and spent on pizza, but the NPV method still assumes that cash flows can be reinvested at the required rate of return, whereas the IRR method assumes reinvestment at the project's IRR.

Which is the better assumption—that cash flows can be reinvested at the required rate of return or that they can be reinvested at the project's IRR? To reinvest at the IRR associated with a capital project, the firm would have to be able to reinvest the project's cash flows in another project with an identical IRR. Such projects generally do not continue to exist, or it is not feasible to reinvest in such projects, because competition in the investment markets drives their prices up and their IRRs down. On the other hand, at the very least, a firm could repurchase the bonds and stock it has issued to raise capital budgeting funds and thus repay some of its investors, which would be the same as investing at its required rate of return. Thus, we conclude that the *more realistic* **reinvestment rate assumption** *is the required rate of return, which is implicit in the NPV method.* This, in turn, leads us to prefer the NPV method, at least for firms willing and able to obtain new funds at a cost reasonably close to their current cost of funds.

**reinvestment rate assumption**
The assumption that cash flows from a project can be reinvested (1) at the cost of capital, if using the NPV method, or (2) at the internal rate of return, if using the IRR method.

---

[8]Of course, it is possible for mutually exclusive projects to differ with respect to both scale and timing. Also, if mutually exclusive projects have different lives (as opposed to different cash flow patterns over a common life), this introduces further complications, and for meaningful comparisons, some mutually exclusive projects must be evaluated over a common life.

We should reiterate that when projects are independent, the NPV and IRR methods both provide exactly the same accept/reject decision. However, when evaluating mutually exclusive projects, especially those that differ in scale or timing, the NPV method should be used to determine which project should be purchased.

### Self-Test Questions

Describe how NPV profiles are constructed.

What is the crossover rate, and how does it affect the choice between mutually exclusive projects?

Why do the NPV and IRR methods always lead to the same accept/reject decisions for independent projects?

What two basic conditions can lead to conflicts between the NPV and IRR methods?

If a conflict exists, should the capital budgeting decision be made on the basis of the NPV or the IRR ranking? Why?

## CASH FLOW PATTERNS AND MULTIPLE IRRs

A project has a *conventional* cash flow pattern if it has cash outflows (costs) in one or more consecutive periods at the beginning of its life followed by a series of cash inflows. If, however, a project has a large cash outflow at the beginning of its life and then another cash outflow (or multiple outflows) either some time during or at the end of its life, then it has an *unconventional* cash flow pattern. Projects with unconventional cash flow patterns present unique difficulties when the IRR method is used, including the possibility of **multiple IRRs**.[9] Following are examples of conventional and unconventional cash flow patterns:

**multiple IRRs**
The situation in which a project has two or more IRRs.

Conventional cash flow patterns:   (1) − + + + + +   (2) − − − + + +
Unconventional cash flow patterns: (1) − + + − + + +   (2) − − + + + − −

There exists an IRR solution for each time the *direction* of the cash flows associated with a project is interrupted—that is, inflows change to outflows. For example, each of the conventional cash flow patterns shown here has only one change in the signs (direction) of the cash flows (is interrupted) from negative (outflow) to positive (inflow); thus, there is only one IRR solution. On the other hand, each of the unconventional cash flow patterns shown here has two "interruptions" and thus two IRR solutions.

Figure 9-3 illustrates the multiple IRR problem with a strip mining project that costs $1.6 million. The mine will produce a cash inflow of $10 million at the end of Year 1, but $10 million must be spent at the end of Year 2 to restore the land to its original condition. Two IRRs exist for this project—25 percent and 400 percent. The NPV profile for the mine shows that the project would have a positive NPV, and thus be acceptable, if the firm's required rate of return is between 25 percent and 400 percent.

---

[9]Multiple IRRs result from the manner in which Equation 9–2 must be solved to arrive at a project's IRR. The mathematical rationale will not be discussed here. Instead, we want you to be aware that multiple IRRs can exist because this possibility complicates capital budgeting evaluation using the IRR method.

## FIGURE 9-3   NPV Profiles for Project M

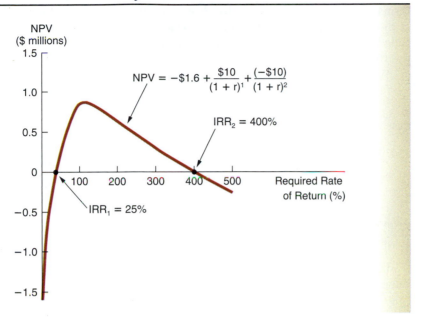

NPV ($ millions)

$$NPV = -\$1.6 + \frac{\$10}{(1+r)^1} + \frac{(-\$10)}{(1+r)^2}$$

$IRR_2 = 400\%$

$IRR_1 = 25\%$

Required Rate of Return (%)

### Self-Test Questions

How would you describe a conventional cash flow pattern? What is an unconventional cash flow pattern?

What is the multiple IRR problem, and what condition is necessary for its occurrence?

## MODIFIED INTERNAL RATE OF RETURN

Despite a strong academic preference for NPV, surveys indicate that many business executives prefer IRR over NPV. It seems that many managers find it intuitively more appealing to analyze investments in terms of percentage rates of return than dollars of NPV. But remember from our earlier discussion that the IRR method assumes the cash flows from the project are reinvested at a rate of return equal to the IRR, which we generally view as unrealistic. Given this fact, can we devise a rate of return measure that is better than the regular IRR? The answer is yes—we can modify the IRR and make it a better indicator of relative profitability, hence better for use in capital budgeting. This "modified" return is called the **modified IRR**, or **MIRR**, and it is defined as follows:

> **modified IRR (MIRR)** The discount rate at which the present value of a project's cost is equal to the present value of its terminal value, where the terminal value is found as the sum of the future values of the cash inflows compounded at the firm's required rate of return.

$$\text{PV of cash outflows} = \frac{\text{TV}}{(1 + \text{MIRR})^n}$$

$$\sum_{t=0}^{n} \frac{\text{COF}_t}{(1-r)^t} = \frac{\sum_{t=0}^{n} \text{CIF}_t(1+r)^{n-t}}{(1 + \text{MIRR})^n}$$

9–3

Here COF refers to cash outflows (all negative numbers) and CIF refers to cash inflows (all positive numbers) associated with a project. The left term in the second line is simply the present value (PV) of the investment outlays (cash *outflows*) when discounted at the project's required rate of return, r, and the numerator of the right term is the future value of the cash *inflows,* assuming that these inflows are reinvested at the project's required rate of return. The future value of the cash inflows is also called the *terminal value,* or TV. The discount rate that forces the PV of the TV to equal the PV of the costs is defined as the MIRR.[10]

We can illustrate the calculation of MIRR with Project S:

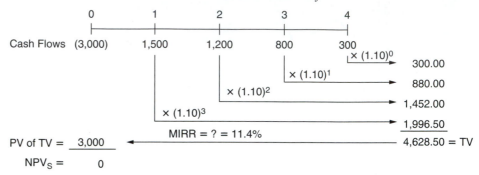

Using the cash flows as set out on the cash flow time line, first find the terminal value by compounding each cash inflow at the 10 percent required rate of return. Then, enter into your calculator PV = −3,000, FV = 4,628.50, and N = 4, and compute I/Y = 11.4% = $MIRR_S$. Similarly, we find $MIRR_L = 11.0\%$.

The modified IRR has a significant advantage over the traditional IRR measure. MIRR assumes that cash flows are reinvested at the required rate of return, whereas the traditional IRR measure assumes that cash flows are reinvested at the project's own IRR. Because reinvestment at the required rate of return (cost of funds) generally is more correct, the MIRR is a better indicator of a project's true profitability. MIRR also solves the multiple IRR problem. To illustrate, with r = 10%, the strip mine project described earlier has MIRR = 5.6% versus the 10 percent required rate of return, so it should be rejected. This is consistent with the decision based on the NPV method because at r = 10%, NPV = −$0.77 million.

Is MIRR as good as NPV for choosing between mutually exclusive projects? If two projects are of equal size and have the same life, then NPV and MIRR will always lead to the same project selection decision. Thus, for any projects like our Projects S and L, if $NPV_S > NPV_L$, then $MIRR_S > MIRR_L$, and the kinds of conflicts we encountered between NPV and the traditional IRR will not occur. Also, if the projects are of equal size but differ in lives, the MIRR will always lead to the same decision as the NPV if the MIRRs for both projects are calculated using as the terminal year the life of the longer project. (Just fill in zeros for the shorter project's missing cash flows.) However, if the projects differ in size, then conflicts can still occur. For example, if we were choosing between a large project and a small mutually exclusive one, then we might find $NPV_{Large} > NPV_{Small}$ and $MIRR_{Large} < MIRR_{Small}$.

Our conclusion is that the MIRR is superior to the regular IRR as an indicator of a project's "true" rate of return or "expected long-term rate of return," but the NPV method is still better for choosing among competing projects that differ in size because it provides a better indicator of the extent to which each project will increase the value of the firm; thus, NPV is still the recommended approach.

---

[10]There are several alternative definitions for the MIRR. The differences relate primarily to whether negative cash flows that occur after positive cash flows begin should be compounded and treated as part of the TV or discounted and treated as a cost. Our definition (which treats all negative cash flows as investments and thus discounts them) generally is the most appropriate procedure. For a complete discussion, see William R. McDaniel, Daniel E. McCarty, and Kenneth A. Jessell, "Discounted Cash Flow with Explicit Reinvestment Rates: Tutorial and Extension," *The Financial Review* (August 1988), 369–385.

**Self-Test Questions**

What is the primary advantage to using MIRR rather than the regular IRR to make capital budgeting decisions?

Whole Wheat Bakery is considering purchasing a new machine that costs $75,000. The machine is expected to generate after-tax cash flows equal to $30,000, $38,000, and $28,000 during its three-year life. Whole Wheat requires such investments to earn a return equal to at least 12 percent. What is the machine's modified internal rate of return (MIRR)? Should the bakery purchase the machine? (*Answers:* MIRR = 13.0%; purchase the project)

# PAYBACK PERIOD—TRADITIONAL (NONDISCOUNTED) AND DISCOUNTED

Many managers like to know how long it will take a project to repay its initial investment (cost) from the cash flows it is expected to generate in the future. Thus, many firms compute a project's **traditional payback period (PB),** which is defined as the expected number of years required to recover the original investment (the cost of the asset). Payback is the simplest and, as far as we know, the oldest *formal* method used to evaluate capital budgeting projects. To compute a project's payback period, simply add up the expected cash flows for each year until the cumulative value equals the amount that is initially invested. The total amount of time, including the fraction of a year if appropriate, that it takes to recapture the original amount invested is the payback period. Figure 9-4 shows the payback calculation process for both Project S and Project L.

The exact payback period can be found using the following formula:

**traditional payback period (PB)**
The length of time it takes for the original cost of an investment to be recovered from its expected cash flows.

$$\text{Payback period (PB)} = \begin{pmatrix} \text{Number of years} \\ before \text{ full recovery} \\ \text{of initial investment} \end{pmatrix} + \dfrac{\begin{pmatrix} \text{Amount of the initial investment} \\ \text{that is } unrecoverd \text{ at the start} \\ \text{of the recovery year} \end{pmatrix}}{\begin{array}{c} \text{Total cash flow generated} \\ \text{during the recovery year} \end{array}}$$

**9-4**

**FIGURE 9-4**   Traditional Payback Period (PB) for Project S and Project L

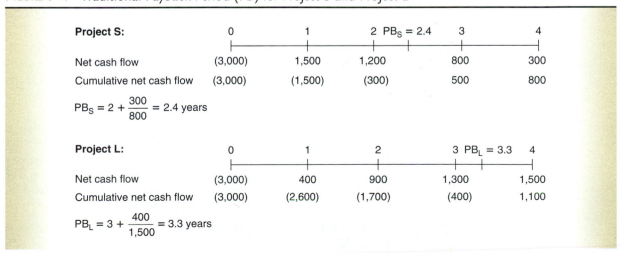

**Project S:**

| | 0 | 1 | 2  PB_S = 2.4 | 3 | 4 |
|---|---|---|---|---|---|
| Net cash flow | (3,000) | 1,500 | 1,200 | 800 | 300 |
| Cumulative net cash flow | (3,000) | (1,500) | (300) | 500 | 800 |

$$PB_S = 2 + \frac{300}{800} = 2.4 \text{ years}$$

**Project L:**

| | 0 | 1 | 2 | 3  PB_L = 3.3 | 4 |
|---|---|---|---|---|---|
| Net cash flow | (3,000) | 400 | 900 | 1,300 | 1,500 |
| Cumulative net cash flow | (3,000) | (2,600) | (1,700) | (400) | 1,100 |

$$PB_L = 3 + \frac{400}{1,500} = 3.3 \text{ years}$$

As Figure 9-4 shows, the payback period for Project S is between two years and three years. Using Equation 9–4, the exact payback period for Project S is computed as follows:

$$\text{PB}_S = 2 + \frac{300}{800} = 2.4\,\text{years}$$

Applying the same procedure to Project L, we find $\text{PB}_L = 3.3$ years.

Using payback to make capital budgeting decisions is based on the concept that it is better to recover the cost of (investment in) a project sooner rather than later. Therefore, Project S is considered better than Project L because it has a lower payback. *As a general rule, a project is considered acceptable if its payback is less than the maximum cost recovery time established by the firm.* In other words, to determine whether a project is acceptable using the traditional payback period method, we apply the following decision rule:

**Traditional Payback Period (PB) Decision Rule:** A project is acceptable if $\text{PB} < n^*$

where $n^*$ is the recovery period that the firm has determined is appropriate. For example, if the firm requires projects to have a payback of three years or less, Project S would be acceptable but Project L would not.

The payback method is simple, which explains why payback traditionally has been one of the most popular capital budgeting techniques. But because payback ignores the time value of money, relying solely on this method could lead to incorrect decisions—at least if our goal is to maximize value. If a project has a payback of three years, we know how quickly the initial investment will be covered by the expected cash flows, but this information does not provide any indication of whether the return on the project is sufficient to cover the cost of the funds invested. In addition, when payback is used, the cash flows beyond the payback period are ignored. For example, even if Project L had a fifth year of cash flows equal to $50,000, its payback would remain 3.3 years, which is less desirable than the payback of 2.4 years for Project S. But with the additional $50,000 cash flow, Project L most likely would be preferred.

**discounted payback period (DPB)**
The length of time it takes for a project's discounted cash flows to repay the cost of the investment.

To correct for the fact that the traditional payback method does not consider the time value of money, we can compute the **discounted payback period (DPB)** for Project S, which is the length of time it takes for a project's *discounted* cash flows to repay the cost of the investment. Using the general payback concept, we can easily compute how long it takes to recapture the initial outlay of $3,000 using the *discounted* cash flows given in the cash flow time line. The sum of the present values of the cash flows for the first three years is $2,956.43 = $1,363.64 + $991.74 + $601.05, so all of the $3,000 cost is not recovered until 3.2 years = 3 years + [($3,000 − $2,956.43)/ $204.90] years. Therefore, on a *present value basis,* it takes 3.2 years for Project S to recover, or pay back, its original cost. The discounted payback for Project L is 3.9 years, so Project S is more acceptable. Figure 9-5 shows the discounted payback computations for Projects S and L.

Unlike the traditional payback computation, the discounted payback computation considers the time value of money. If you look at the cash flow time line that shows the NPV computation for Project S, you can see the reason it has a positive NPV is because the initial investment of $3,000 is recovered on a present value basis prior to the end of the project's life. Thus, using the discounted payback method, a project should be accepted when its discounted payback is less than its expected life.

**Discounted Payback (DPB) Decision Rule:** A project is acceptable if $\text{DPB} < \text{Project's life}$

FIGURE 9-5    Discounted Payback Period (DPB) for Project S and Project L

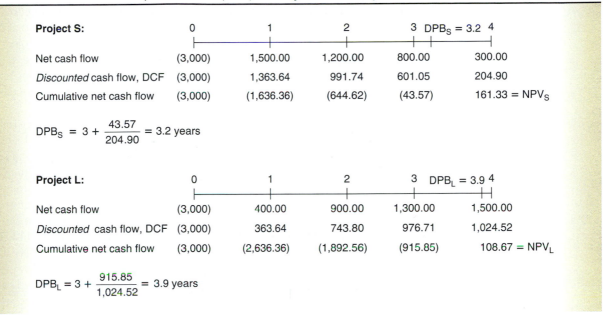

$$\text{DPB}_S = 3 + \frac{43.57}{204.90} = 3.2 \text{ years}$$

$$\text{DPB}_L = 3 + \frac{915.85}{1,024.52} = 3.9 \text{ years}$$

As Figure 9-5 shows, when a project's discounted payback is less than its life, the present value of the future cash flows the project is expected to generate exceeds the initial cost of the asset—that is, NPV > 0.

## Self-Test Questions

How does the traditional payback differ from the discounted payback?

Whole Wheat Bakery is considering purchasing a new machine that costs $75,000. The machine is expected to generate after-tax cash flows equal to $30,000, $38,000, and $28,000 during its three-year life. Whole Wheat requires such investments to earn a return equal to at least 12 percent. What is the machine's traditional payback period (PB) and its discounted payback period (DPB)? Should the bakery purchase the machine? (*Answers:* PB = 2.25 years; DPB = 2.9 years; purchase the project because DPB < machine's life)

## CONCLUSIONS ON THE CAPITAL BUDGETING DECISION METHODS

Earlier in this chapter, we compared the NPV and IRR methods to highlight their relative strengths and weaknesses for evaluating capital projects, and in the process we probably created the impression that "sophisticated" firms should use only one method in the decision process—NPV. However, virtually all capital budgeting decisions are analyzed by computer, so it is easy to calculate and list all the decision measures we discussed: traditional payback, discounted payback, NPV, IRR, and MIRR. In making the accept/reject decision, most large, sophisticated firms such as IBM, General Electric, and General Motors calculate and consider multiple measures because each provides decision makers with a somewhat different piece of relevant information.

Traditional payback and discounted payback provide information about both the risk and the *liquidity* of a project. A long payback means (1) that the investment dollars will be locked up for many years, hence the project is relatively illiquid and (2) that the project's cash flows must be forecast far out into the future, hence the project is probably quite risky.[11] A good analogy for this is the bond valuation process. An investor should never compare the yields to maturity on two bonds without considering their terms to maturity because a bond's riskiness is significantly influenced by its maturity.

NPV is important because it gives a direct measure of the dollar benefit (on a present value basis) to the firm's shareholders, so we regard NPV as the best single measure of *profitability*. IRR also measures profitability, but here it is expressed as a percentage rate of return, which many decision makers, especially nonfinancial managers, seem to prefer. Further, IRR contains information concerning a project's "safety margin," which is not inherent in NPV. To illustrate, consider the following two projects: Project T costs $10,000 at t = 0 and is expected to return $16,500 at the end of one year, whereas Project B costs $100,000 and has an expected payoff of $115,500 after one year. At a 10 percent required rate of return, both projects have an NPV of $5,000, so by the NPV rule we should be indifferent between the two. However, Project T actually provides a much larger margin for error. Even if its realized cash inflow were almost 40 percent below the $16,500 forecast, the firm would still recover its $10,000 investment. On the other hand, if Project B's inflows fell by only 14 percent from the forecasted $115,500, the firm would not recover its investment. Further, if no inflows were generated at all, the firm would lose only $10,000 with Project T, but $100,000 if it took on Project B.

The NPV contains no information about either the safety margin inherent in a project's cash flow forecasts or the amount of capital at risk, but the IRR does provide "safety margin" information: Project T's IRR is a whopping 65 percent, whereas Project B's IRR is only 15.5 percent. As a result, the realized return could fall substantially for Project T, and it would still make money. Note, however, that the IRR method has a reinvestment assumption that probably is unrealistic, and it is possible for projects to have multiple IRRs. Both of these problems can be corrected using the modified IRR calculation, which was discussed earlier.

In summary, the different methods provide different types of information. Because it is easy to calculate them, all should be considered in the decision process. For any specific decision, more weight might be given to one method than another, but it would be foolish to ignore the information provided by any of the methods.

All capital budgeting methods that consider the time value of money provide the same accept/reject decisions, but there could be ranking conflicts, which might lead to different decisions when projects are mutually exclusive, depending on which capital budgeting technique is used.

At this point, we should note that multinational corporations use essentially the same capital budgeting techniques described in this chapter. However, foreign governments, international regulatory environments, and financial and product markets in other countries pose certain challenges to U.S. firms that must make capital budgeting decisions for their foreign operations. We wait to discuss some of these challenges/differences until the next chapter.

---

[11]We generally define liquidity as the ability to convert an asset into cash quickly while maintaining the original investment. Thus, in most cases, short-term assets are considered more liquid than long-term assets. We discuss liquidity in greater detail later in the book.

## THE POSTAUDIT

An important aspect of the capital budgeting process is the **postaudit,** which involves (1) comparing actual results with those predicted by the project's sponsors and (2) explaining why any differences occurred. For example, many firms require that the operating divisions send monthly reports for the first six months after a project goes into operation and quarterly reports thereafter, until the project's results are up to expectations. From then on, reports on the project are handled like those of other operations.

The postaudit has two main purposes:

1. **Improve forecasts.** When decision makers are forced to compare their projections with actual outcomes, there is a tendency for estimates to improve. Conscious or unconscious biases are observed and eliminated; new forecasting methods are sought as the need for them becomes apparent; and people simply tend to do everything better, including forecasting, if they know that their actions are being monitored.

2. **Improve operations.** Businesses are run by people, and people can perform at higher or lower levels of efficiency. When a divisional team has made a forecast about an investment, its members are, in a sense, putting their reputations on the line. If costs are above predicted levels, sales are below expectations, and so on, executives in production, marketing, and other areas will strive to improve operations and to bring results in line with forecasts. In a discussion related to this point, an IBM executive made this statement: "You academicians worry only about making good decisions. In business, we also worry about making decisions good."

The postaudit is not a simple process—a number of factors can cause complications. First, we must recognize that each element of the cash flow forecast is subject to uncertainty, so a percentage of all projects undertaken by any reasonably venturesome firm will necessarily go awry. This fact must be considered when appraising the performances of the operating executives who submit capital expenditure requests. Second, projects sometimes fail to meet expectations for reasons beyond the control of the operating executives and for reasons that no one could realistically be expected to anticipate. For example, poor economic conditions in 2000−2002 adversely affected many projects. Third, it is often difficult to separate the operating results of one investment from those of a larger system. Although some projects stand alone and permit ready identification of costs and revenues, the actual cost savings that result from a new computer system, for example, might be hard to measure. Fourth, it is often hard to hand out blame or praise because the executives who were actually responsible for a given decision might have moved on by the time the results of a long-term investment are known.

Because of these difficulties, some firms tend to downplay the importance of the postaudit. However, observations of both businesses and governmental units suggest that the best-run and most successful organizations are the ones that put the greatest

**postaudit**
A comparison of the actual and expected results for a given capital project.

emphasis on postaudits. Accordingly, we regard the postaudit as being an extremely important element in a good capital budgeting system.

 **Self-Test Questions**

What is done in the postaudit?

Identify several purposes of the postaudit.

What are some factors that can cause complications in the postaudit?

## CAPITAL BUDGETING METHODS USED IN PRACTICE

Many surveys have been conducted over the years to determine which techniques firms rely on when making capital budgeting decisions. The results consistently show that firms rely on each of the methods discussed in this chapter, to some extent, to help make final decisions about the acceptability of capital budgeting projects. As technology has advanced, firms have shifted to using the more sophisticated techniques, such as NPV and IRR. The following table shows to what extent this shift has occurred since the 1970s. The results given in the table were compiled from surveys conducted during each decade.[12] The numbers represent the average percentage of respondents who indicated that their firms "Always" or "Almost Always" use the particular capital budgeting technique. In most cases, those who were surveyed were not asked to indicate the primary and secondary methods that were used.

| Period | Traditional Payback Period | NPV | IRR |
|--------|---------------------------|-----|-----|
| 1970s  | 85%                       | 65% | 80% |
| 1980s  | 78                        | 75  | 88  |
| 1990s  | 60                        | 80  | 79  |
| 2000s  | 53                        | 85  | 77  |

As you can see, the use of the traditional payback period and IRR methods has declined, whereas the use of the NPV method has increased. Prior to the 1970s, many firms relied heavily on the payback period to make capital budgeting decisions. As technology and the understanding of the discounting techniques improved, both NPV and IRR became more popular. It appears that, for the most part, financial managers recognize that these techniques provide correct decisions with respect to value maximization.

For the most part, studies have shown that companies (1) use more sophisticated capital budgeting techniques today than in previous times and (2) do not rely on a

---

[12]Studies that were examined include Lawrence J. Gitman and John R. Forrester, Jr., 1977, "A Survey of Capital Budgeting Techniques Used by Major U.S. Firms," *Financial Management,* Fall, 66–71; David J. Oblak and Roy J. Helm, Jr., 1980, "Survey and Analysis of Capital Budgeting Methods Used by Multinationals, "*Financial Management,* Winter, 37–41; Marjorie T. Stanley and Stanley B. Block, 1984, "A Survey of Multinational Capital Budgeting," *Financial Review,* March, 36–51; Glenn H. Petry and James Sprow, 1993, "The Theory of Finance in the 1990s," *The Quarterly Review of Economics and Finance,* Winter, 359–381; Erika Gilbert and Alan Reichert, 1995, "The Practice of Financial Management among Large United States Corporations," *Financial Practice and Education,* Spring/Summer, 16–23; Patricia Chadwell-Hatfield, Bernard Goitein, Philip Horvath, and Allen Webster, 1996/1997, "Financial Criteria, Capital Budgeting Techniques, and Risk Analysis of Manufacturing Firms," *Journal of Applied Business Research,* Winter, 95–104; John R. Graham and Campbell R. Harvey, 2001, "The Theory and Practice of Corporate Finance: Evidence from the Field," *Journal of Financial Economics,*Vol. 60, No 2–3, 197–243; Patricia A. Ryan and Glenn P. Ryan, 2002, "Capital Budgeting Practices of the Fortune 1000: How Have Things Changed?" *Journal of Business and Management,*Fall, 335–364.

single evaluation method to make decisions about investing in capital projects. Clearly, firms still use payback period in their capital budgeting analyses. But even firms that previously relied on the traditional payback period seem to have switched to the discounted payback period. Thus, indications are that firms do use the methods we profess in finance courses.

**Self-Test Question**
What trend has been observed in practice in the use of capital budgeting methods?

To summarize the key concepts, let's answer the questions that were posed at the beginning of the chapter:

**Chapter *Essentials***
—The Answers

- **How do firms make decisions about whether to invest in costly, long-lived real assets such as buildings and equipment?** To make investment decisions, firms use decision-making methods that are based on the fundamental valuation concepts we discussed in earlier chapters. To make decisions about the acceptability of capital budgeting projects, which generally relate to such real assets as buildings and equipment, firms use techniques to evaluate the assets' values. Although the methods used in capital budgeting analysis have such names as net present value (NPV) and internal rate of return (IRR), they are based on the same concepts we discussed in Chapters 6 through 8. In other words, the decision is based on the present value of the cash flows an asset is expected to generate during its life. An asset's *NPV* is the present value of its expected future cash flows minus the initial investment that must be made to purchase the asset. If NPV > 0, the firm's value will increase if the asset is purchased. An asset's *IRR* is the rate of return that the asset is expected to provide if it is purchased. If IRR > r, which is the firm's required rate of return, the firm's value will increase if the asset is purchased. Most other capital budgeting methods used by firms are based on the same principles as NPV and IRR—that is, time value of money concepts.

- **How does a firm make a choice between two (or more) acceptable investments when only one can be purchased?** When a firm evaluates projects that are independent, all acceptable projects—that is, projects with NPVs > 0—can be purchased. However, when a firm evaluates projects that are mutually exclusive, only one of the acceptable projects can be purchased. If a firm evaluates two mutually exclusive projects, it is possible that the NPV and IRR methods yield conflicting results as to which project should be purchased. In some instances, we find that $NPV_1 > NPV_2$, which suggests that Project 1 is better than Project 2; at the same time, we might find that $IRR_1 < IRR_2$, which suggests that Project 2 is better than Project 1. How should this conflict be resolved? To make a decision that is consistent with the goal of maximizing the value of the firm, the NPV method should be used. As a result, in this case, Project 1 should be purchased.

- **How are different capital budgeting techniques related? Which technique is the best to use?** In this chapter, we discussed five capital budgeting methods—net present value (NPV), internal rate of return (IRR), modified internal rate of return (MIRR), traditional payback period (PB), and discounted payback period (DPB). Except for PB, these methods are based on time value of money concepts. Thus, NPV, IRR, MIRR, and DPB will always yield the same accept/reject decision—that is, if a project is considered acceptable when evaluated using NPV, then it must also be considered acceptable when evaluated using IRR, MIRR, and DPB. As a result, when NPV > 0, IRR > r, MIRR > r, and DPB < the asset's life. Because the traditional payback period (PB) is not based on time value of money concepts, it is not related to the other capital budgeting methods.

- **Which capital budgeting methods do firms actually use?** In practice, firms do not use a single method to evaluate capital budgeting projects; rather, some combination of the techniques discussed in this chapter is used. Most firms rely heavily on NPV and IRR to make investment decisions because decisions made using these methods are consistent with the goal of maximizing shareholders' wealth.

## ETHICAL DILEMMA

### This Is a Good Investment—Be Sure the Numbers Show That It Is!

Oliver Greene is the assistant to the financial manager at Cybercomp Inc., a company that develops software to drive network communications for personal computers. Oliver joined Cybercomp three years ago, following his graduation from college. His primary responsibility has been to evaluate capital budgeting projects and make investment recommendations to the board of directors. Oliver enjoys his job very much; he often finds himself challenged with interesting tasks, and he is paid extremely well.

Last week Oliver started evaluating the capital projects that have been proposed for investment this year. One proposal calls for Cybercomp to purchase NetWare Products, a company that manufactures circuit boards called network cards, which are required to achieve communication connectivity between personal computers. Cybercomp packages network cards with the software that it sells, but it currently purchases those circuit boards from another manufacturer. The proposal, which was submitted by Nadine Wilson, Cybercomp's CEO, suggests that the company might reduce costs and increase profit margins by producing the network cards in house.

Oliver barely had time to scan the proposal when he was summoned to Mrs. Wilson's office. The meeting was short and to the point. Mrs. Wilson instructed Oliver to "make the numbers for NetWare Products look good because we want to buy that company." She also gave Oliver an evaluation of NetWare completed two years ago by an independent appraiser that suggests NetWare might not be worth the amount that Cybercomp is willing to pay. Mrs. Wilson instructed Oliver to find a way to rebut the findings of the report.

Oliver was troubled by the meeting. His gut feeling was that something was wrong, but he hadn't yet had time to carefully examine the proposal. In fact, his evaluation was very cursory, and he was far from making a final decision about the acceptability of the proposed capital budgeting project. Oliver felt he needed much more information before he could make a final recommendation.

Oliver has spent the entire day examining the appraisal report provided by Mrs. Wilson and trying to gather additional information about the proposed investment. The report contains some background information concerning NetWare's operations, but crucial financial data are missing. Further investigation into NetWare Products has produced little information. Oliver has discovered that the company's stock is closely held by a small group of investors. These investors own numerous businesses and contribute generously to the local university, which happens to be Mrs. Wilson's alma mater. In addition, Oliver's secretary has informed him that the gossip around the "water cooler" at Cybercomp suggests that Mrs. Wilson and the owners of NetWare are old college buddies, and she might even have a stake in NetWare.

This morning, Mrs. Wilson called Oliver and repeated her feelings concerning the purchase of NetWare. This time she said: "We really want to purchase NetWare. Some people might not believe so, but it's a very good deal. It's your job to make the numbers work—that's why we pay you the big bucks!" As a result of the conversation, Oliver has the impression that his job might be in jeopardy if he doesn't make the "right" decision. This added pressure has made Oliver very tense.

What should he do? What would you do if you were Oliver? Would your answer change if you knew Mrs. Wilson had recently sold much of her Cybercomp stock?

The concepts presented in this chapter should help you to better understand how to make decisions when investing your money. If you understand the basic concepts we discussed, you should be able to determine whether an investment is acceptable or unacceptable. Following are some ways you can use the concepts presented in this chapter:

- Determine the NPV of such investments as rental property and annuity payments. If you know or can estimate the future cash flows that you expect to receive from a particular investment, you should be able to compute its NPV using the rate of return you would like to earn on your invested funds. You should apply the same decision rule to make your investment decisions as businesses use—that is, purchase investments that have NPVs > 0. Similarly, to provide additional information, an investment's payback period, both traditional and discounted, can be computed when determining whether to invest your money.

- Compute the IRR of your investments. Based on the cash flows you expect to receive from an investment and its current market price, you can compute the investment's IRR. For example, in Chapter 6 we showed how to compute the yield to maturity (YTM) on a bond. In this chapter, you should have discovered that a bond's YTM is also its IRR—that is, the return that an investor expects to earn by purchasing the bond and holding it for the remainder of its life. Similar computations can be performed on other investments. The IRR of an investment can then be compared with the return you want to earn to invest your funds. As we discussed in this chapter, the investment should be purchased if its IRR is greater than your desired rate of return.

- In the chapter, we discussed the reinvestment assumptions that are inherent in the NPV and IRR methods. There is also a reinvestment assumption that applies to individual investors. When you invest your funds, you generally are able to have any income that is earned (interest or dividends) reinvested in the same investment. As a result, you assume that your "new" money is reinvested at the same rate as the money that is already invested. Although it is true that you can reinvest funds received from your existing investments, remember that market interest rates change, which means that the rates at which you can reinvest the income you receive from existing investments also change.

## QUESTIONS

9-1   How is a project classification scheme (for example, replacement, expansion into new markets, and so forth) used in the capital budgeting process?

9-2   Explain why the NPV of a relatively long-term project, defined as one for which a high percentage of its cash flows are expected in the distant future, is more sensitive to changes in the required rate of return than is the NPV of a short-term project.

9-3   Explain why, if two mutually exclusive projects are being compared, the project that generates most of its cash flows in the beginning of its life might have the higher ranking under the NPV criterion if the required rate of return is high, whereas the project that generates most of its cash flows toward the end of its life might be deemed better if the required rate of return is low. Would changes in the required rate of return ever cause a change in the IRR ranking of two such projects? Explain.

**9-4**   Explain the decision rules—that is, under what conditions a project is acceptable—for each of the following capital budgeting methods:

    **a.** Net present value (NPV)

    **b.** Internal rate of return (IRR)

    **c.** Modified internal rate of return (MIRR)

    **d.** Traditional payback (PB)

    **e.** Discounted payback (DPB)

**9-5**   After evaluating a capital budgeting project, Susan discovered that the project's NPV > 0. What does this information tell us about the project's IRR and discounted payback (DPB)? Can anything be concluded about the project's traditional payback period (PB)?

**9-6**   In what sense is a reinvestment rate assumption embodied in the NPV and IRR methods? What is the assumed reinvestment rate of each method?

**9-7**   "If a firm has no mutually exclusive projects, only independent ones, and it also has both a constant required rate of return and projects with conventional cash flow patterns, then the NPV and IRR methods will always lead to identical capital budgeting decisions." Discuss this statement. What does it imply about using the IRR method in lieu of the NPV method? If the projects are mutually exclusive, would your answer be the same?

**9-8**   Are there conditions under which a firm might be better off if it were to choose a machine with a rapid payback rather than one with a larger NPV? Explain.

**9-9**   A firm has $100 million available for capital expenditures. It is considering investing in one of two projects; each has a cost of $100 million. Project A has an IRR of 20 percent and an NPV of $9 million. It will be terminated at the end of one year at a profit of $20 million, resulting in an immediate increase in earnings per share (EPS). Project B, which cannot be postponed, has an IRR of 30 percent and an NPV of $50 million. However, the firm's short-run EPS will be reduced if it accepts Project B because no revenues will be generated for several years.

    **a.** Should the short-run effects on EPS influence the choice between the two projects?

    **b.** How might situations like the one described here influence a firm's decision to use payback as a part of the capital budgeting process?

**9-10**  Following is information for three *mutually exclusive* capital budgeting projects that the CFO of Universal Fire Systems is currently evaluating:

| Project | IRR | NPV | Discounted Payback |
|---------|-----|-----|--------------------|
| K | 21.0% | $5,500 | 3.5 years |
| L | 14.0 | 4,750 | 3.1 |
| M | 10.0 | 6,000 | 4.3 |

    **a.** Which project(s) should be purchased (accepted)?

    **b.** From the information given, what can be concluded about Universal's required rate of return, r?

**9-11** "Two companies examined the same capital budgeting project, which has an internal rate of return equal to 19 percent. One firm accepted the project, but the other firm rejected it. One of the firms must have made an incorrect decision." Discuss the validity of this statement.

**9-12** Following is a table Alice used to construct an NPV profile for Project K.

| Rate of Return (r) | NPV |
|:---:|:---:|
| 5% | $13,609 |
| 10 | 5,723 |
| 15 | 94 |
| 20 | (4,038) |
| 25 | (7,147) |

According to this information, which of the following statements is *incorrect?* Be prepared to discuss your answers.

**a.** Project K should be purchased if a firm has a required rate of return equal to 12 percent.

**b.** To determine whether Project K is acceptable, the internal rate of return (IRR) should be computed.

**c.** Project K has an internal rate of return that is between 15 percent and 20 percent.

**d.** Project K should be rejected if a firm has a required rate of return equal to 20 percent.

**e.** If one firm determines that Project K should be purchased, another firm might determine that it should not be purchased.

## SELF-TEST PROBLEMS

*(Solutions appear in Appendix B at the end of the book.)*

**ST-1** Define each of the following terms:                                                **key terms**

   **a.** Capital budget; capital budgeting

   **b.** Independent projects; mutually exclusive projects

   **c.** Net present value (NPV) method

   **d.** Internal rate of return (IRR) method; IRR

   **e.** NPV profile; crossover rate

   **f.** Unconventional cash flow patterns; multiple IRRs

   **g.** Hurdle rate; required rate of return, r

   **h.** Reinvestment rate assumption; modified IRR (MIRR)

   **i.** Traditional payback period; discounted payback period

   **j.** Postaudit

**ST-2** You are a financial analyst for Damon Electronics Company. The director of       **project analysis** capital budgeting has asked you to analyze two proposed capital investments, Projects X and Y. Each project has a cost of $10,000, and the required rate of return for each project is 12 percent. The projects' expected net cash flows are as follows:

| | Expected Net Cash Flows | |
|---|---|---|
| Year | Project X | Project Y |
| 0 | $(10,000) | $(10,000) |
| 1 | 6,500 | 3,500 |
| 2 | 3,000 | 3,500 |
| 3 | 3,000 | 3,500 |
| 4 | 1,000 | 3,500 |

a. Calculate each project's traditional payback period (PB), net present value (NPV), internal rate of return (IRR), modified internal rate of return (MIRR), and discounted payback period (DPB).

b. Which project or projects should be accepted if they are independent?

c. Which project should be accepted if they are mutually exclusive?

d. How might a change in the required rate of return produce a conflict between the NPV and IRR rankings of these two projects? Would this conflict exist if r were 5 percent? (*Hint:* Plot the NPV profiles.)

e. Why does the conflict exist?

## PROBLEMS

**NPV computation**    **9-1**    A firm is evaluating the acceptability of an investment that costs $90,000 and is expected to generate annual cash flows equal to $20,000 for the next six years. If the firm's required rate of return is 10 percent, what is the net present value (NPV) of the project? Should the project be purchased?

**NPV computation**    **9-2**    If the firm's required rate of return is 14 percent, what is the NPV of the following project?

| Year | Cash Flow |
|---|---|
| 0 | $(75,000) |
| 1 | 50,000 |
| 2 | 40,000 |

**IRR computation**    **9-3**    What is the internal rate of return (IRR) of a project that costs $45,000 if it is expected to generate $15,047 per year for five years?

**IRR computation**    **9-4**    Compute the internal rates of return (IRRs) for the following capital budgeting projects:

| Year | Project G | Project P | Project V |
|---|---|---|---|
| 0 | $(23,000) | $(48,000) | $(36,000) |
| 1 | 7,900 | 0 | (10,000) |
| 2 | 7,900 | 0 | 0 |
| 3 | 7,900 | 0 | 0 |
| 4 | 7,900 | 81,000 | 75,000 |

Based on IRRs, under what conditions should each project be purchased?

**9-5** Plasma Blood Services is deciding whether to purchase a new blood cleansing machine that is expected to generate the following cash flows. What is the machine's IRR?

IRR computation

| Year | Cash Flow |
|------|-----------|
| 0 | $(140,000) |
| 1 | 60,000 |
| 2 | 60,000 |
| 3 | 60,000 |

**9-6** Exit Corporation is evaluating a capital budgeting project that costs $320,000 and will generate $67,910 for the next seven years. If Exit's required rate of return is 12 percent, should the project be purchased?

NPV or IRR computation

**9-7** What is the traditional payback period (PB) of a project that costs $450,000 if it is expected to generate $120,000 per year for five years?

payback period

**9-8** Following is a table that shows the expected cash flows of a machine that QQQ Inc. is currently evaluating for possible purchase. Both the expected annual cash flows ($\hat{CF}$) and the present values (PV) of the cash flows are shown in the table.

payback period

| Year | Expected $\hat{CF}$ | PV of $\hat{CF}$ Using the Firm's Required Rate of Return, r |
|------|---------------------|-------------------------------------------------------------|
| 0 | $(10,000) | $(10,000) |
| 1 | 6,000 | 5,455 |
| 2 | 3,000 | 2,479 |
| 3 | 1,000 | 751 |
| 4 | 5,000 | 3,415 |

Compute both the traditional payback period and the discounted payback period.

**9-9** If the firm's required rate of return is 12 percent, what is the modified internal rate of return (MIRR) for the following project?

MIRR computation

| Year | Cash Flow |
|------|-----------|
| 0 | $(105,000) |
| 1 | 70,000 |
| 2 | 50,000 |

**9-10** Compute the internal rate of return (IRR) and the modified internal rate of return (MIRR) for each of the following capital budgeting projects. Assume that the firm's required rate of return is 14 percent.

MIRR computation

| Year | Project G | Project J | Project K |
|------|-----------|-----------|-----------|
| 0 | $(180,000) | $(240,000) | $(200,000) |
| 1 | 80,100 | 0 | (100,000) |
| 2 | 80,100 | 0 | 205,000 |
| 3 | 80,100 | 375,000 | 205,000 |

Which project(s) should be purchased if they are independent? Which project should be purchased if they are mutually exclusive?

**capital budgeting decision**

**9-11** Following is information about two *mutually exclusive* capital budgeting projects:

| | **Cash Flows** | |
| --- | --- | --- |
| **Year** | **Project Q** | **Project R** |
| 0 | $(4,000) | $(4,000) |
| 1 | 0 | 3,500 |
| 2 | 5,000 | 1,100 |

If the firm's required rate of return is 10 percent, which project should be purchased?

**independent projects— NPVs, IRRs, and PB**

**9-12** Olsen Engineering is considering including two pieces of equipment—a truck and an overhead pulley system—in this year's capital budget. The projects are independent. The cash outlay for the truck is $22,430, and for the pulley system it is $17,100. Each piece of equipment has an estimated life of five years. The annual after-tax cash flow expected to be provided by the truck is $7,500, and for the pulley it is $5,100. The firm's required rate of return is 14 percent. Calculate the NPV, IRR, MIRR, the traditional payback (PB) period, and the discounted payback (DPB) period for each project. Indicate which project(s) should be accepted.

**NPVs and IRRs for mutually exclusive projects**

**9-13** Horrigan Industries must choose between a gas-powered and an electric-powered forklift truck for moving materials in its factory. Because both forklifts perform the same function, the firm will choose only one. (They are mutually exclusive investments.) The electric-powered truck will cost more, but it will be less expensive to operate; it will cost $22,000, whereas the gas-powered truck will cost $17,500. The required rate of return that applies to both investments is 12 percent. The life for both types of truck is estimated to be six years, during which time the net cash flows for the electric-powered truck will be $6,290 per year and those for the gas-powered truck will be $5,000 per year. Calculate the NPV and IRR for each type of truck, and decide which to recommend.

**capital budgeting decisions**

**9-14** Project P costs $15,000 and is expected to produce benefits (cash flows) of $4,500 per year for five years. Project Q costs $37,500 and is expected to produce cash flows of $11,100 per year for five years.

    **a.** Calculate the NPV, IRR, MIRR, discounted payback, and traditional payback period for each project, assuming a required rate of return of 14 percent.

    **b.** If the projects are independent, which project(s) should be selected? If they are mutually exclusive projects, which project should be selected?

**present value of costs**

**9-15** The Cordell Coffee Company is evaluating the within-plant distribution system for its new roasting, grinding, and packing plant. The two alternatives are (1) a conveyor system with a high initial cost but low annual operating costs and (2) several forklift trucks, which cost less but have considerably higher operating costs. The decision to construct the plant has already been made, and the choice here will have no effect on the overall revenues of the project. The required rate of return for the plant is 9 percent, and the projects' expected net costs are listed in the following table:

**Expected Net Cash Flows**

| Year | Conveyor | Forklift |
|------|----------|----------|
| 0 | $(300,000) | $(120,000) |
| 1 | ( 66,000) | ( 96,000) |
| 2 | ( 66,000) | ( 96,000) |
| 3 | ( 66,000) | ( 96,000) |
| 4 | ( 66,000) | ( 96,000) |
| 5 | ( 66,000) | ( 96,000) |

**a.** What is the present value of costs of each alternative? Which method should be chosen? (*Hint:* Be careful—these cash flows are outflows.)

**b.** What is the IRR of each alternative?

**9-16** Your company is considering two mutually exclusive projects—C and R— whose costs and cash flows are shown in the following table:     **NPV and IRR analysis**

**Expected Net Cash Flows**

| Year | Project C | Project R |
|------|-----------|-----------|
| 0 | $(14,000) | $(22,840) |
| 1 | 8,000 | 8,000 |
| 2 | 6,000 | 8,000 |
| 3 | 2,000 | 8,000 |
| 4 | 3,000 | 8,000 |

The projects are equally risky, and their required rate of return is 12 percent. You must make a recommendation concerning which project should be purchased. To determine which is more appropriate, compute the NPV and IRR of each project.

**9-17** The after-tax cash flows for two mutually exclusive projects have been esti- mated, and the following information has been provided:     **NPV and IRR analysis**

**Expected Net Cash Flows**

| Year | Project Y | Project Z |
|------|-----------|-----------|
| 0 | $(25,000) | $(25,000) |
| 1 | 10,000 | 0 |
| 2 | 9,000 | 0 |
| 3 | 7,000 | 0 |
| 4 | 6,000 | 36,000 |

The company's required rate of return is 14 percent, and it can get unlimited funds at that cost. What is the IRR of the *better* project? (*Hint:* Note that the better project might not be the one with the higher IRR.)

**NPV and IRR analysis**    **9-18**   Diamond Hill Jewelers is considering the following independent projects:

| | Expected Net Cash Flows | |
|---|---|---|
| **Year** | **Machine D** | **Machine Q** |
| 0 | $(2,500) | $(2,500) |
| 1 | 2,000 | 0 |
| 2 | 900 | 1,800 |
| 3 | 100 | 1,000 |
| 4 | 100 | 900 |

Which project(s) should be accepted if the required rate of return for the projects is 10 percent? Compute the NPV and the IRR for both projects.

**payback, NPV, and IRR**    **9-19**   Project K has a cost of $52,125, and its expected net cash inflows are $12,000
**calculations**    per year for eight years.

a. What is the project's payback period (to the closest year)?

b. The required rate of return for the project is 12 percent. What is the project's NPV?

c. What is the project's IRR?

d. What is the project's discounted payback period, assuming a 12 percent required rate of return?

**NPV profile**    **9-20**   Derek's Donuts is considering two mutually exclusive investments. The projects' expected net cash flows are as follows:

| | Expected Net Cash Flows | |
|---|---|---|
| **Year** | **Project A** | **Project B** |
| 0 | $(300) | $(405) |
| 1 | (387) | 134 |
| 2 | (193) | 134 |
| 3 | (100) | 134 |
| 4 | 500 | 134 |
| 5 | 500 | 134 |
| 6 | 850 | 134 |
| 7 | 100 | 0 |

a. Construct NPV profiles for Projects A and B.

b. What is each project's IRR?

c. If you were told that each project's required rate of return was 12 percent, which project should be selected? If the required rate of return was 15 percent, what would be the proper choice?

d. Looking at the NPV profiles constructed in part a, what is the *approximate* crossover rate, and what is its significance?

**timing differences**    **9-21**   The Southwestern Oil Exploration Company is considering two mutually exclusive plans for extracting oil on property for which it has mineral rights. Both plans call for the expenditure of $12 million to drill development wells. Under Plan A, all the oil will be extracted in one year, producing a cash flow at the end of Year 1 (t = 1) of \$14.4 million. Under Plan B, cash flows will be \$2.1 million per year for 20 years.

**a.** Construct NPV profiles for Plan A and Plan B, identify each project's IRR, and indicate the approximate crossover rate of return. (To compute the exact crossover rate, see footnote 6 in the chapter.)

**b.** Suppose a company has a required rate of return of 12 percent, and it can get unlimited funds at that cost. Is it logical to assume that it would take on all available independent projects (of average risk) with returns greater than 12 percent? Further, if all available projects with returns greater than 12 percent are purchased, would this mean that cash flows from past investments would have an opportunity cost of only 12 percent because all the firm could do with these cash flows would be to replace money that has a cost of 12 percent? Finally, does this imply that the required rate of return is the correct rate to assume for the reinvestment of a project's cash flows?

**9-22**  The Chaplinsky Publishing Company is considering two mutually exclusive   scale differences
expansion plans. Plan A calls for the expenditure of \$40 million on a large-scale, integrated plant that will provide an expected cash flow stream of \$6.4 million per year for 20 years. Plan B calls for the expenditure of \$12 million to build a somewhat less efficient, more labor-intensive plant that has an expected cash flow stream of \$2.72 million per year for 20 years. Chaplinsky's required rate of return is 10 percent.

**a.** Calculate each project's NPV and IRR.

**b.** Construct the NPV profiles for Plan A and Plan B. Using the NPV profiles, approximate the crossover rate.

**c.** Give a logical explanation, based on reinvestment rates and opportunity costs, as to why the NPV method is better than the IRR method when the firm's required rate of return is constant at some value such as 10 percent.

## Integrative Problem

**9-23**  Your boss, the chief financial officer (CFO) for Southern Textiles, has just   basics of capital budgeting
handed you the estimated cash flows for two proposed projects. Project L involves adding a new item to the firm's fabric line. It would take some time to build up the market for this product, so the cash inflows would increase over time. Project S involves an add-on to an existing line, and its cash flows would decrease over time. Both projects have three-year lives because Southern is planning to introduce an entirely new fabric at that time.

Here are the net cash flow estimates (in thousands of dollars):

| | Expected Net Cash Flows | |
|---|---|---|
| Year | Project L | Project S |
| 0 | \$(100) | \$(100) |
| 1 | 10 | 70 |
| 2 | 60 | 50 |
| 3 | 80 | 20 |

The CFO also made subjective risk assessments of each project, and he concluded that the projects both have risk characteristics that are similar to the firm's average project. Southern's required rate of return is 10 percent. You must now determine whether one or both of the projects should be accepted. Start by answering the following questions:

**a.** What is capital budgeting? Are there any similarities between a firm's capital budgeting decisions and an individual's investment decisions?

**b.** What is the difference between independent and mutually exclusive projects? Between projects with conventional cash flows and projects with unconventional cash flows?

**c. (1)** What is the payback period? Find the traditional payback periods for Project L and Project S.

**(2)** What is the rationale for the payback measure? According to the payback criterion, which project or projects should be accepted if the firm's maximum acceptable payback is two years and Project L and Project S are independent? Mutually exclusive?

**(3)** What is the difference between the traditional payback and the discounted payback? What is each project's discounted payback?

**(4)** What are the main disadvantages of the traditional payback? Is the payback method of any real usefulness in capital budgeting decisions?

**d. (5)** Define the term *net present value (NPV)*. What is each project's NPV?

**(6)** What is the rationale behind the NPV method? According to NPV, which project or projects should be accepted if they are independent? Mutually exclusive?

**(7)** Would the NPVs change if the required rate of return changed?

**e. (8)** Define the term *internal rate of return (IRR)*. What is each project's IRR?

**(9)** How is the IRR on a project related to the YTM on a bond?

**(10)** What is the logic behind the IRR method? According to IRR, which projects should be accepted if they are independent? Mutually exclusive?

**(11)** Would the projects' IRRs change if the required rate of return changed? Explain.

**f. (12)** Construct the NPV profiles for Project L and Project S. At what discount rate do the profiles cross?

**(13)** Look at the NPV profile graph without referring to the actual NPVs and IRRs. Which project or projects should be accepted if they are independent? Mutually exclusive? Explain. Do your answers differ depending on the discount rate used? Explain.

**g. (14)** What is the underlying cause of ranking conflicts between NPV and IRR?

**(15)** What is the *reinvestment rate assumption,* and how does it affect the NPV versus IRR conflict?

**(16)** Which capital budgeting method should be used when NPV and IRR give conflicting rankings? Why?

**h. (17)** Define the term *modified internal rate of return (MIRR)*. What is each project's MIRR?

(18) What is the rationale behind the MIRR method? According to MIRR, which project or projects should be accepted if they are independent? Mutually exclusive?

(19) Would the MIRRs change if the required rate of return changed?

## Computer-Related Problem

*Work the problem in this section only if you are using the problem spreadsheet.*

**9-24** Use the model in File C09 to solve this problem. West Coast Chemical Company (WCCC) is considering two mutually exclusive investments. The projects' expected net cash flows are as follows:

**NPV and IRR analysis**

|  | **Expected Net Cash Flows** | |
| --- | --- | --- |
| **Year** | **Project A** | **Project B** |
| 0 | $(45,000) | $(50,000) |
| 1 | (20,000) | 15,000 |
| 2 | 11,000 | 15,000 |
| 3 | 20,000 | 15,000 |
| 4 | 30,000 | 15,000 |
| 5 | 45,000 | 15,000 |

**a.** Construct NPV profiles for Projects A and B.

**b.** Calculate each project's IRR. Assume the required rate of return is 13 percent.

**c.** If the required rate of return for each project is 13 percent, which project should West Coast select? If the required rate of return is 9 percent, what would be the proper choice? If the required rate of return is 15 percent, what would be the proper choice?

**d.** At what rate do the NPV profiles of the two projects cross?

**e.** Project A has a large cash flow in Year 5 associated with ending the project. WCCC's management is confident of Project A's cash flows in Years 0 to 4 but is uncertain about what its Year 5 cash flow will be. (There is no uncertainty about Project B's cash flows.) Under a worst-case scenario, Project A's Year 5 cash flow will be $40,000, whereas under a best-case scenario, the cash flow will be $50,000. Redo parts a, b, and d for each scenario, assuming a 13 percent required rate of return. If the required rate of return for each project is 13 percent, which project should be selected under each scenario?

**GET REAL WITH** **THOMSON ONE** | Business School Edition

**9-25** Cisco Systems Inc. [CSCO], which is located in San Jose, California, manufactures and sells networking and communication products and provides related services. Cisco is a growing company that makes large capital outlays for plant and equipment to produce its inventory. Cisco's customer base

**capital expenditures**

includes corporations, telecommunication corporations, public institutions, and commercial enterprises.

Using the Thomson ONE database, analyze from a capital budgeting point of view Cisco's capital expenditures compared with its cash flows during the past three years. Answer the following questions:

**a.** What are Cisco's total cash flows for each of the past three years? (*Hint:* You can find this information by clicking on Price/Worldscope Market Data/Market Data Snapshot.)

**b.** How much did Cisco spend on capital expenditures in each of the past three years? (*Hint:* Click on Financials/Thomson Financial Annual Financial Statements.)

**c.** If you make the assumption that Cisco's cost of acquiring capital is 10 percent, determine the present value of the cash flows.

**d.** Calculate the net present value (NPV) of Cisco's capital expenditures.

**e.** Is the NPV positive or negative? What does this result mean for Cisco Systems and its capital budgeting decisions during the past three years? Explain.

# APPENDIX 9A    Using a Spreadsheet to Compute NPV and IRR

You can use a spreadsheet to compute the net present value (NPV) of a capital budgeting project. But you must be careful that you understand what the spreadsheet function actually computes. For example, if you want to compute the NPV for Project S (described in the chapter) using Excel, you could set up the spreadsheet as follows:

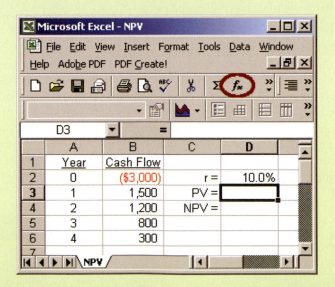

After setting up the spreadsheet, place the cursor in cell **D3** as shown, click on the paste function, which is labeled $f_x$ on the toolbar (circled in the above picture). If $f_x$ is not shown on your toolbar, click on Insert at the top of the toolbar, and then select

Function. When the paste function menu appears, click on the "Financial" function category listed on the left side of the menu (in Function category); then select the NPV function on the right side of the menu. The following table should appear:

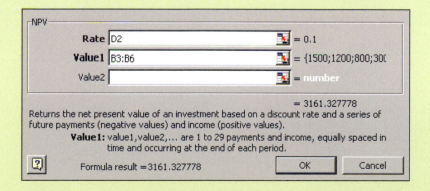

The description of this function, which is shown in the bottom portion of the table, indicates that the result of the computation is the present value of all the *future* cash flows—both inflows and outflows—associated with the investment. What this means is that the Excel function called "NPV" does not compute the net present value as described in this book; rather it computes the present value of all *future* cash flows. As a result, when you enter the cash flows or the locations for the cash flows, the spreadsheet will assume the first cash flow is $\hat{C}F_1$, the second cash flow is $\hat{C}F_2$, and so on. The NPV function actually computes the discounted cash flows (DCF), from which you need to subtract the initial cost to determine the net present value described in the chapter.

Click on the red arrow on the right side of the row labeled "Rate," place the cursor in the cell that contains the value for r (the required rate of return), and then press return. Then click on the arrow on the right side of the row labeled "Value1," use the cursor to highlight the *future cash flows only*—that is, the cash flows from Year 1 through Year 4—located in column B, and then press return. Now the table that originally appeared when you entered the NPV function menu will appear as follows:

You can see the result of the computation at the bottom of the table; it is 3161.327778. If you click the "OK" button, this result will appear in cell **D3** of your spreadsheet. Now place the cursor in cell **D4** and enter the following relationship:

$$= D3 + B2$$

This computation will add the initial investment, which is stated as a negative amount, to the result that is shown in cell **D3.** Your spreadsheet should now appear as follows:

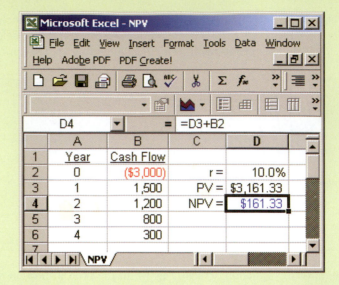

The result of the computation that is shown in cell **D4** is the same as the net present value we computed in the chapter.

To compute the internal rate of return (IRR) for the project using a spreadsheet, set up the problem as before, but type the label "IRR =" in cell **C5.** Place the cursor in cell **D5,** click on the paste function, and then select the IRR function from the financial function category. The following table should appear:

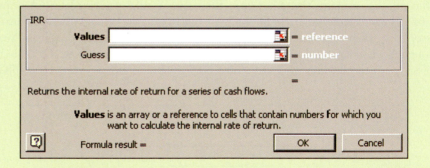

Click on the red arrow on the right side of the row labeled "Values," use the cursor to highlight *all* the cash flows (including $CF_0$) located in column B, and then press return. Now the IRR table will appear as follows:

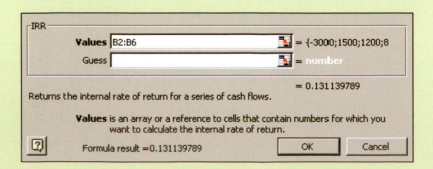

You can see the result of the computation; it is 0.131139789. If you click the "OK" button, this result will appear in cell **D5** of your spreadsheet, which will now appear as follows:

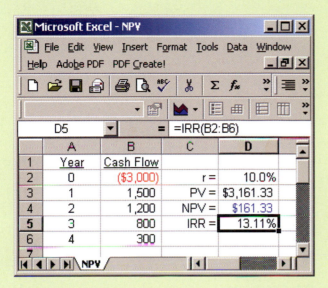

This is the same answer we computed in the chapter.

Now, use the same spreadsheet to compute the NPV and IRR for Project L; all you need to do is change the cash flows in column B. The results given for PV, NPV, and IRR will change as you change the values in the cells **B2** through **B6.** The answers should be the same as we computed in the chapter.

# Project Cash Flows and Risk

**W**hen RJR Nabisco (now R. J. Reynolds Tobacco Company) canceled its smokeless cigarette project, called Premier, *The Wall Street Journal* called it "one of the most stunning new product disasters in recent history." RJR had spent more than $300 million on the product and had test-marketed it for five months. The company had even built a new plant and was all set to produce smokeless cigarettes in huge quantities.

The new cigarette had two fatal flaws—it had to be lit with a special lighter and even then it was hard to light, and many, if not most, smokers didn't like the taste. In addition, it seems smokers didn't like the fact that there was no smoke to blow out or ashes to flick because Premier heated the tobacco rather than burning it. When the cigarette was introduced in 1988, these problems were well known early on, yet RJR still pumped money into the project.

What led RJR's top managers to downplay the flaws and to spend more than $300 million on a bad product? According to industry observers, many people inside the company were aware of the seriousness of the situation, but they were hesitant to voice their concerns because they did not want to offend top managers. The top managers, meantime, were so infatuated with their "new toy" that they assumed consumers would embrace the smokeless cigarette in spite of its obvious flaws. Interestingly, most of the top managers smoked, but none smoked the new smokeless cigarette!

At the time the Premier line was introduced, RJR was not a well-run company, even though it was entrenched in highly profitable markets and was generating billions of dollars of cash each year. The smokeless cigarette project didn't kill the company, but it did contribute to the downfall of the management team that backed the project.

Unfortunately, it seems RJR was intent on salvaging its investment in the first smokeless cigarette it introduced, so in 1996 it introduced a second smokeless cigarette called Eclipse. It invested an additional $150 million in the Eclipse brand, only to discover that it too was a flop.

Even so, in April 2000, RJR once again tested the potential market for Eclipse. But this time, the smokeless cigarette was touted as a smoking alternative that provided a lower chance of contracting some of the maladies that have been associated with traditional tobacco products. The fact that RJR was marketing Eclipse as a "safer" cigarette showed that the company still held hope for salvaging its investment in this project.

In 2003 the Eclipse brand was still alive and kicking. In an effort to make the smokeless cigarette more widely available, RJR began expanding distribution of the product by offering it in convenience stores nationwide.

At the same time, the company continued to test the merits of Eclipse as a safer alternative to the traditional cigarette. The thought was that as people became more health conscious, perhaps the Eclipse brand would find its niche and finally start to pay off for RJR. Unfortunately, tests by independent researchers suggested Eclipse cigarettes contain more harmful amounts of cancer-causing ingredients than some light cigarettes. And in 2005, the attorney general of Vermont filed a lawsuit against R. J. Reynolds for misleading advertising.

Had RJR's top managers followed the procedures set forth in this chapter, perhaps they would not have sunk as much money into the smokeless cigarette projects. Instead, they would have discovered that their project should have been rejected originally because it was not expected to generate the cash flows necessary to make it a viable investment.

**Source:** Various articles available on Dow Jones Interactive ® Publications Library located at http://www.wsj.com.

## Chapter *Essentials*
### —The Questions

After reading this chapter, you should be able to answer the following questions:

- What are the relevant cash flows associated with a capital budgeting project? How are these cash flows identified and used in capital budgeting analysis?
- What is depreciation and how does it affect a project's relevant cash flows?
- How is risk incorporated in capital budgeting analysis?
- How do capital budgeting analyses/decisions differ for multinational firms?

The basic principles of capital budgeting and the methods used to evaluate capital budgeting projects were covered in Chapter 9. In this chapter, we examine some additional issues, including cash flow estimation and incorporating risk into capital budgeting decisions. In addition, we present some of the challenges multinational firms face when applying the capital budgeting decision-making methods described in both Chapter 9 and this chapter.

## CASH FLOW ESTIMATION

**cash flow**
The actual cash, as opposed to accounting net income, that a firm receives or pays during some specified period.

The most important, but also the most difficult, step in the analysis of a capital project is estimating its **cash flows.** The "relevant" cash flows include the investment outlays needed to purchase the project and the net cash flows the project is expected to generate after it is purchased. Many variables are involved in cash flow estimation, and many individuals and departments participate in the process. For example, the forecasts of unit sales and sales prices normally are made by the marketing group based on its knowledge of advertising effects, the state of the economy, competitors' reactions, and trends in consumers' tastes. Similarly, the capital outlays associated with a new product generally are determined by the engineering and product development staffs, whereas operating costs are estimated by cost accountants, production experts, personnel specialists, purchasing agents, and so forth.

Because it is difficult to make accurate forecasts of the costs and revenues associated with a large, complex project, forecast errors can be quite large. For example, in the 1970s, when several major oil companies decided to build the Alaska Pipeline, the original cost estimates were in the neighborhood of $700 million, but the final cost was closer to $8 billion. Similar (or even worse) miscalculations are common in forecasts of product design costs.

As difficult as plant and equipment costs are to estimate, sales revenues and operating costs over the life of the project generally are even more uncertain. For example, several years ago Federal Express developed an electronic delivery service system (ZapMail). It used the correct capital budgeting technique—the net present value (NPV) method—but it incorrectly estimated the project's cash flows. Projected revenues were too high and projected costs were too low; thus, virtually no one was willing to pay the price required to cover the project's costs. As a result, cash flows failed to meet the forecasted levels, and Federal Express ended up losing about $200 million on the venture. This example demonstrates a basic truth: If cash flow estimates are not reasonably accurate, any analytical technique, no matter how sophisticated, can lead to poor decisions and hence to operating losses and lower stock prices. Because of its financial strength, Federal Express was able to absorb losses on the ZapMail venture with no problem, but a similar loss could have forced a weaker firm into bankruptcy.

The financial staff's role in the forecasting process includes (1) coordinating the efforts of the other departments such as engineering and marketing, (2) ensuring that everyone involved with the forecast uses a consistent set of economic assumptions, and (3) making sure that no biases are inherent in the forecasts. This last point is extremely important because division managers often become emotionally involved with pet projects or develop empire-building complexes, both of which can lead to cash flow forecasting biases that make bad projects look good on paper. The RJR smokeless cigarette project discussed previously is an example of this problem.

It is almost impossible to overstate the difficulties one can encounter with cash flow forecasts. Also, it is difficult to overstate the importance of these forecasts. In this chapter, we give you a sense of some of the inputs that are involved in forecasting the cash flows associated with a capital project and in minimizing forecasting errors.

**Self-Test Questions**

What is the most important step in the analysis of a capital project?

What is the financial staff's role in forecasting cash flows for capital projects?

## RELEVANT CASH FLOWS

One important element in cash flow estimation is the determination of **relevant cash flows,** which are defined as the specific set of cash flows that should be considered in the capital budgeting decision. This process can be rather difficult, but two cardinal rules should be followed:

- Capital budgeting decisions must be based on *cash flows after taxes,* not accounting income.
- Only *incremental cash flows*—that is, cash flows that change if the project is purchased—are relevant to the accept/reject decision.

These two rules are discussed in detail in the following sections.

### Cash Flow versus Accounting Income

In capital budgeting analysis, *after-tax cash flows, not accounting profits,* are used—it is cash that pays the bills and can be invested in capital projects, not profits. Cash flows and accounting profits can be very different. To illustrate, consider Table 10-1, which

**relevant cash flows**
The specific cash flows that should be considered in a capital budgeting decision.

| **TABLE 10-1**  Unilate's Accounting Profits versus Net Cash Flow ($ thousands) | | |
|---|---|---|
| | **Accounting Profits** | **Cash Flows** |
| *I. 2010 Situation* | | |
| Sales | $50,000 | $50,000 |
| Costs except depreciation | (25,000) | (25,000) |
| Depreciation | (15,000) | |
| Net operating income or cash flow | $10,000 | $25,000 |
| Taxes based on operating income (30%) | ( 3,000) | ( 3,000) |
| Net income or net cash flow | $ 7,000 | $22,000 |
| Net cash flow = Net income plus depreciation | | |
| = $7,000 + $15,000 = $22,000 | | |
| *II. 2015 Situation* | | |
| Sales | $50,000 | $50,000 |
| Costs except depreciation | (25,000) | (25,000) |
| Depreciation | ( 5,000) | |
| Net operating income or cash flow | $20,000 | $25,000 |
| Taxes based on operating income (30%) | ( 6,000) | ( 6,000) |
| Net income or net cash flow | $14,000 | $19,000 |
| Net cash flow = Net income plus depreciation | | |
| = $14,000 + $5,000 = $19,000 | | |

shows how accounting profits and cash flows are related. We assume that Unilate Textiles, a textile manufacturer based in North Carolina, is planning to start a new division at the end of 2010; that sales and all costs, except depreciation, represent actual cash flows and are projected to be constant over time; and that the division will use accelerated depreciation, which will cause its reported depreciation charges to decline over time.[1]

The top section of the table shows the situation in the first year of operations, 2010. Accounting profits are $7 million, but the division's net cash flow—money that is available to Unilate—is $22 million. The $7 million profit is the *return on the funds* originally invested, whereas the $15 million of depreciation is a *return of part of the funds* originally invested, so the $22 million cash flow consists of both a return *on* and a return *of* part of the invested capital.

The bottom part of the table shows the situation projected for 2015. Here reported profits have doubled because of the decline in depreciation, but net cash flow is down sharply because taxes have doubled. The amount of money received by the firm is represented by the cash flow figure, not the net income figure. And although accounting profits are important for some purposes, only cash flows are relevant for the purposes of setting a value on a project. Cash flows can be reinvested to create value, profits cannot. Therefore, in capital budgeting, we are interested in

---

[1]Depreciation procedures are discussed in detail in accounting courses, but we provide a summary and review in Appendix 10A at the end of this chapter. The tables provided in Appendix 10A are used to calculate depreciation charges used in the chapter examples. In some instances, we simplify the depreciation assumptions to reduce the arithmetic. Because Congress changes depreciation procedures fairly frequently, it is always necessary to consult the latest tax regulations before developing actual capital budgeting cash flows.

net cash flows, not in accounting profits per se. In most cases, we can define net cash flows as[2]

$$\text{Net cash flow} = \text{Net income} + \text{Depreciation}$$
$$= \text{Return } on \text{ capital} + \text{Return } of \text{ capital}$$

## Incremental Cash Flows

In evaluating a capital project, we are concerned only with those cash flows that result directly from the decision to accept the project. These cash flows, called **incremental cash flows,** represent the changes in the firm's total cash flows that occur as a direct result of purchasing the project. To determine whether a specific cash flow is considered incremental, we need to determine whether it is affected by the purchase of the project. Cash flows that will change because the project is purchased are *incremental cash flows* that must be included in the capital budgeting evaluation. Cash flows that are not affected by the purchase of the project are *not* relevant to the capital budgeting decision. Unfortunately, identifying the relevant cash flows for a project is not always as simple as it seems. Some special problems in determining incremental cash flows are discussed next.

**incremental cash flow**
The change in a firm's net cash flow attributable to an investment project.

## Sunk Costs

Sunk costs are not incremental costs, and they should not be included in the analysis. A **sunk cost** is an outlay that has already been committed or that has already occurred and hence is not affected by the accept/reject decision under consideration. To illustrate, in 2008 Unilate Textiles considered building a distribution center in New England in an effort to increase sales in that area of the country. To help with its evaluation, Unilate hired a consulting firm to perform a site analysis and provide a feasibility study for the project; the cost was $100,000, and this amount was expensed for tax purposes. This expenditure is *not* a relevant cost that should be included in the capital budgeting evaluation of the prospective distribution center because Unilate cannot recover this money, regardless of whether the new distribution center is built.

**sunk cost**
A cash outlay that already has been incurred and that cannot be recovered regardless of whether the project is accepted or rejected.

## Opportunity Costs

The second potential problem relates to **opportunity costs,** which are defined as the cash flows that could be generated from assets the firm already owns, provided they are not used for the project in question. To illustrate, Unilate already owns a piece of land that is suitable for a distribution center. When evaluating the prospective center in New England, should the cost of the land be disregarded because no additional cash outlay would be required? The answer is no because there is an opportunity cost inherent in the use of the property. In this case, the land could be sold to yield $150,000 after taxes. Use of the site for the distribution center would require forgoing this

**opportunity cost**
The return on the best alternative use of an asset; the highest return that will not be earned if funds are invested in a particular project.

---

[2]Actually, net cash flow should be adjusted to reflect all noncash charges, not just depreciation. However, for most projects, depreciation is by far the largest noncash charge. Also, note that Table 10-1 ignores interest charges, which would be present if the firm uses debt. Most firms do use debt and hence finance part of their capital budgets with debt. Therefore, the question has been raised as to whether interest charges should be reflected in capital budgeting cash flow analysis. The consensus is that interest charges should not be dealt with explicitly in capital budgeting—rather, the effects of debt financing are reflected in the cost of funds, or required rate of return, which is used to discount the cash flows. If interest is subtracted and cash flows are then discounted, we would be double counting the cost of debt.

inflow, so the $150,000 must be charged as an opportunity cost against the project. Note that the proper land cost in this example is the $150,000 market-determined value, irrespective of whether Unilate originally paid $50,000 or $500,000 for the property. (What Unilate paid would, of course, have an effect on taxes and hence on the after-tax opportunity cost.)

## Externalities: Effects on Other Parts of the Firm

**externalities**

The effect that accepting a project will have on the cash flows in other parts (areas) of the firm.

The third potential problem involves the effects of a project on other parts of the firm; economists call these effects **externalities.** For example, Unilate does have some existing customers in New England who would use the new distribution center because its location would be more convenient than the North Carolina distribution center they have been using. The sales, and hence profits, generated by these customers would not be new to Unilate; rather, they would represent a transfer from one distribution center to another. Thus, the net revenues produced by these customers should not be treated as incremental cash flows in the capital budgeting decision. Although they often are difficult to quantify, externalities such as these should be considered.

## Shipping and Installation Costs

When a firm acquires fixed assets, it often must incur substantial costs for shipping and installing the equipment. These charges are added to the invoice price of the equipment when the total cost of the project is being determined. Also, for depreciation purposes, the *depreciable basis* of an asset, which is the total amount that can be depreciated during the asset's life, includes the purchase price and any additional expenditures required to make the asset operational, including shipping and installation. Therefore, the full cost of the equipment, including shipping and installation costs, is used as the depreciable basis when depreciation charges are calculated. So if Unilate Textiles bought a computer with an invoice price of $100,000 and paid another $10,000 for shipping and installation, then the full cost of the computer, and its depreciable basis, would be $110,000.

Keep in mind that *depreciation is a noncash expense, so there is not a cash outflow associated with the recognition of depreciation expense each year.* But because depreciation is an expense, *it affects the taxable income of a firm, thus the amount of taxes paid by the firm, which is a cash flow.*

## Inflation

Inflation is a fact of life, and it should be recognized in capital budgeting decisions. If expected inflation is not built into the determination of expected cash flows, then the calculated net present value and internal rate of return will be incorrect—both will be artificially low. It is easy to avoid inflation bias—simply build inflationary expectations into the cash flows used in the capital budgeting analysis. Expected inflation should be reflected in the revenue and cost figures, and thus the annual net cash flow forecasts. The required rate of return does not have to be adjusted for inflation expectations because investors include such expectations when establishing the rate at which they are willing to allow the firm to use their funds. Investors decide at what rates a firm can raise funds in the capital markets, and they include an adjustment for inflation when determining the rate that is appropriate. (We discussed this concept in Chapter 5.)

### Self-Test Questions

Briefly explain the difference between accounting income and net cash flow. Which should be used in capital budgeting? Why?

Explain what these terms mean, and assess their relevance in capital budgeting: incremental cash flow, sunk cost, opportunity cost, externalities, shipping and installation costs, and depreciable basis.

Explain why incremental analysis is important in capital budgeting.

How should inflation expectations be included in analysis of capital projects?

## IDENTIFYING INCREMENTAL CASH FLOWS

Generally, when we identify the incremental cash flows associated with a capital project, we separate them according to when they occur during the life of the project. In most cases, we can classify a project's incremental cash flows as follows:

- Cash flows that *occur only at the start* of the project's life—that is, time period 0
- Cash flows that *continue throughout* the project's life—that is, time periods 1 through n
- Cash flows that *occur only at the end,* or the termination, of the project—that is, time period n

We discuss these three incremental cash flow classifications and identify some of the relevant cash flows next. But keep in mind, when identifying the incremental cash flows for capital budgeting, the primary question is which cash flows will be affected by purchasing the project. *If a cash flow does not change, it is not relevant for the capital budgeting analysis.*

### Initial Investment Outlay

The **initial investment outlay,** which we designate $CF_0$, refers to the incremental cash flows that *occur only at the start of a project's life.* $CF_0$ includes such cash flows as the purchase price of the new project and shipping and installation costs. If the capital budgeting decision is a *replacement decision,* then the initial investment must also take into account the cash flows associated with the disposal of the old, or replaced, asset; this amount includes any cash received or paid to scrap the old asset and any tax effects associated with the disposal.

In many cases, the addition or replacement of a capital asset also affects the firm's short-term assets and liabilities, which are known as the *working capital accounts.* For example, additional inventories might be required to support a new operation, and increased inventory purchases will increase accounts payable. The difference between current assets and current liabilities is called *net working capital.* Thus, the difference between the required increase (decrease) in current assets and the spontaneous increase (decrease) in current liabilities is the *change in net working capital.* If this change is positive, as it generally is for expansion projects, then additional financing, over and above the cost of the project, is needed to fund the increase.[3] *Thus, the change*

**initial investment outlay** Includes the incremental cash flows associated with a project that will *occur only at the start of a project's life.*

---

[3]We should note that there are instances in which the change in net working capital associated with a capital project actually results in a decrease in the firm's current funding requirements, which frees up cash flows for investment. Usually this occurs if the project being considered is much more efficient than the existing asset(s).

*in net working capital that results from the acceptance of a project is an incremental cash flow that must be considered in the capital budgeting analysis.* Because the change in net working capital requirements occurs at the start of the project's life, this cash flow impact is an incremental cash flow included as a part of the initial investment outlay.

**incremental operating cash flows**

The changes in day-to-day cash flows that result from the purchase of a capital project and continue until the firm disposes of the asset.

## Incremental Operating Cash Flows

**Incremental operating cash flows** are the changes in day-to-day operating cash flows that result from the purchase of a capital project. These changes occur *throughout the life of the project;* thus, they continue to affect the firm's cash flows until the firm disposes of the asset.

In most cases, the *incremental operating cash flows* for each year can be computed directly by using the following equation:

**10–1**

$$\begin{aligned}
\text{Incremental operating CF}_t &= \Delta\text{Cash revenues}_t - \Delta\text{Cash expenses}_t - \Delta\text{Taxes}_t \\
&= \Delta\text{NOI}_t \times (1 - T) + \Delta\text{Depr}_t \\
&= (\Delta S_t - \Delta OC_t - \Delta\text{Depr}_t) \times (1 - T) + \Delta\text{Depr}_t \\
&= (\Delta S_t - \Delta OC_t) \times (1 - T) + T(\Delta\text{Depr}_t)
\end{aligned}$$

The symbols in Equation 10–1 are defined as follows:

$\Delta$ = Greek letter delta, which indicates the change in something.

$\Delta\text{NOI}_t = \text{NOI}_{t,\ accept} - \text{NOI}_{t,\ reject}$ = Change in net operating income in period t that results from accepting the capital project; the subscript *accept* indicates the firm's operations that would exist if the project is accepted, and the subscript *reject* indicates the level of operations that would exist if the project is rejected (the existing situation *without* the project).

$\Delta\text{Depr}_t = \text{Depr}_{t,accept} - \text{Depr}_{t,reject}$ = Change in depreciation expense in period t that results from accepting the project.

$\Delta S_t = S_{t,accept} - S_{t,reject}$ = Change in sales revenues in period t that results from accepting the project.

$\Delta OC_t = OC_{t,accept} - OC_{t,reject}$ = Change in operating costs, excluding depreciation, in period t that results from accepting the project.

$T$ = Marginal tax rate.

We have emphasized that depreciation is a *noncash* expense. So why is the change in depreciation expense included in the computation of incremental operating cash flow shown in Equation 10–1? The change in depreciation expense needs to be computed because, when depreciation changes, taxable income changes and so does the amount of income taxes paid; and the amount of taxes paid is a cash flow.

**terminal cash flow**

The *net* cash flow that occurs at the end of the life of a project, including the cash flows associated with (1) the final disposal of the project and (2) returning the firm's operations to where they were before the project was accepted.

## Terminal Cash Flow

The **terminal cash flow** *occurs at the end of the life of the project.* It is associated with (1) the final disposal of the project and (2) the return of the firm's operations to where they were before the project was accepted. Consequently, the terminal cash flow includes the salvage value, which could be either positive (selling the asset) or negative (paying for removal), and the tax impact of the disposition of the project. Because we assume the firm returns to the operating level that existed prior to the acceptance of the project, any changes in net working capital that occurred at the beginning of the project's life will be *reversed* at the end of its life. For example, as an expansion project's life approaches termination, inventories will be sold off and not replaced. The firm will therefore receive (invest) an end-of-project cash flow equal to the net working capital requirement, or cash outflow (inflow), that occurred when the project was begun.

## Self-Test Questions

Identify the three classifications for the incremental cash flows associated with a project, and give examples of the cash flows that would be in each category.

Why are the changes in net working capital recognized as incremental cash flows both at the beginning and the end of a project's life?

## CAPITAL BUDGETING PROJECT EVALUATION

Up to this point, we have discussed several important aspects of cash flow analysis. Now we illustrate cash flow estimation for (1) expansion projects and (2) replacement projects.

## Expansion Projects

Remember from Chapter 9 that an **expansion project** is one that calls for the firm to invest in new assets to *increase* sales. We illustrate an expansion project analysis with a project that is being considered by Household Energy Products (HEP), a Dallas-based technology company. HEP's research and development department has created a computerized home appliance control device that will increase a home's energy efficiency by simultaneously controlling all household appliances—large and small, the air-conditioning/heating system, the water heater, the security system, and the filtration and heating systems for pools and spas. At this point, HEP wants to decide whether it should proceed with full-scale production of the appliance control device.

HEP's marketing department plans to target sales of the appliance computer to the owners of larger homes; the computer is cost effective only in homes with 4,000 or more square feet of living space. The marketing vice president believes that annual sales would be 15,000 units if the units are priced at $2,000 each, so annual sales are estimated at $30 million. The engineering department has determined the firm would need no additional manufacturing or storage space; it would need only the equipment to manufacture the devices. The necessary equipment would be purchased and installed late in 2008, and it would cost $9.5 million, not including the $500,000 that would have to be paid for shipping and installation. The equipment would fall into the Modified Accelerated Cost Recovery System (MACRS) 5-year class for the purposes of depreciation (see Appendix 10A at the end of this chapter for depreciation rates and an explanation of MACRS).

The project would require an initial increase in net working capital equal to $4 million, primarily because the raw materials required to produce the devices will significantly increase the amount of inventory HEP currently holds. The investment necessary to increase net working capital will be made on December 31, 2008, when the decision to manufacture the appliance control occurs. The project's estimated economic life is four years. At the end of that time, the equipment would have a market value of $2 million and a book value of $1.7 million. The production department has estimated that variable manufacturing costs would total 60 percent of sales, and fixed overhead costs,

**expansion project**
A project that is intended to increase sales.

**TABLE 10-2** HEP Expansion Project Net Cash Flows, 2008–2012 ($ thousands)

| | 2008 | 2009 | 2010 | 2011 | 2012 |
|---|---|---|---|---|---|
| **I.  Initial Investment Outlay** | | | | | |
| Cost of new asset | $( 9,500) | | | | |
| Shipping and installation | ( 500) | | | | |
| Increase in net working capital | ( 4,000) | | | | |
| Initial investment | $(14,000) | | | | |
| **II.  Incremental Operating Cash Flow**[a] | | | | | |
| Sales revenues | | $ 30,000 | $ 30,000 | $ 30,000 | $ 30,000 |
| Variable costs (60% of sales) | | (18,000) | (18,000) | (18,000) | (18,000) |
| Fixed costs | | ( 5,000) | ( 5,000) | ( 5,000) | ( 5,000) |
| Depreciation on new equipment[b] | | ( 2,000) | ( 3,200) | ( 1,900) | ( 1,200) |
| Earnings before taxes (EBT) | | $ 5,000 | $ 3,800 | $ 5,100 | $ 5,800 |
| Taxes (40%) | | ( 2,000) | ( 1,520) | ( 2,040) | ( 2,320) |
| Net income | | $ 3,000 | $ 2,280 | $ 3,060 | $ 3,480 |
| Add back depreciation | | 2,000 | 3,200 | 1,900 | 1,200 |
| Incremental operating cash flows | | $ 5,000 | $ 5,480 | $ 4,960 | $ 4,680 |
| **III. Terminal Cash Flow** | | | | | |
| Return of net working capital | | | | | $ 4,000 |
| Net salvage value (see Table 10-3) | | | | | 1,880 |
| Terminal cash flow | | | | | $ 5,880 |
| **IV. Incremental Cash Flows** | | | | | |
| Total net cash flow per period | $(14,000) | $ 5,000 | $ 5,480 | $ 4,960 | $ 10,560 |

[a]Using Equation 10–1, the incremental operating cash flows can be computed as follows:

| Year | Incremental Operating Cash Flow Computation |
|---|---|
| 2009 | $5,000 = ($30,000 − $18,000 − $5,000)(1 − 0.4) + $2,000(0.4) |
| 2010 | $5,480 = ($30,000 − $18,000 − $5,000)(1 − 0.4) + $3,200(0.4) |
| 2011 | $4,960 = ($30,000 − $18,000 − $5,000)(1 − 0.4) + $1,900(0.4) |
| 2012 | $4,680 = ($30,000 − $18,000 − $5,000)(1 − 0.4) + $1,200(0.4) |

[b]Depreciation for the new equipment was calculated using MACRS (see Appendix 10A at the end of this chapter):

| Year | 2009 | 2010 | 2011 | 2012 |
|---|---|---|---|---|
| Percent depreciated | 20% | 32% | 19% | 12% |

These percentages are multiplied by the depreciable basis of $10,000 to get the depreciation expense each year.

excluding depreciation, would be $5 million per year. Depreciation expenses would vary from year to year in accordance with the MACRS rates. HEP's marginal tax rate is 40 percent; its cost of funds, or required rate of return, is 15 percent; and, for capital budgeting purposes, the company's policy is to assume that operating cash flows occur at the end of each year. Thus, because manufacture of the new product would begin on January 1, 2009, the first *operating cash flows* would occur on December 31, 2009.

## Analysis of the Cash Flows

The first step in the analysis is to summarize the initial investment outlay required for the project; this is done in the 2008 column of Table 10-2. For HEP's appliance control device project, the initial cash flows consist of the purchase price of the needed equipment, the cost of shipping and installation, and the required investment in net working capital (NWC). Notice that these cash flows do not carry over in the years 2009 through 2012—they occur only at the start of the project. Thus, the *initial investment* outlay is $14 million.

Having estimated the investment requirements, we must now estimate the cash flows that will occur once production begins; these are set forth in the 2009 through 2012 columns of Table 10-2. The operating cash flow estimates are based on information provided by HEP's various departments. The depreciation amounts were obtained by multiplying the depreciable basis, $10 million ($9.5 million purchase price plus $0.5 million shipping and installation), by the MACRS recovery allowance rates as set forth in the footnote to Table 10-2. As you can see, from the values given in footnote a in the table, the incremental operating cash flow differs each year only because the depreciation expense, and thus the impact depreciation has on taxes, differs each year.

The final cash flow component we need to compute is the terminal cash flow. For this computation, remember that the $4 million investment in net working capital will be recovered in 2012. Also, we need an estimate of the net cash flows from the disposal of the equipment in 2012. Table 10-3 shows the calculation of the net salvage value for the equipment. It is expected that the equipment will be sold for more than its book value, which means the company will have to pay taxes on the capital gain because, in essence, the equipment was depreciated too quickly, which allowed HEP to reduce its tax liability by too much in the years 2009–2012. The book value is calculated as the depreciable basis (purchase price plus shipping and installation) minus the accumulated depreciation. The net cash flow from salvage is merely the sum of the salvage value and the tax impact resulting from the sale of the equipment, $1.88 million in this case. Thus, the *terminal cash flow* totals $5.88 million—that is, the $1.88 million cash flow from salvage plus the $4 million cash flow from the return of the investment in net working capital.

Notice that the total net cash flow for 2012 is the sum of the incremental cash flow for the year and the terminal cash flow. In the final year of a project's economic life, the firm incurs two types of cash flows: (1) the incremental operating cash flow attributed to the project's normal operation and (2) the terminal cash flow associated with the

---

**TABLE 10-3**    HEP Expansion Project Net Salvage Value, 2012 ($ thousands)

**I. Book Value of HEP's Project, 2012**

| | |
|---|---:|
| Cost of new asset, 2008 | $ 9,500 |
| Shipping and installation | 500 |
| Depreciable basis of asset | $10,000 |
| Depreciation, 2009–2012 | |
| = $(0.20 + 0.32 + 0.19 + 0.12) \times \$10,000$ | (8,300) |
| Book value, 2012 | $ 1,700 |

**II. Tax Effect of the Sale of HEP's Project, 2012**

| | |
|---|---:|
| Selling price of asset, 2012 | $ 2,000 |
| Book value of asset, 2012 | (1,700) |
| Gain (loss) on sale of asset | $   300 |
| Tax on gain (loss) (40%) | $   120 = $300 × 0.4 |

**III. Net Salvage Value, TCF, 2012**

| | |
|---|---:|
| Cash flow from sale of project | $ 2,000 |
| Tax effect of sale | (   120) |
| Net salvage value cash flow | $ 1,880 |

disposal of the project. For the appliance control device project that HEP is considering, the incremental operating cash flow in 2012 is $4.68 million and the terminal cash flow is $5.88 million, so the total expected net cash flow in 2012 is $10.56 million.

## Making the Decision

A summary of the data and the computation of the project's NPV are provided with the cash flow time line that follows. The amounts are in thousands of dollars, just like in Table 10-2.

**Cash Flow Time Line for HEP's Appliance Control Device Project ($ thousands)**

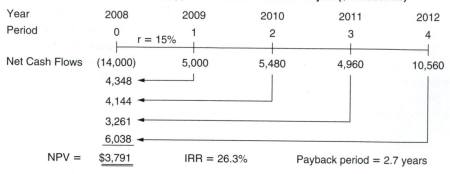

| Year | 2008 | 2009 | 2010 | 2011 | 2012 |
|------|------|------|------|------|------|
| Period | 0 | 1 | 2 | 3 | 4 |
| | | r = 15% | | | |
| Net Cash Flows | (14,000) | 5,000 | 5,480 | 4,960 | 10,560 |
| | 4,348 | | | | |
| | 4,144 | | | | |
| | 3,261 | | | | |
| | 6,038 | | | | |
| NPV = | $3,791 | IRR = 26.3% | | Payback period = 2.7 years | |

The project appears to be acceptable using the NPV and internal rate of return (IRR) methods, and it also would be acceptable if HEP required a maximum payback period of three years. Note, however, that the analysis thus far has been based on the assumption that the project has the same degree of risk as the company's average project. If the project was judged to be riskier than an average project, it would be necessary to increase the required rate of return used to compute the NPV. Later in this chapter, we will extend the evaluation of this project to include a risk analysis.

## Replacement Analysis

All companies make replacement decisions. The analysis relating to replacements is the same as for expansion projects—that is, identify the relevant cash flows and then find the net present value of the project. But to some extent, identifying the *incremental* cash flows associated with a replacement project is more complicated than for an expansion project because the cash flows both from the new asset *and* from the old asset must be considered. We illustrate **replacement analysis** with another HEP example.

**replacement analysis**
An analysis involving the decision as to whether to replace an existing asset with a new asset.

HEP has a lathe for trimming molded plastics that was purchased 10 years ago at a cost of $7,500. The machine had an expected life of 15 years at the time it was purchased, and management originally estimated, and still believes, that the salvage value will be zero at the end of its 15-year life. The machine has been depreciated on a straight-line basis; therefore, its annual depreciation charge is $500, and its current book value is $2,500 = $7,500 − 10($500).

HEP is considering the purchase of a new special-purpose machine to replace the lathe. The new machine, which can be purchased for $12,000 (including shipping and installation), will reduce labor and raw materials usage sufficiently to cut annual operating costs from $8,000 to $4,500. This reduction in costs will cause *before-tax* profits to rise by $8,000 − $4,500 = $3,500 per year.

It is estimated that the new machine will have a useful life of five years, after which it can be sold for $2,000. The old machine's current market value is $1,000, which is below its $2,500 book value. If the new machine is acquired, the old lathe will be sold to another company rather than exchanged for the new machine.

Net working capital requirements will increase by $1,000 if the old lathe is replaced with the new machine; this increase will occur at the time of replacement. By an IRS ruling, the new machine falls into the 3-year MACRS class, and because the risk associated with the new machine is considered average for HEP, the project's required rate of return is 15 percent. Should the replacement be made?

Table 10-4 shows the worksheet format HEP uses to analyze replacement projects. Determining the relevant cash flows for a replacement decision is more involved than for an expansion decision because we need to consider the fact that the cash flows associated with the replaced asset will not continue after the new asset is purchased— that is, *the cash flows associated with the new asset will take the place of the cash flows associated with the old asset.* Because we want to evaluate how the acceptance of a capital budgeting project *changes* cash flows, we must compute the increase or decrease in cash flows that results from the replacement of the old asset with the new asset. Let's examine the cash flows computed in Table 10-4.

## Analysis of Cash Flows

The initial investment outlay of $11,400 includes the cash flows associated with the cost of the new asset and the change in net working capital. But when a replacement asset is purchased, the asset being replaced must be removed from operations. If the asset can be sold to another firm or to a scrap dealer, its disposal will generate a positive cash flow; however, if the firm must pay to have the old asset removed, the cash flow will be negative. And if the firm disposes of the old asset at a value different from its book value (its purchase price less accumulated depreciation), there will be a tax effect. In our example, the old asset has a book value equal to $2,500, but it can be sold for only $1,000. So HEP will incur a capital loss equal to $(1,500) = $1,000 - $2,500 if it replaces the lathe with the new machine. This loss will result in a *tax savings* equal to (Capital loss) × T = $1,500 × 0.4 = $600 to account for the fact that HEP did not adequately depreciate the old asset to reflect its market value. Consequently, the disposal of the old asset will generate a positive cash flow equal to $1,600—the $1,000 selling price plus the $600 tax savings. As a result, disposal of the lathe effectively reduces the amount of cash required to purchase the new machine and thus the initial investment outlay. Any cash flows associated with disposing of the old asset must be included in the computation of the initial investment because they affect the net amount of cash required to purchase the asset.[4]

Next, we need to compute the incremental operating cash flow each year. Section II of Table 10-4 shows these computations. The procedure is the same as before—determine how operating cash flows will change if the new machine is purchased to replace the lathe. Remember, the lathe is expected to decrease operating costs from $8,000 to $4,500, and thus increase operating profits by $3,500—that is, less cash will have to be spent to operate the new machine. Had the replacement resulted in an increase in sales in addition to the reduction in costs—that is, if the new machine had been both larger and more efficient— then this amount would also be reported. Also, note that the $3,500 cost savings is constant over the years 2009–2013. Had the annual savings been expected to change over time, this fact would have to be built into the analysis.

---

[4]If you think about it, the computation of the initial investment outlay for replacement decisions is similar to determining the amount you would need to purchase a new automobile to replace your old one. If the purchase price of the new car is $20,000 and the dealer is willing to give you $5,000 for your old car as a trade-in, then the amount you need is only $15,000. But if you need to pay someone to take your old car out of the garage because that is where you are going to keep the new car at night, then the total amount you need to purchase the new car actually is greater than $20,000.

**TABLE 10-4**    HEP Replacement Project Net Cash Flows, 2008–2012 ($ thousands)

| | 2008 | 2009 | 2010 | 2011 | 2012 | 2013 |
|---|---|---|---|---|---|---|
| **I.    Initial Investment Outlay** | | | | | | |
| Cost of new asset | $(12,000) | | | | | |
| Change in net working capital | (1,000) | | | | | |
| Net cash flow from sale of old asset[a] | 1,600 | | | | | |
| Initial investment | $(11,400) | | | | | |
| **II.    Incremental Operating Cash Flows** | | | | | | |
| Δ Operating costs | | $ 3,500 | $3,500 | $ 3,500 | $ 3,500 | $3,500 |
| Δ Depreciation[b] | | (3,460) | (4,900) | (1,300) | ( 340) | 500 |
| Δ Operating income before taxes (EBT) | | 40 | (1,400) | 2,200 | 3,160 | 4,000 |
| Δ Taxes (40%) | | ( 16) | 560 | ( 880) | (1,264) | (1,600) |
| Δ Net operating income | | 24 | ( 840) | 1,320 | 1,896 | 2,400 |
| Add back Δ depreciation | | 3,460 | 4,900 | 1,300 | 340 | ( 500) |
| Incremental operating cash flows | | $ 3,484 | $4,060 | $ 2,620 | $ 2,236 | $1,900 |
| **III. Terminal Cash Flow** | | | | | | |
| Return of net working capital | | | | | | $1,000 |
| Net salvage value of new asset[c] | | | | | | 1,200 |
| Terminal cash flow | | | | | | $2,200 |
| **IV. Incremental Cash Flows** | | | | | | |
| Total net cash flow per period | $(11,400) | $ 3,484 | $4,060 | $ 2,620 | $ 2,236 | $4,100 |

[a]The net cash flow from the sale of the old (replaced) asset is computed as follows:

| | |
|---|---|
| Selling price (market value) | $1,000 |
| Subtract book value | (2,500) |
| Gain (loss) on sale of asset | (1,500) |
| Tax impact of sale of asset (40%) = (1,500) × 0.4 = | ( 600) = a tax refund |

Net cash flow from the sale of asset = $1,000 + 600 = $1,600

[b]The change in depreciation expense is computed by comparing the depreciation of the new asset with the depreciation that would have existed if the old asset was not replaced. The old asset has been depreciated on a straight-line basis, with five years of $500 depreciation remaining. The new asset will be depreciated using the rates for the 3-year MACRS class (see Appendix 10A at the end of this chapter). The change in annual depreciation would be as follows:

| Year | New Asset Depreciation | | Old Asset Depreciation | | Change in Depreciation |
|---|---|---|---|---|---|
| 2009 | $12,000 × 0.33 = $ 3,960 | − | $500 | = | $3,460 |
| 2010 | 12,000 × 0.45 = 5,400 | − | 500 | = | 4,900 |
| 2011 | 12,000 × 0.15 = 1,800 | − | 500 | = | 1,300 |
| 2012 | 12,000 × 0.07 = 840 | − | 500 | = | 340 |
| 2013 | = 0 | − | 500 | = | ( 500) |
| | Accumulated depreciation = $12,000 | | | | |

[c]The book value of the new asset in 2013 will be zero because the entire $12,000 has been written off. The net salvage value of the new asset in 2013 is computed as follows:

| | |
|---|---|
| Selling price (market value) | $2,000 |
| Subtract book value | ( 0) |
| Gain (loss) on sale of asset | 2,000 |
| Tax impact of sale of asset (40%) | ( 800) = 2,000 × 0.4 |

Net salvage value of the new asset in 2013 = $2,000 − $800 = $1,200

The change in depreciation expense must be computed to determine the impact such a change will have on the taxes paid by the firm. If the new machine is purchased, the $500 depreciation expense of the lathe (old asset) no longer will be relevant for tax purposes; instead, the depreciation expense for the new machine will be used. For example, in 2009, the depreciation expense for the new machine will be $3,960 because, according to the 3-year MACRS classification, 33 percent of the cost of the new asset can be depreciated in the year it is purchased. Because HEP will dispose of the lathe if it buys the new machine, in 2009 it will replace the $500 depreciation expense associated with the lathe with the $3,960 depreciation expense associated with the new machine, and the depreciation expense will increase by $3,460 = $3,960 − $500. The computations for the remaining years are the same. Note that in 2013 the change in depreciation is negative. This results because the new machine will be fully depreciated at the end of 2012, so there is nothing left to write off in 2013; thus, if the lathe is replaced, its depreciation of $500 will be replaced by the new machine's depreciation of $0 in 2013, which is a change of $(500).

The terminal cash flow includes $1,000 for the return of net working capital because the firm's "normal" net working capital level, which is the level that exists with the old machine, will be restored at the end of the new machine's life. Any additional accounts receivable created by the purchase of the new machine will be collected and any additional inventories required by the new machine will be drawn down and not replaced. The net salvage value of the new machine is $1,200—it is expected that the new machine can be sold in 2013 for $2,000, but $800 in taxes will have to be paid on the sale because the new machine will be fully depreciated at the time of the sale.[5] Thus, the terminal cash flow is $2,200 = $1,000 + $1,200.

## Making the Decision

A summary of the data and the computation of the project's NPV are provided with the following cash flow time line:

**Cash Flow Time Line for HEP's Replacement Project ($ thousands)**

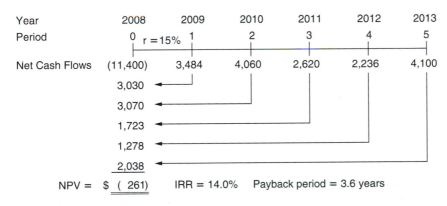

According to the NPV and IRR methods, HEP should not replace the lathe with the new machine.

Before we leave our discussion of replacement decisions, we should note that a replacement decision involves comparing two mutually exclusive projects: retaining

---

[5]In this analysis, the salvage value of the old machine is zero. However, if the old machine was expected to have a positive salvage value at the end of five years, replacing the old machine now would eliminate this cash flow. Thus, the after-tax salvage value of the machine would represent an opportunity cost to the firm, and it would be included as a Year 5 cash outflow in the terminal cash flow section of the worksheet.

the old asset versus buying a new one. To simplify matters, in our replacement example we assumed that the new machine had a life equal to the remaining life of the old machine. If, however, we were choosing between two mutually exclusive alternatives with significantly different lives, an adjustment would be necessary to make the results of the capital budgeting analysis for the two projects comparable. To attain comparability, we can either (1) use a common life for the evaluation of the two projects or (2) compute the annual annuity that could be produced from the dollar amount of the NPV of each project. Both of these procedures are described in Appendix 10B at the end of this chapter. We mention the unequal life problem here to make you aware that the evaluation of mutually exclusive projects with significantly different lives requires a slightly different analysis to ensure that a correct decision is made.

### Self-Test Questions

Explain and differentiate between the capital budgeting analyses required for expansion projects and for replacement projects.

A firm is evaluating a new machine to replace an existing, older machine. The old (existing) machine is being depreciated at $20,000 per year, whereas the new machine's depreciation will be $18,000. The firm's marginal tax rate is 30 percent. Everything else equal, if the new machine is purchased, what effect will the change in depreciation have on the firm's incremental operating cash flows? (*Answer:* $600 reduction in operating CF)

## INCORPORATING RISK IN CAPITAL BUDGETING ANALYSIS

**stand-alone risk**
The risk an asset would have if it were a firm's only asset; it is measured by the variability of the asset's expected returns.

**corporate (within-firm) risk**
Risk that does not take into consideration the effects of stockholders' diversification; it is measured by a project's effect on the firm's earnings variability.

**beta (market) risk**
That part of a project's risk that cannot be eliminated by diversification; it is measured by the project's beta coefficient.

To this point, we have assumed the projects being evaluated have the same risk as the projects that the firm currently possesses. However, three separate and distinct types of project risk need to be examined to determine whether the required rate of return used to evaluate a project should be different from the *average* required rate of the firm. The three risks are (1) the project's own **stand-alone risk,** or the risk it exhibits when evaluated alone rather than as part of a combination, or portfolio, of assets; (2) **corporate,** or **within-firm, risk,** which is the effect a project has on the total, or overall, riskiness of the company, without considering which risk component, systematic or unsystematic, is affected; and (3) **beta,** or **market, risk,** which is project risk assessed from the standpoint of a stockholder who holds a well-diversified portfolio. As we will see, a particular project might have high stand-alone risk, yet taking it on might not have much effect on either the firm's risk or that of its owners because of portfolio, or diversification, effects.

Although more difficult, evaluating the risk associated with a capital budgeting project is similar to evaluating the risk of a financial asset such as a stock. Therefore, much of our discussion in this section relies on the concepts introduced in Chapter 8. As we will see shortly, a project's stand-alone risk is measured by the variability of the project's expected returns, its corporate risk is measured by the project's impact on the firm's earnings variability, and its beta risk is measured by the project's effect on the firm's beta coefficient. Taking on a project with a high degree of either stand-alone risk or corporate risk will not necessarily affect the firm's beta to any great extent. However, if the project has highly uncertain returns, and if those returns are highly correlated with returns on the firm's other assets and also with most other assets in the economy, the project will exhibit a high degree of all three types of risk.

For example, suppose General Motors decides to undertake a major expansion to build solar-powered autos. GM is not sure how its technology will work on a mass production basis, so there are great risks in the venture—its stand-alone risk is high. Management also estimates that the project will have a higher probability of success if the economy is strong because people will have more money to spend on the new autos. This means that the project will tend to do well if GM's other divisions also do well and tend to do badly if other divisions do badly. This being the case, the project will also have high corporate risk. Finally, because GM's profits are highly correlated with those of most other firms, the project's beta coefficient will also be high. Thus, this project will be risky under all three definitions of risk.

### Self-Test Questions

What are the three types of project risk?

How is a project's stand-alone risk measured? How is corporate risk measured? How is beta risk measured?

## STAND-ALONE RISK

To what extent should a firm be concerned with stand-alone risk? In theory, stand-alone risk should be of little or no concern because we know diversification can eliminate some of this type of risk. However, it is of great importance for the following reasons:

1. It is easier to estimate a project's stand-alone risk than either its corporate risk or its beta risk.

2. In the vast majority of cases, all three types of risk are highly correlated. If the general economy does well, so will the firm, and if the firm does well, so will most of its projects. Thus, stand-alone risk generally is a good proxy for hard-to-measure corporate and beta risks.

3. Because of Points 1 and 2, if management wants a reasonably accurate assessment of a project's riskiness, it should spend considerable effort on determining the riskiness of the project's own cash flows—that is, its stand-alone risk.

The starting point for analyzing a project's stand-alone risk involves determining the uncertainty inherent in the project's cash flows. This analysis can be handled in a number of ways, ranging from informal judgments to complex economic and statistical analyses involving large-scale computer models. We illustrate what is involved with Household Energy Products' appliance control computer project that we discussed earlier. Many of the individual cash flows that were shown in Table 10-2 are subject to uncertainty. For example, sales for each year were projected at 15,000 units to be sold at a net price of $2,000 per unit, or $30 million in total. Actual unit sales almost certainly would be somewhat higher or lower than 15,000, however, and also the sales price might turn out to be different from the projected $2,000 per unit. In effect, the sales quantity and the sales price estimates are expected values taken from probability distributions, as are many of the other values that are shown in Table 10-2. The distributions could be relatively "tight," reflecting small standard deviations and low risk, or they could be "flat," denoting a great deal of uncertainty about the final value of the variable in question and hence a high degree of stand-alone risk.

The nature of the individual cash flow distributions, and their correlations with one another, determines the nature of the NPV distribution and, thus, the project's stand-alone risk. We next discuss three techniques for assessing a project's stand-alone risk: (1) sensitivity analysis, (2) scenario analysis, and (3) Monte Carlo simulation.

## Sensitivity Analysis

The cash flows used to determine the acceptability of a project result from forecasts of uncertain events, such as economic conditions in the future and expected demand for a product. Intuitively, then, we know the cash flow amounts used to determine the NPV of a project might be significantly different from what actually happens in the future. But those numbers represent our best, and most confident, prediction concerning the expected cash flows associated with a project. We also know that if a key input variable, such as units sold, changes, the project's NPV will also change.

**sensitivity analysis**
A risk analysis technique in which key variables are changed and the resulting changes in the NPV and the IRR are observed.

**Sensitivity analysis** is a technique that shows exactly how much the NPV will change in response to a given change in an input variable, other things held constant. In a sensitivity analysis, we begin with the base-case situation that was developed using the expected values for each input. Next, each variable is changed by specific percentage points above and below the expected value, holding other things constant; then a new NPV is calculated for each of these values. Finally, the set of NPVs is plotted against the variable that was changed. Figure 10-1 shows sensitivity graphs for HEP's computer project for three of the key input variables. The table below the graphs gives the NPVs that were used to construct the graphs. The slopes of the lines in the graphs show how sensitive NPV is to changes in each of the inputs: *the steeper the slope, the more sensitive the NPV is to a change in the variable.* In the figure, we see that the project's NPV is very sensitive to changes in variable costs, less sensitive to changes in unit sales, and fairly insensitive to changes in the required rate of return. So when

**FIGURE 10-1**    HEP Appliance Computer Sensitivity Analysis ($ thousands)

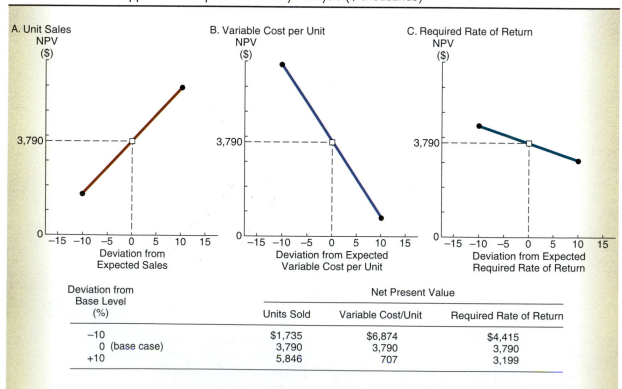

| Deviation from Base Level (%) | Net Present Value | | |
| --- | --- | --- | --- |
| | Units Sold | Variable Cost/Unit | Required Rate of Return |
| −10 | $1,735 | $6,874 | $4,415 |
| 0  (base case) | 3,790 | 3,790 | 3,790 |
| +10 | 5,846 | 707 | 3,199 |

estimating these variables' values, HEP should take extra care to ensure the accuracy of the forecast for variable costs per unit.

If we were comparing two projects, the one with the steeper sensitivity lines would be regarded as riskier because for that project, a relatively small error in estimating an extremely sensitive variable would produce a large error in the project's expected NPV. Thus, sensitivity analysis can provide useful insights into the riskiness of a project.

## Scenario Analysis

Although sensitivity analysis probably is the most widely used risk analysis technique, it does have limitations. Consider, for example, a proposed coal mine project whose NPV is highly sensitive to changes in output, in variable costs, and in sales price. However, if a utility company has contracted to buy a fixed amount of coal at an inflation-adjusted price per ton, the mining venture might be quite safe despite its steep sensitivity lines. *In general, a project's stand-alone risk depends on both (1) the sensitivity of its NPV to changes in key variables and (2) the range of likely values of these variables as reflected in their probability distributions.* Because sensitivity analysis considers only the first factor, it is incomplete.

**Scenario analysis** is a risk analysis technique that considers both the sensitivity of NPV to changes in key variables and the likely range of variable values. In a scenario analysis, the financial analyst asks operating managers to pick a "bad" set of circumstances (low unit sales, low sales price, high variable cost per unit, high construction cost, and so on) and a "good" set of circumstances. The NPVs under the bad and good conditions are then calculated and compared with the expected, or base case, NPV.

As an example, let's return to the appliance control computer project. Assume that HEP's managers are fairly confident of their estimates of all the project's cash flow variables except price and unit sales. Further, they regard a drop in sales below 10,000 units or a rise above 20,000 units as being extremely unlikely. Similarly, they expect the sales price as set in the marketplace to fall within the range of $1,500 to $2,500. Thus, 10,000 units at a price of $1,500 defines the lower bound, or the **worst-case scenario,** whereas 20,000 units at a price of $2,500 defines the upper bound, or the **best-case scenario.** Remember that the **base, or most likely, case** values are 15,000 units and a price of $2,000.

To carry out the scenario analysis, we use the worst-case variable values to obtain the worst-case NPV and the best-case variable values to obtain the best-case NPV.[6] We then use the result of the scenario analysis to determine the *expected* NPV, standard deviation of NPV, and the coefficient of variation. To complete these computations, we need an estimate of the probabilities of occurrence of the three scenarios, the $Pr_i$ values. Suppose management estimates that there is a 20 percent probability of the worst-case scenario occurring, a 60 percent probability of the base case, and a 20 percent probability of the best case. Of course, it is *very difficult* to estimate scenario probabilities accurately. The scenario probabilities and NPVs constitute a probability distribution of returns just like those we dealt with in Chapter 8, except that the returns are measured in dollars instead of in percentages, or rates of return.

We performed the scenario analysis using a spreadsheet model, and Table 10-5 summarizes the results of this analysis. We see that the base case (or most likely case)

**scenario analysis**
A risk analysis technique in which "bad" and "good" sets of financial circumstances are compared with a most likely, or base case, situation.

**worst-case scenario**
An analysis in which all of the input variables are set at their worst reasonably forecasted values.

**best-case scenario**
An analysis in which all of the input variables are set at their best reasonably forecasted values.

**base, or most likely, case**
An analysis in which all of the input variables are set at their most likely values.

[6]We could have included worst- and best-case values for fixed and variable costs, income tax rates, salvage values, and so on. For illustrative purposes, we limited the changes to only two variables. Also, note that we are treating sales price and quantity as independent variables; that is, a low sales price could occur when unit sales are low, and a high sales price could be coupled with high unit sales, or vice versa. As we discuss in the next section, it is relatively easy to vary these assumptions if the facts of the situation suggest a different set of conditions.

**TABLE 10-5**   Scenario Analysis of HEP's Appliance Computer ($ thousands, except sales price)

| Scenario | Sales Volume (Units) | Sales Price | NPV | Probability of Outcome $Pr_i$ | NPV × $Pr_i$ |
|---|---|---|---|---|---|
| Best case | 20,000 | $2,500 | $17,494 | 0.20 | $3,499 |
| Most likely case | 15,000 | 2,000 | 3,790 | 0.60 | 2,274 |
| Worst case | 10,000 | 1,500 | (6,487) | 0.20 | (1,297) |
| | | | | 1.00 | Expected NPV = $4,475* |
| | | | | | $\sigma_{NPV}$ = $7,630 |
| | | | | | $CV_{NPV}$ = 1.7 |

$$\text{Expected NPV} = \sum_{i=1}^{n} Pr_i(NPV_i) = 0.2(\$17,494) + 0.6(\$3,790) + 0.2(-\$6,487) = \$4,475$$

$$\sigma_{NPV} = \sqrt{\sum_{i=1}^{n} Pr_i(NPV_i - \text{Expected NPV})^2}$$

$$= \sqrt{0.2(\$17,494 - \$4,475)^2 + 0.6(\$3,790 - \$4,475)^2 + 0.2(-\$6,487 - \$4,475)^2} = \$7,630$$

$$CV_{NPV} = \frac{\sigma_{NPV}}{\text{Expected NPV}} = \frac{\$7,630}{\$4,475} = 1.7$$

*Rounding difference.

forecasts a positive NPV result; the worst case produces a negative NPV; and the best case results in a large positive NPV. But the expected NPV for the project is $4.5 million and the project's coefficient of variation is 1.7. Now we can compare the project's coefficient of variation with the coefficient of variation of HEP's average project to get an idea of the relative riskiness of the appliance control computer project.

HEP's existing projects, on average, have a coefficient of variation of about 1.0, so, on the basis of this stand-alone risk measure, HEP's managers would conclude that the appliance computer project is riskier than the firm's "average" project.

## Monte Carlo Simulation

**Monte Carlo simulation**
A risk analysis technique in which probable future events are simulated on a computer, generating a probability distribution that indicates the most likely outcomes.

Scenario analysis provides useful information about a project's stand-alone risk. However, it is limited in that it considers only a few discrete outcomes (NPVs) for the project, even though there really are many more possibilities. **Monte Carlo simulation,** so named because this type of analysis grew out of work on the mathematics of casino gambling, ties together sensitivities and input variable probability distributions.

Simulation is more complicated than scenario analysis because the probability distribution of each uncertain cash flow variable has to be specified. Once this has been done, a value from the probability distribution for each variable is randomly chosen to compute the project's cash flows, and then these values are used to determine the project's NPV. Simulation is usually completed using a computer because the process just described is repeated again and again, say, for 500 times, which results in 500 NPVs and a probability distribution for the project's NPV values. Thus, the output produced by simulation is a probability distribution that can be used to determine the most likely range of outcomes to be expected from a project. This provides the decision maker with a better idea of the various outcomes that are possible than is available from a point estimate of the NPV. In addition, simulation software packages can be used to estimate the probability of NPV > 0, of IRR > r, and so on. This additional information can be quite helpful in assessing the riskiness of a project.

Unfortunately, Monte Carlo simulation is not easy to apply because it is often difficult to specify the relationships, or correlations, among the uncertain cash flow variables. The problem is not insurmountable, but it is important not to underestimate the difficulty of obtaining valid estimates of probability distributions and correlations among variables. Such problems have been cited as reasons Monte Carlo simulation has not been widely used in industry.

### Self-Test Questions

List three reasons why, in practice, a project's stand-alone risk is important.

Differentiate between sensitivity and scenario analyses. Why might scenario analysis be preferable to sensitivity analysis?

What is Monte Carlo simulation?

Identify some problems with (1) sensitivity analysis, (2) scenario analysis, and (3) Monte Carlo simulation.

Andy Johnson is considering expanding his bakery. To do so, he must purchase additional equipment. A consulting firm that Andy hired performed a capital budgeting analysis, which produced the following information about the equipment Andy is evaluating:

| Economy | Probability | NPV |
|---------|-------------|-----|
| Boom | 0.3 | $15,000 |
| Normal | 0.5 | 9,000 |
| Recession | 0.2 | (5,000) |

Compute the expected NPV; standard deviation, $\sigma_{NPV}$; and coefficient of variation, $CV_{NPV}$, for the equipment. (*Answers:* $E(NPV) = \$8,000$; $\sigma_{NPV} = \$7,000$; and $CV_{NPV} = 0.875$)

## CORPORATE (WITHIN-FIRM) RISK

To measure corporate, or within-firm, risk, we need to determine how the capital budgeting project is related to the firm's existing assets. Remember from our discussion in Chapter 8 that two assets can be combined to reduce risk if their payoffs move in opposite directions—that is, when the payoff from one asset falls, the payoff from the other asset rises. In reality, it is not easy to find assets with payoffs that move opposite each other. But as we discovered in Chapter 8, as long as assets are *not* perfectly positively related ($\rho = +1.0$), some diversification, or risk reduction, can still be achieved. Many firms use this principle to reduce the risk associated with their operations—adding new projects that are not highly related to existing assets can help reduce corporate risk and reduce fluctuations associated with sales.

Corporate risk is important for three primary reasons:

1. Undiversified stockholders, including the owners of small businesses, are more concerned about corporate risk than about beta risk.

2. Empirical studies of the determinants of required rates of return (r) generally find that both beta and corporate risk affect stock prices. This suggests that investors, even those who are well diversified, consider factors other than beta risk when they establish required returns.

**3.** The firm's stability is important to its managers, workers, customers, suppliers, and creditors, as well as to the community in which it operates. Firms that are in serious danger of bankruptcy, or even of suffering low profits and reduced output, have difficulty attracting and retaining good managers and workers. Also, both suppliers and customers are reluctant to depend on weak firms, and such firms have difficulty borrowing money at reasonable interest rates. These factors tend to reduce risky firms' profitability and hence the prices of their stocks; thus, they also make corporate risk significant.

Therefore, corporate risk is important even if a firm's stockholders are well diversified.

**Self-Test Question**

List three reasons why corporate risk is important.

## BETA (MARKET) RISK

The types of risk analysis discussed thus far in this chapter provide insights into a project's risk and thus help managers make better accept/reject decisions. However, these risk measures do not take account of portfolio risk, and they do not specify whether a project should be accepted or rejected. In this section, we show how the capital asset pricing model (CAPM) can be used to help overcome these shortcomings. Of course, the CAPM has shortcomings of its own, but it nevertheless offers useful insights into risk analysis in capital budgeting.

### Beta (or Market) Risk and Required Rate of Return for a Project

**project required rate of return, $r_{proj}$**
The risk-adjusted required rate of return for an individual project.

In Chapter 8, we developed the concept of beta, $\beta$, as a risk measure for individual stocks. From our discussion, we concluded systematic risk is the relevant risk of a stock because unsystematic, or firm-specific, risk can be reduced significantly or eliminated through diversification. This same concept can be applied to capital budgeting projects because the firm can be thought of as a composite of all the projects it has undertaken. Thus, the relevant risk of a project can be viewed as the impact it has on the firm's systematic risk. This line of reasoning leads to the conclusion that if the beta coefficient for a project, $\beta_{proj}$, can be determined, then the **project required rate of return, $r_{proj}$,** can be found using the following form of the CAPM equation:

$$r_{proj} = r_{RF} + (r_M - r_{RF})\,\beta_{proj}$$

As an example, consider the case of Erie Steel Company, an integrated steel producer operating in the Great Lakes region. For simplicity, let's assume that Erie is all equity financed, so the *average* required rate of return it needs to earn on capital budgeting projects is based solely on the average return demanded by stockholders—that is, there is no debt that might require a different return. Erie's existing beta = $\beta_{Existing}$ = 1.1; $r_{RF}$ = 8%; and $r_M$ = 12%. Thus, Erie's cost of equity is 12.4% = $r_s$ = 8% + (12% – 8%)1.1, which suggests that investors should be willing to give Erie money to invest in *average risk* projects if the company expects to earn 12.4 percent or more on this money.[7] Here again, by average risk we mean projects having risk similar to the firm's existing assets.

---

[7]To simplify things somewhat, we assume at this point that the firm uses only equity capital. If debt is used, the required rate of return used must be a weighted average of the costs of debt and equity. This point is discussed at length in Chapter 11.

Suppose, however, that taking on a particular project will cause a change in Erie's beta coefficient and hence change the company's required rate of return. For example, suppose Erie is considering the construction of a fleet of barges to haul iron ore, and barge operations have betas of 1.5 rather than 1.1. Because the firm itself might be regarded as a "portfolio of assets," just like the beta of any portfolio, Erie's beta is a weighted average of the betas of its individual assets. Thus, taking on the barge project will cause the overall corporate beta to rise to somewhere between the original beta of 1.1 and the barge project's beta of 1.5. The exact value of the new beta will depend on the relative size of the investment in barge operations versus Erie's other assets. If 80 percent of Erie's total funds end up in basic steel operations with a beta of 1.1 and 20 percent in the barge operations with a beta of 1.5, the new corporate beta will increase to $1.18 = 0.8(1.1) + 0.2(1.5)$. This increase in Erie's beta coefficient will cause its stock price to decline unless the increased beta is offset by a higher expected rate of return. Note that taking on the new project will cause the *overall* corporate required rate of return to rise from the original 12.4 percent to 12.7 percent because the new beta will be 1.18. This higher average rate can be earned only if the new project generates a return higher than the existing assets are providing. Because Erie's overall return is based on its portfolio of assets, the return required from the barge project must be sufficiently high so that, in combination with returns of the other assets, the firm's average return is 12.7 percent. Because its beta is higher, the barge project, with $\beta_{Barge} = 1.5$, should be evaluated at a 14 percent required rate of return—that is, $r_{Barge} = 8\% + (4\%)1.5 = 14\%$. On the other hand, a low-risk project such as a new steel distribution center with a beta of only 0.5 would have a required rate of return of 10 percent.

Figure 10-2 gives a graphic summary of these concepts as applied to Erie Steel. Note the following points:

1. The SML is a security market line like the one we developed in Chapter 8. It shows how investors are willing to make trade-offs between risk as measured by beta and expected returns. The higher the beta risk, the higher the rate of

**FIGURE 10-2** **Using the Security Market Line Concept in Capital Budgeting**

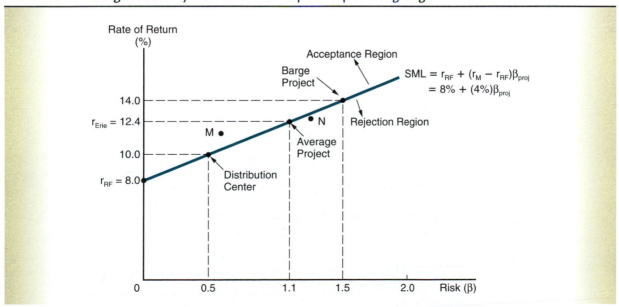

return needed to compensate investors for bearing this risk. The SML specifies the nature of this relationship.

2. Erie Steel initially had a beta of 1.1, so its required rate of return on average-risk investments was 12.4 percent.

3. High-risk investments such as the barge line require higher rates of return, whereas low-risk investments such as the distribution center require lower rates of return. If Erie concentrates its new investments in either high- or low-risk projects rather than average-risk ones, its corporate beta will either rise or fall from the current value of 1.1. Consequently, Erie's required rate of return on common stock would change from its current value of 12.4 percent.

4. If the expected rate of return on a given capital project lies *above* the SML, the expected rate of return on the project is more than enough to compensate for its risk, and the project should be accepted. Conversely, if the project's rate of return lies *below* the SML, it should be rejected. Thus, Project M in Figure 10-2 is acceptable, whereas Project N should be rejected. N has a higher expected return than M, but the differential is not enough to offset its much higher risk.

## Measuring Beta Risk for a Project

**pure play method**
An approach used for estimating the beta of a project in which a firm identifies companies whose only business is the product in question, determines the beta for each firm, and then averages the betas to find an approximation of its own project's beta.

In Chapter 8 we discussed the estimation of betas for stocks, and we indicated that it is difficult to estimate *true* future betas. The estimation of project betas is even more difficult and more fraught with uncertainty. One way a firm can try to measure the beta risk of a project is to find *single-product* companies in the same line of business as the project being evaluated and then use the betas of those companies to determine the required rate of return for the project being evaluated. This technique is termed the **pure play method,** and the single-product companies that are used for comparisons are called *pure play firms.* For example, if Erie could find three existing single-product firms that operate barges, it could use the average of the betas of those firms as a proxy for the barge project's beta.

The pure play approach can be used only for major assets such as whole divisions, and even then it is frequently difficult to implement because it is often impossible to find pure play proxy firms. However, when IBM was considering selling personal computers, it was able to obtain data on Apple Computer and several other essentially pure play personal computer companies. This is often the case when a firm considers a major investment outside its primary field.

 **Self-Test Questions**

What is meant by the term *average-risk project?* How could you find the required rate of return for a project with average risk, low risk, and high risk?

Complete the following sentence: "An increase in a company's beta coefficient would cause its stock price to decline unless..."

Explain why a firm should accept a given capital project if its expected rate of return lies above the SML. What if the expected rate of return lies on or below the SML?

What is the pure play method, and how is it used to estimate a project's beta?

Champion Construction Center, which currently has assets of $200,000 and a beta of 1.5, is evaluating the purchase of a new division that will cost $50,000 and has a beta of 3.0. If the division is purchased, what would be the firm's beta? (*Answer:* 1.8)

## PROJECT RISK CONCLUSIONS

We have discussed the three types of risk normally considered in capital budgeting analysis—stand-alone risk, within-firm (or corporate) risk, and beta (or market) risk—and we have discussed ways of assessing each. However, two important questions remain: (1) Should a firm be concerned with stand-alone risk and corporate risk in its capital budgeting decisions, and (2) what do we do when the stand-alone risk or within-firm risk assessments and the beta risk assessment lead to different conclusions?

These questions do not have easy answers. From a theoretical standpoint, well-diversified investors should be concerned only with beta risk, managers should be concerned only with stock price maximization, and these two factors should lead to the conclusion that beta risk should be given virtually all the weight in capital budgeting decisions. However, if investors are not well diversified, if the CAPM does not operate exactly as theory says it should, or if measurement problems keep managers from having confidence in the CAPM approach in capital budgeting, it might be appropriate to give stand-alone and corporate risk more weight than financial theorists suggest. Note also that the CAPM ignores bankruptcy costs, even though such costs can be substantial, and that the probability of bankruptcy depends on a firm's corporate risk, not on its beta risk. Therefore, one can easily conclude that even well-diversified investors should want a firm's management to give at least some consideration to a project's corporate risk instead of concentrating entirely on beta risk.

Although it would be desirable to reconcile these problems and to measure project risk on some absolute scale, the best we can do in practice is to determine project risk in a somewhat nebulous, relative sense. For example, we can generally say with a fair degree of confidence that a particular project has more or less stand-alone risk than the firm's average project. Then, assuming that stand-alone risk and corporate risk are highly correlated (which is typical), the project's stand-alone risk will be a good measure of its corporate risk. Finally, assuming that beta risk and corporate risk are highly correlated (as is true for most companies), a project with more corporate risk than average will also have more beta risk, and vice versa for projects with low corporate risk.

### Self-Test Questions

In theory, is it correct for a firm to be concerned with stand-alone risk and corporate risk in its capital budgeting decisions? Should the firm be concerned with these risks in practice?

If a project's stand-alone, corporate, and beta risks are highly correlated, would this make the task of measuring risk easier or harder? Explain.

## HOW PROJECT RISK IS CONSIDERED IN CAPITAL BUDGETING DECISIONS

Thus far, we have seen that purchasing a capital project can affect a firm's beta risk, its corporate risk, or both. We also have seen that it is extremely difficult to quantify either type of risk. In other words, although it might be possible to reach the general conclusion that one project is riskier than another, it is difficult to develop a really good measure of project risk. This lack of precision in measuring project risk makes it difficult to incorporate differential risk into capital budgeting decisions.

In reality, most firms incorporate project risk in capital budgeting decisions using the **risk-adjusted discount rate** approach. With this approach, the required rate of

**risk-adjusted discount rate**
The discount rate (required rate of return) that applies to a particular risky stream of income; it is equal to the risk-free rate of interest plus a risk premium appropriate to the level of risk associated with a particular project.

**TABLE 10-6**    Capital Budgeting Decisions Using Risk-Adjusted Discount Rates

| Project | Project Risk | Required Return | Estimated Life | Initial Investment Outlay—$CF_0$ | Incremental Operating Cash Flows— $CF_1 - CF_5$ | NPV | IRR |
|---|---|---|---|---|---|---|---|
| A | Low | 12% | 5 | $(10,000) | $2,850 | $273.61 | 13.1% |
| B | Average | 15 | 5 | (11,000) | 3,210 | (239.58) | 14.1 |
| C | Average | 15 | 5 | ( 9,000) | 2,750 | 218.43 | 16.0 |
| D | High | 20 | 5 | (12,000) | 3,825 | (560.91) | 17.9 |

| Project Risk Classification | Required Rate of Return |
|---|---|
| Low | 12% |
| Average | 15 |
| High | 20 |

return, which is the rate at which the expected cash flows are discounted, is adjusted if the project's risk is substantially different from the average risk associated with the firm's existing assets. Therefore, average-risk projects would be discounted at the rate of return required of projects that are considered "average," or normal for the firm; above-average risk projects would be discounted at a higher-than-average rate; and below-average risk projects would be discounted at a rate below the firm's average rate of return. Unfortunately, because risk cannot be measured precisely, there is no accurate way of specifying exactly how much higher or lower these discount rates should be; given the current state of the art, *risk adjustments are necessarily judgmental and somewhat arbitrary.*

Although the process is not exact, many companies use a two-step procedure to develop risk-adjusted discount rates for use in capital budgeting analysis. First, the overall required rate of return is established for the firm's existing assets. This process is completed on a division-by-division basis for very large firms, perhaps using the CAPM. Second, all projects generally are classified into three categories—high risk, average risk, and low risk. Then, the firm or division uses the average required rate of return as the discount rate for average-risk projects, reduces the average rate by 1 or 2 percentage points when evaluating low-risk projects, and raises the average rate by several percentage points for high-risk projects. For example, if a firm's basic required rate of return is estimated to be 15 percent, a 20 percent discount rate might be used for a high-risk project and a 12 percent rate for a low-risk project. Average-risk projects, which constitute about 80 percent of most capital budgets, would be evaluated at the 15 percent rate of return. Table 10-6 shows an example of the application of risk-adjusted discount rates for the evaluation of four projects. Each of the four projects has a five-year life, and each is expected to generate a constant cash flow stream during its life; therefore, each project's future cash flow pattern represents an annuity. The analysis shows that only Project A and Project C are acceptable when risk is considered. Note, however, that if the average required rate of return is used to evaluate all the projects, Project C and Project D would be considered acceptable because their IRRs are greater than 15 percent, but Project A would not be acceptable because its IRR is less than 15 percent. This example shows that using the average required rate of return would lead to an incorrect decision. Thus, *if project risk is not considered in capital budgeting analysis, incorrect decisions are possible.*

Although the risk-adjusted discount rate approach is far from precise, it does at least recognize that different projects have different risks, and projects with different risks should be evaluated using different required rates of return.

**Self-Test Questions**

How are risk-adjusted discount rates used to incorporate project risk into the capital budgeting decision process?

Briefly explain the two-step process many companies use to develop risk-adjusted discount rates for use in capital budgeting.

When the CFO of Atrium Airplanes evaluates capital budgeting projects, he adjusts the firm's required rate of return, r, to account for risk. He adds 4 percent to r evaluating projects with higher-than-average risk, and he subtracts 2 percent from r when evaluating projects with lower-than-average risk. The CFO just announced that a large capital budgeting project that has an internal rate of return (IRR) equal to 12 percent will be purchased by the firm within two months. If Atrium's r equals 13 percent, what can you conclude about the risk of this project? (*Answer:* This project must have lower risk than the firm's average-risk projects.)

## CAPITAL RATIONING

Capital budgeting decisions are typically made on the basis of the techniques presented in Chapter 9 and applied as described in this chapter: Independent projects are accepted if their NPVs are positive, and choices among mutually exclusive projects are made by selecting the one with the highest NPV. In this analysis, it is assumed that if in a particular year the firm has an especially large number of good projects, management simply will go into the financial markets and raise whatever funds are required to finance all of the acceptable projects. However, some firms do set limits on the amount of funds they are willing to raise, and, if this is done, the capital budget must also be limited. This situation is known as **capital rationing.**

Elaborate and mathematically sophisticated models have been developed to help firms maximize their values when they are subject to capital rationing. However, a firm that subjects itself to capital rationing is deliberately forgoing profitable projects, and hence it is not truly maximizing its value. This point is well known, so few large, sophisticated firms ration capital today. Therefore, we shall not discuss it further, but you should know what the term *capital rationing* means.

**capital rationing**
A situation in which a constraint is placed on the total size of the firm's capital investment.

**Self-Test Questions**

What is meant by the term *capital rationing*?

Why do few sophisticated firms ration capital today?

## MULTINATIONAL CAPITAL BUDGETING

Although the basic principles of capital budgeting analysis are the same for both domestic and foreign operations, some key differences need to be mentioned. First, cash flow estimation generally is much more complex for overseas investments.

**repatriation of earnings**
The process of sending cash flows from a foreign subsidiary back to the parent company.

Most multinational firms set up a separate subsidiary in each foreign country in which they operate, and the relevant cash flows for these subsidiaries are the dividends and royalties **repatriated,** or returned, to the parent company. Second, these cash flows must be converted into the currency of the parent company, and thus are subject to future exchange rate changes. For example, General Motors' Brazilian subsidiary might make a profit of 150 million real (Brazil's monetary unit) in 2008, but the value of these profits to GM will depend on the dollar-to-real exchange rate. Third, dividends and royalties normally are taxed by both foreign and home-country governments. Furthermore, a foreign government might restrict the amount of cash that can be repatriated to the parent company, perhaps to force multinational firms to reinvest earnings in the host country or to prevent large currency outflows, which might affect the exchange rate. Whatever the host country's motivation, the result is that the parent corporation cannot use cash flows blocked in the foreign country to pay current dividends to its shareholders, nor does it have the flexibility to reinvest cash flows elsewhere in the world. Therefore, from the perspective of the parent organization, *the cash flows relevant for the analysis of a foreign investment are the cash flows that the subsidiary legally can send back to the parent.*

In addition to the complexities of the cash flow analysis, *the rate of return required for a foreign project might be different than for an equivalent domestic project because foreign projects might be either riskier or less risky.* A higher risk could arise from two primary sources—(1) exchange rate risk and (2) political risk—whereas a lower risk might result from international diversification.

**exchange rate risk**
The uncertainty associated with the price at which the currency from one country can be converted into the currency of another country.

**Exchange rate risk** reflects the inherent uncertainty about the home currency value of cash flows sent back to the parent. In other words, foreign projects have an added risk element that relates to what the basic cash flows will be worth in the parent company's home currency. The foreign currency cash flows to be turned over to the parent must be converted into U.S. dollars by translating them at *expected* future exchange rates—actual exchange rates might differ substantially from expectations.

**political risk**
The risk of expropriation (seizure) of a foreign subsidiary's assets by the host country or of unanticipated restrictions on cash flows to the parent company.

**Political risk** refers to any action (or the chance of such action) by a host government that reduces the value of a company's investment. It includes at one extreme the expropriation (seizure) without compensation of the subsidiary's assets, but it also includes less drastic actions that reduce the value of the parent firm's investment in the foreign subsidiary, such as higher taxes, tighter repatriation or currency controls, and restrictions on prices charged. The risk of expropriation of U.S. assets abroad is low in traditionally friendly and stable countries such as the United Kingdom or Switzerland. However, in Latin America and Africa, for example, the risk might be substantial.

Generally, political risk premiums are not added to the required rate of return to adjust for this risk. If a company's management has a serious concern that a given country might expropriate foreign assets, it simply will not make significant investments in that country. Expropriation is viewed as a catastrophic or ruinous event, and managers have been shown to be extraordinarily risk averse when faced with ruinous loss possibilities. However, companies can take steps to reduce the potential loss from expropriation in three major ways: (1) by financing the subsidiary with capital raised in the country in which the asset is located, (2) by structuring operations so that the subsidiary has value only as a part of the integrated corporate system, and (3) by obtaining insurance against economic losses from expropriation from a source such as the Overseas Private Investment Corporation (OPIC). In the latter case, insurance premiums would have to be added to the project's cost.

**Self-Test Questions**

List some key differences in capital budgeting as applied to foreign versus domestic operations.

What are the relevant cash flows for an international investment?

Why might the required rate of return for a foreign project differ from that of an equivalent domestic project? Could it be lower?

To summarize the key concepts, let's answer the questions that were posed at the beginning of the chapter:

**Chapter *Essentials***

—The Answers

- **What are the relevant cash flows associated with a capital budgeting project? How are these cash flows identified and used in capital budgeting analysis?** The cash flows that should be analyzed—that is, the relevant cash flows—in capital budgeting analysis are those that are affected by the investment decision. Any cash flow that changes if the firm purchases an asset is considered a relevant cash flow; any cash flow that is not affected by the purchase is irrelevant when looking at the acceptability of the asset being evaluated. Following are the three categories of relevant cash flows associated with a capital budgeting project:

   **(1)** *Initial investment outlay,* which includes cash flows that are associated with the purchase of the asset; these cash flows occur only at the time the asset is purchased.

   **(2)** *Incremental operating cash flows* are cash flows that change because the asset is purchased and continue throughout its life; these changes are generally seen in the day-to-day cash flows.

   **(3)** *Terminal cash flow,* which includes cash flows that are associated with the disposal of the asset; these cash flows occur only at the end of the asset's useful life (to the firm).

- **What is depreciation and how does it affect a project's relevant cash flows?** Depreciation is the means by which a long-term (fixed) asset is expensed over time. Depreciation is used to "match" a decrease in the value of an asset to the revenues it helps to generate. Because the cash flow required to purchase the asset is paid when the asset is bought, depreciation is a noncash expense—that is, depreciation does not require the firm to pay cash at the time the expense is recognized. However, we must consider depreciation when evaluating a capital budgeting project because it is an expense that affects taxes, and taxes must be paid with cash.

- **How is risk incorporated in capital budgeting analysis?** If a firm evaluates a project with a risk that differs significantly from its "average" investments, some adjustment must be made to account for the difference. Generally, projects that are much riskier than average are evaluated with higher required rates of return, whereas projects that have much less risk than average are evaluated with lower required rates of return. Failure to account for risk could lead to incorrect capital budgeting decisions.

- **How do capital budgeting analyses/decisions differ for multinational firms?** Such factors as exchange rate risk, political risk, and the ability to repatriate earnings make capital budgeting decisions more complicated when multinational firms evaluate foreign investments. The relevant cash flows for analysis of a foreign investment are those cash flows that can be sent to the parent company. Often, because the risk is greater, the required rate of return used to evaluate a foreign investment is higher than the required rate of return used to evaluate similar domestic investments.

## ETHICAL DILEMMA

### Mary Mary Quite Contrary, What Makes Your Sales Forecasts Grow?

Saskatchewan Mining and Steel (SMS) Corporation is evaluating whether it should produce a new synthetic steel that will require billions of dollars to develop. According to Bill Bates, the CEO of SMS, the synthetic steel should boost sales such that the company's total net income is increased substantially. Mary, who has worked in the capital budgeting area for six years, was asked to estimate the relevant cash flows that the synthetic steel is expected to generate.

During the past few weeks Mary has had quite a few conversations with the company's engineers, its production manager, and its vice president of marketing. With the information she compiled through her conversations with these people and additional information she received from independent sources, Mary put together a rather detailed forecast of the synthetic steel's relevant cash flows. The final report, which includes only the forecasted cash flows and explanations for the forecasts, was submitted to the chief investment officer yesterday. The report does not include NPV or IRR analyses of the new product because such analyses are conducted by the investment officer.

Today, the investment officer called Mary to tell her that he thought that the forecasts she submitted were incorrect. Mary explained that her forecasts were based on a large amount of information that she had collected and corroborated in combination with analysts' predictions concerning the potential success of the synthetic steel. As she told the investment officer, her forecasts were based on optimistic growth rates in sales for the synthetic steel during the next 15 years. The investment officer said that he thought the growth of such a revolutionary product could be higher than Mary estimated, so he asked her to reconsider her cash flow estimates. Although she had reviewed the numbers dozens of times and she is convinced her forecasts are reliable, Mary agreed to "go over" the forecasts one more time. Being a team player is important to Mary because she wants to move up the corporate ladder as quickly as possible, and she believes that her rise to the executive suite will be enhanced if she cooperates with her superiors, including the investment officer.

Because she set up her forecast on a spreadsheet, Mary knew it would be easy to change the growth rate of sales to get new cash flow forecasts for the synthetic steel. But Mary didn't think that growth rates higher than the ones she used in her original forecasts could be achieved, even if the synthetic steel proved to be a huge success. She did, however, use the higher growth rates that the investment officer had suggested and generated a new set of forecasted cash flows for the synthetic steel. Even though she is convinced that the new growth rates are likely not attainable, Mary sent her new forecasts to the investment officer a little while ago. She figured, "What's the difference? I don't make the final decision anyway."

Do you believe that Mary should have changed her forecasts? What would you have done if you were in Mary's position?

### Chapter *Essentials*
### —Personal Finance

The concepts presented in this chapter should help you to better understand how to determine relevant cash flows and incorporate risk analysis when making investment decisions. If you apply the concepts presented in this chapter, you should be able to make more informed investment decisions.

- When evaluating the purchase of an automobile or a house, you should be able to better estimate the relevant cash flows, especially the initial investment outlay and the incremental operating cash flows. For instance, when considering whether to purchase a new car to replace an older one, you should consider (1) whether you plan to trade in or sell your existing car and (2) the impact your purchase will have on your insurance premiums, gas expenses, and so forth during the time you own the car. If you are replacing an existing car, the purchase price of the new car (initial investment outlay) will be lower if you trade in or sell your existing car. For example, if the trade-in value of your current car is $5,000, and the purchase price of the new car you are considering is $25,000, then you need only $20,000 to purchase the new car. Depending on the type of car you buy and the age and coverage on your old car, your insurance premiums might increase, which will increase the incremental operating cash flows associated with the new car. On the other hand, the new car might be more fuel efficient, which will decrease its incremental operating cash flows compared with the existing car.

You should apply the same reasoning to the purchase of a new house. If the purchase price is $250,000, is that all you need to move in? Generally the answer is no because you need "up-front" funds (cash) for utility deposits, for needed appliances and other furnishings, and for other incidental expenses that must be covered at the time you purchase the house.

- When examining investments, make sure you evaluate the after-tax expected returns. Remember that you cannot spend or reinvest the dollars that must be paid to the government in taxes.

- As we discussed in earlier chapters and continue to discuss throughout the book, you should always consider risk when evaluating investments. An easy way to incorporate risk in your analysis is to use a risk-adjusted required rate of return as suggested in this chapter. You can classify an investment's risk as normal, above normal, or below normal and make an appropriate adjustment to the investment's required rate of return—that is, use a higher required rate of return to evaluate investments with above-normal risk, and vice versa.

## QUESTIONS

**10-1**  Cash flows rather than accounting profits are listed in Table 10-2. What is the basis for this emphasis on cash flows as opposed to net income?

**10-2**  Look at Table 10-4 and answer these questions:
  **a.** Why is the net salvage value shown in Section III reduced for taxes?
  **b.** How is the change in depreciation computed?
  **c.** What would happen if the new machine permitted a reduction in net working capital?
  **d.** Why are the cost savings shown as a positive amount?

**10-3**  Explain why sunk costs should not be included in a capital budgeting analysis but opportunity costs and externalities should be included.

**10-4**  Explain how net working capital is recovered at the end of a project's life and why it is included in a capital budgeting analysis.

**10-5**  In general, is an explicit recognition of incremental cash flows more important in new project analysis or replacement analysis? Why?

**10-6**  Generosity Golf Equipment is considering whether to build a new manufacturing plant in Jacksonville, Florida, in an effort to increase sales of its golf products in the southeast. If it builds the plant, Generosity would not have to buy land because it owns sufficient land in good locations in Jacksonville. The land on which the plant will be built was bought for $100,000 five years ago; its current value is $600,000. Before it decided that Florida would be a good location for a new plant, Generosity hired a company to provide the demographics of the Jacksonville area. The cost of the study was $200,000. It is estimated that $750,000 of the total sales generated by the new plant will be the result of existing customers shifting their business from other plants because Jacksonville is closer to their locations. How should the costs mentioned here be considered when Generosity performs its capital budgeting analysis?

**10-7** Why is it true, in general, that a failure to adjust expected cash flows for expected inflation biases the calculated NPV downward?

**10-8** Define (a) simulation analysis, (b) scenario analysis, and (c) sensitivity analysis. If AT&T were considering two investments, one calling for the expenditure of $20 million to develop a satellite communications system and the other involving the expenditure of $30,000 for a new truck, on which one would the company be more likely to use simulation analysis?

**10-9** Distinguish between beta (or market) risk, within-firm (or corporate) risk, and stand-alone risk for a project being considered for inclusion in the capital budget. Which type of risk do you believe should be given the greatest weight in capital budgeting decisions? Explain.

**10-10** Suppose Reading Engine Company, which has a high beta as well as a great deal of corporate risk, merged with Simplicity Patterns Inc. Simplicity's sales rise during recessions, when people are more likely to make their own clothes, and, consequently, its beta is negative but its corporate risk is relatively high. What would the merger do to the required rates of return in the consolidated company's locomotive engine division and in its patterns division?

**10-11** Suppose a firm estimates its required rate of return for the coming year to be 10 percent. What are reasonable required rates of return for evaluating average-risk projects, high-risk projects, and low-risk projects?

**10-12** How does political risk affect capital budgeting decisions of multinational companies?

**10-13** Should the total cash flows that are expected to be produced by a new international division be included in the analysis that is performed to make a decision as to whether a multinational firm should invest in the division? Explain.

## SELF-TEST PROBLEMS

*(Solutions appear in Appendix B at the end of the book.)*

key terms   **ST-1** Define each of the following terms:

a. Cash flow; accounting income; relevant cash flow

b. Incremental cash flow; sunk cost; opportunity cost; externalities; inflation bias

c. Initial investment outlay; incremental operating cash flow; terminal cash flow

d. Change in net working capital; expansion project

e. Salvage value

f. Replacement analysis

g. Stand-alone risk; within-firm (corporate) risk; beta (market) risk

h. Sensitivity analysis; scenario analysis; Monte Carlo simulation analysis

i. Project beta versus corporate beta

**j.** Pure play method of estimating project betas

**k.** Risk-adjusted discount rate; project required rate of return

**l.** Capital rationing

**m.** Exchange rate risk; political risk

**ST-2** You have been asked by the president of Ellis Construction Company, headquartered in Toledo, to evaluate the proposed acquisition of a new earthmover. The mover's basic price is $50,000, and it will cost another $10,000 to modify it for special use by Ellis Construction. Assume that the earthmover falls into the MACRS 3-year class. (See Table 10A-2 at the end of this chapter for MACRS recovery allowance percentages.) It will be sold after three years for $20,000, and it will require an increase in net working capital (spare parts inventory) of $2,000. The earthmover purchase will have no effect on revenues, but it is expected to save Ellis $20,000 per year in before-tax operating costs, mainly labor. Ellis's marginal tax rate is 40 percent.

   **a.** What is the company's net initial investment outlay if it acquires the earthmover? (That is, what is the Year 0 net cash flow?)

   **b.** What are the incremental operating cash flows in Years 1, 2, and 3?

   **c.** What is the terminal cash flow in Year 3?

   **d.** If the project's required rate of return is 10 percent, should the earthmover be purchased?

*expansion project analysis*

**ST-3** The Dauten Toy Corporation currently uses an injection molding machine that was purchased two years ago. This machine is being depreciated on a straight-line basis toward a $500 salvage value, and it has six years of remaining life. Its current book value is $2,600, and it can be sold for $3,000 at this time. Thus, the annual depreciation expense is ($2,600 – $500)/6 = $350 per year.

   Dauten is offered a replacement machine that has a cost of $8,000, an estimated useful life of six years, and an estimated salvage value of $800. This machine falls into the MACRS 5-year class. (See Table 10A-2 at the end of this chapter for MACRS recovery allowance percentages.) The replacement machine would permit an output expansion, so sales would rise by $1,000 per year. In addition, the new machine's much greater efficiency would cause operating expenses to decline by $1,500 per year. The new machine would require that net working capital be increased by $1,500.

   Dauten's marginal tax rate is 40 percent, and its required rate of return is 15 percent. Should the old machine be replaced?

*replacement analysis*

**ST-4** The staff of Heymann Manufacturing has estimated the following net cash flows and probabilities for a new manufacturing process:

*risk analysis*

**Net Cash Flows**

| Year | $Pr = 0.2$ | $Pr = 0.6$ | $Pr = 0.2$ |
|------|-----------|-----------|-----------|
| 0 | $(100,000) | $(100,000) | $(100,000) |
| 1 | 20,000 | 30,000 | 40,000 |
| 2 | 20,000 | 30,000 | 40,000 |
| 3 | 20,000 | 30,000 | 40,000 |
| 4 | 20,000 | 30,000 | 40,000 |
| 5 | 20,000 | 30,000 | 40,000 |
| 5* | 0 | 20,000 | 30,000 |

Line 0 gives the cost of the process, Lines 1 through 5 give operating cash flows, and Line 5* contains the estimated salvage values. Heymann's required rate of return for an average risk project is 10 percent.

a. Assume that the project has average risk. Find the project's expected NPV. (*Hint:* Use expected values for the net cash flow in each year.)

b. Find the best-case and worst-case NPVs. What is the probability of occurrence of the worst case if the cash flows are perfectly positively correlated over time? If they are independent over time?

c. Assume that all the cash flows are perfectly positively correlated; that is, there are only three possible cash flow streams over time: (1) the worst case; (2) the most likely, or base, case; and (3) the best case, with probabilities of 0.2, 0.6, and 0.2, respectively. These cases are represented by each of the columns in the table. Find the expected NPV, its standard deviation, and its coefficient of variation.

d. The coefficient of variation of Heymann's average project is in the range 0.8 to 1.0. If the coefficient of variation of a project being evaluated is greater than 1.0, 2 percentage points are added to the firm's required rate of return. Similarly, if coefficient of variation is less than 0.8, 1 percentage point is deducted from the required rate of return. What is the project's required rate of return? Should Heymann accept or reject the project?

## Problems

**disposal of an asset**    **10-1**    PowerBuilt Construction is considering whether to replace an existing bulldozer with a new model. If the new bulldozer is purchased, the existing bulldozer will be sold to another company for $85,000. The existing bulldozer has a book value equal to $100,000. If PowerBuilt's marginal tax rate is 35 percent, what will be the net after-tax cash flow that is generated from the disposal of the existing bulldozer?

**disposal of an asset**    **10-2**    A company has collected the following information about a new machine that it is evaluating for possible investment:

| | |
|---|---|
| Purchase price | $340,000 |
| Salvage value at the end of three years | $ 15,000 |
| Shipping and installation | $ 50,000 |
| Book value at the end of three years | $  5,000 |
| Marginal tax rate | 40% |

a. What is the machine's *depreciable basis*—that is, the amount that can be depreciated during its life?

b. In three years, what will be the net cash flow generated by the disposal of the machine?

**replacement analysis**    **10-3**    The Gehr Company is considering the purchase of a new machine tool to replace an obsolete one. The machine being used for the operation has both a book value and a market value of zero; it is in good working order, however, and will last physically for at least another 10 years. The proposed replacement machine will perform the operation so much more efficiently that Gehr engineers estimate it will produce after-tax cash flows (labor savings and the effect of depreciation) of $9,000 per year. The new machine will cost $40,000 delivered and installed, and its economic life is estimated to be 10 years. Its expected salvage value is zero. The firm's required rate of return is 10 percent, and its marginal tax rate is 40 percent. Should Gehr buy the new machine?

**10-4**  Galveston Shipyards is considering the replacement of an eight-year-old riveting machine with a new one that will increase earnings before depreciation from $27,000 to $54,000 per year. The new machine will cost $82,500, and it will have an estimated life of eight years and no salvage value. The new machine will be depreciated over its 5-year MACRS recovery period. (See Table 10A-2 at the end of this chapter for MACRS recovery allowance percentages.) The firm's marginal tax rate is 40 percent, and the firm's required rate of return is 12 percent. The old machine has been fully depreciated and has no salvage value. Should the old riveting machine be replaced by the new one?

*replacement analysis*

**10-5**  The risk-free rate of return is currently 5 percent and the *market risk premium* is 4 percent. The beta of the project under analysis is 1.4, with expected net cash flows estimated to be $1,500 per year for five years. The required investment outlay on the project is $4,500.

*risk adjustment*

   **a.** What is the required risk-adjusted return on the project?

   **b.** Should the project be purchased?

**10-6**  Companioni Computer Corporation (CCC), a producer of office equipment, currently has assets of $15 million and a beta of 1.4. The risk-free rate is 8 percent and the *market risk premium* is 5 percent. CCC would like to expand into the risky home computer market. If the expansion is undertaken, CCC would create a new division with $3.75 million in assets. The new division would have a beta of 2.4.

*beta risk*

   **a.** What is CCC's current required rate of return?

   **b.** If the expansion is undertaken, what would be the firm's new beta? What is the new overall required rate of return, and what rate of return must the home computer division produce to leave the new overall required rate of return unchanged?

**10-7**  The capital budgeting manager of Conscientious Construction Company (CCC) submitted the following report to the CFO:

*risk-adjusted discount rate*

| Project | IRR | Risk |
|---------|------|---------|
| A | 9.0% | Low |
| B | 10.0 | Average |
| C | 12.0 | High |

   CCC generally takes risk into consideration by adjusting its average required rate of return (r), which equals 8 percent, when evaluating projects with risks that are either lower or higher than average. A 5 percent adjustment is made for high-risk projects, and a 2 percent adjustment is made for low-risk projects. If the above projects are *independent*, which project(s) should CCC purchase?

**10-8**  A college intern working at Anderson Paints evaluated potential investments using the firm's average required rate of return (r), and he produced the following report for the capital budgeting manager:

*risk-adjusted discount rate*

| Project | NPV | RR | Risk |
|---------|-----|-----|------|
| LOM | $1,500 | 12.5% | High |
| QUE | 0 | 11.0 | Low |
| YUP | 800 | 10.0 | Average |
| DOG | (150) | 9.5 | Low |

The capital budgeting manager usually considers the risks associated with capital budgeting projects before making her final decision. If a project has a risk that is different from average, she adjusts the average required rate of return by adding or subtracting 2 percentage points. If the four projects listed above are *independent*, which one(s) should the capital budgeting manager recommend be purchased?

**expansion project analysis**    **10-9**   You have been asked by the president of your company to evaluate the proposed acquisition of a spectrometer for the firm's R&D department. The equipment's base price is $140,000, and it would cost another $30,000 to modify it for special use by your firm. The spectrometer, which falls into the MACRS 3-year class, would be sold after three years for $60,000. (See Table 10A-2 at the end of this chapter for MACRS recovery allowance percentages.) Use of the equipment would require an increase in net working capital (spare parts inventory) of $8,000. The spectrometer would have no effect on revenues, but it is expected to save the firm $50,000 per year in before-tax operating costs, mainly labor. The firm's marginal tax rate is 40 percent.

**a.** What is the initial investment outlay associated with this project? (That is, what is the Year 0 net cash flow?)

**b.** What are the incremental operating cash flows in Years 1, 2, and 3?

**c.** What is the terminal cash flow in Year 3?

**d.** If the project's required rate of return is 12 percent, should the spectrometer be purchased?

**expansion project analysis**    **10-10**   The Ewert Company is evaluating the proposed acquisition of a new milling machine. The machine's base price is $108,000, and it would cost another $12,500 to modify it for special use by the firm. The machine falls into the MACRS 3-year class, and it would be sold after three years for $65,000. (See Table 10A-2 at the end of this chapter for MACRS recovery allowance percentages.) The machine would require an increase in net working capital (inventory) of $5,500. The milling machine would have no effect on revenues, but it is expected to save the firm $44,000 per year in before-tax operating costs, mainly labor. Ewert's marginal tax rate is 34 percent.

**a.** What is the initial investment outlay of the machine for capital budgeting purposes? (That is, what is the Year 0 net cash flow?)

**b.** What are the incremental operating cash flows in Years 1, 2, and 3?

**c.** What is the terminal cash flow in Year 3?

**d.** If the project's required rate of return is 12 percent, should the machine be purchased?

**replacement analysis**    **10-11**   Atlantic Control Company (ACC) purchased a machine two years ago at a cost of $70,000. At that time, the machine's expected economic life was six years and its salvage value at the end of its life was estimated to be $10,000.

It is being depreciated using the straight-line method so that its book value at the end of six years is $10,000. In four years, however, the old machine will have a market value of $0.

A new machine can be purchased for $80,000, including shipping and installation costs. The new machine has an economic life estimated to be four years. MACRS depreciation will be used, and the machine will be depreciated over its 3-year class life rather than its five-year economic life. (See Table 10A-2 at the end of this chapter for MACRS recovery allowance percentages.) During its four-year life, the new machine will reduce cash operating expenses by $20,000 per year. Sales are not expected to change. But the new machine will require net working capital to be increased by $4,000. At the end of its useful life, the machine is estimated to have a market value of $2,500.

The old machine can be sold today for $20,000. The firm's marginal tax rate is 40 percent, and the appropriate required rate of return is 10 percent.

**a.** If the new machine is purchased, what is the amount of the initial investment outlay at Year 0?

**b.** What incremental operating cash flows will occur at the end of Years 1 through 4 as a result of replacing the old machine?

**c.** What is the terminal cash flow at the end of Year 4 if the new machine is purchased?

**d.** What is the NPV of this project? Should ACC replace the old machine?

**10-12** The Boyd Bottling Company is contemplating the replacement of one of its bottling machines with a newer and more efficient one. The old machine has a book value of $600,000 and a remaining useful life of five years. The firm does not expect to realize any return from scrapping the old machine in five years, but it can be sold today to another firm in the industry for $265,000. The old machine is being depreciated toward a zero salvage value, or by $120,000 per year, using the straight-line method.    **replacement analysis**

The new machine has a purchase price of $1,175,000, an estimated useful life and MACRS class life of five years, and an estimated market value of $145,000 at the end of five years. (See Table 10A-2 at the end of this chapter for MACRS recovery allowance percentages.) The machine is expected to economize on electric power usage, labor, and repair costs, which will save Boyd $230,000 each year. In addition, the new machine is expected to reduce the number of defective bottles, which will save an additional $25,000 annually.

The company's marginal tax rate is 40 percent, and it has a 12 percent required rate of return.

**a.** What initial investment outlay is required for the new machine?

**b.** Calculate the annual depreciation allowances for both machines, and compute the change in the annual depreciation expense if the replacement is made.

**c.** What are the incremental operating cash flows in Years 1 through 5?

**d.** What is the terminal cash flow in Year 5?

**e.** Should the firm purchase the new machine? Support your answer.

**f.** In general, how would each of the following factors affect the investment decision, and how should each be treated?

**(1)** The expected life of the existing machine decreases.

(2) The required rate of return is not constant but is increasing as Boyd adds more projects into its capital budget for the year.

**risky cash flows**    **10-13** The Singleton Company must decide between two mutually exclusive investment projects. Each project costs $6,750 and has an expected life of three years. Annual net cash flows from each project begin one year after the initial investment is made and have the following probability distributions:

| Project A | | Project B | |
|---|---|---|---|
| **Probability** | **Net Cash Flows** | **Probability** | **Net Cash Flows** |
| 0.2 | $6,000 | 0.2 | $    0 |
| 0.6 | 6,750 | 0.6 | 6,750 |
| 0.2 | 7,500 | 0.2 | 18,000 |

Singleton has decided to evaluate the riskier project at a 12 percent rate and the less risky project at a 10 percent rate.

a. What is the expected value of the annual net cash flows from each project?

b. What is the coefficient of variation ($CV_{NPV}$)? (*Hint:* Use Equation 8–3 from Chapter 8 to calculate the standard deviation of Project A. $\sigma_B = \$5,798$ and $CV_B = 0.76$.)

c. What is the risk-adjusted NPV of each project?

d. If it were known that Project B was negatively correlated with other cash flows of the firm whereas Project A was positively correlated, how would this knowledge affect the decision? If Project B's cash flows were negatively correlated with the gross national product (GNP), would that influence your assessment of its risk?

**CAPM approach to risk adjustments**    **10-14** Goodtread Rubber Company has two divisions: the tire division, which manufactures tires for new autos, and the recap division, which manufactures recapping materials that are sold to independent tire recapping shops throughout the United States. Because auto manufacturing fluctuates with the general economy, the tire division's earnings contribution to Goodtread's stock price is highly correlated with returns on most other stocks. If the tire division were operated as a separate company, its beta coefficient would be 1.5. The sales and profits of the recap division, on the other hand, tend to be countercyclical because recap sales boom when people cannot afford to buy new tires. The recap division's beta is estimated to be 0.5. Approximately 75 percent of Goodtread's corporate assets are invested in the tire division and 25 percent are invested in the recap division.

Currently, the rate of interest on Treasury securities is 6 percent, and the expected rate of return on an average share of stock is 10 percent. Goodtread uses only common equity capital, so it has no debt outstanding.

a. What is the required rate of return on Goodtread's stock?

b. What discount rate should be used to evaluate capital budgeting projects for each division? Explain your answer fully, and, in the process, illustrate your answer with a project that costs $160,000, has a 10-year life, and provides expected after-tax net cash flows of $30,000 per year.

**10-15** Your firm, Agrico Products, is considering the purchase of a tractor that will have a net cost of $72,000, will increase pretax operating cash flows before taking account of depreciation effects by $24,000 per year, and will be depreciated on a straight-line basis to zero over five years at the rate of $14,400 per year, beginning the first year. (Annual cash flows will be $24,000 before taxes plus the tax savings that result from $14,400 of depreciation.) The board of directors is having a heated debate about whether the tractor actually will last five years. Specifically, Joan Lamm insists that she knows of some tractors that have lasted only four years. Alan Grunewald agrees with Lamm, but he argues that most tractors do give five years of service. Judy Maese says she has known some to last for as long as eight years.

scenario analysis

Given this discussion, the board asks you to prepare a scenario analysis to ascertain the importance of the uncertainty about the tractor's life span. Assume a 40 percent marginal tax rate, a zero salvage value, and a required rate of return of 10 percent. (*Hint:* Here straight-line depreciation is based on the MACRS class life of the tractor and is not affected by the actual life. Also, ignore the half-year convention for this problem.)

## Integrative Problems

**10-16** Unilate Textiles is evaluating a new product, a silk/wool blended fabric. Assume you were recently hired as assistant to the director of capital budgeting, and you must evaluate the new project.

expansion analysis

The fabric would be produced in an unused building adjacent to Unilate's Southern Pines, North Carolina plant. Unilate owns the building, which is fully depreciated. The required equipment would cost $200,000, plus an additional $40,000 for shipping and installation. In addition, inventories would rise by $25,000, and accounts payable would go up by $5,000. All of these costs would be incurred at Year 0. By a special ruling, the machinery could be depreciated under the MACRS system as 3-year class property. (See Table 10A-2 at the end of this chapter for MACRS recovery allowance percentages.)

The project is expected to operate for four years, at which time it will be terminated. The cash inflows are assumed to begin one year after the project is undertaken, or at t = 1, and to continue out to t = 4. At the end of the project's life (Year 4), the equipment is expected to have a salvage value of $25,000.

Unit sales are expected to total 100,000 five-yard textile rolls per year, and the expected sales price is $2 per roll. Cash operating costs for the project (total operating costs excluding depreciation) are expected to total 60 percent of dollar sales. Unilate's marginal tax rate is 40 percent, and its required rate of return is 10 percent. Tentatively, the silk/wool blend fabric project is assumed to be of equal risk to Unilate's other assets.

You have been asked to evaluate the project and to make a recommendation as to whether it should be accepted or rejected. To guide you in your analysis, your boss gave you the following set of tasks to complete:

a. Draw a cash flow time line that shows when the net cash inflows and outflows will occur, and explain how the time line can be used to help structure the analysis.

**TABLE IP10-1**   Unilate's Silk/Wool Blend Project ($ thousands)

| End of Year | 0 | 1 | 2 | 3 | 4 |
|---|---|---|---|---|---|
| Unit sales ($ thousands) | | | 100 | | |
| Price/unit | | $ 2.00 | $ 2.00 | | |
| Total revenues | | | | $200.0 | |
| Costs excluding depreciation | | | $(120.0) | | |
| Depreciation | | | | (36.0) | (16.8) |
| Total operating costs | | $(199.2) | $(228.0) | | |
| Earnings before taxes (EBT) | | | | $ 44.0 | |
| Taxes | | ( 0.3) | | | (25.3) |
| Net income | | | | $ 26.4 | |
| Depreciation | | 79.2 | | 36.0 | |
| Incremental operating CF | | $ 79.7 | | | $ 54.7 |
| Equipment cost | | | | | |
| Installation | | | | | |
| Increase in inventory | | | | | |
| Increase in accounts payable | | | | | |
| Salvage value | | | | | |
| Tax on salvage value | | | | | |
| Return of net working capital | | | | | |
| Cash flow time line (Net CF) | $(260.0) | | | | $ 89.7 |
| Cumulative CF for payback | (260.0) | (180.3) | | | 63.0 |
| NPV = | | | | | |
| IRR = | | | | | |
| Payback = | | | | | |

**b.** Unilate has a standard form that is used in the capital budgeting process; see Table IP10-1. Part of the table has been completed, but you must fill in the blanks. Complete the table in the following order:

(1) Complete the unit sales, sales price, total revenues, and operating costs excluding depreciation lines.

(2) Complete the depreciation line.

(3) Now complete the table down to net income and then down to net operating cash flows.

(4) Now fill in the blanks under Year 0 and Year 4 for the initial investment outlay and the terminal cash flows and complete the cash flow time line (net CF). Discuss working capital. What would have happened if the machinery were sold for less than its book value?

**c.** (1) Unilate uses debt in its capital structure, so some of the money used to finance the project will be debt. Given this fact, should the projected cash flows be revised to show projected interest charges? Explain.

(2) Suppose you learned that Unilate had spent $50,000 to renovate the building last year, expensing these costs. Should this cost be reflected in the analysis? Explain.

(3) Now suppose you learned that Unilate could lease its building to another party and earn $25,000 per year. Should this fact be reflected in the analysis? If so, how?

(4) Now assume that the silk/wool blend fabric project would take away profitable sales from Unilate's cotton/wool blend fabric business. Should this fact be reflected in your analysis? If so, how?

d. Disregard all the assumptions made in part c, and assume there was no alternative use for the building over the next four years. Now calculate the project's NPV, IRR, and traditional payback. Do these indicators suggest that the project should be accepted?

e. If this project had been a replacement project rather than an expansion project, how would the analysis have changed? No calculations are needed; just think about the changes that would have to occur in the cash flow table.

f. Assume that inflation is expected to average 3 percent over the next four years, that this expectation is reflected in the required rate of return, and that inflation will increase variable costs and revenues by the same relative amount of 3 percent. Does it appear that inflation has been dealt with properly in the analysis? If not, what should be done, and how would the required adjustment affect the decision?

**10-17** Problem 10-16 contained the details of a new-project capital budgeting evaluation being conducted by Unilate Textiles. Although inflation was considered in the initial analysis, the riskiness of the project was not considered. The expected cash flows considering inflation as they were estimated in Problem 10-16 (in thousands of dollars) are given in Table IP10-2. Unilate's required rate of return is 10 percent.   **risk analysis**

You have been asked to answer the following questions:

a. (1) What are the three levels, or types, of project risk that are normally considered?

(2) Which type of risk is the most relevant?

(3) Which type of risk is the easiest to measure?

(4) How are the three types of risk generally related?

b. (1) What is sensitivity analysis?

(2) Discuss how one would perform a sensitivity analysis on the unit sales, salvage value, and required rate of return for the project. Assume that each of these variables deviates from its base-case, or expected, value by plus and minus 10, 20, and 30 percent. How would you calculate the NPV, IRR, and the payback for each case?

(3) What is the primary weakness of sensitivity analysis? What are its primary advantages?

c. Assume you are confident about the estimates of all the variables that affect the project's cash flows except unit sales. If product acceptance is poor, sales would be only 75,000 units a year, whereas a strong consumer response would produce sales of 125,000 units. In either case, cash costs would still amount to 60 percent of revenues. You believe that there is a 25 percent chance of poor acceptance, a 25 percent chance of excellent acceptance, and a 50 percent chance of average acceptance (the base case).

**TABLE IP10-2**   Unilate's Silk/Wool Blend Project—Inflation Effects ($ thousands)

| | Year | | | | |
|---|---|---|---|---|---|
| | **0** | **1** | **2** | **3** | **4** |
| Investment in: | | | | | |
| Fixed assets | $( 240) | | | | |
| Net working capital | ( 20) | | | | |
| Unit sales (thousands) | | 100 | 100 | 100 | 100 |
| Sales price (dollars) | | $ 2.100 | $ 2.205 | $ 2.315 | $ 2.431 |
| Total revenues | | $ 210.0 | $ 220.5 | $ 231.5 | $ 243.1 |
| Cash operating costs (60%) | | (126.0) | (132.3) | (138.9) | (145.9) |
| Depreciation | | ( 79.2) | (108.0) | ( 36.0) | ( 16.8) |
| Earnings before taxes (EBT) | | $    4.8 | $( 19.8) | $  56.6 | $  80.4 |
| Taxes (40%) | | ( 1.9) | 7.9 | ( 22.6) | ( 32.2) |
| Net income | | $    2.9 | $( 11.9) | $  34.0 | $  48.2 |
| Plus depreciation | | 79.2 | 108.0 | 36.0 | 16.8 |
| Net operating cash flows | | $  82.1 | $  96.1 | $  70.0 | $  65.0 |
| Salvage value | | | | | 25.0 |
| Tax on SV (40%) | | | | | ( 10.0) |
| Recovery of NWC | | | | | 20.0 |
| Net cash flow | $( 260) | $  82.1 | $  96.1 | $  70.0 | $ 100.0 |
| Cumulative cash flow for payback: | ( 260.0) | (177.9) | ( 81.8) | ( 11.8) | 88.2 |
| NPV at 10% coat of capital = $ 15.0 | | | | | |
| IRR           = 12.6% | | | | | |

**(1)** What is the worst-case NPV? The best-case NPV?

**(2)** Use the worst-case, most likely (or base) case, and best-case NPVs and probabilities of occurrence to find the project's expected NPV, standard deviation ($\sigma_{NPV}$), and coefficient of variation ($CV_{NPV}$).

**d. (1)** Assume that Unilate's average project has a coefficient of variation ($CV_{NPV}$) in the range of 1.25 to 1.75. Would the silk/wool blend fabric project be classified as high risk, average risk, or low risk? What type of risk is being measured here?

**(2)** Based on common sense, how highly correlated do you think the project would be to the firm's other assets? (Give a correlation coefficient, or range of coefficients, based on your judgment.)

**(3)** How would this correlation coefficient and the previously calculated $\sigma$ combine to affect the project's contribution to corporate, or within-firm, risk? Explain.

**e. (1)** Based on your judgment, what do you think the project's correlation coefficient would be with respect to the general economy and thus with returns on "the market"?

**(2)** How would correlation with the economy affect the project's market risk?

**f. (1)** Unilate typically adds or subtracts 3 percentage points to the overall required rate of return to adjust for risk. Should the project be accepted?

**(2)** What subjective risk factors should be considered before the final decision is made?

**g.** Define scenario analysis and simulation analysis, and discuss their principal advantages and disadvantages. (Note that you have already done scenario analysis in part c.)

**h. (1)** Assume that the risk-free rate is 10 percent, the market risk premium is 6 percent, and the new project's beta is 1.2. What is the project's required rate of return on equity based on the CAPM?

**(2)** How does the project's market risk compare with the firm's overall market risk?

**(3)** How does the project's stand-alone risk compare with that of the firm's average project?

**(4)** Briefly describe how you could estimate the project's beta. How feasible do you think that procedure actually would be in this case?

**(5)** What are the advantages and disadvantages of focusing on a project's market risk?

## Computer-Related Problem

*Work the problem in this section only if you are using the problem spreadsheet.*

**10-18**   Use the computerized model in the File C10 to work this problem. Golden State Bakers Inc. (GSB) has an opportunity to invest in a new dough machine. GSB needs more productive capacity, so the new machine will not replace an existing machine. The new machine costs $260,000 and will require modifications costing $15,000. It has an expected useful life of 10 years, will be depreciated using the MACRS method over its 3-year class life, and has an expected salvage value of $12,500 at the end of Year 10. (See Table 10A-2 at the end of this chapter for MACRS recovery allowance percentages.) The machine will require a $22,500 investment in net working capital. It is expected to generate additional sales revenues of $125,000 per year, but its use will also increase annual cash operating expenses by $55,000. GSB's required rate of return is 10 percent and its marginal tax rate is 40 percent. The machine's book value at the end of Year 10 will be zero, so GSB will have to pay taxes on the $12,500 salvage value.

*expansion project*

**a.** What is the NPV of this expansion project? Should GSB purchase the new machine?

**b.** Should GSB purchase the new machine if it is expected to be used for only five years and then sold for $31,250?

**c.** Would the machine be profitable if revenues increased by only $105,000 per year? Assume a 10-year project life and a salvage value of $12,500.

**d.** Suppose revenues rose by $125,000 but that expenses rose by $65,000. Would the machine be acceptable under these conditions? Assume a 10-year project life and a salvage value of $12,500.

GET REAL WITH    **THOMSON ONE** Business School Edition

**risk analysis**    **10-19** Imagine you hold a portfolio of three stocks: Coca Cola Company [KO], a manufacturer and distributor of soft drinks; Dell Inc. [DELL], a manufacturer of personal and enterprise computers; and Fifth Third Bank [FITB], a large bank that offers commercial banking, retail banking, and investment advisory services. Each of these companies is preparing to launch a new project.

Coca Cola is launching a new version of Coca Cola with increased caffeine. Dell has produced a new, very low cost personal computer to deliver the basic functions of e-mail, web browsing, and word processing for individuals who do not need all the "bells and whistles." Fifth Third Bank has shifted its investment in marketable securities so as to earn higher returns; this shift has increased the riskiness associated with the bank's investment portfolio.

The following betas were estimated by the companies for the *new projects*:

| Company | Project Beta |
|---|---|
| Coca Cola | 1.19 |
| Dell | 2.01 |
| Fifth Third Bank | 1.20 |

Using the Thomson ONE database, answer these questions:

a. What is the current beta of the three firms? (Click on Price/Interactive Charts.)

b. If the new project causes the corporate beta to rise, how will this impact the company's risk and the shareholders' required rate of return?

c. Can you use the pure play method to determine a more accurate project beta for any or all of these firms? Why or why not?

# APPENDIX 10A    Depreciation

Suppose a firm buys a milling machine for $100,000 and uses it for five years, after which it is scrapped. The cost of the goods produced by the machine each year must include a charge for using the machine and reducing its value. This charge is called *depreciation.* In this appendix, we review some of the depreciation concepts covered in your accounting courses.

Companies often calculate depreciation one way when figuring taxes and another way when reporting income to investors: many use the *straight-line* method for stockholder reporting (or "book" purposes) but use the fastest rate permitted by law for tax purposes.

According to the straight-line method used for stockholder reporting, you normally would take the cost of the asset, subtract its estimated salvage value, and divide the net amount by the asset's useful economic life. For an asset with a five-year life that costs $100,000 and has a $12,500 salvage value, the annual straight-line depreciation charge is ($100,000 − $12,500)/5 = $17,500. Note, however, as we discuss later in this appendix, that salvage value is not considered for tax depreciation purposes.

For tax purposes, Congress changes the permissible tax depreciation methods from time to time. Prior to 1954, the straight-line method was required for tax purposes, but in 1954 accelerated methods (double declining balance and sum-of-years'-digits) were permitted. Then, in 1981, the old accelerated methods were replaced by a simpler procedure known as the Accelerated Cost Recovery System (ACRS). The ACRS system was changed again in 1986 as a part of the Tax Reform Act, and it is now known as the Modified Accelerated Cost Recovery System (MACRS).

**Tax Depreciation Life** For tax purposes, the *entire* cost of an asset is expensed over its depreciable life. Historically, an asset's depreciable life was determined by its estimated useful economic life; it was intended that an asset would be fully depreciated at approximately the same time that it reached the end of its useful economic life. However, MACRS totally abandoned that practice and set simple guidelines that created several classes of assets, each with a more or less arbitrarily prescribed life called a recovery period or class life. The MACRS class life bears only a rough relationship to the expected useful economic life.

A major effect of the MACRS system has been to shorten the depreciable lives of assets, thus giving businesses larger tax deductions and thereby increasing their cash flows available for reinvestment. Table 10A-1 describes the types of property that fit into the different class life groups, and Table 10A-2 sets forth the MACRS recovery allowances (depreciation rates) for selected classes of investment property.

Consider Table 10A-1 first. The first column gives the MACRS class life, whereas the second column describes the types of assets that fall into each category. Property classified with lives equal to or greater than 27.5 years (real estate) must be depreciated by the straight-line method, but assets classified in the other categories can be depreciated either by the accelerated method using rates shown in Table 10A-2 or by an alternate straight-line method.

As we saw earlier in the chapter, higher depreciation expenses result in lower taxes, hence higher cash flows. Therefore, because a firm has the choice of using the alternate straight-line rates or the accelerated rates shown in Table 10A-2, most elect to use the accelerated rates. The yearly recovery allowance, or depreciation expense, is determined

**TABLE 10A-1**    Major Classes and Asset Lives for MACRS

| Class | Type of Property |
|-------|------------------|
| 3-year | Certain special manufacturing tools; a race horse older than two years |
| 5-year | Automobiles, light-duty trucks, computers, office machinery, and certain special manufacturing equipment |
| 7-year | Most industrial equipment, office furniture, and fixtures |
| 10-year | Certain longer-lived equipment, and many water vessels |
| 15-year | Certain land improvement, such as shrubbery, fences, and roads; service station buildings |
| 20-year | Farm buildings |
| 25-year | Property used in water treatment; municipal sewers |
| 27.5-year | Residential rental real property such as apartment buildings |
| 39-year | All nonresidential real property, including commercial and industrial buildings |

**TABLE 10A-2**    Recovery Allowance Percentages for Personal Property

| Ownership Year | Class of Investment | | | |
| --- | --- | --- | --- | --- |
| | 3-Year | 5-Year | 7-Year | 10-Year |
| 1 | 33% | 20% | 14% | 10% |
| 2 | 45 | 32 | 25 | 18 |
| 3 | 15 | 19 | 17 | 14 |
| 4 | 7 | 12 | 13 | 12 |
| 5 | | 11 | 9 | 9 |
| 6 | | 6 | 9 | 7 |
| 7 | | | 9 | 7 |
| 8 | | | 4 | 7 |
| 9 | | | | 7 |
| 10 | | | | 6 |
| 11 | | | | 3 |
| | 100% | 100% | 100% | 100% |

**Note:** These recovery allowance percentages were taken from the Internal Revenue Service Website, which is http://www.irs.gov. The percentages are based on the 200 percent declining balance method prescribed by MACRS, with a switch to straight line depreciation at some point in the asset's life. For example, consider the 5-year recovery allowance percentages. The straight line percentage would be 20 percent per year, so the 200 percent declining balance multiplier is $2.0(20\%) = 40\% = 0.4$. However, because the half-year convention applies, the MACRS percentage for Year 1 is 20 percent. For Year 2, 80 percent of the depreciable basis remains to be depreciated, so the recovery allowance percentage is $0.40(80\%) = 32\%$, and so on. Although the tax tables carry the allowance percentages to two decimal places, we have rounded to the nearest whole number for ease of illustration.

by multiplying each asset's *depreciable basis* by the applicable recovery percentage shown in Table 10A-2. Calculations are discussed in the following sections.

**Half-Year Convention** Under MACRS, it is assumed that property is placed in service in the middle of the first year. Thus, for 3-year class life property, the recovery period begins in the middle of the year the asset is placed in service and ends three years later. The effect of the *half-year convention* is to extend the recovery period out one more year, so 3-year class life property is depreciated over four *calendar* years, 5-year property is depreciated over six calendar years, and so on. This convention is incorporated into Table 10A-2's recovery allowance percentages.[8]

**Depreciable Basis** The *depreciable basis* is a critical element of MACRS because each year's allowance (depreciation expense) depends jointly on the asset's depreciable basis and its MACRS class life. The depreciable basis under MACRS is equal to the purchase price of the asset plus any shipping and installation costs. The basis is not adjusted for salvage value.

**Sale of a Depreciable Asset** If a depreciable asset is sold, the sale price (salvage value) minus the then-existing undepreciated book value is added to operating income and taxed at the firm's marginal tax rate. For example, suppose a firm buys a 5-year class life asset for $100,000 and sells it at the end of the fourth year for $25,000. The

---

[8]The half-year convention also applies if the straight-line alternative is used, with half of one year's depreciation taken in the first year, a full year's depreciation taken in each of the remaining years of the asset's class life, and the remaining half-year's depreciation taken in the year following the end of the class life. You should recognize that virtually all companies have computerized depreciation systems. Each asset's depreciation pattern is programmed into the system at the time of its acquisition, and the computer aggregates the depreciation allowances for all assets when the accountants close the books and prepare the financial statements and tax returns.

asset's book value is equal to $100,000(0.11 + 0.06) = $17,000$. Therefore, $25,000 - $17,000 = $8,000$ is added to the firm's operating income and is taxed. If this difference were negative, the firm would effectively receive a tax refund, which would be recognized as a cash inflow.

**Depreciation Illustration** Assume that Unilate Textiles buys a $150,000 machine that falls into the MACRS 5-year class life asset and places it into service on March 15, 2009. Unilate must pay an additional $30,000 for delivery and installation. Salvage value is not considered, so the machine's depreciable basis is $180,000. (Delivery and installation charges are included in the depreciable basis rather than expensed in the year incurred.) Each year's recovery allowance (tax depreciation expense) is determined by multiplying the depreciable basis by the applicable recovery allowance percentage. Thus, the depreciation expense for 2009 is $0.20($180,000) = $36,000$, and for 2010 it is $0.32($180,000) = $57,600$. Similarly, the depreciation expense is $34,200 for 2011; $21,600 for 2012; $19,800 for 2013; and $10,800 for 2014. The total depreciation expense over the six-year recovery period is $180,000, which is equal to the depreciable basis of the machine.

As noted previously, most firms use straight-line depreciation for stockholder reporting purposes but MACRS for tax purposes. For these firms, for capital budgeting, MACRS should be used because in capital budgeting, we are concerned with cash flows, not reported income.

## PROBLEM

**10A-1** Christina Manning, great-granddaughter of the founder of Manning Tile Products and current president of the company, believes in simple, conservative accounting. In keeping with her philosophy, she has decreed that the company shall use straight-line depreciation, based on the MACRS class lives, for all newly acquired assets. Your boss, the financial vice president and the only nonfamily officer, has asked you to develop an exhibit that shows how much this policy costs the company in terms of market value. Ms. Manning is interested in increasing the value of the firm's stock because she fears a family stockholder revolt that might remove her from office. For your exhibit, assume that the company spends $100 million each year on new capital projects, that the projects have on average a 10-year class life, that the company has a 9 percent required rate of return, and that its marginal tax rate is 34 percent. (*Hint:* Show how much the total NPV of the projects in an average year would increase if Manning used the standard MACRS recovery allowances.)

*depreciation effects*

## Comparing Projects with Unequal Lives    APPENDIX 10B

Two procedures used to compare capital projects with unequal lives are (1) the replacement chain (common life) method and (2) the equivalent annual annuity (EAA) method.

Suppose the company we followed throughout the chapter, HEP, is planning to modernize its production facilities, and, as a part of the process, it is considering either a conveyor system (Project C) or some forklift trucks (Project F) for moving materials

**FIGURE 10B-1    Expected Net Cash Flows for Project C and Project F**

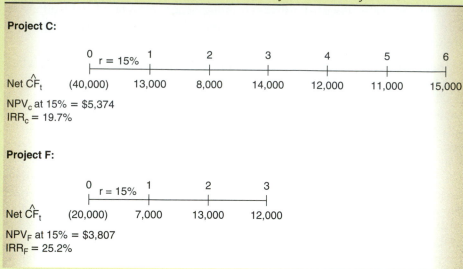

**Project C:**

| | 0 | 1 | 2 | 3 | 4 | 5 | 6 |
|---|---|---|---|---|---|---|---|
| | r = 15% | | | | | | |
| Net $\hat{CF}_t$ | (40,000) | 13,000 | 8,000 | 14,000 | 12,000 | 11,000 | 15,000 |

$NPV_C$ at 15% = $5,374
$IRR_C$ = 19.7%

**Project F:**

| | 0 | 1 | 2 | 3 |
|---|---|---|---|---|
| | r = 15% | | | |
| Net $\hat{CF}_t$ | (20,000) | 7,000 | 13,000 | 12,000 |

$NPV_F$ at 15% = $3,807
$IRR_F$ = 25.2%

from the parts department to the main assembly line. Both the expected net cash flows and the NPVs for these two mutually exclusive alternatives are shown in Figure 10B-1.

We see that Project C, when discounted at a 15 percent required rate of return, has the higher NPV and thus appears to be the better project, despite the fact that Project F has the higher IRR.

**Replacement Chain (Common Life) Approach** Although the analysis in Figure 10B-1 suggests that Project C should be selected, this analysis is incomplete, and the decision to choose Project C actually is incorrect. If we choose Project F, we will have the opportunity to make a similar investment in three years, and if cost and revenue conditions continue at the Figure 10B-1 levels, this second investment will also be profitable. However, if we choose Project C, we will not have this second investment opportunity. Therefore, to make a proper comparison of Projects C and F, we could apply the **replacement chain (common life) approach;** that is, we could find the NPV of Project F over a six-year period and then compare this extended NPV with the NPV of Project C over the same six years.

The NPV for Project C as calculated in Figure 10B-1 is already over the six-year common life. For Project F, however, we must expand the analysis to include the replacement of F in Year 3, resulting in the following six-year cash flow time line[9]:

**replacement chain (common life) approach** A method of comparing projects of unequal lives that assumes each project can be replicated as many times as necessary to reach a common life span; the NPVs over this life span are then compared, and the project with the higher common life NPV is chosen.

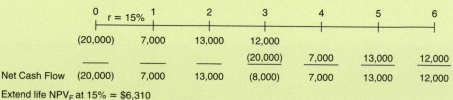

| | 0 | 1 | 2 | 3 | 4 | 5 | 6 |
|---|---|---|---|---|---|---|---|
| | r = 15% | | | | | | |
| | (20,000) | 7,000 | 13,000 | 12,000 | | | |
| | | | | (20,000) | 7,000 | 13,000 | 12,000 |
| Net Cash Flow | (20,000) | 7,000 | 13,000 | (8,000) | 7,000 | 13,000 | 12,000 |

Extend life $NPV_F$ at 15% = $6,310

---

[9]We also could set up Project F's extended time line as follows:

1. The Stage 1 NPV is $3,807.
2. The Stage 2 NPV is also $3,807, but this value will not accrue until Year 3, so its value today, discounted at 15 percent, is $2,503.
3. The extended life NPV is thus $3,807 + $2,503 = $6,310.

Here we make the assumption that Project F's cost and annual cash inflows will not change if the project is repeated in three years and that HEP's required rate of return will remain at 15 percent. Project F's extended NPV is $6,310. This is the value that should be compared with Project C's NPV, $5,374. Because Project F's "true" NPV is greater than that of Project C, Project F should be selected.

**Equivalent Annual Annuity (EAA) Approach** Although the preceding example illustrates why an extended analysis is necessary if we are comparing mutually exclusive projects with different lives, the arithmetic is generally more complex in practice. For example, one project might have a six-year life versus a 10-year life for the other. This would require a replacement chain analysis over 30 years, the lowest common denominator of the two lives. In such a situation, it is often simpler to use a second procedure, the **equivalent annual annuity (EAA) method,** which involves three steps:

**equivalent annual annuity (EAA) method**
A method that calculates the annual payments a project would provide if it were an annuity. When comparing projects of unequal lives, the one with the higher equivalent annual annuity should be chosen.

1. Find each project's NPV over its initial life. In Figure 10B-1, we found $NPV_C$ = $5,374 and $NPV_F$ = $3,807.

2. Find the constant annuity cash flow—the equivalent annual annuity (EAA)— that has the same present value as each project's NPV. For Project F, here is the cash flow time line:

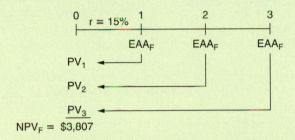

To find the value of $EAA_F$, with a financial calculator, enter –3,807 as the PV, I = r = 15, and N = 3, and solve for PMT. The answer, $1,667, represents the cash flow stream, which, when discounted back three years at 15 percent, has a present value equal to Project F's original NPV of $3,807. The payment figure we found, $1,667, is called the project's *equivalent annual annuity (EAA)*. The EAA for Project C was found similarly to be $1,420. Thus, Project C has an NPV that is equivalent to an annuity of $1,420 per year, whereas Project F's NPV is equivalent to an annuity of $1,667.

3. Assuming that continuous replacements can and will be made each time a project's life ends, these EAAs will continue on out to infinity; that is, they will constitute perpetuities. Recognizing that the value of a perpetuity is PVP = PMT/r, we can find the net present values of the infinite EAAs of Projects C and F as follows:

$$\text{Infinite horizon } NPV_C = \$1,420/0.15 = \$\ 9,467$$
$$\text{Infinite horizon } NPV_F = \$1,667/0.15 = \$11,113$$

In effect, the EAA method assumes that each project, if taken on, will be replaced each time it wears out and will provide cash flows equivalent to the calculated annuity value. The PV of this infinite annuity is then the infinite horizon NPV for the project. Because the infinite horizon NPV of F exceeds that of C, Project F should be accepted. Therefore, the EAA method leads to the same decision as the replacement chain method—accept Project F.

The EAA method often is easier to apply than the replacement chain method, but the replacement chain method is easier to explain to decision makers. Still, the two methods always lead to the same decision if consistent assumptions are used. Also, note that Step 3 of the EAA method is not really necessary—we could have stopped after Step 2 because the project with the higher EAA will always have the higher NPV over any common life *if the same required rate of return is used to evaluate the projects*.

When should we worry about unequal life analysis? As a general rule, the unequal life issue (1) does not arise for independent projects, but (2) can arise if mutually exclusive projects with significantly different lives are being evaluated. However, even for mutually exclusive projects, it is not always appropriate to extend the analysis to a common life. This should be done only if there is a high probability that the projects will actually be replicated beyond their initial lives.

We should note several potentially serious weaknesses inherent in this type of unequal life analysis: (1) If inflation is expected, then replacement equipment will have a higher price, and both sales prices and operating costs will probably change. Thus, the static conditions built into the analysis would be invalid. (2) Replacements that occur down the road would probably employ new technology, which in turn might change the cash flows. This factor is not built into either replacement chain analysis or the EAA approach. (3) It is difficult enough to estimate the lives of most projects, so estimating the lives of a series of projects is often just speculation. (4) If reasonably strong competition is present, the profitability of projects will be eroded over time, and that would reduce the need to extend the analysis beyond the projects' initial lives.

In view of these problems, no experienced financial analyst would be too concerned about comparing mutually exclusive projects with lives of, say, eight years and 10 years. Given all the uncertainties in the estimation process, such projects, for all practical purposes, would be assumed to have the same life. Still, it is important to recognize that a problem does exist if mutually exclusive projects have substantially different lives. When we encounter such problems in practice, we build expected inflation or possible efficiency gains directly into the cash flow estimates and then use the replacement chain approach (but not the equivalent annual annuity method). The cash flow estimation is more complicated, but the concepts involved are exactly the same as in our example.

## PROBLEMS

**unequal lives**    **10B-1**  Keenan Clothes Inc. is considering the replacement of its old, fully depreciated knitting machine. Two new models are available: Machine 190-3, which has a cost of $190,000, a three-year expected life, and after-tax cash flows (labor savings and depreciation) of $87,000 per year, and Machine 360-6, which has a cost of $360,000, a six-year life, and after-tax cash flows of $98,300 per year. Knitting machine prices are not expected to rise because inflation will be offset by cheaper components (microprocessors) used in the machines. Assume that the required rate of return appropriate for evaluating the machines is 14 percent.

    **a.**  Should the firm replace its old knitting machine, and, if so, which new machine should it use?

    **b.**  Suppose the firm's basic patents will expire in nine years, and the company expects to go out of business at that time. Assume further that the firm depreciates its assets using the straight-line method, that its marginal tax rate is 40 percent, and that the used machines can be sold at their book values. Under these circumstances, should the company replace the old machine? Explain.

**10B-2**  Zappe Airlines is considering two alternative planes. Plane A has an expected life of five years, will cost $100, and will produce net cash flows of $30 per year. Plane B has a life of 10 years, will cost $132, and will produce net cash flows of $25 per year. Zappe plans to serve the route for 10 years. Inflation in operating costs, airplane costs, and fares is expected to be zero, and the company's required rate of return is 12 percent. By how much would the value of the company increase if it accepted the better project (plane)? Assume all costs and cash flows are in millions of dollars.

**unequal lives**

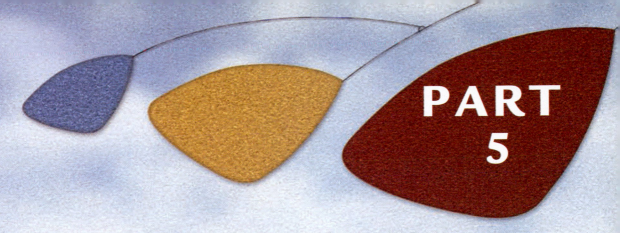

# PART 5

# Cost of Capital, Leverage, and Dividend Policy

# The Cost of Capital

A MANAGERIAL PERSPECTIVE

Firms raise capital in the financial markets, where interest rates and other yields change continuously. As interest rates change, so do the costs associated with the various types of capital. For instance, in 2000 and 2001, interest rates on corporate debt increased while stock prices dropped. As a consequence, companies had to pay higher costs for using investors' funds. Indeed, many companies curtailed their plans to expand or invest funds in long-term projects because the price of the funds needed for such investments had risen so high. For example, Burlington Northern Santa Fe Corporation (BNSF), a railroad company, estimated that if new funds were raised in 2001, the cost to the firm for the funds would be as much as 12 percent. But those same funds could be invested to earn a return of less than 10 percent. Clearly, the firm would lose money if it paid 12 percent for funds that would provide a return of only 10 percent. Would BNSF's stockholders be upset if the company raised funds and knowingly invested those monies in projects that earned returns less than the cost of the funds? Absolutely! For that reason, Burlington Northern postponed a large portion of its planned investments for 2001 until the cost of funds decreased. When interest rates on corporate debt declined in 2002 and 2003, the estimated cost of funds for BNSF had dropped to less

than 7 percent. During the first six months of 2003, interest rates had dropped to levels not seen during the previous 50 years. Although they began to increase slowly at the end of 2003 and the beginning of 2004, rates remained at historically low levels. As a result, not only did BNSF resume its investment program, it also refinanced much of its older, more expensive debt (much like homeowners refinanced their homes during the same period).

As interest rates slowly increased in 2005 and 2006, fewer firms and individuals refinanced their debt. Even so, some firms used other methods to lower their costs of funds. For example, in 2006 both Ford Motor Company and its competitor General Motors (GM) made plans to sell some of their operations in an effort to improve their deteriorating financial positions. The two companies believed that their financing costs would decline if they divested themselves of money-losing operations. Ford and GM were hoping that selling portions of their companies would improve the firms' financial positions, which would decrease the rate of return that investors would demand in the future to provide funds to these companies by investing in their stocks and bonds.

As you read this chapter, keep in mind that firms need funds provided by investors to take advantage of acceptable investment opportunities. The financial marketplace, which consists of investors like you, determines the "price" that firms must pay for these funds. It is essential for us to be able to determine the "price," or the cost, of the capital used by a firm so that we can determine whether the funds are being invested appropriately.

## Chapter *Essentials* —The Questions

After reading this chapter, you should be able to answer the following questions:

- What types of capital do firms use to finance investments?
- What is the cost of capital?
- How is the cost of capital used to make financial decisions?
- Why do funds generated through retained earnings have a cost?
- Who determines a firm's cost of capital?

It is vitally important that a firm knows how much it pays for the funds used to purchase assets. The average return required by the firm's investors determines how much must be paid to attract funds. The firm's required rate of return is its average cost of funds, which more commonly is termed the **cost of capital.** The firm's cost of capital represents the minimum rate of return that must be earned from investments, such as capital budgeting projects, to ensure that the value of the firm does not decrease. In other words, the cost of capital is the firm's **required rate of return, r.** For example, if investors provide funds to a firm for an average cost of 15 percent, wealth will decrease if the funds are used to generate returns less than 15 percent, wealth will not change if exactly 15 percent is earned, and wealth will increase if the firm generates returns greater than 15 percent.

In this chapter, we discuss the concept of cost of capital, how the average cost of capital is determined, and how the cost of capital is used in financial decision making. Most of the models and formulas used in this chapter are the same ones we developed in Chapter 6 and Chapter 7, where we described how stocks and bonds are valued by investors. A firm's cost of funds is based on the return demanded by investors. If the return offered by the firm is not high enough, then investors will not provide sufficient funds. In other words, *the rate of return an investor earns on a corporate security effectively is a cost to the firm of using those funds,* so the same models are used by investors and by corporate treasurers to determine required rates of return.

The first topic in this chapter is the logic of the weighted average cost of capital. Next, we consider the costs of the major types of capital, after which we see how the costs of the individual components of the capital structure are brought together to form a weighted average cost of capital.

**cost of capital**
The firm's average cost of funds, which is the average return required by the firm's investors— what must be paid to attract funds.

**required rate of return, r**
The return that must be earned on invested funds to cover the cost of financing such investments; also called the *opportunity cost rate.*

## THE LOGIC OF THE WEIGHTED AVERAGE COST OF CAPITAL

**capital components**
The particular types of capital used by the firm—that is, its debt, preferred stock, and common equity.

The items in the liability and equity section of a firm's balance sheet—various types of debt, preferred stock, and common equity—are its **capital components.** Any increase in total assets must be financed by an increase in one or more of these capital components. The *costs of capital* represent the rates of return that the firm pays to investors to use various forms of capital funds.

It is possible to finance a firm entirely with equity funds by issuing only stock. In that case, the cost of capital used to analyze capital budgeting decisions should be the company's required return on equity. However, most firms raise a substantial portion of their funds as long-term debt, and some also use preferred stock. For these firms, their cost of capital must reflect the average cost of the various sources of long-term funds used, not just the firms' costs of equity.

Assume that Unilate Textiles has a 10 percent cost of debt and a 13.5 percent cost of equity. Further, assume that Unilate has made the decision to finance next year's projects by selling debt only. The argument is sometimes made that the cost of capital for these projects is 10 percent because only debt will be used to finance them. However, this position is incorrect. If Unilate finances a particular set of projects with debt, the firm will be using up some of its potential for obtaining new debt in the future. As expansion occurs in subsequent years, Unilate will at some point find it necessary to raise additional equity to prevent the proportion of debt from becoming too large.

To illustrate, suppose Unilate borrows heavily at 10 percent during 2010, using up its debt capacity in the process, to finance projects yielding 11.5 percent. In 2011 it has new projects available that yield 13 percent, well above the return on 2010 projects, but it cannot accept them because they would have to be financed with 13.5 percent equity funds. To avoid this problem, Unilate should be viewed as an ongoing concern, and *the cost of capital used in capital budgeting should be calculated as a weighted average, or combination, of the various types of funds generally used, regardless of the specific financing used to fund a particular project.*

### Self-Test Question

Why should the cost of capital used in capital budgeting be calculated as a weighted average of the various types of funds the firm generally uses, regardless of the specific financing used to fund a particular project?

## BASIC DEFINITIONS

*Capital* is a necessary factor of production, and, like any other factor, it has a cost. The cost of each component is called the *component cost* of that particular type of capital. For example, if Unilate can borrow money at 10 percent, its component cost of debt is 10 percent.[1] Throughout this chapter, we concentrate on debt, preferred stock, retained earnings, and new issues of common stock. We use the following symbols to designate specific component costs of capital:

$r_d$ = Interest rate on the firm's debt = Before-tax component cost of debt. For Unilate, $r_d$ = 10.0%.

$r_{dT}$ = $r_d(1 - T)$ = After-tax component cost of debt, where T is the firm's marginal tax rate. $r_{dT}$ is the debt cost used to calculate the weighted average cost of capital. For Unilate, T = 40%, so $r_{dT} = r_d(1 - T) = 10.0\%(1 - 0.4) = 10.0\%(0.6) = 6.0\%$.

$r_{ps}$ = Component cost of preferred stock. Unilate has no preferred stock at this time, but as new funds are raised, the company plans to issue preferred stock. The cost of preferred stock, $r_{ps}$, will be 11 percent.

$r_s$ = Component cost of retained earnings (or internal equity). It is identical to the $r_s$ developed in Chapter 7 and Chapter 8 and defined there as the required rate of return on common stock. As we will see shortly, for Unilate, $r_s$ = 13.5%.

$r_e$ = Component cost of external equity obtained by issuing new common stock as opposed to retaining earnings. As we shall see, it is necessary to distinguish between common equity needs that can be satisfied by retained earnings and the common equity needs that are satisfied by selling new stock. This is why we distinguish between internal and

---

[1]We will see shortly that there is both a before-tax and after-tax cost of debt. For now it is sufficient to know that 10 percent is the before-tax component cost of debt.

external equity, $r_s$ and $r_e$. Further, $r_e$ is always greater than $r_s$. For Unilate, $r_e = 14.5\%$.

**WACC** = Weighted average cost of capital. In the future, when Unilate needs *new* capital to finance asset expansion, it will raise part of the new funds as debt, part as preferred stock, and part as common equity (with common equity coming either from retained earnings or from the issuance of new common stock).[2] We will calculate WACC for Unilate Textiles shortly.

These definitions and concepts are explained in detail in the remainder of the chapter, where we develop a marginal cost of capital (MCC) schedule that can be used to make investment (capital budgeting) decisions. Later, in the next chapter, we will extend the analysis to determine the mix of types of capital, termed the **capital structure,** which will minimize the firm's cost of capital and thereby maximize its value.

**capital structure**
The combination or mix of different types of capital used by a firm.

> **? Self-Test Question**
>
> Identify the firm's four major capital structure components and give their respective component cost symbols.

**after-tax cost of debt, $r_{dT}$**
The relevant cost of new debt, taking into account the tax deductibility of interest.

## COST OF DEBT, $r_{dT}$

The **after-tax cost of debt, $r_{dT}$,** is the interest rate on debt, $r_d$, less the tax savings that result because interest is deductible. This is the same as $r_d$ multiplied by $(1 - T)$, where T is the firm's marginal tax rate:

11–1

$$\begin{aligned} \text{After-tax component} \atop \text{cost of debt} = r_{dT} &= \left( \begin{array}{c} \text{Bondholders' required} \\ \text{rate of return} \end{array} \right) - \left( \begin{array}{c} \text{Tax} \\ \text{savings} \end{array} \right) \\ &= \qquad\qquad r_d \qquad\qquad - \qquad r_d \times T \\ &= r_d(1 - T) \end{aligned}$$

In effect, the government pays part of the cost of debt because interest is tax deductible. Therefore, if Unilate can borrow at an interest rate of 10 percent, and if it has a marginal tax rate of 40 percent, then its after-tax cost of debt is 6 percent:

$$\begin{aligned} r_{dT} = r_d(1 - T) &= 10.0\%(1.0 - 0.4) \\ &= 10.0\%(0.6) = 6.0\% \end{aligned}$$

We use the after-tax cost of debt because the value of the firm's stock, which we want to maximize, depends on *after-tax* cash flows. Because interest is a deductible expense, it produces tax savings that reduce the net cost of borrowing, making the after-tax cost of debt less than the before-tax cost. We are concerned with after-tax cash flows, so after-tax rates of return are appropriate.[3]

---

[2]Firms try to keep their debt, preferred stock, and common equity in optimal proportions. We will learn how firms establish these proportions in the next chapter. However, firms do not try to maintain any proportional relationship between the common stock and retained earnings accounts as shown on the balance sheet—for capital structure purposes, common equity is common equity, whether it comes from selling new common stock or from retaining earnings.

[3]The tax rate is *zero* for a firm with losses. Therefore, for a company that does not pay taxes, the cost of debt is not reduced—that is, in Equation 11–1 the tax rate equals zero, so the after-tax cost of debt is equal to the before-tax interest rate.

Note that the cost of debt is the interest rate on *new* debt, not that on already outstanding debt; in other words, we are interested in the *marginal* cost of debt. Our primary concern with the cost of capital is to use it for capital budgeting decisions—for example, a decision about whether to obtain the capital needed to acquire a new machine tool. The rate at which the firm has borrowed in the past is a sunk cost, and it is irrelevant for cost of capital purposes.

In Chapter 6, we solved the following equation to find $r_d$, the rate of return, or yield to maturity (YTM), for a bond:

$$V_d = \frac{INT}{(1+r_d)^1} + \frac{INT}{(1+r_d)^2} + \cdots + \frac{INT+M}{(1+r_d)^N}$$

**11–2**

Here INT is the dollar coupon interest paid per period, M is the face value repaid at maturity, and N is the number of interest payments remaining until maturity.

Assume that Unilate issued a new bond a few years ago. The bond has face value of $1,000, 20 years left until it matures, and $90 interest is paid annually. Unilate is going to issue new bonds in a couple of days that have the same general characteristics as this outstanding bond. If the market price of the outstanding bond is $915, what should the $r_d$ be for the new bond? We would expect that the return investors demand for the new bond should be approximately the same as for the outstanding bond because both bonds have the same characteristics. The solution for determining $r_d$ is set up as follows:

$$\$915 = \frac{\$90}{(1+r_d)^1} + \frac{\$90}{(1+r_d)^2} + \cdots + \frac{\$1,090}{(1+r_d)^{20}}$$

Whether you use the trial-and-error method or the time value of money functions on your calculator, you should find $r_d$ is 10 percent, which is the before-tax cost of debt for this bond.[4] Unilate's marginal tax rate is 40 percent, so the after-tax cost of debt, $r_{dT}$, is 6.0% = 10.0%(1 – 0.40).

 **Self-Test Questions**

Why is the after-tax cost of debt rather than the before-tax cost used to calculate the weighted average cost of capital?

Is the relevant cost of debt the interest rate on already outstanding debt or that on new debt? Why?

Payment American currently has bonds outstanding that have the following characteristics: maturity value (M) = $1,000, coupon rate of interest (C) = 6%, years to maturity (N) = 5, and interest is paid annually. If the bond's market value is $959, what is its before-tax component cost of debt—that is, its yield to maturity (YTM)? (*Answer:* $r_d = 7\%$)

---

[4]It should also be noted that we have ignored flotation costs (the costs incurred for new issuances) on debt because nearly all debt issued by small and medium-size firms and by many large firms is privately placed and hence has no flotation costs. However, if bonds are publicly placed and do involve flotation costs, the solution value of $r_d$ in the following formula is used as the before-tax cost of debt:

$$V_d(1-F) = \sum_{t=1}^{N} \frac{INT}{(1+r_d)^t} + \frac{M}{(1+r_d)^N}$$

Here F is the percentage amount (in decimal form) of the bond flotation, or issuing, cost; N is the number of periods to maturity; INT is the dollars of interest per period; M is the maturity value of the bond; and $r_d$ is the cost of debt adjusted to reflect flotation costs. If we assume that the bond in the example calls for annual payments, that it has a 20-year maturity, and that F = 2%, then the flotation-adjusted, before-tax cost of debt is 10.23 percent versus 10 percent before the flotation adjustment.

## COST OF PREFERRED STOCK, $r_{ps}$

In Chapter 7, we found that the dividend associated with preferred stock, $D_{ps}$, is constant and that preferred stock has no stated maturity. Thus, $D_{ps}$ represents a perpetuity, and the component **cost of preferred stock, $r_{ps}$,** is the preferred dividend, $D_{ps}$, divided by the net issuing price, NP, or the price the firm receives after deducting the costs of issuing the stock, which are called *flotation costs:*

**11–3**

$$\text{Component cost of preferred stock} = r_{ps} = \frac{D_{ps}}{NP_0} = \frac{D_{ps}}{P_0 - \text{Flotation costs}} = \frac{D_{ps}}{P_0(1 - F)}$$

**cost of preferred stock, $r_{ps}$**
The rate of return investors require on the firm's preferred stock; $r_{ps}$ is calculated as the preferred dividend, $D_{ps}$, divided by the net issuing price, NP.

Here F is the percentage (in decimal form) cost of issuing preferred stock and $P_0$ is the current market price of the stock.

To illustrate, Unilate plans to issue preferred stock that pays a $12.80 dividend per share and sells for $120 per share in the market. It will cost 3 percent, or $3.60 per share, to issue the new preferred stock, so Unilate will net $116.40 per share. Therefore, Unilate's cost of preferred stock is 11 percent:

$$r_{ps} = \frac{\$12.80}{\$120.00(1 - 0.03)} = \frac{\$12.80}{\$116.40}$$
$$= 0.11 = 11.0\%$$

No tax adjustments are made when calculating $r_{ps}$ because preferred dividends, unlike interest expense on debt, are not tax deductible, so there are no tax savings associated with the use of preferred stock.

### Self-Test Questions

Does the component cost of preferred stock include or exclude flotation costs? Explain.

Is a tax adjustment made to the cost of preferred stock? Why or why not?

Payment American has preferred stock that pays a $7.65 dividend per share each year. If the stock currently sells for $88.64 and the company would incur issuing costs of 4 percent, what is Payment American's component cost of preferred stock? (*Answer:* $r_{ps} = 9\%$)

## COST OF RETAINED EARNINGS, OR INTERNAL EQUITY, $r_s$

**cost of retained earnings, $r_s$**
The rate of return required by stock-holders on a firm's existing common stock.

The costs of debt and preferred stock are based on the returns investors require on these securities. Similarly, the **cost of retained earnings, $r_s$,** is the rate of return stockholders require on equity capital the firm obtains by retaining earnings that otherwise could be distributed to common stockholders as dividends.[5]

The reason we must assign a cost to retained earnings involves the *opportunity cost principle.* The firm's after-tax earnings literally belong to its stockholders. Bondholders

---

[5]The term *retained earnings* can be interpreted to mean either the balance sheet item "retained earnings," consisting of all the earnings retained in the business throughout its history, or the income statement item "additions to retained earnings." The income statement item is used in this chapter; for our purpose, *retained earnings* refers to that part of current earnings not paid out in dividends and hence available for reinvestment in the business this year.

are compensated by interest payments, and preferred stockholders by preferred dividends, but the earnings that remain after interest and preferred dividends are paid belong to the common stockholders, and these earnings help compensate stockholders for the use of their capital. Management can either pay out the earnings in the form of dividends or retain earnings and reinvest them in the business. If management decides to retain earnings, there is an opportunity cost involved—stockholders could have received the earnings as dividends and invested this money for themselves in other stocks, in bonds, in real estate, or in anything else. Thus, the firm should earn a return on earnings it retains that is at least as great as the return stockholders themselves could earn on alternative investments of comparable risk.

What rate of return can stockholders expect to earn on equivalent-risk investments? First, recall from Chapter 8 that stocks normally are in equilibrium, with the expected and required rates of return being equal: $\hat{r}_s = r_s$. Therefore, we can assume that Unilate's stockholders expect to earn a return of $r_s$ on their money. *If the firm cannot invest retained earnings and earn at least $r_s$, it should pay these funds to its stockholders and let them invest directly in other assets that do provide this return.*[6]

Whereas debt and preferred stock are contractual obligations that have easily determined costs, it is not as easy to measure $r_s$. However, we can employ the principles developed in Chapter 7 and Chapter 8 to produce reasonably good cost of equity estimates. To begin, we know that if a stock is in equilibrium (which is the typical situation), then its required rate of return, $r_s$, is equal to its expected rate of return, $\hat{r}_s$. Further, its required return is equal to a risk-free rate, $r_{RF}$, plus a risk premium, RP, whereas the expected return on a constant growth stock is equal to the stock's dividend yield, $\hat{D}_1/P_0$, plus its expected growth rate, g. That is

$$\text{Required rate of return} = \text{Expected rate of return}$$
$$r_s = \hat{r}_s$$
$$r_{RF} + RP = \frac{\hat{D}_1}{P_0} + g$$

**11–4**

Because the two must be equal, we can estimate $r_s$ using either the left side or the right side of Equation 11–4. Actually, three methods are commonly used for finding the cost of retained earnings:

- The CAPM approach (left side of Equation 11–4)
- The discounted cash flow (DCF) approach (right side of Equation 11–4)
- The bond-yield-plus-risk-premium approach

These three approaches are discussed next.

## The CAPM Approach (Required Rate of Return, $r_s$)

The capital asset pricing model (CAPM) we developed in Chapter 8 is stated as follows:

$$r_s = r_{RF} + (r_M - r_{RF})\beta_s$$

**11–5**

---

[6]Although some dividends qualify to be taxed at the capital gains rate, which is lower than the rate at which ordinary income is taxed, in this book we assume that the dividends received by investors are non-qualified dividends that are taxed as ordinary income. In this situation, it is beneficial for companies to retain earnings rather than to pay them out as dividends, and that, in turn, results in a relatively low cost of capital for retained earnings. This point is discussed in Chapter 13.

Equation 11–5 shows that the CAPM estimate of $r_s$ begins with the risk-free rate, $r_{RF}$, to which is added a risk premium that is based on the stock's relation to the market as measured by its beta, $\beta_s$, and the magnitude of the market risk premium, $RP_M$, which is the difference between the market return, $r_M$, and the risk-free rate, $r_{RF}$.

To illustrate the CAPM approach, assume $r_{RF} = 6\%$, $r_M = 10.5\%$, and $\beta_s = 1.6$ for Unilate's common stock. Using the CAPM approach, Unilate's cost of retained earnings, $r_s$, is calculated as follows:

$$r_s = 6.0\% + (10.5\% - 6.0\%)(1.6)$$
$$= 6.0\% + 7.2\% = 13.2\%$$

Although the CAPM approach appears to yield an accurate, precise estimate of $r_s$, there actually are several problems with it. First, as we saw in Chapter 8, if a firm's stockholders are not well diversified, they might be concerned with total risk rather than with market risk only (measured by $\beta$); in this case, the firm's true investment risk will not be measured by its beta, and the CAPM procedure will understate the correct value of $r_s$. Further, even if the CAPM method is valid, it is difficult to obtain correct estimates of the inputs required to make it operational because (1) there is controversy about whether to use long-term or short-term Treasury yields for $r_{RF}$ and (2) both $\beta_s$ and $r_M$ should be estimated values, which often are difficult to obtain.

## Discounted Cash Flow (DCF) Approach (Expected Rate of Return, $\hat{r}_s$)

In Chapter 7, we learned that both the price and the expected rate of return on a share of common stock depend, ultimately, on the dividends the stock is expected to pay. The value of a share of stock can be written as follows:

**11–6**

$$P_0 = \frac{\hat{D}_1}{(1+r_s)^1} + \frac{\hat{D}_2}{(1+r_s)^2} + \frac{\hat{D}_3}{(1+r_s)^3} + \cdots + \frac{\hat{D}_\infty}{(1+r_s)^\infty}$$

Here $P_0$ is the current price of the stock, $\hat{D}_t$ is the dividend *expected* to be paid at the end of Year $t$, and $r_s$ is the required rate of return. If dividends are expected to grow at a constant rate, then, as we saw in Chapter 7, Equation 11–6 reduces to

**11–6a**

$$P_0 = \frac{D_0(1+g)}{r_s - g} = \frac{\hat{D}_1}{r_s - g}$$

We can solve Equation 11–6a for $r_s$ to estimate the required rate of return on common equity, which for the marginal investor is also equal to the expected rate of return:

**11–7**

$$r_s = \hat{r}_s = \frac{\hat{D}_1}{P_0} + g$$

Thus, investors expect to receive a dividend yield, $\hat{D}_1/P_0$, plus a capital gain, $g$, for a total expected return of $\hat{r}_s$. In equilibrium, this expected return is also equal to the required return, $r_s$. From this point on, we will assume that equilibrium exists, and we will use the terms $r_s$ and $\hat{r}_s$ interchangeably, so we will drop the "hat," ^, above $r_s$.

It is relatively easy to determine the dividend yield, but it is difficult to establish the proper growth rate. If past growth rates in earnings and dividends have been relatively stable, and if investors appear to be projecting a continuation of past trends, then g can be based on the firm's historical growth rate. However, if the company's past growth has been abnormally high or low, either because of its own unique situation or because of general economic fluctuations, then historical growth probably should not be used. Security analysts regularly make earnings and dividend growth forecasts, looking at such factors as projected sales, profit margins, and competitive factors. For example, *Value Line*, which is available in most libraries, provides growth rate forecasts for approximately 1,700 companies, and Merrill Lynch, Salomon Smith Barney, and other organizations make similar forecasts. Therefore, someone making a cost of capital estimate can obtain several analysts' forecasts, average them, and use the average as a proxy for the growth expectations, g.[7]

To illustrate the DCF approach, suppose Unilate's common stock sells for $15 per share, the common stock dividend expected to be paid in 2010 is $1.40 per share, and its expected long-term growth rate is 4 percent. Unilate's expected and required rate of return, and hence its cost of retained earnings, is 13.3 percent:

$$r_s = \hat{r}_s = \frac{\$1.40}{\$15.00} + 0.04$$
$$= 0.93 + 0.04 = 0.133 = 13.3\%$$

This 13.3 percent is the minimum rate of return that management must expect to earn to justify retaining earnings and plowing them back into the business rather than paying them out to stockholders as dividends.

## Bond-Yield-Plus-Risk-Premium Approach

Although it is a subjective procedure, analysts often estimate a firm's cost of common equity by adding a risk premium of 3 to 5 percentage points to the before-tax interest rate on the firm's own long-term debt. It is logical to think that firms with risky, low-rated, and consequently high-interest-rate debt will also have risky, high-cost equity. Using this logic to estimate the cost of common stock is relatively easy—we simply add a risk premium to a readily observable debt cost. For example, Unilate's cost of equity might be estimated as follows:

$$r_s = \text{Bond yield} + \text{Risk premium}$$
$$= \quad 10.0\% \quad + 4.0\% = 14.0\%$$

Because the 4 percent risk premium is a judgmental estimate, the estimated value of $r_s$ also is judgmental. Empirical work suggests that the risk premium over a firm's own bond yield generally has ranged from 3 to 5 percentage points, so this method is not likely to produce a precise cost of equity—about all it can do is get us "into the right ballpark."

We have used three methods to estimate the cost of retained earnings, which should be a single number. To summarize, we found the cost of common equity to be

---

[7]Analysts' growth rate forecasts are usually for five years into the future, and the rates provided represent the average growth rate over that five-year horizon. Studies have shown that analysts' forecasts represent the best source of growth rate data for DCF cost of capital estimates. See Robert Harris, "Using Analysts' Growth Rate Forecasts to Estimate Shareholder Required Rates of Return," *Financial Management*, Spring 1986, 58–67.

(1) 13.2 percent using the CAPM method; (2) 13.3 percent using the constant growth model, the DCF approach; and (3) 14.0 percent with the bond-yield-plus-risk-premium approach. It is not unusual to get different estimates because each of the approaches is based on different assumptions. The CAPM assumes investors are well diversified, the constant growth model assumes the firm's dividends and earnings will grow at a constant rate far into the future, and the bond-yield-plus-risk-premium approach assumes the cost of equity is closely related to the firm's cost of debt. Which estimate should be used? Probably all of them. Many analysts use multiple approaches to estimate a single value, then average the results. For Unilate, then, the average of the estimates is 13.5% = (13.2% + 13.3% + 14.0%)/3.

People experienced in estimating equity capital costs recognize that both careful analysis and sound judgment are required. It would be nice to pretend that judgment is unnecessary and to specify an easy, precise way of determining the exact cost of equity capital. Unfortunately, this is not possible—finance is in large part a matter of judgment, and we simply must face that fact.

## Self-Test Questions

Why must a cost be assigned to retained earnings?

What are the three approaches for estimating the cost of retained earnings?

Identify some problems with the CAPM approach.

What is the reasoning behind the bond-yield-plus-risk-premium approach?

Which of the components of the constant growth DCF formula is most difficult to estimate? Why?

Payment America has common stock that currently sells for $35. The company's next dividend, $\hat{D}_1$, is expected to be $2.45 and its growth rate is a constant 4 percent. What is Payment America's component cost of retained earnings? (*Answer:* $r_s = 11\%$)

## COST OF NEWLY ISSUED COMMON STOCK, OR EXTERNAL EQUITY, $r_e$

**cost of new common equity, $r_e$**
The cost of external equity; based on the cost of retained earnings but increased for flotation costs.

**flotation costs**
The expenses incurred when selling new issues of securities.

The **cost of new common equity, $r_e$,** or external equity capital, is similar to the cost of retained earnings, $r_s$, except it is higher because the firm incurs *flotation costs* when it issues new common stock. The **flotation costs,** which are the expenses associated with issuing new securities (equity or debt), reduce the amount of funds the firm receives and hence the amount that can be used for investments. Only the amount of funds that is left after paying flotation costs—that is, the *net* amount received by the firm—is available for investment. As a result, *the cost of issuing new common stock (external equity), $r_e$, is greater than the cost of retained earnings, $r_s$,* because there are no flotation costs associated with retained earnings (internal equity) financing.

In general, the cost of issuing new equity, $r_e$, can be found by modifying the DCF formula (Equation 11–7) used to compute the cost of retained earnings, $r_s$, to obtain the following equation:

$$r_e = \frac{\hat{D}_1}{NP_0} + g = \frac{\hat{D}_1}{P_0(1 - F)} + g$$

11

Here F is the percentage flotation cost (in decimal form) incurred in selling the new stock issue, so $P_0(1 - F)$ is the net price per share received by the company.

If Unilate can issue new common stock at a flotation cost of 11 percent, $r_e$ is computed as follows:

$$r_e = \frac{\$1.40}{\$15.00(1 - 0.11)} + 0.04$$

$$= \frac{\$1.40}{\$13.35} + 0.04 = 0.145 = 14.5\%$$

Using the DCF approach to estimate the cost of retained earnings, we found that investors require a return of $r_s = 13.3\%$ on the stock. However, because of flotation costs, the company must earn more than 13.3 percent on funds obtained by selling stock if it is to provide a 13.3 percent return. Specifically, if the firm earns 14.5 percent on funds obtained from new stock, then earnings per share will not fall below previously expected earnings, the firm's expected dividend can be maintained, and, as a result, the price per share will not decline. If the firm earns less than 14.5 percent, then earnings, dividends, and growth will fall below expectations, causing the price of the stock to decline. If it earns more than 14.5 percent, the price of the stock will rise.

The reason for the flotation adjustment can be clearly illustrated using a simple example. Suppose Weaver Realty Company has $100,000 of assets and no debt; it earns a 15 percent return (or $15,000) on its assets; and it pays all earnings out as dividends, so its growth rate is zero. The company has 1,000 shares of stock outstanding, so earnings per share (EPS) equals dividends per share (DPS)— DPS = $15 = $15,000/1,000—and $P_0 = \$100 = \$100,000/1,000$. Weaver's cost of equity is thus $r_s = \$15/\$100 + 0 = 15.0\%$. Now suppose Weaver can get a return of 15 percent on new assets. Should it sell new stock to acquire new assets? If it sold 1,000 new shares of stock to the public for $100 per share, but it incurred a 10 percent flotation cost on the issue, it would net $100 - 0.10(\$100) = \$90$ per share, or $90,000 in total. It would then invest this $90,000 and earn 15 percent, or $13,500. Its new *total* earnings would be $28,500, which would consist of $15,000 generated from the old assets plus $13,500 from the new assets. But the $28,500 would have to be distributed equally to the 2,000 shares of stock now outstanding. Therefore, Weaver's EPS and DPS would decline from $15 to $14.25 = $28,500/2,000. Because its EPS and DPS would fall, the price of the stock would also fall from $P_0 = \$100$ to $P_1 = \$14.25/0.15 = \$95.00$. This result occurs because investors have put up $100 per share, but the company has received and invested only $90 per share. Thus, we see that the $90 must earn more than 15 percent to provide investors with a 15 percent return on the $100 they put up.

We can use Equation 11–8 to compute the return Weaver must earn on the $90,000 of new assets—that is, the amount raised with the new issue:

$$r_e = \frac{\$15}{\$100(1 - 0.10)} + 0.0$$

$$= 0.1667 = 16.67\%$$

If Weaver invests the funds from the new common stock issue at 16.67 percent, here is what would happen:

New total earnings = $15,000 + $90,000(0.16667) = $30,000

New EPS and DPS = $30,000/2,000 = $15

New price = $15/0.15 = $100 = Original price

Thus, if the return on the new assets is equal to $r_e$ as calculated by Equation 11–8, then EPS, DPS, and the stock price will all remain constant. If the return on the new assets exceeds $r_e$, then EPS, DPS, and $P_0$ will rise. Because of flotation costs, the cost of external equity exceeds the cost of equity raised internally from retained earnings—that is, $r_e > r_s$. If $F = 0$, however, then $r_e = r_s$.

### Self-Test Questions

Why is the cost of external equity capital higher than the cost of retained earnings?

How can the DCF model be changed to account for flotation costs?

Payment American has common stock that currently sells for $35. The company's next dividend, $\hat{D}_1$, is expected to be $2.45 and its growth rate is a constant 4 percent. If Payment America issues new common stock, flotation costs will be 12.5 percent. What is Payment America's component cost of new common equity? (*Answer:* $r_s = 12\%$)

## WEIGHTED AVERAGE COST OF CAPITAL, WACC

**target (optimal) capital structure**
The combination (percentages) of debt, preferred stock, and common equity that maximizes the price of the firm's stock.

Each firm has an optimal capital structure—or mix of debt, preferred stock, and common equity—that causes its stock price to be maximized. Therefore, a rational, value-maximizing firm will establish a **target (optimal) capital structure** and then raise new capital in a manner that will keep the actual capital structure on target over time. In this chapter, we assume that the firm has identified its optimal capital structure, that it uses this optimum as the target, and that it raises funds so it constantly remains on target. How the target is established will be examined in Chapter 12.[8]

**weighted average cost of capital (WACC)**
A weighted average of the component costs of debt, preferred stock, and common equity.

The target proportions of debt, preferred stock, and common equity, along with the component costs of capital, are used to calculate the firm's **weighted average cost of capital (WACC).** The WACC simply represents the average cost of each dollar of financing, no matter its source, that the firm uses to purchase assets. That is, WACC represents the minimum return the firm needs to earn on its investments (assets) to maintain its current level of wealth.

To illustrate, suppose Unilate Textiles has determined that in the future it will raise new capital according to the following proportions: 45 percent debt, 5 percent preferred stock, and 50 percent common equity (retained earnings plus new common stock). In the preceding sections, we found that its before-tax cost of debt, $r_d$, is 10 percent, so its *after-tax* cost of debt, $r_{dT}$, is 6 percent; its cost of preferred stock, $r_{ps}$, is 11 percent; and its cost of common equity, $r_s$, is 13.5 percent if all of its equity financing comes from retained earnings. Now we can calculate Unilate's weighted average cost of capital (WACC) as follows:

$$
\begin{aligned}
\text{WACC} &= \left[ \begin{pmatrix} \text{Proportion} \\ \text{of} \\ \text{debt} \end{pmatrix} \times \begin{pmatrix} \text{After-tax} \\ \text{cost of} \\ \text{debt} \end{pmatrix} + \begin{pmatrix} \text{Proportion} \\ \text{of preferred} \\ \text{stock} \end{pmatrix} \times \begin{pmatrix} \text{Cost of} \\ \text{preferred} \\ \text{stock} \end{pmatrix} + \begin{pmatrix} \text{Proportion} \\ \text{of common} \\ \text{equity} \end{pmatrix} \times \begin{pmatrix} \text{Cost of} \\ \text{common} \\ \text{equity} \end{pmatrix} \right] \\
&= \quad w_d \quad \times \quad r_{dT} \quad + \quad w_{ps} \quad \times \quad r_{ps} \quad + \quad w_s \quad \times \quad r_s
\end{aligned}
$$

11

---

[8]Notice that only long-term debt is included in the capital structure. Unilate uses its cost of capital in the capital budgeting process, which involves long-term assets, and it finances those assets with long-term capital. Thus, current liabilities do not enter the calculation. We will discuss this point in more detail in Chapter 12.

Here $w_d$, $w_{ps}$, and $w_s$ are the weights used for debt, preferred stock, and common equity, respectively.

Every dollar of new capital that Unilate raises consists of $0.45 of debt with an after-tax cost of 6 percent, $0.05 of preferred stock with a cost of 11 percent, and $0.50 of common equity (all from additions to retained earnings) with a cost of 13.5 percent. The company's WACC is calculated as follows:

$$\text{WACC} = 0.45(6.0\%) + 0.05(11.0\%) + 0.50(13.5\%) = 10.0\%$$

The average cost of each whole dollar, WACC, is 10 percent as long as these conditions continue. If the component costs of capital change when new funds are raised in the future, then WACC changes. We discuss changes in the component costs of capital in the next section.

Determining a firm's WACC is more complicated than simply plugging numbers into Equation 11–9 and performing the math. Most large firms have numerous types of debt (and sometimes different "classes" of common stock) that have different component costs so that there is not one cost of debt (cost of equity). As a result, in practice, the cost of debt, $r_d$, that is used to compute the firm's WACC is a weighted average of the costs of the various types of debt the firm has issued. Similarly, when a firm raises capital by issuing new common stock, the total amount of equity capital often includes both the amount of earnings retained during the year and the amount raised with the new common stock issue, which means the cost of common equity should be a weighted average of $r_s$ and $r_e$. To simplify our discussions and the subsequent computations, however, we assume that the firm issues only one type of bond each time it raises new funds using debt, and when new common stock is issued that the average cost to the firm for *all* common equity used to finance new investments is the cost of the new common stock, $r_e$, even if retained earnings have provided some of the common equity capital.

## Self-Test Questions

How is the weighted average cost of capital calculated? Write out the equation.

Payment America's capital structure consists of 40 percent debt, 10 percent preferred stock, and 50 percent common equity. The company's component costs of capital are $r_{dT} = 4.2\%$, $r_{ps} = 9\%$, and $r_s = 11\%$. What is Payment America's WACC? (*Answer:* WACC = r = 8.1%)

# THE MARGINAL COST OF CAPITAL, MCC

The marginal cost of any item is the cost of another unit of that item. For example, the marginal cost of labor is the cost of adding one additional worker. The marginal cost of labor might be $25 per person if 10 workers are added but $35 per person if the firm tries to hire 100 new workers because it will be harder to find that many people willing and able to do the work. The same concept applies to capital. As the firm tries to attract more new dollars, at some point, the cost of each dollar will increase. Thus, the **marginal cost of capital (MCC)** *is defined as the cost of the last dollar of new capital that the firm raises, and the marginal cost rises as more and more capital is raised during a given period.*

**marginal cost of capital (MCC)**
The cost of obtaining another dollar of new capital; the weighted average cost of the last dollar of new capital raised.

In the preceding section, we computed Unilate's WACC to be 10 percent. As long as Unilate keeps its capital structure on target, and as long as its debt has an after-tax cost of 6 percent, its preferred stock a cost of 11 percent, and its common equity a cost of 13.5 percent, then its weighted average cost of capital will be 10 percent. Each dollar the firm raises will consist of some long-term debt, some preferred stock, and some common equity, and the cost of the whole dollar will be 10 percent—that is, its marginal cost of capital (MCC) will be 10 percent.

## The MCC Schedule

**MCC (marginal cost of capital) schedule**
A graph that relates the firm's weighted average cost of each dollar of capital to the total amount of new capital raised.

A graph that shows how the WACC changes as more and more new capital is raised by the firm is called the **MCC (marginal cost of capital) schedule.** Figure 11-1 shows Unilate's MCC schedule if the cost of debt, cost of preferred stock, and cost of common equity *never change*. Here the dots represent dollars raised, and because each dollar of new capital will have an average cost equal to 10 percent, the marginal cost of capital (MCC) for Unilate is constant at 10.0 percent under the assumptions we have used to this point.

Do you think Unilate actually could raise an unlimited amount of new capital at the 10 percent cost? Probably not. As a practical matter, as a company raises larger and larger amounts of funds during a given time period, the costs of those funds begin to rise, and as this occurs, the weighted average cost of each new dollar also rises. Thus, companies cannot raise unlimited amounts of capital at a constant cost. At some point, the cost of each new dollar will increase, no matter what its source (debt, preferred stock, or common equity).

**FIGURE 11-1    Marginal Cost of Capital (MCC) Schedule for Unilate Textiles**

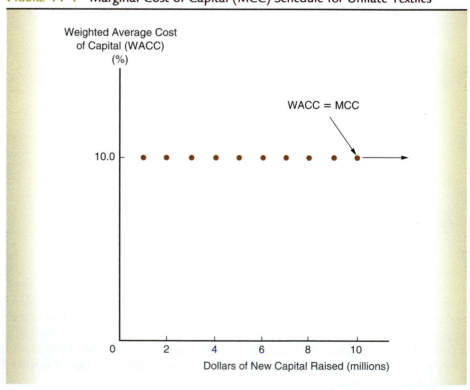

How much can Unilate raise before the cost of its funds increases? As a first step in determining the point at which the MCC begins to rise, recognize that although the company's balance sheet shows total long-term capital of $715 million at the end of 2009, all of this capital was raised in the past, and these funds have been invested in assets that are now being used in operations. If Unilate wants to raise any new (marginal) capital so that the total amount consists of 45 percent debt, 5 percent preferred stock, and 50 percent common equity, then to raise $1,000,000 in new capital, the company should issue $450,000 of new debt, $50,000 of new preferred stock, and $500,000 of additional common equity. The additional common equity could come from two sources: (1) retained earnings, defined as that part of this year's profits that management decides to retain in the business rather than pay out as dividends (but not earnings retained in the past because these amounts have already been invested in existing assets), or (2) proceeds from the sale of new common stock.

We know that Unilate's WACC will be 10.0 percent as long as the after-tax cost of debt is 6 percent, the cost of preferred stock is 11 percent, and the funds needed from common equity can be satisfied by retained earnings with a cost of 13.5 percent ($r_s = 13.5\%$). But what happens if Unilate expands so rapidly that the retained earnings for the year are not sufficient to meet the common equity needs, forcing the firm to sell new common stock? Earlier, we determined that the cost of issuing new common stock, $r_e$, will be 14.5 percent because the flotation costs associated with the new issue will be 11 percent. Because the cost of common equity increases when common stock has to be issued, the WACC also increases at this point.

How much new capital can Unilate raise before it exhausts its retained earnings and is forced to sell new common stock? In other words, where will an increase in the MCC schedule occur?

Assume that Unilate's 2010 net income will be $61 million and that $30.5 million will be paid out as dividends so that $30.5 million will be added to retained earnings (the payout ratio is 50 percent). In this case, Unilate can invest in capital projects to the point where the common equity needs equal $30.5 million before new common stock has to be issued. Remember, though, that when Unilate needs new funds, the target capital structure indicates only 50 percent of the total should be common equity; the remainder of the funds should come from issues of bonds (45 percent) and preferred stock (5 percent). Thus, we know that

$$\text{Common equity} = 0.50 \times \text{Total new capital raised}$$

We can use this relationship to determine how much *total new capital*—that is, debt, preferred stock, and retained earnings (internal equity)—can be raised before the $30.5 million of retained earnings is exhausted and Unilate is forced to sell new common stock. Just set the common equity needs equal to the retained earnings amount, and solve for the total new capital amount:

$$\text{Retained earnings} = \$30.5 \text{ million} = 0.50 \left( \begin{array}{c} \text{Total new} \\ \text{capital raised} \end{array} \right)$$

$$\left( \begin{array}{c} \text{Total new} \\ \text{capital raised} \end{array} \right) = \frac{\$30.5 \text{ million}}{0.50} = \$61.0 \text{ million}$$

Thus, Unilate can raise a total of $61 million before it has to sell new common stock to finance its capital projects.

If Unilate needs exactly $61 million in new capital, the breakdown of the amount that would come from each source of capital and the computation for the weighted average cost of capital (WACC) would be as follows:

| Capital Source | Weight (1) | Amount in Millions $61 × (1) = (2) | After-Tax Component Cost (3) | WACC (1) × (3) = (4) |
|---|---|---|---|---|
| Debt | 0.45 | $27.45 | 6.0% | 2.70% |
| Preferred stock | 0.05 | 3.05 | 11.0 | 0.55 |
| Common equity | 0.50 | 30.50 | 13.5 | 6.75 |
| | 1.00 | $61.00 | | WACC$_1$ = 10.00% |

Therefore, if Unilate needs *exactly* $61 million in new capital in 2010, retained earnings will be just enough to satisfy the common equity requirement, so the firm will not need to sell new common stock and its weighted average cost of capital (WACC) will be 10 percent. But what will happen if Unilate needs more than $61 million in new capital? If Unilate needs $64 million, for example, retained earnings will not be sufficient to cover the $32 million common equity requirements (50 percent of the total funds), so new common stock will have to be sold.

The cost of issuing new common stock, $r_e$, is greater than the cost of retained earnings, $r_s$; hence, the WACC will be greater. If Unilate raises $64 million in new capital, the breakdown of the amount that would come from each source of capital and the computation for the weighted average cost of capital (WACC) would be as follows:

| Capital Source | Weight (1) | Amount in Millions $61 × (1) = (2) | After-Tax Component Cost (3) | WACC (1) × (3) = (4) |
|---|---|---|---|---|
| Debt | 0.45 | $28.80 | 6.0% | 2.70% |
| Preferred stock | 0.05 | 3.20 | 11.0 | 0.55 |
| Common equity | 0.50 | 32.00 | 14.5 | 7.25 |
| | 1.00 | $64.00 | | WACC$_2$ = 10.50% |

The WACC will be greater because Unilate will have to sell new common stock, which has a higher component cost than retained earnings (14.5 percent versus 13.5 percent). Consequently, if Unilate's capital budgeting needs are greater than $61 million, new common stock will need to be sold, and its WACC will increase. The $61 million in total new capital is defined as the *retained earnings break point* because above this amount of total capital, a break, or jump, in Unilate's MCC schedule occurs. In general, a **break point (BP)** is defined as the dollar of *new total capital* that can be raised before an increase in the firm's weighted average cost of capital occurs.

Figure 11-2 graphs Unilate's marginal cost of capital schedule with the retained earnings break point. Each dollar has a weighted average cost of 10.0 percent until the company raises a total of $61 million. This $61 million will consist of $27.45 million of new debt with an after-tax cost of 6 percent, $3.05 million of preferred stock with a cost of 11 percent, and $30.50 million of retained earnings with a cost of 13.5 percent. However, if Unilate raises one dollar over $61 million, each new dollar will contain $0.50 of equity *obtained by selling new common equity at a cost of 14.5 percent.* As a

**break point (BP)**
The dollar value of new capital that can be raised before an increase in the firm's weighted average cost of capital occurs.

FIGURE 11-2    Marginal Cost of Capital Schedule for Unilate Textiles Using Both Retained Earnings and New Common Stock

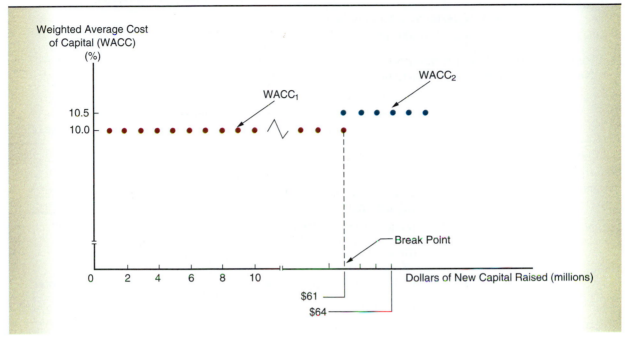

result, WACC jumps from 10.0 percent to 10.5 percent, as calculated previously and shown in Table 11-1.

At this point, we must note two important facts:

- Unilate's cost of equity would not actually jump from 13.5 percent to 14.5 percent because $0.50 of new equity is issued. In reality, the cost of common equity would increase only marginally. However, to simplify our discussion and computations, we assume that once Unilate issues common stock, no matter the amount, the cost of equity increases such that the average cost of each dollar of equity is 14.5 percent. For further simplification, we apply this same logic to all types of capital.

- Because we really don't think the MCC jumps by precisely 0.5 percent when we raise $1 over $61 million, Figure 11-2 should be regarded as an approximation rather than as a precise representation of reality. We will return to this point later in the chapter.

## Other Breaks in the MCC Schedule

There is a jump, or break, in Unilate's MCC schedule at $61 million of new capital because new common stock needs to be sold. Could there be other breaks in the schedule? Yes, there could. For example, suppose Unilate could obtain only $54 million of debt at an after-tax cost of 6.0 percent, with any additional debt costing 7.1 percent (after taxes). This would result in a second break point in the MCC schedule, at the point where the $54 million of 10 percent debt is exhausted. At what amount of total financing would the 10 percent debt be used up? We know that this total financing will amount to $54 million of debt plus some amount of preferred stock and common equity. If we let $BP_{Debt}$ represent the total

**TABLE 11-1** WACC and Break Points for Unilate's MCC Schedule

### I. Break Points

1. $BP_{Retained\ earnings} = \$30,500,000/0.50 = \$61,000,000$
2. $BP_{Debt} = \$54,000,000/0.45 = \$120,000,000$

### II. Weighted Average Cost of Capital (WACC)

**1. New Capital Needs:**     **$0–$61,000,000**

| | Breakdown of Funds at $61,000,000 | Weight | × | After-Tax Component Cost | = | WACC |
|---|---|---|---|---|---|---|
| Debt (10%) | $27,450,000 | 0.45 | | 6.0% | | 2.70% |
| Preferred stock | 3,050,000 | 0.05 | | 11.0 | | 0.55 |
| Common equity (Retained earnings) | 30,500,000 | 0.50 | | 13.5 | | 6.75 |
| | $61,000,000 | 1.00 | | | | $WACC_1 = 10.00\%$ |

**2. New Capital Needs:**     **$61,000,001–$120,000,000**

| | Breakdown of Funds at $120,000,000 | Weight | × | After-Tax Component Cost | = | WACC |
|---|---|---|---|---|---|---|
| Debt (10%) | $ 54,000,000 | 0.45 | | 6.0% | | 2.70% |
| Preferred stock | 6,000,000 | 0.05 | | 11.0 | | 0.55 |
| Common equity (New stock issue) | $ 60,000,000 | 0.50 | | 14.5 | | 7.25 |
| | $120,000,000 | 1.00 | | | | $WACC_2 = 10.50\%$ |

**3. New Capital Needs:**     **Above $120,000,000**

| | Breakdown of Funds at $130,000,000 | Weight | × | After-Tax Component Cost | = | WACC |
|---|---|---|---|---|---|---|
| Debt (12%) | $ 58,500,000 | 0.45 | | 7.1% | | 3.20% |
| Preferred stock | 6,500,000 | 0.05 | | 11.0 | | 0.55 |
| Common equity (New stock issue) | 65,000,000 | 0.50 | | 14.5 | | = 7.25 |
| | $130,000,000 | 1.00 | | | | $WACC_3 = 11.00\%$ |

financing at this second break point, then we know that 45 percent of $BP_{Debt}$ will be debt, so

$$0.45(BP_{Debt}) = \$54\ million$$

Solving for $BP_{Debt}$, we have

$$BP_{Debt} = \frac{\text{Maximum amount of 10\% debt}}{\text{Proportion of debt in the capital structure}}$$

$$= \frac{\$54\ million}{0.45} = \$120\ million$$

As you can see, there will be another break in the MCC schedule after Unilate has raised a total of $120 million, and this second break results from an increase in the cost of debt. The higher after-tax cost of debt (7.1 percent versus 6.0 percent) will result in a higher WACC. For example, if Unilate needs $130 million for capital budgeting projects, the WACC would be 11 percent:

| Capital Source | Weight (1) | Amount in Millions $61 × (1) = (2) | After-Tax Component Cost (3) | WACC (1) × (3) = (4) |
|---|---|---|---|---|
| Debt | 0.45 | $ 58.50 | 7.1% | 3.20% |
| Preferred stock | 0.05 | 6.50 | 11.0 | 0.55 |
| Common equity | 0.50 | 65.00 | 14.5 | 7.25 |
| | 1.00 | $130.00 | | WACC$_3$ = 11.00% |

In other words, the next dollar beyond $120 million will consist of $0.45 of 7.1 percent debt (after taxes), $0.05 of 11 percent preferred stock, and $0.50 of new common stock at a cost of 14.5 percent (retained earnings were used up much earlier), and this marginal dollar will have a cost of WACC$_3$ = 11%.

The effect of this second WACC increase is shown in Figure 11-3. Now there are two break points, one caused by using up all the retained earnings and the other by using up all the 6 percent debt (after taxes). With the two breaks, there are three different WACCs: WACC$_1$ = 10.0% for the first $61 million of new capital; WACC$_2$ = 10.5% in the interval between $61 million and $120 million; and WACC$_3$ = 11.0% for all new capital beyond $120 million.[9]

There could, of course, still be more break points; they would occur if the cost of debt continued to increase with more debt, if the cost of preferred stock increased at some level(s), or if the cost of common equity rose as more new common stock is sold.[10] In general, a break point will occur whenever the cost of one of the capital components increases, and the break point can be determined by the following equation:

**–10**

$$\text{Break point} = \frac{\text{Total amount of lower cost of capital of a given type}}{\text{Proportion of the type of capital in the capital structure}}$$

As you can imagine, numerous break points are possible. At the extreme, an MCC schedule might have so many break points that it rises almost continuously beyond some given level of new financing. Such an MCC schedule is shown in Figure 11-4.

The easiest sequence for calculating MCC schedules is as follows:

1. Use Equation 11–10 to determine each point at which a break occurs. A break will occur any time the cost of one of the capital components rises.

[9]When we use the term *weighted average cost of capital,* we are referring to the WACC, which is the cost of $1 raised partly as debt, partly as preferred stock, and partly as common equity. We could also calculate the average cost of all the capital the firm raised during a given year. For example, if Unilate raised $150 million, the first $61 million would have a cost of 10.0 percent, the next $59 million would cost 10.5 percent, and the last $30 million would cost 11.0 percent. The entire $150 million would have an average cost of

$$\left(\frac{\$61}{\$150}\right) \times (10.0\%) + \left(\frac{\$59}{\$150}\right) \times (10.5\%) + \left(\frac{\$30}{\$150}\right) \times (11.0\%) = 10.4\%$$

*In general, this particular cost of capital should not be used for financial decisions—it usually has no relevance in finance.* The only exception to this rule occurs when the firm is considering a very large asset that must be accepted in total or else rejected, and the capital required for it includes capital with different WACCs. For example, if Unilate were considering one $150 million project, that project should be evaluated with a 10.4 percent cost.

[10]The first break point is not necessarily the point at which retained earnings are used up; it is possible for low-cost debt to be exhausted *before* retained earnings have been used up. For example, if Unilate had available only $22.5 million of 10 percent debt, BP$_{Debt}$ would occur at $50 million:

$$\text{BP}_{Debt} = \frac{\$22.5 \text{ million}}{0.45} = \$50 \text{ million}$$

Thus, the break point for debt would occur before the break point for retained earnings, which occurs at $61 million.

**Figure 11-3**  Marginal Cost of Capital Schedule for Unilate Textiles Using Retained Earnings, New Common Stock, and Higher-Cost Debt

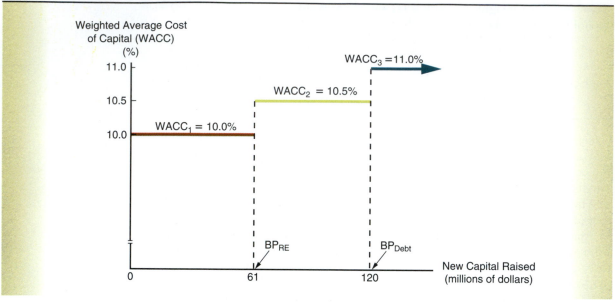

(It is possible, however, that two capital components could both increase at the same point.) After determining the exact break points, make a list of them.

2. Determine the cost of capital for each component in the intervals between breaks.

3. Calculate the weighted averages of these component costs to obtain the WACCs in each interval, as we did in Table 11-1. The WACC is constant within each interval, but it rises at each break point.

Notice that if there are n separate breaks, there will be n + 1 different WACCs. For example, in Figure 11-3 we see two breaks and three different WACCs. Also, we should note again that a different MCC schedule would result if a different capital structure—that is, proportions of debt and equity—is used.

**Figure 11-4**  Smooth, or Continuous, Marginal Cost of Capital Schedule

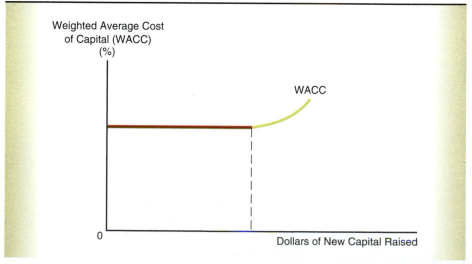

# Constructing an MCC Schedule—An Illustration

To further illustrate the construction of an MCC schedule, let's assume the following information is known about a firm's capital structure, the current market value of its debt and equity, and its financing opportunities:

| Capital Source | Capital Structure | Market Value per Share | Dividend/Interest Payment per Share |
|---|---|---|---|
| Debt | 35.0% | $1,067.10 | $90.00 |
| Preferred stock | 5.0 | 75.00 | 7.20 |
| Common equity | 60.0 | 35.00 | 3.00 |

The face value of the debt is $1,000, and interest is paid annually. The firm is expected to grow at a constant rate of 5 percent far into the future, and retained earnings are forecast to increase by $120 million in the coming year. The flotation costs associated with issuing new debt are negligible, but the costs associated with issuing new preferred stock equal 2 percent of the selling price as long as the amount issued is $15 million or less; amounts of preferred stock exceeding $15 million will have flotation costs of 4 percent. The cost to issue new common stock is 6 percent if $90 million or less is issued; this cost rises to 8 percent for amounts exceeding $90 million. The firm's investment banker estimates that the firm can issue new 10-year debt with the same characteristics as its existing debt up to a maximum of $105 million; any amount in excess of $105 million will have the same characteristics, except that the issue price will match the face value. Preferred stock and common stock can be issued at the current market values given in the preceding table. The firm's marginal tax rate is 40 percent.

Based on the information provided, we construct the MCC schedule as follows:

**Step 1**    Compute the break points. In this case, at most four break points are possible: (a) if the common equity financing needs exceed the $120 million expected retained earnings because new common stock must be issued, and new equity has a higher cost than retained earnings; (b) if the debt financing needs exceed $105 million because additional debt can be sold for the face value ($1,000), which is less than the current market value of the debt ($1,067.10); (c) if preferred stock financing needs exceed $15 million because additional preferred stock will have higher flotation costs; and (d) if the firm needs to issue *new* common equity in excess of $90 million because it will incur higher flotation costs than if lower amounts are issued. If the firm issues new common stock, then its common equity financing needs consist of the $120 million addition to retained earnings plus any new common stock that is issued.

Using Equation 11–10, we can calculate the four break points:

$$BP_{Debt} = \frac{\$105 \text{ million}}{0.35} = \$300 \text{ million}$$

$$BP_{Preferred\ stock} = \frac{\$15 \text{ million}}{0.05} = \$300 \text{ million}$$

$$BP_{Retained\ earnings} = \frac{\$120 \text{ million}}{0.60} = \$200 \text{ million}$$

$$BP_{New\ common\ equity} = \frac{\$120 \text{ million} + \$90 \text{ million}}{0.60} = \$350 \text{ million}$$

In this case, there are three *different* break points. The costs of both debt and preferred stock will increase at the same point, creating a break point at $300 million of total financing.

**Step 2** Next, we compute the cost of capital for each component in the intervals between breaks.

1. *Debt*—$1,000 face; INT = $90, paid annually; N = 10 years; negligible flotation costs:

   a. If the firm's debt financing needs range from $1 to $105 million, a new bond can be sold at a rate that equates to a market value of $1,067.10. Thus $r_d$ is

   $$\$1,067.10 = \frac{\$90}{(1 + r_d)^1} + \frac{\$90}{(1 + r_d)^2} + \cdots + \frac{\$1,090}{(1 + r_d)^{10}}$$

   Using a financial calculator, we find $r_d = 8\%$:

   | Inputs: | 10 | ? | −1,067.10 | 90 | 1,000 |
   |---|---|---|---|---|---|
   | | N | I/Y | PV | PMT | FV |
   | Output: | | = 8.0 | | | |

   $$r_{dT} = 8\%(1 - 0.4) = 4.8\%$$

   b. If debt financing needs are greater than $105 million, the market value of the bond will be $1,000. Thus $r_d$ is

   $$\$1,000 = \frac{\$90}{(1 + r_d)^1} + \frac{\$90}{(1 + r_d)^2} + \cdots + \frac{\$1,090}{(1 + r_d)^{10}}$$

   Using a financial calculator, we find that $r_d = 9\%$:

   | Inputs: | 10 | ? | −1,000 | 90 | 1,000 |
   |---|---|---|---|---|---|
   | | N | I/Y | PV | PMT | FV |
   | Output: | | = 9.0 | | | |

   $$r_{dT} = 9\%(1 - 0.4) = 5.4\%$$

2. *Preferred Stock*—$P_0 = \$75$; $D_{ps} = \$7.20$:

   a. If preferred stock financing needs range from $1 to $15 million, flotation costs are 2 percent. Using Equation 11–3, we find $r_{ps} = 9.8\%$:

   $$r_{ps} = \frac{D_{ps}}{P_0(1 - F)} = \frac{\$7.20}{\$75.00\,(1 - 0.02)} = \frac{\$7.20}{\$73.50} = 0.098 = 9.8\%$$

   b. If preferred stock financing needs are greater than $15 million, flotation costs increase to 4 percent. In this case, $r_{ps} = 10.0\%$:

   $$r_{ps} = \frac{\$7.20}{\$75.00\,(1 - 0.04)} = \frac{\$7.20}{\$72.00} = 0.10 = 10.0\%$$

3. *Common Equity*—$P_0 = \$35$; $D_0 = \$3$; $g = 5\%$:

   a. Expectations are that the addition to retained earnings this year will be $120 million, which represents the amount of internal financing that the firm has available for new investments. Using Equation 11–7, the cost of retained earnings, $r_s$, is

$$r_s = \frac{\hat{D}_1}{P_0} + g = \frac{D_0(1+g)}{P_0} + g = \frac{\$3.00(1.05)}{\$35.00} + 0.05$$
$$= 0.09 + 0.05 = 0.14 = 14.0\%$$

**b.** If common equity financing needs are greater than can be satisfied with retained earnings—that is, greater than $120 million—then the firm must sell new common stock to raise the additional amount. The flotation costs for new common stock in amounts from $1 to $90 million are 6 percent. Using Equation 11–8, the cost of new equity, $r_e$, is

$$r_e = \frac{\hat{D}_1}{P_0(1-F)} + g = \frac{\$3.00(1.05)}{\$35.00(1-0.06)} + 0.05 = \frac{\$3.15}{\$32.90} + 0.05$$
$$= 0.096 + 0.05 = 0.146 = 14.6\%$$

Thus, the cost of common equity is 14.6 percent if the common equity financing needs exceed the $120 million available from retained earnings but are less than or equal to $210 million, which includes the $120 million in retained earnings plus $90 million in new common stock.

**c.** If the amount of new common stock issued exceeds $90 million, the flotation costs are 8 percent. In this case—that is, *total* common equity financing is greater than $210 million—the cost of equity is

$$r_e = \frac{\hat{D}_1}{P_0(1-F)} + g = \frac{\$3.00(1.05)}{\$35.00(1-0.08)} + 0.05 = \frac{\$3.15}{\$32.20} + 0.05$$
$$= 0.098 + 0.05 = 0.148 = 14.8\%$$

**Step 3**    Calculate the weighted averages of these component costs to obtain the WACCs in each interval. Remember, there are three break points:

- At $200 million—the break results from a higher cost of common equity because all internal financing (retained earnings) will be used up at this point.
- At $300 million—the break occurs because cheaper debt *and* cheaper preferred stock will be used up at this point.
- At $350 million—the break occurs because greater amounts of new equity will have a higher cost.

With these break points, the WACC will be constant from $1 to $200 million financing. It will increase to a new level that will remain constant from $200 million plus $1 to $300 million because the firm has exhausted its internal financing and must raise common equity funds by issuing new stock that has a higher cost. It will increase to a higher level that will remain constant from $300 million plus $1 to $350 million because both debt and preferred stock financing are more expensive beyond $300 million. Finally, it will increase to a higher level at $350 million plus $1 because the cost of issuing new common equity is higher.

Table 11-2 shows the computations for the WACCs for each interval of new financing. If you compare the numbers in the column labeled "After-Tax Component Cost" for consecutive intervals, you will see which type of capital caused the WACC to increase from one interval to the next (that is, the highlighted numbers).

## TABLE 11-2    MCC Schedule Illustration ($ million)

### 1. New Capital Needs: Interval = $1 to $200

| | Breakdown of Funds at $200 | Weight | × | After-Tax Component Cost | = | WACC |
|---|---|---|---|---|---|---|
| Debt (8%) | $ 70.0 | 0.35 | | 4.8% | | 1.68% |
| Preferred stock | 10.0 | 0.05 | | 9.8 | | 0.49 |
| Common equity (retained earnings) | 120.0 | 0.60 | | 14.0 | | 8.40 |
| | $200.0 | 1.00 | | | | WACC$_1$ = 10.57% |

### 2. New Capital Needs: Interval = $200+ to $300

| | Breakdown of Funds at $300 | Weight | × | After-Tax Component Cost | = | WACC |
|---|---|---|---|---|---|---|
| Debt (8%) | $105.0 | 0.35 | | 4.8% | | 1.68% |
| Preferred stock | 15.0 | 0.05 | | 9.8 | | 0.49 |
| Common equity (new issue) | 180.0 | 0.60 | | 14.6 | | 8.76 |
| | $300.0 | 1.00 | | | | WACC$_2$ = 10.93% |

### 3. New Capital Needs: Interval = $300+ to $350

| | Breakdown of Funds at $350 | Weight | × | After-Tax Component Cost | = | WACC |
|---|---|---|---|---|---|---|
| Debt (9%) | $122.5 | 0.35 | | 5.4% | | 1.89% |
| Preferred stock | 17.5 | 0.05 | | 10.0 | | 0.50 |
| Common equity (new issue) | 210.0 | 0.60 | | 14.6 | | 8.76 |
| | $350.0 | 1.00 | | | | WACC$_3$ = 11.15% |

### 4. New Capital Needs: Interval = Above $350

| | Breakdown of Funds at $350 | Weight | × | After-Tax Component Cost | = | WACC |
|---|---|---|---|---|---|---|
| Debt (9%) | $126.0 | 0.35 | | 5.4% | | 1.89% |
| Preferred stock | 18.0 | 0.05 | | 10.0 | | 0.50 |
| Common equity (new issue) | 216.0 | 0.60 | | 14.8 | | 8.88 |
| | $360.0 | 1.00 | | | | WACC$_4$ = 11.27% |

### Self-Test Questions

What are break points, and why do they occur in MCC schedules? Write out and explain the equation for determining break points.

How is an MCC schedule constructed? If there are n breaks in the MCC schedule, how many different WACCs are there? Why?

Payment America can issue up to $120,000 of new debt for a cost of 6 percent; amounts above $120,000 will cost 8 percent. If Payment America's capital structure contains 40 percent debt, how much can the company raise in total funds before the cost of debt increases to 8 percent? (*Answer:* BP$_{Debt}$ = $300,000)

# COMBINING THE MCC AND INVESTMENT OPPORTUNITY SCHEDULES (IOS)

Now that we have calculated the MCC schedule, we can use it to develop a discount rate for use in the capital budgeting process—that is, *we can use the MCC schedule to find the cost of capital for determining projects' net present values (NPVs)* as discussed in Chapter 9.

To understand how the MCC schedule is used in capital budgeting, assume that Unilate Textiles has three financial executives: a financial vice president (VP), a treasurer, and a director of capital budgeting (DCB). The financial VP asks the treasurer to develop the firm's MCC schedule, and the treasurer produces the schedule shown earlier in Figure 11-3. At the same time, the financial VP asks the DCB to draw up a list of all projects that are potentially acceptable. The list shows each project's cost, projected annual net cash inflows, life, and internal rate of return (IRR). These data are presented at the bottom of Figure 11-5. For example, Project A has a cost of $39 million, it is expected to produce inflows of $9 million per year for six years, and, therefore, it has an IRR of 10.2 percent. Similarly, Project C has a cost of $36 million, it is expected to produce inflows of $10 million per year for five years, and thus it has an IRR of 12.1 percent. (NPVs cannot be shown yet because we do not yet know the marginal cost of capital.) For simplicity, we assume now that all projects are independent rather than mutually exclusive, that they are equally risky, and that their risks are all equal to those of the firm's average existing assets.

The DCB then plots the IRR data shown at the bottom of Figure 11-5 as the **investment opportunity schedule (IOS)** shown in the graph. The IOS schedule shows, in rank order, how much money Unilate can invest at different rates of return (IRRs). Figure 11-5 also shows Unilate's MCC schedule as it was developed by the treasurer and plotted in Figure 11-3. Now consider Project C: its IRR is 12.1 percent, and it can be financed with capital that costs only 10.0 percent; consequently, it should be accepted. Recall from Chapter 9 that if a project's IRR exceeds its cost of capital, its NPV also will be positive; therefore, Project C must also be acceptable by the NPV criterion. Projects B, D, and E can be analyzed similarly. They are all acceptable because IRR = r > MCC = WACC and hence NPV > 0. Project A, on the other hand, should be rejected because $IRR_A$ < MCC; hence, $NPV_A$ < 0.

People sometimes ask this question: "If we took Project A first, it would be acceptable because its 10.2 percent return would exceed the 10.0 percent cost of money used to finance it. Why couldn't we do this?" The answer is that we are seeking, in effect, to maximize the excess of *returns over costs*, or the area that is above the WACC but below the IOS. We accomplish this by graphing (and accepting) the most profitable projects first.

Another question that sometimes arises is this: What would happen if the MCC cut through one of the projects? For example, suppose the second break point in the MCC schedule had occurred at $100 million rather than at $120 million, causing the MCC schedule to cut through Project E. Should we then accept Project E? If Project E could be accepted in part, we would take on only part of it. Otherwise, the answer would be determined by (1) finding the average cost of the funds needed to finance Project E (some of the money would cost 10.5 percent and some 11.0 percent) and (2) comparing the average cost of this money with the 10.7 percent return on the project. We should accept Project E if its return exceeds the average cost of the $25 million needed to finance it.

The preceding analysis as summarized in Figure 11-5 reveals a very important point: *The cost of capital used in the capital budgeting process as discussed in Chapter 9 and Chapter 10 actually is determined at the intersection of the IOS and MCC schedules. If the cost of capital at the intersection (WACC$_2$ = 10.5% in Figure 11-5) is used, then*

**investment opportunity schedule (IOS)**
A graph of the firm's investment opportunities ranked in order of the projects' internal rates of return.

**FIGURE 11-5**   Combining the MCC and IOS Schedules to Determine the Optimal Capital Budget

Percent

- $IRR_C = 12.1\%$
- 12
- $IRR_D = 11.7\%$
- $IRR_B = 11.5\%$
- $WACC_3 = 11.0\%$   MCC
- 11
- $IRR_E = 10.7\%$
- $WACC_2 = 10.5\%$
- $IRR_A = 10.2\%$   IOS
- $WACC_1 = 10.0\%$
- 10

Optimal Capital
Budget = $115

0    20    40    60    80    100    120    140    160

New Capital Raised and Invested
During the Year (millions of dollars)

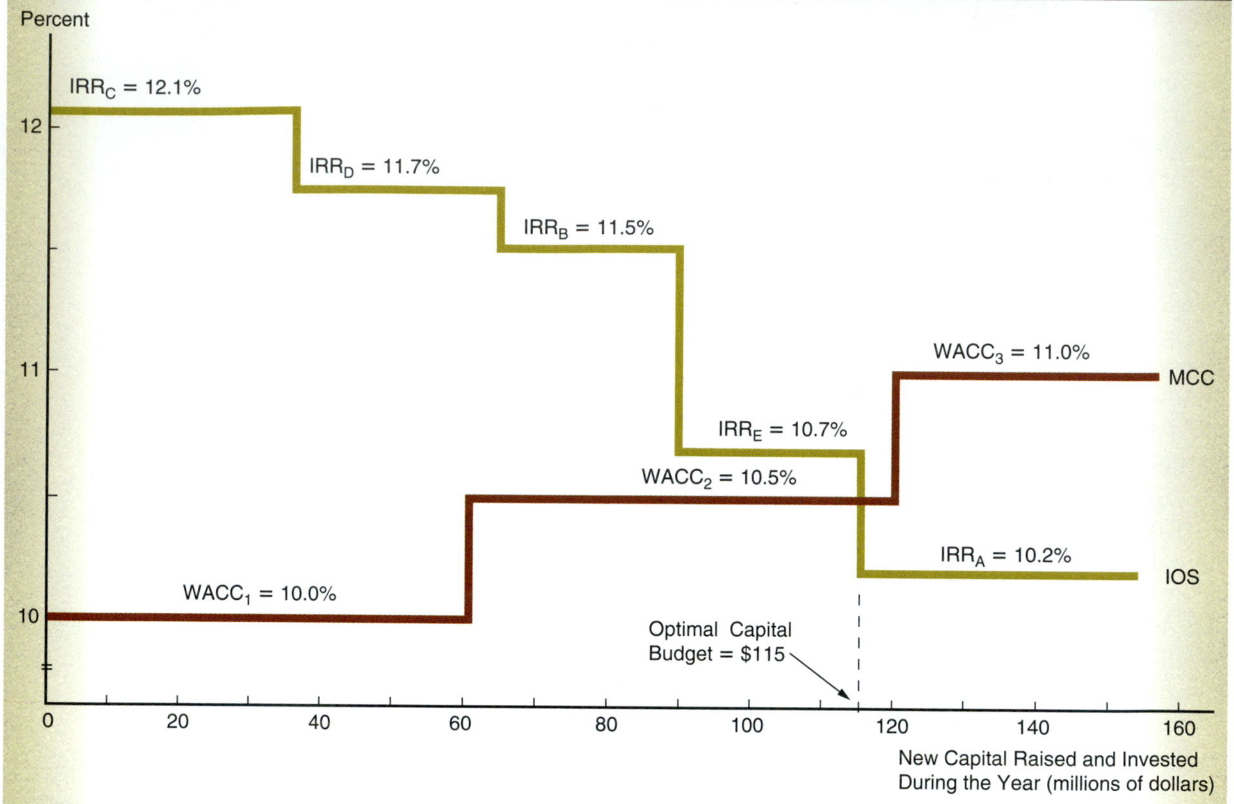

| Project | Initial Cost ($ millions) | Annual Net Cash Flows ($ millions) | Life (years) | IRR |
|---------|---------------------------|-------------------------------------|--------------|------|
| A | $39 | $9 | 6 | 10.2% |
| B | 25 | 6 | 6 | 11.5 |
| C | 36 | 10 | 5 | 12.1 |
| D | 29 | 7 | 6 | 11.7 |
| E | 25 | 8 | 4 | 10.7 |

*the firm will make correct accept/reject decisions, and its level of financing and investment will be optimal. If it uses any other rate, its capital budget will not be optimal.*

The intersection WACC as determined in Figure 11-5 should be used to find the NPVs of new projects that are about as risky as the firm's existing assets, but this corporate cost of capital should be adjusted up or down to find NPVs for projects with higher or lower risk than the average project. This point was discussed in Chapter 10 in connection with the Household Energy Products appliance control computer example.

**Self-Test Questions**

Differentiate between the MCC and IOS schedules.

How is the corporate cost of capital, which is used to evaluate average risk projects to determine their NPVs, found?

As a general rule, do you think a firm's cost of capital as determined in this chapter should be used to evaluate all of its capital budgeting projects? Explain.

# WACC versus Required Rate of Return of Investors

We introduced the concept of risk and rates of return in Chapter 8, where we discovered that investors demand higher rates of return to be compensated for higher levels of risk. In Chapter 6 and Chapter 7, we discovered that, everything else equal, an asset's value is inversely related to the rate of return investors require to invest in it. The following equation, with which you should be familiar by now, shows this relationship:

$$\text{Value} = \frac{\hat{CF}_1}{(1+r)^1} + \frac{\hat{CF}_2}{(1+r)^2} + \cdots + \frac{\hat{CF}_n}{(1+r)^n} = \sum_{t=1}^{n} \frac{\hat{CF}_t}{(1+r)^t}$$

This equation, which was first introduced in Chapter 1, shows that the value of any asset—real or financial—is based on (1) the cash flows that the asset is expected to generate during its life, $\hat{CF}_t$, and (2) the rate of return that investors require to "put up" their money to purchase the investment (asset), r. As a result, we know that investors purchase a firm's stocks and bonds—and thus provide funds to the firm—only if they expect to receive a return that sufficiently compensates them for the risk associated with those stocks and bonds. Consequently, the investors who purchase a firm's stocks and bonds determine the rates of return, or costs, the firm must pay to raise funds to invest in capital budgeting projects.

In Chapter 6 and Chapter 7, we discussed valuation from the standpoint of investors. For example, we described $r_s$ as the required rate of return of investors—that is, the rate of return investors demand to purchase the firm's common stock and thus provide funds to the firm. In this chapter, we described $r_s$ as the cost of internal common equity, which represents the return that the firm must earn to satisfy investors' demands. Which description is correct? They both are. This point can be illustrated with a simple analogy. Assume that Randy borrows money from his credit union to invest in common stocks. The loan agreement requires Randy to repay the amount borrowed plus 10 percent interest at the end of one year. The 10 percent interest rate represents both Randy's cost of borrowing—that is, cost of debt—and his required rate of return. If he does not invest the borrowed funds in stocks that earn at least 10 percent return—that is, have internal rates of return (IRRs) greater than 10 percent—then Randy will lose wealth because he has to pay the credit union, and thus it costs him 10 percent interest to use the money. The 10 percent interest rate also represents the return the credit union demands to lend money to Randy based on his credit risk—that is, 10 percent is the credit union's required rate, or the return it demands to lend money to (invest in) Randy. Although the situation is much more complex, this same relationship exists for firms that use funds provided by investors. Investors are similar to the credit union in the sense that they provide funds to the firms, whereas firms are similar to Randy in the sense that they use the funds provided by investors and must pay a return that is sufficient to attract such funds. And much like the credit union determines the interest rate that Randy must pay for his loan, investors determine the rates that firms must pay to use their funds.

In Chapter 6 and Chapter 7, we showed how financial assets are valued. And then in Chapter 8 we introduced and discussed rates of return. These discussions were developed primarily from the perspective of investors. In this chapter, we used the information introduced earlier in the book to explain the concept of cost of capital, which was discussed from the perspective of the firm. You should have noticed that the general concepts presented in this chapter are similar to the general concepts presented in Chapter 8—that is, determination of required rates of return and the impact on value. In reality, these two chapters present the same relationships from two perspectives—the investor (see Chapter 8) and the firm (this chapter). The rates of return, or component costs of capital, discussed in this chapter, are the same rates that were introduced in Chapter 8. For this reason, we thought it might be a good idea

## TABLE 11-3    WACC versus Required Rates of Return

*Investor's Required Rate of Return/Firm's Cost of Capital:*

$$\text{Investor's required rate of return} = r = r_{RF} + \left[\begin{array}{c}\text{Risk}\\\text{premium}\end{array}\right] = r_d, r_{ps}, \text{or } r_s = \begin{array}{c}\text{Firm's component}\\\text{cost of capital}\end{array}$$

| Financial Asset | Financial Asset's Market Value | Return to Investors | Cost to Firms |
|---|---|---|---|
| *Debt, $r_d$* | $P_0 = \dfrac{INT}{(1+YTM)^1} + \cdots + \dfrac{INT+M}{(1+YTM)^N}$ | $YTM = r_d$ = return investors require to purchase the firm's debt | $r_d = YTM$ = before-tax cost of debt<br><br>$r_{dT} = r_d(1-T)$ = after-tax cost of debt |
| *Preferred Stock, $r_{ps}$* | $P_0 = \dfrac{D_{ps}}{r_{ps}}$ | $r_{ps} = \dfrac{D_{ps}}{P_0}$ = return investors require to purchase the firm's preferred stock | $r_{ps} = \dfrac{D_{ps}}{P_0(1-F)}$ = cost of preferred stock (including flotation costs) |
| *Common Equity, $r_s$ (internal) or $r_e$ (external)* | $P_0 = \dfrac{\hat{D}_1}{r_s - g}$; (constant growth firm) | $r_s = \dfrac{\hat{D}_1}{P_0} + g$ = return investors require to purchase the firm's common stock | $r_s = \dfrac{\hat{D}_1}{P_0} + g$ = cost of retained earnings (internal)<br><br>$r_e = \dfrac{\hat{D}_1}{P_0(1-F)} + g$ = cost of new common equity (external) |

Variable Definitions:

$r_{RF}$ = nominal risk-free rate of return  
$P_0$ = market value of the financial asset  
INT = dollar interest payment  
M = maturity (face) value  
N = number of remaining interest payments  
g = constant growth rate of the firm  

YTM = yield to maturity  
T = the firm's marginal tax rate  
$D_{ps}$ = preferred stock dividend  
$\hat{D}_1$ = next period's expected dividend  
F = cost of issuing new stock (in decimal form)

to summarize these rates here. Table 11-3 shows the rates of return discussed in Chapter 8 and compares them with the component costs of capital discussed in this chapter. Note that the equations shown in the column labeled "Return to Investors" are the same as those shown in the column labeled "Cost to Firms," except for adjustments for taxes and flotation costs.

### Self-Test Questions

Who determines a firm's component costs of capital?

Why is r the required rate of return for both investors and the firm?

**Chapter *Essentials***

—The Answers

To summarize the key concepts, let's answer the questions that were posed at the beginning of the chapter:

- **What types of capital do firms use to finance investments?** When we refer to a firm's capital, we generally mean the sources of long-term funds that are used to purchase plant and equipment (long-term investments). Long-term funds generally are classified as either debt or equity. Debt refers to the firm's bond issues, whereas equity refers to the firm's stock issues. Equity comes in two basic forms—preferred stock and common equity. Common equity includes the common stock that has been issued plus any earnings that have been retained during the life of the firm.

- **What is the cost of capital?** A firm's cost of capital is the average "price" it pays for the funds it uses to purchase (invest in) assets. The cost for each component of capital differs—the after-tax cost of debt, $r_d$, is lower than the cost of preferred stock, $r_{ps}$, which is lower than the cost of common stock, $r_s$. To make decisions, a firm determines the average cost of all of the funds that it uses. Therefore, the firm computes its weighted average cost of capital, WACC, which is simply the average of each dollar of funding based on the proportion of the total funds of each type of capital that the firm uses. In other words, if WACC = 10%, then the firm pays an average cost of 10 percent for each dollar it uses for investments.

- **How is the cost of capital used to make financial decisions?** A firm's WACC is its required rate of return—that is, WACC = r. Thus, when evaluating capital budgeting projects (investments), the firm should invest in projects that are expected to provide returns (internal rates of return, IRRs) greater than its WACC. The WACC is a cost. If a firm does not earn a return that is greater than or equal to its WACC, then the firm's value decreases.

- **Why do funds generated through retained earnings have a cost?** The earnings that a firm retains over time represent amounts that could have been paid to common stockholders in the form of dividends in previous periods. Thus, a firm will be able to retain earnings only if those earnings are reinvested in assets that generate returns greater than the returns that can be earned by the investors to whom those earnings could have been paid as dividends. In other words, firms will be "allowed" to retain earnings as long as the firm can reinvest the earnings at a higher rate than stockholders can earn elsewhere. However, if the firm reinvests the earnings at a rate that is lower than stockholders require, then these investors will demand that the firm pay out the earnings as dividends rather than retaining them.

- **Who determines a firm's cost of capital?** A firm's cost of capital is the rate of return that investors require to provide the funds that are used to purchase assets. Investors will not provide funds to a firm unless they expect to receive returns that are high enough to compensate them for the investment risk they take. Thus, if investors demand a 10 percent return, the firm must earn at least a 10 percent return on its assets.

**ETHICAL DILEMMA**

## How Much Should You Pay to be "Green"?

Tracey works in the capital budgeting department of Sustainable Solutions (SS), which is a company that manufactures products and consults on issues that relate to the protection and preservation of the earth's environment. Tracey's primary responsibility is to estimate the company's cost of capital, which is the "hurdle" rate that is used to make final capital budgeting decisions.

During the 10 years that Tracey has worked at SS, she has been very pleased with the service the company has provided to other companies and environmentalists. Tracey is very compassionate about environmental issues, and she tries to get involved in movements and do everything she can to help clean up and protect the environment.

Last week, Manual, a coworker who works in the capital budgeting department as a project analyst, told Tracey about a project he is currently analyzing. Although he doesn't completely understand the technology, Manual told Tracey that he thought purchasing the project would allow the firm to significantly increase its presence in the "green" industry and it would also propel SS into the leadership role in the quest to clean up and protect the environment.

Tracey was ecstatic after talking with Manual. But her excitement was short-lived because another coworker, one who is part of the team that is evaluating the new project, indicated that the analyses that have been completed to date suggest that the project might not be purchased because its internal rate of return appears to be below the firm's required rate of return. It will be a few weeks until the capital budgeting analyses are complete.

Because she believed that the environmental benefits of the project far outweighed its possible financial drawbacks, Tracey decided to think of ways she could help "sway" the final capital budgeting decision in favor of purchasing the project. As luck would have it, Tracey is close to completing a revised evaluation of the firm's cost of capital. She knows that the results of her evaluation will be used to help decide whether the new project is acceptable. As she pored over her numbers, Tracey realized that if she used a different approach to determine the proportions of debt and equity that are used to compute the firm's weighted average cost of capital (WACC), a higher weight would be given to debt, which has the lowest component cost of capital. It has been the policy of the company to compute the weights for the capital components using the market values of the firm's debt and equity. However, Tracey discovered that debt, which has a substantially lower cost than equity, will have a higher weight if book values are used. If the WAAC is computed using the higher weight given to debt, the required rate of return used to evaluate the new project probably will be low enough to ensure that the new project is accepted. Tracey doesn't feel like she is "cheating" by making the change because she doesn't think that market values should be used to determine the weights for the capital components; she believes that book values are more appropriate. Tracey is convinced she can justify the deviation from policy if her bosses question why she used book values to determine the weights. Do you think it is okay for Tracey to change the way she computes SS's WACC? What would you do if you were Tracey?

## Chapter *Essentials*
### —Personal Finance

The concepts presented in this chapter should help you to better understand how to determine the rate of return that you should demand when investing your money. If you apply the concepts presented in this chapter, you should be able to make more informed borrowing and investment decisions.

- You can apply the techniques presented in the chapter to determine the average interest rate that you are paying for all the loans you have outstanding. If you are like most people, you have a mortgage, an automobile loan, and perhaps other smaller debt. Generally the mortgage represents 75 percent to 80 percent of the total amount of the outstanding loans, so the average interest rate you are paying for your loans is fairly close to the rate on your outstanding mortgage. The average interest you pay on your outstanding loans is your required rate of return.

- If you borrow funds to invest—perhaps to purchase stocks—you should choose investments that you expect to earn a return that is greater than the average interest rate that you are paying on the loan(s). If you invest at a rate that is lower than the average interest rate on the loan(s), your wealth will decrease—the difference between the return you earn on the invested money and the average interest rate on the loan(s) "comes out of your pocket." However, if your investments earn an average return that is greater than the interest you are paying on the loans, the excess "goes in your pocket," and your wealth increases.

- Using the approaches discussed in the chapter, you should be able to compute the "true" costs of your loans. When you borrow funds from a bank, credit union, or any other source, it is comparable to a firm issuing a stock or bond. You as the borrower are effectively issuing debt to the lending institution; the lender is equivalent to an investor who buys a corporate stock or bond. Much like the flotation costs corporations incur when issuing stocks and bonds, you incur issuing costs, which might be referred to as points, service fees, and so forth. For instance, many mortgages require the borrower to pay points at the time the loan is initiated. The amount that must be paid to cover the loan's points simply represents a prepayment of some interest. If the loan requires 1 point to be paid, then 1 percent of the amount borrowed is paid at the time the borrower gets the loan. Often the amount that must be paid for the points is paid out of the amount borrowed such that the amount of money from the loan that the borrower has available for use is decreased. This effect is much like the effect that flotation costs have on the cost of issuing new equity—that is, the cost of new equity is higher when flotation costs are higher. In addition, borrowers generally are required to pay other charges when borrowing money, and these other charges increase the cost of the debt. For example, suppose you want to borrow $100,000 from your bank. The various fees that the bank charges total 2 percent of the loan, or $2,000, and the stated interest rate on the loan is 6 percent. The loan agreement requires you to repay the loan at the end of one year with interest; there will be no interest or principal payments made during the year. What is the cost of the loan? Following the procedure shown in the chapter, the cost of the loan can be computed as follows:

$$\text{Cost of the loan} = \frac{\text{Interest} + \text{fees}}{\text{Net proceeds}} = \frac{\$100,000(0.06) + \$2,000}{\$100,000 - \$2,000} = \frac{\$8,000}{\$98,000}$$
$$= 0.082 = 8.2\%$$

Here the $2,000 of fees that are paid are included as a charge for borrowing the money, which effectively is additional interest, or additional rent that is paid on the borrowed money.

- Because interest paid on a mortgage is tax deductible, the appropriate cost of this form of debt should be stated on an after-tax basis. For example, if the interest rate on your mortgage is 6 percent and you are in the 25 percent tax bracket, then the after-tax cost of the mortgage is $4.5\% = 6\%(1 - 0.25)$. Because the interest paid on the mortgage is tax deductible, the actual cost of the mortgage is less than the stated interest of 6 percent.

# QUESTIONS

**11-1** In what sense does the marginal cost of capital schedule represent a series of average costs?

**11-2** The financial manager of a large national firm was overheard making the following statement: "We try to use as much retained earnings as possible for capital budgeting purposes because there is no *explicit* cost to these funds, and this allows us to invest in relatively low yielding projects that would not be feasible if we had to issue new common stock. We actually use retained earnings to invest in projects with yields below the coupon rate on our bonds." Comment on the validity of this statement.

**11-3** How would each of the following affect a firm's after-tax cost of debt, $r_{dT}$; its cost of equity, $r_s$; and its weighted average cost of capital, WACC? Indicate by a plus (+), a minus (−), or a zero (0) if the factor would increase, decrease, or have an indeterminate effect on the item in question. Assume other things are held constant. Be prepared to justify your answer, but recognize that some of the parts probably have no single correct answer; these questions are designed to stimulate thought and discussion.

| | Effect on | | |
|---|---|---|---|
| | $r_{dT}$ | $r_s$ | WACC |
| **a.** The corporate tax rate is lowered. | _____ | _____ | _____ |
| **b.** The Federal Reserve tightens credit. | _____ | _____ | _____ |
| **c.** The firm significantly increases the proportion of debt it uses. | _____ | _____ | _____ |
| **d.** The dividend payout ratio (percent of earnings paid as dividends) is increased. | _____ | _____ | _____ |
| **e.** The firm doubles the amount of capital it raises during the year. | _____ | _____ | _____ |
| **f.** The firm expands into riskier new areas. | _____ | _____ | _____ |
| **g.** The firm merges with another firm whose earnings are countercyclical both to those of the first firm and to the stock market. | _____ | _____ | _____ |
| **h.** The stock market falls drastically, and the value of the firm's stock falls along with the rest. | _____ | _____ | _____ |
| **i.** Investors become more risk averse. | _____ | _____ | _____ |
| **j.** The firm is an electric utility with a large investment in nuclear plants. Several states propose a ban on nuclear power generation. | _____ | _____ | _____ |

**11-4** Suppose a firm estimates its MCC and IOS schedules for the coming year and finds that they intersect at the point 10 percent, $10 million. What cost of capital should be used to evaluate average projects, high-risk projects, and low-risk projects?

**11-5** Clear Glass Company's investment banker has determined that the following rate schedule would apply if the firm raises funds by issuing new debt (bonds):

| **Amount of New Debt** | **Cost, $r_d$** |
|---|---|
| $1 to $250,000 | 8.0% |
| $250,001 to $1,000,000 | 10.0 |
| $1,000,001 to $5,000,000 | 14.0 |
| Greater than $5,000,000 | 20.0 |

For Clear Glass, how many break points are *associated with debt* when computing the weighted average cost of capital (WACC)?

**11-6** What impact will investors' expectations about inflation have on a firm's cost of debt? Will the firm's cost of equity be affected? Explain.

**11-7** Explain why, for a particular firm, the cost of retained earnings, $r_s$, will always be *less than* the cost of new equity, $r_e$.

**11-8** Suppose a firm invests in projects that are much riskier than its average investments. Do you think the firm's weighted average cost of capital will be affected? Explain.

## SELF-TEST PROBLEMS

*(Solutions appear in Appendix B at the end of the book.)*

**ST-1** Define each of the following terms:                                      **key terms**

  **a.** After-tax cost of debt, $r_{dT}$; capital component cost

  **b.** Cost of preferred stock, $r_{ps}$

  **c.** Cost of retained earnings, $r_s$

  **d.** Cost of new common equity, $r_e$

  **e.** Flotation cost, F

  **f.** Target capital structure; capital structure components

  **g.** Weighted average cost of capital (WACC)

  **h.** Marginal cost of capital (MCC)

  **i.** Marginal cost of capital schedule; break point (BP)

  **j.** Investment opportunity schedule (IOS)

**ST-2** Lancaster Engineering Inc. (LEI) has the following capital structure, which it    **optimal capital budget**
considers to be optimal:

| | |
|---|---|
| Debt | 25% |
| Preferred stock | 15 |
| Common equity | 60 |
| | 100% |

LEI's expected net income this year is $34,285.72; its established dividend payout ratio is 30 percent; its marginal tax rate is 40 percent; and investors expect earnings and dividends to grow at a constant rate of 9 percent in the future. LEI paid a dividend of $3.60 per share last year, and its stock currently sells at a price of $60 per share.

LEI can obtain new capital in the following ways:

*Common:* New common stock has a flotation cost of 10 percent for up to $12,000 of new stock and 20 percent for all common stock over $12,000.

*Preferred:* New preferred stock with a dividend of $11 can be sold to the public at a price of $100 per share. However, flotation costs of $5 per share will be incurred for up to $7,500 of preferred stock, and flotation costs will rise to $10 per share, or 10 percent, on all preferred stock over $7,500.

*Debt:* Up to $5,000 of debt can be sold at an interest rate of 12 percent; debt in the range of $5,001 to $10,000 must carry an interest rate of 14 percent; and all debt over $10,000 will have an interest rate of 16 percent. LEI has the following independent investment opportunities:

| Project | Cost at t = 0 | Annual Net Cash Flow | Project Life | IRR |
|---------|---------------|----------------------|--------------|------|
| A | $10,000 | $2,191.20 | 7 years | 12.0% |
| B | 10,000 | 3,154.42 | 5 | 17.4 |
| C | 10,000 | 2,170.18 | 8 | 14.2 |
| D | 20,000 | 3,789.48 | 10 | 13.7 |
| E | 20,000 | 5,427.84 | 6 | ? |

a. Find the break points in the MCC schedule.

b. Determine the cost of each capital structure component.

c. Calculate the weighted average cost of capital in the interval between each break in the MCC schedule.

d. Calculate the IRR for Project E.

e. Construct a graph showing the MCC and IOS schedules.

f. Which projects should LEI accept?

## PROBLEMS

**cost of debt**  **11-1**  Neotech Corporation's 14 percent coupon rate, semiannual payment, $1,000 par value 30-year bonds currently sell at a price of $1,353.54. If Neotech's marginal tax rate is 40 percent, what is its after-tax cost of debt?

**cost of debt**  **11-2**  The McDaniel Company's financing plans for next year include the sale of long-term bonds with a 10 percent coupon. The company believes it can sell the bonds at a price that will provide a yield to maturity of 12 percent. If the marginal tax rate is 34 percent, what is McDaniel's after-tax cost of debt?

**cost of debt**  **11-3**  A corporation has an outstanding bond with the following characteristics:

| | |
|---|---|
| Coupon interest rate | 6.0% |
| Interest payments | semiannually |
| Face value | $1,000.00 |
| Years to maturity | 8 |
| Current market value | $ 902.81 |

What is the yield to maturity (YTM = $r_d$) for this bond?

**cost of preferred stock**  **11-4**  Maness Industries plans to issue some $100 par preferred stock with an 11 percent dividend. The stock is selling on the market for $97.00, and Maness must pay flotation costs of 5 percent of the market price. What is the cost of the preferred stock for Maness?

**cost of preferred stock**  **11-5**  Hybrid Hydro Plants Inc., which has a marginal tax rate equal to 34 percent, has preferred stock that pays a constant dividend equal to $15 per share. The stock currently sells for $125. If the company incurs a 3 percent flotation cost each time it issues preferred stock, what is the cost of issuing preferred stock?

**11-6**  The common stock of Omega Corporation is currently selling for $50 per share. It is expected that Omega will pay a dividend equal to $5 per share this year. In addition, analysts have indicated that the company has been growing at a constant rate of 3 percent, and this growth is expected to continue forever. What is Omega's cost of retained earnings?

**cost of retained earnings**

**11-7**  Analysts of the ICM Corporation have indicated that the company is expected to grow at a 5 percent rate for as long as it is in business. Currently ICM's stock is selling for $70 per share. The most recent dividend paid by the company was $5.60 per share. If ICM issues new common stock, it will incur flotation costs equal to 7 percent. ICM's marginal tax rate is 35 percent. What is its cost of retained earnings—that is, its internal equity? What is its cost of new equity?

**cost of common equity**

**11-8**  The Choi Company's next expected dividend, $\hat{D}_1$, is $3.18; its growth rate is 6 percent; and its stock currently sells for $36. New stock can be sold to net the firm $32.40 per share.

**cost of new common equity**

    **a.** What is Choi's percentage flotation cost, F?

    **b.** What is Choi's cost of new common stock, $r_e$?

**11-9**  Following is information about the common equity of Funtastic Furniture Company:

**cost of common equity**

| | |
|---|---|
| Current selling price | $68.00 |
| Constant growth rate | 8.0% |
| Most recently paid dividend, $D_0$ | $ 3.50 |
| Flotation costs | 10.0% |
| Marginal tax rate | 40.0% |

    **a.** What is Funtastic's cost of retained earnings?

    **b.** What is Funtastics's cost of new common stock?

**11-10**  A company's 6 percent coupon rate, semiannual payment, $1,000 par value bond that matures in 30 years sells at a price of $515.16. The company's marginal tax rate is 40 percent. What is the firm's component cost of debt for purposes of calculating the WACC? (*Hint:* Base your answer on the simple rate, not the effective annual rate, EAR.)

**cost of debt**

**11-11**  Chicago Paints Corporation has a target capital structure of 40 percent debt and 60 percent common equity. The company expects to have $600 of after-tax income during the coming year, and it plans to retain 40 percent of its earnings. The current stock price is $P_0 = $30, the last dividend paid was $D_0 = $2.00, and the dividend is expected to grow at a constant rate of 7 percent. New stock can be sold at a flotation cost of F = 25%. What will Chicago Paints' marginal cost of equity capital be if it raises a total of $500 of new capital?

**cost of equity**

**11-12**  Magnificent Metal Mining (MMM) expects to generate $60,000 in earnings that will be retained for reinvestment in the firm this year. If MMM's capital structure consists of 25 percent debt and 75 percent common equity, stated in total funds, what is the weighted average cost of capital (WACC) break point that is associated with retained earnings?

**break point**

**11-13**  Roberson Fashion's capital structure consists of 30 percent debt and 70 percent common equity. Roberson is considering raising new capital to

**break points**

finance its expansion plans. The company's investment banker has compiled the following information about the cost of debt if the firm issues debt:

| Amount of Debt | After-Tax Cost of Debt |
|---|---|
| $1 to $150,000 | 6.5% |
| 150,001 to 450,000 | 7.8 |
| 400,001 to 840,000 | 9.0 |
| Above $840,000 | 11.0 |

Roberson expects to generate $350,000 in retained earnings next year. For any new equity that is issued, Roberson will incur flotation costs of 6 percent. What are the break points that Roberson faces when computing its marginal cost of capital?

**marginal cost of capital**    **11-14** The following information is given for Bates Chemical Company (BCC):

| Type of Capital | After-Tax Cost | Proportion of the Capital Structure |
|---|---|---|
| Debt | 5.0% | 20.0% |
| Common equity— retained earnings | 11.0 | 80.0 |
| Common equity— new issue | 14.0 | |

BCC expects to retain $160,000 in earnings this year to invest in capital budgeting projects. If the firm's capital budget is expected to equal $180,000, what required rate of return, or marginal cost of capital, should be used when evaluating capital budgeting projects?

**optimal capital investment**    **11-15** The CFO of Mega Munchies recently received a report that contains the following information:

| Project | Cost | IRR | Capital Structure Type of Capital | Proportion |
|---|---|---|---|---|
| E | $200,000 | 19.0% | Debt | 40.0% |
| F | 300,000 | 17.0 | Preferred stock | 0.0 |
| G | 200,000 | 14.0 | Common equity | 60.0 |

The weighted average cost of capital (WACC) is 12 percent if the firm does *not* have to issue new common equity; if new common equity is needed, the WACC is 15 percent. If Mega Munchies expects to generate $240,000 in retained earnings this year, which project(s) should be purchased? Assume the projects are independent.

**marginal cost of capital**    **11-16** Sam's Orthodontic Services (SOS) will retain for reinvestment $300,000 of the net income it expects to generate next year. Recently, the CFO determined that the firm's after-tax cost of debt, $r_{dT}$, is 5 percent; its cost of internal equity (retained earnings), $r_s$, is 10 percent; and its cost of external equity (new common stock), $r_e$, is 13 percent. Next year, SOS expects to finance capital budgeting projects so as to maintain its current capital structure, which consists of 60 percent debt. SOS has no preferred stock. What will SOS's marginal cost of capital be if its total capital budgeting needs are $700,000 for next year?

**11-17** The Gupta Company's cost of equity is 16 percent. Its before-tax cost of debt is 13 percent, and its marginal tax rate is 40 percent. The stock sells at book value. Using the following balance sheet, calculate Gupta's after-tax weighted average cost of capital:

**weighted average cost of capital**

| Assets | | Liabilities and Equity | |
|---|---|---|---|
| Cash | $ 120 | Long-term debt | $1,152 |
| Accounts receivable | 240 | Equity | 1,728 |
| Inventories | 360 | | |
| Net plant and equipment | 2,160 | | |
| Total assets | $2,880 | Total liabilities and equity | $2,880 |

**11-18** The Mason Corporation's current capital structure, which is also its target capital structure, calls for 50 percent debt and 50 percent common equity. The firm has only one potential project, an expansion program with a 10.2 percent IRR and a cost of $20 million, which is completely divisible—that is, Mason can invest any amount up to $20 million. The firm expects to retain $3 million of earnings next year. It can raise up to $5 million in new debt at a before-tax cost of 8 percent, and all debt after the first $5 million will have a cost of 10 percent. The cost of retained earnings is 12 percent, and the firm can sell any amount of new common stock desired at a constant cost of 15 percent. The firm's marginal tax rate is 40 percent. What is the firm's optimal capital budget?

**optimal capital budget**

**11-19** The management of Ferri Phosphate Industries (FPI) is planning next year's capital budget. FPI projects its net income at $7,500, and its payout ratio is 40 percent. The company's earnings and dividends are growing at a constant rate of 5 percent; the last dividend paid, $D_0$, was $0.90; and the current stock price is $8.59. FPI's new debt will cost 14 percent. If FPI issues new common stock, flotation costs will be 20 percent. FPI is at its optimal capital structure, which is 40 percent debt and 60 percent equity, and the firm's marginal tax rate is 40 percent. FPI has the following independent, indivisible, and equally risky investment opportunities:

**optimal capital budget**

| Project | Cost | IRR |
|---|---|---|
| A | $15,000 | 17% |
| B | 20,000 | 14 |
| C | 15,000 | 16 |
| D | 12,000 | 15 |

What is FPI's optimal capital budget?

**11-20** Refer to Problem 11-19. Management now decides to incorporate project risk differentials into the analysis. The new policy is to add 2 percentage points to the cost of capital of those projects significantly riskier than average and to subtract 2 percentage points from the cost of capital of those that are

**optimal capital budget**

substantially less risky than average. Management judges Project A to be of high risk, Projects C and D to be of average risk, and Project B to be of low risk. None of the projects is divisible. What is the optimal capital budget after adjustment for project risk?

**weighted average cost of capital (WACC)**

**11-21** Florida Electric Company (FEC) uses only debt and equity. It can borrow unlimited amounts at an interest rate of 10 percent as long as it finances at its target capital structure, which calls for 45 percent debt and 55 percent common equity. Its last dividend was $2, its expected constant growth rate is 4 percent, its stock sells at a price of $25, and new stock would net the company $20 per share after flotation costs. FEC's marginal tax rate is 40 percent, and it expects to have $100 million of retained earnings this year. Two projects are available: Project A has a cost of $200 million and an internal rate of return of 13 percent, while Project B has a cost of $125 million and an internal rate of return of 10 percent. All of the company's potential projects are equally risky.

**a.** What is FEC's cost of equity from newly issued stock?

**b.** What is FEC's marginal cost of capital—that is, what WACC cost rate should it use to evaluate capital budgeting projects (these two projects plus any others that might arise during the year, provided the cost of capital schedule remains as it is currently)?

**cost of retained earnings**

**11-22** The earnings, dividends, and stock price of Talukdar Technologies Inc. are expected to grow at 7 percent per year in the future. Talukdar's common stock sells for $23 per share, its last dividend was $2.00, and the company will pay a dividend of $2.14 at the end of the current year.

**a.** Using the discounted cash flow approach, what is its cost of retained earnings?

**b.** If the firm's beta is 1.6, the risk-free rate is 9 percent, and the average return on the market is 13 percent, what will be the firm's cost of equity using the CAPM approach?

**c.** If the firm's bonds earn a return of 12 percent, what will $r_s$ be using the bond-yield-plus-risk-premium approach? (*Hint:* Use the midpoint of the risk premium range discussed in the chapter.)

**d.** Based on the results of parts a through c, what would you estimate Talukdar's cost of retained earnings to be?

**growth and cost of retained earnings**

**11-23** The Shrieves Company's EPS was $6.50 in 2008 and $4.42 in 2003. The company pays out 40 percent of its earnings as dividends, and the stock sells for $36.

**a.** Calculate the past growth rate in earnings. (*Hint:* This is a five-year growth period.)

**b.** Calculate the *next* expected dividend per share, $\hat{D}_1$. [$D_0 = 0.4(\$6.50) = \$2.60$.] Assume that the past growth rate will continue.

**c.** What is the cost of retained earnings, $r_s$, for the Shrieves Company?

**break points**

**11-24** The Simmons Company expects earnings of $30 million next year. Its dividend payout ratio is 40 percent, and its proportion of debt (debt/assets ratio) is 60 percent. Simmons uses no preferred stock.

**a.** What amount of retained earnings does Simmons expect next year?

**b.** At what amount of financing will there be a break point in the MCC schedule?

**c.** If Simmons can borrow $12 million at an interest rate of 11 percent, another $12 million at a rate of 12 percent, and any additional debt at a rate of 13 percent, at what points will rising debt costs cause breaks in the MCC schedule?

**11-25** Rowell Products' stock is currently selling for $60 a share. The firm is expected to earn $5.40 per share this year and to pay a year-end dividend of $3.60.

**growth and earnings**

    **a.** If investors require a 9 percent return, what rate of growth must be expected for Rowell?

    **b.** If Rowell reinvests retained earnings in projects whose average return is equal to the stock's expected rate of return, what will be next year's earnings per share?

**11-26** On January 1, 2008, the total assets of the Dexter Company were $270 million. The firm's current capital structure, which follows, is considered to be optimal. Assume there is no short-term debt.

**weighted average cost of capital**

| | |
|---|---|
| Long-term debt | $135,000,000 |
| Common equity | 135,000,000 |
| Total liabilities and equity | $270,000,000 |

New bonds will have a 10 percent coupon rate and will be sold at par. Common stock, currently selling at $60 a share, can be sold to net the company $54 a share. Stockholders' required rate of return is estimated to be 12 percent, consisting of a dividend yield of 4 percent and an expected growth rate of 8 percent. (The next expected dividend is $2.40, so $2.40/$60 = 4%.) Retained earnings are estimated to be $13.5 million. The marginal tax rate is 40 percent. Assuming that all asset expansion (gross expenditures for fixed assets plus related working capital) is included in the capital budget, the dollar amount of the capital budget, ignoring depreciation, is $135 million.

    **a.** To maintain the current capital structure, how much of the capital budget must Dexter finance by equity?

    **b.** How much of the new equity funds needed will be generated internally? Externally?

    **c.** Calculate the cost of each of the equity components.

    **d.** At what level of capital expenditure will there be a break in Dexter's MCC schedule?

    **e.** Calculate the WACC (1) below and (2) above the break in the MCC schedule.

    **f.** Plot the MCC schedule. Also, draw in an IOS schedule that is consistent with both the MCC schedule and the projected capital budget. (Any IOS schedule that is consistent will do.)

**11-27** The following table gives earnings per share figures for the Brueggeman Company during the preceding 10 years. The firm's common stock, 7.8 million shares outstanding, is now (January 1, 2008) selling for $65 per share, and the expected dividend at the end of the current year (2008) is 55 percent of the EPS expected in 2008. Because investors expect past

**weighted average cost of capital**

trends to continue, g can be based on the earnings growth rate. (Note that nine years of *growth* are reflected in the data.)

| Year | EPS | Year | EPS |
|------|------|------|------|
| 1998 | $3.90 | 2003 | $5.73 |
| 1999 | 4.21 | 2004 | 6.19 |
| 2000 | 4.55 | 2005 | 6.68 |
| 2001 | 4.91 | 2006 | 7.22 |
| 2002 | 5.31 | 2007 | 7.80 |

The current before-tax interest rate on debt is 9 percent. The firm's marginal tax rate is 40 percent. Its capital structure, considered to be optimal, is as follows:

| | |
|------|------|
| Debt | $104,000,000 |
| Common equity | 156,000,000 |
| Total liabilities and equity | $260,000,000 |

a. Calculate Brueggeman's after-tax cost of new debt and of common equity, assuming that new equity comes only from retained earnings. Calculate the cost of equity as $r_s = \hat{D}_1/P_0 + g$.

b. Find Brueggeman's WACC, again assuming that no new common stock is sold and that all debt costs 9 percent.

c. How much can be spent on capital investments before external equity must be sold? (Assume that retained earnings available for 2008 are 45 percent of 2008 earnings. Obtain 2008 earnings by multiplying the expected 2008 EPS by the shares outstanding.)

d. What is Brueggeman's WACC (cost of funds raised in excess of the amount calculated in part c) if new common stock can be sold to the public at $65 a share to net the firm $58.50 a share? The cost of debt is constant.

**optimal capital budget**    **11-28**   Ezzell Enterprises has the following capital structure, which it considers to be optimal under current and forecasted conditions:

| | |
|------|------|
| Debt (long-term only) | 45% |
| Common equity | 55 |
| Total liabilities and equity | 100% |

For the coming year, management expects after-tax earnings of $2.5 million. Ezzell's past dividend policy of paying out 60 percent of earnings will continue. Current commitments from its banker will allow Ezzell to borrow according to the following schedule:

| Loan Amount | Interest Rate |
|------|------|
| $0 to $500,000 | 9% on this increment of debt |
| $500,001 to $900,000 | 11% on this increment of debt |
| $900,001 and above | 13% on this increment of debt |

The company's marginal tax rate is 40 percent, the current market price of its stock is $22 per share, its *last* dividend was $2.20 per share, and the expected growth rate is 5 percent. External equity (new common) can be sold at a flotation cost of 10 percent.

Ezzell has the following investment opportunities for the next year:

| Project | Cost | Annual Cash Flows | Project Life | IRR |
|---|---|---|---|---|
| 1 | $675,000 | $155,401 | 8 years | ? |
| 2 | 900,000 | 268,484 | 5 | 15.0% |
| 3 | 375,000 | 161,524 | 3 | ? |
| 4 | 562,500 | 185,194 | 4 | 12.0 |
| 5 | 750,000 | 127,351 | 10 | 11.0 |

Management asks you to help determine which projects (if any) should be undertaken. You proceed with this analysis by answering the following questions (or performing the tasks) as posed in a logical sequence:

**a.** How many breaks are there in the MCC schedule? At what dollar amounts do the breaks occur, and what causes them?

**b.** What is the weighted average cost of capital in each of the intervals between the breaks?

**c.** What are the IRR values for Projects 1 and 3?

**d.** Graph the IOS and MCC schedules.

**e.** Which projects should Ezzell's management accept?

**f.** What assumptions about project risk are implicit in this problem? If you learned that Projects 1, 2, and 3 were of above-average risk, yet Ezzell chose the projects that you indicated in part e, how would this affect the situation?

**g.** The problem stated that Ezzell pays out 60 percent of its earnings as dividends. How would the analysis change if the payout ratio were changed to zero, to 100 percent, or somewhere in between? (No calculations are necessary.)

## Integrative Problem

**11-29** Assume you were recently hired as assistant to Jerry Lehman, financial VP of Coleman Technologies. Your first task is to estimate Coleman's cost of capital. Lehman has provided you with the following data, which he believes is relevant to your task:

**cost of capital**

    **(1)** The firm's marginal tax rate is 40 percent.

    **(2)** The current price of Coleman's 12 percent coupon, semiannual payment, noncallable bonds with 15 years remaining to maturity is $1,153.72. Coleman does not use short-term interest-bearing debt on a permanent basis. New bonds would be privately placed with no flotation cost.

    **(3)** The current price of the firm's 10 percent, $100 par value, quarterly dividend, perpetual preferred stock is $113.10. Coleman would incur flotation costs of $2.00 per share on a new issue.

**(4)** Coleman's common stock is currently selling at $50 per share. Its last dividend ($D_0$) was $4.19, and dividends are expected to grow at a constant rate of 5 percent in the foreseeable future. Coleman's beta is 1.2, the yield on Treasury bonds is 7 percent, and the market risk premium is estimated to be 6 percent. For the bond-yield-plus-risk-premium approach, the firm uses a risk premium of 4 percentage points.

**(5)** Up to $300,000 of new common stock can be sold at a flotation cost of 15 percent. Above $300,000, the flotation cost would rise to 25 percent.

**(6)** Coleman's target capital structure is 30 percent long-term debt, 10 percent preferred stock, and 60 percent common equity.

**(7)** The firm is forecasting retained earnings of $300,000 for the coming year.

To structure the task somewhat, Lehman has asked you to answer the following questions:

**a.** **(1)** What sources of capital should be included when you estimate Coleman's weighted average cost of capital (WACC)?

   **(2)** Should the component costs be figured on a before-tax or an after-tax basis? Explain.

   **(3)** Should the costs be historical (embedded) costs or new (marginal) costs? Explain.

**b.** What is the market interest rate on Coleman's debt and its component cost of debt?

**c.** **(1)** What is the firm's cost of preferred stock?

   **(2)** Coleman's preferred stock is riskier to investors than its debt, yet the yield to investors is lower than the yield to maturity on the debt. Does this suggest that you have made a mistake? (*Hint:* Think about taxes.)

**d.** **(1)** Why is there a cost associated with retained earnings?

   **(2)** What is Coleman's estimated cost of retained earnings using the CAPM approach?

**e.** What is the estimated cost of retained earnings using the discounted cash flow (DCF) approach?

**f.** What is the bond-yield-plus-risk-premium estimate for Coleman's cost of retained earnings?

**g.** What is your final estimate for $r_s$?

**h.** What is Coleman's cost for up to $300,000 of newly issued common stock, $r_{e1}$? What happens to the cost of equity if Coleman sells more than $300,000 of new common stock?

**i.** Explain in words why new common stock has a higher percentage cost than retained earnings.

**j.** **(1)** What is Coleman's overall, or weighted average, cost of capital (WACC) when retained earnings are used as the equity component?

   **(2)** What is the WACC after retained earnings have been exhausted and Coleman uses up to $300,000 of new common stock with a 15 percent flotation cost?

    **(3)** What is the WACC if more than $300,000 of new common equity is sold?

**k.** **(1)** At what amount of new investment would Coleman be forced to issue new common stock? To put it another way, what is the largest capital budget the company could support without issuing new common stock? Assume that the 30/10/60 target capital structure will be maintained.

    **(2)** At what amount of new investment would Coleman be forced to issue new common stock with a 25 percent flotation cost?

    **(3)** What is a marginal cost of capital (MCC) schedule? Construct a graph that shows Coleman's MCC schedule.

**l.** Coleman's director of capital budgeting has identified the following potential projects:

| Project | Cost | Life | Cash Flow | IRR |
|---------|------|------|-----------|-----|
| A | $700,000 | 5 years | $218,795 | 17.0% |
| B | 500,000 | 5 | 152,705 | 16.0 |
| B* | 500,000 | 20 | 79,881 | 15.0 |
| C | 800,000 | 5 | 219,185 | 11.5 |

Projects B and B* are mutually exclusive, whereas the other projects are independent. All of the projects are equally risky.

    **(1)** Plot the IOS schedule on the same graph that contains your MCC schedule. What is the firm's marginal cost of capital for capital budgeting purposes?

    **(2)** What are the dollar size and the included projects in Coleman's optimal capital budget? Explain your answer fully.

    **(3)** Would Coleman's MCC schedule remain constant at 12.8 percent beyond $2 million regardless of the amount of capital required?

    **(4)** If $WACC_3$ had been 18.5 percent rather than 12.8 percent, but the second WACC break point had still occurred at $1,000,000, how would that have affected the analysis?

**m.** Suppose you learned that Coleman could raise only $200,000 of new debt at a 10 percent interest rate and that new debt beyond $200,000 would have a yield to investors of 12 percent. Trace back through your work and explain how this new fact would change the situation.

## Computer-Related Problem

*Work the problem in this section only if you are using the problem spreadsheet.*

**11-30** Use the model in the File C11 to work this problem.         **optimal capital budget**

    **a.** Refer back to Problem 11-28. Now assume that the debt ratio is increased to 65 percent, causing all interest rates to rise by 1 percentage point, to 10 percent, 12 percent, and 14 percent, and causing g to increase from 5 percent to 6 percent. What happens to the MCC schedule and the capital budget?

    **b.** Assume the facts as in part a, but suppose Ezzell's marginal tax rate falls (1) to 20 percent or (2) to 0 percent. How would this affect the MCC schedule and the capital budget?

**c.** Ezzell's management would now like to know what the optimal capital budget would be if earnings were as high as $3.25 million or as low as $1 million. Assume a 40 percent marginal tax rate.

**d.** Would it be reasonable to use the model to analyze the effects of a change in the payout ratio without changing other variables?

GET REAL WITH   **THOMSON ONE** | Business School Edition

**weighted average cost of capital**

**11-31** Compare the capital structures of the following firms and answer the related questions:

General Motors Corporation [GM], an automobile manufacturing and financing firm; Walt Disney Company [DIS], an entertainment and information company; and Amazon Inc. [AMZN], an online retail sales firm.

**a.** What is the percentage of long-term debt, common stock, retained earnings, and preferred stock in each firm's capital structure? Set up a table to illustrate your answer. (*Hint:* Click on Peers/Financial/Balance Sheet.)

**b.** Which firm has the highest, and lowest, relative amount of long-term debt? Common equity? Retained earnings?

**c.** In one paragraph, describe how you would calculate the weighted average cost of capital for each firm.

**d.** Where does each firm stand in relation to its industry peers with regard to the percentages of debt, common equity, preferred stock, and retained earnings in its capital structure? (Click on Peers and change the peer set to Industry.)

# Capital Structure

Since 1990, Unisys Corporation, a manufacturer of computers and related products for commercial and defense companies, has tried to reduce the amount of debt it uses to finance its assets. When Unisys began the debt-reduction campaign, nearly 75 percent of its total financing was in the form of various types of debt; only 25 percent was in the form of equity. Compared with other firms in its industry, Unisys felt it had much more debt than was appropriate.

One step Unisys took to change its mix of debt and equity was to suspend the payment of future common stock dividends, which allowed Unisys to save $162 million a year and to repurchase, and thus reduce, debt. Unisys was able to reduce its amount of debt substantially—in four years, the debt/assets ratio fell from nearly 75 percent to just over 60 percent. During the same period, net income increased from a loss of a little more than $500 million to a gain of $400 million.

Unfortunately, from 1995 through 1997, the company's debt again increased such that the debt/assets ratio rose above 75 percent. As a result, in September of 1997, Lawrence A. Weinbach was appointed chairman, president, and CEO. One of his first actions was to announce that Unisys would decrease debt by $1 billion by the year 2000. The debt-decreasing actions were so successful that Unisys reached its goal of a $1 billion reduction in debt approximately 18 months ahead of

schedule. Further restructuring of the company's capital from 1999 through 2001 reduced the debt/assets ratio to nearly 62 percent.

Unfortunately, both poor economic conditions in 2002 and 2003 and a pension liability that exceeded $725 million contributed to a significant increase in the relative amount of debt used by Unisys such that the debt/assets ratio increased to greater than 80 percent during this period. During the next few years, Unisys experienced poor performance, much of which was attributed to the high interest costs associated with its debt. As a result, the firm's debt/assets ratio rose to the point where the firm was financed almost entirely with debt by 2006.

Unisys continues to make capital structure changes in an attempt to improve its financial position, which will result in an improvement in shareholder wealth. So how has the stock been affected by the capital structure changes? When Unisys announced the dividend suspension, the price of its common stock dropped by more than 25 percent in one day and by about one-third of its value within one week. Trading at just under $5 per share, the value of Unisys common stock was 76 percent lower than its high value during the previous 12-month period and 90 percent lower than its high value during the previous five years. By 1994, however, Unisys stock was selling for $11 per share; in 1998 the price was nearly $26; and at the end of 1999 the price had climbed to just over $45. During this five-year period, the stock's value grew at a rate of greater than 30 percent per year. Apparently stockholders realized that the capital structure changes benefited the firm's long-run stability and wealth maximization.

Unfortunately, the combination of a poorly performing stock market that existed from 1999 through 2002 and the increase of its debt/assets ratio during this same period resulted in a significant decline in the value of Unisys's stock. In September 2002, the stock sold for less than $7 per share. Efforts by Unisys to improve its capital structure continued, and the company's stock price increased to $15 per share by the end of 2003. However, during the next few years the stock again decreased below $7 as the result of general economic uncertainty and a deteriorating financial position at Unisys. In 2006 the price remained at less than $7 per share. But the future of Unisys was considered bright because (1) analysts' forecasts of future operating profits were favorable, and (2) a new capital restructuring program was "rolled out" in an effort to rebuild the company's image in the financial markets. If investors recognize that the capital structure changes are beneficial to the future value of Unisys, the stock price should rebound.

As you can see from the Unisys example, a firm's capital structure can affect value. As you read this chapter, keep in mind the reasons Unisys wants to decrease the proportion of debt in its capital structure. Consider the effect that a particular capital structure can have on the value of a firm.

## Chapter *Essentials* —The Questions

After reading this chapter, you should be able to answer the following questions:

- What is a firm's capital structure?
- What is a firm's optimal capital structure? Can a firm have too little debt?
- How does a firm's capital structure affect its risk?
- What is leverage? How can information about a firm's leverage position be used to determine its optimal capital structure?
- Why do the capital structures of firms in different industries vary? How do the capital structures of firms vary around the world?

In Chapter 11, when we calculated the weighted average cost of capital for use in capital budgeting, we took the capital structure weights, or the mix of securities the firm uses to finance its assets, as a given. However, if the weights are changed, the calculated cost of capital, and thus the set of acceptable projects, will also change. Further, changing the capital structure will affect the riskiness inherent in the firm's common stock, and this will affect the return demanded by stockholders, $r_s$, and the stock's price, $P_0$. Therefore, the choice of a capital structure is an important decision. In this chapter, we discuss concepts relating to capital structure decisions.

## THE TARGET CAPITAL STRUCTURE

**capital structure**
The combination of debt and equity used to finance a firm.

Firms can choose whatever mix of debt and equity they desire to finance their assets, subject to the willingness of investors to provide such funds. As we shall see, many different mixes of debt and equity, or **capital structures,** exist. In some firms, such as DaimlerChrysler Group, debt accounts for more than 80 percent of the financing, while other firms, such as Microsoft, have little or no long-term debt. In the next few sections, we will discuss factors that affect a firm's capital structure, and we will conclude that a firm should attempt to determine what its optimal, or best, mix of financing should be. It will become apparent that determining the exact optimal capital structure is not a science, so after analyzing a number of factors, a firm establishes a **target capital structure** it believes is optimal that it uses as guidance for raising funds in the future. This target might change over time as conditions vary, but at any given moment the firm's management has a specific capital structure in mind, and individual

**target capital structure**
The mix of debt, preferred stock, and common equity with which the firm plans to finance its investments.

financing decisions should be consistent with this target. If the actual proportion of debt is below the target level, new funds probably will be raised by issuing debt, whereas if the proportion of debt is above the target, stock probably will be sold to bring the firm back in line with the target ratio.

Capital structure policy involves a trade-off between risk and return. Using more debt raises the riskiness of the firm's earnings stream, but a higher proportion of debt generally leads to a higher expected rate of return. From the concepts we discussed in Chapter 11, we know that the higher risk associated with greater debt tends to lower the firm's stock price. At the same time, however, the higher expected rate of return makes the stock more attractive to investors, which, in turn, ultimately increases the stock's price. Therefore, *the optimal capital structure is the one that strikes a balance between risk and return to achieve the ultimate goal of maximizing the price of the stock.*

Four primary factors influence capital structure decisions:

1. The first is the firm's *business risk,* or the riskiness that would be inherent in the firm's operations if it used no debt. The greater the firm's business risk, the lower the amount of debt that is optimal.

2. The second key factor is the firm's *tax position.* A major reason for using debt is that interest is tax deductible, which lowers the effective cost of debt. However, if much of a firm's income is already sheltered from taxes by accelerated depreciation or tax loss carryovers from previous years, its tax rate will be low, and debt will not be as advantageous as it would be to a firm with a higher effective tax rate.

3. The third important consideration is *financial flexibility,* or the ability to raise capital on reasonable terms under adverse conditions. Corporate treasurers know that a steady supply of capital is necessary for stable operations, which in turn are vital for long-run success. They also know that when money is tight in the economy, or when a firm is experiencing operating difficulties, a strong balance sheet is needed to obtain funds from suppliers of capital. Thus, it might be advantageous to issue equity to strengthen the firm's capital base and financial stability.

4. The fourth debt-determining factor has to do with *managerial attitude (conservatism or aggressiveness)* with regard to borrowing. Some managers are more aggressive than others; hence, some firms are more inclined to use debt in an effort to boost profits. This factor does not affect the optimal, or value-maximizing, capital structure, but it does influence the target capital structure a firm actually establishes.

These four points largely determine the target capital structure, but, as we shall see, operating conditions can cause the actual capital structure to vary from the target at any given time. For example, the proportion of debt that Unisys uses clearly has been much higher than its target during most of the past decade, and the company has taken some significant corrective actions to improve its financial position. (See "A Managerial Perspective" at the beginning of this chapter.)

 **Self-Test Questions**

What are the four factors that affect a firm's target capital structure?

In what sense does capital structure policy involve a trade-off between risk and return?

FIGURE 12-1    Bigbee Electronics Company: Trend in Return on Equity (ROE)*

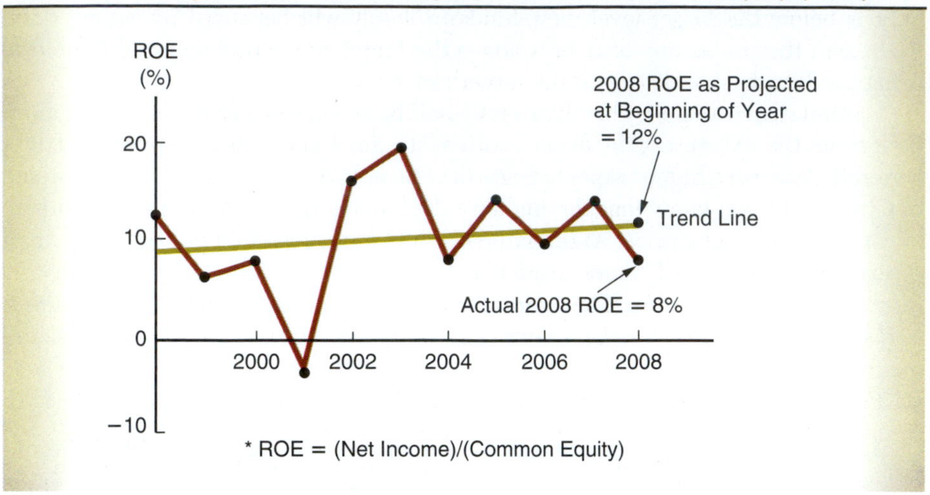

* ROE = (Net Income)/(Common Equity)

## BUSINESS AND FINANCIAL RISK

When we examined risk in Chapter 8, we distinguished between *market risk,* which is measured by the firm's beta coefficient, and *total risk,* which includes both beta risk and a type of risk that can be eliminated by diversification (*firm-specific risk*). In Chapter 10, we considered how capital budgeting decisions affect the riskiness of the firm. There again we distinguished between *beta risk* (the effect of a project on the firm's beta) and *corporate risk* (the effect of the project on the firm's total risk).

Now we introduce two new dimensions of risk:

**business risk**
The risk associated with projections of a firm's future returns on assets (ROA) or returns on equity (ROE) if the firm uses no debt.

1. **Business risk** is defined as the uncertainty inherent in projections of future returns, either on assets (ROA) or on equity (ROE), if the firm uses no debt, or debt-like financing (i.e., preferred stock)—that is, it is the risk associated with the firm's operations, ignoring any financing effects.

2. **Financial risk** is defined as the additional risk, over and above basic business risk, placed on common stockholders that results from using financing alternatives with fixed periodic payments, such as debt and preferred stock—that is, it is the risk associated with using debt or preferred stock.

**financial risk**
The portion of stock-holders' risk, over and above basic business risk, that results from the manner in which the firm is financed.

Conceptually, the firm has a certain amount of risk inherent in its production and sales operations; this is its business risk. When it uses debt, it partitions this risk and concentrates most of it on one class of investors—the common stockholders—this is its financial risk.[1] Both business risk and financial risk affect the capital structure of a firm.

## Business Risk

Business risk is the single most important determinant of capital structure. To illustrate the effects of business risk, consider Bigbee Electronics Company, a firm that currently uses 100 percent equity. Figure 12-1 shows the trend in ROE from 1998 through 2008, and it gives both security analysts and Bigbee's management an idea of the degree to which return on equity (ROE) has varied in the past and might vary in the

_____

[1]Using preferred stock also adds to financial risk. To simplify matters somewhat, in this chapter we shall consider only debt and common equity.

future. Comparing the actual results with the trend line, you can see that Bigbee's ROE has fluctuated significantly since 1998. These fluctuations in ROE were caused by many factors: booms and recessions in the national economy, successful new products introduced both by Bigbee and its competitors, labor strikes, a fire in Bigbee's major plant, and so forth. Similar events will doubtless occur in the future, and when they do, ROE will rise or fall. Further, there always is the possibility that a long-term disaster might strike, permanently depressing the company's earning power. For example, a competitor could introduce a new product that would permanently lower Bigbee's earnings.[2] This element of uncertainty about Bigbee's future ROE is the company's *basic business risk.*

Business risk varies from one industry to another and also among firms in a given industry. Further, business risk can change over time. For example, electric utilities were regarded for years as having little business risk, but a combination of events during the past couple of decades has altered their situation, producing sharp declines in ROE for some companies and greatly increasing the industry's business risk. Today, food processors and grocery retailers frequently are cited as examples of industries with low business risk, whereas cyclical manufacturing industries, such as steel and construction, are regarded as having especially high business risk. Smaller companies, especially single-product firms, also have a relatively high degree of business risk.[3]

Business risk depends on a number of factors, the more important of which include the following:

1. *Sales variability (volume and price).* The more stable the unit sales (volume) and prices of a firm's products, other things held constant, the lower its business risk.

2. *Input price variability.* A firm whose input prices—labor, product costs, and so forth—are highly uncertain is exposed to a high degree of business risk.

3. *Ability to adjust output prices for changes in input prices.* Some firms have little difficulty raising the prices of their products when input costs rise; the greater the ability to adjust selling prices, the lower the degree of business risk. This factor is especially important during periods of high inflation.

4. *The extent to which costs are fixed: operating leverage.* If a high percentage of a firm's operating costs are fixed and hence do not decline when demand falls off, this increases the company's business risk. This factor is called *operating leverage,* which will be discussed in greater detail later in the chapter.

   To illustrate the effects of operating leverage, consider the two companies shown in Table 12-1. Deesen Inc. and Westlex Corporation have identical operating sales/cost structures, and both are financed with stock only. Both companies sell their products for $50 per unit, and the variable operating costs are $30 per unit; hence, the *gross profit* for each unit sold is $20. Deesen's fixed operating costs, however, are twice those of Westlex—$80,000 versus $40,000. Table 12-1 illustrates two important concepts. First, a firm with lower fixed operating costs, or operating leverage (Westlex in this case), does not have to sell as many units to reach the same level of operating income as a firm with higher operating leverage: EBIT equals $120,000 at 8,000 units of sales for

---

[2]Two examples of "safe" industries that turned out to be risky are the railroads just before automobiles, airplanes, and trucks took away most of their business and the telegraph business just before telephones came on the scene.

[3]We have avoided any discussion of market versus company-specific risk in this section. We note now that (1) any action that increases business risk will generally increase a firm's beta coefficient, but (2) a part of business risk as we define it will generally be company specific and hence subject to elimination through diversification by the firm's stockholders.

**TABLE 12-1**  Operating Leverage Example: Deesen Inc. and Westlex Corporation

| | Deesen, Inc. | | | Westlex Corporation | | |
|---|---|---|---|---|---|---|
| | 10% Below Forecast | Forecasted Amounts | 10% Above Forecast | 10% Below Forecast | Forecasted Amounts | 10% Above Forecast |
| Sales in units | 9,000 | 10,000 | 11,000 | 7,200 | 8,000 | 8,800 |
| Sales in dollars | $450,000 | $500,000 | $550,000 | $360,000 | $400,000 | $440,000 |
| Variable operating costs | (270,000) | (300,000) | (330,000) | (216,000) | (240,000) | (264,000) |
| Gross profit | 180,000 | 200,000 | 220,000 | 144,000 | 160,000 | 176,000 |
| Fixed operating costs | ( 80,000) | ( 80,000) | ( 80,000) | ( 40,000) | ( 40,000) | ( 40,000) |
| Earnings before taxes (EBT = EBIT) | 100,000 | 120,000 | 140,000 | 104,000 | 120,000 | 136,000 |
| Taxes (40%) | ( 40,000) | ( 48,000) | ( 56,000) | ( 41,600) | ( 48,000) | ( 54,400) |
| Net income | $ 60,000 | $ 72,000 | $ 84,000 | $ 62,400 | $ 72,000 | $ 81,600 |

**Notes:** 1. Both Deesen and Westlex finance only with equity; thus there is no interest expense, and EBIT = EBT.

2. The sales price per unit equals $50, and the per unit variable cost is $30.

Westlex, but Deesen has to sell 10,000 to produce the same EBIT. Second, when actual sales are different from forecasted, the effect on earnings is greater for the firm with higher operating leverage: EBIT increases (decreases) by $20,000 when Deesen's sales are 10 percent higher (lower) than the forecasted level, whereas Westlex's EBIT increases (decreases) by only $16,000. This finding leads us to conclude that *a firm with greater operating leverage has greater business risk than a firm with lower operating leverage because its earnings will exhibit greater variability when sales vary.*

Each of these factors is determined partly by the firm's industry characteristics, but each also is controllable to some extent by management. For example, most firms can, through their marketing policies, take actions to stabilize both unit sales and sales prices. However, this stabilization might require either large expenditures on advertising or price concessions to induce customers to commit to purchasing fixed quantities at fixed prices in the future. Similarly, firms like Bigbee Electronics can reduce the volatility of future input costs by negotiating long-term labor and materials supply contracts. But they might have to agree to pay prices somewhat above the current market price to obtain these contracts.

## Financial Risk

**financial leverage**
The extent to which fixed-income securities (debt and preferred stock) are used in a firm's capital structure.

*Financial risk* results from using **financial leverage,** which exists when a firm uses fixed income securities, such as debt and preferred stock, to raise capital. When financial leverage is created, a firm intensifies the business risk borne by the common stockholders. To illustrate, suppose 10 people decide to form a corporation to produce operating systems for personal computers. There is a certain amount of business risk in the operation. If the firm is capitalized only with common equity, and if each person buys 10 percent of the stock, then each investor will bear an equal share of the business risk. However, suppose the firm is capitalized with 50 percent debt and 50 percent equity, with five of the investors putting up their capital as debt and the other five putting up their money as equity. In this case, the cash flows received by the debt holders are based on a contractual agreement, so the investors who put up the equity will have to bear essentially all of the business risk, and their position will be twice as risky as it would have been had the firm been financed only with equity. Thus, *the use of debt intensifies the firm's business risk borne by the common stockholders.*

In the next section, we will explain how financial leverage affects a firm's expected earnings per share, the riskiness of those earnings, and, consequently, the price of the firm's stock. As you will see, the value of a firm that has no debt first rises as it substitutes debt for equity, then hits a peak, and finally declines as the use of debt becomes excessive. The objective of our analysis is to determine the capital structure at which *value is maximized;* this point is then used as the target capital structure.[4]

## Self-Test Questions

What is the difference between business risk and financial risk?

Identify and briefly explain some of the more important factors that affect business risk.

Why does business risk vary from one industry to another?

What creates financial risk?

## DETERMINING THE OPTIMAL CAPITAL STRUCTURE

We can illustrate the effects of financial leverage using the data shown in Table 12-2 for a fictional company, which we will call OptiCap. As shown in the top section of the table, the company has no debt. Should it continue the policy of using no debt, or should it start using financial leverage? If it does decide to substitute debt for equity, how far should it go? As in all such decisions, the correct answer is that it should *choose the combination of debt and equity, or a capital structure, that will maximize the price of the firm's stock.*

To answer the questions posed here, we examine the effects of changing OptiCap's capital structure while keeping all other factors, such as the level of operations, constant. To keep all other factors constant, we assume that OptiCap changes its capital structure by *substituting* debt for equity—that is, as new debt is issued, the proceeds are used to repurchase an equal amount of outstanding stock.

## EPS Analysis of the Effects of Financial Leverage

If a firm changes the percentage of debt used to finance existing assets, we would expect the earnings per share (EPS) and, consequently, the stock price to change as well. Remember that debt requires fixed payments, regardless of the firm's level of sales. To understand the relationship between financial leverage and earnings per

---

[4]In this chapter, we examine capital structures on a book value (or balance sheet) basis. An alternative approach is to calculate the market values of debt, preferred stock, and common equity and then to reconstruct the balance sheet on a market value basis. Although the market value approach is more consistent with financial theory, bond rating agencies and most financial executives focus their attention on book values. Moreover, the conversion from book to market values is a complicated process, and because market value capital structures change with stock market fluctuations, they are thought by many to be too unstable to serve as operationally useful targets. Finally, exactly the same insights are gained from the book value and market value analyses. For all these reasons, a market value analysis of capital structure is better suited for advanced finance courses.

**TABLE 12-2**    Financial Information for OptiCap, 2008 ($ thousands, except per-share values)

**I.    Balance Sheet on 12/31/08**

| Current assets | $100 | Debt | $ 0 |
|---|---|---|---|
| Net fixed assets | 100 | Common equity (10,000 shares) | 200 |
| Total assets | $200 | Total liabilities and equity | $200 |

**II.    Income Statement for 2008**

| | |
|---|---|
| Sales | $200 |
| Variable operating costs (60%) | (120) |
| Fixed operating costs | ( 40) |
| Earnings before interest and taxes (EBIT) | $ 40 |
| Interest | 0 |
| Taxable income | $ 40 |
| Taxes (40%) | ( 16) |
| Net income | $ 24 |

**III.    Per-Share Information**

Earnings per share = EPS = $24,000/10,000 shares = $2.40.

Dividends per share = DPS = $24,000/10,000 shares = $2.40. Thus, OptiCap pays out all of its earnings as dividends.

Book value per share = $200,000/10,000 shares = $20.

Market price per share = $P_0$ = $20. Thus, the stock sells at its book value, so (Market price)/(Book price) = M/B = 1.0.

---

share (EPS), we first examine how earnings per share are affected when our illustrative firm changes its capital structure to include greater relative amounts of debt.

First, to simplify our example, we assume that OptiCap's level of operations—that is, production and sales—will not change if its capital structure changes.[5] Table 12-2 shows that OptiCap's level of sales was $200,000, which produced a net operating income (NOI), or earnings before interest and taxes (EBIT), equal to $40,000 in 2008. We expect that the firm's sales will remain at this level when economic conditions are "normal," but sales are expected to be $300,000 when the economy is booming and $100,000 when the economy is in a recession. The probabilities associated with each of these economic states are 0.6, 0.2, and 0.2, respectively. We give the different economic states so that we can see what happens to OptiCap's financial risk when its capital structure is changed.

OptiCap asked its investment banker to help determine what the cost of debt, $r_d$, will be at various levels of debt. The results are shown in Table 12-3. Naturally, we would expect that as a firm increases the percentage of debt it uses, lenders will

---

[5]In the real world, capital structure *does* at times affect EBIT. First, if debt levels are excessive, the firm probably will not be able to finance at all if its earnings are low at a time when interest rates are high. This could lead to stop-start construction and research and development programs, as well as to the necessity of passing up good investment opportunities. Second, a weak financial condition (i.e., too much debt) could cause a firm to lose sales. For example, prior to the time that its huge debt forced Eastern Airlines into bankruptcy, many people refused to buy Eastern tickets because they were afraid the company would go bankrupt and leave them holding unusable tickets. Third, financially strong companies can bargain hard with unions as well as with their suppliers, whereas weaker ones may have to give in simply because they do not have the financial resources to carry on the fight. Finally, a company with so much debt that bankruptcy is a serious threat will have difficulty attracting and retaining managers and employees, or it will have to pay premium salaries. For all these reasons, it is not totally correct to say that a firm's financial policy has no effect on its operating income.

**TABLE 12-3**    Cost of Debt, $r_d$, and Number of Common Shares Outstanding for OptiCap at Different Capital Structures ($ thousands)

| Total Assets | Debt/Assets Ratio | Amount Borrowed[a] | Common Stock | Shares Outstanding[b] | Cost of Debt, $r_d$ |
|---|---|---|---|---|---|
| $200 | 0% | $ 0 | $200 | 10,000 | — |
| 200 | 10 | 20 | 180 | 9,000 | 8.0% |
| 200 | 20 | 40 | 160 | 8,000 | 8.3 |
| 200 | 30 | 60 | 140 | 7,000 | 9.0 |
| 200 | 40 | 80 | 120 | 6,000 | 10.0 |
| 200 | 50 | 100 | 100 | 5,000 | 12.0 |
| 200 | 60 | 120 | 80 | 4,000 | 15.0 |

[a]We assume the firm must borrow in increments of $20 thousand. We also assume that OptiCap cannot borrow more than $120 thousand, or 60 percent of assets, because of restrictions in its corporate charter.

[b]We assume that OptiCap uses the amount of funds raised by borrowing (issuing debt) to repurchase existing common stock at the current market value, which is $20 per share; thus, we assume there are no commissions or other transaction costs associated with repurchasing the stock. For example, if OptiCap's capital structure contains 40 percent debt, then $80 thousand of the $200 thousand total assets is financed with debt. We assume that if OptiCap borrows the $80 thousand, it would repurchase 4,000 shares = $80 million/$20 of its existing shares of common stock; hence 6,000 shares = 10,000 shares − 4,000 shares remain.

perceive the debt to be riskier because the chance of financial distress is higher. As a result, lenders will charge higher interest rates to the firm as its percentage of debt increases, which is the pattern shown in the table.

We assume that OptiCap does not retain any earnings for reinvestment in the firm—that is, all earnings are paid to shareholders, which currently consist of stockholders only. In addition, we assume that the size of the firm remains at its current level. As long as the firm pays all earnings to shareholders and no additional funds are raised, growth will equal zero (g = 0), and future production and sales operations will continue as outlined previously. Thus, any changes in EPS that we observe when the proportion of debt is changed will be a direct result of changing the firm's capital structure, not its level of operations.

Table 12-4 compares OptiCap's expected EPS at two levels of financial leverage: (1) zero debt, which is the existing capital structure, and (2) 50 percent debt. If OptiCap does not change its capital structure, all $200,000 of its assets will be financed with stock, so the interest expense will be zero because no debt exists. Section II of Table 12-4 shows that EPS is expected to be $2.40 with this capital structure—EPS will be as high as $4.80 and as low as $0, but, on average, it will be $2.40. We also calculate the standard deviation of EPS and the coefficient of variation as indicators of the firm's risk with this capital structure: $\sigma_{EPS} = \$1.52$, and $CV_{EPS} = 0.63$.[6]

Section III of Table 12-4 shows the effect on EPS of shifting OptiCap's capital structure so that the mix of financing is 50 percent debt and 50 percent equity—that is, when the $200,000 of assets is financed with $100,000 debt and $100,000 equity. To accomplish this shift, OptiCap would issue $100,000 of debt and repurchase $100,000 of its existing equity. If we assume that stock can be repurchased at its current market price and transaction costs are negligible, then, using the information given in Table 12-2,

[6]See Chapter 8 for a review of procedures for calculating standard deviations and coefficients of variation. Recall that the advantage of the coefficient of variation is that it permits better comparisons when the expected values of EPS vary, as they do here for the two capital structures.

**TABLE 12-4** OptiCap: EPS at Different Capital Structures ($ thousands, except per-share values)

### I. Calculation of EBIT

| | | | |
|---|---:|---:|---:|
| Probability of indicated sales | 0.2 | 0.6 | 0.2 |
| Sales | $ 100.0 | $ 200.0 | $ 300.0 |
| Variable costs (60% of sales) | ( 60.0) | (120.0) | (180.0) |
| Fixed costs | ( 40.0) | ( 40.0) | ( 40.0) |
| Total costs (except interest) | $(100.0) | $(160.0) | $(220.0) |
| Earnings before interest and taxes (EBIT) | $ 0.0 | $ 40.0 | $ 80.0 |

### II. Situation If Debt/Assets (D/A) = 0%

| | | | |
|---|---:|---:|---:|
| EBIT (from Section I) | $ 0.0 | $ 40.0 | $ 80.0 |
| Less interest | ( 0.0) | ( 0.0) | ( 0.0) |
| Earnings before taxes (EBT) | $ 0.0 | $ 40.0 | $ 80.0 |
| Taxes (40%) | ( 0.0) | ( 16.0) | ( 32.0) |
| Net income | $ 0.0 | $ 24.0 | $ 48.0 |
| Earnings per share (EPS) on 10,000 shares[a] | $ 0.0 | $ 2.40 | $ 4.80 |
| Expected EPS | | $ 2.40 | |
| Standard deviation of EPS | | $ 1.52 | |
| Coefficient of variation | | 0.63 | |

### III. Situation If Debt/Assets (D/A) = 50%

| | | | |
|---|---:|---:|---:|
| EBIT (from Section I) | $ 0.0 | $ 40.0 | $ 80.0 |
| Less interest (0.12 × $100) | ( 12.0) | ( 12.0) | ( 12.0) |
| Earnings before taxes (EBT) | $( 12.0) | $ 28.0 | $ 68.0 |
| Taxes (40%; tax credit on losses) | 4.8 | ( 11.2) | ( 27.2) |
| Net income | $( 7.2) | $ 16.8 | $ 40.8 |
| Earnings per share (EPS) on 5,000 shares[a] | $( 1.44) | $ 3.36 | $ 8.16 |
| Expected EPS | | $ 3.36 | |
| Standard deviation of EPS | | $ 3.04 | |
| Coefficient of variation | | 0.90 | |

[a]The EPS figures can be obtained using the following formula, in which the numerator amounts to an income statement at a given sales level laid out horizontally:

$$EPS = \frac{(\text{Sales} - \text{Fixed costs} - \text{Variable costs} - \text{Interest})(1 - \text{Tax rate})}{\text{Shares outstanding}} = \frac{(\text{EBIT} - I)(1 - T)}{\text{Shares outstanding}}$$

For example, with zero debt and Sales = $200,000, EPS is $2.40:

$$EPS_{D/A=0} = \frac{(\$200,000 - \$40,000 - \$120,000 - 0)(0.6)}{10,000} = \$2.40$$

we find that OptiCap can repurchase 5,000 shares = $100,000/$20 per share.[7] Thus, the number of shares outstanding will decrease from 10,000 to 5,000. At the same time, because the firm now has debt, it will have to pay interest, which, according to the schedule given in Table 12-3, will equal $12,000 = $100,000 × 0.12 per year. The

---

[7]We assume in this example that the firm could change its capital structure by repurchasing common stock at the current market value, which is $20 per share. However, if the firm attempts to purchase a large block of its stock, demand pressures might cause the market price to increase, in which case OptiCap would not be able to purchase 5,000 shares with the $100,000 that was raised with its debt issue. Also, we assume the flotation costs associated with the debt issue are negligible so that OptiCap is able to use all $100,000 to repurchase stock. Clearly, the existence of flotation costs would mean OptiCap would have some amount less than $100,000 to repurchase stock. Neither of these assumptions affects the overall concept we are trying to provide through illustration—only the numbers change.

$12,000 interest expense is a fixed cost—it is the same regardless of the level of sales. With a debt/assets ratio of 50 percent, the expected EPS is $3.36, which is $0.96 higher than if the firm uses no debt. The EPS range is also greater; EPS can be as low as −$1.44 when the economy is poor or as high as $8.16 when the economy is booming. Thus, EPS has greater variability when the capital structure is 50 percent debt and 50 percent equity, which suggests that this capital structure is riskier than the capital structure of 100 percent equity financing. The standard deviation of EPS and the coefficient of variation computed for the capital structure with 50 percent debt are $\sigma_{EPS} = \$3.04$ and $CV_{EPS} = 0.90$. As you can see, these computations support our suspicion that this capital structure is riskier than the capital structure shown in Section II of Table 12-4.

Figure 12-2 shows the relationships among expected EPS, risk, and financial leverage for OptiCap for the all-equity capital structure and the various capital structures given in Table 12-3. The tabular data in the lower section were calculated in the manner set forth in Table 12-4, and the graph plots these data. Here we see that expected EPS rises until the firm is financed with 50 percent debt. Interest charges rise, but this effect is more than offset by the declining number of shares outstanding as debt is substituted for equity. EPS peaks at a debt/assets ratio of 50 percent. Beyond this amount, interest rates rise so rapidly that EPS declines despite the smaller number of shares outstanding.

The right panel of Figure 12-2 shows that risk, as measured by the coefficient of variation of EPS, rises continuously and at an increasing rate as debt is substituted for equity.

We see, then, that using leverage has both good and bad effects. Higher leverage increases expected earnings per share (in this example, until the firm is financed with 50 percent debt), but it also increases the firm's risk. Clearly, for OptiCap, the debt/assets ratio should not exceed 50 percent. But where in the range of 0 to 50 percent is the best debt/assets ratio for OptiCap? This issue is discussed in the following sections.

## EBIT/EPS Examination of Financial Leverage

In the previous section, we assumed that OptiCap's EBIT had to be one of three possible values: $0, $40,000, or $80,000. Another way of evaluating alternative financing methods is to plot the EPS of each capital structure at many different levels of EBIT. Figure 12-3 shows such a graph for the two capital structures we considered for OptiCap in Table 12-4—that is, (1) 100 percent stock and (2) 50 percent stock and 50 percent debt. Notice that at low levels of EBIT, and hence low levels of sales, EPS is higher if OptiCap's capital structure includes only stock; at high levels of EBIT, however, EPS is higher with the capital structure that includes debt. Notice also that the "debt" line has a steeper slope, showing that earnings per share will increase more rapidly with increases in EBIT, and hence sales, if the firm uses debt. This relationship exists because the firm has a greater degree of financial leverage with the capital structure that includes 50 percent debt. In this case, the benefits of additional sales need not be shared with debt holders because debt payments are fixed; instead, any profits that remain after debt holders are paid "belong" to stockholders.

The point on the graph where the two lines intersect is called the **EPS indifference point,** which is the level of sales at which EPS is the same no matter which capital structure OptiCap uses. In Figure 12-3, the two lines cross when sales equal $160,000, which corresponds to EBIT equal to $24,000. If sales are below $160,000, EPS would be higher if the firm uses only common stock; above this level, the debt financing alternative would produce higher earnings per share.

If we were certain that sales would never again fall below $160,000, bonds would be the preferred method of financing any increases in assets. We cannot know this for certain, however. In fact, investors know that in a number of previous years, sales have

**EPS indifference point**
The level of sales at which EPS will be the same whether the firm uses debt or common stock financing.

**FIGURE 12-2** OptiCap Relationships among Expected EPS, Risk, and Financial Leverage

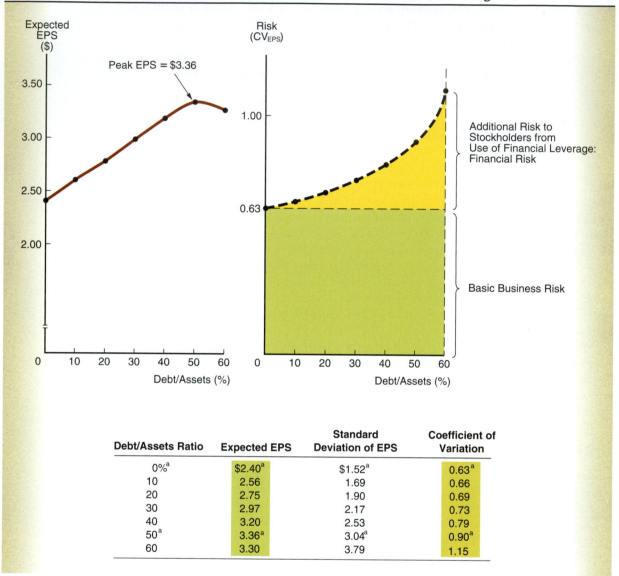

| Debt/Assets Ratio | Expected EPS | Standard Deviation of EPS | Coefficient of Variation |
|---|---|---|---|
| 0%[a] | $2.40[a] | $1.52[a] | 0.63[a] |
| 10 | 2.56 | 1.69 | 0.66 |
| 20 | 2.75 | 1.90 | 0.69 |
| 30 | 2.97 | 2.17 | 0.73 |
| 40 | 3.20 | 2.53 | 0.79 |
| 50[a] | 3.36[a] | 3.04[a] | 0.90[a] |
| 60 | 3.30 | 3.79 | 1.15 |

[a]Values for D/A = 0 and D/A = 50 percent are taken from Table 9-4. Values at other D/A ratios were calculated similarly.

fallen below this critical level, and if any of several detrimental events should occur in the future, sales again would fall below $160,000. On the other hand, if sales continue to expand, higher earnings per share would result from the use of bonds, and this is an advantage that no investor would want to forgo.

## The Effect of Capital Structure on Stock Prices and the Cost of Capital

As we saw in Figure 12-2, OptiCap's expected EPS is maximized at a debt/assets ratio of 50 percent. Does this mean that OptiCap's optimal capital structure calls for 50 percent debt? The answer is a resounding no. *The optimal capital structure is the one that maximizes the price of the firm's stock, and this always calls for a debt/assets ratio that is lower than the one that maximizes expected EPS.* As we shall discover

**FIGURE 12-3**    Earnings per Share of Stock and Debt Financing for OptiCap

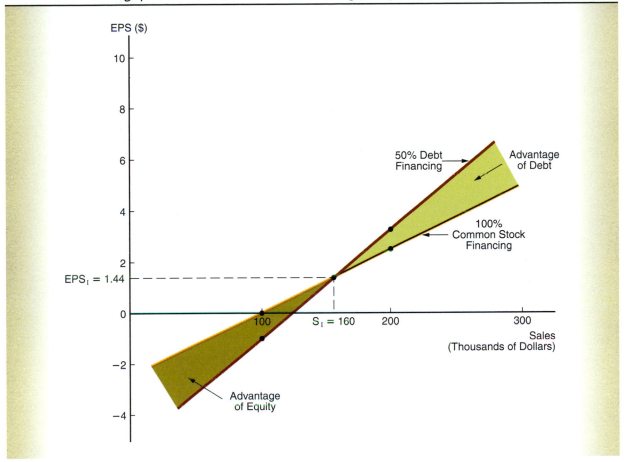

We can develop an equation to find the sales level at which EPS is the same under different degrees of financial leverage:

$$EPS_1 = \frac{S_I - F - VC - I_1}{Shares_1} = \frac{S_I - F - VC - I_2}{Shares_2} = EPS_2$$

Here, $EPS_1$ and $EPS_2$ are the EPSs at two debt levels; $S_I$ is the sales indifference level at which $EPS_1 = EPS_2 = EPS_I$; $I_1$ and $I_2$ are interest charges at the two debt levels; $Shares_1$ and $Shares_2$ are shares outstanding at the two debt levels; F is the fixed costs; and VC = variable costs = Sales $\times$ v, where v is the variable cost percentage. Solving for $S_I$, we obtain this expression:

$$S_I = \left[ \frac{(Shares_2)(I_1) - (Shares_1)(I_2)}{Shares_2 - Shares_1} + F \right] \left( \frac{1}{1 - v} \right)$$

In our example,

$$S_I = \left[ \frac{(5,000)(0) - (10,000)(\$12,000)}{-5,000} + \$40,000 \right] \left( \frac{1}{0.4} \right) = \$160,000$$

shortly, the primary reason this relationship exists is because $P_0$ reflects changes in risk that accompany changes in capital structures and affect cash flows long into the future, whereas EPS generally measures only the expectations for the near term. That is, current EPS generally does not capture future risk, whereas $P_0$ should be indicative of all future expectations. Our analysis to this point has, therefore, indicated that OptiCap's optimal capital structure should contain something less than 50 percent debt. The validity of this statement is demonstrated in Table 12-5, which develops OptiCap's estimated stock price and weighted average cost of capital at different debt/assets ratios. The debt cost and EPS data in columns 2 and 3 were taken from Table 12-3 and Figure 12-2. The beta coefficients shown in column 4

**TABLE 12-5**   Stock Price and Cost of Capital Estimates for OptiCap with Different Debt/Assets Ratios

| Debt/ Assets (1) | $r_d$ (2) | Expected EPS (And DPS)[a] (3) | Estimated Beta (β) (4) | $r_s = [r_{RF} + (r_M − r_{RF})β_s]$[b] (5) | Estimated Price[c] (6) | Weighted Average Cost of Capital, WACC[d] (7) |
|---|---|---|---|---|---|---|
| 0% | — | $2.40 | 1.60 | 12.0% | $20.00 | 12.00% |
| 10 | 8.0% | 2.56 | 1.70 | 12.5 | 20.48 | 11.73 |
| 20 | 8.3 | 2.75 | 1.80 | 13.0 | 21.15 | 11.40 |
| 30 | 9.0 | 2.97 | 2.00 | 14.0 | 21.21 | 11.42 |
| 40 | 10.0 | 3.20 | 2.10 | 14.5 | 22.07 | 11.10 |
| 50 | 12.0 | 3.36 | 2.30 | 15.5 | 21.68 | 11.35 |
| 60 | 15.0 | 3.30 | 2.60 | 17.0 | 19.41 | 12.20 |

**Notes:** [a]OptiCap pays all of its earnings out as dividends, so EPS = DPS.

[b]We assume that $r_{RF} = 4\%$ and $r_M = 9\%$. Therefore, at debt/assets equal to zero, $r_s = 4\% + (9\% − 4\%)1.6 = 4\% + 8\% = 12\%$. Other values of $r_s$ are calculated similarly.

[c]Because all earnings are paid out as dividends, no retained earnings will be plowed back into the business, and growth in EPS and DPS will be zero. Hence, the zero growth stock price model developed in Chapter 7 can be used to estimate the price of OptiCap's stock. For example, at debt/assets = 0,

$$\hat{P}_0 = \frac{\hat{D}_1}{r_s} = \frac{\$2.40}{0.12} = \$20$$

Other prices were calculated similarly.

[d]Column 7 is found by use of the weighted average cost of capital (WACC) equation developed in Chapter 11:

$$WACC = w_d r_d (1 − T) + w_s r_s$$
$$= (D/A)(r_{dT}) + (1 − D/A)r_s$$

For example, at D/A = 40%,

$$WACC = 0.4[(10\%)(0.06)] + 0.06(14.5\%) = 11.10\%$$

were estimated. Recall from Chapter 8 that a stock's beta measures its relative volatility compared with the volatility of an average stock. It has been demonstrated both theoretically and empirically that a firm's beta increases with its degree of financial leverage. The exact nature of this relationship for a given firm is difficult to estimate, but the values given in column 4 do show the approximate nature of the relationship for OptiCap.

If we assume that the risk-free rate of return, $r_{RF}$, is 4 percent and that the required return on an average stock, $r_M$, is 9 percent, we can use the CAPM equation to develop estimates of the required rates of return, $r_s$, for OptiCap as shown in column 5. Here we see that $r_s$ is 12 percent if no financial leverage is used, but $r_s$ rises to 17 percent if the company finances with 60 percent debt, the maximum permitted by its corporate charter.

Figure 12-4 graphs OptiCap's required rate of return on equity at different debt levels. The figure also shows the composition of OptiCap's required return: the risk-free rate of 4 percent and the premiums for both business and financial risk, which were discussed earlier in this chapter. As you can see from the graph, the business risk premium does not depend on the debt level. Instead, it remains constant at 8 percent, which is the difference between the 12 percent WACC when the firm is financed with 100 percent equity and the risk-free rate of 4 percent (8% = 12% – 4%), at all debt levels. However, the financial risk premium varies depending on the debt level—the higher the debt level, the greater the premium for financial risk.

The zero growth stock valuation model developed in Chapter 7 is used in Table 12-5 along with the column 3 values of dividends per share (DPS) and the column 5 values of

**FIGURE 12-4**   OptiCap's Required Rate of Return on Equity at Different Debt Levels

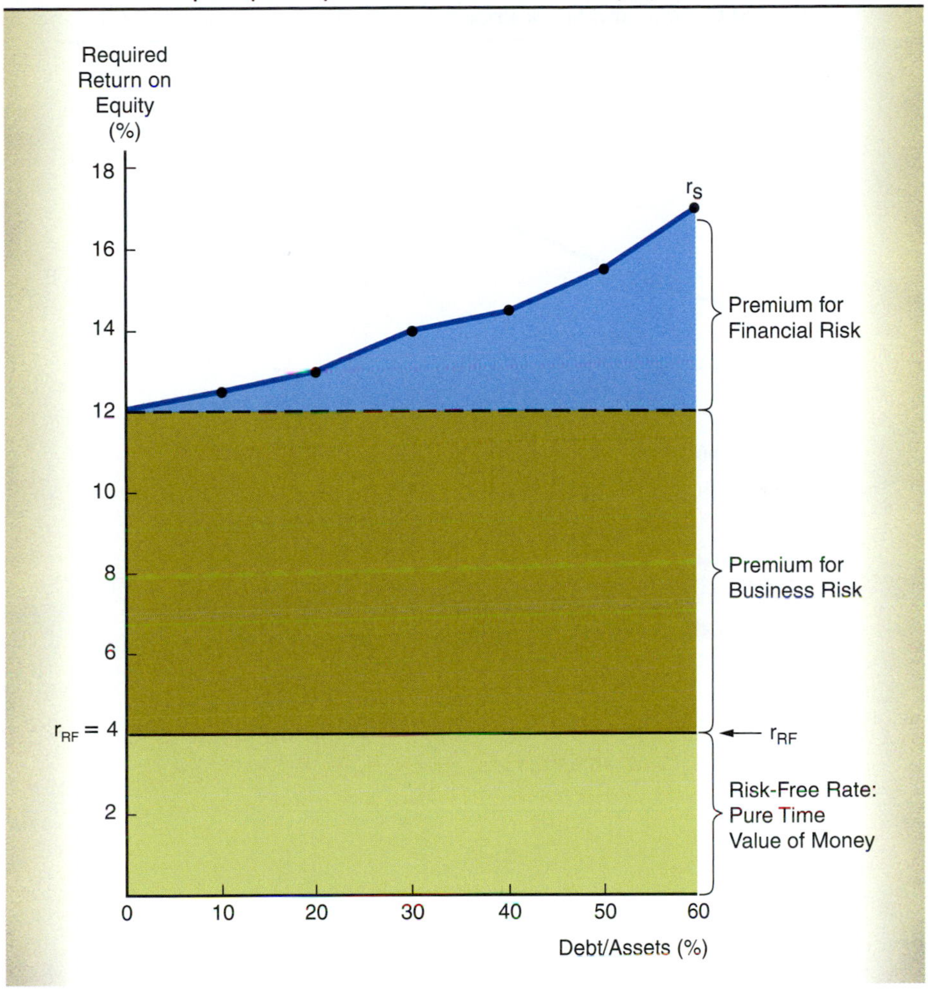

$r_s$, to develop the estimated stock prices shown in column 6. Here we see that the expected stock price first rises with financial leverage, hits a peak of $22.07 at a debt/assets ratio of 40 percent, and then begins to decline. *Thus, OptiCap's optimal capital structure calls for 40 percent debt.*

Finally, column 7 shows OptiCap's weighted average cost of capital (WACC), calculated as described in Chapter 11, at the different capital structures. If the company uses zero debt, its capital is all equity, so WACC = $r_s$ = 12%. As the firm begins to use lower-cost debt, its weighted average cost of capital declines. However, as the debt/assets ratio increases, the costs of both debt and equity rise, and the increasing costs of the two components begin to offset the fact that larger amounts of the lower-cost component are being used. At 40 percent debt, WACC hits a minimum at 11.10 percent, then it begins rising as the debt/assets ratio is increased.

The EPS, cost of capital, and stock price data shown in Table 12-5 are plotted in Figure 12-5. As the graph shows, the debt/assets ratio that maximizes OptiCap's expected EPS is 50 percent. However, the expected stock price is maximized, and the cost of capital is minimized, at a 40 percent debt/assets ratio. Thus, *the optimal capital structure calls for 40 percent debt and 60 percent equity. Management should set its target capital structure at these ratios, and if the existing ratios are off target, it should move toward the target when new security offerings are made.*

FIGURE 12-5    Relationship between OptiCap's Capital Structure and Its EPS, Cost of Capital, and Stock Price

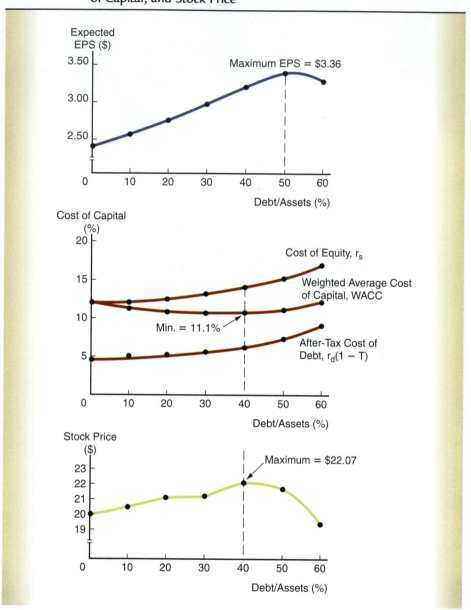

## Self-Test Questions

Explain the following statement: "Using leverage has both good and bad effects." What does the EPS indifference point show? What occurs at sales below this point? What occurs at sales above this point?

Is the optimal capital structure the one that maximizes expected EPS? Explain.

Explain the following statement: "At the optimal capital structure, a firm has minimized its cost of capital." Do stockholders want the firm to minimize its cost of capital?

# DEGREE OF LEVERAGE[8]

Leverage is created when a firm has *fixed costs* associated either with its sales and production operations or with the types of financing it uses. These two types of leverage, called operating leverage and financial leverage, are interrelated. Therefore, if OptiCap *reduced* its operating leverage, this probably would lead to an *increase* in its optimal use of financial leverage. On the other hand, if the firm decided to *increase* its operating leverage, its optimal capital structure probably would call for *less* debt.

The theory of finance has not been developed to the point where we can actually specify simultaneously the optimal levels of operating and financial leverage. However, we can see how operating and financial leverage interact through an analysis of the *degree of leverage concept*.

## Degree of Operating Leverage (DOL)

The **degree of operating leverage (DOL)** is defined as the percentage change in operating income—that is, earnings before interest and taxes, or EBIT—associated with a given percentage change in sales. Thus, the degree of operating leverage is computed as

**degree of operating leverage (DOL)**
The percentage change in operating income (EBIT) associated with a given percentage change in sales.

$$\text{DOL} = \frac{\text{Degree of}}{\text{operating leverage}} = \frac{\%\text{ change in NOI}}{\%\text{ change in sales}} = \frac{\left(\frac{\Delta\text{EBIT}}{\text{EBIT}}\right)}{\left(\frac{\Delta\text{Sales}}{\text{Sales}}\right)} = \frac{\left(\frac{\Delta\text{EBIT}}{\text{EBIT}}\right)}{\left(\frac{\Delta Q}{Q}\right)}$$

**12–1**

According to Equation 12–1, the DOL is an index number that measures the effect of a change in sales on operating income, or EBIT.

DOL for a specific level of production and sales can be computed using the following equation:

$$\text{DOL} = \frac{Q(P-V)}{Q(P-V)-F} = \frac{S-VC}{S-VC-F} = \frac{\text{Gross profit}}{\text{EBIT}}$$

**12–2**

Here, Q is the initial units of output, P is the average sales price per unit of output, V is the variable cost per unit, F is fixed operating costs, S is initial sales in dollars, and VC is total variable costs.

Applying Equation 12-2 to data for OptiCap at a sales level of $200,000 as shown in Table 12-4, we find its degree of operating leverage to be 2.0:

$$\text{DOL}_{\$200,000} = \frac{\$200,000 - \$120,000}{\$200,000 - \$120,000 - \$40,000} = \frac{\$80,000}{\$40,000} = 2.0 \text{ times}$$

Thus, for every 1 percent change (increase or decrease) in sales there will be a 2 percent change (increase or decrease) in EBIT. This situation is confirmed by examining Section I of Table 12-4, where we see that a 50 percent increase in sales,

---

[8]A more detailed discussion of leverage is presented in Chapter 17, and the derivations of the equations contained in this section are included in the footnotes in that chapter.

from \$200,000 to \$300,000, causes EBIT to double. Note, however, that if sales decrease by 50 percent, then EBIT will decrease by 100 percent; according to Table 12-4, EBIT decreases to \$0 if sales decrease to \$100,000.

Note also that the DOL is specific to the initial sales level; thus, if we evaluated OptiCap from a sales base of \$300,000, there would be a different DOL:

$$\text{DOL}_{\$300,000} = \frac{\$300,000 - \$180,000}{\$300,000 - \$180,000 - \$40,000} = \frac{\$120,000}{\$80,000} = 1.5 \text{ times}$$

In general, if a firm is operating at close to its breakeven level, the degree of operating leverage will be high, but DOL declines the higher the base level of sales is above breakeven sales. All else equal, *a lower (higher) DOL suggests that lower (higher) risk is associated with the firm's normal operating activities.*

## Degree of Financial Leverage (DFL)

**degree of financial leverage (DFL)**
The percentage change in earnings per share (EPS) associated with a given percentage change in earnings before interest and taxes.

Operating leverage affects earnings before interest and taxes (EBIT), whereas financial leverage affects earnings after interest and taxes, or the earnings available to common stockholders. In terms of Table 12-4, operating leverage affects the top section (Section I), whereas financial leverage affects the lower section (Section II or Section III). *Financial leverage takes over where operating leverage leaves off, further magnifying the effects on earnings per share of changes in the level of sales.*

The **degree of financial leverage (DFL)** is defined as the percentage change in earnings per share (EPS) that results from a given percentage change in earnings before interest and taxes (EBIT), and it is calculated as follows:[9]

**12–3**

$$\text{DFL} = \frac{\text{Degree of}}{\text{financial leverage}} = \frac{\% \text{ change in EPS}}{\% \text{ change in EBIT}} = \frac{\left(\frac{\Delta \text{EPS}}{\text{EPS}}\right)}{\left(\frac{\Delta \text{EBIT}}{\text{EBIT}}\right)} = \frac{\text{EBIT}}{\text{EBIT} - \text{I}}$$

At sales of \$200,000 and an EBIT of \$40,000, the degree of financial leverage when OptiCap has a 50 percent debt/assets ratio (Section III in Table 12-4) is

$$\text{DFL}_{\$200,000, \text{ Debt/TA}=50\%} = \frac{\$40,000}{\$40,000 - \$12,000} = \frac{\$40,000}{\$28,000} = 1.43 \text{ times}$$

Therefore, a 100 percent change (increase or decrease) in EBIT would result in a $100(1.43) = 143$ percent change (increase or decrease) in earnings per share. This can be confirmed by referring to Section III of Table 12-4. where we see that a 100 percent increase in EBIT, from \$40,000 to \$80,000, produces a 143 percent increase in EPS:

$$\% \Delta \text{EPS} = \frac{\Delta \text{EPS}}{\text{EPS}_0} = \frac{\$8.16 - \$3.36}{\$3.36} = \frac{\$4.80}{\$3.36} = 1.43 = 143\%$$

If no debt were used, the degree of financial leverage would by definition be 1.0, so a 100 percent increase in EBIT would produce exactly a 100 percent increase in EPS. This can be confirmed from the data in Section II of Table 12-4, All else equal, *a lower*

[9]This equation applies only if the firm has no preferred stock. See Chapter 17 for the equation that is appropriate when preferred stock exists.

*(higher) DFL suggests that lower (higher) risk is associated with the firm's financing— that is, its mix of debt and equity.*

## Degree of Total Leverage (DTL)

We have seen that (1) the greater the degree of operating leverage (fixed operating costs), the more sensitive EBIT will be to changes in sales and (2) the greater the degree of financial leverage (fixed financial costs), the more sensitive EPS will be to changes in EBIT. Therefore, if a firm uses a considerable amount of both operating and financial leverage, then even small changes in sales will lead to wide fluctuations in EPS.

Equation 12–2 for the degree of operating leverage can be combined with Equation 12–3 for the degree of financial leverage to produce the equation for the **degree of total leverage (DTL)**, which shows how a given change in sales will affect earnings per share. Here are equivalent equations for computing DTL:

> **degree of total leverage (DTL)**
> The percentage change in EPS that results from a given percentage change in sales; DTL shows the effects of both operating leverage and financial leverage.

**12–4**

$$DTL = \frac{\text{Degree of}}{\text{total leverage}} = \frac{\% \text{ change in sales}}{\% \text{ change in EPS}} = DOL \times DFL$$

$$= \frac{Q(P - V)}{Q(P - V) - F - I} = \frac{S - VC}{S - VC - F - I} = \frac{\text{Gross profit}}{\text{EBIT} - I}$$

For OptiCap at sales of $200,000, we can substitute data from Table 12-4 into Equation 12–4 to find the degree of total leverage if the debt ratio is 50 percent:

$$DFL_{\$200,000, \text{Debt/TA}=50\%} = \frac{\$200,000 - \$120,000}{\$200,000 - \$120,000 - \$40,000 - \$12,000}$$

$$= \frac{\$80,000}{\$28,000} = 2.00 \times 1.43 = 2.86 \text{ times}$$

We can use the degree of total leverage (DTL) to find the new earnings per share ($EPS_1$) for any given percentage increase in sales, proceeding as follows:

**12–5**

$$EPS_1 = EPS_0 + EPS_0(DTL \times \%\Delta Sales)$$

$$= EPS_0[1 + (DTL \times \%\Delta Sales)]$$

For example, a 50 percent increase in sales, from $200,000 to $300,000, would cause $EPS_0$ ($3.36 as shown in Section III of Table 12-4) to increase to $8.16:

$$EPS_1 = \$3.36[1.0 + (2.86)(0.5)] = \$3.36(2.43) = \$8.16$$

This figure agrees with the one for EPS shown in Table 12-4. All else equal, *a lower (higher) DTL suggests that lower (higher) risk is associated with the firm*, both its business risk and financial risk, which in combination represents total risk.

The degree of leverage concept is useful primarily for the insights it provides regarding the joint effects of operating and financial leverage on earnings per share. The concept can be used to show management the effect of financing the firm with debt versus common stock. For example, management might find that the current capital structure is such that a 10 percent decline in sales would produce a 50 percent decline in earnings, whereas with a different financing package, thus a different degree of total leverage, a 10 percent sales decline would cause earnings to decline by perhaps only 20 percent. Having the alternatives stated in this manner gives decision makers a better idea of the ramifications of alternative financing plans, hence different capital structures.[10]

### Self-Test Questions

Give the formula for calculating the degree of operating leverage (DOL), and explain what DOL is.

Why is the DOL different at various sales levels?

Give the formula for calculating the degree of financial leverage (DFL), and explain what this calculation means.

Give the formula for calculating the degree of total leverage (DTL), and explain what DTL is.

Why is the degree of leverage concept useful when making capital structure decisions?

Mayer Manufacturing reported that its gross profit was $144,000 on sales equal to $200,000, its net operating income was $80,000, its interest expense was $40,000, and its net income was $24,000. What is Mayer's degree of operating leverage (DOL), degree of financial leverage (DFL), and degree of total leverage (DTL)? (*Answer:* DOL = 1.8, DFL = 2.0, DTL = 3.6)

## LIQUIDITY AND CAPITAL STRUCTURE

Some practical difficulties are associated with the type of analysis described in the previous section, including the following:

1. It is difficult to determine exactly how either P/E ratios or equity capitalization rates ($r_s$ values) are affected by different degrees of financial leverage.

2. The managers might be more or less conservative than the average stockholder, so management might set a somewhat different target capital structure than the one that would maximize the stock price. The managers of a publicly owned firm never would admit this because, unless they owned voting control, they would be removed from office very quickly. However, in view of the uncertainties about what constitutes the value-maximizing capital structure, management could always say that the target capital structure employed is, in its judgment, the value-maximizing structure, and it would be difficult to prove otherwise. Still, if management is far off target, especially on the low side, then chances are very high that some other firm or management group will take over the company, increase its leverage, and thereby raise its value.

---

[10]The degree of leverage concept is also useful for investors. If firms in an industry are classified as to their degrees of total leverage, an investor who is optimistic about prospects for the industry might favor those firms with high leverage and vice versa if industry sales are expected to decline. However, it is very difficult to separate fixed from variable costs. Accounting statements generally do not contain this breakdown, so the analyst must make the separation in a judgmental manner. Note that costs really are fixed, variable, and "semivariable," for if times get tough enough, firms will sell off depreciable assets and thus reduce depreciation charges (a fixed cost), lay off "permanent" employees, reduce salaries of the remaining personnel, and so on. For this reason, the degree of leverage concept generally is more useful in explaining the general nature of the relationship than in developing precise numbers, and any numbers developed should be thought of as approximations rather than as exact specifications.

**FIGURE 12-6**    **OptiCap: Probability Distributions of Times-Interest-Earned Ratios with Different Capital Structures**

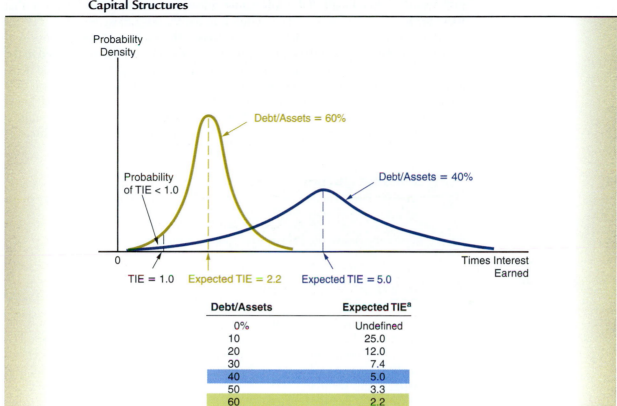

| Debt/Assets | Expected TIE[a] |
|:---:|:---:|
| 0% | Undefined |
| 10 | 25.0 |
| 20 | 12.0 |
| 30 | 7.4 |
| 40 | 5.0 |
| 50 | 3.3 |
| 60 | 2.2 |

[a]TIE = EBIT/Interest. For example, when debt/assets = 50%, TIE = $40,000/$12,000 = 3.3. Data are from Tables 12-2 and 12-3.

**3.** Managers of large firms, especially those that provide vital services such as electricity or telephones, have a responsibility to provide continuous service. Therefore, these firms must refrain from using leverage to the point where long-run survival is endangered. In such instances, long-run viability might conflict with short-run stock price maximization and capital cost minimization.[11]

For all these reasons, managers are concerned about the effects of financial leverage on the risk of bankruptcy, and an analysis of this factor is therefore an important input in all capital structure decisions. Accordingly, managers give considerable weight to financial strength indicators such as the **times-interest-earned (TIE) ratio,** which is computed by dividing earnings before interest and taxes by interest expense. The TIE ratio provides an indication of how well the firm can cover its interest payments with operating income (EBIT)—the lower this ratio, the higher the probability that a firm will default on its debt and be forced into bankruptcy.

The tabular material in the lower section of Figure 12-6 shows OptiCap's expected TIE ratio at several different debt/assets ratios. If the debt/assets ratio was only

**times-interest-earned (TIE) ratio**
A ratio that measures the firm's ability to meet its annual interest obligations; calculated by dividing earnings before interest and taxes by interest charges.

---

[11]Recognizing this fact, most public service commissions require utilities to obtain the commission's approval before issuing long-term securities, and Congress has empowered the SEC to supervise the capital structures of public utility holding companies. However, in addition to concern over the firms' safety, which suggests low debt ratios, both managers and regulators recognize a need to keep all costs as low as possible, including the cost of capital. Because a firm's capital structure affects its cost of capital, regulatory commissions and utility managers try to select capital structures that will minimize the cost of capital, subject to the constraint that the firm's financial flexibility not be endangered.

10 percent, the expected TIE would be very high at 25 times, but the interest coverage ratio would decline rapidly if the debt/assets ratio was increased. Note, however, that these coverages are expected values at different debt/assets ratios; the actual TIE for any debt/assets ratio will be higher if sales exceed the expected $200,000 level but lower if sales fall below $200,000. The variability of the TIE ratio is highlighted in the graph in Figure 12-6, which shows the probability distributions of the TIEs at debt/assets ratios of 40 percent and 60 percent. The expected TIE is much higher if only 40 percent debt is used. In general, we know that with less debt, there is a much lower probability of a TIE of less than 1.0, the level at which the firm is not earning enough to meet its required interest payment and thus is seriously exposed to the threat of bankruptcy.[12]

**Self-Test Questions**

Why do managers give considerable weight to the TIE ratio when they make capital structure decisions?

Why not just use the capital structure that maximizes the stock price?

## CAPITAL STRUCTURE THEORY

Over the years, researchers have proposed numerous theories to explain what firms' capital structures should be and why firms have different capital structures. The general theories of capital structure have been developed along two main lines: (1) tax benefit/bankruptcy cost trade-off theory and (2) signaling theory. These two theories are discussed in this section.

### Trade-Off Theory

Modern capital structure theory began in 1958, when Professors Franco Modigliani and Merton Miller (hereafter MM) published what is considered by many to be the most influential finance article ever written.[13] MM proved—under a very restrictive set of assumptions, including that there exist no personal income taxes, no brokerage costs, and no bankruptcy—that due to the tax deductibility of interest on corporate debt, a firm's value rises continuously as more debt is used, and hence its value will be maximized by financing almost entirely with debt.

Because several of the assumptions outlined by MM obviously were, and are, unrealistic, MM's position was only the beginning of capital structure research. Subsequent researchers, and MM themselves, extended the basic theory by relaxing the assumptions. Other researchers attempted to test the various theoretical models with actual data to see exactly how stock prices and capital costs are affected by capital structure. Both the theoretical and the empirical results have added to our understanding of capital structure, but none of these studies has produced results that can be used to precisely identify a firm's optimal capital structure. A summary of the

---

[12]Note that cash flows can be sufficient to cover required interest payments even though the TIE is less than 1.0. Thus, at least for a while, a firm might be able to avoid bankruptcy even though its *operating income* is less than its interest charges. However, most debt contracts stipulate that firms must maintain the TIE ratio above some minimum level, say, 2.0 or 2.5, or else they cannot borrow any additional funds, which can severely constrain operations. Such potential constraints, as much as the threat of actual bankruptcy, limit the use of debt.

[13]Franco Modigliani and Merton H. Miller, "The Cost of Capital, Corporation Finance, and the Theory of Investment," *American Economic Review,* June 1958, 261–297, and "Corporate Income Taxes and the Cost of Capital," *American Economic Review,* June 1963, 433–443. Modigliani and Miller both won Nobel Prizes for their work.

FIGURE 12-7    Effect of Leverage on the Value of OptiCap's Stock

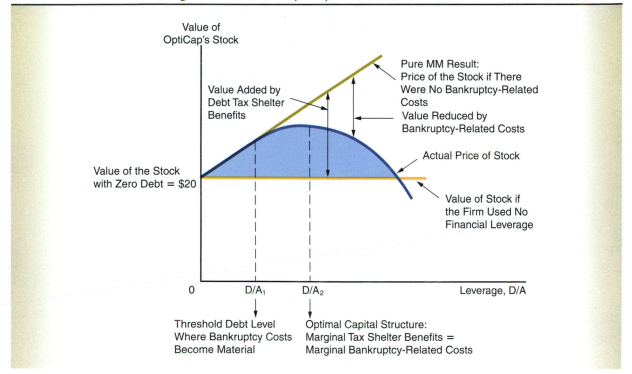

theoretical and empirical research to date is expressed graphically in Figure 12-7. Here are the key points in the figure:

1.  The fact that interest is a tax-deductible expense makes corporate debt less expensive than common or preferred stock. In effect, the government pays, or subsidizes, part of the cost of debt capital; thus, using debt causes more of the firm's operating income (EBIT) to flow through to investors. So the more debt a company uses, the higher its value. Under the assumptions of the original MM paper, their analysis led to the conclusion that the firm's stock price will be maximized if it uses virtually 100 percent debt, and the line labeled "Pure MM Result" in Figure 12-7 expresses their relationship between stock prices and debt.

2.  The MM assumptions do not hold in the real world. First, a firm pays higher interest rates as it uses greater amounts of debt. Second, expected tax rates fall at high debt levels, and this also reduces the expected value of the debt tax shelter. And third, the probability of bankruptcy, which brings with it lawyers' fees and other costs, increases as the debt/assets ratio increases.

3.  There is some threshold level of debt, labeled $D/A_1$ in Figure 12-7, below which the effects noted in Point 2 are immaterial. Beyond $D/A_1$, however, the bankruptcy-related costs, especially higher interest rates on new debt, become increasingly important, and they reduce the tax benefits of debt at an increasing rate. In the range from $D/A_1$ to $D/A_2$, bankruptcy-related costs reduce but do not completely offset the tax benefits of debt, so the firm's stock price rises (but at a decreasing rate) as the debt/assets ratio increases. However, beyond $D/A_2$ bankruptcy-related costs exceed the tax benefits, so from this point on increasing the debt/assets ratio lowers the value of the stock. Therefore, $D/A_2$ is the optimal capital structure.

4. Both theory and empirical evidence support the preceding discussion. However, researchers have not been able to identify points $D/A_1$ and $D/A_2$ precisely, so the graphs shown in Figures 12-5 and 12-7 must be taken as approximations, not as precisely defined functions.

5. Another disturbing aspect of capital structure theory as expressed in Figure 12-7 is the fact that many large, successful firms, such as Microsoft, use far less debt than the theory suggests. This point led to the development of signaling theory, which is discussed next.

## Signaling Theory

**symmetric information**
The situation in which investors and managers have identical information about the firm's prospects.

MM assumed that investors have the same information about a firm's prospects as its managers—this is called **symmetric information** because both those who are inside the firm (managers and employees) and those who are outside the firm (investors) have identical information. However, we know that in fact managers generally have better information about their firms than do outside investors. This is called **asymmetric information,** and it has an important effect on decisions to use either debt or equity to finance capital projects. To see why, consider two situations, one in which the company's managers know that its prospects are extremely favorable (Firm F) and one in which the managers know that the future looks very unfavorable (Firm U).

**asymmetric information**
The situation in which managers have different (better) information about their firm's prospects than do outside investors.

Suppose, for example, that Firm F's research and development labs have just discovered a cure for the common cold, but the product is not patentable. Firm F's managers want to keep the new product a secret for as long as possible to delay competitors' entry into the market. New plants and distribution facilities must be built to exploit the new product, so capital must be raised. How should Firm F's management raise the needed capital? If the firm sells stock, then when profits from the new product start flowing in, the price of the stock will rise sharply and the purchasers of the new stock will have made a bonanza. The current stockholders (including the managers) also will do well, but not as well as they would have if the company had not sold stock before the price increased because then they would not have had to share the benefits of the new product with the new stockholders. *Therefore, one would expect a firm with very favorable prospects to try to avoid selling stock and, rather, to raise any required new capital by other means, including using debt beyond the normal target capital structure.*[14]

Now let's consider Firm U. Suppose its managers have information that new orders are off sharply because a competitor has installed new technology that has improved its products' quality. Firm U must upgrade its own facilities at a high cost just to maintain its existing sales level. As a result, its return on investment will fall (but not by as much as if it took no action, which would lead to a 100 percent loss through bankruptcy). How should Firm U raise the needed capital? Here the situation is just the reverse of that facing Firm F, which did not want to sell stock so as to avoid having to share the benefits of future developments. *A firm with unfavorable prospects would want to sell stock, which would mean bringing in new investors to share the losses!*[15]

The conclusions from all this are that firms with extremely bright prospects prefer not to finance through new stock offerings, whereas firms with poor prospects do like to finance with outside equity. How would you, as an investor, react to these conclusions? You ought to say, "If I see that a company plans to issue new stock, this should worry me

---

[14]It would be illegal for Firm F's managers to purchase more shares on the basis of their inside knowledge of the new product. They could be sent to jail if they did.

[15]Of course, Firm U would have to make certain disclosures when it offered new shares to the public, but it might be able to meet the legal requirements without fully disclosing management's worst fears.

because I know that management would not want to issue stock if future prospects looked good, but it would want to issue stock if things looked bad. Therefore, I should lower my estimate of the firm's value, other things held constant, if I read an announcement of a new stock offering." Of course, the negative reaction would be stronger if the stock sale was by a large, established company such as General Electric or IBM, which surely would have many financing options, than if it were by a small company such as USR Industries. For USR, a stock sale might mean truly extraordinary investment opportunities that were so large that they just could not be financed without a stock sale.

If you gave the preceding answer, your views are consistent with those of many sophisticated portfolio managers of institutions such as Morgan Guaranty Trust. *So, simply stated, the announcement of a stock offering by a mature firm that seems to have multiple financing alternatives is taken as a* **signal** *that the firm's prospects as seen by its management are not bright.* This, in turn, suggests that when a mature firm announces a new stock offering, the price of its stock should decline. Empirical studies have shown that this situation does indeed exist.

What are the implications of all this for capital structure decisions? The answer is that firms should, in normal times, maintain a **reserve borrowing capacity** that can be used in the event that some especially good investment opportunities come along. *This means that firms should generally use less debt than would be suggested by the tax benefit/bankruptcy cost trade-off expressed in Figure 12-7.*

Signaling/asymmetric information concepts also have implications for the marginal cost of capital (MCC) curve as discussed in Chapter 11. There we saw that the weighted average cost of capital (WACC) jumped when retained earnings were exhausted and the firm was forced to sell new common stock to raise equity. The jump in the WACC, or the break in the MCC schedule, was attributed only to flotation costs. However, if the announcement of a stock sale causes a decline in the price of the stock, then $r_e$ as measured by $r_e = \hat{D}_1/P_0(1 - F) + g$ will rise because of the decline in $P_0$. This factor reinforces the effects of flotation costs, and perhaps it is an even more important explanation for the jump in the MCC schedule at the point at which new stock must be issued. For example, assume that $P_0 = \$10, \hat{D}_1 = \$1$, $g = 5\%$, and $F = 10\%$. Therefore, $r_s = 10\% + 5\% = 15\%$, and $r_e$, the cost of external equity, is 16.1 percent:

$$r_e = \frac{\hat{D}_1}{P_0(1 - F)} + g = \frac{\$1}{\$10(1.0 - 0.10)} + 0.05 = 0.161 = 16.1\%$$

Suppose, however, that the announcement of a stock sale causes the current market price of the stock to fall from \$10 to \$8. This will produce an increase in the costs of both retained earnings ($r_s$) and external equity ($r_e$):

$$r_s = \frac{\hat{D}_1}{P_0} + g = \frac{\$1}{\$8} + 0.05 = 0.175 = 17.5\%$$

$$r_e = \frac{\hat{D}_1}{P_0(1 - F)} + g = \frac{\$1}{\$8(1.0 - 0.10)} + 0.05 = 0.189 = 18.9\%$$

This would, of course, have further implications for capital budgeting. Specifically, it would make it even more difficult for a marginal project to show a positive net present value (NPV) if the project required the firm to sell stock to raise capital.

If you find our discussion of capital structure theory somewhat inexact, you are not alone. In truth, no one knows how to identify precisely the optimal capital structure for a firm or how to measure precisely the effect of the firm's capital structure on either its value or its cost of capital. In real life, capital structure decisions must be made more on the basis of judgment than numerical analysis. Nevertheless, an understanding of the theoretical issues as presented here is essential to making sound judgments on capital structure issues.

**signal**
An action taken by a firm's management that provides clues to investors about how management views the firm's prospects.

**reserve borrowing capacity**
The ability to borrow money at a reasonable cost when good investment opportunities arise; firms often use less debt than specified by the MM optimal capital structure to ensure that they can obtain debt capital later if necessary.

## VARIATIONS IN CAPITAL STRUCTURES AMONG FIRMS

As might be expected, wide variations in the use of financial leverage occur both across industries and among the individual firms in each industry. Table 12-6 illustrates differences for selected industries; the ranking is in descending order of common equity ratios, as shown in column 1.

Drug and biotechnology companies do not use much debt (their common equity ratios are high); the uncertainties inherent in industries that are cyclical, oriented toward research, or subject to huge product liability suits normally render the heavy use of debt unwise. On the other hand, utilities traditionally have used large amounts of debt, particularly long-term debt. Their fixed assets make good security for mortgage bonds, and their relatively stable sales make it safe for them to carry more debt than would be true for firms with more business risk.

Particular attention should be given to the times-interest-earned (TIE) ratio because it gives a measure of how safe the debt is and how vulnerable the company is to financial distress. The TIE ratio depends on three factors: (1) the percentage of debt, (2) the interest rate on the debt, and (3) the company's profitability. Generally, the least leveraged industries, such as the drug and biotechnology industries, have the highest coverage ratios, whereas the utility industry, which finances heavily with debt, has a low average coverage ratio. Table 12-6 shows that companies that manufacture drugs and conduct biotechnology research have high average TIEs, whereas utilities have a very low TIE.

Wide variations in capital structures also exist among firms within given industries. For example, although the average pharmaceutical firm had a capital structure

**TABLE 12-6**   Capital Structure Percentages, 2006: Five Industries Ranked by Common Equity Ratios[a]

| Industry | Common Equity (1) | Preferred Stock (2) | Total Debt (3) | Long-Term Debt (4) | Short-Term Debt (5) | Times-Interest-Earned Ratio (6) | Return on Equity[b] (7) |
|---|---|---|---|---|---|---|---|
| Pharmaceuticals | 79.9% | 0.1% | 20.0% | 12.0% | 8.0% | 6.8 | −15.4% |
| Biotechnology | 66.6 | 1.1 | 32.3 | 15.5 | 16.8 | 8.5 | −14.5 |
| Textiles | 54.2 | 1.1 | 44.7 | 23.0 | 21.7 | 5.1 | 9.7 |
| Restaurants | 51.5 | 0.5 | 48.0 | 28.8 | 19.2 | 13.1 | 6.2 |
| Utilities | 27.4 | 0.6 | 72.0 | 54.9 | 17.1 | 2.8 | 9.6 |
| Composite[c] | 47.2 | 0.8 | 52.0 | 29.1 | 22.9 | 4.9 | 5.3 |

**Notes:** [a]These ratios are based on accounting, or book values. Stated on a market value basis, the equity percentages would be higher because most stocks sell at prices that are much higher than their book values.

[b]A negative ROE results because uncertain economic conditions in 2005 resulted in operating losses for many firms in the industry.

[c]These composite ratios include all industries, not just those listed above, except financial and professional service industries.

**Source:** *Standard & Poor's Research Insight, 2006.*

consisting of approximately 20 percent debt in 2006, Genentech had approximately 25 percent debt in its capital structure and GlaxoSmithKline had greater than 70 percent debt in its capital structure. As you can see, factors unique to individual firms, including managerial attitudes, play an important role in setting target capital structures.

### Self-Test Question

Why do wide variations in the use of financial leverage occur both across industries and among the individual firms in each industry?

## CAPITAL STRUCTURES AROUND THE WORLD

As you might expect, when we examine the capital structures of companies around the world, we find wide variations. Table 12-7 illustrates differences for selected countries; the ranking is in descending order of common equity ratios, as shown in column 1. As you can see, companies in Italy and Japan use a much greater proportion of debt than companies in the United States or Canada, and companies in the United Kingdom use the lowest proportion of debt of all the countries listed. Of course, different countries use somewhat different accounting conventions, which makes comparisons difficult. Still, even after adjusting for accounting differences, researchers find that Italian and Japanese firms use considerably more financial leverage than U.S. and Canadian companies. The gap among the countries has narrowed somewhat during the past several decades. In the early 1970s, companies in Canada and the United States had debt/assets ratios of about 40 percent, and companies in Japan and Italy had debt/assets ratios of more than 75 percent (Japanese companies averaged nearly 85 percent leverage).

Why do international differences in financial leverage exist? It seems logical to attribute the differences to dissimilar tax structures. Although the interest on corporate debt is deductible in each country, and individuals must pay taxes on interest received, both dividends and capital gains are taxed differently around the world.

The tax codes in most developed countries encourage personal investing and savings more than the U.S. tax code. For example, Germany, Italy, and many other European countries do not tax capital gains, and in most other developed countries, including Japan, France, and Canada, capital gains are not taxed unless they exceed some minimum amount. Further, in Germany and Italy, dividends are not taxed as income, and in most

| TABLE 12-7 | Capital Structure Percentages for Selected Countries Ranked by Common Equity Ratios, 1995 | | | |
|---|---|---|---|---|
| **Country** | **Equity** | **Total Debt** | **Long-term Debt** | **Short-term Debt** |
| United Kingdom | 68.3% | 31.7% | N/A | N/A |
| United States | 48.4 | 51.6 | 26.8% | 24.8% |
| Canada | 47.5 | 52.5 | 30.2 | 22.3 |
| Germany | 39.7 | 60.3 | 15.6 | 44.7 |
| Spain | 39.7 | 60.3 | 22.1 | 38.2 |
| France | 38.8 | 61.2 | 23.5 | 37.7 |
| Japan | 33.7 | 66.3 | 23.3 | 43.0 |
| Italy | 23.5 | 76.5 | 24.2 | 52.3 |

**Note:** The percentages were computed from financial data that were stated in domestic currency. For example, the amount of total assets for French companies was stated in francs.

**Source:** *OECD Financial Statistics, Part 3: Non-Financial Enterprises Financial Statements, 1996.*

other countries some amount of dividends is tax exempt. Therefore, we can make the following general conclusions: (1) From a tax standpoint, corporations should be equally inclined to use debt in most developed countries. (2) In countries where capital gains are not taxed, investors should show a preference for stocks compared with countries that have capital gains taxes. (3) Investor preferences should lead to relatively low equity capital costs in those countries that do not tax capital gains, and this, in turn, should cause firms in those countries to use significantly more equity capital than their U.S. counterparts. But for the most part, this is exactly the opposite of the actual capital structures we observe, so differential tax laws cannot explain the observed capital structure differences.

If tax rates cannot explain the different capital structures, what might be an appropriate explanation? Another possibility relates to risk, especially bankruptcy costs. Actual bankruptcy, and even the threat of potential bankruptcy, imposes a costly burden on firms with large amounts of debt. Note, however, that the threat of bankruptcy is dependent on the probability of bankruptcy. In the United States, *equity* monitoring costs are comparatively low because corporations produce quarterly reports and must comply with relatively stringent audit requirements. These conditions are less prevalent in other countries. On the other hand, *debt* monitoring costs probably are lower in such countries as Germany and Japan than in the United States because most of the corporate debt consists of bank loans as opposed to publicly issued bonds. More important, though, the banks in many European and developed Asian countries are closely linked to the corporations that borrow from them, often holding major equity positions in, and having substantial influence over, the management of the debtor firms. Given these close relationships, the banks are much more directly involved with the debtor firms' affairs, and as a result they also are more accommodating than U.S. bondholders in the event of financial distress. This, in turn, suggests that any given amount of debt gives rise to a lower threat of bankruptcy than for a U.S. firm with the same amount of business risk. Thus, an analysis of both bankruptcy costs and equity monitoring costs leads to the conclusion that U.S. firms should have more equity and less debt than firms in countries such as Japan and Germany, which is what we typically observe.

We cannot state that one financial system is better than another in the sense of making the firms in one country more efficient than those in another. However, as U.S. firms become increasingly involved in worldwide operations, they must become increasingly aware of worldwide conditions, and they must be prepared to adapt to conditions in the various countries in which they do business.

**Self-Test Question**

Why do international differences in financial leverage exist?

**Chapter *Essentials***
**—The Answers**

To summarize the key concepts, let's answer the questions that were posed at the beginning of the chapter:

- **What is a firm's capital structure?** Capital structure refers to the combination of the long-term funds the firm uses to finance its assets. Thus, its capital structure consists of the proportions of debt, preferred stock, and common equity the firm uses.

- **What is a firm's optimal capital structure? Can a firm have too little debt?** A firm's optimal capital structure is the combination of debt, preferred stock, and common equity that maximizes the value of its stock. A firm's value will be maximized when its weighted average cost of capital (WACC) is minimized.

    The tax deductibility of interest payments makes debt an attractive form of financing. However, the more debt a firm uses, the greater its chances of bankruptcy. As a result, firms find it desirable to finance with some debt. Firms that have little or no debt generally are not operating at their optimal capital structures because they are not taking advantage of the tax deductibility of the interest payments on debt.

- **How does a firm's capital structure affect its risk?** Both debt and preferred stock require fixed financial payments. Because these payments do not vary with sales and operating profits, there is a risk that they cannot be paid when the firm performs poorly. In addition, debt represents a contractual obligation that requires the firm to make payments of specific amounts on specific dates. If debt payments are not made when they are due, debt holders can force the firm into bankruptcy. As a result, everything else equal, we generally consider firms with higher proportions of debt to have riskier financial positions than firms with less debt. Higher risk results in a higher WACC.

- **What is leverage? How can information about a firm's leverage position be used to determine its optimal capital structure?** Leverage refers to fixed costs—both fixed operating costs and fixed financial costs. Because these costs are fixed, they must be paid even when the firm performs poorly. On the positive side, however, the firm gets to keep any earnings that exceed these fixed costs. Everything else equal, firms that have higher proportions of fixed costs are considered riskier than firms with lower proportions of fixed costs. Thus, we can evaluate a firm's capital structure by examining its proportion (degree) of fixed costs, and thus its risk. *Operating leverage* refers to the fixed costs associated with normal operations and *financial leverage* refers to the fixed costs associated with financing. A firm can change its degree, or proportion, of financial leverage by altering its capital structure. Lower financial (operating) leverage suggests lower financial (business) risk, which generally translates into a lower WACC.

- **Why do the capital structures of firms in different industries vary? How do the capital structures of firms vary around the world?** Firms with more stable sales are able to take on greater proportions of debt than firms with more unpredictable sales. In general, then, we observe that firms with fairly predictable earnings have much higher proportions of debt than firms with uncertain earnings.

    An average U.S. firm has a debt/assets ratio equal to approximately 48 percent of its total capital. The average debt ratio of firms in many other countries is above 60 percent. Differences in capital structures around the world can be explained primarily by the relationships firms have with their lenders. In many countries, banks own significant portions of both the stock and the debt of a firm. In such instances, (1) it is easier to change the features of the debt, and (2) the bank is more inclined to lend additional funds to a struggling firm in which it has ownership in an attempt to improve its finances than in the United States where many investors own the company's bonds.

## ETHICAL DILEMMA

### A Bond Is a Bond Is a Bond . . . Is a Stock . . . Is a Bondock?

To fund some of its expansion plans, Ohio Rubber & Tire (ORT) recently issued 30-year bonds with low coupon rates. Investors were willing to purchase the bonds despite the low coupon rates because ORT's ?debt has consistently been rated AAA during the past decade, which means that bond rating agencies consider the company's default risk to be extremely low.

Now ORT is considering raising additional funds by issuing new debt. The company plans to use the new funds to finance additional expansion. Unlike its previous expansion efforts, however, ORT now plans to grow the firm by purchasing young firms that just "went public" that are not in the tire and rubber industry.

Wally, who works closely with ORT's investment banker, has been assigned the task of determining how to best raise the desired funds. After speaking with the investment banker, some friends who work at other companies, and peers in ORT's international subsidiaries, Wally is seriously considering recommending to management that ORT issue a new security that has the characteristics of both debt and equity. The security, which was recently introduced in the U.S. financial markets, is classified as debt because fixed interest payments that are tax deductible are paid every year. Unlike conventional bonds, however, these hybrid bonds, which are called "bondocks," have maturities of 50 to 60 years. In addition, the firm is not considered to be in default if it misses interest payments when the firm's credit rating drops below B+. Most experts consider bondocks to be quite complex financial instruments.

Through his research, Wally discovered that bondocks have been used for quite some time outside of the United States. Compared with conventional debt, companies that have used bondocks have increased their earnings per share (EPS) significantly. A major reason EPS increases is because the cost of a bondock generally is much lower than equity, but the instrument is comparable to equity financing with respect to maturity and default risk. For example, Wally discovered that ORT could issue

bondocks with an after-tax cost equal to 5 percent, which is only slightly higher than the after-tax cost of issuing conventional debt and is approximately one-third the cost of issuing new equity. Although bondocks are considered risky, the actual degree of risk is unknown. The friends and coworkers with whom Wally consulted seem to think there is a slight chance that investors—both stockholders and bondholders—would earn returns significantly lower than would be earned with conventional debt when the company performs extremely poorly. The opposite should occur when the company performs very well.

The major drawback to issuing bondocks is that they will significantly increase the financial leverage of ORT, and thus the value of the recently issued bonds will decrease substantially. On the other hand, Wally thinks that issuing bondocks can be a win-win proposition for ORT and its common stockholders. If the company's expansion plans are successful, stockholders will be nicely rewarded. But if the company's expansion plans are unsuccessful, the market values of both its debt and its equity would decrease to the point that it would be attractive for the firm to repurchase these financing instruments in the capital markets. If this is true, then issuing bondocks would benefit stockholders at the expense of bondholders. ORT's executives are major stockholders because their bonuses and incentives are paid in the company's stock. What should Wally do? What would you do if you were Wally?

## Chapter *Essentials*
### —Personal Finance

The concepts presented in this chapter should help you to better understand how to determine the rate of return that you should demand when investing your money. If you apply the concepts presented in this chapter, you should be able to make more informed borrowing and investment decisions.

- Your capital structure can be defined as the mixture of the various loans (debt) that you have outstanding. Your capital structure determines your overall WACC, which affects your wealth. For example, if you use an expensive type of debt—perhaps credit cards—as a primary source of funds, then your WACC will be high compared to someone who uses less expensive debt. Similar to firms, there are steps you can take to lower your WACC. You can shift your capital structure, or mixture of loans, so that a greater proportion of cheaper debt is used. You can also shift your capital structure to alter your credit risk, which is the single most important variable that financial institutions use to determine the interest rate you are charged for borrowing funds. If you have too many credit cards, discontinue some of them; if you are habitually late (delinquent) with your bill payments, start paying on time; save a portion of your income each week; and don't become too leveraged (borrow too much). If you improve your credit, you will be able to borrow at better rates.

- Many alternative loans with many different interest rates are available to individuals. When you need a loan, you should "shop around" and choose the alternative with the lowest interest rate. Also, because interest rates change continuously, you should monitor your loan portfolio to determine whether it is worthwhile to refinance existing loans when market rates decline. Considering the variety of borrowing alternatives that exist, do you think it is wise to use your credit card as a source of borrowing for an extended period of time? If you think about what is discussed in this chapter, you should conclude that it is better to use other sources to borrow money if possible because the interest rate on loans from credit cards—that is, outstanding balances on which you pay interest—generally is much higher than it is on alternative loans.

## QUESTIONS

**12-1**    "One type of leverage affects both EBIT and EPS. The other type affects only EPS." Explain what this statement means.

**12-2**    Firm A and Firm B are competitors in the same industry. The two firms have similar operating costs, except Firm A has more fixed operating costs than Firm B. As a result, which firm would experience a greater change in operating income as the result of a particular change in sales? Why?

**12-3**    Explain why the following statement is true: "All else the same, firms with relatively stable sales are able to carry relatively high debt/assets ratios."

**12-4**    If a firm went from zero debt to successively higher levels of debt, why would you expect its stock price to first rise, then hit a peak, and then begin to decline?

**12-5**    When Carson's Cars sales increase by 5 percent, its earnings per share increase by 20 percent. Does the firm have leverage? If so, can you tell what kind? Explain.

**12-6**    Why is EBIT generally considered to be independent of financial leverage? Why might EBIT actually be influenced by financial leverage at high levels of debt?

**12-7**    Is the debt level that maximizes a firm's expected EPS the same as the one that maximizes its stock price? Explain.

**12-8**    Explain how a firm might shift its capital structure so as to change its weighted average cost of capital (WACC). What would be the impact on the value of the firm?

**12-9**    Absolute Corporation currently has $50 million in liabilities and common equity in combination. The firm has no preferred stock. After careful evaluation, the CFO constructed the following table to show the CEO the effect of changing the firm's capital structure:

| Amount of Debt in the Capital Structure | Earnings per Share (EPS) | Market Price per Share ($P_0$) |
|---|---|---|
| $10,000,000 | $5.00 | $125.50 |
| 20,000,000 | 5.50 | 130.75 |
| 30,000,000 | 5.70 | 130.00 |
| 40,000,000 | 5.60 | 128.05 |

According to this information, what is Absolute's optimal capital structure? Explain your answer.

**12-10** When the Bell System was broken up, the old AT&T was split into a new AT&T plus seven regional telephone companies. The specific reason for forcing the breakup was to increase the degree of competition in the telephone industry. AT&T had a monopoly on local service, long distance, and the manufacture of all the equipment used by telephone companies, and the breakup was expected to open most of these markets to competition. In the court order that set the terms of the breakup, the capital structures of the surviving companies were specified, and much attention was given to the increased competition telephone companies could expect in the future. Do you think the optimal capital structure after the breakup should be the same as the pre-breakup optimal capital structure? Explain your position.

**12-11** Your firm's R&D department has been working on a new process that, if it works, can produce oil from coal at a cost of about $5 per barrel versus a current market price of $28 per barrel. The company needs $10 million of external funds at this time to complete the research. The results of the research will be known in about a year, and there is about a 50-50 chance of success. If the research is successful, your company will need to raise a substantial amount of new money to put the idea into production. Your economists forecast that although the economy will be depressed next year, interest rates will be high because of international monetary problems. You must recommend how the currently needed $10 million should be raised—as debt or as equity. How would the potential impact of your project influence your decision?

## SELF-TEST PROBLEMS

*(Solutions appear in Appendix B at the end of the book.)*

**key terms**      **ST-1** Define each of the following terms:

a. Target capital structure; optimal capital structure

b. Business risk; financial risk; total risk

c. Financial leverage

d. EPS indifference point

e. Degree of operating leverage; degree of financial leverage; degree of total leverage

f. Times-interest-earned (TIE) ratio

g. Symmetric information; asymmetric information

h. Trade-off theory; signaling theory

i. Reserve borrowing capacity

**financial leverage**    **ST-2** Gentry Motors Inc., a producer of turbine generators, is in this situation: EBIT = $4 million; tax rate = T = 35%; debt outstanding = $2 million; $r_d$ = 10%; $r_s$ = 15%; shares of stock outstanding = 600,000; and book value per share = $10. Because Gentry's product market is stable and the company expects no growth, all earnings are paid out as dividends. The debt consists of perpetual bonds.

a. What are Gentry's earnings per share (EPS) and its price per share ($P_0$)?

b. What is Gentry's weighted average cost of capital (WACC)?

c. Gentry can increase its debt by $8 million, to a total of $10 million, using the new debt to buy back and retire some of its shares of common stock at the current price. Its interest rate on debt will be 12 percent (it will have to call and refund the old debt), and its cost of equity will rise from 15 percent to 17 percent. EBIT will remain constant. Should Gentry change its capital structure?

d. If Gentry did not have to refund the $2 million of old debt, how would this affect things? Assume that the new and the still outstanding debt are equally risky, with $r_d = 12\%$, but that the coupon rate on the old debt is 10 percent.

e. What is Gentry's TIE coverage ratio under the original situation and under the conditions in part c of this question?

## PROBLEMS

**12-1** Expert Analysts Resources (EAR) has provided you with the following information about three companies you are currently evaluating:

**risk analysis**

| Company | Degree of Operating Leverage (DOL) | Degree of Financial Leverage (DFL) |
|---------|------------------------------------|------------------------------------|
| Acme    | 1.5×                               | 6.0×                               |
| Apex    | 3.0×                               | 4.0×                               |
| Alps    | 5.0×                               | 2.0×                               |

According to this information, which firm would be considered *riskiest?*

**12-2** Analysts have evaluated the Sivar Silver Company and discovered that if sales are $800,000, the following will exist:

**operating leverage**

| | |
|---|---|
| Degree of operating leverage (DOL) | 4.0× |
| Degree of financial leverage (DFL) | 2.0× |
| Earnings before interest and taxes (EBIT) | $50,000 |
| Earnings per share (EPS) | $4.00 |

According to this information, what will Sivar's EBIT be if sales actually turn out to be $720,000 rather than $800,000?

**12-3** Super Shoe Store (SSS) has provided the following information:

**operating leverage**

| | |
|---|---|
| Selling price per unit | $50 |
| Variable cost per unit | $30 |
| Fixed operating costs | $120,000 |

If the firm normally sells 10,000 pairs of shoes, what is SSS's degree of operating leverage?

**12-4** Executives of the Donut Shop have determined that the company's degree of operating leverage (DOL) is 3× and its degree of financial leverage (DFL) is 6×. According to this information, how will Donut Shop's earnings per share (EPS) be affected if its amount of earnings before interest and taxes (EBIT) turns out to be 4 percent higher than expected?

**financial leverage**

**total leverage**    **12-5**    Axiom Company's degree of financial leverage is 1.5x. Also, Axiom knows that if *sales* increase by 10 percent, its *earnings per share (EPS)* will increase by 30 percent. What is Axiom's degree of *operating* leverage (DOL)?

**total leverage**    **12-6**    A firm has determined that its degree of operating leverage (DOL) is 2.0x and its degree of financial leverage (DFL) is 1.5x. As a result, what will be the change in its earnings per share if sales are 10 percent lower than expected?

**financial leverage**    **12-7**    The net operating income (EBIT) for Bear Investment Company (BIC) this year is $80,000. During the year, the company paid $20,000 interest on its debt and $25,000 dividends to its common stockholders. If BIC's marginal tax rate is 40 percent, what is the company's degree of financial leverage (DFL)?

**leverage**    **12-8**    Use the following information to compute the firm's degree of operating leverage (DOL), DFL, and degree of total leverage (DTL):

| | |
|---|---:|
| Sales | $ 50,000 |
| Variable operating costs | ( 30,000) |
| Gross profit | $ 20,000 |
| Fixed operating costs | ( 15,000) |
| Net operating income (EBIT) | 5,000 |
| Interest expense | ( 3,000) |
| Earnings before taxes (taxable income) | $ 2,000 |
| Taxes (35%) | ( 700) |
| Net income | 1,300 |

**leverage**    **12-9**    Following is the most recent income statement for Ironworks Railroad. Ironworks has *no preferred stock*.

| | |
|---|---:|
| Sales | $200,000 |
| Variable operating costs (70% of sales) | (140,000) |
| Gross profit | 60,000 |
| Fixed operating costs | ( 40,000) |
| Net operating income (EBIT) | 20,000 |
| Interest expense | ( 10,000) |
| Taxable income | 10,000 |
| Taxes (40%) | ( 4,000) |
| Net income | 6,000 |

**a.** What is Ironworks' degree of *operating* leverage (DOL)?

**b.** What is Ironworks' degree of *financial* leverage (DFL)?

**c.** What is Ironworks' degree of *total* leverage (DTL)?

**financial leverage effects**    **12-10**    The firms HL and LL are identical except for their debt-to-total-assets ratios and interest rates on debt. Each has $20 million in assets, earned $4 million before interest and taxes in 2008, and has a 40 percent marginal tax rate. Firm HL, however, has a debt-to-total-assets ratio of 50 percent and pays 12 percent interest on its debt, whereas LL has a 30 percent debt-to-total-assets ratio and pays only 10 percent interest on debt.

**a.** Calculate the return on equity (net income/equity) for each firm.

**b.** Observing that HL has a higher return on equity, LL's treasurer decides to raise the debt-to-total-assets ratio from 30 to 60 percent, which will increase LL's interest rate on all debt to 15 percent. Calculate the new rate of return on equity (ROE) for LL.

**12-11** The Damon Company wishes to calculate next year's return on equity (ROE) under different leverage ratios. Damon's total assets are $14 million, and its marginal tax rate is 40 percent. The company can estimate next year's earnings before interest and taxes for three possible states of the world: $4.2 million with a 0.2 probability, $2.8 million with a 0.5 probability, and $700,000 with a 0.3 probability. Calculate Damon's expected ROE, standard deviation, and coefficient of variation for each of the debt-to-total-assets ratios in the following list and evaluate the results. ROE = (Net income)/(Common equity).

**financial leverage effects**

| Leverage (Debt/Assets) | Interest Rate |
|:---:|:---:|
| 0% | — |
| 10 | 9% |
| 50 | 11 |
| 60 | 14 |

**12-12 a.** Given the following information, calculate the expected value for Firm C's EPS. $E(EPS_A) = \$5.10$, and $\sigma_A = \$3.61$; $E(EPS_B) = \$4.20$, and $\sigma_B = \$2.96$; and $\sigma_C = \$4.11$.

**risk analysis**

| | Probability | | | | |
|---|:---:|:---:|:---:|:---:|:---:|
| | **0.1** | **0.2** | **0.4** | **0.2** | **0.1** |
| Firm A: $EPS_A$ | ($1.50) | $1.80 | $5.10 | $8.40 | $11.70 |
| Firm B: $EPS_B$ | (1.20) | 1.50 | 4.20 | 6.90 | 9.60 |
| Firm C: $EPS_C$ | (2.40) | 1.35 | 5.10 | 8.85 | 12.60 |

**b.** Discuss the relative riskiness of the three firms' (A, B, and C) earnings.

**12-13** Merville Corporation will begin operations next year to produce a single product at a price of $12 per unit. Merville has a choice of two methods of production: Method A, with variable costs of $6.75 per unit and fixed operating costs of $675,000, and Method B, with variable costs of $8.25 per unit and fixed operating costs of $401,250. To support operations under either production method, the firm requires $2,250,000 in assets, and it has established a debt-to-total-assets ratio of 40 percent. The cost of debt is $r_d = 10$ percent. The tax rate is irrelevant for the problem, and fixed operating costs do not include interest.

**operating leverage effects**

**a.** The sales forecast for the coming year is 200,000 units. Under which method would EBIT be more adversely affected if sales did not reach the expected levels? (*Hint:* Compare DOLs under the two production methods.)

**b.** Given the firm's current debt, which method would produce the greater percentage increase in earnings per share for a given increase in EBIT? (*Hint:* Compare DFLs under the two methods.)

c. Calculate DTL under each method, and then evaluate the firm's total risk under each method.

d. Is there some debt ratio under Method A that would produce the same $DTL_A$ as the $DTL_B$ that you calculated in part c? (*Hint:* Let $DTL_A = DTL_B = 2.90$ as calculated in part c, solve for I, and then determine the amount of debt that is consistent with this level of I. Conceivably, debt could be negative, which implies holding liquid assets rather than borrowing.)

**financial alternatives**    **12-14** Wired Communications Corporation (WCC) supplies headphones to airlines for use with movie and stereo programs. The headphones sell for $288 per set, and this year's sales are expected to be 45,000 units. Variable production costs for the expected sales under current production methods are estimated at $10,200,000, and fixed production (operating) costs are currently $1,560,000. WCC has $4,800,000 of debt outstanding at an interest rate of 8 percent. There are 240,000 shares of common stock outstanding, and there is no preferred stock. WCC pays out 70 percent of earnings and is in the 40 percent marginal tax bracket.

The company is considering investing $7,200,000 in new equipment. Sales would not increase, but variable costs per unit would decline by 20 percent. Also, fixed operating costs would increase from $1,560,000 to $1,800,000. WCC could raise the required capital by borrowing $7,200,000 at 10 percent or by selling 240,000 additional shares at $30 per share.

a. What would be WCC's EPS (1) under the old production process, (2) under the new process if it uses debt, and (3) under the new process if it uses common stock?

b. Calculate the DOL, DFL, and DTL under the existing setup and under the new setup with each type of financing. Assume that the expected sales level is 45,000 units, or $12,960,000.

c. At what unit sales level would WCC have the same EPS, assuming it undertakes the investment and finances it with debt or with stock? (*Hint:* V = Variable cost per unit = $8,160,000/45,000, and EPS = $[(P \times Q - V \times Q - F - I)(1 - T)]$/Shares. Set $EPS_{Stock} = EPS_{Debt}$ and solve for Q.)

d. At what unit sales level would EPS = 0 under the three production/financing setups—that is, under the old plan, the new plan with debt financing, and the new plan with stock financing? (*Hint:* Note that $V_{Old} = \$10,200,000/45,000$, and use the hints for part c, setting the EPS equation equal to zero.)

e. On the basis of the analysis in parts a through c, which plan is the riskiest, which has the highest expected EPS, and which would you recommend? Assume here that there is a fairly high probability of sales falling as low as 25,000 units, and determine $EPS_{Debt}$ and $EPS_{Stock}$ at that sales level to help assess the riskiness of the two financing plans.

**financial alternatives**    **12-15** The Strasburg Company plans to raise a net amount of $270 million to finance new equipment and working capital in early 2009. Two alternatives are being considered: Common stock can be sold to net $60 per share, or bonds yielding 12 percent can be issued. The balance sheet and income statement of the Strasburg Company prior to financing are as follows:

| The Strasburg Company: Balance Sheet as of December 31, 2008 ($ millions) | | | |
|---|---|---|---|
| Current assets | $ 900.00 | Accounts payable | $ 172.50 |
| Net fixed assets | 450.00 | Notes payable to bank | 255.00 |
| | | Other current liabilities | 225.00 |
| | | Total current liabilities | $ 652.50 |
| | | Long-term debt (10%) | 300.00 |
| | | Common stock, $3 par | 60.00 |
| | | Retained earnings | 337.50 |
| Total assets | $1,350.00 | Total liabilities and equity | $1,350.00 |

| The Strasburg Company: Income Statement for Year Ended December 31, 2008 ($ millions) | |
|---|---|
| Sales | $ 2,475.00 |
| Operating costs | (2,227.50) |
| Earnings before interest and taxes (EBIT) (10%) | $   247.50 |
| Interest on short-term debt | (   15.00) |
| Interest on long-term debt | (   30.00) |
| Earnings before taxes (EBT) | $   202.50 |
| Taxes (40%) | (   81.00) |
| Net income | $   121.50 |

The probability distribution for annual sales is as follows:

| Probability | Annual Sales (Millions of Dollars) |
|---|---|
| 0.30 | $2,250 |
| 0.40 | 2,700 |
| 0.30 | 3,150 |

Assuming that EBIT is equal to 10 percent of sales, calculate earnings per share under both the debt financing and the stock financing alternatives at each possible level of sales. Then calculate expected earnings per share and $\sigma_{EPS}$ under both debt and stock financing. Also, calculate the debt-to-total-assets ratio and the times-interest-earned (TIE) ratio at the expected sales level under each alternative. The old debt will remain outstanding. Which financing method do you recommend?

## Integrative Problem

**12-16** Assume you have just been hired by Adams, Garitty, and Evans (AGE), a consulting firm that specializes in analyses of firms' capital structures. Your boss has asked you to examine the capital structure of Campus Deli and Sub Shop (CDSS), which is located adjacent to the campus. According to the owner, sales were $1,350,000 last year, variable costs were 60 percent of sales, and fixed costs were $40,000. As a result, EBIT totaled $500,000. Because the university's enrollment is capped, EBIT is expected to be constant over time. Because no expansion capital is required, CDSS pays out

*optimal capital structure*

all earnings as dividends. The management group owns 50 percent of the stock, which is traded in the over-the-counter market.

CDSS currently has no debt—it is an all-equity firm—and its 100,000 shares outstanding sell at a price of $20 per share. The firm's marginal tax rate is 40 percent. On the basis of statements made in your finance class, you believe that CDSS's shareholders would be better off if some debt financing were used. When you suggested this to your new boss, she encouraged you to pursue the idea but to provide support for the suggestion.

You then obtained from a local investment banker the following estimates of the costs of debt and equity at different debt levels (in thousands of dollars):

| Amount Borrowed | $r_d$ | $r_s$ |
|---|---|---|
| $    0 | — | 15.0% |
| 250 | 10.0% | 15.5 |
| 500 | 11.0 | 16.5 |
| 750 | 13.0 | 18.0 |
| 1,000 | 16.0 | 20.0 |

If the firm were recapitalized, debt would be issued, and the borrowed funds would be used to repurchase stock. You plan to complete your report by asking and then answering the following questions:

a. (1) What is business risk? What factors influence a firm's business risk?

   (2) What is operating leverage, and how does it affect a firm's business risk?

b. (1) What is meant by the terms *financial leverage* and *financial risk?*

   (2) How does financial risk differ from business risk?

c. Now, develop an example that can be presented to CDSS's management. As an illustration, consider two hypothetical firms, Firm U, with zero debt financing, and Firm L, with $10,000 of 12 percent debt. Both firms have $20,000 in total assets and a 40 percent marginal tax rate, and they face the following EBIT probability distribution for next year:

| Probability | EBIT |
|---|---|
| 0.25 | $2,000 |
| 0.50 | 3,000 |
| 0.25 | 4,000 |

   (1) Complete the following partial income statements and the set of ratios for Firm L.

   (2) What does this example illustrate concerning the impact of financial leverage on expected rate of return and risk?

d. With the preceding points in mind, now consider the optimal capital structure for CDSS.

   (1) To begin, define the term *optimal capital structure.*

   (2) Describe briefly, without using numbers, the sequence of events that would occur if CDSS decided to change its capital structure to include more debt.

|  | **Firm U** | | | **Firm L** | | |
|---|---|---|---|---|---|---|
| Assets | $ 20,000 | $ 20,000 | $ 20,000 | $ 20,000 | $ 20,000 | $ 20,000 |
| Equity | $ 20,000 | $ 20,000 | $ 20,000 | $ 10,000 | $ 10,000 | $ 10,000 |
| | | | | | | |
| Probability | 0.25 | 0.50 | 0.25 | 0.25 | 0.50 | 0.25 |
| Sales | $ 6,000 | $ 9,000 | $ 12,000 | $ 6,000 | $ 9,000 | $ 12,000 |
| Operating costs | ( 4,000) | ( 6,000) | ( 8,000) | ( 4,000) | ( 6,000) | ( 8,000) |
| Earnings before | | | | | | |
| interest and taxes | $ 2,000 | $ 3,000 | $ 4,000 | $ 2,000 | $ 3,000 | $ 4,000 |
| Interest (12%) | ( 0) | ( 0) | ( 0) | ( 1,200) | | ( 1,200) |
| Earnings before taxes | $ 2,000 | $ 3,000 | $ 4,000 | $ 800 | $ | $ 2,800 |
| Taxes (40%) | ( 800) | ( 1,200) | ( 1,600) | ( 320) | | ( 1,120) |
| Net income | $ 1,200 | $ 1,800 | $ 2,400 | $ 480 | $ | $ 1,680 |

| | | | | | | |
|---|---|---|---|---|---|---|
| $ROE = \dfrac{\text{Net income}}{\text{Common equity}}$ | 6.0% | 9.0% | 12.0% | 4.8% | % | 16.8% |
| $TIE = \dfrac{\text{EBIT}}{\text{Interest}}$ | ∞ | ∞ | ∞ | 1.7× | × | 3.3× |
| Expected ROE | | 9.0% | | | 10.8% | |
| Expected TIE | | ∞ | | | 2.5× | |
| $\sigma_{ROE}$ | | 2.1% | | | 4.2% | |
| TIE | | 0× | | | 0.6× | |

**(3)** Assume that shares could be repurchased at the current market price of $20 per share. Calculate CDSS's expected EPS and TIE at debt levels of $0, $250,000, $500,000, $750,000, and $1,000,000. How many shares would remain after recapitalization under each scenario? [EPS = (Net income)/(Outstanding shares)]

**(4)** What would be the new stock price if CDSS recapitalizes with $250,000 of debt? $500,000? $750,000? $1,000,000? Recall that the CDSS pays out all earnings as dividends, so g = 0.

**(5)** Considering only the levels of debt discussed, what is CDSS's optimal capital structure?

**(6)** Is EPS maximized at the debt level that maximizes share price? Why?

**(7)** What is the WACC at the optimal capital structure?

**e.** Suppose you discovered that CDSS had more business risk than you originally estimated. Describe how this would affect the analysis. What if the firm had less business risk than originally estimated?

**f.** What is meant by the terms *degree of operating leverage (DOL)*, *degree of financial leverage (DFL)*, and *degree of total leverage (DTL)*? If fixed costs total $40,000 and the company uses $500,000 of debt, what are CDSS's degrees of each type of leverage? Of what practical use is the degree of leverage concept?

**g.** What are some factors that should be considered when establishing a firm's target capital structure?

**h.** Put labels on the following graph, and then discuss the graph as you might use it to explain to your boss why CDSS might want to use some debt.

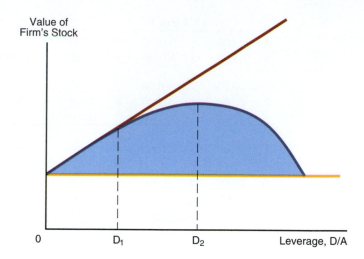

i.  How does the existence of asymmetric information and signaling affect capital structure?

## Computer-Related Problem

*Work the problem in this section only if you are using the problem spreadsheet.*

**effects of financial leverage**

**12-17**  Use the model in File C12 to work this problem.

a.  Rework Problem 12-14, assuming that the old long-term debt will not remain outstanding but, rather, that it must be refinanced at the new long-term interest rate of 12 percent. What effect does this have on the decision to refinance?

b.  What would be the effect on the refinancing decision if the rate on long-term debt fell to 5 percent or rose to 20 percent, assuming that all long-term debt must be refinanced?

c.  Which financing method would be recommended if the stock price (1) rose to $105 or (2) fell to $30? (Assume that all debt will have an interest rate of 12 percent.)

d.  With $P_0 = \$60$ and $r_d = 12\%$, change the sales probability distribution to the following:

| Alternative 1 | | Alternative 2 | |
| --- | --- | --- | --- |
| **Sales** | **Probability** | **Sales** | **Probability** |
| $2,250 | 0.0 | $    0 | 0.3 |
| 2,700 | 1.0 | 2,700 | 0.4 |
| 3,150 | 0.0 | 7,500 | 0.3 |

What are the implications of these changes?

**GET REAL WITH  THOMSON ONE | Business School Edition**

**financial leverage**

**12-18**  Family Dollar Stores [FDO], a firm operating discount retail stores, has no long-term debt in its capital structure, even though the use of financial leverage in the form of long-term debt might increase the firm's earnings per share. Answer the following questions about Family Dollar:

**a.** What was the EBIT—that is, operating income—of Family Dollar for the past three years? [*Hint:* Click on Financials/Financial Statements.]

**b.** Calculate the firm's net income and earnings per share for the past three years.

**c.** What was the average earnings per share during the past three years?

**d.** If the firm borrows $740 million in long-term debt at 10 percent to help finance its operations during the first year, what would be the earnings per share in each year?

**e.** Should Family Dollar start using long-term debt? Explain your answer.

**f.** Based on your findings, make an argument for and against using long-term debt in a firm's capital structure.

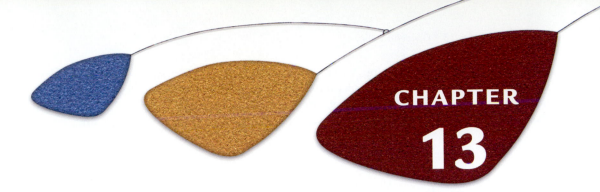

# Dividend Policy

## A MANAGERIAL PERSPECTIVE

The Managerial Perspective at the beginning of Chapter 12 described the actions Unisys Corporation, a manufacturer of computers and related products for commercial and defense companies, took to reduce the relative amount of debt in its capital structure. One of the first actions taken to improve the financial position of the firm was to suspend the payment of common stock dividends. This policy, which directly affected stockholders' cash receipts, has been in effect since the board of directors made the decision in September 1990. Prior to that time, Unisys had paid a regular dividend to common stockholders for nearly 100 years. So why were dividend payments suspended? According to James Unruh, president and CEO at the time (he was replaced by Lawrence A. Weinbach in 1997), the dividend suspension was in the "best interest" of shareholders—the board felt Unisys needed to strengthen its financial condition to improve *shareholder wealth*.

Suspending the common stock dividend saved Unisys more than $162 million a year and allowed the company to use the funds to reduce debt. When Unisys announced the dividend suspension, the price of its common stock dropped more than 25 percent in one day and by about one-third of its preannouncement value within one week. Clearly, the suspension of the dividend payments was not greeted favorably by the stockholders. By 1994, Unisys

stock was selling for $11 per share, and at the end of 1999 the price was above $45. During this five-year period, even though dividends were not being paid, the stock's value grew by nearly 30 percent per year. It seems the stockholders realized the dividend suspension in 1990 was beneficial for long-run stability and wealth maximization. Unfortunately, technology stocks, including Unisys, suffered substantial operating losses in 2000, and this trend continued into 2001. At the end of June 2001, Unisys stock had dropped to less than $15 per share. The decline in share price was compounded by the fact that Unisys had difficulty meeting its earnings expectations. At the beginning of 2004, Unisys projected that its "normal" earnings would increase by 20 percent during the year. Unfortunately, this forecast did not consider the effects of the firm's substantial pension costs on earnings in 2004. And in 2005, continuing reorganization efforts produced substantial losses, which dropped the price of the stock to less than $10 per share. Although the per-share price of the stock remained below $10 in 2006, analysts were encouraged about the company's future, and thus they forecasted that the stock price would increase in future years.

As you can see from this example, a firm's dividend policy can have a significant impact on its market value. Also, from this Managerial Perspective, as well as the one in Chapter 12, it should be clear that a firm's dividend policy affects its capital structure: A firm can use each dollar of earnings to finance projects internally or to pay dividends to stockholders, but not both. As you read this chapter, think about why Unisys suspended its common stock dividend. Consider the impact a particular dividend policy can have on the cash position of a firm and, more important, how a change in the policy can affect the value of a firm.

## Chapter *Essentials*
### —The Questions

After reading this chapter, you should be able to answer the following questions:

- What is an optimal dividend policy?
- What dividend payment policies are followed in practice?
- What factors affect dividend policy decisions?
- How does a stock split (dividend) work? Why would a firm initiate a stock split (pay a dividend in stock)?
- How do dividend payment policies in the United States compare with policies around the world?

We refer to the cash payments, or distributions, made to stockholders from the firm's earnings, whether those earnings were generated in the current period or in previous periods, as **dividends.** Consequently, a firm's *dividend policy* involves the decision to pay out earnings or to retain them for reinvestment in the firm. Remember that, according to the constant dividend growth model given in Chapter 7, the value of common stock can be computed as $P_0 = \hat{D}_1/(r_s - g)$. This equation shows that if the firm adopts a policy of paying out more cash dividends, $\hat{D}_1$ will rise, which will tend to increase the price of the stock. However, everything else equal, if cash dividends are increased, then less money will be available for reinvestment in the firm, and the expected future growth rate, g, will be lowered, which will depress the price of the stock. Thus, changing the dividend has two opposing effects. *The* **optimal dividend policy** *for a firm strikes that balance between current dividends and future growth that maximizes the price of the stock.*

In this chapter, we first examine factors that affect the optimal dividend policy and the types of dividend policies generally used by firms.

**dividends**
Cash distributions made to stockholders from the firm's earnings, whether those earnings were generated in the current period or in previous periods.

**optimal dividend policy**
The dividend policy that strikes a balance between current dividends and future growth and maximizes the firm's stock price.

## DIVIDEND POLICY AND STOCK VALUE

How do dividend policy decisions affect a firm's stock price? Academic researchers have studied this question extensively for many years, and they have yet to reach definitive conclusions. On the one hand, there are those who suggest that dividend policy is *irrelevant* because they argue a firm's value should be determined by the basic earning power and business risk of the firm, in which case value depends only on the income (cash) produced, not on how the income is split between dividends and retained earnings (and hence growth).

Proponents of this line of reasoning, called the **dividend irrelevance theory,** would contend that investors care only about the *total returns* they receive, not whether they receive those returns in the form of dividends, capital gains, or both. Thus, *if the dividend irrelevance theory is correct, there exists no optimal dividend policy because dividend policy does not affect the value of the firm.*[1]

**dividend irrelevance theory**
The theory that a firm's dividend policy has no effect on either its value or its cost of capital.

---

[1]The principal proponents of the *dividend irrelevance theory* are Miller and Modigliani (MM), who outlined their theory in "Dividend Policy, Growth, and the Valuation of Shares," *Journal of Business,* October 1961, 411–433. The assumptions MM made to develop their dividend irrelevance theory are similar to those they introduced in their capital structure theory mentioned in the previous chapter, which include no personal taxes, no brokerage costs, no bankruptcy, and so forth. Such assumptions are made to afford them the ability to develop a manageable theory.

On the other hand, it is quite possible that investors prefer one dividend policy more than another; if so, a firm's dividend policy is *relevant*. For example, it has been argued that investors prefer to receive dividends "today" because current dividend payments are more certain than the future capital gains that *might* result from investing retained earnings in growth opportunities, so $r_s$ should decrease as the dividend payout is increased.[2]

Another factor that might cause investors to prefer a particular dividend policy is the tax effect of dividend receipts. Investors must pay taxes at the time dividends and capital gains are received. Thus, depending on his or her tax situation, an investor might prefer either a payout of current earnings as dividends, which would be taxed in the current period, or capital gains associated with growth in stock value, which would be taxed when the stock is sold, perhaps many years in the future. Investors who prefer to delay the impact of taxes would be willing to pay more for low payout companies than for otherwise similar high payout companies, and vice versa.

Those who believe the firm's dividend policy is relevant are proponents of the **dividend relevance theory,** which asserts that dividend policy can affect the value of a firm through investors' preferences.

> **dividend relevance theory**
> The value of a firm is affected by its dividend policy—the optimal dividend policy is the one that maximizes the firm's value.

**Self-Test Questions**

Differentiate between the dividend irrelevance theory and the dividend relevance theory.

How might taxes affect investors' preferences concerning the receipt of dividends and capital gains?

## INVESTORS AND DIVIDEND POLICY

Although academic researchers have studied the dividend policy issue extensively, the issue remains unresolved; researchers at this time simply cannot tell corporate decision makers exactly how dividend policy affects stock prices and capital costs. But the research has provided some views concerning investors' reactions to dividend policy changes and why firms have particular dividend policies. Three of these views are discussed in this section.

## Information Content, or Signaling

If investors expect a company's dividend to increase by 5 percent per year, and if, in fact, the dividend is increased by 5 percent, then the stock price generally will not change significantly on the day the dividend increase is announced. In Wall Street parlance, such a dividend increase would be "discounted," or *anticipated,* by the market, so the announcement would not be considered newsworthy. However, if investors expect a 5 percent increase, but the company actually increases the dividend by 25 percent—say from $2 to $2.50—this generally would be considered "good," unanticipated news that should be accompanied by an increase in the price of the stock. Conversely, a less-than-expected dividend increase, or an unexpected reduction, generally would result in a price decline.

It is a well-known fact that corporations are extremely reluctant to cut dividends and, therefore, *managers do not raise dividends unless they anticipate higher, or at*

---

[2]Myron J. Gordon, "Optimal Investment and Financing Policy," *Journal of Finance,* May 1963, 264–272, and John Lintner, "Dividends, Earnings, Leverage, Stock Prices, and the Supply of Capital to Corporations," *Review of Economics and Statistics,* August 1962, 243–269.

*least stable, earnings in the future to sustain the higher dividends.* This means that a larger-than-expected dividend increase is taken by investors as a *signal* that the firm's management forecasts improved future earnings, whereas a dividend reduction signals a forecast of poor earnings. Thus, it can be argued investors' reactions to changes in dividend payments do not show that investors prefer dividends to retained earnings; rather, the stock price changes simply indicate that important information is contained in dividend announcements. In effect, dividend announcements provide investors with information previously known only to management. This theory is referred to as the **information content, or signaling, hypothesis.**

**information content (signaling) hypothesis**
The theory that investors regard dividend changes as signals of management's earnings forecasts.

## Clientele Effect

It also has been shown that it is very possible that a firm sets a particular dividend payout policy, which then attracts a *clientele* consisting of those investors who like the firm's dividend policy. For example, some stockholders, such as retired individuals, prefer current income to future capital gains, so they want the firm to pay out a higher percentage of its earnings. Other stockholders have no need for current investment income, so they favor a low payout ratio. If investors could not invest in companies with different dividend policies, it might be very expensive for them to achieve their investment goals—investors who prefer capital gains could reinvest any dividends they receive, but they first would have to pay taxes on the income. In essence, then, a **clientele effect** might exist if stockholders are attracted to companies because they have particular dividend policies. Those investors who desire current investment income can purchase shares in high-dividend-payout firms, whereas those who do not need current cash income can invest in low-payout firms. Consequently, we would expect the stock price of a firm to change if the firm changes its dividend policy because investors will adjust their portfolios to include firms with the desired dividend policy.

**clientele effect**
The tendency of a firm to attract the type of investor who likes its dividend policy.

## Free Cash Flow Hypothesis

If it is the intent of the financial manager to maximize the value of the firm, then investors should prefer that firms pay dividends only if acceptable capital budgeting opportunities do not exist. We know that acceptable capital budgeting projects increase the value of the firm. We also know that, because flotation costs are incurred when issuing new stock, it costs a firm more to raise funds using new common equity than it does using retained earnings. To maximize value, therefore, whenever possible a firm should use retained earnings rather than issue new common stock to finance capital budgeting projects. As a result, dividends should be paid only when *free cash flows* in excess of capital budgeting needs exist. If management does otherwise, the firm's value will not be maximized. According to the **free cash flow hypothesis,** the firm should distribute any earnings that cannot be reinvested at a rate at least as great as the investors' required rate of return, $r_s$—that is, payout, the free cash flows. Everything else equal, firms that retain *free cash flows* will have lower values than firms that distribute *free cash flows* because the firms that retain free cash flows actually decrease investors' wealth by investing in projects with IRR $< r_s$.

**free cash flow hypothesis**
All else equal, firms that pay dividends from cash flows that cannot be reinvested in positive net present value projects, which are termed *free cash flows,* have higher values than firms that retain free cash flows.

The free cash flow hypothesis might help to explain why investors react differently to identical dividend changes made by similar firms. For example, a firm's stock price should not change dramatically if it reduces its dividend for the purposes of investing in capital budgeting projects with positive NPVs. On the other hand, a company that reduces its dividend simply to increase free cash flows should experience a significant decline in the market value of its stock because the dividend reduction is not in the best interests of the stockholders—in this case, an agency problem exists. Thus, the free cash flow hypothesis suggests that a firm's dividend policy can provide information about its behavior with respect to wealth maximization.

**Self-Test Question**

Define (1) information content, (2) the clientele effect, and (3) the free cash flow hypothesis, and explain how each affects dividend policy.

## TYPES OF DIVIDEND PAYMENTS IN PRACTICE

Although no one has been able to develop a formula that can be used to tell management specifically how a given dividend policy will affect a firm's stock price, management still must establish a dividend policy. In this section, we discuss the four dividend payout policies we generally observe in practice.

### Residual Dividend Policy

In practice, dividend policy is very much influenced by investment opportunities and by the availability of funds with which to finance new investments. This fact has led to the development of a **residual dividend policy,** which states that a firm should follow these steps when deciding how much earnings should be paid out as dividends: (1) determine the optimal capital budget for the year, (2) determine the amount of capital needed to finance that budget, (3) use retained earnings to supply the equity component to the extent possible, and (4) *pay dividends only if more earnings are available than are needed to support the optimal capital budget.* The word *residual* means "left over," and the residual policy implies that dividends should be paid only out of "leftover" earnings.

The basis of the residual policy is the fact that *investors prefer to have the firm retain and reinvest earnings rather than pay them out in dividends if the rate of return the firm can earn on reinvested earnings exceeds the rate investors, on average, can themselves obtain on other investments of comparable risk.* For example, if the corporation can reinvest retained earnings at a 12 percent rate of return, whereas the best rate the average stockholder can obtain if the earnings are passed on in the form of dividends is 10 percent, then stockholders should prefer to have the firm retain the profits.

To continue, we saw in Chapter 11 that the cost of retained earnings is an *opportunity cost* that reflects rates of return available to equity investors. If a firm's stockholders can buy other stocks of equal risk and obtain a 12 percent dividend-plus-capital-gains yield, then 12 percent is the firm's cost of retained earnings. The cost of new outside equity raised by selling common stock will be higher than 12 percent because of the costs associated with issuing the new stock (flotation costs).

Most firms have a target capital structure that calls for at least some debt, so new financing is done partly with debt and partly with equity. As long as the firm finances with the optimal mix of debt and equity, and as long as it uses only internally generated equity (retained earnings), its marginal cost of each new dollar of capital will be minimized. Internally generated equity is available for financing a certain amount of new investment, but beyond that amount the firm must turn to more expensive new common stock. At the point where new stock must be sold, the cost of equity, and consequently the marginal cost of capital, rises.

These concepts, which were developed in Chapter 11, are illustrated in Figure 13-1 with data from the Texas and Western (T&W) Transport Company. T&W has a marginal cost of capital (MCC) of 10 percent. However, this cost rate assumes that all additional

**residual dividend policy**
A policy in which the dividend paid is set equal to the actual earnings minus the amount of retained earnings necessary to finance the firm's optimal capital budget.

FIGURE 13-1    Texas and Western Transport Company; Marginal Cost of Capital

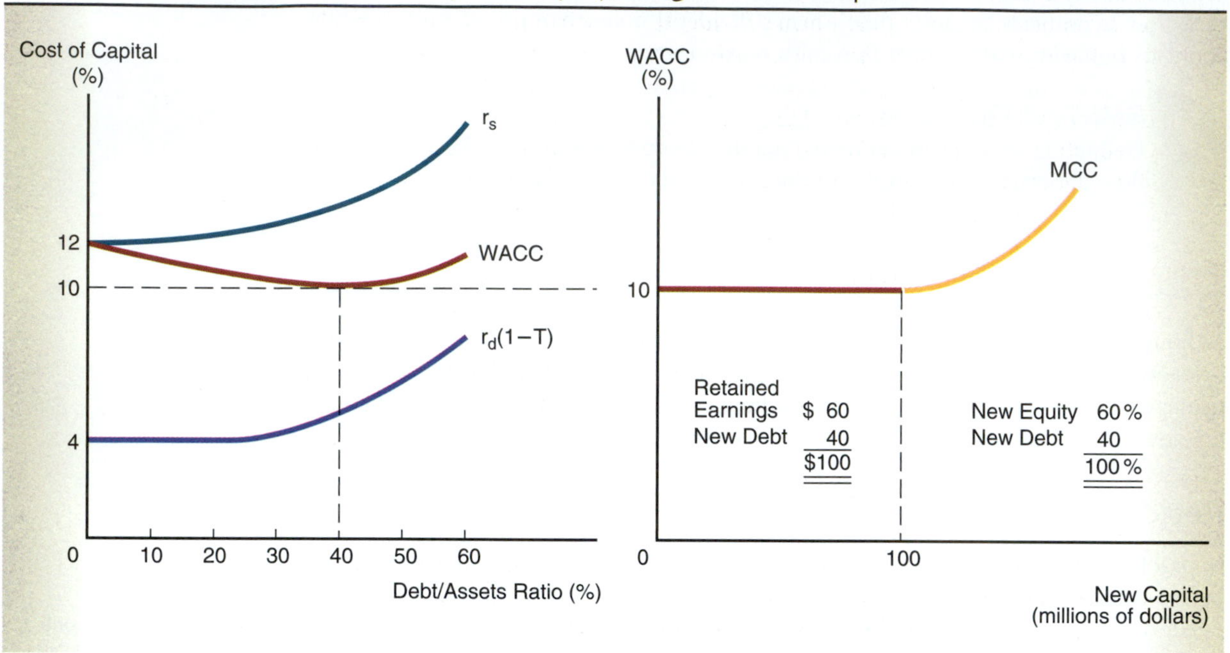

equity comes from retained earnings. Therefore, MCC = 10% as long as retained earnings are available, but the MCC begins to rise at the point where new stock must be sold.

T&W has $60 million of net income and a 40 percent debt ratio at its optimal capital structure. Provided it does not pay cash dividends, T&W can make net investments (investments in addition to asset replacements financed from depreciation) of $100 million, consisting of $60 million from retained earnings plus $40 million of new debt, at a 10 percent marginal cost of capital. Therefore, its MCC is constant at 10 percent up to $100 million of capital, beyond which it rises as the firm begins to use more expensive new common stock.

Suppose T&W's director of capital budgeting has determined that the optimal capital budget requires an investment equal to $70 million. The $70 million will be financed using $28 million debt ($70 million × 0.40) and $42 million in common equity ($70 million × 0.60). So the $60 million in retained earnings will be more than sufficient to cover the common equity financing requirement, and the *residual* of $18 million ($60 million – $42 million) can be paid out as dividends to stockholders.

Now suppose T&W's optimal capital budget is $150 million. Should dividends be paid? Not if T&W follows the residual dividend policy. The $150 million capital budgeting needs will be financed with $60 million debt ($150 million × 0.40) and $90 million common equity ($150 million × 0.60). The common equity financing requirement of $90 million exceeds the $60 million retained earnings available, so $30 million of new common equity will have to be issued. The new, or external, common equity will have a higher cost than retained earnings, so the marginal cost of capital for T&W will be higher. Under these conditions, T&W should not pay dividends to its stockholders. If the company pays part of its earnings in dividends, the marginal cost of capital will be even higher because more common stock will have to be issued to account for the amount of retained earnings paid out as dividends. For example, if T&W pays stockholders $20 million in dividends, it still needs $90 million of common equity to satisfy the capital budgeting requirements. In this case, $50 million of external equity will be required, which means T&W's marginal cost of capital will increase sooner—new common equity will have to be issued when $40 million rather than $60 million of retained earnings are used. So to maximize value, T&W should retain all of its earnings for capital budgeting needs. Consequently, *according to the residual dividend policy, a firm that has to issue new common stock to finance capital budgeting needs does not have residual earnings, and dividends will be zero.*

Because both the earnings level and the capital budgeting needs of a firm vary from year to year, strict adherence to the residual dividend policy would result in dividend variability. One year the firm might declare zero dividends because investment opportunities are good, but the next year it might pay a large dividend because investment opportunities are poor. Similarly, fluctuating earnings would also lead to variable dividends even if investment opportunities were stable over time. Thus, following the residual dividend policy would be optimal only if investors were not bothered by fluctuating dividends. However, if investors prefer stable, dependable dividends, $r_s$ would be higher and the stock price lower, if the firm followed the residual theory in a strict sense rather than attempting to stabilize its dividends over time.

## Stable, Predictable Dividends

In the past, many firms set a specific annual dollar dividend per share and then maintained it, increasing the annual dividend only if it seemed clear that future earnings would be sufficient to allow the new dividend to be maintained. A corollary of that policy was this rule: *Never reduce the annual dividend.*

When the economy expands quickly, inflationary pressures plus reinvested earnings generally tend to push earnings up, so many firms that would otherwise follow the stable dollar dividend payment policy switch to a "stable growth rate" policy. Here the firm sets a target growth rate for dividends—for example, 4 percent per year—and strives to increase dividends by this amount each year. Obviously, earnings must be growing at a reasonably steady rate for this policy to be feasible, but when it can be followed, such a policy provides investors with a stable real income.

A fairly typical dividend policy, that of Eastman Kodak, is illustrated in Figure 13-2. Prior to 1982, Kodak's earnings exhibited relatively stable growth, and so did the payout of dividends. But after 1982, more intense global competition, major litigation, and changing economic periods caused a great deal of volatility in Kodak's earnings. Management stopped increasing the dividend when earnings fell but did not cut the dividend, even when earnings failed to cover it. Maintaining the dividend was Kodak's way of signaling to stockholders that management was confident that any declines in earnings were only temporary and that earnings would soon resume their upward trend. This was indeed the case—since 1992 earnings have fluctuated significantly, but Kodak maintained a nearly constant dividend until September 25, 2003, when the dividend was cut by 72 percent. Kodak cut the dividend to help pay for the estimated $3 billion in capital budgeting investments that the company expected to make during the following three years when it planned to place greater emphasis on digital imaging products to generate future revenues. In addition, cutting the dividend helped Kodak to maintain what it considered to be an appropriate capital structure. On the day that the dividend cut was announced, the market price of Kodak's common stock dropped by nearly 20 percent. During the three months following the dividend cut, however, the stock price increased more than 40 percent because investors became convinced that the decision to cut the dividend was made to improve the company's wealth position—that is, the cut was in the best interests of shareholders. As the result of a realignment of its operations in 2004, Kodak's earnings dropped by 65 percent and dividends were cut by more than 50 percent. Although earnings were expected to increase in 2007 and beyond, the company did not have plans to increase dividends in subsequent years. If Kodak improves its competitive position, especially in digital

**FIGURE 13-2    Eastman Kodak: Earnings per Share (EPS) and Dividends per Share (DPS), 1978–2010**

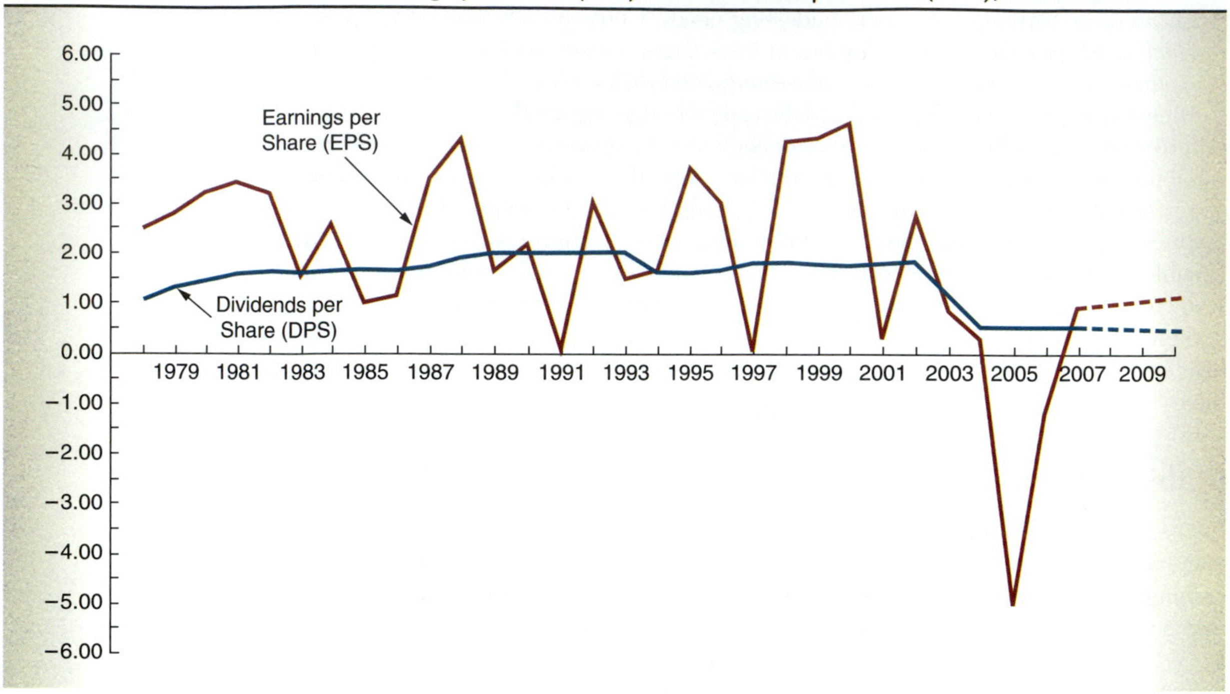

**Note:** Projected values, which are shown as dashed lines, are based on forecasts from sources available in the Internet, including Charles Schwab (located at http://www.schwab.com).

imaging, which accounts for more than 60 percent of its revenues, dividends most likely will be increased to pre-2003 levels at some point.

There are two good reasons for paying **stable, predictable dividends** rather than following the residual dividend policy. First, given the existence of the information content, or signaling, idea, a fluctuating payment policy would lead to greater uncertainty, hence to a higher $r_s$ and a lower stock price, than would exist under a stable policy. Second, many stockholders use dividends for current consumption, and they would be put to trouble and expense if they had to sell part of their shares to obtain cash if the company cut the dividend.

As a rule, stable, predictable dividends imply more certainty than variable dividends, thus a lower $r_s$ and a higher firm value. So it is this dividend policy that most firms favor. Even though the optimal dividend as prescribed by the residual policy might vary somewhat from year to year, a firm might delay some investment projects, depart from its target capital structure during a particular year, or even issue new common stock to avoid the problems associated with unstable dividends and to provide a lower $r_s$ and a higher firm value.

## Constant Payout Ratio

It would be possible for a firm to pay out a constant *percentage* of earnings (dividends per share divided by earnings per share), but because earnings surely will fluctuate, this policy would mean that the dollar amount of dividends would vary. For example, if Eastman Kodak had followed the policy of paying a constant percentage of earnings per share, say 40 percent, the dividends per share paid since 1978 would have fluctuated exactly the same as earnings per share as shown in Figure 13-2, and thus the company would have had to cut its dividend in several different years. Therefore, with the **constant payout ratio** dividend policy, if earnings fluctuate, investors would have

---

**stable, predictable dividends**
Payment of a specific dollar dividend each year, or periodically increasing the dividend at a constant rate—the annual dollar dividend is relatively predictable by investors.

**constant payout ratio**
Payment of a constant *percentage* of earnings as dividends each year.

had much greater uncertainty concerning the expected dividends each year, and chances are $r_s$ also would be greater; hence, its stock price would be lower. Although Kodak's stock price fluctuated somewhat from 1978 to 1997, it showed a general upward trend despite the substantial earnings fluctuations exhibited in Figure 13-2. In an effort to strengthen its financial position, in 1997 Kodak initiated a restructuring program to reduce annual costs by $1.5 billion. Part of the plan was to reduce payroll by laying off nearly 20,000 employees within three years. Because of these factors, Kodak's stock price fell approximately 25 percent in 1997. Since 2001, however, the stock's price has fluctuated between $25 and $35. Had it cut the dividend to keep the payout ratio constant from 1978 to 2006, Kodak's stock price would have "fallen out of bed" several times if investors interpreted the dividend reduction as a signal that management thought the earnings declines were permanent.

## Low Regular Dividend Plus Extras

A policy of paying a low regular dividend plus a year-end extra in good years is a compromise between a stable dividend (or stable growth rate) and a constant payout rate. Such a policy gives the firm flexibility, yet investors can count on receiving at least a minimum dividend. Therefore, if a firm's earnings and cash flows are quite volatile, this policy might be its best choice. The directors can set a relatively low regular dividend—low enough so that it can be maintained even in low-profit years or in years when a considerable amount of retained earnings is needed for investments—and then supplement it with an **extra dividend** in years when excess funds are available. Ford, General Motors, and other auto companies, whose earnings fluctuate widely from year to year, formerly followed such a policy, but in recent years they have joined the crowd and now follow a stable dividend policy.

**extra dividend**
A supplemental dividend paid in years when the firm does well and excess funds are available for distribution.

> ### Self-Test Questions
>
> Explain the logic of the residual dividend policy, the steps a firm would take to implement it, and why it is more likely to be used to establish a long-run payout target than to set the actual year-by-year payout ratio.
>
> Describe the stable, predictable dividend policy, and give two reasons why a firm might follow such a policy.
>
> Describe the constant payout ratio dividend policy. Why is this policy probably not as popular as a constant, or steadily increasing, dividend policy?
>
> Explain what a low-regular-dividend-plus-extras policy is and why a firm might follow such a policy.
>
> Brentford Books has determined that its capital budgeting needs for the year equal $120,000 and earnings are expected to be $90,000. The company's debt/assets ratio is 30 percent. How much will Brentford pay out as dividends if it (1) follows the residual dividend policy or (2) uses a 60 dividend payout ratio to determine dividends? (*Answers:* $6,000; $54,000)

## PAYMENT PROCEDURES

Dividends normally are paid semiannually or quarterly, and, when conditions permit, the dividend is increased. For example, on October 17, 2006, the board of directors of Eastman Kodak declared a $0.25 semiannual common stock dividend. Earlier in the year, Kodak's board indicated that it anticipated the *annual* dividend to be $0.50, which was the same as the dividend paid in 2005. Kodak's stockholders were not surprised when the $0.25 semiannual dividend was announced, but they would have been *shocked* if the dividend had been eliminated because Kodak has paid a dividend since 1902.

When Kodak *declared* the semiannual dividend, it issued the following statement:[3]

### Kodak Board Declares Semi-Annual Cash Dividend

ROCHESTER, N.Y., Oct. 17—Eastman Kodak Company's board of directors today declared a semi-annual cash dividend of 25 cents per share on the outstanding common stock of the company.

The 25-cent per share dividend declared today will be payable December 14, 2006 to shareholders of record at the close of business on November 1, 2006.

The three dates included in this announcement are important to current stockholders. These dates, as well as the ex-dividend date, are defined as follows:

1. **Declaration date.** On the *declaration date,* October 17, 2006, in Kodak's case, the board of directors meets and declares the regular dividend. For accounting purposes, the declared dividend becomes a liability to the firm on the declaration date, and if a balance sheet were constructed, the amount ($0.25 × Number of shares outstanding) would appear as a current liability, and retained earnings would be reduced by a like amount.

2. **Holder-of-record date.** At the close of business on the **holder-of-record date,** or **date of record,** the company closes its stock transfer books and produces a list of shareholders as of that date. Thus, if Kodak was notified of the sale and transfer of some stock before 5 p.m. on Wednesday, November 1, 2006, then the new owner received the dividend. However, if notification was received after November 2, the previous owner of the stock got the dividend check because his or her name appeared on the company's ownership records.

3. **Ex-dividend date.** The securities industry has set up a convention of declaring that the right to the dividend remains with the stock until two business days *prior to* the holder-of-record date. This is to ensure the company is notified of the transfer in time to record the new owner and thus pay the dividend to him or her. The date when the right to receive the next dividend payment no longer goes with the stock—that is, new purchasers will not receive the next dividend—is called the **ex-dividend date.** In the case of Kodak, the *ex-dividend* date was Monday, October 30, 2006, which is two *business days* before the *holder-of-record* date, Wednesday, November 1, 2006. Therefore, any investor who purchased the stock on or after that date did not receive the next dividend payment associated with the stock. All else equal, then, we would expect that the price of Kodak's stock dropped on the ex-dividend date by approximately the amount of the dividend. Assuming no other price fluctuations, the price at which Kodak's stock opened on Monday, October 30, 2006, should have been approximately $0.25 less than

**holder-of-record date (date of record)**
The date the company opens the ownership books to determine who will receive the next dividend; the stockholders of record on this date receive the dividend.

**ex-dividend date**
The date on which the right to the next dividend no longer accompanies a stock; it usually is two working days prior to the holder-of-record date.

---

[3]This statement was the announcement Kodak posted on the company's website, which was located at http://www.kodak.com/.

the close on Friday, October 27.[4] Indeed, at the beginning of the trading day on October 30, 2006, Kodak's stock was trading for 23 cents lower than its closing price on October 27, 2006 ($23.97 versus $24.20).

4. **Payment date.** Kodak paid the common stock dividends on Thursday, December 14, 2006—this is the *payment date.* Many firms now pay dividends electronically.

**payment date**
The date on which a firm actually makes the dividend payment.

## DIVIDEND REINVESTMENT PLANS

Most large companies offer **dividend reinvestment plans (DRIPs),** whereby stockholders can automatically reinvest dividends they receive in the stock of the paying corporation.[5] There are two types of DRIPs (referred to as "drips"): (1) plans that involve only "old" stock that already is outstanding and traded in the financial markets and (2) plans that involve newly issued stock. In either case, the stockholder must pay income taxes on the amount of the dividends even though stock rather than cash is received.

Under the "old-stock" type of plan, the stockholder chooses between receiving dividend checks or having the company use the dividends to buy more stock in the corporation. If the stockholder elects reinvestment, a bank, acting as trustee, takes the total funds available for reinvestment, purchases the corporation's stock on the open market, and allocates the shares purchased to the participating stockholders' accounts on a *pro rata* basis. The transaction costs of buying shares (brokerage costs) are low because of volume purchases, so these plans benefit small stockholders who do not need cash dividends for current consumption.

The "new-stock" type of DRIP provides for dividends to be invested in newly issued stock; hence, these plans raise new capital for the firm. Companies use such plans to raise substantial amounts of new equity capital. No fees are charged to stockholders, and many companies offer stock at a discount of 5 percent below the

**dividend reinvestment plan (DRIP)**
A plan that enables a stockholder to automatically reinvest dividends received back into the stock of the paying firm.

---

[4]Tax effects cause the price decline on average to be less than the full amount of the dividend. Suppose you were an investor in the 40 percent tax bracket. If you bought Kodak's stock on October 27, you would receive the dividend, but you would have to pay 40 percent of it out in taxes within one year. Thus, you would want to wait until after October 27 to buy the stock if you thought you could get it for $0.25 less per share. Your reaction, and those of others, would influence stock prices around dividend payment dates. Here is what would happen:

1. Other things held constant, a stock's price should rise during the six-month period, with the daily price increase (for Kodak) equal to $0.25/180 = $0.0014. Therefore, if the price started at $30 just after its last ex-dividend date, it would rise to $30.25 on October 27.

2. In the absence of taxes, the stock's price would fall to $30 on October 30 and then start up as the next dividend accrual period began. Thus, over time, if everything else were held constant, the stock's price would follow a sawtooth pattern if it were plotted on a graph.

3. Because of taxes, the stock's price would neither rise by the full amount of the dividend nor fall by the full dividend amount when it goes ex-dividend.

4. The amount of the rise and subsequent fall would depend on the average investor's marginal tax rate.

See Edwin J. Elton and Martin J. Gruber, "Marginal Stockholder Tax Rates and the Clientele Effect," *Review of Economics and Statistics,* February 1970, 68–74, for an interesting discussion of this concept.

[5]See Richard H. Pettway and R. Phil Malone, "Automatic Dividend Reinvestment Plans," *Financial Management,* Winter 1973, 11–18, for an excellent discussion of this topic.

actual market price. The companies absorb these costs as a trade-off against the flotation costs that would have been incurred had they sold stock through investment bankers rather than through the dividend reinvestment plans.[6]

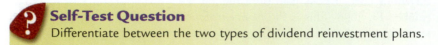

**Self-Test Question**

Differentiate between the two types of dividend reinvestment plans.

## FACTORS INFLUENCING DIVIDEND POLICY

In addition to management's beliefs concerning which dividend theory is most correct, a number of other factors are considered when a particular dividend policy is chosen. The factors firms take into account can be grouped into these five broad categories:

1. **Constraints on dividend payments.** The amount of dividends a firm can pay might be limited due to (1) debt contract restrictions, which often stipulate that no dividends can be paid unless certain financial measures exceed stated minimums; (2) the fact that dividend payments cannot exceed the balance sheet item "retained earnings" (this is known as the *impairment of capital rule,* which is designed to protect creditors by prohibiting the company from distributing assets to stockholders before debt holders are paid); (3) cash availability because cash dividends can be paid only with cash; and (4) restrictions imposed by the Internal Revenue Service (IRS) on improperly accumulated retained earnings. If the IRS can demonstrate that a firm's dividend payout ratio is being held down deliberately to help its stockholders avoid personal taxes, the firm is subject to tax penalties. But this factor generally is relevant only to privately owned firms.

2. **Investment opportunities.** Firms that have large numbers of acceptable capital budgeting projects generally have low dividend payout ratios, and vice versa. But if a firm can accelerate or postpone projects (flexibility), then it can adhere more closely to a target dividend policy.

3. **Alternative sources of capital.** When a firm needs to finance a given level of investments and flotation costs are high, the cost of external equity, $r_e$, will be well above the cost of internal equity, $r_s$, making it better to set a low payout ratio and to finance by retaining earnings rather than through sale of new common stock. Also, if the firm can adjust its debt/assets ratio without raising capital costs sharply, it can maintain a stable dollar dividend, even if earnings fluctuate, by using a variable debt/assets ratio.

4. **Ownership dilution.** If management is concerned about maintaining control, it might be reluctant to sell new stock; hence, the company might retain more earnings than it otherwise would.

5. **Effects of dividend policy on $r_s$.** The effects of dividend policy on $r_s$ might be considered in terms of four factors: (a) stockholders' desire for current versus future income, (b) the perceived riskiness of dividends versus capital

---

[6]One interesting aspect of DRIPs is that they are forcing corporations to reexamine their basic dividend policies. A high participation rate in a DRIP suggests that stockholders might be better off if the firm simply reduced cash dividends, as this would save stockholders some personal income taxes. Quite a few firms survey their stockholders to learn more about their preferences and to find out how they would react to a change in dividend policy. A more rational approach to basic dividend policy decisions might emerge from this research. Also, it should be noted that companies either use or stop using new-stock DRIPs depending on their need for equity capital.

gains, (c) the tax advantage of capital gains over most dividends, and (d) the information content of dividends (signaling). Because we discussed each of these factors earlier, we need only note here that the importance of each factor in terms of its effect on $r_s$ varies from firm to firm, depending on the makeup of its current and possible future stockholders.

It should be apparent from our discussions that dividend policy decisions truly are exercises in informed judgment, not decisions that can be quantified precisely. Even so, to make rational dividend decisions, financial managers must consider all the points discussed in the preceding sections.

**Self-Test Questions**

Identify the five broad categories of factors that affect dividend policy.

What constraints affect dividend policy?

How do investment opportunities affect dividend policy?

How does the availability and cost of outside capital affect dividend policy?

## STOCK DIVIDENDS AND STOCK SPLITS

Stock dividends and stock splits are related to the firm's cash dividend policy. The rationale for stock dividends and splits can best be explained through an example. We will use Porter Electronic Controls Inc., a $700 million electronic components manufacturer, for this purpose. Since its inception, Porter's markets have been expanding, and the company has enjoyed growth in sales and earnings. Some of its earnings have been paid out in dividends, but some are also retained each year, causing earnings per share and market price per share to grow. The company began its life with only a few thousand shares outstanding, and, after some years of growth, each of Porter's shares had very high earnings per share (EPS) and dividends per share (DPS). When a "normal" price/earnings (P/E) ratio was applied, the derived market price was so high that few people could afford to buy a "round lot" of 100 shares. This limited the demand for the stock and thus kept the total market value of the firm below what it would have been if more shares, at a lower price, had been outstanding. To correct this situation, Porter "split its stock," as described next.

### Stock Splits

Although there is little empirical evidence to support the contention, a widespread belief in financial circles holds that an *optimal*, or *psychological*, *price range* exists for stocks. "Optimal" means that if the price is within this range, the P/E ratio, hence the value of the firm, will be maximized. Many observers, including Porter's management, believe that the best range for most stocks is from $20 to $80 per share. Accordingly, if the price of Porter's stock rose to $90, management probably would declare a two-for-one **stock split,** thus doubling the number of shares outstanding, halving the earnings and dividends per share, and thereby lowering the price of the stock. Each stockholder would have more shares, but each share would be worth less. If the post-split price were $45, Porter's stockholders would be exactly as well off as they were before the split because they would have twice as many shares at half the price as before the split. However, if the price of the stock were to stabilize above $45, stockholders would be better off. Stock splits can be of any size—for example, the stock could be split 2-for-1, 3-for-1, 11.2-for-1, or in any other way.

**stock split**
An action taken by a firm to increase the number of shares outstanding and thus decrease the per-share price of the stock.

Reverse splits, which reduce the shares outstanding, can also be used. For instance, a company whose stock sells for $5 might employ a 1-for-5 reverse split, exchanging one new share for five old ones and raising the value of the shares to about $25, which is within the optimal range. On June 16, 2003, for example, Priceline.com Incorporated initiated a 1-for-6 reverse split to avoid being delisted from Nasdaq.

## Stock Dividends

**stock dividend**

A dividend paid in the form of additional shares of stock rather than cash.

**Stock dividends** are similar to stock splits in that they "divide the pie into smaller slices" without affecting the fundamental position of the current stockholders. On a 5 percent stock dividend, the holder of 100 shares would receive an additional five shares (without cost); on a 20 percent stock dividend, the same holder would receive 20 new shares; and so on. Again, the total number of shares is increased, so earnings, dividends, and price per share all decline.

If a firm wants to reduce the price of its stock, should it use a stock split or a stock dividend? Stock splits generally are used after a sharp price run-up to produce a large price reduction. Stock dividends typically are used on a regular annual basis to keep the stock price more or less constrained. For example, if a firm's earnings and dividends were growing at about 10 percent per year, its stock price would tend to go up at about that same rate, and it would soon be outside the desired trading range. A 10 percent annual stock dividend would maintain the stock price within the optimal trading range.

## Balance Sheet Effects

Although the economic effects of stock splits and stock dividends are virtually identical, accountants treat them somewhat differently. On a 2-for-1 split, the shares outstanding are doubled, and the stock's par value is halved. This treatment is shown in Section II of Table 13-1 for Porter Electronic Controls, using a pro forma 2009 balance sheet.

Section III of Table 13-1 shows the effect of a 20 percent stock dividend. With a stock dividend, the par value is not reduced, but an accounting entry is made transferring funds from the retained earnings account to the common stock and paid-in capital accounts. The transfer from retained earnings is calculated as follows:

**13–1**

$$\text{Dollars transferred from retained earnings} = \left[ \left( \begin{array}{c} \text{Number of} \\ \text{shares outstanding} \end{array} \right) \times \left( \begin{array}{c} \text{Percent stock dividend} \\ \text{stated as a decimal} \end{array} \right) \right] \times \left( \begin{array}{c} \text{Market price} \\ \text{of the stock} \end{array} \right)$$

Porter has 5 million shares outstanding, and they sell for $80 each, so a 20 percent stock dividend would require the transfer of $80 million:

$$\text{Dollars transferred} = [(5,000,000)(0.2)](\$80) = \$80,000,000$$

As shown in the table, $1 million of this $80 million is added to the common stock account and $79 million is added to the additional paid-in capital account. The retained earnings account is reduced from $285 million to $205 million.[7]

## Price Effects

Several empirical studies have examined the effects of stock splits and stock dividends on stock prices. These studies suggest that investors see stock splits and stock

---

[7]Note that Porter could not pay a stock dividend that exceeded 71.25 percent; a stock dividend of that percentage would exhaust the retained earnings. Thus, a firm's ability to declare stock dividends is constrained by the amount of its retained earnings. Of course, if Porter had wanted to pay a 50 percent stock dividend, it could have just switched to a 1½-for-1 stock split and accomplished the same thing in terms of the number of shares owned by stockholders.

| **TABLE 13-1** | Porter Electronic Controls Inc.: Stockholders' Equity Accounts, Pro Forma, December 31, 2009 ($ millions, except per share values) |
|---|---|

**I. Before a Stock Split or Stock Dividend**

| | |
|---|---|
| Common stock (5 million shares outstanding, $1 par) | $ 5.0 |
| Additional paid-in capital | 10.0 |
| Retained earnings | 285.0 |
| Total common stockholders' equity | $300.0 |
| Book value per share = $300/5 | $ 60.0 |

**II. After a Two-for-One Stock Split**

| | |
|---|---|
| Common stock (10 million shares outstanding, $0.50 par) | $ 5.0 |
| Additional paid-in capital | 10.0 |
| Retained earnings | 285.0 |
| Total common stockholders' equity | $300.0 |
| Book value per share = $300/10 | $ 30.0 |

**III. After a 20 Percent Stock Dividend**

| | |
|---|---|
| Common stock (6 million shares outstanding, $1 par)[a] | $ 6.0 |
| Additional paid-in capital[b] | 89.0 |
| Retained earnings[b] | 205.0 |
| Total common stockholders' equity | $300.0 |
| Book value per share = $300/6 | $ 50.0 |

[a]Shares outstanding are increased by 20 percent, from 5 million to 6 million.

[b]A transfer equal to the market value of the new shares is made from the retained earnings account to the additional paid-in capital and common stock accounts:

$$\text{Transfer} = [(5,000,000 \text{ shares})(0.2)](\$80) = \$80,000,000.$$

Of this $80 million, ($1 par)(1,000,000 shares) = $1,000,000 goes to common stock and the remaining $79 million to paid-in capital.

dividends for what they are—*simply additional pieces of paper.* If stock dividends and splits are accompanied by higher earnings and cash dividends, then investors will bid up the price of the stock. However, if stock dividends are not accompanied by increases in earnings and cash dividends, the dilution of earnings and dividends per share causes the price of the stock to drop by the same percentage as the stock dividend. Thus, the fundamental determinants of price are the underlying earnings and cash dividends per share, and stock splits and stock dividends merely cut the pie into thinner slices; neither action by itself produces a change in the total economic value of a firm's stock.

**Self-Test Questions**

What is the rationale for a stock split?

Differentiate between the accounting treatments for stock splits and stock dividends.

What is the effect of stock splits and dividends on stock prices?

Suppose that a stock that currently sells for $150 splits 3-for-1. What should the price per share be after the stock split? (*Answer:* $50)

Suppose that a firm "issues" a 5 percent stock dividend. The firm has 100,000 shares of common stock outstanding, its common stock account (it has no paid-in capital) currently equals $200,000, and its retained earnings account equals $100,000. How many shares of stock does the firm have to "issue" when it initiates the stock dividend? If the market value of the stock is $10 per share, what will be the balance in the common stock and retained earnings accounts after the stock dividend? (*Answers:* 5,000 shares; $250,000; $50,000)

## DIVIDEND POLICIES AROUND THE WORLD

The dividend policies of companies around the world vary considerably. Research indicates that the dividend payout ratios of companies range from 10.5 percent in the Philippines to nearly 70 percent in Taiwan.[8] Table 13-2 shows some of the differences in payout ratios. As you can see, as a percent of earnings, the dividends paid out in Canada, France, and the United States range from about 20 percent to 25 percent, in Spain and the United Kingdom the range is from 30 percent to 40 percent, in Germany and Mexico the rate is between 40 percent and 50 percent, and it is more than 50 percent for companies in Japan and Southeast Asian countries. A study of firms in developing countries, such as Zimbabwe and Pakistan, shows that emerging market firms have average payout ratios that range from approximately 30 percent to 60 percent.[9]

Why do international differences in dividend policies exist? As we mentioned in Chapter 12, it seems logical to attribute the differences to dissimilar tax structures because both dividends and capital gains are taxed differently around the world. The tax codes in most developed countries encourage personal investing and savings more than the U.S. tax code. For example, Germany, Italy, and many other European countries do not tax capital gains, and in most other developed countries, including Japan, France, and Canada, capital gains are not taxed unless they exceed some minimum amount. Further, in Germany and Italy, dividends are not taxed as income, and in most other countries some amount of dividends are tax exempt. The general conclusion we can make, then, is that in countries in which capital gains are not taxed, investors should show a preference for companies that retain earnings rather than pay dividends. But it has been found that differences in taxes do not fully explain the differences in dividend payout ratios among the countries.

A study by Rafael La Porta, Florencio Lopez-de-Silanes, Andrei Shleifer, and Robert W. Vishny offers some insight into the dividend policy differences that exist around the world.[10] They suggest that, all else equal, companies pay out greater amounts of earnings as dividends in countries that have measures that help protect the rights of minority stockholders. In such countries, however, firms with many growth opportunities tend to pay lower dividends, which is to be expected because the funds are needed to finance the growth and shareholders are willing to forgo current income in hopes of greater future benefits. On the other hand, in countries where shareholders' rights are not well protected, investors want dividends to be paid because there is great uncertainty about whether management will use earnings for self-gratification rather than for the benefit of the firm. Investors in these countries accept any dividends they can get—that is, they prefer a "bird in hand." Some countries,

---

[8]Rafael La Porta, Florencio Lopez-de-Silanes, Andrei Shleifer, and Robert W. Vishny, "Agency Problems and Dividend Policies around the World," *Journal of Finance*, February 2000, 1–34.

[9]Varouj Aivazian, Laurence Booth, and Sean Cleary, "Do Emerging Market Firms Follow Different Dividend Policies from U.S. Firms?" *Journal of Financial Research*, Fall 2003, 371–387.

[10]Rafael La Porta, Florencio Lopez-de-Silanes, Andrei Shleifer, and Robert W. Vishny, "Agency Problems and Dividend Policies around the World," *Journal of Finance*, February 2000, 1–34.

| **TABLE 13-2** Median Dividend Payout Ratios for Selected Countries |
|---|

### I. Dividend Payout Ratios Less Than 25 Percent

| Country | Payout Ratio |
|---|---|
| Philippines | 10.5 |
| Denmark | 17.3 |
| Canada | 19.8 |
| United States | 22.1 |
| France | 23.6 |

### II. Dividend Payout Ratios between 25 Percent and 40 Percent

| Country | Payout Ratio |
|---|---|
| Switzerland | 25.3 |
| Spain | 30.5 |
| South Africa | 35.6 |
| United Kingdom | 36.9 |
| Portugal | 38.0 |

### III. Dividend Payout Ratios above 40 Percent

| Country | Payout Ratio |
|---|---|
| Germany | 42.9 |
| Mexico | 46.4 |
| India | 49.3 |
| Japan | 52.9 |
| Taiwan | 68.9 |

**Source:** Rafael La Porta, Florencio Lopez-de-Silanes, Andrei Shleifer, and Robert W. Vishny, "Agency Problems and Dividend Policies Around the World," *Journal of Finance*, February 2000, 1–34.

including Brazil, Chile, Colombia, Greece, and Venezuela, have regulations requiring firms to pay dividends. In these countries, minority shareholders have few, if any, legally protected rights.

In summary, it appears the most important factor that determines whether stockholders prefer earnings be retained or paid out as dividends is the level of risk associated with future expected dividends, which is mitigated to some degree by regulations that protect minority shareholders' rights.

 **Self-Test Question**

Why do dividend payout ratios of companies differ among different countries?

**Chapter *Essentials***
**—The Answers**

After reading this chapter, you should be able to answer the following questions:

- **What is an optimal dividend policy?** Because the firm's goal is to maximize shareholders' wealth, the optimal dividend policy is the one that maximizes the value of the firm. When a firm pays dividends, it decreases the amount of earnings that can be used to invest in acceptable capital budgeting projects—that is, the amount that can be used to finance growth. As a result, firms that have many acceptable capital budgeting projects generally pay little or no dividends because earnings are retained to reinvest in the firm. On the other hand, firms with few acceptable capital budgeting projects generally pay out most of their earnings as dividends because not as much internal financing is needed.

- **What dividend payment policies are followed in practice?** The four policies that are observed in practice include (1) residual dividend; (2) stable, predictable dividend; (3) constant payout ratio; and (4) low regular dividend plus extras. According to the residual dividend policy, a firm should pay dividends only when earnings are greater than what is needed to finance the optimal capital budget—that is, earnings should be used to satisfy the firm's capital budgeting needs before dividends are paid. The stable, predictable dividend policy requires a firm to maintain a fairly stable dollar dividend from year to year, regardless of the earnings. If a firm follows the constant payout ratio dividend policy, it pays the same percentage of earnings as dividends each year. The low-regular-plus-extras dividend policy states that the firm should pay a low regular dividend each year, and this regular dividend is supplemented with an extra (bonus) dividend in years when above-normal earnings are generated.

- **What factors affect dividend policy decisions?** Some factors that influence a firm's dividend policy decisions include constraints on payments, investment opportunities, ownership dilution, and the effect on the firm's cost of capital. (1) Factors that limit the amount of dividends that can be paid each year include any restrictions contained in the firm's debt contracts, the amount of cash available to pay dividends, and the firm's retained earnings. (2) Generally the more good investment opportunities a firm has, the lower the proportion of its earnings that is paid as dividends; rather than paying dividends, the firm uses earnings to finance acceptable capital budgeting projects. (3) A firm that is concerned about diluting its ownership generally is inclined to retain earnings rather than to issue new common stock to finance investments. (4) Firms that face high flotation (issuing) costs generally prefer to use retained earnings rather than to issue new stock to fund capital budgeting needs.

- **How does a stock split (dividend) work? Why would a firm initiate a stock split (pay a dividend in stock)?** Both a stock split and a stock dividend increase the number of shares of outstanding stock. Neither action requires stockholders to invest any additional funds. Although both actions reduce the per-share value of the firm's stock, neither action by itself changes the *total* market value of the firm's stock. If a firm initiates a 2-for-1 stock split, then it will replace every one share of existing stock with two shares of new stock. If a firm declares a 10 percent stock dividend, then it "pays" a dividend in the form of stock (not cash) that consists of 10 percent of the firm's outstanding shares of stock.

- **How do dividend payment policies in the United States compare with policies around the world?** Both tax laws and the protection of stockholders' rights differ among countries throughout the world. The proportions of earnings that are paid as dividends generally are higher in countries in which dividends are taxed at low rates and in which stockholders' rights are not well protected.

## ETHICAL DILEMMA

## DRIP, DRIP, DRIP…Should We Call a Plumber?

Freeman Plumbing Supplies has decided to reexamine its existing dividend policy, which was established 30 years ago when the firm first started paying dividends. Freeman's operations have changed significantly during the past 30 years, so the CEO wants to determine whether its dividend policy is still appropriate.

The CEO suggested that it might be a good idea for the firm to begin a dividend reinvestment plan (DRIP) because he believes that the company is a good investment and that most of the firm's stockholders would prefer to have their dividends reinvested in the company's stock rather than paid to them in cash. As a result, Ed Davidson, Freeman's CFO, was assigned the task of evaluating the feasibility of starting a DRIP program.

It is Ed's opinion that Freeman should pay dividends to maintain its market value and thus also maintain stockholders' wealth. Since the tax rate on dividends was lowered a few years ago, most companies in Freeman's industry have either increased their dividends or started paying dividends for the first time. So Ed is convinced that Freeman must continue to pay dividends; in fact, he thinks that the amount of dividends should be increased.

When Ed was assigned the task of evaluating the possibility of starting a DRIP program, he was excited. He knew that the program would be administered in his department, which would give him and his colleagues a chance to showcase the quality of work they perform. As his evaluation progressed, however, Ed started to get concerned that the CEO had a personal ulterior motive in mind when he suggested the DRIP program. Ed's concerns increased when he found out that Freeman's executives receive huge bonuses each year that are normally paid in the form of the company's stock. His research indicates that a DRIP program would permit executives to receive their bonuses in the form of dividends that are reinvested in company's stock, which would have the same effect as the existing bonus-payment system. However, because they actually receive a dividend payment, the executives would be taxed differently if their bonuses "pass through" a DRIP program. If executives are paid their bonuses using the existing plan, any stock they receive is taxed at the same rate as their ordinary, or "regular," income, whereas qualified dividends are taxed at lower rates. In other words, stock that is purchased through a DRIP plan qualifies as a dividend payment that would be taxed at a more favorable rate than ordinary income.

With the additional information that he has collected, Ed is concerned that the CEO wants to initiate a DRIP program only because it will be beneficial to Freeman's executives. Although Ed is still in the beginning stages of his evaluation, he doesn't think the company should initiate programs just because they benefit executives. At this point, Ed is trying to decide whether he should abandon his evaluation and tell the CEO to "go jump in the lake" or continue with an evaluation that might give the CEO the justification he needs to start a program that will benefit top management. What should he do? What would you do if you were Ed?

---

The concepts presented in this chapter should help you to better understand some reasons why stock prices change when management changes the company's dividend policy or splits it stock. If you apply the concepts presented in this chapter, you should be able to make more informed investment decisions.

- Based on the discussion in the chapter, you should understand that firms follow different dividend policies for different reasons. When determining whether to invest in the stock of a company, you should examine its dividend policy. Remember that the total return you earn when investing in a stock includes a yield that is based on dividend payments and a yield that is based on the firm's growth. Often firms that pay high dividends do not have good growth opportunities; thus, they generate high dividend yields but fairly low capital gains (growth) yields. Therefore, you should be aware of the dividend policy of a firm before you purchase its stock.

- When you see the price of a stock drop dramatically from one day to the next, it could be the result of a stock split or a stock dividend. Keep in mind that neither action by itself changes the total market value of the outstanding stock. As a result, when a stock you own splits, your wealth position does not change; the per-share value of the stock declines, but the number of shares increases such that there is no economic effect (change in wealth).

**Chapter *Essentials***
**—Personal Finance**

- You should have a basic understanding of dividend reinvestment plans (DRIPs). Two characteristics you should remember are (1) most large firms offer DRIPs, which permit you to have any dividends paid to you automatically reinvested in the firm's stock, and (2) even though the dividend is reinvested in stock, you must pay taxes on the amount of the dividend you technically receive from the firm.

- As an investor, you should determine the ex-dividend date associated with a firm's stock. On the ex-dividend date, the value of the stock drops by an amount that approximately equals the next dividend payment. The reason for the price decrease is because the ex-dividend date signifies the date when the stock begins to sell "without the next dividend payment"—that is, stockholders who purchase the stock on or after the ex-dividend date will not receive the next dividend payment because there is not enough time to record their names on the company's ownership books before the names of those who will receive the next dividend payment are recorded.

## QUESTIONS

**13-1**   As an investor, would you rather invest in a firm that has a policy of maintaining (a) a constant payout ratio; (b) a stable, predictable dividend per share with a target dividend growth rate; or (c) a constant regular quarterly dividend plus a year-end extra when earnings are sufficiently high or corporate investment needs are sufficiently low? Explain your answer, stating how these policies would affect your required rate of return, $r_s$. Also, discuss how your answer might change if you were a student, a 50-year-old professional with peak earnings, or a retiree.

**13-2**   How would each of the following changes tend to affect the average dividend *payout ratios* for corporations, other things held constant? Explain your answers.

   **a.**   An increase in the personal income tax rate

   **b.**   A liberalization of depreciation for federal income tax purposes—that is, faster tax write-offs

   **c.**   A rise in interest rates

   **d.**   An increase in corporate profits

   **e.**   A decline in corporate investment opportunities

   **f.**   Permission for corporations to deduct dividends for tax purposes as they now can do with interest charges

   **g.**   A change in the tax code so that both realized and unrealized capital gains in any year were taxed at the same rate as dividends

**13-3**   Most firms would like to have their stock selling at a high price/earnings (P/E) ratio, and they would also like to have a large number of different shareholders. Explain how stock dividends or stock splits might help achieve these goals.

**13-4**   What is the difference between a stock dividend and a stock split? As a stockholder, would you prefer to see your company declare a 100 percent stock dividend or a 2-for-1 split? Assume that either action is feasible.

**13-5**   "The cost of retained earnings is less than the cost of new outside equity capital. Consequently, it is totally irrational for a firm to sell a new issue of stock and to pay dividends during the same year." Discuss this statement.

**13-6**   Would it ever be rational for a firm to borrow money to pay dividends? Explain.

**13-7**   If investors have the same information (symmetric information) as the managers/executives of a firm, then which of the dividend policies mentioned in the chapter should the firm follow to maximize value? Explain your answer.

**13-8**   Assume that *asymmetric* information exists in the financial markets. If a firm's earnings fluctuate every year, everything else equal, which of the dividend policies discussed in the chapter should be followed to provide investors with a perception of the least amount of risk? Explain your answer.

**13-9**   Give arguments to support both the relevance and the irrelevance of paying dividends.

**13-10**  One position expressed in the financial literature is that firms set their dividends as a residual after using income to support new investment.

a.   Explain what a residual dividend policy implies, illustrating your answer with a graph showing how different conditions could lead to different dividend payout ratios.

b.   Could the residual dividend policy be consistent with (1) a stable, predictable dividend policy; (2) a constant payout ratio policy; or (3) a low-regular-dividend-plus-extras policy? Answer in terms of both short-run, year-to-year consistency and longer-run consistency.

c.   Think back to Chapter 12, where we considered the relationship between capital structure and the cost of capital. If the WACC-versus-debt-ratio plot was shaped like a sharp V, would this have a different implication for the importance of setting dividends according to the residual policy than if the plot was shaped like a shallow bowl (or a flattened U)?

## SELF-TEST PROBLEMS

*(Solutions appear in Appendix B at the end of the book.)*

**ST-1**   Define each of the following terms:                                       key terms

a.   Optimal dividend policy

b.   Dividend irrelevance theory; dividend relevance theory

c.   Information content, or signaling, hypothesis; clientele effect; free cash flow hypothesis

d.   Residual dividend policy; stable, predictable dividend policy; constant payout ratio policy; low-regular-dividend-plus-extras policy

e.   Declaration date; holder-of-record date; ex-dividend date; payment date

f.   Dividend reinvestment plan (DRIP)

g.   Stock split; stock dividend

**ST-2**   Components Manufacturing Corporation (CMC) has an all-common-equity       alternative dividend
capital structure. It has 200,000 shares of $2 par value common stock out-     policies
standing. When CMC's founder, who was also its research director and most
successful inventor, retired unexpectedly to the South Pacific in late 2008,
CMC was left suddenly and permanently with materially lower growth
expectations and relatively few attractive new investment opportunities.
Unfortunately, there was no way to replace the founder's contributions to the

firm. Previously, CMC found it necessary to plow back most of its earnings to finance growth, which averaged 12 percent per year. Future growth at a 5 percent rate is considered realistic, but that level would call for an increase in the dividend payout. Further, it now appears that new investment projects with at least the 14 percent rate of return required by CMC's stockholders ($r_s = 14\%$) would amount to only $800,000 for 2009 in comparison with a projected $2,000,000 of net income. If the existing 20 percent dividend payout were continued, retained earnings would be $1.6 million in 2009, but, as noted, investments that yield the 14 percent cost of capital would amount to only $800,000.

The one encouraging factor is that the high earnings from existing assets are expected to continue, and net income of $2 million is still expected for 2009. Given the dramatically changed circumstances, CMC's management is reviewing the firm's dividend policy.

**a.** Assuming that the acceptable 2009 investment projects would be financed entirely by earnings retained during the year, calculate DPS in 2009 if CMC follows the residual dividend policy.

**b.** What *payout ratio* does your answer to part a imply for 2009?

**c.** If a 60 percent payout ratio is maintained for the foreseeable future, what is your estimate of the current market price of the common stock? How does this compare with the market price that should have prevailed under the assumptions existing just before the news about the founder's retirement? If the two values of $P_0$ are different, comment on why.

**d.** What would happen to the price of the stock if the old 20 percent payout were continued? Assume that if this payout is maintained, the average rate of return on the retained earnings will fall to 7.5 percent and the new growth rate will be 6 percent.

## PROBLEMS

**external equity financing**  **13-1**  Northern California Heating and Cooling Inc. has a six-month backlog of orders for its patented solar heating system. To meet this demand, management plans to expand production capacity by 40 percent with a $10 million investment in plant and machinery. The firm wants to maintain a 40 percent debt/assets ratio in its capital structure; it also wants to maintain its past dividend policy of distributing 45 percent of last year's net income. In 2008 net income was $5 million. How much external equity must Northern California seek at the beginning of 2009 to expand capacity as desired?

**dividend payout**  **13-2**  The Garlington Corporation expects next year's net income to be $15 million. The firm's debt/assets ratio currently is 40 percent. Garlington has $12 million of profitable investment opportunities, and it wishes to maintain its existing debt ratio. According to the residual dividend policy, how large should Garlington's dividend payout ratio be next year?

**dividend payout**  **13-3**  Open Door Manufacturer earned $100,000 this year. The company follows the residual dividend policy when paying dividends. Open Door has determined that it needs a total of $120,000 for investment in capital budgeting projects this year. If the company's debt/assets ratio is 50 percent, what will its dividend payout ratio be this year?

**dividend payout**  **13-4**  Last year the Bulls Business Bureau (BBB) retained $400,000 of the $1 million net income it generated. This year BBB generated net income equal to $1.2 million. If BBB follows the constant dividend payout ratio dividend policy, how much should be paid in dividends this year?

**13-5**  In 2008, Breaking News Company earned $15 million, and it paid $6 million in dividends. The company follows a constant payout ratio dividend policy. If the company would like to pay $8 million in dividends next year, how much must Breaking News earn?

**dividend payout**

**13-6**  After a 5-for-1 stock split, the Swensen Company paid a dividend of $0.75 per new share, which represents a 9 percent increase over last year's pre-split dividend. What was last year's dividend per share?

**stock split**

**13-7**  HQ Company is considering a 1-for-3 reverse stock split. HQ's stock is currently selling for $3 per share.

**stock split**

    **a.**  What will the price of the stock be after the stock split?

    **b.**  HQ plans to pay a dividend equal to $0.60 per share after the split. The company would like to pay an equivalent dividend per share even if the split does not take place. What would the per-share dividend have to be if the HQ doesn't split the stock?

**13-8**  The Scanlon Company's optimal capital structure calls for 50 percent debt and 50 percent common equity. The interest rate on its debt is a constant 10 percent; its cost of common equity from retained earnings is 14 percent; the cost of equity from new stock is 16 percent; and its marginal tax rate is 40 percent. Scanlon has the following investment opportunities:

**dividend payout**

> Project A: Cost = $5 million; IRR = 20%
> Project B: Cost = $5 million; IRR = 12%
> Project C: Cost = $5 million; IRR =  9%

    Scanlon expects to have net income of $7,287,500. If Scanlon bases its dividends on the residual policy, what will its payout ratio be?

**13-9**  Free Flying Aviation (FFA) just declared a 20 percent stock dividend to be paid three weeks from today. Before the "payment" of the stock dividend, the equity section on FFA's balance sheet appeared as follows:

**stock dividend**

| | |
|---|---:|
| Common stock (10,000 shares outstanding, $5 par value) | $ 50,000 |
| Additional paid-in capital | 20,000 |
| Retained earnings | 30,000 |
| Total common shareholders' equity | $100,000 |

The market value of FFA's stock is $7.00 per share.

    **a.**  How many shares of stock does FFA need to "pay" for the stock dividend?

    **b.**  What will be the amount of FFA's "additional paid-in capital" after the stock dividend is paid?

    **c.**  What will be the amount of retained earnings after the stock dividend is paid?

**13-10**  The McLaughlin Corporation declared a 6 percent stock dividend. Construct a pro forma balance sheet showing the effect of this action. The stock was selling for $37.50 per share, and a condensed version of McLaughlin's balance sheet as of December 31, 2008, before the dividend, follows ($ millions):

**stock dividend**

| Cash | $ 112.5 | Debt | $1,500.0 |
| Other assets | 2,887.5 | Common stock (75 million shares outstanding, $1 par) | 75.0 |
| | | Paid-in capital | 300.0 |
| | | Retained earnings | 1,125.0 |
| Total assets | $3,000.0 | Total liabilities and equity | $3,000.0 |

**alternative dividend policies**

**13-11** In 2008 the Sirmans Company paid dividends totaling $3.6 million on net income of $10.8 million. Sirmans had a normal year in 2008, and for the past 10 years, earnings have grown at a constant rate of 10 percent. However, in 2009 earnings are expected to jump to $14.4 million, and the firm expects to have profitable investment opportunities of $8.4 million. It is predicted that Sirmans will not be able to maintain the 2009 level of earnings growth—the high 2009 earnings level is attributable to an exceptionally profitable new product line introduced that year—and the company will return to its previous 10 percent growth rate. Sirmans's target debt ratio is 40 percent.

**a.** Calculate Sirmans's total dividends for 2009 if it follows each of the following policies:

**(1)** Its 2009 dividend payment is set to force dividends to grow at the long-run growth rate in earnings.

**(2)** It continues the 2008 dividend payout ratio.

**(3)** It uses a pure residual dividend policy (40 percent of the $8.4 million investment is financed with debt).

**(4)** It employs a regular-dividend-plus-extras policy, with the regular dividend being based on the long-run growth rate and the extra dividend being set according to the residual policy.

**b.** Which of the preceding policies would you recommend? Restrict your choices to the ones listed, but justify your answer.

**c.** Assume that investors expect Sirmans to pay total dividends of $9 million in 2009 and to have the dividend grow at 10 percent after 2009. The total market value of the stock is $180 million. What is the company's cost of equity?

**d.** What is Sirmans's long-run average return on equity? [*Hint:* $g = $ (Retention rate) $\times$ (ROE) $= (1.0 -$ Payout rate) $\times$ (ROE)]

**e.** Does a 2009 dividend of $9 million seem reasonable in view of your answers to parts c and d? If not, should the dividend be higher or lower?

**dividend policy and capital structure**

**13-12** Ybor City Tobacco Company has for many years enjoyed a moderate but stable growth in sales and earnings. However, cigar consumption and consequently Ybor's sales have been falling recently, primarily because of an increasing awareness of the dangers of smoking to health. Anticipating further declines in tobacco sales for the future, Ybor's management hopes eventually to move almost entirely out of the tobacco business and into a newly developed, diversified product line in growth-oriented industries. The company is especially interested in the prospects for pollution-control devices because its research department has already done much work on the problems of filtering smoke. Right now the company estimates that an investment of $15 million is necessary to purchase new facilities and to begin operations on these products, but the investment could be earning a return of about 18 percent within a short time. The only other available investment opportunity totals $6 million and is expected to return 10.4 percent.

The company is expected to pay a $3 dividend on its 3 million outstanding shares, the same as its dividend last year. The directors might, however, change the dividend if there are good reasons for doing so. Total earnings after taxes for the year are expected to be $14.25 million, the common stock is currently selling for $56.25, the firm's target debt ratio (debt/assets ratio) is 45 percent, and its marginal tax rate is 40 percent. The costs of various forms of financing are as follows:

New bonds, $r_d = 11\%$. This is a before-tax rate.
New common stock sold at $56.25 per share will net $51.25.
Required rate of return on retained earnings, $r_s = 14\%$.

**a.** Calculate Ybor's expected payout ratio, the break point at which the marginal cost of capital (MCC) rises, and its MCC above and below the point of exhaustion of retained earnings at the current payout. (*Hint:* $r_s$ is given, and $\hat{D}_1/P_0$ can be found. Then, knowing $r_s$ and $\hat{D}_1/P_0$, g can be determined.)

**b.** How large should Ybor's capital budget be for the year?

**c.** What is an appropriate dividend policy for Ybor? How should the capital budget be financed?

**d.** How might risk factors influence Ybor's cost of capital, capital structure, and dividend policy?

**e.** What assumptions, if any, do your answers to the preceding parts make about investors' preferences for dividends versus capital gains (in other words, what are investors' preferences regarding the $\hat{D}_1/P_0$ and g components of $r_s$)?

## Integrative Problem

**13-13** Information Systems Inc. (ISI), which develops software for the health care industry, was founded five years ago by Donald Brown and Margaret Clark, who are still its only stockholders. ISI has now reached the stage at which outside equity capital is necessary if the firm is to achieve its growth targets yet still maintain its target capital structure of 60 percent equity and 40 percent debt. Therefore, Brown and Clark have decided to take the company public. Until now, Brown and Clark have paid themselves reasonable salaries but routinely reinvested all after-tax earnings in the firm, so dividend policy has not been an issue. However, before talking with potential outside investors, they must decide on a dividend policy.

**dividend policy**

Assume you were recently hired by Andrew Adamson & Company (AA), a national accounting firm, which has been asked to help ISI prepare for its public offering. Martha Millon, the senior AA consultant in your group, has asked you to make a presentation to Brown and Clark in which you review the theory of dividend policy and discuss the following questions:

**a. (1)** What is meant by the term *dividend policy?*

   **(2)** The terms *irrelevance* and *relevance* have been used to describe theories regarding the way dividend policy affects a firm's value. Explain what these terms mean, and briefly discuss the relevance of dividend policy.

(3) Explain the relationships between dividend policy and (i) stock price and (ii) the cost of equity under each dividend policy theory.

**b.** Discuss (1) the information content, or signaling, hypothesis; (2) the clientele effect; (3) the free cash flow hypothesis; and (4) their effects on dividend policy.

**c.** (1) Assume ISI has an $800,000 capital budget planned for the coming year. You have determined that its present capital structure (60 percent equity and 40 percent debt) is optimal, and its net income is forecasted at $600,000. Use the residual dividend policy approach to determine ISI's total dollar dividend and payout ratio. In the process, explain what the residual dividend policy is, and use a graph to illustrate your answer. Then explain what would happen if net income were forecasted at $400,000, or at $800,000.

(2) In general terms, how would a change in investment opportunities affect the payout ratio under the residual payment policy?

(3) What are the advantages and disadvantages of the residual policy? (*Hint:* Don't neglect signaling and clientele effects.)

**d.** What are some other commonly used dividend payment policies? What are their advantages and disadvantages? Which policy is most widely used in practice?

**e.** What are dividend reinvestment plans (DRIPs), and how do these plans work?

**f.** What are stock dividends and stock splits? What are the advantages and disadvantages of stock dividends and splits? When should a stock dividend rather than a stock split be used?

### Computer-Related Problem

*Work the problem in this section only if you are using the problem spreadsheet.*

**dividend policy and capital structure**

**13-14** Use the model in the File C13 to work this problem. Refer back to Problem 13-12. Assume that Ybor's management is considering a change in the firm's capital structure to include more debt; thus, management would like to analyze the effects of an increase in the debt ratio to 60 percent. The treasurer believes that such a move would cause lenders to increase the required rate of return on new bonds to 12 percent and that $r_s$ would rise to 14.5 percent.

**a.** How would this change affect the optimal capital budget?

**b.** If $r_s$ rose to 16 percent, would the low-return project be acceptable?

**c.** Would the project selection be affected if the dividend was reduced to $1.88 from $3.00, still assuming $r_s$ = 16 percent?

**GET REAL WITH**   **THOMSON ONE** Business School Edition

**dividend payouts**

**13-15** Compare the dividend payouts of McDonald's Corporation [MCD], a quick-service restaurant firm, and its peers, as denoted by SIC code. Answer the following questions:

**a.** What was the yearly dividend yield during the past five years for McDonald's? [Prices/Overviews/Thomson Market Data/Stock Valuation Overviews]

**b.** How much did McDonald's pay out in dividends to shareholders in each of the five years? State your answer both in total dollars and on a per-share basis. [Click on Financials/Thomson Financials/Cash Flow Statement/5 year Cash Flow Statement.]

**c.** How did McDonald's average dividend compare with that of its peers? [Click on Peers/Overviews/Comparative Profiles.]

**d.** If you analyze the total dividend paid and the dividend yield over the five-year period, would McDonald's or one of its peers be the best investment if you are concerned only with the dividend income generated by the investment?

# PART 6

# Working Capital Management

# CHAPTER 14

# Working Capital Policy

## A MANAGERIAL PERSPECTIVE

In December 1993, Trans World Airlines (TWA) was labeled the best domestic airline for long flights and the second best for short flights by U.S. business travelers. TWA received this accolade just one month after emerging from bankruptcy. The future seemed rosy: Employees had agreed to salary concessions in exchange for an equity position in the company; the airline had restructured its liabilities and lowered its cost structure; and the employees, with their new ownership position, appeared to possess a new found motivation and concern for company success.

Unfortunately, the nation's seventh largest airline at the time soon discovered that its "new lease on life" was not a long-term contract. Because its liquidity position was tenuous, it wasn't long before TWA filed for bankruptcy for a second time. To improve its liquidity, TWA reduced operating costs by laying off employees, eliminating unprofitable flights, and replacing outdated airplanes with more fuel-efficient airplanes.

TWA emerged from its second bankruptcy and regained its status as the best domestic airline for long flights, but its financial position was still very tenuous. Unforeseen circumstances, including a tragic crash and labor difficulties, resulted in large losses in the late 1990s. As a result, TWA again took actions to improve its liquidity position. The benefits of its cost-cutting, revenue-increasing actions were short-lived. TWA filed for bankruptcy a third time at the beginning of 2001, and in April 2001 TWA ceased to exist when it was acquired by American Airlines (AA). But the acquisition did not solve TWA's liquidity problems; it just passed them on to AA.

In 2005, all airlines were still trying to recover from the terrorist attacks of September 11, 2001. AA reported net losses of $0.8 billion, $1.2 billion, $3.5 billion, and $1.8 billion from 2001 through 2004, respectively. As a result of the significant decrease in air travel since the 2001 attacks, AA took measures to improve its liquidity. By improving its liquidity, the cost-cutting measures, which saved AA about $2 billion per year in 2002 and 2003, helped AA, the world's largest airline, to keep its "head above water"—although just barely.

Maintaining a healthy liquidity position is important if AA wants to overcome current financial challenges and continue operating in the future. Although 2006 was a year that saw oil prices increase to record levels, AA's improved liquidity helped the company weather the financial storm. AMR Corporation, AA's parent company, reported a $230 million profit for the year, which was AMR's first annual profit since 2000. Analysts were confident that additional profits would follow in subsequent periods, primarily because AA's liquidity position was fairly strong.

Firms strive to maintain a balance between current assets and current liabilities and between sales and each category of current assets in an effort to provide sufficient liquidity to survive—that is, to live to maximize value in the future. As long as a good balance is maintained, current liabilities can be paid on time, suppliers will continue to provide needed inventories, and companies will be able to meet sales demands. If the financial situation gets out of balance, liquidity problems surface and often multiply into more serious problems, and perhaps even bankruptcy. As you read this chapter, consider how important liquidity—and thus proper management of working capital—is to the survival of a firm. Also, consider the fact that many start-up firms never make it past the first few months of business, primarily because they lack formal working capital policies.

## Chapter *Essentials*
### —The Questions

After reading this chapter, you should be able to answer the following questions:

- What is working capital and why is working capital management critical to the survival of a firm?
- How are working capital accounts related?
- Why is it important for management to understand the firm's cash conversion cycle?
- What working capital investment policy should a firm follow?
- How should the firm finance its working capital needs?

Generally, we divide financial management decisions into the management of assets (investments) and liabilities (sources of financing) in (1) the *long term* and (2) the *short term*. We discussed long-term decisions and analyses in previous chapters. In this and the next two chapters, we discuss *short-term financial management*, also termed **working capital management,** which involves management of the current assets and the current liabilities of a firm. As you read this chapter, you will realize that a firm's value cannot be maximized in the long run unless it survives the short run. In fact, the principal reason firms fail is because they are unable to meet their working capital needs. Thus, *sound working capital management is a requisite for firm survival.*

Much of a financial manager's time is devoted to working capital management, and many of you who get jobs in finance-related fields will find that your first assignment on the job will involve working capital. For these reasons, working capital policy and management is an essential topic of study. In this chapter, we provide an overview of working capital policy, and the next two chapters discuss how current assets and current liabilities should be managed.

**working capital management**
The management of short-term assets (investments) and liabilities (financing sources).

## WORKING CAPITAL TERMINOLOGY[1]

It is useful to begin the discussion of working capital policy by reviewing some basic definitions and concepts:

1. The term **working capital,** sometimes called *gross working capital,* generally refers to current assets.

**working capital**
A firm's investment in short-term assets—cash, marketable securities, inventory, and accounts receivable.

---

[1]The term *working capital* originated with the old Yankee peddler, who would load up his wagon with goods and then go off on his route to peddle his wares. The merchandise was called *working capital* because it was what he actually sold, or "turned over," to produce his profits. The wagon and horse were his fixed assets. He generally owned the horse and wagon, so they were financed with "equity" capital. But to buy the merchandise, he borrowed funds, which were called *working capital* loans, that had to be repaid after each trip to demonstrate to the bank that the credit was sound. If the peddler was able to repay the loan, then the bank would make another loan, and banks that followed this procedure were said to be employing sound banking practices.

2. **Net working capital** is defined as current assets minus current liabilities.

3. The *current ratio,* which was discussed in Chapter 2, is calculated by dividing current assets by current liabilities and is intended to measure a firm's liquidity. However, a high current ratio does not ensure that a firm will have the cash required to meet its needs. If inventories cannot be sold, or if receivables cannot be collected in a timely manner, then the apparent safety reflected in a high current ratio could be illusory.

4. The best and most comprehensive picture of a firm's liquidity position is obtained by examining its *cash budget.* The cash budget, which forecasts cash inflows and outflows, focuses on what really counts, the firm's ability to generate sufficient cash inflows to meet its required cash outflows. Cash budgeting will be discussed in the next chapter.

5. **Working capital policy** refers to the firm's basic policies regarding (a) target levels for each category of current assets and (b) how current assets will be financed.

> **net working capital**
> Current assets minus current liabilities—the amount of current assets financed by long-term liabilities.

> **working capital policy**
> Decisions regarding (1) the target levels for each current asset account and (2) how current assets will be financed.

We must distinguish between those current liabilities that are specifically used to finance current assets and those current liabilities that result from long-term decisions. Such current liabilities include (1) current maturities of long-term debt; (2) financing associated with a construction program that, after the project is completed, will be funded with the proceeds of a long-term security issue; or (3) the use of short-term debt to finance fixed (long-term) assets.

Table 14-1 contains balance sheets for Unilate Textiles constructed at three different dates. According to the definitions given, Unilate's December 31, 2009, working capital—that is, current assets—was $465.0 million, and its net working capital was $335.0 million = $465.0 million – $130.0 million. Also, Unilate's year-end 2009 current ratio was 3.6.

What if the total current liabilities of $130 million at the end of 2009 included the current portion of long-term debt, say $10 million? This account is unaffected by changes in working capital policy because it is a function of past long-term debt financing decisions. Thus, even though we define long-term debt coming due in the next accounting period as a current liability, it is not a working capital decision variable in the current period. Similarly, if Unilate were building a new factory and initially financed the construction with a short-term loan that would be replaced later with mortgage bonds, the construction loan would not be considered part of working capital management. Although such accounts are not part of Unilate's working capital decision process, they cannot be ignored because they are *due* in the current period, and they must be taken into account when Unilate's managers construct the cash budget and assess the firm's ability to meet its current obligations (its liquidity position).

### ? Self-Test Question

Why is it important to properly manage short-term assets and liabilities?

## THE REQUIREMENT FOR EXTERNAL WORKING CAPITAL FINANCING

Unilate's operations and the sale of textile products are seasonal, typically peaking in September and October. Thus, at the end of September Unilate's inventories are significantly higher than they are at the end of the calendar year. Unilate offers

| **TABLE 14-1** | Unilate Textiles: Historical and Projected Balance Sheets (millions of dollars) | | |
| --- | --- | --- | --- |
| | **12/31/09 (Historical)** | **9/30/10 (Projected)** | **12/31/10 (Projected)** |
| Cash and marketable securities | $ 15.0 | $ 30.0 | $ 16.5 |
| Accounts receivable | 180.0 | 251.5 | 198.0 |
| Inventories | 270.0 | 410.0 | 297.0 |
| Total current assets | $465.0 | $ 691.5 | $511.5 |
| Net plant and equipment | 380.0 | 408.5 | 418.0 |
| Total assets | $845.0 | $1,100.0 | $929.5 |
| | | | |
| Accounts payable | $ 30.0 | $ 90.0 | $ 33.0 |
| Accruals | 60.0 | 100.0 | 66.0 |
| Notes payable | 40.0 | 129.0 | 46.8 |
| Total current liabilities | $130.0 | $ 319.0 | $145.8 |
| Long-term bonds | 300.0 | 309.0 | 309.0 |
| Total liabilities | $430.0 | $ 628.0 | $454.8 |
| Common stock | 130.0 | 159.3 | 159.3 |
| Retained earnings | 285.0 | 312.7 | 315.5 |
| Total owners' equity | $415.0 | $ 472.0 | $474.8 |
| Total liabilities and equity | $845.0 | $1,100.0 | $929.5[a] |
| | | | |
| Net working capital | $335.0 | $ 372.5 | $365.7 |
| Current ratio | 3.6 | 2.2 | 3.5 |

[a]Rounding difference. These end-of-year forecasts are derived in Appendix 17A.

significant sales incentives to wholesalers during August and September in an effort to move inventories out of its warehouses and into those of its customers; otherwise, inventories would be even higher than shown in Table 14-1. Because of this sales surge, Unilate's receivables also are much higher at the end of September than at the end of December.

Consider what is expected to happen to Unilate's current assets and current liabilities from December 31, 2009, to September 30, 2010. Current assets are expected to increase from $465.0 million to $691.5 million, or by $226.5 million. Because increases on the asset side of the balance sheet must be financed by identical increases on the liabilities and equity side, the firm must raise $226.5 million to meet the expected increase in working capital over the period. However, the higher volume of purchases, plus labor expenditures associated with increased production, will cause accounts payable and accruals to increase *spontaneously* by only $100 million—from $90 million ($30 million in payables plus $60 million in accruals) to $190 million ($90 million in payables plus $100 million in accruals)—during the first nine months of 2010. This leaves a projected $126.5 million = $226.5 million – $100 million current asset financing requirement, which Unilate expects to finance primarily by an $89 million increase in notes payable. Therefore, for September 30, 2010, notes payable are projected to rise to $129 million. Notice that from December 2009 to September 2010, Unilate's net working capital is expected to increase from $335 million to $372.5 million, but its current ratio is expected to fall from 3.6 to 2.2. This occurs because most, but not all, of the funds invested in current assets are expected to come from current liabilities.[2]

The fluctuations in Unilate's working capital position shown in Table 14-1 result from seasonal variations. Similar fluctuations in working capital requirements, and hence in financing needs, also occur during business cycles—working capital needs typically decline during recessions but increase during booms. For some companies, such as those involved in agricultural products, seasonal fluctuations are much greater than business cycle fluctuations, but for other companies, such as appliance or automobile manufacturers, cyclical fluctuations are larger. In the following sections, we look in more detail at the requirement for working capital financing, and we examine some alternative working capital policies.

**Self-Test Question**

Under normal circumstances, when does the working capital position of a firm change? Explain.

## THE RELATIONSHIPS AMONG WORKING CAPITAL ACCOUNTS

It is important that you understand how the various working capital accounts are related. To illustrate the process of producing and selling inventory and the relationships between current assets and current liabilities, let's assume you open a new textile manufacturing plant to compete with Unilate Textiles. Let's call the new business Global Cloth Products (GCP). Under normal conditions, the new plant is expected to produce and sell 50,000 units each day. Each unit, which will be sold for $14.00, has a direct production cost equal to $11.00. For simplicity we will assume that the $11.00 unit cost can be broken into two components—the cost of raw materials purchased from suppliers (cotton, wool, and so on), which is $6.50, and the cost of labor, which is $4.50—and that there are no other costs associated with the manufacture and sale of the product. GCP will purchase materials from its suppliers on credit, with cash payment due 15 days after the purchase. Likewise, GCP will allow its customers to purchase for credit, and it will require cash payment 15 days after the sale. In our illustration, we assume all GCP customers will pay for their purchases 15 days after the sales, and that GCP will pay its suppliers 15 days after purchasing raw materials. In addition, employees will be paid every 15 days (twice per month).[3] Therefore, all the cash flows associated with the production and sales functions will occur 15 days after the purchase, manufacture, and sale of the products. To simplify the illustration, we assume all cash flows will occur at the beginning of the day, before daily purchasing, producing, and selling activities begin. Thus, at the beginning of Day 16 (1) inventory purchases that were made on the first day of business are paid, (2) the firm collects for the products sold on the first day of business, and (3) the employees are paid for their first 15 days of work.

GCP will use $300,000 in common stock to finance the new processing plant facilities, and the raw materials purchases will be made daily and financed short term with accounts payable (owed to suppliers), wages payable (owed to employees), and short-term bank loans (notes payable). Each day, the raw materials that are purchased will be converted into finished goods and sold before the close of business.

---

[2]Mathematically, when both the numerator and the denominator of a ratio that has a value greater than 1.0 increase by the same amount (magnitude), the value of the ratio decreases. If the ratio's value is less than 1.0, its value will increase when both the numerator and denominator are increased by the same magnitude.

[3]The 15-day period is used for simplicity because there are two 15-day periods in a 30-day month and 24 15-day periods in a 360-day year. If a 14-day period was used, the illustration would become more cumbersome.

On the first day of operations, just *prior to selling any products,* GCP will have 50,000 units in inventory at a cost of $11.00 per unit, so the inventory balance will be $550,000 = 50,000 × $11.00. The inventory cost consists of the raw materials, which amounts to $325,000 = 50,000 × $6.50 owed to suppliers, and the cost of labor, which is $225,000 = 50,000 × $4.50 owed to employees. At this point, then, the balance sheet for GCP's processing plant would be as follows:

| | | | | |
|---|---|---|---|---|
| Cash | $ 0 | Accounts payable | | $325,000 |
| Accounts receivable | 0 | Accrued wages | | 225,000 |
| Inventory | 550,000 | Notes payable | | 0 |
| Current assets | 550,000 | Current liabilities | | 550,000 |
| Fixed assets | 300,000 | Common equity | | 300,000 |
| | | Retained earnings | | 0 |
| Total assets | $850,000 | Total liabilities and equity | | $850,000 |

On the first day, all of the 50,000 units in inventory will be sold for $14.00 each, so the first day's sales will be $700,000 = 50,000 × $14.00. And after the first day's sales are complete, the balance sheet will be as follows:

| | | | | |
|---|---|---|---|---|
| Cash | $ 0 | Accounts payable | | $ 325,000 |
| Accounts receivable | 700,000 | Accrued wages | | 225,000 |
| Inventory | 0 | Notes payable | | 0 |
| Current assets | 700,000 | Current liabilities | | 550,000 |
| Fixed assets | 300,000 | Common equity | | 300,000 |
| | | Retained earnings | | 150,000 |
| Total assets | $1,000,000 | Total liabilities and equity | | $1,000,000 |

Notice that the $150,000 profit on the first day's sales, which is the difference between the inventory cost of $550,000 and the first day's sales of $700,000, is recognized via retained earnings.[4] This shows that not all of the $700,000 in accounts receivable has to be financed because $150,000 represents the profit on the sales.

At the start of the second day, *after inventories are replenished but before daily sales begin,* the inventory balance again will be $550,000 and the balances in accounts payable and accrued wages will *increase* by $325,000 and $225,000, respectively. Thus, the balance sheet will be as follows:

| | | | | |
|---|---|---|---|---|
| Cash | $ 0 | Accounts payable | | $ 650,000 |
| Accounts receivable | 700,000 | Accrued wages | | 450,000 |
| Inventory | 550,000 | Notes payable | | 0 |
| Current assets | 1,250,000 | Current liabilities | | 1,100,000 |
| Fixed assets | 300,000 | Common equity | | 300,000 |
| | | Retained earnings | | 150,000 |
| Total assets | $1,550,000 | Total liabilities and equity | | $1,550,000 |

---

[4]In reality, profits are not posted to retained earnings each day; rather, the recognition of profits (income) occurs at the end of the fiscal period via the income summary account. We recognize the daily profits in this manner for illustrative purposes only.

When the products are sold on the second day, accounts receivable again will increase by $700,000. In fact, the balances in accounts receivable, accounts payable, wages payable, and retained earnings will continue to increase (accumulate) until cash flows affect these accounts' balances. So the balances in receivables, payables, and accrued wages will increase for a total of 15 days, whereas the balance in retained earnings will continue to increase until dividends are paid or losses are incurred.

GCP neither receives nor disburses any cash until 15 days after the first day of business. At that time, GCP will have to *pay* for both the raw materials purchased on the first day of business and the wages owed to employees for the first 15 days of work. In addition, GCP will *receive* payment from those customers who purchased its products on the first day of business. So for the first 15 days of business, the balances in receivables, payables, accruals, and retained earnings continue to increase, reflecting the purchasing and selling activities of GCP prior to the receipt or payment of any cash flows. At the *end* of Day 15, therefore, the balance in each of these accounts would be as follows:

$$\text{Accounts receivable} = \$700,000 \times 15 \text{ days} = \$10,500,000$$
$$\text{Accounts payable} = \$325,000 \times 15 \text{ days} = \$\ 4,875,000$$
$$\text{Accrued wages} = \$225,000 \times 15 \text{ days} = \$\ 3,375,000$$
$$\text{Retained earnings} = \$150,000 \times 15 \text{ days} = \$\ 2,250,000$$

And the balance sheet at the *end* of Day 15 would be as follows:

| | | | |
|---|---|---|---|
| Cash | $            0 | Accounts payable | $ 4,875,000 |
| Accounts receivable | 10,500,000 | Accrued wages | 3,375,000 |
| Inventory | 0 | Notes payable | 0 |
| Current assets | 10,500,000 | Current liabilities | 8,250,000 |
| Fixed assets | 300,000 | Common equity | 300,000 |
| | | Retained earnings | 2,250,000 |
| Total assets | $10,800,000 | Total liabilities and equity | $10,800,000 |

At the *beginning* of Day 16, GCP must pay its employees $3,375,000 for the first 15 days of work, and it also must pay $325,000 to the suppliers for the raw materials purchased on the *first* day of business. But at the same time, GCP will be paid $700,000 for the products that were sold on the first day of business. This cash receipt can be used to pay the $325,000 now due to the suppliers, which leaves only $375,000 to help pay employees' salaries. This means GCP must borrow to meet its cash obligations. If GCP uses the entire $375,000 to help pay employees' salaries, the amount that needs to be borrowed to pay the remaining wages is

$$\text{Loan amount} = \left( \begin{array}{c} \text{Payment owed} \\ \text{to suppliers} \end{array} \right) + \left( \begin{array}{c} \text{Wages owed} \\ \text{employees} \end{array} \right) - \left( \begin{array}{c} \text{Cash} \\ \text{receipts} \end{array} \right)$$
$$= \quad [\$325,000 \quad + \quad \$3,375,000] \quad - \quad \$700,000$$
$$= \quad \$3,700,000 \quad - \quad \$700,000 \quad = \$3,000,000$$

If GCP borrows the funds needed from a local bank, consider what the balance sheet would look like if all of the cash flow activity occurs at the very beginning of Day 16, *prior to the daily materials purchases, inventory production, and product sales*. At this point, GCP would have (1) paid *all* of the $3,375,000 wages owed its employees, so the balance of accrued wages would equal zero; (2) paid $325,000 to its suppliers, so the balance of accounts payable would decrease by $325,000; (3) received a $700,000 payment from its customers, so the balance of accounts receivable would decrease by $700,000; and (4) borrowed $3,000,000 from a local bank to pay employees, so the balance of notes payable would increase by $3,000,000. At this point, the balance sheet would be as follows:

| | | | |
|---|---:|---|---:|
| Cash | $ 0 | Accounts payable | $ 4,550,000 |
| Accounts receivable | 9,800,000 | Accrued wages | 0 |
| Inventory | 0 | Notes payable | 3,000,000 |
| Current assets | 9,800,000 | Current liabilities | 7,550,000 |
| Fixed assets | 300,000 | Common equity | 300,000 |
| | | Retained earnings | 2,250,000 |
| Total assets | $10,100,000 | Total liabilities and equity | $10,100,000 |

But on Day 16, GCP must also conduct its normal daily business—raw materials must be purchased and finished goods must be manufactured and sold. Because no additional cash flows will occur on this day, the purchase of raw materials will increase accounts payable by $325,000, the use of employees to manufacture finished goods will increase accrued wages by $225,000, and credit sales will increase accounts receivable by $700,000. The profit on the day's sales will also increase retained earnings by $150,000. Consequently, at the *end of Day 16,* the balance sheet will be as follows:

| | | | |
|---|---:|---|---:|
| Cash | $ 0 | Accounts payable | $ 4,875,000 |
| Accounts receivable | 10,500,000 | Accrued wages | 225,000 |
| Inventory | 0 | Notes payable | 3,000,000 |
| Current assets | 10,500,000 | Current liabilities | 8,100,000 |
| Fixed assets | 300,000 | Common equity | 300,000 |
| | | Retained earnings | 2,400,000 |
| Total assets | $10,800,000 | Total liabilities and equity | $10,800,000 |

At this point, the accounts payable and accounts receivable balances reflect 15 days' worth of credit activities associated with the production and sales operations that took place from Day 2 through Day 16. On the other hand, because at the beginning of the day the employees were paid the wages due them for the first 15 days of business, accrued wages include only the amount owed to employees for their work to produce inventory on Day 16. And because there have not been any cash disbursements to stockholders, the balance in retained earnings represents the profits from the products sold for all 16 days GCP has been in business—$2,400,000 = $150,000 × 16 days.

At the beginning of Day 17, GCP will pay for the materials it purchased on Day 2. It will also receive payment for the products that were sold on Day 2. This process will continue as long as the purchasing and payment patterns of both GCP and its customers do not change. As a result, GCP will pay out $325,000 every day to pay for materials purchased 15 days earlier (a decrease in payables), but the payables balance will remain the same from this point on because GCP will also purchase on credit raw materials valuing $325,000 (an increase in payables) every day to produce the product needed for that day's sales. Therefore, the accounts payable balance will remain constant at $4,875,000. Similarly, the balance in accounts receivable will remain at $10,500,000 because each day, once this steady state has been reached (after Day 15), GCP will receive cash payments from customers totaling $700,000 (a decrease in receivables) at the same time $700,000 worth of products are sold for credit (an increase in receivables).

At this point, consider the cash flow position of GCP. From Day 16 on, every day, GCP will receive cash payments from its customers that total $700,000, and it will make cash payments to its suppliers that total $325,000. But the employees are paid every 15 days, not every day. Therefore, GCP can accumulate $375,000 = $700,000 − $325,000 in cash each day until employees' salaries need to be paid again. The next time employees' salaries are paid is at the beginning of Day 31, so the cash account balance will increase by $375,000 for 15 days. Therefore, on Day 31, after all cash flows except accrued wages are recognized, GCP will have a cash balance equal to $5,625,000 = $375,000 × 15 days. Accrued wages will equal $3,375,000 = $225,000 × 15 days; so after paying its employees, GCP will still have a cash balance equal to $2,250,000. This amount represents the *total cash profit* GCP has generated during the previous 15 days of business. This amount can be used to pay off a portion of the bank loan, or it could be used to expand operations. In any event, once the balances in receivables and payables have stabilized because the daily adjustments to those accounts are offsetting, GCP actually realizes a *cash* profit of $150,000 per day.

This illustration shows that, in general, once GCP's operations have stabilized so that the credit sales and credit purchasing patterns and the collection and payment activities stay the same day after day, the balances of accounts receivable and accounts payable will remain constant—that is, the daily increase associated with each account will be offset by the daily decrease associated with the account. Therefore, once the firm's operations have stabilized and cash collections from credit sales and cash payments for credit purchases have begun, the balance in accounts receivable and accounts payable can be computed using the following equation:

$$\text{Account balance} = \left( \begin{array}{c} \text{Amount of} \\ \text{daily activity} \end{array} \right) \times \left( \begin{array}{c} \text{Average life} \\ \text{of the account} \end{array} \right)$$

**14–1**

For accounts receivable, the balance would be the daily credit sales times the length of time each account remains outstanding—$700,000 × 15 days = $10,500,000.

The preceding scenario will occur only if GCP's expectations, including forecasted sales, come true. But what happens if GCP's forecasts are too optimistic? If GCP finds it cannot sell 50,000 units each day, its cash collections will decrease, its inventory probably will build up, and perhaps notes payable also will increase. If this pattern continues, GCP eventually might find itself in financial difficulty.

Although the illustration we used here is oversimplified, it should give you an indication of the interrelationships among the working capital accounts. It should be apparent that a decision affecting one working capital account—for example, inventory—will have an impact on other working capital accounts—for example, receivables and payables.

**Self-Test Questions**

If a firm purchases raw materials on credit, which two working capital accounts are affected? What would happen if the purchase was for cash?

Write out the equation that gives the balance in accounts receivable once cash receipts for earlier credit sales begin (assume sales/collection patterns have stabilized).

Suppose Suncrest Orange Juice Manufacturer's sales equal $3.5 million per day. If customers on average pay for their purchases every 10 days, what should the balance in accounts receivable be? (*Answer:* $35 million)

## THE CASH CONVERSION CYCLE

The concept of working capital management originated with the old Yankee peddler who would borrow to buy inventory, sell the inventory to pay off the bank loan, and then repeat the cycle. The previous section illustrates the impact of such activity on the working capital accounts of the firm. That general concept has been applied to more complex businesses, and it is useful when analyzing the effectiveness of a firm's working capital management process.

The working capital management process that Unilate Textiles faces is similar to the process we described in the previous section for GCP, and it can be summarized as follows:

1. Unilate orders and then receives the materials it needs to produce the textile products it sells. Unilate purchases from its suppliers on credit, so an account payable is created for credit purchases. Such purchases have no immediate cash flow effect because payment is not made until some later date, perhaps 20 to 30 days after purchase.

2. Labor is used to convert the materials (cotton and wool) into finished goods (cloth products, thread, and so on ). However, wages are not fully paid at the time the work is done, so accrued wages build up, maybe for a period of one or two weeks.

3. The finished products are sold, but on credit; so sales create receivables, not immediate cash inflows.

4. At some point during the cycle, Unilate must pay off its accounts payable and accrued wages. *If* these payments are made before Unilate has collected cash from its receivables, a net cash outflow occurs and this outflow must be financed.

5. The cycle is completed when Unilate's receivables are collected, perhaps in 30 to 40 days. At that time, the company is in a position to pay off the credit that was used to finance production of the product, and it can then repeat the cycle.

The preceding steps are formalized with the cash conversion cycle model, which focuses on the length of time between when the company makes payments, or invests in the manufacture of inventory, and when it receives cash inflows, or realizes a cash return from its investment in production.[5] The following terms are used in the model:

**inventory conversion period**

The amount of time a product remains in inventory in various stages of completion.

1. The **inventory conversion period** is the average length of time required to convert materials into finished goods and then to sell those goods; it is the

---

[5]See Verlyn Richards and Eugene Laughlin, "A Cash Conversion Cycle Approach to Liquidity Analysis," *Financial Management,* Spring 1980, 32–38.

amount of time the product remains in inventory in various stages of completion. The inventory conversion period, which is the average age of the firm's inventory, is calculated by dividing inventory by the cost of goods sold per day. For example, we can compute the inventory conversion period for Unilate Textiles using the 2009 balance sheet figures shown in Table 14-1. In 2009, Unilate sold $1,500 million of its product with a cost of goods sold equal to $1,230 million, so the inventory conversion period would be

**14–2**

$$\begin{aligned}\text{Inventory} \atop \text{conversion period} &= \frac{\text{Inventory}}{\text{Cost of goods sold per day}} = \frac{\text{Inventory}}{\left(\dfrac{\text{Cost of goods sold}}{360 \text{ days}}\right)} \\[2mm] &= \frac{360 \text{ days}}{\left(\dfrac{\text{Costs of goods sold}}{\text{Inventory}}\right)} = \frac{360 \text{ days}}{\text{Inventory turnover}}\end{aligned}$$

$$= \frac{\$270 \text{ million}}{\left(\dfrac{\$1,230 \text{ million}}{360}\right)} = \frac{\$270 \text{ million}}{\$3.417}$$

$$= 79.0 \text{ days}$$

Thus, according to its 2009 operations, it takes Unilate 79.0 days to convert raw materials into finished goods and then to sell those goods.

Using the form of Equation 14–2 shown in the second line, we find that Unilate's inventory turnover is 4.6 = ($1,230 million)/($270 million). The inventory turnover indicates that Unilate sold, or turned over, its average amount in inventory 4.6 times during the year. As we discovered in Chapter 2, the industry average is 7.4, which means that, compared with its peers, Unilate is not "turning over" its inventory quickly enough.

2.  The **receivables collection period** is the average length of time required to convert the firm's receivables into cash—that is, the time it takes to collect cash following a sale. The receivables collection period is also called the days sales outstanding (DSO), and it is calculated by dividing accounts receivable by the average credit sales per day. Because sales in 2009 equaled $1,500 million, Unilate's receivables collection period (DSO) is

> **receivables collection period**
> The time it takes to collect cash following a sale.

**14–3**

$$\begin{aligned}\text{Receivables} \atop \text{collection period (DSO)} &= \frac{\text{Receivables}}{\text{Daily credit sales}} = \frac{\text{Receivables}}{\left(\dfrac{\text{Annual credit sales}}{360}\right)} \\[2mm] &= \frac{360 \text{ days}}{\left(\dfrac{\text{Annual credit sales}}{\text{Receivables}}\right)} = \frac{360 \text{ days}}{\text{Receivables turnover}}\end{aligned}$$

$$= \frac{\$180 \text{ million}}{\left(\dfrac{\$1,500 \text{ million}}{360}\right)} = \frac{\$180 \text{ million}}{\$4.167} = 43.2 \text{ days}$$

Thus, cash payments associated with credit sales are not collected until 43.2 days after the sales.

Using the form of Equation 14–3 shown in the second line, we find that Unilate's receivables turnover is 8.3 = ($1,500 million)/($180 million), which indicates that the company collected the average amount in receivables 8.3 times during the year. Because its days sales outstanding (DSO), which equals 43.2 days, is greater than the industry average, Unilate is not "turning over" its receivables accounts enough times during the year—that is, the company is not collecting its credit sales quickly enough.

**payables deferral period**
The average length of time between the purchase of raw materials and labor and the payment of cash for them.

3. The **payables deferral period** is the average length of time between the purchase of raw materials and labor and the payment of cash for them. It is computed by dividing accounts payable by the daily credit purchases. Unilate's daily cost of goods sold is $3.417 million, so the payables deferral period for Unilate would be

**14–4**

$$\text{Payables deferral period (DPO)} = \frac{\text{Accounts payable}}{\text{Credit purchases per day}} = \frac{\text{Account payable}}{\left(\dfrac{\text{Cost of goods sold}}{360}\right)}$$

$$= \frac{360 \text{ days}}{\left(\dfrac{\text{cost of goods sold}}{\text{Accounts payable}}\right)} = \frac{360 \text{ days}}{\text{payables turnover}}$$

$$= \frac{\$30 \text{ million}}{\left(\dfrac{\$1,230 \text{ million}}{360}\right)} = \frac{\$30 \text{ million}}{\$3.417} = 8.8 \text{ days}$$

So Unilate pays its suppliers an average of 8.8 days after materials are purchased.[6]

Using the form of Equation 14–4 shown in the second line, we find that Unilate's payables turnover is 41.0 = ($1,230 million)/($30 million), which indicates that the company paid the average amount in payables 41 times during the year. Because the industry average DPO is 18, it appears that Unilate is paying its suppliers much too quickly.

**cash conversion cycle**
The length of time from the payment for the purchase of raw materials to manufacture a product until the collection of accounts receivable associated with the sale of the product.

4. The **cash conversion cycle** computation nets out the three periods just defined, resulting in a value that equals the length of time between the firm's actual cash expenditures to pay for (invest in) productive resources (materials and labor) and its own cash receipts from the sale of products. In other words, the cash conversion cycle represents the length of time between paying for labor and materials and collecting on receivables. The cash conversion cycle thus equals the average length of time a dollar is tied up, or invested, in current assets.

We can now use these definitions to analyze Unilate's cash conversion cycle. The concept is diagrammed in Figure 14-1. The cash conversion cycle can be expressed by this equation:

---

[6]The computation for the payables deferral period shown here is the traditional method used to determine the value used in the calculation of the cash conversion cycle. However, if we recognize that the intent of the computation is to determine the length of time between the purchase of raw materials and the labor used to produce inventory and the payment for these inputs, the payables deferral period might more appropriately be written to include consideration of accrued wages.

**FIGURE 14-1    The Cash Conversion Cycle**

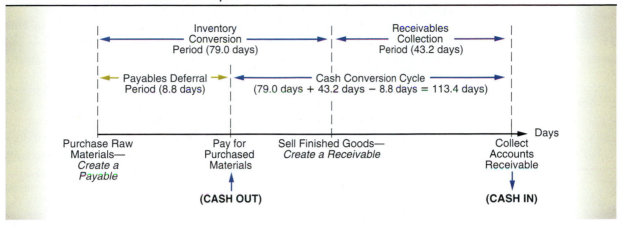

$$\begin{array}{c}\text{Cash} \\ \text{conversion} \\ \text{cycle}\end{array} = \left(\begin{array}{c}\text{Inventory} \\ \text{conversion} \\ \text{period}\end{array}\right) + \left(\begin{array}{c}\text{Receivables} \\ \text{collection} \\ \text{period}\end{array}\right) - \left(\begin{array}{c}\text{Payable} \\ \text{deferral} \\ \text{period}\end{array}\right)$$

14–5

$$\begin{aligned} &= \quad 79.0 \text{ days} \quad + \quad 43.2 \text{ days} \quad - \quad 8.8 \text{ days} \\ &= \quad 113.4 \text{ days} \end{aligned}$$

To illustrate, according to Unilate's 2009 operations, it takes an average of 79.0 days to convert raw materials (cotton, wool, and so on) into finished goods (cloth, thread, and so on) and then sell these products, and then it takes another 43.2 days to collect on the sale (that is, receivables). However, 8.8 days normally elapse between the receipt of raw materials and payment for them. In this case, the cash conversion cycle is 113.4 days. The *receipt* of cash from manufacturing and selling the products will be delayed by approximately 122 days because (1) the product will be "tied up" in inventory for 79 days and (2) the cash from the sale will not be received until 43 days after the selling date. But the *disbursement* of cash for the raw materials purchased will be delayed by nearly 9 days because Unilate does not pay cash for the raw materials when they are purchased. So for Unilate, the net delay in cash receipts associated with an investment (cash disbursement) in inventory is approximately 113 days. What does this mean to Unilate?

Given its cash conversion cycle, Unilate knows when it starts processing its textile products that it will have to finance the manufacturing and other operating costs for a 113-day period, which is nearly one-third of a year. The firm's goal should be to shorten its cash conversion cycle as much as possible without harming operations. This would improve profits because the longer the cash conversion cycle, the greater the need for external, or nonspontaneous, financing, and such financing has a cost.

The cash conversion cycle can be shortened by (1) reducing the inventory conversion period by processing and selling goods more quickly, (2) reducing the receivables collection period by speeding up collections, or (3) lengthening the payables deferral period by slowing down its own payments. To the extent that these actions can be taken *without harming the return* associated with the management of these accounts, they should be carried out. So when taking actions to reduce the inventory conversion period, a firm should be careful to *avoid inventory shortages* that could cause "good" customers to buy from competitors; when taking actions to speed up the collection of receivables, a firm should be careful to *maintain good relations with its "good" credit customers;* and when taking actions to lengthen the payables deferral period, a firm should be careful *not to harm its own credit reputation.*

We can illustrate the benefits of shortening the cash conversion cycle by looking again at Unilate Textiles. Unilate must spend an average of $12.30 on materials and labor to manufacture its products, which are sold for $15.00 per unit. To generate the $1,500 million sales realized in 2009, Unilate turned out 277,778 items per day.

At this rate of production, it must invest $3.417 million = $12.30 × 277,778 units each day to support the manufacturing process. This investment must be financed for 113.4 days—the length of the cash conversion cycle—so the company's working capital financing needs will be $387.5 million = 113.4 × $3.417 million. If Unilate could reduce the cash conversion cycle to 93.4 days—say, by deferring payment of its accounts payable an additional 20 days or by speeding up either the production process or the collection of its receivables—it could reduce its working capital financing requirements by $68.3 million = 20 days × $3.417 million. We see, then, that actions that affect the inventory conversion period, the receivables collection period, and the payables deferral period all affect the cash conversion cycle; hence, they influence the firm's need for current assets and current asset financing. You should keep the cash conversion cycle concept in mind as you go through the remainder of this chapter and the next two chapters.

### Self-Test Questions

What steps are involved in estimating the cash conversion cycle?

Define the terms *inventory conversion period, receivables collection period,* and *payables deferral period.*

What is the cash conversion cycle model? How can it be used to improve current asset management?

Crawford Company has an inventory conversion period of 45 days, a receivables collection period of 32 days, and a payables deferral period of 30 days. What is the length of the firm's cash conversion cycle? (*Answer:* 47 days)

## WORKING CAPITAL INVESTMENT AND FINANCING POLICIES

Working capital policy involves two basic questions: (1) What is the appropriate level for current assets, both in total and by specific accounts, and (2) how should current assets be financed?

### Alternative Current Asset Investment Policies

Figure 14-2 shows three alternative policies regarding the total amount of current assets carried. Essentially, these policies differ in that different amounts of current assets are carried to support any given level of sales. The line with the steepest slope represents a **relaxed current asset investment** (or "fat cat") **policy,** in which relatively large amounts of cash and marketable securities and inventories are carried and in which sales are stimulated by the use of a credit policy that provides liberal financing to customers and a correspondingly high level of receivables. Conversely, with the **restricted current asset investment** (or "lean-and-mean") **policy,** the holdings of cash and marketable securities, inventories, and receivables are minimized. The **moderate current asset investment policy** is between the two extremes.

Under conditions of certainty—when sales, costs, lead times, payment periods, and so on, are known for sure—all firms would hold only minimal levels of current assets. Any larger amounts would increase the need for external funding without a

**relaxed current asset investment policy**
A policy under which relatively large amounts of cash and marketable securities and inventories are carried and under which sales are stimulated by a liberal credit policy that results in a high level of receivables.

**restricted current asset investment policy**
A policy under which holdings of cash and marketable securities, inventories, and receivables are minimized.

**moderate current asset investment policy**
A policy between the relaxed and restricted policies.

FIGURE 14-2   Alternative Current Asset Investment Policies ($ millions)

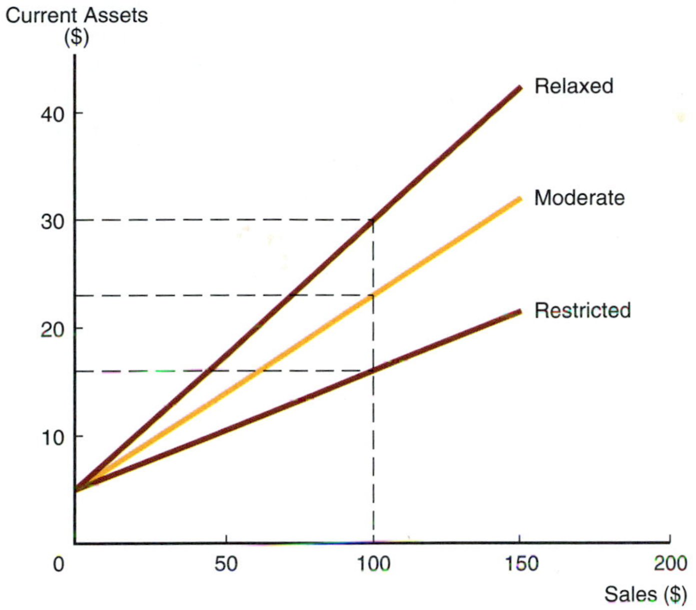

| Policy | Current Assets to Support Sales of $100 |
|--------|-----------------------------------------|
| Relaxed | $30 |
| Moderate | 23 |
| Restricted | 16 |

**Note:** The sales/current assets relationship is shown here as being linear, but the relationship is often curvilinear.

corresponding increase in profits, whereas any smaller holdings would involve late payments to labor and suppliers and lost sales due to inventory shortages and an overly restrictive credit policy.

However, the picture changes when uncertainty is introduced. Here the firm requires some minimum amount of cash and inventories based on expected payments, expected sales, expected order lead times, and so on, plus additional amounts, or *safety stocks*, that enable it to deal with departures from the expected values. Similarly, accounts receivable levels are determined by credit terms, and the tougher the credit terms, the lower the receivables for any given level of sales. With a restricted current asset investment policy, the firm would hold minimal levels of safety stocks for cash and inventories, and it would have a tight credit policy, even though this would mean running the risk of losing sales. A restricted, lean-and-mean current asset investment policy generally provides the highest expected return on investment, but it entails the greatest risk, whereas the reverse is true under a relaxed policy. The moderate policy falls in between the two extremes in terms of both expected risk and return.

In terms of the cash conversion cycle, a restricted investment policy would tend to reduce the inventory conversion and receivables collection periods, which would result in a relatively short cash conversion cycle. Conversely, a relaxed policy would create higher levels of inventories and receivables, longer inventory conversion and receivables collection periods, and a relatively long cash conversion cycle. A moderate policy would produce a cash conversion cycle somewhere between the two extremes.

## Alternative Current Asset Financing Policies

Most businesses experience seasonal fluctuations, cyclical fluctuations, or both. For example, construction firms have peaks in the spring and summer, retailers peak around Christmas, and the manufacturers who supply both construction companies and retailers follow similar patterns. Similarly, virtually all businesses must build up current assets when the economy is strong, but they then sell off inventories and have net reductions of receivables when the economy slacks off. Still, current assets rarely drop to zero, and this realization has led to the development of the idea that some current assets should be considered **permanent current assets** because their levels remain stable no matter the seasonal or economic conditions. Applying this idea to Unilate Textiles, Table 14-1 (presented earlier) suggests that, at this stage in its life, Unilate's total assets are growing at a 10 percent rate, from $845.0 million at the end of 2009 to a projected $929.5 million by the end of 2010, but seasonal fluctuations are expected to push total assets up to $1,100.0 million during the firm's peak season in 2010. Assuming Unilate's permanent assets grow continuously, and at the *same rate*, throughout the year, then 9/12ths (75 percent) of the 10 percent growth in assets will accrue by the end of September and permanent assets would equal $908.4 million = $845.0 million + (9/12)($929.5 million − $845.0 million). But the actual level of assets is expected to be $1,100.0 million because this is Unilate's peak season. So at the end of September, Unilate's total assets of $1,100.0 million consist of $908.4 million of permanent assets and $191.6 million = $1,100.0 million − $908.4 million of seasonal, or **temporary, current assets.** Unilate's temporary current assets fluctuate from zero during the slow season in December to nearly $192 million during the peak season in September. Therefore, temporary current assets are those amounts of current assets that vary with respect to the seasonal or economic conditions of a firm. The manner in which the permanent and temporary current assets are financed is called the firm's *current asset financing policy,* which generally can be classified as one of the three approaches described next.

### *Maturity Matching, or "Self-Liquidating," Approach*

The **maturity matching, or "self-liquidating," approach** calls for matching asset and liability maturities as shown in panel A of Figure 14-3. This strategy minimizes the risk that the firm will be unable to pay off its maturing obligations *if* the liquidations of the assets can be controlled to occur on or before the maturities of the obligations. At the limit, a firm could attempt to match exactly the maturity structure of its assets and liabilities. Inventory expected to be sold in 30 days could be financed with a 30-day bank loan, a machine expected to last for five years could be financed by a five-year loan, a 20-year building could be financed by a 20-year mortgage bond, and so forth. Actually, of course, two factors prevent this exact maturity matching: (1) there is uncertainty about the lives of assets, and (2) some common equity must be used, and common equity has no maturity. To illustrate the uncertainty factor, Unilate might finance inventories with a 30-day loan, expecting to sell the inventories and to use the cash generated to retire the loan. But if sales were slow, the cash would not be forthcoming, and the use of short-term credit could end up causing a problem (for example, look at the cash conversion cycle computed for Unilate in the previous section). Still, if Unilate makes an attempt to match asset and liability maturities, we would define this as a *moderate current asset financing policy.*

### *Aggressive Approach*

Panel B of Figure 14-3 illustrates the **aggressive approach,** used by a firm that (1) finances all of its temporary assets with short-term, nonspontaneous debt and (2) finances its fixed assets with long-term capital, but some of the remainder of its

---

**permanent current assets**
Current assets' balances that remain stable no matter the seasonal or economic conditions; balances that exist no matter the type of business cycle.

**temporary current assets**
Current assets that fluctuate with seasonal or cyclical variations in a firm's business.

**maturity matching, or "self-liquidating," approach**
A financing policy that matches asset and liability maturities. This would be considered a moderate current asset financing policy.

**aggressive approach**
A policy in which all of the fixed assets of a firm are financed with long-term capital but *some* of the firm's permanent current assets are financed with short-term nonspontaneous sources of funds.

**FIGURE 14-3    Alternative Current Asset Financing Policies**

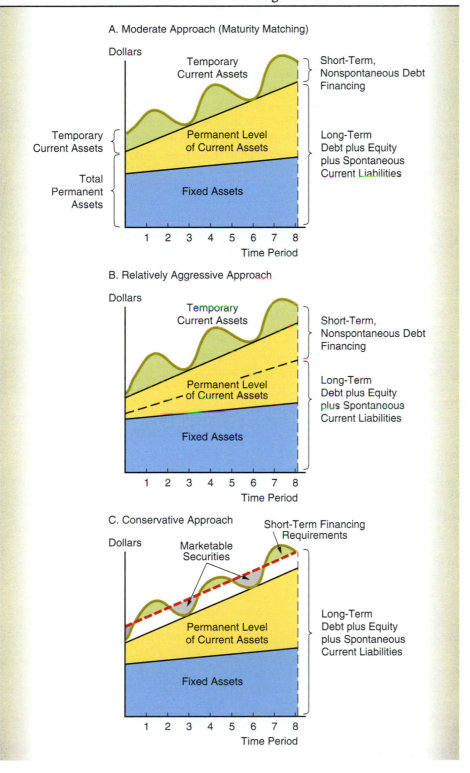

permanent current assets is financed with short-term, nonspontaneous credit. A look back at Table 14-1 shows that Unilate actually follows this strategy. Unilate has $499.9 million in permanent current assets ($908.4 million in permanent assets less $408.5 million fixed assets) projected for September 2010, so its temporary current assets must be $191.6 million = $691.5 million – $499.9 million. However, the firm is projected to have $129.0 million in notes payable as well as temporary financing equal to about $100.0 million from peak levels of accounts payable and accruals (payables are projected to be $60.0 million higher than at the end of 2009, and accruals are projected to be $40.0 million higher). Thus, Unilate's level of temporary financing, which is $229.0 million, exceeds its level of temporary current assets, which is $191.6 million; some part of its permanent assets is financed with temporary capital.

Returning to Figure 14-3, note that we used the term *relatively* in the title for panel B because there can be different *degrees* of aggressiveness. For example, the dashed line in panel B could have been drawn *below* the line designating fixed assets, indicating that all of the permanent current assets and part of the fixed assets were financed with short-term credit; this would be a highly aggressive, extremely nonconservative position, and the firm would be very much subject to dangers from rising interest rates as well as to loan renewal problems. However, short-term debt often is cheaper than long-term debt, and some firms are willing to sacrifice safety for the chance of higher profits.

## Conservative Approach

As shown in panel C of Figure 14-3, the dashed line could also be drawn *above* the line designating permanent current assets, indicating that permanent capital is being used to finance all permanent asset requirements and also to meet some or all of the seasonal, temporary demands. In the situation depicted in our graph, the firm uses a small amount of short-term, nonspontaneous credit to meet its peak requirements, but it also meets a part of its seasonal needs by "storing liquidity" in the form of marketable securities during the off-season. The humps above the dashed line represent short-term financing; the troughs below the dashed line represent short-term security holdings. Panel C represents the **conservative approach,** which is a very safe current asset financing policy that generally is not as profitable as the other two approaches.

**conservative approach**
A policy in which all of the fixed assets, all of the permanent current assets, and some of the temporary current assets of a firm are financed with long-term capital.

**Self-Test Questions**

What two key issues does working capital policy involve?

What is meant by the term *current asset investment policy?*

What is meant by the term *current asset financing policy?*

What are three alternative current asset financing policies? Is one best?

What distinguishes *permanent current assets* from *temporary current assets?*

Which of the three alternative current asset financing policies uses the most short-term debt?

## ADVANTAGES AND DISADVANTAGES OF SHORT-TERM FINANCING

The three possible financing policies described in the previous section were distinguished by the relative amounts of short-term debt used under each policy. The aggressive policy calls for the greatest use of short-term debt, whereas the conservative policy requires the least, and maturity matching falls in between. Although using short-term credit generally is riskier than using long-term credit, short-term credit does have some significant advantages. The pros and cons of short-term financing are considered in this section.

## Speed

A short-term loan can be obtained much faster than long-term credit. Lenders will insist on a more thorough financial examination before extending long-term credit, and the loan agreement will have to be spelled out in considerable detail because much can happen during the life of a 10- or 20-year loan. Therefore, if funds are needed in a hurry, a firm generally looks to short-term sources.

## Flexibility

If the needs for funds are seasonal or cyclical, a firm might not want to commit itself to long-term debt for three reasons. First, the costs associated with issuing long-term debt are significantly greater than the costs of getting short-term credit. Second, some long-term debts carry expensive penalties for prepayments (paying prior to maturity). Accordingly, if a firm thinks its need for funds will diminish in the near future, it should choose short-term debt for the flexibility it provides. Third, long-term loan agreements always contain provisions, or covenants, that constrain the firm's future actions. Short-term credit agreements generally are much less onerous in this regard.

## Cost of Long-Term Versus Short-Term Debt

The yield curve normally is upward sloping, indicating that interest rates generally are lower on short-term than on long-term debt (see Chapter 5). Thus, under normal conditions, interest costs at the time the funds are obtained will be lower if the firm borrows on a short-term rather than on a long-term basis.

## Risk of Long-Term Versus Short-Term Debt

Even though short-term debt is often less expensive than long-term debt, short-term credit subjects the firm to more risk than does long-term financing. This occurs for two reasons: (1) If a firm borrows on a long-term basis, its interest costs will be relatively stable, perhaps even fixed, over time, but if it uses short-term credit, its interest expense will fluctuate widely, at times reaching quite high levels. For example, in 1994, because the Federal Reserve increased rates six times during the year, short-term rates increased by more than 3 percent, which created a significant burden for many firms. (2) If a firm borrows heavily on a short-term basis, it could find itself unable to repay this debt, and it might be in such a weak financial position that the lender will not extend the loan; this too could force the firm into bankruptcy. K-mart found itself in this position not long ago.

**Self-Test Questions**

What are some advantages of short-term debt over long-term debt as a source of capital?

What are some disadvantages of short-term debt?

## MULTINATIONAL WORKING CAPITAL MANAGEMENT

For the most part, the techniques used to manage short-term assets and liabilities in multinational corporations are the same as those used in purely domestic corporations. But multinational corporations face a far more complex task because they operate in many different business cultures, political environments, economic conditions, and so forth. In Chapter 1, we described six factors that complicate managerial finance in general in the international business arena: (1) different currency denominations, (2) differences in economic and legal environments, (3) language differences, (4) cultural differences, (5) governmental role, and (6) political risk. Difficulties with each of these factors are more acute when managing working capital internationally because decisions made in the short run can have significant consequences on the long-run survival of the firm and such decisions are more difficult to adjust or reverse when rules, regulations, and business cultures differ significantly from one business setting to another.

The results of one study provide some indication of how working capital policies of U.S. firms and European firms differ.[7] First, the average cash conversion cycle of European firms (about 263 days) was more than twice the average cash conversion cycle of U.S. firms (about 116 days). A possible explanation for this disparity is that European firms had much higher growth rates than their U.S. counterparts. Second, it appears from the results of the study that U.S. firms follow much more conservative working capital policies than European firms. The average current ratio and the average quick ratio proved to be significantly greater for U.S. firms than for European firms, which suggests that corporations in the United States use significantly more long-term financing alternatives than corporations in Europe. Although a more in-depth study is needed to determine why U.S. firms seem to follow more conservative working capital policies than European firms, one possible explanation might be found in the differences that are apparent in the banking systems in Europe and in the United States. In Chapter 3, we mentioned that U.S. financial institutions generally are at a competitive disadvantage in the global arena because they are subject to more restrictions and regulations than banking organizations in other countries. Foreign banks generally can branch with little or no restrictions and are allowed, in many cases, to own corporations to which they also lend funds. For these reasons, European banks often have very close relationships with their debtor corporations; thus, they tend to be more willing to provide short-term, risky debt than we observe in U.S. banking organizations.

In the next chapter, we discuss some of the techniques used by U.S. firms to manage short-term assets and then we give some indication of how the factors just mentioned affect the methods used by multinational firms.

### Self-Test Question

Which of the factors mentioned in this section do you think has the greatest impact on how working capital methods differ among countries?

## Chapter *Essentials*
### —The Answers

To summarize the key concepts, let's answer the questions that were posed at the beginning of the chapter:

- **What is working capital and why is working capital management important to the survival of a firm?** Working capital refers to the short-term, or current, assets of a firm. Poor working capital management generally results in financial distress, and perhaps bankruptcy. Liquidation of working capital accounts produces the cash that is needed to pay current bills. If a firm cannot pay its current bills, it cannot survive the long term.

- **How are working capital accounts related?** The working capital management process and the relationships of the working capital accounts, which is outlined in Figure 14-1, can be described as follows: (1) A company orders and receives the materials it needs to produce the product its sells. When the materials are received, the amount of inventory increases and, if the materials were purchased on credit, the accounts payable increases. (2) Labor is used to convert the materials into

[7]Chun-Hao Chang, Krishnan Dandapani, and Arun J. Prakish, "Current Assets Policies of European Corporations: A Critical Examination," *Management International Review,* Special Issue 1995/2, 105–117.

finished goods. Because wages are not paid at the time the work is done, accrued wages build up, perhaps for a period of one or two weeks. (3) If the finished product is sold on credit, the accounts receivable increases. (4) At some point, the company must pay off its accounts payable and accrued wages. (5) The cycle is completed when the firm collects cash payment for the products.

- **Why is it important for management to understand the firm's cash conversion cycle?** The cash conversion cycle represents the length of time funds are "tied up," or invested, in current assets. Often a firm has to pay for the materials and labor that are needed to manufacture and sell its products before customers pay for their purchases. During the period from when the firm invests in the product—that is, pays for materials and labor—until it receives cash payment from the sale of the product, external financing is needed to support operations. If a firm reduces its cash conversion cycle, it reduces its need for alternative financing.

- **What working capital investment policy should a firm follow?** More liquid firms are better able to weather financial difficulties, but they also generate lower returns than less liquid firms during prosperous times. Thus, there is a trade-off between liquidity (risk) and return. As a result, a firm must determine whether it should follow a current asset investment policy that is (1) a relaxed, or "fat cat," position, which suggests that large amounts of current assets should be carried, (2) a restricted, or "lean-and-mean," position, which suggests that current assets should be minimized, or (3) a moderate position, which is between the two extremes.

- **How should the firm finance its working capital needs?** Short-term financing generally is riskier but cheaper than long-term financing. Thus, a firm must determine what level of financing risk it can handle. Firms that are able to handle larger amounts of financial risk are likely to finance current assets with more short-term debt—they follow the aggressive approach—than firms that are not able to handle much financial risk—they follow the conservative approach. Most firms follow the maturity matching, or "self-liquidating," approach, which is a moderate approach that is between the aggressive and conservative approaches.

## ETHICAL DILEMMA

### Is a Promotion Liquid?

When examining its financial statements, the CEO of Engeer Manufacturing discovered that the company's cash conversion cycle is more than two times longer than that of the average firm in the industry. The CEO is very concerned because she knows that the cash conversion cycle reflects the firm's liquidity position. Engeer is making plans to raise money in the near future to support operations and to finance its expansion plans. If the firm's liquidity position is considered poor, then it will have difficulty raising the needed funds at a reasonable interest rate.

Because the CEO believes that the cash conversion cycle is an important gauge of the firm's

liquidity position, she has decided that Engeer's cash conversion cycle must be decreased by 10 days as soon as possible. This task was assigned to John, who is Skyler's friend. Although Skyler works in another department, her office is next door to John's office. Because the walls are thin and he speaks very loudly when talking on the phone, Skyler "accidentally" overheard some of the conversations that John had with the CEO and others he consulted for help in completing his task.

The other day John was talking with an acquaintance who works at a competing firm. During the conversation, which took place after regular business hours, John outlined his plans to reduce

Engeer's cash conversion cycle. Skyler was in her office working late to finish a project that was due the next day, so she overheard the entire conversation. What she heard disturbed her very much because she felt John's plans included some "shady" actions. Skyler is convinced that John will take whatever actions are needed to accomplish his assigned task because he recently applied for a promotion to executive vice president.

In essence, Skyler heard John mention three actions that he plans to undertake . These are actions for which he is the decision maker. First, because he believes that Engeer carries too much inventory, John plans to order fewer amounts of raw materials during the next few months. He believes that a lower inventory level will not affect sales but will decrease the firm's inventory conversion period. Second, although he doesn't plan to change when bills are sent to customers, John wants to decrease

by three days the date when the payment is due. Third, John plans to pay Engeer's suppliers three or four days later than he does now. In combination, John believes that these actions will decrease the firm's cash conversion cycle by at least 10 days, which is the CEO's directive.

Skyler is disturbed because she thinks the actions that John proposes will harm the firm's operations and general financial position in the future. One statement she heard John make during the conversation with his friend was particularly disturbing to Skyler. She heard John say "I'm not worried about the fact that these actions might harm the firm because, by the time they do, I will be an executive vice president and I can blame the firm's poor financial position on the person who is in my current position." Skyler is a very loyal employee, but she is also a close friend of John's. What should she do? What would you do if you were Skyler?

## Chapter *Essentials*
### —Personal Finance

The concepts presented in this chapter should help you to understand actions that you can take to better manage your liquidity position and thus to better handle your current obligations.

- Although you do not manufacture products, you do have a "personal" cash conversion cycle. When you purchase items using your credit card, your cash conversion cycle *might* be similar to the following:

In this example, the payment for your credit card purchases is due before you get your next paycheck. When this is the case, to pay your credit card bill you must have alternative sources of funds (for example, savings). Of course, like firms, you prefer to receive cash before you have to use cash. If the situation given here occurs, however, you would want to reduce your cash conversion cycle as much as possible. How can you decrease your cash conversion cycle? In the current example, assuming that you cannot get your employer to pay you sooner, you can delay the credit purchase, delay payment for the credit purchase, or take both actions. If you choose to delay the credit payment, you should make sure that payment is made when it is due—you do not want to harm your credit position.

- One of the concepts discussed in the chapter is the amount of liquidity that a company should have. You should also evaluate your liquidity position. Like firms, if your income is variable and uncertain, you probably should be more liquid than if your income is stable. Because you do not want to jeopardize your ability to pay current bills, you should ensure that you have sufficient liquidity— that is, cash in a checking account, savings, and short-term investments—to be able to meet your current obligations. But you shouldn't be too liquid because short-term investments, which are more liquid, generally earn lower returns than long-term investments, which are less liquid. As a result, you should balance your liquidity position so that you have an appropriate combination of short-term and long-term investments.

- It is tempting to borrow by using loans that have the lowest interest rates. But this strategy is not always wise. In general, it is best to match the maturity of the loan used to finance an asset with the life of the asset. For example, although you could finance a house purchase with a series of one-year loans that are turned over (refinanced) every year for 30 years, such a strategy is very risky. Interest rates change from year to year, and at some point you might not be able to turn over the one-year loan because of personal or economic factors that affect your financial position. As a result, when financing a house, it is better to use a 30-year (15-year) mortgage rather than a one-year mortgage that is renewed every year for 30 years (15 years).

## QUESTIONS

**14-1** How does the seasonal nature of a firm's sales influence its decision regarding the amount of short-term credit to use in its financial structure?

**14-2** Assuming the firm's sales volume remained constant, would you expect it to have a higher cash balance during a tight-money period or during an easy-money period? Why?

**14-3** Describe the relationships among accounts payable, inventories, accounts receivable, and the cash account by tracing the impact on these accounts of a product manufactured and sold by a company. Start with the purchase of raw materials, and conclude with the collection for the sale of the product.

**14-4** Describe the cash conversion cycle. How can a financial manager use knowledge of the cash conversion cycle to better manage the working capital of a firm?

**14-5** What are the advantages of matching the maturities of assets and liabilities? What are the disadvantages?

**14-6** Describe some measures a firm can take to decrease its cash conversion cycle.

**14-7** Can the cash conversion cycle be negative? Explain.

**14-8** From the standpoint of the borrower, is long-term or short-term credit riskier? Explain. Would it ever make sense to borrow on a short-term basis if short-term rates were above long-term rates?

**14-9** If long-term credit exposes a borrower to less risk, why would people or firms ever borrow on a short-term basis?

**14-10** Why is the average cash conversion cycle of European firms more than two times longer than the average cash conversion cycle of U.S. firms?

## SELF-TEST PROBLEMS

*(Solutions appear in Appendix B at the end of the book.)*

**ST-1** Define each of the following terms:                                    key terms

    **a.** Working capital; net working capital; working capital policy

    **b.** Permanent current assets; temporary current assets

    **c.** Cash conversion cycle; inventory conversion period; receivables collection period; payables deferral period

    **d.**  Relaxed current asset investment policy; restricted current asset invest-ment policy; moderate current asset investment policy

    **e.**  Moderate, or maturity matching, current asset financing policy; aggressive current asset financing policy; conservative current asset financing policy

**current asset financing**  **ST-2**  Vanderheiden Press Inc. and Herrenhouse Publishing Company had the following balance sheets as of December 31, 2008 ($ thousands):

|  | Vanderheiden Press | Herrenhouse Publishing |
|---|---|---|
| Current assets | $100,000 | $ 80,000 |
| Fixed assets (net) | 100,000 | 120,000 |
| Total assets | $200,000 | $200,000 |
| Current liabilities | $ 20,000 | $ 80,000 |
| Long-term debt | 80,000 | 20,000 |
| Common stock | 50,000 | 50,000 |
| Retained earnings | 50,000 | 50,000 |
| Total liabilities and equity | $200,000 | $200,000 |

Earnings before interest and taxes (EBIT) for both firms are $30 million, and the marginal tax rate is 40 percent.

    **a.**  What is the return on equity for each firm if the interest rate on current liabilities is 10 percent and the rate on long-term debt is 13 percent?

    **b.**  Assume that the short-term rate rises to 20 percent. While the rate on new long-term debt rises to 16 percent, the rate on existing long-term debt remains unchanged. What would the return on equity be for Vanderhei-den Press and Herrenhouse Publishing under these conditions?

    **c.**  Which company is in a riskier position? Why?

**working capital policy**  **ST-3**  The Calgary Company is attempting to establish a current assets policy. Fixed assets are $600,000, and the firm plans to maintain a 50 percent debt/assets ratio. The interest rate is 10 percent on all debt. The three alter-native current asset policies under consideration are to carry current assets that total 40, 50, and 60 percent of projected sales. The company expects to earn 15 percent before interest and taxes on sales of $3 million. Calgary's marginal tax rate is 40 percent. What is the expected return on equity under each alternative?

## PROBLEMS

**inventory conversion period**  **14-1**  The Cristo Candy Corporation carries an average balance of inventory equal to $400,000. The company's cost of goods sold averages $4.5 million. What are Cristo's (a) inventory turnover and (b) inventory conversion period?

**inventory conversion period**  **14-2**  Wally's Motors generally has inventory that equals $48 million. If the in-ventory turnover for the company is 8, what are its (a) inventory conversion period and (b) cost of goods sold?

**receivables collection period (DSO)**  **14-3**  Small Fry Pools generally carries an amount of receivables equal to $80,000, and its annual credit sales equal $2.4 million. What are Small Fry's (a) receivables turnover and (b) receivables collection period (DSO)?

**14-4**   Unique Uniforms generally has accounts receivable that equal $480,000. If the accounts receivable turnover for the company is 12, what are its (a) receivables collection period (DSO) and (b) annual credit sales?

*receivables collection period (DSO)*

**14-5**   At any point in time, Grandiron Fertilizer generally owes its suppliers $180,000. The company's cost of goods sold averages $2.52 million. What are Grandiron Fertilizer's (a) payables turnover and (b) payables deferral period (DPO)?

*payables deferral period (DPO)*

**14-6**   The accounts payable of Momma's Baby Inc. generally equal $1.6 million. If the turnover of accounts payable is 20, what are the company's (a) payables deferral period (DPO) and (b) annual credit purchases?

*payables deferral period (DPO)*

**14-7**   The Saliford Corporation has an inventory conversion period of 60 days, a receivables collection period of 36 days, and a payables deferral period of 24 days.

*cash conversion cycle*

   **a.**   What is the length of the firm's cash conversion cycle?

   **b.**   If Saliford's annual sales are $3,960,000 and all sales are on credit, what is the average balance in accounts receivable?

   **c.**   How many times per year does Saliford turn over its inventory?

   **d.**   What would happen to Saliford's cash conversion cycle if, on average, inventories could be turned over eight times a year?

**14-8**   The Flamingo Corporation is trying to determine the effect of its inventory turnover ratio and days sales outstanding (DSO) on its cash flow cycle. Flamingo's 2008 sales (all on credit) were $180,000, and it earned a net profit of 5 percent, or $9,000. The cost of goods sold equals 85 percent of sales. Inventory was turned over eight times during the year, and the DSO, or average collection period, was 36 days. The firm had fixed assets totaling $40,000. Flamingo's payables deferral period is 30 days.

*cash conversion cycle and asset turnover*

   **a.**   Calculate Flamingo's cash conversion cycle.

   **b.**   Assuming Flamingo holds negligible amounts of cash and marketable securities, calculate its total assets turnover and return on assets (ROA).

   **c.**   Suppose Flamingo's managers believe that the inventory turnover can be raised to 10. What would Flamingo's cash conversion cycle, total assets turnover, and ROA have been if the inventory turnover had been 10 for 2008?

**14-9**   Go back to the GCP illustration at the beginning of the chapter. Assume the collection and payment patterns of both GCP and its customers do not change.

*working capital accounts relationships*

   **a.**   Construct the balance sheet for GCP at the close of business on Day 31. Remember, the employees' salaries will have been paid at the *beginning* of the day for the *previous* 15 days they have worked, so accrued wages will include only one day of salaries (Day 31).

   **b.**   How long will it take GCP to pay off the bank loan it took out on Day 16 if the *daily cash profits* are used to repay the loan (ignore any interest costs)?

**14-10**  Look back in the chapter to Table 14-1 which showed the balance sheets for Unilate Textiles on three different dates. Unilate's sales fluctuate during the year due to the seasonal nature of its business; however, we can calculate its sales on an average day as total sales divided by 360, recognizing that daily sales will be much higher than this value during its peak selling season and much lower during its slack time. Unilate's projected sales for 2010 are $1,650 million, so daily sales are expected to average $4.583 million. The

*cash conversion cycle*

projected cost of goods sold for 2010 is $1,353 million, so daily credit costs associated with production are expected to average $3.76 million. Assume all sales and all purchases are made on credit.

   a.  Calculate Unilate's inventory conversion period as of September 30, 2010, and December 31, 2010.

   b.  Calculate Unilate's receivables collection period as of September 30, 2010, and December 31, 2010.

   c.  Calculate the payables deferral period as of September 30, 2010, and December 31, 2010.

   d.  Using the values calculated in parts a through c, calculate the length of Unilate's cash conversion cycle on the two balance sheet dates.

   e.  In part d, you should have found that the cash conversion cycle was longer on September 30 than on December 31. Why did these results occur?

   f.  Can you think of any reason why the cash conversion cycle of a firm with seasonal sales might be different during the slack selling season than during the peak selling season?

**working capital investment and cash conversion cycle**

**14-11**  Verbrugge Corporation is a leading U.S. producer of automobile batteries. Verbrugge turns out 1,500 batteries a day at a cost of $6 per battery for materials and labor. It takes the firm 22 days to convert raw materials into a battery. Verbrugge allows its customers 40 days in which to pay for the batteries, and the firm generally pays its suppliers in 30 days.

   a.  What is the length of Verbrugge's cash conversion cycle?

   b.  If Verbrugge always produces and sells 1,500 batteries a day, what amount of working capital must it finance?

   c.  By what amount could Verbrugge reduce its working capital financing needs if it was able to stretch its payables deferral period to 35 days?

   d.  Verbrugge's management is trying to analyze the effect of a proposed new production process on the working capital investment. The new production process would allow Verbrugge to decrease its inventory conversion period to 20 days and to increase its daily production to 1,800 batteries. However, the new process would cause the cost of materials and labor to increase to $7. Assuming the change does not affect the receivables collection period (40 days) or the payables deferral period (30 days), what will be the length of the cash conversion cycle and the working capital financing requirement if the new production process is implemented?

**working capital policy**

**14-12**  The Hawley Corporation is attempting to determine the optimal level of current assets for the coming year. Management expects sales to increase to approximately $2 million as a result of an asset expansion currently being undertaken. Fixed assets total $1 million, and the firm finances 60 percent of its total assets with debt and the rest with equity (common stock). Hawley's interest cost currently is 8 percent on both short-term and longer-term debt (which the firm uses in its permanent structure). Three alternatives regarding the projected current asset level are available to the firm: (1) a tight policy requiring current assets of only 45 percent of projected sales, (2) a moderate policy of 50 percent of sales in current assets, and (3) a relaxed policy requiring current assets of 60 percent of sales. The firm expects to generate earnings before interest and taxes (EBIT) at a rate of 12 percent on total sales.

   a.  What is the expected return on equity under each current asset level? (Assume a 40 percent marginal tax rate.)

**b.** In this problem we have assumed that the level of expected sales is independent of current asset policy. Is this a valid assumption?

**c.** How would the overall riskiness of the firm vary under each policy?

## Integrative Problem

14-13  Daniel Barnes, financial manager of New York Fuels (NYF), a heating oil distributor, is concerned about the company's working capital policy, and he is considering three alternative policies: (1) *a restricted (lean and mean or tight)* policy, which calls for reducing receivables by $100,000 and inventories by $200,000; (2) *a relaxed (loose or fat cat)* policy, which calls for increasing receivables by $100,000 and inventories by $200,000; and (3) a *moderate* policy, which would mean leaving receivables and inventories at their current levels. NYF's 2008 financial statements and key ratios, plus some industry average data, are given in Table IP14-1.

*working capital policy and working capital financing*

**TABLE IP14-1**   Financial Statements and Other Data on NYF ($ thousands)

### A. 2008 Balance Sheet

| | | | |
|---|---|---|---|
| Cash and securities | $  100 | Accounts payable and accruals | $  300 |
| Accounts receivable | 600 | Notes payable (8%) | 500 |
| Inventories | 1,000 | Total current liabilities | $  800 |
| Total current assets | $1,700 | Long-term debt (12%) | 600 |
| Net fixed assets | 800 | Common equity | 1,100 |
| Total assets | $2,500 | Total liabilities and equity | $2,500 |

### B. 2008 Income Statement

| | |
|---|---|
| Sales | $ 5,000.00 |
| Less: Variable costs | (3,700.00) |
| Fixed costs | (1,000.00) |
| EBIT | $   300.00 |
| Interest | ( 112.00) |
| Earnings before taxes | $   188.00 |
| Taxes (40%) | (  75.20) |
| Net income | $   112.80 |
| Dividends (30% payout) | $    33.84 |
| Addition to retained earnings | $    78.96 |

### C. Key Ratios

| | NYF | Industry |
|---|---|---|
| Profit margin | 2.3% | 3.0% |
| Return on equity | 10.3% | 15.0% |
| Days sales outstanding | 43.2 | 30.0 |
| Accounts receivable turnover | 8.3× | 12.0× |
| Inventory turnover | 3.7× | 5.4× |
| Fixed assets turnover | 6.3× | 6.0× |
| Total assets turnover | 2.0× | 2.5× |
| Debt/assets | 56.0% | 50.0% |
| Times interest earned | 2.7× | 4.8× |
| Current ratio | 2.1× | 2.3× |
| Quick ratio | 0.9× | 1.3× |

The cost of long-term debt is 12 percent versus only 8 percent for short-term notes payable. Variable costs as a percentage of sales (74 percent) would not be affected by the firm's working capital policy, but fixed costs would be affected due to the storage, handling, and insurance costs associated with inventory. Here are the assumed fixed costs under the three policies:

| Policy | Fixed Costs |
|---|---|
| Restricted | $   950,000 |
| Moderate | 1,000,000 |
| Relaxed | 1,100,000 |

Sales also would be affected by the policy chosen: Carrying larger inventories and using easier credit terms would stimulate sales, so sales would be highest under the relaxed policy and lowest under the restricted policy. Also, these effects would vary depending on the strength of the economy. Here are the relationships Barnes assumes would have held in 2008:

| | Sales ($ millions) | | |
|---|---|---|---|
| State of the Economy | Restricted | Moderate | Relaxed |
| Weak | $4.3 | $4.5 | $5.0 |
| Average | 4.7 | 5.0 | 5.5 |
| Strong | 5.3 | 5.5 | 6.0 |

Barnes considers the 2008 economy to be average.

You have been asked to answer the following questions to help determine NYF's optimal working capital policy:

a.  How does NYF's current working capital policy as reflected in its financial statements compare with an average firm's policy? Do the differences suggest that NYF's policy is better or worse than that of the average firm in its industry?

b.  Based on the 2008 ratios and financial statements, what were the company's inventory conversion period, its receivables collection period, and, assuming a 29-day payables deferral period, its cash conversion cycle? How could the cash conversion cycle concept be used to help improve the firm's working capital management?

c.  Barnes has asked you to recast the 2008 financial statements, and calculate some key ratios, assuming an average economy and a restricted (tight) working capital policy, and to check some calculations he has made. Construct these statements, and then calculate the new current ratio and return on equity (ROE). Assume that common stock is used to make the balance sheet balance, but do not get into financing feedbacks. (*Hint:* You need to change sales, fixed costs, receivables, inventories, and common equity, plus items affected by those changes, and then calculate new ratios.)

d.  Barnes himself has actually analyzed the situation for each of the policies under each economic scenario; the ROEs he has calculated are shown in Table IP14-2. What are the implications of these data for the working capital policy decision?

| TABLE IP14-2 | ROEs under the Alternative Policies | | |
|---|---|---|---|

| | Working Capital Policy | | |
|---|---|---|---|
| **State of the Economy** | **Tight** | **Moderate** | **Easy** |
| Weak | 4.2% | 3.2% | 3.8% |
| Average | 12.0 | 10.3 | 9.3 |
| Strong | 23.7 | 17.3 | 14.9 |
| Average | 13.3% | 10.3% | 9.3% |

**e.** The working capital policy discussion thus far has focused entirely on current assets and not at all on the current asset financing policy. How would you bring financing policy into the analysis?

## Computer-Related Problem

*Work the problem in this section only if you are using the problem spreadsheet.*

**14-14** Three companies—Aggressive, Moderate, and Conservative—have different working capital management policies as implied by their names. For example, Aggressive employs only minimal current assets, and it finances almost entirely with current liabilities plus equity. This restricted approach has a dual effect. It keeps total assets low, which tends to increase return on assets, but because of stock-outs and credit rejections, total sales are reduced, and because inventory is ordered more frequently and in smaller quantities, variable costs are increased. Condensed balance sheets for the three companies follow:

**working capital financing**

| | **Aggressive** | **Moderate** | **Conservative** |
|---|---|---|---|
| Current assets | $225,000 | $300,000 | $450,000 |
| Fixed assets | 300,000 | 300,000 | 300,000 |
| Total assets | $525,000 | $600,000 | $750,000 |
| Current liabilities (cost = 12%) | $300,000 | $150,000 | $75,000 |
| Long-term debt (cost = 10%) | 0 | 150,000 | 300,000 |
| Total debt | $300,000 | $300,000 | $375,000 |
| Equity | 225,000 | 300,000 | 375,000 |
| Total liabilities and equity | $525,000 | $600,000 | $750,000 |
| Current ratio | 0.75 | 2.0 | 6.0 |

The cost of goods sold functions for the three firms are as follows:

$$\text{Cost of Goods Sold} = \text{Fixed Costs} + \text{Variable Costs}$$

| | | |
|---|---|---|
| *Aggressive:* | Cost of goods sold = $300,000 | + 0.70(Sales) |
| *Moderate:* | Cost of goods sold = $405,000 | + 0.65(Sales) |
| *Conservative:* | Cost of goods sold = $577,500 | + 0.60(Sales) |

Because of the working capital differences, sales for the three firms under different economic conditions are expected to vary as follows:

|  | Aggressive | Moderate | Conservative |
|---|---|---|---|
| Strong economy | $1,800,000 | $1,875,000 | $1,950,000 |
| Average economy | 1,350,000 | 1,500,000 | 1,725,000 |
| Weak economy | 1,050,000 | 1,200,000 | 1,575,000 |

a. Construct income statements for each company for strong, average, and weak economies using the following format:

> Sales
> Less: Cost of goods sold
> Earnings before interest and taxes (EBIT)
> Less: Interest expense
> Earnings before taxes (EBT)
> Less: Taxes (at 40%)
> Net income (NI)

b. Compare the returns on equity for the companies. Which company is best in a strong economy? In an average economy? In a weak economy?

c. Suppose that, with sales at the average-economy level, short-term interest rates rose to 20 percent. How would this affect the three firms?

d. Suppose that because of production slowdowns caused by inventory shortages, the aggressive company's variable cost ratio rose to 80 percent. What would happen to its ROE? Assume a short-term interest rate of 12 percent.

e. What considerations for the management of working capital are indicated by this problem?

**GET REAL WITH**   **THOMSON ONE** | Business School Edition

**working capital policy and financing**

14-15   Office Depot Inc. [ODP] and Staples Inc. [SPLS] both sell office products, supplies, and services. Using the liquidity ratios and asset management ratios, in addition to the firms' financial statements, discuss the following questions:

a. Compare the firms' liquidity positions. [Click on Financials/Fundamental Ratios/Thomson Ratios for each firm.]

b. Evaluate each firm with regard to the management of its current assets and current liabilities. [Click on Financials/Financial Statements and Financials/Fundamental Ratios for each firm.]

c. Based on your analysis in questions a and b, which firm has the more aggressive working capital policy? How would you characterize each firm's working capital policy? Explain your answer.

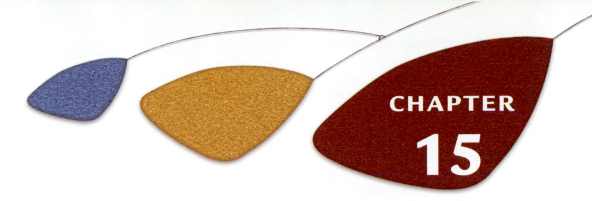

# Managing Short-Term Assets

## A MANAGERIAL PERSPECTIVE

Although Wal-Mart, which is the largest retail store in the world, generated more than $310 billion in sales in 2006, not all of its investors were pleased. Unfortunately, the performance of Wal-Mart's stock was disappointing to both investors and analysts. In fact, Wal-Mart's stock price had declined from a record high of $69 per share at the end of 1999 and the beginning of 2000 to less than $50 per share in 2005 and 2006. One explanation for the price decline was that Wal-Mart's growth had slowed to less than 3.5 percent in 2005, which was about 50 percent of the growth of its major competitor, Target.

As the result of its stagnant growth, in 2006 Wal-Mart announced that it planned to make cuts in its operating costs. One of the areas that management targeted for cost-cutting actions was inventory. Although Wal-Mart was considered to have one of the best inventory control systems in retailing, management thought the efficiency could be improved through better management of the system that was used at the time. If Wal-Mart could decrease inventory costs, it could increase its profit margin, which management felt would translate into a higher stock price.

The challenge to Wal-Mart was how it could make a good inventory control system better. In general, managers felt that the company needed to become "lean" with respect to its inventory practices. One inventory technique that Wal-Mart planned to use heavily was just-in-time (JIT) ordering. A firm that follows JIT places orders at the last possible minute—that is, inventory is ordered so that it arrives "just in time" to be used (sold). Although Wal-Mart had used JIT previously, management believed the application of this inventory management technique could be improved substantially.

Analysts also suggested that Wal-Mart should purchase more of its inventory directly from manufacturers rather than from wholesalers and other third-party organizations. Because many of the products it sells are made in China and Wal-Mart wants to expand its presence in that country from 51 stores to 100 before 2010, it seemed to be a "natural fit" for the company to enter into business relationships with the Chinese firms that manufacture the products it sells. Although in 2006 firms were still learning about Chinese business customs, experts thought that Wal-Mart could benefit by building relationships with its Chinese suppliers. If the chances are high that such relationships will result in lower inventory costs in the future, then it probably is worthwhile for Wal-Mart to pursue this strategy.

If it implements the two strategies mentioned here, Wal-Mart's suppliers will be affected. Following the JIT ordering system more closely will decrease the amount of inventory Wal-Mart purchases at any point in time. Businesses that rely heavily on Wal-Mart for sales will be affected (harmed) substantially. Similarly, if Wal-Mart begins buying directly from companies that manufacture the products it sells, the wholesalers, or "middlemen," will lose all of the sales that previously went through them. Such losses could be devastating for some wholesalers.

As you read this chapter, consider just how critical a firm's inventory management practices really are, as well as how important it is to operate as efficiently as possible while converting short-term assets, such as inventory, into cash in a timely fashion. The lessons to be learned from this chapter apply to the management of short-term assets, which primarily include cash, accounts receivable, and inventory, of individuals as well as to those of businesses. Maybe you will be able to take some of the ideas discussed here and apply them to your personal finances.

**Source:** Parija Bhatnagar, "4 Steps to Get Wal-Mart Back on Track," April 5, 2006, and Parija Bhatnagar, "Wal-Mart Puts the Squeeze on Vendors," April 10, 2006; both articles can be found online at CNNMoney.com at http://money.cnn.com. "Wal-Mart Getting Tougher on Vendors," June 5, 2006, can be found online at Forbes.com at http://www.forbes.com.

## Chapter *Essentials*
### —The Questions

After reading this chapter, you should be able to answer the following questions:

- Why do firms hold cash? What general strategies should be followed to manage cash?
- Why do firms have marketable securities?
- Why do firms sell on credit? What general strategies should be followed to manage credit?
- How should proposed changes in a firm's credit policy be analyzed?
- Why do firms carry inventory? What general strategies should be followed to manage inventory?
- What is the EOQ model and how should it be applied?

As we discovered in the previous chapter, all else equal, the riskiness of the portfolio of assets held by a firm is based on the combination of its short- and long-term investments (assets). The relative amount invested in short-term assets is a function of decisions that are made concerning the management of cash and marketable securities, accounts receivable, and inventories. Of these three assets, we generally consider cash and marketable securities to be least risky, or most *liquid*. But the degree of risk can vary for either accounts receivable or inventories, depending on the general characteristics of the firm's working capital policy. For example, we generally view receivables as relatively safe assets because they represent sales the firm expects to collect in the future. But a firm with an overly aggressive, or relaxed, credit policy might have many slow payers or bad-debt customers that make its receivables extremely risky, thus fairly *illiquid*.

In this chapter, we discuss working capital management policies with respect to the current (short-term) assets of the firm. As you read the chapter, keep in mind that although short-term assets generally are safer than long-term assets, they earn a lower rate of return. Thus, all else equal, firms that hold greater amounts of short-term assets are considered less risky than firms that hold greater amounts of long-term assets; at the same time, firms with more short-term assets earn lower returns than firms with more long-term assets. Consequently, financial managers are faced with a dilemma of whether to forgo higher returns to attain lower risk or to forgo lower risk to achieve higher returns. In general, however, we will see that some amount of short-term assets is required to maintain normal operations.

## CASH MANAGEMENT

In Chapters 6 and 7, we discovered that value, which we want to maximize, is based on cash flows. Thus, managing cash flows is an extremely important task for a financial manager. Part of this task is determining how much cash a firm should have on hand at any time to ensure that normal business operations continue uninterrupted. In this section, we discuss some of the factors that affect the amount of cash firms hold, and we describe some of the cash management techniques currently used by businesses.

For the purposes of our discussion, the term *cash* refers to the funds a firm holds that can be used for immediate disbursement. This includes the amount a firm holds in its checking account as well as the amount of actual coin and currency it holds. Cash is a *nonearning*, or *idle, asset* that is required to pay bills. When possible, cash should be "put to work" by investing in assets that have positive expected returns. Thus, the goal of the cash manager is to minimize the amount of cash the firm must hold for use in conducting its normal business activities, yet, at the same time, to have sufficient cash to (1) pay suppliers, (2) maintain the firm's credit rating, and (3) meet unexpected cash needs.

Firms generally hold cash for the following reasons:

1. Cash balances are necessary in business operations because payments must be made in cash, and receipts are deposited in a cash account. Cash balances associated with routine payments and collections are known as **transactions balances.**

2. A bank often requires a firm to maintain a **compensating balance** on deposit to help offset the costs of providing services such as check clearing and cash management advice.

3. Because cash inflows and cash outflows are somewhat unpredictable, firms generally hold some cash in reserve for random, unforeseen fluctuations in cash flows. These *safety stocks* are called **precautionary balances**—the less predictable the firm's cash flows, the larger such balances should be. However, if the firm has easy access to borrowed funds—that is, if it can borrow on short notice (for example, via a line of credit at the bank)—its need for precautionary balances is reduced.

4. Sometimes cash balances are held to enable the firm to take advantage of bargain purchases that might arise. These funds are called **speculative balances.** As with precautionary balances, though, firms that have easy access to borrowed funds are likely to rely on their ability to borrow quickly rather than to rely on cash balances for speculative purposes.

Although the cash accounts of most firms can be thought of as consisting of transactions, compensating, precautionary, and speculative balances, we cannot calculate the amount needed for each purpose, sum them, and produce a total desired cash balance because the same money often serves more than one purpose. For instance, precautionary and speculative balances can also be used to satisfy compensating balance requirements. Firms do, however, consider all four factors when establishing their target cash positions.

In addition to these four motives, a firm maintains cash balances to preserve its credit rating by keeping its liquidity position in line with those of other firms in the industry. A strong credit rating enables the firm both to purchase goods from suppliers on favorable terms and to maintain an ample line of credit with its bank.

**transactions balance**
A cash balance necessary for day-to-day operations; the balance associated with routine payments and collections.

**compensating balance**
A minimum checking account balance that a firm must maintain with a bank to help offset the costs of services such as check clearing and cash management advice.

**precautionary balances**
A cash balance held in reserve for unforeseen fluctuations in cash flows.

**speculative balance**
A cash balance that is held to enable the firm to take advantage of any bargain purchases that might arise.

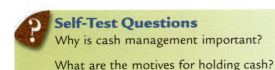

**Self-Test Questions**

Why is cash management important?

What are the motives for holding cash?

# THE CASH BUDGET

Perhaps the most critical ingredient to proper cash management is the ability to estimate the cash flows of the firm so the firm can make plans to borrow when cash is deficient or to invest when cash is in excess of what is needed. Without a doubt, financial managers will agree that the most important tool for managing cash is the cash budget (forecast). *The cash budget helps management plan investment and borrowing strategies,* and it also is used to provide feedback and control to improve the efficiency of cash management in the future.

The firm estimates its general needs for cash as a part of its overall budgeting, or forecasting, process. First, the firm forecasts its operating activities such as expenses and revenues for the period in question. Then, the financing and investment activities necessary to attain that level of operations must be forecasted. Such forecasts entail the construction of *pro forma* financial statements, which we discuss in Chapter 17. The information provided from the *pro forma* balance sheet and income statement is combined with projections about the delay in collecting accounts receivable, the delay in paying suppliers and employees, tax payment dates, dividend and interest payment dates, and so on. All of this information is summarized in the **cash budget,** which shows the firm's projected cash inflows and cash outflows over some specified period. Generally, firms use a monthly cash budget forecasted over the next year plus a more detailed daily or weekly cash budget for the coming month. The monthly cash budgets are used for planning purposes and the daily or weekly budgets are used for actual cash control.

**cash budget**
A schedule showing cash receipts, cash disbursements, and cash balances for a firm over a specified time period.

The cash budget provides much more detailed information concerning a firm's future cash flows than do the forecasted financial statements. For example, when we develop the forecasted financial statements for Unilate Textiles in Chapter 17, in 2010 we project net sales to be $1,650 million and net income to be $61 million. Based on the forecasted financial statements, we can determine that Unilate expects to generate an $80 million cash inflow through normal production and sales operations. Much of this $80 million will be used to satisfy the financing and investment activities of the firm. Even after these activities are considered, Unilate's cash account is projected to increase by $1.5 million in 2010. Does this mean that Unilate will not have to worry about cash shortages during 2010? To answer this question, we must construct Unilate's cash budget for 2010.

To simplify the construction of Unilate's cash budget, we will consider only the last half of 2010 (July through December). Further, we will not list every cash flow that is expected to occur but instead will focus on the operating flows. Remember that Unilate's sales peak is in September and October. All sales are made on credit with terms that allow a 2 percent cash discount for payments made within 10 days, and if the discount is not taken, the full amount is due in 30 days. However, like most companies, Unilate finds that some of its customers delay payment for more than 90 days. Experience has shown that payment on 20 percent of Unilate's *dollar* sales is made during the month in which the sale is made—these are the discount sales. On 70 percent of sales, payment is made during the month immediately following the month of sale, and payment is made on 10 percent of sales two months or more after the initial sales. To simplify the cash budget, however, we will assume that the last 10 percent of sales is collected two months after the sale.

For Unilate, the costs of cotton, wool, and other cloth-related materials average 60 percent of the sales prices of the finished products. These purchases generally are made one month before the firm expects to sell the finished products. In 2010, Unilate's suppliers have agreed to allow payment for materials to be delayed for 30 days after the purchase. Accordingly, if July sales are forecasted at $150 million, then purchases during June will amount to $90 million, and this amount actually will be paid in July.

Other cash expenses such as wages and rent also are built into the cash budget, and Unilate must make estimated tax payments of $16 million on September 15 and $10 million on December 15, while a $20 million payment for a new plant must be made in October. Assuming that Unilate's **target, or minimum, cash balance** is $5 million and that it projects $8 million to be on hand on July 1, 2010, what will the firm's monthly cash surpluses or shortfalls be for the period from July through December?

Unilate's 2010 cash budget for July through December is presented in Table 15-1 The approach used to construct this cash budget generally is termed the **disbursements and receipts method** (also referred to as **scheduling**) because the cash disbursements and cash receipts are estimated to determine the net cash flow expected to be generated each month. The format used in Table 15-1 is quite simple—it is much like balancing a checkbook. The cash receipts are lumped into one category and the cash disbursements are lumped into another category to determine the net effect monthly cash flows have on the cash position of the firm. More detailed formats can be used, depending on how the firm prefers to present the cash budget information.

The first line of Table 15-1 gives the sales forecast for the period from May through December. These estimates are necessary to determine collections for July through December. Similarly, the second line of the table gives the credit purchases expected each month based on the sales forecasts so the monthly payments for credit purchases can be determined.

The Cash Receipts category shows cash collections based on credit sales originating in three months—in the current month and in the previous two months. Take a look at the collections expected in July. Remember that Unilate expects 20 percent of the dollar sales to be collected in the month of the sales, and thus to be affected by the 2 percent cash discount offered; 70 percent of the dollar sales will be collected one month after the sales; and the remaining 10 percent of the dollar sales will be collected two months after the sales (it is assumed there are no bad debts). So in July, $29.4 million $= 0.20 \times (1 - 0.02) \times \$150$ million collections will result from sales in July; $87.5 million $= 0.70 \times \$125$ million will be collected from sales that occurred in June; and $10.0 million $= 0.10 \times \$100$ million will be collected from sales that occurred in May. Thus, the total collections received in July represent 20 percent of July sales (minus the discount) plus 70 percent of June sales plus 10 percent of May sales, or $126.9 million in total.

The Cash Disbursements category shows payments for raw materials, wages, rent, and so forth. Raw materials are purchased on credit one month before the finished goods are expected to be sold, but payments for the materials are not made until one month later—that is the month of the expected sales. The cost of the raw materials is expected to be 60 percent of sales. July sales are forecasted at $150 million, so Unilate will purchase $90 million of materials in June and pay for these purchases in July. Similarly, Unilate will purchase $120 million of materials in July to meet August's forecasted sales of $200 million. Additional monthly cash disbursements include employees' salaries, which equal 22 percent of monthly sales; rent, which remains constant; and other operating expenses, which vary with respect to production levels. Cash disbursements that are not expected to occur monthly include taxes (September and December) and payment for the construction of additional facilities (October).

The line labeled "Net cash flow" shows whether Unilate's operations are expected to generate positive or negative net cash flows each month. But this is only the beginning of the story. We need to examine the firm's cash position based on the cash balance that exists at the beginning of the month and based on the "Target (minimum)

**target (minimum) cash balance**
The minimum cash balance a firm desires to maintain in order to conduct business.

**disbursements and receipts method (scheduling)**
The net cash flow is determined by estimating the cash disbursements and the cash receipts expected to be generated each period.

**TABLE 15-1**  Unilate Textiles: 2010 Cash Budget ($ millions)

|  | May | June | July | Aug. | Sept. | Oct. | Nov. | Dec. |
|---|---|---|---|---|---|---|---|---|
| Credit sales | 100.0 | 125.0 | 150.0 | 200.0 | 250.0 | 180.0 | 130.0 | 100.0 |
| Credit purchases = 60% of next month's sales | | 90.0 | 120.0 | 150.0 | 108.0 | 78.0 | 60.0 | |
| **Cash Receipts** | | | | | | | | |
| Collections from this month's sales = $0.2 \times 0.98 \times$ (current month's sales) | | | 29.4 | 39.2 | 49.0 | 35.3 | 25.5 | 19.6 |
| Collections from previous month's sales = $0.7 \times$ (previous month's sales) | | | 87.5 | 105.0 | 140.0 | 175.0 | 126.0 | 91.0 |
| Collect from sales two months previously = $0.1 \times$ (sales 2 months earlier) | | | 10.0 | 12.5 | 15.0 | 20.0 | 25.0 | 18.0 |
| Total cash receipts | | | $126.9 | $156.7 | $204.0 | $230.3 | $176.5 | $128.6 |
| **Cash Disbursements** | | | | | | | | |
| Payments made for credit purchases (1-month lag) | | | 90.0 | 120.0 | 150.0 | 108.0 | 78.0 | 60.0 |
| Wages and salaries (22% of monthly sales) | | | 33.0 | 44.0 | 55.0 | 39.6 | 28.6 | 22.0 |
| Rent | | | 9.0 | 9.0 | 9.0 | 9.0 | 9.0 | 9.0 |
| Other expenses | | | 7.0 | 8.0 | 11.0 | 10.0 | 5.0 | 4.0 |
| Taxes | | | | | 16.0 | | | 10.0 |
| Payment for plant construction | | | | | | 20.0 | | |
| Total cash disbursements | | | $139.0 | $181.0 | $241.0 | $186.6 | $120.6 | $105.0 |
| ***Net cash flow (Receipts – Disbursements)*** | | | ($ 12.1) | ($ 24.3) | ($ 37.0) | $ 43.7 | $ 55.9 | $ 23.6 |
| ***Beginning cash balance*** | | | $ 8.0 | ($ 4.1) | ($ 28.4) | ($ 65.4) | ($ 21.7) | $ 34.2 |
| ***Ending cash balance*** | | | ( 4.1) | ( 28.4) | ( 65.4) | ( 21.7) | 34.2 | 57.8 |
| ***Target (minimum) cash balance*** | | | 5.0 | 5.0 | 5.0 | 5.0 | 5.0 | 5.0 |
| ***Surplus (shortfall) cash*** | | | ($ 9.1) | ($ 33.4) | ($ 70.4) | ($ 26.7) | $ 29.2 | $ 52.8 |

cash balance " desired by Unilate. The bottom line provides information as to whether Unilate can expect a monthly cash surplus that can be invested temporarily in marketable securities or a monthly cash shortfall that must be financed with external, nonspontaneous sources of funds.

At the beginning of July, Unilate will have cash equal to $8 million. During July, Unilate is expected to generate a negative $12.1 million net cash flow; thus, July cash disbursements are expected to exceed cash receipts by $12.1 million (that is, deficit spending is expected). Because Unilate has only $8 million cash to begin July, the cash balance at the end of July is expected to be overdrawn by $4.1 million if the firm doesn't find additional funding. To make matters worse, Unilate has a target cash balance equal to $5 million, so without any additional financing, its cash balance at the end of July is expected to be $9.1 million short of its target. As a result, Unilate must make arrangements to borrow $9.1 million in July to bring the cash account balance up to the target balance of $5 million. Assuming that this amount is indeed borrowed, loans outstanding will total $9.1 million at the end of July. (We assume that Unilate does not have any bank loans outstanding on July 1 because its beginning cash balance exceeded the target balance.)

The cash surplus or required loan balance (shortfall) is given on the bottom line of the cash budget. A positive value indicates a cash surplus, whereas a negative value (in parentheses) indicates a loan requirement. Note that the *bottom-line* surplus cash or loan requirement shown is a *cumulative amount*. Thus, Unilate must borrow $9.1 million in July. Because it has a cash shortfall during August of $24.3 million as reported on the net cash flow line, Unilate's total loan requirement at the end of August is $33.4 million = $9.1 million + $24.3 million, as reported on the bottom line for August. Unilate's arrangement with the bank permits it to increase its outstanding loans on a daily basis, up to a prearranged maximum, just as you could increase the amount you owe on a credit card. Unilate will use any surplus funds it generates to pay off its loans, and because the loan can be paid down at any time, on a daily basis, the firm never will have both a cash surplus and an outstanding loan balance. If Unilate actually does have a cash surplus, these funds will be invested in short-term, temporary investments.

This same procedure is used in the following months. Sales will peak in September, accompanied by increased payments for purchases, wages, and other items. Receipts from sales will also go up, but the firm will still be left with a $37 million net cash outflow during the month. The total loan requirement at the end of September will hit a peak of $70.4 million, the cumulative cash deficits plus the target cash balance.[1] This amount is also equal to the $33.4 million needed at the end of August plus the $37 million cash deficit for September.

Sales, purchases, and payments for past purchases will fall sharply in October, but collections will be the highest of any month because they will reflect the high September sales. As a result, Unilate will generate a healthy $43.7 million net cash gain during October. This net gain can be used to pay off borrowings, so loans outstanding will decline by $43.7 million, to $26.7 million.

Unilate will generate an even larger cash surplus in November, which will permit the firm to pay off all of its loans. In fact, the company is expected to have $29.2 million in surplus cash by the month's end, and another cash surplus in December will swell

---

[1]This figure is calculated easily as follows:

$$\text{Cash}_{\text{Sept.}} = \binom{\text{Beginning cash}}{\text{balance in July}} + \text{Net CF}_{\text{July}} + \text{Net CF}_{\text{Aug.}} + \text{Net CF}_{\text{Sept.}} - \binom{\text{Target cash}}{\text{balance}}$$

$$= \$8.0 + (-\$12.1) + (-\$24.3) + (-\$37.0) - \$5.0 = -\$70.4$$

the excess cash to $52.8 million. With such a large amount of unneeded funds, Unilate's treasurer certainly will want to invest in interest-bearing securities or to put the funds to use in some other way. Various types of investments into which Unilate might put its excess funds are discussed later in the chapter.

Before concluding our discussion of the cash budget, we should make some additional points:

1. For simplicity, our illustrative budget for Unilate omitted many important cash flows that are anticipated for 2010, such as dividends, proceeds from stock and bond sales, and investments in additional fixed assets. Some of these are projected to occur in the first half of the year, but those that are projected for the July through December period could easily be added to the example. The final cash budget should contain all projected cash inflows and outflows.

2. Our cash budget example does not reflect interest on loans or income from investing surplus cash. This refinement could easily be added.

3. If cash inflows and outflows are not uniform during the month, we could seriously understate the firm's peak financing requirements. The data in Table 15-1 show the situation expected on the last day of each month, but on any given day during the month it could be quite different. For example, if all payments had to be made on the fifth of each month, but collections came in uniformly throughout the month, the firm would need to borrow much larger amounts than those shown in the table. In this case, we would have to prepare a cash budget identifying requirements on a daily basis.

4. Because depreciation is a noncash charge, it does not appear on the cash budget other than through its effect on taxable income, hence on taxes paid.

5. Because the cash budget represents a forecast, all the values in the table are *expected* values. If actual sales, purchases, and so on are different from the forecasted levels, then the projected cash deficits and surpluses will also differ.

6. Computerized spreadsheet programs are particularly well suited for constructing and analyzing cash budgets, especially with respect to the sensitivity of cash flows to changes in sales levels, collection periods, and the like. We could change any assumption—for example, the projected monthly sales or the time that customers pay—and the cash budget would automatically and instantly be recalculated. This would show us exactly how the firm's borrowing requirements would change if various other things changed. Also, with a computer model, it is easy to add features like interest paid on loans, interest earned on marketable securities, and so on.

7. Finally, we should note that the target cash balance will probably be adjusted over time, rising and falling with seasonal patterns and with long-term changes in the scale of the firm's operations. Thus, Unilate probably will plan to maintain larger cash balances during August and September than at other times, and, as the company grows, so will its required cash balance. Also, the firm might even set the target cash balance at zero. This could be done if it carried a portfolio of marketable securities that could be sold to replenish the cash account or if it had an arrangement with its bank that permitted it to borrow any funds needed on a daily basis. In that event, the target cash balance would simply be equal to zero. Note, though, that most firms would find it difficult to operate with a zero-balance bank account, just as you would, and the costs of such an operation would in most instances offset the

costs associated with maintaining a positive cash balance. Therefore, most firms do set positive target cash balances.

 **Self-Test Questions**

What is the purpose of a cash budget?

Suppose a firm's cash flows do not occur uniformly throughout the month. What impact might this have on the accuracy of the forecasted borrowing requirements?

How is uncertainty handled in a cash budget?

Is depreciation reflected in a cash budget? Explain.

## CASH MANAGEMENT TECHNIQUES

Most cash management activities are performed jointly by the firm and its primary bank, but the financial manager ultimately is responsible for the effectiveness of the cash management program. Effective cash management encompasses proper management of both the cash inflows and the cash outflows of a firm, which entails consideration of the factors discussed next.

### Cash Flow Synchronization

It would be ideal if the receipt of a cash payment from a customer occurred at exactly the same time a bill needs to be paid; that portion paid out would never be idle and any excess could be invested quickly to reduce the time it is idle. Recognizing this point, companies try to arrange it so that cash inflows and cash outflows are matched as closely as possible—customers are billed so their billing cycles coordinate with when the firm pays its own bills. Having **synchronized cash flows** enables a firm to reduce its cash balances, decrease its bank loans, lower interest expenses, and boost profits. *The more predictable the timing of the cash flows, the greater the synchronization that can be attained.* Utilities and credit card companies generally have a high degree of cash flow synchronization.

**synchronized cash flows**
A situation in which cash inflows coincide with cash outflows, thereby permitting a firm to hold low transactions balances.

### Check-Clearing Process

When a customer writes and mails a check, this does *not* mean that the funds are immediately available to the receiving firm. Most of us have been told by someone that "the check is in the mail," and we also have deposited a check in an account and then been told that we cannot write checks against the deposit until the **check-clearing process** has been completed. Our bank must first make sure that the deposited check is good and then receive funds itself from the customer's bank before it will give us cash.

As shown on the left side of Figure 15-1, quite a bit of time could be required for a firm to process incoming checks and obtain the use of the money. A *paper* check must first be delivered through the mail and then be cleared through the banking system before the money can be put to use. Checks received from customers in distant cities are especially subject to delays because of mail time and also because more parties are involved in the check-clearing process. For example, assume that you receive a check and deposit it in your bank. Your bank must send the check to the bank on which it was drawn. Only when this latter bank transfers funds to your bank are the funds available

**check-clearing process**
The process of converting a check that has been written and mailed into cash in the payee's (receiver's) account.

**FIGURE 15-1** Diagram of the Check-Clearing Process

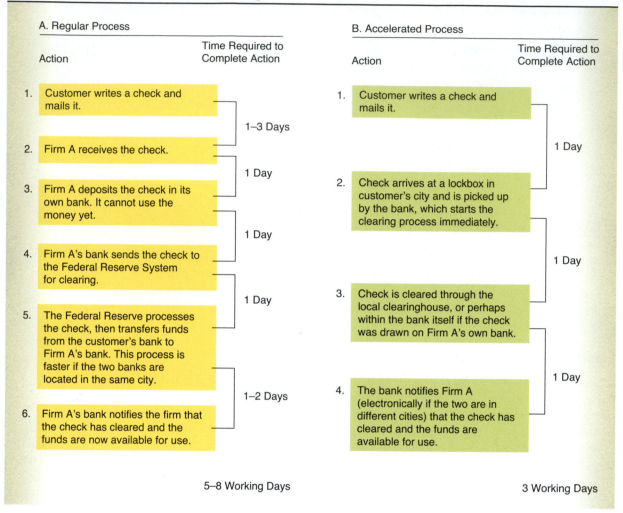

for you to use. If a check is deposited in the same bank on which it was drawn, that bank merely transfers funds by bookkeeping entries from one of its depositors to another. But most deposited checks are drawn from outside banks, so the verification, or clearing process, generally is handled by a check-clearing system, termed a *clearinghouse*, set up by the Federal Reserve or a network of banks in a particular region. The length of time required for checks to clear is a function of the distance between the payer's (check writer's) bank and the payee's (depositor's) bank. In the case of private clearinghouses, it can range from one to three days. The maximum time required for checks to clear through the Federal Reserve System is two days, but mail delays can slow down things on each end of the Fed's involvement in the process.

In an effort to facilitate the check-clearing process, the Check Clearing for the 21st Century Act was signed in October 2003 and became effective one year later. The act, termed Check 21, encourages more efficient processing of payments by allowing financial institutions to convert paper checks into substitutes that can be cleared electronically. The *substitute checks* allow financial intermediaries to clear payments more quickly because they are the electronic and legal equivalents of, and contain the same information as, the original paper checks. As Congress and the Federal Reserve implement more electronically friendly clearing mechanisms and more electronic payment systems are used, the time it takes financial institutions to clear checks or other payment systems will decrease.

## Using Float

**Float** is defined as the difference between the balance shown in a firm's (or individual's) checkbook and the balance on the bank's records. Suppose a firm writes, on average, checks in the amount of $5,000 each day, and it normally takes five days from the time the check is mailed until it is cleared and deducted from the firm's bank account. This will cause the firm's own checkbook to show a balance equal to $25,000 = $5,000 × 5 days smaller than the balance on the bank's records; this difference is called **disbursement float.** Now suppose the firm also receives checks in the amount of $5,000 daily, but it loses three days while they are being deposited and cleared. This will result in $15,000 of **collections float.** In total, the firm's **net float**—the difference between $25,000 positive disbursement float and the $15,000 negative collections float—will be $10,000, which means the balance the bank shows in the firm's checking account is $10,000 greater than the balance the firm shows in its own checkbook.

Delays that cause float arise because it takes time for checks (1) to travel through the mail (*mail delay*), (2) to be processed by the receiving firm (*processing delay*), and (3) to clear through the banking system (*clearing*, or *availability*, *delay*). Basically, the size of a firm's net float is a function of its ability to speed up collections on checks received and to slow down collections on checks written. Efficient firms go to great lengths to speed up the processing of incoming checks, thus putting the funds to work faster, and they try to delay their own payments as long as possible.

## Acceleration of Receipts

A firm cannot use customers' payments until they are received *and* converted into a spendable form, such as cash or an increase in a checking account balance. Thus, it would benefit the firm to accelerate the collection of customers' payments and conversion of those payments into cash.

Although some of the delays that cause float cannot be controlled directly, the techniques described next are used to manage collections.

### Lockboxes

A **lockbox arrangement** requires customers to send their payments to a post office box located in the area near where they live rather than directly to the firm. The firm arranges for a local bank to collect the checks from the post office box, perhaps several times a day, and to immediately deposit them into the company's checking account. By having lockboxes close to the customers, a firm can reduce float because, at the very least, (1) the mail delay is less than if the payment had to travel farther and (2) checks are cleared faster because the banks the checks are written on are in the same Federal Reserve district; thus, fewer parties are involved in the clearing process.

### Preauthorized Debits

If a firm receives regular, repetitious payments from its customers, it might want to establish a **preauthorized debit system** (sometimes called *preauthorized payments*). With this arrangement, the collecting firm and its customer (paying firm) enter into an agreement whereby the paying firm's bank periodically transfers funds from

---

**float**
The difference between the balance shown in a firm's (or individual's) checkbook and the balance on the bank's records.

**disbursement float**
The value of the checks that have been written and *disbursed* but have not yet fully cleared through the banking system and thus have not been deducted from the account on which they were written.

**collections float**
The amount of checks that have been *received* and deposited but have not yet been made available to the account in which they were deposited.

**net float**
The difference between disbursement float and collections float; the difference between the balance shown in the checkbook and the balance shown on the bank's books.

**lockbox arrangement**
A technique used to reduce float by having payments sent to post office boxes located near the customers.

**preauthorized debit system**
A system that allows a customer's bank to periodically transfer funds from its account to a selling firm's bank account for the payment of bills.

the paying firm's account to the collecting firm's account, even if that account is located at another bank. Preauthorized debiting accelerates the transfer of funds because mail and check-clearing delays are completely eliminated, and the processing delay is reduced substantially.

## Concentration Banking

**concentration banking**
A technique used to move funds from many bank accounts to a more central cash pool to more effectively manage cash.

**Concentration banking** is a cash management arrangement used to mobilize funds from decentralized receiving locations, whether they are lockboxes or decentralized company locations, into one or more central cash pools. The cash manager then uses these pools for short-term investing or reallocation among the firm's various bank accounts. By pooling its cash, the firm is able to take maximum advantage of economies of scale in cash management and investment. Often commissions are less per dollar on large investments, and there are instances in which investments of larger dollar amounts earn higher returns than smaller investments.

## Disbursement Control

Accelerating collections represents one side of cash management, and controlling funds outflows, or disbursements, represents the other side. Three methods commonly used to control disbursements include the following:

### Payables Concentration

Centralizing the processing of payables permits the financial manager to evaluate the payments coming due for the entire firm and to schedule the availability of funds to meet these needs on a companywide basis, and it also permits more efficient monitoring of payables and the effects of float. A disadvantage to a centralized disbursement system is that regional offices might not be able to make prompt payment for services rendered, which can create ill will and raise the company's operating costs. But as firms become more electronically proficient, the centralization of disbursements can be coordinated more effectively and such situations should be reduced substantially.

### Zero-Balance Accounts

**zero-balance account (ZBA)**
A special checking account used for disbursements that has a balance equal to zero when there is no disbursement activity.

A **zero-balance account (ZBA)** is a special disbursement account that has a balance equal to zero when there is no disbursement activity. Typically, a firm establishes several ZBAs in its concentration bank and funds them from a master account. As checks are presented to a ZBA for payment, funds are automatically transferred from the master account to ensure the checks are covered.

### Controlled Disbursement Accounts

**controlled disbursement account (CDA)**
A checking account in which funds are not deposited until checks are presented for payment, usually on a daily basis.

Whereas ZBAs typically are established at concentration banks, a **controlled disbursement account (CDA)** can be set up at any bank. Such accounts are not funded until the day's checks are presented against the account. The firm relies on the bank that maintains the CDA to provide information in the morning (before 11 a.m. New York time) concerning the total amount of the checks that will be presented for payment that day. This permits the financial manager to (1) transfer funds to the controlled disbursement account to cover the checks presented for payment or (2) invest excess cash at midday, when money market trading is at a peak.

## Self-Test Questions

What is float? How do firms use float to increase cash management efficiency?

What are some methods firms can use to accelerate receipts?

What are some techniques for controlling disbursements?

Suppose that TIA Industries writes checks for $50,000 per day and it receives checks totaling $60,000 each day. If it takes three days for the checks the company writes, and two days for the checks it receives, to clear through the banking system, what is TIA's net float? (*Answer:* $30,000)

# MARKETABLE SECURITIES

Realistically, the management of cash and marketable securities cannot be separated. Management of one implies management of the other because the amount of marketable securities held by a firm depends on its short-term cash needs.

## Rationale for Holding Marketable Securities

**Marketable securities,** or *near-cash* assets, are extremely liquid, short-term investments that permit the firm to earn positive returns on cash that is not needed to pay bills immediately but will be needed sometime in the near term, perhaps in a few days, weeks, or months. Although such investments typically provide much lower yields than other assets, nearly every large firm has them. The two basic reasons for owning marketable securities are as follows:

> **marketable securities**
> Securities that can be sold on short notice without loss of principal or original investment.

1. Marketable securities serve as a *substitute for cash balances.* Firms often hold portfolios of marketable securities, liquidating part of the portfolio to increase the cash account when cash is needed because the *marketable securities offer a place to temporarily put cash balances to work earning a positive return.* In such situations, the marketable securities could be used as a substitute for transactions balances, for precautionary balances, for speculative balances, or for all three.

2. Marketable securities are also used as a *temporary investment to* (a) finance seasonal or cyclical operations and (b) amass funds to meet financial requirements in the near future. For example, if the firm has a conservative financing policy as we discussed in Chapter 14, then its long-term capital will exceed its permanent assets, and marketable securities will be held when inventories and receivables are low.

## Characteristics of Marketable Securities

A wide variety of securities is available to firms that choose to hold marketable securities. But the characteristics generally associated with marketable securities are as follows:

1. **Maturity.** Firms hold marketable securities to *temporarily* invest cash that otherwise would be idle in the short run. Therefore, marketable securities are short-term investments; often they are held only for a few days or weeks. If the cash budget indicates the funds are not needed in the foreseeable future,

then longer-term investments, which generally earn higher returns, should be used.

2. **Risk.** Recall that in Chapter 5 we developed this equation for determining the nominal interest rate:

$$r = r^* + IP + DRP + LP + MRP$$

Here $r^*$ is the real risk-free rate, IP is a premium for expected inflation, DRP is the default risk premium, LP is the liquidity (or marketability) risk premium, and MRP is the maturity (or interest rate) risk premium. Also, remember from Chapter 5 that the risk-free rate, $r_{RF}$, is equal to $r^* + IP$, and a U.S. Treasury bill comes closest to the risk-free rate. For other instruments considered appropriate as marketable securities, the default and liquidity risks are small, and the interest-rate risk is negligible. These risks are small because marketable securities mature in the short term, and the short run is less uncertain than the long run. Also, recall from Chapter 6 that prices of long-term investments, such as bonds, are much more sensitive to changes in interest rates than are prices of short-term investments. In general, then, the total risk associated with a portfolio of marketable securities (short term) is less than the total risk associated with a portfolio of long-term investments.

3. **Liquidity.** We generally judge an asset's *marketability* according to how quickly and easily it can be bought and sold in the financial markets. If an asset can be sold easily on short notice at a fair price that is not substantially lower than its original purchase price, it is said to be *liquid*. Because marketable securities are held as a substitute for cash and as a temporary investment, such instruments should be very liquid.

4. **Return (Yield).** Because the marketable securities portfolio generally is composed of highly liquid, short-term securities with low risks, the returns associated with such investments are relatively low when compared with other investments. But given the purpose of the marketable securities portfolio, treasurers should not sacrifice safety for higher rates of return.

## Types of Marketable Securities

Table 15-2 lists the major types of securities available for investment, with an indication of how widely the yields on these securities have fluctuated during the past few decades. Depending on how long they will be held, the financial manager decides upon a suitable set of securities, and a suitable maturity pattern, to hold as *near-cash reserves* in the form of marketable securities. As noted in the table, long-term securities are not appropriate investments for marketable securities as we have described in this section. Safety, especially maintenance of principal, should be paramount when putting together a marketable securities portfolio.

 **Self-Test Questions**

What are the characteristics of financial instruments that are considered appropriate marketable securities?

What are some securities commonly held as marketable securities? Why are such securities held by firms?

**TABLE 15-2**    Securities Available for Investment of Surplus Cash

| Security | Typical Maturity at Time of Issue | Approximate Yields | | |
|---|---|---|---|---|
| | | 6/28/82 | 6/27/03 | 6/27/06 |
| **I. Suitable as Near-Cash Reserves** | | | | |
| U.S. Treasury bills | 4 to 26 weeks | 13.3% | 0.9% | 5.1% |
| Commercial paper | Up to 270 days | 15.0 | 0.9 | 5.3 |
| Negotiable CDs | Up to 1 year | 15.7 | 1.1 | 5.6 |
| Money market mutual funds | Instant liquidity | 14.3 | 0.6 | 2.5 |
| Eurodollar time deposits | Up to 1 year | 16.8 | 1.0 | 5.6 |
| **II. Not Suitable as Near-Cash Reserves** | | | | |
| U.S. Treasury notes | 1 to 10 years | 14.7 | 3.6 | 5.3 |
| U.S. Treasury bonds | 10 to 30 years | 14.2 | 3.6 | 5.2 |
| Corporate bonds (AAA)[a] | Up to 40 years | 16.1 | 5.5 | 6.0 |
| Municipal bonds (AAA)[a,b] | Up to 30 years | 12.6 | 4.5 | 4.7 |
| Preferred stocks (AAA)[a,b] | Unlimited | 13.1 | 6.1 | 7.3 |
| Common stocks[c] | Unlimited | −4.8 | 5.0 | 14.9 |

[a]Rates shown for corporate and municipal bonds and for preferred stock are for longer maturities rated AAA. Lower-rated, higher-risk securities have higher yields.

[b]Rates are lower on municipal bonds because the interest they pay is exempt from federal income taxes, and the rate on preferred stocks is low because 70 percent of the dividends paid on them is exempt from federal taxes for corporate owners, who own most preferred stock.

[c]The returns given for common stocks represent the average yield that would have been earned in the stock market during the previous 52-week period. Individual common stock returns vary considerably, even at one point in time.

# CREDIT MANAGEMENT

If you ask financial managers whether they would prefer to sell their products for cash or for credit, you would expect them to respond by saying something like this: "*If sales levels are not affected,* cash sales are preferred because payment is certain and immediate and because the costs of granting credit and maintaining accounts receivable would be eliminated." *Ideally,* then, firms would prefer to sell for cash only. So why do firms sell for credit? The primary reason most firms offer credit sales is because their competitors offer credit. Consider what you would do if you had the opportunity to purchase the same product for the same price from two different firms, but one firm required cash payment at the time of the purchase whereas the other firm allowed you to pay for the product one month after the purchase without any additional cost. From which firm would you purchase? Like you, firms prefer to delay their payments, especially if there are no additional costs associated with the delay.

Effective credit management is extremely important because too much credit is costly in terms of the investment in, and maintenance of, accounts receivable, whereas too little credit could result in the loss of profitable sales. Carrying receivables has both direct and indirect costs, but it also has an important benefit—granting credit should increase profits. Thus, to maximize shareholders' wealth, a financial manager needs to understand how to effectively manage the firm's credit activities.

In this section, we discuss (1) the factors considered important when determining the appropriate credit policy for a firm, (2) procedures for monitoring the credit policy to ensure it is being administered properly, and (3) how to evaluate whether credit policy changes will be beneficial to the firm.

## Credit Policy

**credit policy**
A set of decisions that includes a firm's credit standards, credit terms, methods used to collect credit accounts, and credit monitoring procedures.

The major controllable variables that affect demand for a company's products are sales prices, product quality, advertising, and the firm's **credit policy.** The firm's credit policy, in turn, includes the factors we discuss next.

**credit standards**
Standards that indicate the minimum financial strength a customer must have to be granted credit.

1. **Credit standards** refer to the strength and creditworthiness a customer must exhibit to qualify for credit. The firm's credit standards are applied to determine which customers qualify for the regular credit terms and how much credit each customer should receive. The major factors that are considered when setting credit standards relate to the likelihood that a given customer will pay slowly or perhaps even end up as a bad debt loss. Determining the credit quality, or creditworthiness, of a customer probably is the most difficult part of credit management. But credit evaluation is a well-established practice, and a good credit manager can make reasonably accurate judgments of the probability of default exhibited by different classes of customers by examining a firm's current financial position and evaluating factors that might affect the financial position in the future.

**terms of credit**
The payment conditions offered to credit customers; the terms include the length of the credit period and any cash discounts offered.

2. **Terms of credit** are the conditions of the credit sale, especially with regard to the payment arrangements. Firms need to determine when the **credit period** begins, how long the customer has to pay for credit purchases before the account is considered delinquent, and whether a cash discount for early payment should be offered. An examination of the credit terms offered by firms in the United States would show great variety across industries—credit terms range from cash before delivery (CBD) and cash on delivery (COD) to offering **cash discounts** for early payment. For example, a firm that offers terms of 2/10, net 30 gives its customers a 2 percent discount from the purchase price if the bill is paid on or before Day 10 of the billing cycle; otherwise, the entire bill (the net amount) is due by Day 30. Because of the competitive nature of trade credit, most financial managers follow the norm of the industry in which they operate when setting credit terms.

**credit period**
The length of time for which credit is granted; after that time, the credit account is considered delinquent.

**cash discount**
A reduction in the invoice price of goods offered by the seller to encourage early payment.

3. **Collection policy** refers to the procedures the firm follows to collect its credit accounts. The firm needs to determine when and how notification of the credit sale will be conveyed to the buyer. The quicker a customer receives an invoice, the sooner the bill *can* be paid. In today's world, firms have turned more to the use of electronics to "send" invoices to customers. One of the most important collection policy decisions is how the past-due accounts should be handled. For example, notification might be sent to customers when a bill is 10 days past due; a more severe notice, followed by a telephone call, might be used if payment is not received within 30 days; and the account might be turned over to a collection agency after 90 days.

**collection policy**
The procedures followed by a firm to collect its accounts receivable.

## Receivables Monitoring

**receivables monitoring**
The process of evaluating the credit policy to determine whether a shift in the customers' payment patterns occurs.

Once a firm sets its credit policy, it wants to operate within the policy's limits. Thus, it is important that a firm examine its receivables periodically to determine whether customers' payment patterns have changed such that credit operations are outside the credit policy limits. For instance, if the balance in receivables increases either because the amount of "bad," or uncollectible, sales increases or because the average time it takes to collect existing credit sales increases, the firm should consider making changes in its credit policy. **Receivables monitoring** refers to the process of evaluating the credit policy to determine whether a shift in the customers' payment patterns has occurred.

**TABLE 15-3**  Unilate Textiles: Receivables Aging Schedule for 2009

| Age of Account (In Days) | Net Amount Outstanding | Fraction of Total Receivables | Average Days |
|---|---|---|---|
| 0–30 | $ 72,000 | 40% | 18 |
| 31–60 | 90,000 | 50 | 55 |
| 61–90 | 10,800 | 6 | 77 |
| More than 90 | 7,200 | 4 | 97 |
| | $180,000 | 100% | |

$$DSO = 0.40(18 \text{ days}) + 0.50(55 \text{ days}) + 0.06(77 \text{ days}) + 0.04(97 \text{ days})$$
$$= 43.2 \text{ days}$$

Traditionally, firms have monitored accounts receivable by using methods that measure the amount of time credit remains outstanding. Two such methods are the *days sales outstanding (DSO)* and the *aging schedule.*

## Days Sales Outstanding (DSO)

**Days sales outstanding (DSO),** which is sometimes called the *average collection period,* represents the average time it takes to collect credit accounts. DSO is computed by dividing *annual* credit sales by *daily* credit sales. For example, in the previous chapter, we found that the receivables collection period, or DSO, for Unilate was 43.2 days in 2009. The DSO of 43.2 days can be compared with the credit terms offered by Unilate. If Unilate's credit terms are 2/10, net 30, then we know there are customers that are delinquent when paying their accounts. In fact, if many customers are paying within 10 days to take advantage of the cash discount, the others would, on average, have to be taking much longer than 43.2 days. One way to check this possibility is to use an aging schedule as described next.

**days sales outstanding (DSO)**
The average length of time required to collect accounts receivable; also called the *average collection period.*

## Aging Schedule

An **aging schedule** is a breakdown of a firm's receivables by age of account. Table 15-3 contains the December 31, 2009, aging schedule for Unilate Textiles. The standard format for aging schedules generally includes age categories broken down by month because banks and financial analysts usually want companies to report their receivables' ages in this form. However, more precision, thus better monitoring information, can be attained by using narrower age categories (for example, one or two weeks).

According to Unilate's aging schedule, only 40 percent of its credit sales were collected within the credit period of 30 days; thus, 60 percent of the credit sales collections were delinquent. Some of the payments were delinquent by only a few days, while others were delinquent by three to four times the 30-day credit period.

Management should constantly monitor the days sales outstanding and the aging schedule to detect trends, to see how the firm's collection experience compares with its credit terms and to see how effectively the credit department is operating in comparison with other firms in the industry. If the DSO starts to lengthen or if the aging schedule begins to show an increasing percentage of past-due accounts, then the firm's credit policy might need to be tightened.

We must be careful when interpreting changes in DSO or the aging schedule, however, because if a firm experiences sharp seasonal variations, or if it is growing

**aging schedule**
A report showing how long accounts receivable have been outstanding; the report divides receivables into specified periods, which provides information about the proportion of receivables that is current and the proportion that is past due for given lengths of time.

rapidly, then both measures could be distorted. For example, recall that Unilate's peak selling season is in the fall. Table 14-1 shows that forecasted receivables are expected to be high, at \$251.5 million, at the end of September 2010, while receivables are expected to be much lower, at \$198 million, at the end of December 2010. If sales are expected to be \$1,650 million in 2010, Unilate's DSO will be \$251.5/(\$1,650/360) = 54.9 days on September 30, but \$198/(\$1,650/360) = 43.2 days on December 31, 2010. This decline in DSO would not indicate that Unilate had tightened its credit policy or more efficiently collected its receivables, only that its sales had fallen because of seasonal factors. Similar problems arise with the aging schedule when sales fluctuate widely. Therefore, *a change in either the DSO or the aging schedule should be taken as a signal to investigate further, but not necessarily as a sign that the firm's credit policy has weakened.* If a firm generally experiences widely fluctuating sales patterns, some type of modified aging schedule should be used to correctly account for these fluctuations.[2] Still, days sales outstanding and the aging schedule are useful tools for reviewing the credit department's performance.

### Self-Test Questions

What factors are included in credit policy decisions? Describe how each factor affects sales and profitability.

Define days sales outstanding (DSO). What can be learned from it? How is it affected by sales fluctuations?

What is an aging schedule? What can be learned from it? How is it affected by sales fluctuations?

## ANALYZING PROPOSED CHANGES IN CREDIT POLICY

The key question when deciding on a proposed credit policy change is this: How will the firm's value be affected? Unless the added benefits expected from a credit policy change exceed the added costs on a present value basis, the policy change should *not* be made.

To illustrate how we can evaluate whether a proposed change in a firm's credit policy is appropriate, let's examine what would happen if Unilate Textiles makes changes to reduce its average collection period. Assume that Unilate's financial manager has proposed that this task be accomplished in 2010 by (1) billing customers sooner and exerting more pressure on delinquent customers to pay their bills on time and (2) examining the accounts of existing credit customers and suspending the credit of customers who are considered "habitually delinquent." These actions will result in a direct increase in the costs associated with Unilate's credit policy. At the same time, even though Unilate has an extremely loyal customer base, it is expected that some sales will be lost to competitors as the result of some customers having their credit decreased or even eliminated. But because the credit policy changes will have little, if any, effect on the "good" credit customers, the financial manager does not expect there to be a change in the payments of those customers who currently take advantage of the cash discount. If the proposed credit policy changes are approved, the financial manager believes the average collection period, or DSO,

---

[2]See Eugene F. Brigham and Phillip R. Daves, *Intermediate Financial Management,* 9th ed. (Cincinnati, OH: South-Western College Publishing, 2007), Chapter 21, for a more complete discussion of the problems with the DSO and aging schedule and how to correct for them.

for receivables can be reduced from 43.2 days to 35.6 days, which is more in line with the credit terms offered by Unilate (2/10, net 30) and is closer to the industry average of 32.1 days. Also, if the average collection period is reduced, the amount "carried" in accounts receivable is reduced, which means less funds are "tied up" in receivables.

Table 15-4 provides information relating to Unilate's existing credit policy and the financial manager's proposed changes. According to this information, if the company

**TABLE 15-4**   Unilate Textiles: Existing and Proposed Credit Policies—Expected for 2010

|  | Existing Policy | Proposed Policy |
|---|---|---|
| **I. General Credit Policy Information** | | |
| Credit terms | 2/10 net 30 | 2/10 net 30 |
| Days sales outstanding (DSO) for all customers[a] | 43.2 days | 35.6 days |
| DSO for customers who take cash discount (20%) | 10.0 days | 10.0 days |
| DSO for customers who forgo cash discount (80%) | 51.5 days | 42.0 days |
| **II. Annual Credit Sales and Costs ($ millions)** | | |
| Gross credit sales | $1,656.6 | $1,654.6 |
| Net credit sales[b] | $1,650.0 | $1,648.0 |
| Amount paid by discount customers[c] | $ 324.7 | $ 324.7 |
| Amount paid by nondiscount customers[c] | $1,325.3 | $1,323.3 |
| Variable operating costs (82 percent of net sales)[d] | $1,353.0 | $1,351.4 |
| Bad debts | $ 0.0 | $ 0.0 |
| Credit evaluation and collection costs[d] | $ 16.0 | $ 17.0 |
| **III. Daily Credit Sales and Costs ($ thousands)[e]** | | |
| Net sales | $4,583.3 | $4,577.8 |
| Amount paid by discount customers | $ 901.9 | $ 901.9 |
| Amount paid by nondiscount customers | $3,681.4 | $3,675.8 |
| Variable operating costs (82 percent of net sales) | $3,758.3 | $3,753.9 |
| Bad debts | $ 0.0 | $ 0.0 |
| Credit evaluation and collection costs | $ 44.4 | $ 47.2 |

[a]With the existing policy, 20 percent of the customers take the cash discount and pay on Day 10 and the remaining customers (80 percent) pay on average on Day 51.5; thus the DSO for all customers is 43.2 days = 0.20(10 days) + 0.80(51.5 days).

[b]In Chapter 17, we determine that Unilate's 2010 *net* forecasted sales is $1,650 million, which represents what the firm expects to collect from credit sales, net of cash discounts. The gross sales, which includes cash discounts, can be computed as follows:

$$\text{Net sales} = 0.80(\text{Gross sales}) + (0.20)(1 - 0.02)(\text{Gross sales})$$
$$= (\text{Gross sales})[0.80 + 0.20(0.98)] = \$1,650 \text{ million}$$
$$\text{Gross sales} = \frac{\$1,650 \text{ million}}{0.996} = \$1,656.6 \text{ million}$$

[c]Twenty percent of Unilate's customers pay on Day 10, taking advantage of the 2 percent cash discount. As a result, the amount paid by this group of customers is $324.7 million = 0.20 (1.0 − 0.02) $1,656.6 million. Customers who do not take the discount will pay the full invoice price, or a total of $1,325.3 = 0.80($1,656.6). Because customers who take the discount will not be affected by the credit policy changes that are aimed at delinquent customers, the amount paid by customers who take the discount will be the same under either credit policy—that is, $324.7 million. This means that the $2 million decrease in total sales associated with the proposed credit policy will reduce the amount paid by customers who do not take the discount from $1,325.3 million to $1,323.3 million.

[d]Variable cost of goods sold (CGS) are paid at the time of the credit sale. Fixed operating costs are not included in the analysis because the amount does not change if the credit policy is changed. Expenses related to credit sales (evaluation and collection costs) are also paid at the time of the credit sale. These assumptions are made to simplify the analysis.

[e]Daily figures are required to evaluate whether the proposal should be adopted. See Figure 15-2 for the actual analysis. For consistency, we use a 360-day year to compute the daily figures.

changes its credit policy, its sales will drop by $2 million per year, or by $5,556 per day. Note that only the amount paid by customers who do not take the cash discount will be affected by this decrease because this group of customers includes the "habitually delinquent" payers, which is the category of customers the credit policy change is intended to affect. As a result, on a daily basis, the amount paid by the *nondiscount* customers will decrease by $5,556, from $3,681,333.3 to $3,675,777.8, if the proposed credit policy is adopted; but the amount paid by the discount customers will remain at $901,944 = ($324.7 million)/360.

To determine whether Unilate should adopt the financial manager's proposal, we need to evaluate the effect the proposed changes will have on the value of the firm. Thus, we must compare the net present values (NPVs) of the two credit policies. To complete the analysis, we make two simplifying assumptions: (1) sales occur evenly throughout the year; and (2) each production/selling cycle is constant such that cash inflows and cash outflows occur at the same point in time relative to the credit sale, no matter what time of the year is examined. These assumptions allow us to evaluate the cash inflows and cash outflows associated with the credit sales for one day to determine whether the proposed credit policy change should be made. Table 15-4 gives specific assumptions concerning the timing of the cash flows, and Figure 15-2 shows the

---

**FIGURE 15-2**  Unilate Textiles: NPV Analysis of Credit Policies ($ thousands)

**I. Existing Credit Policy:**

Cash Flow Time Line:

| 0 | r = 10.0%/360 = 0.0278% | 10 | | 51.5 | Days |

(3,758.3) = Operating costs      901.9 = Discount      3,681.4 = Nondiscount
( 44.4) = Credit costs               customers'             customers'
(3,802.7)                        payments             payments

$$NPV_{Existing} = (3,802.7) + \frac{901.9}{(1.000278)^{10}} + \frac{3,681.4}{(1.000278)^{51.5}} = 725.8$$

**II. Proposed Credit Policy:**

Cash Flow Time Line:

| 0 | r = 10.0%/360 = 0.0278% | 10 | | 42 | Days |

(3,753.9) = Operating costs      901.9 = Discount      3,675.8 = Nondiscount
( 47.2) = Credit costs                customers'             customers'
(3,801.1)                        payments             payments

$$NPV_{Existing} = (3,801.1) + \frac{901.9}{(1.000278)^{10}} + \frac{3,675.8}{(1.000278)^{42}} = 731.4$$

**III. Impact on Firm's Value If Proposal Is Adopted**

$$\Delta\ NPV \text{ on a daily basis} = \$731.4 - \$725.8 = \$5.6$$

$$\Delta\ value = \frac{\$5.6}{0.000278} = \$20,143.9$$

results of the NPV analysis assuming Unilate's required rate of return is 10 percent (annually). According to these results, the NPV for the existing credit policy is $725,800 per day, whereas the NPV for the proposed credit policy is $731,400 per day. If the company changes its credit policy, the change in the daily NPV, shown in Section III of Figure 15-2, is $5,600. Given the assumptions we have stated here as well as the assumptions given in Table 15-4 we would expect that this change has a permanent, or continuing, effect on the firm. Thus, the $5,600 change represents a daily perpetuity, which, according to Section III of Figure 15-2, will increase the value of the firm by $20.1 million. Clearly, then, the proposed changes should be made.

The analysis in Table 15-4 provides Unilate's managers with a vehicle for considering the impact of credit policy changes on the firm's value. However, a great deal of judgment must be applied to the decision because both customers' and competitors' responses to credit policy changes are difficult to estimate. Nevertheless, this type of analysis is essential.

## Self-Test Questions

Describe the procedure used to evaluate a change in credit policy.

Rattlefish Manufacturing's annual credit sales equal $1.8 million. If Rattlefish can reduce its days sales outstanding (DSO) from 40 days to 32 days, by how much will its average balance in accounts receivable decrease? (*Answer:* $40,000—A/R will decrease from $200,000 to $160,000)

## INVENTORY MANAGEMENT

If it could, a firm would prefer to have no inventory at all because while products are in inventory they do not generate returns and they must be financed. However, most firms find it necessary to maintain inventory in some form because (1) demand cannot be predicted with certainty and (2) it takes time to transform a product into a form that is ready for sale. And although excessive inventories are costly to the firm, so are insufficient inventories because customers might purchase from competitors if products are not available when demanded, and thus future business could be lost.

Although inventory models are covered in depth in production management courses, it is important to understand the basics of inventory management because proper management requires coordination among the sales, purchasing, production, and finance departments. Lack of coordination among these departments, poor sales forecasts, or both can lead to financial ruin. Therefore, in this section, we describe the concepts of inventory management.

### Types of Inventory

An inventory item can be grouped into one of the following categories:

1. **Raw materials** include new inventory items purchased from suppliers; it is the material a firm purchases to transform into finished products for sale. As long as the firm has an inventory of raw materials, delays in ordering and delivery from suppliers do not affect the production process.

2. **Work-in-process** refers to inventory items that are at various stages in the production process. If a firm has work-in-process at every stage of the production process, then it will not have to completely shut down production if a problem arises at one of the earlier stages.

**raw materials**
The inventories purchased from suppliers that ultimately will be transformed into finished goods.

**work-in-process**
Inventory in various stages of completion; some work-in-process is at the very beginning of the production process while some is at the end of the process.

**finished goods**
Inventories that have completed the production process and are ready for sale.

3. **Finished goods** inventory represents products that are ready for sale. Firms carry finished goods to ensure that orders can be filled when they are received. If there are no finished goods, the firm has to wait for the completion of the production process before inventory can be sold; thus, demand might not be satisfied when it arrives. When a customer arrives and there is no inventory to satisfy that demand, a **stockout** exists, and the firm might lose the demand to competitors, perhaps permanently.

**stockout**
Occurs when a firm runs out of inventory *and* customers arrive to purchase the product.

## Optimal Inventory Level

The goal of inventory management is to provide the inventories required to sustain operations at the lowest possible cost. Thus, the first step in determining the optimal inventory level is to identify the costs involved in purchasing and maintaining inventory, and then we need to determine at what point those costs are minimized.

**carrying costs**
The costs associated with having inventory, which include storage costs, insurance, cost of tying up funds, depreciation costs, and so on; these costs generally increase in proportion to the average amount of inventory held.

### Inventory Costs

We generally classify inventory costs into three categories: those associated with carrying inventory, those associated with ordering and receiving inventory, and those associated with running short of inventory (stockouts). First, let's look at the two costs that are most directly observable—carrying costs and ordering costs.

1. **Carrying costs** include any expenses associated with having inventory, such as rent paid for the warehouse where inventory is stored and insurance on the inventory, and they generally increase in direct proportion to the average amount of inventory carried.

**ordering costs**
The costs of placing an order; the cost of *each* order generally is fixed regardless of the average size of the inventory.

2. **Ordering costs** are those expenses associated with placing and receiving an order for new inventory, which include the costs of generating memos, fax transmissions, and so forth. For the most part, the costs associated with each order are fixed regardless of the order size.[3]

If we assume that the firm knows how much total inventory it needs and sales are distributed evenly during each period, then we can combine the total carrying costs (TCC) and the total ordering costs (TOC) to find total inventory costs (TIC) as follows:

**15–1**

$$
\begin{aligned}
\text{Total inventory costs (TIC)} &= \quad \text{Total carrying costs} \quad + \quad \text{Total ordering costs} \\
&= \begin{pmatrix} \text{Carrying cost} \\ \text{per unit} \end{pmatrix} \times \begin{pmatrix} \text{Average units} \\ \text{in inventory} \end{pmatrix} + \begin{pmatrix} \text{Cost per} \\ \text{order} \end{pmatrix} \times \begin{pmatrix} \text{Number} \\ \text{of orders} \end{pmatrix} \\
&= \quad (C \times PP) \quad \times \quad \left(\frac{Q}{2}\right) \quad + \quad O \quad \times \quad \left(\frac{T}{Q}\right)
\end{aligned}
$$

The variables in Equation 15–1 are defined as follows:

**C** = Carrying costs as a percent (stated as a decimal) of the purchase price of each inventory item

**PP** = Purchase price, or cost, per unit

---

[3]In reality, both carrying and ordering costs can have variable and fixed cost elements, at least over certain ranges of average inventory. For example, security and utilities charges probably are fixed in the short run over a wide range of inventory levels. Similarly, labor costs in receiving inventory could be tied to the quantity received and hence could be variable. To simplify matters, we treat all carrying costs as variable and all ordering costs as fixed.

FIGURE **15-3**   Determination of the Optimal Order Quantity

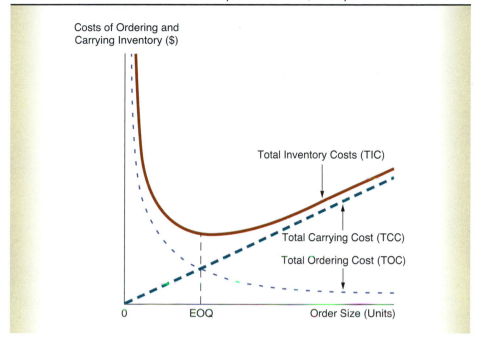

$Q$ = Number of units purchased with each order
$T$ = Total demand, or number of units sold, per period
$O$ = Fixed costs per order

According to Equation 15–1, the average investment in inventory depends on how frequently orders are placed and the size of each order. If we order every day, the average inventory will be much smaller than if we order once a year and inventory carrying costs will be low, but the number of orders will be large and inventory ordering costs will be high. We can reduce ordering costs by ordering greater amounts less often, but then average inventory, thus the total carrying cost, will be high. This trade-off between carrying costs and ordering costs is shown in Figure 15-3. Note from the figure that there is a point at which the total inventory cost (TIC) is *minimized;* this is called the **economic (optimum) ordering quantity (EOQ).**

### The Economic Ordering Quantity (EOQ) Model

The EOQ is determined by using calculus to find the point at which the slope of the TIC curve in Figure 15-3 is perfectly horizontal; thus, it equals zero. The result is the following equation:

**economic (optimum) ordering quantity (EOQ)** The optimal quantity that should be ordered; it is this quantity that will minimize the *total inventory costs.*

**EOQ model** A formula for determining the order quantity that will minimize total inventory costs.

**15–2**

$$\text{Economic ordering quantity} = \text{EOQ} = \sqrt{\frac{2 \times O \times T}{C \times PP}}$$

The primary assumptions of the **EOQ model** given by Equation 15–2 are that (1) sales are evenly distributed throughout the period examined and can be forecasted precisely, (2) orders are received when expected, and (3) the purchase price (PP) of each item in inventory is the same regardless of the quantity ordered.[4]

To illustrate the EOQ model, consider the following data supplied by Cotton Tops Inc., a distributor of custom-designed T-shirts that supplies concessionaires at Daisy World:

$T$ = 78,000 shirts per year.
$C$ = 25 percent of inventory value.
$PP$ = $3.84 per shirt. (The shirts sell for $9, but this is irrelevant for our purposes here.)
$O$ = $260 per order.

Substituting these data into Equation 15–2, we find an EOQ equal to 6,500 units:

$$EOQ = \sqrt{\frac{2 \times \$260 \times 78,000}{0.25 \times \$3.84}}$$
$$= \sqrt{42,250,000} = 6,500 \text{ units}$$

If Cotton Tops orders 6,500 shirts each time it needs inventory, it will place $78,000/6,500 = 12$ orders per year and carry an average inventory of $6,500/2 = 3,250$ shirts. Thus, at the EOQ quantity, Cotton Tops' total inventory costs would equal $6,240:

$$TIC = (C \times PP)\left(\frac{Q}{2}\right) + O\left(\frac{T}{Q}\right)$$
$$= [0.25 \times (\$3.84)]\left(\frac{6,500}{2}\right) + (\$260)\left(\frac{78,000}{6,500}\right)$$
$$= \$3,120 + \$3,120 = \$6,240$$

Note these two points: (1) Because we assume the purchase price of each inventory item does not depend on the amount ordered, TIC does *not* include the $299,520 = 78,000($3.84) annual cost of purchasing the inventory itself. (2) As we see both in Figure 15-3 and in the numbers here, at the EOQ, total carrying cost (TCC) equals total ordering cost (TOC). This property is not unique to our Cotton Tops illustration; it always holds.

Table 15-5 contains the total inventory costs that Cotton Tops would incur at various order quantities, including the EOQ level. Note that (1) as the amount ordered increases, the total carrying costs increase but the total ordering costs decrease, and vice versa; (2) if less than the EOQ amount is ordered, then the higher ordering costs more than offset the lower carrying costs; and (3) if greater than the EOQ amount is ordered, the higher carrying costs more than offset the lower ordering costs.

## EOQ Model Extensions

It should be obvious that some of the assumptions necessary for the basic EOQ to hold are unrealistic. To make the model more useful, we can apply some simple extensions.

---

[4]The EOQ model can also be written as follows:

$$EOQ = \sqrt{\frac{2 \times O \times T}{C^*}}$$

where $C^*$ is the annual carrying cost per unit expressed in dollars.

**TABLE 15-5**    Cotton Tops, Inc.: Total Inventory Costs for Various Order Quantities

|  | Quantity | Number of Orders | Total Ordering Costs | Total Carrying Costs | Total Inventory Costs |
|---|---|---|---|---|---|
|  | 3,000 | 26 | $6,760 | $1,440 | $8,200 |
|  | 5,200 | 15 | 3,900 | 2,496 | 6,396 |
|  | 6,000 | 13 | 3,380 | 2,880 | 6,260 |
| **EOQ** | **6,500** | **12** | **3,120** | **3,120** | **6,240** |
|  | 7,800 | 10 | 2,600 | 3,744 | 6,344 |
|  | 9,750 | 8 | 2,080 | 4,680 | 6,760 |
|  | 13,000 | 6 | 1,560 | 6,240 | 7,800 |
|  | 78,000 | 1 | 260 | 37,440 | 37,700 |

T = Annual sales = 78,000 shirts

C = Carrying cost = 25 percent

PP = Purchase price = $3.84/shirt

O = Ordering cost = $260/order

First, if there is a delay between the time inventory is ordered and when it is received, the firm must reorder before it runs out of inventory. For example, if it normally takes two weeks to receive orders, then Cotton Tops should reorder when two weeks of inventory are left. Cotton Tops sells 78,000/52 = 1,500 shirts per week, so its **reorder point** is when inventory drops to 3,000 shirts. Even if Cotton Tops orders additional inventory at the appropriate reorder point, unexpected demand might cause it to run out of inventory before the new inventory is delivered. To avoid this, the firm could carry **safety stocks,** which represent additional inventory that helps guard against stockouts. The amount of safety stock a firm holds generally *increases* with (1) the uncertainty of demand forecasts, (2) the costs (in terms of lost sales and lost goodwill) that result from stockouts, and (3) the chances that delays will occur in receiving shipments. The amount of safety stock *decreases* as the cost of carrying this additional inventory increases.

Another factor a firm might need to consider when determining appropriate inventory levels is whether its suppliers offer discounts to purchase large quantities. For example, if Cotton Tops' supplier offered a 1 percent discount for purchases equal to 13,000 units or more, the total reduction in the annual cost of purchasing inventory would be [0.01($3.84)] × 78,000 = $2,995.20. Looking at Table 15-5 we see that the total inventory cost (excluding purchase price) at 13,000 units is $7,800, which is $1,560 = $7,800 − $6,240 greater than the cost at the EOQ level of 6,500 units. But the net benefit of taking advantage of the **quantity discount** is $1,435.20 = $2,995.20 − $1,560.00. Therefore, under these conditions, each time Cotton Tops orders inventory it will be more beneficial to order 13,000 units rather than the 6,500 units prescribed by the basic EOQ model.

In cases in which it is unrealistic to assume that the demand for the inventory is uniform throughout the year, the EOQ should not be applied on an annual basis. Rather, it would be more appropriate to divide the year into the seasons within which sales are relatively constant, say, the summer, the spring and fall, and the winter; then the EOQ model can be applied separately to each period.

Although we did not explicitly incorporate the extensions we mentioned here into the basic EOQ, our discussion should give you an idea of how the EOQ amount should be adjusted to determine the optimal inventory level if any of the conditions exist.

**reorder point**
The level of inventory at which an order should be placed.

**safety stocks**
Additional inventory carried to guard against unexpected changes in sales rates or production/shipping delays.

**quantity discount**
A discount from the purchase price offered for inventory ordered in large quantities.

## Inventory Control Systems

**red-line method**
An inventory control procedure in which a *red line* is drawn around the inside of an inventory-stocked bin to indicate the reorder point level.

The EOQ model can be used to help establish the proper inventory level, but inventory management also involves the establishment of an *inventory control system.* Inventory control systems run the gamut from very simple to extremely complex, depending on the size of the firm and the nature of its inventories. For example, one simple control procedure is the **red-line method:** Inventory items are stocked in a bin, a red line is drawn around the inside of the bin at the level of the reorder point, and the inventory clerk places an order when the red line shows. This procedure works well for parts such as bolts in a manufacturing process or for many items in retail businesses.

**computerized inventory control system**
A system of inventory control in which a computer is used to determine reorder points and to adjust inventory balances.

Most firms employ some type of **computerized inventory control system.** Large companies often have fully integrated computerized inventory control systems in which the computer adjusts inventory levels as sales are made, orders inventory when the reorder point is reached, and records the receipt of an order. The computer records also can be used to determine whether the usage rates of inventory items change, and thus adjustments to reorder amounts can be made. Another approach to inventory control that requires a coordinated effort between the supplier and the buyer is called the **just-in-time system,** which was refined by Japanese firms many years ago. With this system, materials are delivered to the company at about the same time they are needed, perhaps a few hours before they are used. Still another important development related to inventories is **outsourcing,** which is the practice of purchasing components rather than making them in-house. Outsourcing often is combined with just-in-time systems to reduce inventory levels.

**just-in-time system**
A system of inventory control in which a manufacturer coordinates production with suppliers so that raw materials of components arrive just as they are needed in the production process.

Inventory control systems require coordination of inventory policy with manufacturing/procurement policies. Companies try to minimize *total production and distribution costs,* and inventory costs are just one part of total costs. Still, they are an important cost, and financial managers should be aware of the determinants of inventory costs and how they can be minimized.

**outsourcing**
The practice of purchasing components rather than making them in-house.

 ### Self-Test Questions

What are the types of inventory?

What are the three categories of inventory costs?

What is the purpose of the EOQ model?

What are safety stocks, and why are they required?

Describe some inventory control systems used in practice.

Suppose that Cotton Tops Inc., the distributor of custom-designed T-shirts that was mentioned in this section, discovered that its cost per shirt was $3.94 rather than $3.84. What would the EOQ be in this situation? (*Answer:* Q = 6,417)

## MULTINATIONAL WORKING CAPITAL MANAGEMENT

As we mentioned in the previous chapter, the methods used to manage short-term assets in multinational corporations are essentially the same as those used in purely domestic corporations. But there are some differences, which we discuss in this section.

## Cash Management

Like a purely domestic company, a multinational corporation wants to (1) speed up collections and slow down disbursements where possible, (2) shift cash as rapidly as possible to those areas where it is needed, and (3) try to put temporary cash balances to work earning positive returns. Multinational companies use the same general procedures for achieving these goals as domestic firms, but because of longer distances and more serious mail delays, lockbox systems and electronic funds transfers are even more important.

One potential problem a multinational company faces that a purely domestic company does not is the chance that a foreign government will restrict transfers of funds out of the country. Foreign governments often limit the amount of cash that can be taken out of their countries because they want to encourage investment domestically. Even if funds can be transferred without limitation, deteriorating exchange rates might make it unattractive for a multinational firm to move funds to its operations in other countries.

Once it has been determined what funds can be transferred out of the various nations in which a multinational corporation operates, it is important to get those funds to locations where they will earn the highest returns. Whereas domestic corporations tend to think in terms of domestic securities, multinationals are more likely to be aware of investment opportunities all around the world. Most multinational corporations use one or more global concentration banks, located in money centers such as London, New York, Tokyo, Zurich, or Singapore, and their staffs in those cities, working with international bankers, are able to take advantage of the best rates available anywhere in the world.

## Credit Management

Credit policy generally is more important for a multinational corporation than for a purely domestic firm for two reasons. First, much U.S. trade is with poorer, less-developed nations, and in such situations granting credit generally is a necessary condition for doing business. Second, and in large part as a result of the first point, developed nations whose economic health depends on exports often help their manufacturing firms compete internationally by granting credit to foreign countries. In Japan, for example, government agencies help firms identify potential export markets and also help potential customers arrange credit for purchases from Japanese firms. The U.S. government has programs that help domestic firms to export products, but it does not provide the degree of financial assistance that other governments offer many multinationals based in other countries.

When granting credit, the multinational firm faces a riskier situation than purely domestic firms because, in addition to the normal risks of default, (1) political and legal environments often make it more difficult to collect defaulted accounts and (2) the multinational corporations must worry about exchange rate changes between the time a sale is made and the time a receivable is collected. We know, however, that hedging can reduce this type of risk, but at a cost.

By pointing out the risks in granting credit internationally, we are not suggesting that such credit is bad. Quite the contrary—the potential gains from international operations far outweigh the risks, at least for companies (and banks) that have the necessary expertise.

## Inventory Management

Inventory management in a multinational setting is more complex than in a purely domestic setting because of logistical problems that arise with handling inventories. For example, should a firm concentrate its inventories in a few strategic centers located worldwide? Such a strategy might minimize the total amount of, thus the investment in, inventories needed to operate the global business, but it also might cause delays in getting goods from central storage locations to user locations all around the world. It is clear, however, that both working stocks and safety stocks will have to be maintained at each user location, as well as at the strategic storage centers.

Exchange rates can significantly influence inventory policy. For example, if a local currency was expected to increase in value against the dollar, a U.S. company operating in that country would want to increase stocks of local products before the rise in the currency, and vice versa. Another factor that must be considered is the possibility of import or export quotas or tariffs. Quotas restrict the quantities of products firms can bring into a country, while tariffs, like taxes, increase the prices of products that are allowed to be imported. Both quotas and tariffs are designed to restrict the ability of foreign corporations to compete with domestic companies; at the extreme, foreign products are excluded altogether.

Another danger in certain countries is the threat of expropriation, or government takeover of the firm's local operations. If the threat of expropriation is large, inventory holdings will be minimized, and goods will be brought in only as needed. Similarly, if the operation involves extraction of raw material, processing plants might be moved offshore rather than located close to the production site.

Taxes also must be considered, and they have two effects on multinational inventory management. First, countries often impose property taxes on assets, including inventories, and when this is done, the tax is based on holdings as of a specific date, say, January 1 or March 1. Such rules make it advantageous for a multinational firm (1) to schedule production so that inventories are low on the assessment date and, (2) if assessment dates vary among countries in a region, to hold safety stocks in different countries at different times during the year.

In general, then, multinational firms use techniques similar to those described in this chapter to manage current assets, but their job is more complex because business, legal, and economic environments can differ significantly from one country to another.

## Self-Test Questions

What are some factors that make cash management especially complicated in a multinational corporation?

Why is granting credit especially risky in an international context?

What are some factors that make inventory management in multinational firms more complex than in purely domestic firms?

## Chapter *Essentials*
### —The Answers

To summarize the key concepts, let's answer the questions that were posed at the beginning of the chapter:

- **Why do firms hold cash? What general strategies should be followed to manage cash?** Firms prefer not to have cash because cash is considered an idle asset that does not earn interest. The primary reason firms hold cash is to ensure that day-to-day obligations can be paid (transactions balances). Firms also hold cash as a precaution to meet unforeseen payments (precautionary balances), to take advantage of bargain purchases that might arise (speculative balances), and to meet minimum cash balances required by the bank (compensating balances).

   When managing cash, a firm should minimize the amount of cash that needs to be held based on normal operations. The firm should construct a cash budget to forecast its cash flows so that funds can be invested when there are cash surpluses and arrangements can be made to borrow funds when there are cash deficiencies. To efficiently manage cash flows, the firm should try to collect funds owed as quickly as possible and try to delay payments of funds as long as possible. Of course, any actions taken should not be detrimental to the value of the firm.

- **Why do firms have marketable securities?** Marketable securities are short-term, highly liquid investments that have little investment risk. As a result, the return on such investments is fairly low. Firms use marketable securities as a temporary "parking place" for cash that is not needed in the current period but will be needed in the near term, perhaps in a few days, weeks, or months. Marketable securities permit firms to invest cash that would otherwise be idle in safe financial instruments that generate positive returns.

- **Why do firms sell on credit? What general strategies should be followed to manage credit?** In simple terms, firms sell on credit because competitors sell on credit. In some instances, customers cannot buy a firm's products unless the purchase is made on credit. A firm that sells on credit must have a credit policy that specifies how customers qualify for credit, the maximum amount of credit that customers are allowed, the terms of credit sales to customers, and what actions will be taken if customers do not pay on time. To ensure that the credit policy is being followed and is achieving the desired objective, a firm's credit policy should be monitored. When customers' payment patterns change significantly, the firm should consider changing its credit policy.

- **How should proposed changes in a firm's credit policy be analyzed?** Like capital budgeting projects and any other investments that are made, proposed changes in a firm's credit policy should be evaluated on a present value basis—that is, the net present value (NPV) of the existing credit policy should be compared with the NPV of the proposed credit policy. Analyzing proposed credit policy changes in this manner will help the firm to maximize its value.

- **Why do firms carry inventory? What general strategies should be followed to manage inventory?** Firms carry inventory to ensure that demand is met when it arrives. If a firm does not have inventory available for sale, then a sale cannot be made when a customer wants to purchase the firm's product. In competitive industries, when a firm does not have inventory available when customers want to purchase its products, the customers often buy from competitors. As a result, firms carry inventories that are ready to sell so that demand can be serviced when it arrives. However, carrying inventory is costly, so firms do not want to have too much inventory on hand at any time. As a result, a firm determines how much inventory to hold by examining the demand for its product, the costs associated with not having enough inventory, and the costs of carrying sufficient inventory to satisfy demand.

- **What is the EOQ model and how should it be applied?** The EOQ, or economic ordering quantity, model is used to determine the optimal amount of inventory that a firm should carry. If the firm orders the amount of inventory specified by the EOQ model, it will minimize the costs associated with carrying inventory. Although the basic EOQ model is based on very restrictive assumptions, extensions to the model make it very useful for inventory management.

## ETHICAL DILEMMA

### Money-Back Guarantee, No Questions Asked

TradeSmart Inc. operates 1,200 discount electronics stores throughout the United States. TradeSmart has been quite successful in a highly competitive industry primarily because it has been able to offer brand-name products at prices lower than can be found at other discount outlets. Because of its size, TradeSmart can purchase bulk inventory directly from manufacturers, and the economies of scale it derives from such purchases can be passed on to consumers in the form of lower prices. In addition to low prices, TradeSmart offers an extremely liberal product return policy. Customers are permitted to return products for virtually any reason and with little regard to the time period covered by manufacturers' warranties. In fact, just a few days ago, a customer returned a digital pager that was more than two years old. TradeSmart gave the customer a full refund even though the pager appeared to have been run over by a car, which, if true, clearly would have voided the manufacturer's warranty. In another instance, a customer was given a refund when he returned the camcorder he had purchased three days earlier to record his daughter's wedding festivities. The customer could not describe the camcorder's malfunction—he said "it just didn't work right." The customer refused an offer to replace the camcorder; instead, he insisted on a full refund, which he was given. The manager of the customer relations department suspected that the customer had "purchased" the camcorder intending all along to return it after his daughter's wedding. But TradeSmart's return policy does not dissuade customers from this practice. According to Ed Davidson, vice president of customer relations, TradeSmart is willing to stand behind every product

it sells, regardless of the problem, because the company believes such a policy is needed to attract and keep loyal customers in such a competitive industry. The company's motto—"Customer Satisfaction Is Our Business"—is displayed prominently throughout TradeSmart stores.

With such a liberal return policy, how does TradeSmart keep its prices so low? Actually, TradeSmart ships the returned products back to the manufacturers as defective products, so the return costs are passed on to the manufacturers. According to the manufacturers, only one out of every six products returned by TradeSmart actually is defective. But when the manufacturers complain about such returns as used products or products that have no mechanical problems, TradeSmart reminds them that the company does not have a service department, so its personnel are not knowledgeable concerning the technical circuitry of the products—the products are returned to the manufacturers with the customers' complaints attached. TradeSmart's inventory manager would contend that the company does not intentionally deceive or take advantage of the manufacturers' return policies and warranties. Do you agree with TradeSmart's return policy? Is it ethical? What action would you take if you were one of TradeSmart's suppliers?

## Chapter *Essentials*
### —Personal Finance

The concepts presented in this chapter should help you to understand actions that you can take to better manage your liquidity position by more effectively managing your short-term assets—that is, cash, short-term investments, and inventory.

- Most of us hold cash in the form of currency or debit cards. We use cash primarily to pay for such daily purchases as gas, lunch, groceries, and so forth (transaction balances). Often we also hold some safety (precautionary) cash in case unexpected purchases arise, and in some cases we hold cash that can be used to take advantage of bargains (speculative balances). Regardless of the reasons you hold cash, you should be aware of the fact that cash is an idle asset that is not working for you to earn a positive return. Thus, you should learn how to effectively manage your cash position.

- A key ingredient in effective cash management is the cash budget. There is a good chance that you already budget your cash, although it might be in a very unsophisticated manner. For example, how do you decide how much cash you should have in your wallet? Often individuals make such decisions by estimating what purchases will be made during the day. Such an estimate represents a rudimentary cash budget. To effectively manage your cash position, however, you should construct a formal cash budget. A cash budget will show you where your money is being spent, when you can expect cash shortfalls that must be financed, and when you might have cash surpluses that can be invested for short periods.

- You should follow the same policies that firms do when collecting monies owed to you and when paying your bills—that is, collect as soon as possible and pay as late as possible. Although you should ensure that all of your bills are paid on time, you do not have to pay them at the time the billing statement arrives. As long as you pay your bills by the due date, you will not harm your credit and you can keep your money working for you earning positive returns for as long as possible.

- Put your money to work earning positive returns. Any funds that you do not need today but you expect to need in the near future should be invested in short-term investments. For example, if you discover that you currently have some surplus cash that you will not need for another six months, invest it in a six-month certificate of deposit (CD). Developing a good cash budget will help you to plan and better time such investments.

- Believe it or not, we can apply the inventory management principles discussed in the chapter to our personal situations. Consider the food and other necessary items that you purchase during the year. You might go to the grocery store every day, whereas your friends might go once each week or every other week. But the question should be: How often should you go to the grocery store? The answer depends on factors such as (1) how much storage space you have in your home or apartment (carrying cost), (2) how convenient it is to go to the grocery store (ordering cost), and (3) how you react when you are hungry and cannot find the food you want in your house or apartment (stockout cost). By considering these factors, you can decide what food inventory management policy is best for you and your family.

## QUESTIONS

**15-1**    What are principal reasons for holding cash? Can a firm estimate its target cash balance by summing the cash held to satisfy each of the reasons?

**15-2**    Explain how each of the following factors probably would affect a firm's target cash balance if all other factors are held constant.

     **a.** The firm institutes a new billing procedure that better synchronizes its cash inflows and outflows.

     **b.** The firm develops a new sales forecasting technique that improves its forecasts.

     **c.** The firm reduces its portfolio of U.S. Treasury bills.

     **d.** The firm arranges to use an overdraft system for its checking account.

     **e.** The firm borrows a large amount of money from its bank and also begins to write far more checks than it did in the past.

     **f.** Interest rates on Treasury bills rise from 3 percent to 6 percent.

**15-3**    What is a cash budget? For what purposes should cash budgets be created?

**15-4**    Why is a cash budget important even when there is plenty of cash in the bank?

**15-5**    Discuss why it is important for a financial manager to understand the concept of float to effectively manage the firm's cash.

**15-6**    Why would a lockbox plan make more sense for a firm that makes sales all over the United States than for a firm with the same volume of business that is concentrated at the same location as the corporate headquarters?

**15-7**    In general, does a firm wish to speed up or slow down collections of payments made by its customers? Why? How does the same firm wish to manage its disbursements? Why?

**15-8** What does the term *liquidity* mean? Which would be more important to a firm that held a portfolio of marketable securities as a precautionary balance against the possibility of losing a major lawsuit—liquidity or rate of return? Explain.

**15-9** Firm A's management is very conservative whereas Firm B's is more aggressive. Is it true that, other things the same, Firm B would probably have larger holdings of marketable securities? Explain.

**15-10** What are the elements of a firm's credit policy? To what extent can firms set their own credit policies rather than having to accept policies that are dictated by the competition?

**15-11** What are aging schedules, and how can they be used to help the credit manager more effectively manage accounts receivable?

**15-12** Indicate by a (+), (−), or (0) whether each of the following events would probably cause accounts receivable (A/R), sales, and profits to increase, decrease, or be affected in an indeterminate manner:

|  | A/R | Sales | Profits |
|---|---|---|---|
| **a.** The firm tightens its credit standards. | _____ | _____ | _____ |
| **b.** The credit terms are changed from 2/10, net 30 to 3/10, net 30. | _____ | _____ | _____ |
| **c.** The credit manager gets tough with past-due accounts. | _____ | _____ | _____ |

**15-13** Describe the three classifications of inventory and indicate the purpose for holding each type.

**15-14** Indicate by a (+), (−), or (0) whether each of the following events would probably cause average annual inventories (the sum of the inventories held at the end of each month of the year divided by 12) to rise, fall, or be affected in an indeterminate manner:

**a.** Our suppliers switch from delivering by train to air freight.    _____

**b.** We change from producing just in time to meet seasonal sales to steady, year-round production. (Sales peak at Christmas.)    _____

**c.** Competition in the markets in which we sell increases.    _____

**d.** The rate of general inflation increases.    _____

**e.** Interest rates rise; other things are constant.    _____

**15-15** "Every firm should use the EOQ model to determine the optimal level of inventory to maintain." Discuss the accuracy of this statement with respect to the form of the EOQ model presented in this chapter.

## SELF-TEST PROBLEMS

*(Solutions appear in Appendix B at the end of the book.)*

key terms    **ST-1** Define each of the following terms:

**a.** Transactions balance; compensating balance; precautionary balance; speculative balance

**b.** Cash budget; target cash balance

**c.** Synchronized cash flows

**d.** Net float; disbursement float; collections float

**e.** Mail delay; processing delay; clearing (availability) delay

**f.** Lockbox arrangement; preauthorized debit; concentration banking

**g.** Zero-balance account (ZBA); controlled disbursement account (CDA)

**h.** Marketable securities; near-cash reserves

**i.** Credit policy; credit terms; collection policy

**j.** Days sales outstanding (DSO); aging schedule

**k.** Carrying costs; ordering costs; total inventory costs

**l.** Economic ordering quantity (EOQ); EOQ model

**m.** Reorder point; safety stock; quantity discount

**n.** Just-in-time system; outsourcing

**ST-2** The Upton Company is setting up a new checking account with Howe National Bank. Upton plans to issue checks in the amount of $1 million each day and to deduct them from its own records at the close of business on the day they are written. On average, the bank will receive and clear the checks at 5 p.m. the third day after they are written; for example, a check written on Monday will be cleared on Thursday afternoon. The firm's agreement with the bank requires it to maintain a $500,000 average compensating balance; this is $250,000 greater than the cash balance the firm would otherwise have on deposit. It makes a $500,000 deposit at the time it opens the account.    **float**

  **a.** Assuming that the firm makes deposits at 4 p.m. each day (and the bank includes them in that day's transactions), how much must it deposit daily to maintain a sufficient balance once it reaches a steady state? (To do this, set up a table that shows the daily balance recorded on the company's books and the daily balance at the bank until a steady state is reached.)

  **b.** Indicate the required deposit on Day 1, Day 2, Day 3, if any, and each day thereafter, assuming that the company will write checks for $1 million on Day 1 and each day thereafter.

  **c.** How many days of float does Upton have?

  **d.** What ending daily balance should the firm try to maintain (1) on the bank's records and (2) on its own records?

**ST-3** The Boca Grande Company expects to have sales of $10 million this year under its current operating policies. Its variable cost ratio is 80 percent, and its cost of short-term funds is 16 percent. Currently, Boca Grande's credit policy is net 25 (no discount for early payment), but its customers pay on average in 30 days. Boca Grande spends $50,000 per year to collect its credit accounts. It collects all receivables (no bad debts), and its marginal tax rate is 40 percent. All costs associated with the manufacture of the product and with the credit department's operations are paid when the product is sold.    **change in credit policy**

The credit manager is considering two alternative proposals for changing Boca Grande's credit policy. Should a change in credit policy be made?

*Proposal 1:* Lengthen the credit period by going from net 25 to net 30. Collection expenditures will remain constant. Under this proposal, sales are expected to increase by $1 million annually, and the DSO is expected to increase from 30 days to 45 days on all sales.

*Proposal 2:* Shorten the credit period by going from net 25 to net 20. Again, collection expenses will remain constant. But sales are expected to decrease by $1 million per year, and the DSO is expected to decline from 30 days to 22 days.

**EOQ and total inventory costs**

**ST-4** The Homemade Bread Company buys and then sells (as bread) 2.6 million bushels of wheat annually. The wheat must be purchased in multiples of 2,000 bushels. Ordering costs are $5,000 per order. Annual carrying costs are 2 percent of the purchase price of $5 per bushel. The delivery time is six weeks.

**a.** What is the EOQ?

**b.** At what inventory level should an order be placed?

**c.** What are the total inventory costs?

## PROBLEMS

**computation of float**

**15-1** Clearwater Glass Company examined its cash management policy and found that it takes an average of five days for checks that the company writes to reach its bank and thus be deducted from its checking account balance—that is, disbursement delay, or float, is five days. On the other hand, it is an average of four days from the time Clearwater Glass receives payments from its customers until the funds are available for use at the bank—that is, collection delay, or float, is four days. On an average day, Clearwater Glass writes checks that total $70,000, and it receives checks from customers that total $80,000.

**a.** Compute the disbursement float, collection float, and net float in dollars.

**b.** If Clearwater Glass has an opportunity cost equal to 10 percent, how much would it be willing to spend each year to reduce collection delay (float) by two days? (*Hint:* Assume any funds that are freed up will be invested at 10 percent annually.)

**receivables balance and DSO**

**15-2** Morrissey Industries sells on terms of 3/10, net 30. Total sales for the year are $900,000. Forty percent of the customers pay on Day 10 and take discounts; the other 60 percent pay, on average, 40 days after their purchases.

**a.** What is the days sales outstanding?

**b.** What is the average amount of receivables?

**c.** What would happen to average receivables if Morrissey tightened its collection policy with the result that all nondiscount customers paid on Day 30?

**tightening credit terms**

**15-3** Helen Bowers, the new credit manager of the Muscarella Corporation, was alarmed to find that Muscarella sells on credit terms of net 50 days whereas industrywide credit terms have recently been lowered to net 30 days. On annual credit sales of $3 million, Muscarella currently averages 60 days' sales in accounts receivable. Bowers estimates that tightening the credit terms to 30 days would reduce annual sales to $2.6 million, but accounts receivable would drop to 35 days of sales, and the savings on investment in them should more than overcome any loss in profit.

Muscarella's variable cost ratio is 70 percent, and its marginal tax rate is 40 percent. If the interest rate on funds invested in receivables is 11 percent, should the change in credit terms be made? All operating costs are paid when inventory is sold.

**credit policy change**

**15-4** The McCollough Company has a variable operating cost ratio of 70 percent, its cost of capital is 10 percent, and current sales are $10,000. All of its sales are on credit, and it currently sells on terms of net 30. Its accounts receivable balance is $1,500. McCollough is considering a new credit policy with terms of net 45. Under the new policy, sales will increase to $12,000, and accounts receivable will rise to $2,500. Compute the days sales outstanding (DSO) under the existing policy and the proposed policy.

**15-5**  Green Thumb Garden Centers sells 240,000 bags of lawn fertilizer annually.         **EOQ**
The optimal safety stock (which is on hand initially) is 1,200 bags. Each bag costs Green Thumb $4, inventory carrying costs are 20 percent, and the cost of placing an order with its supplier is $25.

   **a.** What is the economic ordering quantity (EOQ)?

   **b.** What is the total inventory cost at the EOQ level?

   **c.** What is the maximum inventory of fertilizer?

   **d.** What will Green Thumb's average inventory be?

   **e.** How often must the company order?

**15-6**  The Garvin Company is setting up a new checking account with Barngrover         **disbursement float**
National Bank. Garvin plans to issue checks in the amount of $1.6 million each day and to deduct them from its own records at the close of business on the day they are written. On average, the bank will receive and clear (that is, deduct from the firm's bank balance) the checks at 5 p.m. the fourth day after they are written; for example, a check written on Monday will be cleared on Friday afternoon. The firm's agreement with the bank requires it to maintain a $1.2 million average compensating balance; this is $400,000 greater than the cash balance the firm would otherwise have on deposit. Garvin will make a $1.2 million cash deposit at the time it opens the account.

   **a.** Assuming that the firm makes cash deposits at 2 p.m. each day (and the bank includes them in that day's transactions), how much must it deposit daily to maintain a sufficient balance once it reaches a steady state? (To find the answer, set up a table that shows the daily balance recorded on the company's books and the daily balance at the bank until a steady state is reached.) Indicate the required deposit on Day 1, Day 2, Day 3, Day 4, if any, and each day thereafter, assuming that the company will write checks for $1.6 million on Day 1 and each day thereafter.

   **b.** How many days of float does Garvin carry?

   **c.** What ending daily balance should the firm try to maintain (1) on the bank's records and (2) on its own records?

   **d.** Explain how net float can help increase the value of the firm's common stock.

**15-7**  Patricia Smith recently leased space in the Southside Mall and opened a new         **cash budgeting**
business, Smith's Coin Shop. Business has been good, but Smith frequently runs out of cash. This has necessitated late payment on certain orders, which in turn is beginning to cause a problem with suppliers. Smith plans to borrow from the bank to have cash ready as needed, but first she needs a forecast of just how much she must borrow. Accordingly, she has asked you to prepare a cash budget for the critical period around Christmas, when needs will be especially high.

     Sales are made on a cash basis only. Smith's purchases must be paid for during the month following the purchase. Smith pays herself a salary of $4,800 per month, and the rent is $2,000 per month. In addition, she must make a tax payment of $12,000 in December. The current cash on hand (on

December 1) is $400, but Smith has agreed to maintain an average bank balance of $6,000—this is her target cash balance. (Disregard till cash, which is insignificant because Smith keeps only a small amount on hand to lessen the chances of robbery.)

The estimated sales and purchases for December, January, and February are shown here. Purchases during November amounted to $140,000.

|  | Sales | Purchases |
|---|---|---|
| December | $160,000 | $40,000 |
| January | 40,000 | 40,000 |
| February | 60,000 | 40,000 |

a. Prepare a cash budget for December, January, and February.

b. Now suppose Smith started selling on a credit basis on December 1, giving customers 30 days to pay. All customers accept these terms and pay on time, and all other facts in the problem are unchanged. What would the company's loan requirements be at the end of December in this case? (*Hint:* The calculations required to answer this question are minimal.)

**cash budgeting**     **15-8**    Carol Moerdyk, owner of Carol's Fashion Designs Inc., is planning to request a line of credit from her bank. She has estimated the following sales forecasts for the firm for parts of 2009 and 2010:

| | |
|---|---|
| May 2009 | $180,000 |
| June | 180,000 |
| July | 360,000 |
| August | 540,000 |
| September | 720,000 |
| October | 360,000 |
| November | 360,000 |
| December | 90,000 |
| January 2010 | 180,000 |

Collection estimates obtained from the credit and collection department are as follows: collections within the month of sale, 10 percent; collections the month following the sale, 75 percent; collections the second month following the sale, 15 percent. Payments for labor and raw materials are typically made during the month following the one in which these costs are incurred. Total labor and raw materials costs are estimated for each month as follows:

| | |
|---|---|
| May 2009 | $ 90,000 |
| June | 90,000 |
| July | 126,000 |
| August | 882,000 |
| September | 306,000 |
| October | 234,000 |
| November | 162,000 |
| December | 90,000 |

General and administrative salaries will amount to approximately $27,000 a month; lease payments under long-term lease contracts will be $9,000 a month; depreciation charges will be $36,000 a month; miscellaneous expenses will be $2,700 a month; income tax payments of $63,000 will be due in both September and December; and a progress payment of $180,000 on a new design studio must be paid in October. Cash on hand on July 1 will amount to $132,000, and a minimum cash balance of $90,000 will be maintained throughout the cash budget period.

**a.** Prepare a monthly cash budget for the last six months of 2009.

**b.** Prepare an estimate of the required financing (or excess funds)—that is, the amount of money Carol's Fashion Designs will need to borrow (or will have available to invest)—for each month during that period.

**c.** Assume that receipts from sales come in uniformly during the month (that is, cash receipts come in at the rate of 1/30 each day), but all outflows are paid on the fifth of the month. Will this have an effect on the cash budget—in other words, would the cash budget you have prepared be valid under these assumptions? If not, what can be done to make a valid estimate of peak financing requirements? No calculations are required, although calculations can be used to illustrate the effects.

**d.** Carol's Fashion Designs produces on a seasonal basis, just ahead of sales. Without making any calculations, discuss how the company's current ratio and debt ratio would vary during the year assuming all financial requirements were met by short-term bank loans. Could changes in these ratios affect the firm's ability to obtain bank credit?

**15-9** Durst Corporation began operations five years ago as a small firm serving customers in the Denver area. However, its reputation and market area grew quickly so that today Durst has customers throughout the United States. Despite its broad customer base, Durst has maintained its headquarters in Denver and keeps its central billing system there. Durst's management is considering an alternative collection procedure to reduce its mail time and processing float. On average, it takes five days from the time customers mail payments until Durst is able to receive, process, and deposit them. Durst would like to set up a lockbox collection system, which it estimates would reduce the time lag from customer mailing to deposit by three days— bringing it down to two days. Durst receives an average of $1,400,000 in payments per day.

**lockbox system**

**a.** How many days of collection float now exist (Durst's customers' disbursement float) and what would it be under the lockbox system? What reduction in cash balances could Durst achieve by initiating the lockbox system?

**b.** If Durst has an opportunity cost of 10 percent, how much is the lockbox system worth on an annual basis?

**c.** What is the maximum monthly charge Durst should pay for the lockbox system?

**15-10** The Pettit Corporation has annual credit sales of $2 million. Current expenses for the collection department are $30,000, bad debt losses are 2 percent, and the days sales outstanding is 30 days. Pettit is considering easing its collection efforts so that collection expenses will be reduced to

**relaxing collection efforts**

$22,000 per year. The change is expected to increase bad debt losses to 3 percent and to increase the days sales outstanding to 45 days. In addition, sales are expected to increase to $2.2 million per year.

Should Pettit relax collection efforts if the opportunity cost of funds is 12 percent, the variable cost ratio is 75 percent, and its marginal tax rate is 40 percent? All costs associated with production and credit sales are paid on the day of the sale.

**easing credit terms**    **15-11** Bey Technologies is considering changing its credit terms from 2/15, net 30 to 3/10, net 30 to speed collections. Currently, 40 percent of Bey's paying customers take the 2 percent discount. Under the new terms, discount customers are expected to rise to 50 percent. Regardless of the credit terms, half of the customers *who do not take the discount* are expected to pay on time, whereas the remainder will pay 10 days late. The change does not involve a relaxation of credit standards; therefore, bad debt losses are not expected to rise above their current 2 percent level. However, the more generous cash discount terms are expected to increase sales from $2 million to $2.6 million per year. Bey's variable cost ratio is 75 percent, the interest rate on funds invested in accounts receivable is 9 percent, and the firm's marginal tax rate is 40 percent. All costs associated with production and credit sales are paid on the day of the sale.

**a.** What is the days sales outstanding before and after the change?

**b.** Calculate the costs of the discounts taken before and after the change.

**c.** Calculate the bad debt losses before and after the change.

**d.** Should Bey change its credit terms?

**inventory cost**    **15-12** Computer Supplies Inc. must order diskettes from its supplier in lots of one dozen boxes. Given the information provided here, complete the following table and determine the economic ordering quantity of diskettes for Computer Supplies Inc.

> Annual demand: 26,000 dozen
> Cost per order placed: $30.00
> Carrying cost: 20%
> Price per dozen: $7.80

| Order Size (Dozens) | 250 | 500 | 1,000 | 2,000 | 13,000 | 26,000 |
|---|---|---|---|---|---|---|
| Number of orders | | | | | | |
| Average inventory | | | | | | |
| Carrying cost | | | | | | |
| Order cost | | | | | | |
| Total cost | | | | | | |

**EOQ and inventory costs**    **15-13** The following inventory data have been established for the Thompson Company:

**(1)** Orders must be placed in multiples of 100 units.

**(2)** Annual sales are 338,000 units.

**(3)** The purchase price per unit is $6.

**(4)** Carrying cost is 20 percent of the purchase price of goods.

**(5)** Fixed order cost is $48.

**(6)** Three days are required for delivery.

**a.** What is the EOQ?

**b.** How many orders should Thompson place each year?

**c.** At what inventory level should an order be made?

**d.** Calculate the total cost of ordering and carrying inventories if the order quantity is (1) 4,000 units, (2) 4,800 units, or (3) 6,000 units. (4) What are the total costs if the order quantity is the EOQ?

## Integrative Problems

**15-14** Ray Smith, a retired librarian, recently opened a sportsman's shop called Smitty's Sports Paradise (SSP). Smith decided at age 62 that he wasn't quite ready to stay at home living a life of leisure. It had always been his dream to open an outdoor sportsman's shop, so his friends convinced him to go ahead. Because Smith's educational background was in literature and not in business, he hired you, a finance expert, to help him with the store's cash management. Smith is very eager to learn, so he asked you to develop a set of questions to help him understand cash management. Now answer the following questions:

**cash management**

**a.** What is the goal of cash management?

**b.** For what reasons do firms hold cash?

**c.** What is meant by the terms *precautionary* and *speculative* balances?

**d.** What are some specific advantages for a firm holding adequate cash balances?

**e.** How can a firm synchronize its cash flows, and what good would this do?

**f.** You have been going through the store's checkbook and bank balances. In the process, you discovered that SSP, on average, writes checks in the amount of $10,000 each day and that it takes about five days for these checks to clear. Also, the firm receives checks in the amount of $10,000 daily but loses four days while they are being deposited and cleared. What is the firm's *disbursement float, collections float,* and *net float?*

**g.** How can a firm speed up collections and slow down disbursements?

**h.** Why would a firm hold marketable securities?

**i.** What factors should a firm consider in building its marketable securities portfolio? What are some securities that should and should not be held?

**15-15** Ray Smith also wants you to examine his company's credit policy to determine whether changes are needed because one of his employees, who graduated recently with a finance major, has recommended that the credit terms be changed from 2/10, net 30 to 3/20, net 45 and that both the credit standards and the collection policy be relaxed. According to the employee, such a change would cause sales to increase from $3.6 million to $4.0 million.

**credit policy**

Currently, 62.5 percent of SSP's customers pay on Day 10 of the billing cycle and take the discount, 32 percent pay on Day 30, and 5.5 percent pay (on average) on Day 60. If the new credit policy is adopted, Smith estimated that 72.5 percent of customers would take the discount; 10 percent would pay on Day 45; and 17.5 percent would pay late, on Day 90. Bad debt losses for both policies are expected to be trivial.

Variable operating costs are currently 75 percent of sales, the cost of funds used to carry receivables is 10 percent, and the firm's marginal tax rate is 40 percent. None of these factors would change as a result of a credit policy change.

To help decide whether to adopt the new policy, Smith has asked you to answer the following questions:

a. What variables make up a firm's credit policy? In what direction would each be changed if the credit policy is relaxed? How would each variable tend to affect sales, the level of receivables, and bad debt losses?

b. How are the days sales outstanding (DSO) and the average collection period (ACP) related to one another? What would the DSO be if the current credit policy is maintained? If the proposed policy is adopted?

c. What is the dollar amount of discounts granted under the current and the proposed credit policies?

d. Should SSP make the change? Assume that operating and credit costs are paid on the day of the sale.

e. Suppose the company makes the proposed change, but its competitors react by making changes in their own credit terms, with the net result being that gross sales remain at the $3.6 million level. What would be the effect on the company's value?

f. (1) What does the term *monitoring accounts receivable* mean?

   (2) Why would a firm want to monitor its receivables?

   (3) How might the DSO and the aging schedule be used in this process?

**EOQ model** **15-16** Now Ray Smith wants you to take a look at the company's inventory position because he thinks that inventories might be too high as a result of the manager's tendency to order in large quantities. Smith has decided to examine the situation for one key product—fly rods, which cost $320 each to purchase and prepare for sale. Annual sales of the product are 2,500 units (rods), and the annual carrying cost is 10 percent of inventory value. The company has been buying 500 rods per order and placing another order when the stock on hand falls to 100 rods. Each time SSP orders, it incurs a cost equal to $64. Sales are uniform throughout the year.

a. Smith believes that the EOQ model should be used to help determine the optimal inventory situation for this product. What is the EOQ formula, and what are the key assumptions underlying this model?

b. What is the formula for total inventory costs?

c. What is the EOQ for the fly rods? What will the total inventory costs be for this product if the EOQ is produced?

d. What is SSP's added cost if it orders 500 rods rather than the EOQ quantity? What if it orders 750 rods each time?

e. Suppose it takes three days for SSP to receive its orders and package the rods before they are ready for sale. Assuming certainty in production time and usage, at what inventory level should SSP order? (Assume a 360-day year, that SSP is open every day, and that SSP orders the EOQ amount.)

f. Of course, there is uncertainty in SSP's usage rate, as well as in order delays, so the company must carry a safety stock to avoid running out of the fly rods and having to lose sales. If a safety stock of 50 rods is carried, what effect would this have on total inventory costs?

**g.** For most of SSP's products, inventory usage is not uniform throughout the year; rather, it follows some seasonal pattern. Could the EOQ model be used in this situation? If so, how?

**h.** How would these factors affect the use of the EOQ model?

   **(1)** Just-in-time (JIT) procedures

   **(2)** Use of air freight for deliveries

   **(3)** Computerized inventory control systems

## Computer-Related Problems

*Work the problem in this section only if you are using the problem spreadsheet.*

**15-17** Use the model in File C15 to solve this problem.    **cash budget**

**a.** Refer back to Problem 15-8. Suppose that by offering a 2 percent cash discount for paying within the month of sale, the credit manager of Carol's Fashion Designs Inc. has revised the collection percentages to 50 percent, 35 percent, and 15 percent, respectively. How will this affect the loan requirements?

**b.** Return the payment percentages to their base case values—10 percent, 75 percent, and 15 percent, respectively—and the discount to zero percent. Now suppose sales fall to only 70 percent of the forecasted level. Production is maintained, so cash outflows are unchanged. How does this affect Carol's Fashion Designs' financial requirements?

**c.** Return sales to the forecasted level (100%), and suppose collections slow down to 3 percent, 10 percent, and 87 percent for the three months, respectively. How does this affect financial requirements? If Carol's Fashion Designs went to a cash-only sales policy, how would that affect requirements, other things held constant?

**15-18** Use the model in File C15 to solve this problem.    **tightening credit terms**

**a.** Refer to Problem 15-3. When Bowers analyzed her proposed credit policy changes, she found that they would reduce Muscarella's value and, therefore, should not be enacted. Bowers has reevaluated her sales estimates because all other firms in the industry have recently tightened their credit policies. She now estimates that sales would decline to only $2.8 million if she tightens the credit policy to 30 days. Would the credit policy change be profitable under these circumstances?

**b.** On the other hand, Bowers believes that she could tighten the credit policy to net 45 days and pick up some sales from her competitors. She estimates that sales would increase to $3.3 million and that the days sales outstanding (DSO) would fall to 50 days under this policy. Should Bowers enact this change?

**c.** Bowers also believes that if she leaves the credit policy as it is, sales will increase to $3.4 million and the DSO will remain at 60 days. Should Bowers leave the credit policy alone or tighten it as described in either part a or part b? Which credit policy produces the highest value for Muscarella Corporation?

**credit policy**    **15-19**  Kimberly-Clark [KMB] is a consumer and business-to-business products manufacturing firm. Analyze Kimberly-Clark's credit policy as compared with peers in its industry. Answer the following questions:

**a.** What has been the trend of Kimberly-Clark's receivables turnover during the past five years? [Click on Financials/More/SEC Reports and Charts/Receivables Turnover Ratio.]

**b.** Find the peers of Kimberly-Clark based on its industry group. Pick two of Kimberly-Clark's peers and determine the trend of these firms' receivables turnovers during the past five years.

**c.** What conclusions can you make about Kimberly-Clark's credit policy as compared with other firms in its industry? Explain your answer.

# Managing Short-Term Liabilities (Financing)

**A**lthough they might have large amounts of current assets, many young, fast-growing companies often find themselves in the middle of cash crises where they struggle to pay the bills. It's natural for firms to seek help from their banks when they find themselves in such situations. However, in many cases, these same firms have reached their borrowing limits at the banks, and thus they cannot raise the needed short-term funds through traditional methods. In such cases, the firms often turn to nontraditional borrowing alternatives to finance operations.

Successful small firms that have good sales and high balances in accounts receivable and inventories might find themselves in the middle of a "cash crunch" because their bills are due before receivables can be collected or inventories can be liquidated. When a firm finds itself in such a situation, its short-term assets can be used to raise the cash needed to pay current obligations. Generally, it is easy for a firm to use its liquid assets—for example, receivables and inventories—to generate cash.

Both accounts receivable and inventories are considered good collateral for secured short-term loans. Both of these short-term assets are very liquid, and

because they are "turned into" cash in a short period, perhaps a few days or weeks, it generally is easy to raise funds using receivables loans or inventory loans. In some cases, however, the firm cannot absorb additional debt. Firms that find themselves in this situation can factor their accounts receivable.

When accounts receivable are "factored," they are sold to a firm called a factor for a cash advance. As the accounts are collected, the selling firm receives additional cash. The amount for which the receivables can be sold, the amount of the cash advance, and other arrangements regarding the factoring agreement depend on both the liquidity and the quality of the accounts that are sold.

In this chapter, we discuss factoring, collateralized short-term loans, and other sources of short-term financing that are available to firms, both large and small. As you read this chapter, think about the various sources that are available to companies for financing day-to-day operations. Without such alternatives, many businesses, especially the smaller ones, could not survive. Also, as you will see, the costs and availability of short-term funds can vary widely, both over time and among alternative sources.

After reading this chapter, you should be able to answer the following questions:

- Does trade credit have a cost? For example, does a firm incur a cost when it does not take cash discounts?
- What types of loan arrangements do commercial banks offer?
- What is commercial paper? What types of firms can use commercial paper?
- How is the cost of short-term credit determined? Why is it necessary to compute the cost of credit?
- Which assets generally are considered good security for collateralized short-term loans? What are some of the arrangements that exist with secured short-term loans?

In Chapter 14, we discussed the decisions the financial manager must make concerning alternative current asset financing policies. We also showed how debt maturities can affect both risk and expected returns: Although short-term debt generally is riskier than long-term debt, it generally is also less expensive, and it can be obtained faster and under more flexible terms. The primary purpose of this chapter is to examine the different types of short-term credit that are available to the financial manager. We also examine some of the issues the financial manager must consider when selecting among the various types of short-term credit, or current, liabilities.

## SOURCES OF SHORT-TERM FINANCING

**short-term credit**
Any liability originally scheduled for repayment within one year.

Statements about the flexibility, cost, and riskiness of short-term debt versus long-term debt depend, to a large extent, on the type of short-term credit that actually is used. **Short-term credit** is defined as any liability *originally* scheduled for payment within one year. There are numerous sources of short-term funds, and in the following sections we describe four major types: (1) accruals, (2) accounts payable (trade credit), (3) bank loans, and (4) commercial paper. In addition, we discuss the costs of short-term funds and the factors that influence a firm's choice of a bank.

 **Self-Test Question**
What types of liabilities are included in short-term credit?

## ACCRUALS

Firms generally pay employees on a weekly, biweekly, or monthly basis, so the balance sheet typically will show some accrued wages. Similarly, the firm's own estimated income taxes, the Social Security and income taxes withheld from employee payrolls, and the sales taxes collected generally are paid on a weekly, monthly, or quarterly basis, so the balance sheet typically will show some accrued taxes along with accrued wages.

**accruals**
Continually recurring short-term liabilities; liabilities such as wages and taxes that increase spontaneously with operations.

As we showed in Chapter 14, **accruals** increase automatically, or spontaneously, as a firm's operations expand. Further, this type of debt generally is considered "free" in the sense that no explicit interest is paid on funds generated by accruals. However, a firm ordinarily cannot control its accruals: The timing of wage payments is set by economic forces and industry customs, whereas tax payment dates are established by law. Thus, firms use all the accruals they can, but they have little control over the levels of these accounts.

**Self-Test Questions**

What types of short-term credits are classified as accruals?

What is the *explicit* cost of accruals?

How much control do financial managers have over the dollar amount of accruals?

## ACCOUNTS PAYABLE (TRADE CREDIT)

Firms generally make purchases from other firms (for example, suppliers) on credit, recording the debt as an *account payable*. This type of financing, which is called **trade credit,** is the largest single category of short-term debt, representing about 40 percent of the current liabilities for the average nonfinancial corporation. The percentage is somewhat larger for smaller firms: Because small companies often do not qualify for financing from other sources, they rely especially heavily on trade credit.[1]

Trade credit is a *spontaneous* source of financing in the sense that it arises from ordinary business transactions. For example, suppose a firm makes average purchases of $2,000 per day on terms of net 30, meaning that it must pay for goods 30 days after the invoice date.

As we saw in Chapter 14, on average, the firm will owe 30 times $2,000, or $60,000, to its suppliers. If its sales, and consequently its purchases, were to double, then the firm's accounts payable also would double, to $120,000. So simply by growing, the firm would have spontaneously generated an additional $60,000 of financing. Similarly, if the terms under which it purchases from suppliers are extended from 30 to 40 days, its accounts payable would expand from $60,000 to $80,000.

Thus, lengthening the credit period, as well as expanding sales and purchases, generates additional financing.

**trade credit**
The credit created when one firm buys on credit from another firm.

### The Cost of Trade Credit

As we discussed in Chapter 15, firms that sell on credit have a *credit policy* that includes certain *terms of credit*. For example, Microchip Electronics sells on credit with terms of 2/10, net 30, which means that Microchip gives its customers a 2 percent discount from the invoice price if payment is made within 10 days of the billing date; otherwise, if the discount is not taken, the full invoice amount is due and must be paid within 30 days of the billing date.

Note that the *true* price of the products Microchip offers is the net price, which is 98 percent of the list price, because any customer can purchase an item at a 2 percent "discount" as long as payment is made within 10 days. Consider Personal Computer Company (PCC), which buys its memory chips from Microchip. One commonly used memory chip is listed at $100, so the true cost to PCC is $98. If PCC wants an additional 20 days of credit beyond the 10-day discount period, it will effectively incur a finance charge of $2 per chip for that credit. Thus, the $100 list price can be thought of as follows:

$$\$100 \text{ list price} = \$98 \text{ true price} + \$2 \text{ finance charge}$$

The question that PCC must ask before it takes the additional 20 days of credit from Microchip is whether the firm could obtain similar credit with better terms from

---

[1]In a credit sale, the seller records the transaction as a receivable, whereas the buyer records the transaction as a payable. We examined accounts receivable as an asset investment in Chapter 15. Our focus in this chapter is on accounts payable, a liability item. We should also note that if a firm's payables exceed its receivables, it is said to be *receiving net trade credit,* whereas if its receivables exceed its payables, it is *extending net trade credit.* Smaller firms frequently receive net credit; larger firms generally extend it.

some other lender, say, a bank. In other words, could 20 days of credit be obtained for less than $2 per item?

To answer the question as to whether PCC should take the cash discount, we must compute the cost of using trade credit to finance the firm. The cost of short-term credit is discussed later in this chapter.

## Components of Trade Credit: Free versus Costly

**"free" trade credit**
Credit received during the discount period.

**costly trade credit**
Credit taken in excess of "free" trade credit, whose cost is equal to the discount lost.

On the basis of the preceding discussion, trade credit can be divided into two components: (1) **"free" trade credit,** which involves credit received during the discount period, and (2) **costly trade credit** which involves credit in excess of the free trade credit and whose cost is an implicit one based on the forgone discounts.[2] *Financial managers always should use the free component, but they should use the costly component only after analyzing the cost of this source of financing to make sure that it is less than the cost of funds that could be obtained from other sources.* Under the terms of trade found in most industries, the costly component will involve a relatively high percentage cost (usually greater than 25 percent), so stronger firms will take the cash discounts offered and avoid using trade credit as a source of additional financing.

Firms sometimes can and do deviate from the stated credit terms, thus altering the percentage cost figures cited. For example, a California manufacturing firm that buys on terms of 2/10, net 30, makes a practice of paying in 15 days (rather than 10 days), but it still takes discounts. Its treasurer simply waits until 15 days after receipt of the goods to pay and then writes a check for the invoiced amount less the 2 percent discount. The company's suppliers want its business, so they tolerate this practice. Similarly, a Wisconsin firm that also buys on terms of 2/10, net 30, does not take discounts, but it pays in 60 days rather than in 30 days, thus **stretching** its **accounts payable.** Both practices reduce the cost of trade credit. Neither of these firms is "loved" by its suppliers, and neither could continue these practices in times when suppliers operate at full capacity and have order backlogs, but these practices can and do reduce the costs of trade credit to customers during times when suppliers have excess capacity.

**stretching accounts payable**
The practice of deliberately paying accounts payable late.

> ### Self-Test Questions
> What is trade credit?
>
> What is the difference between free trade credit and costly trade credit?
>
> How does the cost of costly trade credit generally compare with the cost of other short-term sources of funds?

## SHORT-TERM BANK LOANS

Commercial banks, whose loans generally appear on firms' balance sheets as notes payable, are second in importance to trade credit as a source of short-term financing.[3] The influence of banks actually is greater than it appears from the dollar amounts they

---

[2]There is some question as to whether any credit is really "free" because the supplier will have a cost of carrying receivables, which must be passed on to the customer in the form of higher prices. Still, if suppliers sell on standard credit terms such as 2/10, net 30, and if the base price cannot be negotiated downward for early payment, then for all intents and purposes the 10 days of trade credit are indeed "free."

[3]Although commercial banks remain the primary source of short-term loans, other sources are available. For example, in 2006 GE Capital Corporation (GECC) had several billion dollars in commercial loans outstanding. Firms such as GECC, which was initially established to finance consumers' purchases of GE's durable goods, often find business loans to be more profitable than consumer loans.

lend because banks provide *nonspontaneous* funds. As a firm's financing needs increase, it specifically requests additional funds from its bank. If the request is denied, the firm might be forced to abandon attractive growth opportunities. The key features of bank loans are discussed in this section.

## Maturity

Although banks do make longer-term loans, the *bulk of their commercial lending is on a short-term basis.* Bank loans to businesses frequently are written as 90-day notes, so the loan must be repaid or renewed at the end of 90 days. Of course, if a borrower's financial position has deteriorated, the bank might refuse to renew the loan. This can mean serious trouble for the borrower.

## Promissory Note

When a bank loan is approved, the agreement is executed by signing a **promissory note.** The note specifies (1) the amount borrowed; (2) the interest rate; (3) the repayment schedule, which can call for payment either as a lump sum or as a series of installments; (4) any collateral that has to be put up as security for the loan; and (5) any other terms and conditions to which the bank and the borrower have agreed. When the note is signed, the bank credits the borrower's checking account with the amount of the loan, so on the borrower's balance sheet both cash and notes payable increase equally. (See Chapter 14 for an example.)

**promissory note**
A document specifying the terms and conditions of a loan, including the amount, interest rate, and repayment schedule.

## Compensating Balances

Banks sometimes require borrowers to maintain an average demand deposit (checking account) balance equal to from 10 percent to 20 percent of the amount borrowed. This is called a **compensating balance.** In effect, the bank charges borrowers for servicing the loans (bookkeeping, maintaining a line of credit, and so on) by requiring compensating balances, and such balances might increase the effective interest rate on the loans.[4] Calculating the cost of a bank loan is discussed in the next section.

**compensating balance**
A minimum checking account balance that a firm must maintain with a bank to borrow funds—generally 10 to 20 percent of the amount of loans outstanding.

## Line of Credit

A **line of credit** is an agreement between a bank and a borrower indicating the maximum credit the bank will extend to the borrower. For example, on December 31 a bank loan officer might indicate to a financial manager that the bank regards the firm as being "good" for up to $200,000 during the forthcoming year. If on January 10 the financial manager signs a 90-day promissory note for $60,000, this would be called "drawing, or taking, down" $60,000 of the total line of credit. This amount would be credited to the firm's checking account at the bank, and before repayment of the $60,000, the firm could borrow additional amounts up to a *total* of $200,000 outstanding at any one time. So, if the firm has $60,000 "drawn" on its line of credit, it could borrow an additional $140,000 at any time.

When a line of credit is *guaranteed,* it is called a **revolving credit agreement.** A revolving credit agreement is similar to a regular, or general, line of credit, except the

**line of credit**
An arrangement in which a bank agrees to lend up to a specified maximum amount of funds during a designated period.

**revolving (line of) credit agreement**
A formal, committed line of credit extended by a bank or other lending institution.

---

[4]Note, however, that the compensating balance might be set as a minimum monthly *average,* and if the firm generally maintains this average anyway, the compensating balance requirement might not raise the effective interest rate. Also, note that these *loan* compensating balances often are added to any compensating balances that the firm's bank might require for *services performed,* such as clearing checks.

**commitment fee**
A fee charged on the *unused* balance of a revolving credit agreement to compensate the bank for guaranteeing that the funds will be available when needed by the borrower; the fee normally is about 1/4 percent of the unused balance.

bank has a *legal obligation* to provide the funds when requested by the borrower. The bank generally charges a **commitment fee** on the unused balance (sometimes on the total credit commitment) of the credit line for guaranteeing the availability of the funds. To illustrate, in 2006 Dakota Paper Company (DPC) negotiated a revolving credit agreement for $100 million with a group of banks. The banks were formally committed for four years to lend the firm up to $100 million *if the funds were needed*. DPC, in turn, paid an annual *commitment fee* of 1/4 percent on the unused balance of the guaranteed line of credit. Thus, if DPC did not draw down any of the $100 million commitment during a year, it would still be required to pay a $250,000 annual fee (1/4 percent of the $100 million credit agreement), normally in monthly installments of $20,833. If DPC borrowed $60 million on the first day of the agreement, the unused portion of the line of credit would fall to $40 million, and the annual commitment fee would fall to $100,000 = 0.0025 × $40 million. Of course, interest also would have to be paid on the money DPC actually borrowed. As a general rule, the rate of interest on "revolvers" is pegged to the prime rate, so the cost of the loan varies over time as interest rates change.[5] DPC's rate was set at prime plus 1/2 percentage point.

Note that an important feature distinguishes a revolving credit agreement from a general line of credit: The bank has a *legal obligation* to honor a revolving credit agreement, and it receives a commitment fee for guaranteeing that the funds will be available when requested by the borrower. Neither the legal obligation nor the fee exists under the general line of credit.

## The Cost of Bank Loans

The cost of bank loans varies for different types of borrowers at any given point in time and for all borrowers over time. Interest rates are higher for riskier borrowers, and rates also are higher on smaller loans because of the fixed costs involved in making and servicing loans. If a firm can qualify as a "prime credit" because of its size and financial strength, it might be able to borrow at the **prime rate,** which traditionally has been the lowest rate banks charge. Rates on other loans generally are scaled up from the prime rate.[6]

**prime rate**
A published rate of interest charged by banks to short-term borrowers (usually large, financially secure corporations) with the best credit; rates on short-term loans generally are "pegged" to the prime rate.

Bank rates vary widely over time depending on economic conditions and the Federal Reserve policy. When the economy is weak, then (1) loan demand usually is slack, (2) inflation is low, and (3) the Fed also makes plenty of money available to the system. As a result, rates on all types of loans are relatively low. Conversely, when the economy is booming, loan demand typically is strong and the Fed restricts the money supply; the result is high interest rates. As an indication of the kinds of fluctuations that can occur, during 1980 the prime rate exhibited a roller-coaster pattern—it declined from 20 percent in April to 11 percent in July and then rose again to more than 21 percent by the end of the year. In more recent times, the prime rate was 8.25 percent during the latter half of 2006 but only 4 percent in 2003. Interest rates on other bank loans also vary, generally moving with the prime rate.

---

[5]Each bank sets its own prime rate, but because of competitive forces, most banks' prime rates are identical. Further, most banks follow the rate set by the large New York City banks.

[6]In recent years, many banks have been lending to the strongest companies at rates below the prime rate. As we discuss later in this chapter, larger firms have ready access to the commercial paper market, and if banks want to do business with these larger companies, they must match or at least come close to the commercial paper rate. As competition in financial markets increases, as it has been doing because of the deregulation of banks and other financial institutions, "administered" rates such as the prime rate are giving way to flexible, negotiated rates based on market conditions.

## CHOOSING A BANK

Individuals whose only contact with their bank is through the use of its checking services generally choose a bank for the convenience of its location and the competitive cost of its services. However, a business that borrows from banks must look at other criteria, and a potential borrower seeking banking relations should recognize that important differences exist among banks. Some of these differences are considered here.

### Willingness to Assume Risks

Banks have different basic policies toward risk. Some banks are inclined to follow relatively conservative lending practices, whereas others engage in what are properly termed "creative banking practices." These policies reflect partly the personalities of officers of the bank and partly the characteristics of the bank's deposit liabilities. Thus, a bank with fluctuating deposit liabilities in a static community will tend to be a conservative lender, whereas a bank whose deposits are growing with little interruption might follow more liberal credit policies. Similarly, a large bank with broad diversification over geographic regions or across industries can obtain the benefit of combining and averaging risks. Thus, marginal credit risks that might be unacceptable to a small bank or a specialized bank can be pooled by a large branch banking system to reduce the overall risk of a group of marginal accounts.

### Advice and Counsel

Some bank loan officers are active in providing counsel and in stimulating development loans to firms in their early and formative years. Certain banks have specialized departments that make loans to firms expected to grow and thus to become more important customers. The personnel of these departments can provide valuable counseling to customers.

### Loyalty to Customers

Banks differ in the extent to which they will support the activities of borrowers in bad times. This characteristic is referred to as the degree of *loyalty* of the bank. Some banks might put great pressure on a business to liquidate its loans when the firm's outlook becomes clouded, whereas others will stand by the firm and work diligently to help it get back on its feet.

### Specialization

Banks differ greatly in their degrees of loan specialization. Larger banks have separate departments that specialize in different kinds of loans—for example, real estate loans, farm loans, and commercial loans. Within these broad categories, there might be a specialization by line of business, such as steel, machinery, cattle, or textiles. The strengths of banks also are likely to reflect the nature of the business and the economic environment in which the banks operate. For example, some California banks have become specialists in lending to technology companies, whereas many Midwestern banks are agricultural specialists. A sound firm can obtain more creative cooperation and more active support by going to a bank that has experience and familiarity with its particular type of business. Therefore, a bank that is excellent for one firm might be unsatisfactory for another.

## Maximum Loan Size

The size of a bank can be an important factor. Because the maximum loan a bank can make to any one customer is limited to 15 percent of the bank's capital accounts (capital stock plus retained earnings), it generally is not appropriate for large firms to develop borrowing relationships with small banks.

## Merchant Banking

The term *merchant bank* originally was applied to banks that not only loaned depositors' money but also provided customers with equity capital and financial advice. Prior to 1933, U.S. commercial banks performed all types of merchant banking functions. However, about one-third of the U.S. banks failed during the Great Depression, in part because of these activities, so in 1933 the Glass-Steagall Act was passed in an effort to reduce banks' exposure to risk. Recent legislation has allowed commercial banks to get back into merchant banking, in part because their foreign competitors offer such services, and U.S. banks need to be able to compete with their foreign counterparts for multinational corporations' business. Currently, the larger banks, often through holding companies, do offer merchant banking. Thus, corporations will need to consider a bank's ability to provide a full range of commercial and merchant banking services when choosing a bank.

## Other Services

Many banks also provide cash management services such as those described in Chapter 15, assist with electronic funds transfers, help firms obtain foreign exchange, and the like, and the availability of such services should be taken into account when selecting a bank. Also, if the firm is a small business whose manager owns most of its stock, the bank's willingness and ability to provide trust and estate services also should be considered.

**Self-Test Question**

What are some of the factors that should be considered when choosing a bank?

## COMMERCIAL PAPER

**commercial paper**
Unsecured, short-term promissory notes issued by large, financially sound firms to raise funds.

**Commercial paper** is a type of unsecured promissory note issued by large, financially strong firms, and it is sold primarily to other businesses, insurance companies, pension funds, money market mutual funds, and banks. This form of financing has grown rapidly in recent years—in 2006 the amount of commercial paper outstanding was about the same as the amount of regular business loans.

## Use of Commercial Paper

The use of commercial paper is restricted to a comparatively small number of firms that are *exceptionally* good credit risks. Dealers prefer to handle the "paper" of firms whose net worth is $100 million or more and whose annual borrowing exceeds $10 million. One potential problem with commercial paper is that a debtor who is in temporary financial difficulty might receive little help because commercial paper dealings generally are less personal than are bank relationships. Thus, banks generally are more able and willing to help a good customer weather a temporary storm than is a commercial paper dealer. On the other hand, using commercial paper permits a corporation to tap a wider range of credit sources, including financial institutions outside its own area and industrial corporations across the country, and this can reduce interest costs.

## Maturity and Cost

Generally, commercial paper is issued in denominations of $100,000 or greater, so few individuals can afford to invest *directly* in the commercial paper market. Maturities of commercial paper vary from one to nine months, with an average of about five months.[7] The rate on commercial paper fluctuates with supply and demand conditions—it is determined in the marketplace, varying daily as conditions change. Generally, the rates on commercial paper are lower than the stated prime rate of interest. For example, in November 2006, the average rate on 90-day commercial paper was 5.4 percent, which was 2.9 percent less than the prime rate but 0.3 percent greater than 90-day Treasury bill rates.

Commercial paper is called a discount instrument because it is sold at a price below its face, or maturity, value. The cost of using commercial paper as a source of financing is computed the same as for a discount interest loan, which is discussed in the next section.

### Self-Test Questions

What is commercial paper?

What types of companies can use commercial paper to meet their short-term financing needs?

How does the cost of commercial paper compare with the cost of short-term bank loans? With the cost of Treasury bills?

## COMPUTING THE COST OF SHORT-TERM CREDIT

For short-term financing, the percentage cost of using the funds for a given period, $r_{PER}$, can be computed as

$$\frac{\text{Percentage cost}}{\text{per period}} = r_{PER} = \frac{\text{Dollar cost of borrowing}}{\text{Amount of usable funds}}$$

**16–1**

In this equation, the numerator represents the dollar amount that must be paid for using the borrowed funds. This cost includes the interest paid on the loan, application fees, charges for commitment fees, and so forth. The denominator represents the

---

[7]The maximum maturity without SEC registration is 270 days. Also, commercial paper can be sold only to "sophisticated" investors; otherwise, SEC registration would be required even for maturities of 270 days or less.

amount of the loan that actually can be used (spent) by the borrower. This amount is not necessarily the same as the principal amount of the loan because discounts, compensating balances, or other costs might reduce the amount of the loan proceeds that the firm can actually use. We show that *when loan restrictions prevent the borrower from using the entire amount of the loan, the effective annual rate paid for the loan is higher than the stated interest rate.*

Using Equation 16–1 and the concepts described in Chapter 4, the effective annual rate (EAR) and the annual percentage rate (APR) for short-term financing can be computed as follows:

**16–2**

$$\text{Effective annual rate (EAR)} = (1 + r_{PER})^m - 1.0 = r_{EAR}$$

**16-3**

$$\text{Annual percentage rate (APR)} = r_{PER} \times m = r_{SIMPLE}$$

where m is the number of borrowing (interest) periods in one year—that is, if the loan is for one month, m = 12. Recall from our discussion in Chapter 4 that the EAR incorporates interest compounding in the computation, but the APR does not. Both computations adjust the percentage cost per period so that it is stated on an annual basis. We annualize the cost to make it easier to compare short-term credit instruments with different maturities.

Next we illustrate the application of these equations for computing the cost of three short-term financing alternatives: (1) trade credit, (2) bank loans, and (3) commercial paper.

## Computing the Cost of Trade Credit (Accounts Payable)

Consider Microchip's credit terms of 2/10, net 30, which allow its customers, such as Personal Computer Company (PCC), to take a 2 percent discount from the purchase price if payment is made on or before Day 10 of the billing cycle; otherwise, the entire bill is due by Day 30. If the invoice price is $100 and the firm does not take the discount, it effectively pays $2 to borrow $98 for a 20-day period, so the cost of using the funds for the additional 20 days is

$$\text{Periodic rate} = r_{PER} = \frac{\$2}{\$98} = 0.020408 \approx 2.041\%$$

Because there are 18 = 360/20 20-day periods in a 360-day year, the APR, or simple interest rate, associated with the trade credit is

$$\text{APR} = r_{SIMPLE} = 2.041\% \times 18 = 36.7\%$$

The effective annual cost (rate), EAR, of using trade credit with these terms as a source of short-term financing is

$$\text{EAR} = r_{EAR} = (1 + 0.02041)^{18} - 1.0 = 0.439 = 43.9\%$$

According to this computation, if PCC chooses to pay its bill on Day 30, then it will "forgo" the 2 percent cash discount, which is equivalent to borrowing funds at a rate of nearly 44 percent per year.[8] PCC should forgo the cash discount to pay on Day 30 only if alternative financing, such as bank loans, has a cost greater than 43.9 percent.

## Computing the Cost of Bank Loans

A bank loan can take the form of a *simple interest loan,* a *discount loan,* or an *installment loan.* Factors such as a compensating balance or application fees can affect the cost of borrowing for each of these types of loans. Here we give some examples as to how to compute the cost for each of these loans.

### Simple Interest Loan

With a **simple interest loan,** the borrower receives the **face value** of the loan—that is, the amount borrowed, or the principal—and repays both the principal and the interest at maturity. For example, with a simple interest loan of $10,000 at 12 percent interest for nine months, the borrower receives the $10,000 upon approval of the loan and pays back the $10,000 principal plus $900 = $10,000[0.12 × (9/12)] in interest at maturity. Note that interest is paid only for the portion of the year the loan is outstanding, which is nine months in this case. The 12 percent is the **quoted, or simple, interest rate** ($r_{SIMPLE}$).

The nine-month interest rate for this loan is

$$r_{PER} = \frac{\text{Nine-month}}{\text{interest rate}} = \frac{\$10,000 \times \left[0.12 \times \left(\frac{9}{12}\right)\right]}{\$10,000} = 0.090 = 9.00\%$$

The APR for this loan is

$$APR = 9.0\% \times \left(\frac{12}{9}\right) = 12.00\%$$

The EAR is

$$r_{EAR} = (1.09)^{\left(12/9\right)} - 1.0 = 0.1218 = 12.18\%$$

$r_{EAR} > APR$ because this is a nine-month loan, which means interest compounding is assumed to occur every nine months.

### Discount Interest Loan

With a **discount interest loan,** the interest due is deducted "up front" so that the borrower receives less than the principal amount, or face value, of the loan. Assume Unilate Textiles receives a nine-month $10,000 discount interest loan with a 12 percent quoted (simple) interest rate. The interest payment on this loan is $900 = $10,000[0.12 × (9/12)]. Because the interest is paid in advance, Unilate has only

**simple interest loan**
Both the amount borrowed and the interest charged on that amount are paid at the maturity of the loan; there are no payments made before maturity.

**face value**
The amount of the loan, or the amount borrowed; also called the *principal amount* of the loan.

**quoted (simple) interest rate, $r_{EAR}$**
The annual percentage rate (APR) that is used to compute the interest rate per period ($r_{PER}$).

**discount interest loan**
A loan in which the interest, which is calculated on the amount borrowed (principal), is paid at the beginning of the loan period; interest is paid in advance.

---

[8]We assume that the firm pays its supplier on the last day possible. That is, if it takes the discount, payment is made on Day 10; if it doesn't take the discount, payment is made on Day 30. This is rational business behavior. If, however, the firm does not take the discount, but pays on Day 20 (or any other time before the final due date), then the cost associated with using this source of financing is higher than computed here. The funds cost more because the firm uses them for a shorter period.

$9,100 = $10,000 − $900 available for use. Thus, the nine-month interest rate paid for the loan is

$$r_{PER} = \frac{\text{Nine-month}}{\text{interest rate}} = \frac{\$10,000 \times \left[ 0.12 \times \left( \frac{9}{12} \right) \right]}{\$10,000 - \left\{ \$10,000 \left[ 0.12 \times \left( \frac{9}{12} \right) \right] \right\}}$$

$$= \frac{\$900}{\$9,100} = 0.0989 = 9.89\%$$

The APR for this loan is

$$APR = 9.89\% \times \left( \frac{12}{9} \right) = 13.19\%$$

The EAR is

$$r_{EAR} = (1.0989)^{(12/9)} - 1.0 = 0.1340 = 13.40\%$$

What do you think the cost of the loan described here would be if Unilate's bank charged a $50 fee to cover the cost of processing the loan? To answer this question, first take a look at Equation 16–1 and determine whether the payment affects the numerator (that is, the dollar cost of borrowing), the denominator (that is, the amount of usable funds), or both. The general rule is that the numerator is affected by any expense associated with the loan, and the denominator is affected if funds must be put aside (for example, to satisfy a compensating balance requirement) or costs are paid out of the proceeds at the beginning of the loan period. Thus, if Unilate uses the proceeds from the loan to pay the $50 fee, both the numerator and the denominator are affected, and the nine-month interest rate is

$$r_{PER} = \frac{\text{Nine-month}}{\text{interest rate}} = \frac{\$900 + \$50}{\$9,100 - \$50} = \frac{\$950}{\$9,050} = 0.1050 = 10.50\%$$

Check to see that the APR and $r_{EAR}$ are now 14.0 percent and 14.2 percent, respectively.

### Installment Loan: Add-On Interest

**add-on interest**
Interest that is calculated and then added to the amount borrowed to obtain the total dollar amount to be paid back in equal installments.

Lenders often charge **add-on interest** on various types of installment loans. The term *add-on* means that the interest is calculated and then added to the amount borrowed to obtain the total dollar amount to be paid back in equal installments. To illustrate, suppose Unilate borrows $10,000 on an add-on basis at a simple rate of 12 percent, with the loan to be repaid in nine monthly installments. At a 12 percent add-on rate, Unilate will pay a total interest charge of $900 as computed earlier, and a total of $10,900 in nine equal payments. The monthly payments would be $1,211.11 = $10,900/9. Therefore, each month Unilate would pay $100 interest (1/9 of the total interest) and $1,111.11 principal repayment (1/9 of the $10,000 borrowed). Because the loan is paid off in monthly installments, Unilate will have use of the full $10,000 only for the first month, and the outstanding balance declines by $1,111.11 each month such that the remaining principal due at the beginning of the last month of the loan is $1,111.11. As a result, the percent cost of the loan varies each month.

Unilate would pay $900 for the use of approximately 50 percent of the loan's face amount because the average outstanding balance of the loan is only about $5,000 = ($10,000 + $0)/2. (The $10,000 is paid down evenly over the life of the loan.) With this information, we can *approximate* the rate for the nine-month period as follows:

$$\frac{\text{Approximate rate}}{\text{per period}} = \frac{\$900}{\$5,000} = 0.18 = 18.0\%$$

The *approximate* APR would be $24.0\% = 18.0\% \times (12/9)$.

To determine the EAR, recognize that the $1,211.11 payment Unilate makes each month represents an annuity. The cash flow time line for the loan would be

Using a financial calculator, enter N = 9, PV = −10,000, PMT = 1,211.11, and then solve for I. The *monthly* rate equals 1.759. In this case, we assume monthly compounding because the installment payments are made each month. When we annualize the monthly rate, the EAR is

$$r_{EAR} = (1.01759)^{12} - 1.0 = 0.2327 = 23.27\%$$

## Computing the Cost of Commercial Paper

Suppose Unilate issues 270-day commercial paper with a face value equal to $10,000. The simple annual interest rate on the commercial paper is 12 percent, and the total transactions fee, which includes the cost of a backup line of credit, is 1/2 percent of the amount of the issue. Because commercial paper is a discount instrument similar to a discount loan, Unilate will not be able to use the total $10,000 face value. Instead, investors will purchase the commercial paper issue for $9,100 = $10,000 − $10,000[0.12 × (9/12)], and then receive $10,000 at maturity. The transaction fee, which equals $50 = 0.005 × $10,000, is "taken off the top," so Unilate actually would receive only $9,050 = $9,100 − $50 to use from the commercial paper issue. The total dollar cost of borrowing using commercial paper would be $950, which includes interest equal to $900 and the $50 transaction fee. As a result, the nine-month cost of the commercial paper would be

$$r_{PER} = \frac{\text{Nine-month}}{\text{interest rate}} = \frac{\$10,000 \times \left[0.12 \times \left(\frac{9}{12}\right)\right] + (0.005 \times \$10,000)}{\$10,000 - \left\{\$10,000\left[0.12 \times \left(\frac{9}{12}\right)\right]\right\} - (0.005 \times \$10,000)}$$

$$= \frac{\$900 + \$50}{\$9,050} = 0.1050 = 10.50\%$$

The APR for this loan is

$$APR = 10.50\% \times \left(\frac{12}{9}\right) = 14.00\%$$

The EAR is

$$r_{EAR} = (1.1050)^{(12/9)} - 1.0 = 0.1424 = 14.24\%$$

## Borrowed (Principal) Amount versus Required (Needed) Amount

Compensating balances can raise the effective rate on a loan. To illustrate, suppose Unilate *needs* $10,000 to pay for some equipment it recently purchased. Atlantic/Pacific Bank offers to lend Unilate the money for nine months at a 12 percent simple rate, but the company must maintain a *compensating balance* equal to 20 percent of the loan amount (principal, or face value). First, note that Unilate needs to be able to use $10,000 to pay for the equipment. If the firm's checking account balance is not sufficient to cover the compensating balance requirement, then the principal amount of the loan must be greater than $10,000 because some of the amount borrowed must be put aside to satisfy the compensating balance requirement. In this case, the question is: How much must be borrowed so the firm will have $10,000 available for use? To answer this question, first we must determine the *usable funds* from a loan:

**16–4**

$$\text{Usable funds} = \left[\begin{array}{c}\text{Face (principal)}\\\text{amount of the loan}\end{array}\right] - \left(\begin{array}{c}\text{Dollar reductions}\\\text{from the face value}\end{array}\right)$$

If the dollar reductions from the face value of the loan are stated as percentages—for example, compensating balances—Equation 16–4 can be written as follows:

**16-4a**

$$\text{Usable funds} = \left[\begin{array}{c}\text{Face (principal)}\\\text{amount of the loan}\end{array}\right] \times \left[1 - \left(\begin{array}{c}\text{Reductions from the face}\\\text{value stated as a decimal}\end{array}\right)\right]$$

If we know how much of the amount borrowed actually is needed as usable funds, Equation 16–4a can be rearranged to solve for the amount that must be borrowed (principal amount) to provide these needed funds. The computation is

**16–5**

$$\begin{array}{c}\text{Required loan}\\\text{(principal) amount}\end{array} = \dfrac{\text{Amount of usable funds needed}}{1 - \left[\begin{array}{c}\text{Reductions from the principal}\\\text{amount (face) stated as a decimal}\end{array}\right]}$$

If it does not have a checking account at Atlantic/Pacific Bank, then Unilate will have to borrow $12,500 to be able to satisfy the 20 percent compensating balance requirement and have $10,000 available to pay for the equipment. The computation follows:

$$\begin{array}{c}\text{Required loan}\\\text{(principal) amount}\end{array} = \frac{\$10,000}{1 - 0.20} = \$12,500$$

In this case, the nine-month rate for this loan would be

$$r_{PER} = \frac{\text{Nine-month}}{\text{interest rate}} = \frac{\$12{,}500 \times \left[0.12 \times \left(\dfrac{9}{12}\right)\right]}{\$12{,}500 - \$12{,}500(0.20)} = \frac{\$1{,}125}{\$10{,}000} = 0.1125 = 11.25\%$$

The APR and EAR are

$$APR = 11.25\% \times \left(\frac{12}{9}\right) = 15.00\%$$

$$r_{EAR} = (1.1125)^{(12/9)} - 1.0 = 0.1527 = 15.27\%$$

If a firm normally keeps a positive checking account balance at the lending bank, then (1) it needs to borrow less to have a specific amount of funds available for use, and (2) the effective cost of the loan will be lower.

From the examples presented here, you should recognize that the percentage cost of short-term financing is higher when the dollar expenses, such as those associated with interest, clerical efforts, and loan processing, are higher, when the net proceeds from the loan are less than the principal amount, or when both conditions exist. In most cases, then, the effective interest rate (cost) of short-term financing is greater than its stated (quoted) interest rate. *The effective interest rate of a loan is equal to the quoted (simple) rate only if (1) the entire principal amount borrowed can be used by the borrower for one full year and (2) the only dollar cost associated with the loan is interest charged on the outstanding balance.*

### Self-Test Questions

What is the difference between APR and $r_{EAR}$?

All else equal, what causes the APR and $r_{EAR}$ to increase?

How does a discount loan differ from an installment loan?

For what reasons would the amount of a loan that a borrower can actually use be less than the principal amount borrowed?

Everything else equal, how does the effective cost of a loan compare with its simple interest rate if (1) the usable amount is less than the principal amount or (2) the loan period is less than one year?

Suppose you apply for a $5,000 discount loan with an 8 percent quoted interest rate. If this is a six-month loan, what is its APR and $r_{EAR}$? (*Answer:* APR = 8.3%, $r_{EAR}$ = 8.5%)

If a supplier offers terms of 3/20, net 60 to its customers, what is the cost associated with forgoing the cash discount and paying the supplier on Day 60? Compute both the APR and $r_{EAR}$. (*Answer:* APR = 27.8%, $r_{EAR}$ = 31.5%)

## USE OF SECURITY IN SHORT-TERM FINANCING

Thus far we have not addressed the question of whether loans should be secured. Commercial paper is not secured, but all other types of loans can be secured if this is deemed necessary or desirable. Given a choice, it ordinarily is better to borrow on an

**secured loan**
A loan backed by collateral; for short-term loans, the collateral often is inventory, receivables, or both.

unsecured basis because the bookkeeping costs of **secured loans** often are high. However, weak firms might find that they can borrow only if they put up some type of security or that by using security they can borrow at a lower rate.

Several different kinds of security, or collateral, can be used, including marketable securities, land or buildings, equipment, inventory, and accounts receivable. Marketable securities make excellent collateral, but few firms that need loans also hold such portfolios. Similarly, real property (land and buildings) and equipment are good forms of collateral, but they generally are used as security for long-term loans rather than for working capital loans. Therefore, most secured short-term business borrowing involves the use of accounts receivable and inventories as collateral.

To understand the use of security, consider the case of a Chicago hardware dealer who wanted to modernize and expand his store. He requested a $200,000 bank loan. After examining his firm's financial statements, the bank indicated that it would lend him a maximum of $100,000 and that the interest rate would be 12 percent, discount interest, for an effective rate of 13.6 percent. The owner had a substantial personal portfolio of stocks, and he offered to put up $300,000 of high-quality stocks to support the $200,000 loan. The bank then granted the full $200,000 loan, and at a rate of only 11 percent, simple interest. The store owner also might have used his inventories or receivables as security for the loan, but processing costs would have been high.[9]

**Uniform Commercial Code**
A system of standards that simplifies procedures for establishing loan security.

In the past, state laws have varied greatly with regard to the use of security in financing. Today, however, nearly every secured loan is established under the **Uniform Commercial Code,** which has standardized and simplified the procedures for establishing loan security. The heart of the Uniform Commercial Code is the *Security Agreement,* a standardized document on which the specific pledged assets are listed. The assets can be items of equipment, accounts receivable, or inventories. Procedures under the Uniform Commercial Code for using accounts receivable and inventories as security for short-term credit are described in the following sections.

## Accounts Receivable Financing

**pledging receivables**
Using accounts receivable as collateral for a loan.

Accounts receivable financing involves either the pledging of receivables or the selling of receivables (called *factoring*). The **pledging** of accounts receivable is characterized by the fact that the lender not only has a claim against the receivables but also has **recourse** to the borrower: If the person or firm that bought the goods does not pay, the selling firm (borrower), not the lender, must take the loss. Therefore, the risk of default on the pledged accounts receivable remains with the borrowing firm. The customer of the borrowing firm ordinarily is not notified about the pledging of the receivables, and the financial institution that lends on the security of accounts receivable generally is either a commercial bank or one of the large industrial finance companies.

**recourse**
The lender can seek payment from the borrowing firm when receivables accounts used to secure a loan are uncollectible.

**Factoring,** or *selling accounts receivable*, involves the purchase of accounts receivable by the lender (called a factor), generally without recourse to the borrower, which means that if a receivable account that is factored cannot be collected, the lender, not the seller of the goods (borrower), takes the loss. Under factoring, the borrowing firm's customers generally are notified of the transfer and are asked to make payments directly to the lending institution (factor). Because the factor assumes the risk of default on bad accounts, it generally carries out the credit investigation. Accordingly, factors provide not only money but also a credit department for the

**factoring**
The outright sale of receivables.

---

[9]The term *asset-based financing* is often used as a synonym for *secured financing*. In recent years, accounts receivable have been used as security for long-term bonds, and this permits corporations to borrow from lenders such as pension funds rather than being restricted to banks and other traditional short-term lenders.

borrower. Incidentally, the same financial institutions that make loans against pledged receivables also serve as factors. Thus, depending on the circumstances and the wishes of the borrower, a financial institution will provide either type of receivables financing.

## Procedure for Pledging Accounts Receivable

The financing (pledging) of accounts receivable is initiated by a legally binding agreement between the seller of the goods (borrower) and the financing institution (lender). The agreement sets forth in detail the procedures to be followed and the legal obligations of both parties. Once the working relationship has been established, the seller periodically takes a batch of invoices to the financing institution. The lender reviews the invoices and makes credit appraisals of the buyers. Invoices of companies that do not meet the lender's credit standards are not accepted for pledging.

The financial institution seeks to protect itself at every phase of the operation. First, selection of sound invoices is one way the lender safeguards itself. Second, if the buyer of the goods does not pay the invoice, the lender still has recourse against the seller (the borrowing firm). Third, additional protection is afforded the lender because the loan generally will be less than 100 percent of the pledged receivables; for example, the lender might advance the selling firm only 85 percent of the amount of the pledged invoices. The percent advanced depends on the quality of the accounts pledged.

## Procedure for Factoring Accounts Receivable

The procedures used in factoring are somewhat different from those for pledging. Again, an agreement between the seller and the factor specifies legal obligations and procedural arrangements. When the seller receives an order from a customer, a credit approval slip is written and immediately sent to the factoring company for a credit check. If the factor approves the credit, shipment is made and the invoice is stamped to notify the customer to make payment directly to the factoring company. If the factor does not approve the sale, the seller generally refuses to fill the order; if the sale is made anyway, the factor will not buy the account.

The factor normally performs three functions: (1) credit checking, (2) lending, and (3) risk bearing. Consider a typical factoring situation: The goods are shipped, and even though payment is not due for 30 days, the factor immediately makes funds available to the borrower (the firm selling the goods). Suppose $10,000 worth of goods are shipped. Further, assume that the factoring commission for credit checking and risk bearing is $2\frac{1}{2}$ percent of the invoice price, or $250, and that the interest expense is computed at a 9 percent annual rate on the invoice balance, or $75 = $10,000 \times (0.09/360) \times 30$ days. The selling firm would have the following:

| | |
|---|---:|
| Cash | $ 9,175 |
| Interest expense | 75 |
| Factoring commission | 250 |
| Reserve due from factor in collection account | 500 |
| Accounts receivable | $10,000 |

The $500 due from the factor upon collection of the account is a reserve established by the factor to cover disputes between the selling firm and customers over damaged goods, goods returned by customers to the selling firm, and the failure to make an outright sale of goods. The reserve is paid to the selling firm when the factor collects on the account.

Factoring normally is a continuous process instead of the single cycle just described. The firm that sells the goods receives an order; it transmits this order to the factor for approval; upon approval, the firm ships the goods; the factor advances the invoice amount minus withholdings to the selling firm; the buyer (customer) pays the factor when payment is due; and the factor periodically remits any excess in the reserve to the selling firm. Once a routine has been established, a continuous circular flow of goods and funds takes place among the selling firm, the buyers of the goods, and the factor. Thus, once the factoring agreement is in force, funds from this source are *spontaneous* in the sense that an increase in sales automatically generates additional credit.

Visa and MasterCard represent prime examples of nonrecourse factoring. When you purchase from a retailer such as Wal-Mart using Visa or MasterCard, the retailer is paid only 95 percent to 97 percent of the invoice by these credit companies. The reason the 3 percent to 5 percent discount is charged by Visa and MasterCard is because they provide credit-checking services and suffer any losses due to customer nonpayment—the retailer does not incur these costs.

## Cost of Receivables Financing

Both accounts receivable pledging and factoring are convenient and advantageous, but they can be costly. The credit-checking and risk-bearing fee is 1 percent to 5 percent of the amount of invoices accepted by the factor, and it could be even more if the buyers are poor credit risks. The cost of money is reflected in the interest rate (usually 2 to 3 percentage points over the prime rate) charged on the unpaid balance of the funds advanced by the factor.

## Evaluation of Receivables Financing

It cannot be said that accounts receivable financing is categorically either a good or a bad way to raise funds. Among the advantages is, first, the flexibility of this source of financing: As the firm's sales expand, more financing is needed, but a larger volume of invoices, and hence a larger amount of receivables financing, is generated automatically. Second, receivables can be used as security for loans that otherwise would not be granted. Third, factoring can provide the services of a credit department that otherwise might be available only at a higher cost.

Accounts receivable financing also has disadvantages. First, when invoices are numerous and relatively small in dollar amount, the administrative costs involved might be excessive. Second, because receivables represent the firm's most liquid noncash assets, some trade creditors might refuse to sell on credit to a firm that factors or pledges its receivables on the grounds that this practice weakens the firm's financial strength.

## Future Use of Receivables Financing

It is easy to make a prediction at this point: In the future, accounts receivable financing will increase in relative importance. Computer technology has advanced to the point where credit records of individuals and firms are kept on electronic media. For example, one device used by retailers consists of a box that, when an individual's magnetic credit card is inserted, gives a signal that the credit is "good" and that a bank is willing to "buy" the receivable created as soon as the store completes the sale. The cost of handling invoices will be reduced greatly over current costs because the new systems will be so electronically sophisticated. This will make it possible to use accounts receivable financing for very small sales, and it will reduce the cost of all receivables financing. The net result will be a marked expansion of accounts receivable financing.

## Inventory Financing

A substantial amount of credit is secured by business inventories. If a firm is a relatively good credit risk, the mere existence of the inventory might be a sufficient basis for receiving an unsecured loan. However, if the firm is a relatively poor risk, the lending institution might insist on security in the form of a *lien,* or legal claim, against the inventory. Methods for using inventories as security are discussed in this section.

### Blanket Liens

The *inventory blanket lien* gives the lending institution a lien against all of the borrower's inventories. However, the borrower is free to sell inventories, and thus the value of the collateral can be reduced below the level that existed when the loan was granted. A blanket lien generally is used when the inventory put up as collateral is relatively low priced, fast moving, and difficult to identify individually.

### Trust Receipts

Because of the inherent weakness of the blanket lien, another procedure for inventory financing has been developed—the *trust receipt,* which is an instrument acknowledging that the goods are held in trust for the lender. Under this method, the borrowing firm, as a condition for receiving funds from the lender, signs and delivers a trust receipt for the goods. The goods can be stored in a public warehouse or held on the premises of the borrower. The trust receipt states that the goods are held in trust for the lender or are segregated on the borrower's premises on the lender's behalf and that any proceeds from the sale of the goods must be transmitted to the lender at the end of each day. Automobile dealer financing is one of the best examples of trust receipt financing.

One defect of trust receipt financing is the requirement that a trust receipt be issued for specific goods. For example, if the security is automobiles in a dealer's inventory, the trust receipts must indicate the cars by registration number. To validate its trust receipts, the lending institution must send someone to the borrower's premises periodically to see that the auto numbers are listed correctly because auto dealers who are in financial difficulty have been known to sell cars backing trust receipts and then use the funds for other operations rather than to repay the bank. Problems are compounded if the borrower has a number of different locations, especially if they are separated geographically from the lender. To offset these inconveniences, *warehousing* has come into wide use as a method of securing loans with inventory.

### Warehouse Receipts

Warehouse receipt financing is another way to use inventory as security. A *public warehouse* is an independent third-party operation engaged in the business of storing goods. Items that require aging, such as tobacco and liquor, are often financed and stored in public warehouses. When the inventory products used as collateral are moved to public warehouses, the financing arrangement is termed *terminal warehousing.* Sometimes terminal warehousing is not practical because of the bulkiness of goods and the expense of transporting them to and from the borrower's premises. In such cases, a *field warehouse* might be established on the borrower's grounds. To provide inventory supervision, the lending institution employs a third party in the arrangement, the field warehousing company, which acts as its agent.

Field warehousing can be illustrated by a simple example. Suppose a firm that has iron stacked in an open yard on its premises needs a loan. A field warehousing concern can place a temporary fence around the iron, erecting a sign stating, "This is a field warehouse supervised by the Smith Field Warehousing Corporation," and then assign an employee to supervise and control the fenced-in inventory.

This example illustrates the three essential elements for the establishment of a field warehouse: (1) public notification, (2) physical control of the inventory, and (3) supervision by a custodian of the field warehousing concern. When the field warehousing operation is relatively small, the third condition is sometimes violated by hiring an employee of the borrower to supervise the inventory. This practice is viewed as undesirable by most lenders because there is no control over the collateral by a person independent of the borrowing firm.[10]

## Acceptable Products

Canned foods account for nearly 20 percent of all field warehouse loans. In addition, many other types of products provide a basis for field warehouse financing. Some of these are miscellaneous groceries, which represent nearly 15 percent; lumber products, about 10 percent; and coal and coke, about 5 percent. These products are relatively nonperishable and are sold in well-developed, organized markets. Nonperishability protects the lender if it should have to take over the security. For this reason, a bank would not make a field warehousing loan on perishables such as fresh fish; but frozen fish, which can be stored for a long time, can be field warehoused.

## Cost of Financing

The fixed costs of a field warehousing arrangement are relatively high; such financing, therefore, is not suitable for a very small firm. If a field warehousing company sets up a field warehouse, it typically will set a minimum charge of about $25,000 per year, plus about 1 to 2 percent of the amount of credit extended to the borrower. Furthermore, the financing institution will charge an interest rate of 2 to 3 percentage points over the prime rate. An efficient field warehousing operation requires an inventory of at least $1 million.

## Evaluation of Inventory Financing

The use of inventory financing, especially field warehouse financing, as a source of funds has many advantages. First, the amount of funds available is flexible because the financing is tied to the growth of inventories, which in turn is related directly to financing needs. Second, the field warehousing arrangement increases the acceptability of inventories as loan collateral; some inventories simply would not be accepted by a bank as security without such an arrangement. Third, the necessity for inventory control and safekeeping as well as the use of specialists in warehousing often results in improved warehouse practices, which in turn save handling costs, insurance charges, theft losses, and so forth. Thus, field warehousing companies often save money for firms despite the costs of financing that we have discussed. The major disadvantage of field warehousing include the paperwork, physical separation requirements, and, for small firms, the fixed-cost element.

---

[10]The absence of independent control was the main cause of a breakdown that resulted in more than $200 million of losses on loans to the Allied Crude Vegetable Oil Company by Bank of America and other banks. American Express Field Warehousing Company was handling the operation, but it hired men from Allied's own staff as custodians. Their dishonesty was not discovered because of another breakdown—the fact that the American Express touring inspector did not actually take a physical inventory of the warehouses. As a consequence, the swindle was not discovered until losses running into the hundreds of millions of dollars had been suffered.

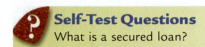 **Self-Test Questions**

What is a secured loan?

What two types of current assets are pledged as security for short-term loans?

Differentiate between pledging accounts receivable and factoring accounts receivable.

Identify the services a factor normally provides.

List the advantages and disadvantages of accounts receivable financing.

Describe three methods of inventory financing.

What are some advantages and disadvantages of inventory financing?

**Chapter *Essentials***
**—The Answers**

To summarize the key concepts, let's answer the questions that were posed at the beginning of the chapter:

- **Does trade credit have a cost? For example, does a firm incur a cost when it does not take cash discounts?** There are two components to trade credit (accounts payable): (1) "free" trade credit and (2) costly trade credit. Companies receive free credit if they take cash discounts by paying within the discount period, whereas companies "pay" for trade credit when they forgo the cash discount and thus pay higher prices for purchases after the discount period. Firms should use the costly portion of trade credit only when the "cost" is less than alternative sources of short-term funds.

- **What types of loan arrangements do commercial banks offer?** Banks offer a variety of short-term loans. Two notable financing arrangements include a note that has a maturity that is less than one year and a line of credit. If a firm borrows a specific amount from a bank, it must sign a promissory note. A line of credit gives the firm the ability to borrow at any time as long as the total amount that is outstanding does not exceed some maximum specified by the bank. Both types of loans are nonspontaneous in the sense that the firm must formally request funds from the bank. Such loans might require the firm to maintain a compensating balance at the bank. The bank uses the compensating balance to earn returns that effectively help to recover fees that would otherwise be charged for the various services it offers.

- **What is commercial paper? What types of firms can use commercial paper?** Commercial paper is an unsecured debt that is issued by large, financially strong companies; it represents an IOU issued by a firm. Most commercial paper is sold to other businesses. Commercial paper is an attractive source of funds for qualified firms because the cost associated with this type of debt generally is lower than the prime rate. Commercial paper does not pay interest; rather, it is sold at a discount— that is, for less than its face value—and then redeemed for face value at maturity.

- **How is the cost of short-term credit determined? Why is it necessary to compute the cost of credit?** The percentage cost of credit per period, $r_{PER}$, is equal to the total dollar cost of borrowing divided by the amount of funds that the borrower can actually use. The percentage cost per period is annualized by computing the APR, which is a noncompounded rate, or the EAR ($r_{EAR}$), which recognizes the effects of compounding. The percentage cost of credit is higher (lower) when the dollar cost of borrowing is higher (lower), the amount available for use is lower (higher), or both. When the entire principal amount of a loan cannot be used by the borrower, the cost of the loan is higher than the quoted, or simple, interest rate.

- **Which assets generally are considered good security for collateralized short-term loans? What are some of the arrangements that exist with secured short-term loans?** Both accounts receivable and inventory are considered good collateral for short-term loans because they are liquid operating assets. Accounts receivable represent sales that have been made but have not been collected. Thus, the accounts receivable balance is an indication of the cash that the firm expects to collect (be paid) in the near future. Firms can use receivables to raise funds before the accounts are actually collected by (1) pledging the accounts as collateral for a loan or (2) factoring the receivables, in which case the receivables are sold to a factor.

   Inventory represents products that the firm expects to sell in the near term. The attractiveness of inventory as collateral depends on its characteristics—nonperishable inventory that is easy to sell is considered better inventory than hard-to-sell inventory that is perishable.

## ETHICAL DILEMMA

### Who Has the Money—The Democrat or The Republican?

Sunflower Manufacturing recently applied for a $10 million loan at The Democrat Federal Bank (known simply as The Democrat). The purpose of the loan is to support its working capital needs during the next nine months. Sunflower has been a loyal customer of the bank for many years and has been extended whatever amount of credit it requested in the past.

Sheli Crocker, who is a new, young loan officer at The Democrat, reviewed Sunflower's loan application and decided to turn down the loan for the requested amount. In her report to Henry, her boss and the senior loan officer, Sheli indicated she thought that Sunflower would have trouble repaying a $10 million loan because its financial position has deteriorated in recent months. Sheli noted that the company's liquidity position is very poor and that analysts are very pessimistic about Sunflower's ability to improve its liquidity during the next two years. As a result, Sheli recommended that Sunflower's request for $10 million be denied. However, she indicated that she thought it would be more appropriate for the bank to lend a smaller amount, up to a maximum of $2 million.

Earlier today Henry called Sheli into his office to discuss her report because he wants her to reconsider her recommendation. Henry told Sheli that he thought the bank should extend the $10 million loan to Sunflower because the company has been a model customer in the past, and the bank should not abandon a loyal customer just because it might have some short-term financial difficulties. Sheli

explained that Sunflower's financial numbers indicate that the firm can handle only a $2 million loan. In addition, she said that the cash budget that was provided with the loan application was "suspicious" because the numbers don't seem to match Sunflower's other financial statements and recent activity in the company's bank accounts.

Henry instructed Sheli to return to her office and reevaluate Sunflower's loan application. He suggested that Sheli should consider the loyalty the company has shown to the bank over the years. In fact, Henry told Sheli that he believes customer loyalty should be the primary consideration when determining to whom the bank should lend money. Further, Henry indicated that he thought Sunflower would go to another bank—perhaps to The Democrat's archrival, The Republican National Bank (affectionately known as The Republican)—for the loan unless The Democrat approved a loan for the entire $10 million that was requested. And if a competing bank grants Sunflower the loan, The Democrat probably will lose all of the company's business, including its checking account, payroll management, and factoring.

After reconsidering the financial numbers, Sheli hasn't changed her mind. In fact, she is even more convinced that the loan should not be made because both Sunflower's financial position and its inability to generate the necessary cash flows in recent months suggest that the bank would be making a big mistake if the loan is granted. But because it is the end of the accounting period and Sheli knows that her department has not generated its quota of loans, she is trying to determine what actions she can take to make the loan application more attractive. In the back of her mind, she can't forget her earlier discussion with Henry in which he reminded her of the importance of meeting loan quotas; he suggested that jobs could be lost if quotas aren't attained.

Another factor Sheli has to consider is that The Democrat is in a somewhat precarious financial position itself. The Democrat has been losing business to competing banks, especially to The Republican, during the past few years. The loss of business has caused a significant decline in The Democrat's growth. What should Sheli do? What would you do if you were in Sheli's position?

The concepts presented in this chapter should help you to understand sources of short-term loans and the costs associated with short-term financing. If you understand the concepts presented in this chapter, you should be able to make more informed decisions about borrowing money on a short-term basis.

## Chapter *Essentials*
—Personal Finance

- At some point in your life, you will borrow money, perhaps to buy a car, to finance a house, or to invest. After reading this chapter, you should realize that the cost of borrowing is significantly affected by application fees, processing costs, and other charges that are included in the loan. In cases in which the stated interest rate is low, look for "hidden" costs that increase the effective rate that you are paying on the loan. You should always evaluate the cost of a loan by computing its $r_{EAR}$.
- Individuals can borrow using lines of credit much like companies. If you are accepted for a line of credit at your credit union or bank, then you are approved to borrow from the bank any amount you want as long as the maximum amount outstanding does not exceed your credit limit.
- Banks often require customers to maintain "compensating balances" to avoid fees and other charges. For example, many banks will charge you a service fee if you don't carry a minimum amount in your checking account. The service fee is a charge for not maintaining a compensating balance at the bank. The amount of the required compensating balance is determined by the bank based on the cost of the services provided to you—for example, with a checking account you receive check-cashing services and the bank clears the checks you write and the checks you deposit.
- Individuals can factor certain receivables just like companies. For example, if you are due a large payoff because you won a lotto that requires annual annuity payments, you can sell the right to receive the annual payments to a third party who will pay a lump-sum amount to you today.

## QUESTIONS

**16-1** "Firms can control their accruals within fairly wide limits; depending on the cost of accruals, financing from this source will be increased or decreased." Discuss.

**16-2** Is it true that both trade credit and accruals represent a spontaneous source of capital for financing growth? Explain.

**16-3** Is it true that most firms are able to obtain some free trade credit and that additional trade credit often is available, but at a cost? Explain.

**16-4** The availability of bank credit often is more important to a small firm than to a large one. Why?

**16-5**    What kinds of firms use commercial paper? Could Mama and Papa Gus's Corner Grocery borrow using this form of credit?

**16-6**    Suppose a firm can obtain funds by borrowing at the prime rate or by selling commercial paper.

    **a.** If the prime rate is 5½ percent, what is a reasonable estimate for the cost of commercial paper?

    **b.** If a substantial cost differential exists, why might a firm like this one actually borrow some of its funds in each market?

**16-7**    Can you think of some firms that might allow you to purchase on credit but probably would factor your receivables account?

**16-8**    On average, which group of borrowers would have to pay a higher effective rate for its short-term loans, those who are required to put up collateral or those who are not? Explain.

**16-9**    What impact does a compensating balance requirement have on the cost of borrowing from a bank if the firm generally holds little or no checking balances at the bank? What would the impact be if the firm holds large checking balances?

**16-10**    What types of inventory make "good" collateral?

**16-11**    Under what circumstances do you think it would be wiser for a firm to factor its accounts receivable rather than pledging them?

**16-12**    Explain why the effective interest rate ($r_{EAR}$) on a loan often is much higher than the simple, or stated, interest rate (APR).

## SELF-TEST PROBLEMS

*(Solutions appear in Appendix B at the end of the book.)*

**key terms**    **ST-1**    Define each of the following terms:

    **a.** Accruals

    **b.** Trade credit; stretching accounts payable; free trade credit; costly trade credit

    **c.** Promissory note; line of credit; revolving credit agreement

    **d.** Prime rate

    **e.** Simple interest; discount interest; add-on interest

    **f.** Compensating balance; commitment fee

    **g.** Commercial paper

    **h.** Secured loan

    **i.** Uniform Commercial Code

    **j.** Pledging receivables; factoring

    **k.** Recourse; without recourse

    **l.** Inventory blanket lien; trust receipt; warehouse receipt financing; field warehouse

**receivables financing**    **ST-2**    The Naylor Corporation is considering two methods of raising working capital: (1) a commercial bank loan secured by accounts receivable and (2) factoring accounts receivable. Naylor's bank has agreed to lend the firm 75 percent of its average monthly accounts receivable balance of $250,000 at an annual interest rate of 9 percent. The bank loan is in the form of a series of

30-day loans. The loan would be discounted, and a 20 percent compensating balance would also be required.

A factor has agreed to purchase Naylor's accounts receivable and to advance 85 percent of the balance to the firm. The 15 percent of receivables not loaned to the firm under the factoring arrangement is held in a reserve account. The factor would charge a 3.5 percent factoring commission and annual interest of 9 percent on the invoice price, less both the factoring commission and the reserve account. The monthly interest payment would be deducted from the advance. If Naylor chooses the factoring arrangement, it can eliminate its credit department and reduce operating expenses by $4,000 per month. In addition, bad debt losses of 2 percent of the monthly receivables will be avoided.

**a.** What is the annual cost associated with each financing arrangement?

**b.** Discuss some considerations other than cost that might influence management's decision between factoring and a commercial bank loan.

## PROBLEMS

**16-1** Calculate the APR of nonfree trade credit under each of following terms. Assume payment is made either on the last due date or on the discount date.
                                                                            *cost of trade credit*

    **a.** 1/15, net 20

    **b.** 2/10, net 60

    **c.** 3/10, net 45

    **d.** 2/10, net 45

    **e.** 2/15, net 40

**16-2** **a.** If a firm buys under terms of 3/15, net 45 but actually pays on the 20th day and still takes the discount, what is the APR of its nonfree trade credit?               *cost of credit*

    **b.** Does the firm receive more or less credit than it would if it paid within 15 days?

**16-3** Susan Visscher, owner of Visscher's Hardware, is negotiating with First Merchant's Bank for a $50,000, one-year loan. First Merchant's has offered Visscher the following alternatives. Calculate the effective interest rate ($r_{EAR}$) for each alternative. Visscher does not have a checking account at Merchant's Bank. Which alternative has the lowest $r_{EAR}$?     *cost of bank credit*

    **a.** A 12 percent annual rate on a simple interest loan with no compensating balance required and interest due at the end of the year.

    **b.** A 9 percent annual rate on a simple interest loan with a 20 percent compensating balance required and interest again due at the end of the year.

    **c.** An 8.75 percent annual rate on a discounted loan with a 15 percent compensating balance.

    **d.** Interest is figured as 8 percent of the $50,000 amount, payable at the end of the year, but the $50,000 is repayable in monthly installments during the year.

**16-4** Howe Industries sells on terms of 2/10, net 40. Gross sales last year were $4.5 million, and accounts receivable averaged $437,500. Half of Howe's customers paid on Day 10 and took discounts. What is the cost of trade     *cost of trade credit*

credit to Howe's nondiscount customers? (*Hint:* Calculate sales per day based on a 360-day year, get the average receivables of discount customers, and then find the DSO for the nondiscount customers.)

**cost of credit**    **16-5**    Boles Corporation needs to raise $500,000 for one year to supply capital to a new store. Boles buys from its suppliers on terms of 3/10, net 90, and it currently pays on Day 10 and takes discounts, but it could forgo discounts, pay on Day 90, and get the needed $500,000 in the form of costly trade credit. Alternatively, Boles could borrow from its bank on a 12 percent discount interest rate basis. What is $r_{EAR}$ of the lower-cost source?

**effective cost of short-term credit**    **16-6**    The Meyer Company must arrange financing for its working capital requirements for the coming year. Meyer can (a) borrow from its bank on a simple interest basis (interest payable at the end of the loan) for one year at a 12 percent simple rate; (b) borrow on a three-month, renewable loan at an 11.5 percent simple rate; (c) borrow on an installment loan basis at a 6.0 percent add-on rate with 12 end-of-month payments; or (d) obtain the needed funds by no longer taking discounts and thus increasing its accounts payable. Meyer buys on terms of 1/15, net 60. What is $r_{EAR}$ of the least expensive type of credit, assuming 360 days per year?

**cash discounts**    **16-7**    Suppose a firm makes purchases of $3.6 million per year under terms of 2/10, net 30 and *takes discounts*.

**a.** What is the average amount of accounts payable net of discounts? (Assume that the $3.6 million of purchases is net of discounts—that is, gross purchases are $3,673,469 and discounts are $73,469. Also, use 360 days in a year.)

**b.** Is there a cost of the trade credit the firm uses?

**c.** If the firm did not take discounts and it paid on time, what would be its average payables and the APR and $r_{EAR}$ of this nonfree trade credit? Assume the firm records accounts payable net of discounts.

**d.** What would be the APR and $r_{EAR}$ of not taking discounts if the firm can stretch its payments to 40 days?

**trade credit versus bank credit**    **16-8**    Gallinger Corporation projects an increase in sales from $1.5 million to $2 million, but it needs an additional $300,000 of current assets to support this expansion. The money can be obtained from the bank at an interest rate of 13 percent, discount interest; no compensating balance is required. Alternatively, Gallinger can finance the expansion by no longer taking discounts, thus increasing accounts payable. Gallinger purchases under terms of 2/10, net 30, but it can delay payment for an *additional* 35 days— paying in 65 days and thus becoming 35 days past due—without a penalty because of its suppliers' current excess capacity problems.

**a.** Based strictly on effective annual interest rate comparisons, how should Gallinger finance its expansion?

**b.** What additional qualitative factors should Gallinger consider before reaching a decision?

**cost of bank credit**    **16-9**    The UFSU Corporation intends to borrow $450,000 to support its short-term financing requirements during the next year. The company is evaluating its financing options at the bank where it maintains its checking account. UFSU's checking account balance, which averages $50,000, can be used to help satisfy any compensating balance requirements the bank might impose.

The financing alternatives offered by the bank include the following:

*Alternative 1:* A discount interest loan with a simple interest of 9¼ percent and no compensating balance requirement.

*Alternative 2:* A 10 percent simple interest loan that has a 15 percent compensating balance requirement.

*Alternative 3:* A $1 million revolving line of credit with simple interest of 9¼ percent paid on the amount borrowed and a ¼ percent commitment fee on the unused balance. No compensating balance is required.

**a.** Compute the effective cost (rate) of each financing alternative assuming UFSU *borrows* $450,000. Which alternative should UFSU use?

**b.** For each alternative, how much would UFSU have to borrow to have $450,000 available for use (to pay the firm's bills)?

**16-10** Gifts Galore Inc. borrowed $1.5 million from National City Bank (NCB). The loan was made at a simple annual interest rate of 9 percent a year for three months. A 20 percent compensating balance requirement raised the effective interest rate because the company does not maintain a checking balance at NCB.

**cost of bank credit**

**a.** The APR on the loan was 11.25 percent. What was $r_{EAR}$?

**b.** What would be $r_{EAR}$ of the loan if the note required discount interest?

**c.** What would be the approximate annual interest rate on the loan if National City Bank required Gifts Galore to repay the loan and interest in three equal monthly installments?

**16-11** Bankston Feed and Supply Company buys on terms of 1/10, net 30, but it has not been taking discounts and has actually been paying in 60 days rather than 30 days. Bankston's balance sheet follows (thousands of dollars):

**short-term financing analysis**

| | | | |
|---|---|---|---|
| Cash | $ 50 | Accounts payable[a] | $ 500 |
| Accounts receivable | 450 | Notes payable | 50 |
| Inventories | 750 | Accruals | 50 |
| Current assets | $1,250 | Current liabilities | $ 600 |
| | | Long-term debt | 150 |
| Fixed assets | 750 | Common equity | 1,250 |
| Total assets | $2,000 | Total liabilities and equity | $2,000 |

[a]Stated net of discounts.

Now Bankston's suppliers are threatening to stop shipments unless the company begins making prompt payments (that is, paying in 30 days or less). The firm can borrow on a one-year note (call this a current liability) from its bank at a rate of 15 percent, discount interest, with a 20 percent compensating balance required. (Bankston's $50,000 in cash is needed for transactions; it cannot be used as part of the compensating balance.)

**a.** Determine what action Bankston should take by calculating (1) the cost of nonfree trade credit and (2) the cost of the bank loan.

**b.** Assume that Bankston forgoes discounts and then borrows the amount needed from the bank to become current on its payables. How large will the bank loan be?

**alternative financing arrangements**

**16-12** Suntime Boats Limited estimates that because of the seasonal nature of its business, it will require an additional $2 million of cash for the month of July. Suntime Boats has the following four options available for raising the needed funds:

(1) Establish a one-year line of credit for $2 million with a commercial bank. The commitment fee will be 1/2 percent per year on the unused portion, and the interest charge on the used funds will be 11 percent per annum. Assume that the funds are needed only in July and that there are 30 days in July and 360 days in the year.

(2) Forgo the cash discount of 2/10, net 40 on $2 million of purchases during July.

(3) Issue $2 million of 30-day commercial paper at a 9 1/2 percent simple annual interest rate. The total transactions fee, including the cost of a backup credit line, on using commercial paper is 1/2 percent of the amount of the issue.

(4) Issue $2 million of 60-day commercial paper at a 9 percent per annum interest rate, plus a transactions fee of 1/2 percent. Because the funds are required for only 30 days, the excess funds ($2 million) can be invested in 9.4 percent per annum marketable securities for the month of August. The total transactions cost of purchasing and selling the marketable securities is 0.4 percent of the amount of the issue.

**a.** What is the *dollar* cost of each financing arrangement?

**b.** Is the source with the lowest expected cost necessarily the one to select? Why or why not?

**factoring receivables**

**16-13** Cooley Industries needs an additional $500,000, which it plans to obtain through a factoring arrangement. The factor would purchase Cooley's accounts receivable and advance the invoice amount, minus a 2 percent commission, on the invoices purchased each month. Cooley sells on terms of net 30 days. In addition, the factor charges a 12 percent annual interest rate on the total invoice amount, to be deducted in advance.

**a.** What amount of accounts receivable must be factored to net $500,000?

**b.** If Cooley can reduce credit expenses by $3,500 per month and avoid bad debt losses of 2.5 percent on the factored amount, what is the total dollar cost of the factoring arrangement?

**c.** What would be the total cost of the factoring arrangement if Cooley's funding needs rose to $750,000? Would the factoring arrangement be profitable under these circumstances?

**field warehousing**

**16-14** Because of crop failures last year, the San Joaquin Packing Company has no funds available to finance its canning operations during the next six months. It estimates that it will require $1,200,000 from inventory financing during the period. One alternative is to establish a six-month, $1,500,000 line of credit with terms of 9 percent annual interest on the used portion, a 1 percent commitment fee on the unused portion, and a $300,000 compensating balance at all times. The other alternative is to use field warehouse financing. The costs of the field warehouse arrangement in this case would be a flat fee of $2,000, plus 8 percent annual interest on all outstanding credit, plus 1 percent of the maximum amount of credit extended.

| Month | Amount |
|---|---|
| July | $  250,000 |
| August | 1,000,000 |
| September | 1,200,000 |
| October | 950,000 |
| November | 600,000 |
| December | 0 |

Expected inventory levels to be financed are as follows:

a. Calculate the dollar cost of funds from using the line of credit. Be sure to include interest charges and commitment fees. Note that each month's borrowings will be $300,000 greater than the inventory level to be financed because of the compensating balance requirement.

b. Calculate the total cost of the field warehousing operation.

c. Compare the cost of the field warehousing arrangement with the cost of the line of credit. Which alternative should San Joaquin choose?

## Integrative Problem

**16-15** C. Charles Smith recently was hired as president of Dellvoe Office Equipment Inc., a small manufacturer of metal office equipment. As his assistant, you have been asked to review the company's short-term financing policies and to prepare a report for Smith and the board of directors. To help you get started, Smith has prepared some questions that, when answered, will give him a better idea of the company's short-term financing policies.

**short-term financing**

a. What is short-term credit, and what are the four major sources of this credit?

b. Is there a cost to accruals, and do firms have much control over them?

c. What is trade credit?

d. Like most small companies, Dellvoe has two primary sources of short-term debt: trade credit and bank loans. One supplier, which supplies Dellvoe with $50,000 of materials a year, offers Dellvoe terms of 2/10, net 50.

(1) What are Dellvoe's net daily purchases from this supplier?

(2) What is the average level of Dellvoe's accounts payable to this supplier if the discount is taken? What is the average level if the discount is not taken? What are the amounts of free credit and costly credit under both discount policies?

(3) What is the APR of the costly trade credit? What is its $r_{EAR}$?

e. In discussing a possible loan with the firm's banker, Smith found that the bank is willing to lend Dellvoe up to $800,000 for one year at a 9 percent simple, or quoted, rate. However, he forgot to ask what the specific terms would be.

(1) Assume the firm will borrow $800,000. What would be the effective interest rate if the loan were based on simple interest? If the loan had been an 8 percent simple interest loan for six months rather than for a year, would that have affected $r_{EAR}$?

(2) What would $r_{EAR}$ be if the loan were a discount interest loan? What would be the face amount of a loan large enough to net the firm $800,000 of usable funds?

(3) Assume now that the terms call for an installment (or add-on) loan with equal monthly payments. The add-on loan is for a period of one year. What would be Dellvoe's monthly payment? What would be the approximate cost of the loan? What would be $r_{EAR}$?

(4) Now assume that the bank charges simple interest, but it requires the firm to maintain a 20 percent compensating balance. How much must Dellvoe borrow to obtain its needed $800,000 and to meet the compensating balance requirement? What is $r_{EAR}$ on the loan?

(5) Now assume that the bank charges discount interest of 9 percent and also requires a compensating balance of 20 percent. How much must Dellvoe borrow, and what is $r_{EAR}$ under these terms?

(6) Now assume all the conditions in Part 4—that is, a 20 percent compensating balance and a 9 percent simple interest loan—but assume also that Dellvoe has $100,000 of cash balances that it normally holds for transactions purposes, which can be used as part of the required compensating balance. How does this affect (i) the size of the required loan and (ii) $r_{EAR}$ of the loan?

f. Dellvoe is considering using secured short-term financing. What is a secured loan? What two types of current assets can be used to secure loans?

g. What are the differences between pledging receivables and factoring receivables? Is one type generally considered better?

h. What are the differences among the three forms of inventory financing? Is one type generally considered best?

i. Dellvoe had expected a really strong market for office equipment for the year just ended, and in anticipation of strong sales, the firm increased its inventory purchases. However, sales for the last quarter of the year did not meet Dellvoe's expectations, and now the firm finds itself short on cash. The firm expects that its cash shortage will be temporary, lasting only three months. (The inventory has been paid for and cannot be returned to suppliers.) Dellvoe has decided to use inventory financing to meet its short-term cash needs. It estimates that it will require $800,000 for inventory financing during this three-month period. Dellvoe has negotiated with the bank for a three-month, $1,000,000 line of credit with terms of 10 percent annual interest on the used portion, a 1 percent commitment fee on the unused portion, and a $125,000 compensating balance at all times. Expected inventory levels to be financed are as follows:

| Month | Amount |
| --- | --- |
| January | $800,000 |
| February | 500,000 |
| March | 300,000 |

Calculate the cost of funds from this source, including interest charges and commitment fees. (*Hint:* Each month's borrowings will be $125,000 greater than the inventory level to be financed because of the compensating balance requirement.)

### Computer-Related Problem

*Work the problem in this section only if you are using the problem spreadsheet.*

**16-16** Use the model in File C16 to work this problem. Refer back to Problem 16-13.

**factoring receivables**

  **a.** Would it be to Cooley's advantage to offer to pay the factor a commission of 2.5 percent if it would lower the interest rate to 10.5 percent annually?

  **b.** Assume a commission of 2 percent and an interest rate of 12 percent. What would be the total cost of the factoring arrangement if Cooley's funding needs rose to $650,000? Would the factoring arrangement be profitable under these circumstances?

## GET REAL WITH     THOMSON ONE | Business School Edition

**16-17** One way to measure whether a firm can meet its short-term debt obligations is to analyze the firm's liquidity. Firms that are growing rapidly often find themselves in a liquidity crisis. Cisco Systems Inc. [CSCO] is a technology firm that manufactures and sells networking and communication products. Answer the following questions:

**liquidity**

  **a.** What have been Cisco's current and quick ratios during the past three years? [Click on Growth Rates/SEC Growth Rates/Annual Ratios.]

  **b.** What has been the trend in Cisco's liquidity position during the three-year time period?

  **c.** Why is there a difference between the current ratio and the quick ratio?

  **d.** How has Cisco compared with peer firms in its industry group with regard to liquidity as measured by the quick and current ratios? Be specific in your answer.

  **e.** Compare the current and quick ratios of Cisco to those of Boeing Company [BA], a more mature defense company. [Click on Peers/Performance/Liquidity Comparison.] What conclusions can you make about the ability of young technology firms such as Cisco to meet their short-term debt obligations as compared with more mature firms like those in the defense industry?

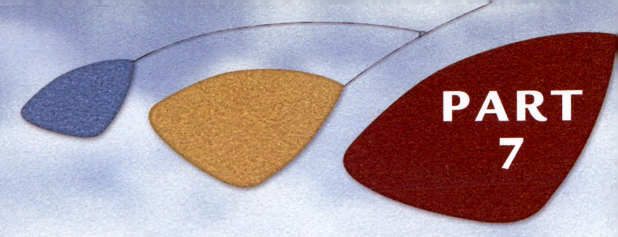

# PART 7

# Strategic Planning and Financing Decisions

# Financial Planning and Control

Benjamin Mays, who was a mentor to Martin Luther King, Jr., once said, "Failure is not reaching your goal, but in having no goal to reach." Over time, this quote has been modified somewhat. Now the adage is "People don't plan to fail, they fail to plan." Applied to business, this maxim would be "Businesses don't plan to fail, they fail to forecast (plan)."

Indeed, planning is a critical ingredient to achieve success in business. Inadequate financial planning is the principal reason businesses fail. Statistics show that approximately 80 percent of business failures can be linked to poor financial planning. Of all the businesses that will begin operations this year, only about 10 percent will still be in business in five years. More than three-quarters of all new businesses fail in their first year. Why? Because the firms either don't have formal business plans or their plans are inadequate.

If you read literature about "how to succeed in business," you will discover a common mantra: "Develop a financial plan that can be used as a 'to-do list' to guide the future of the firm." A financial plan for a business is comparable to a road map for a traveler; it is designed to help the firm stay on course in its attempt to achieve the goal of wealth maximization. Many companies have learned the hard way that a good financial plan is critical to survival, either by going out of business or suffering through difficult financial times.

As you read this chapter, think about businesses with which you might be familiar—perhaps you have read about them in business magazines or newspapers—that have suffered through financial adversity. In nearly every case, you will find that much of the difficulty could have been avoided if the firm had a valid financial plan and a control system in place. The *plan* gives the directions for operating the firm in the future, whereas the *control system* ensures the plan is implemented and modified to account for the dynamic environment the company faces. If you are considering starting your own business some day, *make sure you have a plan so that you have a clue as to which direction the business is headed.*

## Chapter *Essentials*
### —The Questions

After reading this chapter, you should be able to answer the following questions:

- Why is financial planning and control critical to the survival of a firm?
- What are pro forma financial statements? What is the purpose of constructing such statements?
- What are operating breakeven and operating leverage? How are the two related?
- What are financial breakeven and financial leverage? How are the two related?
- How can a firm use knowledge of leverage in the financial forecasting and control process?
- Why is it important to have some understanding of the U.S. Federal Tax Code?

In Chapter 2, we focused on how to use financial statement analysis to evaluate the existing financial position of a firm. In this chapter, we will see how a financial manager can use some of the information obtained through financial statement analysis for financial planning and control of the firm's future operations. Well-run companies generally base their operating plans on a set of forecasted financial statements. The **financial planning** process begins with a sales forecast for the next few years. Then the assets required to meet the sales targets are determined, and a decision is made concerning how to finance the required assets. At that point, income statements and balance sheets can be projected, and earnings and dividends per share, as well as the key ratios, can be forecasted.

Once the "base case" forecasted financial statements and ratios have been prepared, top managers want to know (1) how realistic the results are, (2) how to attain the results, and (3) what impact changes in operations would have on the forecasts. At this stage, which is the **financial control** phase, the firm is concerned with implementing the financial plans, or forecasts, and dealing with the feedback and adjustment process that is necessary to ensure that the goals of the firm are pursued appropriately.

The first part of the chapter is devoted to financial planning using projected financial statements, or forecasts, and the second part of the chapter focuses on financial control using budgeting and the analysis of leverage to determine how changes in operations affect financial forecasts.

**financial planning**
The projection of sales, income, and assets as well as the determination of the resources needed to achieve these projections.

**financial control**
The phase in which financial plans are implemented; control deals with the feedback and adjustment process required to ensure adherence to plans and modification of plans because of unforeseen changes.

**sales forecast**
A forecast of a firm's unit and dollar sales for some future period; generally based on recent sales trends plus forecasts of the economic prospects for the nation, region, industry, and so forth.

## SALES FORECASTS

Forecasting is an essential part of the planning process, and a **sales forecast** is the most important ingredient of financial forecasting. The sales forecast generally starts with a review of sales during the past five to 10 years, which can be expressed in a graph such as that in Figure 17-1. The first part of the graph shows five years of historical sales for Unilate Textiles, the textile and clothing manufacturer we analyzed in Chapter 2. The graph could have contained 10 years of sales data, but Unilate typically focuses on sales figures for the latest five years because the firm's studies have shown that future growth is more closely related to the recent than to the distant past.

Unilate had its ups and downs from 2005 through 2009. In 2007, poor cotton production in the United States and diseased sheep in Australia resulted in low textile production, which caused sales to fall below the 2006 level. Then a significant increase in both the supply of cotton and the supply of wool in 2008 pushed sales up by 15 percent. Based on a regression analysis, Unilate's forecasters determined that the average annual growth rate in sales over the past five years was nearly 10 percent. To determine the forecasted sales growth for 2010, some of the factors that Unilate considered included projections of expected economic activity, competitive conditions, and product development and distribution both in the markets in which Unilate

FIGURE 17-1    Unilate Textiles: 2010 Sales Projection

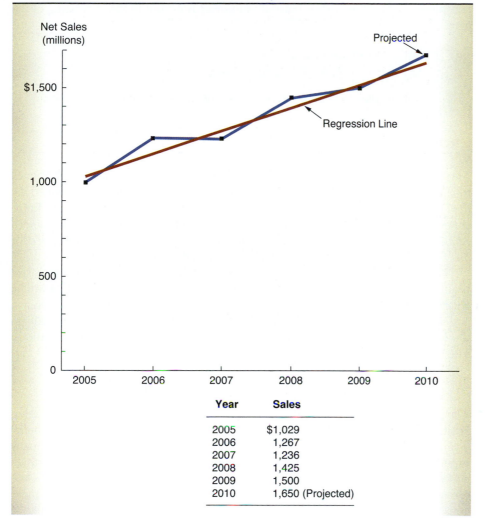

| Year | Sales |
|------|-------|
| 2005 | $1,029 |
| 2006 | 1,267 |
| 2007 | 1,236 |
| 2008 | 1,425 |
| 2009 | 1,500 |
| 2010 | 1,650 (Projected) |

currently operates and in the markets it plans to enter in the future. Often firms develop mathematical models such as regression equations to take into consideration such factors when forecasting future sales. Based on its historical sales trend, plans for new product and market introductions, and Unilate's forecast for the economy, the firm's planning committee has projected a 10 percent growth rate for sales during 2010. So 2010 sales are expected to be $1,650 million, which is 10 percent higher than 2009 sales of $1,500 million.

If the sales forecast is inaccurate, the consequences can be serious. First, if the market expands significantly *more* than Unilate has geared up for, the company probably will not be able to meet demand. Customers will buy competitors' products, and Unilate will lose market share, which will be hard to regain. On the other hand, if the projections are overly optimistic, Unilate could end up with too much plant, equipment, and inventory. This would mean low turnover ratios, high costs for depreciation and storage, and, possibly, write-offs of obsolete or unusable inventory. All of this would result in a low rate of return on equity, which in turn would depress the company's stock price. If Unilate had financed an unnecessary expansion with debt, its problems would, of course, be compounded. Remember from our analysis of its 2009 financial statements in Chapter 2 that Unilate's current financial position is considered poor. Thus, an accurate sales forecast is critical to the well-being of the firm.[1]

 **Self-Test Questions**

How do past trends affect a sales forecast?

Briefly explain why an accurate sales forecast is critical to profitability.

## PROJECTED (PRO FORMA) FINANCIAL STATEMENTS

Any forecast of financial requirements involves (1) determining how much money the firm will need during a given period, (2) determining how much money (funds) the firm will generate internally during the same period, and (3) subtracting the funds generated internally from the required funds to determine the external financial requirements. One method used to estimate external requirements is the *projected,* or *pro forma, balance sheet method,* which is discussed in this section.

The projected balance sheet method is straightforward. Simply project the asset requirements for the coming period, then project the liabilities and equity that will be generated under normal operations—that is, without additional external financing—and subtract the projected liabilities and equity from the required assets to estimate the **additional funds needed (AFN)** to support the level of forecasted operations. The steps in the procedure are explained next.

**additional funds needed (AFN)**
Funds that a firm must raise externally through new borrowing or by selling new stock.

**projected (pro forma) balance sheet method**
A method of forecasting financial requirements based on forecasted financial statements.

## Step 1. Forecast the 2010 Income Statement

The **projected (pro forma) balance sheet method** begins with a forecast of sales. Next, the income statement for the coming year is forecasted to obtain an initial estimate of the amount of retained earnings (internal equity financing) the company expects to generate during the year. This requires assumptions about the operating cost ratio, the tax rate, interest charges, and the dividends paid. In the simplest case, the assumption is made that costs will increase at the same rate as sales; in more complicated situations, cost changes are forecasted separately. Still, the objective of this part of the analysis is to determine how much income the company will earn and then retain for reinvestment in the business during the forecasted year.

Table 17-1 shows Unilate's actual 2009 income statement and the initial forecast of the 2010 income statement if the firm's operating costs change at the same rate as sales. Thus, to create the 2010 income forecast, we assume that sales and variable operating costs will be 10 percent greater in 2010 than in 2009. In addition, it is assumed that Unilate currently *operates at full capacity*, which means it will need to expand its plant capacity in 2010 to handle the additional operations. Thus, to achieve its forecasted growth in 2010, we assume that Unilate will need to increase plant and equipment 10 percent. This assumption is made so that we can simplify the forecasting process. Later in the chapter, we discuss adjustments that are needed when a firm operates at less than full capacity.

Because Unilate is operating at full capacity, in Table 17-1 the 2010 forecasts of sales and *all* operating costs, including depreciation, are 10 percent greater than their

---

[1]A sales forecast is actually the *expected value of a probability distribution* with many possible levels of sales. Because any sales forecast is subject to a greater or lesser degree of uncertainty, for financial planning we are often just as interested in the degree of uncertainty inherent in the sales forecast ($\sigma_{sales}$) as we are in the expected value of sales. The concepts of probability distribution measures as they apply to corporate finance are discussed in Chapter 8.

**TABLE 17-1**   Unilate Textiles: Actual 2009 and Projected 2010 Income Statements ($ millions, except per share data)

|  | 2009 Results | 2010 Forecast Basis[a] | Initial Forecast |
|---|---|---|---|
| Net sales | $ 1,500.0 | ×1.10 | $ 1,650.0 |
| Cost of goods sold | (1,230.0) | ×1.10 | (1,353.0) |
| Gross profit | $ 270.0 |  | $ 297.0 |
| Fixed operating costs except depreciation | ( 90.0) | ×1.10 | ( 99.0) |
| Depreciation | ( 50.0) | ×1.10 | ( 55.0) |
| Earnings before interest and taxes (EBIT) | $ 130.0 |  | 143.0 |
| Interest | ( 40.0) |  | ( 40.0)[b] |
| Earnings before taxes (EBT) | $ 90.0 |  | $ 103.0 |
| Taxes (40%) | ( 36.0) |  | ( 41.2) |
| Net Income | $ 54.0 |  | $ 61.8 |
| Common dividends | ( 29.0) |  | ( 29.0)[b] |
| Addition to retained earnings | $ 25.0 |  | $ 32.8 |
| Earnings per share | $ 2.16 |  | $ 2.47 |
| Dividends per share | $ 1.16 |  | $ 1.16 |
| Number of common shares (millions) | 25.00 |  | 25.00 |

[a]×1.10 indicates "times (1 + g)"; used for items that grow proportionally with sales.

[b]Indicates a 2009 figure carried over for the preliminary forecast.

2009 levels. The result is that earnings before interest and taxes (EBIT) is forecasted to be $143 million in 2010.

To complete the initial forecast of 2010 income, we assume no change in the financing of the firm because, at this point, it is not known whether additional financing is needed. But it is apparent that the 2010 interest expense will change if the amount of debt (borrowing) the firm needs to support the forecasted increase in operations changes. To forecast the 2010 dividends, we simply assume the dividend per share will be the same as it was in 2009—that is, $1.16. So the total common dividends forecasted for 2010 will be $29.0 million if no additional common stock is issued. Like the interest expense amount, however, the amount of total dividends used to create this initial forecast will increase if Unilate decides to sell new stock to raise any additional financing necessary to support the new operations or to raise the dividends per share paid to existing shareholders.

From the initial forecast of 2010 income, we can see that $32.8 million dollars is *expected* to be added to retained earnings in 2010. As it turns out, this addition to retained earnings represents the amount Unilate is expected to invest in itself (internally generated funds) to support the increase in operations in 2010 if the conditions described here exist. So the next step is to determine what impact this level of investment will have on Unilate's forecasted 2010 balance sheet.

## Step 2. Forecast the 2010 Balance Sheet

If we assume the 2009 end-of-year asset levels were just sufficient to support 2009 operations, then in order for Unilate's sales to increase in 2010, its assets must also grow. Because we assume that the company was operating at full capacity in 2009, *each* asset account must increase if the higher sales level is to be attained. In other words, more cash will be needed for transactions, higher sales will lead to higher receivables, additional inventory will have to be stocked, and new plant and equipment must be added to increase production.

Further, if Unilate's assets are to increase, its liabilities and equity must also increase—the additional assets must be financed in some manner. Some liabilities will increase *spontaneously* due to normal business relationships. For example, as sales increase, so will Unilate's purchases of raw materials, and these larger purchases will spontaneously lead to higher levels of accounts payable. Similarly, a higher level of operations will require more labor, and higher sales will result in higher taxable income. Therefore, both accrued wages and accrued taxes will increase. In general, current liabilities that change naturally with sales changes provide **spontaneously generated funds,** which increase at the same rate as sales.

**spontaneously generated funds**

Funds that are obtained from routine business transactions.

Notes payable, long-term bonds, and common stock will not rise spontaneously with sales. Rather, the projected levels of these accounts will depend on conscious financing decisions that will be made once it has been determined how much external financing is needed to support the projected operations. Therefore, for the initial forecast, it is assumed these account balances remain unchanged from their 2009 levels.

Table 17-2 contains Unilate's 2009 actual balance sheet and an initial forecast of its 2010 balance sheet. The mechanics of the balance sheet forecast are similar to those used to develop the forecasted income statement. First, those balance sheet accounts that are expected to increase directly with sales are multiplied by 1.10 to obtain the initial 2010 forecasts. Thus, 2010 cash is projected to be $15.0 \times 1.10 = \$16.5$ million, accounts receivable are projected to be $180.0 \times 1.10 = \$198.0$ million, and so on. In our example, all assets increase with sales, so once the individual assets have been forecasted, they can be summed to complete the asset section of the forecasted balance sheet.

**TABLE 17-2**   Unilate Textiles: Actual 2009 and Projected 2010 Balance Sheets ($ millions)

|  | 2009 Balances | Forecast Basis[a] | 2010 Initial Forecast |
|---|---|---|---|
| Cash | $ 15.0 | ×1.10 | $  16.5 |
| Accounts receivable | 180.0 | ×1.10 | 198.0 |
| Inventories | 270.0 | ×1.10 | 297.0 |
| Total current assets | $465.0 | | $511.5 |
| Net plant and equipment | 380.0 | ×1.10 | 418.0 |
| Total Assets | $845.0 | | $929.5 |
| Accounts payable | $ 30.0 | ×1.10 | $  33.0 |
| Accruals | 60.0 | ×1.10 | 66.0 |
| Notes payable | 40.0 | | 40.0[b] |
| Total current liabilities | $130.0 | | $139.0 |
| Long-term bonds | 300.0 | | 300.0[b] |
| Total liabilities | $430.0 | | $439.0 |
| Common stock | 130.0 | | 130.0[b] |
| Retained earnings | 285.0 | +$32.8[c] | 317.8 |
| Total owners' equity | $415.0 | | $447.8 |
| Total Liabilities and Equity | $845.0 | | $886.8 |
| Additional funds needed (AFN) | | | $  42.7[d] |

[a] ×1.10 indicates "times $(1 + g)$"; used for items which grow proportionally with sales.

[b] Indicates a 2009 figure carried over for the initial forecast.

[c] The $32.8 million represents the "addition to retained earnings" from the 2010 Projected Income Statement given in Table 17-1.

[d] The "additional funds needed (AFN)" is computed by subtracting the amount of total liabilities and equity from the amount of total assets.

Next, the spontaneously increasing liabilities (accounts payable and accruals) are forecasted. Then those liability and equity accounts whose values reflect conscious management decisions—notes payable, long-term bonds, and stock—*initially are not changed from* their 2009 levels. Thus, the amount of 2010 notes payable initially is set at its 2009 level of $40.0 million, the long-term bond account is forecasted at $300.0 million, and so forth. The forecasted 2010 level of retained earnings will be the 2009 level plus the forecasted addition to retained earnings, which was computed as $32.8 million in the projected income statement we created in Step 1 (see Table 17-1).

The forecast of total assets in Table 17-2 is $929.5 million, which indicates that Unilate must add $84.5 million of new assets (compared with 2009 assets) to support the higher sales level expected in 2010. However, according to the initial forecast of the 2010 balance sheet, the total liabilities and equity sum to only $886.8 million, which is an increase of only $41.8 million. So the forecasted amount of total assets exceeds the forecasted amount of total liabilities and equity by $42.7 million = $929.5 million − $886.8 million. This indicates that $42.7 million of the forecasted increase in total assets will not be financed by liabilities that spontaneously increase with sales (accounts payable and accruals) or by an increase in retained earnings. Unilate can raise the additional $42.7 million, which we designate *additional funds needed (AFN)*, by borrowing from the bank as notes payable, by issuing long-term bonds, by selling new common stock, or by some combination of these actions.

The initial forecast of Unilate's financial statements has shown us that (1) higher sales must be supported by higher asset levels; (2) some of the asset increases can be financed by spontaneous increases in accounts payable and accruals and by retained earnings; and (3) any shortfall must be financed from external sources, either by borrowing or by selling new stock.

## Step 3. Raising the Additional Funds Needed

Unilate's financial manager will base the decision of exactly how to raise the $42.7 million additional funds needed on several factors, including the firm's ability to handle additional debt, conditions in the financial markets, and restrictions imposed by existing debt agreements. The decisions concerning how to best finance the firm are discussed in Chapter 12. Regardless of how Unilate raises the $42.7 million AFN, the initial forecasts of both the income statement and the balance sheet will be affected. If Unilate takes on new debt, its interest expenses will increase; if additional shares of common stock are sold, *total* dividend payments will increase if the *same dividend per share* is paid to all common stockholders. Each of these changes, which we term *financing feedbacks,* will affect the amount of additional retained earnings that was originally forecasted, which in turn will affect the amount of additional funds needed that was computed in Step 2.

Our ratio analysis in Chapter 2 showed that Unilate has a below-average debt position. Consequently, Unilate has decided any additional funds needed to support future operations will be raised mainly by issuing new common stock. Following this financing policy should help improve Unilate's debt position as well as its overall profitability.

## Step 4. Financing Feedbacks

As mentioned in Step 3, one complexity that arises in financial forecasting relates to **financing feedbacks.** The external funds raised to pay for new assets create additional financing expenses that must be reflected in the income statement and that lower the initially forecasted addition to retained earnings, which means more external funds than are initially forecasted are needed to make up for the lower amount added to retained earnings. In other words, if Unilate raised the $42.7 million AFN by issuing new debt and new common stock, it would find that both the interest expense and the total dividend

**financing feedbacks**
The effects on the income statement and balance sheet of actions taken to finance forecasted increases in assets.

payments would be higher than the amounts contained in the forecasted income statement shown in Table 17-1. Consequently, after adjusting for the higher interest and dividend payments, the forecasted addition to retained earnings would be lower than the initial forecast of $32.8 million. Because the retained earnings will be lower than projected, a financing shortfall will exist even after the original AFN of $42.7 million is considered. So in reality, Unilate must raise more than $42.7 million to account for the financing feedbacks that affect the amount of internal financing expected to be generated from the increase in operations. To determine the amount of external financing actually needed, we have to adjust the initial forecasts of both the income statement (Step 1) and the balance sheet (Step 2) to reflect the impact of raising the additional external financing. This process has to be repeated until AFN = 0 in Table 17-2, which means Step 1 and Step 2 might have to be repeated several times to fully account for the financing feedbacks.

Table 17-3 contains the adjusted 2010 preliminary forecasts for the income statement and the balance sheet of Unilate Textiles after all of the financing effects (feedbacks) are considered. To generate the adjusted forecasts, it is assumed that of the total external funds needed, 65 percent will be raised by selling new common stock at $23 per share, 15 percent will be borrowed from the bank at an interest rate of 7 percent, and 20 percent will be raised by selling long-term bonds with a coupon interest of 10 percent. Under these conditions, it can be seen from Table 17-3 that Unilate actually needs $45.0 million to support the forecasted increase in operations, not the $42.7 million contained in the initial forecast. The additional $2.3 million is needed because the added amounts of debt and common stock will cause interest and dividend payments to increase, which will decrease the contribution to retained earnings by $2.3 million.[2]

## Analysis of the Forecast

The 2010 forecast as developed here represents a preliminary forecast because we have completed only the first stage of the entire forecasting process. Next, the projected statements must be analyzed to determine whether the forecast meets the firm's financial targets. If the statements do not meet the targets, then elements of the forecast must be changed.

Table 17-4 shows Unilate's 2009 ratios as they were reported back in Table 2-6 in Chapter 2, plus the projected 2010 ratios based on the preliminary forecast and the industry average ratios. As we noted in Chapter 2, the firm's financial condition at the close of 2009 was weak, with many ratios being well below the industry averages. The preliminary final forecast for 2010 (after financing feedbacks are considered), which assumes that Unilate's past practices will continue into the future, shows an improved debt position. But the overall financial position still is somewhat weak, and this condition will persist unless management takes some actions to improve things.

Unilate's management actually plans to take steps to improve its financial condition. The plans are to (1) close down certain operations, (2) modify the credit policy to reduce the collection period for receivables, and (3) better manage inventory so that products are turned over more often. These proposed operational changes will affect both the income statement and the balance sheet, so the preliminary forecast will have to be revised again to reflect the impact of such changes. When this process is complete, management will have its final forecast. To keep things simple, we do not show the final forecast here; instead, for the remaining discussions, we assume the preliminary forecast is not substantially different and use it as the final forecast for Unilate's 2010 operations.

---

[2]Appendix 17A at the end of this chapter gives a more detailed description of the iterations required to generate the final forecasts.

**TABLE 17-3** Unilate Textiles: 2010 Adjusted Forecast of Financial Statements ($ millions)

### Income Statement

|  | Initial Forecast | Adjusted Forecast | Financing Adjustment |
|---|---|---|---|
| Net sales | $ 1,650.0 | $ 1,650.0 | |
| Cost of goods sold | (1,353.0) | (1,353.0) | |
| Gross profit | $ 297.0 | $ 297.0 | |
| Fixed operating costs except depreciation | ( 99.0) | ( 99.0) | |
| Depreciation | ( 55.0) | ( 55.0) | |
| Earnings before interest and taxes (EBIT) | $ 143.0 | $ 143.0 | |
| Less interest | ( 40.0) | ( 41.4) | $(1.4) |
| Earnings before taxes (EBT) | $ 103.0 | $ 101.6 | (1.4) |
| Taxes (40%) | ( 41.2) | ( 40.6) | 0.6 |
| Net income | $ 61.8 | $ 61.0 | (0.8) |
| Common dividends | ( 29.0) | ( 30.5) | (1.5) |
| Addition to retained earnings | $ 32.8 | $ 30.5 | (2.3)[a] |
| Earnings per share | $ 2.47 | $ 2.32 | |
| Dividends per share | $ 1.16 | $ 1.16 | |
| Number of common shares (millions) | 25.00 | 26.27 | |

### Balance Sheet

|  | Initial Forecast | Adjusted Forecast | Financing Adjustment |
|---|---|---|---|
| Cash | $ 16.5 | $ 16.5 | |
| Accounts receivable | 198.0 | 198.0 | |
| Inventories | 297.0 | 297.0 | |
| Total current assets | $511.5 | $511.5 | |
| Net plant and equipment | 418.0 | 418.0 | |
| Total assets | $929.5 | $929.5 | |
| Accounts payable | $ 33.0 | $ 33.0 | |
| Accruals | 66.0 | 66.0 | |
| Notes payable | 40.0 | 46.8 | $ 6.8 |
| Total current liabilities | $139.0 | $145.8 | |
| Long-term bonds | 300.0 | 309.0 | 9.0 |
| Total liabilities | $439.0 | $454.8 | |
| Common stock | 130.0 | 159.2 | 29.2 |
| Retained earnings | 317.8 | 315.5 | (2.3)[a] |
| Total owners' equity | $447.8 | $474.7 | |
| Total liabilities and equity | $886.8 | $929.5 | |
| Additional funds needed (AFN) | $ 42.7 | $ 0.0 | $42.7[b] |

[a]The financing adjustment for the addition to retained earnings in the income statement is the same as the financing adjustment for retained earnings in the balance sheet.

[b]The total AFN, or external funding needs, equal $42.7 million plus the $2.3 million decrease in the change in retained earnings from the initial forecast; thus, total funds needed equal $45.0 million—$6.8 million will be from new bank notes, $9.0 million will come from issuing new bonds, and $29.2 million will be raised by issuing new common stock.

**TABLE 17-4**   Unilate Textiles: Key Ratios

|  | 2009 | Adjusted Preliminary 2010 | Industry Average |
|---|---|---|---|
| Current ratio | 3.6× | 3.5× | 4.1× |
| Inventory turnover | 4.6× | 5.6× | 7.4× |
| Days sales outstanding | 43.2 days | 43.2 days | 32.1 days |
| Total assets turnover | 1.8× | 1.8× | 2.1× |
| Debt ratio | 50.9% | 48.9% | 42.0% |
| Times interest earned | 3.3× | 3.5× | 6.5× |
| Profit margin | 3.6% | 3.7% | 4.9% |
| Return on assets | 6.4% | 6.6% | 10.3% |
| Return on equity | 13.0% | 12.8% | 17.7% |

As we have shown, forecasting is an iterative process, both in the way the financial statements are generated and in the way the financial plan is developed. For planning purposes, the financial staff develops a preliminary forecast based on a continuation of past policies and trends. This provides the executives with a starting point, or "straw man" forecast. Next, the model is modified to see what effects alternative operating plans would have on the firm's earnings and financial condition. This results in a revised forecast.

**Self-Test Questions**

What is the AFN, and how is the projected balance sheet method used to estimate it?

What is a financing feedback, and how do financing feedbacks affect the estimate of AFN?

Why is it necessary for the forecasting process to be iterative?

## OTHER CONSIDERATIONS IN FORECASTING

We have presented a simple method for constructing pro forma financial statements under rather restrictive conditions. In this section, we describe some other conditions that should be considered when creating forecasts.

### Excess Capacity

The construction of the 2010 forecasts for Unilate was based on the assumption that the firm's 2009 operations were at full capacity, so any increase in sales would require additional assets, especially plant and equipment. If Unilate did *not* operate at full capacity in 2009, then plant and equipment would have to be increased only if the additional sales (operations) forecasted in 2010 exceeded the unused capacity of the existing assets. For example, if Unilate actually used only 80 percent of its fixed assets' capacity to produce 2009 sales of $1,500 million, then

$$\$1,500.0 \text{ million} = 0.80 \times (\text{Plant capacity})$$

$$\text{Plant capacity} = \frac{\$1,500 \text{ million}}{0.80} = \$1,875 \text{ million}$$

In this case, then, Unilate could increase sales to $1,875 million, or by 25 percent of 2009 sales, before full capacity is reached and plant and equipment would have to be increased. In general, we can compute the sales capacity of the firm if the percentage of assets used to produce a particular level of sales is known:

$$\text{Full capacity sales} = \frac{\text{Sales level}}{\left(\begin{array}{c}\text{Percent of capacity used}\\\text{to generate sales level}\end{array}\right)}$$

If Unilate does not have to increase plant and equipment, fixed assets would remain at the 2009 level of $380 million, and the amount of AFN would actually be negative, which means that the amount of internally generated funds would be more than sufficient to support (finance) the forecasted 10 percent increase in sales in 2010. In fact, Unilate could increase the per-share dividend it pays to stockholders in 2010 if it does not have to increase fixed assets.

In addition to the excess capacity of fixed assets, the firm could have excesses in other assets that can be used for increases in operations. For instance, in Chapter 2 we concluded that Unilate's inventory level at the end of 2009 probably was greater than it should have been. If true, some increase in 2010 forecasted sales can be absorbed by the above-normal inventory, and production would not have to be increased until inventory levels are reduced to normal. This requires no additional financing.

In general, excess capacity means less external financing is required to support increases in operations than would be needed if the firm previously operated at full capacity.

## Economies of Scale

There are economies of scale in the use of many types of assets, and when such economies occur, a firm's variable cost of goods sold ratio is likely to change as the size of the firm changes (either increases or decreases) substantially. Currently, Unilate's variable cost ratio is 82 percent of sales; but the ratio might decrease to 80 percent of sales if operations increase significantly. If everything else is the same, changes in the variable cost ratio affect the addition to retained earnings, which in turn affects the amount of AFN.

## Lumpy Assets

In many industries, technological considerations dictate that if a firm is to be competitive, it must add fixed assets in large, discrete units; such assets often are referred to as **lumpy assets.** For example, in the paper industry, there are strong economies of scale in basic paper mill equipment, so when a paper company expands capacity, it must do so in large, lumpy increments. Lumpy assets primarily affect the turnover of fixed assets and, consequently, the financial requirements associated with expanding. For instance, if instead of $38 million Unilate needed an additional $50 million in fixed assets to increase operations 10 percent, the AFN would be much greater. With lumpy assets, it is possible that a small projected increase in sales would require a significant increase in plant and equipment, and thus a large financial requirement.

**lumpy assets**
Assets that cannot be acquired in small increments; instead, they must be obtained in large, discrete amounts.

**Self-Test Questions**

Discuss three factors that might cause "spontaneous" assets and liabilities to change at a different rate than sales.

Suppose that a firm that currently operates at 75 percent capacity generates $150 million in sales. What is the firm's level of full-capacity sales? (*Answer:* $200 million)

## FINANCIAL CONTROL—BUDGETING AND LEVERAGE[3]

In the previous section, we focused on financial forecasting, emphasizing how growth in sales requires additional investment in assets, which in turn generally requires the firm to raise new funds externally. In the sections that follow, we consider the planning and control systems used by financial managers when implementing the forecasts. First, we look at the relationship between sales volume and profitability under different operating conditions. These relationships provide information that is used by managers to plan for changes in the firm's level of operations, financing needs, and profitability. Later, we examine the control phase of the planning and control process because a good control system is essential both to ensure that plans are executed properly and to facilitate a timely modification of plans if the assumptions on which the initial plans were based turn out to be different than expected.

The planning process can be enhanced by examining the effects of changing operations on the firm's profitability, both from the standpoint of profits from operations and from the standpoint of profitability after financing effects are considered. In the next few sections, we look at some of the areas financial managers evaluate to provide information about the effects of changing operations.

### Self-Test Question

How can the planning process be enhanced with a good financial control system?

## OPERATING BREAKEVEN ANALYSIS

**operating breakeven analysis**
An analytical technique for studying the relationship among sales revenues, operating costs, and profits.

The relationship between sales volume and *operating profitability* is explored in cost-volume-profit planning, or operating breakeven analysis. **Operating breakeven analysis** is a method of determining the point at which sales will just cover operating costs—that is, the point at which the firm's operations will break even. It also shows the magnitude of the firm's operating profits or losses if sales exceed or fall below that point. Breakeven analysis is important in the planning and control process because the cost-volume-profit relationship can be influenced greatly by the proportion of the firm's investment in assets that are fixed. A sufficient volume of sales must be anticipated and achieved if fixed and variable costs are to be covered, or else the firm will incur losses from operations. In other words, if a firm is to avoid accounting losses, its sales must cover all costs—those that vary directly with production and those that remain constant even when production levels change. Costs that vary directly with the level of production generally include the labor and materials needed to produce and sell the product, whereas the fixed operating costs generally include costs such as depreciation, rent, and insurance expenses that are incurred regardless of the firm's production level.

Operating breakeven analysis deals only with the upper portion of the income statement—the portion from sales to net operating income (NOI), which is also termed earnings before interest and taxes (EBIT). This portion generally is referred to as the *operating section* because it contains only the revenues and expenses associated with the *normal production and selling operations* of the firm. Table 17-5 gives the

---

[3]Because the numbers generated from the computations contained in the rest of the chapter are not rounded until the final result is reported, you might find some slight rounding differences.

**TABLE 17-5**    Unilate Textiles: 2010 Forecasted Operating Income ($ millions)

| | |
|---|---|
| Sales (S) | $ 1,650.0 |
| Variable cost of goods sold (VC) | ( 1,353.0) |
| Gross profit (GP) | $   297.0 |
| Fixed operating costs (F) | (   154.0) |
| Net operating income (NOI-EBIT) | $   143.0 |

**Notes:**

Sales in units = 110 million units.

Selling price per unit = $15.00.

Variable costs per unit = $1,353/110 = $12.30

Fixed operating costs = $154 million, which includes $55 million depreciation and $99 million in other fixed costs such as rent, insurance, and general office expenses.

operating section of Unilate's forecasted 2010 income statement, which was shown in Table 17-3. For the discussion that follows, we assume that all of Unilate's products sell for $15.00 each and the variable cost of goods sold per unit is $12.30, which is 82 percent of the selling price.

## Operating Breakeven Graph

Table 17-5 shows the net operating income for Unilate if 110 million products are produced and sold during the year. But what if Unilate doesn't sell 110 million products? Certainly, the firm's net operating income will be something other than $143 million. Figure 17-2 shows the total revenues and total operating costs for Unilate at various levels of sales, beginning with zero. According to the information given in Table 17-5 Unilate has fixed costs, which include depreciation, rent, insurance, and so forth, equal to $154 million. This amount must be paid even if the firm produces and sells nothing, so the $154 million fixed cost is depicted by a horizontal line. If Unilate produces and sells nothing, its sales revenues will be zero; but *for each unit sold,* the firm's sales will increase by $15. Therefore, the total revenue line starts at the origin of the $x$ and $y$ axes, and it has a slope equal to $15 to account for the dollar increase in sales for each additional unit sold. On the other hand, the line that represents the total operating costs intersects the $y$ axis at $154 million, which represents the fixed costs incurred even when no products are sold, and it has a slope equal to $12.30, which is the cost directly associated with the production of each additional unit sold. The point at which the total revenue line intersects the total operating cost line is the **operating breakeven point** ($Q_{OpBE}$ **and** $S_{OpBE}$) because this is where the revenues generated from sales just cover the *total operating costs* of the firm. Notice that prior to the breakeven point, the total cost line is above the total revenue line, which indicates that Unilate will suffer operating losses because the total costs cannot be covered by the sales revenues. But after the breakeven point, the total revenue line is above the total cost line because revenues are more than sufficient to cover total operating costs, so Unilate will realize operating profits.[4]

**operating breakeven point ($Q_{OpBE}$ and $S_{OpBE}$)** Represents the level of production and sales at which net operating income is zero; it is the point at which revenues from sales just equal total operating costs.

[4]In Figure 17-2, we assume the operating costs can be divided into two distinct groups—fixed costs and variable costs. It should be noted that some costs are considered semivariable (or semifixed). These costs are fixed for a certain range of operations but change if operations are either higher or lower. For the analysis that follows, we have assumed there are no semivariable costs so that the operating costs can be separated into either a fixed component or a variable component.

**FIGURE 17-2** Unilate Textiles: Operating Breakeven Chart

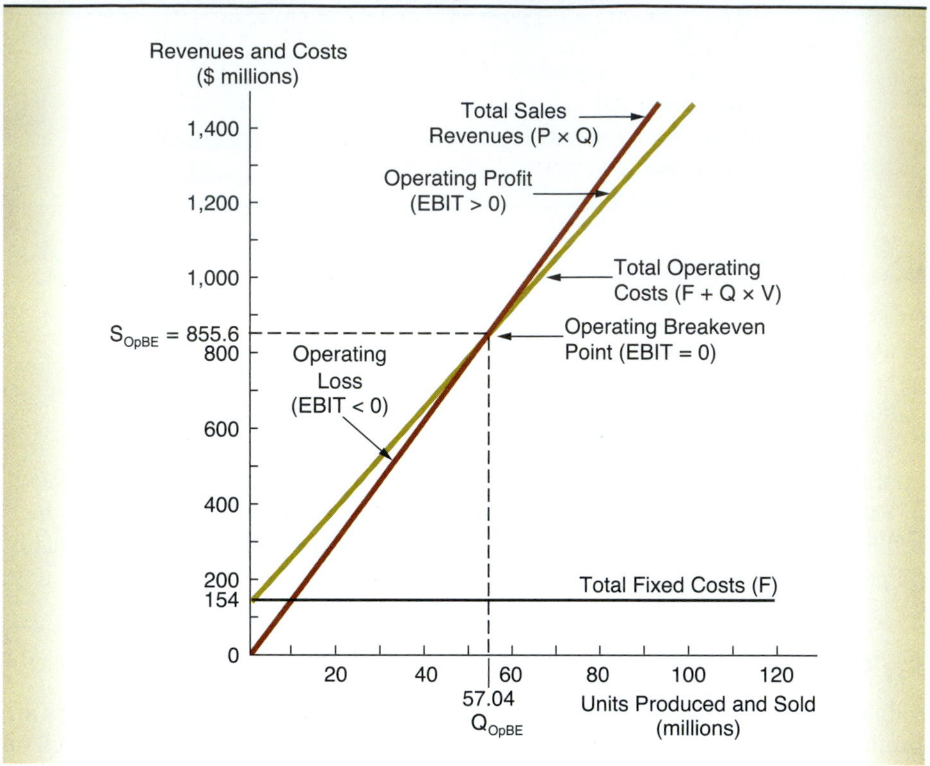

**Notes:**
$S_{OpBE}$ = operating breakeven in dollars
Q = sales in units: $Q_{OpBE}$ = operating breakeven in units
F = fixed costs = $154 million
V = variable costs per unit = $12.30
P = price per unit = $15.00

## Operating Breakeven Computation

Figure 17-2 shows that Unilate must sell 57.04 million units to be at the operating breakeven point. If Unilate sells 57.04 million products, it will generate $855.6 million in sales revenues, which will be just enough to cover the $855.6 million total operating costs—$154 million fixed costs and $701.6 million variable costs (57.04 million units at $12.30 per unit). If we do not have a graph like Figure 17-2, how can the operating breakeven point be computed? Actually, it is rather simple. Remember, the operating breakeven point is where the revenues generated from sales just cover the total operating costs, which include both the costs directly attributable to producing each unit and the fixed operating costs that remain constant regardless of the production level. As long as the selling price of each unit (the slope of the total revenue line) is greater than the variable operating cost of each unit (the slope of the total operating cost line), each unit sold will generate revenues that contribute to covering the fixed operating costs. For Unilate, this contribution (termed the *contribution margin*) is $2.70, which is the difference between the $15 selling price and the $12.30 variable cost of each unit. To compute the operating breakeven for Unilate then, we have to determine how many units need to be sold to cover the fixed operating cost of $154 million if each unit has a contribution margin equal to $2.70. Just divide the $154 million fixed cost by the $2.70 contribution margin and you will discover the breakeven point is 57.04 million units, which equates to $855.6 million in sales revenues.

More formally, the operating breakeven point can be found by setting the total revenues equal to the total operating costs so that net operating income (NOI) is zero. In equation form, NOI = 0 if

$$\frac{\text{Sales}}{\text{revenues}} = \frac{\text{Total operating}}{\text{costs}} = \frac{\text{Total}}{\text{variable costs}} + \frac{\text{Total}}{\text{fixed costs}}$$

$$(P \times Q) = \text{TOC} = (V \times Q) + F$$

where P is the sales price per unit, Q is the number of units produced and sold, V is the variable operating cost per unit, and F is the total fixed operating costs. Solving for the quantity that needs to be sold, Q, produces a formula that can be used to find the number of units that needs to be sold to achieve operating breakeven.

$$Q_{OpBE} = \frac{F}{P - V} = \frac{F}{\text{Contribution margin}}$$

17–1

Thus, the operating breakeven point for Unilate is

$$Q_{OpBE} = \frac{\$154.0 \text{ million}}{\$15.00 - \$12.30} = \frac{\$154.0 \text{ million}}{\$2.70} = 57.04 \text{ million units}$$

In the remainder of the chapter, we omit the word *million* in the computations and include it only in the final answer.

From Equation 17–1, we can see that the operating breakeven point is lower (higher) if the numerator is lower (higher) or if the denominator is higher (lower). Therefore, all else equal, one firm will have a lower operating breakeven point than another firm if its fixed costs are lower, if the selling price of its product is higher, if its variable operating cost per unit is lower, or if some combination of these exists. For instance, if Unilate could increase the sales price per unit from $15 to $15.38 without affecting either its fixed operating costs ($154 million) or its variable operating cost per unit ($12.30), then its operating breakeven point would fall to 50 million units.

The operating breakeven point also can be stated in terms of the total sales revenues needed to cover total operating costs. At this point, we simply need to multiply the sales price per unit by the breakeven quantity we found using Equation 17–1, which yields $855.6 million (= 57.04 × $15.00) for Unilate. Alternatively, we can restate the contribution margin as a percent of the sales price per unit (this is called the *gross profit margin*) and then apply Equation 17–1. In other words,

$$S_{OpBE} = \frac{F}{1 - \left(\dfrac{V}{P}\right)} = \frac{F}{\text{Gross profit margin}}$$

17–2

Solving Equation 17–2 for Unilate, the operating breakeven based on dollar sales is

$$Q_{OpBE} = \frac{\$154.0 \text{ million}}{1 - \left(\dfrac{\$12.30}{\$15.00}\right)} = \frac{\$154.0 \text{ million}}{1 - 0.82} = \frac{\$154.0 \text{ million}}{0.18} = \$855.6 \text{ million}$$

This computation shows that $0.18 of every $1 in sales revenue goes to cover the fixed operating costs, so about $856 million worth of the product must be sold to break even.

Breakeven analysis based on dollar sales rather than on units of output is useful in determining the breakeven volume for a firm that sells many products at varying prices. This analysis requires only that total sales, total fixed costs, and total variable costs at a given level are known.

## Using Operating Breakeven Analysis

Operating breakeven analysis can shed light on three important types of business decisions: (1) When making new product decisions, breakeven analysis can help determine how large the sales of a new product must be for the firm to achieve profitability. (2) Breakeven analysis can be used to study the effects of a general expansion in the level of the firm's operations; an expansion would cause the levels of both fixed and variable costs to rise, but it would also increase expected sales. (3) When considering modernization projects, in which the fixed investment in equipment is increased to lower variable costs, particularly the cost of labor, breakeven analysis can help management analyze the consequences of purchasing these projects.

Care must be taken when using operating breakeven analysis. To apply breakeven analysis as we have discussed here requires that the sales price *per unit,* the variable cost *per unit,* and the *total* fixed operating costs do not change with the level of the firm's production and sales. Within a narrow range of production and sales, this assumption probably is not a major issue. But if the firm expects either to produce a much greater (or fewer) number of products than normal or to expand (reduce) its plant and equipment significantly, these costs will change. Therefore, use of a single breakeven chart like the one presented in Figure 17-2 is impractical. Such a chart provides useful information, but the fact that it cannot deal with changes in the price of the product, with changing variable cost rates, and with changes in fixed cost levels suggests the need for a more flexible type of analysis. Today, such analysis is provided by computer simulation and other sophisticated models. Functions such as those expressed in Equation 17–1 and Equation 17–2 (or more complicated versions of them) can be put into a spreadsheet or similarly modeled with other computer software, and then variables such as sales price, P; the variable cost per unit, V; and the level of fixed costs, F, can be changed. The model can instantaneously produce new versions of Figure 17-2, or a whole set of such graphs, to show what the operating breakeven point would be under different production setups and price-cost situations.

### Self-Test Questions

Is interest paid considered in operating breakeven analysis? Why or why not?

Give the equations used to calculate the operating breakeven point in units and in dollar sales.

Give some examples of business decisions for which operating breakeven analysis might be useful.

Identify some limitations to the use of a single operating breakeven chart.

Suppose that Nixon Hardware sells screwdrivers for $12 each. The screwdrivers cost $9.60 to produce, and Nixon's fixed operating costs equal $144,000. What is Nixon's operating breakeven point? (*Answer:* $Q_{OpBE} = 60,000$; $S_{OpBE} = \$720,000$)

## OPERATING LEVERAGE

If a high percentage of a firm's total operating costs are fixed, the firm is said to have a high degree of **operating leverage.** In physics, leverage implies the use of a lever to raise a heavy object with a small amount of force. In politics, people who have leverage can accomplish a great deal with their smallest word or action. *In business terminology, a high degree of operating leverage, other things held constant, means that a relatively small change in sales will result in a large change in operating income.*

Operating leverage arises because the firm has *fixed operating costs* that must be covered no matter the level of production. The impact of the leverage, however, depends on the actual operating level of the firm. For example, Unilate has $154.0 million in fixed operating costs, which are covered rather easily because the firm currently sells 110 million products; thus, it is well above its operating breakeven point of 57.04 million units. But what would happen to the operating income if Unilate sold more or less than forecasted? To answer this question, we need to determine the **degree of operating leverage (DOL)** associated with Unilate's forecasted 2010 operations.

Operating leverage can be defined more precisely in terms of the way a given change in sales volume affects operating income (NOI). To measure the effect of a change in sales volume on NOI, we calculate the degree of operating leverage, which is defined as the percentage change in NOI (or EBIT) associated with a given percentage change in sales:

> **operating leverage**
> The existence of fixed operating costs, such that a change in sales will produce a larger change in operating income (EBIT).

> **degree of operating leverage (DOL)**
> The percentage change in NOI (or EBIT) associated with a given percentage change in sales.

$$\text{Degree of operating leverage} = \text{DOL} = \frac{\%\Delta \text{ in NOI}}{\%\Delta \text{ in sales}} = \frac{\left(\frac{\Delta\text{NOI}}{\text{NOI}}\right)}{\left(\frac{\Delta\text{Sales}}{\text{Sales}}\right)} = \frac{\left(\frac{\text{NOI}^* - \text{NOI}}{\text{NOI}}\right)}{\left(\frac{\text{Sales}^* - \text{Sales}}{\text{Sales}}\right)} \qquad \textbf{17–3}$$

The symbol $\Delta$—the Greek letter for "delta"—means *change*. The term with the asterisk (*) indicates the actual outcome, whereas the term without the asterisk is the forecasted result. Thus, $\text{NOI}^* - \text{NOI}$ represents the actual NOI minus the forecasted NOI. In effect, the DOL is an index number that measures the effect of a change in sales on operating income or EBIT.

Table 17-5 shows that the NOI for Unilate is $143.0 million at production and sales equal to 110 million units. If the number of units produced and sold increases to 121 million (a 10 percent increase), the operating income (in millions of dollars) would be

$$\text{NOI} = 121(\$15.00 - \$12.30) - \$154.0 = \$172.7$$

So the degree of operating leverage associated with this change is 2.08:

$$\text{DOL} = \frac{\left(\frac{\$172.7 - \$143.0}{\$143.0}\right)}{\left[\frac{\$15.00(121 - 110)}{\$15.00(110)}\right]} = \frac{\left(\frac{\$29.7}{\$143.0}\right)}{\left(\frac{11}{110}\right)} = \frac{0.208}{0.100} = \frac{20.8\%}{10.0\%} = 2.08\times$$

To interpret the meaning of the value of the degree of operating leverage, remember we computed the percent change in operating income and then divided the result by the percent change in sales. Taken literally then, Unilate's DOL of 2.08× indicates that the percent change in operating income will be 2.08 times the percent

**TABLE 17-6** Unilate Textiles: Operating Income at Sales Levels of 110 Million Units and 121 Million Units ($ millions)

|  | 2010 Forecasted Operations | Sales Increase | Unit Change | Percent Change |
|---|---|---|---|---|
| Sales in units (millions) | 110 | 121 | 11 | +10.0% |
| Sales revenues | $1,650.0 | $1,815.0 | $ 165.0 | +10.0% |
| Variable cost of goods sold | (1,353.0) | (1,488.3) | (135.3) | +10.0% |
| Gross profit | $ 297.0 | $ 326.7 | $ 29.7 | +10.0% |
| Fixed operating costs | ( 154.0) | ( 154.0) | ( 0.0) | 0.0% |
| Net operating income (EBIT) | $ 143.0 | $ 172.7 | $ 29.7 | +20.8% |

change in sales from the current 110 million units ($1,650.0 million). So if the number of units sold increases from 110 million to 121 million, or by 10 percent, Unilate's operating income should increase by $2.08 \times 10\% = 20.8\%$. At 121 million units, *operating income* should be 20.8 percent greater than the $143.0 million generated at 110 million units of sales; the new operating income should be $172.7 million $= 1.208 \times \$143$ million. Table 17-6, which compares the operating incomes generated at the two different sales levels, confirms this result.

The results contained in Table 17-6 show that Unilate's *gross profit* would increase by $29.7 million, or by 10 percent, if sales increase 10 percent. The fixed operating costs remain constant at $154.0 million, so EBIT also increases by $29.7 million, and the total impact of a 10 percent increase in sales is a 20.8 percent increase in operating income. If the fixed operating costs were to increase in proportion to the increase in sales—that is, 10 percent—then the net operating income would also increase by 10 percent because all revenues and costs would have changed by the same proportion. In reality, fixed operating costs will not change (a zero percent increase); so a 10 percent increase in Unilate's forecasted 2010 sales will result in an *additional* 10.8 percent increase in operating income. The total increase is 20.8 percent, which results because operating leverage exists.

Equation 17–3 can be simplified so that the degree of operating leverage at *a particular level of operations* can be calculated as follows:[5]

---

[5]Equation 17–4 can be derived by restating Equation 17–3 in terms of the variables we have defined previously and then simplifying the result. Starting with Equation 17–3, we have

$$\text{DOL} = \frac{\%\Delta \text{ in NOI}}{\%\Delta \text{ in sales}} = \frac{\left(\frac{\Delta \text{NOI}}{\text{NOI}}\right)}{\left(\frac{\Delta \text{Sales}}{\text{Sales}}\right)}$$

NOI can be stated as the gross profit, $Q(P-V)$, minus the fixed operating costs, F. So if we use Q to indicate the level of operations forecasted for 2010 and $Q^*$ to indicate the level of operations that would exist if operations were different, the percent change in NOI is stated as

$$\%\Delta \text{ in NOI} = \frac{[Q^*(P-V) - F] - [Q(P-V) - F]}{Q(P-V) - F} = \frac{(Q^* - Q)(P-V)}{Q(P-V) - F}$$

Substituting into Equation 17–3, restating the denominator, and solving, yields

$$\text{DOL} = \frac{\left[\frac{(Q^*-Q)(P-V)}{Q(P-V)-F}\right]}{\left[\frac{P(Q^*-Q)}{P(Q)}\right]} = \frac{(Q^* - Q)(P-V)}{Q(P-V) - F} \times \left(\frac{Q}{Q^* - Q}\right) = \frac{Q(P-V)}{Q(P-V) - F}$$

$$DOL_Q = \frac{Q(P - V)}{Q(P - V) - F}$$

Or, rearranging the terms, DOL can be stated in terms of sales revenues as follows:

$$DOL_Q = \frac{(Q \times P) - (Q \times V)}{(Q \times P) - (Q \times V) - F} = \frac{S - VC}{S - VC - F} = \frac{\text{Gross profit}}{\text{EBIT}}$$

To compute DOL using Equation 17–4 or Equation 17–4a, we only need information from Unilate's forecasted operations; we do not need information about the possible change in forecasted operations. So Q represents the forecasted 2010 level of production and sales, and S and VC are the sales and variable operating costs, respectively, at that level of operations. For Unilate, the equation solution for DOL would be

$$DOL_{Q=110} = \frac{110(\$15.00 - \$12.30)}{110(\$15.00 - \$12.30) - \$154} = \frac{\$1,650 - \$1,353}{\$1,650 - \$1,353 - \$154} = \frac{\$297}{\$143} = 2.08\times$$

Equation 17–4 normally is used to analyze a single product, whereas Equation 17–4a is used to evaluate an entire firm with many types of products and, hence, for which "quantity in units" and "sales price" are not meaningful.

The DOL of 2.08× indicates that *each* 1 percent *change* in sales will result in a 2.08 percent *change* in operating income. What would happen if Unilate's sales decrease, say, by 10 percent? According to the interpretation of the DOL figure, Unilate's operating income would be expected to decrease by 20.8 percent. Table 17-7 shows that this actually would be the case. Therefore, *the DOL value indicates the change (increase or decrease) in operating income resulting from a change (increase or decrease) in the level of operations.* It should be apparent that the greater the DOL, the greater the impact of a change in operations on operating income, whether the change is an increase or a decrease.

The DOL value found by using Equation 17–4 is the degree of operating leverage only for a specific initial sales level. For Unilate, that sales level is 110 million units, or $1,650 million. The DOL value would differ if the initial (existing) level of operations differed. For example, if Unilate's operating cost structure was the same but only 65 million units were produced and sold, the DOL would have been

$$DOL_{Q=65} = \frac{65(\$15.00 - \$12.30)}{65(\$15.00 - \$12.30) - \$154} = \frac{\$175.5}{\$21.5} = 8.16\times$$

**TABLE 17-7**    Unilate Textiles: Operating Income at Sales Levels of 110 Million Units and 99 Million Units ($ millions)

| | 2010 Forecasted Operations | Sales Decrease | Unit Change | Percent Change |
|---|---|---|---|---|
| Sales in units (millions) | 110 | 99 | ( 11) | −10.0% |
| Sales revenues | $1,650.0 | $1,485.0 | $(165.0) | −10.0% |
| Variable cost of goods sold | (1,353.0) | (1,217.7) | 135.3 | −10.0% |
| Gross profit | $ 297.0 | $ 267.3 | $( 29.7) | −10.0% |
| Fixed operating costs | ( 154.0) | ( 154.0) | ( 0.0) | 0.0% |
| Net operating income (EBIT) | $ 143.0 | $ 113.3 | $( 29.7) | −20.8% |

The DOL at 65 million units produced and sold is nearly four times greater than the DOL at 110 million units. Thus, from a base sales of 65 million units, a 10 percent increase in sales, from 65 million units to 71.5 million units, would result in an $8.16 \times 10\% = 81.6\%$ increase in operating income, from $21.5 million to $39.05 million. This shows that when Unilate's operations are closer to its operating breakeven point of 57.04 million units, its degree of operating leverage is higher.

In general, given the same operating cost structure, if a firm's level of operations is decreased, its DOL increases; or, stated differently, the closer a firm is to its operating breakeven point, the greater is its degree of operating leverage. This occurs because, as Figure 17-2 indicates, the closer a firm is to its operating breakeven point, the more likely it is to incur an operating loss due to a decrease in sales. There is not a large buffer in operating income to absorb a decrease in sales and still be able to cover the fixed operating costs. Similarly, at the same level of production and sales, a firm's degree of operating leverage will be higher if the contribution margin for its products is lower. The lower the contribution margin, the less each product sold is able to help cover the fixed operating costs, and the closer the firm is to its operating breakeven point. Therefore, the higher the DOL for a particular firm, it generally can be concluded the closer the firm is to its operating breakeven point, and the more sensitive its operating income is to a change in sales volume. *Greater sensitivity generally implies greater risk; thus, it can be stated that firms with higher DOLs generally are considered to have riskier operations than firms with lower DOLs.*

## Operating Leverage and Operating Breakeven

The relationship between operating leverage and the operating breakeven point is illustrated in Figure 17-3, in which various levels of operations are compared for Unilate and two other textile manufacturers. One firm has a higher contribution margin than Unilate and the other firm has lower fixed operating costs, so we know the other two firms have operating breakeven points that are less than Unilate's. Allied Cloth has the lowest operating breakeven point because it has the highest contribution margin relative to its fixed costs. Unilate has the highest operating breakeven point because it uses the greatest relative amount of operating leverage of the three firms. Consequently, all else equal, of the three textile manufacturers, Unilate's operating income would be magnified the most if actual sales turned out to be greater than forecasted; but it also would experience the greatest decrease in operating income if actual sales turned out to be less than expected.

### Self-Test Questions

What does the term *high degree of operating leverage* imply, and what are some implications of having a high degree of operating leverage?

What is the general equation used to calculate the degree of operating leverage?

What is the association between the concepts of operating breakeven and operating leverage?

Premier Putters expects to produce and sell 5,000 sets of golf clubs next year. Premier sells each set of clubs for $350, the variable cost to produce each set is $200, and fixed operating costs are $250,000. What is Premier's degree of operating leverage (DOL)? (*Answer:* DOL = 1.5×)

## FIGURE 17-3    Operating Leverage

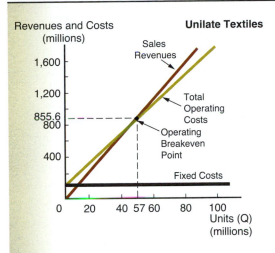

Selling price = $15.00
Variable cost per unit = $12.30
Fixed costs = $154 million
Operating breakeven = 57.04 million units
= $855.6 million

| SALES LEVEL | | TOTAL | OPERATING | |
|---|---|---|---|---|
| UNITS (Q) | REVENUES ($) | OPERATING COSTS | PROFIT (EBIT) | DOL |
| 30 | $ 450 | $ 523 | $ (73) | |
| 60 | 900 | 892 | 8 | 20.3 |
| 110 | 1,650 | 1,507 | 143 | 2.1 |
| 150 | 2,250 | 1,999 | 251 | 1.6 |

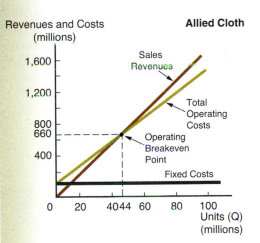

Selling price = $15.00
Variable cost per unit = $11.50
Fixed costs = $154 million
Operating breakeven = 44 million units
= $660 million

| SALES LEVEL | | TOTAL | OPERATING | |
|---|---|---|---|---|
| UNITS (Q) | REVENUES ($) | OPERATING COSTS | PROFIT (EBIT) | DOL |
| 30 | $ 450 | $ 499 | $ (49) | |
| 60 | 900 | 844 | 56 | 3.8 |
| 110 | 1,650 | 1,419 | 231 | 1.7 |
| 150 | 2,250 | 1,879 | 371 | 1.4 |

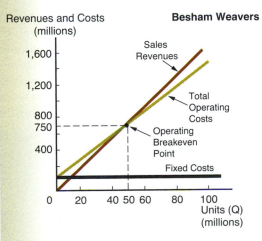

Selling price = $15.00
Variable cost per unit = $12.30
Fixed costs = $135 million
Operating breakeven = 50 million units
= $750 million

| SALES LEVEL | | TOTAL | OPERATING | |
|---|---|---|---|---|
| UNITS (Q) | REVENUES ($) | OPERATING COSTS | PROFIT (EBIT) | DOL |
| 30 | $ 450 | $ 504 | $ (54) | |
| 60 | 900 | 873 | 27 | 6.0 |
| 110 | 1,650 | 1,488 | 162 | 1.8 |
| 150 | 2,250 | 1,980 | 270 | 1.5 |

**TABLE 17-8**    Unilate Textiles: 2010 Forecasted Earnings per Share ($ millions)

| | |
|---|---:|
| Earnings before interest and taxes (EBIT) | $ 143.0 |
| Interest | (41.4) |
| Earnings before taxes (EBT) | $ 101.6 |
| Taxes (40%) | (40.6) |
| Net income | $ 61.0 |
| Preferred dividends | ( 0.0) |
| Earnings available to common stockholders | $ 61.0 |

**Notes:**

$\text{Shrs}_C$ = Number of common shares = 26.3 million

EPS = Earnings per share = $61.0/26.3 = $2.32

## FINANCIAL BREAKEVEN ANALYSIS

**financial breakeven analysis**
Determining the operating income (EBIT) the firm needs to just cover all of its financing costs and produce earnings per share equal to zero.

Operating breakeven analysis deals with evaluation of production and sales to determine at what level the firm's sales revenues will just cover its operating costs—the point at which the operating income is zero. **Financial breakeven analysis** is used to determine the operating income, or EBIT, the firm needs to just cover all of its *financing costs* and produce earnings per share equal to zero. Typically, the financing costs involved in financial breakeven analysis consist of the interest payments to bondholders and the dividend payments to preferred stockholders. Usually these financing costs are fixed, and, in every case, they must be paid before dividends can be paid to common stockholders.

Financial breakeven analysis deals with the lower section of the income statement—the portion from operating income (EBIT) to earnings available to common stockholders. This portion of the income statement generally is referred to as the *financing section* because it contains the expenses associated with the financing arrangements of the firm. The financing section of Unilate's forecasted 2010 income statement is shown in Table 17-8.

### Financial Breakeven Graph

**financial breakeven point (EBIT$_{\text{FinBE}}$)**
The level of EBIT at which EPS equals zero.

Figure 17-4 shows the earnings per share (EPS) for Unilate at various levels of EBIT. The point at which EPS equals zero is referred to as the **financial breakeven point (EBIT$_{\text{FinBE}}$).** As the graph indicates, the financial breakeven point for Unilate is where EBIT equals $41.4 million. At this EBIT level, the income generated from operations is just sufficient to cover the financing costs and income taxes; thus, EPS equals zero. To see this, we can compute the EPS when EBIT is $41.4 million:

| | |
|---|---:|
| Earnings before interest and taxes (EBIT) | $ 41.4 |
| Interest | (41.4) |
| Earnings before taxes (EBT) | 0.0 |
| Taxes (40%) | ( 0.0) |
| Net income | 0.0 |
| Preferred stock dividends | 0.0 |
| Earnings available to common stockholders (EAC) | $ 0.0 |
| EPS = $0/26.3 = $0 | |

FIGURE 17-4   Unilate Textiles: Financial Breakeven Chart

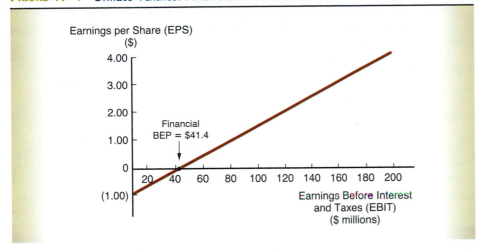

## Financial Breakeven Computation

The results obtained from Figure 17-4 can be translated algebraically to produce a relatively simple equation that can be used to compute the financial breakeven point of any firm. First, remember the financial breakeven point is defined as the level of EBIT that generates EPS equal to zero. Therefore, at the financial breakeven point,

**17–5**

$$EPS = \frac{\text{Earnings available to common stockholders}}{\text{Number of common shares outstanding}} = 0$$
$$= \frac{(EBIT - I)(1 - T) - D_{ps}}{Shrs_c} = 0$$

where EBIT is the earnings before interest and taxes, I represents the interest payments on debt, T is the marginal tax rate, $D_{ps}$ is the amount of dividends paid to preferred stockholders, and $Shrs_C$ is the number of shares of common stock outstanding. Notice that EPS equals zero if the numerator in Equation 17–5, which is the earnings available to common stockholders, equals zero; so the financial breakeven point also can be stated as follows:

$$(EBIT - I)(1 - T) - D_{ps} = 0$$

Rearranging this equation to solve for EBIT gives the solution for the level of EBIT needed to produce EPS equal to zero. Therefore, the computation for a firm's financial breakeven point is

**17–6**

$$EBIT_{FinBE} = I + \frac{D_{ps}}{(1 - T)}$$

Using Equation 17–6, the financial breakeven point for Unilate Textiles in 2010 is

$$EBIT_{FinBE} = \$41.4 + \frac{\$0.0}{(1 - 0.4)} = \$41.4$$

which is the same result shown in Figure 17-4.

According to Equation 17–6, the amount of preferred stock dividends must be stated on a before-tax basis to determine the financial breakeven point. If a firm has no preferred stock, though, the firm needs to cover only its interest payments, so the financial breakeven point simply equals the interest expense. This is the case for Unilate because it has no preferred stock. Because most corporations in the United States do not have preferred stock outstanding, we will not include preferred dividends in the discussions that follow.

## Using Financial Breakeven Analysis

Financial breakeven analysis can be used to help determine the impact of the firm's financing mix on the earnings available to common stockholders.[6] When the firm uses financing alternatives that require fixed financing costs such as interest, financial leverage exists. *Financial leverage affects the financing section* of the income statement like *operating leverage affects the operating section.* This point is discussed in the next section.

**Self-Test Questions**

Define the financial breakeven point. How does the financial breakeven point differ from the operating breakeven point?

Why is it important to carry out financial breakeven analysis?

Suppose that a firm pays interest equal to $120,000 and preferred dividends equal to $70,000. If the firm's marginal tax rate is 30 percent, what is its financial breakeven point? (*Answer:* $EBIT_{FinBE} = $220,000$)

**financial leverage**
The existence of fixed financial costs such as interest and preferred dividends; when a change in EBIT results in a larger change in EPS.

**degree of financial leverage (DFL)**
The percentage change in EPS that results from a given percentage change in EBIT.

## FINANCIAL LEVERAGE

Operating leverage considers how changing sales volume affects operating income, whereas **financial leverage** considers how changing operating income affects earnings per share, or earnings available to common stockholders. Operating leverage affects the operating section of the income statement, whereas financial leverage affects the financing section of the income statement. *Financial leverage takes over where operating leverage leaves off, magnifying the effects on earnings per share of changes in operating income.*

Like operating leverage, financial leverage arises because fixed costs exist, but, in this case, the fixed costs are associated with how the firm is financed. The **degree of financial leverage (DFL)** is defined as the percent change in earnings per share (EPS) that results from a given percent change in earnings before interest and taxes (EBIT). DFL is computed as follows:

17–7

$$\text{Degree of financial leverage} = \text{DFL} = \frac{\%\Delta \text{ in EPS}}{\%\Delta \text{ in EBIT}} = \frac{\left(\frac{\Delta \text{EPS}}{\text{EPS}}\right)}{\left(\frac{\Delta \text{EBIT}}{\text{EBIT}}\right)} = \frac{\left(\frac{\text{EPS}^* - \text{EPS}}{\text{EPS}}\right)}{\left(\frac{\text{EBIT}^* - \text{EBIT}}{\text{EBIT}}\right)}$$

The term with the asterisk (*) indicates the actual outcome, whereas the term without the asterisk is the forecasted result. Thus, EPS* – EPS represents the actual EPS minus the forecasted EPS.

---

[6]The effect of financing the firm with various proportions of debt and equity is discussed in greater detail in Chapter 12.

**TABLE 17-9**   Unilate Textiles: Earnings per Share at Sales Levels of 110 Million Units and 121 Million Units ($ millions, except per share data)[a]

| | 2010 Forecasted Operations | Sales Increase | Dollar Change | Percent Change |
|---|---|---|---|---|
| Sales in units (millions) | 110 | 121 | | +10.0% |
| Earnings before interest and taxes (EBIT) | $ 143.0 | $ 172.7 | $ 29.7 | +20.8% |
| Interest (I) | (41.4) | (41.4) | ( 0.0) | + 0.0% |
| Earnings before taxes (EBT) | $ 101.6 | $ 131.3 | $ 29.7 | +29.2% |
| Taxes (40%) | (40.6) | (52.5) | (11.9) | +29.2% |
| Net income | $ 61.0 | $ 78.8 | $ 17.8 | +29.2% |
| Earning per share (26.3 million shares) | $ 2.32 | $ 3.00 | $ 0.68 | +29.2% |

[a]A spreadsheet was used to generate the results in this table. Only the final results are rounded; thus, there will be some rounding differences if you rely on some of the values in the table, which are rounded to one decimal place, to compute the other values.

Table 17-9 shows the results of increasing Unilate's EBIT 20.8 percent. The increase in EPS is 29.2 percent, which is 1.41 times the change in EBIT; so the DFL for Unilate equals 1.41.

The degree of financial leverage at a particular level of EBIT can be computed easily by using the following equation:[7]

$$DFL = \frac{EBIT}{EBIT - EBIT_{FinBE}}$$

$$= \frac{EBIT}{EBIT - I} \qquad \text{when } D_{ps} = 0$$

17–8

---

[7]Equation 17–8 can be derived easily by expanding Equation 17–7, rearranging the terms, and then simplifying the results. If we use EPS and EBIT to indicate the forecasted 2010 EPS and EBIT, respectively, and EPS* and EBIT* to indicate the EPS and EBIT that would exist after a change in sales volume, then

$$DLF = \frac{\left(\frac{\Delta EPS}{EPS}\right)}{\left(\frac{\Delta EBIT}{EBIT}\right)} = \frac{\left(\frac{EPS^* - EPS}{EPS}\right)}{\left(\frac{EBIT^* - EBIT}{EBIT}\right)}$$

The computation for 2010 forecasted earnings per share is

$$EPS = \frac{(EBIT - I)(1 - T)}{Shrs_C}$$

where $Shrs_C$ is the number of common shares outstanding. The percent change in EPS can be written and simplified as follows:

$$\Delta EPS = \frac{\left[\frac{(EBIT^* - I)(1 - T)}{Shrs_C}\right] - \left[\frac{(EBIT - I)(1 - T)}{Shrs_C}\right]}{\left[\frac{(EBIT - I)(1 - T)}{Shrs_C}\right]} = \frac{[(EBIT^* - I)(1 - T)] - [(EBIT - I)(1 - T)]}{(EBIT - I)(1 - T)} = \frac{EBIT^* - EBIT}{EBIT - I}$$

Substituting this relationship into the computation of DFL, we have

$$DFL = \frac{\left(\frac{EBIT^* - EBIT}{EBIT - I}\right)}{\left(\frac{EBIT^* - EBIT}{EBIT}\right)} = \frac{EBIT^* - EBIT}{EBIT - I} \times \frac{EBIT}{EBIT^* - EBIT} = \frac{EBIT}{EBIT - I} = \frac{EBIT}{EBIT - [\text{Financial BEP}]}$$

If a firm has preferred stock, the relationship given in Equation 17–6 should be substituted in this equation for the [Financial BEP].

Using Equation 17–8, the DFL for Unilate Textiles at EBIT equal to $143.0 million (sales of 110 million units) is

$$\text{DLF}_{Q=110} = \frac{\$143.0}{\$143.0 - \$41.4} = \frac{\$143.0}{\$101.6} = 1.41\times$$

The interpretation of the DFL value is the same as for the degree of operating leverage, except the starting point for evaluating financial leverage is the earnings before interest and taxes (EBIT) and the ending point is earnings per share (EPS). Because the DFL for Unilate is 1.41×, the company can expect a 1.41 percent change in EPS for every 1 percent change in EBIT; a 20.8 percent increase in EBIT results in approximately a 29.2 percent (20.8 percent × 1.41) increase in earnings available to common stockholders, thus the same percent increase in EPS (the number of common shares outstanding does not change). Unfortunately, the opposite also is true—if Unilate's 2010 EBIT is 20.8 percent below expectations, its EPS will be 29.2 percent below the forecast of $2.32. To prove that this result is correct, construct the financing section of Unilate's income statement when EBIT equals $113.3 million = (1 − 0.208) × $143.0 million, and you will find EPS = $1.64, which is 29.2 percent lower that the forecasted amount of $2.32.

The value of the degree of financial leverage found using Equation 17–8 pertains to one specific initial EBIT level. If the level of sales changes, and thus the EBIT changes, so does the value computed for DFL. For example, at sales equal to 80 million units, Unilate's EBIT would be

$$\text{DLF}_{Q=80} = \frac{80(\$15.00 - \$12.30) - \$154}{80(\$15.00 - \$12.30) - \$154 - 41.4} = \frac{\$62.0}{\$62.0 - \$41.4} = \frac{\$62.0}{\$20.6} = 3.01\times$$

Compared with sales equal to 110 million units, at sales equal to 80 million units Unilate would have greater difficulty covering the fixed financing costs, so its DFL is much greater. At EBIT equal to $62.0 million, Unilate is close to its financial breakeven point—EBIT equal to $41.4 million—and its degree of financial leverage is high. So the more difficulty a firm has covering its fixed financing costs with operating income, the greater its degree of financial leverage. In general then, the higher the DFL for a particular firm, it can be concluded the closer the firm is to its financial breakeven point, and the more sensitive its earnings per share is to a change in operating income. *Greater sensitivity implies greater risk; thus, it can be stated that firms with higher DFLs generally are considered to have greater financial risk than firms with lower DFLs.*

### Self-Test Questions

What does the term *high degree of financial leverage* imply, and what are some implications of having a high degree of financial leverage?

Give the general equation used to calculate the degree of financial leverage. Compare the equation for DFL with the equation for the times-interest-earned ratio given in Chapter 2.

Suppose a firm normally generates operating income, EBIT, equal to $440,000. The firm pays interest equal to $120,000 and preferred dividends equal to $70,000. If the firm's marginal tax rate is 30 percent, what is its degree of financial leverage? *(Answer:* DFL = 2.0×)

## COMBINING OPERATING AND FINANCIAL LEVERAGE (DTL)

Our analysis of operating leverage and financial leverage has shown that *(1) the greater the degree of operating leverage, or fixed operating costs for a particular level of operations, the more sensitive EBIT will be to changes in sales volume, and (2) the greater the degree of financial leverage, or fixed financial costs for a particular level of operations, the more sensitive EPS will be to changes in EBIT.* Therefore, if a firm has a considerable amount of both operating leverage and financial leverage, then even small changes in sales will lead to wide fluctuations in EPS. Look at the impact leverage has on Unilate's forecasted 2010 operations. We found that if the sales volume increases by 10 percent, Unilate's EBIT would increase by 20.8 percent; and if EBIT increases by 20.8 percent, its EPS would increase by 29.2 percent. So in combination, a 10 percent increase in sales volume would result in a 29.2 percent increase in EPS. This shows the impact of total leverage, which is the combination of both operating leverage and financial leverage, with respect to Unilate's current operations.

**degree of total leverage (DTL)**
The percentage change in EPS that results from a 1 percent change in sales.

The **degree of total leverage (DTL)** is defined as the percent change in EPS resulting from a 1 percent change in sales volume. This relationship can be written as follows:

$$\text{Degree of total leverage} = \text{DTL} = \frac{\left(\dfrac{\Delta \text{EPS}}{\text{EPS}}\right)}{\left(\dfrac{\Delta \text{Sales}}{\text{Sales}}\right)} = \frac{\left(\dfrac{\Delta \text{EBIT}}{\text{EBIT}}\right)}{\left(\dfrac{\Delta \text{Sales}}{\text{Sales}}\right)} \times \frac{\left(\dfrac{\Delta \text{EPS}}{\text{EPS}}\right)}{\left(\dfrac{\Delta \text{EBIT}}{\text{EBIT}}\right)} = \text{DOL} \times \text{DLF} \qquad \textbf{17--9}$$

Combining the equations for DOL (Equations 17–4 and 17–4a) and for DFL (Equation 17–8), Equation 17–9 can be restated as follows:

$$\text{DTL} = \frac{\text{Gross profit}}{\text{EBIT}} \times \frac{\text{EBIT}}{\text{EBIT} - \text{EBIT}_{\text{FinBE}}} = \frac{\text{Gross profit}}{\text{EBIT} - \text{EBIT}_{\text{FinBE}}} \qquad \textbf{17--10}$$

$$= \frac{\text{S} - \text{VC}}{\text{EBIT} - \text{I}} = \frac{\text{Q}(\text{P} - \text{V})}{[\text{Q}(\text{P} - \text{V}) - \text{F}] - \text{I}} \quad \text{when } \text{D}_{\text{ps}} = 0$$

Using Equation 17–10, the degree of total leverage for Unilate would be

$$\text{DTL}_{\text{Q}=110} = \frac{110(\$15.00 - \$12.30)}{[110(\$15.00 - \$12.30) - \$154.0] - \$41.4} = \frac{\$297.0}{\$101.6} = 2.92\times$$

$$= \qquad \text{DOL} \qquad \times \qquad \text{DFL}$$

$$= \frac{\$297.0}{\$297.0 - \$154.0} \times \frac{\$297.0 - \$154.0}{\$297.0 - \$154.0 - \$41.4}$$

$$= 2.077 \times 1.407 = 2.92\times$$

This value indicates that for every 1 percent change in sales volume, Unilate's EPS will change by 2.92 percent; a 10 percent increase in sales will result in a 29.2 percent increase in EPS. This is exactly the impact expected.

The value of DTL can be used to compute the new earnings per share (EPS*) after a change in sales volume. We already know that Unilate's EPS will change by 2.92 percent for every 1 percent change in sales. So EPS* resulting from a 10 percent increase in sales can be computed as follows:

$$\text{EPS}^* = \text{EPS}[1 + (0.10)(2.92)] = \$2.32 \times (1 + 0.292) = \$3.00$$

which is the same result given in Table 17-9.

The degree of combined (total) leverage concept is useful primarily for the insights it provides regarding the joint effects of operating and financial leverage on earnings per share. The concept can be used to show management, for example, that a decision to finance new equipment with debt would result in a situation in which a 10 percent decline in sales would result in a nearly 30 percent decline in earnings, whereas with a different operating and financial package, a 10 percent sales decline would cause earnings to decline by only 15 percent. Having the alternatives stated in this manner gives decision makers a better idea of the ramifications of alternative actions with respect to the firm's level of operations and how those operations are financed.

## Self-Test Questions

What information is provided by the degree of total (combined) leverage?

What does the term *high degree of total leverage* imply?

Suppose that when a firm generates a gross profit equal to $660,000, its operating income is $440,000. The firm pays interest equal to $120,000 and preferred dividends equal to $70,000. If the firm's marginal tax rate is 30 percent, what is its degree of operating leverage, degree of financial leverage, and degree of total leverage? *(Answer:* DOL = 1.5×, DFL = 2.0×, DTL = 3.0×*)*

## USING LEVERAGE AND FORECASTING FOR CONTROL

From the discussion in the previous sections, it should be clear what the impact on income would be if the 2010 sales forecast for Unilate Textiles is different than expected. If sales are greater than expected, both operating and financial leverage will magnify the "bottom line" effect on EPS (DTL = 2.92). But the opposite also holds.

Consequently, if Unilate does not meet its forecasted sales level, leverage will result in a magnified loss in income compared with what is expected. This will occur because production facilities might have been expanded too greatly, inventories might be built up too quickly, and so on; the end result might be that the firm suffers a significant income loss. This loss will result in a lower-than-expected addition to retained earnings, which means the plans for additional external funds needed to support the firm's operations will be inadequate. Likewise, if the sales forecast is too low, then, if the firm is at full capacity, it will not be able to meet the additional demand, and sales opportunities will be lost—perhaps forever. In the previous sections, we showed only how changes in operations (2010 forecasts) affect the income generated by the firm; we did not continue the process to show the impact on the balance sheet and the financing needs of the firm. To determine the impact on the financial statements, the financial manager needs to repeat the steps discussed in the first part of this chapter. At this stage, the financial manager needs to evaluate and act on the feedback received from the forecasting and budgeting processes. In effect, then, the forecasting (planning) and control of the firm is an ongoing activity, a vital function to the long-run survival of any firm.

The forecasting and control functions described in this chapter are important for several reasons. First, if the projected operating results are unsatisfactory, management can "go back to the drawing board," reformulate its plans, and develop more reasonable targets for the coming year. Second, it is possible that the funds required to meet the sales forecast simply cannot be obtained; if so, it obviously is better to know this in advance and to scale back the projected level of operations than to suddenly run out of cash and have operations grind to a halt. Third, even if the required funds can be raised, it is desirable to plan for their acquisition well in advance. Finally, any deviation from the projections needs to be dealt with to improve future forecasts and the predictability of the firm's operations to ensure that the goals of the firm are being pursued appropriately.

### Self-Test Question
Why is it important that the forecasting and control of the firm be an ongoing activity?

## THE FEDERAL INCOME TAX SYSTEM

In this and earlier chapters, we discovered that after-tax cash flows should be evaluated when making financial decisions. In this section, we summarize some important points about the tax system in the United States. The points discussed here apply only to federal taxes; state tax codes often contain somewhat different rules.

### U.S. Federal Tax Code[8]

The U.S. Federal Tax Code is divided into two sections: (1) tax laws that are applicable to individuals, and (2) tax laws that are applicable to corporations. As the name implies, the corporate tax code applies to businesses that are organized as corporations. Other types of businesses, including proprietorships and partnerships, are taxed according to the individual tax code. Most states also tax income for both individuals and businesses. As a result, the average tax rate paid by both corporations and individuals generally is higher than the federal tax rate.

### Taxable Income

**Taxable income** is defined as gross income less deductions and exemptions that are allowed by the tax code. Most expenses incurred by businesses are tax deductible, whereas few expenses incurred by individuals are tax deductible. Because the individual section of the tax code applies to income generated by proprietorships and partnerships, it is important to understand the difference between business expenses that are tax deductible and personal expenses that are not tax deductible. Generally speaking, an allowable business expense is a cost incurred to generate business revenues. On the other hand, if an expense is incurred for personal benefit (use), it is considered a personal expense, which is not tax deductible. For instance, Loretta Kay owns a house in which she lived until last month, at which time she moved and rented the house to a group of college students. Three months ago, the plumbing burst in the kitchen, and Loretta had to call the plumber for repairs. The repairs cost $1,000. Is this a tax-deductible expense? No, because the house was Loretta's personal residence at the time. Last night, Loretta had to call the plumber again to fix pipes that had burst in the same house. The repairs cost $1,200. Is this a tax-deductible expense? Yes, the expense was incurred for business purposes because the house now is rental property, which is considered a business operation.

> **taxable income**
> Gross income minus exemptions and allowable deductions as set forth in the tax code.

### Tax Rates

In 2007, federal income tax rates for individuals ranged from 10 percent to approximately 35 percent, and corporate profits were subject to federal income tax rates that

---

[8]For more information about taxes, visit the Internal Revenue Service Website at http://www.irs.gov.

**progressive tax**
A tax that requires a higher percentage payment on higher incomes.

**marginal tax rate**
The tax applicable to the last unit of income; the tax payer's tax bracket.

ranged from 15 percent to 39 percent. Thus, our tax rates are **progressive** because higher dollars of income are taxed at higher rates.

The "tax bracket" of a company (or individual) is its **marginal tax rate,** which is defined as the tax on the last unit of income. A corporation's (individual's) average tax rate is the percent of taxable income that the firm (person) pays in taxes, which equals the total taxes paid divided by the taxable income.

## Interest Income

Most interest income received by corporations and individuals is taxable. One exception is interest earned on municipal bonds—that is, bonds issued by states and local governments—which is not subject to federal income taxes. Thus, investors get to keep all of the interest received from most municipal bonds but only a fraction of the interest received from bonds issued by corporations or by the U.S. government.

## Interest Expense

Interest payments made by businesses on loans are tax deductible when computing taxable income. On the other hand, with the exception of interest on mortgages, most interest paid by individuals on loans is not tax deductible.

## Dividend Income

Dividends received by both individuals and corporations are considered income for tax purposes. Dividends received by individuals that qualify are taxed at 15 percent if the individual's tax rate is 25 percent or higher; if the individual's tax rate is lower than 25 percent, dividends are taxed at 5 percent. Because firms pay dividends from income after paying corporate taxes and individuals pay taxes on dividends they receive, there is a double taxation of dividends—first at the corporation and then again when the individual receives the dividend.

When one corporation receives a dividend payment from another corporation, 70 percent of the dividend is excluded for tax purposes. As a result, only 30 percent of a dividend received by a corporation is taxed at the ordinary rate. The reason for this exclusion is because dividends received by corporations can be subject to triple taxation: (1) the corporation that pays the original dividend is taxed first, (2) the second corporation is taxed on the dividend it receives, and (3) the individual who receives the dividend from the second corporation is taxed again.

## Dividends Paid

Dividend payments are not tax-deductible expenses. Thus, because interest on debt is a tax-deductible expense, our tax system favors debt financing over equity financing. Although it generally is not possible to finance exclusively with debt and the risk of doing so would offset the tax benefits, it is clear that the tax treatment of interest payments versus dividend payments has a profound effect on the way businesses are financed. This point was discussed in detail in Chapters 11 and 12.

**capital gain (loss)**
The profit (loss) from the sale of a capital asset for more (less) than its depreciated value.

## Capital Gains

When an individual or corporation buys a capital asset and later sells it for more than its depreciated value, the profit is called a **capital gain;** if the asset is sold for less than its depreciated value, a **capital loss** is incurred. An asset sold within one year of the time it was purchased produces a *short-term gain (loss),* whereas a capital asset that was held for one year or longer produces a *long-term gain (loss).*

For an individual, a short-tem capital gain is taxed at the marginal tax rate of the taxpayer, whereas a long-term capital gain is taxed at 15 percent (5 percent if the individual's regular tax rate is lower than 25 percent). A corporate capital gain, whether it is long-term or short-term, is taxed at the same rate as the firm's operating income.

## Corporate Loss Carryback and Carryover

Ordinary corporate *operating losses* can be carried back (termed a **carryback**) to each of the preceding two years and carried over (termed a **carryover**) for the next 20 years to offset taxable income in those years. The loss is applied first to the earliest year, then to the next earliest year, and so on, until losses have been used up or the 20-year carryover limit has been reached. The purpose of permitting firms to treat losses like this is to avoid penalizing corporations whose incomes fluctuate substantially from year to year.

**tax loss carryback and carryover**
Operating losses that can be carried backward or forward in time to offset taxable income in a given year.

## Depreciation

Depreciation plays an important role in income tax calculations. Congress specifies, in the tax code, the life over which assets can be depreciated for tax purposes and the methods of depreciation that can be used. Because these factors have a major influence on the amount of depreciation a firm can take in a given year, and thus on the firm's taxable income, depreciation has an important effect on taxes paid and cash flows from operations. We discussed how depreciation is calculated and how it affects income and cash flows when we discussed the subject of capital budgeting in Chapter 9 and Chapter 10.

## Small Businesses

Generally a small business takes the form of either a proprietorship or a partnership, and it is taxed according to the rules that apply to individuals. A small corporation that meets certain restrictions as spelled out in the tax code, including having fewer than 75 stockholders, can elect to be taxed as a proprietorship or partnership rather than as a corporation. These corporations are called **S corporations.** An S corporation receives the benefits of the corporate form of organization—including limited liability—but its income is reported as personal income by the owners. Because the firm's income is taxed only once at the individual level, S-corporation status is preferred by owners of small corporations in which all or most of the income earned each year is distributed as dividends.

A small corporation that does not qualify for S corporation status is termed a C corporation, and it is required to follow the corporate tax code when computing taxes.

**S corporation**
A small corporation that elects to be taxed as a proprietorship or a partnership yet retains limited liability and other benefits of the corporate form of organization.

**Self-Test Questions**

Explain what is meant by the statement: "Our tax rates are progressive."

What are capital gains and losses?

Differentiate between the tax treatment of dividends received by corporations and the tax treatment of dividends received by individuals. Why is there a difference?

Briefly explain how tax loss carryback and carryover procedures work.

What is the difference between an S corporation and a C corporation?

## Chapter *Essentials*
### —The Answers

To summarize the key concepts, let's answer the questions that were posed at the beginning of the chapter:

- **Why is financial planning and control critical to the survival of a firm?** Financial planning requires the firm to forecast future operations. Such forecasts are needed so that the firm can make arrangements for expected changes in production, future financing needs, and so forth. A financial plan represents a "road map" for the firm to follow to attain future goals. The process doesn't stop when financial forecasts are completed because the firm needs to monitor operations as the financial plan is implemented to determine whether modifications are needed.

- **What are pro forma financial statements? What is the purpose of constructing such statements?** Pro forma financial statements represent a firm's projections about future operations. The firm projects what it thinks the balance sheet and income statement will look like if future expectations come true. It is important for a firm to construct pro formas so that it can make plans to raise any needed external funds, to expand plant and equipment, and so forth to attain forecasted growth.

- **What are operating breakeven and operating leverage? How are the two related?** The operating breakeven point is the level of production and sales that a firm needs to attain so that operating income (EBIT = NOI) equals zero—that is, it is the level of sales at which the firm just covers its operating expenses. Operating leverage represents the fixed operating costs of the firm. The degree of operating leverage (DOL) states these operating costs on a relative basis, and it indicates by what percent the firm's operating income will change if sales change. Everything else equal, because firms with higher DOLs operate closer to their operating breakeven points, they are considered riskier than firms with lower DOLs.

- **What are financial breakeven and financial leverage? How are the two related?** The financial breakeven point is the level of EBIT that a firm must generate so that EPS equals zero—that is, it is the level of operating income at which the firm's financial costs are covered and its net income is zero. Financial leverage represents the fixed financial costs of the firm. The degree of financial leverage (DFL) states these financial costs on a relative basis, and it indicates by what percent the firm's EPS will change if EBIT changes. Everything else equal, because firms with higher DFLs operate closer to their financial breakeven points, they are considered riskier than firms with lower DFLs.

- **How can a firm use knowledge of leverage in the financial forecasting and control process?** In general, a firm that has a higher degree of leverage is considered riskier than a similar firm that has a lower degree of leverage. A firm uses the concept of leverage to estimate how fixed costs, both operating and financial, affect its "bottom line" net income. Everything else equal, a firm can decrease its risk by decreasing its relative fixed costs, increasing sales, or by attaining both actions. Remember from our discussions in previous chapters that when a firm reduces its risk, its cost of capital decreases, and thus its value increases.

- **Why is it important to have some understanding of the U.S. Federal Tax Code?** Simply stated, taxes must be paid in cash. As a result, a firm's financial plans must consider the effects of taxes. Whereas taxes reduce the cash flows generated from operations that can be reinvested in the firm, taxes also decrease the effective cost of borrowing to finance the firm.

## ETHICAL DILEMMA

### Competition-Based Planning—Promotion or Payoff?

A few months ago, Kim Darby, financial manager of Republic Communications Corporation (RCC), contacted you about a job opening in the financial planning division of the company. RCC is a well-established firm that has offered long-distance phone service in the United States for more than three decades. But recent deregulation in the telecommunications industry has RCC concerned because competition has increased significantly—today many more firms offer long-distance services than five years ago. In fact, RCC has seen its profits decline along with market share since deregulation began. Kim Darby indicated that RCC wants to reverse this trend by improving the company's planning function so that long-distance rates can be set to better attract and keep customers in the future. Kim says that is the reason she contacted you.

When she first called, Kim told you RCC would like to hire you because you are one of the "up-and-comers" in the telecommunications industry. You have worked at National Telecommunications Inc. (NTI), one of RCC's fiercest competitors, since you graduated from college four years ago, helping to develop their rate-setting program, which many consider the best in the industry.

Taking the position at RCC would be comparable to a promotion with a $30,000 salary increase and provide greater chances for advancement than your current position at NTI. So, after interviewing with RCC and talking to friends and family, a couple of days ago you informally accepted the job at RCC. You have not yet notified NTI of your decision.

Earlier today, Kim called to see whether you could start your new position in a couple of weeks. RCC would like you to start work as soon as possible because it wants to begin a redesign of its rate-setting plan in an effort to regain market share. During the conversation, Kim mentioned that it would be helpful if you could bring NIT's rate-setting program and some rate-setting information with you to your new job—it will help RCC rewrite its rate-setting program. In an attempt to allay any reservations you might have, Kim told you that NTI sells its software to other companies and any rate-setting information is available to the public through states' public service commissions, so everything you bring really is well known in the industry and should be considered in the public domain. And, according to Kim, RCC is not going to copy the rate-setting program; her attitude is "what is wrong with taking a look at it as long as we don't copy the program?" If you provide RCC with NTI's rate-setting program, you know it will help the company to plan better, and better planning will lead to increased market share and higher stock prices. An improved rate-setting plan might net RCC as much as $200 million each year, and RCC has a very generous bonus system to reward employees who help the company improve its market position.

If you do not provide the software, you might start off your new job "on the wrong foot." What should you do?

---

The concepts presented in this chapter should help you to understand the importance of financial planning. If you understand the concepts presented in this chapter, you should be able to develop a financial plan that will help you make more informed financial decisions.

- Like firms, it is important for you to develop "sales" forecasts so that you can plan your financial future. In your case, however, a "sales" forecast is a prediction of your future income. Such forecasting is important to your financial survival. For example, if you want to purchase a house, you must determine the "amount of house" you can afford, which is dependent on the income you expect to generate in the future. Even if you construct an unsophisticated financial plan, it is important that you plan your financial future; otherwise, you might find yourself in financial distress. Your financial

## Chapter *Essentials*
### —Personal Finance

plan should include more than your expectations about purchasing such high-price items as a house or an automobile; it should also include plans for retirement, plans for a child's education, plans for the financial security of dependents, and so forth. Financial plans necessarily become more complicated as you grow in your career and your family ages because your finances become more complicated.

If we slightly change the mantra that is included in the A Managerial Perspective at the beginning of the chapter, we can say, "People don't plan to fail financially, they fail to develop financial plans." You should keep these words in mind when dealing with financial matters.

- As we discovered in the chapter, firms want to determine their breakeven points so that they know what levels of operations must be attained to earn profits. You too should want to determine your breakeven point so that you know when you have funds available to invest in your retirement fund, to buy a car, or to take a dream vacation. Determining your breakeven point should be an integral part of your financial plan.

- In the chapter, we discussed how leverage affects the income generated by a firm. Consider how you can use leverage to your advantage, as well as how leverage can be harmful to your financial position. Remember that when leverage exists, returns are magnified. Consequently, when a person uses leverage, his or her returns are magnified; when returns are positive, there is a "good" magnification, but when returns are negative, there is a "bad" magnification. For example, suppose you borrow $1,000 at 10 percent and you add the borrowed money to $1,000 of your own money to invest in a stock. If the $2,000 earns a 15 percent return, the *total dollar return* from the investment is $300. Because you have to pay the lender only $100 interest for the money that you borrowed, you get to keep $200 of the amount that is earned. Thus, the percent return on *your* $1,000 is 20% = $200/$1,000. The 20 percent return you earn on your $1,000 is much greater than the 10 percent return that the $2,000 investment earned because you do not have to share your additional profits with the lender—that is, you have a fixed financial cost equal to $100. But, if the $2,000 earns only 6 percent, then the *total dollar return* would be $120. You still have to pay the lender $100 interest, thus you earn only $20 on your $1,000 investment. This translates to a 2 percent rate of return (= $20/$1,000). The 2 percent return you earn on your $1,000 is much less than the 6 percent return that the $2,000 investment earns because you have to pay the lender $100 interest regardless of what you do with the money—that is, you have a fixed financial cost equal to $100. As you can see, the fixed financial cost—that is, $100 in interest—magnifies the return you earn, regardless of whether you earn a "good" return or you earn a "bad" return.

- When investing or borrowing, you should always consider the effects of taxes before making decisions. Except for tax-exempt investments, taxes reduce the return that is earned on investments. For example, suppose that you are in the 25 percent tax bracket and you invest $1,000 in a stock that you sell six months later for $1,100. For tax purposes, you must include $100 as taxable income, which means you will pay $25 = $100(0.25) taxes on your investment income. As a result, your after-tax investment income is $75 and your after-tax return is 7.5 percent, which is lower than the 10 percent return that was earned before taxes. When making investment decisions, you should always compare the after-tax returns of investments. The same logic applies when comparing loan alternatives.

# QUESTIONS

**17-1**  Certain liability and net worth items generally increase spontaneously with increases in sales. Put a check mark (✔) by those items that typically increase spontaneously:

Accounts payable            _____
Notes payable to banks      _____
Accrued wages               _____
Accrued taxes               _____
Mortgage bonds              _____
Common stock                _____
Retained earnings           _____

**17-2**  Suppose a firm makes the following policy changes. If the change means that external, nonspontaneous financial requirements (AFN) will increase, indicate this by a plus sign (+); indicate a decrease by a negative sign (−); and indicate indeterminate or no effect by a zero (0). Think in terms of the immediate, short-run effect on funds requirements.

  **a.** The dividend payout is increased.                                          _____

  **b.** The firm contracts to buy, rather than make, certain components used in its products.                                  _____

  **c.** The firm decides to pay all suppliers on delivery, rather than after a 30-day delay, to take advantage of discounts for rapid payment.                          _____

  **d.** The firm begins to sell on credit (previously all sales had been on a cash basis).                              _____

  **e.** The firm's profit margin is eroded by increased competition; sales are steady.                           _____

  **f.** Advertising expenditures are increased.                _____

  **g.** A decision is made to substitute long-term mortgage bonds for short-term bank loans.                          _____

  **h.** The firm begins to pay employees on a weekly basis (previously it had paid at the end of each month).      _____

**17-3**  What benefits can be derived from breakeven analysis, both operating and financial? What are some problems with breakeven analysis?

**17-4**  Explain how profits or losses will be magnified for a firm with high operating leverage as opposed to a firm with lower operating leverage.

**17-5**  Explain how profits or losses will be magnified for a firm with high financial leverage as opposed to a firm with lower financial leverage.

**17-6**  What data are necessary to construct an operating breakeven chart?

**17-7**  What data are necessary to construct a financial breakeven chart?

**17-8**  What would be the effect of each of the following on a firm's operating and financial breakeven point? Indicate the effect in the space provided by placing a plus sign (+) for an increase, a negative sign (−) for a decrease, and a zero (0) for no effect. When answering this question, assume everything except the change indicated is held constant.

| | Operating Breakeven | Financial Breakeven |
|---|---|---|
| **a.** An increase in the sales price | _____ | _____ |
| **b.** A reduction in the variable cost ratio | _____ | _____ |
| **c.** A decrease in fixed operating costs | _____ | _____ |
| **d.** Issuing new bonds | _____ | _____ |
| **e.** Issuing new preferred stock | _____ | _____ |
| **f.** Issuing new common stock | _____ | _____ |

**17-9** Assume that a firm is developing its long-run financial plan. What period should this plan cover—one month, six months, one year, three years, five years, or some other period? Justify your answer.

**17-10** What does *double taxation of corporate income* mean?

**17-11** If you were starting a business, what tax considerations might cause you to prefer to set it up as a proprietorship or a partnership rather than as a corporation? Would you consider the average or the marginal tax rate more relevant?

**17-12** Explain how the federal income tax structure affects the choice of financing (use of debt versus equity) of U.S. businesses.

## SELF-TEST PROBLEMS

*(Solutions appear in Appendix B at the end of the book.)*

**key terms**

**ST-1** Define each of the following terms:

    **a.** Sales forecast

    **b.** Projected balance sheet method

    **c.** Spontaneously generated funds

    **d.** Dividend payout ratio

    **e.** Pro forma financial statement

    **f.** Additional funds needed (AFN)

    **g.** Financing feedback

    **h.** Financial planning; financial control

    **i.** Operating breakeven analysis; operating breakeven point, $Q_{OpBE}$

    **j.** Financial breakeven analysis; financial breakeven point ($EBIT_{FinBE}$)

    **k.** Operating leverage; degree of operating leverage (DOL)

    **l.** Financial leverage; degree of financial leverage (DFL)

    **m.** Combined (total) leverage; degree of total leverage (DTL)

    **n.** Progressive tax; marginal tax rate

    **o.** Capital gain; capital loss

    **p.** Tax loss carryback and carryforward

    **q.** S corporation

**operating leverage and breakeven analysis**

**ST-2** Olinde Electronics Inc. produces stereo components that sell for P = $100. Olinde's fixed costs are $200,000; 5,000 components are produced and sold each year; EBIT is currently $50,000; and Olinde's assets (all equity financed) are $500,000. Olinde estimates that it can change its production process, adding $400,000 to investment and $50,000 to fixed operating costs. This change will (1) reduce variable costs per unit by $10 and (2) increase output by 2,000 units, but (3) the sales price on all units will have to be lowered to $95 to sell the 7,000 components. Olinde has tax loss carryovers, so its current tax rate equals zero. Olinde uses no debt, and its average cost of capital is 10 percent.

**a.** Should Olinde make the change?

**b.** Would Olinde's degree of operating leverage increase or decrease if it made the change? What about its operating breakeven point?

**c.** Suppose Olinde was unable to raise additional equity financing and had to borrow the $400,000 to make the investment at an interest rate of 8 percent. Use the DuPont equation (see Chapter 2) to find the expected return on total assets (ROA) of the investment. Should Olinde make the change if debt financing must be used?

**d.** What would Olinde's degree of financial leverage be if the $400,000 was borrowed at the 8 percent interest rate?

## PROBLEMS

**17-1** Following is information about the Super Shoe Store (SSS):

*operating leverage and breakeven*

| | |
|---|---|
| Selling price per unit | $ 50 |
| Variable cost per unit | $ 30 |
| Fixed operating costs | $120,000 |

**a.** What is SSS's operating income (NOI) when sales are 10,000 units (boxes of shoes)?

**b.** How many pairs of shoes does SSS have to sell to break even with its operations?

**c.** If the firm normally sells 10,000 pairs of shoes, what is SSS's degree of operating leverage?

**17-2** Premier Primer Pumps (PPP) sells sump pumps for $2,500 each. The variable costs associated with the manufacture of each pump are $1,750 and fixed operating costs are $150,000 annually. PPP normally sells 300 pumps each year, has an interest expense equal to $30,000, and its marginal tax rate is 40 percent. Given this information, what is PPP's operating breakeven point?

*operating breakeven*

**17-3** Analysts have evaluated the Sivar Silver Company and discovered that if sales are $800,000 the following will exist:

*leverage analysis*

| | |
|---|---|
| Degree of operating leverage (DOL) | 4.0× |
| Degree of financial leverage (DFL) | 2.0× |
| Earnings before interest and taxes (EBIT) | $50,000 |
| Earnings per share (EPS) | $ 4.00 |

According to this information, what will Sivar's EBIT be if sales actually turn out to be $720,000 rather than $800,000? What will the EPS be?

**17-4** The Niendorf Corporation produces tea kettles, which it sells for $15 each. Fixed costs are $700,000 for up to 400,000 units of output. Variable costs are $10 per kettle.

*operating leverage*

**FIGURE 17-5**   **Breakeven Charts for Problem 17-5**

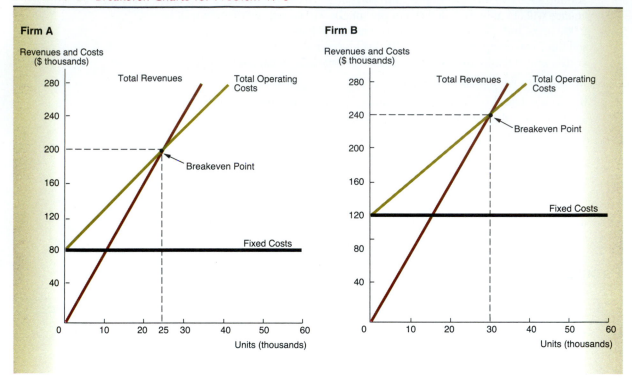

a. What is the firm's gain or loss at sales of 125,000 units? Of 175,000 units?

b. What is the operating breakeven point? Illustrate by means of a chart.

c. What is Niendorf's degree of operating leverage at sales of 125,000 units? Of 150,000 units? Of 175,000 units?

**degree of operating leverage**   **17-5**   a. Given the graphs shown in Figure 17-5, calculate the total fixed costs, variable costs per unit, and sales price for Firm A. Firm B's fixed costs are $120,000, its variable costs per unit are $4, and its sales price is $8 per unit.

b. Which firm has the higher degree of operating leverage? Explain.

c. At what sales level, in units, do both firms earn the same profit?

**long-term financing needs**   **17-6**   At year-end 2009, total assets for Shome Inc. were $1.2 million and accounts payable were $375,000. Sales, which in 2009 were $2.5 million, are expected to increase by 25 percent in 2010. Total assets and accounts payable are proportional to sales, and that relationship will be maintained. Shome typically uses no current liabilities other than accounts payable. Common stock amounted to $425,000 in 2009, and retained earnings were $295,000. Shome plans to sell new common stock in the amount of $75,000. The firm's profit margin on sales is 6 percent, and 40 percent of earnings will be paid out as dividends.

a. What was Shome's total debt in 2009?

b. How much new, long-term debt financing will be needed in 2010? (*Hint:* AFN − New stock = New long-term debt.) Do not consider any financing feedback effects.

**17-7**  The McGill Company's sales are forecasted to increase from $1,000 in 2009     **additional funds needed**
to $2,000 in 2010. Here is the December 31, 2009, balance sheet:

| | | | |
|---|---|---|---|
| Cash | $ 100 | Accounts payable | $ 50 |
| Accounts receivable | 200 | Notes payable | 150 |
| Inventories | 200 | Accruals | 50 |
| Current assets | $ 500 | Current liabilities | $ 250 |
| Net fixed assets | 500 | Long-term debt | 400 |
| | | Common stock | 100 |
| | | Retained earnings | 250 |
| Total assets | $1,000 | Total liabilities and equity | $1,000 |

McGill's fixed *assets were used to only 50 percent of capacity* during 2009, but its current assets were at their proper levels. All assets except fixed assets increase at the same rate as sales, and fixed assets would also increase at the same rate if the current excess capacity did not exist. McGill's after-tax profit margin is forecasted to be 5 percent, and its payout ratio will be 60 percent. What is McGill's additional funds needed (AFN) for the coming year? Ignore financing feedback effects.

**17-8**  Straight Arrow Company manufactures golf balls. The following income     **breakeven analysis**
statement information is relevant for Straight Arrow in 2010:

| | |
|---|---|
| Selling price per sleeve of balls (P) | $ 5.00 |
| Variable cost of goods sold (% of price, P) | 75% |
| Fixed operating costs (F) | $50,000 |
| Interest expense (I) | $10,000 |
| Preferred dividends ($D_{PS}$) | $ 0.00 |
| Marginal tax rate (T) | 40% |
| Number of common shares | 20,000 |

a. What level of sales does Straight Arrow need to achieve in 2010 to break even with respect to *operating income?*

b. At its operating breakeven, what will be the EPS for Straight Arrow?

c. How many sleeves of golf balls (units) does Straight Arrow need to sell in 2010 to attain the financial breakeven point? [*Hint:* An easy way to look at this problem is to consider how many sleeves of balls (units) *beyond those needed for operating breakeven* Straight Arrow needs to sell to cover its fixed financial charges.]

d. If Straight Arrow expects its sales to be $300,000 in 2010, what is its degree of operating leverage, its degree of financial leverage, and its degree of total (combined) leverage? Based on the degree of total leverage, compute the earnings per share you would expect in 2010 if sales actually turn out to be $270,000.

**17-9**  Magee Computers makes bulk purchases of small computers, stocks     **pro forma and ratios**
them in conveniently located warehouses, and ships them to its chain of retail stores. Magee's balance sheet as of December 31, 2009, is shown here ($ millions):

| | | | |
|---|---|---|---|
| Cash | $ 3.5 | Accounts payable | $ 9.0 |
| Receivables | 26.0 | Notes payable | 18.0 |
| Inventories | 58.0 | Accruals | 8.5 |
| Current assets | $ 87.5 | Current liabilities | $ 35.5 |
| Net fixed assets | 35.0 | Long-term bonds | 6.0 |
| | | Common stock | 15.0 |
| | | Retained earnings | 66.0 |
| Total assets | $122.5 | Total liabilities and equity | $122.5 |

Sales for 2009 were $350 million, while net income for the year was $10.5 million. Magee paid dividends of $4.2 million to common stock-holders. Sales are projected to increase by $70 million, or 20 percent, during 2010. The firm is operating at full capacity. Assume that the profit margin and dividend payout ratios remain constant.

**a.** Construct Magee's pro forma balance sheet for December 31, 2010. Assume that all external capital requirements are met by bank loans and are reflected in notes payable. Do not consider any financing feedback effects.

**b.** Now calculate the following ratios, based on your projected December 31, 2010, balance sheet. Magee's 2009 ratios and industry average ratios are shown here for comparison:

| | Magee Computers | | Industry Average |
|---|---|---|---|
| | **12/31/10** | **12/31/09** | **12/31/09** |
| Current ratio | | 2.5 | 3.0 |
| Debt/total assets | | 33.9% | 30.0% |
| Return on equity | | 13.0% | 12.0% |

**c.** **(1)** Now assume that Magee grows by the same $70 million but that the growth is spread over five years—that is, that sales grow by $14 million each year. Do not consider any financing feedback effects. Construct a pro forma balance sheet as of December 31, 2010, using notes payable as the balancing item.

**(2)** Calculate the current ratio, debt/assets ratio, and rate of return on equity as of December 31, 2014. [*Hint:* Be sure to use total sales, which amount to $1,960 million, to calculate retained earnings but 2014 profits to calculate the rate of return on equity—that is, return on equity = (2014 profits)/(12/31/14 equity).]

**d.** Do the plans outlined in parts a or c seem feasible to you? That is, do you think Magee could borrow the required capital, and would the company be raising the chance of its bankruptcy to an excessive level in the event of some temporary misfortune?

**additional funds needed**   **17-10** Following are Noso Textile's 2009 financial statements.

**a.** Suppose 2010 sales are projected to increase by 15 percent over 2009 sales. Determine the additional funds needed. Assume that the company was operating at *full capacity* in 2009, that it cannot sell off any of its fixed assets, and that any required financing will be borrowed as notes payable. Also, assume that assets, spontaneous liabilities, and operating costs are expected to increase by the same percentage as sales. Use the

**Noso Textile: Balance Sheet as of December 31, 2009 ($ thousands)**

| | | | |
|---|---|---|---|
| Cash | $ 1,080 | Accounts payable | $ 4,320 |
| Receivables | 6,480 | Accruals | 2,880 |
| Inventories | 9,000 | Notes payable | 2,100 |
| Current assets | $16,560 | Current liabilities | $ 9,300 |
| Net fixed assets | 12,600 | Long-term bonds | 3,500 |
| | | Common stock | 3,500 |
| | | Retained earnings | 12,860 |
| Total assets | $29,160 | Total liabilities and equity | $29,160 |

**Noso Textile: Income Statement for December 31, 2009 ($ thousands)**

| | |
|---|---|
| Sales | $ 36,000 |
| Operating costs | (32,440) |
| Earnings before interest and taxes | $ 3,560 |
| Interest | ( 560) |
| Earnings before taxes | $ 3,000 |
| Taxes (40%) | ( 1,200) |
| Net income | $ 1,800 |
| Dividends (45%) | $ 810 |
| Addition to retained earnings | $ 990 |

projected balance sheet method to develop a pro forma balance sheet and income statement for December 31, 2010. (Do not incorporate any financing feedback effects. Use the pro forma income statement to determine the addition to retained earnings.)

**b.** Use the financial statements developed in part a to incorporate the financing feedback as a result of the addition to notes payable. (That is, do the next financial statement iteration.) For the purpose of this part, assume that the notes payable interest rate is 10 percent. What is the AFN for this iteration?

**17-11** Van Auken Lumber's 2009 income statement is shown here:

**degree of leverage**

**Van Auken Lumber: Income Statement for December 31, 2009 ($ thousands)**

| | |
|---|---|
| Sales | $36,000 |
| Cost of goods sold | (25,200) |
| Gross profit | $10,800 |
| Fixed operating costs | ( 6,480) |
| Earnings before interest and taxes | $ 4,320 |
| Interest | ( 2,880) |
| Earnings before taxes | $ 1,440 |
| Taxes (40%) | ( 576) |
| Net income | $ 864 |
| Dividends (50%) | $ 432 |

**a.** Compute the degree of operating leverage (DOL), degree of financial leverage (DFL), and degree of total leverage (DTL) for Van Auken Lumber.

**b.** Interpret the meaning of each of the numerical values you computed in part a.

c. Briefly discuss some ways Van Auken can reduce its degree of total leverage.

**external financing requirements**

**17-12** The 2009 balance sheet and income statement for the Woods Company are shown here:

**Woods Company: Balance Sheet as of December 31, 2009 ($ thousands)**

| | | | |
|---|---|---|---|
| Cash | $    80 | Accounts payable | $  160 |
| Accounts receivable | 240 | Accruals | 40 |
| Inventories | 720 | Notes payable | 252 |
| Current assets | $1,040 | Current liabilities | $  452 |
| Fixed assets | 3,200 | Long-term debt | 1,244 |
| | | Common stock | 1,605 |
| | | Retained earnings | 939 |
| Total assets | $4,240 | Total liabilities and equity | $4,240 |

**Woods Company: Income Statement for the Year Ending December 31, 2009 ($ thousands)**

| | |
|---|---|
| Sales | $ 8,000 |
| Operating costs | (7,450) |
| Earnings before interest and taxes | $    550 |
| Interest | (   150) |
| Earnings before taxes | $    400 |
| Taxes (40%) | (   160) |
| Net income | $    240 |
| *Per-Share Data* | |
| Common stock price | $ 16.96 |
| Earnings per share (EPS) | $   1.60 |
| Dividends per share (DPS) | $   1.04 |

a. The firm operated at full capacity in 2009. It expects sales to increase by 20 percent during 2010 and expects 2010 dividends per share to increase to $1.10. Use the projected balance sheet method to determine how much outside financing is required, developing the firm's pro forma balance sheet and income statement, and use AFN as the balancing item.

b. If the firm must maintain a current ratio of 2.3 and a debt ratio of 40 percent, how much financing, after the first pass, will be obtained using notes payable, long-term debt, and common stock?

c. Construct the second-pass financial statements incorporating financing feedbacks, using the ratios in part b. Assume that the interest rate on debt averages 10 percent.

**operating breakeven analysis**

**17-13** The Weaver Watch Company manufactures a line of ladies' watches that is sold through discount houses. Each watch is sold for $25; the fixed costs are $140,000 for 30,000 watches or less; variable costs are $15 per watch.

a. What is the firm's gain or loss at sales of 8,000 watches? Of 18,000 watches?

b. What is the operating breakeven point? Illustrate by means of a chart.

c. What is Weaver's degree of operating leverage at sales of 8,000 units? Of 18,000 units? (*Hint:* Use Equation 17–4 to solve this problem.)

   **d.** What happens to the operating breakeven point if the selling price rises to $31? What is the significance of the change to the financial manager?

   **e.** What happens to the operating breakeven point if the selling price rises to $31 but variable costs rise to $23 a unit?

**17-14** The following relationships exist for Dellva Industries, a manufacturer of electronic components. Each unit of output is sold for $45; the fixed costs are $175,000, of which $110,000 are annual depreciation charges; and variable costs are $20 per unit.

**operating breakeven analysis**

   **a.** What is the firm's gain or loss at sales of 5,000 units? Of 12,000 units?

   **b.** What is the operating breakeven point?

   **c.** Assume Dellva is operating at a level of 4,000 units. Are creditors likely to seek the liquidation of the company if it is slow in paying its bills?

**17-15** Gordon's Plants has the following partial income statement for 2009:

**financial leverage**

   **a.** If Gordon's has no preferred stock, what is its financial breakeven point?

| | |
|---|---:|
| Earnings before interest and taxes | $4,500 |
| Interest | ( 2,000) |
| Earnings before taxes | $2,500 |
| Taxes (40%) | ( 1,000) |
| Net income | $1,500 |
| Number of common shares | 1,000 |

   Show that the amount you come up with actually is the financial breakeven by re-creating the portion of the income statement shown here for that amount.

   **b.** What is the degree of financial leverage for Gordon's? What does this value mean?

   **c.** If Gordon's actually has preferred stock that requires payment of dividends equal to $600, what would be the financial breakeven point? Show that the amount you compute is the financial breakeven by re-creating the portion of the income statement shown here for that amount. What is the degree of financial leverage in this case?

## Integrative Problem

**17-16** Sue Wilson is the new financial manager of Northwest Chemicals (NWC), an Oregon producer of specialized chemicals sold to farmers for use in fruit orchards. She is responsible for constructing financial forecasts and for evaluating the financial feasibility of new products.

**forecasting, breakeven, and leverage**

## Part I. Financial Forecasting

Sue must prepare a financial forecast for 2010 for Northwest. NWC's 2009 sales were $2 billion, and the marketing department is forecasting a 25 percent increase for 2010. Sue thinks the company was operating at full capacity in 2009, but she is not sure about this. The 2009 financial statements, plus some other data, are given in Table IP17-1.

**TABLE IP17-1**    Financial Statements and Other Data on NWC ($ millions)

**A. 2009 Balance Sheet**

| | | | | |
|---|---|---|---|---|
| Cash and securities | $ 20 | Accounts payable and accruals | $ 100 |
| Accounts receivable | 240 | Notes payable | 100 |
| Inventories | 240 | Total current liabilities | $ 200 |
| Total current assets | $ 500 | Long-term debt | 100 |
| Net fixed assets | 500 | Common stock | 500 |
| | | Retained earnings | 200 |
| Total assets | $1,000 | Total liabilities and equity | $1,000 |

**B. 2009 Income Statement**

| | |
|---|---|
| Sales | $ 2,000.00 |
| Less: Variable costs | ( 1,200.00) |
| Fixed costs | ( 700.00) |
| Earnings before interest and taxes | $ 100.00 |
| Interest | ( 16.00) |
| Earnings before taxes | $ 84.00 |
| Taxes (40%) | ( 33.60) |
| Net income | $ 50.40 |
| Dividends (30%) | ( 15.12) |
| Addition to retained earnings | $ 35.28 |

**C. Key Ratios**

| | NWC | Industry | Comment |
|---|---|---|---|
| Profit margin | 2.52 | 4.00 | |
| Return on equity | 7.20 | 15.60 | |
| Days sales outstanding (360 days) | 43.20 days | 34.00 days | |
| Inventory turnover | 5.00× | 8.00× | |
| Fixed assets turnover | 4.00× | 5.00× | |
| Total assets turnover | 2.00× | 2.50× | |
| Total debt ratio | 30.00% | 36.00% | |
| Times interest earned | 6.25× | 9.40× | |
| Current ratio | 2.50× | 3.00× | |
| Payout ratio | 30.00% | 30.00% | |

Assume you were recently hired as Sue's assistant, and your first major task is to help her develop the forecast. She asked you to begin by answering the following set of questions:

a. *Assume that NWC was operating at full capacity in 2009* with respect to all assets. Estimate the 2010 financing requirements using the projected financial statement approach, making an initial forecast plus one additional "pass" to determine the effects of "financing feedbacks." Assume that (1) each type of asset, as well as payables, accruals, and fixed and variable costs, grow at the same rate as sales; (2) the dividend payout ratio is held constant at 30 percent; (3) external funds needed are financed 50 percent by notes payable and 50 percent by long-term debt (no new common stock will be issued); and (4) all debt carries an interest rate of 8 percent.

b. Calculate NWC's forecasted ratios, and compare them with the company's 2009 ratios and with the industry averages. How does NWC compare with the average firm in its industry, and is the company expected to improve during the coming year?

c. Suppose you now learn that NWC's 2009 receivables and inventories were in line with required levels, given the firm's credit and inventory policies, but that excess capacity existed with regard to fixed assets. Specifically, fixed assets were operated at only 75 percent of capacity.

   **(1)** What level of sales could have existed in 2009 with the available fixed assets? What would the fixed assets/sales ratio have been if NWC had been operating at full capacity?

   **(2)** How would the existence of excess capacity in fixed assets affect the additional funds needed during 2010?

d. Without actually working out the numbers, how would you expect the ratios to change in the situation in which excess capacity in fixed assets exists? Explain your reasoning.

e. Based on comparisons between NWC's days sales outstanding (DSO) and inventory turnover ratios with the industry average figures, does it appear that NWC is operating efficiently with respect to its inventories and accounts receivable? If the company was able to bring these ratios into line with the industry averages, what effect would this have on its AFN and its financial ratios?

f. How would changes in these items affect the AFN? (1) The dividend payout ratio, (2) the profit margin, (3) the plant capacity, and (4) NWC begins buying from its suppliers on terms that permit it to pay after 60 days rather than after 30 days. (Consider each item separately and hold all other things constant.)

## Part II. Breakeven Analysis and Leverage

One of NWC's employees recently submitted a proposal that NWC should expand its operations and sell its chemicals in retail establishments such as Home Depot and Lowe's. To determine the feasibility of the idea, Sue needs to perform a breakeven analysis. The fixed costs associated with producing and selling the chemicals to retail stores would be $60 million, the selling price per unit is expected to be $10, and the variable cost ratio would be the same as it is currently.

a. What is the operating breakeven point both in dollars and in number of units for the employee's proposal?

b. Draw the operating breakeven chart for the proposal. Should the employee's proposal be adopted if NWC can produce and sell 20 million units of the chemical?

c. If NWC can produce and sell 20 million units of its product to retail stores, what would be its degree of operating leverage? What would be NWC's percent increase in operating profits if sales actually were 10 percent higher than expected?

d. Assume NWC has excess capacity, so it does not need to raise any additional external funds to implement the proposal—that is, its 2010 interest payments remain the same as in 2009. What would be its degree of financial leverage and its degree of total leverage? If the actual sales turned out to be 10 percent greater than expected, as a percent, how much greater would the earnings per share be?

e. Explain how breakeven analysis and leverage analysis can be used for planning the implementation of this proposal.

## Computer-Related Problem

*Work the problem in this section only if you are using the problem spreadsheet.*

**forecasting**  **17-17**  Use the model in File C17 to solve this problem. Stendardi Industries' 2009 financial statements are shown in the following table:

| Stendardi Industries: Balance Sheet as of December 31, 2009 ($ millions) | | | |
|---|---|---|---|
| Cash | $ 4.0 | Accounts payable | $ 8.0 |
| Receivables | 12.0 | Notes payable | 5.0 |
| Inventories | 16.0 | Current liabilities | $13.0 |
| Current assets | $32.0 | Long-term debt | 12.0 |
| Net fixed assets | 40.0 | Common stock | 20.0 |
| | | Retained earnings | 27.0 |
| Total assets | $72.0 | Total liabilities and equity | $72.0 |

| Stendardi Industries: Income Statement for December 31, 2009 ($ millions) | |
|---|---|
| Sales | $80.0 |
| Operating costs | (71.3) |
| Earnings before interest and taxes | $ 8.7 |
| Interest | ( 2.0) |
| Earnings before taxes | $ 6.7 |
| Taxes (40%) | ( 2.7) |
| Net income | $ 4.0 |
| Dividends (40%) | $ 1.60 |
| Addition to retained earnings | $ 2.40 |

Assume that the firm *has no excess capacity in fixed assets*, that the average interest rate for debt is 12 percent, and that the projected annual sales growth rate for the next five years is 15 percent.

a. Stendardi plans to finance its additional funds needed with 50 percent short-term debt and 50 percent long-term debt. Using the projected balance sheet method, prepare the pro forma financial statements for 2010 through 2014, and then determine (1) additional funds needed, (2) the current ratio, (3) the debt ratio, and (4) the return on equity.

b. Sales growth could be 5 percentage points above or below the projected 15 percent. Determine the effect of such variances on AFN and the key ratios.

c. Perform an analysis to determine the sensitivity of AFN and the key ratios for 2010 to changes in the dividend payout ratio as specified in the following, assuming sales grow at a constant 15 percent. What happens to AFN if the dividend payout ratio (1) is raised from 40 percent to 70 percent or (2) is lowered from 40 percent to 20 percent?

**17-18** Gillette Company [G], a company that manufactures and sells consumer products, uses only debt and common stock to finance the firm. The firm's EBIT and interest expense have fluctuated during the past five years. Answer the following questions about Gillette:    **financial leverage**

  **a.** What is the degree of financial leverage (DFL) for Gillette in each of the past five years? [Click on Financials/Financial Statements.]

  **b.** How has the change in EBIT from year to year affected Gillette's earnings per share in each of the past five years?

  **c.** Choose two of Gillette's industry peers that do not have preferred stock in their capital structures and compare these companies with Gillette in regard to their degree of financial leverage? Explain what your comparison means. [Click on Peers/Financials.]

# Projected Financial Statements, Including Financing Feedbacks

**APPENDIX 17A**

In the chapter, we discussed the procedure used to construct pro forma financial statements. The first step is to estimate the level of operations and then project the impact such operations will have on the financial statements of the firm. We found that when a firm needs additional external financing, its existing interest and dividend payments will change; thus, the values initially projected for the financial statements will be affected. Therefore, to recognize these *financing feedbacks*, the construction of projected financial statements needs to be an iterative process. In this appendix, we give an indication of the iterative process for constructing the pro forma statements for Unilate. Table 17A-1 contains the initial projected statements shown in  Table 17-1 and Table 17-2 of the chapter, and some of the subsequent "passes" used to adjust the forecasted statements are given. According to the discussion given in the chapter, the forecasted statements first are constructed assuming that only changes in retained earnings and spontaneous financing are available to support the forecasted operations. This "first pass" is necessary to provide an indication of the additional external funds that are needed. Unilate needs $42.7 million. But if Unilate raises this additional amount by borrowing from the bank and by issuing new bonds and new common stock, then its interest and dividend payments will increase. This can be seen by examining the income statement, which was constructed in the second pass to show the effects of raising the $42.7 million additional funds needed. Because Unilate would have additional debt, it would have to pay $1.30 million more interest; and because it has more shares of common stock outstanding, it would have to pay $1.40 million more dividends. Consequently, as the second-pass balance sheet shows, if Unilate raises only the $42.7 million AFN (additional funds needed) initially computed, it would find there still would be a need for funds—the AFN would be $2.18 million—because the addition to retained earnings would be lower than expected originally. As it turns out, Unilate actually would need to raise $45.0 million to support the forecasted 2010 operations—$6.75 million from notes, $9.0 million from bonds, and $29.25 million from stock.

**TABLE 17A-1**   Unilate Textiles: 2010 Forecast of Financial Statements ($ millions)

### Income Statement

| | Initial Pass | Feedback | Second Pass | | Final Pass |
|---|---|---|---|---|---|
| Earnings before interest and taxes (EBIT) | $143.00 | | $143.00 | | $143.00 |
| Less interest | (40.00) | +1.30 | (41.30) | +0.07 | (41.37) |
| Earnings before taxes (EBT) | $103.00 | | $101.70 | | $101.63 |
| Taxes (40%) | (41.20) | −0.52 | (40.68) | −0.03 | (40.65) |
| Net Income | $ 61.80 | | $ 61.02 | | $ 60.98 |
| Common dividends | (29.00) | +1.40 | (30.40) | +0.08 | (30.48) |
| Addition to retained earnings | $ 32.80 | −2.18 | $ 30.62 | −0.12 | $ 30.50 |
| Earnings per share | $   2.47 | | $   2.33 | | $   2.32 |
| Dividends per share | $   1.16 | | $   1.16 | | $   1.16 |
| Number of common shares (millions) | 25.00 | | 26.21 | | 26.27 |

### Balance Sheet

| | Initial Pass | Feedback | Second Pass | | Final Pass |
|---|---|---|---|---|---|
| Cash | $ 16.50 | | $ 16.50 | | $ 16.50 |
| Accounts receivable | 198.00 | | 198.00 | | 198.00 |
| Inventories | 297.00 | | 297.00 | | 297.00 |
| Total current assets | $511.50 | | $511.50 | | $511.50 |
| Net plant and equipment | 418.00 | | 418.00 | | 418.00 |
| Total assets | $929.50 | | $929.50 | | $929.50 |
| Accounts payable | $ 33.00 | | $ 33.00 | | $ 33.00 |
| Accruals | 66.00 | | 66.00 | | 66.00 |
| Notes payable | 40.00 | +6.41 | 46.41 | +0.34 | 46.75 |
| Total current liabilities | $139.00 | | $145.41 | | $145.75 |
| Long-term bonds | 300.00 | +8.54 | 308.54 | +0.46 | 309.00 |
| Total liabilities | $439.00 | | $453.95 | | $454.75 |
| Common stock | 130.00 | +27.76 | 157.76 | +1.49 | 159.25 |
| Retained earnings | 317.80 | −2.18 | 315.62 | −0.12 | 315.50 |
| Total owners' equity | $447.80 | | $473.37 | | $474.75 |
| Total liabilities and equity | $886.80 | +40.52 | $927.32 | +2.18 | $929.50 |
| Additional funds needed (AFN) | $ 42.70 | | $   2.18 | | $   0.00 |

**Note:** The results in this table are carried to two decimal places to show some of the more subtle changes that occur. Even so, you will find some rounding differences when summing the feedback amounts.

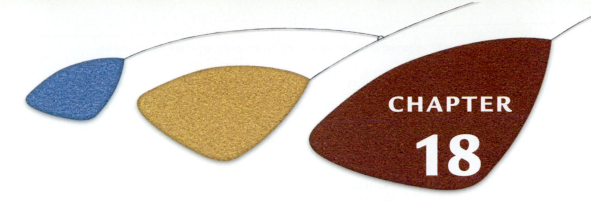

# CHAPTER 18

# Alternative Financing Arrangements and Corporate Restructuring

The growth of convertible securities, which are debt or preferred stock issues that can be exchanged for companies' common stocks, has been extraordinary during the past decade. Many firms use convertibles because they feel that funds can be raised more cheaply than with "straight" debt or preferred stock. For example, in 1999 Amazon.com issued $1.25 billion in convertible notes that had a 4.75 percent coupon rate, which was below the rate on many Treasury notes. The debt, which matures in 2009, allows investors to convert each $1,000 bond into 12.816 shares of common stock. Consequently, as long as the price of the stock is above $78.03 per share (its *conversion price*), it would be worthwhile to convert the bonds into common stock. The convertible also includes a call provision that allows Amazon.com to recall the bonds at a price of $1,080.75 for each $1,000 bond. Although bondholders would get 8.075 percent more than the face value of the bonds at call, they would lose the opportunity to convert their bonds into stock.

At the end of 1999, at $88 per share, Amazon.com was selling for more than the conversion price; thus, analysts speculated that it wouldn't be long before the convertible notes were called by the company. A few months later, however, Amazon.com announced earnings that were lower (more negative) than expected; thus, the stock price dropped substantially. On the day of the announcement, the stock lost about 14.6 percent of its value, whereas the convertible notes lost 17.8 percent during the week. At the end of 2006, Amazon.com's stock was selling for $40 per share, which is well below the conversion price of the notes. Therefore, it seems unlikely that the company will call the bonds any time soon.

Convertibles are attractive to investors because they offer the opportunity to earn the substantial returns available with stocks, but they also offer the stability associated with debt or preferred stock. For the past decade, convertibles have generated a return equal to more than 11 percent compared with the 16 percent return provided by large stocks and the 7 percent to 12 percent return associated with small stocks.

As the financial markets strengthen, convertibles gain popularity; but when the financial markets weaken, selling pressure results and convertibles lose favor with investors. Like other financial assets, convertibles are risky—most experts would caution investors not to put large portions of their investments into convertible securities; instead, they should diversify. Once you have read this chapter and understand the concepts presented, you should be able to make informed decisions regarding convertibles, as well as other hybrid securities.

## Chapter *Essentials*

### —The Questions

After reading this chapter, you should be able to answer the following questions:

- Why do firms lease rather than purchase assets? How should a firm determine whether to lease or purchase an asset?
- What types of leases exist? Do all leases have the same effect on a firm's financial statements?
- What are stock options? Why would an investor buy an option?
- How does a stock option differ from a warrant?
- What is a convertible security? Why do firms use convertibles?
- Why do firms merge or take over other firms?
- Why would a firm pay off (refund) its bonds before maturity?

In Chapter 6 and Chapter 7, we examined the use of common stock and various types of debt. In this chapter, we examine some other types of long-term financing arrangements used by financial managers. We give only fundamental descriptions of these alternative sources of financing to enlighten you about the variety of means by which a firm can raise funds. The fact is, many variations and combinations of financial assets exist today, and it would take multiple volumes to describe them all. Firms often engage in "creative financing" when seeking different ways to attract investors, so you should not be surprised to see new forms of financing emerge on a continuous basis. In addition, because firms have become extremely "creative" when determining how to finance mergers and acquisitions, we briefly discuss mergers and merger activity at the end of the chapter.

The purpose of this chapter is to provide you with a basic understanding of (1) some financing techniques we have not discussed in previous chapters and (2) corporate restructuring through mergers and leveraged buyouts. If you want more in-depth discussions, you should look in either an upper-level corporate finance text or an investments text.

## LEASING

Firms generally own fixed assets and report them on their balance sheets, but it is the *use* of buildings and equipment that is important, not their ownership per se. One way of obtaining the use of assets is to buy them, but an alternative is to lease them. Prior to the 1950s, leasing generally was associated with real estate—that is, land and buildings. Today, however, it is possible to lease virtually any kind of fixed asset, and in 2006 more than 25 percent of all new capital equipment acquired by businesses was leased. In fact, it is estimated that 70 percent of firms listed in the Fortune 1000 lease some equipment.

### Types of Leases

Leasing takes three different forms: (1) sale-and-leaseback arrangements, (2) operating leases, and (3) straight financial, or capital, leases.

### *Sale and Leaseback*

**sale and leaseback**
Situation in which a firm sells land, buildings, or equipment and simultaneously leases the property back for a specified period under specific terms.

Under a **sale and leaseback,** a firm that owns land, buildings, or equipment sells the property and simultaneously executes an agreement to lease the property back for a particular period under specific terms. The purchaser could be an insurance company, a commercial bank, a specialized leasing company, or even an individual investor. The sale-and-leaseback plan is an alternative to taking out a mortgage loan. The firm that sells the property, or the **lessee,** immediately receives the purchase price from the buyer, or the **lessor.**[1] At the same time, the seller-lessee firm retains the use of the property just as if it had borrowed and mortgaged the property to secure the loan. Note that under a mortgage loan arrangement, the financial institution normally would receive a series of equal payments just sufficient to amortize the loan while providing a specified rate of return to the lender on the outstanding balance. Under a sale-and-leaseback arrangement, the lease payments are set up in exactly the same way; the payments are set so the investor-lessor recoups the purchase price and earns a specified rate of return on the investment.

**lessee**
The party that uses, rather than the one that owns, the leased property.

**lessor**
The owner of leased property.

## Operating Leases

**Operating leases,** sometimes called *service leases,* provide for both *financing* and *maintenance.* IBM is one of the pioneers of the operating lease contract, and computers and office copying machines, together with automobiles and trucks, are the primary types of equipment involved. Ordinarily, these leases call for the lessor to maintain and service the leased equipment, and the cost of providing maintenance is built into the lease payments.

Another important characteristic of operating leases is the fact that they frequently are *not fully amortized;* in other words, the payments required under the lease contract are not sufficient to recover the full cost of the equipment. However, the lease contract is written for a period considerably shorter than the expected economic life of the leased equipment, and the lessor expects to recover all investment costs through subsequent renewal payments, through subsequent leases to other companies (lessees), or by selling the leased equipment.

A final feature of operating leases is that they frequently contain a *cancellation clause,* which gives the lessee the right to cancel the lease before the expiration of the basic agreement. This is an important consideration for the lessee because it means that the equipment can be returned if it is rendered obsolete by technological developments or if it no longer is needed because of a decline in the lessee's business.

**operating lease**
A lease under which the lessor maintains and finances the property; also called a *service lease.*

## Financial, or Capital, Leases

**Financial leases,** sometimes called *capital leases,* are differentiated from operating leases in three respects: (1) they do *not* provide for maintenance services; (2) they are *not* cancelable; and (3) they are *fully amortized*—that is, the lessor receives rental payments that are equal to the full price of the leased equipment plus a return on the investment. In a typical financial lease arrangement, the firm that will use the equipment (the lessee) selects the specific items it requires and negotiates the price and delivery terms with the manufacturer. The user firm then negotiates terms with a leasing company and, once the lease terms are set, arranges to have the lessor buy the equipment from the manufacturer or the distributor. When the equipment is purchased, the user firm simultaneously executes the lease agreement.

Financial leases are similar to sale-and-leaseback arrangements, except that the leased equipment is new and the lessor buys it from a manufacturer or a distributor instead of from the user-lessee. A sale and leaseback might thus be thought of as a

**financial lease**
A lease that does not provide for maintenance services, is not cancelable, and is fully amortized over its life; also called a *capital lease.*

---

[1]The term *lessee* is pronounced "less-ee," and *lessor* is pronounced "less-or."

**TABLE 18-1**    Balance Sheet Effects of Leasing

| Before Asset Increase | | | After Asset Increase | | | | | |
|---|---|---|---|---|---|---|---|---|
| **Firms B and L** | | | **Firm B—Purchases Asset** | | | **Firm L—Leases Asset** | | |
| Current assets | $ 50 | Debt | $ 50 | Current assets | $ 50 | Debt | $150 | Current assets | $ 50 | Debt | $ 50 |
| Fixed assets | 50 | Equity | 50 | Fixed assets | 150 | Equity | 50 | Fixed assets | 50 | Equity | 50 |
| Total | $100 | | $100 | Total | $ 200 | | $200 | Total | $100 | | $100 |
| | | Debt ratio = 50% | | | | Debt ratio = 75% | | | | Debt ratio = 50% | |

special type of financial lease, and both sale-and-leaseback leases and financial leases are analyzed in the same manner.[2]

## Financial Statement Effects

**off-balance-sheet financing**
Financing in which the assets and liabilities involved do not appear on the firm's balance sheet.

Lease payments are shown as operating expenses on a firm's income statement, but under certain conditions, neither the leased assets nor the liabilities under the lease contract appear on the firm's balance sheet. For this reason, leasing is often called **off-balance-sheet financing.** This point is illustrated in Table 18-1 by the balance sheets of two hypothetical firms, B (for Buy) and L (for Lease). Initially, the balance sheets of both firms are identical, and both have debt ratios of 50 percent. Each firm then decides to acquire fixed assets that cost $100. Firm B borrows $100 to make the purchase, so both an asset and a liability are recorded on its balance sheet, and its debt ratio is increased to 75 percent. Firm L leases the equipment, so its balance sheet is unchanged. The lease might call for fixed charges as high as or even higher than those on the loan, and the obligations assumed under the lease might be equally or more dangerous from the standpoint of financial safety, but the firm's debt ratio remains at 50 percent.

**FASB #13**
The statement of the Financial Accounting Standards Board (FASB) that details the conditions and procedures for capitalizing leases.

To correct this problem, the Financial Accounting Standards Board (FASB) issued **FASB #13,** which requires that for an unqualified audit report, firms that enter into financial (or capital) leases must restate their balance sheets to report leased assets as fixed assets and the present value of future lease payments as a debt. This process is called *capitalizing the lease,* and its net effect is to cause Firms B and L to have similar balance sheets, both of which will resemble the one shown for Firm B after the asset increase.[3]

The logic behind FASB #13 is as follows. If a firm signs a lease contract, its obligation to make lease payments is just as binding as if it had signed a loan agreement. The failure to make lease payments can bankrupt a firm just as surely as can the failure to make principal and interest payments on a loan. Therefore, for all intents and purposes, a financial lease is identical to a loan.[4] This being the case, when a firm signs

[2]For a lease transaction to qualify as a lease for *tax purposes,* and thus for the lessee to be able to deduct the lease payments, the life of the lease must not exceed 80 percent of the expected life of the asset, and the lessee cannot be permitted to buy the asset at a nominal value. These conditions are IRS requirements, and they should not be confused with the FASB requirements discussed in the next section concerning the capitalization of leases. It is important to consult lawyers and accountants to ascertain whether a prospective lease meets current IRS regulations.

[3]FASB #13, "Accounting for Leases," November 1976, spells out in detail the conditions under which leases must be capitalized and the procedures for doing so.

[4]There are, however, certain legal differences between loans and leases. For example, in a bankruptcy liquidation, the lessor is entitled to take possession of the leased asset, and if the value of the asset is less than the required payments under the lease, the lessor can enter a claim (as a general creditor) for one year's lease payments. In a bankruptcy reorganization, the lessor receives the asset plus three years' lease payments if needed to bring the value of the asset up to the remaining investment in the lease.

a lease agreement, it has, in effect, raised its "true" debt ratio and thereby changed its "true" capital structure. Accordingly, if the firm previously had established a target capital structure, and if there is no reason to think that the optimal capital structure has changed, then using lease financing requires additional equity backing in exactly the same manner as does the use of debt financing.

If a disclosure of the lease in the Table 18-1 example were not made, then investors could be deceived into thinking that Firm L's financial position is stronger than it actually is. Even if the lease were disclosed in a footnote, investors might not fully recognize its impact and might not see that Firm B and Firm L essentially are in the same financial position. If this were the case, Firm L would have increased its true amount of debt through a lease arrangement, but its required return on debt, $r_d$; its required return on equity, $r_s$; and consequently its weighted average cost of capital would have increased less than those of Firm B, which borrowed directly. Thus, investors would be willing to accept a lower return from Firm L because they would view it as being in a stronger financial position than Firm B. These benefits of leasing would accrue to stockholders at the expense of new investors, who were, in effect, being deceived by the fact that the firm's balance sheet did not fully reflect its true liability situation. This is why FASB #13 was issued.

A lease will be classified as a capital lease, and hence be capitalized and shown directly on the balance sheet, if any one of the following conditions exists:

1. Under the terms of the lease, ownership of the property effectively is transferred from the lessor to the lessee.

2. The lessee can purchase the property or renew the lease at less than a fair market price when the lease expires.

3. The lease runs for a period equal to or greater than 75 percent of the asset's life. Thus, if an asset has a 10-year life and if the lease is written for more than 7½ years, the lease must be capitalized.

4. The present value of the lease payments is equal to or greater than 90 percent of the initial value of the asset.[5]

These rules, together with strong footnote disclosures for operating leases, are sufficient to ensure that no one will be fooled by lease financing. Thus, leases are recognized to be essentially the same as debt, and they have the same effects as debt on the firm's required rate of return. Therefore, leasing generally will not permit a firm to use more financial leverage than could be obtained with conventional debt.

## Evaluation by the Lessee

Any prospective lease must be evaluated by both the lessee and the lessor. The lessee must determine whether leasing an asset will be less costly than buying it, and the lessor must decide whether the lease will provide a reasonable rate of return. Because our focus in this text primarily is on managerial finance rather than investments, we restrict our analysis to that conducted by the lessee.[6]

---

[5]The discount rate used to calculate the present value of the lease payments must be the lower of (1) the rate used by the lessor to establish the lease payments or (2) the rate of interest that the lessee would have paid for new debt with a maturity equal to that of the lease.

[6]The lessee typically is offered a set of lease terms by the lessor, which generally is a bank, a finance company such as General Electric Capital (the largest U.S. lessor), or some other institutional lender. The lessee can accept or reject the lease, or shop around for a better deal. In this chapter, we take the lease terms as given for purposes of our analysis. See Chapter 19 of Eugene F. Brigham and Phillip R. Daves, *Intermediate Financial Management,* 9th ed. (Cincinnati, OH: South-Western College Publishing, 2007), for a discussion of lease analysis from the lessor's standpoint, including a discussion of how a potential lessee can use such an analysis in bargaining for better terms.

In the typical case, the events leading to a lease arrangement follow the sequence described in the following list. We should note that a great deal of theoretical literature exists about the correct way to evaluate lease-versus-purchase decisions, and some complex decision models have been developed to aid in the analysis. The analysis given next, however, leads to the correct decision in every case we have encountered.

1. The firm decides to acquire a particular building or piece of equipment. This decision is based on regular capital budgeting procedures, and it is not an issue in the typical lease analysis. In a lease analysis, we are concerned simply with whether to finance the machine by a lease or by a loan.

2. Once the firm has decided to acquire the asset, the next question is how to finance it. Well-run businesses do not have large amounts of excess cash, so new assets must be financed in some manner.

3. Funds to purchase the asset could be obtained by borrowing, by retaining earnings, or by issuing new stock. Alternatively, the asset could be leased. Because of the FASB #13 capitalization/disclosure provision for leases, we assume that a lease would have the same capital structure effect as a loan.

As indicated earlier, a lease is comparable to a loan in the sense that the firm is required to make a specified series of payments, and a failure to make these payments can result in bankruptcy. Thus, it is most appropriate to compare the cost of lease financing with that of debt financing.[7] The lease-versus-borrow-and-purchase analysis is illustrated with data on the Richards Electronics Company. The following conditions are assumed:

1. Richards plans to acquire equipment with a four-year life that has a cost of $10,000 delivered and installed.

2. Richards can either purchase the equipment using a four-year, 10 percent loan or lease the equipment for four years at a rental charge of $3,000 per year, payable at the end of each year. If Richards leases the equipment, the lessor will own it upon the expiration of the lease.[8]

3. The equipment definitely will be used for four years, at which time its estimated net salvage value will be $600. Richards plans to continue using the equipment, so (a) if it purchases the equipment, the company will keep it, and (b) if it leases the equipment, the company will exercise an option to buy it at its estimated salvage (residual) value, $600.

4. The lease contract stipulates that the lessor will maintain the equipment. However, if Richards borrows and buys, it will have to bear the cost of maintenance, which will be performed by the equipment manufacturer at a fixed contract rate of $400 per year, payable at the end of each year.

5. The equipment falls in the MACRS 3-year class life, and for this analysis we assume that Richards' effective marginal tax rate is 40 percent.

## Net Present Value (NPV) Analysis

Table 18-2 shows the cash flows that would be incurred each year under the two financing plans. All cash flows occur at the end of the year, and the $\hat{CF}_t$ values are shown on lines 5 and 10 of Table 18-2 for buying and leasing, respectively.

---

[7]The analysis should compare the cost of leasing to the cost of debt financing regardless of how the asset is actually financed. The asset might be purchased with available cash if it is not leased, but because leasing is a substitute for debt financing, a comparison between the two is still appropriate.

[8]Lease payments can occur at the beginning of the year or at the end of the year. In this example, we assume end-of-year payments, but we demonstrate beginning-of-year payments in Self-Test Problem ST-2.

**TABLE 18-2**    Richards Electronics Company: NPV Lease Analysis

| | | | Year | | |
|---|---|---|---|---|---|
| | **0** | **1** | **2** | **3** | **4** |
| **I. Cost of Owning** | | | | | |
| 1. Net purchase price | $(10,000.0) | | | | |
| 2. Maintenance cost | | $( 400) | $( 400) | $( 400) | $( 400) |
| 3. Maintenance cost tax savings | | 160 | 160 | 160 | 160 |
| 4. Depreciation tax savings | | 1,320 | 1,800 | 600 | 280 |
| 5. Net cash flow | $(10,000.0) | $ 1,080 | $ 1,560 | $ 360 | $ 40 |
| 6. Present value of owning (r = 6%) | $( 7,258.8) | | | | |
| **II. Cost of Leasing** | | | | | |
| 7. Lease payment | | $(3,000) | $(3,000) | $(3,000) | $(3,000) |
| 8. Lease payment tax savings | | 1,200 | 1,200 | 1,200 | 1,200 |
| 9. Purchase option price | | | | | ( 600) |
| 10. Net cash flow | $ 0.0 | $(1,800) | $(1,800) | $(1,800) | $(2,400) |
| 11. Present value of leasing (r = 6%) | $( 6,712.4) | | | | |
| **III. Cost Comparison** | | | | | |
| 12. Net advantage to leasing | $ 546.4 = | | $7,258.8 − $6,712.4 | | |

NOTES: A line-by-line explanation of the table follows:

1. If Richards buys the equipment, it will have to spend $10,000 on the purchase. Alternatively, we could show all the financing flows associated with a $10,000 loan, net of taxes, but the result would be the same because the PV of those flows would be exactly $10,000.

2. If the equipment is owned, Richards must pay $400 at the end of each year for maintenance.

3. The $400 maintenance expense is tax deductible, so it will produce a tax savings of $160 = 0.4($400) each year.

4. If Richards buys the equipment, it can depreciate the equipment for tax purposes and thus lower the taxes paid through lower taxable income. The tax savings in each year is equal to Tax rate × (Depreciation expense) = 0.4 (Depreciation expense). As shown in Appendix 10A, the MACRS rates for 3-year class property are 0.33, 0.45, 0.15, and 0.07 in Years 1 through 4, respectively. To illustrate the calculation of the depreciation tax savings, consider Year 2. The depreciation expense is 0.45($10,000) = $4,500, and the tax savings is 0.4($4,500) = $1,800.

5. Sum Lines 1 through 4 to find the net cash flows associated with owning the equipment.

6. The PV of the Line 5 cash flows, discounted at $r_{dT} = 10\%(1 − 0.4) = 6\%$, is − $7,258.8.

7. The annual end-of-year lease payment is $3,000.

8. Because the lease payment is tax deductible, a tax savings of $1,200 = 0.4($3,000) results for each year.

9. Because Richards plans to continue to use the equipment after the lease expires, it must purchase the equipment for $600 at the end of Year 4 if it leases.

10. Sum Lines 7 through 9 to find the net cash flows associated with leasing.

11. The PV of the Line 10 cash flows, discounted at $r_{dT} = 10\%(1 − 0.4) = 6\%$, is −$6,712.4.

12. The net advantage to leasing is the difference between the PV cost of owning and the PV cost of leasing = $7,258.8 − $6,712.4 = $546.4. Because the NAL is positive, leasing is favored over borrowing and buying.

The top section of the table (lines 1 to 6) is devoted to the cost of owning (borrowing and buying). Lines 1 to 4 show the individual cash flow items. Line 5 summarizes the annual net cash flows that Richards will incur if it finances the equipment with a loan. The present values of these cash flows are summed to find the present value of the cost of owning, which is shown on line 6 in the Year 0 column. Section II of the table calculates the present value cost of leasing. The cash flows associated with the lease are shown on lines 7 to 9, and line 10 gives the annual net cash flow. The present value of the cash flows is shown on line 11. Finally, the net advantage to leasing, which is the difference between the present value of purchasing and the present value of leasing, is shown on line 12. The result of the analysis shown in Table 18-2 indicates that Richards should lease rather than purchase the equipment because the net advantage to leasing is positive.

The rate used to discount the cash flows is a critical issue. In Chapter 8, we saw that the riskier a cash flow, the higher the required return associated with a series of cash flows. This same principle was observed in our discussion of capital budgeting, and it also applies in lease analysis. Just how risky are the cash flows under consideration here? Most of them are relatively certain, at least when compared with the types of cash flow estimates that were developed in capital budgeting. For example, the loan payment schedule is set by contract, as is the lease payment schedule. The depreciation expenses are established by law and generally are not subject to change, and, in many cases, the annual maintenance cost is fixed by contract as well. The tax savings are somewhat uncertain because tax rates can change, although tax rates do not change significantly very often. The residual, or salvage, value is the least certain of the cash flows, but even here Richards' management is fairly confident that it will want to acquire the property and also that the cost of doing so will be close to $600. Because the cash flows under both the lease and the borrow-and-purchase alternatives are reasonably certain, they should be discounted at a relatively low rate. Most analysts recommend that the company's cost of debt be used, and this rate seems reasonable in our example. Further, because all the net cash flows are on an after-tax basis, *the after-tax cost of debt, which is 6 percent, should be used.*

## Factors That Affect Leasing Decisions

The basic method of analysis set forth in Table 18-2 is sufficient to handle most situations. However, certain factors warrant additional comments.

### Estimated Residual Value

**residual value**
The value of leased property at the end of the lease term.

It is important to note that the lessor will own the property upon the expiration of the lease. The estimated end-of-lease value of the property is called the **residual value.** Superficially, it would appear that if residual value is expected to be large, owning would have an advantage over leasing. However, if the expected residual value is large—as it might be under inflation for certain types of equipment as well as if real estate property is involved—then competition among leasing companies will force leasing rates down to the point where potential residual value will be fully recognized in the lease contract rate. Thus, the existence of a large residual value on equipment is not likely to bias the decision against leasing.

### Increased Credit Availability

As noted earlier, leasing sometimes is said to have an advantage for firms that are seeking the maximum degree of financial leverage. First, it sometimes is argued that a firm can obtain more money, and for a longer period, under a lease arrangement than under a loan secured by the asset. Second, because some leases do not appear on the balance sheet, lease financing has been said to give the firm a stronger appearance in a superficial credit analysis, thus permitting it to use more leverage than it could if it did not lease. There might be some truth to these claims for smaller firms. However, because larger firms are required to capitalize major leases and to report them on their balance sheets, this point is of questionable validity.

# OPTIONS

An **option** is a contract that gives its holder the right to buy (or sell) an asset at some predetermined price within a specified period of time. "Pure options" are instruments that are created by outsiders (generally investment banking firms) rather than by the firm itself; they are bought and sold primarily by investors (or speculators). However, financial managers should understand the nature of options because this will help them structure warrant and convertible financings, both of which have similar characteristics.

## Option Types and Markets

There are many types of options and option markets. To understand how options work, suppose you owned 100 shares of IBM stock that, on November 14, 2006, sold for $92 per share. You could sell to someone else the right to buy your 100 shares at any time during the next three months at a price of, say, $90 per share. The $90 is called the **strike,** or **exercise, price.** Such options exist, and they are traded on a number of exchanges, with the Chicago Board of Options Exchange (CBOE) being the oldest and largest. This type of option is known as a **call option** because the option holder can "call" in 100 shares of stock for purchase any time during the option period. The seller of a call option is known as an option writer. An investor who writes a call option against stock held in his or her portfolio is said to be selling *covered options;* options sold without the stock to back them up are called *naked options.*

On November 14, 2006, IBM's three-month, 90 call options sold on the CBOE for $4.07 each. Thus, for ($4.07)(100) = $407, you could buy an option contract that would give you the right to purchase 100 shares of IBM at a price of $90 per share at any time during the following three months. If the stock stayed below $90 during that period, you would lose your $407, but if the stock's price rose to $100, your $407 investment would be worth ($100−$90)(100) = $1,000. That translates into a healthy rate of return on your $407 investment. Incidentally, if the stock price did go up, you probably would not actually exercise your options to buy the stock; rather, you would sell the options to another option buyer, at a price greater than or equal to $10 per option—you originally paid only $4.07.

You also can buy an option that gives you the right to sell a stock at a specified price during some period in the future. This is called a **put option.** For example, suppose you expect IBM's stock price to decline from its current level some time during the next five months. For $380 = $3.80 × 100, you could buy a three-month put option giving you the right to sell 100 shares (which you would not necessarily own) at a price

**option**
A contract that gives the option holder the right to buy (or sell) an asset at some predetermined price within a specified period of time.

**strike (exercise) price**
The price that must be paid (buying or selling) for a share of common stock when an option is exercised.

**call option**
An option to buy, or "call," a share of stock at a certain price within a specified period.

**put option**
The option to sell a specified number of shares of stock at a prespecified price during a particular period.

of $95 per share ($95 is the put option strike price). If you bought a 100-share put contract for $380 and IBM's stock price actually fell to $85, you would make ($95−$85)(100) = $1,000, minus the $380 you paid for the put option, for a net profit (before taxes and commissions) of $620.

Stock option trading is very active in the United States. The leverage involved makes it possible for speculators with just a few dollars to make a fortune almost overnight. Also, investors with sizable portfolios can sell options against their stocks and earn the value of the options (minus brokerage commissions) even if the stocks' prices remain constant. Still, those who have profited most from the development of options trading are security firms, which earn very healthy commissions on such trades.

The corporations on whose stocks options are written, such as IBM, have nothing to do with the options market. They neither raise money in that market nor have any direct transactions in it, and option holders neither receive dividends nor vote for corporate directors (unless they exercise their options to purchase the stock, which few actually do). There have been studies by the Securities and Exchange Commission (SEC) and others as to whether option trading stabilizes or destabilizes the stock market and whether it helps or hinders corporations seeking to raise new capital. The studies have not been conclusive, but option trading is here to stay, and many regard it as the most exciting game in town.

## Option Values

The value of an option is closely related to the value of the *underlying* stock, which is the stock on which the option is written, and the strike price. For example, an investor who purchases call options hopes that the value of the underlying stock goes above the strike price during the option period because then the option could be exercised at a gross profit equal to the market value of the stock less the strike price. In this case, the investor is said to have an **in-the-money option** because he or she can make money by exercising the option—that is, by purchasing the stock at the strike price and immediately selling it for a higher market price. For example, if IBM's stock sells for $95 at the beginning of 2007, call options with a strike price of $90 would be in the money because the option holder could exercise the options by paying the option seller $9,000 for 100 shares of IBM stock, and then the stock could be sold on the NYSE for $9,500—the financial benefit of exercising to the option holder would be $500 before commissions and taxes. If the market value of IBM's stock is $85, or any other amount below the strike price, the call is said to be an **out-of-the-money option** because it would not be favorable for the option holder to exercise the call. If the investor were to exercise the call option, there would be a financial loss because the stock would be purchased at a value (the $90 strike price) greater than it could be sold (the $85 market value).

The opposite relationship holds for put options because the strike price represents the price at which an investor can *sell* the stock to the put option writer (seller). To be able to sell to the put option writer, the investor first must *buy* the stock in the market (for example, on the NYSE). Thus, for a put option to be in the money, the strike price must be above the market value of the underlying stock.

As you can see, both the value of the underlying stock and the strike price of the option are important in determining whether an option is in the money or out of the money. If an option is out of the money on its expiration date, it is worthless. Therefore, the stock price and the strike price are important for determining the market value of an option. In fact, options are called *derivative securities* because their values are dependent on, or derived from, the value of the underlying asset and the strike price.

**in-the-money option**
When it is beneficial financially for the option holder to exercise the option—a profit would be earned if the option is exercised.

**out-of-the-money option**
When it is *not* beneficial financially for the option holder to exercise the option—a loss would be incurred if the option is exercised.

In addition to the stock price and the strike price, the value of an option also depends on (1) the option's time to maturity and (2) the variability of the underlying stock's price, as explained here:

1. The longer an option has to run, the greater its value. If a call option expires at 4 p.m. today, there is not much chance that the stock price will go way up. Therefore, the option will sell at close to the difference between the stock price and the strike price ($P_s$−strike price), or zero if this difference is negative. On the other hand, if it has a year to go, the stock price could rise sharply, pulling the option's value up with it. For this reason, in such a case, the option generally sells for greater than the difference between the stock price and the strike price.

2. An option on an extremely volatile stock will be worth more than one on a stable stock. We know that an option on a stock whose price rarely moves will not offer much chance for a large gain. On the other hand, an option on a stock that is highly volatile could provide a large gain, so such an option is valuable. Note also that because losses on options are limited, large declines in a stock's price do not have a correspondingly bad effect on call option holders. Therefore, stock price volatility can only enhance the value of an option.[9]

If everything else were held constant, then the longer an option's life, the higher its market price would be, no matter the type of option. Also, the more volatile the price of the underlying stock, the higher the option's market price, regardless of the option type.

### Self-Test Questions

Differentiate between a call option and a put option.

Do the corporations on whose stock options are written raise money in the options market? Explain.

Explain how these factors affect the value of an option: (1) the time remaining before the option expires and (2) the volatility of the underlying stock.

How is the value of a call option affected by the value of the underlying stock and the strike price? How is the value of a put option affected by these factors?

---

[9]To illustrate this point, suppose that for $2 you could buy a call option on a stock now selling for $20. The strike price is also $20. Now suppose the stock is highly volatile, and you think it has a 50 percent probability of selling for either $10 or $30 when the option expires in one month. What is the expected value of the option? If the stock sells for $30, the option will be worth $30−$20 = $10; but, if the stock sells for $10, the option will be worthless. Because there is a 50-50 chance that the stock will be worth $10 or $30, the expected value of the option is $5:

$$\text{Expected value of option} = 0.5(0) + 0.5(\$10) = \$5$$

To be exactly correct, we would have to discount the $5 back for one month.

Now suppose the stock was more volatile, with a 50-50 chance of the option being worth zero or $20 (the stock value might be $0 or $40). Here the option would be worth

$$\text{Expected value option} = 0.5(0) + 0.5(\$20) = \$10$$

This demonstrates that the greater the volatility of the stock, the greater the value of the option. The reason this result occurs is because the large loss on the stock ($20) had no more of an adverse effect on the option holder than the small loss ($10). Thus, option holders benefit greatly if a stock goes way up, but they do not lose too badly if it drops all the way to zero. These concepts have been used to develop formulas for pricing options, with the most widely used formula being the Black-Scholes model, which is discussed in most investments texts.

# WARRANTS

A **warrant** is an option *issued by a company* that gives the holder the right to buy a stated number of shares of the company's stock at a specified price. Generally, warrants are distributed along with debt, and they are used to induce investors to buy a firm's long-term debt at a lower interest rate than otherwise would be required. For example, when Key Isles Transport (KIT) wanted to sell $100 million of 20-year bonds in 2006, the company's investment bankers informed the financial vice president that straight bonds would be difficult to sell and that an interest rate of 11 percent would be required. However, the investment bankers suggested as an alternative that investors would be willing to buy bonds with an annual coupon rate as low as 8 percent if the company would offer 30 warrants with each $1,000 bond, each warrant entitling the holder to buy one share of common stock at a price of $12 per share. The stock was selling for $10 per share at the time, and the warrants would expire in 2016 if they had not been exercised previously.

Why would investors be willing to buy KIT's bonds at a yield of only 8 percent in an 11 percent market just because warrants were offered as part of the package? The answer is that warrants are long-term options, and they have a value for the reasons set forth in the previous section. In the KIT case, this value offset the low interest rate on the bonds and made the entire package of low interest bonds plus warrants attractive to investors.

## Use of Warrants in Financing

Warrants generally are used by small, rapidly growing firms as "sweeteners" to help sell either debt or preferred stock. Such firms frequently are regarded as being very risky, and their bonds can be sold only if the firms are willing to pay extremely high rates of interest and to accept very restrictive indenture (contract) provisions. To avoid this, firms such as KIT often offer warrants along with their bonds. However, some strong firms also have used warrants.

Getting warrants along with bonds enables investors to share in a company's growth if that firm does in fact grow and prosper; therefore, investors are willing to accept a lower bond interest rate and less restrictive indenture provisions. A bond with warrants has some characteristics of debt and some of equity. It is a hybrid security that provides the financial manager with an opportunity to expand the firm's mix of securities and to appeal to a broader group of investors, thus lowering the firm's cost of capital. Virtually all warrants today are **detachable warrants,** meaning that after a bond with attached warrants has been sold, the warrants can be detached and traded separately from the bond. Further, when these warrants are exercised, the bonds themselves (with their low coupon rate) will remain outstanding. Thus, the warrants will bring in additional equity capital while leaving low interest rate debt on the books.

The warrants' exercise price generally is set from 10 percent to 30 percent above the market price of the stock on the date the bond is issued. For example, if the stock sells for $10, the exercise price will probably be set in the $11 to $13 range. If the firm does grow and prosper, and if its stock price rises above the exercise price at which shares can be purchased, warrant holders will turn in their warrants, along with cash equal to the stated exercise price, in exchange for stock. Without some incentive, however, many warrants would never be exercised until just before expiration. Their value in the market would be greater than their exercise value; thus, holders would sell warrants rather than exercise them.

Three conditions encourage holders to exercise their warrants:

1. Warrant holders surely will exercise warrants and buy stock if the warrants are about to expire with the market price of the stock above the exercise price. This means that if a firm wants its warrants exercised soon to raise capital, it should set a relatively short expiration date.

2. Warrant holders will tend to exercise voluntarily and buy stock if the company raises the dividend on the common stock by a sufficient amount. Because no dividend is paid on the warrant, it provides no current income. However, if the common stock pays a high dividend, it provides an attractive dividend yield. Therefore, the higher the stock's dividend, the greater the opportunity cost of holding the warrant rather than exercising it. Thus, if a firm wants its warrants exercised, it can raise the common stock's dividend.

3. Warrants sometimes have **stepped-up exercise prices,** which prod owners into exercising them. For example, Mills Agricorp has warrants outstanding with an exercise price of $25 until December 31, 2012, at which time the exercise price will rise to $30. If the price of the common stock is over $25 just before December 31, 2012, many warrant holders will exercise their options before the stepped-up price takes effect.

> **stepped-up exercise price**
> An exercise price that is scheduled to increase if a warrant is exercised after a designated date.

Another useful feature of warrants is that they generally bring in funds only if such funds are needed. If the company grows, it probably will need new equity capital. At the same time, this growth will cause the price of the stock to rise and the warrants to be exercised, thereby allowing the firm to obtain additional cash. If the company is not successful and cannot profitably employ additional money, the price of its stock probably will not rise sufficiently to induce exercise of the warrants.

### Self-Test Questions

What three conditions would encourage holders to exercise their warrants?

Do warrants bring in additional funds to the firm when exercised? Explain.

Explain how a firm can use warrants to issue debt with a lower cost than similar debt without warrants.

## CONVERTIBLES

**Convertible securities** are bonds or preferred stocks that can be exchanged for common stock at the option of the holder (investor). Unlike the exercise of warrants, which provides the firm with additional funds, conversion does not bring in additional capital—debt or preferred stock simply is replaced by common stock. Of course, this reduction of debt or preferred stock will strengthen the firm's balance sheet and make it easier to raise additional capital, but this is a separate action.

> **convertible security**
> A security, usually a bond or preferred stock, that is exchangeable at the option of the holder for the common stock of the issuing firm.

### Conversion Ratio and Conversion Price

One of the most important provisions of a convertible security is the **conversion ratio, CR,** defined as the number of shares of stock the convertible holder receives upon conversion. Related to the conversion ratio is the conversion price, $P_c$, which is

> **conversion ratio (CR)**
> The number of shares of common stock that can be obtained by converting a convertible bond or a share of convertible preferred stock.

the effective price paid for the common stock obtained by converting a convertible security. The relationship between the conversion ratio and the conversion price can be illustrated by the convertible debentures issued at par value by Bee TV Inc. in 2006. At any time prior to maturity on July 1, 2026, a debenture holder can exchange a bond for 20 shares of common stock; therefore, CR = 20. The bond has a par value of $1,000, so the holder would be relinquishing this amount upon conversion. Dividing the $1,000 par value by the 20 shares received gives a conversion price of $P_c = \$50$ a share:

**18–1**

$$\text{Conversion price} = P_c = \frac{\text{Par value of bond}}{\text{Conversion ratio}}$$

Like a warrant's exercise price, the conversion price usually is set at from 10 percent to 30 percent above the prevailing market price of the common stock at the time the convertible issue is sold. Generally, the conversion price and ratio are fixed for the life of the bond, although sometimes a stepped-up conversion price is used.

Another factor that might cause a change in the conversion price and ratio is a standard feature of almost all convertibles—the clause protecting the convertible against dilution from stock splits, stock dividends, and the sale of common stock at prices below the conversion price. The typical provision states that if common stock is sold at a price below the conversion price, the conversion price must be lowered (and the conversion ratio raised) to the price at which the new stock was issued. Also, if the stock is split (or if a stock dividend is declared), the conversion price must be lowered by the percentage of the stock split (or stock dividend). If this protection was not contained in the contract, a company could completely thwart conversion by the use of stock splits. Warrants are similarly protected against such dilution.

## Use of Convertibles in Financing

Convertibles offer three important advantages from the *issuer's* standpoint. First, convertibles, like bonds with warrants, permit a company to sell debt with a lower interest rate and with less restrictive covenants than straight bonds. Second, convertibles generally are subordinated to mortgage bonds, bank loans, and other senior debt, so financing with convertibles leaves the company's access to "regular" debt unimpaired. Third, convertibles provide a way of selling common stock at prices higher than those that currently prevail. Many companies actually want to sell common stock and not debt, but they believe that the price of their stock is temporarily depressed. The financial manager might know, for example, that earnings are depressed because of start-up costs associated with a new project, but he or she might expect earnings to rise sharply during the next year or so, pulling the price of the stock along. In this case, if the company sold stock now, it would be giving up too many shares to raise a given amount of money. However, if the firm sets the conversion price at 20 percent to 30 percent above the current market price of its stock, then 20 percent to 30 percent fewer shares must be given up when the bonds are converted. Notice, however, that management is counting on the stock's price rising sufficiently above the conversion price to make the bonds attractive in conversion. If earnings do not rise and pull the stock price up, and hence if conversion does not occur, the company could be saddled with debt in the face of low earnings, which could be disastrous.

How can the company be sure that conversion will occur if the price of the stock rises above the conversion price? Typically, convertibles contain a call provision that enables the issuing firm to force bondholders to convert. Suppose the conversion price is $50, the conversion ratio is 20, the market price of the common stock has risen to $60, and the call price on the convertible bond is $1,050. If the company calls the bond, bondholders could either convert into common stock with a market value of $1,200 or allow the company to redeem the bond for $1,050. Naturally, bondholders prefer $1,200 to $1,050, so conversion will occur. The call provision therefore gives the company a means of *forcing* conversion, but only if the market price of the stock is greater than the conversion price.

Convertibles are useful, but they do have three important disadvantages:

1. The use of a convertible security might, in effect, give the issuer the opportunity to sell common stock at a price higher than it could sell stock otherwise. However, if the common stock increases greatly in price, the company probably would have been better off if it had used straight debt despite its higher interest rate and then later sold common stock to refund the debt.

2. If the company truly wants to raise equity capital, and if the price of the stock does not rise sufficiently after the bond is issued, then the firm will be stuck with debt.

3. Convertibles typically have a low coupon interest rate, an advantage that will be lost when conversion occurs. Warrant financings, on the other hand, permit the company to continue to use the low-coupon debt for a longer period.

### Self-Test Questions

Does the exchange of convertible securities for common stock bring in additional funds to the firm? Explain.

How do you calculate the conversion price?

What are the key advantages and disadvantages of convertibles?

Suppose that the Bee TV convertible bond issue described in this section has a conversion ratio equal to 50 rather than 20. What is the bond's conversion price in this case? (*Answer:* $P_c$ = $20)

## REPORTING EARNINGS WHEN WARRANTS OR CONVERTIBLES ARE OUTSTANDING

If warrants or convertibles are outstanding, a firm theoretically can report earnings per share (EPS) in one of three ways:

1. **Simple EPS.** The earnings available to common stockholders are divided by the average number of shares *actually* outstanding during the period.

2. **Primary EPS.** The earnings available are divided by the average number of shares that would have been outstanding if warrants and convertibles *likely to be converted* in the near future had actually been exercised or converted.

3. **Fully diluted EPS.** This is similar to primary EPS except that all warrants and convertibles are *assumed to be exercised or converted,* regardless of the likelihood of either occurring.

Simple EPS is virtually never reported by firms that have warrants or convertibles likely to be exercised or converted; the SEC prohibits use of this figure, and it requires that primary and fully diluted earnings be shown on the income statement.

### Self-Test Questions

Differentiate among simple EPS, primary EPS, and fully diluted EPS.

Suppose a firm has 10,000 shares of common stock outstanding. In addition, it has convertible debt that can be converted into 2,000 shares of common stock. If the firm's net income for the year is $24,000, what are its simple EPS and its fully diluted EPS? (*Answers:* simple EPS = $2.40, fully diluted EPS = $2.00)

## LEVERAGED BUYOUTS (LBOs)

**leveraged buyout (LBO)**
A transaction in which a firm's publicly owned stock is bought up in a mostly debt-financed tender offer, and a privately owned, highly leveraged firm results.

With the extraordinary merger activity that took place in the 1980s, we witnessed a huge increase in the popularity of **leveraged buyouts,** or **LBOs.** The number and size of LBOs jumped significantly during this period. This development occurred for the same reasons that mergers and divestitures occurred—the existence of potential bargains; situations in which companies were using insufficient leverage; and the development of the junk bond market, which facilitated the use of leverage in takeovers.

LBOs can be initiated in one of two ways: (1) The firm's own managers can set up a new company whose equity comes from the managers themselves, plus some equity from pension funds and other institutions. This new company then arranges to borrow a large amount of money by selling junk (low-rated) bonds through an investment banking firm. With the financing arranged, the management group then makes an offer to purchase all the publicly owned shares through a tender offer. (2) A specialized LBO firm, with Kohlberg Kravis Roberts & Co. (KKR) being one of the best known, will identify a potential target company, go to the management, and suggest that an LBO deal be done. KKR and other LBO firms have billions of dollars of equity, most put up by pension funds and other large investors, available for the equity portion of the deals, and they arrange junk bond financing just as a management-led group would. Generally, the newly formed company will have at least 80 percent debt, and sometimes the debt ratio is as high as 98 percent. Thus, the term *leveraged* is most appropriate.

To illustrate an LBO, consider the $25 billion leveraged buyout of RJR Nabisco by KKR in 1989. RJR, a leading producer of tobacco and food products with such brands as Winston, Camel, Planters, Ritz, and Oreo, was trading at about $55 a share. Then F. Ross Johnson, RJR Nabisco's president and CEO at the time, announced a $75 per share, or $17.6 billion, offer to take the firm private. The day after the announcement, RJR's stock soared to $77.25, which indicated that investors thought that the final price would be even higher than Johnson's opening bid. A few days later, KKR offered $90 per share, or $20.6 billion, for the firm. The battle between the two bidders continued until late November, when RJR's board accepted a revised KKR bid of cash and securities worth about $109 per share, for a total value of about $25.1 billion.

Was RJR worth $25 billion, or did Henry Kravis and his partners let their egos govern their judgment? At the time the LBO was initiated, analysts believed that the deal was workable, but barely. Six years after the deal, KKR had disposed of all its interest in RJR Nabisco, and many experts called the biggest LBO of its time the biggest financial flop in history.

It is not clear whether LBOs are, on balance, a good or a bad idea. Some government officials and others have stated a belief that the leverage involved might destabilize the economy. On the other hand, LBOs certainly have stimulated some lethargic management teams, and that is good. Good or bad, however, LBOs have helped reshape the face of corporate America.

**Self-Test Questions**

Identify and briefly explain the two ways in which an LBO can be initiated.

How has the development of the junk bond market affected the use of LBOs?

## MERGERS

**Mergers** have taken place at a feverish pace during the past couple of decades. The brief discussion in this section will help you understand the motivations behind all this activity.[10]

**merger**
The combination of two or more firms to form a single firm.

### Rationale for Mergers

Two or more firms are merged to form a single firm for five principal reasons.

1. **Synergy.** The primary motivation for most mergers is to increase the value of the combined enterprise—the hope is that *synergy* exists so that the value of the company formed by the merger is greater than the sum of the values of the individual companies taken separately. Synergistic effects can arise from four sources: (a) *operating economies of scale* occur when cost reductions result from the combination of the companies; (b) *financial economies* might include a higher price/earnings ratio, a lower cost of debt, or a greater debt capacity; (c) *differential management efficiency* generally results when one firm is relatively inefficient, so the merger improves the profitability of the acquired assets; and (d) *increased market power* occurs if reduced competition exists after the merger. Operating and financial economies are socially desirable, as are mergers that increase managerial efficiency, but mergers that reduce competition are both undesirable and often illegal.[11]

2. **Tax considerations.** Tax considerations have stimulated a number of mergers. For example, a firm that is highly profitable and in the highest corporate tax bracket could acquire a company with large accumulated tax losses, then use those losses to shelter its own income.[12] Similarly, a company with large losses could acquire a profitable firm. Also, tax considerations could cause mergers to

---

[10]The purpose of this section is to provide you with a general understanding of mergers, the motivations for mergers, and merger activity in the United States. Merger analysis, which is the evaluation of the attractiveness of a merger, should be conducted in the same manner as capital budgeting analysis (if the present value of the cash flows expected to result from the merger exceeds the price that must be paid for the company being acquired, then the merger has a positive net present value and the acquiring firm should proceed with the acquisition). Because the very nature of the merger process is complex, we choose not to discuss the specifics of merger analysis in this section. For a detailed discussion of merger analysis, see Chapter 26 of Eugene F. Brigham and Philip R. Daves, *Intermediate Financial Management,* 9th ed. (Cincinnati, OH: South-Western College Publishing, 2007).

[11]In the 1880s and 1890s, many mergers occurred in the United States, and some of them clearly were directed toward gaining market power at the expense of competition rather than increasing operating efficiency. As a result, Congress passed a series of acts designed to ensure that mergers are not used as a method of reducing competition. Today, the principal acts include the Sherman Act (1890), the Clayton Act (1914), and the Celler Act (1950). These acts make it illegal for firms to combine in any manner if the combination will lessen competition. They are administered by the antitrust division of the Justice Department and by the Federal Trade Commission.

[12]Mergers undertaken only to use accumulated tax losses probably would be challenged by the IRS. However, because many factors are present in any given merger, it is hard to prove that a merger was motivated only, or even primarily, by tax considerations.

be a desirable use for excess cash. For example, if a firm has a shortage of internal investment opportunities compared with its cash flows, it will have excess cash, and its options for disposing of this excess cash are to (a) pay an extra dividend, (b) invest in marketable securities, (c) repurchase its own stock, or (d) purchase another firm. If the firm pays an extra dividend, its stockholders will have to pay taxes on the distribution. Marketable securities such as Treasury bonds provide a good temporary parking place for money, but the rate of return on such securities is less than that required by stockholders. A stock repurchase might result in a capital gain for the remaining stockholders, but it could be disadvantageous if the company has to pay a high price to acquire the stock, and, if the repurchase is designed solely to avoid paying dividends, it might be challenged by the IRS. However, using surplus cash to acquire another firm has no immediate tax consequences for either the acquiring firm or its stockholders, and this fact has motivated a number of mergers.

3. **Purchase of assets below their replacement cost.** Sometimes a firm will become an acquisition candidate because the replacement value of its assets is considerably higher than its market value. For example, in the 1980s, oil companies could acquire reserves more cheaply by buying out other oil companies than by exploratory drilling. This factor was a motive in Chevron's acquisition of Gulf Oil. The acquisition of Republic Steel (the sixth largest steel company) by LTV (the fourth largest) provides another example of a firm being purchased because its purchase price was less than the replacement value of its assets. LTV found that it was less costly to purchase Republic Steel for $700 million than it would have been to construct a new steel mill. At the time, Republic's stock was selling for less than one-third of its book value. However, the merger did not help LTV's inefficient operations—ultimately, the company filed for bankruptcy.

4. **Diversification.** Managers often claim that diversification helps to stabilize the firm's earnings and thus reduces corporate risk. Therefore, diversification often is given as a reason for mergers. Stabilization of earnings certainly is beneficial to a firm's employees, suppliers, and customers, but its value to stockholders and debt holders is less clear. If an investor is worried about earnings variability, he or she probably could diversify through stock purchases (investment portfolio adjustment) more easily than the firm could through acquisitions.

5. **Maintaining control.** Some mergers and takeovers are considered *hostile* because the management of the acquired firm opposes the merger. One reason for the hostility is that the managers of the acquired companies generally lose their jobs, or at least their autonomy. Therefore, managers who own less than 50 percent plus one share of the stock in their firms look to devices that will lessen the chances of their firms being taken over. Mergers can serve as such a device. For example, in 1985, when InterNorth of Omaha was under attack, it arranged to merge with Houston Natural Gas Company, paying for Houston primarily with debt. That merger made the combined company, which was renamed Enron in 1986, much larger and hence harder for any potential acquirer to "digest." Also, the much higher debt level resulting from the merger made it hard for any acquiring company to use debt to buy Enron. Such **defensive mergers** are difficult to defend on economic grounds. The managers involved invariably argue that synergy, not a desire to protect their own jobs, motivated the acquisition, but there can be no question that many mergers have been designed more for the benefit of managers than for stockholders.

**defensive merger**
A merger designed to make a company less vulnerable to a takeover.

# Types of Mergers

Economists classify mergers into four groups: (1) horizontal, (2) vertical, (3) congeneric, and (4) conglomerate. A **horizontal merger** occurs when one firm combines with another in its same line of business. For example, the acquisition of Chrysler by Daimler-Benz AG in 1998 was a horizontal merger because both firms are automobile manufacturers. An example of a **vertical merger** is a steel producer's acquisition of one of its own suppliers, such as an iron or coal mining firm. The 1993 merger of Merck & Co., a manufacturer of health care products, and Medco Containment, the largest mail-order pharmacy service, is an example of a vertical merger. Congeneric means "allied in nature or action"; hence, a **congeneric merger** involves related enterprises but not producers of the same product (horizontal) or firms in a producer-supplier relationship (vertical). Examples of congeneric mergers include Viacom's acquisitions of Paramount Communications and Blockbuster Entertainment in 1994. Viacom owns several television stations and cable systems and distributes television programming; Paramount produces movies and other entertainment shown both on television and in theaters, and Blockbuster's principal business is the rental of movies, most of which have been shown previously in theaters. A **conglomerate merger** occurs when unrelated enterprises combine, as illustrated by the merger of Philip Morris, a tobacco company, and Kraft General Foods, a food processor, in 1989.

Operating economies (and also anticompetitive effects) are dependent on the type of merger involved. Vertical and horizontal mergers generally provide the greatest synergistic operating benefits, but they also are the ones most likely to be attacked by the U.S. Department of Justice. In any event, it is useful to think of these economic classifications when analyzing the feasibility of a prospective merger.

**horizontal merger**
A combination of two firms that produce the same type of good or service.

**vertical merger**
A merger between a firm and one of its suppliers or customers.

**congeneric merger**
A merger of firms in the same general industry, but for which no customer or supplier relationship exists.

**conglomerate merger**
A merger of companies in totally different industries.

# Merger Activity

Four major "merger waves" have occurred in the United States. The first was in the late 1800s, when consolidations occurred in the oil, steel, tobacco, and other basic industries. The second was in the 1920s, when the stock market boom helped financial promoters consolidate firms in a number of industries, including utilities, communications, and autos. The third was in the 1960s, when conglomerate mergers were the rage. The fourth began in the early 1980s, and it is still going strong. Many of the recent mergers have been horizontal mergers.

The current "merger mania" has been sparked by several factors: (1) at times, the depressed level of the dollar relative to Japanese and European currencies has made U.S. companies look cheap to foreign buyers; (2) the unprecedented level of inflation that existed during the 1970s and early 1980s, which increased the replacement value of firms' assets even while a weak stock market reduced their market values; (3) the general belief among the major natural resource companies that it is cheaper to "buy reserves on Wall Street" through mergers than to explore and find them in the field; (4) attempts to ward off raiders by use of defensive mergers; (5) the development of the junk bond market, which has made it possible to use far more debt in acquisitions than had been possible earlier; and (6) the increased globalization of business, which has led to increased economies of scale and to the formation of worldwide corporations.

For the past decade, the pace of merger activity can best be described as furious. Each year from 1995 through 2000, a new record was set for the values of announced mergers, with the peak of $3.4 trillion occurring in 2000. An economic slump decreased merger activity by 53 percent in 2001 and another 25 percent in 2002, but a positive economic outlook in 2003 resulted in a reversal, and merger activity started a new upward trend. The trend has continued such that in 2006 the total value of mergers was approximately equal to the record-setting level in 2000.

During the current merger frenzy, many of the largest mergers have been in financial services (for example, BankAmerica and NationsBank and J. P. Morgan Chase & Company and Bank One), telecommunications (for example, WorldCom and MCI Communications and AT&T and Tele-Communications), and technology (for example, Oracle and PeopleSoft). As mergers in these industries continue, the companies' and industries' infrastructures will be reshaped.

Often, large, well-publicized mergers fail because the combination of the two companies is counterproductive. For example, two of the most celebrated and costly mergers—RJR Nabisco and AOL Time Warner—ultimately ended in divorce, and those involved in the mergers ended up losing large amounts of wealth.

Many of the mergers in the 1990s resulted either because the acquired firms were considered undervalued or because it was felt economies of scale could produce less costly combined operations. Increased global competition and governmental reforms were the major reasons for merger activities in the telecommunications and financial services industries, which accounted for nearly 50 percent of the mergers in 1998. Experts expect these industries and other industries, such as defense, consumer products, and natural resources, to become significantly reshaped as merger activity continues in the future.

### Self-Test Questions

What are the five primary motives behind most mergers?

From what sources do synergistic effects arise?

How have tax considerations stimulated mergers?

Is diversification to reduce stockholder risk a valid motive for mergers? Explain.

Explain briefly the four economic classifications of mergers.

What factors have sparked the most recent *merger mania*?

## BANKRUPTCY AND REORGANIZATION

During recessions, bankruptcies normally rise, and the recessions of 1991–1992 and 2001 were no exceptions. The 1991–1992 casualties included Pan Am, Continental Airlines, and R. H. Macy & Company; the 2001 casualties included Kmart, UAL, and Pacific Gas and Electric. Because of its importance, at least a brief discussion of bankruptcy is warranted in the book.

When a business becomes *insolvent,* it does not have enough cash to meet scheduled interest and principal payments—that is, the firm cannot service its debt. A decision must then be made whether to dissolve the firm through *liquidation* or to permit it to *reorganize* and thus stay alive. These issues are addressed in Chapter 7 and Chapter 11 of the federal bankruptcy statutes, and the final decision is made by a federal bankruptcy court judge.

The decision to force a firm to liquidate or to permit it to reorganize depends on whether the value of the reorganized firm is likely to be greater than the value of the firm's assets if they were sold off piecemeal. In a reorganization (Chapter 11 bankruptcy), a committee of unsecured creditors is appointed by the court to negotiate with management on the terms of a potential reorganization. The reorganization plan might call for a *restructuring* of the firm's debt, in which case the interest rate might be reduced, the term to maturity lengthened, or some of the debt might be exchanged for equity. The point of the restructuring is to reduce the financial charges to a level that the firm's cash flows can support. Of course, the common stockholders also have to give up something—they normally see their position eroded as a result of additional shares being given to debt holders in exchange for accepting a reduced amount of debt principal and interest. A trustee might be appointed by the court to oversee the reorganization, or the existing management might be allowed to retain control.

Liquidation occurs if the company is deemed to be too far gone to be saved—that is, if it is worth more dead than alive. If the bankruptcy court orders a liquidation, assets are distributed as specified in Chapter 7 of the Bankruptcy Act. As a rule, proceeds are distributed to secured creditors first, then wages and taxes are paid; the remaining proceeds are distributed in order to unsecured creditors, to preferred stockholders, and finally to common stockholders, if anything is left. The priority of claims established by federal bankruptcy statutes *must* be followed when distributing the proceeds from a liquidated firm.

### Self-Test Questions

When a business becomes insolvent, what two alternatives are available?

Differentiate between a liquidation and a reorganization.

In the case of liquidation, who gets paid first and who gets paid last?

## REFUNDING OPERATIONS

A great deal of long-term debt was issued at high interest rates during the late 1970s and early 1980s. Since then, interest rates have fallen, and the call protection periods of many bonds have expired. As a result, corporations and government units have retired old bonds and have replaced them with new bonds with lower interest rates. In fact, most long-term debt that exists today was issued in 2003 or later when interest rates were at historically low levels—many older debt issues were refinanced (refunded) at that time.

Bond refunding analysis is similar to capital budgeting analysis, as discussed in Chapter 9 and Chapter 10. Also, bond refunding can be compared with the process individuals go through to refinance a house: An existing debt (mortgage) with a high interest rate is replaced by a new debt (mortgage) with a lower interest rate.

The refunding decision actually involves two separate questions: (1) Would it be profitable to call an outstanding issue now and to replace it with a new issue? (2) Even if refunding currently is profitable, would it be better to call now or to postpone the refunding to a later date?

As we noted, refunding decisions are similar to capital budgeting decisions, and the net present value method is the primary tool. In essence, the costs of undertaking the refunding operation (the investment outlay) are compared with the present value of the interest that will be saved if the bond with the high interest rate is called and replaced with a new bond with a low interest rate. If the net present value of refunding is positive, then the refunding should take place. The costs of the refunding operation consist primarily of the call premium on the old bond issue and the flotation costs associated with selling the new issue. The cash flow benefits consist primarily of the interest expenses that will be saved if the company replaces high-cost debt with low-cost debt. The discount rate used to find the present value of the interest savings is the after-tax cost of *new* debt: The interest saved is the difference between two relatively certain cash flow streams, so the difference essentially is without risk. Therefore, a low discount rate should be used, and that rate is today's after-tax cost of new debt in the market.

To illustrate the refunding decision, consider Strasburg Communications Corporation, which has a $100 million, 13 percent, semiannual coupon bond outstanding with 10 years remaining to maturity. The bond has a call provision that permits the company to retire the issue by calling in the bonds at an 8 percent call premium. Investment bankers have assured Strasburg that it could issue an additional $100 million of new 10 percent coupon, 10-year bonds that pay interest semiannually. Flotation costs on the new refunding issue will amount to $4 million. Predictions are that long-term interest rates are unlikely to fall below 10 percent. Strasburg's marginal tax rate is 40 percent. Should the company refund the $100 million of 13 percent semiannual coupon bonds?

Strasburg's refunding analysis is presented in Table 18-3. Because the marginal tax rate is 40 percent, the company's after-tax cost of new debt is equal to 6 percent, or 3 percent per six-month period. And because the bonds have semiannual coupons, there will be 20 semiannual periods in the analysis.

The net present value of refunding is positive, so Strasburg should refund the old bond issue—the firm's value will be increased by $1,389,727 if the old bond is retired.

**TABLE 18-3**  NPV Refunding Analysis

*Cost of Refunding at t = 0*

| | |
|---|---:|
| Call premium on old bond (0.08 × $100 million) | $( 8,000,000) |
| Flotation costs on new issue | ( 4,000,000) |
| Total initial outlay | $(12,000,000) |

*Semiannual Interest Savings Due to Refunding: t = 1 to 20*
*(10 years of payments twice a year)*

| | |
|---|---:|
| Interest on old bond (0.065 × $100 million) | $ 6,500,000 |
| Interest on new bond (0.050 × $100 million) | ( 5,000,000) |
| Interest savings per period | $ 1,500,000 |
| Increased taxes due to lower interest payment[a] (0.40 × $1,500,000) | $( 600,000) |
| Net interest savings | $ 900,000 |

*Refunding Cash Flow Time Line*

| | | | | 1 | 10 Years |
|---|---|---|---|---|---|
| Interest period | 0 | r = 3% | 1 | 2 | 20 Interest payments |
| Initial outlay | (12,000,000) | | | | |
| Interest savings | 0 | | 900,000 | 900,000 . . . | 900,000 |
| Net cash flow | (12,000,000) | | 900,000 | 900,000 . . . | 900,000 |

NPV of refunding at $r_{dt}/2 = 3\%$ is $1,389,727

---

[a]Strasburg's interest expense will decrease by $1,500,000, thus taxable income will increase by $1,500,000, if the new bond is issued. Strasburg will have to pay 0.40 × $1,500,000 = $600,000 additional taxes on this increased taxable income.

**Self-Test Questions**

How is bond refunding analysis similar to capital budgeting analysis?

What two questions are involved in the bond refunding decision?

What are the primary costs and the primary benefits in a bond refunding analysis?

Why is the after-tax cost of debt used as the discount rate in a bond refunding analysis?

After reading this chapter, you should be able to answer the following questions:

**Chapter *Essentials***
—The Answers

- **Why do firms lease rather than purchase assets? How should a firm determine whether to lease or purchase an asset?** Most firms will lease rather than purchase an asset when the benefits of leasing are greater than the benefits of purchasing—that is, an asset should be leased when this action increases the firm's value. In some cases, firms lease assets because they are unable to borrow the capital that is needed to purchase the assets. To determine whether an asset should be leased or purchased, a firm should use the same techniques that are used to evaluate capital budgeting projects, which we discuss in Chapter 9. In other words, an NPV analysis should be conducted to determine whether the value of leasing is greater than the value of purchasing.

- **What types of leases exist? Do all leases have the same effect on a firm's financial statements?** The basic types of leases include (1) a sale-and-leaseback arrangement, which is a situation in which a firm sells an asset it owns and then arranges to lease it back from the purchaser; (2) an operating lease, which is a short-term, cancelable arrangement in which the lessor (the owner of the leased asset) generally provides maintenance for the asset; and (3) a capital lease, which is a long-term, noncancelable arrangement in which the lessee (the firm using the asset) is responsible for the maintenance of the asset. If a leasing arrangement qualifies as a capital lease, then the transaction appears on the financial statements the same as if the lessee had purchased the asset. Although the lease payments represent a tax-deductible expense, operating leases generally are not reported on the balance sheet.

- **What are stock options? Why would an investor buy an option?** A stock option gives the owner the right to buy (sell) a specified number of shares of a particular stock at some predetermined price within a specified time period. The two basic types of stock options include a call option and a put option. A call option gives an investor the right to buy stock at a predetermined price, whereas a put option gives an investor the right to sell stock at a predetermined price. Because the price of an option is relatively low compared with the price of the underlying stock on which it is written and the price at which the option is executed is contractually set, the most an investor can lose on an option position is the purchase price of the option contract. Thus, investors buy (sell) options for one of two reasons: (1) risk management or (2) speculation. An investor can use an option as investment insurance by entering a position that effectively "pays off" when the position in the stock incurs losses. For example, if an investor owns the stock of Microsoft, he or she can buy a put option on Microsoft. If the value of Microsoft declines significantly, the option position will be profitable, which will help the investor recover some of the losses from owning Microsoft stock. An example of this arrangement is contained in Chapter *Essentials*—Personal Finance. Investors who think a stock's value will move in a specific direction might purchase an option to try to capitalize on the stock's price movement. In this case, investors are speculating that the stock will move in the forecasted direction.

- **How does a stock option differ from a warrant?** A warrant, which is created and issued by a firm, represents an option to purchase shares of stock from the issuing firm. When a warrant is exercised, the investor buys the stock from the issuing firm. As a result, the issuing firm receives funds that can be invested in capital budgeting projects. On the other hand, an option technically is created, or written, by an investor. When an option is exercised, the transaction takes place between investors, and the firm of the underlying stock on which the option is written is not involved.

- **What is a convertible security? Why do firms use convertibles?** A convertible security is a financial instrument—generally either a bond or preferred stock—that can be converted into the common stock of the issuing firm. It is the investor who decides whether to convert the instrument into common stock. Generally an investor will "convert" when the market value of the common stock he or she will receive is greater than the value of the convertible instrument. Because the conversion feature benefits investors, a firm generally uses a convertible to attract investors to purchase its bonds or preferred stock and to issue bonds or preferred stock at lower rates (everything else equal).

- **Why do firms merge or take over other firms?** A firm might merge or take over another firm (1) because the combination of the two firms is more valuable than the sum of the two firms separately—this is called *synergy;* (2) because the acquired firm is in a beneficial tax position; (3) because the acquired firm has assets that can be purchased at bargain prices; (4) to diversify into other industries; and (5) to maintain control of the firm by increasing its size so that an undesirable firm cannot afford to acquire the new merged firm.

- **Why would a firm pay off (refund) its bonds before maturity?** Firms refund bonds to save interest expenses. To refund its bonds, a firm issues a new bond at a lower interest rate than existing bonds, and then uses the proceeds of the new bond issue to pay off the existing bond. In other words, the firm refinances its debt.

## ETHICAL DILEMMA

### Should Maria Take a SINful Cruise?

Maria Santos was recently promoted to senior vice president and assistant to the CFO at Paradise Environmental Designs (PED). In her new position, Maria is responsible for raising external funds for PED. When the firm needs to raise capital, her team recommends the type of financial instrument that should be issued, completes the appropriate paperwork, negotiates with PED's investment bankers, and so forth. In a departmental meeting a couple of days ago, the CEO stated that he thought the rate at which PED has been raising capital has been much too high, and he wants any future funds

that are raised to have substantially lower costs. Although he blamed her predecessor, the comments were clearly directed at Maria and the members of her department. As a result, Maria felt that she had to come up with some means by which PED can lower the costs of funds in the future.

Because she is fairly new to her position, Maria thought it would be a good idea to meet with others who are more experienced in raising funds for corporations. One of the people who offered Maria some ideas is Roger, a close friend of hers, who works at Superior Investment Networks (SIN), which is one of the investment banking organizations used by PED. Roger suggested that PED consider issuing convertible bonds rather than straight, or traditional, bonds. He explained that a convertible bond can be issued at a lower interest rate than an identical bond that is not convertible because the conversion feature is a benefit to investors rather than issuers. Roger also explained that convertibles are somewhat complex hybrid securities. Other than the information that Roger gave her, Maria knows nothing about convertibles. But because Roger is a friend and his description of convertibles was intriguing, she decided to investigate whether it would be appropriate for PED to use convertibles.

When she arrived at work this morning, Maria was told that PED plans to raise $400 million as soon as possible to invest in capital budgeting projects that the CEO wants to purchase within one year. Unfortunately, Maria hasn't had a chance to collect more information about convertibles. Even so, she thinks that a convertible might be an appropriate instrument to issue at this time. As a result, Maria called Roger and asked him how she could learn more about convertibles in a very short time period. Roger told her that SIN presents a conference each year at which invited participants discuss various aspects of convertibles. The topics that are covered at the conference range from the basics of convertible securities to more complex topics. The conference seems to be exactly what Maria needs to become more informed about the advantages and disadvantages of issuing convertibles, so she asked Roger to provide her with specific information about the conference, including the dates, costs, specific session topics, and so forth.

One hour ago, Roger called with details about the SIN conference. The seven-day conference will be held aboard a cruise ship as it sails to exotic ports in the Mediterranean Sea. The sessions are scheduled during the time the ship is traveling from one port to another, which generally takes four or five hours. When the ship is in port, the conference coordinator has arranged for the participants to take tours, play golf and tennis, lounge at the beach, and enjoy the local entertainment. The conference sounds great to Maria because she can work and relax at the same time. One thing bothers her, however—all of the costs, including recreation, relaxation, and entertainment activities, will be paid for by SIN.

Maria is convinced she will get the information she needs at the SIN conference. But she is concerned that attending the conference might be considered a conflict of interest because she knows that SIN representatives will try to convince her to use the company's services to issue convertibles. She also knows that Roger will earn substantial commissions if PED uses SIN to issue convertibles. Further, Maria is concerned that material/information she receives at the conference will be one-sided (biased).

If she is going to attend the conference, Maria needs to register within the next couple of days. As a result, she needs to make a decision soon. What should she do? What would you do if you were Maria?

The concepts presented in this chapter should give you an idea as to what alternative investments are available in the financial markets. There are many types of investment opportunities that range from basic stocks and bonds to complex, exotic combinations of options and convertibles. You should be careful, however, when investing your money. You should not invest in securities that you don't understand; if you do, you might be left wondering why you lost your money.

Following are concepts from this chapter that can be applied to personal finance:

## Chapter *Essentials*
—Personal Finance

- When you want to purchase a new car, you should consider whether leasing might be a better alternative. Under certain circumstances, purchasing a car is more appropriate, whereas there are other circumstances in which leasing is more appropriate. To make a decision, you must first estimate the expenses, including maintenance and repairs, insurance, and so forth, associated with both options during the period you expect to use the automobile, and then use NPV analysis to determine which alternative is preferable.

- Options provide some protection against "bad" risk, which means that they can be used to reduce the risks associated with investment positions. Consider, for example, an investor who owns 100 shares of IBM stock. Suppose the current market value of IBM stock is $92 per share. Perhaps the investor believes that the price of IBM stock is likely drop during the next few months. Although she does not want to sell the stock today, she does plan to sell the stock within two months. To protect against the risk of a significant price decrease, she can purchase a three-month put option on the IBM stock she owns. The cost to purchase a put position to cover the 100 shares of IBM stock is $380, and the strike price for each put is $95. Consider what happens if the price of IBM's stock declines to $80. The investor will lose $1,200 = 100($80−$92) on her current position in the stock, but she will realize a net gain equal to $1,120 = 100($95−$80)−$380 on the put position. As a result, her net loss on the combined position is $80 = $1,120−$1,200, which is much less than if she did not have the put position. If the price of IBM increases to $100 per share, the investor will let the put options expire because they are worthless. In this case, it effectively costs the investor $380 to insure the 100 shares of IBM stock that she holds from "downside" risk.
- Similar to firms, people can declare bankruptcy when the value of their debt exceeds the value of their assets. However, it is not a good idea for individuals to think of bankruptcy as a means to "get out from under" their financial obligations. If you declare bankruptcy, your credit will be harmed substantially, and the "bankruptcy blemish" will follow you for a very long period. If you find yourself in financial difficulty, it is generally better to try to work with creditors to pay off your debt than to declare bankruptcy.
- Like firms, individuals refinance debt to reduce their interest expenses when interest rates decline. Just because interest rates drop, however, you should not automatically refinance. To determine whether you should refinance your debt, you should conduct an NPV analysis similar to the one shown in Table 18-3.

## QUESTIONS

**18-1**   Distinguish between operating leases and financial leases. Would a firm be more likely to finance a fleet of trucks or a manufacturing plant with an operating lease?

**18-2**   One alleged advantage of leasing voiced in the past was that it kept liabilities off the balance sheet, thus making it possible for a firm to obtain more leverage than it otherwise could have. This raised the question of whether both the lease obligation and the asset involved should be capitalized and shown on the balance sheet. Discuss the pros and cons of capitalizing leases and related assets.

**18-3**   Suppose there were no IRS restrictions on what constitutes a valid lease. Explain in a manner that a legislator might understand why some restrictions should be imposed.

**18-4**   Suppose Congress changed the tax laws in a way that (a) permitted equipment to be depreciated over a shorter period, (b) lowered corporate tax rates, and (c) reinstated the investment tax credit. Discuss how each of these changes would affect the relative use of leasing versus conventional debt in the U.S. economy.

**18-5**   What effect does the expected growth rate of a firm's stock price (subsequent to issue) have on its ability to raise additional funds through (a) convertibles and (b) warrants?

**18-6**   **a.** How would a firm's decision to pay out a higher percentage of its earnings as dividends affect each of the following?

  **(1)** The value of its long-term warrants

  **(2)** The likelihood that its convertible bonds will be converted

  **(3)** The likelihood that its warrants will be exercised

  **b.** If you owned the warrants or convertibles of a company, would you be pleased or displeased if it raised its payout rate from 20 percent to 80 percent? Why?

**18-7**   Suppose a company simultaneously issues $50 million of convertible bonds with a coupon rate of 9 percent and $50 million of pure bonds with a coupon rate of 12 percent. Both bonds have the same maturity. Does the fact that the convertible issue has the lower coupon rate suggest that it is less risky than the pure bond? Would you regard the cost of capital as being lower on the convertible than on the pure bond? Explain. (*Hint:* Although it might appear at first glance that the convertible's cost of capital is lower, this is not necessarily the case because the interest rate on the convertible understates its cost. Think about this.)

**18-8**   How does a firm "force" investors to convert their convertible bonds (or convertible preferred stock) into its common stock?

**18-9**   Describe how LBOs are used to finance mergers.

**18-10**  Distinguish between a congeneric merger and a vertical merger. Give examples of existing companies that if merged would be classified in each category.

## SELF-TEST PROBLEMS

*(Solutions appear in Appendix B at the end of the book.)*

**ST-1** Define each of the following terms:                                                   key terms

  **a.** Lessee; lessor

  **b.** Sale and leaseback; operating lease; financial lease

  **c.** Off-balance-sheet financing

  **d.** FASB #13

  **e.** Residual value

  **f.** Option; strike, or exercise, price; call option; put option

  **g.** Warrant; detachable warrant; stepped-up exercise price

  **h.** Convertible security; conversion ratio (CR)

  **i.** Simple EPS; primary EPS; fully diluted EPS

  **j.** Leveraged buyout (LBO)

  **k.** Merger; synergy

**ST-2** The Olsen Company has decided to acquire a new truck. One alternative is to    lease analysis
lease the truck on a four-year contract for a lease payment of $10,000 per year, with payments to be made at the beginning of each year. The lease would include maintenance. Alternatively, Olsen could purchase the truck outright for $40,000, financing with a bank loan for the net purchase price, amortized over a four-year period at an interest rate of 10 percent per year, payments to be made at the end of each year. Under the borrow-to-purchase arrangement, Olsen would have to maintain the truck at a cost of $1,000 per

year, payable at year-end. The truck falls into the MACRS 3-year class. It has a salvage value of $10,000, which is the expected market value after four years, at which time Olsen plans to replace the truck irrespective of whether it leases or buys. Olsen has a marginal tax rate of 40 percent.

**a.** What is Olsen's PV cost of leasing?

**b.** What is Olsen's PV cost of owning? Should the truck be leased or purchased?

**c.** The appropriate discount rate for use in Olsen's analysis is the firm's after-tax cost of debt. Why?

**d.** The salvage value is the least certain cash flow in the analysis. How might Olsen incorporate the higher riskiness of this cash flow into the analysis?

## PROBLEMS

**convertible bond**    **18-1**    The Swift Company was planning to finance an expansion in the summer of 2009. The principal executives of the company agreed that an industrial company like theirs should finance growth by means of common stock rather than by debt. However, they believed that the price of the company's common stock did not reflect its true worth, so they decided to sell a convertible bond.

**a.** What conversion price should be set by the issuer? The conversion rate will be 5.0; that is, each $1,000 face-value convertible bond can be converted into five shares of common stock.

**b.** Do you think the convertible bond should include a call provision? Why or why not?

**balance sheet effects of leasing**    **18-2**    Two textile companies, Grimm Manufacturing and Wright Mills, began operations with identical balance sheets. A year later, both required additional manufacturing capacity at a cost of $200,000. Grimm obtained a five-year, $200,000 loan at an 8 percent interest rate from its bank. Wright, on the other hand, decided to lease the required $200,000 capacity from American Leasing for five years; an 8 percent return was built into the lease. The balance sheet for each company, before the asset increases, is as follows:

|              |          | Debt                           | $200,000 |
|--------------|----------|--------------------------------|----------|
|              |          | Equity                         | 200,000  |
| Total assets | $400,000 | Total liabilities and equity   | $400,000 |

**a.** Show the balance sheet of each firm after the asset increase, and calculate each firm's new debt ratio. (Assume Wright's lease is kept off the balance sheet.)

**b.** Show how Wright's balance sheet would have looked immediately after the financing if it had capitalized the lease.

**c.** Would the rate of return (1) on assets and (2) on equity be affected by the choice of financing? How?

**lease analysis**    **18-3**    As part of its overall plant modernization and cost reduction program, the management of Teweles Textile Mills has decided to install a new automated weaving loom. In the capital budgeting analysis of this equipment, the IRR of the project was found to be 20 percent versus a project required return of 12 percent.

The loom has an invoice price of $250,000, including delivery and installation charges. The funds needed could be borrowed from the bank through a four-year amortized loan at a 10 percent interest rate, with payments to be made at the *end* of each year. In the event that the loom is purchased, the manufacturer will contract to maintain and service it for a fee of $20,000 per year paid at the end of each year. The loom falls in the MACRS 5-year class, and Teweles's marginal tax rate is 40 percent.

Apilado Automation Inc., maker of the loom, has offered to lease the loom to Teweles for $70,000 upon delivery and installation (at t=0) plus four additional annual lease payments of $70,000 to be made at the ends of Years 1 through 4. (Note that there are five lease payments in total.) The lease agreement includes maintenance and servicing. Actually, the loom has an expected life of eight years, at which time its expected salvage value is zero; however, after four years, its market value is expected to equal its book value of $42,500. Teweles plans to build an entirely new plant in four years, so it has no interest in either leasing or owning the proposed loom for more than that period.

**a.** Should the loom be leased or purchased?

**b.** The salvage value clearly is the most uncertain cash flow in the analysis. Assume that the appropriate salvage value pretax discount rate is 15 percent. What would be the effect of a salvage value risk adjustment on the decision?

**c.** The original analysis assumed that Teweles would not need the loom after four years. Now assume that the firm will continue to use it after the lease expires. Thus, if it leased, Teweles would have to buy the asset after four years at the then-existing market value, which is assumed to equal the book value. What effect would this requirement have on the basic analysis? (No numerical analysis is required; just verbalize.)

18-4 The city of Gainesville issued $1,000,000 of 14 percent coupon, 30-year, semiannual payment, tax-exempt muni bonds 10 years ago. The bonds had 10 years of call protection, but now Gainesville can call the bonds if it chooses to do so. The call premium would be 10 percent of the face amount. New 20-year, 12 percent, semiannual payment bonds can be sold at par, but flotation costs on this issue would be 2 percent, or $20,000. What is the net present value of the refunding? (*Hint:* Approach this problem just like the capital budgeting problems in Chapter 9 and Chapter 10.)

**NPV of refunding**

18-5 The Cox Computer Company has grown rapidly during the past five years. Recently its commercial bank urged the company to consider increasing its permanent financing. Its bank loan under a line of credit has risen to $150,000, carrying a 10 percent interest rate, and Cox has been 30 to 60 days late in paying trade creditors.

**financing alternatives**

Discussions with an investment banker have resulted in the decision to raise $250,000 at this time. Investment bankers have assured Cox that the following alternatives are feasible (flotation costs will be ignored):

*Alternative 1:* Sell common stock at $10 per share.

*Alternative 2:* Sell convertible bonds at a 10 percent coupon, convertible into 80 shares of common stock for each $1,000 bond (that is, the conversion price is $12.50 per share).

*Alternative 3:* Sell debentures with a 10 percent coupon; each $1,000 bond will have 80 warrants to buy one share of common stock at $12.50.

Charles Cox, the president, owns 80 percent of Cox's common stock and wishes to maintain control of the company; 50,000 shares are outstanding. The following are summaries of Cox's latest financial statements:

### Balance Sheet

|              |           | Current liabilities          | $200,000 |
|--------------|-----------|------------------------------|----------|
|              |           | Common stock, $1 par         | 50,000   |
|              |           | Retained earnings            | 25,000   |
| Total assets | $275,000  | Total liabilities and equity | $275,000 |

### Income Statement

| Sales                    | $550,000   |
|--------------------------|------------|
| All costs except interest | (495,000) |
| EBIT                     | $ 55,000   |
| Interest                 | ( 15,000)  |
| EBT                      | $ 40,000   |
| Taxes at 40%             | ( 16,000)  |
| Net income               | $ 24,000   |
|                          |            |
| Shares outstanding       | 50,000     |
| Earnings per share       | $0.48      |
| Price/earnings ratio     | 18 ×       |
| Market price of stock    | $8.64      |

a. Show the new balance sheet under each alternative. For Alternatives 2 and 3, show the balance sheet after conversion of the debentures or exercise of the warrants. Assume that $150,000 of the funds raised will be used to pay off the bank loan and the rest to increase total assets.

b. Show Charles Cox's control position under each alternative, assuming that he does not purchase additional shares.

c. What is the effect on earnings per share of each alternative if it is assumed that earnings before interest and taxes will be 20 percent of total assets?

d. What will be the debt ratio under each alternative?

e. Which of the three alternatives would you recommend to Charles Cox and why?

**lease versus buy**    18-6 Maltese Mining Company must install $1.5 million of new machinery in its Nevada mine. It can obtain a bank loan for 100 percent of the required amount. Alternatively, a Nevada investment banking firm that represents a group of investors believes that it can arrange for a lease financing plan. Assume that the following facts apply:

(1) The equipment falls in the MACRS 3-year class.

(2) Estimated maintenance expenses are $75,000 per year.

(3) Maltese's marginal tax rate is 40 percent.

(4) If the money is borrowed, the bank loan will be at a rate of 15 percent, amortized in four equal installments to be paid at the end of each year.

(5) The tentative lease terms call for end-of-year payments of $400,000 per year for four years.

**(6)** Under the proposed lease terms, the lessee must pay for insurance, property taxes, and maintenance.

**(7)** Maltese must use the equipment if it is to continue in business, so it will almost certainly want to acquire the property at the end of the lease. If it does, then under the lease terms it can purchase the machinery at its fair market value at that time. The best estimate of this market value is the $250,000 salvage value, but it could be much higher or lower under certain circumstances.

To assist management in making the proper lease-versus-buy decision, you are asked to answer the following questions:

**a.** Assuming that the lease can be arranged, should Maltese lease or should it borrow to buy the equipment? Explain.

**b.** Consider the $250,000 estimated salvage value. Is it appropriate to discount it at the same rate as the other cash flows? What about the other cash flows—are they all equally risky? (*Hint:* Riskier cash flows are normally discounted at higher rates, but when the cash flows are *costs* rather than *inflows*, the normal procedure must be reversed.)

## Integrative Problem

**18-7** Kris Crawford, capital acquisitions manager for Heath Financial Services Inc., has been asked to perform a lease-versus-buy analysis on a new stock price quotation system for Heath's Sarasota branch office. The system would receive current prices, record the information for retrieval by the branch's brokers, and display current prices in the lobby.

**lease analysis**

The equipment costs $1,200,000, and, if it is purchased, Heath could obtain a term loan for the full amount at a 10 percent cost. The loan would be amortized over the four-year life of the equipment, with payments made at the end of each year. The equipment is classified as special purpose, and hence it falls into the MACRS 3-year class. If the equipment is purchased, a maintenance contract must be obtained at a cost of $25,000, payable at the beginning of each year.

After four years, the equipment will be sold, and Crawford's best estimate of its residual value at that time is $125,000. Because technology is changing rapidly in real-time display systems, however, the residual value is uncertain.

As an alternative, National Leasing is willing to write a four-year lease on the equipment, including maintenance, for payments of $340,000 at the *beginning* of each year. Heath's marginal tax rate is 40 percent. Help Crawford conduct her analysis by answering the following questions:

**a.** **(1)** Why is leasing sometimes referred to as *off-balance-sheet* financing?

   **(2)** What is the difference between a capital lease and an operating lease?

   **(3)** What effect does leasing have on a firm's capital structure?

**b.** **(1)** What is Heath's present value cost of owning the equipment? (*Hint:* Set up a table whose bottom line is a time line that shows the net cash flows over the period $t=0$ to $t=4$, and then find the PV of these net cash flows, or the PV cost of owning.)

   **(2)** Explain the rationale for the discount rate you used to find the present value.

c. **(1)** What is Heath's present value cost of leasing the equipment? (*Hint:* Again, construct a cash flow time line.)

**(2)** What is the net advantage to leasing? Does your analysis indicate that Heath should buy or lease the equipment? Explain.

d. Now assume that Crawford believes the equipment's residual value could be as low as $0 or as high as $250,000, but she stands by $125,000 as her expected value. She concludes that the residual value is riskier than the other cash flows in the analysis, and she wants to incorporate this differential risk into her analysis. Describe how this could be accomplished. What effect would it have on Heath's lease decision?

e. Crawford knows that her firm has been considering moving to a new downtown location for some time, and she is concerned that these plans might come to fruition prior to the expiration of the lease. If the move occurs, the company would obtain completely new equipment, and hence Crawford would like to include a cancellation clause in the lease contract. What effect would a cancellation clause have on the riskiness of the lease?

### Computer-Related Problem

*Work the problem in this section only if you are using the problem spreadsheet.*

**lease versus buy**   **18-8** Use the model in File C18 to work this problem.

a. Refer to Problem 18-6. Determine the lease payment at which Maltese would be indifferent to buying or leasing—that is, find the lease payment that equates the NPV of leasing to that of buying. (*Hint:* Use trial and error.)

b. Using the $400,000 lease payment, what would be the effect if Maltese's tax rate fell to 20 percent? What would be the effect if the tax rate fell to zero percent? What do these results suggest?

**GET REAL WITH**   **THOMSON ONE** | Business School Edition

**preferred stock**   **18-9** Issuing preferred stock is one method that firms use to finance their operations. But not all firms issue preferred stock. Allstate Corporation [ALL], an insurance and investments firm, does have preferred stock in its capital structure. Answer the following questions about Allstate:

a. Has the amount of preferred stock Allstate has outstanding increased or decreased during the past three years? [Click on Financials/Financial Statements.]

b. Compare the relative amount of preferred stock Allstate uses with the relative amount used by its peers. [Click on Peers/Market Sector.]

c. In general, did the use of preferred stock in this market sector increase or decrease during the three-year time period?

d. What are the advantages and disadvantages of using preferred stock financing?

e. Explain why companies in this market sector use preferred stock as a method of financing whereas companies in other industries do not?

# Appendix A
# Using Spreadsheets to Solve Financial Problems

Like calculators, spreadsheets were developed to make mathematical computations easier to solve. In this appendix, we provide a brief tutorial on how to use spreadsheets to solve the problems discussed in this book.

## SETTING UP MATHEMATICAL RELATIONSHIPS

It is easy to set up relationships to solve mathematical problems that require you to use such arithmetic operators as addition, subtraction, multiplication, division, and so forth. Following are the common arithmetic operators used by Excel:

| Operator | Description | Function |
|---|---|---|
| + | Plus sign | Addition |
| − | Minus sign | Subtraction |
| * | Asterisk | Multiplication |
| / | Forward slash | Division |
| ^ | Caret | Exponentiation |

To solve a problem, put the cursor in the cell that you want to contain the final answer, type an equal sign (=), enter the relationship that you want to solve, and then press "enter" to generate the result. For example, suppose you want to compute to how much $100 invested today will grow to in three years if it earns 6 percent interest compounded annually. This problem can be easily solved by entering into one of the cells of a spreadsheet the relationship shown in Equation 4–1 in Chapter 4. Following is the solution:

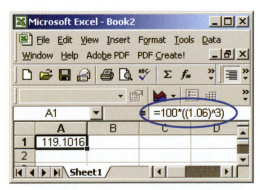

The equation that was input into cell **A1,** which is shown in the circled area, is FV = $100(1.06)^3$, and the solution is 119.1061.

Although it is easy to a solve problem by defining the relationship and entering numbers in a cell, it is better to create a table that contains the values needed to solve a particular relationship and then set up a general solution that refers to the locations of the specific cells that contain the needed values. For example, for the current computation, the spreadsheet might be set up as follows:

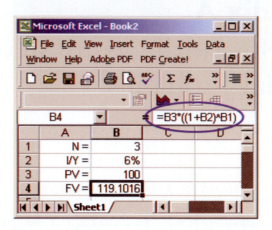

As you can see by the equation shown in the circled area, cell **B4** contains the relationship that computes the future value of the $100 investment. But the equation that is contained in cell **B4** refers to the cells in which the values that are needed to solve the problem are located. By setting up the solution in this manner, you can change any of the input values and the answer using the new value will be shown immediately. Try setting up your spreadsheet as shown here. You should get the answer shown above. Now change the interest rate to 10 percent. When you input 0.10 and press enter, you will see the result in cell **B4** change to 133.1, or $133.10. Note that when you input a percent into the spreadsheet, you must either enter the number in decimal form—for example, 0.10—or as a number followed by a % sign—for example, 10%. If you enter the percentage without a % sign, the spreadsheet interprets the number literally, and solves the problem accordingly. For example, if you enter 6 rather than 0.06 or 6% in the original computation, the result shown in cell **B4** will be:

$$FV = 100(1 + 6)^3 = 100(7)^3 = 34,300$$

which is an incorrect answer.

Although it is fairly easy to set up relationships for most of the problems presented in Chapter 4, it is even easier to use the pre-programmed functions contained in the spreadsheet. In the remainder of this appendix we show you how to use the time value of money functions that are programmed into spreadsheets to solve the problems introduced in Chapter 4.

## SOLVING TIME VALUE OF MONEY (TVM) PROBLEMS USING PRE-PROGRAMMED FUNCTIONS

The functions that are programmed into spreadsheets are the same as those programmed into financial calculators. In this section, we show how to use an Excel spreadsheet to solve some of the examples given in Chapter 4. Remember that in Chapter 4 we showed only the spreadsheet set up and the final solution to each problem. Here we show the specific steps that should be followed when using the TVM functions. Note that we label the values entered into the cells of the spreadsheet (column A) the same as the TVM keys on a Texas Instruments BAIIPlus financial calculator, which is the same calculator that was used to solve the problems presented in Chapter 4.

To access the TVM functions, click on the "Paste Function," which is found in the Insert menu on the toolbar. The Paste Function is designated $f_x$. When you click on $f_x$ the following menu will appear:

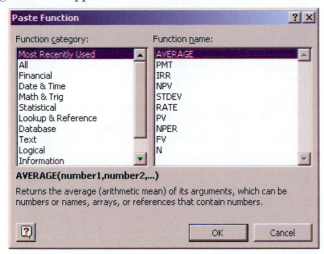

On the left side of the menu, click on "Financial" in the Function Category. This will give you access to the financial functions that are needed to solve the time value of money problems.

## Solving for Future Value (FV): Lump-Sum Amount and Annuity

The same function—FV—is used to solve for the future value of a lump-sum amount and an annuity.

### FV of a Lump-Sum Amount

If you want to find the FV in three years of $100 invested today at 6 percent compounded annually, you might want to set up your spreadsheet as follows:

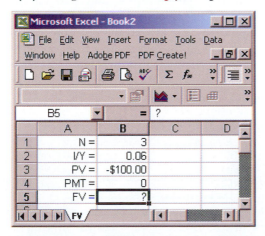

Note that in this case, we entered the interest rate as a decimal. Also, the amount invested, $100, is entered as a negative number, just as it is when solving this problem using a financial calculator—that is, the $100 investment is a cash outflow.

To solve for the future value, place the cursor in cell **B5**, click on the Paste Function (you should have clicked on the "Financial" category earlier), and scroll down the list you see on the right side of the menu until you reach FV.

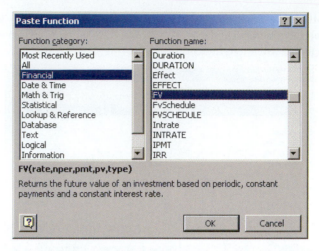

When you click OK or double click on FV, the following table will appear:

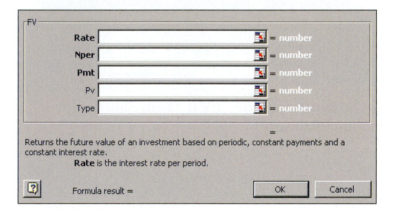

"Rate" represents the interest rate per period, "Nper" is the number of periods interest is earned, "Pmt" is the periodic, or annuity, payment (we will use this later), "Pv" is the present value of the amount, and "Type" refers to the type of annuity payment (0 = ordinary annuity; 1 = annuity due). To solve our problem, you need to refer to the appropriate cells in the spreadsheet that contain the value requested. As a result, you should insert **B2** in the first row of the table (Rate), **B1** in the second row (Nper), **B4** in the third row (Pmt), **B3** in the fourth row (Pv), and leave the last row (Type) blank so that the table looks like the following:

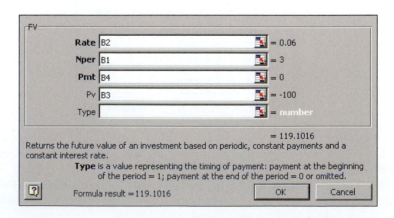

Note that you can also insert the appropriate location for each row of the box shown above by clicking ■ (the red arrow to the right of the row), placing the cursor in the cell that contains the value, and then pressing return. When enough information is entered, you will see the result of the computation at the bottom of the box shown above.

Once the locations of all the appropriate values are in the table, click "OK," and the answer will appear in cell **B5** in the spreadsheet. The spreadsheet will now be as follows:

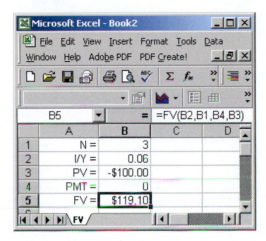

The future value amount we computed here, $119.10, is the same result we found in the previous section. If you press the F2 key, you will see the contents of **B5,** which should be **=FV(B2,B1,B4,B3).**

## FV of an Annuity

To solve for the future value of an annuity, we use the same financial function—that is, FV. For example, in Chapter 4, we solved for a three-year $100 annuity with an opportunity cost equal to 5 percent. Using the same spreadsheet set up shown earlier, change the values so that N = 3, I/Y = 0.05, PV = 0, and PMT = −100. You will see that the value for FV changes so that it is equal to $315.25, which is the same result we found in the chapter—that is, FVA = $315.25.

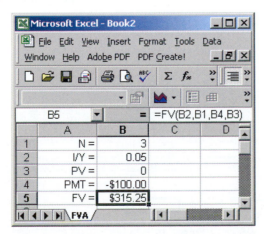

The result given here is the future value of an ordinary annuity. To find the future value of an annuity due, place the cursor in cell **B5** and click on Paste Function—that is, $f_x$. When the menu appears, place a 1 in the last row so that the inputs are as follows:

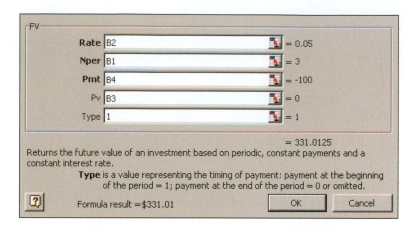

You will notice that the result shown in the menu changes to $331.01 and when you click on OK the result appears in cell **B5.** As you can see on the menu, when you enter 1 in the last row you change the timing of the cash flows from the end of the period to the beginning of the period for the purposes of the computation. The result found here is the same as we found in Chapter 4.

## SOLVING FOR PRESENT VALUE (PV): LUMP-SUM AMOUNT AND ANNUITY

To find the PV using a spreadsheet, you follow the same steps as described to solve for FV except you use the PV financial function. The menus are the same as in the previous section, except the value for the future value (labeled "Fv" in the menu) is a required input rather than the present value (labeled "Pv") that was required previously. For example, if you want to determine the present value of $315.25 to be received in three years if your opportunity cost is 5 percent, the spreadsheet set-up and the PV function table would be:

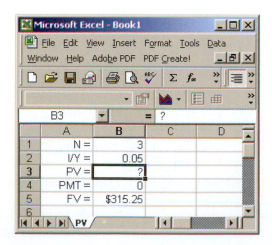

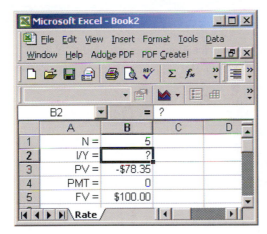

The result is the same as was reported in Chapter 4, PV = $272.32.

## SOLVING FOR r: LUMP-SUM AMOUNT AND ANNUITY

Suppose you want to determine the rate of return that would be earned if you purchase an investment for $78.35 that will pay $100 after five years. To solve this problem using a spreadsheet, use the "RATE" function. The spreadsheet might be set up as follows:

Once the appropriate cell locations are entered, the "RATE" function table would be as follows:

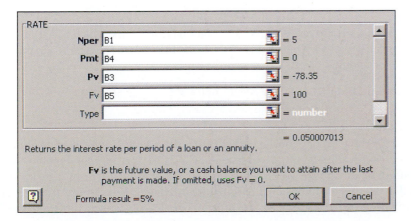

As you can see, the result of the computation is 5 percent, which will appear in cell **B2** when you press OK. You would use the same function to find the interest rate, r, for an annuity.

## SOLVING FOR **n**: LUMP-SUM AMOUNT AND ANNUITY

Suppose you want to determine how many years it will take $68.30 invested today to grow to $100 if the interest rate is 10 percent. To solve this problem using a spreadsheet, use the "NPER" function. The spreadsheet might be set up as follows:

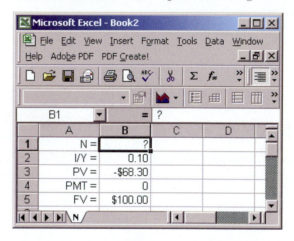

Once the appropriate cell locations are entered, the "NPER" function table will be as follows:

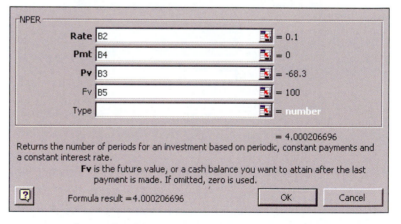

As you can see, the result of the computation is four years, which will appear in cell **B1** when you press OK. You would use the same function to solve for n, the number of periods, for an annuity.

## SOLVING FOR PRESENT VALUE AND FUTURE VALUE: UNEVEN CASH FLOWS

To solve for the PV of an uneven cash flow stream, use the NPV function. Take care, however, to ensure that you understand what this spreadsheet function actually computes. In this book, NPV represents the net present value of a series of cash flows that include the initial amount that is invested and the future cash flows that the investment is expected to generate. In the Excel spreadsheet, however, the NPV function computes the present value of the *future* cash flows only; thus, the current investment should not be included when using the spreadsheet's NPV function. Here we use the NPV function to compute the present value of a series of uneven cash flows. Appendix 9A at the end of Chapter 9 shows how to use the NPV function to compute the net present value of a capital asset.

Suppose that you are considering purchasing an investment that promises to pay $500, $800, and $300 at the end of the next three years, respectively. If your opportunity cost is 8 percent, how much should you pay for the investment? To answer this question, you need to determine the present value of the series of cash flows that the investment will generate in the future.

To compute the present value of a series of uneven cash flows using a spreadsheet, we must use the NPV function. For the current situation, we can set up the spreadsheet as follows:

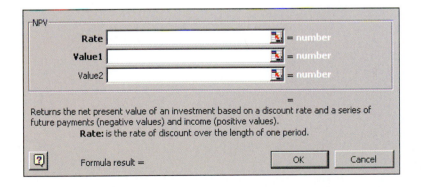

Place the cursor in cell **E4** as shown, select the NPV function in the financial category of the paste function, and the following table should appear:

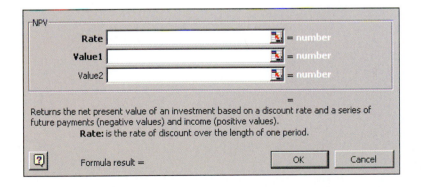

The description of this function indicates that the result of the computation is the present value of all the *future* cash flows—both inflows and outflows—associated with the investment. Enter the appropriate cell locations for the values that are needed to compute the present value of the cash flows given in the spreadsheet. In the table, **Value 1** refers the series of cash flows. After clicking on the arrow on the right side of the row labeled **Value 1,** use the cursor to highlight the cells **B2** through **B4.** Now the table that shows the cell locations of the needed values will look as follows:

The result of the computation, which is shown at the bottom of the table, is $1,386.98. If you click the "OK" button, this result will appear in cell **E4** of the spreadsheet. Thus, the present value of the series of cash flows is $1,386.98, which is the same result we found in Chapter 4 using a financial calculator.

To compute the future value of the series of uneven cash flows, first compute its present value and then compound this value to the future period at the appropriate opportunity cost. For our example, the future value would be:

$$FV = \$1,386.98(1.08)^3 = \$1,747.20$$

This relationship can be entered into the spreadsheet so that it is automatically computed.

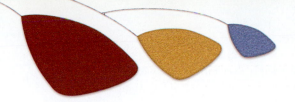

# Appendix B
## Solutions to Self-Test Problems

Note: Except for Chapter 1, we do not show an answer for ST-1 problems because they are verbal rather than quantitative in nature.

### CHAPTER 1

**ST-1** Refer to the marginal glossary definitions or relevant chapter sections to check your responses.

### CHAPTER 2

**ST-2** Billingsworth paid $2 in dividends and retained $2 per share. Because total retained earnings rose by $12 million, there must be 6 million shares outstanding. With a book value of $40 per share, total common equity must be $40(6 million) = $240 million. Because Billingsworth has $120 million of debt, its debt ratio must be 33.3 percent:

$$\text{Debt ratio} = \frac{\text{Debt}}{\text{Assest}} = \frac{\text{Debt}}{\text{Debt} + \text{Equity}} = \frac{\$120\text{ million}}{\$120\text{ million} + \$240\text{ million}}$$

$$= 0.333 = 33.3\%$$

**ST-3** **(1)** Operating cash flow = Net income + Depreciation

$$= \$120,000 + \$25,000 = \$145,000$$

**(2)** Free cash flow = Operating cash flow − Investments

$$= \$145,000 - \$150,000 = -\$5,000$$

**(3)** $\text{EVA} = \text{NOI}(1 - \text{Tax rate}) - \left[\left(\begin{array}{c}\text{Invested} \\ \text{capital}\end{array}\right) \times \left(\begin{array}{c}\text{After-tax cost} \\ \text{of funds}\end{array}\right)\right]$

$$= \$120,000(1 - 0.40) - [\$500,000(0.12)]$$

$$= \$72,000 - \$60,000 = \$12,000$$

**ST-4** **a.** In answering questions such as this, always begin by writing down the relevant definitional equations, then start filling in numbers. Note that the extra zeros indicating millions have been deleted in the calculations below. The results are not rounded until the final answer.

**(1)** $$\text{DSO} = \frac{\text{Accounts receivable}}{\left(\text{Sales}/360\right)}$$

$$40 = \frac{\text{Accounts receivable}}{\left(\$1,000/360\right)}$$

$$\text{A/R} = 40(\$2.778) = \$111.1\text{ million}$$

**(2)** $\text{Quick ratio} = \dfrac{\text{Current assets} - \text{Inventories}}{\text{Current liabilities}} = \dfrac{\text{Cash \& securities} + \text{A/R}}{\text{Current liabilities}} = 2.0$

$$2.0 = \dfrac{\$100 + \$111.1}{\text{Current liabilities}}$$

$$\text{Current liabilities} = (\$100 + 111.1)/2 = \$105.55$$

**(3)** $\text{Current ratio} = \dfrac{\text{Current assets}}{\text{Current liabilities}} = \dfrac{\text{CA}}{\$105.55} = 3.0$

$$\text{Current assets} = 3.0(\$105.55) = \$316.65$$

**(4)** $\text{Total assets} = \text{Current assets} + \text{Fixed assets}$

$$= \$316.7 + \$283.5 = \$600.2 \text{ million.}$$

**(5)** $\text{ROA} = \text{Profit margin} \times \text{Total assets turnover}$

$$= \dfrac{\text{Net income}}{\text{Sales}} \times \dfrac{\text{Sales}}{\text{Total assets}} = \dfrac{\$50}{\$1,000} \times \dfrac{\$1,000}{\$600.1}$$

$$= 0.05 \times 1.667 = 0.0833 = 8.33\%$$

**(6)** $\text{ROE} = \dfrac{\text{Net income}}{\text{Equity}}$

$$12.0\% = \dfrac{\$50}{\text{Equity}} = 0.12$$

$$\text{Equity} = \dfrac{\$50}{0.12} = \$416.7 \text{ million}$$

**(7)** $\qquad\qquad \text{Total assets} = \text{Total claims} = \$600.1 \text{ million}$

$$\text{Current liabilities} + \text{Long-term debt} + \text{Equity} = \$600.1 \text{ million}$$

$$\$105.6 + \text{Long-term debt} + \$416.7 = \$600.1 \text{ million}$$

$$\text{Long-term debt} = \$600.1 - \$105.6 - \$416.7 = \$\ 77.8 \text{ million}$$

**b.** Kaiser's average sales per day were $\$1,000/360 = \$2.778$ million. Its DSO was 40, so A/R $= 40(\$2.778) = \$111.1$ million. Its new DSO of 30 would result in A/R $= 30(\$2.778) = \$83.3$ million. The reduction in receivables would be $\$111.1 - \$83.3 = \$27.8$ million, which would equal the amount of cash generated.

**(1)** $\qquad\quad \text{New equity} = \text{Old equity} - \text{Stock bought back}$

$$= \$416.7 - \$27.8 = \$388.9 \text{ million.}$$

Thus,

$$\text{New ROE} = \dfrac{\text{Net income}}{\text{New equity}} = \dfrac{\$50}{\$388.9}$$

$$= 12.86\% (\text{versus old ROE of } 12.0\%)$$

**(2)** $\text{New ROA} = \dfrac{\text{Net income}}{\text{Total assets} - \text{Reduction in A/R}} = \dfrac{\$50}{\$600.1 - \$27.8}$

$$= 8.74\% \text{ (versus old ROS of } 8.33\%)$$

**(3)** The old debt is the same as the new debt:

$$\text{Debt} = \text{Total claims} - \text{Equity}$$

$$= \$600.1 - \$416.7 = \$183.4 \text{ million.}$$

$$\text{Old total assets} = \$600.1 \text{ million}$$

$$\text{New total assets} = \text{Old total assets} - \text{Reduction in A/R}$$

$$= \$600.1 - \$27.8$$

$$= \$572.3 \text{ million.}$$

Therefore,

$$\frac{\text{Debt}}{\text{Old total assets}} = \frac{\$183.4}{\$600.1} = 0.306 = 30.6\%$$

while

$$\frac{\text{New debt}}{\text{New total assets}} = \frac{\$183.4}{\$572.3} = 0.32 = 32.0\%$$

# CHAPTER 3

**ST-2** **a.** Net proceeds $= \$150,000,000 - 0.07(\$150,000,000) - \$225,000$

$$= \$139,275,000.$$

**b.** Number of shares $= \$150,000,000/\$25 = 6,000,000$

**c.** 

Needs $= \$150,000,000$

$= $ Amount issued $- 0.07($Amount issued$) - \$225,000$

$= ($Amount issued$) \times (1.0 - 0.07) - \$225,000$

$\$150,000,000 + \$225,000 = 0.93($Amount issued$)$

Amount issued $= \$150,225,000/0.93 = \$161,532,258.10$

Number of shares $= \$161,532,258.10/\$25 = 6,461,290.3 \approx 6,461,291$

To see that this is the correct number of shares to issue, compute the net proceeds the firm would receive if 6,461,291 shares were issued at \$25 per share:

Net proceeds $= (6,461,291 \times \$25) - 0.07(6,461,291 \times \$25) - \$225,000$

$$= \$161,532,275 - \$11,532,259.25 = \$150,000,015.80.$$

The additional \$15.80 results because the firm has to issue a full share rather than 0.3 shares.

# CHAPTER 4

**ST-2** **a.** **(1)**

$$\text{FV}_n = \text{PV}(1 + r)^n$$

$$\$7,020 = \$5,500(1 + r)^5$$

$$(1 + r)^5 = \frac{\$7,020}{\$5,500} = 1.2764$$

To solve for the rate, use your calculator or solve algebraically. Using your calculator, enter N = 5, FV = 7,020, PV = −5,500, and then press the I ≠ Y key—you should find the result is 5.001. To solve algebraically, recognize that, according to the above computations, $(1 + r)^5 = 1.276364$ (carried to 6 places). Therefore,

$$(1 + r)^5 = 1.276364$$

$$r = (1.276364)^{1/5} = 0.05001 = 5.001\%$$

(2)

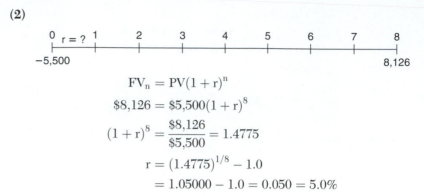

$$FV_n = PV(1 + r)^n$$

$$\$8,126 = \$5,500(1 + r)^8$$

$$(1 + r)^8 = \frac{\$8,126}{\$5,500} = 1.4775$$

$$r = (1.4775)^{1/8} - 1.0$$

$$= 1.05000 - 1.0 = 0.050 = 5.0\%$$

Using your calculator or solving algebraically will yield the same result. Because both investments yield the same return, you should be indifferent between them.

**b.** If you believe there is greater uncertainty about whether the eight-year investment will pay the amount expected ($8,126) than about whether the five-year investment will pay the amount expected ($7,020), then you should prefer the shorter-term investment. We discuss the effects of risk on value in Chapter 8.

**ST-3 a.**

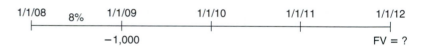

$1,000 is being compounded for three years, so your balance on January 1, 2012 is $1,259.71:

$$FV_n = PV(1 + r)^n = \$1,000(1 + 0.08)^3 = \$1,259.71.$$

Using a financial calculator, input N = 3, I ≠ Y = 8, PV = −1,000, PMT = 0, and FV = ? = $1,259.71.

**b.**

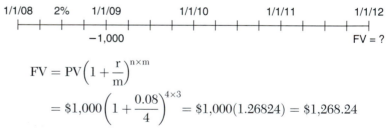

$$FV = PV\left(1 + \frac{r}{m}\right)^{n \times m}$$

$$= \$1,000\left(1 + \frac{0.08}{4}\right)^{4 \times 3} = \$1,000(1.26824) = \$1,268.24$$

Using a financial calculator, input N = 12, I ≠ Y = 2, PV = −1,000, PMT = 0, and FV = ?; FV = $1,268.24.

**c.**

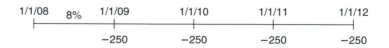

Using a financial calculator, input N = 4, I ≠ Y = 8, PV = 0, PMT = −250, and FV = ? = $1,126.53.

**d.**

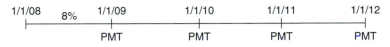

$$FV = 1,259.71$$

$$N = 4; \ I = 8\%; \ PV = 0; \ FV = \$1,259.71; \ PMT = ? = \$279.56.$$

Therefore, you would have to make 4 payments of $279.56 each to have a balance of $1,259.71 on January 1, 2012.

**ST-4  a.** Set up a timeline like the one in the preceding problem:

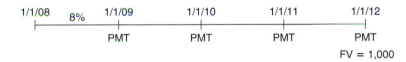

Note that your deposit will grow for three years at 8 percent. The fact that it is now January 1, 2008 is irrelevant. The deposit on January 1, 2009 is the PV, and the FV is $1,000. Here is the solution:

$$N = 3; \ I \neq Y = 8\%; \ PMT = 0; \ FV = \$1,000; \ PV = ? = \$793.83.$$

$$PV = \$1,000 \left[ \frac{1}{(1.08)^3} \right] = \$1,000(0.79383) = \$793.83$$

**b.**

Here we are dealing with a four-year annuity whose first payment occurs one year from today, on 1/1/09, and whose future value must equal $1,000. You should modify the time line to help visualize the situation. Here is the solution:

$$N = 4; \ I \neq Y = 8\%; \ PV = 0; \ FV = \$1,000; \ PMT = ? = \$221.92.$$

$$FVA_4 = PMT \left[ \frac{(1.08)^4 - 1}{0.08} \right] = \$1,000$$

$$PMT = \frac{\$1,000}{4.50611} = \$221.92$$

**c.** This problem can be approached in several ways. Perhaps the simplest is to ask this question: "If I received $750 on 1/1/09 and deposited it to earn 8 percent, would I have $1,000 on 1/1/12?" The answer is no:

$$FV_3 = \$750(1.08)^3 = \$944.78$$

$$N = 3; \ I \neq Y = 8\%; \ PV = -\$750; \ PMT = 0; \ FV = ? = \$944.78.$$

This indicates that you should let your father make the payments rather than accept the lump sum of $750.

You could also compare the $750 with the PV of the payments:

$$N = 4; \ I \neq Y = 8\%; \ PMT = -\$221.92; \ FV = 0; \ PV = ? = \$735.03$$

$$PVA_4 = \$221.92 \left[ \frac{1 - \frac{1}{(1.08)^4}}{0.08} \right] = \$221.92(3.31212) = \$735.03$$

This is less than the $750 lump sum offer, so your initial reaction might be to accept the lump sum of $750. However, this would be a mistake. The problem is that when you found the $735.03 PV of the annuity, you were finding the value of the annuity *today*, on January 1, 2008. You were comparing $735.03 today with the lump sum of $750 one year from now. This is, of course, invalid. What you should have done was take the $735.03, recognize that this is the PV of an annuity as of January 1, 2008, multiply $735.03 by 1.08 to get $793.83, and compare $793.83 with the lump sum of $750. You would then take your father's offer to make the payments rather than take the lump sum on January 1, 2009. If you solved the PV for an annuity due, you would find the same answer.

**d.**

| 1/1/08 | r = ? | 1/1/09 | 1/1/10 | 1/1/11 | 1/1/12 |
|--------|-------|--------|--------|--------|--------|
|        |       | −750   |        |        | 1,000  |

$$N = 3; \ PV = -\$750; \ PMT = 0; \ FV = \$1,000; \ I \neq Y = ? = 10.0642\%$$

**e.**

| 1/1/08 | r = ? | 1/1/09 | 1/1/10 | 1/1/11 | 1/1/12 |
|--------|-------|--------|--------|--------|--------|
|        |       | −186.29 | −186.29 | −186.29 | −186.29 |
|        |       |        |        |        | FV =1,000 |

$$N = 4; \ PV = 0; \ PMT = -186.29; \ FV = \$1,000; \ I \neq Y = ? = 20.00\%.$$

You might be able to find a borrower willing to offer you a 20 percent interest rate, but there would be some risk involved—he or she might not actually pay you your $1,000 on January 1, 2012.

**f.**

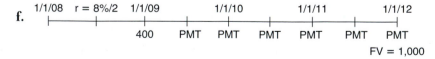

Find the future value of the original $400 deposit: $FV_6 = 400(1.04)^6 = \$400(1.26532) = \$506.13$. This means that on January 1, 2012, you need an additional sum of $493.87:

$$\$1,000.00 - \$506.13 = \$493.87$$

This will be accumulated by making six equal payments that earn 8 percent compounded semiannually, or 4 percent each six months: $N = 6$; $I \neq Y = 4\%$; $PV = 0$; $FV = \$493.87$; $PMT = ?$; $PMT = 74.46$.

**g.**

$$\text{Effective annual rate} = \left(1 + \frac{r_{\text{SIMPLE}}}{m}\right)^m - 1.0$$

$$= \left(1 + \frac{0.08}{2}\right)^2 - 1.0$$

$$= 1.0816 - 1 = 0.0816 = 8.16\%$$

**ST-5**   Bank A's effective annual rate is 8.24 percent:

$$\text{Effective annual rate} = \left(1 + \frac{0.08}{4}\right)^4 - 1.0$$

$$= (1.02)^4 - 1 = 1.0824 - 1$$

$$= 0.0824 = 8.24\%$$

Now Bank B must have the same effective annual rate:

$$\left(1 + \frac{r}{12}\right)^{12} - 1.0 = 0.0824$$

$$\left(1 + \frac{r}{12}\right)^{12} = 1.0824$$

$$1 + \frac{r}{12} = (1.0824)^{1/12}$$

$$1 + \frac{r}{12} = 1.00662$$

$$\frac{r}{12} = 0.0062$$

$$r = 0.07944 = 7.944\%$$

Thus, the two banks have different quoted rates—Bank A's quoted rate is 8 percent, while Bank B's quoted rate is 7.94 percent; however, both banks have the same effective annual rate of 8.24 percent. The difference in their quoted rates is due to the difference in compounding frequency.

# CHAPTER 5

**ST-2**   Purchase price of the stock $= \$80(100) = \$8,000$

**a.**   Dollar return $= [\$75(100) - \$8,000] + \$5(100) = -\$500 + \$500 = 0$

**b.**   $\text{Yield} = \dfrac{\text{Dollar return}}{\text{Amount invested}} = \dfrac{\$0}{\$8,000} = 0.00 = 0\%$

**ST-3   a.**   Average $= (2\% + 3\% + 5\% + 6\%)/4 = 16\%/4 = 4.0\%$.

**b.**   $r_{\text{T-bond}} = r^* + IP = 3.0\% + 4.0\% = 7.0\%$.

**c.**   If the five-year T-bond rate is 8 percent, the inflation rate is expected to average approximately $8\% - 3\% = 5\%$ during the next five years. Thus, the implied Year 5 inflation rate is 9 percent:

$$5\% = (2\% + 3\% + 5\% + 6\% + I_5)/5$$

$$25\% = 16\% + I_5$$

$$\text{Infl}_5 = 9\%.$$

## CHAPTER 6

**ST-2  a.**  Conversion price = $1,000/50 = $20

**b.**  If the bond is converted, investors would be able to sell the stock for $20.50 per share, which would yield a total of $1,025 = $30.50 × 50. Thus, it would be better to redeem the bond for $1,100.

**ST-3  a.**  Pennington's bonds were sold at par; therefore, the original YTM equaled the coupon rate of 12%.

**b.**
$$V_d = \sum_{t=1}^{50} \frac{\$120/2}{\left(1 + \frac{0.10}{2}\right)^t} + \frac{\$1,000}{\left(1 + \frac{0.10}{2}\right)^{50}} = \$60 \left[\frac{1 - \frac{1}{(1.05)^{50}}}{0.05}\right] + \$1,000 \left[\frac{1}{(1.05)^{50}}\right]$$

$$= \$60(18.25593 + \$1,000(0.08720) = \$1,095.36 + \$87.20$$

$$= \$1,182.56$$

Alternatively, with a financial calculator, input the following: N = 50, I ≠ Y = 5, PMT = 60, FV = 1,000, and PV = ? = $1,182.56.

**c.**
$$\text{Current yield} = \text{Annual coupon payment/Price}$$
$$= \$120/\$1,182.56$$
$$= 0.1015 = 10.15\%.$$

$$\text{Capital gains yield} = \text{Total yield} - \text{Current yield}$$
$$= 10\% - 10.15\% = -0.15\%.$$

**d.**
$$\$891.64 = \sum_{t=1}^{19} \frac{\$60}{\left(1 + \frac{r_d}{2}\right)^t} + \frac{\$1,000}{\left(1 + \frac{r_d}{2}\right)^{19}}$$

Using a financial calculator, input the following: N = 19, PV = − 891.64, PMT = 60, FV = 1,000, and $r_d/2$ = I ≠ Y = ? Calculator solution = $r_d/2$ = 7.05%; therefore, $r_d$ = 14.1%.

**e.**
$$\text{Current yield} = \$120/\$891.64 = 13.46\%.$$
$$\text{Capital gains yield} = 14.1\% - 13.46\% = 0.64\%$$

**ST-4  a.**  $100,000,000/10 = $10,000,000 per year, or $5 million every 6 months. Because the $5 million will be used to retire bonds immediately, no interest will be earned on it.

**b.**  The debt service requirements will decline. As the amount of bonds outstanding declines, so will the interest requirements (amounts given in millions of dollars):

| Semiannual Payment Period (1) | Sinking Fund Payment (2) | Outstanding Bonds On Which Interest Is Paid (3) | Interest Payment[a] (4) | Total Bond Service (2) + (4) = (5) |
|---|---|---|---|---|
| 1 | $5 | $100 | $6.0 | $11.0 ⎫ Req. in Year 1 |
| 2 | 5 | 95 | 5.7 | 10.7 ⎬ = $21.7 |
| 3 | 5 | 90 | 5.4 | 10.4 |
| . | . | . | . | . |
| . | . | . | . | . |
| . | . | . | . | . |
| 20 | 5 | 5 | 0.3 | 5.3 |

[a]Interest is calculated as [(0.12)/2](Column 3); for example: interest in Period 2 = (0.06)($95) = $5.7.

The company's total cash bond service requirement will be $21.7 million for the first year. The requirement will decline by 0.12($10,000,000) = $1,200,000 per year for the remaining years.

c. Here we have a 10-year, 9 percent annuity whose compound value is $100 million, and we are seeking the annual payment, PMT. The solution can be obtained with a financial calculator. Input N = 10, I = 9, PV = 0, and FV = 100,000,000, and press the PMT key to obtain $6,582,009. We could also find the solution using this equation:

$$FVA = PMT \left[ \frac{(1+r)^n - 1}{r} \right]$$

$$100,000,000 = PMT \left[ \frac{(1.09)^{10} - 1}{0.09} \right] = PMT(15.19293)$$

$$PMT = \frac{100,000,000}{15.19293} = 6,582,009$$

Annual debt service costs will be $100,000,000(0.12) + $6,582,009 = $18,582,009.

d. If interest rates rose, causing the bond's price to fall, the company would use open market purchases. This would reduce its debt service requirements.

# CHAPTER 7

ST-2  a. This is not necessarily true. Because G plows back two-thirds of its earnings, its growth rate should exceed that of D, but D pays higher dividends ($6 versus $2). We cannot say which stock should have the higher price.

b. Again, we just do not know which price would be higher.

c. This is false. The changes in $r_d$ and $r_s$ would have a greater effect on G— its price would decline more.

d. The total expected return for D is $\hat{r}_D = \hat{D}_1/P_0 + g = 15\% + 0\% = 15\%$. The total expected return for G will have $\hat{D}_1/P_0$ less than 15 percent and g greater than 0 percent, but $\hat{r}_G$ should be neither greater nor smaller than D's total expected return, 15 percent, because the two stocks are stated to be equally risky.

e. We have eliminated a, b, c, and d, so e should be correct. On the basis of the available information, D and G should sell at about the same price, $40; thus, $\hat{r}_s = 15\%$ for both D and G. G's current dividend yield is $2/$40 = 5%. Therefore, $g = 15\% - 5\% = 10\%$.

ST-3  The first step is to solve for g, the unknown variable, in the constant growth equation. Because $\hat{D}_1$ is unknown but $D_0$ is known, substitute $D_0(1 + g)$ as follows:

$$\hat{P}_0 = P_0 = \frac{\hat{D}_1}{r_s - g} = \frac{D_0(1 + g)}{r_s - g}$$

$$\$36 = \frac{\$2.40(1 + g)}{0.12 - g}$$

Solving for g, we find the growth rate to be 5 percent:

$$\$4.32 - \$36g = \$2.40 + \$2.40g$$
$$\$38.4g = \$1.92$$
$$g = 0.05 = 5\%.$$

The next step is to use the growth rate to project the stock price five years hence:

$$\hat{P}_5 = \frac{D_0(1+g)^6}{r_s - g}$$

$$= \frac{\$2.40(1.05)^6}{0.12 - 0.05} = \frac{\$3.2162}{0.07}$$

$$= \$45.95$$

Therefore, Ewald Company's expected stock price five years from now, $\hat{P}_5$, is $45.95.

**ST-4  a. (1)** Calculate the PV of the dividends paid during the supernormal growth period:

$$\hat{D}_1 = \$1.1500(1.15) = \$1.3225.$$

$$\hat{D}_2 = \$1.3225(1.15) = \$1.5209.$$

$$\hat{D}_3 = \$1.5209(1.13) = \$1.7186.$$

$$\text{PV of } \hat{D} = \$1.3225(0.89286) + \$1.5209(0.79719) + \$1.7186(0.71178)$$

$$= \$1.1809 + \$1.2124 + \$1.2233$$

$$= \$3.6167 \approx \$3.62.$$

**(2)** Find the PV of Snyder's stock price at the end of Year 3:

$$\hat{P}_3 = \frac{\hat{D}_4}{r_s - g} = \frac{\hat{D}_3(1+g)}{r_s - g}$$

$$= \frac{\$1.7186(1.06)}{0.12 - 0.06}$$

$$= \$30.36$$

$$\text{PV of } \hat{P}_3 = \$30.36(0.71178) = \$21.61$$

**(3)** Sum the two components to find the value of the stock today:

$$\hat{P}_0 = \$3.62 + \$21.61 = \$25.23.$$

Alternatively, the cash flows can be placed on a time line as follows:

$$\hat{P}_3 = \$1.8217/(0.12 - 0.06) = \underline{30.3617}$$
$$= \underline{32.0803}$$

Enter the cash flows into the cash flow register, I = 12, and press the NPV key to obtain $P_0$ = $25.23.

**b.** $\quad \hat{P}_1 = \$1.5209(0.89286) + \$1.7186(0.79719) + \$30.36(0.79719)$

$\quad\quad\quad = \$1.3580 + \$1.3701 + \$24.2027 = \$26.9308 = \$26.93.$

$\quad\quad\quad\quad$ (Calculator solution: \$26.93.)

$\quad\quad \hat{P}_2 = \$1.7186(0.89286) + \$30.36(0.89286)$

$\quad\quad\quad = \$1.5345 + \$27.1072 = \$28.6418 = \$28.64.$

$\quad\quad\quad\quad$ (Calculator solution: \$28.64.)

**c.**

| Year | Dividend Yield | + | Capital Gains Yield | = | Total Return |
|------|---------------|---|---------------------|---|--------------|
| 1 | $\dfrac{\$1.3225}{\$25.23} \approx 5.24\%$ | + | $\dfrac{\$26.93 - 25.23}{\$25.23} \approx 6.74\%$ | = | 12% |
| 2 | $\dfrac{\$1.5209}{\$26.93} \approx 5.65\%$ | + | $\dfrac{\$28.64 - 26.93}{\$26.93} \approx 6.35\%$ | = | 12% |
| 3 | $\dfrac{\$1.7186}{\$28.64} \approx 6.00\%$ | + | $\dfrac{\$30.36 - 28.64}{\$28.64} \approx 6.00\%$ | = | 12% |

**ST-5  a.** $\quad$ EVA = EBIT$(1 - T)$ − (Average cost of funds × Invested capital)

$\quad\quad\quad = \$600,000(1 - 0.40) - (0.08 \times \$2,000,000)$

$\quad\quad\quad = \$360,000 - \$160,000$

$\quad\quad\quad = \$200,000$

**b.** $\quad$ EVA dividend = EVA/(Shares outstanding)

$\quad\quad\quad = \$200,000/100,000$

$\quad\quad\quad = \$2.00$

**c.** First, we must compute the net income for AT:

| | |
|---|---:|
| EBIT | \$600,000 |
| Interest | (80,000) |
| Earnings before taxes | 520,000 |
| Taxes (40%) | (208,000) |
| Net income | \$312,000 |

$\quad\quad$ EPS = (Net income)/(Shares outstanding)

$\quad\quad\quad = \$312,000 \neq 100,000$

$\quad\quad\quad = \$3.12$

$\quad\quad\quad\quad\quad \hat{P}_0 = \text{EPS} \times \text{P/E}$

$\quad\quad\quad\quad\quad\quad = \$3.12 \times 15$

$\quad\quad\quad\quad\quad\quad = \$46.80$

# CHAPTER 8

**ST-2  a.** $\quad \beta_P = W_A\beta_A + W_B\beta_B$

$\quad\quad 0.95 = 0.3(2.0) + 0.7(\beta_B)$

$\quad\quad \beta_B = (0.95 - 0.6)/0.7$

$\quad\quad\quad = 0.5$

**ST-3**    $r_s = r_{RF} + (r_M - r_{RF})\beta_s$
$= 4\% + (12\% - 4\%)2.5$
$= 4\% + 20\%$
$= 24\%$

**ST-4    a.**    Returns

| Year | Stock A | Stock B | 50/50 Portfolio | |
|------|---------|---------|-----------------|---|
| 2004 | −10.00% | −3.00% | −6.50% | $= 0.5(-10.00\%) + 0.5(-3.00\%)$ |
| 2005 | 18.50 | 21.29 | 19.90 | $= 0.5(\ 18.50\%) + 0.5(\ 21.29\%)$ |
| 2006 | 38.67 | 44.25 | 41.46 | $= 0.5(\ 38.67\%) + 0.5(\ 44.25\%)$ |
| 2007 | 14.33 | 3.67 | 9.00 | $= 0.5(\ 14.33\%) + 0.5(\ 3.67\%)$ |
| 2008 | 33.00 | 28.30 | 30.65 | $= 0.5(\ 33.00\%) + 0.5(\ 28.30\%)$ |
| r̈ | 18.90% | 18.90% | 18.90% | $= 0.5(\ 18.90\%) + 0.5(\ 18.90\%)$ |

$$\ddot{r}_A = \frac{-10.0\% + 18.50\% + 38.67\% + 14.33\% + 33.00\%}{5 - 1} = 18.90\%$$

**b.**   The standard deviation of returns is estimated as follows:

$$\text{Estimated } \sigma = s = \sqrt{\frac{\sum\limits_{t=1}^{n}(\ddot{r}_t - \bar{r})^2}{n - 1}}$$

or Stock A, the estimated $\sigma$ is 19.0 percent:

$$s_A = \sqrt{\frac{(-10.00 - 18.9)^2 + (18.50 - 18.9)^2 + (38.67 - 18.9)^2 + (14.33 - 18.9)^2 + (33.00 - 18.9)^2}{4}}$$

$$= \sqrt{\frac{1,445.92}{4}} = \sqrt{361.48} = 19.01\%$$

The standard deviation of returns for Stock B and the portfolio are similarly determined, and they are as follows:

| | Stock A | Stock B | Portfolio AB |
|---|---------|---------|--------------|
| Standard deviation | 19.0% | 19.0% | 18.6% |

**c.**   Because the risk from diversification is small—the standard deviation falls only from 19.0 percent to 18.6 percent—the most likely value of the correlation coefficient is 0.9. If the correlation coefficient was −0.9, the risk reduction would be much larger. In fact, the correlation coefficient between Stock A and Stock B is 0.92.

**ST-5    a.**    $\hat{r}_R = 0.5(-2\%) + 0.1(10\%) + 0.4(15) = 6.0\%$
$\hat{r}_S = 0.5(20\%) + 0.1(12\%) + 0.4(2\%) = 12.0\%$

**b.**    $\hat{r}_P = w_R\hat{r}_R + w_S\hat{r}_S$
$\hat{r}_P = 0.5(6.0\%) + 0.5(12.0\%) = 9.0\%$

Alternative computation: Compute the portfolio return for each possible stock outcome.

| | | Returns | |
|---|---|---|---|
| Probability | Stock R | Stock S | 50/50 Portfolio |
| 0.5 | −2% | 20% | 9.0% = 0.5 (−2%) + 0.5 (20%) |
| 0.1 | 10 | 12 | 11.0  = 0.5 ( 10%) + 0.5 (12%) |
| 0.4 | 15 | 2 | 8.5  = 0.5 ( 15%) + 0.5 ( 2%) |

Then compute the expected return based on the probability of the outcome.

$$\hat{r}_P = 0.5(9.0\%) + 0.1(11.0\%) + (0.4)(8.5\%) = 9.0\%$$

c.  Standard deviation $= \sigma = \sqrt{\sigma^2} = \sqrt{\sum_{i=1}^{n}(r_i - \hat{r})^2 Pr_i}$

$$\sigma_R = \sqrt{0.5(-2\% - 6\%)^2 + 0.1(10\% - 6\%)^2 + 0.4(15\% - 6\%)^2}$$
$$= \sqrt{32 + 1.6 + 32.4} = \sqrt{66} = 8.12\%$$

$$\sigma_S = \sqrt{0.5(20\% - 12\%)^2 + 0.1(12\% - 12\%)^2 + 0.4(2\% - 12\%)^2}$$
$$= \sqrt{32 + 0 + 40} = \sqrt{72} = 8.49\%$$

$$\sigma_P = \sqrt{0.5(9\% - 9\%)^2 + 0.1(11\% - 9\%)^2 + 0.4(8.5\% - 9\%)^2}$$
$$= \sqrt{0 + 0.4 + 0.1} = \sqrt{0.5} = 0.71\%$$

Stock S is riskier because its standard deviation is higher than that of Stock R. Clearly, however, the portfolio, or combination of the two stocks, has the lowest risk.

d.  Coefficient of variation $= CV = \dfrac{\text{Risk}}{\text{Return}} = \dfrac{\sigma}{\hat{r}}$

$$CV_R = 8.12\%/6\%  = 1.35$$
$$CV_S = 8.49\%/12\% = 0.71$$

According to the coefficient of variations computed here, Stock R is riskier than Stock S. Although Stock S has a higher amount of total risk, it also has a much higher expected return than Stock R. The coefficient of variation for the portfolio is 0.08 = 0.71%/9%, which is much lower than for either stock.

e.  Because the risk reduction from diversification is large—that is, $\sigma_P$ is close to zero—it is more likely that the correlation coefficient is −0.9 rather than 0.9. If the correlation coefficient was 0.9, the risk reduction would be much smaller.

f.  In this case, because the standard deviation for the two-stock portfolio is close to zero, we would expect that, initially, there would be little change in the riskiness of the portfolio as additional stocks are added. But, as the number of stocks in the portfolio increases substantially, we would expect that the risk associated with the portfolio should approach the standard deviation of the market, or average, portfolio, which is near 15 percent. See Figure 8-8.

## CHAPTER 9

**ST-2  a.** *Payback*

To determine the payback, construct the cumulative cash flows for each project:

| | Project X | | Project Y | |
|---|---|---|---|---|
| **Year** | **Cash Flows** | **Cumulative CF** | **Cash Flows** | **Cumulative CF** |
| 0 | ($10,000) | ($10,000) | ($10,000) | ($10,000) |
| 1 | 6,500 | ( 3,500) | 3,500 | ( 6,500) |
| 2 | 3,000 | ( 500) | 3,500 | ( 3,000) |
| 3 | 3,000 | 2,500 | 3,500 | 500 |
| 4 | 1,000 | 3,500 | 3,500 | 4,000 |

$$\text{Payback}_X = 2 + \frac{\$500}{\$3,000} = 2.17\,\text{years}$$

$$\text{Payback}_Y = 2 + \frac{\$3,000}{\$3,500} = 2.86\,\text{years}$$

*Net present value (NPV):*

$$\text{NPV}_X = -\$10,000 + \frac{\$6,500}{(1.12)^1} + \frac{\$3,000}{(1.12)^2} + \frac{\$3,000}{(1.12)^3} + \frac{\$1,000}{(1.12)^4}$$

$$= -\$10,000 + \$5,803.57 + \$2,391.58 + \$2,135.34 + \$635.52$$

$$= \$966.02$$

$$\text{NPV}_Y = -\$10,000 + \frac{\$3,500}{(1.12)^1} + \frac{\$3,500}{(1.12)^2} + \frac{\$3,500}{(1.12)^3} + \frac{\$3,500}{(1.12)^4}$$

$$= -\$10,000 + \$3,125.00 + \$2,790.18 + \$2,491.23 + \$2,224.31$$

$$= \$630.72$$

Alternatively, using a financial calculator, input the cash flows into the cash flow register, enter I = 12, and then press the NPV key to obtain $\text{NPV}_X = \$966.01$ and $\text{NPV}_Y = \$630.72$.

*Internal rate of return (IRR):*
To solve for each project's IRR, find the discount rates that equate each NPV to zero:

$$\text{IRR}_X = 18.0\%.$$
$$\text{IRR}_Y = 15.0\%.$$

*Modified internal rate of return (MIRR):*

$$\text{PV of cash outflows} = \frac{\text{TV}}{(1 + \text{MIRR})^n}$$

$$\text{Cost} = \frac{\sum_{t=1}^{n} \text{CIF}_t (1 + r)^{n-t}}{(1 + \text{MIRR})^n}$$

$$\$10{,}000 = \frac{\$6{,}500(1.12)^3 + \$3{,}000(1.12)^2 + \$3{,}000(1.12)^1 + \$1{,}000(1.12)^0}{(1 + \text{MIRR}_X)^4}$$

$$\$10{,}000 = \frac{\$17{,}255.23}{(1 + \text{MIRR}_X)^4}$$

$$(1 + \text{MIRR}_X)^4 = \frac{\$17{,}255.23}{\$10{,}000} = 1.725523$$

$$\text{MIRR}_X = (1.725523)^{1/4} - 1.0$$

$$= 0.1481 = 14.81\%$$

$$\$10{,}000 = \frac{\$3{,}500(1.12)^3 + \$3{,}500(1.12)^2 + \$3{,}500(1.12)^1 + \$3{,}500(1.12)^0}{(1 + \text{MIRR}_Y)^4}$$

$$\$10{,}000 = \frac{\$16{,}727.65}{(1 + \text{MIRR}_Y)^4}$$

$$(1 + \text{MIRR}_Y)^4 = \frac{\$16{,}727.65}{\$10{,}000} = 1.672765$$

$$\text{MIRR}_Y = (1.672765)^{1/4} - 1.0$$

$$= 0.1373 = 13.73\%$$

*Discounted Payback Period* ($PB_{Disc}$):
To determine the discounted payback, construct the cumulative discounted cash flows for each project:

| | **Project X** | | **Project Y** | |
|---|---|---|---|---|
| **Year** | **PV CF @ 12%** | **Cumulative CF** | **PV CF @ 12%** | **Cumulative CF** |
| 0 | ($10,000.00) | ($10,000.00) | ($10,000.00) | ($10,000.00) |
| 1 | 5,803.57 | ( 4,196.43) | 3,125.00 | ( 6,875.00) |
| 2 | 2,391.58 | ( 1,804.85) | 2,790.18 | ( 4,084.82) |
| 3 | 2,135.34 | 330.49 | 2,491.23 | ( 1,593.59) |
| 4 | 635.52 | 966.01 | 2,224.31 | 630.72 |

$$\text{PB}_{DiscX} = 2 + \frac{\$1{,}804.85}{\$2{,}135.34} = 2.85 \text{ years}$$

$$\text{PB}_{DiscY} = 3 + \frac{\$1{,}593.59}{\$2{,}224.31} = 3.72 \text{ years}$$

**b.** The following table summarizes the project rankings by each method:

| | **Project that Ranks Higher** |
|---|---|
| Traditional Payback | X |
| NPV | X |
| IRR | X |
| MIRR | X |
| $PB_{Disc}$ | X |

Note that all methods rank Project X over Project Y. In addition, both projects are acceptable under the NPV, IRR, MIRR, and $PB_{Disc}$ criteria. Thus, both projects should be accepted if they are independent.

**c.** In this case, we would choose the project with the higher NPV at r = 12%, or Project X.

**d.** To determine the effects of changing the cost of capital, plot the NPV profiles of each project. The crossover rate occurs at about 6 percent (6.2%).

   If the firm's required rate of return is less than 6 percent, a conflict exists because $NPV_Y > NPV_X$, but $IRR_Y < IRR_X$. Therefore, if r were 5 percent, a conflict would exist.

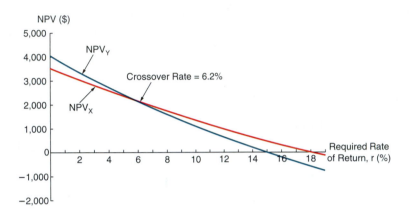

| Required Rate of Return | NPVₓ | NPVᵧ |
|:---:|:---:|:---:|
| 0% | $3,500 | $4,000 |
| 4 | 2,545 | 2,705 |
| 8 | 1,707 | 1,592 |
| 12 | 966 | 631 |
| 16 | 307 | (206) |
| 18 | 5 | (585) |
| 20 | (281) | (939) |

**e.** The basic cause of the conflict is differing reinvestment rate assumptions between NPV and IRR. NPV assumes that cash flows can be reinvested at the cost of the funds the firm uses, whereas IRR assumes reinvestment at the (generally) higher IRR. The high reinvestment rate assumption under IRR makes early cash flows especially valuable, and hence short-term projects look better under IRR.

## CHAPTER 10

**ST-2   a.** *Estimated investment outlay:*

| | |
|:---|---:|
| Price | ($50,000) |
| Modification | ( 10,000) |
| Change in net working capital | ( 2,000) |
| Total investment outlay | ($62,000) |

**b.** *Incremental operating cash flows:*

|  | Year 1 | Year 2 | Year 3 |
|---|---|---|---|
| 1. After-tax cost savings[a] | $12,000 | $12,000 | $12,000 |
| 2. Depreciation[b] | 19,800 | 27,000 | 9,000 |
| 3. Depreciation tax savings[c] | 7,920 | 10,800 | 3,600 |
| Net CF = (1 + 3) | $19,920 | $22,800 | $15,600 |

[a]$20,000 (1 − T).

[b]Depreciable basis = $60,000; the MACRS percentage allowances are 0.33, 0.45, and 0.15 in Years 1, 2, and 3, respectively; hence, depreciation in Year 1 = 0.33($60,000) = $19,800, and so on. There will remain $4,200, or 7 percent, undepreciated after Year 3; it would normally be taken in Year 4.

[c]Depreciation tax savings = T(Depreciation) = 0.4($19,800) = $7,920 in Year 1, and so on.

**c.** *Terminal cash flow:*

| | |
|---|---|
| Salvage value | $20,000 |
| Tax on salvage value[a] | (6,320) |
| Net working capital recovery | 2,000 |
| Terminal CF | $15,680 |

| | |
|---|---|
| Sales price | $20,000 |
| Less book value[a] | (4,200) |
| Taxable amount | $15,800 |
| Tax at 40% | $ 6,320 |

Book value = Depreciable basis − Accumulated depreciation
= $60,000 − ($19,800 + $27,000 + $9,000) = $4,200.

**d.** *Project NPV:*

$$NPV = -\$62,000 + \frac{\$19,920}{(1.10)^1} + \frac{\$22,800}{(1.10)^2} + \frac{\$31,280}{(1.10)^3}$$
$$= -\$62,000 + \$18,109.09 + \$18,842.98 + \$23,501.13$$
$$= \$1,546.80$$

Alternatively, using a financial calculator, input the cash flows into the cash flow register, enter I = 10, and then press the NPV key to obtain NPV = −$1,546.81. Because the earthmover has a negative NPV, it should not be purchased.

**ST-3** *First determine the initial investment outlay:*

| | |
|---|---|
| Purchase price | ($8,000) |
| Sale of old machine | 3,000 |
| Tax on sale of old machine | ( 160)[a] |
| Change in net working capital | ( 1,500) |
| Total investment | ($6,660) |

[a]The market value is $3,000 − $2,600 = $400 above the book value. Thus, there is a $400 recapture of depreciation, and Dauten would have to pay 0.40($400) = $160 in taxes.

*Now, examine the operating cash inflows:*

| | |
|---|---|
| Sales increase | $1,000 |
| Cost decrease | 1,500 |
| Increase in pretax operating revenues | $2,500 |
| After-tax operating revenue increase: | $1,500 = $2,500(1 − T) = $2,500(0.60) |

Depreciation:

| Year | 1 | 2 | 3 | 4 | 5 | 6 |
|---|---|---|---|---|---|---|
| New[a] | $1,600 | $2,560 | $1,520 | $960 | $880 | $480 |
| Old | 350 | 350 | 350 | 350 | 350 | 350 |
| Change | $1,250 | $2,210 | $1,170 | $610 | $530 | $130 |
| Depreciation Tax savings[b] | $ 500 | $ 884 | $ 468 | $244 | $212 | $ 52 |

[a]Depreciable basis = $8,000. Depreciation expense in each year equals depreciable basis times the MACRS percentage allowances of 0.20, 0.32, 0.19, 0.12, 0.11, and 0.06 in Years 1–6, respectively.

[b]Depreciation tax savings = T(Depreciation) = 0.4(Depreciation).

Now recognize that at the end of Year 6 Dauten would recover its net working capital investment of $1,500, and it would also receive $800 from the sale of the replacement machine. However, because the machine would be fully depreciated, the firm must pay 0.40($800) = $320 in taxes on the sale. Also, by undertaking the replacement now, the firm forgoes the right to sell the old machine for $500 in Year 6; thus, this $500 in Year 6 must be considered an opportunity cost in that year. No tax would be due because the $500 salvage value would equal the old machine's Year 6 book value.

*Finally, place all the cash flows on a time line:*

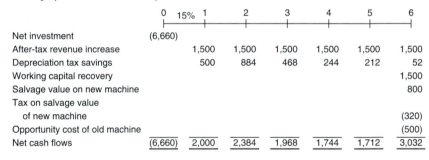

NPV = $1,335

The net present value of this incremental cash flow stream, when discounted at 15 percent, is $1,335. Thus, the replacement should be made.

**ST-4  a.**  First, find the expected cash flows:

| Year | Expected Cash Flows |
|---|---|
| 0 | 0.2(−$100,000) + 0.6(−$100,000) + 0.2(−$100,000) = ($100,000) |
| 1 | 0.2($20,000) + 0.6($30,000) + 0.2($40,000) = $30,000 |
| 2 | $30,000 |
| 3 | $30,000 |
| 4 | $30,000 |
| 5 | $30,000 |
| 5* | 0.2($0) + 0.6($20,000) + 0.2($30,000) = $18,000 − $48,000 |

Next, determine the NPV based on the expected cash flows:

$$NPV = -\$100,000 + \frac{\$30,000}{(1.10)^1} + \frac{\$30,000}{(1.10)^2} + \frac{\$30,000}{(1.10)^3} + \frac{\$30,000}{(1.10)^4} + \frac{\$48,000}{(1.10)^5}$$

$$= -\$100,000 + \$27,272.73 + \$24,793.39 + \$22,539.44$$

$$+ \$20,490.40 + \$29,804.22$$

$$= \$24,900.18$$

Using a financial calculator, input the cash flows in the cash flow register, enter I = 10, and then press the NPV key to obtain NPV = $24,900.19.

**b.** For the worst case, the cash flow values from the cash flow column farthest on the left are used to calculate NPV:

```
 0     10%   1         2         3         4         5
 ├───────────┼─────────┼─────────┼─────────┼─────────┤
(100,000)  20,000    20,000    20,000    20,000    20,000
```

Next, determine the NPV based on the expected cash flows:

$$NPV = -\$100,000 + \frac{\$20,000}{(1.10)^1} + \frac{\$20,000}{(1.10)^2} + \frac{\$20,000}{(1.10)^3} + \frac{\$20,000}{(1.10)^4} + \frac{\$20,000}{(1.10)^5}$$

$$= -\$100,000 + 18,181.82 + 16,528.93 + 15,026.30$$

$$+ 13,660.27 + 12,418.43$$

$$= -\$24,184.25$$

Using a financial calculator, input the cash flows in the cash flow register, enter I = 10, and then press the NPV key to obtain NPV = −$24,184.26.

Similarly, for the best case, use the values from the column farthest on the right. Here the NPV is $70,259.

If the cash flows are perfectly dependent, then the low cash flow in the first year will mean a low cash flow in every year. Thus, the probability of the worst case occurring is the probability of getting the $20,000 net cash flow in Year 1, or 20 percent. If the cash flows are independent, the cash flow in each year can be low, high, or average, and the probability of getting all low cash flows will be

$$0.2(0.2)(0.2)(0.2)(0.2) = 0.2^5 = 0.00032 = 0.032\%.$$

**c.** The base case NPV is found using the most likely cash flows and is equal to $26,142. This value differs from the expected NPV of $24,900 because the Year 5 cash flows are not symmetric. Under these conditions, the NPV distribution is as follows:

| Pr | NPV |
| --- | --- |
| 0.2 | ($24,184) |
| 0.6 | 26,142 |
| 0.2 | 70,259 |

Thus, the expected NPV is $0.2(-\$24,184) + 0.6(\$26,142) + 0.2(\$70,259)$ $= \$24,900$. As is generally the case, the expected NPV is the same as the NPV of the expected cash flows found in part a. The standard deviation is $29,904:

$$\sigma_{NPV}^2 = 0.2(-\$24,184 - \$24,900)^2 + 0.6(\$26,142 - \$24,900)^2$$
$$+ 0.2(\$70,259 - \$24,900)^2$$
$$= 894,261,126.$$
$$\sigma_{NPV} = \sqrt{894,261,126} = \$29,904.$$

The coefficient of variation, CV, is $29,904/\$24,900 = 1.20$.

d.  Because the project's coefficient of variation is 1.20, the project is riskier than average, and hence the project's risk-adjusted required rate of return is $10\% + 2\% = 12\%$. The project now should be evaluated by finding the NPV of the expected cash flows, as in part a, but using a 12 percent discount rate. The risk-adjusted NPV is $18,357, and therefore the project should be accepted.

# Chapter 11

ST-2  a.  A break point will occur each time a low-cost type of capital is used up. We establish the break points as follows, after first noting that LEI has $24,000 of retained earnings:

$$\text{Retained earnings} = (\text{Total earnings})(1.0 - \text{Payout})$$
$$= \$34,285.72(0.7)$$
$$= \$24,000.$$

$$\text{Break point} = \frac{\text{Maximum amount of low-cost capital of a given type}}{\text{Proportion of this type of capital in the capital structure}}$$

| Type of Capital | Break Point Calculation | Break Point | Break Number |
|---|---|---|---|
| Retained earnings | $BP_{RE} = \dfrac{\$24,000}{0.60}$ | $= \$40,000$ | 2 |
| 10% flotation common equity | $BP_{10\%E} = \dfrac{\$24,000 + \$12,000}{0.60}$ | $= \$60,000$ | 4 |
| 5% flotation preferred stock | $BP_{5\%PS} = \dfrac{\$7,500}{0.15}$ | $= \$50,000$ | 3 |
| 12% debt | $BP_{12\%D} = \dfrac{\$5,000}{0.25}$ | $= \$20,000$ | 1 |
| 14% debt | $BP_{14\%D} = \dfrac{\$10,000}{0.25}$ | $= \$40,000$ | 2 |

*Summary of break points*

(1) There are three common equity costs and hence two changes and, therefore, two equity-induced breaks in the MCC. There are two preferred costs and hence one preferred break. There are three debt costs and hence two debt breaks.

(2) The numbers in the fourth column of the table designate the sequential order of the breaks, determined after all the break points

were calculated. Note that the second debt break and the break for retained earnings both occur at $40,000.

(3) The first break point occurs at $20,000, when the 12 percent debt is used up. The second break point, $40,000, results from using up both retained earnings and the 14 percent debt. The MCC curve also rises at $50,000 and $60,000, as preferred stock with a 5 percent flotation cost and common stock with a 10 percent flotation cost, respectively, are used up.

**b.** Component costs within indicated total capital intervals are as follows:
Retained earnings (used in interval $0 to $40,000):

$$r_s = \frac{\hat{D}_1}{P_0} + g = \frac{\hat{D}_0(1+g)}{P_0} + g = \frac{\$3.60(1.09)}{\$60} + 0.09$$

$$= 0.0654 + 0.09 = 0.1554 \qquad = 15.54\%$$

Common with $F = 10\%$ ($40,001 to $60,000):

$$r_e = \frac{\hat{D}_1}{P_0(1.0 - F)} + g = \frac{\$3.924}{\$60(0.9)} + 0.09$$

$$= 0.0727 + 0.09 = 0.1627 \qquad = 16.27\%$$

Common with $F = 20\%$ (over $60,000):

$$r_e = \frac{\$3.924}{\$60(0.8)} + 0.09$$

$$= 0.08175 + 0.09 = 0.17175 \qquad = 17.18\%$$

Preferred with $F = 5\%$ ($0 to $50,000):

$$r_{ps} = \frac{D_{ps}}{P_0(1.0 - F)} = \frac{\$11}{\$100(0.95)}$$

$$= 0.1158 \qquad = 11.58\%$$

Preferred with $F = 10\%$ (over $50,000):

$$r_{ps} = \frac{\$11}{\$100(0.9)}$$

$$= 0.1222 \qquad = 12.22\%$$

Debt at $r_d = 12\%$ ($0 to $20,000): $r_{dT} = r_d(1 - T) = 12\%(0.6) = 7.20\%$

Debt at $r_d = 14\%$ ($20,001 to $40,000): $r_{dT} = 14\%(0.6) \qquad = 8.40\%$

Debt at $r_d = 16\%$ (over $40,000): $r_{dT} = 16\%(0.6) \qquad = 9.60\%$

**c.** WACC calculations within indicated total capital intervals:

(1) $0 to $20,000(debt = 7.2%, preferred = 11.58%, and retained earnings [RE] = 15.54%):

$$WACC_1 = w_d r_{dT} + w_{ps} r_{ps} + w_s r_s$$

$$= 0.25(7.2\%) + 0.15(11.58\%) + 0.60(15.54\%) = 12.86\%.$$

(2) $20,001 to $40,000(debt = 8.4%, preferred = 11.58%, and RE = 15.54%):

$$WACC_2 = 0.25(8.4\%) + 0.15(11.58\%) + 0.60(15.54\%) = 13.16\%.$$

(3) $40,001 to $50,000(debt = 9.6%, preferred = 11.58%, and equity = 16.27%):

$$WACC_3 = 0.25(9.6\%) + 0.15(11.58\%) + 0.60(16.27\%) = 13.90\%.$$

**(4)** $50,001 to $60,000(debt = 9.6%, preferred = 12.22%, and equity = 16.27%):

$$\text{WACC}_4 = 0.25(9.6\%) + 0.15(12.22\%) + 0.60(16.27\%) = 14.00\%.$$

**(5)** Over $60,000(debt = 9.6%, preferred = 12.22%, and equity = 17.18%):

$$\text{WACC}_5 = 0.25(9.6\%) + 0.15(12.22\%) + 0.60(17.18\%) = 14.54\%.$$

**d.** IRR calculation for Project E using a financial calculator:

$$N = 6, \ PV = -20,000, \ PMT = 5,427.84, \ \text{and} \ l \neq Y = ? = 16.00\%.$$

**e.** See the graph of the MCC and IOS schedules for LEI.

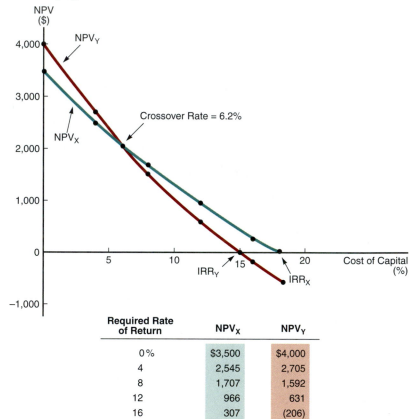

| Required Rate of Return | NPV$_X$ | NPV$_Y$ |
|:---:|:---:|:---:|
| 0% | $3,500 | $4,000 |
| 4 | 2,545 | 2,705 |
| 8 | 1,707 | 1,592 |
| 12 | 966 | 631 |
| 16 | 307 | (206) |
| 18 | 5 | (585) |

**f.** LEI should accept Projects B, E, and C. It should reject Projects A and D because their IRRs do not exceed the marginal costs of funds needed to finance them. The firm's capital budget would total $40,000.

## CHAPTER 12

**ST-2   a.**

| EBIT | $ 4,000,000 |
|:---|---:|
| Interest($2,000,000 × 0.10) | ( 200,000) |
| Earnings before taxes(EBT) | $ 3,800,000 |
| Taxes(35%) | (1,330,000) |
| Net income | $ 2,470,000 |

$$\text{EPS} = \$2,470,000/600,000 = \$4.12.$$
$$P_0 = \$4.12/0.15 = \$27.47.$$

**b.**
$$\text{Equity} = 600,000 \times (\$10) = \$6,000,000.$$
$$\text{Debt} = \$2,000,000.$$
$$\text{Total capital} = \$8,000,000.$$
$$\text{WACC} = w_d[r_d(1 - T)] + w_s r_s$$
$$= (2/8)[(10\%)(1 - 0.35)] + (6/8)(15\%)$$
$$= 1.63\% + 11.25\%$$
$$= 12.88\%.$$

**c.**

| | |
|---|---|
| EBIT | $4,000,000 |
| Interest($10,000,000 × 0.12) | (1,200,000) |
| Earnings before taxes(EBT) | $2,800,000 |
| Taxes(35%) | ( 980,000) |
| Net income | $1,820,000 |

Shares bought and retired:

$$\Delta\text{Shares} = \Delta\text{Debt}/P_0 = \$8,000,000/\$27.47 = 291,227.$$

New outstanding shares:

$$\text{Shares}_1 = \text{Shares}_0 - \Delta\text{Shares} = 600,000 - 291,227 = 308,773.$$

New EPS:

$$\text{EPS} = \$1,820,000/308,773 = \$5.89.$$

New price per share:

$$P_0 = \$5.89/0.17 = \$34.65 \text{ versus } \$27.47.$$

Therefore, Gentry should change its capital structure.

**d.** In this case, the company's net income would be higher by $(0.12 - 0.10)$ $(\$2,000,000)(1 - 0.35) = \$26,000$ because its interest charges would be lower. The new price would be

$$P_0 = \frac{(\$1,820,000 + \$26,000)/308,733}{0.17} = \$35.17$$

In the first case, in which debt had to be refunded, the bondholders were compensated for the increased risk of the higher debt position. In the second case, the old bondholders were not compensated; their 10 percent coupon perpetual bonds would now be worth

$$\$100/0.12 = \$833.33,$$

or $1,666,667 in total, down from the old $2 million, or a loss of $333,333. The stockholders would have a gain of

$$(\$35.17 - \$34.65)(308,773) = \$160,562.$$

This gain would, of course, be at the expense of the old bondholders. (There is no reason to think that bondholders' losses would exactly offset stockholders' gains.)

**e.**

$$\text{TIE} = \frac{\text{EBIT}}{\text{I}}$$

$$\text{Original TIE} = \frac{\$4,000,000}{\$200,000} = 20\times$$

$$\text{New TIE} = \frac{\$4,000,000}{\$1,200,000} = 3.33\times$$

# Chapter 13

**ST-2  a.**

| | |
|---|---:|
| Projected net income | $2,000,000 |
| Less projected capital investments | (800,000) |
| Available residual | $1,200,000 |
| Shares outstanding | 200,000 |
| DPS = $1,200,000/200,000 shares = $6 = $\hat{D}_1$ | |

**b.**  EPS = $2,000,000/200,000 shares = $10.

Payout ratio = DPS/EPS = $6/$10 = 60%, or

Total dividends/NI = $1,200,000/$2,000,000 = 60%.

**c.**  Currently, $P_o = \dfrac{\hat{D}_1}{r_s - g} = \dfrac{\$6}{0.14 - 0.05} = \dfrac{\$6}{0.09} = \$66.67$

Under the former circumstances, $\hat{D}_1$ would be based on a 20 percent payout on $10 EPS, or $2. With $r_s = 14\%$ and $g = 12\%$, we solve for $P_0$:

$$P_o = \frac{\hat{D}_1}{r_s - g} = \frac{\$2}{0.14 - 0.12} = \frac{\$2}{0.02} = \$100$$

Although CMC has suffered a severe setback, its existing assets will continue to provide a good income stream. More of these earnings should now be passed on to the shareholders, as the slowed internal growth has reduced the need for funds. However, the net result is a 33 percent decrease in the value of the shares.

**d.**  If the payout ratio were continued at 20 percent, even after internal investment opportunities had declined, the price of the stock would drop to $2/(0.14 − 0.06) = $25 rather than to $66.67. Thus, an increase in the dividend payout is consistent with maximizing shareholder wealth.

Because of the downward-sloping IOS curve, the greater the firm's level of investment, the lower the average ROE. Thus, the more money CMC retains and invests, the lower its average ROE will be. We can determine the average ROE under different conditions as follows:

*Old situation (with founder active and 20 percent payout):*

$$g = (1.0 - \text{Payout ratio})(\text{Average ROE})$$
$$12\% = (1.0 - 0.2)(\text{Average ROE})$$
$$\text{Average ROE} = 12\%/0.8 = 15\% > \quad r_s = 14\%.$$

Note that the *average* ROE is 15 percent, whereas the *marginal* ROE is presumably equal to 14 percent.

*New situation (with founder retired and a 60 percent payout):*

$$g = 6\% = (1.0 - 0.6)(\text{ROE})$$
$$\text{ROE} = 6\%/0.4 = 15\% > r_s = 14\%.$$

This suggests that the new payout is appropriate and that the firm is taking on investments down to the point at which marginal returns are equal to the cost of capital.

# CHAPTER 14

**ST-2  a.** and **b.**  Income Statements for Year Ended December 31, 2008 ($ Thousands)

|  | Vanderheiden | | Herrenhouse Press Publishing | |
|---|---|---|---|---|
|  | **a** | **b** | **a** | **b** |
| EBIT | $ 30,000 | $ 30,000 | $ 30,000 | $ 30,000 |
| Interest | (12,400) | (14,400) | (10,600) | ( 18,600)* |
| Taxable income | $ 17,600 | $ 15,600 | $ 19,400 | $ 11,400 |
| Taxes (40%) | ( 7,040) | ( 6,240) | ( 7,760) | ( 4,560) |
| Net income | $ 10,560 | $ 9,360 | $ 11,640 | $ 6,840 |
| Equity | $100,000 | $100,000 | $100,000 | $100,000 |
| Return on equity | 10.56% | 9.36% | 11.64% | 6.84% |

*Interest = $80,000(0.20) + $20,000(0.13) = $18,600

The Vanderheiden Press has a higher ROE when short-term interest rates are high, whereas Herrenhouse Publishing does better when rates are lower.

**c.**  Herrenhouse's position is riskier. First, its profits and return on equity are much more volatile than Vanderheiden's. Second, Herrenhouse must renew its large short-term loan every year, and if the renewal comes up at a time when money is very tight, when its business is depressed, or both, then Herrenhouse could be denied credit, which could put it out of business.

**ST-3**  The Calgary Company: Alternative Balance Sheets

|  | Restricted (40%) | Moderate (50%) | Relaxed (60%) |
|---|---|---|---|
| Current assets | $1,200,000 | $1,500,000 | $1,800,000 |
| Fixed assets | 600,000 | 600,000 | 600,000 |
| Total assets | $1,800,000 | $2,100,000 | $2,400,000 |
|  |  |  |  |
| Debt | $ 900,000 | $1,050,000 | $1,200,000 |
| Equity | 900,000 | 1,050,000 | 1,200,000 |
| Total liabilities and equity | $1,800,000 | $2,100,000 | $2,400,000 |

The Calgary Company: Alternative Income Statements

|  | Restricted | Moderate | Relaxed |
|---|---|---|---|
| Sales | $3,000,000 | $3,000,000 | $3,000,000 |
| EBIT (15% of sales) | 450,000 | 450,000 | 450,000 |
| Interest (10%) | (90,000) | (105,000) | (120,000) |
| Earnings before taxes (EBT) | $ 360,000 | $ 345,000 | $ 330,000 |
| Taxes (40%) | (144,000) | (138,000) | (132,000) |
| Net income | $ 216,000 | $ 207,000 | $ 198,000 |
| ROE | 24.0% | 19.7% | 16.5% |

# CHAPTER 15

**ST-2  a.** First determine the balance on the firm's checkbook and the bank's records as follows:

|  | Firm's Checkbook | Bank's Records |
|---|---|---|
| Day 1: Deposit $500,000; write check for $1,000,000 | ($ 500,000) | $500,000 |
| Day 2: Write check for $1,000,000 | ($1,500,000) | $500,000 |
| Day 3: Write check for $1,000,000 | ($2,500,000) | $500,000 |
| Day 4: Write check for $1,000,000; deposit $1,000,000 | ($2,500,000) | $500,000 |

After Upton has reached a steady state, it must deposit $1,000,000 each day to cover the checks written three days earlier.

**b.** The firm has three days of float; not until Day 4 does the firm have to make any additional deposits.

**c.** As shown above, Upton should try to maintain a balance on the bank's records of $500,000. On its own books it will have a balance of −$2,500,000.

**ST-3**  Analysis of change:

|  | Current | Proposal 1 | Proposal 2 |
|---|---|---|---|
| *Annual amounts:* |  |  |  |
| Sales | $10,000,000 | $11,000,000 | $9,000,000 |
| Operating expenses (80%) | ($ 8,000,000) | ($ 8,800,000) | ($7,200,000) |
| Collection expense* | ($ 50,000) | ($ 50,000) | ($ 50,000) |
| Bad debt losses* | ($ 0) | ($ 0) | ($ 0) |
| Days sales outstanding (DSO) | 30 days | 45 days | 22 days |
| Required return, r | 16      % | 16      % | 16      % |
| *Daily amounts:* |  |  |  |
| Sales = (Annual sales)/360 | $ 27,778 | $ 30,556 | $ 25,000 |
| Operating costs (80%) | ($ 22,222) | ($ 24,444) | ($ 20,000) |
| Required return = 12%/360 | 0.0444% | 0.0444% | 0.0444% |

*Because bad debt losses and collection expenses do not change, they are not considered in the analysis.

*Current Policy:*

$$
\begin{array}{ll}
& \quad 0 \qquad r = 0.0444\% \qquad\qquad\qquad\qquad 30 \\
\text{Production costs} & (22{,}222) \qquad\qquad\qquad\qquad\qquad 27{,}778
\end{array}
$$

$$
\text{NPV}_{\text{Current}} = -\$22{,}222 + \frac{\$27{,}778}{\left(1 + \dfrac{0.16}{360}\right)^{30}} = \$5{,}188
$$

*Proposal 1:*

$$
\begin{array}{ll}
& \quad 0 \qquad r = 0.0444\% \qquad\qquad\qquad\qquad\qquad\qquad 45 \\
\text{Production costs} & (24{,}444) \qquad\qquad\qquad\qquad\qquad\qquad\qquad 30{,}556
\end{array}
$$

$$
\text{NPV}_{\text{Proposal 1}} = -\$24{,}444 + \frac{\$30{,}556}{\left(1 + \dfrac{0.16}{360}\right)^{45}} = \$5{,}507
$$

*Proposal 2:*

$$
\begin{array}{ll}
& \quad 0 \qquad r = 0.0444\% \qquad\qquad\qquad\qquad 22 \\
\text{Production costs} & (20{,}000) \qquad\qquad\qquad\qquad\qquad 25{,}000
\end{array}
$$

$$
\text{NPV}_{\text{Proposal 2}} = -\$20{,}000 + \frac{\$25{,}000}{\left(1 + \dfrac{0.16}{360}\right)^{22}} = \$4{,}757
$$

The NPV is greatest with Proposal 1, so the firm should change its term of credit from net 25 to net 30.

**ST-4   a.**

$$
\text{EOQ} = \sqrt{\frac{2 \times O \times T}{C \times PP}}
$$

$$
= \sqrt{\frac{2(\$5{,}000)(2{,}600{,}000)}{(0.02)(\$5.00)}}
$$

$$
= 509{,}902 \text{ bushels}
$$

Because the firm must order in multiples of 2,000 bushels, it should order in quantities of 510,000 bushels.

**b.**

$$
\begin{aligned}
\text{Average weekly sales} &= 2{,}600{,}000/52 \\
&= 50{,}000 \text{ bushels.} \\
\text{Reorder point} &= 6 \text{ weeks' sales} \\
&= 6(50{,}000) \\
&= 300{,}000 \text{ bushels}
\end{aligned}
$$

**c.** Total inventory costs:

$$
\begin{aligned}
\text{TIC} &= (C)PP\left(\frac{Q}{2}\right) + O\left(\frac{T}{Q}\right) \\
&= (0.02)(\$5)\left(\frac{510{,}000}{2}\right) + \$5{,}000\left(\frac{2{,}600{,}000}{510{,}000}\right) \\
&= \$25{,}500 + \$25{,}490.20 \\
&= \$50{,}990.20
\end{aligned}
$$

# CHAPTER 16

**ST-2  a.**  *Commercial bank loan*

| | | |
|---|---|---|
| Amount loaned | = (0.75)($250,000) | = $ 187,500 |
| Discount | = (0.09/12)($187,500) | = ( 1,406) |
| Compensating balance | = (0.20)($187,500) | = ( 37,500) |
| Amount received | = | 148,594 |
| | | |
| Interest expense | = (0.09)($187,500) | = ($ 16,875) |
| Credit department* | = ($4,000)(12) | = ( 48,000) |
| Bad debts* | = (0.02)($250,000)(12) | = ( 60,000) |
| Total annual costs | = | ($124,875) |

*The costs of the credit department and bad debts are expenses that will be incurred if a bank loan is used, but these costs will be avoided if the firm accepts the factoring arrangement.

*Factoring*

| | | |
|---|---|---|
| Amount loaned | = (0.85)($250,000) | = $212,500 |
| Commission for period | = (0.035)($250,000) | = ( 8,750) |
| Prepaid interest | = (0.09/12)($203,750) | = ( 1,528) |
| Amount received | = | $202,222 |
| | | |
| Annual commission | = ($8,750)(12) | = ($105,000) |
| Annual interest | = (0.09)($203,750) | = ( 18,338) |
| Total annual costs | = | ($123,338) |

**b.**  The factoring costs are slightly lower than the cost of the bank loan, and the factor is willing to advance a significantly greater amount. On the other hand, the elimination of the credit department could reduce the firm's options in the future.

# CHAPTER 17

**ST-2  a.  (1)**  Determine the variable cost per unit at present, using the following definitions and equations:

$$Q = \text{units of output (sales)} = 5,000.$$
$$P = \text{averages sales price per unit of output} = \$100.$$
$$F = \text{fixed operating costs} = \$200,000.$$
$$EBIT = \text{operating income} = \$50,000$$
$$V = \text{variable costs per unit.}$$

$$EBIT = P(Q) - F - V(Q)$$
$$\$50,000 = \$100(5,000) - \$200,000 - V(5,000)$$
$$5,000V = \$250,\ 000$$
$$V = \$50.$$

(2) Determine the new EBIT level if the change is made:

$$\text{New EBIT} = P_2(Q_2) - F_2 - V_2(Q_2)$$
$$= \$95(7,000) - \$250,000 - \$40(7,000)$$
$$= \$135,000.$$

(3) Determine the incremental EBIT:

$$\Delta\text{EBIT} = \$135,000 - \$50,000 = \$85,000.$$

(4) Estimate the approximate rate of return on the new investment:

$$\Delta\text{ROA} = \frac{\Delta\text{EBIT}}{\text{Investment}} = \frac{\$85,000}{\$400,000} = 0.2125 = 21.25\%.$$

Because the ROA exceeds Olinde's average cost of capital, this analysis suggests that Olinde should go ahead and make the investment.

b.

$$\text{DOL} = \frac{Q(P-V)}{Q(P-V) - F}$$

$$\text{DOL}_{Old} = \frac{5,000(\$100 - \$50)}{5,000(\$100 - \$50) - \$200,000} = 5.00\times$$

$$\text{DOL}_{New} = \frac{7,000(\$95 - \$40)}{7,000(\$95 - \$40) - \$250,000} = 2.85\times$$

This indicates that operating income will be less sensitive to changes in sales if the production process is changed; thus the change would reduce risks. However, the change would increase the breakeven point. Still, with a lower sales price, it might be easier to achieve the higher new breakeven volume.

$$Old: Q_{OpBE} = \frac{F}{P - V} = \frac{\$200,000}{\$100 - \$50} = 4,000 \text{ units}$$

$$New: Q_{OpBE} = \frac{F_2}{P_2 - V_2} = \frac{\$250,000}{\$95 - \$40} = 4,545 \text{ units}$$

c. The incremental ROA is:

$$\Delta\text{ROA} = \frac{\Delta\text{Profit}}{\Delta\text{Sales}} \times \frac{\Delta\text{Sales}}{\Delta\text{Assets}}$$

Using debt financing, the incremental profit associated with the investment is equal to the incremental profit found in part a minus the interest expense incurred as a result of the investment:

$$\Delta\text{Profit} = \text{New profit} - \text{Old profit} - \text{Interest}$$
$$= \$135,000 - \$50,000 - 0.08(\$400,000)$$
$$= \$53,000.$$

The incremental sales is calculated as:

$$\Delta\text{Sales} = P_2 Q_2 - P_1 Q_1$$
$$= \$95(7,000) - \$100(5,000)$$
$$= \$665,000 - \$500,000$$
$$= \$165,000.$$

$$\text{ROA} = \frac{\$53,000}{\$165,000} \times \frac{\$165,000}{\$400,000} = 0.1325 = 13.25\%$$

The return on the new equity investment still exceeds the average cost of funds, so Olinde should make the investment.

**d.**
$$\text{DFL} = \frac{\text{EBIT}}{\text{EBIT} - \text{I}}$$

$$= \frac{\$135,000}{\$135,000 - \$32,000} = 1.31\times$$

$$\text{EBIT}_{\text{FinBE}} = \$32,000 = 0.08(\$400,000)$$

## CHAPTER 18

**ST-2  a.**  *Cost of leasing:*

| | Beginning of Year | | | |
| --- | --- | --- | --- | --- |
| | **0** | **1** | **2** | **3** |
| Lease payment (AT)[a] | ($ 6,000) | ($6,000) | ($6,000) | ($6,000) |
| PV of leasing @ 6%[b] | ($ 6,000) | ($5,660) | ($5,340) | ($5,038) |
| Total PV cost of leasing = | ($22,038) | | | |

[a]After-tax payment = $10,000(1 − T) = $10,000(0.60) $6,000.

[b]This is the after-tax cost of debt: 10%(1 − T) = 10%(0.60) = 6.0%.

Alternatively, using a financial calculator, input the following data after switching your calculator to "BEG" mode: N = 4, I ≠ Y = 6, PMT = −6,000, and FV = 0. Then press the PV key to arrive at the answer of ($22,038). Remember to switch your calculator back to "END" mode.

**b.**  *Cost of owning:*
Depreciable basis = $40,000.
Here are the cash flows under the borrow-and-buy alternative:

| | End of Year | | | | |
| --- | --- | --- | --- | --- | --- |
| | **0** | **1** | **2** | **3** | **4** |
| 1. Depreciation schedule | | | | | |
| (a) Depreciable basis | | $ 40,000 | $ 40,000 | $ 40,000 | $40,000 |
| (b) Allowance | | 0.33 | 0.45 | 0.15 | 0.07 |
| (c) Depreciation | | 13,200 | 18,000 | 6,000 | 2,800 |
| 2. Cash outflows | | | | | |
| (d) Net purchase price | ($40,000) | | | | |
| (e) Depreciation tax savings[a] | | 5,280 | 7,200 | 2,400 | 1,120 |
| (f) Maintenance (AT)[b] | | (600) | (600) | (600) | (600) |
| (g) Salvage value (AT)[c] | | | | | 6,000 |
| (h) Total cash outflows | ($40,000) | $ 4,680 | $ 6,600 | $ 1,800 | $ 6,520 |
| PV of owning | ($40,000) | $ 4,415 | $ 5,874 | $ 1,511 | $ 5,164 |
| Total PV cost of owning = | ($23,036) | | | | |

[a]Depreciation(T) = $13,200(0.40) = $5,280 in Year.

[b]After-tax cost = $1,000(1 − 0.4) = $600

[c]Because the asset will be fully depreciated, the after tax salvage = $10,000(1 − 0.4) = $6,000.

Alternatively, input the cash flows for the individual years in the cash flow register and input I = 6, then press the NPV button to arrive at the answer of −$23,035. Because the present value of the cost of leasing is less than that of owning, the truck should be leased: $23,035 − $22,038 = $997, net advantage to leasing.

c. The discount rate is based on the cost of debt because most cash flows are fixed by contract and, consequently, are relatively certain. Thus, the lease cash flows have about the same risk as the firm's debt. Also, leasing is considered to be a substitute for debt. We use an after-tax cost rate because the cash flows are stated net of taxes.

d. Olsen could increase the discount rate on the salvage value cash flow. This would increase the PV cost of owning and make leasing even more advantageous.

# Appendix C
## Answers to End-of-Chapter Problems

We present here some answers to selected end-of-chapter problems. Please note that your answer might differ slightly from ours due to rounding differences. Also, although we hope not, some of the problems may have more than one correct solution, depending upon what assumptions are made in working the problems. Finally, many of the problems involve some verbal discussion as well as numerical calculations; this verbal material is not presented here

**2-1**    $262,500; 1.19×

**2-2**    Sales = $2,511,628; DSO = 37 days

**2-3**    TIE = 3.5

**2-4**    ROE = 24.5%; ROA = 9.8%

**2-5**    $230,000

**2-6**    **a.** $2.8 million

       **b.** $950,000

**2-7**    −$20,000

**2-8**    Net profit margin = 2%; Debt/Assets = 40%

**2-9**    **a.** 5.54%

       **b.** 2) 3.21%

**2-10**   Total sources = $102; Net increase in cash & marketable securities = $19

**2-11**   **a.** NOI = $150,000; CF = $2,400,000

       **b.** CF = $3,000,000

**2-13**   **a.** Current ratio = 1.98×; DSO = 75 days; Total assets turnover = 1.7×; Debt ratio = 61.9%

**2-14**   A/P = $90,000; Inv = $67,500; FA = $160,500

**2-16**   **a.** Quick ratio = 0.85×; DSO = 37.8 days; ROE = 13.1%; Debt ratio = 54.8%

**3-1**    **a.** $1,050,000

       **c.** ($3,450,000)

**3-2**    600,000

**3-3**    5 million

**3-4**    77,784 bonds

**3-5**    **a.** $2.73 million

       **c.** $41,935,484

**3-6**    **a.** $10,325,000

**3-7**    **a.** $4.2 million

**3-8**   **a.**  $35,280,000

      **b.**  10 million

**4-1**   $561.80

**4-2**   $747.26

**4-3**   **(1)** $499.99

      **(2)** $867.13

**4-4**   **(1)** n $\approx$ 10 years

**4-5**   $1,000 today is worth more

**4-6**   **a.**  14.87%

**4-7**   **a.**  $6,374.97

**4-8**   **a.**  $7,012.47

**4-9**   **a.**  $2,457.83

      **b.**  $865.90

**4-10**  **a.**  $2,703.61

**4-11**  PV@7% = $1,428.57; PV@14% = $714.29

**4-12**  **a.**  Stream A: $973.57

**4-13**  **a.**  $881.17

      **b.**  $895.42

      **c.**  $903.06

      **d.**  $908.35

**4-14**  **b.**  $279.20

      **c.**  $276.84

      **d.**  $275.22

**4-15**  **a.**  $5,272.32

      **b.**  $5,374.07

**4-16**  **a.**  $2,944.03

      **b.**  $2,975.49

**4-17**  **a.**  $33,872.11

      **b.**  **(1)** $26,243.16; **(2)** $0

**4-18**  $1,205.55

**4-19**  n $\approx$ 15 years

**4-20**  5 years; $1,885.09

**4-21**  PVA = $46.8 million; take the annuity

**4-22**  **a.**  PVA = $51.1 million; take the lump-sum payment

      **b.**  5.4%

**4-23**  **b.**  7%

      **c.**  9%

      **d.**  15%

**4-24**  **a.**  1st City = 7%; 2nd City = 6.66%

**4-25**  APR = 8.0%; EAR = 8.24%

**4-26**  12%

**4-27**   9%

**4-28**   **a.**   $6,300

      **b.**   PMT(Bank of South Alaska) = $1,600

      **c.**   3.8%

**4-29**   $984.88

**4-30**   **a.**   PMT = $6,594.94

      **b.**   $13,189.87

**4-31**   **a.**   Z = 9%; B = 8%

      **b.**   Z = $558.39; $135.98; 32.2%; B = $548.33; $48.33; 9.7%

**4-32**   **a.**   $260.73

      **b.**   $263.34

**4-33**   $r_{SIMPLE}$ = 15.19%

**4-34**   **a.**   26.5 months

      **c.**   9.8 months

**4-35**   **a.**   $854.74

      **c.**   14.3 years

**4-36**   **b.**   $493.19

      **d.**   Credit union loan: $16,211.66

**4-37**   **a.**   $61,204

      **b.**   $11,020

      **c.**   $6,841

**4-38**   **a.**   $176,792

      **b.**   $150,259

**4-39**   $1,901

**4-40**   $4,971

**5-1**   57.1%

**5-2**   −10%

**5-3**   **a.**   $r_2$ = 10%

**5-4**   $r_2$ = 15%; Year 2 inflation = 11%

**5-5**   6.0%

**5-6**   $Infl_2$ = 3.4%

**5-7**   DRP = 5.0%

**5-8**   $r_{2013}$ = 5.4%

**5-9**   $r_{2013}$ = 7.0%

**5-10**   **a.**   $r_1$ = 9.2%; $r_5$ = 7.2%

**5-11**   **a.**   $Infl_5$ = 4.6%

      **b.**   $MRP_5$ = 0.8%

      **c.**   $r_5$ = 8.4%

      **d.**   $r_{10}$ = 8.4%

**5-12**   **a.**   0.3%

      **c.**   $r^*$ = 1.5%

**5-13**    **a.**   11.1%

        **c.**   3.7%

**5-15**    **a.**   4.8%

        **b.**   6.8%

        **c.**   5-yr bond = 7.3%

**6-1**     **a.**   7,931

        **c.**   12%

**6-2**     **a.**   $40

**6-3**     $823.32

**6-4**     12%

**6-5**     7.65%

**6-6**     **a.**   $1,251.22

**6-7**     $841.15

**6-8**     $813.07

**6-9**     **a.**   $V_L$ at 5 percent = $1,518.99; $V_L$ at 7 percent = $1,273.24; $V_L$ at 11 = percent = $928.09

**6-10**   8%

**6-11**   **a.**   YTM at $829 = 15%

**6-12**   0.5%

**6-13**   **a.**   10.54%

        **c.**   Capital gains = 17.2%; total return = 26.2%

**6-14**   Capital gains = −0.7%; total return = 7%

**6-15**   **a.**   13.3%

        **b.**   10%

        **c.**   8%

        **d.**   5.3%

**6-16**   IBM bond = 9.33%

**6-17**   10.2%

**6-18**   **a.**   $1,250

        **b.**   $833.33

        **d.**   At 8%, Vd = $1,196.36

**6-19**   **a.**   $1,000

        **b.**   $V_{GM}$ = $888.42

        **c.**   GM capital gains = −11.2%

        **d.**   GM current yield = 5.0%

        **e.**   GM total return = −6.2%

        **g.**   $V_{GM}$ = $907.05

**7-1**     46%

**7-2**     15%

**7-3**     $85

**7-4**     $150

**7-5**     $100

**7-6**   $65

**7-7**   $15.30

**7-8**   $23.75

**7-9**   $30

**7-10**   $1.96

**7-11**   EVA = $0

**7-12**   **a.**   $140,000

　　　　**b.**   −$50,000

**7-13**   **a.**   $4.08

　　　　**b.**   $122.40

**7-14**   $\hat{D}_1 = \$2.10, \hat{D}_2 = \$2.21, \hat{D}_3 = \$2.32, \hat{P}_3 = \$34.73$

**7-15**   $25.03

**7-16**   $P_0 = \$19.89$

**7-17**   $35.28

**7-18**   **a.**   $20

**7-19**   12%

**7-20**   5%

**7-21**   **a.**   7%

　　　　**b.**   5%

　　　　**c.**   12%

**7-22**   **a.**   **(1)**   $9.50

　　　　　　　**(2)**   $13.33

　　　　**b.**   **(1)**   Undefined

**7-23**   **a.**   $22.50

　　　　**b.**   $27.79

　　　　**d.**   $42.59

**7-24**   **a.**   Dividend 2010 = $2.66

　　　　**b.**   $P_0 = \$39.43$

　　　　**c.**   Dividend yield 2008 = 5.10%; 2012 = 7.00%

**7-25**   **a.**   $\hat{P}_0 = \$54.11$

**8-1**   15%

**8-2**   10%

**8-3**   2.0

**8-4**   15.5%

**8-5**   14%

**8-6**   $CV_E = 0.667$

**8-7**   $r_{RF} = 2.5\%$

**8-8**   17%

**8-9**   **a.**   $\hat{r}_M = 13.5\%$; $\hat{r}_S = 11.6\%$

　　　　**b.**   $\sigma_M = 3.85\%$; $\sigma_S = 6.22\%$

　　　　**c.**   $CV_M = 0.29$; $CV_S = 0.54$

**8-10**   19%

**8-11**  **a.** $\hat{r}_Y = 14\%$

  **b.** $\sigma_X = 12.20\%$

**8-12**  $r_K = 19\%$

**8-13**  $\beta_{New} = 1.4$

**8-14**  $\beta_{Stock} = 1.2$

**8-15**  **a.** $\beta_B = 2$

  **b.** $r_B = 12.5\%$

**8-16**  **a.** $r_X = 15.5\%$

  **b.** **(1)** $r_X = 16.5\%$

  **c.** **(1)** $r_X = 18.1\%$

**8-17**  $\beta_{New} = 1.16$

**8-18**  4.5%

**8-19**  $\beta_P = 0.7625$; $r_p = 12.1\%$

**8-20**  **a.** $\hat{r}_C = 8\%$

  **b.** $\sigma_A = 9\%$

  **c.** $CV_A = 0.50$; $CV_B = 0.97$; $CV_C = 0.41$

**8-21**  **a.** $0.5 million

  **d.** **(2)** 15%

**8-22**  **a.** 13.5%

  **b.** 1.8

  **c.** $r_F = 8\% + 5.5\% \beta_F$

  **d.** 17.9%

**8-23**  **a.** $\bar{r}_A = 11.3\%$

  **c.** $s_A = 20.8\%$

  **d.** $CV_A = 1.84$

**9-1**  −$2,894.79

**9-2**  −$361.65

**9-3**  20%

**9-4**  $IRR_G = 14.04\%$; $IRR_P = 13.98\%$; $IRR_V = 13.75\%$

**9-5**  13.7%

**9-6**  $NPV = -\$10,075.29$

**9-7**  3.75 years

**9-8**  $PB_{Disc} = 3.39$ years

**9-9**  $MIRR = 10.3\%$

**9-10**  $IRR_G = 15.96\%$; $MIRR_G = 15.25\%$
$IRR_J = 16.04\%$; $MIRR_J = 16.04\%$
$IRR_K = 15.53\%$; $MIRR_K = 15.10\%$

**9-11**  $NPV_Q = \$132.23$; $IRR_Q = 11.80\%$
$NPV_R = \$90.91$; $IRR_R = 12.04\%$

**9-12**  $NPV_P = \$409$; $IRR_P = 15\%$; $MIRR_P = 14.5\%$; $PB_P = 3.4$ years; $DPB_P = 4.9$ years; Accept

**9-13**  $NPV_E = \$3,861$; $IRR_E = 18\%$; $NPV_G = \$3,057$; $IRR_G = 18\%$; Purchase electric-powered forklift; it has a higher NPV

**9-14**   $NPV_P = \$448.86$; $NPV_Q = \$607.20$; $IRR_P = 15.24\%$; $IRR_Q = 14.67\%$; $DPB_P = 4.67$ years; $DPB_Q = 4.89$ years; $MIRR_P = 14.7\%$; $MIRR_Q = 14.4\%$

**9-15**   **a.**   $PV_C = -\$556,717$; $PV_F = -\$493,407$; Forklift should be chosen

**9-16**   $NPV_C = \$1,256$; $IRR_C = 17.3\%$; $NPV_R = \$1,459$

**9-17**   $IRR_Q = 15.6\%$

**9-18**   $NPV_Y = \$886$; accept Project Y

**9-19**   **b.**   $NPV = \$7,486.68$

      **d.**   $DPB = 6.51$ yrs

**9-20**   **a.**   $IRR_A = 17.8\%$; $IRR_B = 24.0\%$

**9-21**   **a.**   $IRR_A = 20\%$; $IRR_B = 16.7\%$; Crossover rate $\approx 16\%$

**9-22**   **a.**   $NPV_A = \$14,486,808$; $NPV_B = \$11,156,893$; $IRR_A = 15.03\%$; $IRR_B = 22.26\%$

**10-1**   $\$90,250$

**10-2**   **a.**   $\$390,000$

      **b.**   $\$11,000$

**10-3**   $NPV = 15,301$; Buy the new machine

**10-4**   $NPV = \$22,329$; Replace the old machine

**10-5**   **a.**   $10.6\%$

      **b.**   $NPV = \$1,100$; Accept

**10-6**   **a.**   $15\%$

      **b.**   $\beta = 1.48$; $r_{firm} = 15.4\%$; $r_{division} = 17.0\%$

**10-7**   Accept A and B

**10-8**   Accept QUE and DOG

**10-9**   **a.**   ($\$178,000$)

      **b.**   $\$52,440$; $\$60,600$; $\$40,200$

      **c.**   $\$48,760$

      **d.**   $NPV = -\$19,549$; Do not purchase

**10-10**   **a.**   ($\$126,000$)

      **b.**   $\$42,560$; $\$47,477$; $\$35,186$

      **c.**   $\$51,268$

      **d.**   $NPV = \$11,385$; Purchase

**10-11**   **a.**   ($\$52,000$)

      **b.**   $\$18,560$; $\$22,400$; $\$12,800$; $\$10,240$

      **c.**   $\$1,500$

      **d.**   $NPV = \$1,021$; Replace the old machine

**10-12**   **a.**   ($\$776,000$)

      **c.**   $\$199,000$; $\$255,400$; $\$194,300$; $\$161,400$; $\$156,700$

      **d.**   $\$115,200$

      **e.**   $NPV = \$436.77$; Purchase the new machine

**10-13**   **a.**   Expected $CF_A = \$6,750$; Expected $CF_B = \$7,650$

      **b.**   $CV_A = 0.0703$

      **c.**   $NPV_A = \$10,036$; $NPV_B = \$11,624$

**10-14**   **a.**   $11\%$

**10-15** $NPV_5 = \$4,422$; $NPV_4 = -\$4,161$; $NPV_8 = \$26,658$

**10A-1** $PV = \$1,273,389$

**10B-1 a.** $NPV_{190-3} = \$20,070$; $NPV_{360-6} = \$22,256$

**10B-2** $NPV_A = \$12.76$ million

**11-1** 6.12%

**11-2** 7.92%

**11-3** 7.64%

**11-4** 11.94%

**11-5** 12.37%

**11-6** 13.0%

**11-7** $r_e = 14.0\%$

**11-8** **a.** F = 10%

     **b.** $r_e = 15.8\%$

**11-9** **a.** 13.6%

     **b.** 14.2%

**11-10** 7.2%

**11-11** $r_e = 16.5\%$

**11-12** $80,000

**11-13** $BP_{RE} = \$500,000$; $BP_{7.8\% \text{ debt}} = \$1,500,000$

**11-14** 9.8%

**11-15** 15%

**11-16** 7.0%

**11-17** WACC = 12.72%

**11-18** $10 million

**11-19** $42,000

**11-20** $62,000

**11-21** **a.** 14.40%

     **b.** $WACC_2 = 10.62\%$

**11-22** **a.** 16.3%

     **b.** 15.4%

     **c.** 16%

**11-23** **a.** 8%

     **b.** $2.81

     **c.** 15.8%

**11-24** **a.** $18 million

     **b.** BP = $45 million

     **c.** $BP_1 = \$20$ million; $BP_2 = \$40$ million

**11-25** **a.** g = 3%

     **b.** EPS = $5.562

**11-26** **a.** $67,500,000

     **c.** $r_s = 12\%$; $r_e = 12.4\%$

    **d.** $27,000,000

    **e.** $WACC_1 = 9\%$; $WACC_2 = 9.2\%$

**11-27 a.** $r_{dT} = 5.4\%$; $r_s = 15.1\%$

    **b.** $WACC = 11.22\%$

    **d.** $WACC = 11.70\%$

**11-28 a.** Three breaks; $BP_{D1} = \$1,111,111$; $BP_{RE} = \$1,818,182$; $BP_{D2} = \$2,000,000$

    **b.** $WACC_1 = 10.96\%$; $WACC_2 = 11.50\%$; $WACC_3 = 12.14\%$; $WACC_4 = 12.68\%$

    **c.** $IRR_1 = 16\%$; $IRR_3 = 14\%$

**12-1** Apex has $DTL = 12\times$

**12-2** $30,000

**12-3** $2.5\times$

**12-4** 24%

**12-5** $2.0\times$

**12-6** 30%

**12-7** $1.33\times$

**12-8** $DOL = 4.0x$; $DTL = 10.0\times$

**12-9** $DOL = 3.0x$; $DTL = 6.0\times$

**12-10 a.** $ROE_{LL} = 14.6\%$; $ROE_{HL} = 16.8\%$

    **b.** $ROE_{LL} = 16.5\%$

**12-11** No leverage: $ROE = 10.5\%$; $\sigma = 5.4\%$; $CV = 0.515$; 60% leverage: $ROE = 13.7\%$; $\sigma = 13.5\%$; $CV = 0.987$

**12-12 a.** $5.10

**12-13 a.** $DOL_A = 2.80$; $DOL_B = 2.15$; Method A

    **b.** $DFL_A = 1.32$; $DFL_B = 1.35$; Method B

    **d.** Debt = $129,310; $D/A = 5.75\%$

**12-14 a.** $EPS_{Old} = \$2.04$; New: $EPS_D = \$4.74$; $EPS_S = \$3.27$

    **b.** $DOL_{Old} = 2.30$; $DOL_{New} = 1.60$; $DFL_{Old} = 1.47$; $DFL_{New,Stock} = 1.15$; $DTL_{New,Debt} = 2.53$

    **c.** 33,975 units

    **d.** $Q_{New,Debt} = 27,225$ units

**12-15** Debt used: $E(EPS) = \$5.78$; $\sigma_{EPS} = \$1.05$; $E(TIE) = 3.49\times$; Stock used: $E(EPS) = \$5.51$; $\sigma_{EPS} = \$0.85$; $E(TIE) = 6.00\times$

**13-1** $3,250,000

**13-2** Payout = 52%

**13-3** $40,000

**13-4** $720,000

**13-5** $20,000,000

**13-6** $D_0 = \$3.44$

**13-7** $0.20

**13-8** Payout = 31.39%

**13-9**  **a.** 2,000

    **b.** $24,000

    **c.** $16,000

**13-10** CS = $79.50; PIC = $464.25; RE = $956.25

**13-11** **a.** **(1)** $3,960,000

       **(2)** $4,800,000

       **(3)** $9,360,000

       **(4)** Regular = $3,960,000; Extra = $5,400,000

    **c.** 15%

    **d.** 15%

**13-12** **a.** Payout = 63.16%; $BP_{with\ dividend}$ = $9.55 million; $WACC_1$ = 10.67%; $WACC_2$ = 10.96%

    **b.** $15 million

**14-1**  **a.** 11.25×

    **b.** 32 days

**14-2**  **a.** 45.0 days

    **b.** $384,000,000

**14-3**  **a.** 30.0×

    **b.** 12 days

**14-4**  **a.** 30 days

    **b.** $5,760,000

**14-5**  **a.** 14.0×

    **b.** 25.7 days

**14-6**  **a.** 18 days

    **b.** $32,000,000

**14-7**  **a.** 72 days

    **b.** $396,000

    **d.** Decrease to 57

**14-8**  **a.** 51 days

    **b.** Turnover = 2.33× ROA = 11.67%;

    **c.** CCC = 42 days; TA turnover = 2.46; ROA = 12.3%

**14-9**  **b.** 20 days

**14-10** **a.** **(1)** 109 days

       **(2)** 79 days

    **d.** **(1)** 140 days

       **(2)** 113 days

**14-11** **a.** 32 days

    **b.** $288,000

    **c.** $45,000

    **d.** **(1)** 30 days

       **(2)** $378,000

**14-12** **a.** $ROE_{Tight}$ = 11.75%; $ROE_{Moderate}$ = 10.80%; $ROE_{Relaxed}$ = 9.16%

**15-1**  **a.**  Net float = $30,000

 **b.**  $16,000

**15-2**  **a.**  DSO = 28 days

 **b.**  $70,000

**15-3**  $NPV_{Existing}$ = $2,349, $NPV_{Proposal}$ = $2,089

**15-4**  $DSO_{Existing}$ = 54 days, $DSO_{Proposal}$ = 75 days

**15-5**  **a.**  EOQ = 3,873

 **b.**  5,073 bags

 **c.**  3,137 bags

 **d.**  Every 6 days

**15-6**  **a.**  $1,600,000

 **c.**  Bank = $1,200,000; Books = −$5,200,000

**15-7**  **b.**  $164,400

**15-8**  **b.**  Oct. loan = $22,800

**15-9**  **b.**  $420,000

 **c.**  $35,000

**15-10**  $NPV_{Existing}$ = $1,141, $NPV_{Proposal}$ = $1,196

**15-11**  **a.**  $DSO_{Old}$ = 27 days; $DSO_{New}$ = 22.5 days

 **b.**  $D_{Old}$ = $15,680; $D_{New}$ = $38,220

 **c.**  $BD_{Old}$ = $40,000; $BD_{New}$ = $52,000

 **e.**  $NPV_{Old}$ = $1,197, $NPV_{New}$ = $1,514

**15-12**  EOQ = 1000

**15-13**  **a.**  EOQ = 5,200

 **b.**  65

 **c.**  Every 5.5 days

 **d.**  (1)  TIC = $6,456

**16-1**  **b.**  14.69%

 **d.**  20.99%

**16-2**  **a.**  44.54%

**16-3**  **a.**  12%

 **b.**  11.25%

 **c.**  11.48%

 **d.**  16%

**16-4**  APR = 14.69%; EAR = 15.65%

**16-5**  N/P = 13.64%

**16-6**  **b.**  12.01%

 **d.**  8.37%

**16-7**  **a.**  $100,000

 **b.**  $300,000

 **c.**  Approximate cost = 36.73%; EAR = 43.86%

**16-8**  **a.**  $EAR_{Disc}$ = 14.94%

**16-9** **a.** Alternative 3 EAR = 9.56%

   **b.** Alternative 2 $470,588

**16-10** **a.** 11.73%

   **b.** 12.09%

   **c.** 18%

**16-11** **b.** $384,615

   **c.** Cash = $126.9; NP = $434.6

**16-12** **a.** (**1**) $27,500

   (**2**) $25,833

**16-13** **a.** $515,464

**16-14** **a.** $46,167

   **b.** $40,667

**17-1** **a.** $80,000

   **b.** $Q_{OpBE}$ = 6,000

**17-2** $Q_{OpBE}$ = 200

**17-3** $30,000

**17-4** **a.** (**1**) −$75,000

   (**2**) $175,000

   **b.** $Q_{OpBE}$ = 140,000

   **c.** (**1**) −8.3

   (**2**) 15.0

   (**3**) 5.0

**17-5** **a.** $FC_A$ = $80,000; $VC_A$ = $4.80/unit; $P_A$ = $8.00/unit

**17-6** **a.** $480,000

   **b.** $18,750

**17-7** AFN = $360

**17-8** **a.** 40,000

   **b.** ($0.30)

   **c.** 48,000

   **d.** DOL = 3.0; DFL = 1.7

**17-9** **a.** Notes payable = $31.44 million

   **b.** Current ratio = 2.0×; ROE = 14.2%

   **c.** (**1**) −$14.28 million

   (**2**) Total assets = $147 million; Notes payable = $3.72 million

   (**3**) Current ratio = 4.25×; ROE = 10.84%

**17-10** **a.** Total assets = $33,534; AFN = $2,128

   **b.** Notes payable = $4,228; AFN = $70; ΔInterest = $213

**17-11** **a.** DOL = 2.5×; DFL = 3.0×

**17-12** **a.** First pass AFN = $667

   **b.** Increase in notes payable = $51; Increase in CS = $368

**17-13** **a.** (**1**) −$60,000

     **b.**  $Q_{OpBE} = 14,000$

     **c.**  **(1)** $-1.33$

**17-14**  **a.**  **(2)** $125,000

     **b.**  $Q_{OpBE} = 7,000$

**17-15**  **a.**  $2,000

     **b.**  $DFL = 1.8$

     **c.**  $3,000

**18-1**  **a.**  $200

**18-2**  **a.**  $D/A_W = 50\%$; $D/A_G = 67\%$

**18-3**  **a.**  PV cost of owning = $-$185,112; PV cost of leasing = $-$187,534; Purchase loom

**18-4**  $30,463

**18-5**  **b.**  Percent ownership: Original $= 80\%$; Plan $1 = 53\%$; Plans 2 and $3 = 57\%$

     **c.**  $EPS_0 = \$0.48$; $EPS_1 = \$0.60$; $EPS_2 = \$0.64$; $EPS_3 = \$0.86$

     **d.**  $D/A_1 = 13\%$; $D/A_2 = 13\%$; $D/A_3 = 48\%$

**18-6**  **a.**  PV cost of owning = ($991,845); PV cost of leasing = ($954,639); Lease equipment

# Appendix D
## Selected Equations

### CHAPTER 1

Value = Current (present) value of *expected* cash flows $\hat{CF}$ based on the return demanded by investors (r)

$$= \frac{\hat{CF}_1}{(1+r)^1} + \frac{\hat{CF}_2}{(1+r)^2} + \cdots + \frac{\hat{CF}_N}{(1+r)^N} = \sum_{t=1}^{N} \frac{\hat{CF}_t}{(1+r)^t}$$

### CHAPTER 2

Net cash flow = Net income + Depreciation and amortization

Net working capital = NWC = Current assets − Current Liabilities

$$\begin{array}{c}\text{Net operating}\\\text{working capital}\end{array} = \text{NOWC} = \left(\begin{array}{c}\text{Current assets}\\\text{required for operations}\end{array}\right) - \left(\begin{array}{c}\text{Non − interest bearing}\\\text{current liabilities}\end{array}\right)$$

Operating cash flow = NOI(1 − Tax rate) + Depreciation and amortization expense

$$= \begin{array}{c}\text{Net operating}\\\text{profit after taxes}\end{array} + \begin{array}{c}\text{Depreciation and}\\\text{amortization expense}\end{array}$$

Free Cash Flow (FCF) = Operating cash flow − Investments

$$= \text{Operating cash flow} - (\Delta \text{ in fixed assets} + \Delta \text{ NOWC})$$

$$\text{EVA} = \text{NOI}(1 - \text{Tax rate}) - [(\text{Invested capital}) \times (\text{After- tax cost of funds})]$$

$$\text{Current ratio} = \frac{\text{Current assets}}{\text{Current liabilities}}$$

$$\text{Quick, or acid test, ratio} = \frac{\text{Current assets} - \text{Inventory}}{\text{Current liabilities}}$$

$$\text{Inventory turnover} = \frac{\text{Cost of goods sold}}{\text{Inventory}}$$

$$\text{Days sales outstanding (DSO)} = \frac{\text{Accounts Receivable}}{\left[\dfrac{\text{Annual sales}}{360}\right]}$$

$$\text{Fixed assets turnover} = \frac{\text{Sales}}{\text{Net fixed assets}}$$

$$\text{Total assets turnover} = \frac{\text{Sales}}{\text{Total assets}}$$

$$\text{Debt ratio} = \text{Debt to total assets} = \frac{\text{Total liabilities}}{\text{Total assets}}$$

$$\text{Times interest earned (TIE)} = \frac{\text{EBIT}}{\text{Interest charges}}$$

$$\text{Fixed charge coverage} = \frac{\text{EBIT} + \text{Lease payments}}{\underset{\text{charges}}{\text{Interest}} + \underset{\text{payments}}{\text{Lease}} + \left[\dfrac{\text{Sinking fund payments}}{(1 - \text{Tax rate})}\right]}$$

$$\text{Net profit margin} = \frac{\text{Net profit}}{\text{Sales}}$$

$$\text{Return on total assets (ROA)} = \frac{\text{Net income}}{\text{Total assets}} = \frac{\text{Net income}}{\text{Sales}} \times \frac{\text{Sales}}{\text{Total assets}}$$

$$\text{Return on equity (ROE)} = \frac{\left(\begin{array}{c}\text{Net income available to}\\\text{common stockholders}\end{array}\right)}{\text{Common equity}}$$

$$= \frac{\text{Net income}}{\text{Total assets}} \times \frac{\text{Total assets}}{\text{Common equity}}$$

$$\text{Price/Earnings(P/E)} = \frac{\text{Market price per share}}{\text{Earnings per share}}$$

$$\text{Market/Book(M/B)} = \frac{\text{Market price per share}}{\text{Book value per share}}$$

# CHAPTER 3

$$\text{Shares to issue} = \frac{\text{Amount to be raised}}{\text{Market price per share}}$$

# CHAPTER 4

$$FV_n = PV(1 + r)^n$$

$$PV = FV_n\left[\frac{1}{(1 + r)^n}\right]$$

$$FVA_n = PMT\left[\sum_{t=0}^{n-1}(1 + r)^n\right] = PMT\left[\frac{(1 + r)^n - 1}{r}\right]$$

$$FVA(DUE)_n = PMT\left[\sum_{t=1}^{n}(1 + r)^t\right] = PMT\left[\left\{\frac{(1 + r)^n - 1}{r}\right\} \times (1 + r)\right]$$

$$PVA_n = PMT\sum_{t=1}^{n}\left[\frac{1}{(1 + r)^t)}\right] = PMT\left[\frac{1 - \frac{1}{(1 + r)^n}}{r}\right]$$

$$PVA(DUE)_n = PMT \sum_{t=0}^{n-1} \left[ \frac{1}{(1+r)^t)} \right] = PMT \left[ \left\{ \frac{1 - \frac{1}{(1+r)^n}}{r} \right\} \times (1+r) \right]$$

$$PVP = \frac{\text{Payment}}{\text{Interest rate}} = \frac{PMT}{r}$$

$$PV = \frac{CF_1}{(1+r)^1} + \frac{CF_2}{(1+r)^2} + \cdots + \frac{CF_n}{(1+r)^n} = \sum_{t=1}^{n} \frac{CF_t}{(1+r)t}$$

$$\frac{\text{Periodic}}{\text{rate}} = r_{PER} = \frac{\text{Stated annual interest rate}}{\text{Number of interest payments per year}} = \frac{r_{SIMPLE}}{m}$$

$$\frac{\text{Number of}}{\text{interest periods}} = n_{PER} = \text{Number of years} \times \text{Interest payments per year}$$

$$= n_{YRS} \times m$$

$$APR = r_{SIMPLE} = r_{PER} \times m$$

$$\text{Effective annual rate}(EAR) = r_{EAR} = \left(1 + \frac{r_{SIMPLE}}{m}\right)^m - 1.0 = (1 + r_{PER})^m - 1.0$$

# CHAPTER 5

$$\text{Dollar return} = (\text{Dollar income}) + (\text{Capital gains})$$

$$= (\text{Dollar income}) + (\text{Ending value} - \text{Beginning value})$$

$$\text{Yield} = \frac{\text{Total dollar return}}{\text{Beginning value}} = \frac{\text{Dollar income} + \text{Capital gains}}{\text{Beginning value}}$$

$$= \frac{\text{Dollar income} + (\text{Ending value} - \text{Beginning value})}{\text{Beginning value}}$$

$$\text{Rate of return} = r = \text{Risk-free rate} + \text{Risk premium} = r_{RF} + RP$$

$$= r_{RF} + [DRP + LP + MRP]$$

$$= [r^* + IP] + [DRP + LP + MRP]$$

$$r_{Treasury} = r_{RF} + MRP = [r^* + IP] + MRP$$

$$\frac{\text{Yield on a}}{\text{two-year bond}} = \frac{\left(\begin{array}{c}\text{Interest rate}\\\text{in Year 1}\end{array}\right) + \left(\begin{array}{c}\text{Interest rate}\\\text{in Year 2}\end{array}\right)}{2} = \frac{R_1 + R_2}{2}$$

$$\text{Inflation premium} = IP_n = \frac{Infl_1 + \cdots + Infl_n}{n}$$

$$\text{Value of an asset} = \frac{\hat{CF}_1}{(1+r)^1} + \frac{\hat{CF}_2}{(1+r)^2} + \cdots + \frac{\hat{CF}_n}{(1+r)^n} = \sum_{t=1}^{n} \frac{\hat{CF}_t}{(1+r)^t}$$

## CHAPTER 6

$$\text{Bond Value} = V_d = \left[\frac{INT}{(1+r_d)^1} + \frac{INT}{(1+r_d)^2} + \cdots + \frac{INT}{(1+r_d)^N}\right] + \frac{M}{(1+r_d)^N}$$

$$= \left[\sum_{t=1}^{N} \frac{INT}{(1+r_d)^t}\right] + \frac{M}{(1+r_d)^N} = INT\left[\frac{1 - \frac{1}{(1+r_d)^N}}{r_d}\right] + M\left[\frac{1}{(1+r_d)^N}\right]$$

$$= \frac{INT}{(1+YTM)^1} + \cdots + \frac{INT}{(1+YTM)^n}$$

$$V_d = \left(\frac{INT}{2}\right)\left[\frac{1 - \frac{1}{\left(1 + {r_d}/{2}\right)^{2 \times N}}}{\left({r_d}/{2}\right)}\right] + \frac{M}{\left(1 + {r_d}/{2}\right)^{2 \times N}} \quad \text{(semiannual compounding)}$$

$$\text{Approximate yield to maturity} = \frac{\left(\substack{\text{Annual} \\ \text{interest}}\right) + \left(\substack{\text{Accrued} \\ \text{capital gains}}\right)}{\text{Average value of the bond}} = \frac{INT + \left(\frac{M - V_d}{N}\right)}{\left[\frac{2(V_d) + M}{3}\right]}$$

$$\text{Price of a callable bond, } V_d = \frac{INT}{(1+r_d)^1} + \frac{INT}{(1+r_d)^2} + \cdots + \frac{INT + \text{Call price}}{(1+r_d)^{N_c}}$$

$$= \frac{INT}{(1+YTC)^1} + \frac{INT}{(1+YTC)^2} + \cdots + \frac{INT + \text{Call price}}{(1+YTC)^{N_c}}$$

$$\text{Bond yield} = \text{Current (interest) yield} + \text{Capital gains yield}$$

$$= \frac{INT}{V_{d,\text{Begin}}} + \frac{V_{d,\text{End}} - V_{d,\text{Begin}}}{V_{d,\text{Begin}}} = YTM$$

## CHAPTER 7

$$\hat{r}_s = \frac{\hat{D}_1}{P_0} + \frac{\hat{P}_1 - P_0}{P_0}$$

$$\text{Stock Value} = V_s = \hat{P}_0 = \frac{\hat{D}_1}{(1+r_s)^1} + \frac{\hat{D}_2}{(1+r_s)^2} + \cdots + \frac{\hat{D}_{\infty-1}}{(1+r_s)^{\infty-1}} + \frac{\hat{D}_\infty}{(1+r_s)^\infty} = \sum_{t=1}^{\infty} \frac{\hat{D}_t}{(1+r_s)^t}$$

$$\text{Value of a zero growth stock} = \hat{P}_0 = \frac{D}{r_s}$$

Value of a constant growth stock, where $g_1 = g_2 = \cdots = g_\infty$,

$$\hat{P}_0 = \frac{D_0(1+g)}{r_s - g} = \frac{\hat{D}_1}{r_s - g}$$

$$\hat{r}_s = \frac{\hat{D}_1}{P_0} + g$$

$$\begin{array}{ccc} \text{Expected rate} \\ \text{of return} \end{array} = \begin{array}{c} \text{Expected} \\ \text{dividend yield} \end{array} + \begin{array}{c} \text{Expected growth rate,} \\ \text{or capital gains yield} \end{array}$$

$$\text{Capital gains yield} = \frac{\hat{P}_1 - P_0}{P_0}$$

$$\begin{array}{c} \text{Economic} \\ \text{value added} \end{array} = EVA = EBIT(1 - T) - \left[ \left( \begin{array}{c} \text{Percent cost} \\ \text{of funds} \end{array} \right) \times \left( \begin{array}{c} \text{Invested} \\ \text{capital} \end{array} \right) \right]$$

# CHAPTER 8

$$\text{Expected rate of return} = \hat{r} = Pr_1 r_1 + Pr_2 r_2 + \cdots + Pr_n r_n = \sum_{i=1}^{n} Pr_i r_i$$

$$\text{Variance} = \sigma^2 = (r_1 - \hat{r})^2 Pr_1 + (r_2 - \hat{r})^2 Pr_2 + \cdots + (r_n - \hat{r})^2 Pr_n$$
$$= \sum_{i=1}^{n} (r_i - \hat{r})^2 Pr_i$$

$$\text{Standard deviation} = \sigma = \sqrt{(r_1 - \hat{r})^2 Pr_1 + (r_2 - \hat{r})^2 Pr_2 + \cdots + (r_n - \hat{r})^2 Pr_n}$$
$$= \sqrt{\sum_{i=1}^{n} (r_i - \hat{r})^2 Pr_i} = \sqrt{\sigma^2}$$

$$\text{Estimated } \sigma = \sqrt{\frac{\sum_{t=1}^{n} (\ddot{r}_t - \bar{r})^2}{n - 1}} = S$$

$$\bar{r} = \frac{\ddot{r}_1 + \ddot{r}_2 + \cdots + \ddot{r}_n}{n} = \frac{\sum_{t-1}^{n} \ddot{r}}{n}$$

$$\text{Coefficient of variation} = CV = \frac{\text{Risk}}{\text{Return}} = \frac{\sigma}{\hat{r}}$$

$$\text{Portfolio return} = \hat{r}_p = w_1 \hat{r}_1 + w_2 \hat{r}_2 + \cdots + w_N \hat{r}_N = \sum_{j-1}^{N} w_j \hat{r}_j$$

$$\text{Portfolio beta} = \beta_p = w_1 \beta_1 + w_2 \beta_2 + \cdots + w_N \beta_N = \sum_{j=1}^{N} w_j \beta_j$$

$$\text{Total risk} = \text{Systematic risk} + \text{Unsystematic risk}$$

$$\text{Risk premium for Stock j} = RP_M \times \beta_j$$

$$\text{Stock return} = r_j = \text{Risk-free rate} + \text{Risk premium}$$

$$r_j = r_{RF} + (RP_m)\beta_j = \text{Capital Asset Pricing Model (CAPM)}$$

$$= r_{RF} + (r_m - r_{RF})\beta_j$$

$$\text{Value} = \frac{\hat{CF}_1}{(1+r)^1} + \frac{\hat{CF}_2}{(1+r)^2} + \cdots + \frac{\hat{CF}_n}{(1+r)^n} = \sum_{t-1}^{n} \frac{\hat{CF}_t}{(1+r)^t}$$

## CHAPTER 9

$$\text{NPV: } \hat{CF}_0 + \frac{\hat{CF}_1}{(1+r)^1} + \frac{\hat{CF}_2}{(1+r)^2} + \cdots + \frac{\hat{CF}_n}{(1+r)^n} = \sum_{t=0}^{n} \frac{\hat{CF}_t}{(1+r)^t}$$

$$\text{IRR: } \hat{CF}_0 + \frac{\hat{CF}_1}{(1+IRR)^1} + \frac{\hat{CF}_2}{(1+IRR)^2} + \cdots + \frac{\hat{CF}_n}{(1+IRR)^n} = \sum_{t=0}^{n} \frac{\hat{CF}_t}{(1+IRR)^t} = 0$$

$$\text{MIRR: } \sum_{t=0}^{n} \frac{COF_t}{(1+r)^t} = \frac{\sum_{t=0}^{n} CIF_t(1+r)^{n-t}}{(1+MIRR)^n}$$

$$\text{Payback period} = \left( \begin{array}{c} \text{Number of years} \\ \textit{before} \text{ full recovery} \\ \text{of initial investment} \end{array} \right)$$

$$+ \left( \frac{\begin{array}{c}\text{Amount of the initial investment that is} \\ \textit{unrecovered} \text{ at the start of the recovery year}\end{array}}{\begin{array}{c}\text{Total cash flow generated} \\ \text{during the recovery year}\end{array}} \right)$$

## CHAPTER 10

$$\text{Net cash flow} = \quad \text{Net income} \quad + \quad \text{Depreciation}$$

$$= \text{Return } \textit{on} \text{ capital} + \text{Return } \textit{of} \text{ capital}$$

$$\text{Incremental operating } CF_t = \Delta\text{Cash revenues}_t - \Delta\text{Cash expenses}_t - \Delta\text{Taxes}_t$$

$$= \Delta NOI_t \times (1-T) + \Delta Depr_t$$

$$= (\Delta S_t - \Delta OC_t - \Delta Depr_t) \times (1-T) + \Delta Depr_t$$

$$= (\Delta S_t - \Delta OC_t) \times (1-T) + T(\Delta Depr_t)$$

$$E(NPV) = \sum_{i=1}^{n} Pr_i(NPV_i)$$

$$\sigma_{NPV} = \sqrt{\sum_{i=1}^{n} Pr_i[NPV_i - E(NPV)]^2}$$

$$CV_{NPV} = \frac{\sigma_{NPV}}{E(NPV)}$$

$$r_{proj} = r_{RF} + (r_M - r_{RF})\beta_{proj}$$

# CHAPTER 11

$$\text{After} - \text{tax component} \atop \text{cost of debt} = r_{dT} = r_d - r_d \times T = r_d(1 - T)$$

$$V_d = \frac{INT}{(1 + r_d)^1} + \frac{INT}{(1 + r_d)^2} + \cdots + \frac{INT + M}{(1 + r_d)^N}; \quad r_d = YTM$$

$$\text{Component cost} \atop \text{of preferred stock} = r_{ps} = \frac{D_{ps}}{NP_0} = \frac{D_{ps}}{P_0 - \text{Flotation costs}} = \frac{D_{ps}}{P_0(1 - F)}$$

$$\text{component cost of} \atop \text{retained earnings} = r_s = r_{RF} + RP = \frac{\hat{D}_1}{P_0} + g$$

$$r_s = r_{RF} + (r_M - r_{RF})\beta_s$$

$$r_s = \text{Bond yield} + \text{Risk premium} = r_d + RP$$

$$\text{component cost of new} \atop \text{common equity} = r_e = \frac{\hat{D}_1}{NP_0} + g = \frac{\hat{D}_1}{P_0(1 - F)} + g$$

$$WACC = w_d r_{dT} + w_{ps} r_{ps} + w_s(r_s \text{ or } r_e)$$

$$\text{Break point} = \frac{\text{Total amount of lower cost of capital of a given type}}{\text{Proportion of the type of capital in the capital structure}}$$

$$Value = \frac{\hat{CF}_1}{(1 + r)^1} + \frac{\hat{CF}_2}{(1 + r)^2} + \cdots + \frac{\hat{CF}_n}{(1 + r)^n} = \sum_{t=1}^{n} \frac{\hat{CF}_t}{(1 + r)^t}$$

$$= \frac{\hat{CF}_1}{(1 + WACC)^1} + \cdots + \frac{\hat{CF}_n}{(1 + WACC)^n} = \sum_{t=1}^{n} \frac{\hat{CF}_t}{(1 + WACC)^t}$$

## CHAPTER 12

$$DOL = \frac{Q(P-V)}{Q(P-V)-F} = \frac{S-VC}{S-VC-F} = \frac{\text{Gross profit}}{\text{EBIT}}$$

$$DFL = \frac{\text{EBIT}}{\text{EBIT}-L} \quad \text{(when there is no preferred stock)}$$

$$DTL = DOL \times DFL = \frac{Q(P-V)}{Q(P-V)-F-I} = \frac{S-VC}{S-VC-F-I} = \frac{\text{Gross profit}}{\text{EBIT}-L}$$

$$EPS_1 = EPS_0 + EPS_0(DTL \times \%\Delta Sales)$$
$$= EPS_0[1 + (DTL \times \%\Delta Sales)]$$

## CHAPTER 13

$$\begin{matrix} \text{Dollars transferred from} \\ \text{retained earnings} \end{matrix} = \left[ \begin{pmatrix} \text{Number of shares} \\ \text{outstanding} \end{pmatrix} \times \begin{pmatrix} \text{Percent stock dividend} \\ \text{stated as a decimal} \end{pmatrix} \right]$$
$$\times \begin{pmatrix} \text{Market price} \\ \text{of the stock} \end{pmatrix}$$

## CHAPTER 14

$$\text{Account balance} = \begin{pmatrix} \text{Amount of} \\ \text{daily activity} \end{pmatrix} \times \begin{pmatrix} \text{Average life} \\ \text{of the account} \end{pmatrix}$$

$$\begin{matrix} \text{Inventory} \\ \text{conversion} \\ \text{period} \end{matrix} = \frac{\text{Inventory}}{\left( \dfrac{\text{Cost of goods sold}}{360 \text{ days}} \right)} = \frac{360 \text{ days}}{\text{Inventory turnover}}$$

$$\begin{matrix} \text{Receivables} \\ \text{collection} \\ \text{period (DSO)} \end{matrix} = \frac{\text{Receivables}}{\left( \dfrac{\text{Annual credit sales}}{360} \right)} = \frac{360 \text{ days}}{\text{Receivables turnover}}$$

$$\begin{matrix} \text{Payables} \\ \text{deferral} \\ \text{period(DPO)} \end{matrix} = \frac{\text{Accounts payable}}{\left( \dfrac{\text{Cost of goods sold}}{360} \right)} = \frac{360 \text{ days}}{\text{Payables turnover}}$$

$$\begin{matrix} \text{Cash} \\ \text{conversion} \\ \text{cycle} \end{matrix} = \begin{pmatrix} \text{Inventory} \\ \text{conversion} \\ \text{period} \end{pmatrix} + \begin{pmatrix} \text{Receivables} \\ \text{collection} \\ \text{period} \end{pmatrix} - \begin{pmatrix} \text{Payable} \\ \text{deferral} \\ \text{period} \end{pmatrix}$$

# CHAPTER 15

$$\text{Total inventory costs (TIC)} = (C \times PP)\left(\frac{Q}{2}\right) + O\left(\frac{T}{Q}\right)$$

$$\text{Total carrying costs} = (C \times PP)\left(\frac{Q}{2}\right)$$

$$\text{Total ordering costs} = O\left(\frac{T}{Q}\right)$$

$$\text{Economic ordering quantity} = \text{EOQ} = \sqrt{\frac{2 \times O \times T}{C \times PP}}$$

# CHAPTER 16

$$\text{Percentage cost per period} = r_{\text{PER}} = \frac{\text{Dollar cost of borrowing}}{\text{Amount of usable funds}}$$

$$\text{Effective annual rate (EAR)} = (1 + r_{\text{PER}})^m - 1.0$$

$$\text{Annual percentage rate (EAR)} = r_{\text{PER}} \times m = r_{\text{SIMPLE}}$$

$$\text{Compensating balance requirement} = CB = (\text{Principal amount})\left(\begin{array}{c}\text{Compensating balance} \\ \text{as a decimal}\end{array}\right)$$

$$\text{Usable funds} = \left[\begin{array}{c}\text{Face (principal)} \\ \text{amount of the loan}\end{array}\right] - \left(\begin{array}{c}\text{Dollar reductions} \\ \text{from the face value}\end{array}\right)$$

$$= \left[\begin{array}{c}\text{Face (principal)} \\ \text{amount of the loan}\end{array}\right] \times \left[1 - \left(\begin{array}{c}\text{Reductions from the face} \\ \text{value stated as a decimal}\end{array}\right)\right]$$

$$\text{Required loan (principal) amount} = \frac{\text{Amount of usable funds needed}}{1 - \left[\begin{array}{c}\text{Reductions from the principal} \\ \text{amount (face) stated as a decimal}\end{array}\right]}$$

# CHAPTER 17

$$\text{Full capacity sales} = \frac{\text{Sales level}}{\left(\begin{array}{c}\text{Percent of capacity used} \\ \text{to generate sales level}\end{array}\right)}$$

$$\underset{\text{revenues}}{\text{Sales}} = \underset{\text{costs}}{\text{Total operating}} = \underset{\text{variable costs}}{\text{Total}} + \underset{\text{fixed costs}}{\text{Total}}$$

$$(P \times Q) = \quad TOC \quad = \quad (V \times Q) \quad + \quad F$$

$$Q_{\text{OpBE}} = \frac{F}{P - V} = \frac{F}{\text{Contribution margin}}$$

$$S_{\text{OpBE}} = \frac{F}{1 - \left(\dfrac{V}{P}\right)} = \frac{F}{\text{Gross profit margin}}$$

$$DOL = \frac{\left(\dfrac{\Delta NOI}{NOI}\right)}{\left(\dfrac{\Delta Sales}{Sales}\right)}$$

$$DOL_Q = \frac{Q(P - V)}{Q(P - V) - F} = \frac{S - VC}{S - VC - F} = \frac{\text{Gross profit}}{\text{EBIT}}$$

$$\text{At financial BEP, } EPS = \frac{(EBIT - I)(1 - T) - D_{ps}}{Shrs_c} = 0$$

$$EBIT_{\text{FinBE}} = I + \frac{D_{ps}}{(1 - T)}$$

$$DFL = \frac{\left(\dfrac{\Delta EPS}{EPS}\right)}{\left(\dfrac{\Delta EBIT}{EBIT}\right)}$$

$$DFL = \frac{EBIT}{EBIT - EBIT_{\text{FinBE}}}$$
$$= \frac{EBIT}{EBIT - I} \qquad \text{When } D_{ps} = 0$$

$$DTL = \frac{\left(\dfrac{\Delta EPS}{EPS}\right)}{\left(\dfrac{\Delta Sales}{Sales}\right)} = \frac{\left(\dfrac{\Delta EBIT}{EBIT}\right)}{\left(\dfrac{\Delta Sales}{Sales}\right)} \times \frac{\left(\dfrac{\Delta EPS}{EPS}\right)}{\left(\dfrac{\Delta EBIT}{EBIT}\right)} = DOL \times DFL$$

$$DTL = \frac{\text{Gross profit}}{EBIT} \times \frac{EBIT}{EBIT - EBIT_{\text{FinBE}}} = \frac{\text{Gross profit}}{EBIT - EBIT_{\text{FinBE}}}$$
$$= \frac{S - VC}{EBIT - I} = \frac{Q(P - V)}{[Q(P - V) - F] - I} \qquad \text{when } D_{ps} = 0$$

## CHAPTER 18

$$\text{Conversion price} = P_c = \frac{\text{Par value of bond}}{\text{Conversion ratio}}$$

# Index

Page numbers followed by an f indicate material found within a figure; numbers followed by a t indicate material found within a table.